Quakertown Christian School
50 East Paletown Road
Quakertown, PA 18951

Literature

and the Language Arts

Discovering Literature

THE EMC MASTERPIECE SERIES

SECOND EDITION

EMCParadigm Publishing Saint Paul, Minnesota

Staff Credits

Editorial

Laurie Skiba
Editor

Lori Ann Coleman
Associate Editor

Brenda Owens
Associate Editor

Diana Moen
Associate Editor

Gia Marie Garbinsky
Assistant Editor

Jennifer Joline Anderson
Assistant Editor

Janice Johnson
Curriculum Specialist

Paul Spencer
Art and Photo Researcher

Chris Bohen
Editorial Assistant

Katherine S. Link
Editorial Assistant

Design

Shelley Clubb
Production Manager

Jennifer Wreisner
Senior Designer

C. Vern Johnson
Senior Designer

Michelle Lewis
Senior Design Specialist

Julie L. Hansen
Design Specialist

Bill Connell
Design Specialist

Cover Credits

Cover Designer: C. Vern Johnson

Rooftops (No. 1, This is Harlem) [Detail], 1943. Jacob Lawrence.
Saint George and the Dragon [Detail], c.1400s. Spanish artist.
The Fate of Animals [Detail], 1913. Franz Marc.
Tornado Over Kansas [Detail], 1929. John Stuart Curry.

ISBN 0-8219-2019-7
©2007, 2005 by EMC Publishing, LLC

875 Montreal Way
St. Paul, Minnesota 55102
800-328-1452
www.emcp.com
E-mail: educate@emcp.com

Printed in the United States of America.
10 9 8   XXX 10 09 08 07

Literature
and the Language Arts

SECOND EDITION

REDWOOD LEVEL
DISCOVERING LITERATURE

WILLOW LEVEL
UNDERSTANDING LITERATURE

CEDAR LEVEL
EXPLORING LITERATURE

PINE LEVEL
THE AMERICAN TRADITION

OAK LEVEL
RESPONDING TO LITERATURE

MAPLE LEVEL
THE BRITISH TRADITION

BIRCH LEVEL
EXPERIENCING LITERATURE

CYPRESS LEVEL
WORLD LITERATURE

Consultants and Writers

Senior Consultant
Dr. Edmund J. Farrell
Emeritus Professor of English Education
University of Texas at Austin
Austin, Texas

Maria Backus
Educational Writer
Arvada, Colorado

Amy Bergstrom
Instructor
Education Department
University of Minnesota
Duluth, Minnesota

Diana Blythe
Senior Content Manager
Humanities Software, a division
of Advantage Learning
    Systems, Inc.
Hood River, Oregon

Cherie Boen
National Board Certified
    Teacher
Educational Consultant
Minneapolis, Minnesota

Jamy Bond
Educational Writer
Washington, DC

Walker Brents III
Instructor
Berkwood-Hedge School
Berkeley, California

Nancy Campbell
Educational Writer
Richfield, Minnesota

Linda Christopherson
Educational Writer
Charlotte, North Carolina

Dr. Mary Curfman
Language Arts Supervisor
Department of Curriculum and
    Professional Development
Clark County Schools
Las Vegas, Nevada

Lisa De Leon
Educational Writer
Northfield, Minnesota

Rebecca Gander
Educational Consultant
Anoka, Minnesota

Sara Hyry
Educational Writer
Easthampton, Massachusetts

Christina Kolb
Educational Writer
Newton, Massachusetts

Sharon Kremer
English Department Chair
A. O. Calhoun Middle School
Denton, Texas

Jon Madian
Senior Instructional Designer
Humanities Software, a division
of Advantage Learning
    Systems, Inc.
Hood River, Oregon

Beverly Martin
Managing Editor
Humanities Software, a division
of Advantage Learning
    Systems, Inc.
Hood River, Oregon

Danielle Martin
Educational Writer
Brooklyn, New York

Kristi McGee
Educational Writer
Brooklyn, New York

Mertys Mrvos
Language Arts/Reading
    Instructor
South View Middle School
Edina, Minnesota

Carol Satz
Clinician
Center for Reading and Writing
Rider University
Lawrenceville, New Jersey

Karen Schwabach
Itinerant Literacy Leader
Lower Kuskokwim School
    District
Bethel, Alaska

Elnora Shields
Educational Consultant
Durham, North Carolina

Dr. Jane Shoaf
Educational Consultant
Edenton, North Carolina

Kendra Sisserson
Research Associate
University of Chicago
Chicago, Illinois

Jim Swanson
Educational Consultant
Minneapolis, Minnesota

Shannon Taylor
Educational Writer
Eagan, Minnesota

Anne Todd
Educational Writer
Walnut Creek, California

Jan Toth
Language Arts Instructor
Whitman Middle School
Seattle, Washington

Geraldine Troutman
Reading Mentor
Hollywood Beach Elementary
    School
Advisor, Curriculum Council
    Advisory Committee
Hueneme School District
Oxnard, California

Anita Usmiani
Language Arts Supervisor
Hamilton Township School
    District
Hamilton, New Jersey

The Sunflower Quilting Bee at Arles, 1991. Faith Ringgold.

Windy Day in Atchison, 1952. John Philip Falter.

Hercules Fighting with the Lernaean Hydra, 1600s.
Francisco de Zurbaran.

Little Sweet, 1944. William H. Johnson.

Washington Square, 1900. Paul Cornoyer.

Man Looking into Outer Space, c.1500s. French artist.

PART THREE • LANGUAGE ARTS SURVEY

1   READING RESOURCE

Dead End, Lyonel Feininger.

The Mountain-path, 1937. J. R. R. Tolkien.

Howl, 1977. Luis Jimenez.

To the Student

Features of Your Textbook

A GUIDE FOR READING

When you open your *EMC Masterpiece Series* textbook, you will find great literature, both classic and contemporary, by a wide variety of authors. You will also find useful step-by-step study strategies for each selection, helpful background information, and activities that allow you to relate the literature to your own experiences and share your point of view.

The **Guided Reading** program in this *EMC Masterpiece Series* book gives you tips before, during, and after you read each selection. Read on for a description of the features you will find in your textbook.

- **Reader's Resource** gives you background and other information you'll need for the reading.

- **Reader's Toolbox** features point out and explain literary techniques that are used in the selection.

- A **Graphic Organizer** is provided to help you sort out the important points on paper.

- **Guided Reading Questions** within the selection help you check your understanding of the reading.

- **Words for Everyday Use** includes the definition and pronunciation for new vocabulary. A sample sentence demonstrates the use of the word in context.

- **Footnotes** explain unfamiliar terms or unusual words.

- **ArtSmart** features provide information about the history, culture, or artistic technique of the fine art throughout the textbook and foster critical viewing of the art.

- **Respond to the Selection** allows you to relate the literature to your own experiences.

- **Investigate, Inquire, and Imagine** contains questions you need to perfect your understanding of the reading, from basic recalling and interpreting questions to ones that ask you to analyze, synthesize, evaluate, and extend your ideas. Some questions also ask you to look at a specific point of view, or examine a different perspective.

- **Understanding Literature** follows up on the literary techniques introduced in Reader's Toolbox and asks you questions to further your understanding.

- **Writer's Journal** gives you three quick-writing options to help you build writing skills.

- **Skill Builders** contain creative activities that tie literature to other language arts areas such as grammar, vocabulary development, public speaking, study and research, collaborative learning, media literacy, and applied English.

A GUIDE FOR WRITING

At the end of each unit of your textbook you will find a **Guided Writing** activity that takes you through the steps of the writing process. The lesson includes models from professional writers and students. Also included are graphic organizers, questions to get you thinking, and an integrated **Language, Grammar, and Style** lesson to help you brush up on grammar points.

A GUIDE FOR LANGUAGE ARTS SKILLS

The **Language Arts Survey** in the back of your textbook is your resource for information about how to use the English language effectively. It includes tips on what you need to know to write, speak, and read effectively. There are six sections in the Language Arts Survey: the **Reading Resource**, the **Writing Resource**, the **Language, Grammar, and Style Resource**, the **Speaking and Listening Resource**, the **Study and Research Resource**, and the **Applied English Resource**. Do you need to correct a passive sentence? include an Internet site in a research paper? interview someone in the community? write a letter? It's all here for you.

Themes in Literature
PART ONE

Van Gogh Painting, 1888. Paul Gauguin. Private Collection.

Finding Your True SELF

echoes

Keep company with those who may make you better.
—English proverb

No one can make you feel inferior without your consent.
—Eleanor Roosevelt

When you were born, you cried and the world rejoiced. Live your life so that when you die, the world cries and you rejoice.
—Cherokee proverb

Then the time came when the risk it took to remain tight in a bud was more painful than the risk it took to blossom.
—Anaïs Nin

I like being unconventional.
—Florence Griffith Joyner

I didn't belong as a kid, and that always bothered me. If only I'd known that one day my differentness would be an asset, then my early life would have been much easier.
—Bette Midler

This above all: to thine own self be true.
—William Shakespeare, Hamlet

You are your most valuable asset. Don't forget that. You are the best thing you have.
—Gary Paulsen

Prereading

"The Goodness of Matt Kaizer" by Avi

Reader's TOOLBOX

CONFLICT. A **conflict** is a struggle between two people or things in a literary work. A story's plot is formed around conflict. A conflict can be internal or external. A struggle that takes place between a character and some outside force—such as another character, society, or nature—is called an **external conflict**. A struggle that takes place within a character is called an **internal conflict**. As you read "The Goodness of Matt Kaizer," decide whether the conflict in this story is external or internal.

CHARACTER. A **character** is a person (or sometimes an animal) who takes part in the action of a literary work. A one-dimensional character, flat character, or caricature is one who exhibits a single quality, or character trait. A three-dimensional, full, or rounded character is one who seems to have all the complex qualities of an actual human being. The main character in a story is the most important one. In this story, Matt is the main character. As you read the story, note what you learn about Matt. Use the graphic organizer below to keep track of each detail.

Graphic *Organizer*

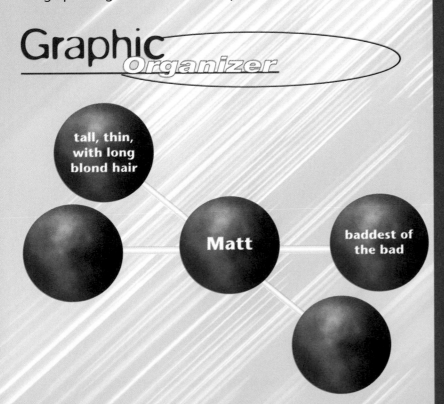

tall, thin, with long blond hair

Matt

baddest of the bad

Reader's *Journal*

How do you react when someone dares you to do something?

Reader's *Resource*

- Originally the word *gang* had no negative connotation. In Old English, *gang* simply referred to a "number of people who went around together—a group." Today a gang can be defined in four basic ways: 1) an organized group with a leader; 2) a unified group that usually remains together during peaceful times as well as times of conflict; 3) a group whose members show unity through clothing and/or language; and 4) a group whose activities are criminal or threatening to the larger society.

- Peer pressure is the social influence a peer group exerts on its individual members as each member attempts to conform to the expectations of the group. Sometimes, members of such a social group might taunt or ridicule other members or would-be members to pressure them into certain behavior. Depending on the situation, conforming to peer pressure can have a positive or negative impact on an individual.

The Goodness Of Matt

Avi

People are always saying, "Nothing's worse than when a kid goes bad." Well, let me tell you, going good isn't all that great either. Tell you what I mean.

Back in sixth grade there was a bunch of us who liked nothing better than doing bad stuff. I don't know why. We just liked doing it. And the baddest of the bad was Matt Kaizer.

Matt was a tall, thin kid with long, light blond hair that reached his shoulders. He was twelve years old—like I was. His eyes were pale blue and his skin was a vanilla cream that never—no matter the season—seemed to darken, except with dirt. What with the way he looked—so pale and all—plus the fact that he was into wearing extra large blank white T-shirts that reached his knees, we called him "Spirit."

Now, there are two important things you need to know about Matt Kaizer. The first was that as far as he was concerned there was nothing good about him at all. Nothing. The second thing was that his father was a minister.[1]

Our gang—I'm Marley, and then there was Chuck, Todd, and Nick—loved the fact that Matt was so bad and his father a minister. You know, we were always daring him to do bad things. "Hey, minister's kid!" we'd taunt. "Dare you to . . ." and we'd challenge him to do something, you know, really gross. Thing is, we could always count on Matt—who wanted to show he wasn't good—to take a dare.

For instance: Say there was some dead animal out on the road. We'd all run to Matt and say, "Dare you to pick it up."

Matt would look at it—up close and personal—or more than likely poke it with a stick, then pick it up and fling it at one of us.

Disgusting stories? Someone would tell one and then say, "Dare you to tell it to Mary Beth Bataky"—the class slug—and Matt would tell it to her—better than anyone else, too.

TV and movies? The more blood and gore there was, the more Matt ate it up—if you know what I mean. MTV, cop shows, all that bad stuff, nothing was too gross for him.

And it didn't take just dares to get Matt going. No, Matt would do stuff on his own. If anyone blew a toot—even in class—he would bellow, "Who cut the cheese?" He could

> **GUIDED READING**
>
> According to the narrator, what are the two important things to know about Matt Kaizer?

> **GUIDED READING**
>
> What is the gang always doing to Matt?

---

1. **minister.** One who leads the church, a clergyperson

words for everyday use   **taunt** (tont') v., challenge in a mocking or insulting manner. *They began to taunt the boy by mocking him about his haircut.*

Kaizer

belch whenever he wanted to, and did, a lot. Spitballs, booger flicking, wedgie yanking, it was all wicked fun for Matt. No way was he going to be good! Not in front of us.

Now, his father, the minister, "Rev. Kaizer" we called him, wasn't bad. In fact just the opposite. The guy was easygoing, always dressed decently, and as far as I knew, never raised his voice or acted any way than what he was, a nice man, a good man. Sure, he talked a little funny, like he was reading from a book, but that was all.

Did Matt and his father get along? In a way. For example, once I was with Matt after he did something bad—I think he blew his nose on someone's lunch. Rev. Kaizer had learned about it. Instead of getting mad he just gazed at Matt, shook his head, and said, "Matt, I do believe there's goodness in everyone. That goes for you too. Someday you'll find your own goodness. And when you do you'll be free."

"I'm not good," Matt insisted.

"Well, I think you are," his father said, patiently.

GUIDED READING
What do Matt and his father disagree about?

Matt grinned. "Long as my friends dare me to do bad things, I'll do 'em."

"Never refuse a dare?" his father asked, sadly.

"Never," Matt said with pride.

Rev. Kaizer sighed, pressed his hands together, and looked toward heaven.

So there we were, a bunch of us who knew we were bad and that it was doing bad things that held

GUIDED READING
What holds the gang together?

us together. And the baddest of the bad, like I said, was Matt—the Spirit—Kaizer. But then…oh, man, I'll tell you what happened.

One day after school we were hanging out in the playground. The five of us were just sitting around telling disgusting stories, when suddenly Chuck said, "Hey, hear about Mary Beth Bataky?"

"What about her?" Matt asked.

"Her old man's dying."

Right away Matt was interested. "Really?"

"It's true, man," Chuck insisted. "He's just about had it."

"How come?" I asked.

"Don't know," said Chuck. "He's sick. So sick they sent him home from the hospital. That's why Mary Beth is out. She's waiting for him to die."

"Cool," said Matt.

Now, Mary Beth was one small straw of a sad slug. She had this bitsy face with pale eyes and two gray lines for lips all framed in a pair of frizzy braids. Her arms were thin and always crossed over her chest, which was usually bundled in a brown sweater. The only bits of color on her were her fingernails, which, though chewed, were spotted with bright red nail polish—chipped.

So when we heard what was going on with Mary Beth and her father, we guys eyed one another, almost knowing what was going to happen next. But, I admit, it was me who said, "Hey, Spirit, I dare you to go and see him."

GUIDED READING
What does Marley dare Matt to do?

Matt pushed the blond hair out of his face and looked at us with those pale blue, cool-as-ice eyes of his.

"Or maybe," Todd said, "you're too chicken, being as you're a minister's kid and all."

That did it. Course it did. No way Matt could resist a dare. He got up, casual like. "I'll do it," he said. "Who's coming with me?"

To my disgust the other guys backed off. But I accepted. Well, actually, I really didn't think he'd do it.

But then, soon as we started off, I began to feel a little nervous. "Matt," I warned. "I think Mary Beth is very religious."

"Don't worry. I know about all that stuff."

"Yeah, but what would your father say?"

"I don't care," he bragged. "Anyway, I'm not going to do anything except look. It'll be neat. Like a horror movie. Maybe I can even touch the guy. A dying body is supposed to be colder than ice."

GUIDED READING

What does Matt answer when Marley asks him what his father would say?

That was Matt. Always taking up the dare and going you one worse.

The more he talked the sorrier I was we had dared him to go. Made me really uncomfortable. Which I think he noticed, because he said, "What's the matter, Marley? You scared or something?"

"Just seems…"

"I know," he taunted, "you're too good!" He belched loudly to make his point that he wasn't. "See you later, dude." He started off.

I ran after him. "Do you know where she lives?"

"Follow me."

"They might not let you see him," I warned.

He pulled out some coins. "I'm going to buy some flowers and bring them to him. That's what

GUIDED READING

What does Matt decide to buy?

my mother did when my aunt was sick." He stuffed his mouth full of bubble gum and began blowing and popping.

Mary Beth's house was a wooden three-decker with a front porch. Next to the front door were three bell buttons with plastic name labels. The Batakys lived on the first floor.

By the time Matt and I got there he had two wilted carnations in his hand. One was dyed blue, the other green. The flower store guy had sold them for ten cents each.

"You know," I said in a whisper, as we stood before the door, "her father might already be dead."

GUIDED READING

What does Marley whisper as they stand before the door?

"Cool," Matt replied, blowing another bubble, while cleaning out an ear with a pinky and inspecting the earwax carefully before smearing it on his shirt. "Did you know your fingernails still grow when you're dead? Same for your hair. I mean, how many really dead people can you get to see?" he said and rang the Batakys' bell.

From far off inside there was a buzzing sound.

I was trying to get the nerve to leave when the door opened a crack. Mary Beth—pale eyes rimmed with red—peeked out. There were tears on her cheeks and her lips were crusty. Her small hands—with their spots of red fingernail polish—were trembling.

"Oh, hi," she said, her voice small and tense.

I felt tight with embarrassment.

Matt spoke out loudly. "Hi, Mary Beth. We heard your old man was dying."

"Yes, he is," Mary Beth murmured. With one hand on the doorknob it was pretty clear she wanted to <u>retreat</u> as fast as possible. "He's <u>delirious</u>."

"Delirious?" Matt said. "What's that?"

"Sort of . . . crazy. "

"Oh . . . wow, sweet! " he said, giving me a nudge of appreciation. Then he held up the blue and green carnations, popped his gum, and said, "I wanted to bring him these."

Mary Beth stared at the flowers, but didn't move to take them. All she said was, "My mother's at St. Mary's, praying."

Now I really wanted to get out of there. But Matt said, "How about if I gave these to your father?" He held up the flowers again. "Personally."

words for everyday use

re • treat (ri trēt′) v., draw or lead back, withdraw. *Alice began to <u>retreat</u> as she withdrew away from the barking dog.*

de • lir • i • ous (di lir′ ē əs) adj., state of being confused, having disordered speech and hallucinations. *The medicine the old man took made him <u>delirious</u> and confused about his surroundings.*

"My mother said he may die any moment," Mary Beth informed us.

"I know," Matt said. "So I'd really like to see him before he does."

Mary Beth gazed at him. "He's so sick," she said, "he's not up to visiting."

"Yeah," Matt pressed, "but, you see, the whole class elected me to come and bring these flowers."

GUIDED READING

What lie does Matt tell Mary Beth?

His lie worked. "Oh," Mary Beth murmured, and she pulled the door open. "Well, I suppose . . ."

We stepped into a small entrance way. A low-watt bulb dangled over our heads from a wire. Shoes, boots, and broken umbrellas lay in a plastic milk crate.

Mary Beth shut the outside door then pushed open an inner one that led to her apartment. It was gloomy and stank of medicine.

Matt bopped me on the arm. "Who cut the cheese!" he said with a grin. I looked around at him. He popped another bubble.

"Down this way," Mary Beth whispered.

We walked down a long hallway. Two pictures were on the walls. They were painted on black velvet. One was a scene of a mountain with snow on it and the sun shining on a stag² with antlers. The second picture was of a little girl praying by her bed. Fuzzy gold light streamed in on her from a window.

At the end of the hall was a closed door. Mary Beth halted. "He's in here," she whispered. "He's really sick," she warned again. "And he doesn't notice anyone. You really sure you want to see him?"

"You bet," Matt said with enthusiasm.

"I mean, he won't say hello or anything," Mary Beth said in her low voice. "He just lies there with his eyes open. I don't even know if he sees anything."

"Does he have running sores?" Matt asked. I almost gagged.

"Running *what?*" Mary Beth asked.

"You know, wounds."

"It's his liver," Mary Beth explained sadly, while turning the door handle and opening the door. "The doctor said it was all his bad life and drinking."

Dark as the hall had been, her father's room was darker. The air was heavy and really stank. A large bed took up most of the space.

On one side of the bed was a small chest of drawers. On top of the chest was a lit candle and a glass of water into which a pair of false teeth had been dropped. On the other side of the bed was a wooden chair. Another burning candle was on that.

On the bed—beneath a brown blanket—lay Mr. Bataky. He was stretched out on his back perfectly straight, like a log. His head and narrow chest were propped up on a pile of four pillows with pictures of flowers on them. At the base of the bed his toes poked up from under the blanket. He was clothed in pajamas dotted with different colored hearts. His hands—looking like a bunch of knuckles—were linked over his chest. His poorly shaven face—yellow in color—was thin. With his cheeks sunken, his nose seemed enormous. His thin hair was uncombed. His breathing was drawn

"It's . . . it's . . . an angel . . ." Mr. Bataky said in a low, rasping voice. "An angel . . . from heaven has come to save me."

---

2. **stag.** Adult male deer

out, almost whistling, and collapsed into throat gargles[3]—as if he were choking.

Worst of all, his eyes were open but he was just staring up, like he was waiting for something to happen in heaven.

GUIDED READING

What is the worst thing about Mr. Bataky's appearance?

Mary Beth stepped to one side of the bed. Matt stood at the foot, with me peering over his shoulder. We stared at the dying man. He really looked bad. Awful.

"I don't think he'll live long," Mary Beth murmured, her sad voice breaking, her tears dripping.

Matt lifted the blue and green carnations. "Mr. Bataky," he shouted, "I brought you some flowers to cheer you up."

"His hearing isn't good," Mary Beth said apologetically.

Matt looked about for a place to put the flowers, saw the glass with the teeth near Mr. Bataky's head, and moved to put them into the water. In the flickering candlelight, Matt's pale skin, his long blond hair, seemed to glow.

Now, just as Matt came up to the head of the bed, Mr. Bataky's eyes shifted. They seemed to fasten on Matt. The old man gave a start, made a <u>convulsive</u> twitch as his eyes positively bulged. Matt, caught in the look, froze.

"It's . . . it's . . . an *angel* . . ." Mr. Bataky said in a low, <u>rasping</u> voice. "An angel . . . from heaven has come to save me."

GUIDED READING

Who does Mr. Bataky think Matt is? What does he think Matt is going to do?

Matt lifted his hand—the one that held the carnations—and tried to place them in the glass of water. Before he could, Mr. Bataky made an unexpected jerk with one of his knobby hands and took hold of Matt's arm. Matt was so surprised he dropped the flowers.

"Father!" Mary Beth cried.

"Thank . . . you . . . for coming, Angel," Mr. Bataky rasped.

"No . . . really," Matt stammered, "I'm not—"

"Yes, you're an angel," Mr. Bataky whispered. His eyes—full of tears—were hot with joy.

Matt turned red. "No, I'm not . . ."

"Please," Mr. Bataky cried out with amazing energy, "I don't want to die bad." Tears gushed down his hollow cheeks. "You got to help me. Talk to me. Bless[4] me."

GUIDED READING

What does Mr. Bataky not want to do?

Matt, speechless for once, gawked at the man.

With considerable effort he managed to pry Mr. Bataky's fingers from his arm. Soon as he did he <u>bolted</u> from the room.

"Don't abandon me!" Mr. Bataky begged, somehow managing to lift himself up and extend his arms toward the doorway. "Don't!"

Frightened, I hurried out after Matt.

My buddy was waiting outside, breathing hard. His normally pale face was paler than ever. As we walked away he didn't say anything.

Now, according to Matt—he told us all this later—what happened was that night Rev. Kaizer called him into his study.

"Matt, please sit down."

Matt, thinking he was going to get a lecture about visiting Mary Beth's house, sat.

His father said, "Matt, I think it's quite wonderful what you've done, going to the

---

3. **gargles.** Sound of liquid or air in the throat
4. **Bless.** Speak well of or approve, to endow happiness or prosperity upon someone

---

words for everyday use

con • vul • sive (kən vəl' siv) *adj.*, producing involuntary and uncontrolled movement of the muscles. *Her hand moved in a <u>convulsive</u> twitch as it began to shake uncontrollably.*
rasp • ing (ras' piŋ) *adj.*, producing a harsh, irritating sound. *Because the man had laryngitis, his <u>rasping</u> voice was harsh and grating.*
bolt (bōlt') *v.*, move or break away suddenly or rapidly. *The deer suddenly ran into the woods as they <u>bolted</u> from the hunters.*

home of your classmate's dying father to comfort him."

"What do you mean?" Matt asked.

Rev. Kaizer smiled sweetly. "A woman by the name of Mrs. Bataky called me. She said her husband was very ill. Dying. She said you—I gather you go to school with her daughter—came to visit him today. Apparently her husband thought you were an…angel. It's the first real sign of life her poor husband has shown in three days. And now, Matt, he's quite desperate to see the angel—you—again."

"It's not true," Matt rapped out.

"Now, Matt," his father said, "I found the woman's story difficult to believe, too. 'Madam,' I said to her, 'are you quite certain you're talking about *my* son? And are you truly saying your husband really thought he was…an angel?'

"And she said, 'Rev. Kaizer—you being a minister I can say it—my husband led a bad, sinful life. But there's something about your son that's making him want to talk about it. Sort of like a confession.[5] Know what I'm saying? I mean, it would do him a lot of good. What I'm asking is, could you get your son to come again? I'm really scared my husband will get worse if he doesn't.'

GUIDED READING
What does Mrs. Bataky tell Matt's father? What does she ask him to do?

"Matt," said Rev. Kaizer, "I'm proud of you. I think it would be a fine thing if you visited him again."

"I'm not an angel," Matt replied in a <u>sulky</u> voice.

"I never said *you* were an angel," his father said. "But as I've told you many times, there is goodness inside you as there is in everyone. And now you are in the fortunate position of being able to help this sinful man."

"I don't want to."

"Son, here is a sick man who needs to unburden himself of the unhappy things he's done. I know your <u>reputation</u>. Are you fearful of hearing what Mr. Bataky has to say for himself?"

"I don't want to."

Rev. Kaizer sat back in his chair, folded his hands over his stomach, smiled gently, and said, "I dare you to go back and listen to Mr. Bataky. I dare you to do goodness. "

GUIDED READING
What does Rev. Kaizer dare Matt to do?

Alarmed, Matt looked up. "But…"

"Or are you, being a minister's son, afraid to?"

Matt shifted uncomfortably in his seat and tried to avoid his father's steady gaze.

Rev. Kaizer offered up a faint[6] smile. "Matt, I thought you never refused a dare."

Matt squirmed. Then he said, "I'll go."

Anyway, that's the way Matt explained it all. And as he said to me, sadly, "What choice did I have? He dared me."

We all saw then that Matt was in a bad place.

So the next day when Matt went to visit Mr. Bataky, the bunch of us—me, Chuck, Todd, and Nick—tagged along. We all wanted to see what Matt would do. We figured it *had* to be gross.

Mary Beth opened the door. I think she was surprised to see all of us. But she looked at Matt with hope. "Thank you for coming," she said in her tissue paper voice. "He's waiting for you."

GUIDED READING
How does Mary Beth look at Matt when she opens the door?

---

5. **confession.** Act of acknowledging one's guilt or wrongs done
6. **faint.** Weakly accomplished, lacking distinctiveness

---

words for everyday use

sulk • y (səl′ kē) *adj.*, indicating a moody silence. *The toy was taken from the child, so he got into a <u>sulky</u> mood by being quiet and withdrawn.*

re • pu • ta • tion (re pyə tā′ shən) *n.*, overall character as seen or judged by people. *Sarah had a good <u>reputation</u> because people saw her as being nice and friendly.*

Matt gave us an <u>imploring</u> look. There was nothing we could do. He disappeared inside. We waited outside.

Half an hour later, when he emerged, there was a ton of worry in his eyes. We waited him out, hoping he'd say something <u>ghastly</u>. Didn't say a word.

Two blocks from Mary Beth's house I couldn't hold back. "Okay, Matt," I said. "What's happening?"

Matt stopped walking. "He really thinks I'm a good angel."

"How come?" Nick asked.

"I don't know." There was puzzlement in Matt's voice. "He thinks I'm there to give him a second chance at living."

"I don't get it," Todd said.

Matt said, "He thinks, you know, if he tells me all his bad stuff, he'll get better."

We walked on in silence. Then I said—easy like, "He tell you anything, you know . . . really bad?"

Matt nodded.

"Oooo, that's so cool," Nick crowed, figuring Matt would—as he always did—pass it on. "Like what?"

Instead of answering, Matt remained silent. Finally, he said, "Not good."

"Come on!" we cried. "Tell us!"

"He dared me to forgive him. To give him a second chance."

"Forgive him for what?" I asked.

"All the stuff he's done."

"Like what?"

"He said he was talking to me . . . in confidence."

GUIDED READING

What does Mr. Bataky think will happen if he tells Matt all his bad stuff?

GUIDED READING

What does Mr. Bataky dare Matt to do?

"What's that mean?"

"Angels can't tell secrets."

"You going to believe that?" Todd asked after a bit of silence.

Matt stopped walking again. "But . . . what," he stammered. "What . . . if it's true?"

"What if *what's* true?" I asked.

"What if I'm really good inside?"

"No way," we all assured him.

"But he thinks so," Matt said with real trouble in his voice. "And my father is always saying that too."

"Do *you* think so?" Chuck asked.

Matt got a <u>flushed</u> look in his eyes. Then he said, "If it is true, it'll be the grossest thing ever."

"Hey, maybe it's just a phase," I suggested, hopefully. "You know, something you'll grow out of."

Matt gave a shake to his head that suggested he was really seriously confused.

Anyway, every afternoon that week, Matt went to see Mr. Bataky. Each time we went with him. For support. We felt we owed him that, though really, we were hoping we'd get to hear some of the bad stuff. But I think we were getting more and more upset, too. See, Matt was changing. Each time he came out of the sick man's room, he looked more and more haggard. And silent.

"What did he say this time?" someone would finally ask.

"Really bad," he'd say.

"Worse than before?"

"Much worse."

We'd go on for a bit, not saying anything. Then the pleading would erupt. "Come on! Tell us! What'd he say?"

GUIDED READING

Why won't Matt tell the others about the bad parts of Mr. Bataky's life?

---

words for everyday use

im • plor • ing (im plō′ riṇ) *adj.*, cry or call out earnestly, beg. *The baby begged for her bottle as she gave an <u>imploring</u> cry.*

ghast • ly (gast′ lē) *adj.*, frightening, terrifying. *The girls let out a <u>ghastly</u> scream because they were terrified of the spider.*

flush (flŭsh′) *v.*, blush; be lively. *Her face <u>flushed</u> after she made the winning field goal.* **flushed,** *adj.*

"Can't."

"Why?"

"I told you: He thinks I'm an angel," Matt said and visibly shuddered. "Angels can't tell secrets."

As the week progressed, Matt began to look different from before. He wasn't so grubby. His clothes weren't torn. Things went so fast that by Friday morning, when he came to school, he was actually wearing a tie! Even his hair was cut short and combed. It was awful.

"What's the matter with Matt?" we kept asking one another.

"I think he's beginning to think he really is an angel," was the only explanation I could give.

GUIDED READING

What's the only explanation Marley can give for Matt's change in appearance?

Finally, on Friday afternoon, when Matt came out of Mary Beth's house, he sat on the front steps, utterly beat. By that time he was dressed all in white: white shirt, pale tie, white pants, and even white sneakers. Not one smudge on him. I'm telling you, it was eerie. Nothing missing but wings.

"What's up?" I asked.

"The doctor told Mr. Bataky he's better."

"You cured him!" cried Nick. "Cool! That mean you don't have to visit him again?"

"Right." But Matt just sat there looking as sad as Mary Beth ever did.

"What's the matter?" I asked.

"I've been sitting and listening to that guy talk and talk about all the things he's done. I mean, I used to think I was bad. But, you know what?"

"What?"

"I'm not bad. No way. Not compared to him. I even tried to tell him of some of the things I've done."

"What did he say?"

"He laughed. Said I was only a young angel. Which was the reason I didn't have wings."

GUIDED READING

What does Matt think about how bad he is in comparison to Mr. Bataky?

Matt stared down at the ground for a long time. We waited patiently. Finally he looked up. There were tears trickling down his pale face.

"I have to face it," he said, turning to look at us, his pals, with real grief in his eyes. "The more I heard that stuff Mr. Bataky did, the more I knew that deep down, inside, I'm just a good kid. I mean, what am I going to do? Don't you see, I'm just like my father said. I'm *good*."

GUIDED READING

What does Matt have to face?

You can't believe how miserable he looked. All we could do was sit there and pity him. I mean, just to look at him we knew there weren't going to be any more wicked grins, belches, <u>leers</u>, sly winks, wedgies, or flying boogers.

Life went on, but with Matt going angel on us, our gang couldn't hold together. We were finished. Busted.

So I'm here to tell you, when a guy turns good, hey, it's rough. ■

Respond *to the* SELECTION

If you had been thinking about joining Matt's gang when Matt began to change, how would that have influenced your decision to join or not?

words for everyday use

leer (lēr') *n.*, knowing, wanton look. *The prisoner's <u>leer</u> did not frighten the prison guards.*

About *the* AUTHOR

Avi was born in New York City in 1937 but was raised in Brooklyn. His twin sister gave him his name when they were about a year old. He doesn't give out his real name because "Avi" is the only name he uses. As a child, he struggled with school. In elementary school, he had trouble writing. In high school, he failed all his courses. At that point, his parents put him in a smaller school that focused on reading and writing. Even then, he still needed special tutoring. Despite the struggle, he stuck with writing because he wanted to prove to everyone around him that he could write. It wasn't until he had children that he began to write for young people. He has written all types of books including animal tales, historical fiction, mystery, adventure, and fantasy books. His favorite book out of all he has written is *Ereth's Birthday*. For those people who want to write, he says that "reading is the key to writing. The more you read, the better your writing can be."

Investigate, Inquire, and Imagine

Recall: GATHERING FACTS

1a. Who in the story is the "baddest of the bad"? What kinds of things does he or she do?

2a. What does Rev. Kaizer do when Matt says he doesn't want to go back to Mr. Bataky's?

3a. What nickname does the gang use for Matt? What does Mr. Bataky call Matt?

Interpret: FINDING MEANING

1b. Why do you think the person is behaving this way?

2b. What Rev. Kaizer does may seem a bit unusual for a minister. Why might he have done this?

3b. How are these names alike? What might be important about this?

Analyze: TAKING THINGS APART

4a. What evidence can you find that Matt is not always being bad anymore?

Synthesize: BRINGING THINGS TOGETHER

4b. How do you think Matt will continue to change? Imagine a few possible situations that will help demonstrate your answer.

Evaluate: MAKING JUDGMENTS

5a. To what degree did Mr. Bataky influence Matt? Explain your answer.

Extend: CONNECTING IDEAS

5b. Think of a time when someone caused you to change part of how you think about yourself. How did you feel at the time? How did your behavior change to match your new view of yourself? How do you feel about the experience now?

Understanding Literature

CONFLICT. A **conflict** is a struggle between two people or things in a literary work. A plot is formed around the conflict. A conflict can be internal or external. For example, a struggle that takes place between a character and some outside force—such as another character, society, or nature—is called an **external conflict;** a struggle that takes place within a character is called an **internal conflict.** In "The Goodness of Matt Kaizer," someone besides the main character is struggling with conflict. Mr. Bataky is also struggling with something. What is his struggle, and is it internal or external?

CHARACTER. A **character** is a person (or sometimes an animal) who takes part in the action of a literary work. A one-dimensional character, flat character, or caricature is one who exhibits a single quality, or character trait. A three-dimensional, full, or rounded character is one who seems to have all the complexities of an actual human being. In pairs or small groups, fill in the chart below based on what you've learned about Matt throughout the story. Refer to your lists about Matt made earlier and/or scan the story again.

Graphic Organizer

Matt	Physical Appearance	Clothing	Habits and Behaviors	Thoughts and Feelings
during first half of story:	• tall and thin • •	• • •	• watches MTV and cop shows • tells disgusting stories with buddies	• •
during second half of story:	•	• tie	•	• puzzlement

After completing the chart, discuss in class whether Matt—as a character—has only one quality or character trait, or many varied qualities (some unpredictable, some changing) much as a real person might have.

Writer's Journal

1. Write a brief **note** to a classmate across the aisle that Marley might write to explain how the gang works.
2. Imagine that Mr. Bataky dies. Write a short **remembrance** about him that Matt might write in a sympathy card he's sending to Mary Beth and Mrs. Bataky.
3. Imagine that Matt, in a continuation of this story, is asking his father questions about the goodness in people. Write a short **dialogue** of two of Matt's questions and Rev. Kaizer's responses to each.

Skill Builders

Applied English

WRITING AN AD. Pretend you are Mrs. Bataky and you have just broken your leg in a bad fall. You need to advertise in the local paper for someone to assist you part-time in caring for Mr. Bataky. In as few words as possible, write the ad, being sure to include the following information: description of job, days and hours needed, qualifications desired, and salary.

Collaborative Learning

GROUP DISCUSSION. As young people realize that almost everyone not only notices peer pressure but has to deal with it, they find it much easier to recognize and talk about. In small groups of four or five, discuss what you know about peer pressure. First, come up with a definition of peer pressure that you all can agree on. Then have each member of the group offer a real example of peer pressure that he or she has noticed or heard about. As a group, come up with two strong examples of peer pressure: one that has a negative influence on an individual and another that has a positive influence on an individual. (These last two examples can be real or imaginary.)

Language, Grammar, and Style

LOOKING AT SLANG. Slang is the informal, nonstandard vocabulary peculiar to a particular group. Such vocabulary, often temporary, consists typically of made-up or invented words, existing words that are used in new ways, and words that have been changed or exaggerated. Because slang is colorful and changes over time, it can be interesting to study and compare.

The author uses many slang words in "The Goodness of Matt Kaizer." Some of these words have been listed in the center column of the chart below. Look over these words and fill in their probable meanings. Then fill in the first column with slang that you've heard was popular in the past. You may want to ask your parents, grandparents, and other older people what slang words they used when they were young—and what these words meant! Finally, fill in the last column with slang (and their meanings) you and your friends use today. For fun, make up a few new slang words and their meanings for this column as well. Place a star by your inventions.

Of the slang words used in the past, which are still used today and which are no longer used? Of the slang words used today, which will probably be around for a while and which are being used less often or replaced by new slang? Which of all the slang words on the chart are your favorites?

Slang used in the past		Slang used in the story		Slang used now (and in the future)	
word	meaning	word	meaning	word	meaning
		cool			
		neat			
		sweet			

Prereading

"Eleven" by Sandra Cisneros

Reader's Resource

- **SOCIAL STUDIES CONNECTION.** All over the world, people have songs and traditions honoring the stages of a person's life. In the United States, a birthday is often a time of gift-giving and celebration.

- Birthdays in other cultures usually also involve celebrations, but the rituals may be different. For example, piñatas are a part of most birthday parties in Mexico. In England, cake batter contains symbolic objects. If your piece of cake has a coin, you will supposedly become rich. In China people usually eat noodles for a birthday lunch; in Japan the birthday girl or boy wears all new clothes. In Denmark flags fly in front of a house in which someone is celebrating a birthday, and in the Philippines blinking lights brighten a birthday home. In many different cultures, as young adults reach a certain age, they are called upon to prove that they are developing the strength, knowledge, or independence needed in adulthood.

- The preteen and teenage years can be the most challenging years of all in a person's life. Like the narrator in "Eleven," young people begin to realize that the world is not always as simple or fair as it might have seemed. A person might blow out the candles of a birthday cake and know that he or she is another year older but not feel more mature. With each year, and with each birthday, a person is expected to grow farther from childhood and closer to adulthood. Growing up is a long but exciting process.

Reader's Journal

When do you feel most grown up and able to handle anything? When do you feel young and unsure of yourself?

Reader's TOOLBOX

DESCRIPTION. Description is a type of writing that portrays a character, object, or scene. Descriptions make use of sensory details—words and phrases that describe how things look, sound, smell, taste, or feel. Effective descriptions contain precise—or concrete—nouns, verbs, adverbs, and adjectives. Descriptive writing can be found in short stories, poems, essays, and other works. Note places in "Eleven" where the author uses descriptive writing to give the reader a better sense of how things look, sound, smell, taste, or feel.

SIMILE. A **simile** is a comparison using *like* or *as*. Sandra Cisneros uses a variety of similes in "Eleven." One example is "the way you grow old is kind of like an onion." In this simile, *the way you grow old* is compared to *an onion. Like* is the word that links the two parts of the simile. As you read "Eleven," look for more examples of similes.

Portrait of Virginia, 1925. Frida Kahlo. Private Collection.

Eleven

Sandra Cisneros

What they don't understand about birthdays and what they never tell you is that when you're eleven, you're also ten, and nine, and eight, and seven, and six, and five, and four, and three, and two, and one. And when you wake up on your eleventh birthday, you expect to feel eleven, but you don't. You open your eyes and everything's just like yesterday, only it's today. And you don't feel eleven at all. You feel like you're still ten. And you are—underneath the year that makes you eleven.

Like some days you might say something stupid, and that's the part of you that's still ten. Or maybe some days you might need to sit on your mama's lap because you're scared, and that's the part of you that's five. And maybe one day when you're all grown up, maybe you will need to cry like if you're three, and that's OK. That's what I tell Mama when she's sad and needs to cry. Maybe she's feeling three.

Because the way you grow old is kind of like an onion or like the rings inside a tree trunk or like my little wooden dolls that fit one inside the other, each year inside the next one. That's how being eleven years old is.

You don't feel eleven. Not right away. It takes a few days, weeks even, sometimes even months before you say Eleven when they ask you. And you don't feel smart eleven, not until you're almost twelve. That's the way it is.

Only today I wish I didn't have only eleven years rattling inside me like pennies in a tin Band-Aid box. Today I wish I was one hundred and two instead of eleven because if I was one hundred and two, I'd have known what to say when Mrs. Price put the

red sweater on my desk. I would've known how to tell her it wasn't mine instead of just sitting there with that look on my face and nothing coming out of my mouth.

"Whose is this?" Mrs. Price says, and she holds the red sweater up in the air for all the class to see. "Whose? It's been sitting in the coatroom for a month."

"Not mine," says everybody. "Not me."

"It has to belong to somebody," Mrs. Price keeps saying, but nobody can remember. It's an ugly sweater with red plastic buttons and a collar and sleeves all stretched out like you could use it for a jump rope. It's maybe a thousand years old, and even if it belonged to me, I wouldn't say so.

Maybe because I'm skinny, maybe because she doesn't like me, that stupid Sylvia Saldívar says, "I think it belongs to Rachel." An ugly sweater like that, all raggedy and old, but Mrs. Price believes her. Mrs. Price takes the sweater and puts it right on my desk, but when I open my mouth, nothing comes out.

"That's not, I don't, you're not . . . Not mine," I finally say in a little voice that was maybe me when I was four.

"Of course it's yours," Mrs. Price says. "I remember you wearing it once." Because she's older and the teacher, she's right and I'm not.

Not mine, not mine, not mine, but Mrs. Price is already turning to page thirty-two, and math problem number four. I don't know why, but all of a sudden I'm feeling sick inside, like the part of me that's three wants to come out of my eyes, only I squeeze them shut tight and bite down on my teeth real hard and try to remember today I am eleven, eleven. Mama is making a cake for me for tonight, and when Papa comes home, everybody will sing Happy birthday, happy birthday to you.

GUIDED READING
What does Rachel try to remember?

But when the sick feeling goes away and I open my eyes, the red sweater's still sitting there like a big red mountain. I move the red sweater to the corner of my desk with my ruler. I move my pencil and books and eraser as far from it as possible. I even move my chair a little to the right. Not mine, not mine, not mine.

In my head I'm thinking how long till lunchtime, how long till I can take the red sweater and throw it over the schoolyard fence, or leave it hanging on a parking meter, or bunch it up into a little ball and toss it in the alley. Except when math period ends, Mrs. Price says loud and in front of everybody, "Now, Rachel, that's enough," because she sees I've shoved the red sweater to the tippy-tip corner of my desk and it's hanging all over the edge like a waterfall, but I don't care.

"Rachel," Mrs. Price says. She says it like she's getting mad. "You put that sweater on right now and no more nonsense."

"But it's not—"

"Now!" Mrs. Price says.

GUIDED READING
What does Mrs. Price say in front of the whole class?

This is when I wish I wasn't eleven, because all the years inside of me—ten, nine, eight, seven, six, five, four, three, two, and one—are pushing at the back of my eyes when I put one arm through one sleeve of the sweater that smells like cottage cheese, and then the other arm through the other and stand there with my arms apart like if the sweater hurts me and it does, all itchy and full of germs that aren't even mine.

That's when everything I've been holding in since this morning, since when Mrs. Price put the sweater on my desk, finally lets go, and all of a sudden I'm crying in front of everybody. I wish I was invisible, but I'm not. I'm eleven and it's my birthday today and I'm crying like I'm three in front of everybody. I put my head down on the desk and bury my face in my stupid clown-sweater arms. My face all hot and spit coming out of my mouth because I can't stop the little animal noises from coming out of me, until there aren't any more tears left in my eyes, and it's just my body shaking like when you have the hiccups, and my whole head hurts like when you drink milk too fast.

GUIDED READING
Why does Rachel start crying?

But the worst part is right before the bell rings for lunch. That stupid Phyllis Lopez, who is even dumber than Sylvia Saldívar, says she remembers the red sweater is hers! I take it off right away and give it to her, only Mrs. Price pretends like everything's OK.

Today I'm eleven.

GUIDED READING
What does Phyllis Lopez remember? What does Mrs. Price pretend?

There's a cake Mama's making for tonight, and when Papa comes home from work, we'll eat it. There'll be candles and presents, and everybody will sing Happy birthday, happy birthday to you, Rachel, only it's too late.

I'm eleven today. I'm eleven, ten, nine, eight, seven, six, five, four, three, two, and one, but I wish I was one hundred and two. I wish I was anything but eleven, because I want today to be far away already, far away like a runaway balloon, like a tiny o in the sky, so tiny-tiny you have to close your eyes to see it. ■

Describe your last birthday and how you felt about it.

About *the* AUTHOR

Sandra Cisneros (b.1954), a poet and novelist born in Chicago, is from a large Mexican-American family that includes her mother, her father, and six brothers. Cisneros has worked as a teacher, a college recruiter, and an arts administrator. She has published a volume of poetry and a collection of fictional pieces called *The House on Mango Street,* about a girl named Esperanza growing up in the Hispanic quarter of Chicago. "Eleven" is taken from her collection of short stories, *Woman Hollering Creek.*

Investigate, Inquire, and Imagine

Recall: GATHERING FACTS

1a. According to Rachel, what don't people understand about birthdays?

2a. What does Mrs. Price hold up for the class to see? What does she ask the class? How does the class respond?

3a. What does Sylvia Saldívar say to Mrs. Price? How do Rachel and Mrs. Price respond?

4a. What does Mrs. Price tell Rachel to do with the sweater?

Interpret: FINDING MEANING

1b. Does Rachel feel older when she wakes up on her birthday? Why, or why not?

2b. Why does Rachel say "even if it belonged to me, I wouldn't say so"?

3b. What does Rachel do when the sweater is placed on her desk? What does she try to remember to feel better?

4b. Why does Rachel obey Mrs. Price?

Analyze: TAKING THINGS APART

5a. Identify the words and actions of Mrs. Price that affect Rachel's day.

Synthesize: BRINGING THINGS TOGETHER

5b. Why might Mrs. Price do and say these things? Why does Rachel react the way she does?

Perspective: LOOKING AT OTHER VIEWS

6a. What do you think Rachel does after school on this day? What do you think she tells her parents about the day? How do you think her mood might change, if at all?

Empathy: SEEING FROM INSIDE

6b. If you had been in Rachel's position, what would you have done? How would you have acted if you were Mrs. Price?

Understanding *Literature*

DESCRIPTION. Description is a type of writing that portrays a character, object, or scene. Descriptions make use of sensory details—words and phrases that describe how things look, sound, smell, taste, or feel. What objects or actions in "Eleven" are described in detail? How do those descriptions contribute to the story?

SIMILE. A **simile** is a comparison using *like* or *as.* Find examples of simile in "Eleven" and note them in a graphic organizer like the one that follows.

Graphic Organizer

the way you grow old — like → an onion

Writer's Journal

1. Imagine you are an advice columnist and that Rachel writes to you about the day of her eleventh birthday and about how she wishes she were older. Write a **letter of advice** back to her, expressing your thoughts.

2. Write three **similes** that compare items you own or see every day with other things.

3. Write a detailed **description** of a room in your home. Include details that appeal to all of the senses, revealing how things in the room look, sound, feel, smell, and taste.

Skill Builders

Collaborative Learning
GROUP DISCUSSION. Form small groups to discuss how you imagine your life will be in ten years, in 20 years, and in 50 years. What about your lives will change? What will remain the same? Make sure everyone in your group has a chance to contribute to the discussion.

Applied English & Media Literacy
MAKING A POSTER. In "Eleven," Mrs. Price tries to find the owner of a lost sweater. One good way to try to locate the owners of missing valuables, articles of clothing, pets, or other items is to make and post "found" posters. Read the Language Arts Survey 6.11, "Displaying Effective Visual Information." Then create an effective "found" poster that has the ability to catch the eye of passersby. Include all important information describing what was lost and how a person can locate it if he or she is the owner.

Vocabulary
USING A THESAURUS. Review the Language Arts Survey 5.21. Next, using a thesaurus, find as many synonyms for the verb *age* as you can. Then write a paragraph explaining what *age* or *aging* means to you.

Reader's *Journal*

List the people who have been important teachers in your life. These people might be friends, family members, or school teachers. What have you learned about yourself and the world from these people?

Reader's TOOLBOX

PERSONAL ESSAY. An **essay** is a short nonfiction work that expresses a writer's thoughts about a single subject. A **personal essay** is one that relates to the life of the writer. It is written from the author's point of view using the pronouns *I* and *me*. A good essay develops a single idea, or thesis, and is organized into an introduction, a body, and a conclusion. As you read "Why?," decide what the topic of the essay is and then identify the author's thesis, or idea about that topic.

Prereading

"Why?"
by Anne Frank

Reader's Resource

- **HISTORY CONNECTION.** Anne Frank was a Jewish German teenager who lived and wrote during a dark period in the history of Europe. The Nazi party, led by Adolf Hitler, rose to power in Germany in 1933. Hitler promised jobs and prosperity for a troubled Germany, but he was a ruthless and cruel dictator. He blamed Germany's problems on the Jews, and his mission was to destroy the Jewish population. Frank was born in Germany in 1929. Her family moved to Holland in 1933 when it became clear to her parents that, as German Jews, their lives would be in danger. In 1940, German soldiers invaded Holland, bringing the anti-Jewish laws that already existed in Germany. Jews were forced to wear yellow stars to identify themselves as Jews, and they were no longer allowed to ride bikes, ride trains, or drive. They were ordered indoors by eight o'clock in the evening, and Jewish children were forbidden to attend school with other children. Jews were not allowed to hold certain jobs, so many of them could no longer make a living. In addition to being forced to live by these rules, Jewish men, women, and children were brought to prison-like work camps called concentration camps.

- Frank's older sister, Margot, was ordered to be sent to a concentration camp. To avoid separating, the Frank family moved with another family to some hidden rooms in an office building. These rooms became known as "the secret annex." After two years in hiding, the group was discovered by Hitler's secret police. Anne Frank, her mother, and her sister died of disease in the Nazi camps. Today, Frank is known all over the world for her diary, which tells of the two years she spent in hiding. Her diary and her other writings were found in the secret annex by friends who had been helping to hide the family. They were later given to Anne's father, the only member of the family to survive. He published them so that his family would be remembered. Since then, Anne Frank's writings have been published in many languages, inspiring courage around the world.

1950 Winter

Why?

ANNE FRANK

v.l.n.r.

Martha v.d. Berg — juf.
Godron — Anne — Rela
Salomon.

The little word "why" has been a very strong thing with me ever since I was a tiny little girl and couldn't even speak properly. It is a well-known fact that little children ask questions about everything because they are unfamiliar with everything. This was very much the case with me, but even when I grew older I couldn't wait to ask all kinds of questions, whether they could be answered or not. This is not so terrible in itself and I must say that my parents tried to answer every one of my questions very patiently, until . . . I began even badgering strangers, and they generally can't stand "children's endless questions." I must admit that this can be very tiresome, but I console myself with the idea that there is a saying that "you must ask in order to know," which couldn't be completely true, otherwise I'd be a professor by now.

When I grew older, I realized that it is not possible to ask every kind of question to everyone and that there are many "why's" that cannot be answered. It then followed from that that I tried to help myself by starting to think out these questions on my own. So I came to the important discovery that questions which one mustn't ask can be solved by oneself. Therefore, the little word "why"

GUIDED READING
What was true of Anne Frank ever since she was a little girl?

taught me not only to ask but to think.

Now as to the second part of the word "why." How would it be if everyone who did anything asked himself first, "Why?" I think they would then become more honest and much, much better people. For the best way to become honest and good is to keep examining oneself without stopping. I can imagine that the last thing people like to do is to confess to themselves their faults and their bad side (which everybody has). This is the case with children as well as grownups—in that respect I don't see any difference. Most people think parents should try to educate their children and see to it themselves that their characters develop as well as possible. This is certainly untrue. Children ought to educate themselves from their earliest youth and must try to show real character by themselves. Many will think this is crazy, but it isn't. Even a very small child is a little personality and has a conscience and should be brought up by being treated in this way, so that it will feel that its own conscience is punishing it in the harshest way possible. When children reach the age of fourteen or fifteen, every punishment is

GUIDED READING
What makes Frank believe that a person should ask "Why?" before doing something?

GUIDED READING
What does Frank believe that everyone has?

words for everyday use

bad • ger (baj' ər) v., bother. "If you badger mom, she'll never say yes," said Raoul to his whining little brother.

char • ac • ter (kar' ək tər) n., person's behavior, thoughts, and personality. Michael had a difficult life as a child, but he developed a strong character as a result of it.

con • science (kän' shəns) n., thoughts and feelings about right and wrong. Sabrina's conscience told her that it was wrong to cheat even though she wanted to do well on the test.

ridiculous. Such a child knows very well that no one, not even its own parents, can get anywhere with punishments and spankings. By arguing <u>reasonably</u> and by showing the child the mistakes it is making, one would get much better results than by strong punishments.

GUIDED READING

Why might reasons be more effective than punishments?

But here, I don't want to sound <u>pedantic</u>, but only to say that in the life of every child and every man, the little word "why" plays a big part, and rightly so. The saying, "You must ask in order to know," is true in so far as it leads to thinking about things, and by thinking nobody can ever get worse but will only get better. ■

GUIDED READING

What does Anne believe would make anyone better?

Respond *to the* SELECTION

How does Anne Frank believe that children should be raised? Do you agree? Why, or why not?

About *the* AUTHOR

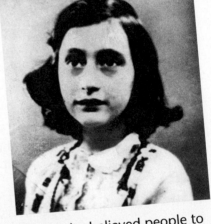

Anne Frank (1929–1945) was born in Frankfurt, Germany. Her middle-class family included a mother, a father, and an older sister. Frank received her diary as a thirteenth birthday present less than a month before the Frank family went into hiding. Frank loved to read and write, and she kept a careful record of her family's ordeal. In her diary she recorded her ideas about life and the books she read, as well as her hopes for the future. In addition to her diary entries, she wrote stories and essays including the essay "Why?" People who read Frank's work are often amazed by the thoughtfulness and strong spirit she had even after living for two years in hiding. A few weeks before the family's discovery by the Nazis, Anne wrote in her diary that she could not give up hope because she believed people to be "good at heart." She also wrote that she was anxious to go out into the world again and make a difference. Frank, however, died at Bergen-Belsen, a concentration camp, just three months before her sixteenth birthday.

words for everyday use

rea • son • a • ble (rē′ zən ə bəl) *adj.*, agreeable; logical. *When he spoke in a <u>reasonable</u> way and told me what had upset him, I understood.* **reasonably**, *adj.*

pe • dan • tic (ped an′ tik) *adj.*, paying too much attention to unimportant details. *Mr. Robinson thought it was <u>pedantic</u> to require students to memorize and recite the Pledge of Allegiance without discussing what it means.*

Investigate, Inquire, and Imagine

Recall: GATHERING FACTS

1a. What was a "very strong thing" with Frank ever since she was a little girl? What does she say is a "well-known fact"?

2a. What did Frank realize about questions as she got older? What discovery did Frank make about questions that she did not feel she could ask or that she did not believe others could answer?

3a. According to Frank, what must a person ask of himself or herself before doing anything?

4a. According to Frank, what should children do from their earliest youth? What does even a small child have?

Interpret: FINDING MEANING

1b. Why do children need to ask questions?

2b. What valuable skill did Frank learn by trying to answer her own questions?

3b. Why is it important for people to use this type of questioning?

4b. What does Frank believe should be encouraged and developed in children?

Analyze: TAKING THINGS APART

5a. What different points does Frank make about the word "why"? What different points does she make about asking questions?

Synthesize: BRINGING THINGS TOGETHER

5b. How can asking "why" and thinking things through for yourself make you a better person? How can it help to develop your conscience?

Evaluate: MAKING JUDGMENTS

6a. Do you agree with Frank's statements about asking questions and learning? Why, or why not?

Extend: CONNECTING IDEAS

6b. Think of a time in your life when you learned by asking questions. What did you learn? How might you learn something new today by asking questions?

Understanding Literature

PERSONAL ESSAY. An **essay** is a short nonfiction work that expresses a writer's thoughts about a single subject. A **personal essay** is one that relates to the life of the writer. It is written from the author's point of view using the pronouns *I* and *me*. How do you know that Frank's essay is a personal essay? How does she relate her topic to her life?

Graphic Organizer

Use a graphic organizer like this one to examine your thoughts about this essay.

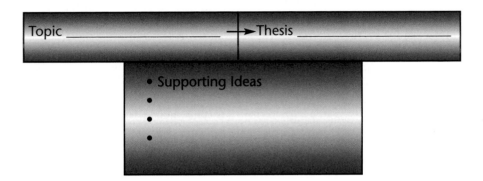

Topic _____ → Thesis _____

- Supporting Ideas
-
-
-

Writer's Journal

1. Write a **topic sentence** that you could use for a personal essay. Then write a **list of questions** that your essay could answer or explore.

2. Write a **letter** to Anne Frank, telling her your thoughts about her essay and about asking questions.

3. Write **song lyrics** that use the word *why*.

Skill Builders

Applied English
RESPONDING TO INTERVIEW QUESTIONS. Imagine that you are interviewing for the position of tour guide for a student exchange program. Review the Language Arts Survey 4.1, "Verbal and Nonverbal Communication," and 4.7, "Communicating with Another Person." Then answer in writing the following questions. After you have finished, get together with a partner to practice responding orally to the questions.

1. Why did you respond to our job advertisement?
2. Why are you interested in this student exchange program?
3. Why do you feel you are the right person for the position?
4. Are you planning to pursue a career in tourism? Why, or why not?
5. In what field do you intend to pursue your education? Why?
6. Ask the interviewer three "why" questions about the organization or position.

Language, Grammar, and Style

PRONOUNS. A **pronoun** is a word used in place of a noun. Two types of pronouns in the English language are the personal pronoun and the interrogative pronoun. Read the Language Arts Survey 3.41, "Using *I* and *Me*," and 3.52, "Types of Pronouns." Then underline the pronouns in each of the following sentences.

1. The little word "why" has been a very strong thing with me ever since I was a tiny little girl and couldn't even speak properly.
2. It is a well-known fact that little children ask questions about everything because they are unfamiliar with everything.
3. This was very much the case with me, but even when I grew older I couldn't wait to ask all kinds of questions, whether they could be answered or not.
4. This is not so terrible in itself and I must say that my parents tried to answer every one of my questions very patiently.
5. I console myself with the idea that there is a saying that says, "you must ask in order to know," which couldn't be completely true, otherwise I'd be a professor by now.
6. How would it be if everyone who did anything asked himself first, "Why?"
7. I can imagine that the last thing people like to do is to confess to themselves their faults and their bad side (which everybody has).
8. Most people think parents should try to educate their children and see to it themselves that their characters develop as well as possible.
9. By arguing reasonably and by showing the child the mistakes it is making, one would get much better results than by strong punishments.
10. The saying "you must ask in order to know," is true in so far as it leads to thinking about things, and by thinking nobody can ever get worse but will only get better.

Collaborative Learning

DEVELOPING A PLOT. Form a small group. Together, brainstorm and discuss ideas for a story that demonstrates how asking questions enables a character (or characters) to become a better person. After you have developed a basic plot, begin writing the story down. Elect one person to type or print the story. Working together as a group, fill in the details as you work to get the story written. To help you get started, see the Language Arts Survey 2.9, "Brainstorming."

"TA-NA-E-KA"

by Mary Whitebird

Reader's TOOLBOX

DIALOGUE. Dialogue is conversation involving two or more people or characters. In fiction, dialogue is enclosed in quotation marks (" "). Through dialogue, a reader learns a lot about the characters. As you read "Ta-Na-E-Ka," closely examine the dialogue to see what it reveals about the main characters and their beliefs.

PLOT. A **plot** is a series of events related to a central conflict, or struggle. A plot usually involves the introduction of a conflict, its development, and its eventual resolution. As you read, keep track of the main events that happen in this story by recording them in the following graphic organizer.

Graphic *Organizer*

EVENTS THAT OCCUR IN "TA-NA-E-KA"

EARLY EVENTS:	The narrator is having nightmares about having to participate in Ta-Na-E-Ka.
MIDDLE EVENTS:	
MID-to-LATE EVENTS:	

Reader's *Journal*

What do you think about the traditions your family observes?

Reader's Resource

- This story features a Kaw Indian girl who, by following her own instincts as well as the directions of her grandfather, manages to lessen the discomforts usually associated with Ta-Na-E-Ka— a rite of passage for boys and girls moving into adulthood.

- **SOCIAL STUDIES CONNECTION.** Rites of passage, which take place in all societies, usually involve ritual activities and teachings designed to prepare young people for new roles. Rites of passage also reaffirm and honor the values of a society.

- **AMERICAN HISTORY CONNECTION.** The Kaw, also known as the Kansa Indians, are Native Americans who speak a dialect of the Dakota, or Sioux, language. The group originally lived along the lower Kansas River. The Kaw obtained social prestige and honor only in combat, and their chiefs were chosen for bravery and wisdom. By 1840 the lands of the Kaw had been acquired by the U.S. government. In 1846 the Kaw were moved to a reservation at Council Grove in Kansas. In 1873 the tribe was moved once more, this time to the so-called Indian Territory within the present borders of Oklahoma, where they have since remained. Charles Curtis was a celebrated tribal member who served as vice president of the United States under President Herbert Hoover.

TA-NA-E-KA

Mary Whitebird

As my birthday drew closer, I had awful nightmares about it. I was reaching the age at which all Kaw Indians had to participate in Ta-Na-E-Ka. Well, not all Kaws. Many of the younger families on the reservation were beginning to give up the old customs. But my grandfather, Amos Deer Leg, was devoted to tradition. He still wore handmade beaded moccasins instead of shoes, and kept his iron gray hair in tight braids. He could speak English, but he spoke it only with white men. With his family he used a Sioux dialect.

Rustic Landscape, 1927. Carlo Carra. Private Collection.

Grandfather was one of the last living Indians (he died in 1953 when he was eighty-one) who actually fought against the U.S. Cavalry.[1] Not only did he fight, he was wounded in a skirmish at Rose Creek—a famous encounter in which the celebrated Kaw chief Flat Nose lost his life. At the time, my grandfather was only eleven years old.

Eleven was a magic word among the Kaws. It was the time of Ta-Na-E-Ka, the "flowering of adulthood." It was the age, my grandfather informed us hundreds of times, "when a boy could prove himself to be a warrior and a girl took the first steps to womanhood."

GUIDED READING

Why was eleven a magic word among the Kaws?

"I don't want to be a warrior," my cousin, Roger Deer Leg, confided to me. "I'm going to become an accountant."

"None of the other tribes make girls go through the endurance ritual," I complained to my mother.

"It won't be as bad as you think, Mary," my mother said, ignoring my protests. "Once you've gone through it, you'll certainly never forget it. You'll be proud."

I even complained to my teacher, Mrs. Richardson, feeling that, as a white woman, she would side with me.

She didn't. "All of us have rituals of one kind or another," Mrs. Richardson said. "And look at it this way: how many girls have the opportunity to compete on equal terms with boys? Don't look down on your heritage."

GUIDED READING

How did Mrs. Richardson suggest looking at Ta-Na-E-Ka?

Heritage, indeed! I had no intention of living on a reservation for the rest of my life. I was a good student. I loved school. My fantasies were about knights in armor and fair ladies in flowing gowns being saved from dragons. It never once occurred to me that being Indian was exciting.

But I've always thought that the Kaw were the originators of the women's liberation movement.[2] No other Indian tribe—and I've spent half a lifetime researching the subject—treated women more "equally" than the Kaw. Unlike most of the subtribes of the Sioux Nation, the Kaw allowed men and women to eat together. And hundreds of years before we were "acculturated,"[3] a Kaw woman had the right to refuse a prospective husband even if her father arranged the match.

The wisest women (generally wisdom was equated with age) often sat in tribal councils. Furthermore, most Kaw legends revolve around "Good Woman," a kind of supersquaw, a Joan of Arc[4] of the high plains. Good Woman led Kaw warriors into battle after battle from which they always seemed to emerge victorious.

GUIDED READING

What do most Kaw legends revolve around?

And girls as well as boys were required to undergo Ta-Na-E-Ka.

The actual ceremony varied from tribe to tribe, but since the

---

1. **U.S. Cavalry.** Early mounted troops
2. **women's liberation movement.** A movement for political, social, and educational equality of women with men. Its roots in America date back to 1848, but women were not granted equal rights until the 1920s.
3. **acculturated.** Adapting to or borrowing traits from another culture
4. **Joan of Arc.** French saint and national heroine who was ultimately burned at the stake for standing up for her beliefs

---

words for everyday use

skir • mish (skər' mish) n., minor fight in war. *My brother got hurt in a skirmish during WWII.*

her • i • tage (her' ə tij) n., something that is passed on to an heir; tradition. *Wearing our hair in braids is a tradition in my heritage.*

equate (ē kwāt') v., make equal. *People sometimes equate a doctor with a healer.*

Indians' life on the plains was dedicated to survival, Ta-Na-E-Ka was a test of survival.

"Endurance is the loftiest <u>virtue</u> of the Indian," my grandfather explained. "To survive, we must endure. When I was a boy, Ta-Na-E-Ka was more than the mere symbol it is now. We were painted white with the juice of a <u>sacred</u> herb and sent naked into the wilderness without so much as a knife. We couldn't return until the white had worn off. It wouldn't wash off. It took almost eighteen days, and during that time we had to stay alive, trapping food, eating insects and roots and berries, and watching out for enemies. And we did have enemies—both the white soldiers and the Omaha[5] warriors, who were always trying to capture Kaw boys and girls undergoing their endurance test. It was an exciting time."

"What happened if you couldn't make it?" Roger asked. He was born only three days after I was, and we were being trained for Ta-Na-E-Ka together. I was happy to know he was frightened too.

"Many didn't return," Grandfather said. "Only the strongest and <u>shrewdest</u>. Mothers were

GUIDED READING

How long was Ta-Na-E-Ka in Grandfather's boyhood, and what had to be done?

GUIDED READING

When Grandfather was a boy, which participants returned?

not allowed to weep over those who didn't return. If a Kaw couldn't survive, he or she wasn't worth weeping over. It was our way."

"What a lot of hooey," Roger whispered. "I'd give anything to get out of it."

"I don't see how we have any choice," I replied.

Roger gave my arm a little squeeze. "Well, it's only five days."

Five days! Maybe it was better than being painted white and sent out naked for eighteen days. But not much better.

GUIDED READING

How long was Ta-Na-E-Ka for Mary and Roger, and what had to be done?

We were to be sent, barefoot and in bathing suits, into the woods. Even our very traditional parents put their foot down when Grandfather suggested we go naked. For five days we'd have to live off the land, keeping warm as best we could, getting food where we could. It was May, but on the northernmost reaches of the Missouri River the days were still chilly and the nights were fiercely cold.

Grandfather was in charge of the month's training for Ta-Na-E-Ka. One day he caught a grasshopper and demonstrated how to pull its legs and wings off in one flick of the fingers and how to swallow it.

I felt sick, and Roger turned green. "It's a darn good thing it's 1947," I told Roger teasingly. "You'd make a terrible warrior." Roger just grimaced.

I knew one thing. This particular Kaw Indian girl wasn't going to swallow a grasshopper, no matter how hungry she got. And then I had an idea. Why hadn't I thought

---

5. **Omaha.** North American Plains Indians who migrated from the Ohio valley to the Missouri and Mississippi River valleys and finally settled in Iowa

---

words for everyday use

vir • tue (vər' chü) *n.,* particular strength or moral excellence. *A <u>virtue</u> my dad has is honesty, because he never lies.*

sa • cred (sā' krəd) *adj.,* highly valued, important. *Saffron is a <u>sacred</u> type of spice and it is highly valued.*

shrewd (shrüd') *adj.,* clever, having a high degree of common sense. *Jill, who solved the hardest riddle, is one of the <u>shrewdest</u> people I know.*

of it before? It would have saved nights of bad dreams about squooshy grasshoppers.

I headed straight for my teacher's house. "Mrs. Richardson," I said, "would you lend me five dollars?"

"Five dollars!" she exclaimed. "What for?"

"You remember the ceremony I talked about?"

"Ta-Na-E-Ka. Of course. Your parents have written me and asked me to excuse you from school so you can participate in it."

"Well, I need some things for the ceremony," I replied, in a half-truth. "I don't want to ask my parents for the money."

GUIDED READING

How does Mary reply when Mrs. Richardson asks what she needs the five dollars for?

"It's not a crime to borrow money, Mary. But how can you pay it back?"

"I'll baby-sit for you ten times."

"That's more than fair," she said, going to her purse and handing me a crisp new five-dollar bill. I'd never had that much money at once.

"I'm happy to know the money's going to be put to a good use," Mrs. Richardson said.

A few days later, the ritual began with a long speech from my grandfather about how we had reached the age of decision, how we now had to <u>fend</u> for ourselves and prove that we could survive the most horrendous of <u>ordeals</u>. All the friends and relatives who had gathered at our house for dinner made jokes about their own Ta-Na-E-Ka experiences. They all advised us to fill up now, since for the next five days we'd be gorging ourselves on crickets. Neither Roger nor I was very hungry. "I'll probably laugh about this when I'm an accountant," Roger said, trembling.

"Are you trembling?" I asked.

"What do you think?"

"I'm happy to know boys tremble too," I said.

At six the next morning we kissed our parents and went off to the woods. "Which side do you want?" Roger asked. According to the rules, Roger and I would stake out "territories" in separate areas of the woods, and we weren't to communicate during the entire ordeal.

GUIDED READING

What couldn't Roger and Mary do during their Ta-Na-E-Ka?

"I'll go toward the river, if it's okay with you," I said.

"Sure," Roger answered. "What difference does it make?"

To me, it made a lot of difference. There was a marina a few miles up the river and there were boats moored there. At least, I hoped so. I

ALL OF A SUDDEN I REALIZED I WAS NO LONGER FRIGHTENED. TA-NA-E-KA MIGHT BE MORE FUN THAN I'D ANTICIPATED.

figured that a boat was a better place to sleep than under a pile of leaves.

"Why do you keep holding your head?" Roger asked.

"Oh, nothing. Just nervous," I told him. Actually, I was afraid I'd

---

words for everyday use

fend (fend) v., provide for, support. *Now that the baby bird can fly, it will have to <u>fend</u> for itself.*

or • deal (or dēl') n., severe test or trial. *Training camp is one of many <u>ordeals</u> a soldier must go through to become an officer.*

lose the five-dollar bill, which I had tucked into my hair with a bobby pin. As we came to a fork in the trail, Roger shook my hand.

"Good luck, Mary."

"*N'ko-n'ta*," I said. It was the Kaw word for courage.

The sun was shining and it was warm, but my bare feet began to hurt immediately. I spied one of the berry bushes Grandfather had told us about. "You're lucky," he had said. "The berries are ripe in the spring, and they are delicious and nourishing." They were orange and fat and I popped one into my mouth.

Argh! I spat it out. It was awful and bitter, and even grasshoppers were probably better tasting, although I never intended to find out.

I sat down to rest my feet. A rabbit hopped out from under the berry bush. He nuzzled the berry I'd spat out and ate it. He picked another one and ate that too. He liked them. He looked at me, twitching his nose. I watched a redheaded woodpecker bore into an elm tree and I caught a glimpse of a civet cat[6] waddling through some twigs. All of a sudden I realized I was no longer frightened. Ta-Na-E-Ka might be more fun than I'd <u>anticipated</u>. I got up and headed toward the marina.

> **GUIDED READING**
>
> What did Mary realize as she watched a rabbit, a redheaded woodpecker, and a civet cat?

"Not one boat," I said to myself <u>dejectedly</u>. But the restaurant on the shore, "Ernie's Riverside," was open. I walked in, feeling silly in my bathing suit. The man at the counter was big and tough-looking. He wore a sweat shirt with the words "Fort Sheridan, 1944," and he had only three fingers on one of his hands. He asked me what I wanted.

"A hamburger and a milk shake," I said, holding the five-dollar bill in my hand so he'd know I had money.

"That's a pretty heavy breakfast, honey," he murmured.

"That's what I always have for breakfast," I lied.

"Forty-five cents," he said, bringing me the food. (Back in 1947, hamburgers were twenty-five cents and milk shakes were twenty cents.) "Delicious," I thought. "Better'n grasshoppers—and Grandfather never once mentioned that I couldn't eat hamburgers."

While I was eating, I had a grand idea. Why not sleep in the restaurant? I went to the ladies' room and made sure the window was unlocked. Then I went back outside and played along the riverbank, watching the water birds and trying to identify each one. I planned to look for a beaver dam the next day.

> **GUIDED READING**
>
> Why did Mary make sure the ladies' room window was unlocked?

The restaurant closed at sunset, and I watched the three-fingered man drive away. Then I climbed in the unlocked window. There was a night light on, so I didn't turn on any lights. But there was a radio on the

---

6. **civet cat.** Small spotted skunk of western North America

words for everyday use

an • tic • i • pate (an ti' sə pāt) *v.*, look forward to, expect. *I've <u>anticipated</u> the coming of my birthday, and it's finally here.*

de • ject • ed (di jek' təd) *adj.*, be cast down in spirits, depressed. *Brett looked at the crowd of <u>dejected</u> people after he missed the touchdown pass.* **dejectedly,** *adv.*

bet you never ate one of those rotten berries yourself."

Grandfather laughed! He laughed aloud! My mother and father and aunt and uncle were all dumbfounded. Grandfather never laughed. Never.

"Those berries—they are terrible," Grandfather admitted. "I could never swallow them. I found a dead deer on the first day of my Ta-Na-E-Ka—shot by a soldier, probably—and he kept my belly full for the entire period of the test!"

Grandfather stopped laughing. "We should send you out again," he said.

I looked at Roger. "You're pretty smart, Mary," Roger groaned. "I'd never have thought of what you did."

"Accountants just have to be good at arithmetic," I said comfortingly. "I'm terrible at arithmetic."

Roger tried to smile, but couldn't. My grandfather called me to him. "You should have done what your cousin did. But I think you are more alert to what is happening to our people today than we are. I think you would have passed the test under any circumstances, in any time. Somehow, you know how to exist in a world that wasn't made for Indians. I don't think you're going to have any trouble surviving."

Grandfather wasn't entirely right. But I'll tell about that another time. ■

GUIDED READING

What does Grandfather think about Mary's Ta-Na-E-Ka and her chances for surviving?

Respond *to the* SELECTION

Imagine you participated in a rite of passage like Ta-Na-E-Ka when you turned eleven, and describe what would have happened.

Investigate, Inquire, and Imagine

Recall: GATHERING FACTS

1a. What are Mary's fantasies about?

2a. What is Mary's reaction when Ernie says Ta-Na-E-Ka is a "pretty silly thing to do to a kid"?

3a. How did Grandfather easily endure the entire period of his Ta-Na-E-Ka test?

→ **Interpret:** FINDING MEANING

1b. What is she probably looking for in these fantasies?

2b. Why does she react this way when she herself had be thinking the same thing for months?

3b. What is similar about Mary's and Grandfather's experiences of Ta-Na-E-Ka?

Analyze: TAKING THINGS APART

4a. Examine the events in the story that show Mary's careful honesty about money. Then examine the events that show her being dishonest about other matters—for example, her half-truths, lies, and sneaking actions. Rank the seriousness of her deceptions on a scale of one (least serious) to ten (most serious).

→ **Synthesize:** BRINGING THINGS TOGETHER

4b. What are the main causes for Mary's dishonest behavior? Why doesn't she feel guilty or uncomfortable about it?

Evaluate: MAKING JUDGMENTS

5a. How effective is the author in creating a believable plot? How strong of a person does Mary seem to you, and why? To what extent, if any, did her making friends with Ernie impress Grandfather?

→ **Extend:** CONNECTING IDEAS

5b. Tests of endurance occur throughout life in all cultures. What strategies and attitudes from the story would you choose to apply to the tests you will face? Why do you think these strategies might work in more than one situation?

Understanding Literature

DIALOGUE. Dialogue is conversation involving two or more people or characters. In fiction, dialogue is enclosed in quotation marks (" "). Through dialogue, a reader learns a lot about the characters. What did you learn about Grandfather and his beliefs from what he says? What did you learn about Ernie and his beliefs? about Mary and her beliefs?

PLOT. A **plot** is a series of events related to a central conflict, or struggle. A plot usually involves the introduction of a conflict, its development, and its eventual resolution. Look again at the events recorded on your graphic organizer. What is the main conflict in "Ta-Na-E-Ka"? What part or parts of the story introduce you to the plot and characters? How do events within the middle section of the story help to develop the plot? How do events at the end of the story bring a conclusion to the story? How are problems or conflicts resolved at the end?

Writer's Journal

1. Pretend you are Roger. Write a **diary entry** about some of the details and experiences of your five-day Ta-Na-E-Ka.

2. Imagine you are Mary in her sixties and you are training your granddaughter for her Ta-Na-E-Ka. Make an **outline** for your granddaughter that lists the topics you will cover in the training.

3. Imagine that you are an editor at a medium-sized newspaper. Write an **editorial** for the newspaper that explains your views on the value of taking wilderness survival training.

Skill Builders

Language, Grammar, and Style

PARTS OF SPEECH. The *parts of speech* are: noun, verb, pronoun, adjective, adverb, preposition, conjunction, and interjection. Review the definitions and examples given for each part of speech in the Language Arts Survey 3.7, "Grammar Reference Chart—Parts of Speech Overview." Then, on your own paper, identify the part of speech of each underlined word in the sentences below.

EXAMPLE Roger would <u>give</u> anything to get out of participating in <u>Ta-Na-E-Ka</u>.

give: verb   Ta-Na-E-Ka: noun

1. Many of the younger <u>families</u> on the <u>reservation</u> were beginning to give up the old customs.
2. <u>They</u> all advised us to fill up <u>now</u>, since for the next five days we'd be gorging ourselves on crickets.
3. He wore a sweat shirt with the words "Fort Sheridan, 1944," <u>and</u> he had only three fingers on one of <u>his</u> hands.
4. "I'll probably laugh about this when I'm an accountant," <u>Roger</u> said, <u>trembling</u>.
5. What if Grandfather <u>asks</u> me <u>about</u> the berries and the grasshoppers?
6. It never once <u>occurred</u> to me that being <u>Indian</u> was exciting.
7. It would have saved nights of bad dreams about <u>squooshy</u> grasshoppers.
8. He could speak English, <u>but</u> he spoke it <u>only</u> with white men.
9. "That's the <u>lost-and-found</u> closet," he <u>said</u>.
10. I sucked in my breath and blurted out the <u>truth</u>: "<u>Hamburgers</u> and milk shakes."
11. <u>Argh!</u> I <u>spat</u> it out.
12. Somehow, you know how to exist in a world <u>that</u> wasn't made <u>for</u> Indians.

Applied English

CREATING A MENU. Imagine you are the owner of a brand new restaurant located in Kansas City, Kansas, in 1947. Plan the design and contents of your menu, including the name of your restaurant, its address and hours of operation, the listing of foods with their descriptions and prices, and the daily specials. Base your prices on the examples used in the story. When all your ideas about the menu are determined, make a final version to display with the menus of other class members.

Speaking and Listening & Collaborative Learning

DEVELOPING DIALOGUE. With a partner, develop and outline a dialogue between Mary and Roger describing and comparing the specifics of each of their Ta-Na-E-Kas. With one of you being Mary and the other Roger, role play the conversation, extemporaneously extending the dialogue as you think it might have happened. Enhance the descriptive dialogues with facial expressions, changes in tone of voice, and body language. Then, switch roles and see how much more can be conveyed about each experience.

Media Literacy

EXAMINING RITES OF PASSAGE IN THE MEDIA. Rites of passage recognize and celebrate or honor the passage of an individual from one stage of his or her life to another. Common rites of passage are connected to being born, becoming an adult, marrying, and dying. In small groups, come up with as many ways that rites of passage have been depicted in the media as possible. (For example, the film *Breaking Away* is an example of the rite of passage into adulthood.) Remember to consider media such as cartoons, songs, and slogans as well as books, plays, poems, films, and videos.

Collaborative Learning

RESEARCH. In small groups, gather and analyze four or five examples of treaties and/or purchase agreements that involved the transfer of Native American lands to the United States. First, pool ideas on the best sources for finding the information you need. After each group member has brought an example to the group, make a listing of the key points of each, including the date of the document, the name of the Indian tribe(s), a description of the size of the land, and the terms and any conditions. Plot the areas of land on a U.S. map. Then study each example more closely. What money or goods were given by the U.S. government for the purchase of the lands? What arrangements are specified (or not specified) for the people currently living on the land? Are there parts of the agreements that the Native Americans might not understand? Can you find loopholes or fuzzy or vague wording in the documents? In a brief report, summarize your findings.

Reader's *Journal*

What have you done when you were with new people and weren't sure of the correct eating procedures or manners?

Reader's TOOLBOX

ONOMATOPOEIA.
Onomatopoeia is the use of words or phrases like *meow* or *beep* that sound like what they name. There are several examples of onomatopoeia in this story. As you read "The All-American Slurp," make a list of these words and, at the same time, notice if other examples of onomatopoeia come to your mind.

THEME. A **theme** is a central idea in a literary work. As you read, try to find the central ideas in this story. To help find the central ideas, create a flow chart of the main events and actions in the story. At the end of the chart, you will probably be able to describe at least two themes of the story.

Prereading

"The All-American Slurp"
by Lensey Namioka

Reader's Resource

- **GEOGRAPHY CONNECTION.** China is a country of eastern Asia. Beijing is the capital and Shanghai is the largest city. China is the most populous country of the world, and the third largest in area after the Soviet Union and Canada. As of the early 1990s, the population of China reached well over one billion.

- The words *emigrate* and *immigrate* are often confused. Both refer to a people's permanent move, usually across a political border. *Emigrate*, which describes the move as it relates to the point of departure, means "to <u>leave</u> one's home country or region to settle in another." *Immigrate*, which describes the move as it relates to the destination, means "to <u>arrive</u> and settle in a country or region to which one is not native."

- **CULTURAL CONNECTION.** There are many reasons people decide to leave their homeland and move to another country. The decision to move is usually not an easy one to make. When people move away from their homeland, they often move away from extended family, friends, and familiar things and places. Some of the reasons for moving to a new homeland include freedom (political and/or religious); new adventures, new opportunities, new jobs; escaping a war, a famine, or a drought; and the scarcity of jobs or land. Chinese culture, which has a long history, is very strong, and many Chinese do not want to leave China to live elsewhere. But when people go through hard times such as having no money because there is no work, or because there is famine, drought, or war, they will move. This happened to many Chinese people.

family embarrassed by dinner at the Gleasons → □ → □ → theme / theme

Still Life #25, 1963. Tom Wesselmann. Rose Art Museum, Waltham, Massachusetts.

The All-American SLURP

Lensey Namioka

The first time our family was invited out to dinner in America, we <u>disgraced</u> ourselves while eating celery. We had emigrated to this country from China, and during our early days here we had a hard time with American table manners.

In China we never ate celery raw, or any other kind of vegetable raw. We always had to disinfect the vegetables in boiling water first. When we were presented with our first relish tray, the raw celery caught us unprepared.

We had been invited to dinner by our neighbors, the Gleasons. After arriving at the house, we shook hands with our hosts and packed ourselves into a sofa. As our family of four sat stiffly in a row, my younger brother and I stole glances at our parents for a clue as to what to do next.

Mrs. Gleason offered the relish tray to Mother. The tray looked pretty, with its tiny red radishes, curly sticks of carrots, and long, slender stalks of pale green celery. "Do try some of the celery, Mrs. Lin" she said. "It's from a local farmer, and it's sweet."

Still Life #25, 1963. Tom Wesselman. Rose Art Museum, Waltham, Massachusetts.

Tom Wesselman (b.1931) is a Pop artist, meaning that his work derives from popular culture, especially advertising. The aim of advertising is to make products desirable, so that ordinary objects look like beautiful artworks. Pop artists often exaggerate those aspects. In this picture several items are exactly repeated. What does that suggest to you?

Mother picked up one of the green stalks, and Father followed suit.[1] Then I picked up a stalk, and my brother did too. So there we sat, each with a stalk of celery in our right hand.

Mrs. Gleason kept smiling. "Would you like to try some of the dip, Mrs. Lin? It's my own recipe: sour cream and onion flakes, with a dash of Tabasco sauce."

Most Chinese don't care for dairy products, and in those days I wasn't even ready to drink fresh milk. Sour cream sounded perfectly <u>revolting</u>. Our family shook our heads in <u>unison</u>.

Mrs. Gleason went off with the relish tray to the other guests, and we carefully watched to see what they did. Everyone seemed to eat the raw vegetables quite happily.

Mother took a bite of her celery. *Crunch.* "It's not bad!" she whispered.

Father took a bite of his celery. *Crunch.* "Yes, it is good," he said, looking surprised.

I took a bite, and then my brother. *Crunch, crunch.* It was more than good; it was delicious. Raw celery has a slight sparkle, a <u>zingy</u> taste that you don't get in cooked celery. When Mrs. Gleason came around with the relish tray, we each took another stalk of celery, except my brother. He took two.

> **GUIDED READING**
> How is raw celery different from cooked celery?

There was only one problem: long strings ran through the length of the stalk, and they got caught in my teeth. When I help my mother in the kitchen, I always pull the strings out before slicing celery.

> **GUIDED READING**
> What is the one problem with celery?

---
1. **followed suit.** Copied or imitated

I pulled the strings out of my stalk. *Z-z-zip, z-z-zip.* My brother followed suit. *Z-z-zip, z-z-zip.* To my left, my parents were taking care of their own stalks. *Z-z-zip, z-z-zip, z-z-zip.*

Suddenly I realized that there was dead silence except for our zipping. Looking up, I saw that the eyes of everyone in the room were on our family. Mr. and Mrs. Gleason, their daughter Meg, who was my friend, and their neighbors the Badels—they were all staring at us as we busily pulled the strings of our celery.

That wasn't the end of it. Mrs. Gleason announced that dinner was served and invited us to the dining table. It was lavishly covered with platters of food, but we couldn't see any chairs around the table. So we helpfully carried over some dining chairs and sat down. All the other guests just stood there.

Mrs. Gleason bent down and whispered to us, "This is a buffet[2] dinner. You help yourselves to some food and eat it in the living room."

Our family beat a <u>retreat</u> back to the sofa as if chased by enemy soldiers. For the rest of the evening, too <u>mortified</u> to go back to the dining table, I nursed a bit of potato salad on my plate.

Next day Meg and I got on the school bus together. I wasn't sure how she would feel about me after the <u>spectacle</u> our family made at the party. But she was just the same as usual, and the only reference she made to the party was, "Hope you and your folks got enough to eat last night. You certainly didn't take very much. Mom never tries to figure out how much food to prepare. She just puts everything on the table and hopes for the best."

I began to relax. The Gleasons' dinner party wasn't so different from a Chinese meal after all. My mother also puts everything on the table and hopes for the best.

Meg was the first friend I had made after we came to America. I eventually got acquainted with a few other kids in school, but Meg was still the only real friend I had.

My brother didn't have any problems making friends. He spent all his time with some boys who were teaching him baseball, and in no time he could speak English much faster than I could—not better, but faster.

I worried more about making mistakes, and I spoke carefully, making sure I could say everything right before opening my mouth. At least I had a better accent than my parents, who never really got rid of their Chinese accent, even

GUIDED READING

What does the narrator worry about when speaking English?

---

2. **buffet.** Meal set out on a table for informal service

years later. My parents had both studied English in school before coming to America, but what they had studied was mostly written English, not spoken.

Father's approach to English was a scientific one. Since Chinese verbs have no tense, he was fascinated by the way English verbs changed form according to whether they were in the present, past imperfect, perfect, pluperfect, future, or future perfect tense.[3] He was always making diagrams of verbs and their <u>inflections</u>, and he looked for opportunities to show off his mastery of the pluperfect and future perfect tenses, his two favorites. "I shall have finished my project by Monday," he would say smugly.

> **GUIDED READING**
>
> How does the father show off?

Mother's approach was to memorize lists of polite phrases that would cover all possible social situations. She was constantly muttering things like "I'm fine, thank you. And you?" Once she accidentally stepped on someone's foot, and hurriedly blurted, "Oh, that's quite all right!" Embarrassed by her slip, she resolved to do better next time. So when someone stepped on her foot, she cried, "You're welcome!"

In our own different ways, we made progress in learning English. But I had another worry, and that was my appearance. My brother didn't have to worry, since Mother bought him blue jeans for school, and he dressed like all the other boys. But she insisted that girls had to wear skirts. By the time she saw that Meg and the other girls were wearing jeans, it was too late. My school clothes were bought already, and we

> **GUIDED READING**
>
> What is another worry of the narrator?

didn't have money left to buy new outfits for me. We had too many other things to buy first, like furniture, pots, and pans.

The first time I visited Meg's house, she took me upstairs to her room, and I wound up trying on her clothes. We were pretty much the same size, since Meg was shorter and thinner than average. Maybe that's how we became friends in the first place. Wearing Meg's jeans and T-shirt, I looked at myself in the mirror. I could almost pass for an American—from the back, anyway. At least the kids in school wouldn't stop and stare at me in the hallways, which was what they did when they saw me in my white blouse and navy blue skirt that went a couple of inches below the knees.

When Meg came to my house, I invited her to try on my Chinese dresses, the ones with a high collar and slits up the sides. Meg's eyes were bright as she looked at herself in the mirror. She struck several <u>sultry</u> poses, and we nearly fell over laughing.

The dinner party at the Gleasons' didn't stop my growing friendship with Meg. Things were getting better for me in other ways too. Mother finally bought me some jeans at the end of the month, when Father got his paycheck. She wasn't in any hurry about buying them at first, until I worked on her. This is what I did. Since we didn't have a car in those days, I often ran down to the neighborhood store to pick up things for her. The groceries cost less at a big supermarket, but the closest one was many

> **GUIDED READING**
>
> Why does the narrator "work on" her mother?

---

3. **present, past imperfect, perfect, pluperfect, future, future perfect tense.** Verb variations that indicate time

---

words for everyday use

in • flec • tion (in flek' shən) n., change of form words undergo to distinguish case, gender, number, tense, person, or mood. *Words that change in tense are one form of <u>inflections</u>.*

sul • try (səl' trē) adj., expressing strong sexual desire or passion. *The eye make-up the woman wore made her look <u>sultry</u>.*

blocks away. One day, when she ran out of flour, I offered to borrow a bike from our neighbor's son and buy a ten-pound bag of flour at the big supermarket. I mounted the boy's bike and waved to Mother. "I'll be back in five minutes!"

Before I started pedaling, I heard her voice behind me. "You can't go out in public like that! People can see all the way up to your thighs!"

"I'm sorry," I said innocently. "I thought you were in a hurry to get the flour." For dinner we were going to have pot-stickers (fried Chinese dumplings), and we needed a lot of flour.

"Couldn't you borrow a girl's bicycle?" complained Mother. "That way your skirt won't be pushed up."

GUIDED READING

Why does Mrs. Lin want her daughter to borrow a girl's bicycle?

"There aren't too many of those around," I said. "Almost all the girls wear jeans while riding a bike, so they don't see any point buying a girl's bike."

We didn't eat pot-stickers that evening, and Mother was thoughtful. Next day we took the bus downtown and she bought me a pair of jeans. In the same week, my brother made the baseball team of his junior high school, Father started taking driving lessons, and Mother discovered rummage sales. We soon got all the furniture we needed, plus a dart board and a 1,000-piece jigsaw puzzle (fourteen hours later, we discovered that it was a 999-piece jigsaw puzzle). There was hope that the Lins might become a normal American family after all.

Then came our dinner at the Lakeview restaurant.

The Lakeview was an expensive restaurant, one of those places where a headwaiter[4] dressed in tails[5] conducted you to your seat, and the only light came from candles and flaming desserts. In one corner of the room a lady harpist played tinkling melodies.

GUIDED READING

What is the Lakeview restaurant like?

Father wanted to celebrate, because he had just been promoted. He worked for an <u>electronics</u> company, and after his English started improving, his superiors decided to appoint him to a position more suited to his training. The promotion not only brought a higher salary but was also a tremendous boost to his pride.

GUIDED READING

What were two positive outcomes of Mr. Lin's promotion?

Up to then we had eaten only in Chinese restaurants. Although my brother and I were becoming fond of hamburgers, my parents didn't care much for western food, other than chow mein.

But this was a special occasion, and Father asked his coworkers to recommend a really elegant restaurant. So there we were at the Lakeview, stumbling after the headwaiter in the murky dining room.

---

4. **headwaiter.** Head of the dining room staff of a hotel or restaurant
5. **tails.** Two long tapering skirts on the back part of a tuxedo coat

words for everyday use

e • lec • tron • ics (i lek trä' niks) n., electronic devices or equipment. The <u>electronics</u> store sells car radios and stereos.

At our table we were handed our menus, and they were so big that to read mine I almost had to stand up again. But why bother? It was mostly in French, anyway.

Father, being an engineer, was always <u>systematic</u>. He took out a pocket French dictionary. "They told me that most of the items would be in French, so I came prepared." He even had a pocket flashlight, the size of a marking pen. While Mother held the flashlight over the menu, he looked up the items that were in French.

GUIDED READING

How does Mr. Lin prepare for the French menu?

"*Pâté en croûte*," he muttered. "Let's see…*pâté* is paste…*croûte* is crust…hmm…a paste in crust."

The waiter stood looking patient. I squirmed and died at least fifty times.

At long last Father gave up. "Why don't we just order four complete dinners at random?" he suggested.

"Isn't that risky?" asked Mother. "The French eat some rather peculiar things, I've heard."

"A Chinese can eat anything a Frenchman can eat," Father declared.

The soup arrived in a plate. How do you get soup up from a plate? I glanced at the other diners, but the ones at the nearby tables were not on their soup course, while the more distant ones were invisible in the darkness.

Fortunately my parents had studied books on western <u>etiquette</u> before they came to America. "Tilt your plate," whispered my mother. "It's easier to spoon the soup up that way."

She was right. Tilting the plate did the trick. But the etiquette book didn't say anything about what you did after the soup reached your lips. As any respectable Chinese knows, the correct way to eat your soup is to slurp. This helps to cool the liquid and prevent you from burning your lips. It also shows your appreciation.

GUIDED READING

What is the correct way to eat soup according to the Chinese?

We showed our appreciation. *Shloop*, went my father. *Shloop*, went my mother. *Shloop, shloop*, went my brother, who was the hungriest.

The lady harpist stopped playing to take a rest. And in the silence, our family's <u>consumption</u> of soup suddenly seemed unnaturally loud. You know how it sounds on a rocky beach when the tide goes out and the water drains from all those little pools? They go *shloop, shloop, shloop*. That was the Lin family, eating soup.

At the next table a waiter was pouring wine. When a large *shloop* reached him, he froze. The bottle continued to pour, and red wine flooded the tabletop and into the lap of a customer. Even the customer didn't notice anything at first, being also hypnotized by the *shloop, shloop, shloop*.

It was too much. "I need to go to the toilet," I mumbled, jumping to my feet. A waiter, sensing my <u>urgency</u>, quickly directed me to the ladies' room.

I splashed cold water on my burning face, and as I dried myself with a paper towel, I stared into the mirror. In this perfumed ladies' room, with its pink-and-silver wallpaper and marbled sinks, I looked completely out of place. What was I doing here? What was our family doing in the Lakeview restaurant? In America?

GUIDED READING

What thoughts go through the narrator's mind as she looks in the mirror in the ladies' room?

words for everyday use

sys • tem • a • tic (sis tə ma′ tik) *adj.*, methodical in procedure or plan. *My dad has a <u>systematic</u> and organized way of doing the dishes.*

et • i • quette (e′ ti kət) *n.*, conduct prescribed by authority to be observed in social life. *In Asian countries, it is proper <u>etiquette</u> to slurp your soup.*

con • sump • tion (kən səm[p]′ shən) *n.*, act of eating or drinking in great quantity. *There is much <u>consumption</u> of food during holidays.*

The door to the ladies' room opened. A woman came in and glanced curiously at me. I retreated into one of the toilet cubicles and latched the door.

Time passed—maybe half an hour, maybe an hour. Then I heard the door open again, and my mother's voice. "Are you in there? You're not sick, are you?"

There was real concern in her voice. A girl can't leave her family just because they slurp their soup. Besides, the toilet cubicle had a few drawbacks as a permanent <u>residence</u>. "I'm all right," I said, undoing the latch.

Mother didn't tell me how the rest of the dinner went, and I didn't want to know. In the weeks following, I managed to push the whole thing into the back of my mind, where it jumped out at me only a few times a day. Even now, I turn hot all over when I think of the Lakeview restaurant.

But by the time we had been in this country for three months, our family was definitely making progress toward becoming Americanized. I remember my parents' first PTA meeting. Father wore a neat suit and tie, and Mother put on her first pair of high heels. She stumbled only once. They met my homeroom teacher and beamed as she told them that I would make honor roll soon at the rate I was going. Of course Chinese etiquette forced Father to say that I was a very stupid girl and Mother to protest that the teacher was showing <u>favoritism</u> toward me.

But I could tell they were both very proud.

The day came when my parents announced that they wanted to give a dinner party. We had invited Chinese friends to eat with us before, but this dinner was going to be different. In addition to a Chinese-American family, we were going to invite the Gleasons.

"Gee, I can hardly wait to have dinner at your house," Meg said to me. "I just *love* Chinese food."

That was a relief. Mother was a good cook, but I wasn't sure if people who ate sour cream would also eat chicken gizzards[6] stewed in soy sauce.

Mother decided not to take a chance with chicken gizzards. Since we had western guests, she set the table with large dinner plates, which we never used in Chinese meals. In fact we didn't use individual plates at all, but picked up food from the platters in the middle of the table and brought

GUIDED READING

What does Chinese etiquette force Mr. and Mrs. Lin to do when the teacher praises their daughter's progress?

GUIDED READING

What do the Chinese use in place of large dinner plates?

6. **gizzards.** Thick, muscular walls in the digestive systems of birds used for grinding food

words for everyday use

res • i • dence (re' zə dən[t]s) *n.,* place where one lives or dwells. *Our dog sleeps with me sometimes, but his permanent <u>residence</u> is his doghouse in the backyard.*

fa • vor • it • ism (fā' vər ti zəm) *n.,* showing of special favor. *My parents treat my sister and I equally, so there is no <u>favoritism</u> shown between us.*

it directly to our rice bowls. Following the practice of Chinese-American restaurants, Mother also placed large serving spoons on the platters.

The dinner started well. Mrs. Gleason exclaimed at the beautifully arranged dishes of food: the colorful candied fruit in the sweet-and-sour pork dish, the noodle-thin shreds of chicken meat stir-fried with tiny peas, and the glistening pink prawns[7] in a ginger sauce.

> **GUIDED READING**
> What foods does Mrs. Lin serve at the dinner party?

At first I was too busy enjoying my food to notice how the guests were doing. But soon I remembered my duties. Sometimes guests were too polite to help themselves and you had to serve them with more food.

I glanced at Meg, to see if she needed more food, and my eyes nearly popped out at the sight of her plate. It was piled with food: the sweet-and-sour meat pushed right against the chicken shreds, and the chicken sauce ran into the prawns. She had been taking food from a second dish before she finished eating her helping from the first! Horrified, I turned to look at Mrs. Gleason. She was dumping rice out of her bowl and putting it on her dinner plate. Then she <u>ladled</u> prawns and gravy on top of the rice and mixed everything together, the way you mix sand, gravel, and cement to make concrete.

I couldn't bear to look any longer, and I turned to Mr. Gleason. He was chasing a pea around his plate. Several times he got it to the edge, but when he tried to pick it up with his chopsticks, it rolled back toward the center of the plate again. Finally he put down his chopsticks and picked up the pea with his fingers. He really did! A grown man!

All of us, our family and the Chinese guests, stopped eating to watch the activities of the Gleasons. I wanted to giggle. Then I caught my mother's eyes on me. She frowned and shook her head slightly, and I understood the message: the Gleasons were not used to Chinese

> **GUIDED READING**
> Why doesn't the narrator giggle when she and the others are watching the Gleasons eat?

ways, and they were just coping the best they could. For some reason I thought of celery strings.

When the main courses were finished, Mother brought out a platter of fruit. "I hope you weren't expecting a sweet dessert," she said. "Since the Chinese don't eat dessert, I didn't think to prepare any."

"Oh, I couldn't possibly eat dessert!" cried Mrs. Gleason. "I'm simply stuffed!"

Meg had different ideas. When the table was cleared, she announced that she and I were going for a walk. "I don't know about you, but I feel like dessert," she told me, when we were outside. "Come on, there's a Dairy Queen down the street. I could use a big chocolate milkshake!"

Although I didn't really want anything more to eat, I insisted on paying for the milkshakes. After all, I was still hostess.

Meg got her large chocolate milkshake and I had a small one. Even so, she was finishing hers while I was only half done. Toward the end she pulled hard on her straws and went *shloop, shloop.*

"Do you always slurp when you eat a milkshake?" I asked, before I could stop myself.

Meg grinned. "Sure. All Americans slurp." ∎

---

7. **prawns.** Edible crustaceans that resemble shrimps

la • dle (lā′ dəl) *v.*, take or dip using a ladle or oversized spoon. *My grandma <u>ladled</u> gravy onto my mashed potatoes.*

If you had to move to a new country, learn a new language, and make all new friends, what do you think your main worries might be? What kinds of things would discourage you? What would help you along?

About *the*
AUTHOR

Lensey Namioka was born on June 14, 1929, in Beijing, China. Her family moved to the United States when she was eight years old. Namioka's early experiences as an immigrant to America form the basis for some of her books, including the Yang family chronicles, *April and the Dragon Lady*, and the latter part of *Ties that Bind, Ties that Break*. Namioka hasn't always been a writer. She taught mathematics at Cornell University and worked as a translator for the American Mathematical Society. Her husband, Isaac Namioka, is also a mathematician. They live in Seattle and have two daughters and two grandchildren.

Books for young people by Lensey Namioka include: *Coming of the Bear, Island of the Ogres, Den of the White Fox,* and *April and the Dragon Lady.*

How to Eat Like a Child

Delia Ephron

Peas:
Mash and flatten into thin sheet on plate. Press the back of the fork into the peas. Hold fork vertically, prongs up, and lick off peas.

Mashed Potatoes:
Pat mashed potatoes flat on top. Dig several little depressions. Think of them as ponds or pools. Fill the pools with gravy. With your fork, sculpt rivers between pools and watch the gravy flow between them. Decorate with peas. Do not eat.

Alternative method: Make a large hole in center of mashed potatoes. Pour in ketchup. Stir until potatoes turn pink. Eat as you would peas.

Animal Crackers:

Eat each in this order—legs, head, body.

Sandwich:
Leave the crusts. If your mother says you have to eat them because that's the best part, stuff the crusts into your pants pocket or between the cushions of the couch.

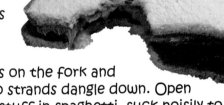

Spaghetti:
Wind too many strands on the fork and make sure at least two strands dangle down. Open your mouth wide and stuff in spaghetti, suck noisily to inhale the dangling strands. Clean plate, ask for seconds, and eat only half. When carrying your plate to the kitchen, hold it tilted so that the remaining spaghetti slides off and onto the floor.

Ice-Cream Cone:
Ask for a double scoop. Knock the top scoop off while walking out the door of the ice-cream parlor. Cry. Lick the remaining scoop slowly so that ice cream melts down the outside of the cone and over your hand. Stop licking when the ice cream is even with the top of the cone. Be sure it is absolutely even. Eat a hole in the bottom of the cone and suck the rest of the ice cream out the bottom. When only the cone remains with ice cream coating the inside, leave on car dashboard.

Ice-Cream in Bowl:
Grip spoon upright in fist. Stir ice cream vigorously to make soup. Take a large helping on a spoon, place spoon in mouth, and slowly pull it out, sucking only the top layer of ice cream off. Wave spoon in air. Lick its back. Put in mouth again and suck off some more. Repeat until all ice cream is off spoon and begin again.

Cooked Carrots:

On way to mouth, drop in lap. Smuggle to garbage in napkin.

Spinach:

Divide into little piles. Rearrange into new piles. After five or six maneuvers, sit back and say you are full.

Chocolate-Chip Cookies:

Half-sit, half-lie on the bed, propped up by a pillow. Read a book. Place cookies next to you on the sheet so that crumbs get in the bed. As you eat the cookies, remove each chocolate chip and place it on your stomach. When all the cookies are consumed, eat the chips one by one, allowing two per page.

Milk Shake:

Bite off one end of the paper covering the straw. Blow through straw to shoot paper across table. Place straw in shake and suck. When the shake just reaches your mouth, place a finger over the top of the straw—the pressure will keep the shake in the straw. Lift straw out of shake, put bottom end in mouth, release finger, and swallow.

Do this until the straw is squished so that you can't suck through it. Ask for another. Open it the same way, but this time shoot the paper at the waitress when she isn't looking. Sip your shake casually—you are just minding your own business—until there is about an inch of shake remaining. Then blow through the straw until bubbles rise to the top of the glass. When your father says he's had just about enough, get a stomachache.

Chewing Gum:

Remove from mouth and stretch into spaghetti-like strand. Swing like a lasso. Put back in mouth. Pulling out one end and gripping the other end between teeth, have your gum meet your friend's gum and press them together. Think that you have just done something really disgusting.

Baked Apple:

With your fingers, peel skin off baked apple. Tell your mother you changed your mind, you don't want it. Later, when she is harassed and not paying attention to what she is doing, pick up the naked baked apple and hand it to her.

French Fries:

Wave one French fry in air for emphasis while you talk. Pretend to conduct orchestra. Then place four fries in your mouth at once and chew. Turn to your sister, open your mouth and stick out your tongue coated with potatoes. Close mouth and swallow. Smile.

Investigate, Inquire, and Imagine

Recall: Gathering Facts

1a. What do the people in China do to all their vegetables before eating them?

2a. What does Mr. Lin say in the fancy restaurant after his wife says, "The French eat some rather peculiar things, I've heard"?

3a. How does the Lin family eat their soup in the restaurant?

→ **Interpret:** Finding Meaning

1b. Why do you think they do this?

2b. What does Mr. Lin's response tell you about him?

3b. Why might this behavior cause others in the restaurant to freeze and stare?

Analyze: Taking Things Apart

4a. List the specific things the narrator worries about in this story.

→ **Synthesize:** Bringing Things Together

4b. What is the biggest worry the narrator has but never talks about?

Evaluate: Making Judgments

5a. In your opinion, how well is the Lin family adjusting to life in America?

→ **Extend:** Connecting Ideas

5b. The related reading, "How to Eat Like a Child," also looks at ways to eat like someone else does, but the overall message is not the same as that in "The All-American Slurp." How do the messages differ?

Understanding *Literature*

THEME. A **theme** is a central idea in a literary work. It is often found by looking for the meaning behind the things that happen in a selection. You usually won't find a sentence in the selection that actually states the theme. What themes did you discover in "The All-American Slurp"? Which theme do you think is stressed the most? In what ways do the events support your choice?

ONOMATOPOEIA. Onomatopoeia is the use of words or phrases like *meow* or *beep* that sound like what they name. Look at your examples from the story. Now take about five minutes to list as many other examples of onomatopoeia as you can.

Writer's Journal

1. Imagine you are the narrator and you are writing a **postcard** to your best friend back in China. Tell your friend what you like most and least about living in the U.S.

2. Pretend you are the author of "How to Eat Like a Child." For future readers, write a **description** of how to eat one more food like a child.

3. Write a personal **diary entry** that the narrator might write after finding out that all Americans slurp their milkshakes.

Skill Builders

Language, Grammar, and Style

ONOMATOPOEIA. Words of onomatopoeia—like *splash, wow, gush, kerplunk*—are fun because they bring out the full flavor of words. Such words also make the meaning of the word much easier to understand, because an example is built right into the word. Find at least five examples of onomatopoeia in a comic book or the comic strip section of a newspaper. Next, think of a high-action scene, such as a soccer game. Write a description of your scene using as many onomatopoeia words as possible. If appropriate, use some of the words from the comics.

Study and Research

RESEARCHING PEOPLE. Research famous Chinese-Americans and the contributions they have made. Using 3-by-5-inch note cards, put the person's name, date of birth, and place of U.S. residence on the top line of the card. Then, write the person's contributions in the center of the card. Try to cover a broad range of occupations, such as: computer programmers, conductors, composers, architects, lawyers, artists, money managers, astronomers, musicians, authors, biologists, comedians, chefs, singers, environmentalists, teachers, actors and actresses, doctors, poets, designers, craftspeople, athletes, city planners, inventors, manufacturers, owners of businesses, photographers, and so on. When everyone has completed his or her cards, make a master list that can be sorted and studied—for example, by state, gender, age, type of contribution, and award-winners. You might want to show your master list to your social studies teacher and ask for his or her comments.

Speaking and Listening

IMMIGRATION INTERVIEW. Locate someone you or your parents know from another country who is relatively new to the United States. (If you have difficulty finding someone new to this country, interview the older members of your own family for the reasons their ancestors came to the United States.) Interview this person using the interview sheet on the next page. If possible and if the interviewee does not mind, take a Polaroid or regular photograph of the person.

Person's name: _____

Native country: _____

Immigration date: _____

Transportation used: _____

How long the trip took: _____

Special events of the trip: _____

_____

Special things brought along: _____

_____

Reasons person emigrated: _____

_____

_____

Who else came: _____

Arrival place in USA: _____

First USA sight: _____

First USA memory: _____

_____

_____

_____

Language issues: _____

_____

Feelings about the move: _____

_____

_____

_____

How USA is different from native land: _____

_____

_____

_____

Any other notes of interest: _____

_____

_____

After the interview, share your information with the class. If time permits, create a newspaper feature about immigration including all of the interviews and pictures that were taken. To summarize your data, chart or graph the reasons people emigrated, the countries they came from, and any other variables the class finds interesting.

for your READING LIST

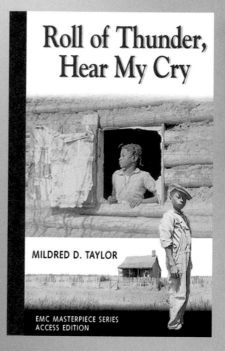

Roll of Thunder, Hear My Cry, by Mildred D. Taylor, is a Newbery Medal-winning novel about the Logans, an African-American family struggling against poverty and racism in Mississippi in the 1930s. The main character of the novel, Cassie Logan, has always felt loved and valued by her family and the members of the African-American community in which she lives, but several events make Cassie realize that most of the white people she encounters believe they are superior to her simply because of their color. As she struggles to understand herself and discover her identity, Cassie must also try to understand where she fits in an increasingly hostile world that includes the horrors of burnings, lynchings, and night men. The strength and love of her family and community sustain Cassie and teach her valuable lessons about life and tolerance. Taylor has said it is her hope for those who read her books that "the Logans will provide those heroes missing from the schoolbooks of my childhood, Black men, women, and children of whom they can be proud."

CREATING A CIVIL RIGHTS EXHIBIT

Even though slavery had been abolished for more than half a century when the events in *Roll of Thunder, Hear My Cry* took place, life had not changed much for African-Americans in the rural South. Based on Mildred D. Taylor's real family, the Logans and other African-Americans like them laid the groundwork for the signing of the Civil Rights Bill in 1964, almost one century after Lincoln declared freedom for the slaves in the Emancipation Proclamation. Working in small groups, create a Civil Rights exhibit for your library or media center. Select any of the following—speeches, essays, photos, art reproductions, and other images, videotapes, or written works—to capture the spirit of the Civil Rights movement of the 1960s.

Other books you may want to read:
A Wrinkle in Time by Madeleine L'Engle
The Birchbark House by Louise Erdrich
The Diary of Anne Frank by Anne Frank
Adventures of Huckleberry Finn by Mark Twain

Guided Writing

"When you are writing about yourself, the problem is what to leave out."

—Russell Baker

Examining the Model

In "Eleven" by Sandra Cisneros, the narrator expresses her feelings of being embarrassed in front of all her classmates. Cisneros never has the character say, "I was embarrassed," but she shows that she was. How does she do that? She does it by giving details to describe the situation. She says, "It's an ugly sweater with red plastic buttons and a collar and sleeves all stretched out like you could use it for a jump rope. It's maybe a thousand years old." The reader can see that ugly thing and understand why her character doesn't want to claim it. She also has her character express her frustration at being eleven years old and not knowing what to do. She doesn't say, "I didn't want to cry." Instead she shows what it looks like when someone is trying not to cry: "I squeeze them shut tight and bite down on my teeth real hard and try to remember today I am eleven." She also writes what the young girl was saying to herself: "Not mine, not mine, not mine." Those are all effective ways to write about your feelings.

PREPARING AN AUTOBIOGRAPHICAL INCIDENT

Rob was looking forward to seeing his cousin Bill at the family reunion. All sorts of people he hadn't seen since his family had moved to California three years ago would be there, including his older cousin Bill, whom he really admired. When Bill saw him, he looked surprised. "Rob, is that you?" Bill looked at him in pretend horror, teasing him. "You're not a little kid any more. You've gotten—maybe six inches taller!" Rob grinned back. "I guess you can't call me 'shrimp' any more."

You may have had an experience like Rob's. Someone you haven't seen in a while notices that there's something different about you. And while it can be easy to see signs of change in the way you look, it can take some time to figure out who the person on the *inside* of you is becoming. What are your thoughts and feelings? Part of growing up is learning who you are and what you believe.

One way you can come to know yourself better is by writing down your thoughts and feelings. This type of writing is called **expressive writing**. Expressive writing is primarily done for oneself, not for a reader. Expressive writing can take many forms, including a journal or diary entry. For this lesson, you will complete some expressive writing.

Professional Model

from "Eleven" by Sandra Cisneros, page 21

Today I wish I was one hundred and two instead of eleven because if I was one hundred and two, I'd have known what to say when Mrs. Price put the red sweater on my desk. I would've known how to tell her it wasn't mine instead of just sitting there with that look my face and nothing coming out of my mouth.

"Whose is this?" Mrs. Price says, and she holds the red sweater up in the air for all the class to see. "Whose? It's been sitting in the coatroom for a month."

"Not mine," says everybody. "Not me."

"It has to belong to somebody," Mrs. Price keeps saying, but nobody can remember. It's an ugly sweater with red plastic buttons and a collar and sleeves all stretched out like you could use it for a jump rope. It's maybe a thousand years old, and even if it belonged to me, I wouldn't say so....

Mrs. Price takes the sweater and puts it right on my desk, but when I open my mouth, nothing comes out.

"That's not, I don't, you're not… Not mine," I finally say in a little voice that was maybe me when I was four.

"Of course it's yours," Mrs. Price says. "I remember you wearing it once." Because she's older and the teacher, she's right and I'm not.

Not mine, not mine, not mine, but Mrs. Price is already turning to page thirty-two, and math problem number four. I don't know why, but all of a sudden I'm feeling sick inside, like the part of me that's three wants to come out of my eyes, only I squeeze them shut tight and bite down on my teeth real hard and try to remember today I am eleven.

Prewriting

WRITING WITH A PLAN. What will you write about? To get ideas, think of an event or an experience that happened to you recently or when you were younger. For example, did your best friend move away? How did that affect you? Have you worked hard and improved your grades? How do you feel about that? Have you camped out under the stars? How did that experience influence you? What has impressed you? What did you think about it at the time? Has your perspective of it changed over time? What are your dreams and hopes for the future?

To get your ideas flowing, try freewriting on a piece of your own paper. Copy one or two of the sentence starters below. Then, just write whatever comes to mind for several minutes. I remember . . . I feel . . . I think . . .

After you freewrite, decide on a topic for your expressive writing. Then fill in the graphic organizer below to help you recall specific ideas about your topic. Madison filled in the graphic organizer about learning to ride a bicycle.

Student Model—Graphic Organizer

My perspective at the time
no training wheels - looked hard on 2 wheels - just in front of house seems like other kids were learning faster than I was

Feelings
Fun with training wheels with my hair flying back, but when I got them off I didn't want to do it because I kept falling down

Memories
age 6 or 7? - it was hard to learn how to ride. I fell off many times. I had got my sister's old bike. It was pink and white. I didn't like the pink, but it would do. on sidewalk, uneven rocky parts. Summer - blue jeans - helmet (styrofoam)

Topic
Learning to Ride Bike

My perspective now
Why didn't I just get up and ride it. It seems so easy now. Glad I kept at it.

Specific details
scraped my knee shoelaces got caught in the chain

IDENTIFYING YOUR AUDIENCE. For this lesson, you are your audience. The purpose of your writing is to clarify your thoughts about an event or an incident that happened to you. Your writing can help you sort out your thoughts, air your feelings, or formulate your hopes and plans for the future.

You may want to share your polished writing with a parent, a grandparent, an older sibling, or a friend. Your writing will help that person know and understand you better, too. If you want to share your writing, keep that particular person in mind as you write.

IDENTIFYING YOUR VOICE. Voice is the way a writer uses language to reflect his or her personality and attitude toward topic, form, and audience. The purpose of expressive writing is to help you know yourself better or gain some perspective about your life. Since you are writing to explore your thoughts and feelings, your voice should be personal and sincere.

Look at the two sentences below. Which one shows a personal and sincere voice?

When I was four years old, I would lie on my back and just watch the clouds float by.

Clouds are cool.

Language, Grammar, and Style
Writing

Complete Sentences

A **sentence** is a group of words that expresses a complete thought. Simple sentences can be divided into two parts: the subject and the predicate. In the most common English sentences, the first part of the sentence tells what or who the sentence is about. This is the **complete subject.** Then it gives information about the subject; this second part of the sentence is called the **complete predicate.** In the following examples, the complete subject is underlined once. The complete predicate is underlined twice.

The red sweater was ugly.

No one claimed the sweater.

It had been in the coatroom for a month.

A sentence **fragment** is a phrase or clause that does not express a complete thought but has been punctuated as though it does. A fragment means a "part." A sentence fragment is only "part" of a sentence. It does not make sense by itself.

SENTENCE FRAGMENTS

Wearing the red sweater.

Not mine.

No way.

After you copy the graphic organizer onto a sheet of your own paper, note your topic, then list feelings, memories, and specific details about the topic.

The last, and in many ways, most important part of the writing asks you to think about the incident. Has your perspective about the event or experience changed over time? What did you learn? What does the experience reveal about you when it happened? What does it have to do with you now? This forms the last paragraph of your writing.

Drafting

Use the information from your freewriting and your graphic organizer to guide you as you write your rough draft. You do not have to focus on spelling or mechanics now—that can come later. Instead, concentrate on capturing your experience. Put in details that will help you bring this incident back to life. Include your perspective at the time; that is, tell how you reacted then.

Try to include a simile in your writing. A simile is a comparison of unlike things using *like* or *as.* In "Eleven," Sandra Cisneros compares the way a person grows old to an onion, to the rings inside a tree trunk, and to "little wooden dolls that fit one inside the other, each year inside the next one." Her simile helps her clarify how she feels about getting older. You can help clarify your own thoughts by thinking about how one thing is similar to something else and expressing your idea as a simile.

Be sure in your last paragraph to write about your perspective on the incident as you now look back on it. What did you learn from it? How did it help you? What do you now do or think differently as a result of this experience? All of this goes in your conclusion.

Student Model—Draft

~~When~~ I Got My Wheels

My hair was flying behind me. I felt the wind rush Against my face. I was riding on my bike that my sister had handed down to me. It was pink and white ~~(now an off white)~~. I was six and I loved it. It wasn't too big. Or too small. It fit just right!

Soon my birthday had come and my father said it was probably time to

take ^off the training wheels ~~off~~. I ^had never
really paid any attention to them, so I
said o.k. It wasn't very hard to ride
my bike with them on, how hard could it
be to ride with them off? *Good-shows what you were thinking.*

   I woke up the next day and was ready
~~to ride my bike~~. My dad had already
~~taken~~ ^removed the training wheels ~~off~~, so I
pushed my bike up our driveway. I got
to the top ~~of the driveway~~ and looked
down the sidewalk. I ^had only ~~rode~~ ridden my bike
a small portion of it so my mom or
dad could see me ride. The sidewalk was
cement on most parts, ~~but on~~ some of ~~the~~
~~sidewalk~~ it was covered in pebbles. ^Those ~~The~~
~~pebbles~~ were hard to ride on even with
the training wheels ~~on~~. I got on my
bike and realized it was wobbly ~~without~~
~~the training wheels on~~. Dad held the
back of the bike so I wouldn't fall, ^but I
~~keep~~ ^kept tipping from one side to another.
This was going to be hard!~~!!!~~

I had on my styrofoam helmet. -nice blue overalls

What did you have on? Help us visualize you.

Student Model—Revised

I Got My Wheels
by Madison Kyger

   My hair was flying behind me, and the
wind was rushing against my face. It
probably looked like the mane of a lion
when he's running very fast. I was
riding on my pink and white bike that
my sister handed down to me. I was six
and I loved it. It wasn't too big or
too small. It fit just right!

IDENTIFYING COMPLETE SENTENCES. Identify the complete subject and the complete predicate in each complete sentence below.

   The teacher placed the red sweater on her desk.

   The narrator in "Eleven" tried to explain the situation.

   The teacher could have apologized.

FIXING SENTENCE FRAGMENTS. Look at part of Madison's first draft and revise any sentence fragments so they are complete sentences.

   My hair was flying behind me. I felt the wind rush. Against my face. I was riding on my bike that my sister handed down to me. It was pink and white (now an off white). I was 6 and I loved it. It wasn't too big. Or too small. It fit just right!

USING COMPLETE SENTENCES. Look at your own writing and examine each of your sentences. Does each sentence contain a complete subject and a complete predicate? If you have any sentence fragments, rewrite them as complete sentences.

Self- and Peer Evaluation

After you finish your first draft, complete a self-evaluation of your writing. You may also want to get one or two peer evaluations. For more information, see the Language Arts Survey 2.37, "Self- and Peer Evaluation."

As you evaluate your writing, answer the following questions.

- What feelings or thoughts are expressed in the writing? What words communicate these feelings or thoughts? Which words are the strongest? Which words are the weakest?
- What perspective do you express about the event or experience? Has your perspective changed over time?
- Check each sentence. Are there any fragments that you could rewrite as complete sentences?

Look at Madison's evaluation of her first draft. Then notice the changes she made to her revised draft. What other changes would you suggest for her?

Soon my birthday had come and my father said it was probably time to take off the training wheels. I had never really paid any attention to them, so I said o.k. It wasn't very hard to ride my bike with them on, how hard could it be to ride with them off?

I woke up the next day and was all ready to ride my bike. I put on some nice blue overalls and my Styrofoam helmet. My dad had already removed the training wheels so I pushed my bike up our driveway. I got to the top and looked down the sidewalk. Up until now, I had only ridden my bike on a small portion of the walk so my mom or dad could see me ride. The sidewalk was cement on most parts, but on some parts it was covered in pebbles. Those were hard to ride on even with the training wheels. I got on my bike and realized it was wobbly without the training wheels. Dad held the back of the bike so I wouldn't fall. I kept tipping from one side to another like a top. This was going to be hard!

After a while I started not to wobble as much. Then for what seemed to be the hundredth time of my going up and down the sidewalk, Dad let go of the bike.

"WWWHHHOOOOOO!" Crash! I fell. I felt so mad, my eyes started to well up with tears.

"It's ok, dear, get up and try again," my dad said, trying to comfort me.

"No!" I stamped my foot and then I let it out.

I just stood there crying. I kicked my bike I was so mad and went back to my house. I went outside every day and tried to ride. It seemed like everyone else knew how to ride a bike! Once my friend Erin called me and asked if I wanted to ride bikes together.

"Uuuummm...well... I don't think I'm free today," I lied. I don't know why I said that. I should have just said I didn't know how to ride my bike yet. Then I had to make up excuses or lie when the subject came to bikes.

One day when I woke up I was determined to ride my bike without training wheels. I got outside, pushed my bike up to the top of the driveway, and started to ride without Dad holding on to me. I fell a lot and even cried, but I kept going. Then on my 14th or 20th or 75th run I got it. It was great! It was even faster without training wheels. But then...BANG I fell. I had forgotten about the pebbles! After I went a couple more times I even got past the pebbles and was fine. Later, on my seventh birthday I got a new pink and teal Huffy with sparkles on it. Soon after I acquired the name *Scooter!*

I learned something from this experience that helps me any time I'm trying to learn something new. I know that I can learn new things after a lot of practice, just like I did with my bike. I learned to keep on trying.

Revising and Proofreading

As you consider your writing and self-evaluation, think about the changes that would help clarify your thoughts and express your ideas. Try to include a simile that compares two unlike ideas. Make revisions according to your decisions.

Next, proofread your draft for errors in spelling, grammar, usage, punctuation, and capitalization. Check each sentence. Rewrite any sentence fragments as complete sentences.

For more information, see the Language Arts Survey 2.45, "A Proofreading Checklist." Then prepare your final version using the Language Arts Survey 2.46, "Proper Manuscript Form."

Publishing and Presenting

You might wish to share your final copy of your writing with a parent, grandparent, older sibling, or a friend. Sharing your expressive writing is a way you can let others know and understand you better.

Reflecting on Your Writing

As you reflect on your expressive writing, ask yourself these questions:

- What have I learned in writing this essay?
- What kind of voice does my writing have?
- What strengths have I discovered in my work? In myself?

UNIT ONE *review*

Review: Words for Everyday Use

Check your knowledge of the following vocabulary words. Choose ten words that you would like to incorporate into your own daily language. For each word, write a short sentence that includes the word in context. To review a word, look back to the page number(s) indicated.

- anticipate (39)
- audacity (41)
- badger (28)
- bolt (11)
- character (28)
- conscience (28)
- consumption (52)
- convulsive (11)
- dejected (39)
- delirous (9)
- disgrace (48)
- electronics (51)
- equate (36)
- etiquette (52)
- favoritism (53)
- fend (38)

- flush (13)
- ghastly (13)
- heritage (36)
- hospitality (40)
- hostility (41)
- imploring (13)
- inflection (50)
- ladle (54)
- leer (14)
- mortified (49)
- ordeal (38)
- pedantic (29)
- rasping (11)
- reasonable (29)
- reputation (12)
- residence (53)

- retreat (9, 49)
- revolting (48)
- sacred (37)
- shrewd (37)
- skirmish (36)
- spectacle (49)
- sulky (12)
- sultry (50)
- systematic (52)
- taunt (6)
- unison (48)
- unsightly (41)
- virtue (37)
- zingy (48)

Review: Literary Tools

Define each of the following terms, giving concrete examples when possible. To review a term, refer to the page number(s) indicated.

- character (5)
- conflict (5)
- description (19)

- dialogue (33)
- onomatopoeia (46)
- personal essay (26)

- plot (33)
- simile (19)
- theme (46)

Reflecting
on your *reading*

Theme

The selections in this unit are all written in the first person. They are personal accounts, from a first-person point of view. The authors come from a wide range of cultural backgrounds— Native American Indian, Anglo, Chinese, Jewish, and Mexican American. Through the stories they tell, the authors try to describe what it was like to grow up in their culture. They describe their own personal heritage. The main character in each story changes and grows as a result of his or her thoughts and actions. In "The Goodness of Matt Kaizer," for example, Matt is challenged to be "good" and to be kind to other people. Because his father dares him, he is kind to Mr. Bataky. Matt helps Mr. Bataky get well and discovers that he truly is a good person. What do the other characters in this unit discover about themselves? What do they learn about growing up?

Graphic *Organizer*

For the main character of each selection in this unit, create a graphic organizer like this one. Write the character's name on the person, and in the mirror, list what that character learned about himself or herself and about life in general. Compare the mirrors for each character. All together, what do these self-discoveries and life lessons have in common?

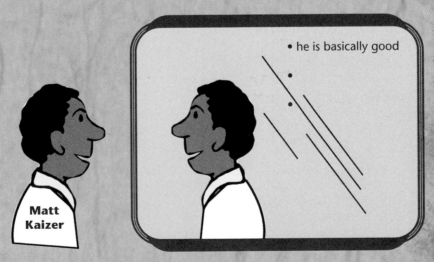

"Sitting Bull Returns" at the Drive-in, 1976. Willard Midgette. National Museum of American Art, Washington, DC.

Learning from HEROES

echoes

Self-trust is the essence of heroism.
—*Ralph Waldo Emerson*

One must think like a hero to behave like a merely decent human being.
—*May Sarton*

My heroes have always been cowboys.
—*Willie Nelson*

We are the hero of our own story.
—*Mary McCarthy*

It's not bravery. It's a question of doing what you have to do. You can go ahead with what you're doing or you can run away.
—*Aung San Suu Kyi*

Being a hero is about the shortest-lived profession on earth.
—*Will Rogers*

All these were honoured in their generations and were the glory of their times.
—*Ecclesiastes 44:7 (Engraved on a government building in Ottawa, Canada)*

Just as my accident and its aftermath caused me to redefine what a hero is, I've had to take a hard look at what it means to live as fully as possible in the present.
—*Christopher Reeve,* Still Me

Prereading

"How Robin Hood Saved the Widow's Three Sons" by Sara Hyry

Reader's T O O L B O X

ORAL TRADITION. An **oral tradition** is a body of works that are passed by way of mouth over generations. Stories of Robin Hood have circulated for hundreds of years. They first circulated as part of the oral tradition of England. Ballads about the adventures of Robin Hood began circulating as early as the 14th century. Like all stories that were passed orally, many versions of these stories exist. Later they were written down. These stories have even made their way to television and have become movies.

HERO. A hero is a character whose actions are inspiring and courageous. Robin Hood is a legendary hero.

Graphic *Organizer*

Make a chart to keep track of inspiring and courageous actions of Robin Hood. Next to the action, write his motivation, or reason for acting as he does.

Action	Motivation
• stops to speak with the woman	•
•	•

Reader's *Journal*

What would you do if a friend was accused of doing something that he or she did not do?

Reader's Resource

- Historians debate whether Robin Hood was in fact a real person. Various records mention men with the name Robin Hood, or something similar. Those who believe Robin Hood existed suggest that he lived during the thirteenth century. Not everything in the tales of Robin Hood support this theory, but that may be because of details added as the stories were passed through the ages.

- Robin Hood, the legendary figure, is perhaps best known as the leader of a bunch of merry men, including Little John, Friar Tuck, and Will Scarlet. This band of outlaws reigned in Sherwood Forest, in Nottingham, England. Robin and his followers were said to "steal from the rich and give to the poor." They challenged a corrupt system of government and tried to help the less fortunate, who had few rights in the England of their time.

- Robin Hood is also linked romantically with Maid Marion. In one tale, Marion sets out in disguise to find Robin. He also is in disguise, so she does not recognize him when she finds him. They begin to fight. Marion is getting the best of him, until she hears him cry out and realizes who he is.

how Robin Hood
Saved the Widow's Three Sons

Sara Hyry

One fine morning, Robin Hood was walking down a lane toward Nottingham town. He was dressed in the colors of green and brown. A fine figure he made as he wandered down. But as he continued, he heard a terrible wailing. Turning a corner, he found a widow weeping.

"What, pray tell, is troubling you?" Robin asked the woman. He knew her well, for he had often dined at her hearth with her sons, who were counted among his followers.

"Down the way, my three sons are to be hanged today," she replied.

"What have they done to deserve such a punishment? Have they stolen? Have they killed a priest? Have they burned down a church?"

"No, none of those have they done. They are to be killed because they killed the king's deer. Following your ways, they shot it with their longbows[1] and 'twas their bad fortune that the sheriff should happen by," she cried.

---

1. **longbows.** Bows used to shoot arrows. Robin Hood was an expert marksman with this weapon.

"That's no crime as I see it," said Robin. "You have told me just in time. If they are to be hanged today, I must be along quickly now." And he hurried off, towards the site of gallows. As he walked, he <u>pondered</u> how to save the widow's sons.

GUIDED READING

Why are the three men to be killed?

"I need some sort of disguise, to get me in to the town without the sheriff knowing," he thought. At that moment, he happened upon an old man dressed in rags, a palmer[2] back from his journey to the Holy Land. "What news have you?" Robin asked the man.

"There's to be a hanging today—three hangings to be exact. And a shame it is. For the three who are to be hanged are no villains, I say."

"Why then are they to be hanged?" asked Robin.

"The sheriff finds killing the king's deer to be a crime. He wishes to make an example, for he is charged with stopping the hunting of the king's beasts. Yet, he sees nothing wrong with the likes of me and the likes of the three going hungry for want of meat, when a bit of venison would be a treat."

Robin looked at the man shrewdly. "Thank you for the news, good man. And for your troubles, I propose a trade. I will give you my clothes and thirty silver coins in exchange for your clothes. What say you?"

"Don't poke fun at an old man, who has but little in this life," he protested.

"I am in <u>earnest</u>. Come, come, I haven't all day," urged Robin. "I'll give you these pieces of gold for your hat and your cloak, and your tattered old breaches."

"'Tis not a fair trade," thought the man, "but it

GUIDED READING

What disguise does Robin wear when he goes to save the three men?

will do me a world of good." So he did not protest when Robin plucked the hat from his head and placed it on his own. Robin dressed himself in the patched breeches and the threadbare cloak. He tucked his arrows under his clothes, unstrung his bow and leaned upon it as a staff. He had his disguise, and he thought, perhaps, a plan.

Robin continued down the road, looking for all the world like the worn, old palmer he pretended to be. He reached the town and found that quite a crowd had gathered in the square. He asked some of those near him what all the hubbub was about.

"The sheriff is to hang three men today."

"For what crime?" asked Robin.

"For poaching on the king's land," came the reply.

"And this is a spectacle for all the town to see. Does nobody protest such action? For shame!" Robin cried.

"We dare not protest the sheriff, for he would have our heads as well. Besides, the fellows did break the law. And there's the sheriff now."

Robin caught sight of the sheriff and began to move through the crowd. He neared the gallows and approached the sheriff. "What price do you pay your hangman today?" Robin asked. "Might you permit this old man to do the job?"

"Clothes of the hanged, of course, and by the looks of it you could use them," said the sheriff with a laugh. "Plus sixpence, two pence per man—the usual hangman's price. The job is yours if you do it right quick."

"Allow me first to take the last confessions of the men; they should not die without that."

---

2. **palmer.** Person who had made a pilgrimage to Jerusalem, often wearing a palm leaf as a sign of his or her religious journey

---

pon • der (pän′ dər) v., think hard upon something. *Horace <u>pondered</u> carefully before making his next move.*

ear • nest (ər′ nest) adj., serious, not joking. *We all laughed until we realized Ling was <u>earnest</u> when she told us she wanted to be a rock star.*

"Very well, but be speedy, old man," said the sheriff impatiently.

GUIDED READING
What two requests does Robin make of the sheriff?

"And mind you if I string up my bow that I might end their misery once they begin to swing from the ropes?"

"Fine, but again I say be quick about it."

So Robin prepared his bow and approached the widow's sons. The prisoners were bound at the hands with the nooses ready round their necks. Robin leaned in to the first man, as though to hear his confession and give him absolution.[3] But what he said was this: "Stand still, my good man, as I cut your hands free. When I throw off my cloak, pull the noose from your neck and run quickly to the forest."

GUIDED READING
What does Robin tell the men to do?

To each man in turn Robin did the same. Then turning from the last, he faced the crowd and the sheriff and shouted, "I'm no hangman, nor do I wish to be!" He pulled a horn from under his rags and blew it long and loud. Then with a flourish, he tossed off his cloak. At this sign, the three men pulled the nooses from their necks and scrambled for the forest.

"After them," ordered the sheriff.

"Halt!" shouted Robin. He had an arrow ready on his bow. "The first man to approach will have my arrow for a souvenir. And any who have seen me shoot know I can hit my mark."

"Yet, even you cannot shoot all at once," laughed the sheriff. "I have you now, Robin Hood." But at that moment, a hundred men in green streamed into the square, for Robin's men had heard the blast of his horn.

"Stop them," the sheriff shouted into the confusion. But the sheriff's men could not stop the men in green. Robin leapt down into the crowd. He and his men let off a shower of arrows as they edged backward out of the town. They disappeared into the forest, as the widow's sons had done before them.

GUIDED READING
How does Robin escape from the sheriff?

And that is how Robin saved three of his men from wrongly losing their lives. ∎

---

3. **absolution.** Forgiveness of sins

Respond *to the* SELECTION

If you were one of the three men, what would you say to Robin the next time you saw him?

About *the* AUTHOR

Sara Hyry grew up in Rockport, Massachusetts. Hyry has loved reading as long as she can remember. "My interest in writing grew out of my love of reading. I wanted to be able to create connections for others as my favorite authors had done for me," says Hyry. Hyry majored in English and also studied literature in other languages at Mount Holyoke College and in Florence, Italy. Hyry's interests include cooking, and she has studied regional cuisine in her travels. She also plays and coaches field hockey. Currently, Hyry is a writer and editor living in Massachusetts.

Investigate, Inquire, and Imagine

Recall: GATHERING FACTS → **Interpret:** FINDING MEANING

1a. What crime have the widow's three sons committed? What punishment are they to receive?

1b. Does the punishment fit the crime? Explain your answer.

2a. What disguise does Robin Hood wear to save the three men?

2b. In what way is his disguise important to his plan?

3a. What does Robin tell the men to do? Who comes to his aid?

3b. How do you think the sheriff feels at the end of the day?

Analyze: TAKING THINGS APART → **Synthesize:** BRINGING THINGS TOGETHER

4a. Analyze the reactions Robin Hood receives when he asks about the fate of the three men. What do people think of this punishment?

4b. What do the punishment and people's reaction to it tell you about the sheriff and his power?

Evaluate: MAKING JUDGMENTS → **Extend:** CONNECTING IDEAS

5a. Evaluate the relationship between Robin Hood and his men. What is each willing to do for the other?

5b. Identify one or more relationships outside the story that are similar to that of Robin Hood and his men. Explain why you think the relationships are similar.

Understanding Literature

ORAL TRADITION. An **oral tradition** is a body of works that are passed by way of mouth over generations. Stories of Robin Hood have circulated for hundreds of years. These types of stories are called legends. Why do you think Robin Hood is a popular legendary figure?

HERO. A **hero** is a character whose actions are inspiring and courageous. Explain why Robin is a hero.

Writer's Journal

1. Write a **thank you note** from the widow to Robin Hood for saving her sons.
2. Write a **news article** about the rescue of the three men. Your article may present Robin Hood as a hero who saved the three men, or as an outlaw who defied the law.
3. Write an **adventure tale** about another heroic deed of Robin Hood.

Skill Builders

Language, Grammar, and Style

USING QUOTATION MARKS. In dialogue, quotation marks are used to show what a person said. Take a look at the dialogue in this story about Robin Hood. Then review the rules for using quotation marks in the Language Arts Survey 3.82, "Quotation Marks." Rewrite the following sentences, adding quotation marks as needed.

1. I would like to dress up as a beggar and have an adventure as you have, said Little John with a pout.
2. Robin Hood replied, It's a risky business, and the sheriff is now on his guard.
3. Still, I'd like to try, said Little John. And there's a beggar now. I'll get his clothes.

Speaking and Listening

COMPARING AND CONTRASTING DISCUSSION. Discuss with your classmates other stories you have heard of Robin Hood. Describe the actions he took in other stories. Then discuss whether his character was similar to or very different from the character in this story.

Applied English

CREATING A POSTER. Imagine you work for the Sheriff of Nottingham. Create a wanted poster for Robin Hood. On your poster include a description of Robin Hood, a list of actions for which he is wanted, and any reward for his capture. You may also wish to include a picture of Robin Hood or a map showing where he was last seen.

Study and Research

DEVELOPING A BIBLIOGRAPHY. Using a library catalog and the Internet, find at least five resources that relate to Robin Hood. These might be collections of stories about Robin Hood, video or films about Robin Hood, Internet sites related to the legend or study of Robin Hood, or any other material. Create a bibliography of these resources. For more information, see the Language Arts Survey 5.39, "Making Bibliographies and Bibliography Cards."

Prereading

from Still Me
by Christopher Reeve

Reader's T O O L B O X

POINT OF VIEW. Point of view is the vantage point from which a story is told. If a story is told from a **first-person point of view**, the narrator uses the pronouns *I* and *we* and is a part of or a witness to the action. When a story is told from a **third-person point of view**, the narrator is outside the action; uses words such as *he, she, it,* and *they;* and avoids the use of *I* and *we.* As you read, note whether the point of view is first- or third-person.

AUTOBIOGRAPHY. An **autobiography** is the story of a person's life, written by that person. The selection you are about to read is from Christopher Reeve's autobiography entitled *Still Me.* Look over the following chart and fill in any facts about Reeve's life that you already know. Then, as you read, notice what events and memories of Reeve's life are covered in this section of his autobiography. Fill in what you have learned about Reeve and his life from this reading.

Graphic Organizer

	AGES birth-5	AGES 6-12	AGES 13-19	AGES 20-29	AGES 30-39	AGES 40+
Relatives and friends						
Activities and interests						
Schooling						
Jobs						
Ideas						
Goals						
Awards						
Special or unusual events						

Reader's Journal

What part of your life would you most hate to lose due to a serious injury, and why?

Reader's Resource

- Christopher Reeve gained worldwide fame for his starring role in the *Superman* movies of the 1970s and 1980s. Born in 1952, Reeve's life has been full of action, discipline, energy, and productivity. At age 13, he went to the McCarter Theater in Princeton, New Jersey, where he would play any part they would give to a kid. At 15, he was accepted by the Williamstown Theater Festival in Massachusetts. After graduating from Cornell University in 1974, he went on to study acting at Juilliard.

- On Memorial Day weekend, 1995, Reeve was competing in an equestrian event in Virginia. Without warning, his horse balked on the third jump, and Reeve, who had been riding at about 500 yards per minute, went flying over the horse's head. His six-foot-four-inch, 215-pound body landed head first. In seconds he was paralyzed from the neck down, choking for air. Examination found that Reeve had broken his top two cervical vertebrae; fortunately, his head was intact and his brain stem appeared unharmed. Nine days later he was scheduled for a perilous operation to reconnect his skull to his spinal column.

from

Still Me

Christopher Reeve

People often ask me what it's like to have <u>sustained</u> a spinal cord injury and be confined to a wheelchair. Apart from all the medical complications, I would say the worst part of it is leaving the physical world—having had to make the transition from participant to observer long before I would have expected. I think most of us are prepared to give up <u>cherished</u> physical activities gradually as we age. I certainly wouldn't be competing in combined training events in my sixties or skiing nearly as fast as I used to. If I went sailing in my later years I wouldn't go single-handed. Stronger arms and more agile bodies would be needed to raise and trim the sails or steer in a heavy sea.

The difference is that I would have had time to prepare for other ways of enjoying the things I love to do most. But to have it all change and have most of it taken away at age forty-two is <u>devastating</u>. As much as I remind myself that being is more important than doing, that the quality of relationships is the key to happiness, I'm actually putting on a brave face. I do believe those things are true, but I miss freedom, <u>spontaneity</u>, action, and adventure more than I can say. Sometimes when we're up in Williamstown I sit out on the deck looking across our pastures to Mount Greylock, and I remember how I used to be a

GUIDED READING

What does Reeve miss more than he can say?

---

words for everyday use

sus • tain (sə stān') v., bear or withstand. *The pain of cutting my finger was more than I could <u>sustain</u>.*
cher • ish (cher' ish) v., hold dear, treasure. *I <u>cherish</u> my football because it is autographed by my favorite pro-football player.*
dev • as • tate (de' və stāt) v., overwhelm with grief; destroy violently. *The flood <u>devastated</u> many homes.* **devastating,** *adj.*
spon • ta • ne • i • ty (spän tə nā' ə tē) n., voluntary or undetermined action or movement. *Sometimes practicing too much is bad because you lose <u>spontaneity</u>.*

part of it. We hiked up the mountain, swam in the streams, rode our horses across the open fields, chopped our own Christmas tree from the woods above the house. Now it's just scenery—still beautiful, but almost as if <u>cordoned</u> off behind velvet ropes. I feel like a visitor at a spectacular outdoor museum.

When I first moved to the Williamstown house in the summer of '87, the trailer for my sailplane was parked beside the barn. As soaring gave way to riding, a horse trailer took its place. Over the next few years the three stalls were home in turn to Valentine, Abby, Hope, Dandy, Denver, and Buck. I taught Al to ride, and we spent many happy hours cleaning tack[1] together, bringing the horses in from their turnout,[2] getting up at six for the morning feed. Bill Stinson kept all his gardening equipment in the other half of the barn, so he was always coming and going. Many times Matthew and Al would play with their friends in the hayloft above, making forts out of bales of hay and attacking each other with tennis balls. The barn was always cool and inviting on humid August days.

Now the stalls are empty. The barn is all closed up, and my van, full of ramps, oxygen tanks, and emergency supplies, is parked where the horse trailer used to be. We all remember how it was, but we don't talk about it much. The barn, too, has become scenery. Al continued to ride for about a year after my accident, and I coached her once at a local show, but now she's given it up. As I write this she's just turned fourteen. Her schoolwork takes much more of her time, she enjoys spending weekends with her friends, and the phone is ringing more and more as

Reeve starred in this and other *Superman* movies in the 1970s and 1980s.

boys her age are beginning to work up the courage to ask her out. There may be other reasons why she's stopped, but I don't ask. Dana doesn't ride anymore either because it was something we did together.

When the first Superman movie came out, I gave dozens of interviews to promote it. The most frequently asked question was: "What is a hero?" I remember how easily I'd talk about it, the <u>glib</u> response I repeated so many times. My answer was that a hero is someone who commits a courageous action without considering the consequences. A soldier who crawls out of a foxhole to drag an

> **GUIDED READING**
>
> What is the author's van full of and where is it parked?

---

1. **tack.** Stable gear such as saddles and bridles used to ride horses
2. **turnout.** Time spent out at pasture

injured buddy back to safety, the prisoners of war who never stop trying to escape even though they know they may be executed if they're caught.

GUIDED READING

What was the most frequently asked question in Reeve's interviews? How did he answer it?

And I also meant individuals who are slightly larger than life: Houdini[3] and Lindbergh[4] of course, John Wayne and JFK, and even sports figures who have taken on <u>mythical</u> proportions, such as Babe Ruth or Joe DiMaggio.[5]

Now my definition is completely different. I think a hero is an ordinary individual who finds the

GUIDED READING

What is Reeve's definition of a hero now?

strength to persevere and endure in spite of overwhelming obstacles. The fifteen-year-old boy down the hall at Kessler who had landed on his head while wrestling with his brother, leaving him paralyzed and barely able to swallow or speak. Travis Roy, paralyzed in the first eleven seconds of a hockey game in his freshman year at college. Henry Steifel, paralyzed from the chest down in a car accident at seventeen, completing his education and working on Wall Street at age thirty-two, but having missed so much of what life has to offer. These are real heroes, and so are the families and friends who have stood by them.

At UVA and at Kessler, I always kept the picture of the Pyramid of Quetzalcoatl[6] in front of me. I would look at the hundreds of steps leading up to the clouds and

GUIDED READING

What picture does Reeve keep with him at UVA and Kessler?

imagine myself climbing slowly but surely to the top. That desire sustained me in the early days after my injury, but during the next couple of years I had to learn to face

the reality: you manage to climb one or two steps, but then something happens and you fall back three. The worst of it is the unpredictability. Several times I've made a commitment to appear at a function or give a speech, but the night before, or even that morning, a skin tear, or dysreflexia,[7] or a lung infection suddenly developed and I had to go to the hospital instead.

Climbing up the steps, I've appeared at the Oscars,[8] spoken at the Democratic Convention,[9] directed a film, written this book, worked on political issues, and traveled more extensively than most high-level quadriplegics.[10] But, falling backwards, I've been hospitalized

GUIDED READING

What has Reeve done that he considers "climbing up the steps"? What has happened to Reeve that he considers "falling backwards"?

eleven times for dysreflexia, pneumonia, a collapsed lung, a broken arm, two blood clots, a possible hip fracture, and the infection in my left ankle that nearly resulted in the partial amputation[11] of my leg.

---

3. **Houdini.** American magician and writer (1874-1926) world famous for escaping locks, handcuffs, straitjackets, and sealed chests

4. **Lindbergh.** American aviator (1902-1974) who made the first solo, nonstop transatlantic flight

5. **Babe Ruth or Joe DiMaggio.** Both in the Baseball Hall of Fame. They both played for the New York Yankees and are revered as top American baseball players of all time.

6. **Pyramid of Quetzalcoatl.** Pyramid in Mexico. Quetzalcoatl means "feathered serpent" in Toltec and is considered the god of Toltec civilization.

7. **dysreflexia.** Potentially dangerous complication of a spinal cord injury in which blood pressure may rise to dangerous levels

8. **Oscars.** Award ceremony that focuses mainly on films

9. **Democratic Convention.** Event during which the Democratic Party nominates a candidate for president

10. **quadriplegics.** People who are affected with paralysis of both arms and legs

11. **amputation.** Removal of a limb from the body (i.e. arms, legs)

words for everyday use

myth • i • cal (mith' i kəl) *adj.*, having qualities suitable to myth. *Michael Jordon has become a <u>mythical</u> figure in America because of his extreme athleticism.*

I was told by so many "experts"—doctors, psychologists,[12] physical therapists,[13] other patients, and well-meaning friends and family members—that as time went by not only would I become more stable physically but I would become well adjusted psychologically to my condition. I have found exactly the opposite to be true. The longer you sit in a wheelchair, the more the body breaks down and the harder you have to fight against it. Psychologically, I feel I have established a workable baseline: I have my down days, but I haven't been <u>incapacitated</u> by them. This doesn't mean, though, that I accept paralysis, or that I'm at peace with it.

The sensory deprivation[14] hurts the most: I haven't been able to give Will a hug since he was two years old, and now he's five and a half. This is the reason Dana and I decided not to have another child; it would be too painful not to be able to hold and embrace this little creature the way I did with the others. The physical world is still very meaningful to me; I have not been able to detach myself from it and live entirely in my mind. While I believe it's true that we are not our bodies, that our bodies are like houses we live in while we're here on earth, that concept is more of an intellectual <u>construct</u> than a philosophy[15] I can live by on a daily basis. I'm jealous when someone talks about a recent skiing vacation, when friends embrace each other, or even when Will plays hockey in the driveway with someone else.

If someone were to ask me what is the most difficult lesson I've learned from all this, I'm very clear about it: I know I have to give when sometimes I really want to take. I've realized

GUIDED READING

What does Reeve believe is the most difficult lesson he's learned from all this?

<u>instinctively</u> that it's part of my job as a father now not to cause Will to worry about me. If I were to give in to self-pity or express my anger in front of him, it would place an unfair burden on this carefree five-year-old. If I were to turn inward and spend my time mourning the past, I couldn't be as close to Matthew and Alexandra, two teenagers who naturally need to turn to me for advice. And what kind of life would it be for Dana if I let myself go and became just a depressed hulk in a wheelchair? All of this takes effort on my part, because it's still very difficult to accept the turn my life has taken, simply because of one unlucky moment.

When I was in California in September 1997 for the dedication of the building that will house the Reeve-Irvine Research Center, I had another MRI.[16] There was concern that a cyst[17] could have developed on my spinal cord, or that there might be a cavity—sometimes the cord splits open long after the initial injury, causing further damage to the nerves. Fortunately, the pictures were clean, meaning that even after two and a half years there had been no more deterioration. This was excellent news and caused a lot of excitement among the doctors who studied the film, but I came away sobered by the comments of the chief radiologist.[18] He

---

12. **psychologists.** People who study mental or behavioral characteristics of an individual or group or counsel those who are mentally and psychologically challenged
13. **physical therapists.** Health professionals who treat people with physical disabilities by exercise, massage, and hydrotherapy
14. **sensory deprivation.** Inability to feel bodily sensations
15. **philosophy.** System of beliefs and values
16. **MRI.** Magnetic Resonance Imaging, a device used to scan detailed sectional images of the internal body
17. **cyst.** Closed sac having a distinct membrane and developing abnormally in the body
18. **radiologist.** Physician specializing in the use of radiant energy for diagnostic and therapeutic purposes

---

words for everyday use

in • ca • pac • i • tate (in kə pa′ sə tāt) v., become incapable or disabled. *The injury <u>incapacitated</u> John—he had casts on both legs.*
con • struct (kən′ strəkt) n., something constructed by the mind, concept. *Freud introduced a psychological <u>construct</u> that explained how the mind processes information.*
in • stinc • tive (in stiŋk′ tiv) adj., prompted by natural instinct or spontaneity. *A bird's <u>instinctive</u> reaction to danger is to fly away.* **instinctively,** adv.

showed me that the damage to my spinal cord was only one centimeter wide, and said that if I had landed with my head twisted only a fraction further to the left, I would have been killed instantly. If I had landed with my head slightly more to the right, I probably would have sustained a bruise and

GUIDED READING

What probably would have happened if Reeve had landed with his head slightly more to the right?

been up on my feet within a few weeks. I just happened to hit the rail at an angle that turned me into a C2 vent-dependent[19] quadriplegic. The irony of it hit me very hard, although I kept my emotions to myself. I knew there was no point in dwelling on it. But now I knew on a <u>visceral</u> level how fragile our existence is. ∎

---

19. **C2 vent-dependent.** Needing pumped oxygen

Respond *to the* SELECTION

What would you, as a teenager, most likely feel and do if one of your parents became a quadriplegic because of an accidental injury?

About *the* AUTHOR

Christopher Reeve was born on September 25, 1952 in New York City. Reeve traces his love of acting back to the early years of his childhood when he and his younger brother would climb inside cardboard grocery cartons and pretend they were pirate ships. By age eight, he had appeared in school plays, became interested in music, and was taking piano lessons. At age nine, he was chosen to be in an operetta at McCarter Theatre, a professional theater in Princeton, New Jersey. By the age of sixteen, he had an agent. He went to Cornell University where he majored in Music Theory and English. During his college years, he spent time studying theater in Britain and France. And in his final year at Cornell, he was one of two students (the other being Robin Williams) accepted to New York's famous Julliard School of Performing Arts.

Reeve has been in a total of 17 feature films, a dozen TV movies, and about 150 plays. Since his years after his accident in 1995, Reeve has gradually regained sensation in parts of his body—notably down the spine, in his left leg, and areas of his left arm. He continues to schedule many speaking engagements and is considering several projects to direct in the spring while tirelessly raising money for spinal cord injury research. He looks to the future with characteristic enthusiasm, saying: "I'm realistically optimistic. I don't plan to spend the rest of my life like this."

words for everyday use

vis • cer • al (vi′ sə rəl) *adj.,* felt deeply in the heart, not intellect. *I felt pain on a <u>visceral</u> level when my cat died.*

SPEECH AT THE 1996 DEMOCRATIC NATIONAL CONVENTION

Thank you. Thank you. Thank you very, very much. Well, I just have to start with a challenge to the President. Sir, I have seen your train go by, and I think I can beat it.

I'll even give you a head start.

(Over) the last few years we have heard a lot about something called "family values." And like many of you, I have struggled to figure out what that means, and since my accident, I have found a definition that seems to make sense. I think it means that we are all family.

And that we all have value.

Christopher Reeve talks with senators after a Labor, Health and Human Services committee meeting, 1999.

Now, if that's true, if America really is a family, then we have to recognize that many members of our family are hurting. And just to take one aspect of it, one in five of us has some kind of disability. You may have an aunt with Parkinson's disease, a neighbor with a spinal cord injury, or a brother with AIDS, and if (we're) really committed to this idea of family, we have got to do something about it.

Now first of all, our nation cannot tolerate discrimination of any kind.

And that's why the Americans with Disabilities Act is so important.

It must be honored everywhere. It is a Civil Rights Law that is tearing down barriers, both in architecture and in attitude.

Its purpose—its purpose is to give the disabled access not only to buildings but to every opportunity in society.

Now, I strongly believe our nation must give its full support to the caregivers, who are helping people with disabilities live independent lives.

Now, of course we have to balance the budget. And we will. We have to be extremely careful with every dollar we spend. But we have also got to take care of our family.

And not slash programs that people need. We should be enabling and healing and curing.

Now, one of the smartest things we can do about disability is to invest in research that will protect us from diseases and lead to cures.

This country already has a long history of doing it. When we put our minds to a problem, we find solutions. But our scientists can do more. We have got to give them the chance. And that means more funding for research.

Right now, for example, about a quarter million Americans have a spinal cord injury, and our government spends about $8.7 billion a year just maintaining these members of our family. But we only spend $40 million a year on research that would actually improve the quality of their lives, and get them off public assistance, or even cure them. We have got to be smarter and do better.

The money we invest in research today is going to determine the quality of life of members of our family tomorrow.

Now, during my rehabilitation, I met a young man named Gregory Patterson. He was innocently driving through Newark, New Jersey, and a stray bullet, from a gang shooting, went through a car window, right into his neck and severed his spinal cord. Five years ago, he might have died. Today, because of research, he is alive.

But merely being alive—merely being alive is not enough. We have a moral and an economic responsibility to ease his suffering and to prevent others from experiencing such pain.

And to do that, we don't need to raise taxes.

We just need to raise our expectations.

Now America has a tradition that many nations probably envy. We frequently achieve the impossible.

That's part of our national character. That's what got us from one coast to another, that's what got us the largest economy in the world. That's what got us to the moon.

Now on the wall of my room while I was in rehab, there was a picture of the Space Shuttle blasting off, and it was autographed by every astronaut now at NASA, and on the top of that picture, it says, "We found nothing is impossible."

Now that, that should be our motto. It's not a Democratic motto, not a Republican motto, it's an American motto.

It's not something one Party can do alone. It's something we as a nation have to do together.

So many of our dreams, so many dreams at first seem impossible. And then they seem improbable. And then when we summon the will, they soon become inevitable.

So if we can conquer outer space, we should be able to conquer inner space, too.

And that's the frontier of the brain, the central nervous system, and all the afflictions of the body that destroy so many lives, and rob our country of so much potential.

Research can provide hope for people who suffer from Alzheimer's. We have already discovered the gene that causes it. Research can provide hope for people like Muhammed Ali and the Reverend Billy Graham, who suffer from Parkinson's. Research can provide hope for Americans like Kirk Douglas, who suffer from stroke. We can ease the pain of people like Barbara Jordan, who battled multiple sclerosis. We can find treatments for people like Elizabeth Glaser, whom we lost to AIDS. And now that we know that (nerves in) the spinal cord can regenerate, we are on the way to getting millions of people around the world, millions of people around the world like me, up and out of these wheelchairs.

Now, 56 years ago, FDR dedicated new buildings for the National Institutes of Health. He said that, "The defense this nation seeks involves a great deal more than building airplanes, ships, guns, and bombs.

We cannot be a strong nation unless we are a healthy nation."

He could have said that today. President Roosevelt showed us that a man who could barely lift himself out of a wheelchair could still lift this nation out of despair.

And I believe, and so does this administration, in the most important principle, the most important principle that FDR taught us: America does not let its needy citizens fend for themselves.

America is stronger when all of us take care of all of us. Giving new life to that ideal is the challenge before us tonight. Thank you very much. Thank you. ■

ABOUT THE RELATED READING
Christopher Reeve gave this speech at the Democratic National Convention in 1996. Reeve has done much public speaking since his accident in an effort to raise public awareness about disabilities and to advocate for increased spending on research to fight paralysis. Reeve is also chairman of the board of the Christopher Reeve Paralysis Foundation (CRPF), which encourages and supports research to develop effective treatments and a cure for paralysis caused by spinal cord injury and other central nervous system disorders.

Investigate, *Inquire*, and Imagine

Recall: GATHERING FACTS

1a. What reasons does the author give for his daughter Al's giving up riding a year after his accident?

2a. What memories cause Reeve to feel "like a visitor at a spectacular outdoor museum"?

3a. Does Reeve "accept" paralysis? Is he "at peace" with it?

→ Interpret: FINDING MEANING

1b. What might be a deeper, more personal reason Al gave up riding?

2b. Why do you think Reeve lets himself have these memories?

3b. Do his answers make sense to you? Why do you think he answers these questions as he does?

Analyze: TAKING THINGS APART

4a. Identify Reeve's thoughts, words, and actions that show how he feels about his family and close friends. Is he bitter or protective? withdrawn or available? angry or thoughtful?

→ Synthesize: BRINGING THINGS TOGETHER

4b. Discuss what his thoughts, words, and actions reveal about Reeve's personal character.

Evaluate: MAKING JUDGMENTS

5a. How effective are Reeve's strategies for coping with his situation? What kinds of things has he learned, and what adjustments has he made?

→ Extend: CONNECTING IDEAS

5b. What strategies have you seen people use to deal with serious losses?

Understanding *Literature*

POINT OF VIEW. Point of view is the vantage point from which a story is told. If a story is told from a **first-person point of view**, the narrator uses the pronouns *I* and *we* and is a part of or a witness to the action. When a story is told from a **third-person point of view**, the narrator is outside the action; uses words such as *he, she, it,* and *they;* and avoids the use of *I* and *we.* Now that you have determined whether the point of view in *Still Me* is first- or third-person, what do you think are some advantages of using this person's point of view for a story of this type?

AUTOBIOGRAPHY. An **autobiography** is the story of a person's life, written by that person. Look again at your chart, filled in with what you already knew and what you learned from the reading about Christopher Reeve's life. Since this story is only a part of Reeve's entire autobiography, there are probably time periods on the chart that are less filled in. Which of these periods would you like to know more about? How could you find out about them?

Writer's Journal

1. Write the front and inside copy for a **greeting card** of encouragement that you could send to Christopher Reeve.

2. Design and write information for a **poster** to advertise to the public a fundraising dinner for research that would benefit quadriplegics.

3. What is your definition of a hero? Write a **statement of belief** about what a hero is, and read it to one or two of your classmates.

Skill Builders

Vocabulary

SENTENCE COMPLETION. Following is a list of words used in the selection from *Still Me.* Choose the word that best completes each of the following sentences and write it in the blank.

burden	spontaneity	sobered	cordoned	glib
sustained	unpredictability	fragile	visceral	self-pity
executed	incapacitated	depressed	amputation	cherished

1. Even though she would be bedridden for three years, the teenager refused to become negative and fall into _____ .

2. The front row of seats was _____ off for the relatives of the bride and groom.

3. He wondered how long he could carry the _____ of caring for his younger brothers and sisters.

4. Although we couldn't afford a vacation, I had a _____ need to visit the ocean.

5. The excited fans quickly _____ when the umpire called the hit a foul ball.

6. Because of needing to follow a standard set of questions in a limited time, the interview lacked _____ .

7. While starting to cross the mall, the grandmother suddenly froze, realizing her _____ three-year-old granddaughter was nowhere to be seen.

8. Her quick answer seemed too _____ given the seriousness of the situation.

9. How were they ever going to mend the _____ vase?

10. He much preferred a set routine, so he was frustrated by the _____ of his new schedule.

11. The skate-boarder crashed into the wall and _____ a broken shoulder.

12. _____ by the scorching heat, the woman could only drag herself slowly along the road.

Speaking and Listening

ROLE-PLAYING. Imagine you are Christopher Reeve, and prepare a short presentation to be given to new patients with spinal cord injuries. Be sure to include: a) simple facts on spinal cord injuries, b) the importance of rehabilitation and support groups, and c) encouragement. Working in pairs, give your presentation to your partner who will assume the role of one of the new patients. The new patient listens closely and asks a few questions about the presentation. Try to answer any questions the patient has. Then switch roles, repeating the activity.

Study and Research

REPORTING ON SCIENTIFIC RESEARCH. Scientists have made some important advances in the past few years on the way to finding a cure for victims of paralysis. Using library materials and the Internet, research and write a report on what some of these advances are. Be sure to include any statistics and facts about paralysis that you come across as well. Two Internet sites that might help you get started are: The Christopher Reeve Paralysis Foundation at http://www.APACURE.com, and Cure Paralysis Now at http://www.cureparalysis.org.

Collaborative Learning & Media Literacy

ANALYZING THE MEDIA. Working in small groups of three to five, explore and analyze different news media (magazines, newspapers, press releases, television news, radio news, Internet news) to see how they cover accidents causing severe long-term injury (spinal cord injuries, sudden blindness or deafness, full-body burns). Find news about long-term injuries to famous and non-famous people of any age. (The news can be from current or past times.) What differences in coverage do you notice? Which type of media goes into more detail? Which is briefer, with essential facts only? Do any of the media track the progress of the victim over time? Which of the media tries to educate the public about the injury beyond the accident being reported on? Most importantly, for each of the media, how is its coverage of long-term injuries the same as or different from its coverage of news of a less serious nature—such as athletic competitions, performances by popular musical groups, the opening of a mega-mall, and so on?

Prereading

"JOYRIDING"
by Jim Naughton

Reader's T O O L B O X

DESCRIPTION. A **description** gives a picture in words of a character, object, or scene. Descriptions make use of **sensory details**—words and phrases that describe how things look, sound, smell, taste, or feel. As you read "Joyriding," notice the many sensory details and list them under the headings LOOK, SOUND, SMELL, TASTE, and FEEL.

CHARACTERIZATION. Characterization is the act of creating or describing a character. Writers create characters in three major ways: by showing what characters say, do, and think; by showing what other characters say about them; and by showing what physical features, dress, and personality the characters display. The author of "Joyriding" uses all three techniques in characterizing the two boys in this story. As you read, find examples of these techniques and record them on the following graphic organizer.

Graphic *Organizer*

	Peter Whitney	Kevin McGrail
DIRECTLY DESCRIBING THE CHARACTER:	• Flat nose • • •	• Tall, lean, and broad-shouldered •
PORTRAYING THE CHARACTER'S BEHAVIOR, THOUGHTS, & EMOTIONS:	• He left his music and went out on the porch to watch the runner race by •	• At first Kevin felt kind of spooked when the music stopped . . . •
SHOWING WHAT OTHER CHARACTERS SAY OR THINK ABOUT THEM:	• The kid was obviously never going to be a runner, Kevin thought... •	• The way the boy moved reminded him of music. •

Reader's *Journal*

Which of your activities seem like work and which seem like play?

Reader's *Resource*

• **SPORTS CONNECTION.** Cross-country is a long-distance running sport in which competitors run a distance of 5 kilometers (3.1 miles) on an outdoor course (instead of on a track). Cross-country competitions occur on the high school, college, and amateur levels.

• Individuals have many skills and talents. They may range from writing music, creating works of art, or playing a certain game to singing or dancing or acting, surfing the Internet, cooking, swimming, or solving puzzles. Sociologists and psychologists are now studying the outcomes of how people approach their skills and talents. For example, some people perform a skill or talent for the simple pleasure of doing so, while others work hard at the same skill or talent in order to excel. Be on the watch for news on these studies and think about how it might apply to you and your own skills and talents.

JOYRIDING

Jim Naughton

Peter glanced at the clock on the bookshelf. It was quarter after four. "Fifteen minutes to freedom," he said to himself. Fifteen minutes until he could turn off the metronome[1]—*two, three, four*—and stop moving his fingers across the keys.

For Peter the best part of the day began at the moment he stopped practicing the piano. Beginning at four-thirty each day he had an entire hour to himself. He could read science fiction. He could play video games in the den. He just couldn't leave the house.

This had never really bothered him until the afternoon three weeks earlier when he'd seen the runner gliding up Putnam Street hill. Something about the way the older boy looked, something about the way he moved, drew Peter away from his music and out onto the porch to watch the runner race by in his maroon and gold Darden High School sweat suit.

That night at dinner his mother had said, "Mrs. Kennedy says she saw you on the porch this afternoon. I hope you weren't neglecting your music."

---

1. **metronome.** Instrument that makes repeated clicking sounds at an adjustable pace, used to mark rhythm, especially in practicing music

"I was just saying hello to a friend," Peter lied. He didn't even know the other boy's name.

Intimidated by his mother's intelligence network, Peter had not <u>ventured</u> back onto the porch for three weeks, content to watch from his bench as the older boy churned up the hill and off to the oval behind Peter's junior high school. But the previous afternoon, as he'd watched the second hand on the parlor clock ticking away the final seconds of his captivity, *two, three, four,* Peter had decided to go back out on the porch. He thought he might wave as the runner strode by, but instead he studied the older boy in silence.

The runner was tall, lean, and broad-shouldered. *I am none of that stuff,* Peter thought.

The runner had sharp features. Peter's nose looked like he had flattened it against a window and it had stayed that way. The runner had a clear, steady gaze. Peter was near-sighted[2] and tended to squint. The runner had a shock of copper-colored hair. Peter had a frizz so fine it was hard to say what color it was.

In spite of these differences, Peter could have imagined himself in the other boy's place were it not for the runner's grace. The way the boy moved reminded him of music. His legs had the spring of a sprightly melody. His arms pumped a <u>relentless</u> rhythm. He ascended the hill almost effortlessly, as though gravity were no greater <u>hindrance</u> on this steep incline than it had been on the prairie-flat main street below.

He must never lose, Peter thought.

> **GUIDED READING**
>
> What does the way the runner moves remind Peter of?

That was another way in which they were different. Peter had just come in third in the piano competition sponsored by the university, after coming in second in the contest sponsored by the orchestra and third in the contest sponsored by the bank.

"Peter," his mother said, "you are a <u>perpetual</u> runner-up." Then she decided that rather than practice for one hour every day, he should practice for two. Two hours!

> **GUIDED READING**
>
> What does Peter's mother call him when he comes in third in the piano competition sponsored by the university?

But two hours were now up. And as Peter stopped the metronome, he spotted a familiar figure in a maroon sweat suit at the bottom of the hill.

Who is this kid? Kevin asked himself. Kevin McGrail had not yet reached the crest of Putnam Street when he noticed the pudgy boy in the orange T-shirt on the porch of the white stucco[3] house.

At least he's on the porch today, Kevin thought. For three weeks the kid had watched him from his piano bench. Every day as he pounded up the hill Kevin would hear this weird tinkly music coming from the stucco house across the street. Then there would be a pause as he passed by, and he would see the little frizzy-headed kid looking at him through the window. Then the weird tinkly music would begin again.

At first Kevin felt kind of spooked when the music stopped, like maybe Freddy Krueger

---

2. **near-sighted.** Ability to see near, but not far
3. **stucco.** Exterior finish composed of cement, sand, and lime mixed with water

---

words for everyday use

ven • ture (ven[t]′ shər) *v.,* undertake and be exposed to risks and dangers. *My brave brother <u>ventured</u> out into the snowstorm to fetch our dog.*

re • lent • less (ri lent′ ləs) *adj.,* showing no sign of decrease in intensity, strength, or pace. *Even though he had run five miles, he was <u>relentless</u> in refusing to take a break.*

hin • drance (hin′ drənts) *n.,* something that interferes. *The hail was a <u>hindrance</u> in getting the players excited to play.*

per • pet • u • al (pər pe′ chə wəl) *adj.,* occurring continually. *Sharon is a <u>perpetual</u> talker, always gabbing about something.*

was going to jump out of the bushes or something. But after a while he just wondered why the kid was so interested in him.

It wasn't like he was a big star or anything. Kevin was the number three man on the Darden cross-country team, a nice steady runner who could be counted on to come in ahead of the number three man on the opposing team. Coach Haggerty always told him he could be the number two man if he worked at it, but Kevin thought working at something was the surest way to turn it from a pleasure into a chore.

GUIDED READING

What does Kevin think when Coach Haggerty tells him he could be the number two man if he worked at it?

Just look at what happened with Mark Fairbanks. He and Kevin used to hang out together, but that was before Haggerty had convinced Mark that if he devoted his entire life to cross-county he could be a star. Well, Markie was a star all right. He was the fastest guy on the team and one of the top runners in the district. But he was also the biggest drone in the school. Every day at the beginning of practice he would shout, "Okay, men, it's time to go to *work!*"

Kevin felt the strain on his legs lighten as he reached the top of the hill. He saw the road flatten before him and felt the crisp autumn air tingling pleasantly in his lungs. *As soon as this becomes work*, he said to himself, *I quit*.

"Mom," Peter said at dinner, "I want to go out for the football team."

His mother looked up from her Caesar salad with an expression of exaggerated horror. "Think of your hands!" she said.

Peter had known she would say that. "Well, maybe basketball then," he replied.

"That is every bit as dangerous."

Peter had kind of figured she would say that too. "Well, I want to do something," he said. "Something where there's people. Where there's guys."

His mother put down her fork, pressed her palms together in front of her face, hooked her thumbs under her chin, and regarded him from over her fingertips. *Now we are getting serious*, Peter thought.

"What about choir?" his mother proposed. "I haven't wanted you exposed to a lot of influences. Musically, I mean. But I am not insensitive to your need for companionship."

Peter shook his head. "How about cross-country?" he asked. "It's only running. How about that?"

GUIDED READING

What does Peter's mother say when he asks if he can go out for cross-country?

"Sports are nothing but trouble," his mother said. "Trouble and disappointment. I think you will agree it is much more satisfying to devote yourself to something at which you can really excel."

"There is a boy on the high-school team who runs up at the oval every day," Peter said. "He told me I could practice with him."

His mother pursed her lips. If Peter could only have explained his plan to her, he was certain she would have said yes. But he wasn't ready to try that. He could barely make sense of it himself.

One thing he was sure of: That boy who ran past the house every day was a champion. He would know what separates winners from perpetual runners-up. And if Peter

GUIDED READING

What is one thing Peter is sure of?

could learn that, well then, his mother would be happy, and if his mother was happy, well then, everything would be okay again. All she had to do was say yes.

"You still owe me two hours at that piano every day," she said.

Kevin was surprised to see the little piano player up at the oval the next day. The kid was dressed in one of those shapeless sweat suits they wore in junior-high-school gym class.

Looks like he's already winded, Kevin thought as he watched the kid struggle through about a dozen jumping jacks. *I hope he doesn't hurt himself.*

Kevin was beginning his second lap when the kid fell in beside him.

"Hi," the boy said.

"Hey," said Kevin without slowing down.

"I'm getting in shape for next season," said the boy, who was already breathing heavily and losing ground.

"It's good to give yourself a lot of time," Kevin said, not meaning to sound quite so smart.

"See you around," the boy called as Kevin opened up the space between them.

Every day for the next three weeks the routine was the same: The kid was always waiting when Kevin arrived. He would puff along beside Kevin for a few strides, try to start a gasping conversation, and then fall hopelessly behind. The kid was obviously never going to be a runner, Kevin thought, and he sure didn't look like he was enjoying himself. Yet there he was, grinding away, just like Fairbanks only without the talent.

You're a better man than I am, Kevin thought. *Or a sicker one.*

That Friday when Kevin got to the oval the chubby kid took one look at him and started to run. It was as though he were giving himself a head start in some kind of private race. The thought of

GUIDED READING

Why does Kevin laugh at the thought of some competition between himself and Peter?

some competition between the two of them made Kevin laugh, because he generally lapped the kid at least five or six times each session.

He put the little piano player out of his mind and tried to focus on the rhythm of his own footfalls. The following weekend he and the rest of the Darden team would be competing in the district championships, and Kevin had begun to think it might be a good time to answer a question that had been nagging at him for the last month. He wanted to know how good he was—not how good he could be if he devoted his entire life to cross-country, but how good he was at that moment. What would happen, he wondered, if he ran one race as hard as he could?

Part of him did not want to know. Suppose he beat out Billy Kovacs, the number two man on the Darden team. That would mean Coach Haggerty would be all over him. He'd expect Kevin to have a big season in his senior year, maybe even make it to the state championships. Just thinking about the way Haggerty put his <u>gaunt</u> face up next to yours and shouted "Go for the goal!" was enough to stop Kevin in his tracks.

On the other hand he might not beat Billy Kovacs, and that would be depressing too. Kevin liked to think of himself as somebody who *could* run faster if he *wanted* to run faster. But if he went all out and still finished in the middle of the pack, it would mean he was just another <u>mediocre</u> high-school runner.

Maybe I should just run a nice easy race and forget about this, Kevin thought. *It would be less complicated.*

GUIDED READING

What is the question that has been nagging at Kevin for the last month?

words for everyday use

gaunt (gänt') *adj.*, excessively thin and angular. *The man's <u>gaunt</u> face was thin and hollow-looking.*

me • di • o • cre (mē dē ō' kər) *adj.*, of moderate or low quality, value, ability or performance. *My singing is <u>mediocre</u> because it is neither the best nor the worst.*

As he began the seventh of his eight laps, Kevin noticed that the chubby kid was still running—puffing and panting and <u>lurching</u> from one foot to another. "This is my bell lap,"[4] he gasped as Kevin trotted by.

Kevin chuckled at the idea of the little piano player in a race, but when he finished his workout he stopped to watch the other boy circle the track one last time. This was the kid's fourth lap. Kevin had never seen him run a mile before, and he felt a sneaky sense of pride in his training partner's accomplishment.

> **GUIDED READING**
>
> How did Kevin feel when he saw Peter run his first mile?

The kid came chugging down the track, gulping huge bites of air and clutching his right side. But when he reached his imaginary finish line, he threw both hands into the air and held that pose for a moment before collapsing onto the grass. Kevin was about to jog over when he heard a voice in the stands announce: "And the winner in the Pudge Ball Olympics: Peter Whitney."

Kevin turned quickly and recognized three kids from the freshman class at school. "Hey, why don't you bozos take off," he said sharply, and looked at them long enough for the kids to understand that he meant it.

The piano player was still lying flat on his back when Kevin reached him and extended a hand to help him to his feet.

"Thanks," the boy said, in a barely <u>audible</u> voice.

Hours after he had gotten home, Peter kept replaying the details in his head to see if there was something he had missed. First the fudge-brains from the ninth grade had made fun of him and the runner had taken his side. Next the older boy had waited around while Peter caught his breath. Then they'd walked down the hill together all the way to Peter's house. It was almost like they were friends.

But things had begun to go wrong as soon as Peter tried to ask him his secret. The trouble was he couldn't figure out how to put the question in his own words, and so he began talking like the books his mother read to help her get ahead at her office.

"Do you visualize your goals?" he blurted.

The boy looked at him <u>quizzically</u>.

"Some people do that," Peter continued, eager to fill the silence. "But other people, they say that you should concentrate on developing the habits of a highly effective person."

The runner didn't respond, so Peter felt compelled to keep talking. "Do you think your habits are effective? I mean, are they consistent with your aspirations? You know?"

The other boy shrugged. "You still play the piano?" he asked.

"Two hours a day," Peter said.

"You like it?"

"No," Peter said. "I mean, yes. I used to."

"But now you don't?"

Peter did not want to waste time talking about himself, but the older boy seemed genuinely interested. "Before we came here I had a different teacher," he said, and as he did every time he sat down at the piano, he began to think of Mickey Ray.

---

4. **bell lap.** Final lap, usually signaled by the ringing of a bell during a race

words for everyday use

lurch (lərch′) *v.*, roll or tip abruptly; stagger. *The toddler began to <u>lurch</u> while taking its first staggering steps.*

au • di • ble (ä′ də bəl) *adj.*, pertaining to the sense of hearing. *It was hard to hear what was said over the intercom because the words were not <u>audible</u>.*

quiz • zi • cal (kwi′ zi kəl) *adj.*, questioning or puzzled expression. *Because the boy didn't understand, he looked up at the teacher with a <u>quizzical</u> expression.* **quizzically,** *adv.*

Mickey was his teacher back in Rochester. He taught part-time at the university and at night he played in clubs. Peter's mother didn't like him because he wore a ponytail. But everybody told her that he was the best teacher in town. She let Peter take lessons from him on one condition: that they play only "performance pieces"—compositions Peter might later play in a competition.

But Mickey did not always abide by this condition. Every once in a while he would pull a new piece of music from his satchel, wink <u>conspiratorially</u> at Peter, and ask him to give it a try. This is how Peter got to know jazz and ragtime and gospel music.

After Peter played through the piece once, Mickey would sit down on the bench beside him. "Next time," he would say, "a little more like this." And off he would go, playing the same notes in the same order, but making the piece sound more <u>fluid</u>, more powerful, more alive.

"It is not about hitting the right key at the right time," Mickey used to say. "It is about taking this baby for a ride." Peter began to tell the other boy about Mickey Ray.

"He sounds cool," the runner said.

"My teacher now is better," Peter said. Actually he wasn't sure if that was true. "Mr. Brettone is a superior musical pedagogue,"[5] his mother had said. But lately Peter had found himself imagining that Mr. Brettone had tiny pickaxes attached to his fingertips and that each time he struck a key it would crack and crumble.

GUIDED READING

How did Mickey explain how he made the piece sound more fluid, more powerful, more alive?

GUIDED READING

What has Peter imagined lately about his new teacher, Mr. Brettone?

They were standing in front of the house by the time Peter finished the story, and he was no closer to learning the other boy's secret than he had before all those grueling afternoons on the oval. Finally, just as the other boy was about to leave, he blurted: "How do you do it?"

"Do what?"

"Win."

"I don't know anything about winning," the runner said. "I just know about running."

GUIDED READING

What does Kevin say when Peter asks him how he wins?

Then came what Peter found the most puzzling exchange of all. "I hope you win at the districts," he said as the boy jogged away.

"Now what would I want to do that for?" the runner called back.

Kevin stood among the <u>throng</u> of two hundred runners packed into a clearing just off the first fairway at the Glen Oaks Golf Club. At the crack of the starter's pistol they would all surge forward onto the manicured expanse of the fairway. The sight of all those bodies churning and all those bright uniforms bobbing up and down was so captivating that during his first two seasons Kevin had hung back at the beginning just to take in the spectacle.

Not this year, though. He had decided to run the race of his life, and moments after the gun was fired, he found himself in the first fourth of the great mob of runners struggling for position as they tore toward the first

---

5. **pedagogue.** Teacher

words for everyday use

con • spir • a • to • ri • al (kən spir ə tōr′ ē əl) *adj.*, plotting, conspiring, scheming. *The <u>conspiratorial</u> enemy looked over his plan of attack.* **conspiratorially,** *adv.*

flu • id (flü′ əd) *adj.*, changing or shifting smoothly. *The cat walked with <u>fluid</u> grace over the glass.*

throng (thrôŋ′) *n.*, multitude of people crowded or assembled together. *There was a <u>throng</u> of people crowded together at the rock concert.*

green, where the course cut sharply downhill and into the woods. As he hit what he thought was a good cruising speed for the first stage of the race, Kevin couldn't help wondering if he would wear himself out too quickly or collapse on the grass at the finish line like that crazy little piano player.

It was strange to be thinking of him at a time like this. Or maybe it wasn't. Because what Kevin had been trying to figure out all along was whether excelling at his sport would somehow ruin it for him, the way excelling at the piano had ruined it for Peter. He half suspected that it would, but something the kid had told him that day Kevin had walked him home had given him a . . . kind of hope.

GUIDED READING

What has Kevin been trying to figure out all along?

In the pack just ahead of him Kevin picked out Mark Fairbanks, Kovacs, and a couple of the top runners from other schools he had raced against during the year. No question—he was a lot closer to them than he usually was at the half-mile mark.

As the runner streaked by, Peter cheered and pointed his friend out to his mother. It had taken heroic persuasion to get Mom to come out to a cross-country meet on a Saturday morning, but now he was sure that everything would go just the way he planned. His friend would win the race and then Peter would introduce him to Mom.

He wasn't really certain what would happen after that. He couldn't really explain why he wanted them to meet. It wasn't so that Mom could see that he was making friends at school, because she thought friends only distracted him from his piano. And it wasn't because he thought she would be impressed by a cross-country champion, since Mom didn't really appreciate sports.

Peter wanted them to meet so that Mom could see that he had a little of the runner in him, a little bit of the champion, a little bit of something that would lift him beyond the status of a "perpetual runner-up." If he could only convince her of that, maybe it wouldn't be so hard to keep sitting down alone at the piano. Or to keep sitting down to dinner with her.

GUIDED READING

Why does Peter want his mother and Kevin to meet?

"He's not winning," Peter's mother said as they watched the runners cut off the fairway and into the woods.

"It's strategy, Mom," Peter told her, though he too was wondering why his friend was not at the head of the pack.

They were tearing along an old railroad bed at the top of a ridge near the fourth tee. Kevin's legs still felt strong. His breath came easily. Fairbanks, who was fighting for the lead, was just a speck up along the train tracks, but Billy Kovacs was only twenty yards or so ahead of Kevin.

I can take him, Kevin thought, *but then I'll have to hold him off the rest of the way.* He hesitated for a second, and then decided to pick up his pace.

A single runner in the maroon Darden uniform came streaking out of the woods and onto the tenth fairway. There was only a half mile remaining in the race.

"That isn't your friend," Peter's mother said.

Another runner in red and white charged out of the woods a few yards behind. In a few moments there were six, seven, and then eight other runners pounding the last half mile toward the finish line. Peter didn't recognize any of them.

"I'm sorry, dear," his mother said, rummaging in her purse for her car keys.

Peter felt as though he had bet a lifetime of allowances on the wrong horse.

GUIDED READING

How does Peter feel as he doesn't recognize any of the runners in the last half mile of the cross-country race?

🎹

As he tore out of the woods and onto the tenth fairway, Kevin began counting the people ahead of him, a feat made more difficult by the sweat dripping into his eyes. There were fifteen of them, as nearly as he could tell. The top ten finishers went on to the state finals. Somewhere up along the railroad tracks the desire to be in that group had seized him and he had picked up his pace. Now the wind burned in his lungs and the acid burned in his calves. His Achilles tendons[6] felt like guitar strings being tightened with each footfall. He had less than half a mile to make up six places.

He glanced quickly across the fairway and saw Fairbanks dueling for the lead with Pat Connors of Tech. In the crowd behind them he saw the little piano player. He was gazing in Kevin's direction, disappointment etched on his face.

GUIDED READING

How does Kevin react when he sees disappointment etched in Peter's face?

I'm running the race of my life and it isn't good enough for him, Kevin thought. He could feel the anger rising inside him. The race was ruined for him now, and he began to doubt his motives. Was he really running all out just to see what it felt like, or had the

GUIDED READING

How is the race now ruined for Kevin?

attention of this peculiar little kid made him hungry for more?

Kevin wanted his sense of purity back. He wanted to stop caring whether he finished in the top ten. Something inside him whispered, "Slow down," but instead he emptied his mind and kept running.

Into that emptiness floated the memory of the conversation he and the little piano player had had just a few days before. The kid had been talking about his old teacher, the one who liked to take the piano "for a ride." *I can't play*, Kevin thought, *but I can run. This can be my ride.*

GUIDED READING

What does Kevin think when he remembers Peter's old teacher who liked to take the piano "for a ride"?

Imagining that he was Mickey Ray, Kevin focused his eyes on the ground in front of him and sprinted the last two hundred yards, unaware of the screaming fans or the other runners on the course.

🎹

Peter couldn't understand what the big fuss was about. The kid had come in eleventh. That wasn't even good enough to qualify for the state finals, yet people were acting like that was a bigger deal than Mark Fairbanks, who had come in second. It was pretty cool to take a minute off your best time, he supposed, but still, eleventh place wasn't worth all the cheering the Darden fans did when the kid crossed the finish line.

Besides that, Kevin McGrail looked like hell. When he had glided up Putnam Street six weeks ago he had been so smooth, so

---

6. **Achilles tendons.** Tendons joining the calf muscles to the heel bone

---

words for everyday use

mo • tive (mō′ təv) *n.*, something that causes a person to act a certain way. *Because his motive was to become rich, he chose to be a doctor.*

<u>poised</u>. Now he was bent over, walking like he had a sunburn on the bottoms of his feet.

Peter saw the boy's coach, a gaunt man wearing a baseball cap, put an arm around Kevin's shoulder. "You dug down deep and you came up big," the coach barked.

Kevin drew a few rapid breaths. "I was joyriding," he said.

"Joyriding," Peter repeated to himself as he sat at his piano later that afternoon. "Joyriding lands you in eleventh place." He stood up, opened the piano bench, and withdrew the exercises Mr. Brettone had assigned for that week. Beneath it he found *The Fats Waller Songbook*. Mickey had given it to him as a going-away present. Peter thumbed through the pages until he found "Your Feet's Too Big." Just the title made him laugh. And the way Mickey used to play it—

He looked up to see his mother standing in the doorway. "What are we featuring this afternoon?" she asked.

"Exercises for the left hand," Peter said, and he sat down to work. ∎

Respond *to the* SELECTION

Do you think Peter is going to forget about Mickey Ray's suggestion to take the music "for a ride"? Why, or why not?

About *the* AUTHOR

As a sports reporter, **Jim Naughton** covered the Mets for the New York Daily News in 1986, the year the Mets won the World Series. The holder of a B.A. in journalism and an M.A. in American history from Syracuse University, he has also covered sports for *The New York Times* and worked as a feature writer for *The Post-Standard* in Syracuse and *The Washington Post*. He is the author of three sports books for young adults: two novels and a biography of Michael Jordon. Naughton's most recent novel, *Where the Frost Has Its Home*, features a seventh-grade hockey player. In high school, Naughton helped found his school's cross-country team. But he says, when he was growing up, "my heart belonged to baseball. Unfortunately, I wasn't much good at it." As an adult living in Washington DC, he now walks and swims for exercise.

words for everyday use   **poised** (poizd') *adj.*, dignified, self-confident. *The film star looked <u>poised</u> as he received his award for Best Actor.*

Investigate, Inquire, and Imagine

Recall: GATHERING FACTS

1a. Why does Peter's mother increase his practice time from one to two hours?

2a. What does Kevin think after he compares Peter's efforts at running to those of Mark Fairbanks?

3a. Why couldn't Peter understand what the fuss over Kevin was all about at the end of the race?

→ **Interpret:** FINDING MEANING

1b. How do you think Peter feels about this?

2b. What do you think this means?

3b. What do you think caused Peter to react this way?

Analyze: TAKING THINGS APART

4a. Identify some of the things Peter does that help Kevin decide to give the race his best shot.

→ **Synthesize:** BRINGING THINGS TOGETHER

4b. Predict whether Kevin will view his last-quarter-mile sprint as work or enjoyment.

Evaluate: MAKING JUDGMENTS

5a. Decide whether Peter views Kevin as a hero. Then decide whether you think Kevin is a hero. Explain.

→ **Extend:** CONNECTING IDEAS

5b. How do you think Peter will apply his experiences with Kevin to his own life? Who will have a stronger influence on him, Kevin, or his mother?

Understanding Literature

DESCRIPTION. A **description** gives a picture in words of a character, object, or scene. Descriptions make use of **sensory details**—words and phrases that describe how things look, sound, smell, taste, or feel. In your opinion, what were some of the most effective sensory details in "Joyriding"?

CHARACTERIZATION. Characterization is the act of creating or describing a character. Writers use three major techniques to create a character: direct description, portraying the character's behavior, and presenting the thoughts and emotions of the character. Looking at your entries on the graphic organizer, summarize the characterization of Peter. Summarize the characterization of Kevin. How are these two characters different? How are they similar?

Writer's Journal

1. Describe for a friend a kind of food you like by **listing** five sensory details about it.

2. Pretend you are Peter's mother and that you have an advice column in your city's newspaper. Write your **advice** to a reader who asks how he can move from second to first place in a piano competition.

3. Imagine you are Peter. Write a **dream report** for Mickey Ray that tells about last night's dream in which you won a piano competition by taking your well-practiced performance piece "for a ride."

Skill Builders

Language, Grammar, and Style

CORRECTING USAGE ERRORS. Review "Correcting Common Usage Problems" in the Language Arts Survey 3.44. Then identify the correct word from the two given in parentheses in each of the following sentences.

1. Peter was (altogether, all together) convinced that Kevin was a champion.
2. Peter's mother said, "You (can, may) have an hour's time to yourself after you practice for two hours."
3. Kevin enjoyed running (accept, except) when it became work.
4. At first, Peter always did (fewer, less) laps than four.
5. (Among, Between) those five runners and himself, Kevin felt he could put in the best time.
6. Coach Haggerty often told Kevin, "You (can, may) be the number two man if you work at it."
7. The large audience clapped (altogether, all together) as the pianist finished playing.
8. Peter wanted his mother to (accept, except) that he had a little bit of something that would lift him beyond the status of a "perpetual runner-up."
9. The walk after practice was usually a good time for some talking (among, between) Kevin and Peter.
10. Peter sometimes wanted to do (fewer, less) practicing than his mother requested.

Speaking and Listening

DISCUSSION AND ROLE-PLAY. Sit with a partner and give each other examples of something you've been trying to learn and how you've been going about it. Be sure to explain how the learning is enjoyable, how it seems like work, or both. After each of you listens carefully to the other's example, give him or her some feedback—for instance, some other ways to learn it, some encouragement, some cautions, or your own reactions (admiration, surprise, whether you're trying to learn the same thing, and so on).

With your partner, take the roles of Mickey Ray and Mr. Brettone and have a conversation on how to play a piece of music on the piano. Remembering to stay in character, try to use as many sensory details (how things look, taste, sound, feel, and smell) as possible and have the conversation grow into an argument. Then switch roles and do the same, except have the speakers be agreeable.

Applied English

GIVING DIRECTIONS. Every day people all over the world face the challenge of doing something they have never done before. Despite their inexperience, many succeed because some-one else is able to give them clear, precise directions. Review the guidelines for "Giving Directions," found in Language Arts Survey 6.3. Write a set of directions for how best to do one of the following:

- Sprint as far as you can
- Read a short story and understand it
- Memorize a song, a poem, or a jingle
- Catch a ball
- Your choice of topic

Collaborative Learning and Study and Research

EXAMINING ACHIEVEMENTS. In small groups, use library resources and the Internet to find and read about some of the star performers in various fields of activity, such as business, teaching, politics, military, or law. Discuss whether each person who excels in each field appears to be more technical (precise, accurate), more expressive/creative (taking the activity "for a ride"), or both. Chart your data and look for any patterns that might begin to emerge. For each field of activity, report whether most of its "stars" seem to be known for technical expertise, expressive/creative talents, or both. Can you think of reasons for your findings in each field?

Reader's Journal

How do you feel and react when someone cuts in line in front of you? when someone tries to force you to do something?

Reader's TOOLBOX

DIALOGUE. Dialogue is conversation involving two or more people or characters. Plays are made up of dialogue and stage directions. In a play, dialogue appears after the names of characters. As you read "A Woman Called Truth," notice that not all the words after the names of characters are dialogue. Try to identify examples of dialogue by looking for conversations involving more than one character.

STAGE DIRECTIONS. Stage directions are notes included in a play to describe how something should look, sound, or be performed. Stage directions describe setting, lighting, music, sound effects, entrances and exits, props, and the movements of characters. They are usually printed in italics and enclosed in brackets or parentheses. As you read "A Woman Called Truth," look for such descriptions in its stage directions. See the Elements of Drama on page 694 for more information.

Prereading

A Woman Called Truth

by Sandra Fenichel Asher

Reader's Resource

- **HISTORY CONNECTION.** Sojourner Truth was born into slavery in 1797 in Ulster County, New York. In 1827, Sojourner escaped from her master, and the following year she was freed under the New York State Anti-Slavery Act. As a free woman she took on the name of Sojourner Truth and began speaking out against slavery and for women's rights. At six feet tall, Sojourner was an excellent speaker with a booming voice. Traveling on foot, she took her ideas on freedom as far west as Ohio. Her speeches upset many and sometimes put her in great personal danger. Sojourner's most famous speech, "Ain't I a Woman?"—delivered in Akron, Ohio, in 1851—made even a white and prejudiced audience pay attention. In 1864 Sojourner was appointed counselor with the National Freedmen's Relief Association. She died on November 26, 1883, in Battle Creek, Michigan.

- Most African-American slaves toiled endlessly on huge plantations under brutal conditions. Out of their pain and suffering, slaves created and sang spirituals, or religious folk songs, to give them hope, faith, and courage to go on living. With short lines repeating over and over, spirituals were sung in a rich, rhythmic harmony, usually in choral rather than solo form. These deeply sorrowful songs gave slaves a means of communication as well as a way to ease the burden of their imprisonment. Many of the songs contained coded messages that only the slaves could understand. Spirituals flourished in the 1800s.

Graphic Organizer

In each cluster, jot down stage directions that reveal information about the cluster's label.

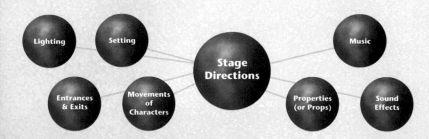

A Woman CALLED TRUTH

Sandra Fenichel Asher

A WOMAN CALLED TRUTH
A Play in One Act
For One Woman and Others*

CHARACTERS

SOJOURNER TRUTH . . . . also referred to as BELLE, a tall, muscular, handsome black woman with a forceful speaking and singing voice

*OTHERS

Two women and three men play a variety of roles as follows:

FIRST WOMAN . . . . black, also plays MAMA, SISSY, and OLD WOMAN

SECOND WOMAN . . . . white, also plays MRS. NEELY, MARIA, MRS. GEDNEY, and MRS. WHITING

FIRST MAN . . . . .white, also plays BAUMFREY, NEELY, CATLIN, ISAAC, CHIP, OLD MAN, and FIRST REVEREND

SECOND MAN . . . . white, also plays AUCTIONEER, DUMONT, GEDNEY, OFFICER, and SECOND REVEREND

THIRD MAN . . . . black, also plays brother PETER, BOB, son PETE, and SLAVE BOY

TIME: Approximately 1810–1855

PLACE: In and around Ulster County, New York, New York City, and Akron, Ohio.

AT RISE: *The stage is bare except for six cubes or stools, a lectern,*[1] *a prop table, and hat racks. Five cubes are arranged U. The lectern is DR; the sixth cube, DR of it. The table and racks are at the sides of stage and hold props and costume changes.* OTHERS *are seated on U cubes in shadow.* FIRST WOMAN *and* THIRD MAN *wear slave cloth; the rest, street dress suggesting the 1800s.*

SOJOURNER, *also in slave cloth, a rough strip of undyed material with a neck hole, sits on DR cube in a pool of light.* OTHERS' *voices are heard out of darkness.*

FIRST WOMAN. Tell your story. It must be told.

SECOND WOMAN (*disdainfully*). Well, wouldn't you just know it?

FIRST MAN. Is something wrong?

THIRD MAN. Tell your story.

SECOND WOMAN. Don't you see her? Sitting on the steps of the <u>podium</u> as if she owned the place? This is no woman's rights convention. This is an abolitionist[2] affair. Get her down from there.

FIRST WOMAN. Tell your story.

SOJOURNER. But who will listen? Who will hear?

FIRST WOMAN. They'll listen. They'll hear.

(SOJOURNER *rises as* OTHERS *sing first verse of* "Somebody Callin' My Name.")

OTHERS.

HUSH, HUSH, SOMEBODY
    CALLIN' MY NAME,

HUSH, HUSH, SOMEBODY
    CALLIN' MY NAME,

HUSH, HUSH, SOMEBODY
    CALLIN' MY NAME,

OH, MY LORD, OH, MY LORD,
    WHAT SHALL I DO?

SOJOURNER (*moves behind lectern and begins her <u>narrative</u> in a mature but not overly aged voice*). My name? (*Laughs, shakes her head.*)

---

1. **lectern.** Stand with a slanted top used to hold papers and books for speeches
2. **abolitionist.** Person who supported the abolishing of slavery

---

dis • dain • ful (dis dān' fəl) *adj.,* to be full of scorn or contempt. *She gave a <u>disdainful</u> speech about the unfair treatment of animals.* **disdainfully,** *adv.*

po • di • um (pō' dē əm) *n.,* small platform for a speaker or conductor. *The speaker put his notes on the <u>podium</u> before he began his speech.*

nar • ra • tive (nar' ə tiv) *n.,* story or account of events and experiences. *My grandpa's <u>narrative</u> included stories about his childhood.*

Which one is that, I wonder? Oh, I've had a bunch of them in my day. And a bunch of days for each of them. Yes, indeed, I've lived a life, I have. "What if there is no heaven?" a fellow once asked me. "What if you never get there? What'll you say then?" "I'll say, 'Bless the Lord,'" I told him, I had a good time thinking I would! (OTHERS *ad lib[3] responses of* "Amen," *etc., as if at a lecture or tent meeting.*) I was born a slave in Ulster County, New York. Oh, yes, there were slaves up there, too. Not so many as in the south, and not so profitable, so there was talk going on about changing the laws. Took its time doing me any good. Must have been seventeen ninety-something I came into this world. On a bed of straw in the slave cellar. We were part of the livestock, Mama, Papa, my brother Peter, and me. There were other children, too, but I never knew them. All sold away. Mama called me Isabelle, but that got shortened to Belle. My last name belonged to my master, just like me. Belle Hardenburgh. Master Hardenburgh's Belle. Papa's name was Baumfrey, a Dutch word. Ulster County was Dutch country, you see. Everybody spoke Dutch up there, master and slave alike. Baumfrey means tall, strong tree.

> **GUIDED READING**
>
> What does the narrator first say about her birth?

> **GUIDED READING**
>
> Except for her brother Peter, why did the narrator never know the other children in her family?

> **GUIDED READING**
>
> Who spoke Dutch in Ulster County, New York?

MAMA (*in darkness*). Where are you going, Baumfrey?

SOJOURNER (*continuing narrative*). Master Hardenburgh was a kindly man, but he was getting old.

BAUMFREY (*in darkness*). Up to the sickroom, Mama Betts. I've been called.

MAMA. Is Master that bad?

BAUMFREY. Bad, Mama Betts. Bad sick. I've got to go.

SOJOURNER. There was an awful quiet in the slave cellar that night. Families huddled together, waiting. Peter and I fell asleep, but Mama kept watch.

(PETER *comes forward into light as* SOJOURNER *moves in front of lectern. They huddle on floor, asleep.* OTHERS *sing following verse of* "Somebody Callin' My Name.")

OTHERS.

> EARLY ONE MORNIN', DEATH
>   CAME KNOCKIN' AT MY DOOR,
> EARLY ONE MORNIN', DEATH
>   CAME KNOCKIN' AT MY DOOR,
> EARLY ONE MORNIN', DEATH
>   CAME KNOCKIN' AT MY DOOR,
> OH, MY LORD, OH, MY LORD,
>   WHAT SHALL I DO?

(MAMA *hurries forward into light whispering.*)

MAMA. Isabelle! Peter! Wake up.

SOJOURNER (*in a child's voice*). Mama? What is it?

MAMA. Just listen to me, child. Pay attention now. I want you to show me you remember everything I've been teaching you.

PETER. I'm tired, Mama. I want to sleep.

MAMA. No time for that now. You must swear to me that you will never lie.

SOJOURNER. Mama, why are you—

MAMA. Isabelle, do as I say!

SOJOURNER. Yes, Mama.

MAMA. Will you ever lie?

SOJOURNER and **PETER.** No, Mama.

MAMA. And you will never steal?

SOJOURNER and **PETER.** No, Mama.

MAMA. And you will always obey your master?

---

3. *ad lib.* Improvise lines

SOJOURNER and **PETER.** Yes, Mama.

MAMA. Good. Now, children, listen hard to what I tell you tonight, even if I have told it all before. I want you to remember it always, because you will be told many things after I am gone.

SOJOURNER. Where are you going, Mama?

MAMA. Just listen. There is a God, and he sees everything and he knows everything. You must never forget him, you hear? He lives in the sky, high, high up in the sky. And if ever you are beaten or cruelly treated—

SOJOURNER. Master doesn't beat us, Mama.

MAMA. Isabelle, will you hush? *Listen to me.*

SOJOURNER. Yes, Mama.

MAMA. Whenever you fall into any kind of trouble, you must ask God for help. Talk to him. Listen to him. He will always hear you and help you, if you remember to ask. Will you?

GUIDED READING What does Mama tell Sojourner and Pete to do if they ever fall into trouble?

PETER. Yes, Mama.

SOJOURNER. I'll remember.

MAMA. Good. Now, look. Look up at the stars. Do you see them?

SOJOURNER. I see them.

MAMA. Those are the same stars that shine down on your brothers and sisters, the very stars they see as they look up, though they are far away from us and from each other. Remember them. Remember us here, right now, warm and close. No matter where we go, when we look up at those stars, we will be together.

GUIDED READING What does Mama say about the stars?

(MAMA *sings "African Lullaby."*)

MAMA.

> DO BANA COBA
> GE-NE ME, GE-NE ME!
> DO BANA COBA

GE-NE ME, GE-NE ME!
BEN D'NU-LI, NU-LI, NU-LI, NU-LI, BEN D'LE.

SOJOURNER. What does it mean, Mama, that song you sing?

MAMA. It means I remember.

SOJOURNER. Remember what?

MAMA. My mama, who sang it to me. It means she remembered, way back to Africa, where she was born—and the song was, too.

GUIDED READING How does Mama explain the meaning of the song "African Lullaby"?

SOJOURNER. The words say all that?

MAMA. I don't know what the words say. Only what they mean.

BAUMFREY (*in darkness*). Mama Betts?

MAMA. Baumfrey? Is that you?

BAUMFREY. Ya, it's me. Master Hardenburgh— he's dead.

GUIDED READING What happens to Master Hardenburgh?

MAMA (*clutching* PETER *and* SOJOURNER). So soon? Oh, Lord, so soon!

(*Lights come up on* AUCTIONEER, *who places a cube C and immediately begins his spiel.[4]* MAMA, SOJOURNER, *and* PETER *rise.* PETER *and* MAMA *move away, holding* SOJOURNER *as long as they can.*)

AUCTIONEER. I want to thank you folks for coming here today.

SOJOURNER. Mama?

AUCTIONEER. You all knew Charles Hardenburgh, and he knew quality. He demanded it. Keep that in mind while bidding on the goods we are offering you today. (*Pushes* SOJOURNER *toward cube.*) Get on up there, girl.

---

4. *spiel.* Extravagant speech

SOJOURNER. Mama?

AUCTIONEER. The very best Gold Coast[5] stock. Pure African. Nothing but the best for Charles Hardenburgh. Nothing but the best for you. Who bids, gentlemen? What do you bid for her? Five dollars! Do I hear ten? Come, gentlemen, how much do you bid? Ten dollars! Who'll bid fifteen? Look at that arm, near strong as a man's. Turn around, girl. A broad back. A strong back. Go on, keep turning. Now, I know all about the rumbling up in the capital. Old laws, new laws—doesn't mean a thing. This girl will serve you long, she'll serve you well, I'll <u>warrant</u> her. Let me hear fifteen. Tell you what I'll do. Got a fine flock of sheep. Give me a hundred for the sheep, take the girl for ten. Take them both, or don't take either. A hundred and ten for a fine flock of sheep and a sturdy wench[6] to tend them.

(NEELY *steps forward, speaks reluctantly*).

NEELY. I'll give you a hundred for both.

GUIDED READING

What is the final selling bid on the sheep and Sojourner?

AUCTIONEER. Sold to Mr. John Neely for one hundred dollars! *(Turns and leaves scene.)*

NEELY (*to* SOJOURNER, *uncomfortably*). Well, come on then, girl. Get those sheep moving.

SOJOURNER. Mama!

MAMA. Better go, Isabelle. You belong to Master Neely now.

(OTHERS *sing "Goodbye, Brother" as* MAMA *and* SOJOURNER *embrace.)*

OTHERS.

GOODBYE, BROTHER,
GOODBYE, SISTER
IF I DON'T SEE YOU MORE,

NOW GOD BLESS YOU, NOW
GOD BLESS YOU,

IF I DON'T SEE YOU MORE.

WE PART IN BODY, BUT MEET
IN SPIRIT,

IF I DON'T SEE YOU MORE,

WE'LL MEET IN HEAVEN, THE
BLESSED KINGDOM,

IF I DON'T SEE YOU MORE.

SOJOURNER (*returning to narrative and mature voice*). Now my name was Belle Neely—and the war was begun. Master Neely beat me often, he beat me hard, and I never knew why. He and his wife, they came from Massachusetts. They spoke English; I spoke Dutch. If they sent me for a frying pan, not knowing what they meant, perhaps I'd carry them the pothooks. Then oh! how angry they'd be. (*Drops to her knees beside lectern, hands above her head as if tied.*)

GUIDED READING

How does language cause a problem between Sojourner and Mr. and Mrs. Neely?

MRS. NEELY (*in darkness*). John Neely, look at this pan. Look at it!

NEELY (*in darkness*). Woman, what is it you want of me now?

SOJOURNER. One day, Master Neely dragged me out to the barn, tied my hands to a post, and whipped me till the blood stood in pools on the ground. (*A pause. She tries to rise, sinks back down, her hands freed now.*) Mama? Mama, I see you there. Don't go!

GUIDED READING

What does Mr. Neely do to Sojourner one day?

---

5. **Gold Coast.** Former British territory in West Africa, now a part of Ghana
6. **wench.** Young woman

words for everyday use

war • rant (wär′ ənt) v., give a guarantee or promise. *I'll <u>warrant</u> that he will pay me back the money.*

Mama, please. I'm afraid! He hurt me, Mama. Master Neely hurt me bad. Mama? *(Pause.)* Gone. *(She calms herself, realizes, in a childlike way, that she has an alternative.)* God? God, you know it isn't right for Master to beat me like that. I'm trying to learn English, but I can't learn it fast enough. Mama told me to do what's right. I'm trying. Why isn't he? *(Pause.)* Could you find me another Master? I'll be waiting for your answer. Mama says, if I ask, you'll always hear me, so now it's up to you.

(MRS. NEELY steps forward into light.)

MRS. NEELY. I asked that girl three times to wash out this pan and she hasn't touched it. Now everything's stuck on there. John!

(NEELY steps into light.)

NEELY. I've already beaten the child till there's no place left on her to bleed. It does no good. She doesn't understand. She knows no English.

GUIDED READING

What does Mr. Neely realize about Sojourner when beating her does not change her behavior?

MRS. NEELY. She *does.* She must. She pretends to be ignorant to spite us.

NEELY *(emphatically).* It's the Dutch who spite us, not the girl. For God's sake, hear me! She knows no English.

MRS. NEELY *(appalled at the ramifications of this).* Oh, John, what have we done?

NEELY. All that we could and more. And still these stubborn New York Dutch want no part of us. I thought surely owning a slave as they do would help, but no. They never change. They go miles out of their way to trade with one of their own.

MRS. NEELY. They never change, but we do.

NEELY. What?

MRS. NEELY. We've been changing ever since we came here. Changing and changing, and it's all been for the worse. We've never owned slaves. We've never raised a hand in anger to anyone. It's this place. We mustn't stay here any longer. Take me home, John. I want to go home.

GUIDED READING

Why does Mrs. Neely want to go home?

NEELY. This is the only home we've got.

MRS. NEELY. Sell it. Sell the land, the store, the girl. Let them have it all and get us out of here before there's nothing left of us worth saving. *(She clings to his arm, pleading.)* Sell it, John, please, and let us go...

(NEELY regards her for a moment, then pats her hand and nods. She relaxes against him. Lights dim on them and come up on SOJOURNER.)

SOJOURNER *(with a child's, delight and awe).* I thank you, God. *(As she slips on a dress and apron, OTHERS hum "Round the Corn, Sally." They continue as she returns to lectern and narrative.)* Once again, I was walking down a country road, following a flock of sheep, barefoot and weary. I had no idea where I was headed, but it had to be better than where I'd been. I was Belle Scriver for a while. Master Scriver owned a tavern. Oh, times were lively there!

(OTHERS sing and dance to "Round the Corn, Sally.")

GUIDED READING

How does Sojourner describe her time with Master Scriver?

OTHERS.

> HOORAY, HOORAY, HO! ROUND
>   THE CORN, SALLY,
> HOORAY FOR ALL THE LOVELY
>   LADIES,
> ROUND THE CORN, SALLY.

---

words for everyday use

spite (spīt') v., harm, annoy, or frustrate. *My sister purposely broke my glasses to spite me.*
em • pha • tic (im fa' tik) adj., strongly expressive, using emphasis to make a point. *She answered the question with an emphatic "No!"* **emphatically,** adv.
ap • pall (ə pàl') v., overcome with dismay. *Horror movies appall my parents, who won't let me watch them.* **appalled,** adj.
ram • i • fi • ca • tion (ra' mə fə kā' shən) n., consequence or outgrowth of something. *The ramifications of snacking before dinner included a stomachache.*

THIS LOVE'S THE THING
   THAT'S SURE TO HAVE YOU,
ROUND THE CORN, SALLY.
HE HOLDS YOU TIGHT WHEN
   ONCE HE GRABS YOU,
ROUND THE CORN, SALLY.

HOORAY, HOORAY, HO! ROUND
   THE CORN, SALLY,
HOORAY FOR ALL THE LOVELY
   LADIES,
ROUND THE CORN, SALLY.

SOJOURNER. Word got out about Master Scriver's Belle, big and strong as a tree—just like Papa! Smart and hard-working, too, with a singing voice some folks thought was worth the listening. A quiet-speaking man named John Dumont happened by. Offered Master Scriver three hundred dollars for me. Master Scriver hated to see me go, but three hundred dollars? Well. My name was Belle Dumont now.

> **GUIDED READING**
> How does Sojourner become Belle Dumont?

(She takes up a laundry basket and begins sorting clothes. An African drum is heard, slow and faint at first, then rising in <u>intensity</u>, reaching full crescendo[7] at Bob's entrance. SISSY *steps forward.)*

SISSY. Put that laundry away, Belle. No work today. It's Pinxter.

SOJOURNER. Pinxter?

SISSY. Slaves' holiday. Don't you hear that drum?

SOJOURNER. Yes, I hear it.

SISSY. That means Bob Catlin's getting ready to dance. No man, woman, or child can out-dance that boy. Don't they have Pinxter where you come from?

> **GUIDED READING**
> How does Sissy describe Pinxter to Sojourner?

SOJOURNER. Uh-uh.

SISSY. Oooh, come along with me, child. You have got a treat in store.

SOJOURNER. What about Master's shirts?

SISSY. No masters today, child. No master all week. This is Pinxter, hear? Come on!

*(*BOB *leaps into C. Dressed in rags and bits of colored ribbon, he performs a dance to the primitive drumbeat meant to exorcise[8] the past 51 weeks of slavery, if not the past 100 years. When he finishes,* SISSY *and* OTHERS *move U to dance in shadows.* BOB *moves D to* SOJOURNER.*)*

> **GUIDED READING**
> What is the purpose of the rising African drumbeat to which Bob Catlin dances during Pinxter?

BOB. I'm Bob, from Catlin's place.

SOJOURNER. I'm Belle, from Dumont's.

BOB. Do you dance?

SOJOURNER. No.

BOB. Do you walk?

SOJOURNER. Sure, I walk.

BOB *(laughing, takes her hand).* Then, let's walk.

(They move off. OTHERS *continue and conclude their dance.* BOB *and* SOJOURNER *re-enter.)*

SOJOURNER. Oh, I am <u>ranting</u> on so! I don't talk like this to anyone but you, Bob, you know that?

BOB. I like to listen to you talk.

SOJOURNER. That's good, because I don't seem to be able to stop. Before you, there'd be days go by sometimes when I never said a

---

7. *crescendo.* Gradual increase in force, volume, and intensity
8. *exorcise.* Expel or cast out evil spirits or influences

---

words for everyday use

in • ten • si • ty (in ten′ sə tē) *n.,* great energy, a feeling of high degree. *In the final seconds of the ballgame, the <u>intensity</u> of the game grew.*

rant (rant′) *v.,* talk in a noisy, excited, wild manner. *My brother <u>ranted</u> and raved about the amusement park.*

word to anybody, except "yes, sir" and "no, ma'am."

BOB (*playfully*). Is that so?

SOJOURNER (*laughing*). I know you don't believe me, but it's so. (*Growing serious.*) I don't seem to fit in at the Dumonts', Bob. Never have fit in anywhere. Not with the white folks, not with the black. I'm different and I don't know why.

GUIDED READING

What does Sojourner say to Bob about "fitting in"?

BOB. You are different. I knew that right off, when I saw you standing there all alone, back at Pinxter time.

SOJOURNER. Well, I just wonder why.

BOB. Belle, I've got to tell you something.

SOJOURNER. What?

BOB. We can't stay up here so long, like we sometimes do. Like now. We've been up here too long. We better get back.

SOJOURNER. Bob, what is it? Nobody's ever seen us here—

BOB. Master Catlin says he'll kill me if he catches me coming to see you again.

SOJOURNER. He knows?

BOB. He doesn't want Dumont getting my children. He's picked out a girl for me on his own place. Belle, I have to take care. He'll kill me, just like he says.

SOJOURNER. But he'd never catch us up here. You just have to stay away from the house. Isn't that right?

BOB. I don't know. Maybe. I want to see you, but—

SOJOURNER. You have to! This little bit of time we've been together, it's . . . I forgot how

to be lonely, Bob. I can't be that way again. I won't be able to stand it.

BOB (*holding and rocking her*). I know. I know. (*They kiss; he pulls away.*) I've got to go now, Belle. I'm sorry. (*He moves out of scene.* SOJOURNER *returns sadly to laundry basket and takes up her work.*)

(DUMONT *steps into light.*)

DUMONT. Feeling a little better today, Belle?

SOJOURNER. Yes, Master. Almost back to my old self.

DUMONT. You take it easy one more day. I don't want you down with that fever all over again.

SOJOURNER. Yes, sir.

DUMONT. Uh—Belle, have you seen Bob?

SOJOURNER (*concerned, but <u>wary</u>*). No, sir. Bob has no reason to come here.

DUMONT. Well, if he should turn up, tell him to watch his step. Catlin's been looking for him.

GUIDED READING

Who warns Sojourner about Mr. Catlin?

SOJOURNER. Yes, sir.

(As DUMONT *turns to go,* BOB *appears DL. A second later,* CATLIN *appears at R.*)

SOJOURNER. Bob!

BOB. I heard you were sick, Belle—

CATLIN. Stand where you are, you black dog! (BOB *freezes.* CATLIN *beats him with a cane.* SOJOURNER *screams.* BOB *falls.*)

DUMONT. Catlin, stop! Stop, I say!

CATLIN. This is no business of yours, Dumont.

DUMONT. I'll have no slave beaten to death on my property! Get your boy up and get out

words for everyday use

wary (wār′ ē) *adj.*, watchful, careful. *The boy was <u>wary</u> of walking across the busy street.*

of here! (CATLIN *pulls* BOB *to his feet, pushes him out of scene.*)

SOJOURNER. Master, please. He'll kill my Bob.

DUMONT. I'm sorry, Belle. I've done all I can.

SOJOURNER. NO! (DUMONT *exits. She doubles over in grief, then slowly pulls herself up, returns to lectern and narrative.*) There were other Pinxters, but no Bob to dance at them. I heard Catlin beat him so bad, he was never the same. Master Dumont gave me a husband named Tom and I bore children: Hannah, Elizabeth, and a little boy I named for my brother, Peter. My brother, close to me still as Mama's stars, and just as far away. Never did see him again. Saw Mama once, and Papa, too. They'd been set free. Set free because they were old and tired and weak. Too old to work, too old to sell. Set free to wander homeless, free to get sick, free to be cold and hungry and alone. The day Papa came to see me, we stood by Master's gate in the snow. (*Steps to side of lectern.*)

> **GUIDED READING**
> Why doesn't Bob dance at other Pinxters?

> **GUIDED READING**
> Why are Sojourner's parents set free?

BAUMFREY (*in darkness*). Who'll care for us, Belle? Who'll do for us now that we can't do for ourselves?

SOJOURNER. I will, Papa. Just as soon as I'm free.

BAUMFREY. Can't wait that long, girl.

SOJOURNER (*returning to narrative*). Every day after that, I came to the gate and put my feet in the snowy prints Papa's feet had made. Every day I came, until my Papa's prints just melted away.

(DUMONT *steps into scene.*)

DUMONT. Belle?

SOJOURNER (*joining him, away from lectern*). Yes, Master Dumont?

DUMONT. You've heard about the state law that's going to set you free in two years—

SOJOURNER. Yes, Master?

DUMONT. Well, I've got a proposition for you, Belle. I've never had anyone work as hard for me as you do, slave or hired hand. Give me one more year of that kind of work, and I'll sign your freedom papers a year early. This time next summer.

> **GUIDED READING**
> What state law does Dumont mention to Sojourner?

> **GUIDED READING**
> What proposition does Dumont make to Sojourner?

SOJOURNER. My freedom?

DUMONT (*moving out of scene*). One more year, Belle. That's a promise.

SOJOURNER. My freedom! (*She returns to narrative, but remains in scene, grabbing up a broom and sweeping.*) I'd work like twenty men, I told Master Dumont, and I did. Field work in the heat of the sun. Laundry by the light of the moon. An hour or two of sleep sometimes; other times, none at all. Never mind if my back ached and my feet blistered, and my hands got bruised and sore. I had plans!

(PETE *steps into scene.*)

PETE. Tell me about the house, Mama.

SOJOURNER. Already told you, Pete.

PETE. Tell me again.

SOJOURNER. No, Pete. I've got work to do.

PETE. Tell me anyway.

SOJOURNER. You sure are a pesky child! (*A pause, then she gives in.*) We're going to have

words for everyday use
prop • o • si • tion (prä pə zi' shən) *n.,* act of offering or suggesting something to be considered. *The proposition of going to the party instead of studying was tempting.*

our own little house someday, Pete. High on a hill, close to the stars. Soon as I'm free, I can work for wages. Then I'll buy your freedom, too.

GUIDED READING

What does Sojourner tell her son Pete about a house?

PETE. And Hannah's? And Elizabeth's?

SOJOURNER. And Hannah's and Elizabeth's. And my mama and papa will live with us, too.

PETE. We'll take good care of them!

SOJOURNER. That's right! All of us close and warm. Would you like that, Pete?

PETE. I'd like that, Mama.

SOJOURNER. Then move yourself along so I can get to my work! (PETE *exits.* SOJOURNER *sweeps, humming.*)

(SISSY *steps into scene.*)

SISSY. Mmmmm-hmmmmm. There she is now, our fine Mistress Isabelle, queen of the slave cellar. You'll be wanting the spot closest to the fire, I suppose? Wouldn't do for you to catch a chill. What would Master say if his Belle caught a chill? I'll tell you what. He'd say, "Look at my Belle. Sick as a dog and see her work. Nothing stops my Belle. No, sir!"

SOJOURNER. What's the matter with you, Sissy?

SISSY. What's the matter with *you*, girl? Can't you see you're hurting the rest of us when you work like that? Next thing you know Master will have us all up night and day. What'll happen to our children then? And the old folks, when will they rest?

SOJOURNER. Master promised me my freedom if I—

SISSY. Promised you, did he? And you believe it? When's a master ever kept a promise to a slave?

GUIDED READING

What does Sissy think of Mr. Dumont's promise to Sojourner?

SOJOURNER. Master Dumont's always been fair to me.

SISSY. Fair? We're slaves and he's the master. What's fair about that? I thought you were smart, girl, but I was wrong. You are stupid. Horses work till they drop and so do you. It's stupid in a horse and it's stupid in a slave. Working hard won't free a one of us. Just kill us sooner, that's all. (*She spits at* SOJOURNER *and exits scene.*)

SOJOURNER (*after a pause*). Look at the stars, Mama said. Same stars for all of us. Mama and Papa and Peter—and Bob. (*Pause.*) Folks tell me Bob's dead. Is that right, God? They say he just gave up and died. A dancing man like that. A laughing man like that. Just gave up and died. (*Pause.*) I'm not going to listen to Sissy and the others, God. I can't let them stop me. But I get so lonely sometimes.

GUIDED READING

What do folks tell Sojourner about Bob?

(SOJOURNER *sings "Lord, Make Me More Patient."*)

SOJOURNER.

LORD, MAKE ME MORE PATIENT,
LORD, MAKE ME MORE PATIENT,
LORD, MAKE ME MORE PATIENT,
UNTIL WE MEET AGAIN.
PATIENT, PATIENT, PATIENT,
UNTIL WE MEET AGAIN.
LORD, MAKE ME MORE
  PEACEFUL,
LORD, MAKE ME MORE
  PEACEFUL,
LORD, MAKE ME MORE
  PEACEFUL,
UNTIL WE MEET AGAIN.
PEACEFUL, PEACEFUL,
  PEACEFUL,
UNTIL WE MEET AGAIN.

(*Returns to lectern.*) Fall came, and then winter, and spring. And then one day, the planting was done and the sun poured down hot as fire on my face, and I knew the year was over. (*Turns toward* DUMONT.) Master Dumont?

(DUMONT *steps into scene.*)

DUMONT. What is it, Belle?

SOJOURNER. It's time, sir. Your promise—

DUMONT (*he has honestly forgotten*). My promise?

SOJOURNER. That I'd go free. A year before the law. This summer.

DUMONT. Oh. Oh, yes.

SOJOURNER. I've worked hard for you, Master.

DUMONT. Yes, Belle, you've worked hard.

SOJOURNER. Yes, I have.

DUMONT (*sincerely*). We depend on you, Belle. I don't see how we can get through summer and the harvest without you—

SOJOURNER. But, Master, you promised.

DUMONT. Is it so bad for you here? I've given you a home, clothing, food, a husband—

SOJOURNER. This is not my home, these are not my clothes, my food is not my own. The children old Tom has given me are slaves he's given you! I want my freedom, Master. I have earned it.

DUMONT (*moving out of scene*). I'm sorry, Belle. We need you. It's only one more year.

SOJOURNER. One more year! Is that right? Is that fair?

SISSY (*out of darkness*). Fair? You stupid girl. Working hard won't free a one of us. Just kill us sooner, that's all.

SOJOURNER (*returning to narrative*). I stayed on through the summer and helped with the livestock and the crops and the kitchen garden. I stayed on through the fall. I did their spinning[9] and put up their preserves and smoked their meats for the winter store. But after the first frost, when the busy time was over, I took what was not given to me, but

GUIDED READING

What does Sojourner do before the year is up?

what was mine still, sure as I had earned it—my freedom.

(PETE *rushes over to her.*)

PETE. Mama, don't go!

SOJOURNER. I have to, Pete. You know I do. I have to leave you for a little while so we can all be together later.

PETE. But I'm afraid.

SOJOURNER. No need to be. You and your sisters will be safe here with the Dumonts. For all their faults, they'll never harm you. Look at the stars, you hear? And *remember*. (*She kisses him and watches him walk away, then—*) Mama? Up there with the stars now. Papa, too. Never lived to see me free. (*Shaking her head, she returns to narrative.*) I left just before dawn and walked toward the rising sun.

(*She sings "Many Thousand Go."*)

SOJOURNER.

> NO MORE PECK O' CORN FOR ME,
>   NO MORE, NO MORE;
> NO MORE PECK O' CORN FOR ME,
>   MANY THOUSAND GO.
> NO MORE PINT OF SALT FOR ME,
>   NO MORE, NO MORE;
> NO MORE PINT OF SALT FOR ME,
>   MANY THOUSAND GO.
> NO MORE MISTRESS' CALL FOR
>   ME, NO MORE, NO MORE;
> NO MORE MISTRESS' CALL FOR
>   ME,
> MANY THOUSAND GO.

(*Speaks.*) When the sun had met me halfway, I stopped, and before me was the home of some Quaker[10] folks. They talked in a peculiar way, but there was nothing wrong with their thinking.

---

9. **spinning.** Making yarn by drawing out, twisting, and winding fibers

10. **Quaker.** Member of the Religious Society of Friends

(ISAAC *steps forward, followed by* MARIA. *Both wear stark black and white Quaker garb.*)

ISAAC. Yes, what is it?

SOJOURNER (*unsure of her* reception). I'm Belle. From Dumont's place.

ISAAC. Yes, Belle? Is there something we can do for thee?

SOJOURNER (*blurting it out*). Master Dumont, he told me I'd be free if I worked extra hard all year. And I did. And then he said I had to stay.

ISAAC (*understands she has run away. He nods and gestures her over to where three of the cubes have been placed as if around a dining table*). Come in, Belle. (*She hesitates.*) Do not be afraid. We will not harm thee. I am Isaac Van Wagener. This is my wife, Maria.

MARIA. Sit down, Belle. Thee must be tired.

SOJOURNER. No, ma'am! I'll work. I'll do good work for you.

ISAAC. We may have work for thee here. But not now. Now thee must have something to eat. (*He nods to* MARIA, *who goes for food.*) Thee has walked many miles.

SOJOURNER. Not so very many. I know Master Dumont will come after me, growing angrier every step of the way. I thought it best not to go too far.

ISAAC (*laughing*). A wise thought, Belle. (MARIA *returns with a plate of food.* SOJOURNER *tries to rise, but* ISAAC *stops her.*) It is all right. Stay here, with us.

MARIA I hope this will please thee, Belle.

SOJOURNER. Oh, yes, ma'am.

GUIDED READING

Where does Sojourner stop first after she walks away from the Dumonts' place?

(DUMONT *steps into scene.*)

DUMONT. So, Belle, you've run away.

SOJOURNER (*jumps to her feet, as do* ISAAC *and* MARIA). No, Master, I did not run away. I walked away, because you promised me a year of my time. You said I could go free, and I did. That's all.

DUMONT. You'll have to come straight home with me.

SOJOURNER. No, Master, I won't.

DUMONT. I'll not have this, Belle.

ISAAC. Mister Dumont, I'm not in the habit of buying or selling human beings. But rather than have thee take Belle back to a place she does not wish to be, I will buy her services from thee for the rest of the year.

DUMONT. Ah, very well. How much, then?

ISAAC. Name it, sir. I'll not bargain with thee for a human life. I have no heart for it.

DUMONT. Twenty dollars.

ISAAC. As you wish. (MARIA *takes a purse from her apron pocket.* ISAAC *removes the coins and hands them to* DUMONT.)

DUMONT. So be it. Belle— (*He raises a hand as if to say goodbye to a friend, then lets it fall.* SOJOURNER *does the same, then bows her head.* DUMONT *exits scene.*)

SOJOURNER (*to* ISAAC). Master, I—

ISAAC. I am not thy master, Belle. There is but one master in this house. He who is thy master is mine as well. It is not right that thee should be a slave. God does not want it.

GUIDED READING

When Dumont tries to take Sojourner back home, what does Isaac Van Wagener do?

words for everyday use   **re • cep • tion** (rē sep' shən) *n.*, act of being received. *The* reception *for Buddy was to welcome him back home.*

SOJOURNER. No, sir, *God* does not want it. (ISAAC *and* MARIA *move out of scene.* SOJOURNER *resumes narrative and dons a white cap and shawl like Maria's before returning to lectern.*) Now I was known as Isabelle Van Wagener. From the Van Wageners, I learned to love the goodness that lies in the hearts of white folks and black folks alike, and that what Mama called doing right was called "justice" in fancy talk. I listened to those good people as we sat long winter nights by the fire, and learned about the law. How the law was supposed to be for everybody: men and women, black and white, young and old. Shouldn't be laws for some people and not others. On July 4, 1827, the law set me free, but not my children.

(MARIA *re-enters scene.*)

GUIDED READING

What does Sojourner learn from the Van Wageners?

GUIDED READING

What happens on July 4, 1827?

MARIA. What will thee do, Belle, on this great freedom day?

SOJOURNER. I'd like to see my boy, Peter.

MARIA. By all means, thee must go to the Dumonts' and visit him and your daughters.

SOJOURNER. Pete's not with the Dumonts, anymore, ma'am. The girls tell me he's with a man named Solomon Gedney.

MARIA. Sold? But that cannot be. The new law states—

SOJOURNER. Not sold, ma'am. Given. As a gift.

MARIA. How long have thee known this?

SOJOURNER. Been some time, ma'am. Right after the first thaw.

MARIA. Why did thee not tell us?

SOJOURNER. You never asked, ma'am.

MARIA. When something is wrong, Belle, people must be told. Told and told and told again, until the wrong is righted. Go to this Solomon Gedney and find out about your son. God be with thee.

(MARIA *turns away, changes hats, etc., then joins* OTHERS *as they step forward to block* SOJOURNER'S *way.*)

SOJOURNER. Yes, ma'am, I believe He is.

SLAVE BOY. What do you want here, woman?

SOJOURNER. Is this Master Solomon Gedney's place?

SLAVE BOY. Yeah, this is Master Solomon Gedney's place.

SOJOURNER. I'm looking for my boy, Peter.

SLAVE BOY (*obviously afraid*). Peter? There's no one here named Peter.

SOJOURNER. But there's got to be. Master Dumont—

SLAVE BOY. Never heard of any boy named Peter.

SOJOURNER. You have! I know you have. I could see it as soon as I said his name.

SLAVE BOY. I don't know him, you hear? Leave me alone. (*He leaves scene.*)

SOJOURNER. Something is wrong here. Oh, Lord, something is very wrong. What have they done with my boy?

OLD WOMAN. You looking for Peter Dumont? They sent him on south.

SOJOURNER. South?

OLD WOMAN. Alabama.

SOJOURNER. That can't be.

OLD WOMAN. Can be and is.

SOJOURNER. You're crazy, old woman. I won't listen to you.

OLD WOMAN. I'm not crazy, girl. I'm not scared, either. Not anymore. (*Gestures toward* SLAVE BOY.) Now that one, he's got to serve Master Gedney seven more years. He's got to watch what he says and who he says it to. Master Gedney's got ways to find out what's been said and ways to make a body sorry. But I'm a free woman now. Got no cause to lie to you. Master Gedney's sister married a man from Alabama, name of Fowler. When the marriage party left here a few months back, your boy went with them. Too late. Too bad. (*She leaves scene.*)

GUIDED READING

What does Sojourner learn from an old woman about Pete's whereabouts?

SOJOURNER. No. Oh, no. NO!

(MRS. GEDNEY *enters scene.*)

MRS. GEDNEY. Who are you, and what do you mean by barging in here?

SOJOURNER. Mrs. Gedney, you've sent my boy south. Don't you know what that means? He'll never be free down there. Never!

GUIDED READING

According to Sojourner, what does being sent to the South mean for Pete?

MRS. GEDNEY. Oh, what a fine fuss you're making! And what for? Haven't you more than enough children to tend to?

SOJOURNER. Mrs. Gedney, I will have my child back again.

MRS. GEDNEY. And just how do you intend to get him? Do you have any money?

SOJOURNER. No, ma'am. I have no money. But I can earn it. Mrs. Gedney, my mama lost every one of her children, sold away from her one by one, and nothing she could do about it but cry. For her sake, I will do more than cry. I will have my child again!

GUIDED READING

What reason does Sojourner give for saying she will do more than cry to have her child back again?

MRS. GEDNEY. Fine words, I must say. But there's nothing you can do, girl. Nothing. (*She exits scene.*)

SOJOURNER (*stunned, and then determined*). God, this time I got to ask you for everything.

If I were you and you were me, I'd help you, you know I would. Show them that you're my helper. Or if you can't show them, show me, and that'll give me the strength I need to go on. Help me, God. Help me. I'll never leave you alone till you do.

(DUMONT *steps forward.*)

DUMONT. Belle!

SOJOURNER. Master Dumont. I didn't know where else to go. You must help me get Pete back.

DUMONT. I never dreamed Gedney would send the boy south. Believe me, Belle. But it's too late now. I can't help you.

SOJOURNER (*frantic*). Who else can I ask? Where else can I go? Master Dumont—

DUMONT (*wanting to quiet her and his own conscience*). Oh, now, Belle, calm down. There must be something. There . . . may be . . . something . . .

SOJOURNER. Yes?

DUMONT. You know the old white house on the road to town?

SOJOURNER. I know it.

DUMONT. A man named Chip lives there, Squire Chip. He's a lawyer. He may be able to do something for you. But, Belle—

SOJOURNER. Oh, thank you, Master Dumont!

GUIDED READING

Why does Dumont tell Sojourner she is never to tell anyone he sent her to see Squire Chip?

DUMONT. Belle, listen to me. You're never to tell anyone I sent you there, do you hear? Solomon Gedney is a neighbor, and a powerful man, and I cannot have it known that I've gone against him. Promise me you'll never say a word?

SOJOURNER. Yes, sir. I promise.

DUMONT. Good. Now, go—before anyone sees us talking here. (*He starts off.*)

SOJOURNER. Master Dumont? *(He turns back.)* I keep *my* promises, sir. *(Stung,* DUMONT *shakes his head and exits scene.)*

*(*CHIP *appears behind lectern, which represents his desk.)*

CHIP. Well? What is it? What do you want?

SOJOURNER. I want my son, Peter.

CHIP. Is he in some kind of trouble? We can't get your boy out of jail if he's in trouble. Don't waste our time.

SOJOURNER. He's in trouble, sir, but he's not in jail. Master Dumont gave him to Master Gedney. Master Gedney sold him to Master Fowler. And Master Fowler took the boy south. My son is supposed to go free when he's twenty-five years old. But in Alabama, he'll be a slave the rest of his days.

CHIP. What are you babbling about, woman? *(Realizing what she's said.)* Are you saying somebody sold your boy out of this state? Are you accusing someone of defying New York state law?

SOJOURNER. Yes, I am.

CHIP *(interested).* Are you willing to swear the child you speak of is your son?

SOJOURNER. Why else would I be troubling so about him?

CHIP *(holds out Bible).* You have to make it official and swear by this.

SOJOURNER. I can't read.

CHIP. You don't have to read it. You just have to swear by it. It's the Bible. Put your hand on top.

SOJOURNER. That's all right, then. I know the Bible.

CHIP. Fine. Now then, do you swear that the child, Peter, is your own son, by birth?

SOJOURNER. I swear he is.

CHIP. Good. *(Shuffles through papers, finds one and writes.)* What is your name?

SOJOURNER. Isabelle.

CHIP. Isabelle. *(Writes, then waits.)* Isabelle what?

SOJOURNER. Isabelle whatever my master's name is. The last was Van Wagener. But I'm a free woman now. I need to get me a free name. That'll take some thinking, won't it?

CHIP. Indeed it will. But let's use Van Wagener for now. Is there a husband? Could the boy's father appear in court to identify him?

SOJOURNER. Haven't seen Tom since last fall. He's free now, too. I don't expect to see him again.

CHIP. Never mind. We'll make do. *(Finishes writing.)* Take this writ[11] to Solomon Gedney. He's broken the law. That's what this paper says. And it tells him he must bring your son back to New York.

GUIDED READING

How does Chip explain the writ to Sojourner?

SOJOURNER. Yes, sir! I do thank you, sir.

(Lights fade on CHIP; GEDNEY *steps forward.)*

SOJOURNER. Good morning, Master Gedney.

GEDNEY. Morning. *(*SOJOURNER *hands him the writ.)* What's this? Who are you?

SOJOURNER. That's a writ, sir. It says you have to bring back my son, Peter.

GEDNEY. Oh, does it now? Since when do the likes of you practice law?

SOJOURNER. The law is for everybody, Master Gedney.

GEDNEY. I'll have to spend months traveling to get that boy.

SOJOURNER. And months in jail if you don't, sir.

---

11. **writ.** Formal document in letter form

GEDNEY. How dare you! You will regret this, woman. You are going to <u>rue</u> the day you ever thought to cross me. *(He and* OTHERS *close in on her, repeating and alternating their phrases several times, a rising cacophony[12] that drives her to her knees.)* You will rue this day.

SLAVE BOY. I don't know any boy named Peter.

OLD WOMAN. That boy is gone. Too late. Too bad.

MRS. GEDNEY. There is nothing you can do.

ALL *(together and in turn).* You will rue this day. I don't know any boy named Peter. That boy is gone. Too late. Too bad. There is nothing you can do.

SOJOURNER *(covers her ears and cowers at first, until assault reaches its peak, then rises, shouting).* NO!

(ALL retreat into darkness; lights up on CHIP.*)*

SOJOURNER. Squire Chip!

CHIP. You again, Isabelle? What's it been, four times this week? And it's only Wednesday.

SOJOURNER. You keep telling me to be patient, but I can't be patient anymore. Master Gedney's been gone for months. Haven't you had any word at all about my boy?

CHIP. As a matter of fact, I have. Just last night. Gedney's back in town, and he has your son with him.

SOJOURNER. He has? Oh, my!

(Lights fade on CHIP, *come up on* GEDNEY*)*

SOJOURNER. Master Gedney! I've come for my son!

GEDNEY. Have you? I wonder why?

SOJOURNER. Why? But… he's here, isn't he?

GUIDED READING

How does Gedney react when Sojourner says he'll have to spend months in jail if he doesn't get her son back?

GEDNEY. Oh, yes, he's here. With me. He belongs… to me. Not that I'm so very pleased with him, you understand. Oh, no. Quite a bit of trouble he's caused me. Quite … a bit … of trouble.

(He turns away. Light comes up on CHIP.*)*

SOJOURNER *(stunned).* Squire Chip?

CHIP *(impatiently).* Oh, Isabelle, look here, your son is home from Alabama, isn't he?

SOJOURNER. He's *back* from Alabama. But he's not home. He's not safe.

CHIP. Of course he is. Gedney has posted $600 in bond money, promising to appear in court when the time comes. With the boy. He's not going to risk <u>defaulting</u> on that money. And even if he does, half will be yours. Three hundred dollars.

SOJOURNER. Squire Chip, you do not understand me. I do not want Master Gedney's money. I want my son. You say you can call Master Gedney to court. Well, call him.

CHIP. I have every intention of doing so, but not now. Court is <u>adjourned</u>.

SOJOURNER. Adjourned?

CHIP. The next session will begin in just a few months. You've waited this long, you can wait a little longer, can't you?

SOJOURNER. No, sir, I cannot. Master Gedney is madder than a hornet about bringing Pete back. He'll take it out on my boy. I must have my child. I must have him now.

CHIP *(losing patience).* Do you have any idea how much trouble you've put us to? Do you think it's a simple matter to bring a case against a <u>prominent</u> citizen like Solomon

---

12. ***cacophony.*** Harsh dissonance of sound

rue (rü′) *v.,* repent over or regret bitterly. *You will <u>rue</u> the day you skipped practice.*

de • fault (də fawlt′) *v.,* fail to fulfill an agreement. *Bill failed to make the monthly payments and <u>defaulted</u> on his car loan.*

ad • journ (ə jərn′) *v.,* postpone or defer to a future time. *The staff meeting was <u>adjourned</u> to reconvene on Wednesday.*

prom • i • nent (prä′ mə nənt) *adj.,* standout, important, well known. *The mayor is a <u>prominent</u> citizen in our community.*

Gedney? A case on behalf of a slave—and a woman? The least you can do now is to be reasonable and wait as I tell you to. There's nothing to be done until next session. Go home! (SOJOURNER *folds her arms and stays put.*) What do you think you are doing?

SOJOURNER. I won't leave until you bring Master Gedney to court. I'll stay right here all day every day until you bring Master Gedney to court.

CHIP. You can't do that.

SOJOURNER. Is there a law says I can't?

CHIP. No.

SOJOURNER. Then I can. And I will.

CHIP (*exasperated, but admiring her* tenacity). Oh, very well. There is something I can do.

SOJOURNER. I thought maybe there was.

CHIP. I can call a special session of the court. But prepare yourself, Isabelle. It won't be an easy day.

GUIDED READING

What does Chip finally admit he can do?

SECOND MAN (*a voice out of darkness*). His Honor will see you in his chambers.[13] Please follow me.

(SOJOURNER *and* CHIP *approach "judge," who is in direction of audience,* GEDNEY *and* PETE *enter scene from opposite side.*)

SOJOURNER. I've never had an easy day in my life, and I don't expect any very soon. But I feel the power of a nation within me today. The law, Squire Chip, the law is for everybody.

CHIP. Let's hope so, Isabelle.

SOJOURNER (*seeing* PETE *who cries out and falls to the floor, cowering against* GEDNEY). Pete! Pete, what is it? Are you hurt?

GEDNEY (*smugly*). Is that your mama, boy?

PETE (*terrified*). No, sir. That's not my mama. My mama doesn't look like that. My mama doesn't live around here.

GUIDED READING

How does Sojourner's son Pete react when Sojourner sees him in court?

SOJOURNER. Pete!

CHIP (*pulling her aside*). What do you make of it, Isabelle? Is that your son?

SOJOURNER. Don't you think I know my own boy? (*She moves toward* PETE, *who cringes and clings to* GEDNEY, *whimpering.*) Pete, what's wrong with you?

PETE. Master Gedney, please don't let them take me away. I want to stay with you, Master. Please.

GEDNEY. Nobody's going to take you away, boy.

CHIP (*as if speaking to judge*). Your Honor, may I question the child? Thank you. (*He kneels beside* PETE, *lifts Pete's chin.* PETE winces *and pulls away.*) What's that scar on your forehead, Pete?

PETE (*looks at* GEDNEY, *who nods permission to speak*). Master's horse kicked me, sir.

CHIP. Your master's horse kicked you. Your master in Alabama or your master in New York? (*Confused,* PETE *looks at* GEDNEY.)

GEDNEY. Fowler's horse kicked him.

CHIP. It's the boy I'm asking, Mr. Gedney. But thank you. (*Regards* PETE *thoughtfully again.*) This bruise on your cheek? Where did that come from?

PETE. I ... I ran against the carriage, sir.

---

13. **chambers.** Private office of a judge where he hears matters not requiring action in open court

CHIP (*turns toward judge with a meaningful look*). He says he ran against a carriage, Your Honor.

PETE. Please, Master Gedney, let me stay with you.

CHIP. Forget your master for now, boy, and pay attention to me. (*Indicates* SOJOURNER.) Do you know that woman?

PETE. No, sir! She's not my mama!

CHIP. Stand up, Pete. (PETE *cringes against* GEDNEY) Stand up, I say! And remove your shirt. Stand here where the judge can see you. (PETE *rises reluctantly and removes his shirt.*)

SOJOURNER. Oh, Pete! What have they done to you? Your Honor! Squire Chip! My child has welts on his body as big as the fingers of my hand.

CHIP. It wasn't a horse that kicked you, was it, Pete? You didn't run into any carriage. Well? Who did this to you?

PETE (*terrified, he runs to* GEDNEY *and sinks to the floor beside him*). Master Gedney! Help me!

> **GUIDED READING**
> What is seen on Pete's body after he removes his shirt?

GEDNEY. The boy has no reason to lie.

CHIP. The boy has every reason to lie. His life depends on it. Your Honor, by his own admission,[14] Solomon Gedney sold this boy in clear <u>defiance</u> of New York state law, thinking, no doubt, that no one would have the interest or the courage to stop him. And, indeed, few would, except the boy's mother. Granted, Gedney has brought the child back. At considerable expense and inconvenience, he tells us. And, having re-established himself as the

> **GUIDED READING**
> How does Chip explain Pete's lying?

boy's rightful owner, he feels he is entitled to his labor until the age of twenty-five. You have seen the child's wounds. You have witnessed his terror. You know my client's story. And a law *was* broken. We have nothing more to add, Your Honor. We await your decision.

(FIRST WOMAN *sings two verses of "My Father, How Long?" as* OTHERS *in scene freeze and lights dim slightly.*)

FIRST WOMAN.

> MY FATHER, HOW LONG? MY
>   FATHER, HOW LONG?
> MY FATHER, HOW LONG, POOR
>   CHILDREN SUFFER HERE?
> MY MOTHER, HOW LONG? MY
>   MOTHER, HOW LONG?
> MY MOTHER, HOW LONG,
>   POOR CHILDREN SUFFER
>   HERE?

(*She continues to hum through Chip's line.*)

CHIP (*reacting as if to judge*). Yes? Yes! He's yours, Isabelle. He's free. Take him home.

SOJOURNER. Oh, thank you, Squire Chip! Thank you, Your Honor. Thank you, God! (CHIP *pats her shoulder, leaves scene.* SOJOURNER *faces* GEDNEY, *who also leaves.*)

PETE. Master! Don't go! (SOJOURNER *reaches out to him, but he dodges her and tries to hide. Finally, she catches up to him, kneels, and touches the scars on his forehead and cheek.* PETE *whimpers.*)

SOJOURNER. Oh, Pete, no need to cry now. We're together. (*Offers him a bag of candy from her pocket.*) Look here! See what your mama brought you? Sucking candy. You always did

---

14. **admission.** A voluntary acknowledgment of truth

---

words for everyday use

de • fi • ance (də fīʹ əns) *n.*, open disregard to authority. *The girls' <u>defiance</u> to the rules led them to suspension.*

love candy, now didn't you? (PETE *turns away, refusing candy.*) Don't you remember me, Pete? Say you remember me.

PETE. When will they take me back to Alabama?

SOJOURNER. Is that what Master Gedney told you? Listen, child, you'll never go back there. Never.

PETE. Master Fowler can take me away from you anytime. You can't protect me. But Master Gedney would have.

SOJOURNER. Was it Master Fowler who beat you, child? (PETE *nods.*) Nobody's going to take you away again, you hear me? It's the law that brought you back, and the law will protect you. It's stronger than Master Fowler and it's stronger than Master Gedney. (*A pause, then she tries another approach.*) Your mama's here with you, Pete. And God's going to show your mama the way. He always has, and he always will. You do know me. Say you do.

GUIDED READING

Who had beaten Pete?

PETE. Yes, ma'am. (*Weeping quietly now, he lets her hold him.*)

SOJOURNER. That's right. That's all right.

(*She sings "African Lullaby."*)

SOJOURNER.

> DO BA-NA CO-BA
> GE-NE ME, GE-NE ME.
>
> DO BA-NA CO-BA
> GE-NE ME, GE-NE ME.
>
> BEN D'NU-LI, NU-LI, NU-LI,
> BEN D'LE.

(*She offers* PETE *candy. He takes it. She kisses him and watches as he leaves scene, then returns to lectern and narrative.*) The law is for everybody. I took two more arrogant men to court in my time, and won my cases against them. One tried to shove me off a streetcar he didn't think I ought to be riding. The

other accused me of murder, all the while looking mighty guilty himself. No one believed I'd done it, of course, but I wanted the law to clear my name. My name. Isabelle Hardenburgh. Belle Neely. Belle Scriver. Belle Dumont. Isabelle Van Wagener. I was all of those—and none of them. Who was I then? Years rolled by, and I took myself off to New York City, where I could send my boy to school. My girls were fine at the Dumonts, and I was still dreaming of that house high up on a hill. But times were hard and jobs were scarce. I found work cooking and cleaning for a Mrs. Whiting, a good woman, with a special love for the needy. (*Removes a coin from her apron.*) Every day, she left fifty cents with me and told me if some poor soul came along and offered to clear the snow off her steps, I was to let him do it and pay him the money. And every day, I cleared those steps myself and kept the money, for who was poorer than me? (*Drops coin back into pocket.*)

GUIDED READING

What two other court cases does Sojourner win?

GUIDED READING

By what names had Sojourner been known?

GUIDED READING

After she moves to New York City, what kind of work does Sojourner find?

(OFFICER *pushes* PETE *toward her.*)

OFFICER. There you go, Pete. Get on home.

SOJOURNER. Officer, what's wrong?

OFFICER. Better keep an eye on this one, Belle. He's smarter than those friends of his. Oughtn't to follow them into trouble. (*He leaves scene, leaving* PETE *with head bowed.*)

SOJOURNER. Oh, Pete, what ails you, child? In and out of school. In and out of trouble. Why? (PETE *says nothing.* SOJOURNER *lifts his chin and touches his scars as before.*) This is where Master's horse kicked me. And this is where I ran into a carriage. It never leaves you, does it, Pete? That time in Alabama?

(PETE *yanks himself away*.) What am I going to do with you, child?

PETE. You don't have to do anything, Mama. I can do for myself.

SOJOURNER. Pete! Don't go!

PETE (*moving farther from her*). There's nothing for me here, Mama. I've signed aboard a whaling boat.

SOJOURNER. You're too young.

GUIDED READING

Why does Pete sign aboard a whaling boat?

PETE. They don't know. Don't care. I'm big for my age and strong.

SOJOURNER. Oh, Lord, I'm afraid!

PETE. I'll be all right, Mama. There's nothing they can do to me that hasn't already been done.

SOJOURNER. Pete!

PETE (*alone in a spotlight now, as if writing a letter*). My dear and beloved mother, I take this opportunity to write to you and inform you that I am well and in hopes for to find you the same. I am got on board that same unlucky ship, Zone of Nantucket. I have been punished once severely, for shoving my head in the fire for other folks. I would like to know how my sisters are. I wish you would write to me and answer me as soon as possible. Mother, I hope you do not forget me. I hope you all will forgive me for all that I have done. Your son, Peter Van Wagener.

SOJOURNER. I wrote to my boy. Time and again, Mrs. Whiting took down my words as I spoke them and sent them off to sea.

GUIDED READING

Who helps Sojourner answer her son's letters?

PETE. My dear mother, this is the fifth letter that I have wrote to you and have received no answer and it makes me very uneasy. So pray write as quick as you can.

(MRS. WHITING *joins in the reading, her voice gradually becoming the stronger, until the light fades from* PETE *as letter ends*.)

PETE and **MRS. WHITING.** We are out from home 23 months, and in hopes to be back home in 15 months. I have had very bad luck. I should like if my sisters are well and all the people around the neighborhood. I want to know what sort of a time it is at home. So write as quick as you can, won't you?

SOJOURNER. I never saw my boy again.

GUIDED READING

Does Sojourner ever see her son again?

(OLD MAN *steps into scene*.)

OLD MAN. Any work today, Missus? (*Numb from Pete's loss,* SOJOURNER *shakes her head "no."*) Clear the snow off the steps for you. I'm a poor man, Missus. I need the money for my family.

SOJOURNER (*takes coin from pocket, clutches it in her fist, speaking in a hollow, weary voice*). I'm poor, too, and need the money for mine. (OLD MAN *leaves scene. As she watches him go, her feelings return in a dizzying rush. She drops the coin, crying out as if it had burned through her hand. As* OTHERS *sing, she slowly lifts the injured hand toward heaven*.)

GUIDED READING

What happens when Sojourner refuses to allow an old man to clear snow off the steps for money?

(OTHERS *sing first verse of* "Somebody Callin' My Name.")

OTHERS.

HUSH, HUSH, SOMEBODY
   CALLIN' MY NAME,
HUSH, HUSH, SOMEBODY
   CALLIN' MY NAME,
HUSH, HUSH, SOMEBODY
   CALLIN' MY NAME,
OH, MY LORD, OH, MY LORD,
   WHAT SHALL I DO?
(*Continue under following dialogue*.)

SOJOURNER. Oh, God, forgive me. Have I not suffered enough to know the weight of it? The rich rob the poor, and the poor rob each other. But no more! No more. I will give back all I have taken away. I am no longer Isabelle!

(MRS. WHITING steps into scene.)

MRS. WHITING. Belle, what are you doing?

SOJOURNER *(handing over purse from her pocket).* Take this money, Mrs. Whiting. Take it all and give it to the poor. I have no more need of it. My girls are settled. My boy is gone. My old dream is dead. I must move on.

GUIDED READING

What does Sojourner give to Mrs. Whiting?

MRS. WHITING. Are you sure?

SOJOURNER. Oh, yes, ma'am. I am sure. *(Sings with OTHERS as MRS. WHITING leaves scene.)*

> HUSH, HUSH, SOMEBODY
> CALLIN' MY NAME,
> HUSH, HUSH, SOMEBODY
> CALLIN' MY NAME,
> HUSH, HUSH, SOMEBODY
> CALLIN' MY NAME,
> OH, MY LORD, OH, MY LORD,
> WHAT SHALL I DO?

FIRST WOMAN *(in darkness).* Tell your story. It must be told.

SOJOURNER. But who will listen? Who will hear?

FIRST MAN. They'll listen. They'll hear.

SECOND WOMAN. Look at Frederick Douglass.[15]

SOJOURNER. Frederick Douglass is an educated man. I can't read or write.

THIRD MAN. Just tell it your way.

SOJOURNER *(at lectern).* I began walking east again, as I'd walked before toward freedom. "Sojourner" I became, a wanderer among the people. 'Lord,' I cried, 'Thy name is truth,' and I took for my own the name of my last and greatest and only master. My name, my free name, my own name: Sojourner Truth. *(Speaks as if addressing public meeting. OTHERS ad lib responses as at opening.)* Children, I have come here tonight, like the rest of you, to hear what I have got to say. *(Laughs at her own joke.)* Children, I talk to God and God talks to me. I go out and talk to God in the fields and the woods. This morning I was walking out, and I got over the fence. I saw the wheat holding up its head, looking very big. I went up and took hold of it. You believe it? There was no wheat there! I said, 'God, what is the matter with this wheat?' And he says to me, "Sojourner, there's a little weevil in it." Now, I hear talk about the Constitution and the rights of man. I come up and I take hold of this Constitution. It looks mighty big and I feel for my rights, but there aren't any there. Then I say, 'God, what ails this Constitution?' and he says to me, "Sojourner, there's a little weevil in it." Well, now, don't these little weevils just eat up this country's crop? *(OTHERS applaud. She returns to cube DR of lectern.)*

GUIDED READING

How does Sojourner come to have her own name?

GUIDED READING

When Sojourner questions God, how does God respond?

(SECOND WOMAN enters scene.)

SECOND WOMAN. Well, wouldn't you just know it.

FIRST REVEREND. Something wrong?

SECOND WOMAN. Over there, Reverend. Don't you see her? Sitting right on the steps of the podium as if she owned the place.

FIRST REVEREND. That's Sojourner Truth, isn't it? I've seen her picture.

---

15. **Frederick Douglass.** Ex-slave, abolitionist, orator

SECOND WOMAN. In the abolitionist papers, no doubt. This is no woman's rights convention. This is an abolitionist affair.

FIRST REVEREND. Is there such a difference? Shall we insist on justice for one group and deny it to another?

SECOND WOMAN. My point exactly, and I want no part of it. If my husband knew I was here with the likes of her—! This is Ohio, not New York. We're not <u>accustomed</u> to this sort of thing. *(They exit scene.)*

(SECOND REVEREND enters scene.)

SECOND REVEREND. And I maintain the Lord intended man to have superior rights and privileges. Did not the Lord make man's <u>intellect</u> superior to that of women? *(OTHERS ad lib responses to him. SOJOURNER listens, but does not join in shouting.)*

GUIDED READING

What does the second reverend maintain?

FIRST MAN. I agree with you, Reverend. What is it these women want, anyway? Don't they have enough privileges as it is? Do they suppose men will help them into carriages or over mud puddles or save them the best places everywhere when they become our rivals in business and politics?

SECOND REVEREND. Precisely. And therefore, as a man of the cloth, I feel it is my duty to refer you all to your Bible. If God had indeed desired the equality of women, would he not have given some token of his will through the birth, life, and death of his son, our savior? *(Boos and cheers. As SOJOURNER rises, all fall momentarily silent. She moves to lectern.)*

SECOND WOMAN. Do something! Get her down from there! *(Another outcry, both pro and con.)*

SOJOURNER *(calmly awaiting their attention).* Well, children, where there's so much racket, there must be something out of kilter.[16] I think that twixt[17] the Negroes of the South and the women of the North all talking about rights, the white men will be in a fix pretty soon. *(OTHERS ad lib responses and move closer.)* But what's all this here talking about? *(Points to FIRST MAN.)* That man over there says that women need to be helped into carriages and lifted over ditches and to have the best place everywhere. Nobody ever helps me into carriages or over mud puddles, or gives me any best place—and aren't I a woman? I could work as much as a man, and eat as much, too, when I could get it, and bear the lash as well—and aren't I a woman? I have borne children and seen them sold into slavery and when I cried out with a mother's grief, none but the Lord heard me—and aren't I a woman? Then they talk about this thing in the head—what's that they call it?

FIRST WOMAN *(drawing closer with interest, as are ALL except SECOND REVEREND).* Intellect.

SOJOURNER. That's it, honey. What's intellect got to do with woman's rights or Negro's rights? If my cup won't hold but a pint and yours holds a quart, wouldn't you be mean not to let me have my little half-measure *full*? *(Pointing at SECOND REVEREND.)* Then that little man in black there, he says women can't have as much rights as men because Christ wasn't a woman. Where did your Christ come from? *(ALL are silent.)* Where did he come from? From God and a *woman*. Man had nothing to do with it. *(Applause from ALL except SECOND REVEREND.)* If the first woman

---

16. **out of kilter.** Out of balance; not right
17. **twixt.** Between

---

words for everyday use

ac • cus • tomed (ə kəs′ təmd) *adj.*, customary, habitual, usual. *We are <u>accustomed</u> to eat an apple a day because it keeps us healthy.*

in • tel • lect (in′ təl ekt′) *n.*, capacity for thinking and gaining knowledge. *Kim is smart and has a strong amount of <u>intellect</u>.*

God ever made was strong enough to turn the world upside down all alone, these women together ought to be able to turn it back and get it right side up again. And now that they are asking to do it, the men better let them. *(She stops, then smiles sweetly.)* Obliged to you for hearing me. (ALL *except* SECOND REVEREND *applaud enthusiastically.* SECOND REVEREND *stands apart and approaches* SOJOURNER *as she leaves lectern.)*

SECOND REVEREND. You think your talk does any good, old woman? Why, I don't care any more for it than for a flea bite!

SOJOURNER. A flea bite, you say? Well, the good Lord willing, sir, I am going to keep you scratching!

(OTHERS begin to sing "My Father, How Long?" SOJOURNER and SECOND MAN join in.)

ALL.

MY FATHER, HOW LONG? MY
FATHER, HOW LONG?
MY FATHER, HOW LONG, POOR
CHILDREN SUFFER HERE.
MY MOTHER, HOW LONG? MY
MOTHER, HOW LONG?
MY MOTHER, HOW LONG,
POOR CHILDREN SUFFER
HERE.
MY BROTHER, HOW LONG? MY
SISTER, HOW LONG?
MY BROTHER, HOW LONG,
POOR CHILDREN SUFFER
HERE?
AND IT WON'T BE LONG, AND
IT WON'T BE LONG,
AND IT WON'T BE LONG, POOR
CHILDREN SUFFER HERE
AND WE'LL SOON BE FREE, AND
WE'LL SOON BE FREE,
AND WE'LL SOON BE FREE,
POOR CHILDREN SUFFER
HERE.

(Lights fade. FINAL CURTAIN.) ■

Respond *to the* SELECTION

Imagine Sojourner Truth is living today. What might she say in a speech about the rights of African Americans and women in the twenty-first century?

About *the* AUTHOR

Sandra Fenichel Asher was born in Philadelphia, Pennsylvania, on October 16, 1942. As a child, she knew she wanted to do three things: dance, act, and write. Dance lessons began at the age of four. She also began acting in school plays at the age of six, and continued to play parts in amateur productions as she grew older. While she was in grade school, she began to write plays. By the time she was a senior in high school, she had written, directed, and narrated her own productions. Asher received her college degree from Indiana University in 1964 and married professor Harvey Asher the following year. She has written numerous books and plays for young adults and has taught creative writing at several colleges. She lives with her husband in Springfield, Missouri.

THE Sunflower QUILTING BEE AT ARLES

The Sunflower Quilting Bee at Arles, 1991. Faith Ringgold. Private Collection.

The text around the women's quilt says "The Sunflower Quilters Society of America, March 22, 1992. Madam C. J. Walker, Sojourner Truth, Ida Wells, Fannie Lou Hamer, Harriet Tubman, Rosa Parks, Mary McLeod Bethune, Ella Baker. An International symbol of our dedication to change the world." The text at the top and bottom of the quilt is reprinted on the facing page.

The National Sunflower Quilters Society of America are having quilting bees in sunflower fields around the world to spread the cause of freedom. Aunt Melissa has written to inform me of this and to say: "Go with them to the sunflower fields in Arles. And please take care of them in that foreign country, Willa Marie. These women are our freedom," she wrote.

2. Today the women arrived in Arles. They are Madame Walker, Sojourner Truth, Ida Wells, Fannie Lou Hamer, Harriet Tubman, Rosa Parks, Mary McLeod Bethune and Ella Baker, a fortress of African American women's courage, with enough energy to transform a nation piece by piece.

3. Look what they've done in spite of their oppression: Madame Walker invented the hair straightening comb and became the first self-made American-born woman millionaire. She employed over 3,000 people. Sojourner Truth spoke up brilliantly for women's rights during slavery, and could neither read nor write. Ida Wells made an exposé of the horror of lynching in the South.

4. Fannie Lou Hamer braved police dogs, water hoses, brutal beatings, and jail in order to register thousands of people to vote. Harriet Tubman brought over 300 slaves to freedom in 19 trips from the South on the Underground Railroad during slavery and never lost a passenger. Rosa Parks became the mother of the Civil Rights Movement when she sat down in the front of a segregated bus and refused to move to the back.

5. Mary McLeod Bethune founded Bethune Cookman College and was special advisor to Presidents Harry Truman and Franklin Delano Roosevelt. Ella Baker organized thousands of people to improve the condition of poor housing, jobs, and consumer education. Their trip to Arles was to complete *The Sunflower Quilt*, an international symbol of their dedication to change the world.

6. The Dutch painter, Vincent van Gogh came to see the black women sewing in the sunflower fields. "Who is this strange looking man," they said. "He is un grand peintre," I told them, "though he is greatly troubled in his mind." He held a vase of sunflowers, no doubt une nature morte, a still life, for one of his paintings.

7. "He's the image of the man hit me in the head with a rock when I was a girl," Harriet said. "Make him leave. He reminds me of slavers." But he was not about to be moved. Like one of the sunflowers, he appeared to be growing out of the ground. Sojourner wept into the stitches of her quilting for the loss of her thirteen children mostly all sold into slavery.

8. One of Sojourner's children, a girl, was sold to a Dutch slaver in the West Indies who then took her to Holland. "Was that something this Dutch man might know something about? He should pay for all the pain his people has given us. I am concerned about you, Willa Marie. Is this a natural setting for a black woman?" Sojourner asked.

9. "I came to France to seek opportunity," I said. "It is not possible for me to be an artist in the States." "We are all artists. Piecing is our art. We brought it straight from Africa," they said. "That was what we did after a hard day's work in the fields to keep our sanity and our beds warm and bring beauty into our lives. That was not being an artist. That was being alive."

10. When the sun went down and it was time for us to leave, the tormented little man just settled inside himself and took on the look of the sunflowers in the field as if he were one of them. The women were finished piecing now. "We need to stop and smell the flowers sometimes," they said. "Now we can do our real quilting, our real art: making this world piece up right."

11. "I got to get back to that railroad," Harriet said. "Ain't all us free yet, no matter how many them laws they pass. Sojourner fighting for women's rights. Fannie for voter registration. Ella and Rosa working on civil rights. Ida looking out for mens getting lynch. Mary Bethune getting our young-uns' education, and Madame making money fixing hair and giving us jobs. Lord, we is sure busy."

12. "I am so thankful to my aunt Melissa for sending you wonderful women to me," I said. "Art can never change anything the way you have. But it can make a picture so everyone can see and know our true history and culture from the art. Some day I will make you women proud of me, too. Just wait, you'll see." "We see, Willa Marie," they said. "We see." ∎

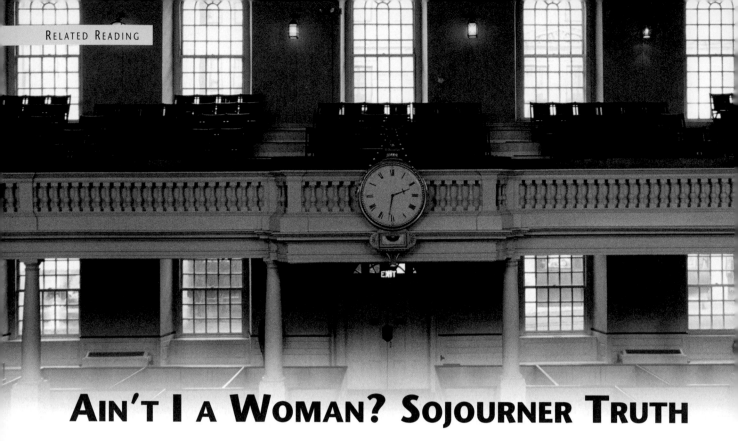

AIN'T I A WOMAN? SOJOURNER TRUTH

Well, children, where there is so much racket there must be something out of kilter. I think that 'twixt the negroes of the South and the women at the North, all talking about rights, the white men will be in a fix pretty soon. But what's all this here talking about?

That man over there says that women need to be helped into carriages, and lifted over ditches, and to have the best place everywhere. Nobody ever helps me into carriages, or over mud-puddles, or gives me any best place! And ain't I a woman? Look at me! Look at my arm! I have ploughed and planted, and gathered into barns, and no man could head me! And ain't I a woman? I could work as much and eat as much as a man—when I could get it—and bear the lash as well! And ain't I a woman? I have borne thirteen children, and seen most all sold off to slavery, and when I cried out with my mother's grief, none but Jesus heard me! And ain't I a woman?

Then they talk about this thing in the head; what's this they call it? [member of audience whispers, "intellect"] That's it, honey. What's that got to do with women's rights or negroes' rights? If my cup won't hold but a pint, and yours holds a quart, wouldn't you be mean not to let me have my little half-measure full?

Then that little man in black there, he says women can't have as much rights as men, 'cause Christ wasn't a woman! Where did your Christ come from? Where did your Christ come from? From God and a woman! Man had nothing to do with Him.

If the first woman God ever made was strong enough to turn the world upside down all alone, these women together ought to be able to turn it back, and get it right side up again! And now they is asking to do it, the men better let them.

Obliged to you for hearing me, and now old Sojourner ain't got nothing more to say. ■

Sojourner Truth delivered this famous speech at the Women's Convention in Akron, Ohio, in 1851. One newspaper, the Anti-Slavery Bugle, reported the following. "One of the most unique and interesting speeches of the Convention was made by Sojourner Truth, an emancipated slave. It is impossible to transfer it to paper, or convey any adequate idea of the effect it produced upon the audience. Those only can appreciate it who saw her powerful form, her whole-souled, earnest gesture, and listened to her strong and truthful tones."

The president of the convention was an activist named Frances Dana Gage. Gage allowed Truth to speak and later recounted Truth's words as they appear here. There is debate about the accuracy of this account, because Gage did not record it until 1863 and her record differs somewhat from newspaper accounts of 1851. Nevertheless, the speech has endured for more than a century as a classic expression of women's rights. About Truth's speech, Gage later said, "I have never in my life seen anything like the magical influence that subdued the mobbish spirit of the day, and turned the sneers and jeers of an excited crowd into notes of respect and admiration."

Faith Ringgold's painted story quilt, *The Sunflower Quilting Bee at Arles,* is one of many such works of art. On these quilts, a central picture is surrounded by a border in which the story appears. Her story quilts are in the collections of many museums. Ringgold has also written and illustrated children's books, such as *Tar Beach, Aunt Harriet's Underground Railroad in the Sky*, and *The Invisible Princess*. Ringgold is married and has two daughters and three granddaughters. She is a professor at the University of California in San Diego.

Investigate, Inquire, and Imagine

Recall: GATHERING FACTS

1a. Early in the play, what does Mama tell Sojourner and Pete to do if they are ever beaten or cruelly treated?

2a. What does Bob do to make Mr. Catlin angry?

3a. How do Isaac and Maria Van Wagener help Sojourner?

4a. What happens when Chip and Sojourner go to court?

Interpret: FINDING MEANING

1b. Why do you think Mama tells them this at this time?

2b. Would Mr. Catlin care about that?

3b. Why do the Van Wageners do this? What does Sojourner learn from them?

4b. Why does Pete react the way he does in court?

Analyze: TAKING THINGS APART

5a. What does Sojourner dream about for most of the play?

Synthesize: BRINGING THINGS TOGETHER

5b. How does Sojourner change through the course of the play?

Evaluate: MAKING JUDGMENTS

6a. In what ways does Sojourner favorably impress Squire Chip? How effective are these ways in influencing him?

Extend: CONNECTING IDEAS

6b. Think of a situation in which you tried to influence someone to change his or her mind about something. Did you exaggerate the truth or try to trick the person into changing? Did you clearly state your honest thoughts about the matter? How could that be more powerful?

Understanding Literature

DIALOGUE. Dialogue is conversation involving two or more people or characters. Plays are made up of dialogue and stage directions. In a play, dialogue appears after the names of characters. Think about the dialogues you found in this play. How do you know where they begin and end?

STAGE DIRECTIONS. Stage directions are notes included in a play to describe how something should look, sound, or be performed. Stage directions describe setting, lighting, music, sound effects, entrances and exits, properties, and the movements of characters. They are usually printed in italics and enclosed in brackets or parentheses. Look over your examples of stage directions in "A Woman Called Truth." How would the play be confusing without them?

Writer's Journal

1. Write a **name** for yourself that describes something about you. Provide a reason for your choice.

2. Imagine you are Isaac or Maria Van Wagener, running a farm with no outside help. Write out a **schedule** of chores you need to accomplish daily. Include start times for each task.

3. Write an **epitaph** for Sojourner's tombstone, using words that describe her impact on U.S. history and culture.

Skill Builders

Study and Research

RESEARCHING SPIRITUALS. Using the Internet and materials from your school's media center, research several African-American spirituals to uncover their meanings and any coded messages. For example, the song titled "Many Thousand Go" (found in the play you've just read) includes the phrases "peck o' corn" and "pint of salt." These phrases refer to slaves' rations. That same spiritual was sung in secret to avoid detection during the anti-slavery rebellion. To start your search, use the key words "Negro+Spirituals."

Collaborative Learning

ACTING. With a partner, make up a dialogue in which a mother and her fifteen-year-old son are discussing the disappearance of another family member. Then, working individually, each of you add stage directions describing the setting, lighting, music, sound effects, entrances and exits, props, and the movements of the mother and son. Look over each other's stage directions and then role-play the dialogue twice, each time using a different set of stage directions. Notice the differences in meaning, mood, and detail.

Media Literacy

READING A MAGAZINE ARTICLE. Find and summarize a magazine article about one of the following topics: Mary McCloud Bethune, Rosa Parks, Madam C. J. Walker, women and slavery, prejudice (in general), women's rights, the Bill of Rights. Whatever your topic, point out how the ideas in the article are similar to or different from the ideas in the play *A Woman Called Truth*.

Applied English

WRITING AN ARTICLE. Imagine you work at one of the main newspapers in Akron, Ohio, in 1851. Sojourner has just delivered her famous speech "Ain't I a Woman?" at the Women's Convention there, and your job is to get the news out. Write an article, including quotations from the speech, for your readers. You may want to review rules for the punctuation of direct quotations in the Language Arts Survey 3.82, "Quotation Marks."

Reader's Journal

What have you or some of your classmates done when intimidated by a bully or gang member?

Reader's Resource

- **AMERICAN HISTORY CONNECTION.** The earliest identified American gangs formed after the Revolutionary War (1775–1783). These gangs were known as Smith's Vly gang, the Bowery Boys, the Broadway Boys, the Long Bridge Boys, and the Fly Boys. Members were in their teens and early twenties.

- **GEOGRAPHY CONNECTION.** Although today's American gangs are more common in metropolitan areas such as Los Angeles, Chicago, and New York, gang activity also occurs in mid-size cities and small towns. In 1984 Los Angeles had an estimated 450 gangs and 40,000 members; by the mid-1990s those estimates had grown to 900 gangs and more than 100,000 members. In 1987, the city of Louisville, Kentucky, reported 1,000 gang members; Albuquerque, New Mexico, 1,757 members; and Fort Wayne, Indiana, 50 members.

Prereading

"Priscilla and the Wimps"
by Richard Peck

Reader's TOOLBOX

CHARACTER. A **character** is a person or animal who takes part in the action of a literary work. The main character is called the **protagonist**. A character who struggles against the main character is called an **antagonist**. Characters can also be classified as **major characters** or **minor characters**. Major characters are ones who play important roles in a work. Minor characters are ones who play less important roles. A **one-dimensional character**, **flat character**, or **caricature** is one who exhibits a single quality, or character trait. A **three-dimensional**, **full**, or **rounded character** is one who seems to have all the complexities of an actual human being. As you read "Priscilla and the Wimps," determine for each character whether he or she is: 1) the protagonist, antagonist, or neither; 2) a major or minor character; and 3) a one-dimensional character or a three-dimensional character. To help keep track of your findings, you may want to place checkmarks in a graphic organizer like the one below. Below, the narrator has been done for you as an example.

HYPERBOLE. A **hyperbole** is an exaggeration made for effect. Look for hyperboles as you read.

Graphic Organizer

	Type of Character	Narrator	Monk Klutter	Priscilla Roseberry	Melvin Detweiler
I.	protagonist				
	antagonist				
	neither	✔			
II.	major character				
	minor character	✔			
III.	one-dimensional character	✔			
	three-dimensional character				

PRISCILLA
and the wimps

Richard Peck

Listen, there was a time when you couldn't even go to the *rest room* around this school without a pass. And I'm not talking about those little pink tickets made out by some teacher. I'm talking about a pass that could cost anywhere up to a buck, sold by Monk Klutter.

Not that Mighty Monk ever touched money, not in public. The gang he ran, which ran the school for him, was his collection agency. They were Klutter's Kobras, a name spelled out in nailheads on six well-known black plastic windbreakers.

GUIDED READING

Who runs the gang that runs the school?

HYPERBOLE. A **hyperbole** is an exaggeration made for effect. Some hyperboles in "Priscilla and the Wimps" are mainly descriptive; others add humor to the story. Look back at the story and identify those hyperboles that add humor.

Writer's Journal

1. To serve as an illustration for "Priscilla and the Wimps," draw a **cartoon** of one or more of the characters and add a humorous caption below it.

2. For a **newspaper advice column**, write a response to a reader who is asking what to do when hassled by a gang at school.

3. As an extension to the story, write a **telephone dialogue** that Priscilla and Melvin might have had on the second day of the school's closing because of the icy blizzard.

Skill Builders

Speaking and Listening

READING ALOUD. Form small groups. Each group member will write a one-page continuation about what happens after the original ending of "Priscilla and the Wimps." Listen closely as each member reads his or her continuation. After all of the readings are complete, discuss which continuation is the most realistic and which is the most far-fetched. Give examples of how each reading maintained or deviated from the behavior and speech of the characters, as established by the author in the original story.

Study and Research & Collaborative Learning

GROUP RESEARCH. Individually, select one of the following four topics: 1) intimidation tactics, 2) gender bias, 3) school gangs, 4) weapons at school. Form groups of those who selected the same topic. Each group will research and compile factual data on its topic. Use fairly current resources from the library, the Internet, or both. Select a representative from each group to orally present their group's data to the class. As a class, expand on the data for each topic by raising questions and bringing up any additional data known about the topic.

Applied English

LOGGING INFORMATION. Imagine you are a middle school social studies teacher who is also serving as monitor in the school cafeteria. After about six weeks as monitor, you begin to notice glimpses of various students' facial expressions and behavior and to overhear snatches of conversations that cause you to worry that something might be wrong. As you begin to see a pattern, you suspect a certain small group of students could be intimidating other students. Then you notice similarly troublesome student interactions in your classroom, in the hallways, and on the school grounds, and you decide to inform the vice-principal. She requests that you prepare a log of what you've seen and heard that makes you suspicious. Write up such a log, listing what you've observed, who the students were, and the approximate date of each happening.

for your READING LIST

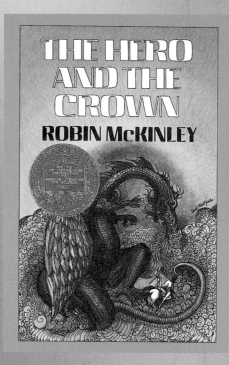

The Hero and the Crown by Robin McKinley is the story of Aerin, a young princess and member of the royal family that rules over the kingdom of Damar. Aerin has been haunted since childhood by stories of the mother she never knew. Told that her mother was a witch who ensnared the king and then died of disappointment after giving birth to a daughter, rather than the son she believed could save the kingdom, Aerin struggles to discover the truth about her mother and herself. Aerin is uncomfortably aware that she is the only member of her family who does not appear to have the "Gift," the special, magical ability that has always marked royalty in Damar. Little does awkward, unconfident Aerin realize that she is destined to be the hero who will one day wield the powerful blue sword and save her country from the forces of evil.

WRITING A SCREENPLAY

Imagine that you are a Hollywood screenwriter. You have just read *The Hero and the Crown,* and you believe it would make a great movie. Write a letter to a movie producer, explaining in detail why the story, characters, and conflicts would translate well from the book to the screen. You should discuss filming locations, as well as actors to play the main roles. Write a sample scene to include as part of your proposal. For help with writing your screenplay, you might wish to search the Internet for sites that give ideas on script basics, such as proper format.

Other books you may want to read:
The Door in the Wall by Marguerite de Angeli
The Ear, the Eye and the Arm by Nancy Farmer
Number the Stars by Lois Lowry
The Adventures of Charlotte Doyle by Avi
The Giver by Lois Lowry

Guided Writing

> "What a hero one can be without moving a finger!"
>
> —Henry David Thoreau

A **persuasive essay** is a short nonfiction work that expresses a writer's thoughts about a single subject. A good essay develops a single idea or thesis, and is organized into an introduction, a body, and a conclusion. A persuasive essay is written to advance or promote an opinion.

Examining the Model

In the excerpt from *Still Me*, Christopher Reeve writes persuasively about his changing definition of a hero. Reeve once thought that a hero was "someone who commits a courageous action without considering the consequences." After his accident, however, Reeve realized that a hero is someone who perseveres in spite of great obstacles. Writing about his own experience and about people like Travis Roy and Henry Steifel reinforces his point that a hero is an ordinary individual who perseveres despite "overwhelming obstacles." Notice also that Reeve strengthens this point when he says that "the family and friends who have stood by them" are heroes as well. By carefully taking the reader from his old idea of what a hero is to his new

continued on page 143

NOMINATING A HERO

Just as Christopher Reeve once thought that a hero was "someone who commits a courageous action without considering the consequences," that's exactly what Nina had thought, too. After his accident, however, Mr. Reeve realized that a hero was someone who perseveres in spite of great obstacles. His new definition of a hero inspired Nina to rethink her ideas and to nominate Christopher Reeve as a true hero.

Most people have a hero—someone they admire, respect and want to be like. Perhaps you admire someone well known like Mohandas Gandhi who practiced nonviolent resistance. Or perhaps you hold a teacher or coach in your community in high esteem. You might admire a member of your family who is courageous or patient or who has some quality that inspires you to do your best. For this assignment, you will write a persuasive essay in which you nominate someone as a hero.

Professional Model

from *Still Me* by Christopher Reeve, pages 81–82

When the first Superman movie came out, I gave dozens of interviews to promote it. The most frequently asked question was: "What is a hero?" I remember how easily I'd talk about it, the glib response I repeated so many times. My answer was that a hero is someone who commits a courageous action without considering the consequences. A soldier who crawls out of a foxhole to drag an injured buddy back to safety, the prisoners of war who never stop trying to escape even though they know they may be executed if they're caught. And I also meant individuals who are slightly larger than life: Houdini[3] and Lindbergh[4] of course, John Wayne and JFK, and even sports figures who have taken on mythical proportions, such as Babe Ruth or Joe DiMaggio.[5]

Now my definition is completely different. I think a hero is an ordinary individual who finds the strength to persevere and endure in spite of overwhelming obstacles. The fifteen-year-old boy down the hall at Kessler who had landed on his head while wrestling with his brother, leaving him paralyzed and barely able to swallow or speak. Travis Roy, paralyzed in the first eleven seconds of a hockey game in his freshman year at college. Henry Steifel, paralyzed from the chest down in a car accident at seventeen, completing his education and working on Wall Street at age thirty-two, but having missed so much of what life has to offer. These are real heroes, and so are the families and friends who have stood by them.

Prewriting

WRITING WITH A PLAN. You probably can think of several people that you admire, respect, and value. On a separate piece of paper, write down the names of at least two people that you could nominate as a hero. Then freewrite three or four sentences next to each name telling why that person would be a good candidate for a hero. After you freewrite, select the person that you want to write about.

Nina decided to nominate Christopher Reeve as a hero. To prepare for her draft, she filled in the graphic organizer below. She wrote notes about why he was a hero and gave supporting evidence. She told how he had inspired her to do her best and included an anecdote about him. An **anecdote** is a usually short narrative of an interesting, amusing, or biographical incident. Plan to include at least one anecdote in your writing that will help persuade your readers that your person is a hero.

Student Model—Graphic Organizer

Copy the graphic organizer onto your own paper. Fill in the graphic organizer with information about the person you have nominated as a hero.

<u>Who I nominate as a hero:</u>
Christopher Reeve

↓

<u>Why I nominate this person as a hero:</u>
• He tries hard not to let his problems affect his family too much.
• He works hard to increase research for disabilities and to help others, not just himself.

<u>Supporting Evidence:</u>
• He tries to keep his young son Will carefree and to be a good father to his teenage children.
• He won't let himself become a drepressed "hulk" in a wheelchair because he cares about his wife.
• He lobbies hard by speaking about the need for more research for people with disabilities

<u>Interesting Anecdote:</u>

<u>How this person inspired me:</u>
I'm going to do the best I can and help others, too.

understanding, Reeve persuades his audience that many people with disabilities and the people who support them are heroes.

FINDING YOUR VOICE. Voice is the way a writer uses language to reflect his or her unique personality and attitude toward his or her topic and audience. Since you will be trying to persuade your peers that the person you nominated is a hero, your voice needs to be convincing, yet honest.

Which example below uses a convincing and honest voice?

> My dad is my hero because he never stops trying, even when things are really tough for him.

> My dad is my hero. He's the greatest dad there ever was.

IDENTIFYING YOUR AUDIENCE. The audience for this assignment will be your peers. Your task will be to convince them why the person you are writing about is truly a hero. Since your essay is also a tribute to the person you are writing about, you may want to share your writing with that person.

DRAFTING CHECKLIST FOR A PERSUASIVE ESSAY

Introduction
- Name the person you are nominating
- Include a thesis statement

Body Paragraphs
- Give supporting evidence for the thesis statement
- Explain why this person inspires you
- Relate an anecdote about the person

Conclusion
- Restate your thesis and major supporting ideas in different words
- Finish your essay with impact

"Heroes and heroines serve as models and leaders of people and nations because they reflect the feelings, dreams, fantasies, and need of individuals and of society itself."

—Ray B. Browne

continued on page 145

Drafting

Using the information from your freewriting and your graphic essay, the next step is to organize these ideas in a useful way. Your essay should start with an introduction. The introduction should include your thesis statement. A **thesis statement** is simply a sentence that presents the main point or the position you will take in your essay. Nina included the following thesis statement in her persuasive essay:

```
After reading Still Me, I think
Christopher Reeve is a hero because he
has worked so hard not to let his
problems fall too heavily on his family
and because.
```

You can use the notes in your graphic organizer to help you write your thesis statement. Include your thesis statement in your introduction.

Next, in the first body paragraph of her essay, Nina gave supporting evidence for her thesis statement. She describes how Christopher Reeve tries to help his family and speak out for people with disabilities.

In the first body paragraph of your essay, give **supporting evidence** for your thesis. You can also include a paragraph that explains how this person has inspired you.

Include an **anecdote** about the person. An anecdote is a usually short narrative of an interesting, amusing, or biographical incident. This anecdote should show your hero in action. It should show why this person can be considered a hero. It will help you to persuade your readers.

Write the **conclusion** to your essay. Restate your thesis and major supporting ideas in different words.

Student Model—Draft

```
    I would like to nominate Christopher
Reeve as a true hero. Many people
thought he was pretty heroic when he        reword
played Superman in the movies. But in
1995, Mr. Reeve had an unfortunate
accident: he was thrown from his
horse, and his spinal cord is injured.
                                   was
```

He has to use a wheelchair now. I have just recently read Christopher Reeve's book, *Still Me*. After reading this book, I think he is now a real hero, not just a pretend hero in the movies, because he has worked so hard not to *add more specific supporting evidence* let his problems fall too heavily on his family. And also, he works hard to improve the lives of many people with disabilities, not just himself.

Self- and Peer Evaluation

After you finish your first draft, complete a self-evaluation of your review and get one or two peer evaluations. For more information, see the Language Arts Survey 2.37, "Self- and Peer Evaluation."

As you evaluate your essay and those of your peers, answer the following questions. Write notes on the draft that can be used later at the revision stage.

- How persuasive is the essay? What additional information would help it be more persuasive?
- Does the introduction to the essay contain a thesis statement? Try to restate the thesis statement clearly. What additional information would help clarify it?
- Does the body of the essay contain enough supporting evidence for the thesis statement? What details could be added to support the thesis? What details should be deleted because they do not support the thesis?
- Does the body of the essay offer an anecdote about the person? How effectively does it persuade the reader that the person is a hero?
- How well does the conclusion restate the thesis and major supporting ideas in different words?
- Which words and sentences present the most honest and convincing voice? Which words present the least honest and convincing voice?

Revising and Proofreading

Review your self- and peer evaluations. Revise your writing after considering these comments. Finally, proofread your revised draft for spelling, capitalization, and usage errors. If you are unsure about the spelling of a word, circle it and look it up in the dictionary. Check to see if you are using verb tense correctly in each sentence.

Language, Grammar, and Style
Using Verb Tenses Correctly

Verbs carry a concept of time, called tense. Two kinds of tenses are the **simple tenses**—these express simple past, present, and future—and the **perfect tenses** that give information about actions that took place over time.

SIMPLE TENSES

Present tense verbs show that something is happening now. Past tense verbs talk about something that happened before now, and future tense verbs talk about something that will happen in the future.

Present tense
Today I <u>play</u> soccer.
Today I <u>do play</u> soccer.
Today I <u>am playing</u> soccer.

Past tense
Yesterday I <u>played</u> soccer.
Yesterday I <u>did play</u> soccer.
Yesterday I <u>was playing</u> soccer.

Future tense
Tomorrow I <u>will play</u> soccer.
Tomorrow I <u>will be playing</u> soccer.

PERFECT TENSES

The perfect tenses express past, present, and future, but they add information about actions that continued over a period of time and were completed in the past or will be competed in the present

continued on page 146

or future. All perfect tenses use some form of the helping verb *to have*.

Present perfect tense

Today I <u>have played</u> soccer. Today I <u>have been playing</u> soccer.

Past perfect tense

Yesterday I <u>had played</u> soccer. Yesterday I <u>had been playing</u> soccer.

Future perfect tense

Tomorrow I <u>will have played</u> soccer. I <u>will have been playing</u> soccer.

One error that student writers make is to shift tense in the middle of a piece of writing. Each piece needs to maintain a consistent tense.

IDENTIFYING CONSISTENT VERB TENSE. Reread the sentences below from "Why Christopher Reeve Is a True Hero." Identify the verb tenses for the verbs that are underlined. How does Nina use verb tense consistently and to convey action happening over time?

After Reeve's accident, he <u>learned</u> that a hero is "an ordinary individual who <u>finds</u> the strength to persevere and endure in spite of over-whelming obstacles." I <u>agree</u> with that definition. Christopher Reeve <u>played</u> a hero in the *Superman* movie, but he actually <u>is</u> a hero because of the way he <u>perseveres</u> and <u>helps</u> his family and others with disabilities.

Student Model—Revised

"Why Christopher Reeve Is a True Hero"
by Nina Brandt

Christopher Reeve was the hero of the first *Superman* movie. Then, in 1995, Mr. Reeve had an unfortunate accident: he was thrown from his horse, and his spinal cord was injured. He is confined to a wheelchair now. After reading his book *Still Me*, I think he is a real hero because he has worked so hard not to let his problems fall too heavily on his family. He also works hard to increase research for disabilities. This may help thousands of people in the future.

It has been very difficult for Christopher Reeve to adjust to suddenly being in a wheelchair. In *Still Me*, he says he misses his "freedom, spontaneity, action, and adventure." Yet, in spite of that, he realizes how important it is not to cause his family too much worry. He tries to keep his young son carefree. He tries to be close to his two teenagers, Matthew and Alexandra, and to give them fatherly advice. He won't let himself become a "depressed hulk" in a wheelchair because he cares about his wife. So he tries very hard not to spend too much time turning inward and mourning the past.

As you know, I use a wheelchair, too. It's so frustrating not to be able to do so many of the things that most of you can do. Mr. Reeve's story has really inspired me, though. I'm going to do whatever I can, and I'm going to do it well. I'm going to help others, too.

Before Reeve's accident, he spent much of his time helping others. He helped lead a demonstration to free imprisoned artists in Chile, encouraged the United Nations to ban drift-net tuna fishing, and lobbied to protect the Hudson River. He worked with Amnesty International, Save the Children, and the Creative Coalition. Even after his accident, Reeve has continued to work to help other people. His fame has allowed him to raise public awareness about spinal injuries, and his drive for success has pushed him to participate in many programs and appear before many audiences, despite his disabilities.

In an interview with Steve Younis, webmaster of The Christopher Reeve Homepage, at http://www.geocities.com/Hollywood/Studio/4071/frameset.html, June Fox—the editor who assisted Reeve in transcribing Reeve's words for *Still Me*—tells about Reeve's determination. When confined to his bed for health reasons, Reeve would not stop working. She says, "One day his doctor told him that he would have to stay in bed for a month in order for a wound to heal. Chris was so depressed about this that he sent me home. He asked me to do what I could on the current chapter on my own, and to come back the next morning. By the next day, he was in complete control of his emotions and we were able to continue working. . . . I have tremendous respect for the way Chris always overcomes these emotional and physical setbacks. He does it through the sheer force of his own will and self-discipline. He refuses to give in to self-pity. I don't think many people could do what he does." "More than anyone else I know, he has taken responsibility for his life and what he chooses to do with it," Fox relates, "Everything he does is because he knows its value, from lobbying for scientific research to listening to his wife to playing with Will."

FIXING INCONSISTENT VERB TENSE. You need to keep verb tenses consistent; that is, if you are talking about something that happened in the past, the verb tense must show that. Switching tenses thoughtlessly mars good writing. Explain how you would fix the errors in tense that appear below.

He also thought people like Houdini or Lindbergh are heroes.
Most kids today sit around and watched television.
My grandparent start the restaurant years ago.

USING CONSISTENT VERB TENSE. Look at each sentence in your persuasive essay. Underline the verbs and identify which tense they use. Correct any improper verb tenses and make the verbs reflect consistent tense. Make sure your verbs accurately depict the passage of time. For more information, see the Language Arts Survey 3.60, "Verb Tenses."

Publishing and Presenting

You can write your final copy in ink or print it from a computer. Add a cover to your essay and include a photograph or sketch of the person. Try to show the person in some context. For example, if you are writing about Neil Armstrong, you might want to show a picture of the moon in the background. You can download pictures of many well-known people from the Internet. Plan to read the essays in class or create a book of class essays that can be copied for everyone to take home.

Reflecting

After listening to your classmates read their essays about their heroes, reflect on what you know now about heroes. How would you define a hero? Who can be a hero? Do some people change when they become heroes? Why might they? Should they? How do heroes help others reach their potential? How does your hero inspire you to become a better citizen of your school or community?

UNIT TWO *review*

Review: Words for Everyday Use

Check your knowledge of the following vocabulary words. Choose ten words that you would like to incorporate into your own daily language. For each word, write a short sentence that includes the word in context. To review a word, look back to the page number(s) indicated.

- accustomed (126)
- adjourn (120)
- appall (110)
- audible (96)
- bar (136)
- behalf (121)
- cherish (80)
- conspiratorial (97)
- construct (83)
- cordon (81)
- default (120)
- defiance (122)
- devastate (80)
- disdainful (106)
- earnest (75)
- emphatic (110)
- fate (138)
- fluid (97)
- gaunt (95)

- glib (81)
- hindrance (93)
- incapacitate (83)
- instinctive (83)
- intellect (126)
- intensity (111)
- laceration (136)
- lurch (96)
- mediocre (95)
- motive (99)
- mythical (82)
- narrative (106)
- perpetual (93)
- podium (106)
- poised (100)
- ponder (75)
- prominent (120)
- proposition (113)
- pun (137)

- quizzical (96)
- ramification (110)
- rant (111)
- reception (116)
- relentless (93)
- rue (120)
- slither (136)
- smug (121)
- spite (110)
- spontaneity (80)
- subtle (136)
- sustain (80)
- tenacity (121)
- throng (97)
- venture (93)
- visceral (84)
- warrant (109)
- wary (112)
- wince (121)

Review: Literary Tools

Define each of the following terms, giving concrete examples when possible. To review a term, refer to the page number(s) indicated.

- antagonist (134)
- autobiography (79)
- character (134)
- characterization (91)

- description (91)
- dialogue (104)
- hero (73)
- oral tradition (73)

- point of view (79)
- protagonist (134)
- stage directions (104)

Reflecting on your reading

Theme

Heroes are fun to read about in literature. Readers find heroes in myths and legends, throughout history, among the famous, and in everyday life. There are many heroes in your own neighborhood. They are people who stand up for what they believe in and who work to help others. Sometimes just being yourself is a heroic act. Heroes help others to see their own potential and inspire them to fight for their own causes. Who do you consider a hero? What makes that person a hero? Write—in a literary form of your choice—about someone you consider a hero.

Group Project

With the members of your group make a list of heroes. Share them with each other and discuss the qualities and acts that make them heroes. Your hero could be a sports figure, like Magic Johnson; a cartoon character, like Batman; a historical figure, like Harriet Tubman; or someone you know, like your grandfather. Look back at the picture of the story quilt that Faith Ringgold created (page 128). Based on that, make a painting together of your group's heroes. What would it be like if they all got together in the same room? What would they be doing?

art smart

"Sitting Bull Returns" at the Drive-in, 1976. Willard Midgette.

Look back at the painting on pages 70–71. Sitting Bull was a chief of the Lakota tribe who fought to retain his homeland and preserve Lakota traditions. Although they defeated General Custer at the Battle of Little Big Horn in 1876, the Lakota were eventually forced by law to abandon their traditional way of life. This painting is a picture within a picture: real, contemporary Native Americans are watching a Hollywood version of their past. What do you think the artist is saying in making this comparison?

Tornado Over Kansas, 1929. John Stuart Curry. Muskegon Museum of Art, Muskegon, Michigan.

ADVENTURES and DISASTERS

echoes

Bygone troubles are good to tell.
—*Yiddish proverb*

We did not begin to understand the situation till we were perhaps a mile away from the *Titanic* . . .
—*Colonel Archibald Gracie,* The Story of the Titanic

Calamity is the test of integrity.
—*Samuel Richardson*

When one has too great a dread of what is impending, one feels some relief when the trouble has come.
—*Joseph Joubert*

This is still a world in which too many of the wrong things happen somewhere. But this is a world in which we now have the means to make a great many more of the right things happen everywhere.
—*Margaret Mead*

Action springs not from thought, but from a readiness for responsibility.
—*Dietrich Bonhoeffer*

One of the basic causes for all the trouble in the world today is that people talk too much and think too little.
—*Margaret Chase Smith*

Nature reserves the right to inflict upon her children the most terrifying jests.
—*Thornton Wilder*

I wanted you to see what real courage is, instead of getting the idea that courage is a man with a gun in his hand. It's when you know you're licked before you begin, but you begin anyway and you see it through no matter what.
—*Harper Lee,* To Kill a Mockingbird

Prereading

"The Face of the Deep Is Frozen"

by Jennifer Armstrong

Reader's Resource

- **HISTORY CONNECTION.** In August 1914, Ernest Shackleton and 27 men sailed from England in an attempt to become the first team of explorers to cross the Antarctic continent from one side to the other. Five months later and still 100 miles from land, their ship, *Endurance*, became trapped. The expedition survived an Antarctic winter in the icebound ship, but then the *Endurance* sank and the men were forced to camp on the ice for five months. In a desperate effort to save themselves, the men made a perilous boat journey through storms and icebergs to Elephant Island. From there, their only hope was for someone to fetch help. Shackleton and five others navigated 800 miles of the treacherous open ocean in a 20-foot boat and then hiked across the unmapped, glacier-strewn interior of South Georgia Island to a whaling station. In August 1916, 19 months after *Endurance* first became icebound, Shackleton led a rescue party back to Elephant Island for his men. All of the members of Shackleton's expedition survived. Shackleton became well known for his ability to lead his crew successfully to safety.

Graphic Organizer

Create a story web with the chapter title at center. Make branches at the right to name events. Use branches at the top and bottom for the setting and descriptions.

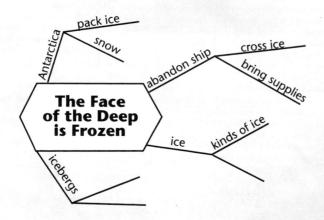

Reader's Journal

What would you do if you found yourself the leader of a crew forced to abandon their ship in the dangerous cold of Antarctica?

Reader's TOOLBOX

SETTING. The **setting** of a literary work is the time and place in which it happens. In fiction and in drama, writers create setting using what they know about the time and place they wish to represent. In nonfiction, writers try to stay true to the particular time and place in which a person lived or in which an event took place. Writers use description to develop in the reader's mind an accurate picture of the setting. As you read "The Face of the Deep Is Frozen," look for information on the setting.

DESCRIPTION. Description is a type of writing that portrays a character, object, or scene. Descriptions make use of sensory details—words and phrases that describe how things look, sound, smell, taste, or feel. Effective descriptions contain precise—or concrete—nouns, verbs, adverbs, and adjectives. In what ways does Jennifer Armstrong, the author of this selection, describe the setting? Identify some of the descriptions she offers about the setting.

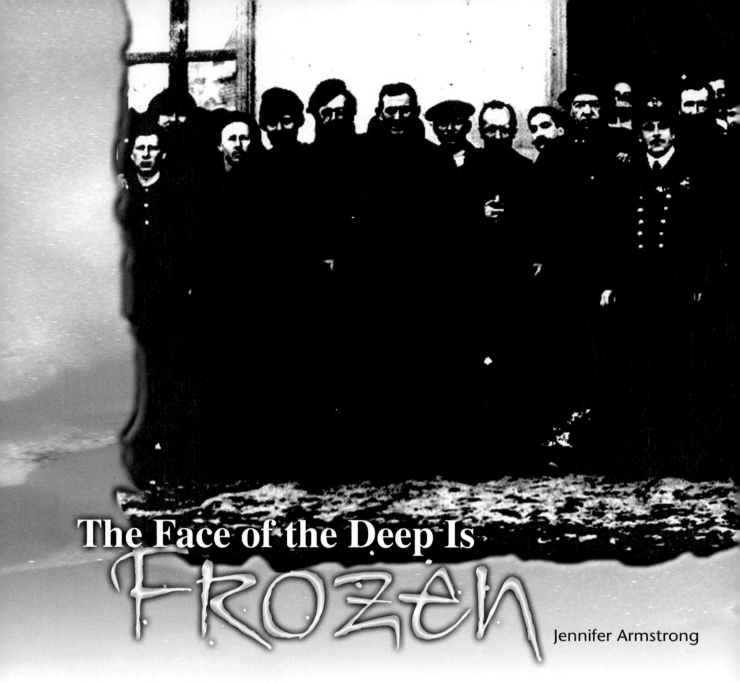

The Face of the Deep Is
FROZEN

Jennifer Armstrong

GUIDED READING

How much of the world's snow and ice does the Antarctic contain?

The Antarctic contains ninety percent of the world's snow and ice, and there are more than eighty kinds of it. There's brash ice, pancake ice, bullet ice, green ice, frazil, nilas, breccia, shuga, slush ice, rotten ice, pressure ice, grease ice, ice dust, shorefast ice, ice flowers, ice haycocks, ice saddles, floes, calf bergs, growlers, and sastrugi, to name just a few.

And when it comes to icebergs, there are whole family trees to study. In the family of tabular bergs, there are domed, horizontal, blocky, tilted, and uneven bergs; in the tribe of rounded bergs, there are surrounded, well-rounded, and rounded bergs; and when it comes to irregular bergs, there are tabular remnant, pinnacled, pyramidal, drydock, castellate, jagged, slab, and roof bergs.

Much of the ice on the continent of Antarctica is actually a form of

Members of the *Endurance* expedition after their rescue. Shackleton is to the left of the man in uniform—Captain Pardo—who sailed the rescue ship to Elephant Island.

<u>consolidated</u> snow called firn. As snow accumulates, it begins to compact, forcing out the air between the snowflakes. Eventually, all the air is squeezed out, and the snow is a <u>dense</u>,

> **GUIDED READING**
>
> How does snow become dense, heavy ice?

heavy ice. This <u>compression</u> also makes much of the ice blue.

These masses of ice form glaciers that reach the edge of the continent, where every year 5,000 to 10,000 icebergs "calve," or break off, from the ice sheets into the surrounding

words for everyday use

con • sol • i • date (kən säl' lə dāt) *v.*, join together into one whole. *Our group gathered our thoughts together and <u>consolidated</u> our ideas.* **consolidated,** *adj.*

dense (den[t]s') *adj.*, compact; crowding together of parts. *Pound cake is more compact than angel food cake because it is more <u>dense</u>.*

com • pres • sion (kəm pre' shən) *n.*, act of pressing together. *When snow is under <u>compression</u>, it becomes hard like ice.*

ocean. Many icebergs are so large that they create their own weather systems. The largest iceberg ever recorded was one the size of Belgium (close to 12,000 square miles), spotted in 1956, and the most northerly iceberg reached twenty-six degrees south latitude[1] in the Atlantic Ocean, in 1894. This is the latitude of Rio de Janeiro, in Brazil, just south of the Tropic of Capricorn.[2] As the icebergs drift, the seawater <u>erodes</u> them from below, until the berg <u>abruptly</u> topples over and continues its journey upside down. The erosion continues until the berg flips again, and then again, and eventually it is eroded and melted away.

As the icebergs calve from the glaciers on the continent, they bring with them mineral deposits scraped up from the ground, and release these nutrients into the water. As they melt, the bergs also release <u>atmospheric</u> nutrients that have been trapped in the ice for centuries. It is this steady deposit of nutrients from icebergs that makes the waters of the Southern Ocean[3] so rich and full of life.

Of course, the ocean around the continent also turns to ice. Salt water freezes at a lower temperature than fresh water, around twenty-seven degrees Fahrenheit, depending on the concentration of salt and other minerals. As the water on the surface cools, it begins to condense, and individual ice crystals act as seeds, causing the water to <u>congeal</u> around them, squeezing the salt out into the water below. On the surface, the water seems to stiffen and turn greasy. This layer of thick, flexible ice is called nilas. If the nilas is disturbed by wind, the ice forms rounded discs called pancakes, which

> **GUIDED READING**
>
> What does it mean for an iceberg to calve?

> **GUIDED READING**
>
> How is nilas formed?

look something like white lily pads with their edges turned up. As the air temperature drops and the water continues to freeze, the pancakes mass together and harden into a single sheet, or ice field. Because the water forces out salt as it freezes, the water below the ice field is saturated with salt and minerals, and the ice itself is clean enough to melt into drinking water.

This process of turning seawater into drinking water is important—it means that a shipwreck on the frozen sea does not *necessarily* mean certain death.

When the exhausted crew of *Endurance* gave up the battle against the pressure and abandoned the ship, the ice field around her was not a sight to inspire confidence. The ship itself was a mess of snapped rigging and broken spars. Beside her on the ice was Dump Camp, a junk pile of most of the stores and equipment the men had. The dogs milled around, straining at their tethers,[4] snapping and snarling at one another. The crew staggered like dead men, utterly beaten from their labors, trying to pitch tents so they could crawl in to sleep. There were only eighteen sleeping bags, originally meant for the overland journey, and the men drew straws to see who would get them. The rest of the men had to make do with wool blankets. Tom

> **GUIDED READING**
>
> What happens to the ship *Endurance* that causes the crew to abandon it?

---

1. **latitude.** Angular distance north or south from the earth's equator measured through 90 degrees
2. **Tropic of Capricorn.** The parallel of latitude that is about 23 degrees south of the equator and that is the southernmost latitude reached by the overhead sun
3. **Southern Ocean.** Ocean in the subantarctic region of Antarctica
4. **tethers.** Ropes or chains fastened onto an animal to keep it within a certain range

---

words for everyday use

erode (i rōd′) v., wear away or cause deterioration. *After many years, waves eventually <u>erode</u> rocks into sand.*
ab • rupt (ə brəpt′) adj., without preparation or warning; unexpected. *An <u>abrupt</u> storm unexpectedly forced our picnic indoors.* **abruptly,** adv.
at • mo • spher • ic (at məs fir′ ik) adj., relating to or occurring in the atmosphere. *We breathe in <u>atmospheric</u> elements such as oxygen and nitrogen.*
con • geal (kən jēl′) v., turn fluid into a more solid state; solidify. *Water <u>congeals</u> to ice when you freeze it.*

> "The task is to
> reach land with all
> the members of
> the expedition."

Crean was suffering from snow blindness (a temporary condition that often affects polar travelers when they are exposed to the glare of sunlight on snow); he had to be helped into a tent. That night, the ice beneath the tents quivered as whales rubbed up against it from below.

"Though we have been compelled to abandon the ship, which is crushed beyond all hope of ever being righted, we are alive and well, and we have stores and equipment for the task that lies before us. The task is to reach land with all the members of the expedition," Shackleton wrote in his diary the next morning.

GUIDED READING

What is the task that Shackleton writes in his diary?

There were precious few options available to the Boss. Already the ship had drifted 1,000 miles north and west with the pack ice. The tip of South America was more than 2,000 miles away, and there was no way of reaching it on foot. They had ample food, guns, matches, and dogs. But, after all, they were in the Antarctic, not Hyde Park[5] in London. The circumstances were <u>dire</u>, to say the least.

After a quiet conference with Wild, Shackleton announced his plan to the crew: they would march across the frozen sea with two of the three lifeboats to Paulet Island, 346 miles to the northwest. To the best of Shackleton's knowledge, there was a <u>cache</u> of stores in a hut on Paulet Island from a 1902 Swedish expedition. What they would do once they reached this destination was not specified: it was enough to have a goal. He would plan the next step when they got there. But 346 miles is more than the distance between Boston and New York City, almost as far as from Los Angeles to San Francisco,

GUIDED READING

What does Shackleton announce is his plan after a quiet conference with Wild?

---

5. **Hyde Park.** Park in London, England. Races used to be held there in the 1800s.

---

words for everyday use

dire (dīr') *adj.*, terrifying, desperately urgent. *Because we hadn't eaten for ten days, we were in <u>dire</u> need of food.*

cache (kash') *n.*, hiding place for preserving necessities. *I asked John to store the canned goods in the <u>cache</u> downstairs.*

about the entire width of Iowa. They would have to walk the whole way, hauling their gear and the two boats. The men knew they were doomed without the boats; eventually they would reach open water. They would need the boats, no matter how burdensome they were to drag over the ice. Shackleton gave the men a couple of days' rest. October 30 was the appointed day of departure.

In the meantime, there was much to get ready. Mrs. Chippy, the carpenter's cat, had to be shot, because without the protection of the ship the dogs would have eaten him. The youngest of the puppies, who were too small to pull with a team, also had to be killed.

GUIDED READING

Why do Mrs. Chippy, the carpenter's cat, and the youngest puppies have to be killed?

While McNeish and McLeod began fitting the lifeboats onto sledges, the rest of the crew began sorting their equipment. The men were given a two-pound limit on personal gear, which allowed them to keep only the items that were essential for survival—although the Boss did allow them to keep their diaries and their tobacco, and the doctors were allowed their medical supplies. In a dramatic gesture, Shackleton took his gold cigarette case and a handful of gold coins from his pocket and dropped them on the snow. Gold was useless for the task ahead.

GUIDED READING

What does Shackleton do with his gold?

He then opened the Bible inscribed to him by Queen Alexandra and ripped out a page from the Book of Job:[6]

Out of whose womb came the ice?
And the hoary frost of Heaven, who hath gendered it?
The waters are hid as with a stone,

And the face of the deep is frozen.

Then he folded the page into a pocket and dropped the heavy Bible on the cigarette case and gold coins, showing the crew the route they must take. If they wanted to survive, they must travel light, harden their hearts against sentimental keepsakes, and trust that they could make do with the bare bones of equipment. Shackleton the improviser believed that it was foolish to burden themselves with equipment for *every* possible emergency. As the day wore on, the pile of discards grew. Extra clothes, books, scientific instruments and specimens, chess sets, flags, lanterns, tools, sewing kits, lucky talismans, razors, barometers, combs, scissors, playing cards, dishes, silverware, photographs—each man added to the heap. Some of the men saved leather suitcases to use for boot repairs later on. Hussey kept his toothbrush, and Shackleton ordered him to keep the banjo, because they would need the comfort of music in the hard months ahead. Each man kept a spoon and a knife.

The journey was ready to begin at 2:00 P.M. on October 30 under heavy gray skies. It had already snowed on and off during the day, and it threatened to continue. That didn't pose much of a problem, but the road ahead did. If they only had to trek across 346 miles of flat ice field, the journey would have been bearable. But stretching ahead of them into the white horizon was a scene of utter devastation and chaos. It was as if a giant hand had smashed down onto the frozen face

GUIDED READING

What stretched ahead of the men into the white horizon?

6. **Book of Job.** A narrative and poetic book of the Bible that tells about Job, a man who endures afflictions with fortitude and faith

words for everyday use

im • pro • vis • er (im' prə vīz ər) *n.*, one who makes or invents things offhand. *Mary is a good improviser because she is able to make up music while she plays the piano.*

trek (trek') *v.*, go on a journey. *Our journey required us to trek 200 miles across the ocean.*

And the face of the deep is frozen.

The crew drags the *James Caird* over the ice to the next camp.

of the deep and broken it into a million shards. Jagged floes[7] tilted up at all angles. Pressure ridges reared up like wrinkles in a huge white blanket. If the sea had been frozen at the height of a tempest, and every storm-tossed wave locked into place, the scene could not have been more jumbled and uneven. There were 346 miles of *that* to cross—assuming the drift of the pack didn't change course and carry them helplessly in another direction.

On the lead sled went Shackleton, Wordie, Hussey, and Hudson, looking for the best route among the pressure ridges and tumbled ice floes. They were equipped with shovels, picks, and axes to chop a path through the chaos of ice. Behind them came the other dog teams pulling sleds that were each loaded with 900 pounds of stores and gear.

> **GUIDED READING**
> What are the men on the lead sled equipped with?

Bringing up the rear was the remainder of the crew pulling the boats on sledge runners. Loaded with food and equipment, the boats weighed in at more than a ton apiece. Fifteen men in harness dragged one boat at a time across the wet snow and over the ice, stopping every quarter mile to rest, before going back to haul the second boat forward. Shackleton was in constant anxiety over continuing pressure in the ice. If a crack opened up between one team and another, the result could be disastrous. So he kept the men and sleds and boats close together, relaying forward one agonizing quarter mile at a time. Frequently, one of the dog teams had to be unharnessed from its sled and then hitched to a lifeboat to help the men drag it up and over a hummock[8] or ridge.

After two hours of backbreaking labor, hauling the boats through wet, heavy snow, detouring around piles of broken floe, they were only one mile from *Endurance*. Soaked, and numb with fatigue, the men swallowed a hasty dinner and fell into their tents. It began to snow during the night. When the men resumed their burdens the next day, they had a new layer of heavy, wet slush to trudge through, and more wet snow was falling steadily. After another three hours and only an additional three quarters of a mile, the

> **GUIDED READING**
> How far have the men gone after two hours of back-breaking labor?

---

7. **floes.** Floating ice formed in a large sheet on the surface of a body of water
8. **hummock,** Ridge of ice

Boss called a halt. He and Worsley were worried about damaging the boats as they knocked their way across the ice. They were getting nowhere.

At the moment they were on a very large, level floe, more than a half a mile in diameter. There wasn't another good, solid, flat floe in sight, and Shackleton felt they could not do better for a camping place. The men pitched their tents on the wet snow and crawled into their sleeping bags. Shackleton anxiously scouted ahead and found it impossible to advance.

Next morning, he announced that they would stay where they were and let the drifting pack carry them northward into a better position to make for Paulet Island. There was no alternative. Shackleton told Green to start adding large chunks of blubber to the crew's food. The thick seal fat that kept the animals warm would provide valuable calories in the men's diets and keep them from freezing. It was time to get used to it. ∎

GUIDED READING

After camping for the night, what does Shackleton announce the next morning?

Respond *to the* SELECTION

If you were one of the crew members forced to abandon the *Endurance*, how would you face the prospect of trekking over snow and ice for 346 miles?

About *the* AUTHOR

Jennifer Armstrong is the author of over 50 books for young readers, including *The Dreams of Mairhe Mehan, Mary Mehan Awake, Pockets, Chin Yu Min and the Ginger Cat,* and *Black-eyed Susan.* "The Face of the Deep Is Frozen" is from the book *Shipwreck at the Bottom of the World: The Extraordinary True Story of Shackleton and the* Endurance. The book was a 1999 Boston Globe-Horn Book Honor Book and is on many recommended reading lists. Armstrong did months of research and even traveled to England to select the photographs for the book. Apart from that book, Armstrong usually writes fiction because she likes to make up stories and create her own characters. She started to make up stories when she was in the first grade. It was then that she knew she wanted to be an author. Armstrong lives with her husband in Saratoga Springs, New York. The couple has three dogs named Minch, Chloe, and Posy.

Investigate, Inquire, and Imagine

Recall: GATHERING FACTS

1a. How does the Antarctic ice become clean enough to drink even though it has come from salty seawater?

2a. What does Shackleton write in his diary when the crew of the expedition is forced to abandon ship? What is "the task that lies ahead"?

3a. What is the weight limit that Shackleton places on the items each member of the expedition can carry?

→ Interpret: FINDING MEANING

1b. What does the author mean when she writes, "a shipwreck on the frozen sea does not *necessarily* mean certain death"? In addition to understanding that they can melt the ice for drinking water, what else will the men need to do in order to avoid death?

2b. How does Shackleton come to this conclusion? What other options do the men have? Do you think Shackleton has chosen the best option available?

3b. What is the purpose of this weight limit? How do the men decide what's important and what's not important? What does the author mean when she writes that the men must "harden their hearts against sentimental keepsakes"? Why does Shackleton leave his gold in the snow?

Analyze: TAKING THINGS APART

4a. Examine the character of Ernest Shackleton by his words and actions. What are the qualities that make him a good leader?

→ Synthesize: BRINGING THINGS TOGETHER

4b. Why do you think the members of the crew follow the guidance of Shackleton? Is there any guarantee that they will survive if they follow his orders? What about his character helps you understand why the members of the crew want to follow his lead?

Evaluate: MAKING JUDGMENTS

5a. How do the words from the Book of Job reflect the situation of Shackleton and his expedition? Why does Shackleton find these words comforting? Who is the passage referring to when it asks, "Out of whose womb came the ice"? Why does Shackleton keep this page from his Bible?

→ Extend: CONNECTING IDEAS

5b. If the men are only allowed to carry with them those things essential to their survival, why do you think Shackleton carries this page from the Book of Job? How is this essential to his survival? If you were the leader of this expedition, what would you take that would be essential to your survival?

Understanding *Literature*

SETTING AND DESCRIPTION. The **setting** of a literary work is the time and place in which it happens. In fiction and in drama, a writers create setting using what they know about the time and place they wish to represent. In nonfiction, a writer tries to stay true to the particular time and place in which a person lived or in which an event took place. Writers use **description** to develop in the reader's mind an accurate picture of the setting. Now that you have read the selection, summarize the setting in your own words.

Writer's Journal

1. Imagine that you are one of the crewmembers on the expedition. You decide to write a **message**, put it in a bottle, and drop the bottle into the water, hoping that if you don't reach land, at least the bottle with your message will. Write what you would say in your message.

2. A news flash has just come in that Ernest Shackleton and his crew from the lost ship, *Endurance*, have just been found off Elephant Island. Write a brief **news report** to be read on the radio announcing this discovery.

3. Imagine that you are Ernest Shackleton on the eve before you are to lead your expedition on the perilous journey across the snow and ice. Write a brief **inspirational speech** to deliver to the crew just before departure.

Skill Builders

Applied English

DESIGN AN ADVERTISEMENT. Review the following advertisement that Ernest Shackleton placed in London newspapers in 1900 in preparation for the National Antarctic Expedition.

Men wanted for hazardous journey. Small wages, bitter cold, long months of complete darkness, constant danger, safe return doubtful. Honor and recognition in case of success.

Imagine that you are planning an expedition of your own. Perhaps you are sailing across the Antarctic, climbing to the top of Mt. Everest, flying a balloon around the world, or riding camels across the desert. Design an advertisement to be placed in newspapers around the country, recruiting other men and women to join your expedition.

Collaborative Learning

SETTING UP AN EXPEDITION. Form a small group to plan your own expedition. You must choose your method of travel—boat, animal, bicycle, or other—and state the objective of your journey. For example, one expedition could be to be the first group of men and women to walk across the United States from Washington State to Florida. Use a map to mark the path of your expedition. Develop a plan that includes everything you must carry, how many miles to be traveled each day, where you will stop at night, and how long you expect the entire journey to take.

Prereading

"Pompeii" by Robert Silverberg

Reader's Resource

- **SCIENCE CONNECTION.** A volcano is a break, or vent, in the earth's crust where heat, gas, and molten rock can escape. Volcanoes can take many shapes, including a cone, which forms when lava and solid matter are ejected through the vent from the interior of the earth. Solid materials fall around the vent, while lava streams from the vent. The lava and other materials harden into a cone that slopes outward away from the vent. Mount Vesuvius is an example of a cone-shaped volcano. Many volcanoes are born underwater on the sea floor. Mount Vesuvius—like the vast cones of the Hawaiian Islands—began as an underwater volcano.

- In a violent eruption of a volcano, lava is highly charged with steam and other gases, such as carbon dioxide, hydrogen, carbon monoxide, and sulfur dioxide. The steam and other gases continuously escape from the surface of the lava with violent explosions. Lava shoots up and forms a fiery fountain of drops of ash. The lava rises in the vent and flows over the rim of the crater. After an eruption the volcano may return to an inactive, or dormant, state. Mount Vesuvius is one of many active volcanoes in the world today, having exploded many times since the fateful explosive eruption that hit Pompeii, Italy, in AD 79. The most recent eruption occurred in 1944.

art smart

When the ashes and lava fell on Pompeii, they covered people and animals. The bodies of these people and animals decayed, leaving pockets, or holes, in the ground in the shapes of the bodies. Later, archeologists recovered the body shapes by filling the holes with plaster and then allowing the plaster to harden. The process of creating a mold and filling it with a liquefied material that hardens is called casting. Imagine you are one of the archeologists working at Pompeii. What thoughts and feelings would you be experiencing while working there?

Reader's Journal

Write about a natural disaster you have experienced or heard about.

Reader's TOOLBOX

ESSAY. An **essay** is a short nonfiction work that expresses a writer's thoughts about a single subject. A good essay develops a single idea, or thesis, and is organized into an introduction, a body, and a conclusion. As you read the essay, identify the thesis.

CHRONOLOGICAL ORDER. Events arranged in order of the time when they happened are said to be in **chronological order**. This organization is used in informative nonfiction writing that describes processes, cause-and-effect relationships, and historical events. As you read, look for the main part of the essay where the author uses chronological order.

Statue from the Temple of Apollo, Pompeii, Italy.

Pompeii

Robert Silverberg

Not very far from Naples a strange city sleeps under the hot Italian sun. It is the city of Pompeii and there is no other city quite like it in all the world. No one lives in Pompeii but crickets and beetles and lizards, yet every year thousands of people travel from distant countries to visit it.

Pompeii is a dead city. No one has lived there for nearly two thousand years, not since the summer of the year AD 79, to be exact.

GUIDED READING

Why is Pompeii a unique city?

Until that year Pompeii was a prosperous city of twenty-five thousand people. Nearby was the Bay of Naples, an arm of the blue Mediterranean. Rich men came down from wealthy Rome, 125 miles to the north, to build luxurious seaside villas. Fertile farmlands occupied the fields surrounding Pompeii. Rising sharply behind the city was the four-thousand-foot bulk of Mount Vesuvius, a grass-covered slope where the shepherds of Pompeii took their goats to graze. Pompeii was a busy city and a happy one.

It died suddenly, in a terrible rain of fire and ashes.

The tragedy struck on the twenty-fourth of August, AD 79. Mount Vesuvius, which had slumbered quietly for centuries, exploded with savage violence. Death struck on a hot summer afternoon. Tons of hot ashes fell on Pompeii, smothering it, hiding it from sight. For three days the sun did not break through the cloud of volcanic ash that filled the sky. And when the eruption ended, Pompeii was buried deep. A thriving city had perished in a single day.

GUIDED READING

What destroyed the city of Pompeii?

Centuries passed. Pompeii was forgotten. Then, fifteen hundred years later, it was discovered again. Beneath the protecting shroud of ashes, the city lay intact. Everything was as it had been the day Vesuvius erupted. There were still loaves of bread in the ovens of the bakeries. In the wine shops, the wine jars were in place, and on one counter could be seen a stain where a customer had thrown down his glass and fled.

Modern archaeology began with the discovery of buried Pompeii. Before then, the digging of treasures from the ground had been a haphazard and unscholarly affair. But the excavation of Pompeii was done in a systematic, scientific manner, and so the science of serious archaeology can be said to have begun there. Since the year 1748, generations of skilled Italian workmen have been carefully removing the ashes that buried Pompeii, until today almost four-fifths of the city has been uncovered.

GUIDED READING

In what way was the excavation of Pompeii different from other excavations?

Other Roman cities died more slowly. Wind and rain and fire wore them away. Later peoples tore down the ancient monuments, using the stone to build houses and churches. Over the centuries, the cities of the Caesars[1] vanished, and all that is left of them today are scattered fragments.

Not so with Pompeii. It was engulfed in an instant, and its people's tragedy was our great gain. The buildings of Pompeii still stand as they stood two thousand years ago, and within the houses we can still see the pots and pans, the household tools, the hammers and nails. On the walls of the buildings are election slogans and the scrawlings of unruly boys. Pompeii is like a photograph in three dimensions. It shows us exactly what a city of the Roman Empire was like, down to the smallest detail of everyday life.

GUIDED READING

Why can we learn more from Pompeii than we can from other ruins? What can we discover?

---

1. **Caesars.** Emperors of ancient Rome

words for everyday use

shroud (shroud) n., something that covers or protects. *A shroud covered the body in the coffin.*
hap • haz • ard (hap′ haz ´ərd) adj., not planned; casual. *Haphazard planning ensured that the wedding would be a disaster.*
ex • ca • va • tion (eks kə vā´shən) n., something unearthed by digging. *Excavation for the new house uncovered pieces of old pottery.*
en • gulf (in gulf´) v., swallow up; overwhelm. *The huge waves threatened to engulf the small boat.*
un • rul • y (un rōō´lē) adj., hard to control. *Ralph's unruly hair always stuck up in the morning.*

Pompeii is a dead city.

To go to Pompeii today is to take a trip backward in a time machine. The old city comes to vivid life all around you. You can almost hear the clatter of horses' hoofs on the narrow streets, the cries of children, the loud, hearty laughter of the shopkeepers. You can almost smell meat sizzling over a charcoal fire. The sky is cloudlessly blue, with the summer sun almost directly overhead. The grassy slopes of great Vesuvius pierce the heavens behind the city, and sunlight shimmers on the water of the bay a thousand yards from the city walls. Ships from every nation are in port, and the babble of strange languages can be heard in the streets.

Such was Pompeii on its last day. And so it is today, now that the volcanic ash has been cleared away. A good imagination is all you need to restore it to bustling vitality. . . .

At dawn on the twenty-fourth of August in the year 79, Pompeii's twenty-five thousand people awakened to another hot day in that hot summer. There was going to be a performance in the arena that night, and the whole town was looking forward to the bloody contests of the gladiators.[2] The rumble of heavy wooden wheels was heard as carts loaded with grain entered the city from the farms outside the walls. Over the centuries the steady stream of carts had worn ruts deep into the pavement of Pompeii's narrow streets.

Wooden shutters were drawn back noisily. The grocers and sellers of fruit opened their shops, displaying their wares on trays set out on the sidewalk. In the wine shops, the girls who sold wine to the thirsty sailors got ready for another busy day. . . .

Outside, children headed toward school, carrying slates and followed by their dogs. Nearly everyone in Pompeii had a dog, and barking could be heard everywhere as the Pompeiian pets greeted one another. A small boy who had just learned the Greek alphabet stopped in front of a blank wall and took a piece of charcoal from his

---

2. **gladiators.** In ancient Rome, men who fought other men or animals with weapons in an arena for the entertainment of spectators

tunic. Hastily he scribbled the Greek letters: *alpha*, *beta*, *gamma*.

In the Forum, the town's important men had gathered after breakfast to read the political signs that were posted during the night. Elsewhere in the Forum, the wool merchants talked business, and the men who owned the vineyards were smiling to each other about the high quality of this year's wine, which would fetch a good price in other countries. . . .

The quiet morning moved slowly along. There was nothing very unusual about Pompeii. . . .

But tragedy was on its way. Beneath Vesuvius' vine-covered slopes, a mighty force was about to break loose.

GUIDED READING

Did people know that something unusual was about to happen?

No one in Pompeii knew the dangerous power imprisoned in Vesuvius. For fifteen hundred years the mountain had slept quietly, but far beneath the crest a boiling fury of <u>molten</u> lava had gradually been gathering strength. The solid rock of Vesuvius held the hidden forces in check. An earthquake sixteen years before had been the first sign that the trapped fury beneath

GUIDED READING

What is happening under the surface of the earth while people go about their usual lives?

the mountain was struggling to break free. Pressure was building up. In the city at the base of the mountain, life went on in complete ignorance of the looming <u>catastrophe</u>.

At one o'clock in the afternoon on the twenty-fourth of August, AD 79, the <u>critical</u> point was reached. The walls of rock could hold no longer.

The mountain exploded, raining death on thousands.

Like many tragedies, this one was misunderstood at first. Down in Pompeii, four miles from Vesuvius, a tremendous explosion was heard, echoing ringingly off the mountains on the far side of the city.

"What was that?" people cried from one end of town to another. They stared at each other, puzzled, troubled. Were the gods fighting in heaven? Is that what the loud explosion was?

"Look!" somebody shouted. "Look at Vesuvius!"

Thousands of eyes swiveled upward. Thousands of arms pointed. A black cloud was rising from the shattered crest of the mountain. Higher and higher it rose. An eyewitness, the Roman philosopher Pliny, described the cloud as he saw it from Misenum, twenty-two miles from Pompeii on the opposite side of the bay.

"Better than any other tree, the pine can give an idea of the shape and appearance of this cloud," Pliny wrote in his notebook later that day. "In fact it was <u>projected</u> into the air like an enormous trunk and then spread into many branches, now white, now black, now spotted, according to whether earth or ashes were thrown up."

Minutes passed. The sound of the great explosion died away, but it still tingled in everyone's ears. The cloud over Vesuvius still rose, black as night, higher and higher.

"The cloud is blotting out the sun!" someone cried in terror.

Still no one in Pompeii had perished. The fragments of rock thrown up when the mountain exploded all fell

words for everyday use

mol • ten (mōl´tən) *adj.,* melted or liquefied by heat. *The ironworker poured <u>molten</u> metal into the mold to harden.*

ca • tas • tro • phe (kə tas´trə fē) *n.,* any great or sudden disaster or misfortune. *The flood was a huge <u>catastrophe</u> in this town.*

crit • i • cal (krit´i kəl) *adj.,* of or forming a crisis or turning point. *The final stretch of the race was <u>critical</u> in determining the winner.*

pro • ject (prō jekt´) *v.,* throw or hurl forward. *The slingshot could <u>project</u> water balloons across the road.*

back on the volcano's slopes. Within the crater, sizzling masses of molten rock were rushing upward, and upwelling gas drove small blobs of liquefied stone thousands of feet into the air. They cooled high above the gaping mouth of the volcano and plummeted earthward.

GUIDED READING
What happened after the initial explosion? Was the initial explosion very damaging? Why, or why not?

A strange rain began to fall on Pompeii—a rain of stone.

The stones were light. They were pumice stones, consisting mostly of air bubbles. They poured down as though there had been a sudden cloudburst. The pumice stones, or lapilli, did little damage. They clattered against the wooden roofs of the Pompeiian houses. They fell by the hundreds in the streets. The people who had rushed out of houses and shops and thermopolia[3] to see what had caused the explosion now scrambled to take cover as the weird rain of lapilli continued.

"What is happening?" Pompeiians asked one another. They rushed to the temples— the Temple of Jupiter, the Temple of Apollo, the Temple of Isis. Bewildered priests tried to calm bewildered citizens. Darkness had come at midday, and a rain of small stones fell from the sky, and who could explain it?

Some did not wait for explanation. In a tavern near the edge of the city, half a dozen gladiators who were scheduled to compete in that night's games decided to flee quickly. They had trumpets with them that were used to sound a fanfare at the amphitheater.[4] But they tossed the trumpets aside, leaving them to be found centuries later. Covering their heads with tiles and pieces of wood, the gladiators rushed out into the hail of lapilli and sprinted toward the open country beyond the walls, where they hoped they would be safe.

Vesuvius was rumbling ominously now. The sky was dark. Lapilli continued to pour down, until the streets began to clog with them.

"The eruption will be over soon!" a hopeful voice exclaimed.

But it did not end. An hour went by, and darkness still shrouded everything; and still the lapilli fell. All was confusion now. Children struggled home from school, panicky in the midday darkness.

The people of Pompeii knew that doom was at hand now. Their fears were doubled when an

GUIDED READING
What added to the fear of the people of Pompeii?

enormous rain of hot ashes began to fall on them, along with more lapilli. Pelted with stones, half smothered by the ashes, the Pompeiians cried out to the gods for mercy. The wooden roofs of some of the houses began to catch fire as the heat of the ashes reached them. Other buildings were collapsing under the weight of the pumice stones that had fallen on them.

In those first few hours, only the quick-witted managed to escape. Vesonius Primnus, a wealthy wool merchant, called his family together and piled jewelry and money into a

---

3. **thermopolia.** Shops selling wine
4. **amphitheater.** Round building with an open space surrounded by rising rows of seats

---

sack. Lighting a torch, Vesonius led his little band out into the nightmare of the streets. Overlooked in the confusion was Vesonius's black watchdog, chained in the courtyard. The terrified dog barked wildly as lapilli struck and drifting white ash settled around him. The animal struggled with his chain, battling fiercely to get free; but the chain held, and no one heard the dog's cries. The humans were too busy saving themselves.

Many hundreds of Pompeiians fled in those first few dark hours. Stumbling in the darkness, they made their way to the city gates, then out, down to the harbor. They boarded boats and got away, living to tell the tale of their city's destruction. Others preferred to remain within the city, huddling inside the temples or in the public baths or in the cellars of their homes. They still hoped that the nightmare would end—that the tranquillity of a few hours ago would return. . . .

> **GUIDED READING**
>
> About how many people managed to escape? How did they escape?

It was evening now, and new woe was in store for Pompeii. The earth trembled and quaked! Roofs that had somehow withstood the rain of lapilli went crashing in ruin, burying hundreds who had hoped to survive the eruption. In the Forum, tall columns toppled as they had in AD 63. Those who remembered that great earthquake screamed in new terror as the entire city seemed to shake in the grip of a giant fist.

Three feet of lapilli now covered the ground. Ash floated in the air. Gusts of poisonous gas came drifting from the belching crater, though people could still breathe. Roofs were collapsing everywhere. The cries of the dead and dying filled the air. Rushing throngs, blinded by the darkness and the smoke, hurtled madly up one street and down the next, trampling the fallen in a crazy, fruitless dash toward safety. Dozens of people plunged into dead-end streets and found themselves trapped by crashing buildings. They waited there, too frightened to run farther, expecting the end.

> **GUIDED READING**
>
> How do the citizens of Pompeii behave once they sense the danger?

The rich man Diomedes was another of those who decided not to flee at the first sign of alarm. Rather than risk being crushed by the screaming mobs, Diomedes calmly led the members of his household into the solidly built basement of his villa. Sixteen people altogether, as well as his daughter's dog and her beloved little goat. They took enough food and water to last for several days.

But for all his shrewdness and foresight, Diomedes was undone anyway. Poison gas was creeping slowly into the underground shelter! He watched his daughter begin to cough and struggle for breath. Vesuvius was giving off vast quantities of deadly carbon monoxide that was now settling like a blanket over the dying city. . . .

> **GUIDED READING**
>
> What did Diomedes do during the danger? Why did his plan fail?

The poison gas thickened as the terrible night continued. It was possible to hide from the lapilli but not from the gas, and Pompeiians died by the hundreds. Carbon monoxide gas keeps the body from absorbing oxygen. Victims of carbon monoxide poisoning get sleepier and sleepier until they lose consciousness, never to regain it. All over Pompeii, people lay down in the beds of lapilli, overwhelmed by the gas, and death came quietly to them. . . .

Two prisoners, left behind in the jail when their keepers fled, pounded on the sturdy

---

words for everyday use

tran • quil • li • ty (traŋ kwil´ə tē) *n.*, quality or state of being calm. *Reading outside gives me a sense of tranquility.*

belch (belch´) *v.*, throw forth contents rapidly. *The smokestack belched black smoke into the sky.*

fruit • less (frōōt´ ləs) *adj.*, without results. *My search for the missing watch was fruitless.*

shrewd • ness (shrōōd´nəs) *n.*, cleverness. *Margie's shrewdness as a pitcher led her to strike out many opponents.*

By morning, few remained alive.

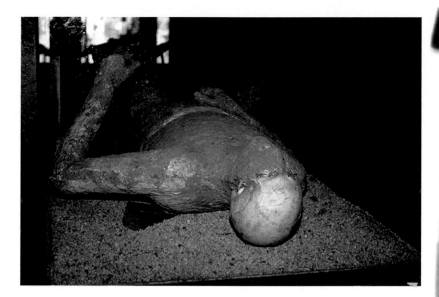

wooden doors. "Let us out!" they called. But no one heard, and the gas entered. They died, not knowing that the jailers outside were dying as well.

In a lane near the Forum, a hundred people were trapped by a blind-alley wall. Others hid in the stoutly built public bathhouses, protected against collapsing roofs but not against the deadly gas. Near the house of Diomedes, a beggar and his little goat sought shelter. The man fell dead a few feet from Diomedes' door; the faithful goat remained by his side, its silver bell tinkling, until its turn came.

All through the endless night, Pompeiians wandered about the streets or crouched in their ruined homes or clustered in the temples to pray. By morning, few remained alive. Not once had Vesuvius stopped hurling lapilli and ash into the air, and the streets of Pompeii were filling quickly. At midday on August 25, exactly twenty-four hours after the beginning of the holocaust,[5] a second eruption racked the volcano. A second cloud of ashes rose above Vesuvius' summit. The wind blew ash as far as Rome and Egypt. But most of the new ashes descended on Pompeii.

The deadly shower of stone and ashes went unslackening into its second day. But it no longer mattered to Pompeii whether the eruption continued another day or another year. For by midday on August 25, Pompeii was a city of the dead. . . .

Arriving at Pompeii today, you leave your car outside and enter through an age-old gate. Just within the entrance is a museum that has been built in recent years to house many of the smaller antiquities found in the ruins. Here are statuettes and toys, saucepans and loaves of bread. The account books of the banker Caecilius Jucundus are there, noting all the money he had lent at steep interest rates. Glass cups, coins, charred beans and peas and turnips, baskets of grapes and plums and figs, a box of chestnuts—the little things of Pompeii have all been miraculously preserved for your startled eyes.

Then you enter the city proper. The streets are narrow and deeply <u>rutted</u> with the tracks of chariot wheels. Only special

5. **holocaust.** Great or total destruction of life

words for everyday use   rut • ted (rut´əd) *adj.*, grooved or carved out surface. *The <u>rutted</u> path cut through the trees.*

narrow Pompeiian chariots could travel inside the town. Travelers from outside were <u>obliged</u> to change vehicles when they reached the walls of the city. This provided a profitable <u>monopoly</u> for the Pompeiian equivalent of cab drivers twenty centuries ago!

GUIDED READING

Why were Pompeiian chariots narrower than other chariots?

At each intersection, blocks of stone several feet high are mounted in the roadway, so designed that chariot wheels could pass on either side of them.

"Those are steppingstones for the people of Pompeii," your guide tells you. "Pompeii had no sewers, and during heavy rainfalls the streets were flooded with many inches of water. The Pompeiians could keep their feet dry by walking on those stones." . . .

The houses and shops are of stone. The upper stories, which were wooden, were burned away in the holocaust or simply crumbled with the centuries. The biggest of the shops are along the Street of Abundance, which must have been the Fifth Avenue of its day. Silversmiths, shoemakers, manufacturers of cloth—all had their shops here. And every few doors, there is another thermopolium, or wine shop. In many of these, the big jars of wine are still intact, standing in holes in marble counters just the way bins of ice cream are stored in a soda fountain today. . . .

The center of the city's life was the Forum, a large square which you enter not far from the main gate of the city. Before the earthquake of AD 63, Pompeii's Forum must have been a truly <u>imposing</u> place, enclosed on three sides by a series of porticoes[6] supported by huge columns. At the north

end, on the fourth side, stood the temple of Jupiter, Juno, and Minerva, raised on a podium ten feet high. But the earthquake toppled the temple and most of the columns, and not much rebuilding had been done at the time of the eruption. Pompeii's slowness to rebuild was our eternal loss, for little remains of the Forum except the stumps of massive columns. . . .

GUIDED READING

Why is it especially difficult to tell what the Forum was like in Pompeii?

Many public buildings were on the main square: the headquarters of the wool industry and several other temples, including one dedicated to Vespasian (father of Titus), a Roman emperor who was worshiped as a deity.[7] Near the Forum was a macellum, or market, where foodstuffs were sold and where beggars wandered.

Pompeii had many beggars. One of them was found in April 1957 at the gate of the road leading to the town of Nocera. A cast taken of him shows him to have been less than five feet tall and deformed by the bone disease known as rickets. On the last day of Pompeii's life, this beggar had gone about asking for alms,[8] and some generous citizen had given him a bone with a piece of meat still adhering to it. When the eruption came, the beggar tried to flee, jealously guarding his precious sack containing the cutlet and he was found with it two thousand years later.

Pompeii was a city of many fine temples, both around the Forum and in the outlying streets. One of the most interesting is one

---

6. **porticoes.** Porch-like sheltered areas supported by roof-to-floor columns
7. **deity.** God
8. **alms.** Money, food, or clothing given to poor people

words for everyday use

o • blige (ə blīj´) v., compel or force. *My mother <u>obliged</u> me to do my homework.*

mo • nop • o • ly (mə näp´ə lē) n., exclusive possession or control over something. *The company has a <u>monopoly</u> over the railroad business.*

im • pos • ing (im pō´ziŋ) adj., making a strong impression because of great size or strength. *The <u>imposing</u> figure of the bear scared me silly.*

dating from the sixth century BC, the oldest building in the city. Only the foundation and a few fragmented columns remain, but this temple was evidently regarded with great reverence, since it was located in the center of a fairly large triangular space adjoining the main theater. Nearby is the Temple of Isis, which was rebuilt after the earthquake and so is in fairly good preservation. Isis, an Egyptian goddess, was one of the many foreign gods and goddesses who had come to be worshiped in the Roman Empire by the time of the destruction of Pompeii. Her gaudily decorated temple at Pompeii is the only European temple of Isis that has come down to us from the ancient world.

But many temples, bathhouses, amphitheaters, and government buildings have survived in other places. What makes Pompeii uniquely significant is the wealth of knowledge it gives us about the *private* lives of its people. Nowhere else do we have such complete information about the homes of the ancients, about their customs and living habits, their humble pots and pans.

GUIDED READING

What makes Pompeii different from other ruins?

The houses in Pompeii show the evolution of styles over a period of several centuries. Many of the houses are built to the same simple plan: a central court, known as the atrium, around which a living room, bedrooms, and a garden are arrayed. This was the classic Roman style of home. Some of the later and more impressive houses show the influence of Greek styles, with paintings and mosaic[9] decorations as well as baths, reception rooms, huge gardens, and sometimes a second atrium.

The houses of Pompeii are known by name, and a good deal is known of their occupants. One of the most famous is the House of the Vetti Brothers, which is lavishly decorated with paintings, mosaics, and sculptures. The inscriptions on these houses are often amusing today. One businessman had written on the walls of his villa WELCOME PROFITS! Another greeted his visitors with the inscribed words PROFITS MEAN JOY!

At the so-called House of the Tragic Poet, a mosaic shows a barking dog, with the inscription *cave canem*— "Beware of the dog." On the building known as the House of the Lovers, which received its name because the newly married Claudius Elogus lived there, someone had written a line of verse, dedicated to the newlyweds, on the porch: *Amantes, ut apes, vitam mellitem exigunt.* ("Lovers, like bees, desire a life full of honey.")

One interesting house uncovered since World War II is the Villa of Giulia Felix ("Happy Julia"), which was of exceptional size. Apparently Giulia found the expense of this elegant house too much for her budget because she had opened her baths to the public and advertised the fact with a sign on the gate. For a fee, Pompeiians who scorned the crowds at the public baths could bathe at Giulia's in privacy and comfort. Even this income does not seem to have been enough, for another sign uncovered in 1953 announced that the magnificent villa was for rent. . . .

GUIDED READING

What two interesting facts are known about the Villa of Giulia Felix? How do we know these things?

One of the truly fascinating aspects of Pompeii is the multitude of scribbled street signs. Notices were painted directly on the

---

9. **mosaic.** Design made by inlaying small bits of stone or glass to a surface

stone and have come down to us. At the big amphitheater, an inscription tells us, "The troupe of gladiators owned by Suettius Centus will give a performance at Pompeii on May 31st. There will be an animal show. The awnings[10] will be used." And at the theater where plays were given, a message to a popular actor reads, "Actius, beloved of the people, come back soon; fare thee well!"

There are inscriptions at the taverns, too. "Romula loves Staphyclus" is on one wall. Elsewhere there is a poem that sounds like one of today's hit tunes: "Anyone could as well stop the winds blowing, / And the waters from flowing, / As stop lovers from loving." . . .

Wherever you turn in Pompeii, echoes of the dead city strike you. In one rich house, a breakfast-set in silver, complete with two egg cups, was found. Shopping lists were discovered. Wall paintings show religious ceremonies, games, and everyday amusements. The vats used for bleaching cloth for togas still remain. In some of the twenty bakeries, newly baked loaves stand on the counters.

To enter Pompeii is to step into the Rome of the Caesars. An entire city, forever frozen in the last moment of its life by a terrible cataclysm,[11] awaits the visitor. Thanks to the painstaking work of generations of devoted Italian archaeologists, we can experience today the most minute details of life twenty centuries ago in a Roman city. So much do we know of the people of Pompeii that they take on vivid life for us—the banker Jucundus, the wool merchant Vesonius, the newlywed Claudius Elogus, the nobleman Diomedes. The dreadful eruption that snatched the life of these people and this city in a single day also gave it a kind of immortality. Pompeii and its people live on today in timeless permanence, their city transformed by Vesuvius' fury into a miraculous survivor of the ancient world. ∎

> **GUIDED READING**
>
> What does the author say visiting Pompeii allows us to do? Why do the people of Pompeii seem real and vivid to us?

---

10. **awnings.** Structures of canvas or metal over doors to protect from rain or sun
11. **cataclysm.** Any great upheaval that causes sudden and violent changes

Respond *to the* SELECTION

If you could go back in time, what time and place would you visit? Why?

About *the* AUTHOR

Robert Silverberg (b.1935) has written over fifty science fiction and nonfiction books. He was born in New York and attended Columbia University. His favorite subjects are archaeology, space exploration, and military history. *Lost Cities and Vanished Civilizations,* from which this selection was taken, is an example of his nonfiction work that draws upon his interest in archeology. *Needle in a Timestack* is one of his works of science fiction. Silverberg, who has also written under the name of Walker Chapman, won the World Science Fiction "Hugo" award in 1955.

Fire and Ice

Robert Frost

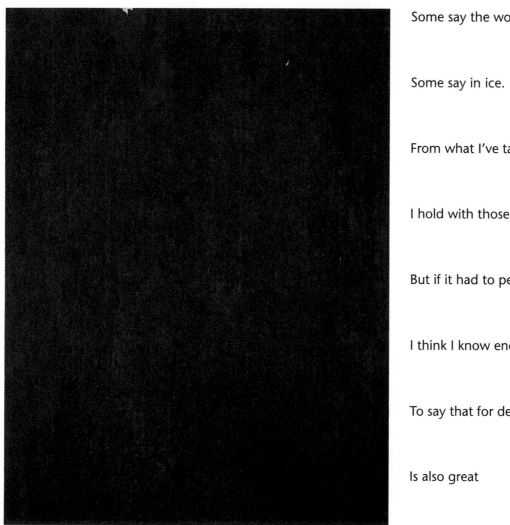

1951–N, 1951. Clyfford Still. National Gallery of Art, Washington, DC.

Some say the world will end in fire,

Some say in ice.

From what I've tasted of desire

I hold with those who favor fire.

But if it had to perish twice,

I think I know enough of hate

To say that for destruction ice

Is also great

And would suffice. ■

ABOUT THE RELATED READING

Robert Frost (1874–1963) was one of the most popular poets of the 1900s. Born in San Francisco, Frost lived in New England before moving to Britain in 1912. He returned to the United States, where he taught and wrote. He published many collections of poetry, including *New Hampshire,* from which this poem comes. Frost won four Pulitzer Prizes and recited a poem at John F. Kennedy's presidential inauguration.

Investigate, Inquire, and Imagine

Recall: GATHERING FACTS

1a. Where is the city of Pompeii? How much time passed after Pompeii's destruction before the city was rediscovered?

2a. What happened after the volcano's initial explosion? What did the people who stayed in town do to try to survive?

3a. What is unusual about entering Pompeii?

4a. What kinds of street signs existed in Pompeii?

→ Interpret: FINDING MEANING

1b. Why do you think it took so long to rediscover the lost city?

2b. Why do you think so many people chose to stay in Pompeii?

3b. Why do you think the Pompeiians developed the gates and roads this way?

4b. Why do you think people put up signs like these?

Analyze: TAKING THINGS APART

5a. List the different things archeologists have learned about Pompeii and its destruction.

→ Synthesize: BRINGING THINGS TOGETHER

5b. In what ways is this information important? How can we use information about the way Pompeiians lived? How can we use information about the way the city was destroyed?

Evaluate: MAKING JUDGMENTS

6a. What do you think about how the people of Pompeii reacted to the initial explosion, the black cloud, and the falling stones? Why do you think more people didn't run away?

→ Extend: CONNECTING IDEAS

6b. As the poem "Fire and Ice" imagines the end of the world, the people of Pompeii may have envisioned the end of the world as they knew it. How do you envision the end of the world?

Understanding Literature

ESSAY. An **essay** is a short nonfiction work that expresses a writer's thoughts about a single subject. A good essay develops a single idea, or thesis, and is organized into an introduction, a body, and a conclusion. As a narrative essay, "Pompeii" tells a true story to make some point. Reread the essay and identify the introduction, the body, and the conclusion. What is the author's point in writing about Pompeii and Mount Vesuvius?

CHRONOLOGICAL ORDER. Events arranged in order of the time when they happened are said to be in **chronological order.** This organization is used in informative nonfiction writing that describes processes, cause-and-effect relationships, and historical events. What part (or parts) of the essay—introduction, body, or conclusion—uses chronological order? Why is important to use this organizational pattern in that part of the essay?

Writer's Journal

1. Imagine you were a reporter in Rome in AD 79. Write a **news article** about the destruction of Pompeii.

2. Review the examples of messages that appeared on ancient street signs in Pompeii and write five additional **street sign** messages that might have existed.

3. Write what you think would be a typical **shopping list** for a family in ancient Pompeii.

Skill Builders

Vocabulary

MATCHING. From the choices provided, identify the word or phrase that most closely matches the given term.

1. fertile
   a. desert sands
   b. farmland
2. shroud
   a. cloth placed over a corpse
   b. folk costume
3. engulf
   a. rain shower
   b. tidal wave
4. unruly
   a. choir
   b. mob
5. molten
   a. water
   b. glass
6. haphazard
   a. branches fallen from a tree
   b. rows of desks in a classroom

7. catastrophe
   a. sunlight
   b. earthquake
8. monopoly
   a. retail clothing store
   b. taxi company with exclusive rights for a city
9. shrewdness
   a. figuring out how to make money in the stock market
   b. failing an exam
10. imposing
   a. a leprechaun
   b. the Great Pyramid at Giza

Reader's Journal

In what situation would you be most frightened: atop a very tall building, in a small tight space, or lost in the pitch-black dark? Why?

Reader's TOOLBOX

RHYME AND REPETITION. Writers of song lyrics use many of the same devices that poets use, such as rhyme and repetition. **Rhyme** is the repetition of sounds at the ends of words. **Repetition** is more than one use of a sound, word, or group of words. Identify where rhyme and repetition are used in these lyrics.

MOOD. Mood, or atmosphere, is the feeling or emotion the writer creates in a literary work. By working carefully with descriptive language, a writer can evoke in the reader an emotional response such as fear, discomfort, longing, or anticipation. How would you describe the mood in "The Springhill Disaster"?

Prereading

"The Springhill Disaster"

by Peggy Seeger

Reader's Resource

- **GEOGRAPHY CONNECTION.** Springhill is a town in northern Nova Scotia, Canada. Coal was first mined commercially in Springhill in 1872. One of the mines is 4,000 feet deep and is considered the deepest in Canada. Like many deep mines, those of Springhill have been plagued by disaster. In 1891, 125 people died in a mining accident. In another accident in 1956, 39 people died. In 1958, part of the mine collapsed and buried miners alive; 76 people died but some were rescued. The 1956 and 1958 accidents prompted the closing of mining facilities in Springhill, where light industry now fuels the economy. The song you are about to read was written after the accident of 1958.

- **HISTORY CONNECTION.** People have mined the earth for minerals, stone, and metal for thousands of years. Coal mining became an important industry in the Middle Ages (400s–1500s). By the end of the Middle Ages, surface deposits of coal were used up. Miners dug shafts—deep vertical openings—into the earth. Until recently, miners went underground to dig and chop the coal with pickaxes. People, mules, and horses dragged the coal back up to the surface.

- **SCIENCE CONNECTION.** In deep mines, groundwater must be continually drained. Pockets of dangerous flammable gas can explode or poison miners without warning. Because of the pressure of gravity, the underground tunnels of deep mines can collapse if not properly engineered.

art smart

Miners' Wives, c.1948. Ben Shahn. Philadelphia Museum of Art.

Ben Shahn addressed social problems with his art. He shared the same concern for the hard life of miners as did the writer of "Springhill Disaster." How might this scene relate to the poem?

Miners' Wives, c.1948.
Ben Shahn. Philadelphia
Museum of Art.

THE
SPRINGHILL
DISASTER

Peggy Seeger

1

In the town of Springhill, Nova Scotia,
Down in the dark of the Cumberland Mine
There's blood on the coal and the miners lie
In the roads that never saw sun nor sky.
The roads that never saw sun nor sky.

2

In the town of Springhill, you don't sleep easy
Often the earth will tremble and roll.
When the earth is restless, miners die,
Bone and blood is the price of coal.
Bone and blood is the price of coal.

GUIDED READING

What does the earth often do in Springhill?

3

In the town of Springhill, Nova Scotia,
Late in the year of fifty-eight
Day still comes and the sun still shines
But it's dark as the grave in the Cumberland Mine.
But it's dark as the grave in the Cumberland Mine.

4

Down at the coal face, miners working
Rattle of the belt and the cutter's blade.
Rumble of rock and the walls close round
The living and the dead men two miles down.
The living and the dead men two miles down.

GUIDED READING

What happens in the mine?

5

Twelve men lay two miles from the pitshaft
Twelve men lay in the dark and sang.
Long hot days in a miners' tomb,
It was three feet high and a hundred long.
It was three feet high and a hundred long.

6

Three days passed and the lamps gave out
And Caleb Rushton he up and says,
"There's no more water or light or bread
So we'll live on songs and hope instead.
So we'll live on songs and hope instead."

GUIDED READING

What solution does Caleb Rushton suggest to the trapped miners?

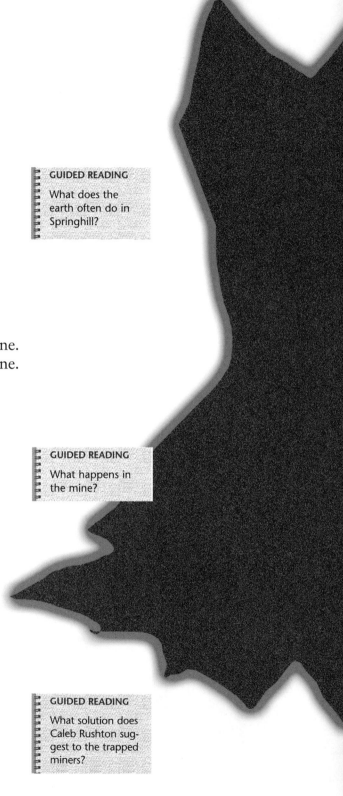

7

Listen for the shouts of the bareface miners
Listen through the rubble for a rescue team,
Six hundred feet of coal and slag
Hope imprisoned in a three-foot seam.
Hope imprisoned in a three-foot seam.

8

Eight long days and some were rescued,
Leaving the dead to lie alone,
Through all their lives they dug their grave
Two miles of earth for a marking stone.
Two miles of earth for a marking stone. ■

GUIDED READING

What is imprisoned underground besides the miners?

In the town of Spring-hill, Nov-a Sco-tia,
In the town of Spring-hill you don't sleep eas-y,

Down in the dark of the Cum-ber-land Mine There's
Of-ten the earth will trem-ble and roll when the

blood on the coal and the min-ers lie in the
earth is rest-less min-ers die

roads that ne-ver saw sun nor sky The
Bone and blood are the price of coal-

roads that nev-er saw sun nor sky.
Bone and blood are the price of coal.

If you were a miner who survived the 1958 disaster, would you go back to work in the mine?

About *the* AUTHOR

Peggy Seeger is a singer and songwriter. She was born in 1935 in New York City into a musical family. Both her mother, Ruth Crawford Seeger, and her father, Charles Louis Seeger, were musicians. Her brothers Pete and Mike are well-known folk musicians. Peggy Seeger was married to and worked with Ewan MacColl from 1956 to 1989, when MacColl died. Seeger has three children and seven grandchildren.

The best-known of Peggy's songs are "Gonna Be an Engineer" (which has become one of the anthems of the women's movement) and "The Ballad of Springhill." Her songs have been recorded on numerous records, most of them made with Ewan MacColl. She also has made many solo albums of her own compositions, the most recent of which is *An Odd Collection*.

Investigate, *Inquire,* and Imagine

Recall: GATHERING FACTS   →   Interpret: FINDING MEANING

1a. What does the speaker say is on the coal? What does the earth do in Springhill? What does the speaker say is the price of coal?

1b. Why don't people sleep easy in Springhill? How does the speaker feel about the price of coal?

2a. What happens to the miners? Where are the survivors trapped?

2b. Why might rescuing the miners be difficult?

3a. What does Caleb Rushton suggest that the miners do?

3b. Why might he have made this suggestion?

4a. What happens to the living men? What happens to the dead?

4b. Why does the speaker say "Through all their lives they dug their grave"?

Analyze: TAKING THINGS APART   →   Synthesize: BRINGING THINGS TOGETHER

5a. List the fifth line of each section.

5b. What is similar about all eight lines? What effect does this repetition have on the mood?

Evaluate: MAKING JUDGMENTS   →   Extend: CONNECTING IDEAS

6a. Do you think the title is appropriate for this selection? Why, or why not?

6b. If the title of this selection was "The Springhill Rescue," how would the language in this poem be different? What do you think the mood would be like?

Understanding *Literature*

RHYME AND REPETITION. Rhyme is the repetition of sounds at the ends of words. **Repetition** is more than one use of a sound, word, or group of words. What effect do rhyme and repetition have on these lyrics?

MOOD. Mood, or atmosphere, is the feeling or emotion the writer creates in a literary work. Descriptive language helps create a gloomy, foreboding, frightening mood in this song. What other literary elements contribute to the mood of the song?

Writer's Journal

1. Write the copy that would appear on a **compact disc packaging label** for a collection of songs that includes "The Springhill Disaster."

2. Write the ninth **stanza** following the same pattern and rhyme scheme of the other eight stanzas.

3. Imagine a **plaque** is being installed at the mouth of the old Cumberland Mine in Springhill. Write a few lines in memory of the miners, including the year of the disaster mentioned in the song and the number of people trapped.

Skill Builders

Critical Thinking

CREATING MOOD. Think about a situation in which you have recently found yourself. What mood did the situation create for you? Write a couple of paragraphs that create a certain mood, such as joyful, angry, frightening, lazy, or creepy. Mood, created through descriptive language, relies on sensory details—details about how things look, feel, taste, smell, and sound. Make a sensory detail chart like the one below to jot down some of the specific descriptions you can use within each of those categories.

Sensory Detail Chart				
Sight	Sound	Touch	Taste	Smell

Speaking and Listening

RECORDING A SONG. Form a small group of classmates interested in music. Work together to read the music and sing the song. You may want to find instrumental sheet music for the song so you can accompany the vocals with a piano, a guitar, or other instruments. After you have practiced the song, record it on a cassette tape.

Language, Grammar, and Style

ADJECTIVES AND ADVERBS. Descriptive language requires the use of adjectives and adverbs. Adjectives describe nouns or pronouns (*he, she, we, it*). Adverbs describe verbs. Underline the adjective or adverb in each sentence and mark "adj" if it is an adjective or "adv" if it is an adverb. Then circle the noun or verb that it describes.

1. It was a beautiful, sunny day.
2. My eyes are weary and heavy from staying out all night.
3. The ice skater skated gracefully along the pond.
4. The manager's duty is to see that the office runs smoothly.
5. The couple sang the song quietly and mysteriously.

Prereading

"The Cutoff: The Story of the Donner Party"

by Catherine Gourley

Reader's Resource

- **HISTORY CONNECTION.** In the 1840s, thousands of people traveled over land from the eastern United States to the newly acquired territories of Oregon and California. They followed the advice of guidebooks, such as *The Emigrants' Guide to Oregon and California* by Lansford Hastings. They gathered supplies and wagons and set off during springtime, hoping to reach their destination before the next winter.

- **GEOGRAPHY CONNECTION.** To get from Springfield, Illinois, to California, the Donner family crossed several mountain ranges within the Rocky Mountain system as well as the Wasatch Mountains in Utah and the Sierra Nevada Mountains on the eastern border of California. They also had to cross a number of big rivers, including the Platte and the Green, and vast deserts in Nevada and Utah.

Graphic *Organizer*

To help you organize the facts and the fiction in this selection, copy and complete the chart below onto your own paper.

What really happened/Facts	What things are made up/Fiction

Reader's Journal

If you were making a nine-month journey, what would you pack?

Reader's TOOLBOX

HISTORICAL FICTION. Fiction is prose writing about imagined events or characters. **Historical fiction** is fiction that is based on real people and events. This short story contains many elements that are real. The author filled in some of the details of the story, such as the dialogue, with her imagination. As you read, try to figure out what in the story really happened and what the author imagines happened. Use the graphic organizer on this page to help you.

DIALOGUE. Dialogue is conversation involving two or more people or characters. Fiction is made up of dialogue, narration, and description. Look for dialogue in "The Cutoff: The Story of the Donner Party."

THE CUTOFF: The Story of the DONNER PARTY

Catherine Gourley

The journey begins in the winter of 1845 with wind and snow and a book.

Outside, the wind howls across the frozen Sangamon River near Springfield, Illinois. Snow drifts against the farmhouse. Inside, two elderly brothers sit by a hearth fire and read the well-thumbed pages of *The Emigrants' Guide to Oregon and California*. "Hollyhocks and Sweet William[1] bloom even in winter," says George Donner, quoting the book. "Clover stands five feet high and cattle never go hungry."

"It is a dangerous journey," his brother Jacob argues. "You cannot deny that. Are you willing to risk our land, our families' welfare, based on the word of just one man?"

George stares at the book's leather cover. For two years the overland trail to California and Oregon has been traveled by covered wagons. Now the author of the book, a man named

> **GUIDED READING**
>
> What does Lansford Hastings claim?

---

1. **Hollyhocks and Sweet William.** Wildflowers

Donner Pass today.

Lansford Hastings, claims to have found a shorter way west.

"I am sixty-two years old," George answers at last. "I have children and grandchildren and money enough to live the rest of my life in comfort. But oh, the Illinois winters! Lately, I've felt the wind and snow in my bones."

George looks hopefully at his wife, Tamsen. She has been sitting quietly in the room, listening.

"What do you say? Are you up for it?"

"I suppose I could study the land and draw the plants we discover as we travel," she began. Then she adds, with growing enthusiasm, "Once in California I could start a school for girls. Of course, I'd have to bring my books and maybe some watercolors to teach painting."

George smiles. Tamsen is younger than he by almost twenty years. The former schoolteacher stands barely five feet tall and weighs less than one hundred pounds, but she shares his sense of adventure. George turns to his brother. "Yes, Jacob. I would risk it."

GUIDED READING

What does Tamsen share with George?

Not far away, in another house, James Reed has also read Hastings's book. Reed is in his forties, a former soldier who fought in the Black Hawk War. Like the Donner brothers, James Reed is considered wealthy by those who live in the town. He enjoys fine wines and fast horses. But the last few years have been hard. He's lost some money in his furniture business.

"Opportunity is elsewhere now—beyond the prairie, beyond the mountains," he tells his wife.

GUIDED READING
Where does James Reed say opportunity is?

"And just what is beyond the prairie?" Margaret Reed asks. "You don't know. No one does. It's a wilderness."

"It's all in Hastings's book. <u>Perpetual</u> summer. Snowclad mountains. Green valleys."

"*If* we get there," Margaret argues. "Mother's too ill to take such a hard trip, and I won't leave her behind."

James stands and stares from his window at the wind whipping the snow across an open field. "I can build a fine wagon, Margaret. It'll be a palace on wheels. We'll outfit it with a stove and beds and spring seats just like in a stagecoach."[2]

Margaret knows her husband's mind is set. They will go to California by way of Hastings's cutoff.

What James Reed does not know—nor do the Donners—is that Hastings is a <u>fraud</u>. The cutoff he describes in his book is nothing more than a guess.

And so the journey begins, on a winter night in Springfield, Illinois, in 1845, with wind and snow, a book . . . and <u>betrayal</u>.

May 1846. The wagon train out of Independence, Missouri, is one month on the trail and already falling behind schedule.

Accidents and <u>bickering</u> among the emigrants have slowed the journey.

GUIDED READING
What slows the journey?

Eight-year-old Patty Reed clutches her little doll as she watches the men dig a grave under the spreading branches of a tree. Her mother—Margaret Reed—weeps quietly. The morning's sorrow is caused by the death of the little girl's grandmother. Earlier that morning, inside their wagon, Patty and her older sister Virginia watched as Margaret snipped a lock of their grandmother's hair and folded it inside a handkerchief. "It's to remember her by," Margaret explained to her daughters. "It is all we can take with us."

"But why must we leave Grandma behind?" Patty asked.

"Because we're too far along the trail to turn back," Virginia answered for her grieving mother. "You don't want to go home to Illinois, do you, Patty?"

The girl shook her head and hugged her doll tighter.

Patty Reed's doll

After the burial, the journey begins again. One by one, past the oak tree and the wooden grave marker, roll the wagons of the emigrants—the Patrick Breen family with seven children, the Lewis Kesebergs, the William Eddys, the Donners, and more. The last to leave are the Reeds. Their three wagons overflow with fine things—bolts of silk,

GUIDED READING
What will the Reeds's wagon have in it?

2. **stagecoach.** Horse-drawn passenger and mail coach running on a regular schedule between established stops

---

words for everyday use

per • pet • u • al (pər pe′ chə wəl) *adj.*, continuing forever. *In Minnesota, the <u>perpetual</u> winters seem to be never ending.*

fraud (frod′) *n.*, person who is not what he or she pretends to be. *The man said he was Elvis, but he was a <u>fraud</u>.*

be • tray (be trā′) *v.*, lead astray, mislead. *Sinbad <u>betrayed</u> me by revealing my secrets to others.* **betrayal,** *n.*

bick • er (bik′ ər) *v.*, quarrel. *My brother and I always <u>bicker</u> over who gets to sit in the front seat.* **bickering,** *n.*

bottles of brandy, furniture, and extra <u>provisions</u> should the journey prove hard. The death and burial of the grandmother has caused still another troubling delay for the entire wagon train.

The others in the train may not speak of it openly, but they see a difference between themselves and the Reeds and the Donners. Those two families have hired men to drive their oxen and cattle. And the Reeds' third wagon is truly a palace car, with a side door and a stove inside. Its pipe rises through the top of the canvas.

GUIDED READING

What makes the Reeds and Donners different from the others?

James rides a high-stepping gray mare named Glaucus after a Roman aristocrat. Thirteen-year-old Virginia Reed has her own pony, too. She gallops across the prairie while the other children must walk alongside the wagons in the dust. But there is more about James Reed that troubles them. He has a <u>fiery</u> Irish temper. The first to feel the fire of that hot temperament is Lewis Keseberg.

GUIDED READING

What about James Reed troubles the other families?

Keseberg proudly displays the buffalo robe in front of the others, who sit smoking by a campfire one night. "I took it from a dead Sioux," Keseberg brags. "His burial platform is on the back side of that hill."

"You stole it?" James Reed asks.

Keseberg turns on him. "Who are you to criticize me? You spend all day hunting buffalo on your fancy Roman horse. Not for food. For sport!"

"You robbed a sacred Indian burial ground!" Reed glares angrily through the sparks of the campfire. "Do you realize what that means?"

GUIDED READING

What had Keseberg done?

"They're savages. What do I care about burial grounds? The robe, though, will come in handy once the weather cools."

Reed lunges across the fire at him. Lilburn Boggs and two other men hurry to separate the two struggling men. Lilburn is the captain of the train, the man the emigrants have elected to keep order. Once the two men are apart, restrained by the others, Lilburn speaks.

"Reed's right. You've put the safety of the entire train at risk. What if Sioux warriors discover that one of their dead has been disturbed?"

Keseberg stares at the fire-brightened faces of the men. After a moment, he kicks the robe across the ground, <u>relinquishing</u> his claim on it. Reed picks it up and shoves it into Keseberg's arms again. "Take it back."

GUIDED READING

What does Reed want Keseberg to do with the robe?

Keseberg starts in alarm. "Back? Are you crazy?"

Again Lilburn sides with Reed. He forces Keseberg to ride back to the burial scaffold[3] and wrap the dead warrior in his robe. Even so, Reed still isn't satisfied. Keseberg must be punished, Reed argues, to set an example for the others. He must be <u>banished</u> from the train for one full week.

"But that could be suicide!" Keseberg cries. "If the Sioux see a single wagon, without the protection of the others—"

---

3. **scaffold.** Platform at a height above ground or floor level

words for everyday use

pro • vi • sion (pro vi′ zhun) n., stock of needed materials or supplies. *As we trekked across the desert, our main provision was water.*
fi • ery (fi′ rē) adj., easily provoked, full of emotion or spirit. *Because of his fiery nature, he lashed out in anger without thinking.*
re • lin • quish (ri lin′ kwish) v., give up possession or control; release. *The president relinquished his position after the scandal.*
ban • ish (ban′ ish) v., drive out or remove something. *My dog was banished from the house after chewing up our shoes.*

Again Lilburn decides for the others. "You will be banished."

GUIDED READING
What is Keseberg's punishment?

For seven days, the Keseberg wagon rolls along a mile behind the other wagons, dangerously alone on the prairie.

In late June, a single horseman from out of the west rides into Fort Laramie. James Clyman is a mountain man—a hunter and a trapper. At the fort are hundreds of emigrants heading for the golden land Clyman has just left. Among them, he recognizes now, is an old friend—from the Black Hawk War.

"James Reed? Is that really you?"

"Clyman? You old mountain goat!" The two men grip each other's arms in welcome. "What are you doing here?" Reed asks.

"Going home," says Clyman. "I've a bellyful of California."

That night, the men sit around a fire. Reed opens a bottle of brandy and passes it along. This night, the old mountain man sits and drinks with them.

"What about the cutoff?" Lilburn Boggs asks him. "Is it really 300 miles shorter like the book says?"

"Can't say that it is, not with all the twistings and turnings through canyons," says Clyman. "I've just come that way on horseback with Hastings. I wouldn't try it with covered wagons."

GUIDED READING
What does Clyman say about the cut-off?

The men frown. This is not what they want to hear.

"Whom do we believe—this old vagabond[4] or Hastings?" asks Patrick Breen.

"Any fool can write a book for profit," says Clyman. "Getting over the mountains and across the desert is another thing entirely. It's a long, dry pull, and oxen aren't camels. Take the regular wagon track and never leave it. It's barely possible to get through if you follow it—and may be impossible if you don't."

Lilburn stands. His mind is made up. "I go the tried way. Whoever wishes can join me."

GUIDED READING
What does Lilburn Boggs decide to do?

Without waiting for an answer, he leaves. The others who had put their trust in Boggs as their leader soon stand and follow him from the circle.

"What about you, Jim?" Clyman asks, swigging one more mouthful from the brandy bottle.

"Hastings is waiting at Fort Bridger to lead us over the mountains. Does his book count for nothing?"

"Does the advice of an old friend count for nothing?"

The two men stare at each other. Reed stands. "Hastings has found a shorter route. It makes no sense to follow the longer course."

"You always were a hot-tempered, stubborn Irishman," says Clyman. "But this time, Jim, you are making a bad mistake."

The next morning, Lilburn and those who will follow him leave for Fort Hall. Tamsen Donner frowns as she watches the wagons depart. "We know nothing about Hastings, George," she confides in her husband. "I'm uneasy about this."

"That's the first words of doubt I've heard from you," George says, surprised. "But you have no need to fear. Hastings is waiting for us at Fort Bridger and has promised to show us the way."

---

4. **vagabond.** One who is irresponsible and wanders around from place to place

con • fide (kən fīd') v., have confidence or trust in something. *Best friends* confide *in each other by sharing their secrets.*

words for everyday use

As the wagons in the Boggs party lumber away, Tamsen whispers, "I pray you are right."

Before leaving for Fort Bridger, the remaining wagons must elect a new train captain. "The way I see it," says William Eddy, "either we go with George Donner or Jim Reed."

Reed stands with his arms crossed, <u>anxious</u> to be on the road. He is years younger than George and without question, courageous. But his <u>arrogance</u> has offended many. The vote is taken.

"That settles it, then," announces Patrick Breen, having made the count. "The company elects George Donner."

GUIDED READING

Who is elected the new train captain?

And so the journey begins again with a new leader. From now on the company will be known as the Donner Party.

The first disappointment comes days later at Fort Bridger. The "fort" is nothing more than two log cabins and a corral. Mountain man Jim Bridger has built his outpost to cash in on the new flow of emigrants—especially those who decide to take Hastings's cutoff. He speaks highly of Hastings and the new route. "You'll find good grass. Plenty of

GUIDED READING

What is Fort Bridger like?

Patty Reed

water. Except for that one dry stretch."

The second disappointment is learning that Hastings is not at the fort, waiting as he had promised, to guide the party through the canyons.

"What do you mean he pulled out?" George Donner asks Bridger.

"He had sixty-six wagons in his party already. Couldn't wait for you. Season is getting late, you know. I recommend you folks waste no time picking up whatever supplies you need right here from me, and get started after him."

Tamsen's eyes narrow. "Your prices are high, sir."

"Take it or leave it," snips Bridger. "Ain't nothing between here and California. Like they say, last chance."

On the last day of July, the Donner Party leaves Fort Bridger, following the tracks of Hastings's wagons.

The journey continues—into the Wasatch Mountains, past soda springs with foul-tasting water and mineral springs with water the color of blood,[5] over stone ridges, and into canyons so steep the oxen cannot keep their feet. Then comes a hard blow to the

---

5. **soda springs…color of blood.** The water in the area was colored by the red rocks that dominate the landscape.

words for everyday use

an • xious (ank' shəs) *adj.*, worried or eager. *I was <u>anxious</u> to receive news from the college.*

ar • ro • gance (ar' ə gəns) *n.*, feeling or impression of superiority. *Her <u>arrogance</u> led her to believe that she was the best singer in the choir.*

weary emigrants—a note from Hastings nailed on a tree.

GUIDED READING
What do the emigrants find?

Tamsen frees the paper from the bark. "Passage hard," she reads. "Many delays. Recommend you find a more northern route." She looks up at her husband and James Reed. Reed volunteers to scout an easier passage to the north. He rides ahead on his sleek horse, searching for a way over the mountains. What is passable for a man on horseback, he soon discovers, is impossible for wagons. He returns with grim news. The emigrants have no choice. They must hack a road out of the wilderness.

GUIDED READING
What do the emigrants have to do?

The men use picks and shovels and axes to clear boulders and thick brush wide enough to allow passage of the wagons. At one point, the men must lower each wagon down the side of a canyon wall, then up the other side. Their hands are raw and bleeding. Worse, they make only a mile or two a day.

Finally, by the end of August, the wagons make it through the mountains. Yet what lies ahead fills the emigrants with <u>despair</u>—a sea of salt and sand stretching in all directions.

At the end of the salt desert is a wagon board with tattered bits of paper stuck to it. "It's another message from Hastings," Tamsen says as she reads. "Two days, two nights, hard driving to reach the next grass and water."

GUIDED READING
What does the message from Hastings say?

"He says forty miles at most," says George.

"*If* you believe him," says Tamsen. "He broke his pledge to wait for us at the fort and deceived us about the mountains."

George looks grim. Tamsen knows what he is thinking, for it is what she is thinking as well. They have come too far to turn back. The only possibility is to push on.

A trap has closed behind the exhausted emigrants. The only way out is across the burning desert. The men fill all available barrels with water and pack extra grass for the animals. At daybreak, the party sets out. Sun burns down on the dazzling white plain. The wagon wheels break through the thin crust of salt and sink inches into slush. The oxen strain against the yokes.

To lighten the load, everyone walks. Some families discard furniture and boxes of books from the wagons. Patty Reed hides her doll inside her clothing, afraid her mother will make her

GUIDED READING
What do people do to lighten the loads in their wagons?

leave it behind with the crate of wine. The animals cannot survive the strain without water, without rest. But to stop is certain death for human and animal both. And so the wagons push on . . .

Three days, three nights they plod slowly forward. All water is gone, but still the party is miles out on the salt plain. Oxen lie down in their harnesses to die. Reed confides in George Donner, the elected leader of the train, "We must unhitch the animals and drive them forward to the water."

"And leave the wagons behind?"

"We'll water and rest the animals, then drive them back for the wagons."

George sees the logic in this, but still he is fearful. "What about the women, the children?"

Reed is firm. If the train is to cross the salt desert, then the animals must be

GUIDED READING
What do George Donner and James Reed decide?

words for everyday use

de • spair (di spār') *n.*, utter loss of hope. *John was in <u>despair</u> because didn't make the honor roll.*

set free of the wagons. "The women and children must stay behind."

George nods. It is a dreadful decision. As the men and oxen depart, Patty Reed stares with terrified eyes from inside the covered wagon. "Where's Papa going?" she cries.

"For water," Virginia answers. "He'll come back for us. Don't you worry."

The desert night is freezing. A white moon glares over the salt plain. Alone in the wagons, the women and children huddle together, waiting, waiting.

At last, James returns, but there are not enough oxen remaining alive to pull his three wagons. The grand palace car with all its silks and springs must be left behind in the desert. It stands alone, a sad <u>remnant</u> of the hopes for a new life in California.

> **GUIDED READING**
>
> What does James Reed have to leave behind?

Autumn. Days are shorter. Nights are colder. The animals—those that have survived the desert crossing—are weak and starving. Even for humans, provisions are alarmingly low. The cutoff is behind them, and they are once again on the main road, but Hastings has lied. The cutoff has added miles and precious days to the journey. Now the party follows a scrawny stream leading into the Sierra Nevadas. Overhead, a string of honking geese heads south.

> **GUIDED READING**
>
> What is behind the Donner Party? How did it affect their journey?

Virginia shades her eyes, watching them migrate across the October sky. "How far to the Sierras, Pa?"

"I don't know," Reed answers. "Two hundred miles, maybe more."

"We're the last train on the trail, aren't we?" she asks.

He nods <u>grimly</u>. Ahead is a steep sand hill. As one wagon tries to pass another, the oxen become unruly and tangle. One emigrant cracks his whip over his oxen's heads. "Get on there. Gee! GEE!" he shouts.

Reed approaches him on horseback. "Ease up, John!" he says. "The animals are played out. No use in beating them to death."

The emigrant resents Reed's interference. "Move out of my way, Jim. You're not captain of this company. Move or I'll whip you, too!"

Furious, James dismounts and pulls out his hunting knife. At once, the emigrant attacks. With the butt of the whip, he cracks Reed violently across the head, drawing blood. Reed dives forward, plunging his knife under the man's collarbone.

"James!" Margaret screams. "John! Stop!"

She rushes between the two men, but the enraged emigrant strikes her, then Reed again, knocking him to his knees.

Suddenly, the emigrant staggers backward, clutching his bloody shirt. "Patrick. I'm dead!" The emigrant falls to his knees.

Reed kneels beside the dying man. The emigrant reaches up for him. "Reed, I am to blame."

"No, no," Reed cries. "It was a mistake. It shouldn't have happened."

The emigrant collapses.

"He's dead," Patrick Breen says. He glares with hatred at Reed. "You've killed him!"

> **GUIDED READING**
>
> What has James Reed done?

Reed himself is covered with blood from the blows of the man's whip. <u>Anguished</u>, he turns away and throws his knife into the river. Behind him, the company is in confusion.

---

words for everyday use

rem • nant (rem′ nənt) *n.*, small surviving group; trace remaining. *There was a <u>remnant</u> of cookie crumbs left on the plate.*

grim (grim′) *adj.*, somber, gloomy. *The sky looked <u>grim</u> as the clouds became darker.* **grimly,** *adv.*

an • guish (aŋ′ gwish) *n.*, extreme pain or distress. *The cat cried out in <u>anguish</u> as I accidentally stepped on its tail.*

Lewis Keseberg, who <u>harbors</u> his own grudge against James, cries for justice.

"It was murder!" shouts Keseberg. "You all saw what he did! I say hang him!"

Keseberg props up his wagon tongue with an ox yoke.[6] Another emigrant grabs a rope.

"Hold on here!" argues William Eddy. "Reed acted out of self-defense."

The captain of the train—George Donner—is a day's ride ahead of these few straggling wagons. In his absence, chaos is about to rule.

GUIDED READING

Where is George Donner?

"Give me the rope!" Keseberg roughly grabs it.

"Have mercy, please!" sobs Margaret.

"There is another way," William Eddy states. He looks apologetically at Margaret and then at Reed. "Banishment."

"What?" cries Reed. "Leave camp? No! I won't abandon my family."

William Eddy, the one man who remains calm, turns to him and tries to reason with him. "For your own safety and theirs," he nods to the Reed children, "go! I'll watch out for them. Alone you'll make better time. Get over the mountains to Sutter's Fort and bring back help."

Keseberg steps forward. "If he goes, he takes no provisions. And no weapons."

Now Virginia intercedes for her father. "But there are Indians. Without a weapon, he'll die."

Patrick Breen cares little for her pleas. "John Snyder was a good man, well-liked. But Reed—he's always lording it over us, riding that fancy horse, hunting buffalo while we drive the oxen."

The company agrees. Banishment is the punishment, just as Reed had called for Keseberg's banishment months ago on the prairie. Reed mounts the haggard Glaucus. The once proud horse is so weak now that it can barely carry a rider. Reed rides away slowly, once again leaving his family behind.

GUIDED READING

On what does the company agree?

Later that day, as the men struggle to drive the oxen and wagons over the sand hill, Virginia mounts her pony and steals away, following her father's tracks. She overtakes him and gives him a gun and ammunition. Gratefully, he takes it. "You must go back now, Virginia. Your ma and the others need you."

"You'll make it to Sutter's Fort, Pa. I know it. Then you'll come for us. I'll watch for you every day, Pa!" she swears.

She rides away in one direction, and he goes in another.

The journey continues—into another desert. White clouds of alkaline[7] soil rise around the wagons as they roll onward. The chalky dust covers the bony hides of the animals and the faces of the people, making them all ghostlike. Weird steaming geysers[8] erupt from holes in the ground, but the water is too hot, too bitter to drink. Children with tongues swollen from thirst beg for water.

"Breen," pleads William Eddy, "for the love of God. Give us some of your water. My children are dying!"

GUIDED READING

Why can't the people drink the water?

"If I give you water, what will my children drink?"

---

6. **wagon tongue...ox yoke.** Wagon tongue is a rod that fastens on to the harness (yoke) that an ox wears.

7. **alkaline.** Containing or having the properties of alkali or alkali metal (having a pH of over 7)

8. **steaming geysers.** Springs that emit jets of heated water and steam

words for everyday use

har • bor (här′ bər) v., hold on to, especially in the mind. *My dad developed an ulcer because he <u>harbored</u> his anger.*

The Donner Party is rescued.

Eddy dives for the water cask, pulling a gun on Patrick. "God help me, I'll kill you if you try to stop me!" Breen backs off. Eddy's children drink.

The journey continues, but the Donner Party is no longer a train of families working together to reach the golden land. It is a single file of souls—each family for itself, hoping to cross the Sierras before heavy snows and starvation stop them.

Death is a walker now among the wagons.

Late October. A deep lake. Tall pines. Plenty of grass.

"We should push on," Patrick Breen advises. "Attempt the pass now."

"The animals will die if we do," says William Eddy.

Camped near a lake high in the Sierra Nevadas, the emigrants are just one thousand feet from the summit. Even so, they are scraping the bottom of their flour barrels.

George Donner studies the cloudy sky that threatens to storm.

"Hastings crossed the pass in December last year," he tells the others. "He made it through. We might as well take one more night to rest the animals."

And so the journey is delayed still one day more. George's decision is a fateful one, for that afternoon, snow begins to fall.

GUIDED READING

Where have the emigrants camped?

GUIDED READING

What happens the day George Donner decides to wait?

The journey began with wind and snow. With wind and snow it shall end—snow so deep it buries the hastily built shelters roofed with animal hides. Inside his shelter, Patrick Breen writes in his diary: *Friday, Nov. 20, 1846 Came to this place on the 31st of last month . . . we climbed to the pass . . . the snow so deep we were unable to find the road . . .*

Nearby in another shelter, Virginia Reed also writes: *. . . the mules kept falling down in the snow head foremost[9] . . . the women were all so tired carrying their children.*

Within 3 miles of the summit, according to Patrick Breen's record, the emigrants were forced to turn back to their shanties on the lake. They had come 2,500 miles in 7 months to lose the race against winter by a single day.

GUIDED READING

What are the emigrants forced to do? How far had they traveled until that point?

The first death from starvation comes in December. With each break in the storms, groups of emigrants desperately try to cross the pass. Each time, the waist-deep snow forces them back to the lake.

Dec. 1st, writes Patrick Breen. *Still snowing . . . difficult to get wood, no going from the house . . . our cattle are all killed but three or four, the horses and mules supposed lost in the snow, no hopes of finding them alive.*

On a clear day, men and women chisel steps in the snow from their doorways up to the surface. With long poles, they poke in the sea of white, hoping to discover the dead cattle and horses. The search fails.

Each day, the desperation of their lives is recorded in the diaries they keep. *We have not had the first thing to eat*, writes Virginia. *We had to kill little Cash the dog and eat him. We ate his entrails and feet and hide and everything.*

The weakest—the very young, the very old—die first.

Sad news, writes Patrick Breen. *Jacob Donner is dead. Buried him in the snow . . . Jan. 17 . . . Provisions scarce. Hides are the only article we depend on.*

The animal hides are boiled into a thick, gluey paste. The women cook it with anything they can swallow—leaves, twigs, bark.

Ma went down to the other cabin and got half a hide, carried it in snow up to waist. I can hardly eat the hide, but have not eaten anything in three days, writes Virginia.

Each day begins with the hope that a rescue party still might find them. But each day ends in despair and hunger. Always hunger. The threat of cannibalism[10] creeps closer. At last, the unspeakable is spoken.

"We shall go mad!" cries Keseberg. "We shall all die! It is useless to hunt for cattle. But the *dead* might keep us alive."

"No," Margaret Reed states emphatically. "Not as long as we have hides left to eat."

Sometime in late winter, it happens. Those who first eat the flesh avert their faces from one another and they weep.

GUIDED READING

What are people in the party forced to do to survive?

In the dark of his sad shelter, Patrick Breen writes, *May God send us help.*

After a week of struggling through the snow, the relief team from Sutter's Fort crosses through the pass in the jagged peaks and descends the mountain. At dusk, they wade across the deep snow on the frozen lake. They see no cabins, no life, and fear they have come too late. And then, like an animal crawling out of a hole in the snow, a human figure appears.

"Are you men from California?" Virginia Reed asks in a thin voice. "Or do you come from heaven?"

Other humans appear, <u>gaunt</u> with hunger. They weep. They laugh hysterically. Some give prayers of thanksgiving. The relief team

---

9. *foremost.* First
10. **cannibalism.** Practice of eating human flesh

---

words for everyday use

gaunt (gänt') *adj.*, excessively thin. *She had a <u>gaunt</u> look about her because she was so thin.*

gives what food they can spare, then selects the strongest who will leave and attempt to cross the mountains on foot. George Donner is too weak, and Tamsen refuses to leave him. Keseberg, his eyes blazing with madness, is bedridden and must stay behind too. Margaret Reed and all her children go. But two miles out, Patty and little Tommy begin to fail. To carry them is to risk the lives of the others. "If they go back, I go back," Margaret announces.

The relief team argues with her. There is not enough food back at the lake for her and her children. No, the children must return, but Margaret will go forward over the pass. She knows the decision is the right one, the best one for her children's survival. Her own matters little. Still, she hesitates.

"You promise, you swear? You'll come back for my children?" She pleads with the relief team.

The men nod.

Anguished, she hugs Tommy, then Patty. She gives the little girl a handkerchief. Folded inside is the lock of the grandmother's hair.

Patty looks up at her with brave eyes. "Well, Ma. If you never see me again, do the best you can," she says.

GUIDED READING

What does Patty Reed tell her mother?

For four days, the relief team and the survivors struggle through the mountain pass. On the fifth day, they see a file of men on the trail ahead. It is the second relief team.

"Halloo!" a voice calls through the cold. "Is Mrs. Reed with you? Tell her Mr. Reed is here."

Margaret hears the voice. "Jim? He's alive!"

Overcome, she collapses in the snow. Virginia stumbles ahead and falls into her father's arms. "Your mother," Reed cries. "Your mother? Where is she?"

Virginia points. Reeds goes to her and kneels in the snow beside Margaret. After months of separation and starvation, of not knowing what had become of one another, the Reeds are a family again.

Except, Margaret tells him, for Patty and Tommy.

March 3, 1847. Rain falls gently at Sutter's Fort in the Sacramento Valley of California. Margaret stands in the doorway and stares at the mountain peaks. "If it is raining here, then it must be snowing up there," she murmurs to no one in particular.

GUIDED READING

What does Margaret Reed say about the mountains?

Far away, on the other side of the mountain, in the valley by the lake, Patty sits on the roof of a cabin, her feet buried in the snow. She sees a person coming across the still-frozen and snow-drifted lake. She tries to stand and wave, but falls. Her father gathers her into his arms. In the folds of her clothes are her two treasures—the lock of hair in the handkerchief and her doll.

"I brought her all the way from Springfield, Pa, and I didn't once lose her."

Tommy, too, is alive, but a near skeleton with deep-sunken eyes that do not recognize his father. Reed rocks his two children in his arms.

In another day or two, he will bundle them and, with the others who are still alive, cross the mountain one more time.

And then, the journey will be over at last.

■

NOTE

Bad judgment. The members of the Donner Party cursed Hastings and his cutoff. But bad luck also played a role in this true and tragic story. In another year, another winter, they could have crossed the mountain passes before the coming of heavy snows. The winter of 1846–47 was the worst ever recorded in the Sierra Nevadas.

When the fourth and final relief team arrived at the camp by the lake, the men found only Lewis Keseberg alive. George Donner was dead. His wife had wrapped his body in a sheet. But Tamsen Donner was missing. Her body was never discovered. In total, of the eighty-seven people who had made up the Donner Party, five women, fourteen children, and twenty-two men had died of starvation in the mountains.

On April 25, 1847, the last survivor of the Donner Party—Keseberg—was brought into Sutter's Fort. Almost one year to the day had passed since the emigrants had set out from Independence, Missouri.

Respond *to the* SELECTION

If you had been in the Donner Party, would you ever have traveled back east again? Why, or why not?

About *the* AUTHOR

Catherine Gourley is an award-winning author of stories for young adults. Her books include *Island in the Creek, Never Turn Back,* and *Beryl Mehan,* which is a historical fiction novel. She attended Rutgers University in New Jersey and even played in the orchestra there. Her many jobs have included being a former editor at Weekly Reader Corporation and a journalist for various Canadian and American newspapers and magazines, including *The Wall Street Journal.* "The Cutoff: The Story of the Donner Party" is an example of the simplistic yet well-crafted and compelling writing style for which she is well known.

Investigate, *Inquire,* and Imagine

Recall: GATHERING FACTS → **Interpret:** FINDING MEANING

1a. Who do the emigrants see at Fort Laramie? What does this person tell them?

1b. Why do you think James Reed ignores the advice of his friend?

2a. What happens after the Donner Party leaves Fort Bridger? What notes do they get from Hastings?

2b. Why is the only possibility to push on through the desert?

3a. Why does George Donner delay the party at the lake in the Sierra Nevadas instead of pushing on through the pass?

3b. How might things have gone differently if they had left?

4a. How do people react when the relief team arrives at their camp?

4b. Why do they react this way?

Analyze: TAKING THINGS APART → **Synthesize:** BRINGING THINGS TOGETHER

5a. List all the choices and events that lead up to the failure of the Donner Party to get across the pass. Then rank these items from most important to least important.

5b. Looking at the disaster that the Donner Party lived, determine how much of it was due to human error and how much of it was due to nature.

Perspective: LOOKING AT OTHER VIEWS → **Empathy:** SEEING FROM INSIDE

6a. How do you think Patty Reed felt when the family left on their journey? What might she have been thinking about during the months she waited to be rescued?

6b. In Springfield, Illinois, Patty Reed lived a sheltered and pampered life. If you were Patty Reed, how would you feel different after your journey to California? How would the journey have affected your views of the world? How would it have changed your personality, if at all?

Understanding *Literature*

HISTORICAL FICTION. Fiction is prose writing about imagined events or characters. **Historical fiction** is fiction that is based on real people and events. What elements of "The Cutoff: The Story of the Donner Party" reveal that it is historical fiction?

DIALOGUE. Dialogue is conversation involving two or more people or characters. Fiction is made up of dialogue, narration, and description. How would this story be different if it didn't contain dialogue?

Writer's Journal

1. Pretend you are a member of the Keseberg family. Write a **journal entry** about how you feel being banished from the train.

2. Imagine you are Clyman, James Reed's old friend. Write a **letter** to James, telling him why he should go the longer way and not the way Hastings tells him to go in the book. Try to convince him not to listen to Hastings.

3. Imagine you are a person who followed Hastings's way and found that he was a fraud. Write an **editorial** to the newspaper about his book and how it is misleading.

Skill Builders

Speaking and Listening

LEGAL ARGUMENTS. Split students into two groups: one group believes that Reed is innocent in the death of James and the other group believes that Reed is a murderer. Have each group gather details from the selection that support their decision. After both groups have presented their case, let the appointed judge make a ruling on whether or not Reed is guilty for James's death.

Media Literacy

FURTHER STUDY. Research at the library to find articles or information about Lansford W. Hastings's book, *The Emigrants' Guide to Oregon and California*. See if you can find commentaries or critiques that were written about the book. Present their finding to the rest of the class.

Applied English

OFFERING CRITIQUE. Write a letter to the publishers of Hastings's book stating why it should never have been published and why it should no longer be in print. Use examples from the selection to defend your position. You should also find other stories about families who experienced some of the same things as the Donner Party. The more examples you have of the negative effects of his book on travelers, the stronger and more convincing your argument.

Language, Grammar, and Style

DIRECT OBJECTS. A sentence must have a subject and a verb, but sometimes a sentence has other parts that complete the meaning—such as direct objects. Underline the verb and identify the direct object for each of the sentences below. For more information, see the Language Arts Survey 3.20, "Completers for Action Verbs: Direct and Indirect Objects."

EXAMPLE   *I will bring my books.*
            will bring what? *books*
            verb: *will bring*
            direct object: *books*

1. He enjoys fast horses.
2. James rides a gray mare.
3. He kicks the robe across the ground.
4. Tamsen watches the wagons.
5. The Donner Party follows the tracks of Hastings's wagons.

Prereading

"THE WRECK OF THE HESPERUS"

by Henry Wadsworth Longfellow

Reader's Resource

- **AMERICAN HISTORY CONNECTION.** In December 1839, 20 bodies from the schooner *Hesperus* washed ashore. One of the bodies was tied to the mast of the ship. The schooner was destroyed on the rocks of Norman's Reef, or Norman's Woe, off Gloucester, Massachusetts. Longfellow wrote in his journal about his horror upon hearing of this disaster, and a few days later wrote the poem.

- Commercial fishing has played a major role in the history of Gloucester, which was first settled in 1623. As a monument to the many lives lost at sea, Gloucester erected the Fisherman's Memorial, a statue of a fisherman at the wheel of a ship with the inscription, "They that go down to the sea in ships."

- **MATH AND SCIENCE CONNECTION.** Sailing ships need wind to move, but very strong winds can be dangerous. Sir Francis Beaufort devised a scale, based on ocean conditions, to classify winds. In the Beaufort Scale there are 13 force levels. At Force 0, the ocean is calm with a mirrorlike surface. The forces rise gradually in intensity. At Force 12, hurricane-force winds blow above an extremely turbulent sea. Force 12 winds begin at 74 miles per hour; gusts can reach 220 miles per hour. Winds are fiercest near the eye, or center, of the storm. Hurricanes often cause damage because of the force of their winds, torrential rains, and storm surges along the coast. Storm surges are walls of water that can be sucked up to 25 feet high in the eye of the storm.

Graphic Organizer

Write the following stanza. Place an X next to each of the two lines that rhyme. Do the same for other stanzas in the poem.

> It was the schooner Hesperus,
> That sailed the wintry sea;
> And the skipper had taken his little daughter,
> To bear him company.

Reader's Journal

Have you ever seen a shipwreck or a smashed-up automobile? What did viewing such destruction make you think about?

Reader's TOOLBOX

NARRATIVE POEM AND BALLAD. A **narrative poem** is any verse that tells a story. A **ballad** is a simple poem that tells a story. Most ballads have four-line stanzas, and the second and fourth lines usually rhyme. As you read "The Wreck of the Hesperus," think about how the poem is telling a story.

STANZA. A **stanza** is a group of lines in a poem. Stanzas are usually separated by spaces from other stanzas. Look at the first stanza of the poem. Which lines rhyme? Use the graphic organizer at left to help.

Vessels Close Hauled, c.1672. Willem van de Velde the Younger. National Gallery, London.

THE WRECK OF THE HESPERUS

Henry Wadsworth Longfellow

It was the schooner[1] Hesperus,
    That sailed the wintry sea;
And the skipper had taken his little daughter,
    To bear him company.

5   Blue were her eyes as the fairy-flax,
    Her cheeks like the dawn of day,

---

1. **schooner.** Ship with two or more masts

And her bosom white as the hawthorn buds
    That ope in the month of May.

The skipper he stood beside the helm,
10   His pipe was in his mouth,
And he watched how the veering flaw[2] did blow
    The smoke now West, now South.

Then up and spake an old Sailor,
    Had sailed the Spanish Main,[3]
15 "I pray thee, put into yonder port,
    For I fear a hurricane.

"Last night the moon had a golden ring,
    And tonight no moon we see!"
The skipper he blew a whiff from his pipe,
20   And a scornful laugh laughed he.

Colder and colder blew the wind,
    A gale from the North-east;
The snow fell hissing in the brine,[4]
    And the billows frothed like yeast.

25 Down came the storm, and <u>smote</u> amain,
    The vessel in its strength;
She shuddered and paused, like a frightened steed,
    Then leaped her cable's length.

"Come hither! come hither! my little daughter,
30   And do not tremble so;
For I can weather the roughest gale,
    That ever wind did blow."

He wrapped her warm in his seaman's coat
    Against the stinging blast;
35 He cut a rope from a broken spar,[5]
    And bound her to the mast.

GUIDED READING

Who is at sea with the skipper? How is this person described?

---

2. **veering flaw.** Gust of wind that changes direction
3. **Spanish Main.** Coastal region of the Americas along the Caribbean Sea
4. **brine.** Salt water
5. **spar.** Pole supporting the sail of a ship

words for everyday use

smite (smīt') v., hit or strike hard. *The valiant knight <u>smote</u> his enemy with his sword.*

"O father! I hear the church-bells ring,
    O say, what may it be?"
"'Tis a fog-bell on a rock-bound coast!"
40   And he steered for the open sea.

"O father! I hear the sound of guns,
    O say, what may it be?"
"Some ship in distress, that cannot live
    In such an angry sea!"

45 "O father! I see a gleaming light,
    O say, what may it be?"
But the father answered never a word,
    A frozen corpse was he.

Lashed to the helm, all stiff and stark,
50   With his face turned to the skies,
The lantern gleamed through the gleaming snow
    On his fixed and glassy eyes.

Then the maiden clasped her hands and prayed
    That savèd she might be;
55 And she thought of Christ, who stilled the wave,
    On the Lake of Galilee.

And fast through the midnight dark and drear,
    Through the whistling sleet and snow,
Like a sheeted ghost, the vessel swept
60   Towards the reef of Norman's Woe.

And ever the fitful gusts between
    A sound came from the land;
It was the sound of the trampling surf,
    On the rocks and the hard sea-sand.

65 The breakers were right beneath her bows,
    She drifted a dreary wreck,
And a whooping billow swept the crew
    Like icicles from her deck.

She struck where the white and fleecy waves
70   Looked soft as carded[6] wool,
But the cruel rocks, they gored[7] her side
    Like the horns of an angry bull.

GUIDED READING

What has happened to the skipper?

---

6. **carded.** Combed
7. **gored.** Punctured

Her rattling shrouds, all sheathed in ice,
　　With the masts went by the board;
75　Like a vessel of glass, she stove[8] and sank,
　　Ho! ho! the breakers roared!

At daybreak, on the bleak sea-beach,
　　A fisherman stood aghast,[9]
To see the form of a maiden fair,
80　Lashed close to a drifting mast.

The salt sea was frozen on her breast,
　　The salt tears in her eyes;
And he saw her hair, like the brown sea-weed,
　　On the billows fall and rise.

85　Such was the wreck of the Hesperus,
　　In the midnight and the snow!
Christ save us all from a death like this
　　On the reef of Norman's Woe! ■

8. **stove.** Broke
9. **aghast.** Horrified

Respond *to the* SELECTION

Did the skipper of the *Hesperus* act wisely and do the best he could do in a bad situation? Why, or why not? What would you have done if you were the skipper?

About *the* AUTHOR

Henry Wadsworth Longfellow (1807–1882) was born in Portland, Maine, to an old New England family. Longfellow published his first poem at age thirteen. At the age of fifteen, he attended Bowdoin College where he was a classmate of Nathaniel Hawthorne. Longfellow excelled as a student and later taught modern language—French, Spanish, and Italian—at Bowdoin College and at Harvard. His poem *The Song of Hiawatha* sold over one million copies during his lifetime and helped establish him as a writer. He also wrote "Paul Revere's Ride" and several books of poetry, including *Evangeline* and *The Courtship of Miles Standish*.

The Wreck of the Edmund Fitzgerald

Gordon Lightfoot

The legend lives on from the Chippewa on down
Of the big lake they called "Gitche Gumee"
The lake, it is said, never gives up her dead
When the skies of November turn gloomy

With a load of iron ore twenty-six thousand tons more
Than the Edmund Fitzgerald weighed empty.
That good ship and true was a bone to be chewed
When the "Gales of November" came early.

The ship was the pride of the American side
Coming back from some mill in Wisconsin
As the big freighters go, it was bigger than most
With a crew and good captain well seasoned

Concluding some terms with a couple of steel firms
When they left fully loaded for Cleveland
And later that night when the ship's bell rang
Could it be the north wind they'd been feelin'?

The wind in the wires made a tattle-tale sound
And a wave broke over the railing
And every man knew, as the captain did too,
'Twas the witch of November come stealin'.

The dawn came late and the breakfast had to wait
When the Gales of November came slashin'.
When afternoon came it was freezin' rain
In the face of a hurricane west wind.

When suppertime came, the old cook came on deck sayin',
"Fellas, it's too rough to feed ya."
At seven pm a main hatchway caved in, he said
"Fellas, it's been good t'know ya."

The captain wired in he had water comin' in
And the good ship and crew was in peril.
And later that night when his lights went outta sight
Came the wreck of the Edmund Fitzgerald.

Does anyone know where the love of God goes
When the waves turn the minutes to hours?
The searchers all say they'd have made Whitefish Bay
If they'd put fifteen more miles behind her.

They might have split up or they might have capsized;
May have broke deep and took water.
And all that remains is the faces and the names
Of the wives and the sons and the daughters.

Lake Huron rolls, Superior sings
In the rooms of her ice-water mansion.
Old Michigan steams like a young man's dreams;
The islands and bays are for sportsmen.

And farther below Lake Ontario
Takes in what Lake Erie can send her,
And the iron boats go as the mariners all know
With the Gales of November remembered.

In a musty old hall in Detroit they prayed
In the "Maritime Sailors' Cathedral."
The church bell chimed till it rang twenty-nine times
For each man on the Edmund Fitzgerald.

The legend lives on from the Chippewa on down
Of the big lake they call "Gitche Gumee."
"Superior," they said, "never gives up her dead
When the Gales of November come early!" ■

ABOUT THE RELATED READING
Gordon Lightfoot wrote "The Wreck of the Edmund Fitzgerald" in 1976,
after the ship *Edmund Fitzgerald* sank into Lake Superior in November 1975.
The crew of 29 was lost with the ship.

Investigate, *Inquire,* and Imagine

Recall: GATHERING FACTS

1a. Who does the skipper of the *Hesperus* take along to sea for company? What description is given of that person?

2a. What causes the skipper to laugh a "scornful laugh"? What does he say he can do?

3a. What two things does the other character hear? What does that person see?

4a. What does the fisherman see from the beach?

→ **Interpret:** FINDING MEANING

1b. How does the description of this character affect the outcome in this ballad?

2b. What do the skipper's actions tell you about the skipper's attitude and character?

3b. What is the significance of each of these three things?

4b. Would the fisherman have guessed what happened? Why, or why not?

Analyze: TAKING THINGS APART

5a. In what ways does Longfellow describe the different parts of this tragic accident?

→ **Synthesize:** BRINGING THINGS TOGETHER

5b. What do you think is the theme, or main idea, that Longfellow offers in this poem?

Evaluate: MAKING JUDGMENTS

6a. Longfellow chose to tell the story of the wreck of the *Hesperus* in a ballad—a type of poetry—instead of using another form. How is (or isn't) the ballad form fitting for the subject of the shipwreck? How does it create a certain mood or atmosphere?

→ **Extend:** CONNECTING IDEAS

6b. Compare the mood of "The Wreck of the Hesperus" to that of "The Wreck of the Edmund Fitzgerald." In what ways are they different? How are they alike?

Understanding *Literature*

NARRATIVE POEM AND BALLAD. A **narrative poem** is any verse that tells a story. A **ballad** is a simple poem that tells a story. Most ballads have four-line stanzas, and the second and fourth lines usually rhyme. What story does "The Wreck of the Hesperus" tell? Why do you think the author chose to write it?

STANZA. A **stanza** is a group of lines in a poem. Stanzas are usually separated by spaces from other stanzas. Besides the spaces between stanzas, what else makes each stanza stand apart from the others?

Writer's Journal

1. Write a list of **interview questions** you would like to have asked Henry Wadsworth Longfellow or the skipper of the *Hesperus*.
2. Imagine you were one of the searchers looking for the *Edmund Fitzgerald* in Lake Superior. Write an **official report** about your fruitless search.
3. Write a short **ballad** of four stanzas, in each of which the second and fourth stanzas rhyme.

Skill Builders

Collaborative Learning

DEVELOPING A BOARD GAME. Form small groups to create a board game in which the object is to safely sail your boat to an island during a storm. Use a piece of flat wood, cardboard, or posterboard for the game board, and add details using any other art supplies available to you. When you have finished, play the game in your group to work out any problems. Remember to create a title for the game and to list the rules in clear and simple steps. Review the Language Arts Survey 6.3, "Giving Directions," to help you write directions. Then present your game to others in your class. You may want to take turns playing the games of other groups.

Language, Grammar, and Style

CAPITALIZATION. Using capital letters is called capitalization. It is important always to capitalize proper nouns and adjectives. Review the Language Arts Survey 3.85, "Proper Nouns and Adjectives." Then make three underline marks under each letter that needs capitalization in the following sentences. The three underline marks are a proofreading symbol to indicate a need for capitalization.

EXAMPLE   Mr. jefferson and grandfather went to the dooley café.

1. My sister named her boat *young ambition*.
2. I was surprised to learn that uncle pete is getting married on kay's yacht.
3. Jesse usually docks his boat in late may.
4. I think it was around memorial day that we got that big storm.
5. The hammonds just took in a russian exchange student who loves to swim.

Reader's Journal

What things do you like to watch and help grow? What about those things most interests you?

Reader's Resource

- **SCIENCE CONNECTION.** Greenhouses are buildings in which fragile or out-of-season plants are grown. Modern greenhouses, made almost entirely of glass, are carefully controlled environments for raising particular plants. Glass can transmit the sunlight that plants need and it can hold in heat. The frame of a greenhouse can be made of metal or of woods such as cypress, redwood, or cedar. Most greenhouses cannot rely on the sun alone to provide heat and so are heated artificially, often by steam, hot air, or hot water.

- There are three types of greenhouses: cool, warm, and tropical. At night, cool greenhouses are usually kept at temperatures around 45°–50°. Plants such as irises, daffodils, tulips, and geraniums are grown there. Warm greenhouses are 50°–55° at night. African violets, ferns, cacti, and roses are grown in warm greenhouses. Tropical greenhouses are 60°–70° at night, and begonias, gardenias, palms, and orchids are grown there.

Prereading

"BIG WIND"

and "Child on Top of a Greenhouse"

by Theodore Roethke

Reader's TOOLBOX

FIGURES OF SPEECH. A **figure of speech** is writing or speech meant to be understood imaginatively instead of literally. Many writers, especially poets, use figures of speech to help readers to see things in new ways. Figures of speech include metaphor, simile, and personification. A **metaphor** is a figure of speech in which one thing is spoken or written about as if it were another. This figure of speech invites the reader to make a comparison between the two things. A metaphor works because the things to be compared have one or more qualities in common. A **simile** is a comparison using *like* or *as*. **Personification** is a figure of speech in which something not human is described as if it were human. Keep track of the figures of speech you find in "Big Wind" and "Child on Top of a Greenhouse" by using a graphic organizer like the one showing the examples below.

Graphic Organizer

Figure of speech	What is it?	Explanation
The black canopy of the nighttime sky was painted with dazzling jewels.	Metaphor	The nighttime sky is spoken about as if it were a black canopy; the stars are called dazzling jewels.

Windy Day in Atchison, 1952.
John Philip Falter.
Sheldon Memorial Art Gallery,
Lincoln, Nebraska.

BIG WIND

Theodore Roethke

Where were the greenhouses going,
Lunging into the lashing
Wind driving water
So far down the river
5　　All the faucets stopped?—
So we drained the manure-machine
For the steam plant,
Pumping the stale mixture
Into the rusty boilers,
10　　Watching the pressure gauge
Waver over to red,
As the seams hissed
And the live steam
Drove to the far
15　　End of the rose-house,
Where the worst wind was,
Creaking the cypress window-frames,
Cracking so much thin glass
We stayed all night,
20　　Stuffing the holes with burlap;
But she rode it out,
That old rose-house,
She hove[1] into the teeth of it,
The core and pith[2] of that ugly storm,
25　　Ploughing with her stiff prow,[3]
Bucking into the wind-waves
That broke over the whole of her,
Flailing her sides with spray,
Flinging long strings of wet across the roof-top,
30　　Finally veering, wearing themselves out, merely
Whistling thinly under the wind-vents;
She sailed until the calm morning,
Carrying her full cargo of roses.　■

GUIDED READING

What is the weather like?

GUIDED READING

Why does the speaker stay in the greenhouse all night?

GUIDED READING

To what does the speaker compare the greenhouse?

GUIDED READING

What is the greenhouse carrying as it "sails"?

---

1. **hove.** Alternate past tense of *heave*, a nautical term meaning to proceed or to move forward
2. **pith.** Center; force or strength
3. **prow.** The front, or forward, part of a ship

words for everyday use

flail (flāl') *v.*, whip. *The heron flailed its wings and rose up over the lake.*

veer (vir') *v.*, change direction. *We had to veer off the road to avoid the squirrel.*

Child
on top of a
Greenhouse

Theodore Roethke

The wind billowing out the seat of my britches,
My feet crackling splinters of glass and dried putty,[1]
The half-grown chrysanthemums staring up like accusers,
Up through the streaked glass, flashing with sunlight,
A few white clouds all rushing eastward,
A line of elms plunging and tossing like horses,
And everyone, everyone pointing up and shouting!

■

---

1. **putty.** Doughlike material used to fasten glass in window frames and to fill crevices in
woodwork

What would you see if you were atop a greenhouse in your community?

About *the* AUTHOR

Theodore Roethke (1908–1963) was born in Saginaw, Michigan, where his father owned a greenhouse. Growing up around greenhouses influenced Roethke's poetry—greenhouses, plants, and images of growth appear in many of his poems. Roethke attended Harvard University and the University of Michigan and later became a college professor. One of the best-known American poets, Roethke won many awards for his work, including two Guggenheim Fellowships, two National Book Awards, the Bollingen Prize, and a Pulitzer Prize.

Investigate, Inquire, and Imagine

Recall: GATHERING FACTS

1a. What is going on outside the greenhouse in "Big Wind"?

2a. What words does the speaker use to describe the greenhouse as if it were a ship?

3a. Where is the speaker in "Child on Top of a Greenhouse"?

4a. What is everyone doing?

→ **Interpret:** FINDING MEANING

1b. What are the effects of this event on the greenhouse?

2b. Why might the greenhouse seem like a ship to the speaker?

3b. Why might the speaker have gone there?

4b. Why are they doing this? How does the speaker's mood probably differ from that of the people?

Analyze: TAKING THINGS APART

5a. What words and phrases does Roethke use to describe the weather in "Big Wind"? What words and phrases does he use to describe the weather in "Child on Top of a Greenhouse"? Contrast the weather descriptions of the two poems.

→ **Synthesize:** BRINGING THINGS TOGETHER

5b. In what ways does Roethke use weather descriptions to help create a certain mood?

Evaluate: MAKING JUDGMENTS

6a. How well do these poems encourage you to "see" the scene described?

→ **Extend:** CONNECTING IDEAS

6b. If the scenes described in these two poems were in a film, which scene would be more suspenseful? Which would be more surprising? Which would be the bigger spectacle?

Understanding Literature

FIGURES OF SPEECH. A **figure of speech** is writing or speech meant to be understood imaginatively instead of literally. Many writers, especially poets, use figures of speech to help readers to see things in new ways. Figures of speech include metaphor, simile, and personification. A **metaphor** is a figure of speech in which one thing is spoken or written about as if it were another. This figure of speech invites the reader to make a comparison between the two things. A metaphor works because the things to be compared have one or more qualities in common. A **simile** is a comparison using *like* or *as*. **Personification** is a figure of speech in which something not human is described as if it were human. What figures of speech did you find in "Big Wind" and "Child on Top of a Greenhouse"? Which of those did you think was the most powerful? Why?

Writer's Journal

1. Write a **metaphor** describing an element of weather, such as wind, rain, snow, heat, sunshine, or cold.
2. Write a short **play** about what might have happened after the scene described in "Child on Top of a Greenhouse."
3. Write an **invitation** to the public to view a flower show at a local greenhouse.

Skill Builders

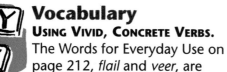

Vocabulary

USING VIVID, CONCRETE VERBS. The Words for Everyday Use on page 212, *flail* and *veer*, are examples of vivid, concrete verbs that give specific information about a particular action. For example, *veer* reveals much more about the action of the "wind-waves" than *move* would have revealed. In addition, *flail* gives a more specific description than *hit* would. In a small group, brainstorm a list of vivid verbs that could be used in place of *move*. Then do the same for the word *hit*.

Cooperative Learning

GROWING PLANTS. Get into groups of four to design a garden. First, ask your principal for permission to use a small area for planting somewhere on school grounds. Then in your group, decide on the type of seeds you want to plant. Finally, gather any gardening equipment you may need and plant your seeds. Some of the equipment may include a shovel, gloves, hoe, and a watering hose.

Language, Grammar, and Style

PREPOSITIONS, CONJUNCTIONS, AND INTERJECTIONS. Do you know the difference between prepositions, conjunctions, and interjections? Review the Language Arts Survey 3.66, "Prepositions," 3.67, "Conjunctions," and 3.70, "Interjections". Then identify the underlined words in the sentences below as one of the three.

1. I watched the pressure gauge waver over <u>to</u> red.
2. The water flailed her sides <u>with</u> spray.
3. The roof <u>and</u> walls wavered <u>in</u> the storm.
4. <u>Hey</u>, help me stuff the holes <u>with</u> burlap!
5. Splinters of glass <u>and</u> dried putty stung my feet.
6. I climbed <u>upon</u> the greenhouse.
7. <u>Oh</u>, but I forgot my shoes <u>and</u> hat <u>in</u> there.
8. I will help you <u>or</u> Dad with the planting.
9. The elms plunged <u>and</u> tossed like horses.
10. Everyone went <u>inside</u>.

for your READING LIST

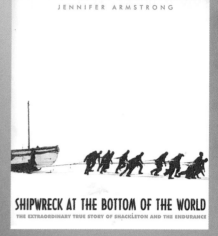

JENNIFER ARMSTRONG

SHIPWRECK AT THE BOTTOM OF THE WORLD
THE EXTRAORDINARY TRUE STORY OF SHACKLETON AND THE ENDURANCE

Shipwreck at the Bottom of the World: The Extraordinary True Story of Shackleton and the Endurance by Jennifer Armstrong tells the story of English explorer Sir Ernest Shackleton and his ill-fated ship, the *Endurance*. Shackleton and his crew of 27 men sailed from England in August of 1914 with the goal of becoming the first team of explorers to cross the frozen Antarctic continent. The men could never have imagined the challenges and hardships that lay before them: seven months spent cramped onboard ship while trapped in an ice pack, the destruction of the *Endurance* just one hundred miles from its final destination, sea lion attacks, unimaginable cold, and harrowing sea journeys in small, open boats. With vivid details, including accounts from many of the crew members' diaries and more than 40 fascinating photographs by expedition photographer Frank Hurley, Armstrong creates a compelling tale of heroism, daring, and loyalty—"one of the most incredible feats of survival ever recorded."

INTERVIEWING AN ANTARCTIC EXPLORER

After you have read *Shipwreck at the Bottom of the World*, work with a partner to conduct a talk show-style interview with Sir Ernest Shackleton or one of the members of his crew. Before you begin, review the Language Arts Survey 4.14, "Conducting an Interview," for guidelines. Develop a list of questions that would be appropriate to ask the person you select. You should base your questions and responses on information from the book, but you might also want to use your imagination to create questions and responses about issues that are not included in the book. The following topics may be helpful to you in developing your questions:

- reason for organizing (or joining) the expedition
- mood of the crew from the day the voyage began to the day the rescue boat arrived on Elephant Island
- worst moment of the 19-month adventure
- best moment of the 19-month adventure
- first thing you did when you arrived home in England
- how you would feel about returning to the Antarctic
- what effect this experience had on you

When you have developed your list of questions, decide which of you will portray the explorer and which will play the interviewer. You may want to videotape or tape record the interview to share with the rest of your class.

Other books you may want to read:
The Adventures of Sojourner: The Mission to Mars That Thrilled the World by Susi Trautmann Wunsch
Black Whiteness: Admiral Byrd Alone in the Antarctic by Robert Burleigh

Examining the Model

In the excerpt below from "The Face of the Deep Is Frozen," the author points out Shackleton's perspective of the disaster. Shackleton writes in his journal that the task before them is to reach land with all the members of the expedition. The rest of the story chronicles their struggle to do just that. The excerpt also provides lively details that let you feel like you are almost there with the men, hauling the boats through the heavy wet snow.

Reflecting

Before you begin to write your story, think about the best "disaster" story you have ever read. What was it about that story that made it so powerful? Was it someone's ability to endure great hardships? Was it someone's attitude toward the disaster? Was it someone's cleverness at solving a problem? How did the story pull you in and keep your attention? Why are stories one of the best ways for people to share their experiences?

Prewriting

IDENTIFYING YOUR AUDIENCE. Who will read your disaster story? The audience for this story will be your peers. As your write, consider which feelings, thoughts, and observations will be most interesting and captivating for that audience.

Guided Writing

NARRATIVE WRITING: DESCRIBING A DISASTER

Annele asked Jake if he remembered what happened when the tornado hit his hometown last summer. "I don't think I'll ever forget that. I still can't believe how fast and powerful a tornado can be!" replied Jake. "First, I watched the sky turn a peculiar shade of green. Then the wind suddenly picked up, and the lawn chairs on our west-facing front porch lifted off, rounded the corner, and flew east. As we ran down to the basement, we heard the wind roaring and things crashing above us. It was all over so fast. When we went upstairs, some of our windows were broken and we had parts of the neighbor's roof inside our house. Outside, the streets were flooded with a foot of rain; huge tree limbs lay scattered about like pick-up sticks thrown by a kid who was mad. We were lucky that nobody was hurt."

You, too, may have experienced a natural disaster. Perhaps you have lived through a tornado, hurricane, blizzard, or flood. Or, you may have experienced a personal disaster. You may have broken a bone or suffered an injury. A personal disaster might also include something that frightened you in some way.

What has been your experience of a natural, personal, or community disaster? What happened to you and your family? How did you react? How did it affect you at the time and later? Your experience of the disaster is unique to you. No one else has exactly the same perspective or insight that you have. You can preserve your experience and perspective of the disaster by writing it down in a story.

Professional Model

from "The Face of the Deep Is Frozen," from *Shipwreck at the Bottom of the World: The Extraordinary True Story of Shackleton and the Endurance*, by Jennifer Armstrong, pages 157–159

As you read the following excerpt, consider how Shackleton and the crew struggled to continue their journey on foot after they abandoned the *Endurance*.

Though we have been compelled to abandon the ship, which is crushed beyond all hope of ever being righted, we are alive and well, and we have stores and equipment for the task that lies before us. The task is to reach land with all the members of the expedition," Shackleton wrote in his diary the next morning....

The journey was ready to begin at 2:00 P.M. on October 30 under heavy gray skies. It had already snowed on and off during the day, and it threatened to continue. That didn't pose much of a problem, but the road ahead did. If they only had to trek across 346 miles of flat ice field, the journey would have been bearable. But stretching ahead of them into the white horizon was a scene of utter devastation and chaos. It was as if a giant hand had smashed down onto the frozen face of the deep and broken it into a million shards. Jagged floes tilted up at all angles. Pressure ridges reared up like wrinkles in a huge white blanket. If the sea had been frozen at the height of a tempest, and every storm-tossed wave locked into place, the scene could not have been more jumbled and uneven. There were 346 miles of *that* to cross…

After two hours of backbreaking labor, hauling the boats through wet, heavy snow, detouring around piles of broken floe, they were only one mile from *Endurance*. Soaked, and numb with fatigue, the men swallowed a hasty dinner and fell into their tents. It began to snow during the night. When the men resumed their burdens the next day, they had a new layer of heavy wet slush to trudge through, and more wet snow falling steadily.

Student Model—Graphic Organizer

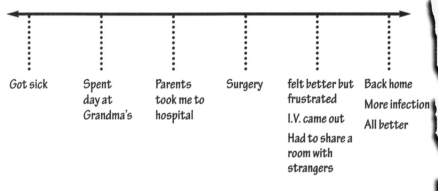

Got sick | Spent day at Grandma's | Parents took me to hospital | Surgery | felt better but frustrated / I.V. came out / Had to share a room with strangers | Back home / More infection / All better

Copy the time line onto a piece of paper. Fill in the events that happened at the beginning, middle, and end of the disaster.

Drafting

As you start to write your draft, concentrate on getting your ideas down in **chronological order**. You want your readers to know what happened to you at the beginning, middle, and end of the disaster. Your goal is not just to relate the events in order, though. You want to write a story that pulls in and keeps the attention of your readers.

One way you can engage your readers is by providing **lively details**. In the Professional Model, the details help you understand the men's increasing exhaustion as they detour around the piles of broken floe. You can sympathize with the crew who are "soaked, and numb with fatigue." Try to include lively details as you write your rough draft.

FINDING YOUR VOICE. You can pull in and keep your readers' attention by using a natural, personal voice to share your experience and perspective. By using a first-person point of view, you can show your involvement in and reaction to the disaster.

To help you practice using your natural, personal voice, imagine that you have just experienced each disaster below. On your own piece of paper, write three or four sentences that express your personal response to each disaster. Use the first-person point of view.

- Your house is flooded with a foot of water. The carpeting and much of the furniture is ruined. Your library books and your photo album that you left on your bedroom floor are also ruined.

- Your neighborhood has been burglarized lately.

- You broke your ankle playing soccer the night before the tournament.

WRITING WITH A PLAN. You may already know what you want to write about. Lisa still needed a topic, so she brainstormed with her friends and family.

Once you know your topic, think about the events that happened at the beginning, middle, and end of the disaster. Tyrone filled in the time line at the left to help him organize the events in the order that they happened.

continued on page 220

As you write your rough draft, you do not have to worry about grammar or spelling. You can go back later and check for errors. At this point, focus on:

- Developing a controlling idea that expresses your perspective
- Describing events in chronological order
- Including lively details about the events
- Creating a simile
- Writing dialogue

Self- and Peer Evaluation

After finishing your rough draft, you can do a self-evaluation of your work. If time allows, you may also want to do peer evaluations. For more information, see the Language Arts Survey 2.37, "Self- and Peer Evaluation."

As you evaluate your draft, ask yourself the following questions:

- What disaster does the story relate?
- What insight or perspective does the author have about the disaster? What could be added to clarify the perspective?
- How well does each paragraph contribute to the controlling idea?
- Does the story follow chronological order?
- Which details help hold the reader's attention? Which details could be added to make the story more interesting to the reader?
- How could dialogue enhance the story?
- What simile could be added to the story?

Another way you can engage your readers is to include an occasional **simile**. In the Professional Model, the author compared the pressure ridges to "wrinkles in a huge white blanket." At the beginning of this lesson, Jake compared the scattered tree limbs to "pick-up sticks thrown by a kid who was mad." What simile could you include in your story? On a piece of paper, write down a detail from the disaster and compare it to another idea or image. Plan to use at least one simile in your story.

A third way to engage your readers is to include some **dialogue** from the situation. If you can't remember the exact words that someone said, give an approximation of those words.

You will also want to let your readers know your **perspective** or insight about what happened. In the opening of this lesson, Jake expressed his insight that tornadoes are incredibly fast and powerful. All the rest of his story supports that insight.

In "The Face of the Deep Is Frozen," Shackleton's perspective was that he was determined to reach land with all the members of the expedition. The rest of the story describes the crew's struggle to do just that.

What is your perspective or insight about the disaster you experienced? You can express your perspective toward the beginning of your story. Your perspective will form the **controlling idea**—the main point—of your story. The rest of your story should support your controlling idea.

Student Model—Draft

How old were you?

This whole disaster started on a Friday in 1995 when I woke up and didn't feel well. My dad ~~brought~~ me to my grandma's house for the day. *took* I ~~laid~~ *lay* down on her couch and watched movies. *All morning* At lunch I tried to get off the couch but there was ~~this~~ *a* terrible pain in my side and I could hardly use my stomach muscles at all with out feeling ~~this~~ *a* searing pain in my side. I sat down at the table for lunch and couldn't even get close enough to my soup to eat any of it.

When I was back home my parent's decided that they should take me to a doctor to see if there was anything *really?*

wrong. When I got to the emergency room the doctors ran a lot of tests on me. after an hour or so the doctor came in and said that there was either something wrong with my appendix or I had a bladder infection. ~~It turned out it was a very bad case of a rotting appendix (we found out after surgery).~~ *Out of order here*

next the doctor put an i.v. in my left hand, and that so far was the most painful thing. *Even worse than your searing pain?*

I went into surgery late at night. All I can remember about the surgery is that the doctor's put ~~this~~ mask over my mouth and told me it was fresh air. *Use dialogue here* Next they told me to count to ten I know I said something like 1-2-5-3-6-4-7-9-8 if I even got that far. It seemed like seconds and I woke up. The nurses ~~or someone~~ was wheeling me into a hospital room, but I remember the electronic bed didn't work so they put me into a different room. I also got a teddy bear ~~(from the hospital)~~ and that made me feel a lot better. I think the next day I was up and slowly but surely I was able to walk more easily. *Expand from here*

Revising and Proofreading

If possible, wait a day before you revise your writing. That way, you will be able to see your writing with "new eyes." Read your story and check to see if your perspective is clearly expressed. Does the rest of your story support your perspective?

Try reading your story out loud to yourself. Listen to the words that you used. Focus on changing the words and adding the details that will sound good to your listeners.

- Do any corrections need to be made to show the correct form of plurals and possessives?

Tyrone did a self-evaluation of his story about his surgery.

> "It is not the voice that commands the story: it is the ear."
> —*Italo Calvino*

Language, Grammar, and Style
Forming Plurals Correctly

IDENTIFYING PLURAL NOUNS AND POSSESSIVE NOUNS. Most nouns form their plurals by simply adding –*s* to the end of the word.

Singular	Plural
telephone	telephone**s**
computer	computer**s**
modem	modem**s**

The plurals of nouns that end in *o, s, x, z, ch,* or *sh* should be formed by adding –*es.*

Singular	Plural
potato	potatoes
bus	buses
fox	foxes
topaz	topazes
church	churches
rash	rashes

An exception to the rule above is that musical terms (and certain other words that end in *o*) are usually pluralized by adding –*s.*

continued on page 222

Singular	Plural
piano	pianos
solo	solos
radio	radios

Form the plurals of nouns that end in *y* following a vowel by adding *–s*.

boy + s = boys
valley + s = valleys
Monday + s = Mondays

Form the plurals of nouns that end in *y* following a consonant by changing the *y* to an *i* and adding *–es*.

city + s = cities
necessity + s = necessities
story + s = stories

USING POSSESSIVES CORRECTLY.
An apostrophe is used to form the possessive of nouns. To form the possessive of a singular noun, you should add an apostrophe and an *–s* to the end of the word.

The planet's moon can be seen in a telescope.

(planet + 's = planet's)

The girl's mother is in the hospital.

(girl + 's = girl's)

The possessive of a plural noun is formed two different ways. If the plural noun does not end in *–s*, you add an apostrophe and an *–s* to the end of the word. If the plural noun ends with an *–s*, add only an apostrophe.

The children's clothing department is upstairs.

(children + 's = children's)

I have three dollars' worth of change.

(dollars + ' = dollars')

Proofread your revised draft for errors in spelling, grammar, punctuation, capitalization, and other details. Be sure you have written the plural and possessive forms of nouns correctly.

Student Model—Revised

One Appendix is Enough

One Friday when I was only seven years old, I woke up and didn't feel well. My dad took me to my grandma's house instead of school for the day. All morning I lay on her couch and watched movies. At lunch I tried to get off the couch but I could hardly use my stomach muscles at all without feeling a searing pain in my side. I sat down at the table for lunch and couldn't even get close enough to my soup to eat any of it.

When I was back home my parents decided that they should take me to a doctor to see if there was anything seriously wrong. When I got to the emergency room the doctors ran a lot of tests on me. After an hour or so the doctor came in and said that there was either something wrong with my appendix or I had a bladder infection. Next the doctor put an I.V. in my left hand, and that so far was an even more painful thing. I guess it hurt more because it involved a needle, and because I knew, in advance, it would hurt.

I went into surgery late at night. All I can remember about the surgery is that the doctors put a mask over my mouth and told me, "This is just fresh air, Lisa. Now I want you to count to ten for me. Can you do that?" I said something like "1-2-5-3-6-4-7-9-8," if I even got that far! It seemed like just seconds and I woke up. The nurse was wheeling me into a hospital room, but I remember the electronic bed didn't work, so they put me into a different room. I also got a teddy bear from the hospital and that made me feel a lot better. The doctor said my appendix was rotting inside of me, so they took it out.

I think the next day I was up and slowly but surely I was able to walk more easily. I remember several unpleasant things happened while I was in the hospital. Once my I.V. came out and a nurse had to put it into my other arm. Another time, my parents had gone to get lunch and I was in my bed watching television. I stayed in the same position for a long time. Later, when I attempted to move, it was as though my muscles had just gone on strike! I got very frustrated because I wanted to move and I felt unable to do it. The most uncomfortable experience was the last night when I had to be moved into another room. The people I was in a room with weren't loud or anything, but I couldn't sleep very well that night. I felt nervous among strangers and maybe a little bit homesick. But I got over that and the next day I went home.

I had to sleep in our living room for a while because I couldn't walk upstairs to my bedroom yet without my side hurting a lot. One disappointing part was that a few days after I got home the infection that caused this whole ordeal started to drain out. Luckily, that didn't last long, and within months I was allowed to run again. I'm just glad I only have one appendix!

Publishing and Presenting

Rewrite your final copy in ink or print it from a computer. Create a cover that illustrates a part of your story. If you are writing about a natural or community disaster, you may be able to find pictures to cut out of old newspapers.

Stories are best when they are shared out loud with other students. Plan to meet in small groups and take turns reading your stories.

Identify the correct plural form of the nouns below.

womans	women
concertoes	concertos
brushs	brushes
spys	spies

Identify the correct singular possessive of the nouns below.

<u>Jacob's</u> homework   or
<u>Jacobs'</u> homework

The <u>stores'</u> window   or
The <u>store's</u> window

Identify the correct plural possessive of the nouns below.

<u>children's</u> concert   or
<u>childrens'</u> concert

<u>churches'</u> council   or
<u>church's</u> council

FIXING PLURAL AND POSSESSIVE NOUNS. Look at the sentences in Tyrone's rough draft. Fix any errors that you find in the plural and possessive forms of nouns. Then check to see how the writer fixed the errors in the final copy.

My dad brought me to my grandmas house for the day. Back home my parents' decided that they should take me to the hospital. All I can remember about the surgery is that the doctor's put a mask over my mouth and told me it was fresh air.

USING PLURAL AND POSSESSIVE NOUNS EFFECTIVELY. Examine each noun in your story. Check to see that there are no errors in the plural forms of the nouns or in the singular or plural possessive forms of the nouns in your story. Rewrite any nouns that are incorrect.

UNIT THREE *review*

Review: Words for Everyday Use

Check your knowledge of the following vocabulary words. Choose ten words that you would like to add to your own daily language. For each word, write a short sentence that includes the word in context. To review a word, look back to the page number(s) indicated.

- abrupt (156)
- anguish (193)
- anxious (191)
- arrogance (191)
- atmospheric (156)
- banish (189)
- belch (170)
- betray (188)
- bewilder (169)
- bicker (188)
- cache (157)
- catastrophe (168)
- compression (155)
- confide (190)
- congeal (156)
- consolidate (155)
- critical (168)
- dense (155)

- despair (192)
- dire (157)
- emigrant (186)
- engulf (166)
- erode (156)
- excavation (166)
- fiery (189)
- flail (212)
- fraud (188)
- fruitless (170)
- gaudy (173)
- gaunt (196)
- grim (193)
- haphazard (166)
- harbor (194)
- imposing (172)
- improviser (158)
- molten (168)

- monopoly (172)
- oblige (172)
- ominous (169)
- perpetual (188)
- project (168)
- provision (189)
- relinquish (189)
- remnant (193)
- rutted (171)
- shrewdness (170)
- shroud (166)
- smite (203)
- tranquility (170)
- trek (158)
- unruly (166)
- veer (212)
- vitality (167)

Review: Literary Tools

Define each of the following terms, giving concrete examples when possible. To review a term, refer to the page number(s) indicated.

- ballad (201)
- chronological order (163)
- description (153)
- dialogue (185)
- essay (163)

- figures of speech (210)
- historical fiction (185)
- mood (178)
- narrative poem (201)
- repetition (178)

- rhyme (178)
- setting (153)
- stanza (201)

Reflecting on your reading

Theme

Most selections in this unit are about disasters that occurred in history: the Antarctic voyage of the *Endurance,* the destruction of Pompeii, the Springhill Mine disaster, the wreck of the *Hesperus,* and the grueling and deadly journey of the Donner Party. Theodore Roethke's poem "Big Wind" describes a violent storm like the many that seriously affect communities from time to time. In each selection, people face horrifying situations and endure great hardship. If you were to write about a time in which you faced an extraordinary challenge or hardship, what would you write about?

Genre

There are many ways of retelling history. A popular genre is the epic poem or song. From about AD 1000 to 1300, troubadours traveled from one town to the next, singing songs and retelling stories of battles and adventures. In this way, people would learn history. Early American folk songs also recount tales that inform us of our heritage and history. Rhyming songs and poems are easy to remember, so they are good ways to learn facts. Make a list of other disasters that you can think of. Choose one of those events and write a short rhyming song or poem to describe it. Include details and facts in your song so that others can learn about the event.

Group Project

Get into groups of four or five students. Pretend that members of your group are among the Donner Party stuck crossing the mountain or part of the crew of Shackleton's frozen ship, the *Endurance.* What would you be experiencing right now? Write a group memoir reflecting on your thoughts and ideas that you might leave for others to find in case you don't make it.

Critical Thinking

In the accounts of these disasters, many people died, but many also survived. Some risked their own lives to save others. Ernest Shackleton, for example, was committed to keeping the spirits of his men strong. He was determined that not one of them would die, and none did. On the other hand, almost everyone in Pompeii died, but the wealth of information we have learned from that city is invaluable. Perhaps they did not die in vain. Their deaths had meaning, as did their lives. Review the selections in the unit. What did people learn from each disaster that could prevent similar disasters in the future?

The Fate of Animals, 1913. Franz Marc, Kunstmuseum, Basel, Germany.

Insights from Animals

echoes

Where is man without the beasts? If all the beasts were gone, man would die from a great loneliness of spirit.

—Chief Seattle

You think that these dogs will not be in Heaven! I tell you they will be there long before any of us.

—Robert Louis Stevenson

A Robin red breast in a cage
Puts all of heaven in a rage.
—William Blake

[Concern for animals] is a matter of taking the side of the weak against the strong, something the best people have always done.

—Harriet Beecher Stowe

Perhaps, in some way, I owe my gold medals to the dolphins. In their trusting and playful way, they taught me the subtleties of swimming technique.
—Olympic gold medalist Matt Biondi

The animals of the world exist for their own reasons. They were not made for humans any more than black people were made for whites, or women created for men.

—Alice Walker

Cats have the most beautiful moves of any animal. They never think about it—they simply do it. I watch my cat all the time. I love to study him. If I could run like a cat, I'd be the greatest runner in the world.
—Notre Dame halfback Eric Penick

If you will talk with the animals they will talk with you and you will know each other. If you do not talk to them, you will not know them, and what you do not know, you will fear. What one fears one destroys.
—Chief Dan George

We must never permit the voice of humanity within us to be silenced. It is humanity's sympathy with all creatures that first makes us truly human.
—Albert Schweitzer

Prereading

"My Friend Flicka"

by Mary O'Hara

Reader's Resource

- **SCIENCE CONNECTION.** The horse originated in North America about 50 million years ago. About 2.5 million years ago, ancestors of modern horses crossed the then-existing land bridge into Asia. Later the horse died out in North America and did not reappear until it was introduced by Spanish explorers in the 1500s.

- **HISTORY CONNECTION.** No one knows for certain when wild horses were first tamed, or domesticated. By 2000 BC, the Scythian peoples of Central Asia were riding horses and using both saddles and stirrups. The Scythians introduced the horse to ancient Greece, where riding and managing horses became a passion. Throughout the later history of Europe and Asia, horses were extremely important as draft animals, used to pull wagons, plows, and other burdens. Horses were also used for transportation, for sport, and in warfare. Herds of wild horses descended from domestic horses that escaped from their European owners. Some of these still exist in the American West. Many Native peoples of the American West, and particularly of the prairies, became accomplished riders of wild horses that they captured and trained. Training a wild horse to accept a rider is a difficult, demanding undertaking.

- For thousands of years, people have bred horses to meet particular needs. Such breeding resulted in three main types of horses: large, heavy draft horses like the Belgian; light saddle or riding horses like the Arabian and the Thoroughbred; and very small ponies like the Shetland. A male horse is a stallion; a female is a mare. Young horses are called foals. Male foals are called colts, and female foals are called fillies. A foal that has reached the age of one year is known as a yearling. The height of a horse is measured in units known as hands. A hand is equal to four inches.

Reader's Journal

If you could have any realistic wish come true, what would it be? What does this wish reveal about you?

Reader's TOOLBOX

CHARACTER. A **character** is a person (or sometimes an animal) who takes part in the action of a literary work. Major characters are ones who play important roles in a literary work. Minor characters are ones who play less important roles. The main character of a literary work is the protagonist. As you read this story, try to determine who the main character is and who the other major characters are.

SUSPENSE. Suspense is a feeling of anxiousness or curiosity. Writers create suspense by raising questions in the reader's mind and by using details that create strong emotions. Look for points in this story that are suspenseful.

My friend Flicka

Mary O'Hara

Report cards for the second semester[1] were sent out soon after school closed in mid-June.

Kennie's was a shock to the whole family.

"If I could have a colt all for my own," said Kennie, "I might do better."

Rob McLaughlin glared at his son. "Just as a matter of curiosity," he said, "how do you go about it to get a *zero* in an examination? Forty in arithmetic; seventeen in history! But a *zero*? Just as one man to another, what goes on in your head?"

"Yes, tell us how you do it, Ken," chirped Howard.

"Eat your breakfast, Howard," snapped his mother.

Kennie's blond head bent over his plate until his face was almost hidden. His cheeks burned.

---

1. **semester.** One half of a school year

McLaughlin finished his coffee and pushed his chair back. "You'll do an hour a day on your lessons all through the summer."

Nell McLaughlin saw Kennie wince as if something had actually hurt him.

GUIDED READING

Why does Kennie wince?

Lessons and study in the summertime, when the long winter was just over and there weren't hours enough in the day for all the things he wanted to do!

Kennie took things hard. His eyes turned to the wide-open window with a look almost of despair.

The hill opposite the house, covered with arrow-straight jack pines, was sharply etched in the thin air of the eight-thousand-foot altitude.[2] Where it fell away, <u>vivid</u> green grass ran up to meet it; and over <u>range</u> and upland poured the strong Wyoming sunlight that stung everything into burning color. A big jack rabbit[3] sat under one of the pines, waving his long ears back and forth.

Ken had to look at his plate and blink back tears before he could turn to his father and say carelessly, "Can I help you in the corral with the horses this morning, Dad?"

"You'll do your study every morning before you do anything else." And McLaughlin's scarred boots and heavy spurs clattered across the kitchen floor. "I'm disgusted with you. Come, Howard."

Howard strode after his father, nobly refraining from looking at Kennie.

"Help me with the dishes, Kennie," said Nell McLaughlin as she rose, tied on a big apron, and began to clear the table.

Kennie looked at her in despair. She poured steaming water into the dishpan and sent him for the soap powder.

"If I could have a colt," he muttered again.

"Now get busy with that dish towel, Ken. It's eight o'clock. You can study till nine and then go up to the corral. They'll still be there."

GUIDED READING

What does Kenny want?

At supper that night Kennie said, "But Dad, Howard had a colt all of his own when he was only eight. And he trained it and schooled it all himself; and now he's eleven, and Highboy is three, and he's riding him. I'm nine now, and even if you did give me a colt now I couldn't catch up to Howard, because I couldn't ride it till it was a three-year-old, and then I'd be twelve."

Nell laughed. "Nothing wrong with that arithmetic."

But Rob said, "Howard never gets less than seventy-five average at school and hasn't disgraced himself and his family by getting more demerits than any other boy in his class."

Kennie didn't answer. He couldn't figure it out. He tried hard; he spent hours <u>poring</u> over his books. That was supposed to get you good marks, but it never did. Everyone said he was bright. Why was it that when he studied he didn't learn? He had a vague feeling that perhaps he looked out the window too much, or looked through the walls to see clouds and sky and hills and wonder what was happening out there. Sometimes it wasn't even a wonder, but just a pleasant drifting feeling of nothing at all, as if nothing mattered, as if there was always plenty of time, as if the lessons

GUIDED READING

What seems to be Kennie's problem in school?

---

2. **altitude.** Height above sea level
3. **jack rabbit.** Large rabbit found in the western United States

---

words for everyday use	
de • spair (di spār') *n.*, lack of hope. *Although the odds were against her, Andrea did not feel <u>despair</u>.*
viv • id (viv' id) *adj.*, bright. *His shirt was a very <u>vivid</u> red until he washed it and it faded.*
range (rānj') *n.*, land for grazing cattle, sheep, or horses. *The stretch of <u>range</u> he bought was excellent land for grazing cattle.*
pore (pôr') *v.*, study thoroughly. *Jeannie <u>pored</u> over the new novel by her favorite author.*

would get done of themselves. And then the bell would ring, and study period was over.

If he had a colt . . . .

When the boys had gone to bed that night, Nell McLaughlin sat down with her overflowing mending basket and glanced at her husband.

He was at his desk as usual, working on account books and inventories.[4]

Nell threaded a darning needle and thought, "It's either that whacking big bill from the vet for the mare that died or the last half of the tax bill."

It didn't seem just the <u>auspicious</u> moment to plead Kennie's cause. But then, these days there was always a line between Rob's eyes and a harsh note in his voice.

"Rob," she began.

He flung down his pencil and turned around.

"Darn that law!" he exclaimed.

"What law?"

"The state law that puts high taxes on pedigreed[5] stock. I'll have to do as the rest of 'em do—drop the papers."

"Drop the papers! But you'll never get decent prices if you don't have registered horses."

"I don't get decent prices now."

"But you will someday if you don't drop the papers."

"Maybe." He bent again over the desk.

Rob, thought Nell, was a lot like Kennie himself. He set his heart. Oh, how stubbornly he set his heart on just some one thing he wanted above everything else. He had set his heart on horses and ranching way back when he had been a crack rider at West Point; and he had resigned and thrown away his army

GUIDED READING

In what ways is Kennie like his father?

If he had a colt . . . .

career just for the horses. Well, he'd got what he wanted . . . .

She drew a deep breath, snipped her thread, laid down the sock, and again looked across at her husband as she unrolled another length of darning cotton.

To get what you want is one thing, she was thinking. The three-thousand-acre ranch and the hundred head of horses. But to make it pay—for a dozen or more years they had been trying to make it pay. People said ranching hadn't paid since the beef barons[6] ran their herds on public land; people said the only <u>prosperous</u> ranchers in Wyoming were the dude ranchers; people said . . .

But suddenly she gave her head a little <u>rebellious</u>, gallant shake. Rob would always be fighting and struggling against something, like Kennie—perhaps like herself, too. Even those first years when there was no water piped into the house, when every day brought a new difficulty or danger, how she had loved it! How she still loved it!

She ran the darning ball into the toe of a sock, Kennie's sock. The length of it gave her a shock. Yes, the boys were growing up fast, and now Kennie— Kennie and the colt . . .

---

4. **inventories.** Lists of things belonging to a person
5. **pedigreed.** Known to be purebred
6. **beef barons.** Wealthy owners of large herds of cattle

words for everyday use

aus • pi • cious (äs pish' əs) *adj.,* favorable. *The farmers saw the rains as an <u>auspicious</u> sign of a successful growing season.*

pros • per • ous (präs' per əs) *adj.,* successful. *The market was <u>prosperous</u> because of its fair prices.*

re • bel • lious (ri bel' yəs) *adj.,* defiant. *My <u>rebellious</u> cousin never listens to her parents.*

After a while she said, "Give Kennie a colt, Rob."

"He doesn't deserve it." The answer was short. Rob pushed away his papers and took out his pipe.

"Howard's too far ahead of him, older and bigger and quicker, and has his wits about him, and—"

"Ken doesn't half try, doesn't stick at anything."

She put down her sewing. "He's crazy for a colt of his own. He hasn't had another idea in his head since you gave Highboy to Howard."

"I don't believe in bribing children to do their duty."

"Not a bribe." She hesitated.

"No? What would you call it?"

She tried to think it out. "I just have the feeling Ken isn't going to pull anything off, and"—her eyes sought Rob's— "it's time he did. It isn't the school marks alone, but I just don't want things to go on any longer with Ken never coming out at the right end of anything."

"I'm beginning to think he's just dumb."

"He's not dumb. Maybe a little thing like this—if he had a colt of his own, trained him, rode him—"

Rob interrupted. "But it isn't a little thing, nor an easy thing, to break and school a colt the way Howard has schooled Highboy. I'm not going to have a good horse spoiled by Ken's careless ways. He goes woolgathering.[7] He never knows what he's doing."

"But he'd *love* a colt of his own, Rob. If he could do it, it might make a big difference in him."

GUIDED READING

Why does Kennie's mother think he should have a colt of his own?

"*If* he could do it! But that's a big if."

At breakfast next morning Kennie's father said to him, "When you've done your study, come out to the barn. I'm going in the car up to section twenty-one this morning to look over the brood mares.[8] You can go with me."

"Can I go, too, Dad?" cried Howard.

McLaughlin frowned at Howard. "You turned Highboy out last evening with dirty legs."

Howard wriggled. "I groomed him—"

"Yes, down to his knees."

"He kicks."

"And whose fault is that? You don't get on his back again until I see his legs clean."

The two boys eyed each other, Kennie secretly <u>triumphant</u> and Howard <u>chagrined</u>. McLaughlin turned at the door. "And, Ken, a week from today I'll give you a colt. Between now and then you can decide what one you want."

Kennie shot out of his chair and stared at his father. "A—a spring colt, Dad, or a yearling?"

McLaughlin was somewhat taken aback, but his wife concealed a smile. If Kennie got a yearling colt, he would be even up with Howard.

"A yearling colt, your father means, Ken," she said smoothly. "Now hurry with your lessons. Howard will wipe."

Kennie found himself the most important <u>personage</u> on the ranch. <u>Prestige</u> lifted his head, gave him an inch more of height and a bold stare, and made him feel

GUIDED READING

How does Kennie feel about being able to decide which colt to choose?

---

7. **woolgathering.** Daydreaming
8. **brood mares.** Female horses used for breeding

---

words
for
everyday
use

tri • um • phant (trī um′ fənt) *adj.*, overjoyed with success. *The <u>triumphant</u> horse and rider pranced to the winner's circle.*

cha • grined (shə grind′) *adj.*, ashamed. *The child looked <u>chagrined</u> when his mother caught him taking cookies from the cookie jar before dinner.*

per • son • age (pər′ sən ij) *n.*, person of fame. *Such an important <u>personage</u> should realize that people expect her to be dignified.*

pres • tige (pres tēzh′) *n.*, reputation, fame. *Once elected, politicians have great responsibilities as well as <u>prestige</u> and power.*

different all the way through. Even Gus and Tim Murphy, the ranch hands, were more interested in Kennie's choice of a colt than anything else.

Howard was fidgety with suspense. "Who'll you pick, Ken? Say—pick Doughboy, why don't you? Then when he grows up he'll be sort of twins with mine, in his name anyway. Doughboy, Highboy, see?"

The boys were sitting on the worn wooden step of the door which led from the tack room[9] into the corral, busy with rags and polish, shining their bridles.

Ken looked at his brother with scorn. Doughboy would never have half of Highboy's speed.

"Lassie, then," suggested Howard. "She's black as ink, like mine. And she'll be fast—"

"Dad says Lassie'll never go over fifteen hands."

Nell McLaughlin saw the change in Kennie, and her hopes rose. He went to his books in the morning with determination and really studied. A new alertness took the place of the daydreaming. Examples in arithmetic were neatly written out, and as she passed his door before breakfast, she often heard the <u>monotonous</u> drone of his voice as he read his American history aloud.

Each night when he kissed her, he flung his arms around her and held her fiercely for a moment, then, with a <u>winsome</u> and blissful smile into her eyes, turned away to bed.

He spent days inspecting the different bands of horses and colts. He sat for hours on

Study for Fairman Rogers Four-in-Hand, c.1879.
Thomas Eakins. Hirshhorn Museum, Washington, DC.

the corral fence, very important, chewing straws. He rode off on one of the ponies for half the day, wandering through the mile-square pastures that ran down toward the Colorado border.

And when the week was up he announced his decision. "I'll take that yearling filly[10] of

---

9. **tack room.** Room for storage of horseback-riding equipment
10. **filly.** Young female horse

Rocket's. The sorrel[11] with the cream tail and mane."

His father looked at him in surprise. "The one that got tangled in the barbed wire? That's never been named?"

In a second all Kennie's new pride was gone. He hung his head defensively. "Yes."

"You've made a bad choice, son. You couldn't have picked a worse."

GUIDED READING

Why does Kennie hang his head? Why is his new pride gone?

"She's fast, Dad. And Rocket's fast—"

"It's the worst line of horses I've got. There's never one amongst them with real sense. The mares are hellions and the stallions outlaws; they're untamable."

"I'll tame her."

Rob <u>guffawed</u>. "Not I, nor anyone, has ever been able to really tame any one of them."

Kennie's chest heaved.

"Better change your mind, Ken. You want a horse that'll be a real friend to you, don't you?"

"Yes." Kennie's voice was unsteady.

"Well, you'll never make a friend of that filly. She's all cut and scarred up already with tearing through barbed wire after that mother of hers. No fence'll hold 'em—"

"I know," said Kennie, still more faintly.

"Change your mind?" asked Howard briskly.

"No."

Rob was grim and put out. He couldn't go back on his word. The boy had to have a reasonable amount of help in breaking and taming the filly, and he could <u>envision</u> precious hours, whole days, wasted in the struggle.

Nell McLaughlin despaired. Once again Ken seemed to have taken the wrong turn and was back where he had begun; <u>stoical</u>, silent, defensive.

But there was a difference that only Ken could know. The way he felt about his colt. The way his heart sang. The pride and joy that filled him so full that sometimes he hung his head so they wouldn't see it shining out of his eyes.

GUIDED READING

How does Kennie feel about the colt?

He had known from the very first that he would choose that particular yearling because he was in love with her.

The year before, he had been out working with Gus, the big Swedish ranch hand, on the irrigation ditch,[12] when they had noticed Rocket standing in a gully on the hillside, quiet for once and eyeing them cautiously.

"Ay bet she got a colt," said Gus, and they walked carefully up the draw. Rocket gave a wild snort, thrust her feet out, shook her head wickedly, then fled away. And as they reached the spot, they saw standing there the <u>wavering</u>, pinkish colt, barely able to keep its feet. It gave a little squeak and started after its mother on crooked, wobbling legs.

"Yee whiz! Luk at de little *flicka!*" said Gus.

"What does *flicka* mean, Gus?"

"Swedish for little gurl, Ken."

Ken announced at supper, "You said she'd never been named. I've named her. Her name is Flicka."

The first thing to do was to get her in. She was running with a band of yearlings on the saddleback,[13] cut with ravines and gullies, on section twenty.

---

11. **sorrel.** Horse that is light reddish-brown
12. **irrigation ditch.** Channel dug to carry water to crops planted in dry soil
13. **saddleback.** Ridge connecting two peaks

words for everyday use

guf • faw (gu fô′) v., laugh loudly and suddenly. *Craig <u>guffawed</u> loudly at the joke, although I did not think it was funny at all.*

en • vi • sion (en vizh′ ən) v., imagine. *Whenever Lucy was feeling stressed, she would <u>envision</u> herself on a warm sandy beach.*

sto • i • cal (stō i kəl) adj., showing no feeling. *With <u>stoical</u> determination, the injured football player insisted on continuing to play.*

wa • ver (wā′ vər) v., sway unsteadily. *The milk-carton boats <u>wavered</u> on the flowing water.* **wavering,** adj.

They all went out after her, Ken, as owner, on old Rob Roy, the wisest horse on the ranch.

Ken was <u>entranced</u> to watch Flicka when the wild band of youngsters discovered that they were being pursued and took off across the mountain. Footing made no difference to her. She floated across the ravines, always two lengths ahead of the others. Her pink mane and tail whipped in the wind. Her long, delicate legs had only to aim, it seemed, at a particular spot for her to reach it and sail on. She seemed to Ken a fairy horse.

GUIDED READING
What seems exceptional about Flicka?

He sat motionless, just watching and holding Rob Roy in, when his father thundered past on Sultan and shouted, "Well, what's the matter? Why didn't you turn 'em?"

Kennie woke up and galloped after.

Rob Roy brought in the whole band. The corral gates were closed, and an hour was spent shunting the ponies in and out and through the chutes, until Flicka was left alone in the small round corral in which the baby colts were branded.[14] Gus drove the others away, out the gate, and up the saddleback.

But Flicka did not intend to be left. She hurled herself against the poles which walled the corral. She tried to jump them. They were seven feet high. She caught her front feet over the top rung, clung, scrambled, while Kennie held his breath for fear the slender legs would be caught between the bars and snapped. Her hold broke; she fell over backward, rolled, screamed, tore around the corral. Kennie had a sick feeling in the pit of his stomach, and his father looked disgusted.

One of the bars broke. She hurled herself again. Another went. She saw the opening

"Her name is Flicka."

and, as neatly as a dog crawls through a fence, inserted her head and forefeet, scrambled through, and fled away, bleeding in a dozen places.

As Gus was coming back, just about to close the gate to the upper range, the sorrel whipped through it, sailed across the road and ditch with her <u>inimitable</u> floating leap, and went up the side of the saddleback like a jack rabbit.

From way up the mountain Gus heard excited whinnies as she joined the band he had just driven up, and the last he saw of them they were strung out along the crest, running like deer.

"Yee whiz!" said Gus, and stood motionless and staring until the ponies had disappeared over the ridge. Then he closed the gate, remounted Rob Roy, and rode back to the corral.

Rob McLaughlin gave Kennie one more chance to change his mind. "Last chance, son. Better pick a horse that you have some hope of riding one day. I'd have got rid of this whole line of stock if they weren't so fast that I've had the fool idea that someday there

---

14. **branded.** Marked on the hide with a hot iron shaped in the symbol of the ranch. Branding shows ownership of livestock and is done to prevent stealing.

---

words for everyday use

en • tranced (en transt') *adj.*, absorbed; filled with wonder. *Claire was so <u>entranced</u> with the novel she was reading at the beach that she did not even notice that it was beginning to rain.*

in • im • i • ta • ble (in im' i tə bəl) *adj.*, unique. *The artist had a certain <u>inimitable</u> quality that made her work much different than that of her contemporaries.*

might turn out one gentle one in the lot—and I'd have a racehorse. But there's never been one so far, and it's not going to be Flicka."

"It's not going to be Flicka," chanted Howard.

"Perhaps she *might* be gentled," said Kennie; and Nell, watching, saw that although his lips quivered, there was <u>fanatical</u> determination in his eye.

"Ken," said Rob, "it's up to you. If you say you want her, we'll get her. But she wouldn't be the first of that line to die rather than give in. They're beautiful, and they're fast, but let me tell you this, young man, they're *loco!*"[15]

Kennie flinched under his father's direct glance.

"If I go after her again, I'll not give up whatever comes; understand what I mean by that?"

"Yes."

"What do you say?"

"I want her."

They brought her in again. They had better luck this time. She jumped over the Dutch half door of the stable and crashed inside. The men slammed the upper half of the door shut, and she was caught.

The rest of the band was driven away, and Kennie stood outside of the stable, listening to the wild hoofs beating, the screams, the crashes. His Flicka inside there! He was drenched with perspiration.

"We'll leave her to think it over," said Rob when dinnertime came. "Afterward we'll go up and feed and water her."

But when they went up afterward, there was no Flicka in the barn. One of the windows, higher than the mangers, was broken.

GUIDED READING

What does Kennie's father mean when he says, "I'll not give up whatever comes"?

The window opened onto a pasture an eighth of a mile square, fenced in barbed wire six feet high. Near the stable stood a wagonload of hay. When they went around the back of the stable to see where Flicka had hidden herself, they found her between the stable and the hay wagon, eating.

At their approach she leaped away, then headed east across the pasture.

"If she's like her mother," said Rob, "she'll go right through the wire."

"Ay bet she'll go over," said Gus. "She yumps like a deer."

"No horse can jump that," said McLaughlin.

Kennie said nothing because he could not speak. It was, perhaps, the most terrible moment of his life. He watched Flicka racing toward the eastern wire.

A few yards from it she swerved, turned, and raced diagonally south.

"It turned her! It turned her!" cried Kennie, almost sobbing. It was the first sign of hope for Flicka. "Oh, Dad! She has got sense. She has! She has!"

Flicka turned again as she met the southern boundary of the pasture, again at the northern; she avoided the barn.

Without <u>abating</u> anything of her whirlwind speed, following a precise, accurate <u>calculation</u> and turning each time on a dime,[16] she investigated every possibility. Then, seeing that there was no hope, she raced south toward the range where she had spent her life, gathered herself, and shot into the air.

GUIDED READING

What is the first "sign of hope" for Flicka?

---

15. *loco.* (Spanish) Crazy, out of control
16. **on a dime.** In a small circle

---

words for everyday use

fa • nat • i • cal (fə nat′ ik əl) *adj.*, unreasonably enthusiastic or determined. *Samuel was so <u>fanatical</u> about cleaning his house that he seldom let guests inside to make it untidy.*

a • bate (ə bāt′) *v.*, decrease. *When the sea <u>abates</u> at low tide, we can look for seashells along the shore.*

cal • cu • la • tion (kal kyoo lā′ shən) *n.*, plan; estimate. *After a quick <u>calculation</u>, we determined we did not have enough money to take a taxi, so we took the bus instead.*

Each of the three men watching had the impulse to cover his eyes, and Kennie gave a sort of a howl of despair.

Twenty yards of fence came down with her as she hurled herself through. Caught on the upper strands, she turned a complete somersault, landing on her back, her four legs dragging the wires down on top of her, and tangling herself in them beyond hope of escape. . . .

Kennie followed the men miserably as they walked to the filly. They stood in a circle watching while she kicked and fought and thrashed until the wire was tightly wound and knotted about her, cutting, piercing, and tearing great three-cornered pieces of flesh and hide. At last she was unconscious, streams of blood running on her golden coat and pools of crimson widening and spreading on the grass beneath her.

With the wire cutter which Gus always carried in the hip pocket of his overalls, he cut all the wire away, and they drew her into the pasture, repaired the fence, placed hay, a box of oats, and a tub of water near her, and called it a day.

"I don't think she'll pull out of it," said McLaughlin.

Next morning Kennie was up at five, doing his lessons. At six he went out to Flicka.

She had not moved. Food and water were untouched. She was no longer bleeding, but the wounds were swollen and caked over.

Kennie got a bucket of fresh water and poured it over her mouth. Then he leaped away, for Flicka came to life, scrambled up, got her balance, and stood swaying.

Kennie went a few feet away and sat down to watch her. When he went in to breakfast she had drunk deeply of the water and was mouthing the oats.

There began then a sort of recovery. She ate, drank, limped about the pasture, stood for hours with hanging head and weakly splayed-out legs under the clump of cottonwood trees. The swollen wounds scabbed and began to heal.

Kennie lived in the pasture too. He followed her around; he talked to her. He, too, lay snoozing or sat under the cottonwoods; and often, coaxing her with hand outstretched, he walked very quietly toward her. But she would not let him come near her.

Often she stood with her head at the south fence, looking off to the mountain. It made the tears come to Kennie's eyes to see the way she longed to get away.

Still Rob said she wouldn't pull out of it. There was no use putting a halter on her. She had no strength.

One morning as Ken came out of the house, Gus met him and said, "De filly's down."

Kennie ran to the pasture, Howard close behind him. The right hind leg, which had

words for everyday use

im • pulse (im' puls) n., sudden wish or desire. *Janie had an impulse for fresh-squeezed orange juice.*

coax (kōks') v., try to persuade with a gentle manner. *Because Joe was shy about his talent, we usually needed to coax him to play the piano for us.*

been badly swollen at the knee joint, had opened in a festering[17] wound, and Flicka lay flat and motionless, with staring eyes.

"Don't you wish now you'd chosen Doughboy?" asked Howard.

"Go away!" shouted Ken.

Howard stood watching while Kennie sat down on the ground and took Flicka's head on his lap. Though she was conscious and moved a little, she did not struggle or seem frightened. Tears rolled down Kennie's cheeks as he talked to her and petted her. After a few moments Howard walked away.

"Mother, what do you do for an infection when it's a horse?" asked Kennie.

"Just what you'd do if it was a person. Wet dressings. I'll help you, Ken. We mustn't let those wounds close or scab over until they're clean. I'll make a poultice for that hind leg and help you put it on. Now that she'll let us get close to her, we can help her a lot."

"The thing to do is see that she eats," said Rob. "Keep up her strength."

But he himself would not go near her. "She won't pull out of it," he said. "I don't want to see her or think about her."

Kennie and his mother nursed the filly. The big poultice was bandaged on the hind leg. It drew out

GUIDED READING

Why doesn't Kennie's father want to go near Flicka?

much poisoned matter, and Flicka felt better and was able to stand again.

She watched for Kennie now and followed him like a dog, hopping on three legs, holding up the right hind leg with its huge knob of a bandage in comical fashion.

"Dad, Flicka's my friend now; she likes me," said Ken.

His father looked at him. "I'm glad of that, son. It's a fine thing to have a horse for a friend."

Kennie found a nicer place for her. In the lower pasture the brook ran over cool stones. There was a grassy bank the size of a corral, almost on a level with the water. Here she could lie softly, eat grass, drink fresh running water. From the grass a twenty-foot hill sloped up, crested with overhanging trees. She was <u>enclosed</u>, as it were, in a green open-air nursery.

Kennie carried her oats morning and evening. She would watch for him to come, eyes and ears pointed to the hill. And one evening, Ken, still some distance off, came to a stop, and a wide grin spread over his face. He had heard her nicker.[18] She had caught sight of him coming and was calling to him!

GUIDED READING

Why does Kennie grin?

He placed the box of oats under her nose, and she ate while he stood beside her, his hand smoothing the satin-soft skin under her mane. It had a nap as deep as plush.[19] He played with her long, cream-colored <u>tresses</u>, arranged her forelock neatly between her eyes. She was a bit dish faced, like an Arab,[20] with eyes set far apart. He lightly <u>groomed</u> and brushed her while she stood turning her head to him whichever way he went.

He spoiled her. Soon she would not step to the stream to drink but he must hold a bucket for her. And she would drink, then lift her dripping muzzle, rest it on the shoulder of his blue chambray shirt, her

---

17. **festering.** Infected
18. **nicker.** Whinny softly and repeatedly
19. **nap as deep as plush.** Like velvet
20. **Arab.** Breed of horse native to Arabia

---

en • close (en klōz') v., contain; shut in. *If we <u>enclose</u> the deck with glass, we will be able to sit out there all year round, not just in summer*

tress (tres') n., hair. *She brushed her black <u>tresses</u> until her hair shone.*

groom (grōōm') v., clean and comb. *To <u>groom</u> a horse, you need a hoof pick, a curry comb, and a brush.*

golden eyes dreaming off into the distance, then daintily dip her mouth and drink again.

When she turned her head to the south and pricked her ears and stood tense and listening, Ken knew she heard the other colts galloping on the upland.

"You'll go back there someday, Flicka," he whispered. "You'll be three, and I'll be eleven. You'll be so strong you won't know I'm on your back, and we'll fly like the wind. We'll stand on the very top where we can look over the whole world and smell the snow from the Neversummer Range. Maybe we'll see antelope. . . ."

This was the happiest month of Kennie's life.

GUIDED READING

Why is this "the happiest month of Kennie's life"?

With the morning, Flicka always had new strength and would hop three-legged up the hill to stand broadside to the early sun, as horses love to do.

The moment Ken woke he'd go to the window and see her there, and when he was dressed and at his table studying, he sat so that he could raise his head and see Flicka.

After breakfast she would be waiting for him and the box of oats at the gate, and for Nell McLaughlin with fresh bandages and buckets of <u>disinfectant</u>; and all three would go together to the brook, Flicka hopping along ahead of them as if she were leading the way.

But Rob McLaughlin would not look at her.

One day all the wounds were swollen again. Presently they opened one by one, and Kennie and his mother made more poultices.

Still the little filly climbed the hill in the early morning and ran about on three legs. Then she began to go down in flesh and almost overnight wasted away to nothing. Every rib showed; the glossy hide was dull

He spoiled her.

and brittle and was pulled over the skeleton as if she were a dead horse.

Gus said, "It's de fever. It burns up her flesh. If you could stop de fever she might get vell."

McLaughlin was standing in his window one morning and saw the little skeleton hopping about three-legged in the sunshine, and he said, "That's the end. I won't have a thing like that on my place."

Kennie had to understand that Flicka had not been getting well all this time; she had been slowly dying.

"She still eats her oats," he said mechanically.

GUIDED READING

What does Kennie have to understand?

They were all sorry for Ken. Nell McLaughlin stopped disinfecting and dressing the wounds. "It's no use, Ken," she said gently, "you know Flicka's going to die, don't you?"

"Yes, Mother."

Ken stopped eating. Howard said, "Ken doesn't eat anything any more. Don't he have to eat his dinner, Mother?"

But Nell answered, "Leave him alone."

Because the shooting of wounded animals is all in the day's work on the western plains, and sickening to everyone, Rob's voice, when he gave the order to have Flicka shot, was as

---

words for everyday use **dis • in • fect • ant** (dis in fec′ tənt) *n.*, substance that prevents infection. *Alice winced when her mother put <u>disinfectant</u> upon her scraped knee.*

flat as if he had been telling Gus to kill a chicken for dinner.

"Here's the Marlin, Gus. Pick out a time when Ken's not around and put the filly out of her misery."

Gus took the rifle. "*Ja*, boss. . . ."

Ever since Ken had known that Flicka was to be shot, he had kept his eye on the rack which held the firearms. His father allowed no firearms in the bunkhouse. The gun rack was in the dining room of the ranch house, and going through it to the kitchen three times a day for meals, Ken's eye scanned the weapons to make sure that they were all there.

GUIDED READING

Why does Ken keep an eye on the gun rack?

That night they were not all there. The Marlin rifle was missing.

When Kennie saw that, he stopped walking. He felt dizzy. He kept staring at the gun rack, telling himself that it surely was there—he counted again and again—he couldn't see clearly. . . .

Then he felt an arm across his shoulders and heard his father's voice.

"I know, son. Some things are awful hard to take. We just have to take 'em. I have to, too."

Kennie got hold of his father's hand and held on. It helped steady him.

Finally he looked up. Rob looked down and smiled at him and gave him a little shake and squeeze. Ken managed a smile too.

"All right now?"

"All right, Dad."

They walked in to supper together.

Ken even ate a little. But Nell looked thoughtfully at the ashen color of his face and at the little pulse that was beating in the side of his neck.

After supper he carried Flicka her oats, but he had to coax her, and she would only eat a little. She stood with her head hanging, but when he stroked it and talked to her, she pressed her face into his chest and was content.

He could feel the burning heat of her body. It didn't seem possible that anything so thin could be alive.

Presently Kennie saw Gus come into the pasture carrying the Marlin. When he saw Ken he changed his direction and <u>sauntered</u> along as if he was out to shoot some cottontails.

Ken ran to him. "When are you going to do it, Gus?"

"Ay was goin' down soon now, before it got dark. . . ."

"Gus, don't do it tonight. Wait till morning. Just one more night, Gus."

"Vell, in de morning den, but it got to be done, Ken. Yer fader gives de order."

"I know. I won't say anything more."

An hour after the family had gone to bed, Ken got up and put on his clothes. It was a warm, moonlit night. He ran down to the brook, calling softly. "Flicka! Flicka!"

But Flicka did not answer with a little nicker; and she was not in the nursery nor

words for everyday use

saun • ter (sôn′ tər) *v.,* walk slowly or casually. *It was a glorious spring day, so we <u>sauntered</u> about as if we hadn't a care in the world.*

hopping about the pasture. Ken hunted for an hour.

At last he found her down the creek, lying in the water. Her head had been on the bank, but as she lay there the current of the stream had sucked and pulled at her, and she had had no strength to resist; and little by little her head had slipped down, until when Ken got there only the muzzle was resting on the bank, and the body and legs were swinging in the stream.

Kennie slid into the water, sitting on the bank, and he hauled at her head. But she was heavy, and the current dragged like a weight; and he began to sob because he had no strength to draw her out.

Then he found a leverage for his heels against some rocks in the bed of the stream, and he braced himself against these and pulled with all his might; and her head came up onto his knees, and he held it cradled in his arms.

He was glad that she had died of her own accord, in the cool water, under the moon, instead of being shot by Gus. Then, putting his face close to hers and looking searchingly into her eyes, he saw that she was alive and looking back at him.

GUIDED READING

What does Ken think has happened to Flicka?

And then he burst out crying and hugged her and said, "Oh, my little Flicka, my little Flicka."

The long night passed.

The moon slid slowly across the heavens.

The water rippled over Kennie's legs and over Flicka's body. And gradually the heat and fever went out of her. And the cool running water washed and washed her wounds.

When Gus went down in the morning with the rifle they hadn't moved. There they were, Kennie sitting in water over his thighs and hips, with Flicka's head in his arms.

Gus seized Flicka by the head and hauled her out on the grassy bank and then, seeing that Kennie couldn't move, cold and stiff and half paralyzed as he was, lifted him in his arms and carried him to the house.

"Gus," said Ken through chattering teeth, "don't shoot her, Gus."

"It ain't fur me to say, Ken. You know dat."

"But the fever's left her, Gus."

"Ay wait a little, Ken. . . ."

Rob McLaughlin drove to Laramie to get the doctor, for Ken was in violent chills that would not stop. His mother had him in bed wrapped in hot blankets when they got back.

He looked at his father imploringly as the doctor shook down the thermometer.

"She might get well now, Dad. The fever's left her. It went out of her when the moon went down."

"All right, son. Don't worry. Gus'll feed her, morning and night, as long as she's—"

"As long as I can't do it," finished Kennie happily.

The doctor put the thermometer in his mouth and told him to keep it shut.

All day Gus went about his work, thinking of Flicka. He had not been back to look at her. He had been given no more orders. If she was alive, the order to shoot her was still in effect. But Kennie was ill, McLaughlin making his second trip to town, taking the doctor home, and would not be back till long after dark.

After their supper in the bunkhouse, Gus and Tim walked down to the brook. They did not speak as they approached the filly, lying stretched out flat on the grassy bank, but their eyes were straining at her to see if she was dead or alive.

She raised her head as they reached her.

"By the powers!" exclaimed Tim. "There she is!"

She dropped her head, raised it again, and moved her legs and became tense as if struggling to rise. But to do so she must use her right hind leg to brace herself against the earth. That was the damaged leg, and at the first bit of <u>pressure</u> with it she gave up and fell back.

"We'll swing her onto the other side," said Tim. "Then she can help herself."

"*Ja*...."

Standing behind her, they leaned over, grabbed hold of her left legs, front and back, and gently hauled her over. Flicka was as lax and willing as a puppy. But the moment she found herself lying on her right side, she began to scramble, braced herself with her good left leg, and tried to rise.

"Yee whiz!" said Gus. "She got plenty strength yet."

"Hi!" cheered Tim. "She's up!"

But Flicka wavered, slid down again, and lay flat. This time she gave notice that she would not try again by heaving a deep sigh and closing her eyes.

Gus took his pipe out of his mouth and thought it over. Orders or no orders, he would try to save the filly. Ken had gone too far to be let down.

GUIDED READING

Why does Gus decide to disobey McLaughlin's orders?

"Ay'm goin' to rig a blanket sling fur her, Tim, and get her on her feet and keep her up."

There was bright moonlight to work by. They brought down the posthole digger and set two aspen poles deep into the ground either side of the filly, then, with ropes attached to the blanket, hoisted her by a pulley.

Not at all disconcerted, she rested comfortably in the blanket under her belly, touched her feet on the ground, and reached for the bucket of water Gus held for her.

Kennie was sick a long time. He nearly died. But Flicka picked up. Every day Gus passed the word to Nell, who carried it to Ken. "She's cleaning up her oats." "She's out of the sling." "She bears a little weight on the bad leg."

Tim declared it was a real miracle. They argued about it, eating their supper.

"Na," said Gus. "It was de cold water, washin' de fever outa her. And more dan dat—it was Ken—you tink it don't count? All night dot boy sits dere and says, 'Hold on, Flicka, Ay'm here wid you. Ay'm standin' by, two of us togedder.'..."

Tim stared at Gus without answering, while he thought it over. In the silence a coyote yapped far off on the plains, and the wind made a rushing sound high up in the jack pines on the hill.

Gus filled his pipe.

"Sure," said Tim finally. "Sure. That's it."

Then came the day when Rob McLaughlin stood smiling at the foot of Kennie's bed and said, "Listen! Hear your friend?"

Ken listened and heard Flicka's high, eager whinny.

"She don't spend much time by the brook any more. She's up at the gate of the corral half the time, nickering for you."

"For me!"

Rob wrapped a blanket around the boy and carried him out to the corral gate.

Kennie gazed at Flicka. There was a look of marveling in his eyes. He felt as if he had been living in a world where everything was dreadful and hurting but awfully real; and *this* couldn't be real; this was all soft and happy, nothing to struggle over or worry about or fight for any more. Even his father was proud of him! He could feel it in the way Rob's big arms held him. It was all like a

words for everyday use   **pres • sure** (presh′ ər) *n.*, force pressing down. *When I sprained my ankle, it was painful at first to put any <u>pressure</u> on it.*

dream and far away. He couldn't, yet, get close to anything.

But Flicka—Flicka— alive, well, pressing up to him, recognizing him, nickering. . . .

Kennie put out a hand—weak and white— and laid it on her face. His thin little fingers straightened her forelock the way he used to do, while Rob looked at the two with a

GUIDED READING

Why does Ken feel as if he's in a dream?

strange expression about his mouth and a glow in his eyes that was not often there.

"She's still poor, Dad, but she's on four legs now."

"She's picking up."

Ken turned his face up, suddenly remembering. "Dad! She did get gentled, didn't she?"

"Gentle—as a kitten. . . ."

They put a cot down by the brook for Ken, and boy and filly got well together. ■

Respond *to the* SELECTION

What do you think saved Kennie? What helped Flicka survive?

About *the* AUTHOR

Mary O'Hara (1885–1980) was born in New Jersey and grew up in New York. After living in California and working as a screenwriter, she moved to Wyoming, where she wrote several works that became classics, including *My Friend Flicka*. That book began as a short story, but a magazine editor saw potential in it and urged O'Hara to expand the story into a full-length novel. As a novel, it became quite popular with both critics and readers. In the book, O'Hara describes the beautiful and wild Wyoming ranch land that was her home. Other books by Mary O'Hara include *Green Grass of Wyoming* and *Wyoming Summer*.

ABOUT THE RELATED READING (next page) ➤
Bruce Kiskaddon (1878–1950) wrote poems about life in the West. He described his friends and the way of life in the West, remaining true to the ranch and range realities of the time. His poems tell of cattle stampedes, horse roundups, neighborly get-togethers, and trips to the town.

The Gentle HOSS

Bruce Kiskaddon

Of all the things you come across,
　　the best one is a gentle hoss.
A man don't have to git a rope
　　and ketch him on the flyin' lope,
And mebby have to ear him down,
　　and git all shook and jerked around.
And mebbyso git kicked or throwed
　　before he gits the critter rode.

A gentle hoss is shore a pal.
　　You walk into the hoss corral,
You take yore bridle in yore hand
　　and he's so gentle that he'll stand.
He doesn't fight the bit aytall,
　　and when you put on the head stall,
He doesn't seem to have no fears.
　　He knows you won't rough up his ears.

He doesn't fret and fight and fuss,
　　like some ill tempered onery cuss.
He's with you all the long day through
　　to help with what you have to do.
And any time you rope and tie,
　　he'll hold the slack and shore stand by.
In case you're workin' on the ground,
　　jest drop the reins, he'll stick around.

Jest think the time and work he saves;
　　this gentle pony that behaves.
A cow boy mighty soon will find
　　he's worth three of the other kind.
He wants to work and do his share
　　and never quits you any where.
Of all the things you come across,
　　the best one is a gentle hoss. ■

Investigate, *Inquire,* and Imagine

Recall: GATHERING FACTS

1a. On what does Kennie have his heart set? Why does Ken's father not want to grant his wish?

2a. Who persuades Rob McLaughlin to give Ken a horse of his own?

3a. Which horse does Ken choose? How does his father feel about this choice? How does the filly act when she is put in the corral?

4a. How does Ken make the filly gentle? How does he save the filly from death?

→ Interpret: FINDING MEANING

1b. Do you think that Kennie's father is being reasonable in denying him this wish? Why, or why not?

2b. Why does this person believe that a horse will be good for Ken? How does Ken prove that this person is right?

3b. Why does Ken choose that filly? Why doesn't the filly's wild behavior make him change his mind about keeping her?

4b. Why does Ken's father finally change his mind about both Ken and the filly? In what way does he change?

Analyze: TAKING THINGS APART

5a. In what specific ways does Ken demonstrate that he is becoming more responsible?

→ Synthesize: BRINGING THINGS TOGETHER

5b. How does the filly become a factor in Ken's becoming more responsible? What does this story say about the value of owning and caring for animals?

Evaluate: MAKING JUDGMENTS

6a. Which person do you think is wiser in Kennie's parenting, Kennie's mother or his father? Why?

→ Extend: CONNECTING IDEAS

6b. What specific things do you tell yourself you will or will not do if and when you become a parent?

Understanding *Literature*

CHARACTER. A **character** is a person or animal who takes part in the action of a literary work. Major characters are ones who play important roles in a literary work. Minor characters are ones who play less important roles. A static character does not change. A dynamic character does change. Use the graphic organizer on the next page to determine which characters in the story are dynamic and which are static. Is there any pattern between the major and minor characters and the dynamic and static characters?

Graphic Organizer

Write the names of the main character and the major and minor characters in "My Friend Flicka." Then determine for each character whether he or she is static or dynamic.

Main character		
Major characters	Flicka	dynamic: wild at beginning of story; tame by the end
Minor characters	Tim	static

Writer's Journal

1. Write a **list** of chores that need to be done every day at the McLaughlins' horse ranch.

2. Think up **names** for colts that match the following descriptions: a high-spirited jet-black filly; a large, gallant, chestnut (gold) Arabian; a friendly pair of white Appaloosas.

3. Write a **true or false quiz**, along with answers, about the story "My Friend Flicka."

Skill Builders

Critical Thinking

DECISION MAKING. In "My Friend Flicka," the main characters face a variety of difficult decisions. Throughout your life, you will make important decisions. When making a decision, you often must weigh several factors. To do this, you may want to make a pro-con chart. Think of two things you have to decide between, and make a pro-con chart to see the reasons for and against deciding each way.

PROS AND CONS		
Painting Yearbook Illustration or Drawing It in Pencil		
	Painting	**Drawing in Pencil**
Pros	colorful	easier less expensive
Cons	more expensive more difficult	not colorful

Study and Research

LEARNING ABOUT COWBOY POETRY. Find out more about the history of cowboy poetry, cowboy poetry gatherings, and famous poets of the genre. Gather information, asking yourself *who, what, when, where, why,* and *how* questions about cowboy poetry. See the Language Arts Survey 2.14, "Questioning," for more information. Report your findings to your class. You may want to try looking on the Internet at the following sites—Western Folklife Center: Cowboy Poets on the Internet at http://www.westfolk.org/ and Voices of Youth: A Program of the Western Folklife Center at http://www.westernfolklife.org/voy/.

Prereading
"Rikki-tikki-tavi"

by Rudyard Kipling

Reader's Resource

- **SCIENCE CONNECTION.** This story features an Indian, or gray, mongoose. A small, short-legged animal, the mongoose belongs to the civet family and is found in Africa, Asia, and southern Europe. The mongoose has a pointed nose, small ears, and a long, furry tail. Rikki-tikki-tavi is a brave and determined mongoose who fights two deadly cobras. Courage is typical of the mongoose, which is known as a bold predator of poisonous snakes.

- **HISTORY CONNECTION.** In the late 1700s and early 1800s, the British East India Company, a powerful shipping and trading organization, took control of much of India. Then, in 1858, the administration of India was transferred to the British Crown. After World War I, Mohandas Gandhi led Indian citizens in a peaceful revolt against British authority. India finally won its independence from Britain in 1947.

Graphic Organizer

To help distinguish personification in the animal characters, fill in the chart below:

Character's Name	Type of Animal	Human Characteristics
Darzee	tailorbird	speaks; warns Rikki-tikki

Reader's Journal

Have you ever seen an animal commit a courageous act? Write about any unusual animal behavior you have seen.

Reader's TOOLBOX

PERSONIFICATION. **Personification** is a figure of speech in which something not human is described as if it were human. In "Rikki-tikki-tavi," the animal characters take on human characteristics. Find examples of this as you read.

CONFLICT. A **conflict** is a struggle between two people or things in a literary work. An external conflict is one that involves a character and some outside force. As you read this story, try to identify the external conflict.

Rikki-tikki-tavi

Rudyard Kipling

This is the story of the great war that Rikki-tikki-tavi fought single-handed, through the bathrooms of the big bungalow in Segowlee cantonment.[1] Darzee, the tailorbird, helped him, and Chuchundra, the muskrat, who never comes out into the middle of the floor, but always creeps round by the wall, gave him advice; but Rikki-tikki did the real fighting.

He was a mongoose, rather like a little cat in his fur and his tail, but

GUIDED READING

Who is the protagonist, or main character, in this story?

quite like a weasel in his head and his habits. His eyes and the end of his restless nose were pink; he could scratch himself anywhere he pleased, with any leg, front or back, that he chose to use; he could fluff up his tail till it looked like a bottle brush, and his war cry as he scuttled through the long grass, was: "*Rikk-tikk-tikki-tikki-tchk!*"

One day, a high summer flood washed him out of the burrow where

---

1. **Segowlee cantonment.** Living quarters for British troops in Segowlee, India

he lived with his father and mother, and carried him, kicking and clucking, down a roadside ditch. He found a little wisp of grass floating there, and clung to it till he lost his senses. When he revived, he was lying in the hot sun on the middle of a garden path, very draggled indeed, and a small boy was saying: "Here's a dead mongoose. Let's have a funeral."

"No," said his mother; "let's take him in and dry him. Perhaps he isn't really dead."

They took him into the house, and a big man picked him up between his finger and thumb and said he was not dead but half choked; so they wrapped him in cotton wool, and warmed him, and he opened his eyes and sneezed.

"Now," said the big man (he was an Englishman who had just moved into the bungalow); "don't frighten him, and we'll see what he'll do."

It is the hardest thing in the world to frighten a mongoose, because he is eaten up from nose to tail with curiosity. The motto of all the mongoose family is, "Run and find out"; and Rikki-tikki was a true mongoose. He looked at the cotton wool, decided that it was not good to eat, ran all round the table, sat up and put his fur in order, scratched himself, and jumped on the small boy's shoulder.

GUIDED READING

Why is it hard to frighten a mongoose?

"Don't be frightened, Teddy," said his father. "That's his way of making friends."

"Ouch! He's tickling under my chin," said Teddy.

Rikki-tikki looked down between the boy's collar and neck, snuffed at his ear, and climbed down to the floor, where he sat rubbing his nose.

GUIDED READING

How does Rikki-tikki act toward the humans?

"Good gracious," said Teddy's mother, "and that's a wild creature! I suppose he's so tame because we've been kind to him."

"All mongooses are like that," said her husband. "If Teddy doesn't pick him up by the tail, or try to put him in a cage, he'll run in and out of the house all day long. Let's give him something to eat."

They gave him a little piece of raw meat. Rikki-tikki liked it immensely, and when it was finished he went out into the veranda and sat in the sunshine and fluffed up his fur to make it dry to the roots. Then he felt better.

"There are more things to find out about in this house," he said to himself, "than all my family could find out in all their lives. I shall certainly stay and find out."

GUIDED READING

Why does the mongoose decide to stay?

He spent all that day roaming over the house. He nearly drowned himself in the bathtubs, put his nose into the ink on a writing table, and burned it on the end of the big man's cigar, for he climbed up in the big man's lap to see how writing was done. At nightfall he ran into Teddy's nursery to watch how kerosene lamps were lighted, and when Teddy went to bed Rikki-tikki climbed up too; but he was a restless companion, because he had to get up and attend to every noise all through the night, and find out what made it. Teddy's mother and father came in, the last thing, to look at their boy, and Rikki-tikki was awake on the pillow. "I don't like that," said Teddy's mother; "he may bite the child." "He'll do no such thing," said the father. "Teddy's safer with that little beast than if he had a bloodhound to watch him. If a snake came into the nursery now—"

But Teddy's mother wouldn't think of anything so awful.

Early in the morning Rikki-tikki came to early breakfast in the veranda riding on Teddy's shoulder, and they gave him banana and some boiled egg; and he sat on all their laps one after the other, because every well-brought-up mongoose always hopes to be a house mongoose some day and have rooms to run about in, and Rikki-tikki's mother (she used to live in the General's house at Segowlee) had carefully told Rikki what to do if ever he came across Englishmen.

Then Rikki-tikki went out into the garden to see what was to be seen. It was a large garden, only half cultivated, with bushes as big as summer houses of Marshal Niel roses, lime and orange trees, clumps of bamboos, and thickets of high grass. Rikki-tikki licked his lips. "This is a splendid hunting ground," he said, and his tail grew bottle-brushy at the thought of it, and he scuttled up and down the garden, snuffing here and there till he heard very sorrowful voices in a thornbush.

It was Darzee, the tailorbird, and his wife. They had made a beautiful nest by pulling two big leaves together and stitching them up the edges with fibers, and had filled the hollow with cotton and downy fluff. The nest swayed to and fro, as they sat on the rim and cried.

"What is the matter?" asked Rikki-tikki.

"We are very miserable," said Darzee.

"One of our babies fell out of the nest yesterday and Nag ate him."

"H'm!" said Rikki-tikki. "That is very sad—but I am a stranger here. Who is Nag?"

Darzee and his wife only cowered down in the nest without answering, for from the thick grass at the foot of the bush there came a low hiss—a horrid cold sound that made Rikki-tikki jump back two clear feet. Then inch by inch out of the grass rose up the head and spread hood of Nag, the big black cobra, and he was five feet long from tongue to tail. When he had lifted one third of himself clear of the ground, he stayed balancing to and fro exactly as a dandelion tuft balances in the wind, and he looked at Rikki-tikki with the wicked snake's eyes that never change their expression, whatever the snake may be thinking of.

"Who is Nag?" he said. "*I* am Nag. The great god Brahm[2] put his mark upon all our people when the first cobra spread his hood to keep the sun off Brahm as he slept. Look, and be afraid!"

He spread out his hood more than ever, and Rikki-tikki saw the spectacle mark on the back of it that looks exactly like the eye part of a hook-and-eye fastening. He was afraid for the minute; but it is impossible for a mongoose to stay frightened for any length of time, and though Rikki-tikki had never met a live cobra before, his mother had fed him on dead ones, and he knew that all a grown mongoose's business in life was to fight and eat snakes. Nag knew that too, and at the bottom of his cold heart he was afraid.

"Well," said Rikki-tikki, and his tail began to fluff up again, "marks or no marks, do you think it is right for you to eat fledglings out of a nest?"

Nag was thinking to himself and watching the least little movement in the grass behind Rikki-tikki. He knew that mongooses in the garden meant death sooner or later for him and his family; but he wanted to get Rikki-tikki off his guard. So he dropped his head a little, and put it on one side.

> **GUIDED READING**
> What is impossible for a mongoose?

> **GUIDED READING**
> What does Nag know about mongooses?

---

2. **Brahm.** Short for Brahma, the creator of the universe according to Hindu religion

---

words for everyday use

cul • ti • vate (kul' tə vāt') v., prepare for growing plants. *Dad cultivated a garden in our yard with plenty of room for your tomato plants.* **cultivated**, *adj.*

cow • er (kou' ər) v., shrink and tremble as from someone's anger, threats, or blows. *The mouse is sure to cower in the corner when it sees the large cat.*

"Let us talk," he said, "You eat eggs. Why should not I eat birds?"

"Behind you! Look behind you!" sang Darzee.

Rikki-tikki knew better than to waste time in staring. He jumped up in the air as high as he could go, and just under him whizzed by the head of Nagaina, Nag's wicked wife. She had crept up behind him as he was talking, to make an end of him; and he heard her savage hiss as the stroke missed. He came down almost across her back, and if he had been an old mongoose he would have known that then was the time to break her back with one bite; but he was afraid of the terrible lashing return stroke of the cobra. He bit, indeed, but did not bite long enough, and he jumped clear of the whisking tail, leaving Nagaina torn and angry.

GUIDED READING

What does Rikki-tikki do to Nagaina?

"Wicked, wicked Darzee!" said Nag, lashing up as high as he could reach toward the nest in the thornbush; but Darzee had built it out of reach of snakes; and it only swayed to and fro.

Rikki-tikki felt his eyes growing red and hot (when a mongoose's eyes grow red, he is angry), and he sat back on his tail and hind legs like a little kangaroo, and looked all around him, and chattered with rage. But Nag and Nagaina had disappeared into the grass. When a snake misses its stroke, it never says anything or gives any sign of what it means to do next. Rikki-tikki did not care to follow them, for he did not feel sure that he could manage two snakes at once. So he trotted off to the gravel path near the house, and sat down to think. It was a serious matter for him.

GUIDED READING

What is Rikki-tikki unsure about?

If you read the old books of natural history, you will find they say that when the mongoose fights the snake and happens to get bitten, he runs off and eats some herb that cures him. That is not true. The victory is only a matter of quickness of eye and quickness of foot—snake's blow against mongoose's jump—and as no eye can follow the motion of a snake's head when it strikes, that makes things much more wonderful than any magic herb. Rikki-tikki knew he was a young mongoose, and it made him all the more pleased to think that he had managed to escape a blow from behind. It gave him confidence in himself, and when Teddy came running down the path, Rikki-tikki was ready to be petted.

GUIDED READING

Why is Rikki-tikki pleased?

But just as Teddy was stooping, something flinched a little in the dust, and a tiny voice said: "Be careful. I am death!" It was Karait, the dusty brown snakeling that lies for choice on the dusty earth; and his bite is as dangerous as the cobra's. But he is so small that nobody thinks of him, and so he does the more harm to people.

Rikki-tikki's eyes grew red again, and he danced up to Karait with the peculiar rocking, swaying motion that he had inherited from his family. It looks very funny, but it is so perfectly balanced a gait that you can fly off from it at any angle you please; and in dealing with snakes this is an advantage. If Rikki-tikki had only known, he was doing a much more dangerous thing than fighting Nag, for Karait is so small, and can turn so quickly, that unless Rikki bit him close to the back of the head, he would get the return stroke in his eye or lip. But Rikki did not know; his eyes were all red, and he rocked back and forth, looking for a good place to hold. Karait struck out. Rikki jumped sideways and tried to run in, but the wicked little dusty gray head lashed within a fraction of his shoulder, and he had to jump over the body, and the head followed his heels close.

Teddy shouted to the house: "Oh, look here! Our mongoose is killing a snake"; and Rikki-tikki heard a scream from Teddy's mother. His father ran out with a stick, but by the time he came up, Karait had lunged out once too far, and Rikki-tikki had sprung, jumped on the snake's back, dropped his head far between his forelegs, bitten as high up the back as he could get hold, and rolled away. That bite paralyzed Karait, and Rikki-tikki was just going to eat him up from the tail, after the custom of his family at dinner, when he remembered that a full meal makes a slow mongoose, and if he wanted all his strength and quickness ready, he must keep himself thin.

GUIDED READING
Why doesn't Rikki-tikki eat Karait?

He went away for a dust bath under the castor-oil bushes, while Teddy's father beat the dead Karait. "What is the use of that?" thought Rikki-tikki. "I have settled it all"; and then Teddy's mother picked him up from the dust and hugged him, crying that he had saved Teddy from death, and Teddy's father said that he was a <u>providence</u>, and Teddy looked on with big scared eyes. Rikki-tikki was rather amused at all the fuss, which, of course, he did not understand.

GUIDED READING
What amuses Rikki-tikki?

Teddy's mother might just as well have petted Teddy for playing in the dust. Rikki was thoroughly enjoying himself.

That night, at dinner, walking to and fro among the wineglasses on the table, he could have stuffed himself three times over with nice things; but he remembered Nag and Nagaina, and though it was very pleasant to be patted and petted by Teddy's mother, and to sit on Teddy's shoulder, his eyes would get red from time to time, and he would go off into his long war cry of "*Rikktikk-tikki-tikki-tchk!*"

Teddy carried him off to bed, and insisted on Rikki-tikki sleeping under his chin. Rikki-

tikki was too well bred to bite or scratch, but as soon as Teddy was asleep he went off for his nightly walk round the house, and in the dark he ran up against Chuchundra, the muskrat, creeping round by the wall. Chuchundra is a brokenhearted little beast. He whimpers and cheeps all the night, trying to make up his mind to run into the middle of the room, but he never gets there.

"Don't kill me," said Chuchundra, almost weeping. "Rikki-tikki don't kill me."

"Do you think a snake-killer kills muskrats?" said Rikki-tikki scornfully.

"Those who kill snakes get killed by snakes," said Chuchundra, more sorrowfully than ever. "And how am I to be sure that Nag won't mistake me for you some dark night?"

GUIDED READING
What does Chuchundra say about snake killers?

"There's not the least danger," said Rikki-tikki; "but Nag is in the garden, and I know you don't go there."

"My cousin Chua, the rat, told me—" said Chuchundra, and then he stopped.

"Told you what?"

"H'sh! Nag is everywhere, Rikki-tikki. You should have talked to Chua in the garden."

"I didn't—so you must tell me. Quick, Chuchundra, or I'll bite you!"

Chuchundra sat down and cried till the tears rolled off his whiskers. "I am a very poor man," he sobbed. "I never had spirit enough to run out into the middle of the room. H'sh! I mustn't tell you anything. Can't you *hear*, Rikki-tikki?"

Rikki-tikki listened. The house was as still as still, but he thought he could just catch the faintest *scratch-scratch* in the world—a noise as

words for everyday use
prov • i • dence (präv′ ə dəns) *n.*, valuable gift, godsend. *The family felt that the much-needed rain after months of drought was a <u>providence</u>.*

faint as that of a wasp walking on a windowpane—the dry scratch of a snake's scales on brickwork.

"That's Nag or Nagaina," he said to himself; "and he is crawling into the bathroom <u>sluice</u>. You're right, Chuchundra; I should have talked to Chua."

He stole off to Teddy's bathroom, but there was nothing there, and then to Teddy's mother's bathroom. At the bottom of the smooth plaster wall there was a brick pulled out to make a sluice for the bath water, and as Rikki-tikki stole in by the masonry curb where the bath is put, he heard Nag and Nagaina whispering together outside in the moonlight.

"When the house is emptied of people," said Nagaina to her husband, "*he* will have to go away, and then the garden will be our own again. Go in quietly, and remember that the big man who killed Karait is the first one to bite. Then come out and tell me, and we will hunt for Rikki-tikki together."

"But are you sure that there is anything to be gained by killing the people?" said Nag.

"Everything. When there were no people in the bungalow, did we have any mongoose in the garden? So long as the bungalow is empty, we are king and queen of the garden; and remember that as soon as our eggs in the melon bed hatch (as they may tomorrow), our children will need room and quiet."

"I had not thought of that," said Nag. "I will go, but there is no need that we should hunt for Rikki-tikki afterward. I will kill the big man and his wife, and the child if I can, and come away quietly. Then the bungalow will be empty, and Rikki-tikki will go."

GUIDED READING

What are Nagaina and Nag planning to do?

words for everyday use

sluice (slōōs') *n.,* valve through which water is run. *Is the water coming out of the <u>sluice</u> clean and fresh?*

Rikki-tikki tingled all over with rage and hatred at this, and then Nag's head came through the sluice, and his five feet of cold body followed it. Angry as he was, Rikki-tikki was very frightened as he saw the size of the big cobra. Nag coiled himself up, raised his head, and looked into the bathroom in the dark, and Rikki could see his eyes glitter.

"Now, if I kill him here, Nagaina will know;—and if I fight him on the open floor the odds are in his favor. What am I to do?" said Rikki-tikki-tavi.

GUIDED READING

What question does Rikki-tikki consider?

Nag waved to and fro, and then Rikki-tikki heard him drinking from the biggest water jar that was used to fill the bath. "That is good," said the snake. "Now, when Karait was killed, the big man had a stick. He may have that stick still, but when he comes in to bathe in the morning he will not have a stick. I shall wait here till he comes. Nagaina—do you hear me?—I shall wait here in the cool till daytime."

There was no answer from outside, so Rikki-tikki knew Nagaina had gone away. Nag coiled himself down, coil by coil, round the bulge at the bottom of the waterjar, and Rikki-tikki stayed still as death. After an hour he began to move, muscle by muscle, toward the jar. Nag was asleep, and Rikki-tikki looked at his big back, wondering which would be the best place for a good hold. "If I don't break his back at the first jump," said Rikki, "he can still fight; and if he fights—O Rikki!" He looked at the thickness of the neck below the hood, but that was too much for him; and a bite near the tail would only make Nag savage.

"It must be the head," he said at last; "the head above the hood; and, when I am once there, I must not let go."

Then he jumped. The head was lying a little clear of the water jar, under the curve of it; and, as his teeth met, Rikki braced his back against the bulge of the red earthenware to hold down the head. This gave him just one second's purchase,[3] and he made the most of it. Then he was battered to and fro as a rat is shaken by a dog—to and fro on the floor, up and down, and round in great circles; but his eyes were red, and he held on as the body cartwhipped over the floor, upsetting the tin dipper and the soap dish and the fleshbrush, and banged against the tin side of the bath. As he held he closed his jaws tighter and tighter, for he made sure he would be banged to death, and, for the honor of his family, he preferred to be found with his teeth locked. He was dizzy, aching, and felt shaken to pieces when something went off like a thunderclap just behind him; a hot wind knocked him senseless and red fire singed his fur. The big man had been wakened by the noise, and had fired both barrels of a shotgun into Nag just behind the hood.

Rikki-tikki held on with his eyes shut, for now he was quite sure he was dead; but the head did not move, and the big man picked him up and

GUIDED READING

What happens to Nag?

said: "It's the mongoose again, Alice, the little chap has saved *our* lives now." Then Teddy's mother came in with a very white face, and saw what was left of Nag, and Rikki-tikki dragged himself to Teddy's bedroom and spent half the rest of the night shaking himself tenderly to find out whether he really was broken into forty pieces, as he fancied.

When morning came he was very stiff, but well pleased with his doings. "Now I have Nagaina to settle with, and she will be worse than five Nags, and there's no knowing when the eggs she spoke of will hatch. Goodness! I must go and see Darzee," he said.

Without waiting for breakfast, Rikki-tikki ran to the thornbush where Darzee was singing a song of triumph at the top of his voice. The news of Nag's death was all over

---

3. **purchase.** Firm hold

the garden, for the sweeper had thrown the body on the rubbish heap.

"Oh, you stupid tuft of feathers!" said Rikki-tikki, angrily. "Is this the time to sing?"

"Nag is dead—is dead—is dead!" sang Darzee. "The valiant Rikki-tikki caught him by the head and held fast. The big man brought the bang-stick and Nag fell in two pieces! He will never eat my babies again."

GUIDED READING
What does Darzee sing?

"All that's true enough; but where's Nagaina?" said Rikki-tikki, looking carefully round him.

"Nagaina came to the bathroom sluice and called for Nag," Darzee went on; "and Nag came out on the end of a stick—the sweeper picked him up on the end of a stick and threw him upon the rubbish heap. Let us sing about the great, the red-eyed Rikki-tikki!" and Darzee filled his throat and sang.

"If I could get up to your nest, I'd roll all your babies out!" said Rikki-tikki. "You don't know when to do the right thing at the right time. You're safe enough in your nest there, but it's war for me down here. Stop singing a minute, Darzee."

"For the great, the beautiful Rikki-tikki's sake, I will stop," said Darzee. "What is it, O Killer of the terrible Nag!"

"Where is Nagaina, for the third time?"

"On the rubbish heap by the stables, mourning for Nag. Great is Rikki-tikki with the white teeth."

"Bother my white teeth! Have you ever heard where she keeps her eggs?"

"In the melon bed, on the end nearest the wall, where the sun strikes nearly all day. She had them there weeks ago."

GUIDED READING
Where are Nagaina's eggs?

"And you never thought it worthwhile to tell me? The end nearest the wall, you said?"

"Rikki-tikki, you are not going to eat her eggs?"

"Not eat exactly; no. Darzee, if you have a grain of sense you will fly off to the stables and pretend that your wing is broken, and let Nagaina chase you away to this bush! I must get to the melon bed, and if I went there now she'd see me."

Darzee was a featherbrained little fellow who could never hold more than one idea at a time in his head; and just because he knew that Nagaina's children were born in eggs like his own, he didn't think at first that it was fair to kill them. But his wife was a sensible bird, and she knew that cobra's eggs meant young cobras later on; so she flew off from the nest, and left Darzee to keep the babies warm, and continue his song about the death of Nag. Darzee was very like a man in some ways.

GUIDED READING
Why does Darzee's wife agree to help Rikki-tikki?

She fluttered in front of Nagaina by the rubbish heap, and cried out, "Oh, my wing is broken! The boy in the house threw a stone at me and broke it." Then she fluttered more desperately than ever.

Nagaina lifted up her head and hissed, "You warned Rikki-tikki when I would have killed him. Indeed and truly, you've chosen a bad place to be lame in." And she moved toward Darzee's wife, slipping along over the dust.

"The boy broke it with a stone!" shrieked Darzee's wife.

"Well! It may be some consolation to you when you're dead to know that I shall settle accounts with the boy. My husband lies on the rubbish heap this morning, but before night the boy in the house will lie very still. What is the use of running away? I am sure to catch you. Little fool, look at me!"

Darzee's wife knew better than to do *that*, for a bird who looks at a snake's eyes gets so frightened that she cannot move. Darzee's wife fluttered on, piping sorrowfully, and never

GUIDED READING
What is Darzee's wife attempting to do?

leaving the ground, and Nagaina quickened her pace.

Rikki-tikki heard them going up the path from the stables, and he raced for the end of the melon patch near the wall. There, in the warm litter about the melons, very cunningly hidden, he found twenty-five eggs, about the size of a bantam's eggs, but with whitish skin instead of shell.

"I was not a day too soon," he said; for he could see the baby cobras curled up inside the skin, and he knew that the minute they were hatched they could each kill a man or a mongoose. He bit off the tops of the eggs as fast as he could, taking care to crush the young cobras, and turned over the litter from time to time to see whether he had missed any. At last there were only three eggs left, and Rikki-tikki began to chuckle to himself, when he heard Darzee's wife screaming:

"Rikki-tikki, I led Nagaina toward the house, and she has gone into the veranda, and—oh, come quickly—she means killing!"

Rikki-tikki smashed two eggs, and tumbled backward down the melon bed with the third egg in his mouth, and scuttled to the veranda as hard as he could put foot to the ground. Teddy and his mother and father were there at early breakfast; but Rikki-tikki saw that they were not eating anything. They sat stonestill, and their faces were white. Nagaina was coiled up on the matting by Teddy's chair, within easy striking distance of Teddy's bare leg, and she was swaying to and fro singing a song of triumph.

"Son of the big man that killed Nag," she hissed, "stay still. I am not ready yet. Wait a little. Keep very still, all you three. If you move I strike, and if you do not move I strike. Oh, foolish people, who killed my Nag!"

GUIDED READING

What does Rikki-tikki know about baby cobras?

GUIDED READING

Where is Nagaina? What danger does she pose?

Teddy's eyes were fixed on his father, and all his father could do was to whisper. "Sit still, Teddy. You mustn't move. Teddy, keep still."

Then Rikki-tikki came up and cried: "Turn round, Nagaina; turn and fight!"

"All in good time," said she, without moving her eyes. "I will settle my account with *you* presently. Look at your friends, Rikki-tikki. They are still and white; they are afraid. They dare not move, and if you come a step nearer I strike."

"Look at your eggs," said Rikki-tikki, "in the melon bed near the wall. Go and look, Nagaina."

The big snake turned half round, and saw the egg on the veranda. "Ah-h! Give it to me," she said.

Rikki-tikki put his paws one on each side of the egg, and his eyes were blood-red. "What price for a snake's egg? For a young cobra? For a young king cobra? For the last—the very last of the brood? The ants are eating all the others down by the melon bed."

Nagaina spun clear round, forgetting everything for the sake of the one egg; and Rikki-tikki saw Teddy's father shoot out a big hand, catch Teddy by the shoulder, and drag him across the little table with the teacups, safe and out of reach of Nagaina.

"Tricked! Tricked! Tricked! *Rikk-tck-tck!*" chuckled Rikki-tikki. "The boy is safe, and it was I—I—I that caught Nag by the hood last night in the bathroom." Then he began to jump up and down, all four feet together, his head close to the floor. "He threw me to and fro, but he could not shake me off. He was dead before the big man blew him in two. I did it. *Rikki-tikki-tck-tck!* Come then, Nagaina. Come and fight with me. You shall not be a widow long."

Nagaina saw that she had lost her chance of killing Teddy, and the egg lay between Rikki-tikki's paws. "Give me the egg, Rikki-

GUIDED READING

What does Rikki-tikki do to stop Nagaina?

tikki. Give me the last of my eggs, and I will go away and never come back," she said, lowering her hood.

"Yes, you will go away, and you will never come back; for you will go to the rubbish heap with Nag. Fight, widow! The big man has gone for his gun! Fight!"

GUIDED READING

What threat does Rikki-tikki make?

Rikki-tikki was bounding all round Nagaina, keeping just out of reach of her stroke, his little eyes like hot coals. Nagaina gathered herself together, and flung out at him. Rikki-tikki jumped up and backward. Again and again and again she struck, and each time her head came with a whack on the matting of the veranda and she gathered herself together like a watchspring. Then Rikki-tikki danced in a circle to get behind her, and Nagaina spun round to keep her head to his head, so that the rustle of her tail on the matting sounded like dry leaves blown along by the wind.

He had forgotten the egg. It still lay on the veranda, and Nagaina came nearer and nearer to it, till at last, while Rikki-tikki was drawing breath. She caught it in her mouth, turned to the veranda steps, and flew like an arrow down the path, with Rikki-tikki behind her. When the cobra runs for her life, she goes like a whiplash flicked across a horse's neck.

Rikki-tikki knew that he must catch her, or all the trouble would begin again. She headed straight for the long grass by the thornbush, and as he was running Rikki-tikki heard Darzee still

GUIDED READING

What does Rikki-tikki know?

singing his foolish little song of triumph. But Darzee's wife was wiser. She flew off her nest as Nagaina came along, and flapped her wings about Nagaina's head. If Darzee had helped they might have turned her; but Nagaina only lowered her hood and went on. Still, the instant's delay brought Rikki-tikki up to her, and as she plunged into the rat hole where she and Nag used to live, his little

white teeth were clenched on her tail, and he went down with her—and very few mongooses, however wise and old they may be, care to follow a cobra into its hole. It was dark in the hole; and Rikki-tikki never knew when it might open out and give Nagaina room to turn and strike at him. He held on savagely, and struck out his feet to act as brakes on the dark slope of the hot, moist earth.

Then the grass by the mouth of the hole stopped waving, and Darzee said: "It is all over with Rikki-tikki! We must sing his death song. Valiant Rikki-tikki is dead! For Nagaina will surely kill him underground."

So he sang a very mournful song that he made up all on the spur of the minute, and just as he got to the most touching part the grass quivered

GUIDED READING

What does Darzee assume will happen underground? What really happens?

again, and Rikki-tikki, covered with dirt, dragged himself out of the hole leg by leg, licking his whiskers. Darzee stopped with a little shout. Rikki-tikki shook some of the dust out of his fur and sneezed. "It is all over," he said. "The widow will never come out again." And the red ants that live between the grass stems

GUIDED READING

What happens underground?

heard him, and began to troop down one after another to see if he had spoken the truth.

Rikki-tikki curled himself up in the grass and slept where he was—slept and slept till it was late in the afternoon, for he had done a hard day's work.

"Now," he said, when he awoke, "I will go back to the house. Tell the Coppersmith, Darzee, and he will tell the garden that Nagaina is dead."

The Coppersmith is a bird who makes a noise exactly like the beating of a little hammer on a copper pot; and the reason he is always making it is because he is the town crier to every Indian garden, and tells all the news to everybody who cares to listen. As Rikki-tikki went up the path, he heard his "attention" notes like a tiny dinner gong; and then the steady "*Ding-dong-tock!* Nag is dead—*dong!* Nagaina is dead! *Ding-dong-tock!*" That set all the birds in the garden singing, and the frogs croaking; for Nag and Nagaina used to eat frogs as well as little birds.

GUIDED READING

What does Coppersmith do?

When Rikki got to the house, Teddy and Teddy's mother and Teddy's father came out and almost cried over him; and that night he ate all that was given him till he could eat no more, and went to bed on Teddy's shoulder, where Teddy's mother saw him when she came to look late at night.

"He saved our lives and Teddy's life," she said to her husband. "Just think, he saved all our lives."

Rikki-tikki woke up with a jump, for all the mongooses are light sleepers.

"Oh, it's you," said he. "What are you bothering for? All the cobras are dead; and if they weren't, I'm here."

Rikki-tikki had a right to be proud of himself; but he did not grow too proud, and he kept that garden as a mongoose should keep it, with tooth and jump and spring and bite, till never a cobra dared show its head inside the walls. ∎

GUIDED READING

How does Rikki-tikki keep the garden?

Respond *to the* SELECTION

Besides a mongoose, what animal would be useful to have around the house? Why?

About *the* AUTHOR

Rudyard Kipling (1865–1936) was born in India but educated in England. When he returned to India at the age of seventeen, Kipling worked as a journalist on a British newspaper. During this time, he began writing his first stories about life in India, stories that were to make him famous. "Rikki-tikki-tavi" is a story in one of Kipling's most popular works, *The Jungle Book*, his first collection of animal stories. Like the animal characters in "Rikki-tikki-tavi," the animals throughout *The Jungle Book* personify many human characteristics and teach readers about life experiences. In 1907, Kipling became the first English writer to be awarded the Nobel Prize for literature.

Investigate, Inquire, and Imagine

Recall: GATHERING FACTS

1a. What is the motto of the mongoose family?

2a. Who is Nag?

3a. What is the plan that Nag and Nagaina come up with to regain the garden as their territory?

4a. Who helps Rikki-tikki catch Nagaina?

Interpret: FINDING MEANING

1b. What does this motto tell you about Rikki-tikki?

2b. Why are Nag and Rikki-tikki enemies?

3b. Why would the plan get rid of Rikki-tikki?

4b. What makes Rikki-tikki particularly brave?

Analyze: TAKING THINGS APART

5a. Examine Rikki-tikki's words and actions. Which of these reveal something about his character?

Synthesize: BRINGING THINGS TOGETHER

5b. Why does Rikki-tikki fight Nag and Nagaina? How would you describe Rikki-tikki's character?

Perspective: LOOKING AT OTHER VIEWS

6a. Summarize this story from Nagaina's point of view.

Empathy: SEEING FROM INSIDE

6b. If you were Nagaina, would you have gone in the house to attack Teddy, or would you have left the garden with your children? Explain your answer.

Understanding Literature

PERSONIFICATION. Personification is a figure of speech in which something not human is described as if it were human. In "Rikki-tikki-tavi," the animal characters take on human characteristics. What human characteristics do they take on? How would this story be different if the animal characters displayed no human characteristics?

CONFLICT. A conflict is a struggle between two people or things in a literary work. An external conflict is one that involves a character and some outside force. Which character or characters are involved in the conflict in "Rikki-tikki-tavi"? What is that conflict?

Writer's Journal

1. Suppose Teddy's family could understand and communicate with Rikki-tikki. Create a **dialogue** in which Teddy, his mother, and his father thank Rikki-tikki for saving their lives. Include Rikki-tikki's responses.

2. Imagine you are Rikki-tikki, the mongoose. Send a **postcard** to your friends and family describing your experiences with Teddy and his family.

3. Pretend you are the author of this story and you want to change the title. Come up with three different **titles** for this story. Make sure your titles are creative so they catch the reader's eye.

Skill Builders

Language, Grammar, and Style

COMBINING SENTENCES. If you have several short sentences in a paragraph, your writing might sound choppy. It is very useful to know how to combine sentences that have the same main idea. Review the Language Arts Survey 3.34, "Combining and Expanding Sentences." Then revise the sentences below by combining them.

1. We thought that the mongoose was dangerous. It was really friendly.
2. The mongoose ran as fast as it could. It wanted to escape the snake.
3. The cobra was trying to scare the birds in the tree. The birds in the tree called out to the mongoose for help.
4. Do you prefer the mongoose? Do you prefer the cobra?
5. Cameron's pet monkey used to sleep only a few hours a day. Now he takes several naps throughout the day and sleeps through the night.

Study and Research & Media Literacy

RESEARCHING ANIMALS. Using your library's resources, research one of the animals from the story—the mongoose, cobra, tailorbird, or Coppersmith. Keeping track of the resources you use, try to find answers to the following questions:

- What is the animal's habitat? What does it eat? Where does it sleep? Does the animal sleep in the day or in the night?
- How much does the animal weigh? What is its lifespan? How many babies does it usually have at a time? What unique physical characteristics does the animal have?
- What behaviors are unique to the animal? With what other animals does it interact? What animals are its enemies or predators?

After you have answered these questions, evaluate the sources you used. Which source provided the most valuable information?

Prereading

"Zlateh the Goat"

by Isaac Bashevis Singer

Reader's Resource

Reader's Journal

Have you ever had a special relationship with an animal? What can you learn about yourself through a relationship with an animal?

- **CULTURAL CONNECTION.** Hanukkah is an eight-day Jewish festival celebrated in December. During Hanukkah, Jewish people remember the victory of the first Jews who fought to defend their religion against a Syrian king. The festival honors the 165 BC rededication of the Second Temple of Jerusalem that followed this victory. According to the Talmud, a Jewish text, there was only enough lamp oil to burn for one night during the rededication ceremony, but miraculously it lasted for eight nights. As a symbol of the small amount of oil burned in the temple for eight full days, a menora with nine candles, one extra used for lighting the other candles, is lit during Hanukkah. In addition to the lighting of candles, gifts are exchanged, and holiday games are played by children. A common Hanukkah game is *dreidel*. The game is played with a toy that revolves like a spinning top.

- **SCIENCE CONNECTION.** Goats are related to sheep. Male goats are called rams or billies. Female goats are called does or nannies, and young goats are called kids. Some goats are raised for meat or wool, but most goats are raised for their milk, which can also be used to make cheese. In very hot and very cold climates, goats are more useful for large-scale milk production than cows.

Reader's TOOLBOX

SENSORY DETAILS. Sensory details are words and phrases that describe how things look, sound, smell, taste, or feel. As you read "Zlateh the Goat," look for details that appeal to all of the five senses.

PLOT AND CLIMAX. A plot is a series of events related to a central conflict, or struggle. A plot usually involves the introduction of a conflict, its developments, and its eventual resolution. The **climax** of a story is the high point of interest or suspense in the story. Look for the climax as you read this story.

Graphic Organizer

You may want to use a story strip like the following to keep track of the sequence of events in "Zlateh the Goat." Use each box to draw a picture that represents each event in the story. Write a caption under each box.

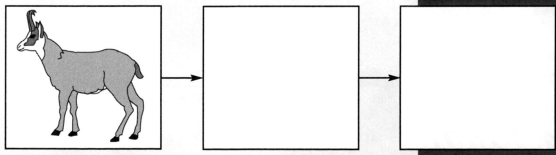

Reuven decides to sell Zlateh.

Illustration for *Zlahteh the Goat*, 1966. Maurice Sendak.

the Goat

Isaac Bashevis Singer

t Hanukkah time, the road from the village to the town is usually covered with snow, but this year the winter had been a mild one. Hanukkah had almost come, yet little snow had fallen. The sun shone most of the time. The peasants complained that because of the dry weather there would be a poor harvest of winter grain. New grass sprouted, and the peasants sent their cattle out to pasture.

For Reuven, the furrier,[1] it was a bad year, and after long hesitation he decided to sell Zlateh the goat. She was old and gave little milk. Feyvel, the town butcher, had offered eight gulden[2] for her. Such a sum would buy Hanukkah candles, potatoes and oil for pancakes, gifts for the children, and other holiday necessaries for the house. Reuven told his oldest boy, Aaron, to take the goat to town.

GUIDED READING

Why does Reuven plan to sell Zlateh?

Aaron understood what taking the goat to Feyvel meant, but he had to obey his father. Leah, his mother, wiped the tears from her eyes when she heard the news. Aaron's younger sisters, Anna and Miriam, cried loudly. Aaron put on his quilted jacket and a cap with earmuffs, bound a rope around Zlateh's neck, and took along two slices of bread with cheese to eat on the road. Aaron was supposed to deliver the goat by evening, spend the night at the butcher's, and return the next day with the money.

GUIDED READING

What is the family's reaction to Reuven's decision?

While the family said goodbye to the goat, and Aaron placed the rope around her neck, Zlateh stood as patiently and good-naturedly as ever. She licked Reuven's hand. She shook her small white beard. Zlateh trusted human beings. She knew that they always fed her and never did her any harm.

When Aaron brought her out on the road to town, she seemed somewhat astonished. She'd never been led in that direction before.

She looked back at him questioningly, as if to say, "Where are you taking me?" But after a while she seemed to come to the conclusion that a goat shouldn't ask questions. Still, the road was different. They passed new fields, pastures, and huts with thatched roofs. Here and there a dog barked and came running after them, but Aaron chased it away with his stick.

The sun was shining when Aaron left the village. Suddenly the weather changed. A large black cloud with a bluish center appeared in the east and spread itself rapidly over the sky. A cold wind blew in with it. The crows flew low, croaking. At first it looked as if it would rain, but instead it began to hail as in summer. It was early in the day, but it became dark as dusk. After a while, the hail turned to snow.

GUIDED READING

How does the weather change?

In his twelve years, Aaron had seen all kinds of weather, but he had never experienced a snow like this one. It was so dense it shut out the light of the day. In a short time their path was completely covered. The wind became as cold as ice. The road to town was narrow and winding. Aaron no longer knew where he was. He could not see through the snow. The cold soon penetrated his quilted jacket.

At first Zlateh didn't seem to mind the change in weather. She too was twelve years old and knew what winter meant. But when her legs sank deeper and deeper into the snow, she began to turn her head and look at Aaron in wonderment. Her mild eyes seemed to ask, "Why are we out in such a storm?" Aaron hoped that a peasant would come along with his cart, but no one passed by.

The snow grew thicker, falling to the ground in large, whirling flakes. Beneath it Aaron's boots touched the softness of a

---

1. **furrier.** Dealer in furs
2. **gulden.** Unit of money

plowed field. He realized that he was no longer on the road. He had gone astray. He could no longer figure out which was east or west, which way was the village, the town. The wind whistled, howled, whirled the snow about in <u>eddies</u>. It looked as if white imps[3] were playing tag on the fields. A white dust rose above the ground. Zlateh stopped. She could walk no longer. Stubbornly she anchored her <u>cleft</u> hooves in the earth and bleated[4] as if pleading to be taken home. Icicles hung from her white beard, and her horns were glazed with frost.

GUIDED READING

What happens to Aaron and Zlateh on the road?

Aaron did not want to admit the danger, but he knew just the same that if they did not find shelter, they would freeze to death. This was no ordinary storm. It was a mighty blizzard. The snowfall had reached his knees. His hands were numb, and he could no longer feel his toes. He choked when he breathed. His nose felt like wood, and he rubbed it with snow. Zlateh's bleating began to sound like crying. Those humans in whom she had so much confidence had dragged her into a trap. Aaron began to pray to God for himself and for the innocent animal.

GUIDED READING

What danger does the blizzard present?

Suddenly he made out the shape of a hill. He wondered what it could be. Who had piled snow into such a huge heap? He moved toward it, dragging Zlateh after him. When he came near it, he realized that it was a large haystack which the snow had blanketed.

Aaron realized immediately that they were saved. With great effort he dug his way through the snow. He was a village boy and knew what to do. When he reached the hay, he hollowed out a nest for himself and the goat. No matter how cold it may be outside, in the hay it is always warm. And hay was food for Zlateh. The moment she smelled it, she became contented and began to eat. Outside the snow continued to fall. It quickly covered the passageway Aaron had dug. But a boy and an animal need to breathe, and there was hardly any air in their hideout. Aaron bored a kind of a window through the hay and snow and carefully kept the passage clear.

GUIDED READING

What saves Aaron and Zlateh?

Zlateh, having eaten her fill, sat down on her hind legs and seemed to have regained her confidence in man. Aaron ate his two slices of bread and cheese, but after the difficult journey he was still hungry. He looked at Zlateh and noticed her udders were full. He lay down next to her, placing himself so that when he milked her, he could squirt the milk into his mouth. It was rich and sweet. Zlateh was not accustomed to being milked that way, but she did not resist. On the contrary, she seemed eager to reward Aaron for bringing her to a shelter whose very walls, floor, and ceiling were made of food.

Through the window Aaron could catch a glimpse of the chaos outside. The wind carried before it whole drifts of snow. It was completely dark, and he did not know whether night had already come or whether it was the darkness of the storm. Thank God

---

3. **imps.** Young demons
4. **bleated.** Made the cry of a goat or sheep

words for everyday use

eddy (ed′ ē) *n.*, whirlwind; whirlpool. *The rocks tumbled about in the swirling <u>eddy</u> of foaming water.*

cleft (kleft′) *adj.*, split; divided. *Sheila used the crevice in the <u>cleft</u> rock as a handhold while climbing.*

that in the hay it was not cold. The dried hay, grass, and field flowers exuded the warmth of the summer sun. Zlateh ate frequently; she nibbled from above, below, from the left and right. Her body gave forth an animal warmth, and Aaron cuddled up to her. He had always loved Zlateh, but now she was like a sister. He was alone, cut off from his family, and wanted to talk. He began to talk to Zlateh.

"Zlateh, what do you think about what has happened to us?" he asked.

"Maaaa," Zlateh answered.

"If we hadn't found this stack of hay, we would both be frozen stiff by now," Aaron said.

"Maaaa," was the goat's reply.

"If the snow keeps falling like this, we may have to stay here for days," Aaron explained.

"Maaaa," Zlateh bleated.

"What does 'Maaaa' mean?" Aaron asked. "You'd better speak up clearly."

"Maaaa. Maaaa," Zlateh tried.

"Well, let it be 'Maaaa' then," Aaron said patiently. "You can't speak, but I know you understand. I need you and you need me. Isn't that right?"

> **GUIDED READING**
> What one response does Zlateh give?

"Maaaa."

Aaron became sleepy. He made a pillow out of some hay, leaned his head on it, and dozed off. Zlateh too fell asleep.

When Aaron opened his eyes, he didn't know whether it was morning or night. The snow had blocked up his window. He tried to clear it, but when he had bored through to the length of his arm, he still hadn't reached the outside. Luckily he had his stick with him and was able to break through to the open air. It was still dark outside. The snow continued to fall and the wind wailed, first with one voice and then with many. Sometimes it had the sound of devilish laughter. Zlateh too awoke, and when Aaron greeted her, she answered, "Maaaa." Yes, Zlateh's language consisted of only one word, but it meant many things. Now she was saying, "We must accept all that God gives us—heat, cold, hunger, satisfaction, light, and darkness."

Aaron had awakened hungry. He had eaten up his food, but Zlateh had plenty of milk.

For three days Aaron and Zlateh stayed in the haystack. Aaron had always loved Zlateh, but in these three days he loved her more and more. She fed him with her milk and helped him keep warm. She comforted him with her patience. He told her many stories, and she always cocked her ears and listened. When he patted her, she licked his hand and his face. Then she said, "Maaaa," and he knew it meant, I love you too.

> **GUIDED READING**
> In what ways does Aaron take care of Zlateh in the haystack? In what ways does Zlateh take care of Aaron?

The snow fell for three days, though after the first day it was not as thick, and the wind quieted down. Sometimes Aaron felt that there could never have been a summer, that the snow had always fallen, ever since he could remember. He, Aaron, never had a father or mother or sisters. He was a snow child, born of the snow, and so was Zlateh. It was so quiet in the hay that his ears rang in the stillness. Aaron and Zlateh slept all night and a good part of the day. As for Aaron's dreams, they were all about warm weather. He dreamed of green fields, trees covered with blossoms, clear brooks, and singing birds. By the third night the snow had stopped, but Aaron did not dare to find his way home in the darkness. The sky became clear, and the moon shone, casting silvery nets on the snow. Aaron dug his way out and looked at the world. It was all white, quiet, dreaming dreams of heavenly splendor. The stars were large and close. The moon swam in the sky as in a sea.

> **GUIDED READING**
> What does it look like outside?

On the morning of the fourth day Aaron heard the ringing of sleigh bells. The haystack was not far from the road. The peasant who drove the sleigh pointed out the way to him— not to the town and Feyvel, the butcher, but home to the village. Aaron had decided in the haystack that he would never part with Zlateh.

Aaron's family and their neighbors had searched for the boy and the goat but had found no trace of them during the storm. They feared they were lost. Aaron's mother and sisters cried for him; his father remained silent and gloomy. Suddenly one of the neighbors came running to their house with the news that Aaron and Zlateh were coming up the road.

There was great joy in the family. Aaron told them how he had found the stack of hay and how Zlateh had fed him with her milk. Aaron's sisters kissed and hugged Zlateh and gave her a

> **GUIDED READING**
> How does the family greet Zlateh?

special treat of chopped carrots and potato peels, which Zlateh gobbled up hungrily.

Nobody ever again thought of selling Zlateh, and now that the cold weather had finally set in, the villagers needed the services of Reuven, the furrier, once more. When Hanukkah came, Aaron's mother was able to fry pancakes every evening, and Zlateh got her portion too. Even though Zlateh had her own pen, she often came to the kitchen, knocking on the door with her horns to indicate that she was ready to visit; and she was always admitted. In the evening Aaron, Miriam, and Anna played dreidel. Zlateh sat near the stove watching the children and the flickering of the Hanukkah candles.

Once in a while Aaron would ask her, "Zlateh, do you remember the three days we spent together?"

And Zlateh would scratch her neck with a horn, shake her white bearded head, and come out with the single sound which expressed all her thoughts, and all her love. ■

Respond *to the* SELECTION

Do you think Zlateh means different things when she says, "Maaaa"? Why, or why not?

About *the* AUTHOR

Isaac Bashevis Singer (1904–1991) wrote his novels and short stories in Yiddish, the language of his birthplace, Radzymin, Poland. Singer came from a family of rabbis and studied at a rabbinical seminary. He finally decided, however, on writing as a career and moved to the United States in 1935. Singer's folk stories are usually set in 19th-century *shtetls*, small Jewish villages in Poland. In 1978, Singer received the Nobel Prize in literature. His works include *The Manor*, *The Magician of Lublin*, *The Family Moskat*, and *Zlateh the Goat and Other Stories*.

Investigate, Inquire, and Imagine

Recall: GATHERING FACTS → **Interpret:** FINDING MEANING

1a. Why does Reuven decide to sell the goat to the butcher?

1b. Why do the other family members react strongly to this plan?

2a. How does Zlateh act around human beings?

2b. Why does she act this way?

3a. What stops Aaron and Zlateh from reaching town?

3b. How does Aaron feel about this? How does he feel when he finds the haystack?

4a. What decision does Aaron reach while staying in the haystack?

4b. Why does no one ever think of selling Zlateh again?

Analyze: TAKING THINGS APART → **Synthesize:** BRINGING THINGS TOGETHER

5a. In what ways does Zlateh assist Aaron during the time they spend in the haystack? In what ways does Aaron help Zlateh?

5b. Which of the two is most responsible for saving the other's life?

Perspective: LOOKING AT OTHER VIEWS → **Empathy:** SEEING FROM INSIDE

6a. Why does Aaron become so attached to the goat during the time they spend together in the haystack?

6b. If you experienced a life-threatening situation like this one and lived through it with an animal, how might you feel about animals in general afterwards?

Understanding *Literature*

SENSORY DETAILS. Sensory details are words and phrases that describe how things look, sound, smell, taste, or feel. Find at least one example of sensory details that appeal to each of the five senses, and write them on your own paper like shown.

Smell: _____ Sight: _____ Hearing: _____ Taste: _____ Touch: _____

PLOT AND CLIMAX. A **plot** is a series of events related to a central conflict, or struggle. A plot usually involves the introduction of a conflict, its developments, and its eventual resolution. The **climax** of a story is the high point of interest or suspense in the story. What is the conflict in this story? Identify the place in the story where the conflict is introduced. Then identify the climax, or high point of suspense. Lastly, identify the place in the story where the conflict is resolved.

Writer's Journal

1. Write an **advertisement** for a traditional food you eat with your family. Make use of sensory details to create an appetizing description of the food.

2. Imagine you are a reporter for the newspaper in the town near Aaron's house. Write a brief **article** about the blizzard and about how Aaron survived it.

3. Refer back to page 267. Pretend you are Zlateh, the goat, and that you can speak English. Finish the dialogue between Aaron and Zlateh (you) by writing your **response** to Aaron's questions and comments.

Skill Builders

Collaborative Learning

FINDING AND FOLLOWING A RECIPE. Ask your teacher to help you find a time you can use a kitchen area in your school. In small groups, search in your library or on the Internet for a recipe for potato pancakes. After finding a recipe, gather the necessary ingredients from home or from the supermarket. As a group, assign roles in preparing the pancakes. Work together to make sure you follow the recipe, cook the pancakes for the proper amount of time, and afterwards, clean up. Enjoy your potato pancakes! When you are finished in the kitchen, evaluate the recipe and your group's ability to follow it.

Speaking and Listening

ROLE-PLAYING A SCENE. Form groups of four or five. As a group, discuss what you think probably went on at Aaron's house while he and Zlateh were away. Imagine what Reuven (Aaron's father), Leah (Aaron's mother), and Anna and Miriam (Aaron's sisters) were saying and doing. Develop ideas for a scene that you could role-play as a group. If you have five people in your group, include a phone call to Feyvel the butcher, asking if he had seen Aaron. After some practice, role-play your scene for the class.

Prereading

"Shelter Shock"

by Elizabeth Hess

Reader's T O O L B O X

DESCRIPTION. A **description** gives a picture in words of a character, object, or scene. Descriptions make use of **sensory details**—words and phrases that describe how things look, sound, smell, taste, or feel. As you read "Shelter Shock," pay attention to the many sensory details that contribute to the descriptions of animals, workers, pet owners, rooms, and procedures. Notice which descriptions give you the most lifelike, complete picture.

TONE. Tone is a writer's or speaker's emotional attitude toward the subject or the reader. Examples of the different tones that a writer might create include angry, playful, sarcastic, serious, and sincere. As you read this selection, think about the emotional attitudes the author has about the animals and the shelter. What tone does she create by expressing her thoughts and feelings about what she is learning in the animal shelter? Fill out the graphic organizer below to help you identify the tone of this selection.

Graphic Organizer

Unusual facts and situations described by the author:	How the author thinks or feels about the fact or situation:	What tone is the author creating?
Shelter's efforts to check on the stability of the author's lifestyle	Thought it was a little excessive; almost put off; was amazed	Surprise
After time is up, animals are either put up for adoption or euthanized.		
Spotting the cardboard box sitting in a flower bed	Expects the worst; stands back a bit	Fear
Kittens under six weeks old are usually euthanized		

Reader's Journal

What do you think a person must be willing to do to be a good owner of a pet?

Reader's Resource

- The Humane Society of the United States (HSUS) was founded in 1954 to promote the humane treatment of animals and to foster respect, understanding, and compassion for all creatures. With nine regional offices and more than five million members, the HSUS is the nation's largest animal-protection organization.

- Besides the Humane Society, many other organizations and shelters exist around the country. Some organizations focus on caring for a specific breed of dog. Shelters range from pounds in large cities to small "no-kill" establishments that pledge not to put to sleep any animal they take in.

SHELTER SHOCK

Elizabeth Hess

The cramped office of the Columbia-Greene Humane Society is covered with cat hair. There are files, folders, messages written on scraps of paper, copies of forms, dog biscuits, and cat toys chaotically scattered all over the place. Hand-painted wooden silhouettes of cats frolic around the walls, carelessly suggesting that life is one big playground. A two-way radio, which looks like it barely survived World War II, sits on a desk near an antiquated[1] answering machine. The place is momentarily quiet. The only noise comes from a standing fan in the corner, as it circulates the sticky summer air as well as several large tufts of cat hair. Grace, a slender calico[2] who is a full-time resident here, is curled up in a ball on the copy machine. Pebbles, a gray-and-white longhair with a bushy striped tail and a mask across her face, has just slipped out the door for her morning stroll. These two cats run the front office.

Peace and quiet are rare <u>commodities</u> at Columbia-Greene. At eight in the morning, when the doors are not yet open, there is a sense of calm before the usual run of emergencies. The dog kennels are in the process of being scrubbed in a routine and laborious procedure that begins each day, seven days a week. Laura-Ann Cammisa, the director, is straightening up, annoyed at the mess that has been left from the previous evening. Smells of bleach and dog food mingle in the air.

When I first met Laura-Ann three years ago in the month of August, I was applying for a longhaired terrier mix who had been in the facility for almost two weeks. The dog, a shaggy, <u>bereft</u> creature as cute as could be,

> **GUIDED READING**
>
> What routine, laborious procedure begins each day at the Columbia-Greene Humane Society?

was to be a gift for my daughter. I was immediately informed that "live surprises" were a bad idea; I agreed to bring my daughter and husband to meet the dog. My next hurdle was a three-page application that asked a number of detailed questions about my attitude toward animals and required three personal references.[3] The shelter also wanted authorization to phone my veterinarian to find out if I had consistently cared for my previous pets. These people were being careful—very careful. I had to convince them that I was capable of taking care of this dog.

> **GUIDED READING**
>
> What does the narrator learn about giving an animal as a "live surprise"?

In the beginning, I thought Cammisa was a little excessive. I wasn't exactly put off by the adoption process, but I was amazed by the thoroughness of the shelter's efforts to check on the stability of my lifestyle. The director even phoned the head of the tenants' association[4] in my building in New York City when my landlord could not be reached (then or ever) and asked him if we were good neighbors. From Cammisa's point of view, my daughter was a little young to be getting a dog. Moreover, since I was not a full-time resident of Columbia County, Snowy would be commuting back and forth between the country and the city. I promised I wouldn't let the dog drive. Cammisa didn't laugh.

Weekenders, or "212's" as we are commonly called, are as <u>prevalent</u> as mosquitoes in the

---

1. **antiquated.** Being out of style; old
2. **calico.** Spotted animal with white, orange, and black patches.
3. **references.** People to whom inquiries as to character or ability can be made
4. **tenants' association.** An organization made up of people who rent living space

---

words for everyday use

com • mod • i • ty (kə mä′ də tē) n., something useful or valued. *In many countries, money is a valuable <u>commodity</u>.*

be • reft (bi reft′) adj., deprived or lacking something needed; wanting. *After the fire, we were <u>bereft</u> of our most cherished photographs.*

prev • a • lent (pre′ və lənt) adj., widespread; generally accepted or practiced. *The flu was <u>prevalent</u> in schools during the month of January.*

Hudson River Valley,[5] only a few hours north of New York City, and about as welcome, so far as some locals are concerned. Laura-Ann is not fond of commuters, despite the fact that she used to be one herself. When I first began volunteering at the shelter, I suggested to her that I might change her poor opinion of New Yorkers. She shot me a skeptical look. "Give it a few months and you'll see why I gave you a hard time with Snowy," she said, smirking. "The weekenders will begin abandoning their animals at the end of August, before they head back for the winter." I found this hard to believe. I had a lot to learn.

GUIDED READING

Why does Laura-Ann dislike commuters, or weekenders?

Laura-Ann Cammisa is not exactly what she appears. She is certainly not the kind of person one expects to meet in an animal shelter. This morning she is wearing a vintage Laura Ashley dress that ends at her calves and a white cardigan sweater that is covered with tiny white beads. A pair of plastic basset hounds dangles from her ears. Her waist-length hair falls down her back in perfect ringlets that look as if she slept all night in rollers. (She did.) With the exception of the dog earrings, Cammisa looks like she's dressed for lunch at the country club rather than a day of holding, chasing, or just hugging a wide variety of homeless animals. No one would ever guess that this prim, delicate woman is an unrelenting defender of animals.

Laura-Ann switches off the answering machine in the office. The first call of the day comes through like a bullet. She grabs the phone with a crisp gesture before it rings twice. It is a woman who lost her dog three days ago and has finally realized that Nevada is not coming home. The dog, as it turns out, has been a guest at the shelter for two days. He's the color of ripe cantaloupe and almost as big as a Saint Bernard;[6] a dark blue tongue hangs out of his mouth. The woman tells the director he's a purebred golden retriever purchased from a breeder for five hundred dollars.

When Laura-Ann reveals that Nevada is present and accounted for, the woman does not seem pleased. Their conversation starts to get heated as they spar back and forth about the shelter's procedures for releasing the dog. The director listens patiently to the woman's protests and asks her to wait a moment. Then she puts the caller on hold while she explains the situation to me, part of my training as a volunteer.

"The woman is demanding her dog back—right away," Cammisa begins. "But there's a problem. She doesn't want to pay the required fees to the shelter, and she doesn't feel like getting the dog a rabies shot and then a license, which are required by state law." The director has a knowing look on her face. "This is what we get all the time instead of 'Thanks for taking care of my dog.'"

Laura-Ann gets back on the phone and explains in an official tone that the shelter is legally obligated to follow certain protocol[7] before releasing stray dogs to their rightful owners. The state requires verification of a license and a minimum impoundment fee. (A rabies vaccination is a prerequisite[8] for a

---

5. **Hudson River Valley.** Area along the Hudson River that stretches from New York City to Albany, NY
6. **Saint Bernard.** Swiss alpine breed of tall, powerful working dogs
7. **protocol.** Set of rules
8. **prerequisite.** Requirement necessary in carrying out something

words for everyday use

skep • ti • cal (skep' ti kəl) adj., being doubtful or uncertain. My mom gave me a skeptical look when I told her I cleaned my room.
vin • tage (vin' tij) adj., being old-fashioned, dating from the past. The vintage store is filled with old clothes and shoes.
prim (prim') adj., stiffly formal and proper. The professor looked prim as he stood in his suit and tie.
un • re • len • ting (ən ri len' tiŋ) adj., not letting up or yielding in determination. Kirk's unrelenting strength drove him to finish the marathon race.

license.) But the woman could care less about these details. "I just want my dog!" she shouts into the phone.

Laura-Ann removes the receiver from her ear as the woman continues to blast her. "If you want your dog back," the director says sternly, "you

GUIDED READING

What legal requirements must the shelter meet before releasing stray dogs to their rightful owners?

have to pay ten dollars for a rabies shot, get an up-to-date license from a town clerk, and pay a ten-dollar impoundment fee. There's an additional ten-dollar charge if I have to transport your dog to a veterinarian's office for the shot. You have two more days to comply, or Nevada will be put up for adoption." Then, in a more <u>conciliatory</u> tone, she adds, "Why don't you start the process by coming in to identify the dog?" The woman reluctantly agrees, but doesn't know when she will be able to get to the shelter. Then she hangs up.

Laura-Ann is steaming. "This woman is looking for an excuse to get rid of her dog. So she's going to blame us for holding him and charging fees, as if we're purposely making it difficult for her to get him back. I guarantee you, if I give her a graceful way out, she will allow us to keep him and put the dog up for adoption. She doesn't want him."

Cammisa turns out to be absolutely right.

I quickly learn the state laws that govern most shelter policies. Stray animals in New York must be held for five days. After their stray time is up, they can either be put up for adoption or euthanized,[9] at the shelter's <u>discretion</u>. The animals go through an evaluation process that determines which road they take. The only exception to the five-day rule is New York City where, as a

result of an <u>inordinately</u> high volume of animals, strays are held for only two days. But stray time, whether two days or five, is appallingly short. Owners attempting to find lost pets must move quickly. Those who wait a week, hoping their dogs or cats will come home, often find out they have been put to sleep, a popular <u>euphemism</u> for

GUIDED READING

Why must owners attempting to find lost pets move quickly?

euthanasia. Small newspapers across the country are filled with poignant stories about angry pet owners who lose their animals to overburdened shelters simply because they did not get to a facility in time.

The oddest thing about this situation is that no one is searching for most of the strays. When I first go through the dog kennels and cat rooms, I cannot comprehend why the owners of all these lost animals have failed to locate them. It's no secret that strays frequently end up at the pound. When I begin to read through shelter files and track specific animals over time, it turns out that many of them have had numerous stray and

---

9. **euthanized.** Put to sleep

THE ANIMALS EITHER DISAPPEAR OR ARE GIVEN AWAY IN A VICIOUS CIRCLE THAT FREQUENTLY LEADS THEM TO A SHELTER.

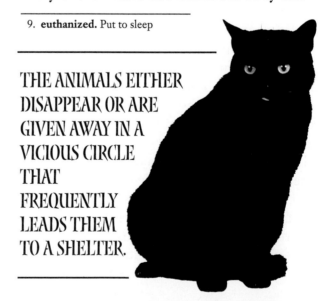

---

words for everyday use

con • cil • i • a • to • ry (kən sil′ ye tōr ē) *adj.,* friendly or agreeable. *Lisa was mad at first, but she become more <u>conciliatory</u>.*
dis • cre • tion (dis kre′ shən) *n.,* individual choice or judgment. *The teacher asked us to use <u>discretion</u> when choosing movies.*
in • or • di • nate (i nor′ dən ət) *adj.,* exceeding reasonable limits. *My dad cooked an <u>inordinate</u> amount of food during the family reunion.* **inordinately,** *adv.*
eu • phe • mism (yü′ fə mi zəm) *n.,* substitution of inoffensive expression for one that may be unpleasant. *The doctor did not want to scare his patient, so he spoke in <u>euphemisms</u>.*

owned chapters of their lives, passing from one set of hands to another. The animals either disappear or are given away in a vicious circle that frequently leads them to a shelter. The lucky ones make it back out again into long-term homes.

Assessing a person's attitude toward an animal is a critical piece of Laura-Ann's work. She lives in fear of placing dogs in homes where they will be chained outside twenty-four hours a day, which is the way many of them live in Columbia and Greene Counties. People here commonly treat dogs like livestock. Many of these dogs are so loyal that they learn to survive under the grimmest conditions, but this is not the case for all of them. Some slip their collars at every opportunity and arrive at the shelter in terrible condition, eager to shift their <u>allegiances</u>. They become enormously contented once they are treated with kindness and fed on a regular schedule. I come to realize that stray dogs and cats are sometimes not just running, but running away. I no longer view them as lost pets but as refugees looking for new identities and new homes. The shelter offers them a witness-protection program.

GUIDED READING

Why is assessing a person's attitude toward an animal a critical piece of Laura-Ann's work?

GUIDED READING

What does the narrator realize that stray dogs and cats are sometimes doing besides running?

Laura-Ann and I go into the back building where the strays are initially kept to take a peek at Nevada. The dog looks old, maybe eight or nine, walks with difficulty, and is covered with some kind of crusty rash. (This turns out to be severe dermatitis, an inflammation of the skin.) He's also much larger than the average retriever. The <u>affable</u> fellow arrived at the shelter dragging a four-foot chain around his neck. The chain, much too tight, had to be cut out of his hair and then clipped off with a wire cutter. "We'll find him a much better home than the one he came from," Laura-Ann assures me. That, I assume, will not be difficult.

GUIDED READING

What is the retriever named Nevada dragging from his neck?

Laura-Ann likes dogs but loves cats. She shares her home with five of the furry creatures (and two horses). When the director can't be found in her office, she is more likely to be in one of the cat rooms than <u>cavorting</u> with a dog in a kennel. Nevertheless, Cammisa has recently invited an old terrier named Nicholas to share the front office with Grace and Pebbles. When the dog, a stray, first arrived, he was aged at about six years old. A week later, he was recognized in the kennel by a friend of the family who had originally owned him. Nicholas was really Sparky. When Laura-Ann researched his vet records, she discovered that Nicholas was fourteen years old. He had been in one family his whole life. The old sweet dog was made King of the Pound—shelter mascot. St. Nick lies on the floor in front of the director's office, sleeping most of the day. He loves doughnuts.

GUIDED READING

Who becomes the shelter mascot?

Grace, the calico, pops into Cammisa's lap as she hits PLAY on the answering machine to check the morning's calls. As the messages start, Laura-Ann grabs the cat, kissing and hugging her to the point where Grace leaps out of her arms and runs away, her head covered with bright-red lipstick kisses.

words for everyday use

al • le • giance (ə lē′ jəns) *n.*, devotion or loyalty to a person or a cause. *Dogs are said to be "a man's best friend" because of their <u>allegiance</u> to their owner.*

af • fa • ble (a′ fə bəl) *adj.*, gracious, friendly. *The <u>affable</u> host greeted everyone with a warm smile.*

ca • vort (kə vort′) *v.*, prance or engage in extravagant behavior. *My brother began to <u>cavort</u> around the house when he got all As on his report card.*

Cammisa wants me to learn how to answer the phones and deal with the public. I have no idea how complicated these generally simple tasks can be in an animal shelter. "Take these down," she tells me as the messages spill out of the machine. I can barely <u>decipher</u> the words, but she is used to the rumble of muffled voices. The first call is from a hysterical woman in Ghent, a nearby town, with an uninvited flock of Canadian geese in her backyard; the geese are terrifying her children and French poodle. She is so upset that she fails to leave a return number. "There's not much you can do about geese, short of getting a Border collie,"[10] says Laura-Ann. "There's probably a pond in her backyard. They'll swim, rest, and when they're ready, continue on their way north."

The second call is from Dr. Johnson's office; two cats who were just spayed[11] are ready to be picked up. The third call is from a person reporting a dead dog by the side of the road; a fourth is from a landlord in Catskill, just across the river, complaining about a tenant breeding pit bulls in one of his apartments; the fifth is from a woman in Hudson reporting a vicious, <u>albeit</u> muzzled, German shepherd[12] wandering around her backyard. She sounds frightened and repeats her number twice.

There are more messages, but Laura-Ann suddenly tunes in to a faint sound of crying that seems to be coming from outside. The dogs are making so much noise in their kennels that it's difficult to hear anything through the barking. Laura-Ann turns off the phone machine so we can listen more carefully. The cries are real.

We go outside, and she immediately spots a cardboard box sitting in a flower bed to the right of the shelter door. I expect the worst, even stand back a little, as Laura-Ann rushes over and opens it up. Surprise packages are about as welcome here as a mink coat at a PETA demonstration. (PETA stands for People for the <u>Ethical</u> Treatment of Animals, the largest animal rights organization in the country.)

Inside the box there are nine tiny kittens, maybe one week old, all huddled together on a frayed red towel. Fleas are hopping all over them. The kittens are squealing for food, but there is no mother cat in sight. "Will they survive?" I ask Laura-Ann. "I doubt it," she answers <u>impassively</u>.

____

10. **Border collie.** Breed of medium-sized sheepdogs of British origin
11. **spayed.** Having underwent a procedure in which the ovaries of a female animal are removed
12. **German shepherd.** Breed of working dogs of German origin

> **GUIDED READING**
>
> What is the fourth call from a landlord in Catskill about?

---

words for everyday use

de • ci • pher (dē sī' fər) v., make out the meaning. *If you can <u>decipher</u> the riddle, you win the game!*
al • be • it (ol bē' ət) conj., even though. *Jeremy was happy, <u>albeit</u> tired, after the weekend hiking trip.*
e • thi • cal (e' thi kəl) adj., conforming to accepted practices of conduct. *The lawyer was <u>ethical</u> by being completely honest with his client.*
im • pas • sive (im pa' siv) adj., giving no sign of feeling or emotion. *Tari was <u>impassive</u> about her parents' decision to move.* **impassively,** adv.

The director picks up the box and takes it inside without saying a word. She already has about fifty cats and kittens in residence, which is not unusual in June. The Humane Society of the United States has made June "Adopt-a-Cat Month" because so many kittens are born in the spring. (According to HSUS, the average female cat hits puberty at around 10 months old and can have up to three litters a year. Over a period of seven years, one female cat and her offspring can produce 420,000 cats.) There are four other large litters in the shelter, which is already more kittens than Laura-Ann can put in her main adoption area. "If I fill the cat rooms with kittens, none of our adults will be chosen by adopters," she explains. But the more pressing problem is how this group is going to survive without their mother to nurse them.

GUIDED READING

Why did the Humane Society of the United States make June "Adopt-a-Cat Month"?

The staff is arriving, grabbing the phones as they sit down at their desks. There are three people in the front office, taking calls, accepting surrendered animals, and working on adoptions. A team of four part-time kennel workers cares for the <u>transient</u> population, which ranges from about 50 to 100 animals. At full capacity, the Hudson shelter can hold about 150 animals. While this is the main facility, there is a second smaller shelter across the river in Athens (Greene County), which usually has around 40 dogs and cats for the public to choose from. Space is always kept open for new arrivals in both shelters, which accept animals twenty-four hours a day; no animal is

GUIDED READING

What would happen if Laura-Ann filled the cat rooms with kittens?

ever turned away. This is the cornerstone of Columbia-Greene's philosophy on animal welfare. Cammisa explains that "people who don't want their animals either neglect them, give them away to inappropriate people, or chain them up in inhumane conditions." She lists these scenarios as if she has repeated them countless times before. "Shelters are the last resort," she adds.

GUIDED READING

What is the cornerstone of Columbia-Greene's philosophy on animal welfare?

Sometimes Cammisa sounds like an animal rights advocate, but she's not particularly sympathetic to their demands. She supports proactive legislative campaigns but does not engage in local protests against pigeon shoots or the scientific use of animals for research. One of the largest suppliers of laboratory rats and mice in the nation is a breeding facility near the shelter. It's of little concern to the director. She has her hands full taking care of the cats and dogs in the county.

Andrea Walker, the animal-care supervisor, is under twenty-five, has long blond hair, and often dresses in shorts and combat boots; there are no required staff uniforms—yet. Andrea brings the found box of kittens to the examination room. It is her job to examine all the incoming animals and assess their adoptability, which is to say, their health and <u>temperament</u>. After each cat is checked out, he or she is given a distemper[13] shot. Dogs are also vaccinated against parvo, a highly contagious, particularly nasty, and often fatal disease. The dogs and cats are treated for fleas, ear mites, and worms, which plague virtually every

GUIDED READING

What is Andrea Walker's job?

---

13. **distemper.** Highly contagious virus, especially seen in dogs and cats

---

words for everyday use

tran • si • ent (tran' sē ənt) *adj.,* passing quickly into and out of existence. *My uncle lives a <u>transient</u> lifestyle, traveling around the country and working odd jobs.*

tem • per • a • ment (tem' prə mənt) *n.,* distinguishing mental or physical character or quality. *A puppy's <u>temperament</u> is usually wild and rambunctious.*

incoming animal. Worms are especially hard to get rid of in a shelter environment. There are four common varieties—whip, round, hook, and tape—that can require different treatments. Even though the shelter administers three doses of Panacur, the broadest spectrum anthelmintic[14] available, the animals frequently pick up another bug during their stay at the shelter and bring it to their adoptive homes. At the moment, Walker is experimenting with a new Bordetella vaccine, which is supposed to protect the dogs from kennel cough. Upon receiving the dosage, administered through the nose, some of them are coming down with hacking coughs. It takes a few days before their <u>immune</u> systems kick in. Laura-Ann is afraid that the cough will turn off potential adopters, hindering the animals' chances of getting out.

Walker is one of those people born with an extraordinary ability to relate to animals. Not everyone in this line of work has this talent; some eventually acquire it. Walker, however, is a natural. She grew up locally in a close-knit family that included pets. "My parents were permissive," she says. "Our dogs were allowed on the beds." Within the first six months of Andrea's employment, her parents took home two dogs who were in danger of being put down. The first, Marmaduke, was a large, uncontrollable brown dog with some mastiff[15] in the mix, who was going cage-crazy. When Mr. Walker took Marmaduke out for a walk his first night home, the dog pulled him down onto the ground and ran away. Mr. Walker went to the emergency room with a shattered kneecap.

> **GUIDED READING**
>
> What happened within the first six months of Andrea's employment?

(Later that evening, Andrea found the dog.) A week later, Mrs. Walker harnessed herself to Marmaduke, her insurance against losing him, and went for a walk. The dog suddenly took off after a rabbit and Mrs. Walker fell. She was taken away in an ambulance with a bad concussion. The Walkers, undaunted, kept the dog, whom they adore. They even went back for another one. Basil, their second rescue, was a purebred basset hound with a nasty temper. "He's still a monster," adds Andrea. "But they love him." Walker never imagined herself in a career that would require her to scoop out dog kennels and learn how to inject animals with needles. She wanted to be a stage actress and had even landed a few choice roles in regional productions. But she could not have stumbled onto a more dramatic stage than an animal shelter. She came over one afternoon on a <u>fluke</u> to walk a few dogs—and never left.

This morning's kittens are too young for inoculations. Andrea explains that they won't survive without their mother. She checks to see if there's a nursing cat in the shelter; there are two, but they are busy feeding their own kittens. The other young mothers have been separated from their litters, so their milk is drying up. Still, Walker is determined to figure out some way to save this litter. She asks me to go outside and search the grounds, just in case the mother ran away in fear. "It's their only hope," she tells me.

I spend about twenty minutes looking around. It is a spectacular morning on Humane Society Road; the cows in the field

---

14. **anthelmintic.** Destroying parasitic worms especially in the intestine
15. **mastiff.** Any of a breed of large, powerful dogs often used as guard dogs

words for everyday use

im • mune (i myūn′) *adj.,* having a high degree to resistance to disease or illness. *My aunt is <u>immune</u> to chicken pox because she's had them before.*

fluke (flük′) *n.,* chance occurrence. *It was a <u>fluke</u> that we won the lottery.*

across from the shelter are grazing, and the road is lined with Queen Anne's lace, wild black-eyed Susans, and daisies. There's a red barn in the back and a small paddock[16] where two goats, Billy and Willy, are munching on their breakfast of grain. Billy, the older goat, has swirling horns that jut out of his forehead. Both were seized during cruelty investigations years ago; in exchange for not pressing charges, custody of the animals was given to the shelter—par for the course.[17]

GUIDED READING

How did the shelter get custody of the two goats named Billy and Willy?

There are several regular outside cats who eat at the shelter's kitchen door. Princess, an eight-year-old black-and-white long-hair, is exceptionally beautiful but not too friendly. Fred, an orange male, is completely antisocial. The shelter's outside cats were fixed[18] and released by a previous director; Cammisa doesn't approve of keeping "kitchen cats," as they're called. She feels they set a bad example for the public. The shelter recommends keeping cats inside—all the time—to prolong their lives and keep them from straying. Princess and Fred, however, look perfectly content lying in the sun, licking themselves. Pebbles, who is allowed outside, is another exception to this dictum.[19] A few lonely chickens, strays who became permanent residents, are marching around the animal cemetery, poking at the grass between the

THE SHELTER RECOMMENDS KEEPING CATS INSIDE—ALL THE TIME—TO PROLONG THEIR LIVES AND KEEP THEM FROM STRAYING.

headstones. The cemetery is available to the public to bury their animals, but it is so full that there is only room to put ashes in small plots.

The missing mother cat is nowhere to be seen. What if she is hiding in the woods? It's more likely that the person who dropped off this box kept the mother.

GUIDED READING

What is likely to have happened to the missing mother cat?

When I go back inside to give Walker the bad news, she is crushed. The kittens have been removed from their filthy box, and Andrea is washing the fleas off each of their tiny bodies. She has tried to place them in a cage with one of the lactating[20] mothers, but the cat rejected the orphans. The animal-care supervisor is pressed for time; there are eighteen new animals waiting for their incoming examinations, eight others who need their morning medications, and three cats who need to be transported to the vet for surgery. They've been adopted and are getting spayed or neutered[21] before they go home. There's no time to even begin hand-feeding the kittens. "Laura-Ann doesn't encourage us to keep them alive if there's no mother and they are too small to eat on their own," she says sadly. "Kittens under six weeks old are usually euthanized." It takes me a while to understand the consequences of this piece of reality for kittens in Columbia County.

GUIDED READING

What usually happens to kittens under six weeks old who arrive at the shelter with no mother and are too small to eat on their own?

During the summer, almost three hundred cats arrive each month, a figure that can rise or fall dramatically, depending on whether a

---

16. **paddock.** Enclosed area used for pasturing or exercising animals
17. **par for the course.** Not unusual; normal
18. **fixed.** Euphemism for neutered
19. **dictum.** Authoritative pronouncement of a principle or opinion
20. **lactating.** Secreting milk
21. **neutered.** Having underwent a procedure removing male sex organs

collector shows up. "Collectors," in shelter vernacular,[22] are not people who buy art. They are people who take in large numbers of homeless animals regardless of their ability to care for them. Most collectors are eventually turned in to the Humane Society by disgruntled neighbors or landlords when the noise or smell becomes intolerable. Caring for a population of animals is expensive; it's also a full-time job. Collectors usually can't afford to spay and neuter, so their homes become breeding colonies. There are several well-known collectors in Columbia County. When complaints periodically reach a critical mass, a humane officer will get a search warrant and go into their homes to take out the animals. After a bust, collectors frequently move to a new town, where they are unknown, and start collecting all over again. Investigators talk about "depopulating" the same collectors over and over. These cases are extreme, yet they seem to have created a general distrust of all pet owners at the shelter, which I don't quite understand. Again, I have a lot to learn.

"You have to see the most adorable litter that just came in," Walker tells me, lighting up at the very thought of these critters. She wants an excuse to visit with them and takes me into a <u>dilapidated</u> building called "Cat Boarding" that from the outside looks like an abandoned shed. The paint is peeling, the exterior kennels are rusting, and the windows look as if they might fall out of their frames any second. Inside, there's an ancient washer and dryer, several towering piles of frayed blankets, and a large tub used for bathing animals. In another open area, there's a collection of antiquated, jury-rigged[23] cages for about twenty to forty cats, depending on how many can bunk together. Entire litters are kept in the larger cages, while single adults have smaller spaces. The goal is to keep buddies together: the cats are happier, and the shelter can conserve space. There's always a new arrival coming up Humane Society Road.

This is the building where incoming cats initially live. Their first few days are key. The staff interacts with the cats, making notes that will seriously affect whether they live or die. Can they be handled? Do they have any long-term or short-term health problems? Are they making the necessary adjustments to survive shelter life? When a space opens up in the main adoption area, the cats are moved along, one by one, in a system that is geared to getting them out, either through the front door or the back.

The PTS ("put to sleep") rooms occupy an inconspicuous area on one side of the shelter. In one, euthanasia is performed on a table. Then the bodies are taken next door and put in a sealed cold room, where they are stored until they can be cremated. The furnace is in yet another room about ten feet away. This is not a place I visit for months.

Walker leads me directly to a cage filled with a large, stunning longhaired orange-and-white cat. She has almond-shaped green eyes, and she is unusually friendly for a nursing mother. Her four multicolored fur balls are contentedly sucking. "They're all Manxes," she says. "None of them have tails. They came in at about five weeks old, so we've been taking care of them for a few

GUIDED READING

What happens in the PTS rooms?

---

22. **vernacular.** Language relating to a particular group, region, or community
23. **jury-rigged.** Constructed in a makeshift fashion

weeks." The litter is so <u>diverse</u>, it's amazing they came from the same uterus; there's a tiger, a buff, an orange-and-white, and a tortie (orange-and-black). "Female cats can get caught by more than one male when they're in heat," Andrea explains. It's difficult to say how many fathers are in this mix. "Laura-Ann has a real weakness for orange cats," she adds, offering me a shelter secret. "Now these babies are eight weeks old and ready to be weaned. They're going into main adoption today. Probably go like hotcakes," she adds, like a proud mother.

We walk back to the office. Andrea reports to Laura-Ann that the "box-kittens" are not doing well and they need to see a vet. "Two cats are waiting to be picked up at Dr. Johnson's office," says the director. "Pick them up, and take the kittens with you." Andrea nods and disappears. I later learn they were too far gone to be saved and the vet euthanized them.

Just as Laura-Ann picks up the phone to make a call, two attractive men in their mid-thirties walk into the shelter. They seem upset. I can tell from their clothes—L. L. Bean and Eddie Bauer—that they are weekenders, probably up from New York. Bill Stone, a redhead, catches my eye and says, "I really feel terrible about this." Laura-Ann looks up from her desk and recognizes him

> **GUIDED READING**
> What is unusual about the bodies of Manx cats?

immediately. "Bill, what's the matter with Bandit?" (She remembers the name of virtually every animal she places.)

"Nothing is the matter with him," says Stone. "It's us."

"Are you bringing him back?"

Stone nods solemnly. They've had the dog for only one week. There is nothing more discouraging than an animal being returned, but this dog is coming back for the third time. Bandit looks like an adult, but he's only five months old. A dalmatian-Akita cross, he's white with a sprinkling of black spots across his thick, short fur. Bandit is the kind of dog that everyone falls in love with because he is so <u>gregarious</u>, but no one wants to bring home. He's huge. At five months, he weighs about eighty pounds. The dog was difficult to place because Akitas have nasty reputations for being animal-aggressive, although people-friendly, while dalmatians, now the flavor-of-the-week thanks to Walt Disney, frequently turn into biters. ("I would rather leave an infant in a room with a pit bull than a dalmatian," a veterinarian once told me.) Bandit's breed combination is not particularly desirable, but he looks like a large version of the RCA dog, which is in his favor. Moreover, his personality is <u>beguiling</u>, the reason he is still alive.

> **GUIDED READING**
> What does Laura-Ann remember about every animal she places?

---

words for everyday use

di • verse (dī vərs´) *adj.*, differing from one another. *The school is <u>diverse</u> because the student body represents many different countries.*

gre • gar • i • ous (gri gar´ ē əs) *adj.*, sociable; seeks companionship. *John has many friends because he is <u>gregarious</u>.*

be • guile (bi gīl´) *v.*, amuse or charm; delight. *The salesman was <u>beguiling</u> while trying to sell the car.* **beguiling,** *adj.*

"Phillip is allergic to the dog," Bill tells Laura-Ann. "He had no trouble until we gave Bandit a bath, but a half hour later he had an asthma attack." Bandit, ironically, is happy to be back, wagging his long tail and jumping up on the counter. But Cammisa looks miserable. The more a dog bounces back to the shelter, the harder it is to send him out again. Bill and Phillip are Bandit's fourth owners. Some dogs come back to the shelter and sink into depression; this is not Bandit's problem. The last time he was returned, he kept wagging his tail against the cement walls of his kennel so hard that his tail began to bleed. I soon learn this is a common problem for large exuberant dogs.

As Bill and Phillip leave, a young woman in a nurse's uniform comes rushing through the front door. "I've come to claim my dog," she tells me, frantic. She's late for work at Columbia Memorial Hospital, which is in Hudson, about five minutes from the shelter. "It's a cocker spaniel." I recall an overweight stray cocker sitting in the back kennel. "Is the dog a large blond female?' I ask. "Yes, how long have you had Candy?" I grab the paperwork to try to figure this out.

"How long has she been missing?"

"I just noticed she was gone this morning."

The dog has been at the shelter for four days. One more and she would have been legally available for adoption or euthanasia.

The woman has her act together. She gives me the dog's license, vet records, and enough cash to pay the boarding fees. While she fills out the appropriate forms, I go get Candy, a rolypoly, sweet little creature with a silky coat. When she wags her stubby tail, her entire body vibrates with delight. The dog might be neglected, but she's certainly well fed.

When I bring her out, Candy completely ignores her owner. It's hard to tell if the dog even knows her. But she does know her car and is frantic to jump in and go home.

Purebred cockers—in all colors—come in regularly to Columbia-Greene, usually because they have begun nipping at the youngest child in the household. If cockers were once considered to be one of the most child-friendly breeds, they are so no longer; these dogs have been vastly overbred in puppy mills, which produce the majority of purebred dogs. The term "puppy mill" describes a facility where dogs are bred for quantity, not quality, often in filthy conditions. Pet stores are stocked by these mills, largely because professional breeders would never allow their pups to be sold over-the-counter like shoes. In the animal world, where there is little consensus on most issues, there is general agreement among shelters, breeders, rescuers, and activists that puppy mills should be outlawed. Not only are breed lines ruined, but the dogs are often born with congenital[24] illnesses and poor temperaments. Million-dollar lawsuits over dog bites are not uncommon.

I begin to wonder if the nippy cockers and cranky terriers whom I meet at Columbia-Greene were produced in factorylike puppy mills. These smaller breeds, regardless of their personalities, get adopted first. But they

---

GUIDED READING
Why do Bill and Phillip have to return Bandit to the shelter?

GUIDED READING
Why do purebred cockers come in regularly to Columbia-Greene?

GUIDED READING
What does the term "puppy mill" describe?

---

24. **congenital.** Existing or dating from birth

---

words for everyday use

i • ron • ic (ī rä′ nik) adj., curious or surpising. *It was ironic that my dad wasn't mad when I told him I didn't do my chores.* **ironically,** adv.

ex • u • ber • ant (ig zü′ bə rənt) adj., joyously unrestrained and enthusiastic. *Tim let out an exuberant shout after throwing a touchdown pass.*

are far outnumbered by the larger Labrador and shepherd mixes who make up the bulk of the population. This week at Columbia-Greene, there are three adult black Labs and a litter of ten-week-old Lab mixes, a dime a dozen during the summer months. The pups are solid black and look about 90 percent pure. It's impossible to tell what breeds are in the mix when they're so young. There are three males, Picasso, Cezanne, and Mondrian, and one female, O'Keefe. Females are more popular largely because people incorrectly assume they're more <u>docile</u> and sweeter. O'Keefe is adopted her first day out.

GUIDED READING

Why are female dogs more popular?

All animals in the shelter get named, either when they arrive or at the moment of their incoming exam. The staff will change an animal's name if he or she arrives with one like Devil Dog or Killer. If the animals know their names, the shelter will attempt to find something that sounds similar. If a second Jake or Bear shows up, the newcomer becomes Smiling Bear or Teddy Bear; Jake turns into Jacques or Jacob. You can always count on finding a Bandit or a Lady in the house. One dog who came in named Budweiser became Buddy; a cat named Jerky became Jack; a dog named Stupid became Cupid. I have never met so many black dogs named Blackie or white cats named Casper.

Judging from the population in this shelter, Labradors and shepherds are spreading their seed faster than kudzu.[25] People who breed these dogs don't seem to have noticed the so-called "animal population crisis." But Laura-Ann has. She does not allow dogs, cats, or even rabbits to leave the shelter without

being sterilized. Rodents, including hamsters and gerbils, can also be a problem because some vets don't want to operate on them. They're just too small.

GUIDED READING

What is Laura-Ann doing about the "animal population crisis"?

When a local vet sterilizes a potbellied pig for the shelter, she tells Laura-Ann that she does not want to do the procedure again because it is too traumatic for the pigs. "Besides," she says, "they live indoors. They're not even kept outside." Laura-Ann explains that the pig she just neutered had been found stray, walking down the road.

Mary Grady bursts through the front door saying, "I know I'm early, but I just couldn't wait." She has an appointment to pick up her new dog, an Italian greyhound[26] named Elmo who is eight months old. The little gray dog has been in the shelter for five days. He was originally surrendered by Jim Cooper, who had purchased Elmo at a mall in nearby Albany. The Coopers just couldn't housebreak him or get him to eat. The dog arrived looking like a Giacometti[27] skeleton.

"Elmo has American Kennel Club papers that came with him at the pet store," Laura-Ann tells Grady. "Would you like to have a copy?"

"What would I use them for, toilet paper?" she responds <u>cynically</u>. Laura-Ann laughs. "People usually want these," she says, waving the certificate around over her

---

25. **kudzu.** Fast-growing Asian vine that is considered a weed in the United States
26. **Italian greyhound.** Breed of dogs resembling a small greyhound
27. **Giacometti.** Swiss sculptor and painter (1901–1966)

words for everyday use

do • cile (dä' səl) *adj.*, easily led or managed. *This dog is more <u>docile</u> than a sleeping baby.*

cyn • i • cal (si' ni kəl) *adj.*, having an attitude of distrust or pessimism. *My mom can be <u>cynical</u> towards doctors because she doesn't trust them.*

head like a flag. "Registering a litter is about as difficult as registering a car, " the director informs me, tossing the papers in the garbage. Cammisa thinks the American Kennel Club has promoted casual and rampant breeding; litters, regardless of their size, can be registered for the price of eighteen dollars. (Both parents must also be registered.) She considers breeders to be her worst enemies. She used to have a policy against allowing them to adopt from Columbia-Greene. But over the years she has lightened up. There are many different kinds of breeders, and some of them make outstanding pet owners. In

GUIDED READING

How has Camissa lightened up about breeders in recent years?

recent years a couple of them have even joined the board of directors.

Andrea walks in with Elmo in her arms. The dog is shaking. Every rib is visible. "I've been feeding him baby food with a spoon," she tells Grady. "He won't eat anything else."

Grady takes one look at this scrawny bundle and sighs with pleasure. She scoops Elmo up in her arms and says, "You have to rock them like babies. I've had a couple of them." A little cloud passes over Laura-Ann's face. "Did you give the others away?" the director casually inquires.

"I've had four husbands," Mary answers right away. "I got rid of each of them, but I'd never give up a dog!" Elmo is already licking her face. ∎

Respond *to the* SELECTION

What experiences have you had or seen that involve people adopting pets?

About *the* AUTHOR

Elizabeth Hess is a New York City arts critic and journalist. She has written for the *Village Voice* and the *Washington Post,* among other publications. Her most recent book, *Lost and Found: Dogs, Cats, and Everyday Heroes at a Country Animal Shelter,* is an eye-opening record of true events about a team of dedicated volunteers who fight for the lives of numerous castoff dogs, cats, rabbits, and even traumatized horses. This book was inspired when she and her daughter visited the rural animal shelter in upstate New York to adopt a dog. Hess was horrified at what she saw, so she decided to write a book about her experiences. Presently, she volunteers at the Colombia-Greene Humane Society and lives in New York City with her ten-year-old daughter; they are both dog lovers.

Purebred Husky male, $100, loves to run. Blue eyes. 1 year old. 555-1243

Beagle mix, great with kids, loves attention, 3 yrs old. Free to good home. 555-9732.

Dogs of all kinds want loving homes. Adopt a lifelong friend today. 555-2938.

Bulldo— ,200, 1 year owner r— 555-6578

Chocola— great with kids, loves kids, ve— to good home. 555-099—

Golden R— —ppies, only 3 left, shots, —55-3490.

Boxer pups —ixed. 1st. shots, wormed, extra —125.

German Shep— 2 years.

Bulldog, $200 owner mo—

Chocola— kids, very— 555-099—

Gold— left,

Cr— —er— b—

Choosing *a* DOG

Choosing a dog can be challenging. It can also be one of the most rewarding experiences of your life if you know what steps to follow. Your choice—wise or unwise—will affect you, your family, and the dog for years to come, so choose wisely. Here are some tips:

1. Know what you want. Would you like a dog small enough to curl up in your lap? Do you prefer Labrador Retrievers that love retrieving Frisbees for hours? Do you  want a dog that can keep up with you on long runs? Do you want a puppy or a grown dog? a purebred or a mixed breed? Remember that purebreds registered with the American Kennel Club can cost up to several hundred dollars. If owning a purebred isn't important to you, know what shelters and other sources charge for a dog.

2. Know what you can offer a dog. Do you have a large farm where a dog can run or a small apartment where you will need to take it for several walks a day? Is someone home all day to give a dog attention, or will you only be home at night and on weekends? Some dogs don't mind a small space with enough exercise. Others, like Huskies, feel best when they can run for miles every day. Some dogs don't mind being left to themselves for large parts of the day, but others whine, bark, or shred everything in sight while they wait for their owner to come home.

3. Research. Read dog books. Talk to dog owners, especially people who have dogs like the one you want. Find out what owning that particular dog has been like for them. What are the pros of having a dog like that? What are the cons?

4. Once you have decided on what kind of dog you are looking for, it's time to look for one that meets your requirements. Decide where you will and will not look in your search. Do you want to try animal shelters? Do you need to go through a breeder? Will a careful screening of the classified ads' pet section lead you to some good choices? The more you have done your homework in steps 1–3, the more likely you will avoid wasting your time searching.

5. Once you go to the source that has the dog, interview the seller. Why is the dog for sale? How long has the owner had it? How does the owner describe the dog? Observe how the dog and owner get along. If there are children or other people in contact with the dog, watch how the dog and people interact. Any fear or hostility on the dog's part spells trouble.

6. Mostly, see how the dog reacts around you. Here are several tests you should do:
   a. The health test. Does the dog look healthy? Is its coat shiny and soft? Are its eyes bright? Is its nose free of discharge? Are the insides of its ears pink and healthy? Does the dog scratch excessively, cough, or show signs of diarrhea or other ill health?
   b. The curiosity test. Stand behind the dog and drop a set of car keys. Does the dog come over to see what you dropped? Does it run and hide? Does it ignore the sound? A dog that shows interest  or curiosity is usually pretty smart. See if the dog comes when you call it. If it responds to your voice, you've got a great prospect. Walk away, still calling the dog. If the dog follows you, you've got an even better possibility.
   c. The socializing test. Pet the dog and let it get familiar with you. After a few minutes, gently have the dog lie down and turn it so it is belly up. A dog that cowers in this position may be too shy. A dog that fights you may be too aggressive. A dog that gently resists without fighting or cowering is a dog likely to listen to you since it is already showing trust.

If you've gotten this far and the dog you want has passed all of these tests, you're well on your way to being a happy dog owner. Proceed with caution—and good luck!

Investigate, Inquire, and Imagine

Recall: GATHERING FACTS

1a. What is the narrator doing at the Columbia-Greene Humane Society?

2a. Why does Laura-Ann Cammisa say she doesn't want to fill the cat room with kittens?

3a. How are time and space major considerations at an animal shelter?

→ **Interpret:** FINDING MEANING

1b. What does this tell you about the narrator?

2b. Why would people rather take kittens than adult cats?

3b. Why should pet owners know about these considerations?

Analyze: TAKING THINGS APART

4a. Identify situations in which the shelter operates strictly according to rules and guidelines. Identify situations in which the shelter is more flexible.

→ **Synthesize:** BRINGING THINGS TOGETHER

4b. How do you think shelters decide whether to be strict or flexible? Explain your answer.

Evaluate: MAKING JUDGMENTS

5a. How well does the narrator explain the operations of the Columbia-Greene Humane Society? Support your answer with evidence from the text. To what extent do you think the average person knows about the information given in this selection?

→ **Extend:** CONNECTING IDEAS

5b. According to Insights: Choosing a Dog, on pages 286–287, dashing out to get the first pet that strikes your fancy may not be the wisest approach. Write out a plan for how you would go about selecting your first (or next) pet.

Understanding Literature

DESCRIPTION. A **description** gives a picture in words of a character, object, or scene. Descriptions make use of **sensory details**—words and phrases that describe how things look, sound, smell, taste, or feel. Select one of the most complete descriptions in "Shelter Shock" and identify the sensory details that are used to create that description.

TONE. Tone is a writer's or speaker's emotional attitude toward the subject. Examples of the different tones that a writer might create include angry, playful, sarcastic, serious, and sincere. Looking back at the information in your graphic organizer, think about the overall tone used by Elizabeth Hess in this selection. In what ways does this tone relate to the title of the selection?

Writer's Journal

1. Create a new advertising **slogan** that the Humane Society of the United States might use to increase responsible pet ownership.

2. Imagine you are the owner of a missing cat. Write a **"Lost Cat" sign** to be posted in public places. Provide a full description of the cat, include information about how to contact you, and post a reward for its return.

3. Write a brief **newspaper editorial** giving your opinion about animal "collectors."

Skill Builders

Collaborative Learning & Speaking and Listening

DEBATE ON PUPPY MILLS. In pairs, prepare a debate on the pros and cons of puppy mills. One of you should play the role of a pet store owner who is strongly in favor of puppy mills because they are the most economical source of dogs you can find for your store. The other debater should take the role of a professional breeder who sees puppy mills only in their most negative light. Prior to debating, together find out some current information about how puppy mills and professional breeders operate. During the debate, keep the following points in mind:

- Listen actively when your partner is speaking. Maintain frequent eye contact, and think critically about whether you agree or disagree with what he or she is saying and why.
- Be polite. Wait your turn to speak, without interrupting.
- Stick to the topic.

For more information, see the Language Arts Survey 4.21, "Participating in a Debate."

Study and Research

LEGAL RESEARCH. Research how state laws affect the animal shelters in your state. Use the Internet and resources in your library. Call animal shelters and talk to the director or to his or her assistant. Find out what the shelter must do before releasing a stray to its rightful owner. Find out how many days strays must be kept before they can either be put up for adoption or euthanized. What other policies must be followed? If possible, find out what opinions the animal shelter owners have about these regulations. If they disagree with any of the laws, find out why and what laws they think would be more useful.

Language, Grammar, and Style

TYPES OF NOUNS. A **noun** is the name of a person, place, thing, or idea.

> **EXAMPLES** *Susannah* (person), *gymnasium* (place), *CD* (thing), *energy* (idea)

A **compound noun** is a noun made up of two or more words. Some compound nouns are written as one word, some as two words, and some as hyphenated words.

> **EXAMPLES** *bee-keeper, horseback, pool hall, lily pad, step-brother*

A **proper noun** names a specific person, place, or thing and begins with a capital letter.

> **EXAMPLES** *Charlie Brown, Mexico, New Year's Eve*

A **common noun** names any person, place, thing, or idea.

> **EXAMPLES** *boy, city, book, fear*

A **concrete noun** names a thing that can be touched, seen, heard, smelled, or tasted—something that can be perceived with any of your five senses.

> **EXAMPLES** *cornflower, apple pie, car horn, wind, coffee*

An **abstract noun** names an idea, a theory, a concept, or a feeling—something that cannot be touched or seen.

> **EXAMPLES** *perfection, history, fear*

On your own paper, list all the nouns in the following sentences. Tell whether each noun is common or proper. Then tell whether it is concrete or abstract. If a noun is compound, draw a line between its parts.

> **EXAMPLE** A two-way radio, which looks as if it barely survived World War II, sits on a desk near an antiquated answering machine.
> *radio:* common, concrete
> *World War II:* proper, abstract, compound (*World* | *War* | *II*)
> *desk:* concrete
> *answering machine:* concrete, compound (*answering* | *machine*)

1. The shelter also wanted authorization to phone my veterinarian to find out whether I had consistently cared for my previous pets.
2. The chain, much too tight, had to be cut out of his hair and then clipped off with a wire cutter.
3. People here commonly treat dogs like livestock.
4. The first call is from a hysterical woman in Ghent, a nearby town, with an uninvited flock of Canadian geese in her backyard.
5. This is the cornerstone of our philosophy on animal welfare.
6. Mr. Walker went to the emergency room with a shattered kneecap.
7. Basil, their second rescue, was a purebred basset hound with a nasty temper.
8. It is a spectacular morning on Humane Society Road.
9. Most collectors are eventually turned in to the Humane Society by disgruntled neighbors or landlords when the noise or smell becomes intolerable.
10. Some dogs come back to the shelter and sink into depression; this is not Bandit's problem.
11. Million-dollar lawsuits over dog bites are not uncommon.
12. Grady takes one look at this scrawny bundle and sighs with pleasure.

Prereading

"Cat on the Go"

by James Herriot

Reader's Resource

- **SCIENCE CONNECTION.** Surgery is a branch of medicine in which diseases and injuries are treated, often through cutting and sewing, using the hands and various instruments. In 1846 anesthetics were discovered, and major surgery became standard practice. Anesthetics are gases or other medications used to induce sleep and numb pain.

- In the late 1800s the French scientist Louis Pasteur developed the germ theory of disease. Pasteur showed that infections were caused by tiny creatures called bacteria. Building on the work of Pasteur, Joseph Lister developed ways to keep wounds from becoming infected by cleaning them and sterilizing them to kill bacteria. Bacteria-free dressings, instruments, hands, and wounds are said to be antiseptic. Anesthetics and antiseptic methods made modern surgery possible.

- Today surgeons routinely perform operations that would have seemed like miracles in earlier days, repairing and even replacing major organs of the body. Even veterinarians are able to practice sophisticated procedures that 100 years ago were unavailable to humans.

Graphic Organizer

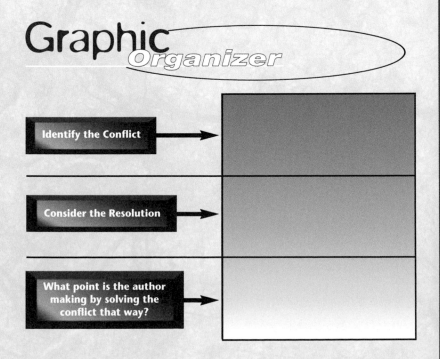

Identify the Conflict →

Consider the Resolution →

What point is the author making by solving the conflict that way? →

Reader's Journal

What causes certain people and animals to behave in ways that most people find unusual? Why are some individuals so different?

Reader's TOOLBOX

PERSONAL ESSAY. A **personal essay** is a short nonfiction work on a single topic related to the life of the writer. Although based on real events, personal essays sometimes include specific details and dialogue that may or may not reflect exactly the way things happened in real life. These details and the dialogue help create an interesting perspective on the events in the story. What details in this story help make it particularly interesting?

THEME. A **theme** is a central idea in a literary work. In a personal essay, a writer may be freer to express his or her views on a given topic than a writer of another literary form. As you read "Cat on the Go," think about what the main topics are. What is the author saying about those topics? There are three main steps in finding a story's theme. Fill in the chart at left to help you find the theme of this selection.

Woman with a Cat, 1875. Pierre-Auguste Renoir. National Gallery of Art, Washington, DC.

CAT on the Go

James Herriot

One winter evening Tristan shouted up the stairs from the passage far below.

"Jim! Jim!"

I went out and stuck my head over the bannisters. "What is it, Triss?"

"Sorry to bother you, Jim, but could you come down for a minute?" The upturned face had an anxious look.

I went down the long flights of steps two at a time and when I arrived slightly breathless on the ground floor Tristan beckoned me through to the consulting room at the back of the house. A teenage girl was standing by the table, her hand resting on a stained roll of blanket.

"It's a cat," Tristan said. He pulled back a fold of the blanket and I looked down at a large, deeply striped tabby. At least he would have been large if he had had any flesh on his bones, but ribs and pelvis stood out painfully through the fur and as I passed my hand over the motionless body I could feel only a thin covering of skin.

Tristan cleared his throat. "There's something else, Jim."

I looked at him curiously. For once he didn't seem to have a joke in him. I watched as he gently lifted one of the cat's hind legs and rolled the abdomen into view. There was a gash on the ventral[1] surface through which a coiled cluster of intestines spilled <u>grotesquely</u> onto the cloth. I was still shocked and staring when the girl spoke.

GUIDED READING

What is wrong with the cat?

"I saw this cat sittin' in the dark, down Brown's yard. I thought 'e looked skinny, like, and a bit quiet and I bent down to give 'im a pat. Then I saw 'e was badly hurt and I went home for a blanket and brought 'im round to you."

"That was kind of you," I said. "Have you any idea who he belongs to?"

The girl shook her head. "No, he looks like a stray to me."

"He does indeed." I dragged my eyes away from the terrible wound. "You're Marjorie Simpson, aren't you?"

"Yes."

"I know your Dad well. He's our postman."

"That's right." She gave a half smile then her lips trembled.

"Well, I reckon I'd better leave 'im with you. You'll be going to put him out of his misery. There's nothing anybody can do about . . . about that?"

I shrugged and shook my head. The girl's eyes filled with tears, she stretched out a hand

---

1. **ventral.** Abdominal side of the body

words for everyday use

gro • tesque (grō tesk´) *adj.*, misshapen, distorted. *The rotting pumpkin looked <u>grotesque</u>.* **grotesquely,** *adv.*

and touched the <u>emaciated</u> animal then turned and walked quickly to the door.

"Thanks again, Marjorie," I called after the retreating back. "And don't worry—we'll look after him."

In the silence that followed, Tristan and I looked down at the shattered animal. Under the surgery lamp it was all too easy to see. He had almost been disemboweled and the pile of intestines was covered in dirt and mud.

"What d'you think did this?" Tristan said at length. "Has he been run over?"

"Maybe," I replied. "Could be anything. An attack by a big dog or somebody could have kicked him or struck him." All things were possible with cats because some people seemed to regard them as fair game for any cruelty.

GUIDED READING

What might have caused the cat's injuries?

Tristan nodded. "Anyway, whatever happened, he must have been on the verge of starvation. He's a skeleton. I bet he's wandered miles from home."

"Ah well," I sighed. "There's only one thing to do. Those guts are perforated in several places. It's hopeless."

Tristan didn't say anything but he whistled under his breath and drew the tip of his forefinger again and again across the furry cheek. And, unbelievably, from somewhere in the scraggy chest a gentle purring arose.

GUIDED READING

What action do the two men think they must take? What does the cat do as they are discussing this action?

The young man looked at me, round eyed. "My God, do you hear that?"

"Yes . . . amazing in that condition. He's a good-natured cat."

Tristan, head bowed, continued his stroking. I knew how he felt because,

although he preserved a cheerfully hard-boiled attitude to our patients he couldn't kid me about one thing; he had a soft spot for cats. Even now, when we are both around the sixty mark, he often talks to me about the cat he has had for many years. It is a typical relationship—they tease each other <u>unmercifully</u>—but it is based on real affection.

GUIDED READING

How does Tristan feel toward cats?

"It's no good, Triss," I said gently. "It's got to be done." I reached for the syringe but something in me rebelled against plunging a needle into that mutilated body. Instead I pulled a fold of the blanket over the cat's head.

"Pour a little ether onto the cloth," I said. "He'll just sleep away."

Wordlessly, Tristan unscrewed the cap of the ether bottle and poised it above the head. Then from under the shapeless heap of blanket we heard it again: the deep purring which increased in volume till it boomed in our ears like a distant motorcycle.

Tristan was like a man turned to stone, hand gripping the bottle rigidly, eyes staring down at the mound of cloth from which the purring rose in waves of warm friendly sound.

At last he looked up at me and gulped. "I don't fancy this much, Jim. Can't we do something?"

"You mean, put that lot back?"

"Yes."

GUIDED READING

What does Tristan want to do?

"But the bowels are damaged—they're like a sieve in parts."

"We could stitch them, couldn't we?"

I lifted the blanket and looked again. "Honestly, Triss, I wouldn't know where to start. And the whole thing is filthy."

words for everyday use

e • ma • ci • at • ed (ē mā' shē āt əd) *adj.*, abnormally thin, as from disease or starvation. *The stray cat was <u>emaciated</u> when we first found her, but now she is plump and healthy.*

un • mer • ci • ful (un mər' si fəl) *adj.*, without mercy, without stopping. *We bothered Shana with <u>unmerciful</u> begging until she agreed to show us her artwork.* **unmercifully,** *adv.*

periods. His favorite ploy was to push his leg round the corner of the table and withdraw it repeatedly just as the cat pawed at it.

Oscar was justifiably irritated by this teasing but showed his character by lying in wait for Tristan one night and biting him smartly in the ankle before he could start his tricks.

From my own point of view Oscar added many things to our menage.[6] Sam was delighted with him and the two soon became firm friends, Helen adored him and each evening I thought afresh that a nice cat washing his face by the hearth gave extra comfort to a room.

Oscar had been established as one of the family for several weeks when I came in from a late call to find Helen waiting for me with a stricken face.

"What's happened?" I asked.

"It's Oscar—he's gone!"

"Gone? What do you mean?"

"Oh, Jim, I think he's run away."

I stared at her. "He wouldn't do that. He often goes down to the garden at night. Are you sure he isn't there?"

GUIDED READING

What happens to Oscar? How do the Herriots feel about this? How do you know?

"Absolutely. I've searched right into the yard. I've even had a walk round the town. And remember." Her chin quivered. "He . . . he ran away from somewhere before."

I looked at my watch. "Ten o'clock. Yes, that is strange. He shouldn't be out at this time."

As I spoke the front door bell jangled. I galloped down the stairs and as I rounded the corner in the passage I could see Mrs. Heslington, the vicar's wife, through the glass. I threw open the door. She was holding Oscar in her arms.

"I believe this is your cat, Mr. Herriot," she said.

"It is indeed, Mrs. Heslington. Where did you find him?"

She smiled. "Well it was rather odd. We were having a meeting of the Mothers' Union at the church house and we noticed the cat sitting there in the room."

GUIDED READING

Where has the cat been? What was he doing there?

"Just sitting . . . ?"

"Yes, as though he were listening to what we were saying and enjoying it all. It was unusual. When the meeting ended I thought I'd better bring him along to you."

"I'm most grateful, Mrs. Heslington." I snatched Oscar and tucked him under my arm. "My wife is <u>distraught</u>—she thought he was lost."

It was a little mystery. Why should he suddenly take off like that? But since he showed no change in his manner over the ensuing week we put it out of our minds.

GUIDED READING

What does Herriot think is mysterious?

Then one evening a man brought in a dog for a distemper inoculation and left the front door open. When I went up to our flat I found that Oscar had disappeared again. This time Helen and I scoured the marketplace and side alleys in vain and when we returned at half past nine we were both despondent. It was nearly eleven and we were thinking of bed when the doorbell rang.

It was Oscar again, this time resting on the ample stomach of Jack Newbould. Jack was a gardener at one of the big houses. He hiccuped gently and gave me a huge

---

6. **menage.** Household

words for everyday use

dis • traught (di strôt') *adj.*, extremely troubled. *My family was <u>distraught</u> when we were unable to find our dog Harry.*

benevolent smile. "Brought your cat, Mr. Herriot."

"Gosh, thanks, Jack!" I said, scooping up Oscar gratefully. "Where the devil did you find him?"

"Well, s'matter o' fact 'e sort of found me."

"What do you mean?"

Jack closed his eyes for a few moments before <u>articulating</u> carefully. "Thish is a big night, tha knows, Mr. Herriot. Darts championship. Lots of t'lads round at t'Dog and Gun—lotsh and lotsh of 'em. Big gatherin'."

"And our cat was there?"

"Aye, he were there, all right. Sitting among t'lads. Shpent t'whole evenin' with us."

"Just sat there, eh?"

"That 'e did." Jack giggled reminiscently. "By gaw 'e enjoyed 'isself. Ah gave 'em a drop out of me own glass and once or twice ah thought 'e was going to have a go at chuckin' a dart. He's some cat." He laughed again.

As I bore Oscar upstairs I was deep in thought. What was going on here? These sudden desertions were upsetting Helen and I felt they could get on my nerves in time.

I didn't have long to wait till the next one. Three nights later he was missing again. This time Helen and I didn't bother to search—we just waited.

He was back earlier than usual. I heard the door bell at nine o'clock. It was the elderly Miss Simpson peering through the glass. And she wasn't holding Oscar—he was prowling on the mat waiting to come in.

Miss Simpson watched with interest as the cat stalked inside and made for the stairs. "Ah, good, I'm so glad he's come home safely. I knew he was your cat and I've been <u>intrigued</u> by his behavior all evening."

"Where . . . may I ask?"

"Oh, at the Women's Institute. He came in shortly after we started and stayed there till the end."

"Really? What exactly was your program, Miss Simpson?"

"Well, there was a bit of committee stuff, then a short talk with lantern slides by Mr. Walters from the water company and we finished with a cake-making competition."

"Yes . . . yes . . . and what did Oscar do?"

She laughed. "Mixed with the company, apparently enjoyed the slides and showed great interest in the cakes."

"I see. And you didn't bring him home?"

"No, he made his own way here. As you know, I have to pass your house and I merely rang your bell to make sure you knew he had arrived."

"I'm obliged to you, Miss Simpson. We were a little worried."

I mounted the stairs in record time. Helen was sitting with the cat on her knee and she looked up as I burst in.

"I know about Oscar now," I said.

"Know what?"

"Why he goes on these nightly outings. He's not running away—he's visiting."

"Visiting?"

"Yes," I said. "Don't you see? He likes getting around, he loves people, especially in groups, and he's interested in what they do. He's a natural mixer."

Helen looked down at the attractive mound of fur curled on her lap.
"Of course . . . that's it . . . he's a socialite!"

"Exactly, a high stepper!"

"A cat-about-town!"

GUIDED READING

What is special about Oscar?

words for everyday use

ar • tic • u • late (är tik′ yōō lāt) v., speak clearly. *I must learn to <u>articulate</u> my opinions clearly.*

in • trigue (in trēg′) v., excite interest or curiosity. *The new exhibit at the science museum <u>intrigues</u> me.*

It all afforded us some innocent laughter and Oscar sat up and looked at us with evident pleasure, adding his own throbbing purr to the merriment. But for Helen and me there was a lot of relief behind it; ever since our cat had started his excursions there had been the gnawing fear that we would lose him, and now we felt secure.

From that night our delight in him increased. There was endless joy in watching this facet of his character unfolding. He did the social round meticulously, taking in most of the activities of the town. He became a familiar figure at whist drives, jumble sales, school concerts and scout bazaars. Most of the time he was made welcome, but was twice ejected from meetings of the Rural District Council who did not seem to relish the idea of a cat sitting in on their deliberations.

At first I was apprehensive about his making his way through the streets but I watched him once or twice and saw that he looked both ways before tripping daintily across. Clearly he had excellent traffic sense and this made me feel that his original injury had not been caused by a car.

Taking it all in all, Helen and I felt that it was a kind stroke of fortune which had brought Oscar to us. He was a warm and cherished part of our home life. He added to our happiness.

When the blow fell it was totally unexpected.

I was finishing the evening surgery. I looked round the door and saw only a man and two little boys.

"Next, please," I said.

The man stood up. He had no animal with him. He was middle-aged, with the rough weathered face of a farm worker. He twirled a cloth cap nervously in his hands.

"Mr. Herriot?" he said.

"Yes, what can I do for you?"

He swallowed and looked me straight in the eyes. "Ah think you've got ma cat."

"What?"

"Ah lost ma cat a bit since." He cleared his throat. "We used to live at Missdon but ah got a job as plowman to Mr. Horne of Wederly. It was after we moved to Wederly that t'cat went missin'. Ah reckon he was tryin to find 'is way back to his old home."

GUIDED READING

What news does the visitor have about the cat?

Of course . . . that's it . . . he's a socialite!

"Wederly? That's on the other side of Brawton—over thirty miles away."

"Aye, ah knaw, but cats is funny things."

"But what makes you think I've got him?"

He twisted the cap around a bit more. "There's a cousin o' mine lives in Darrowby and ah heard tell from 'im about this cat that goes around to meetin's. I 'ad to come. We've been huntin' everywhere."

"Tell me," I said. "This cat you lost. What did he look like?"

"Gray and black and sort o' gingery. Right bonny 'e was. And 'e was allus goin' out to gatherin's."

GUIDED READING

How can Herriot be sure that the man is discussing the same cat?

A cold hand clutched at my heart. "You'd better come upstairs. Bring the boys with you."

Helen was putting some coal on the fire of the bed-sitter.

"Helen," I said. "This is Mr.—er—I'm sorry, I don't know your name."

"Gibbons, Sep Gibbons. They called me Septimus because ah was the seventh in family and it looks like ah'm goin' t'same way 'cause we've got six already. These are our two youngest." The two boys, obvious twins of about eight, looked up at us solemnly.

I wished my heart would stop hammering. "Mr. Gibbons thinks Oscar is his. He lost his cat some time ago."

My wife put down her little shovel. "Oh . . . oh . . . I see." She stood very still for a moment then smiled faintly. "Do sit down. Oscar's in the kitchen, I'll bring him through."

She went out and reappeared with the cat in her arms. She hadn't got through the door before the little boys gave tongue.

"Tiger!" they cried. "Oh, Tiger, Tiger!"

The man's face seemed lit from within. He walked quickly across the floor and ran his big work-roughened hand along the fur.

"Hullo, awd lad," he said, and turned to me with a radiant smile. "It's 'im, Mr. Herriot. It's 'im awright, and don't 'e look well!"

"You call him Tiger, eh?" I said.

"Aye," he replied happily. "It's them gingery stripes. The kids called 'im that. They were brokenhearted when we lost 'im."

As the two little boys rolled on the floor our Oscar rolled with them, pawing playfully, purring with delight.

Sep Gibbons sat down again. "That's the way 'e allus went on wi' the family. They used to play with 'im for hours. By gaw we did miss 'im. He were a right favorite."

I looked at the broken nails on the edge of the cap, at the decent, honest, uncomplicated Yorkshire face so like the many I had grown

to like and respect. Farm men like him got thirty shillings a week in those days and it was reflected in the threadbare jacket, the cracked, shiny boots and the obvious hand-me-downs of the boys.

But all three were scrubbed and tidy, the man's face like a red beacon, the children's knees gleaming and their hair carefully slicked across their foreheads. They looked like nice people to me. I didn't know what to say.

Helen said it for me. "Well, Mr. Gibbons." Her tone had an unnatural brightness. "You'd better take him."

The man hesitated. "Now then, are ye sure, Missis Herriot?"

"Yes . . . yes, I'm sure. He was your cat first."

"Aye, but some folks 'ud say finders keepers or summat like that. Ah didn't come 'ere to demand 'im back or owt of t'sort."[7]

"I know you didn't, Mr. Gibbons, but you've had him all those years and you've searched for him so hard. We couldn't possibly keep him from you."

He nodded quickly. "Well, that's right good of ye." He paused for a moment, his face serious, then he stooped and picked Oscar up. "We'll have to be off if we're goin' to catch the eight o'clock bus."

GUIDED READING

What makes Helen willing to let the cat go?

Helen reached forward, cupped the cat's head in her hands and looked at him steadily for a few seconds. Then she patted the boys' heads. "You'll take good care of him, won't you?"

"Aye, missis, thank ye, we will that." The two small faces looked up at her and smiled.

"I'll see you down the stairs, Mr. Gibbon," I said.

On the descent I tickled the furry cheek resting on the man's shoulder and heard for the last time the rich purring. On the front door step we shook hands and they set off

---

7. **owt of t'sort.** Anything of the sort

down the street. As they rounded the corner of Trengate they stopped and waved, and I waved back at the man, the two children and the cat's head looking back at me over the shoulder.

It was my habit at that time in my life to mount the stairs two or three at a time but on this occasion I trailed upwards like an old man, slightly breathless, throat tight, eyes prickling.

I cursed myself for a sentimental fool but as I reached our door I found a flash of consolation. Helen had taken it remarkably well. She had nursed that cat and grown deeply attached to him, and I'd have thought an unforeseen calamity like this would have upset her terribly. But no, she had behaved calmly and rationally.

It was up to me to do as well. I adjusted my features into the <u>semblance</u> of a cheerful smile and marched into the room.

Helen had pulled a chair close to the table and was slumped face down against the wood. One arm cradled her head while the other was stretched in front of her as her body shook with an utterly abandoned weeping.

I had never seen her like this and I was appalled. I tried to say something comforting but nothing stemmed the flow of racking sobs.

Feeling helpless and inadequate I could only sit close to her and stroke the back of her head. Maybe I could have said something if I hadn't felt just about as bad myself.

You get over these things in time. After all, we told ourselves, it wasn't as though Oscar had died or got lost again—he had

gone to a good family who would look after him. In fact he had really gone home.

And of course, we still had our much-loved Sam, although he didn't help in the early stages by sniffing disconsolately where Oscar's bed used to lie then collapsing on the rug with a long <u>lugubrious</u> sigh.

There was one other thing, too. I had a little notion forming in my mind, an idea which I would spring on Helen when the time was right. It was about a month after that shattering night and we were coming out of the cinema at Brawton at the end of our half day. I looked at my watch.

"Only eight o'clock," I said. "How about going to see Oscar?"

Helen looked at me in surprise. "You mean—drive on to Wederly?"

"Yes, it's only about five miles."

A smile crept slowly across her face. "That would be lovely. But do you think they would mind?"

"The Gibbons? No, I'm sure they wouldn't. Let's go."

Wederly was a big village and the plowman's cottage was at the far end a few yards beyond the Methodist chapel. I pushed open the garden gate and we walked down the path.

A busy-looking little woman answered my knock. She was drying her hands on a striped towel.

"Mrs. Gibbons?" I said.

"Aye, that's me."

"I'm James Herriot—and this is my wife."

Her eyes widened uncomprehendingly. Clearly the name meant nothing to her.

"We had your cat for a while," I added.

Suddenly she grinned and waved her towel at us. "Oh aye, ah remember now. Sep told me about you. Come in, come in!"

GUIDED READING

What keeps the Herriots from feeling great grief over the loss of their cat?

---

words for everyday use

sem • blance (sem′ bləns) *n.*, outward appearance. *The teacher would not speak until there was some <u>semblance</u> of order in the classroom.*

lu • gu • bri • ous (lə goo′ brē əs) *adj.*, very sad, especially in an exaggerated way. *The actor on the show gave a <u>lugubrious</u> moan and began to sob into a tissue.*

The big kitchen-living room was a tableau of life with six children and thirty shillings a week. Battered furniture, rows of much-mended washing on a pulley, black cooking range and a general air of chaos.

Sep got up from his place by the fire, put down his newspaper, took off a pair of steel-rimmed spectacles and shook hands.

He waved Helen to a sagging armchair. "Well, it's right nice to see you. Ah've often spoke of ye to t'missis."

His wife hung up her towel. "Yes, and I'm glad to meet ye both. I'll get some tea in a minnit."

She laughed and dragged a bucket of muddy water into a corner. "I've been washin' football jerseys. Them lads just handed them to me tonight—as if I haven't enough to do."

As she ran the water into the kettle I peeped <u>surreptitiously</u> around me and I noticed Helen doing the same. But we searched in vain. There was no sign of a cat. Surely he couldn't have run away again? With a growing feeling of dismay I realized that my little scheme could backfire devastatingly.

It wasn't until the tea had been made and poured that I dared to raise the subject.

"How—" I asked diffidently. "How is—er—Tiger?"

"Oh, he's grand," the little woman replied briskly. She glanced up at the clock on the mantelpiece. "He should be back any time now, then you'll be able to see 'im."

As she spoke, Sep raised a finger. "Ah think ah can hear 'im now."

He walked over and opened the door and our Oscar strode in with all his old grace and majesty. He took one look at Helen and leaped onto her lap. With a cry of delight she put down her cup and stroked the beautiful fur as the cat arched himself against her hand and the familiar purr echoed round the room.

"He knows me," she murmured. "He knows me."

Sep nodded and smiled. "He does that. You were good to 'im. He'll never forget ye, and we won't either, will we mother?"

"No, we won't, Mrs. Herriot," his wife said as she applied butter to a slice of gingerbread. "That was a kind thing ye did for us and I 'ope you'll come and see us all whenever you're near."

"Well, thank you," I said. "We'd love to—we're often in Brawton."

I went over and tickled Oscar's chin, then I turned again to Mrs. Gibbons. "By the way, it's after nine o'clock. Where has he been till now?"

She poised her butter knife and looked into space.

"Let's see, now," she said. "It's Thursday, isn't it? Ah yes, it's 'is night for the Yoga class." ■

> **GUIDED READING**
> What do James and Helen do?

> **GUIDED READING**
> What has the cat been doing? What makes this unusual behavior for a cat?

Respond *to the* SELECTION

What exceptional qualities does the cat in this selection have?

About *the* AUTHOR

James Herriot (1916–1995) is the pen name of Alfred Wight, who was a practicing veterinarian in rural England. This story is taken from *All Things Wise and Wonderful*, one of Herriot's immensely popular books about his experiences as a Yorkshire veterinarian. His other books include *All Creatures Great and Small*, which was made into a television series, and *The Lord God Made Them All*. Herriot began writing at the prompting of his friends. They encouraged him to write a book based on his experiences as a veterinary surgeon of over 40 years. After two publishers turned him down, the third accepted. His books are now printed in 26 languages and sell in the millions. In March 1999, a new state of the art visitor's center called "The World of James Herriot" opened in the Hambleton District of England as a tribute to the "world's most famous vet." You can visit the Hambleton's Herriot Country site online at http://www.hambleton.gov.uk/.

Backyard, Greenwich Village, 1914. John Sloan.
Whitney Museum of Art, New York.

CAT
& the Weather
May Swenson

ABOUT THE RELATED READING
May Swenson was born in 1913 to Swedish immigrants in
Utah. She was the oldest of eight children. Her first work in
writing was for a newspaper. In 1954 she published her first
book of poems, *Another Animal.* Swenson is known for the
keen observations she describes in her poetry. She won many
awards for her work, including Guggenheim and Rockefeller
Fellowships. Swenson passed away in 1989 and is buried in
Logan, Utah.

Cat takes a look at the weather:
snow;
puts a paw on the sill;
his perch is piled, is a pillow.

Shape of his pad appears:
will it dig? No,
not like sand,
like his fur almost.

But licked, not liked:
too cold.
Insects are flying, fainting down.
He'll try

to bat one against the pane.
They have no body and no buzz,
and now his feet are wet;
it's a puzzle.

Shakes each leg,
then shakes his skin
to get the white flies off;
looks for his tail,

tells it to come on in
by the radiator.
World's turned queer
somehow: all white,

no smell. Well, here
inside it's still familiar.
He'll go to sleep until
it puts itself right. ■

Investigate, *Inquire,* and Imagine

Recall: GATHERING FACTS

1a. What is wrong with the cat when it is first brought to Herriot?

2a. What remarkable thing does the cat do despite its ailments?

3a. Why do Herriot and his wife give up Oscar?

4a. What does Oscar do when he runs off?

Analyze: TAKING THINGS APART

5a. In what ways does Oscar change through the course of this essay? In what ways does he stay the same?

Evaluate: MAKING JUDGMENTS

6a. How does Herriot inform the reader that the cat in "Cat on the Go" is unusual without saying so directly? How does the cat's personality affect the reader?

→ **Interpret:** FINDING MEANING

1b. What convinces Herriot to try to save the cat?

2b. What does this reveal about the cat? How does this action affect Herriot and Tristan?

3b. Did Herriot and his wife have to give up Oscar? Why, or why not?

4b. Why does this make the cat unusual?

→ **Synthesize:** BRINGING THINGS TOGETHER

5b. Why is Herriot so fond of this cat? Why does he write about this experience?

→ **Extend:** CONNECTING IDEAS

6b. How does Oscar in "Cat on the Go" differ from the cat in "Cat & the Weather"? Do you think the cat in the poem would be as likely to do a lot of visiting? Why, or why not?

Understanding *Literature*

PERSONAL ESSAY. A **personal essay** is a short nonfiction work on a single topic related to the life of the writer. Why do you think Herriot chose to write about this cat in this personal essay? Why do you think the topic of pets is important to him?

THEME. A **theme** is a central idea in a literary work. In a personal essay, a writer may be freer to express his or her views on a given topic than a writer of another literary form. What theme or themes do you find in "Cat on the Go"?

Writer's Journal

1. Write a **public notice** to post in stores and public places around town. The purpose of the public notice or announcement is to request donations for a veterinarian who treats stray animals for free.

2. Write a **poem** about something funny that you have seen an animal do.

3. Write a **thank-you note** from the Gibbonses to the Herriots, thanking them for taking care of Tiger (Oscar).

Skill Builders

Collaborative Learning & Study and Research

RESEARCHING LOCAL EVENTS. Recall that in James Herriot's essay, Oscar is said to enjoy attending all of the public meetings and events in town. Form groups to find out about the activities and meetings being held this month in your town. Consult the following resources to help you in your search: your town's chamber of commerce; the local phone directory; the arts calendar; the local newspaper; a community activity newsletter. When you have finished your search, add the events and activities to an oversized calendar. You and your group may decide on a local event to attend.

Vocabulary

ANTONYMS. An antonym is a word that has the opposite meaning of another word. For example, *down* is an antonym for *up*. Review the Words for Everyday Use in "Cat on the Go." Then choose the description that is most opposite in meaning to the word in italics.

1. comradely
   a. hostile
   b. friendly
   c. strangely

2. manipulate
   a. handle or use
   b. throw
   c. leave alone

3. emaciated
   a. portly
   b. abnormally thin
   c. delicate

4. articulate
   a. enunciate
   b. communicate
   c. mumble

5. intrigue
   a. bore
   b. excite
   c. detest

6. distraught
   a. troubled
   b. happy
   c. silly

7. unfathomable
   a. able to be figured out
   b. incapable of being understood
   c. confusing

8. lugubrious
   a. happy
   b. distraught
   c. very sad

9. grotesque
   a. misshapen
   b. distorted
   c. normal

Prereading

from **Ranch of Dreams**
by Cleveland Amory

Reader's T O O L B O X

ANECDOTE. An **anecdote** is a brief story, usually told to make a point. The author of *Ranch of Dreams* includes several anecdotes. As you read, determine which paragraphs are used as anecdotes.

AIM. A writer's **aim** is his or her purpose, or goal. People may write with the following aims:
*   to inform (expository/informational writing);
*   to tell a story, either true or invented, about an event or sequence of events (narrative writing);
*   to reflect (personal/expressive writing);
*   to share a perspective by using an artistic medium, such as fiction or poetry, to entertain, enrich, or enlighten (imaginative writing);
*   to persuade readers or listeners to respond in some way, such as to agree with a position, change a view on an issue, reach an agreement, or perform an action (persuasive/argumentative writing)

Although writers can have more than one aim in a given piece of writing, one is usually more important than the others. As you read this selection from *Ranch of Dreams,* determine the primary aim the author has in writing it. To help you decide, list examples of passages from the selection under the appropriate headings in the graphic organizer below.

Graphic Organizer

Identifying Aim in *Ranch of Dreams*				
INFORMING	**TELLING A STORY**	**REFLECTING**	**SHARING A PERSPECTIVE**	**PERSUADING**

Reader's Journal

How important is it to preserve wildlife?

Reader's Resource

*   The Fund for Animals, founded in 1967 by Cleveland Amory, is headquartered in New York. Using the mottoes "We speak for those who can't" and "Animals have rights, too," the Fund has far-reaching influence in protecting animals. Among the Fund's many victories are passage of the federal Airborne Hunting Act, the Marine Mammal Protection Act, and the Endangered Species Act (our nation's strongest wildlife protection law).

*   The world-famous Black Beauty Ranch in eastern Texas is operated by The Fund for Animals. This 1,430-acre refuge is home to many hundreds of animals—from chimpanzees to burros to elephants. Here, free from harassment and harm, animals get a helping hand and healthy food.

from

RANCH
OF DREAMS

———————————— Cleveland Amory

We had not, of course, acquired the Ranch as a home for cats and dogs. We had indeed acquired it primarily to be, first and foremost, a home for—of all animals— burros. The reason for this was something that

GUIDED READING

Why had the ranch been acquired?

happened some distance from Texas, in the State of Arizona, in the Grand Canyon.[1] What had happened was that the Grand Canyon National Park Service had, in its <u>finite</u> wisdom, declared war on the burros in the Canyon. In fact they had decided, on information conveyed to us by Richard Negus, the Fund for Animals' Arizona correspondent, to shoot the burros.

At that time we had no definite plans about what to do about their plan, except one. And that was that if the Grand Canyon National Park was going to declare war on their burros, then we were going to declare war on the Grand Canyon National Park. As a first step, we decided to sue the Park Service. We knew we had very little chance of success in this, but our plan had at least the <u>virtue</u> of being able to give us time, in the event of failure, to plan what our next step would be. This, we shortly but firmly decided, would be to try to rescue the burros. And,

GUIDED READING

What would be their next step?

before we had any idea of how to do this, we did one very practical thing—we put down our first payment on the Black Beauty Ranch. After that we knew that if we ever did get to

---

1. **Grand Canyon.** Gorge of the Colorado River in northwestern Arizona

---

words for everyday use

fi • nite (fī′ nīt) *adj.*, having definite limits. *Samantha has a <u>finite</u> list of excuses she uses to avoid babysitting for her little brother.*

vir • tue (vər′ chü) *n.*, quality; merit. *Sun, water, and shopping were some of the <u>virtues</u> of a holiday in Mexico.*

rescue the burros, we would have a place to put them.

When I said that the Park people were going to shoot the burros, I am not talking about the mules that people ride when they go down into the Grand Canyon. I am talking about burros or, as they are also called, donkeys—which, <u>incidentally</u>, is a word they dislike almost as much as they dislike the other name that they are also called, which is better known for being the backside of people than it is for anything having to do with an animal and which we will not dignify by even mentioning. In any case, the Grand Canyon people called their burros "wild burros," which I suppose was their privilege since the burros lived in their Canyon. Over the years, however, I have become very suspicious of a lot of animals that are called "wild" as if they were wild in the sense of being fierce, when in reality the only reason they are wild is that they have no home with people.

GUIDED READING

Why is the narrator very suspicious of a lot of animals that are called "wild"?

They are not wild; they are feral,[2] and they have returned to be wild only because they had to. Anyway, then and there we decided, before we began our war with the Park people, that if we did not win our suit, we would go for the possibility of rescuing the burros and afterwards adopting them out as, if not pets, at least companion animals.

As the Park people pointed out to us, no previous group who had ever tried to get burros out of the Park—and there were, incidentally, very few of these—had ever had much success. A few animals here and there had been taken out by <u>literally</u> being pulled and pushed up the long trail, but only one group had ever come close to succeeding with many burros. This was a group that used not only people on horseback but also dogs to pursue the burros. And, actually, they did get within sight of their objective—the top of the Canyon. But when the burros too saw the objective, they simply turned around and bolted past both the people on horseback and the dogs and went all the way down to the bottom—from whence[3] they had come.

That bottom, incidentally, was seven thousand feet down, and considering not only this fact, but also all the other failed rescues, we soon decided that we would not try either to pull the burros up the trail or to push them up by pursuit and pressure.

GUIDED READING

What is the depth of the Grand Canyon?

Instead, we resolved to lift them up by helicopter, burro by burro and helicopter by helicopter, with a sling underneath the helicopter to carry each burro. We knew perfectly well that the whole thing would be a very expensive operation.

GUIDED READING

How do they plan to get the burros out of the canyon?

Helicopter time does not come cheap, nor do helicopter pilots, particularly when you are, as we were, determined to get the best. Besides all this, we had to figure out a way of getting the helicopters to the burros or, <u>conversely</u>, the burros to the helicopters.

In the end we decided on roping them, and to do this I set out to find not just good ropers but, again, like the helicopter pilots, the best ones. It was an interesting search, particularly

---

2. **feral.** Not domesticated by humans; or, domesticated and later escaped or were abandoned to the wild

3. **from whence.** From what place, source, or cause

in • ci • den • tal • ly (in sə den' təl ē) adv., by way of interjection, by the way. *Rover was named, <u>incidentally</u>, for his hometown of Rover, Arkansas.*

lit • er • al • ly (li' tə rə lē) adv., actually. *Jane <u>literally</u> pulled the rug out from under my feet.*

con • verse (kən vərs') adj., reversed in order or action. *Unlike the wild ride to school, the <u>converse</u> ride home was calm.* **conversely,** adv.

as it soon involved close attention to a sport I had long <u>detested</u> for its cruelty—rodeo. However, I soon realized that if we were not going to practice cruelty ourselves we would have to get ropers who could operate in that incredibly

GUIDED READING

What does the narrator realize they will need to do so that they are not cruel?

difficult environment of savagely steep slopes and frighteningly high ridges—not only ropers who were highly skilled but also ones who had practiced their skills without, of course, killing but also without even inflicting any harm. And the very first job of all was to find someone who would not only find such people but also actually lead them.

After a long search I was directed to a former World Champion roper by the name of Dave Ericsson. I found him in a small town in Arizona named Wickiup. I had been told before I met him that he was a man who could do anything with a rope, but the one thing he could do which impressed me the most was that he had, I was told, once roped a rabbit. When I

GUIDED READING

What was one of things about Dave Ericsson that most impressed Amory?

faced him with this achievement or rather, from my point of view, with this charge,[4] he was clearly nervous about it because he had obviously been informed about the Fund for Animals' beliefs. At first he tried to get out of it by saying that it wasn't all that big a deal, that the rabbit had been quite near, and anyway he had done it on a bet, and finally that he was lucky. I was immediately impressed with his modesty, but far more so when he also <u>solemnly</u> promised me that he had not hurt the rabbit and that, after roping

it, he turned it loose and, as he put it, "Cleveland, it ran off just fine."

In the talks Dave and I afterwards had at his ranch, one of the things I liked best about him was the way he talked about animals. For one thing, he told me that he wished people would leave wild horses and wild burros alone out there, because he wanted his children to be able to see them when they grew up. For another thing, he told me that he had brought up his children to believe that at his ranch no one should sit down to eat breakfast in the morning—or dinner at night, or for that matter, any meal—without having first been certain that every animal on the place had been fed.

After that talk I knew I had my man, and I told him exactly what we intended to do to stop the Park people from

GUIDED READING

What is Dave's response after the narrator tells him what they intended to do?

shooting the burros by offering them the alternative of allowing us to rescue them. For a long time Dave said nothing, and then he asked me what I was paying. This time it was my turn to say nothing for a while. The Fund for Animals had been in existence for only a decade, and we were by no means long on money. But we did have one ace in our hole—the same advertising firm who had helped us get started, and who had coined the phrase "Animals Have Rights, Too." The firm of Young and Rubicam had, I told Dave, come up with what I thought was a wonderful ad which they agreed to run for a <u>nominal</u> price on a whole page in *Parade*. The ad, I

GUIDED READING

What would the new ad show?

---

4. **charge.** Criticism

words for everyday use

de • test (dē test´) *v.*, hate. *Frank <u>detests</u> squash soup.*

sol • emn (sä´ləm) *adj.*, serious; somber. *Amber looked <u>solemn</u> as she told her mother the truth.* **solemnly,** *adv.*

nom • i • nal (nä´ mə nəl) *adj.*, insignificant. *Joan paid a <u>nominal</u> fee to enter the contest.*

explained, would show me holding a baby burro on the rim of the Canyon and the copy would read simply, "If You Turn This Page, This Burro Will Be Shot." Dave was very impressed by the ad and I told him luckily other people had been, too.

The response to the ad enabled us to pay Dave not what he wanted, but at least enough to get him. Dave promised me that he would put together a team that would not only do the job but also do it, he also promised, the right way. He also told me that for the roping he would have to have not only horses, but also mules. When I asked him why he would need mules, he told me because mules were smarter than horses and would only put their hooves down where they knew it was safe. He said they would have to ride along a lot of tough ridges in the Canyon, and unless they knew where to put their hooves down they not only might be hurt, they could also be killed. "Mules always know where to put their hooves down; horses don't," he said. When I asked him why, Dave smiled. "The reason mules are smarter than horses," he said, "is because their fathers were burros." He looked at one of his children, who was doing something he didn't like. "And another reason they are smarter," he added, "is because they don't have children."

One piece of news that galvanized our determination to do the job was that we learned that the Park people had made their decision to shoot the burros based on a report from a wildlife biologist. We were, of course, by then well aware that

> **GUIDED READING**
> Why does Dave need mules as well as horses for the roping?

> **GUIDED READING**
> What news increases their determination to do the job?

wildlife biologists in general have one answer to any problem involving wildlife, and that is to shoot it—not the problem, unfortunately, but the wildlife. But what made this report so especially infuriating to us was that we also learned that the man who had written the report, and was therefore the man primarily responsible for the Park people having decided to shoot the burros, was the same man who was going to be paid for running the shooting—indeed, he himself would be one of the ones doing the shooting.

That was really too much. We well knew, to begin with, that the burros are very difficult animals to shoot. For one thing, they are extremely intelligent, and the minute the shooting started they could be counted upon to find every possible hiding place in a terrain far more familiar to them than to their prospective murderers. For another thing, the burro has only two vital[5] areas—the brain and the heart—and the shooters, who would obviously have had little experience with either, would certainly wind up wounding many more burros than they would kill outright. Dave himself told me that he had witnessed one shoot in which he saw a burro, as he put it, "one who had ten bullets in him"—trying to die.

> **GUIDED READING**
> How does being extremely intelligent make burros difficult animals to shoot?

By the time we had been granted permission to attempt our rescue, the relations between us and the Park people had become severely strained. This was not

---

5. **vital.** Necessary to the maintenance of life

just because of us, either; it was because we had become to them indelibly identified with the burros, and to them anyone or indeed anything that had anything to do with the burros, or particularly anything to do with being in favor of them, was an enemy. A remarkable example of this was a little book written back in 1951 by an author named Marguerite Henry. It was a touching fictional story of a lonely burro in the Canyon named Brighty who befriended, and was in turn befriended by, as the book jacket says, "a grizzled old miner, a big-game hunter, and even President Teddy Roosevelt."

GUIDED READING

How do the Park people view anyone who had anything to do with being in favor of the burros?

"But," this jacket copy goes on, "when a ruthless claim jumper[6] murdered the prospector, loyal Brighty risked everything to bring the killer to justice." Actually, of course, being befriended by a big-game hunter, and then by President Teddy Roosevelt, who shot everything in sight apparently, with the exception of little Brighty, was a tough enough life to begin with, never mind the murder. But in any case the saga of Brighty for many years had been a local classic in the Grand Canyon area and did a brisk business in the Park people's shops. Indeed, they even put up a statue to Brighty, which someone had given to them, in an extremely prominent place.

Once they had decided to shoot the burros, however, all this came to a crashing halt. No more could you find hide nor hair of the story of little Brighty in any of the shops and, as for the statue of little Brighty, it was nowhere to be seen. Once we had rescued the burros, however, back came little Brighty to the stores again and, sure enough, back up went the statue on a prominent Canyon rim. Even today, long after the rescue, if you should go back to the Canyon and ask the Park people whatever happened to the burros who used to be down in the Canyon, they will tell you that they were all rescued. And if you go on and ask them who rescued the burros, they will tell you that, too. They will tell you they did.

GUIDED READING

What happens to the book about Brighty after the burros had been rescued?

GUIDED READING

If the Park people are asked about who rescued the burros, what do they say?

Not only did the Park people never rescue so much as one burro, they also put every possible obstacle and roadblock in our path that they could think of. Perhaps the most ingenious of these was the "quota"[7] they gave us. Although no previous rescue had ever, in any length of time, gotten out more than twenty burros, our "quota" was fixed at thirty burros within a month—otherwise there would be no more rescue.

GUIDED READING

What is the quota that the Fund for Animals had to meet in the first month if the rescue was to continue, and why does it seem unfair?

On top of that, and as a further way of trying to make sure we did not succeed, they set our starting date for the first day of the rescue on the ninth of August, the hottest time of the year in the Canyon and what turned out to be further bad luck for us, the hottest time of one of the hottest summers in Canyon history. It was so hot indeed that down there on the floor of the Canyon,

---

6. **claim jumper.** Historically, one who illegally settled on another's property
7. **quota.** Assigned number, share, or proportion of something

---

words for everyday use

in • del • i • ble (in de′ lə bəl) adj., lasting; unerasable. *I have indelible memories of my summer with the horses.* **indelibly,** adv.

prom • i • nent (prä′ mə nənt) adj., standing out; conspicuous. *The statue was the most prominent feature in the park.*

in • ge • nious (in jēn′ yəs) adj., clever. *Clara's ingenious essay answer earned her the top score on the test.*

where the temperature was as high as 120 degrees, even if we had been able to work in the

GUIDED READING

Why can't a burro be taken up in the middle of the day?

middle of the day we could not have taken a burro up with a helicopter—the heat would not have permitted us the necessary lift. Our only hope was to work in the early morning, as soon as there was at least enough light to see, or late in the afternoon when, again, there was just enough coolness and at least some light. We worked indeed, as Texan Sid Richardson used to put it, "from can to cain't."

As if this was not enough proof of their opposing us, they even put up a further obstacle. We had early found out that they regularly broke promise after promise and agreement after agreement, but this was the worst. It was so bad that it almost made the first day of our rescue also the last. What the Park people had promised us was that we could use, to get our men and horses and

mules and equipment down to the bottom of the Canyon, the relatively wide tourist trail to the bottom of the Canyon floor. At the last moment, however, the Park instead gave us a trail that, as I first looked at it that morning, seemed to me to be one that in some places was close to nonexistent and, in other places, straight down. Our men and

GUIDED READING

What trail are the resuers allowed to use?

horses and mules were still within sight of the top of the Canyon when suddenly one horse slipped and fell right into the horse in front of him, who in turn fell right into a third horse in front of that one. Only incredibly quick thinking on the part of Ericsson and one of his best riders saved the day, as well as the animals and our rescue. Despite the way that first day had started, the second day, our first working day, was memorable. Working, as I said, just early in the morning and late in the

GUIDED READING

How is their first working day memorable?

afternoon, because of the 120-degree heat, our team managed to rope, tie, put into slings, and helicopter up to the Canyon top no fewer than twenty-seven burros. In one day we had gotten ninety percent of our first month's quota.

Our success began attracting sizable crowds of people, who would gather around our corrals at the top of the Canyon to look at the burros, protected from them by a fence. At once, at the sound of the helicopter, with a burro in a net underneath, a cry would go up, "Burro coming up!" and more people would gather to watch. What they saw was a pilot who would gently and expertly let the burro down on his back in the net. Immediately the corral workers would rush to untie the sling and throw it back up to the helicopter. Then, while the helicopter took off, the corral workers and the vet would approach the burro, the vet would give him an examination, and then the corral workers would untie his legs.

It was a moving experience, and while at first the cowboys poked a lot of fun at the "Bambi lovers," as they delighted in calling us, as time went on they did less and less of this. Indeed, one day at the end of the first week when I had come from another part of the Canyon down to the Canyon floor, I noticed a group of cowboys standing around the helicopter. As I came closer I saw that they had that day, for the first time, captured both a mother and a baby burro. I also learned that a spirited debate was in progress about this—one concerning whether the mother or the baby should be lifted by the helicopter first.

One cowboy was <u>adamantly</u> insisting that it would be better to lift the baby first. The

> **GUIDED READING**
>
> How do cowboys poke fun at the group of rescuers?

mother would then, he said, at least see what was happening and would be relieved when the helicopter returned for her. Another cowboy was equally adamant that the mother be lifted first. That way, he said, she would at least know she wasn't being hurt, and that maybe her baby wouldn't be either. Finally it remained for Ericsson himself to settle the matter. First he asked the helicopter pilot what was the heaviest male burro we had lifted so far. "One was close to six hundred fifty pounds," the pilot replied. Ericsson next asked the weight of the heaviest female burro he had carried. "About four hundred pounds," came the response. "Okay," Ericsson said. "How much does a baby weigh?" "I'd say a hundred fifty," said the pilot. "Hell," said Ericsson, "let's build two slings and lift them together."

Our "Bambi loving" had apparently spread. In any case, we were told by several veteran[8] rescue authorities up at the corral that we had engineered the first helicopter rescue of large animals ever when the mother and the baby had been lifted together. Altogether the operation took two years and involved saving 577 burros. We had some close calls, but to my knowledge not a single burro, horse, mule, or rider was badly injured. This was due in no small part to the extraordinary skill of the helicopter pilots who, day after day, braved terrifyingly different conditions and dangerous swirls and eddies[9] of winds to land every single one of their precious cargoes lightly and with pinpoint accuracy. The skill

> **GUIDED READING**
>
> How long does the rescue operation take, and how many burros are saved?

---

8. **veteran.** Long-time
9. **eddies.** Circular current of water or air

of the riders, too, and the courage of their horses and mules, going over the difficult ground, was awesome. As for the ropers, their talent too was superb.

I have never forgotten one example of this. My assistant, Marian Probst, came out to view the rescue and Dave Ericsson rode up to her as she was sitting on the grass down on the floor of the Canyon and told her to stay right where she was. He said he would soon have a burro for her to pat right at her feet. He was showing off, of course, but it turned out to be true. Only a few moments later a burro came running by, trailed by Ericsson and his horse. Then, at the very moment the burro shot by Marian and me, out curled Dave's rope, and the next instant there was the burro, quietly standing only a few feet from our feet. So near, indeed, that all Marian had to do was to stand up to pat him. And then still, just a few moments later, the helicopter appeared, one of the cowboys grabbed the sling, the burro's hooves were tied, he was trussed[10] into the sling, and then the next moment he was sailing off from us, up into the sky.

There were also many humorous moments. One of these occurred at the Indian corral on the Colorado River, an area where the burros did not have to be helicoptered out but were merely roped, placed in barges, and sailed down the river to the corral. But the corral was not on Park land; it was on Indian land. While we generally had much better relations with the Indians than we had with the Park people, they were not in the slightest way shy about getting as much money from the Fund for Animals, charity or no charity, as possible. They had decided, for example, that since the corral was on their land they would charge us ten dollars for bringing a car down to the corral area and parking it. One day I came to it for the second time that day. The Indian sitting, as usual, by a chain across the gate asked me for ten dollars. I told him I had

been there earlier—as I knew he well knew—and I confidently started to go by him. It was no use. It was Indian property, he explained, and it was ten dollars each *time*, not each *day*.

He had me. But I am from Boston and, when it comes to money, Indian or no Indian, I had not given up. I pointed over to the corral where there were many Indians, some of them looking at the burros and others just taking pictures. Who are those people, I asked him, and what are they doing? "They're our people," he said, "and they're taking pictures." Oh, I said. What are they taking pictures of? "The burros," he said. Oh, I said again. And whose burros are those? For the first time, he actually smiled. "I guess they're yours now," he said. I told him indeed they were, and furthermore I wanted to know who had given the Indians at the corral permission to take pictures of our burros for nothing? I started to go on, but I did not need to. He smiled broadly, and from that time on it was no longer ten dollars per trip for me, it was ten dollars per day.

GUIDED READING

Who are the real heroes of the Grand Canyon rescue?

The real heroes of the Grand Canyon rescue were, of course, the burros themselves. Those of us who became intimate with burros in the Canyon rescue for the first time never forgot the affection for these animals which started quickly and then, as you got to know them better, continued to grow. The Fund's second large burro rescue a few years later, in another National Park, the Death Valley National Monument, was far larger in numbers than the Canyon rescue, involving thousands of burros. But even being associated with that rescue and getting to know so many of them did nothing to lessen the individual affection and

GUIDED READING

What are the details of the Fund's second largest burro rescue?

10. **trussed.** Secured tightly

respect we had for each and every one of them. Indeed it made it, if anything, grow even more.

To many animal activists, the Fund for Animals' attention to burros seemed out of all proportion in terms of cost to how much we could do to help save other animals in trouble. But to this we had one answer— this was that the burro was the beast of burden for the whole world, and that the case could easily and effectively be made that no other animal had ever suffered so much, for so long, and so unfairly as the burro, that the overworking, the overloading, the underfeeding, and the underwatering had been undoubtedly as bad and perhaps even worse throughout the years for burros than for any other animal on Earth. All in all, we reasoned, if we could make a highly publicized statement for that animal—as indeed we felt we had—then it would be well worth it, no matter what the cost. In our opinion, no animal deserved it more.

Respond *to the* SELECTION

Imagine you have been asked to help out with the rescue of the burros, and describe in a paragraph what you would most like to do.

About *the* AUTHOR

Cleveland Amory was a well-known author who made his mark with three books about his famous cat, *Polar Bear—The Cat Who Came for Christmas, The Cat and the Curmudgeon,* and *The Best Cat Ever.* Earlier books by Amory include *The Proper Bostonians,* which is still considered a classic, and *Man Kind? Our Incredible War on Wildlife.* During Amory's writing career, he worked as editor at the *Saturday Evening Post,* chief critic for *TV Guide,* social commentator for *The Today Show,* and senior contributing editor of *Parade* magazine.

In 1967 Amory founded The Fund for Animals, an organization that has spearheaded many important environmental movements. In 1980 the Fund for Animals purchased lands for the Black Beauty Ranch, an animal sanctuary that became home to burros, dogs, cats, chimpanzees, buffalo, horses, pigs, sheep, deer, goats, monkeys, wolves, llamas, kinkajous, elephants, bobcats, prairie dogs, pumas,

and more. *Ranch of Dreams,* of which this selection is a part, was published in 1997. Amory died in 1998.

Investigate, Inquire, and Imagine

Recall: GATHERING FACTS

1a. What made the report of the wildlife biologist so infuriating to the narrator and his group?

2a. When did the Canyon park shops display the little book about Brighty? When did they remove it from the shops?

3a. What enabled the Fund for Animals to pay Dave Ericsson for his roping services?

Analyze: TAKING THINGS APART

4a. The Park people placed many obstacles in the path of the rescuers. Make a list of these obstacles.

Evaluate: MAKING JUDGMENTS

5a. Do you agree with Cleveland Amory that the extremely high cost of saving the 577 burros was as important or even more important than saving other animals in trouble? Explain.

Interpret: FINDING MEANING

1b. How might the payment for the shooting have influenced the biologist's report?

2b. What might be the reasoning behind whether or not to display the book?

3b. In what way do you think people responded to the ad that was placed in *Parade*?

Synthesize: BRINGING THINGS TOGETHER

4b. Why would the Park people want to stop the rescuers? What might the Park people be trying to protect?

Extend: CONNECTING IDEAS

5b. How might the goals of the rescuers of the burros in this excerpt and those of other animal activists be different? How might they be similar? How might full, clear, and respectful communication help improve such situations?

Understanding Literature

ANECDOTE. An **anecdote** is a brief story, usually told to make a point. The author of *Ranch of Dreams* includes several anecdotes. In your opinion, which is the most effective anecdote and what is the point being made?

AIM. A writer's **aim** is his or her purpose, or goal. People may write with the following aims:
- to inform (expository/informational writing);
- to tell a story, either true or invented, about an event or sequence of events (narrative writing);
- to reflect (personal/expressive writing);
- to share a perspective by using an artistic medium, such as fiction or poetry, to entertain, enrich, or enlighten (imaginative writing);

- to persuade readers or listeners to respond in some way, such as to agree with a position, change a view on an issue, reach an agreement, or perform an action (persuasive/argumentative writing)

Although writers can have more than one aim in a given piece of writing, one is usually more important than the others. What do you believe is Cleveland Amory's primary aim in *Ranch of Dreams*? Referring to your tally of examples in your chart, support your answer with evidence from the text.

Writer's Journal

1. Pretend you are a Grand Canyon tourist who saw one of the rescues. Write a **postcard** about it to one of your best friends.

2. Imagine you are narrator Cleveland Amory. Write a **notice** to Canyon park tourists that explains what the rescue work is all about.

3. Pretend you are one of the helicopter pilots. Write a **descriptive paragraph** about flying one of the burros to the top of the Canyon.

Skill Builders

Study and Research and Collaborative Learning

GROUP RESEARCH PROJECT. Form small groups to research the Black Beauty Ranch. You may want to access the ranch's Internet site at: http://www.blackbeautyranch.org or check for articles in the library. Find out as much as you can about what animals are there (and what their names are), what their environments are like, how injured animals are cared for, which animals are friends, what some of their habits and behaviors are like, and where the burros are kept. Determine a special assignment for each group member, such as: draw a detailed map or diagram of the ranch with identifying labels, make a list of all the animals (include definitions of ones not familiar), find pictures to illustrate each type of animal, classify the animals (mammal, bird, fish, reptile, or amphibian), form a list of questions and suggestions about the ranch and its

operation. Assemble the completed assignments into one report and present it to the class. If you wish, send a class letter or e-mail to the ranch, reporting some of your thoughts and feelings about it.

Media Literacy

LOOKING AT SLOGANS. The slogan "Animals have rights, too" has helped make animal rights a huge issue worldwide. Explore as many media as possible for examples that champion the rights of animals. Remember to check sources such as song lyrics, T-shirts, paintings, photographs, billboards, and comics as well as newspapers, magazines, TV shows, and movies. Make a chart of your findings using the following headings: Media Source, Date, General Description, Animal Rights Message. Display all the charts together in the classroom and see the variety of coverage.

for your
READING LIST

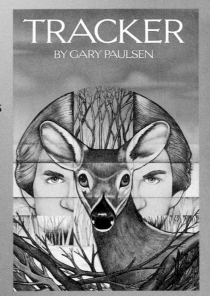

TRACKER
BY GARY PAULSEN

Tracker by Gary Paulsen is a moving story about a young man named John Borne, who must somehow come to terms with the fact that his grandfather is dying of cancer. Every year John and his grandfather go hunting for deer so they will have meat to last through the winter. But this year his grandfather is too ill for the rigorous trip, and John must go alone. While making his way across the frozen Minnesota marsh, John comes upon the trail of a young doe. Certain that he has seen her before and that she has been waiting for him, John finds himself unable to shoot the doe and instead begins to track her. John begins to believe that the creature he has been stalking has the power to cure his grandfather—if he can just get close enough to touch her. Paulsen's lyrical storytelling captures the essence of the struggle all people must go through when confronted with the loss of someone they love.

BOOK CLUB

After everyone in your book club has finished reading the book, decide on a time to meet for discussion. You may find it helpful to use these questions as you get started. Read a question aloud and make sure each member of your group has the opportunity to respond. Your discussion will probably move beyond the questions listed here as you respond to one another's comments. For help preparing for your book club, see the Language Arts Survey 1.8, "Guidelines for Discussing Literature in a Book Club."
* Did the story seem believable to you? Why, or why not?
* Describe John Borne's relationship with his grandfather.
* What is the conflict that John Borne faces?
* How would you describe the mood of this book?
* Why do you think John believes the doe has special powers?
* Why does John think the doe can help him cheat death?
* How did you feel about John's pursuit of the doe?
* How does this experience change John's ideas about hunting?
* What do you think will happen to John's grandfather? How do you think John will react?

Other books you may want to read:
Shiloh by Phyllis Reynolds Naylor
The Incredible Journey by Sheila Burnford
The Call of the Wild by Jack London
Where the Red Fern Grows by Wilson Rawls
Animal Stories and **Dog Stories** by James Herriot

Guided Writing

Examining the Model

In the introduction, the author uses a friendly tone and directly addresses the audience by using the word *you*. The author gives specific information for you to think about before you even go see a dog that you might want as a pet. The information is logical, clear, and easy for the audience to understand. Clear visuals (shown below) illustrate the text.

RELATING A PROCESS

Drex was an expert at origami, the art of Japanese paper folding. He could take a square piece of paper and transform it into a leaping frog, a crane, a flying pigeon, a rabbit, or even a grasshopper. His friend Lynn asked him how he learned all the steps needed to make each creature. Drex took out a small book from his backpack and replied, "This origami book gives you step by step diagrams that show you how to fold the paper. It's not too hard to learn."

Like Drex, you probably can do something well, too. Is it grooming a horse? Repairing your bicycle? Taking care of your pet? Setting up a tent? Launching a rocket? Preparing a fancy dessert? Sketching a landscape? What can you do really well?

This assignment will give you the opportunity to share your expertise with your classmates. You will write about a **process** you already know how to do, or one that you would like to learn to do. You will relate how to do that process, step by step. You will also prepare a visual that illustrates the process. Then, using your visual, you will make an oral presentation to your class.

Professional Model

from Insights: Choosing a Dog on pages 286–287

Choosing a dog can be challenging. It can also be one of the most rewarding experiences of your life if you know what steps to follow. Your choice—wise or unwise—will affect you, your family, and the dog for years to come, so choose wisely. Here are some tips:

Know what you want. Would you like a dog small enough to curl up in your lap? Do you prefer Labrador Retrievers that love retrieving Frisbees for hours? Do you want a dog who can keep up with you on long runs? Do you want a puppy or a grown dog? a purebred or a mixed breed? How much can you pay? Remember that purebreds registered with the American Kennel Club can cost up to several hundred dollars. If owning a purebred isn't important to you, know what shelters and other sources charge for a dog.

Know what you can offer a dog. Do you have a large farm where a dog can run or a small apartment where you will need to take it for several walks a day? Is someone home all day to give a dog attention, or will you only be home at night and on weekends? Some dogs don't mind a small space with enough exercise. Others, like Huskies, feel their best when they can run for miles every day. Some dogs don't mind being left to themselves for large parts of the day, and others whine, bark, or shred everything in sight while they wait for their owner to come home.

Research. Read dog books. Talk to dog owners, especially people who have dogs like the one you want. Find out what owning that particular dog has been like for them. What are the pros of having a dog like that? What are the cons?

Student Model—Graphic Organizer

Folding an Origami Paper Cup

Steps to Explain	Visuals to Use
Step #1: Tell size of paper and explain how to fold it diagonally. Tell how to mark points A, C, D.	Visual #1: Diagram showing a paper folded as a triangle with the points marked.
Step #2: Explain how to find Point B.	Visual #2: Diagram showing how the triangle looks with Point A indicating location of Point B.
Step #3: Explain how to fold Point D to Point B.	Visual #3: Diagram showing how Point D is folded to Point B.
Step #4: Explain how to put the nearest flap A into the pocket	Visual #4: Diagram showing how to put flap A in the pocket.
Step #5: Explain how to flip paper and fold Point C to the diagonally opposite corner and tuck in the remaining flap.	Visual #5: Diagram showing the back of cup with flap tucked in.
Step #6: Explain how to open cup.	Visual #6: Diagram showing how to open the cup.
Step #7:	Visual #7:

Copy the graphic organizer onto a piece of your own paper. List the steps and the visuals you will use for your presentation.

Drafting

Depending on your topic, you will need to decide what kind of **introduction** to write. You could give some history or background about your topic. You might tell the story of how you became interested in this topic. Or, you could explain how this information will be beneficial to your classmates. For example, you might tell how someone's life was saved or improved with this information. Use your introduction to connect with your audience.

Next, write the **body** of your informational piece. Explain the process to your classmates step-by-step. You can include your

Prewriting

FINDING YOUR VOICE. Voice is the way you use language to reflect your unique personality and attitude toward your topic and your audience. You can express your voice through tone, word choice, and sentence structure.

For this lesson, you will be explaining a process to your classmates. Therefore, you will want your voice to be confident and to reflect your knowledge of your topic and the process. You will also want your voice to be friendly and to show your genuine enthusiasm. Consider the two statements below. Which statement is confident, friendly, and enthusiastic?

Would you like to see this square piece of paper turn into a jumping frog?

Origami is great fun.

IDENTIFYING YOUR AUDIENCE. Your classmates will be your audience. Therefore, you will need to pick a topic that is of genuine interest to you *and* to your audience. The visuals that you prepare should be appropriate for your classmates. Finally, your classmates will expect you to be informed and enthusiastic about your topic.

As you prepare for your presentation, keep in mind how much knowledge your classmates already have about your topic. For example, if you are writing about how to search the Internet, you would not need to explain what a *computer* is. You might need to explain other terms, though.

WRITING WITH A PLAN.
Perhaps you already have a topic in mind that you could write about. If not, consider your answers to these questions:

- What do you know that others should know because it might save a life?
- What do you know that might make your classmates' lives more enjoyable?
- What do you know that might make your classmates' lives more interesting?
- What do you know that might save them some money?

After you select your topic, think through each step in the process. You will need to describe each step precisely. Define any terms you use that may not be known to your audience. Then place those steps in the proper order. Nothing is more confusing than a misplaced step in a set of directions. Finally, think about what visuals will help explain the process to your classmates. You might consider charts, tables, diagrams, posters, overheads, or slides.

Since Drex loved origami, he decided to explain how to fold a paper cup. He filled in the graphic organizer on page 321 to help him separate the process into steps and to determine the visuals he would need to make.

continued on page 323

audience by using words such as *you, yours, yourself, we, ours,* and *ourselves.*

Wrap up your writing with a lively **conclusion**. It is often a good idea to refer back to something you wrote in your introduction. You want the last words to leave an impact on your audience.

You will *not* be reading your piece to your classmates although you may want to memorize your opening lines and your concluding lines. What you will be doing is presenting a step-by-step explanation of a process to your classmates. You should refer to your visuals during your presentation. If you can demonstrate your process, do so for your classmates. Drex planned not only to explain how to fold a paper cup, but also to demonstrate the process.

Self- and Peer Evaluation
Once you have finished the draft, let someone outside class read your explanation and observe your presentation. (You don't want to give your speech ahead of time to your audience.) As you look over your work, ask yourself these questions:

- How does the introduction draw the audience into the topic?
- Are technical terms adequately explained?
- Were any steps of the process missing or not in order?
- Was the audience included by the use of words such as *you, yours, yourself, we, ours, ourselves?*
- Did the visuals help provide information about the steps in the process?
- What errors, if any, were there in the visuals?
- What are the most effective parts of the visuals? What could be added to make the visuals more effective? (Consider color, lettering, spacing, and size.)
- What is the impact of the last sentence in the presentation?

Drex's rough draft on the facing page explains how to fold a square piece of paper into a paper cup. The visuals he plans to use are shown below.

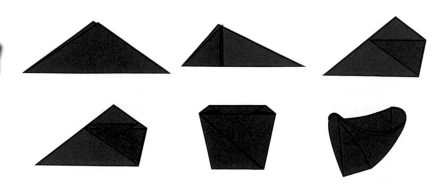

Student Model—Draft

Can you imagine this setting? It is a hot summer day. There is a pitcher of ice-cold lemonade ∧ on the back porch. You desperately want a glass of that lemonade but all the glasses in your house are in the dishwasher being washed. What should you do? Drink from the pitcher? No∧that's gross. Wait an hour for the dishwasher to finish? No∧ you'd die of thirst. Your answer∧of course∧is to make yourself a paper cup from a clean square piece of paper.∧

Your voice sounds natural. You have my interest.

You need a transition to lead to the next paragraph.

All you have to do is fold your paper into a triangle like this. Mark the corners with Points A, C, and D as you can see in Diagram #1. Next, you need to find Point B. To find Point B, just bring Point A down to the fold line C-D. Fold the edge at Point B to show the position. You can see how to do this in Diagram #2. The next step is easy. All you have to do is open the paper back to the single diagonal fold. Then fold Point D over to Point B. Check this out in Diagram #3. The next step is to tuck the nearest flap with Point A into the pocket.∧Diagram #4 shows what your paper should look like now. (I forgot to tell you that you were supposed to firm the edge after you tucked that flap into the pocket.) For the next step, just turn the paper

Good. I like the way you refer to your visuals.

Put it here!

Rewrite— put it where it belongs

Before you decide to use a visual, ask yourself:
- Is it attention-grabbing?
- Is it simple and neat?
- Does it serve a real purpose?
- Does it fit smoothly into the presentation?

Guidelines for Displaying Visuals

- Keep visual information simple. Do not clutter your visual with different styles and sizes of lettering. Do not use too many small images, or too much textual or graphic information.
- Include a title or caption, labels for different parts, and simple, main points when needed.
- Make the visual visible. Stand back and see if you can see it clearly from the back of the room or wherever your audience members will be.
- Use bullets or numbering to organize any text. For simple presentations, use either one or the other; don't use both.
- Use color carefully. Do not let the color distract your audience or make the graphic or text area hard to see.
- Document all sources of graphic information. The ideas in visual information are someone's intellectual property, just like the ideas in text material.
- Make sure you give proper credit for all work not your own.

Language, Grammar, and Style
Using Commas Correctly

When you write, use **commas** to separate words or groups of words within a sentence. Commas tell the reader to pause at certain spots in the sentence. These pauses help keep the reader from running certain words and phrases together when they should be kept apart. Use commas to separate items in a series. Three or four words make a series.

EXAMPLE

Good foods to eat include rice, pasta, bread, and cereal.

Use commas when you combine sentences using *and, but, or, nor, yet, so,* or *for.* Place the comma before these words.

EXAMPLE

I wanted to go to the beach, but it started to rain.

Use a comma to set off words or phrases that interrupt sentences. Use two commas if the word or phrase falls in the middle of the sentence. Use

continued on page 325

over. Fold Point C to the diagonally opposite corner. Tuck the remaining flap into this pocket. Diagram #5 shows how it should look. All you have to do now is open up the cup by putting your finger into the space. Voila! You should now have a cup that looks like Diagram
and-?
#6. Pick up lemonade from 1st ¶.

Revising and Proofreading

Review your self- and peer evaluations. Revise your writing after considering these comments. Make sure you've considered the audience's level of knowledge and have explained any technical terms. Look over your visuals. Double check that they are accurate, clear, and necessary. Then practice your presentation aloud in the kind of voice you will use for your audience.

After considering his self- and peer evaluation notes, Drex revised his writing by adding a sentence to the end of the introduction that helped him make a smooth transition to the next part. He fixed up several errors in comma usage in the introduction, as well. In the body of his writing, Drex separated the steps into separate paragraphs. Again, he fixed errors in comma usage. He made sure all the steps were in order and added the diagrams. Finally, Drex added two sentences in his conclusion that referred back to the ideas in the introduction.

Student Model—Revised

Can you imagine this setting? It is a *hot* summer day. There is a pitcher of ice-cold lemonade on the back porch. You desperately want a glass of that lemonade, but all the glasses in your house are in the dishwasher being washed. What should you do? Drink from the pitcher? No, that's gross. Wait an hour for the dishwasher to finish? No, you'd die of thirst. Your answer, of course, is to make yourself a paper cup from a clean square piece of paper. In six easy steps, you can be drinking lemonade.

Step 1

All you have to do 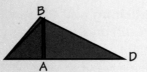 is fold your paper into a triangle like this. Mark the corners with Points A, C, and D as you see in the diagram.

Step 2

Next, you need to find Point B. To find Point B, just bring Point A down to the fold line C-D. Fold the edge at Point B to show the position. You can see how to do this in the diagram.

Step 3

This step is easy. All you have to do is open the paper back to the single diagonal fold. Then fold Point D over to Point B. Check this out in the diagram.

Step 4

The next step is to tuck the nearest flap with Point A into the pocket. Firm the edge. The diagram shows what the paper should look like now.

Step 5

For the next step, just turn the paper over. Fold Point C to the diagonally opposite corner. Tuck the remaining flap into this pocket. The diagram shows how it should look.

Step 6

All you have to do now is open up the

one comma if the word or phrase comes at the beginning or at the end of a sentence.

EXAMPLES

My friend Melissa, who is in seventh grade, gave me this book to read.

After the clock struck midnight, the new millennium began.

Use commas to separate the parts of a date. Do not use a comma between the month and the year.

EXAMPLES

Picasso painted this picture on February 14, 1958.

Hank goes to the dentist on Wednesday, March 5.

Use commas to separate items in addresses. (Do not put a comma between the state and the ZIP code.)

EXAMPLES

She visited Miami, Florida last summer.

Barb lives at 368 Parker Street, Fond du Lac, Wisconsin 54935.

IDENTIFYING CORRECT COMMA USAGE. Read the following sentences from the Professional Model. Then explain why the commas are placed correctly.

Others, like huskies, feel their best when they can run for miles every day.
Some dogs don't mind being left to themselves for large parts of the day, and others whine, bark, or shred everything in

continued on page 326

sight while they wait for their owner to come home.

FIXING COMMAS. Read through the following paragraph from Drex's rough draft. Where should he place commas? On your own piece of paper, rewrite Drex's paragraph correctly.

Imagine this setting. It is a hot summer day. There is a pitcher of ice-cold lemonade on the back porch. You desperately want a glass of that lemonade but all the glasses in your house are in the dishwasher being washed. What should you do? Drink from the pitcher? No that's gross. Wait an hour for the dishwasher to finish? No you'd die of thirst. Your answer of course is to make yourself a paper cup from a clean square piece of paper.

USING COMMAS CORRECTLY. Read back through your own informational piece. Be sure to correct any errors in comma usage.

```
cup by putting your finger
into the space and opening
it. You should have a cup
that looks like the one in the diagram.
     Voila! There's the paper cup. Now if
we only had that ice-cold lemonade!
```

Publishing and Presenting
Have fun presenting your topic to your classmates. Just begin with the opening lines you have memorized. You should have your visuals displayed where they can be clearly seen by the audience. If you have more than one visual, display only the visual you are referring to. That way, the audience will not be distracted from your speech. Talk directly to your classmates and refer to the visuals as you explain each step in the process. If you can demonstrate the process, do so. Conclude your presentation with your memorized lines.

You may wish to deliver the speech to other audiences. Consider who else might be interested in this information. For instance, if you've done an informative piece on building a terrarium, what elementary school science class would be interested in this very subject?

Reflecting
Should you have any "flash" in your presentation or should it be all "substance"? How do you feel when someone gives a presentation that is all "flash"? How do you feel when someone gives a presentation that is all "substance"? How can you balance substance and flash in your presentation? What do you think Duke Ellington meant when he said, "It don't mean a thing if it ain't got that zing"?

UNIT FOUR *review*

Review: Words for Everyday Use

Check your knowledge of the following vocabulary words. Choose ten words that you would like to add to your own daily language. For each word, write a short sentence that includes the word in context. To review a word, look back to the page number indicated.

- abate (238)
- adamant (314)
- affable (276)
- albeit (277)
- allegiance (276)
- articulate (298)
- auspicious (233)
- beguile (282)
- bereft (273)
- calculation (238)
- cavort (276)
- chagrined (234)
- cleft (266)
- coax (239)
- commodity (273)
- comrade (295)
- conciliatory (275)
- converse (309)
- cower (252)
- cultivate (252)
- cynical (284)
- decipher (277)
- despair (232)
- detest (310)
- dilapidated (281)
- discretion (275)
- disinfectant (241)
- distraught (297)
- diverse (282)
- docile (284)
- eddy (266)

- emaciated (294)
- enclose (240)
- entranced (237)
- envision (236)
- ethical (277)
- euphemism (275)
- exuberant (283)
- fanatical (238)
- finite (308)
- fluke (279)
- galvanize (311)
- gregarious (282)
- groom (240)
- grotesque (293)
- guffaw (236)
- immune (279)
- impassive (277)
- impulse (239)
- incidentally (309)
- indelible (312)
- infuriate (311)
- ingenious (312)
- inimitable (237)
- inordinate (275)
- intrigue (298)
- ironic (283)
- literally (309)
- lugubrious (301)
- manipulate (295)
- monotonous (235)
- nominal (310)

- personage (234)
- pore (232)
- pressure (244)
- prestige (234)
- prevalent (273)
- prim (274)
- prominent (312)
- prospective (311)
- prosperous (233)
- providence (254)
- range (232)
- rebellious (233)
- saunter (242)
- semblance (301)
- skeptical (274)
- sluice (255)
- solemn (310)
- stoical (236)
- surreptitious (302)
- temperament (278)
- transient (278)
- tress (240)
- triumphant (234)
- unfathomable (296)
- unmerciful (294)
- unrelenting (274)
- vintage (274)
- virtue (308)
- vivid (232)
- waver (236)
- winsome (235)

Review: Literary Tools

Define each of the following terms, giving concrete examples when possible. To review a term, refer to the page number(s) indicated.

- aim (307)
- anecdote (307)
- character (229)
- climax (263)
- conflict (249)

- description (271)
- personal essay (291)
- personification (249)
- plot (263)

- sensory details (263)
- suspense (229)
- theme (291)
- tone (271)

Reflecting
on your *reading*

Theme

A lot of literature is written about animals or has animals in it. Humans share the world with animals, and being aware of and respecting the relationships between humans and animals benefits all. The selections in this unit are about relationships between human beings and animals. In some, the humans benefit from the relationships as much as or more than the animals. By fostering mutual understanding, through language or otherwise, the characters form ways to communicate. In some of these selections, the author has used personification, which means giving an animal human characteristics. A common use of personification is to give animals the ability to speak. In other cases, humans try to interpret what they are thinking or saying. Have you ever tried to communicate in some way with an animal? How?

Group Project

Give words and voices to a group of animals. For example, pretend that members of your group are horses in a riding stable, a flock of geese in the winter, a pack of wild dogs, or deer during hunting season. As a group, choose the animals and situation you would like to work with. What kind of conversations would you have? How would you communicate your feelings and thoughts to human beings?

Critical Thinking

The relationship between human beings and animals is quite special. We do not share a common language. We have to use different methods to figure out, or interpret, what animals are trying to communicate. It almost seems to make the bond of love between humans and animals more pure. Some people are more in tune to what animals are "saying" than others. Review each of the stories. Using the chart below recall some of the animals from these stories. Make a list of their actions, and how humans, either the other characters in the story or the author, interpreted those actions.

Graphic Organizer

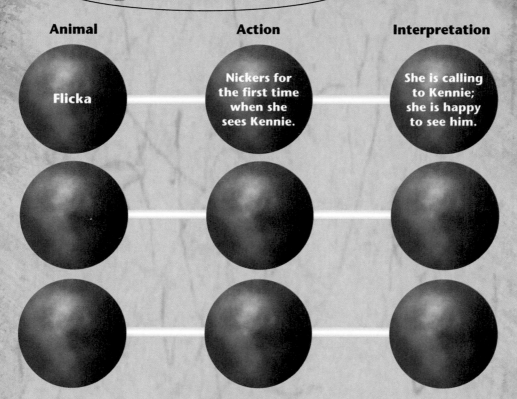

Animal	Action	Interpretation
Flicka	Nickers for the first time when she sees Kennie.	She is calling to Kennie; she is happy to see him.

On Your Own

Write a short essay describing the actions of an animal, and give words and voice to its behavior. You can write about one of your pets at home, a school pet, or an animal that you have watched outside, such as a mother bird, a fat squirrel or rabbit, or a lonely neighbor dog.

 art smart.

Fate of the Animals, 1913. Franz Marc.

At the time that Franz Marc (1880–1916) made the painting on pages 226–227, some people felt that modern life was destroying humans' spirit and they could foresee the coming world war. Marc felt that animals were morally and spiritually superior to humans and in this painting he is concerned with the fate of the animals in that conflict. Ironically, he was killed in World War I (1914–1918).

Composition X, 1929. Wassily Kandinsky. Private Collection.

DO YOU HEAR THE Music?

echoes

My voice is like a house I'm keeping up. You know you don't just build a house and do nothing to it. You're always washing the windows, painting, adding a room.

—Ray Charles

There are no wrong notes.
—Thelonious Monk

Music is your own experience—your thoughts, your wisdom. If you don't live it, it won't come out of your horn.

—Charlie Parker

To me the art of music is magnificent and I cannot bear to see it treated in a shabby way.

—Maria Callas

You've got to find some way of saying it without saying it.
—Duke Ellington

When you play, do not trouble yourself as to who is listening, yet always play as though a master listened to you.

—Robert Schumann

I thought my singing was pretty much hollering, but a bandleader named Chuck Webb didn't.

—Ella Fitzgerald

The main thing is to be original—to play a way of your own.
—Coleman Hawkins

The whole basis for my singing is feeling. Unless I feel something, I can't sing.

—Billie Holiday

I feel everyone has a song inside. It's a matter of whether it can be brought out.

—June Kuramoto

Through music you learn not to care about the color of someone's skin.
—Vince Gill

Prereading

"The Creation of Music"

by Donna Rosenberg

Reader's TOOLBOX

MYTH. A **myth** is a story that explains the beginnings of things in the natural world. These natural objects or events are explained as the result of the action of some supernatural force or being. As you read "The Creation of Music," notice the actions of supernatural forces or beings that contribute to the beginning of music on Earth.

SETTING. The **setting** of a literary work is the time and place in which it happens. Writers create settings in many different ways. In drama, the setting is usually made plain by the stage set and the costumes. In fiction, setting is most often revealed by means of descriptions of landscape, scenery, buildings, furniture, clothing, the weather, and the season. It can also be revealed by how characters talk and behave. As you read "The Creation of Music," use a cluster chart like the one below to show how one of its settings—Earth—is created. A few of the descriptions are already in place.

Graphic Organizer

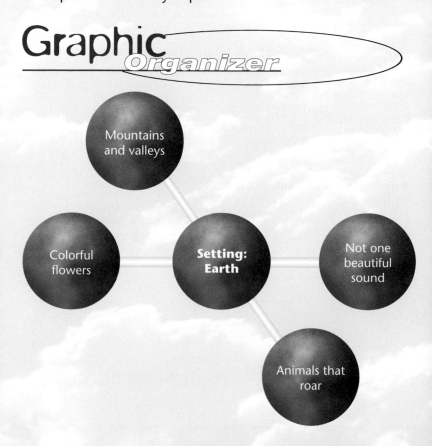

Mountains and valleys

Colorful flowers

Setting: Earth

Not one beautiful sound

Animals that roar

Reader's Journal

If suddenly all song and music in the world were eliminated, what might you be noticing and how might you feel after a month or two?

Reader's Resource

- **HISTORY CONNECTION.** A Native American people known as the Aztecs ruled Mexico before Spaniards conquered the region in the 1500s. The Aztecs, who had built up an advanced civilization and empire, worshiped many gods. Each god was connected with some aspect of the universe and helped explain the natural world. Tezcatlipoca and Quetzalcoatl were two of the most powerful gods worshiped by the Aztecs.

- The Aztecs depicted music and dance as well as battles and ceremonies in their detailed artworks. Four common instruments in these scenes are the drum, flute, rattle, and conch-shell trumpet.

The Creation of Music

Donna Rosenberg

One day Tezcatlipoca,[1] God of the Heavens, came down to earth and wandered from place to place, observing all the beauties of nature. As he walked, he said to himself, "Earth Monster has brought forth mountains and valleys, rivers and streams, forests and meadows. In the light of Sun's rays, her flowers sparkle like brilliant jewels among her blades of grass. Clearly, there is much on Earth to please the hearts of human beings. Yet creation is not complete. Something is missing. Animals roar and people talk, but I hear no music! My heart is heavy with sadness, for music delights the soul as nothing else can."

So Tezcatlipoca summoned Quetzalcoatl,[2] in his form as Wind. "Wind, hear my voice and come to me!" he called to each of the four corners of the world.

Wind groaned complainingly and <u>reluctantly</u>

> **GUIDED READING**
>
> Who is Tezcatlipoca?

> **GUIDED READING**
>
> What is missing in the creation of Earth?

> **GUIDED READING**
>
> Why does Tezcatlipoca call to each of the four corners of the world?

---

1. **Tezcatlipoca.** Aztec god of Creation
2. **Quetzalcóatl.** Powerful Aztec god, identified with the wind and life

words for everyday use

re • luc • tant (ri lək′ tənt) *adj.*, not in the mood, disinclined. *Susan was <u>reluctant</u> to tell her mother about the broken vase.* **reluctantly,** *adv.*

gathered himself together from where he lay scattered over Earth's surface. He rose higher than the tallest tree and the mightiest mountain, and in the form of a great black bird, he came forth to meet the god of the heavens.

Tezcatlipoca heard the waves rise in tumult[3] from the ocean depths and crash with a roar upon the sandy shore. He heard the branches of the trees creak and moan as their leaves tossed and touched. He smiled. Quetzalcoatl had heard his voice, and he was coming.

Quetzalcoatl arrived quickly. As usual, his <u>tempestuous</u> <u>disposition</u> gave him an angry look even when he was quiet. He rested at Tezcatlipoca's feet without complaint.

"Quetzalcoatl," Tezcatlipoca began, "I find that ripe fruits, colorful flowers, and the brightness of Sun's rays make the whole earth beautiful. Yet, in spite of such beauty, Earth is sick with sadness! Not one beautiful sound fills the silence. Not one animal, bird, or human being can sing! Even you know only how to whine and howl, or moan and groan!

"Life must contain music! Music must accompany the awakening dawn. It must inspire the dreaming man. It must comfort the waiting mother. One must be able to hear it in the wings of the bird overhead and in the waters of the nearby brook.

"You must travel high above to the roof of the universe, find the house of Sun, Father of All Life, and ask him to give you musicians to live on Earth and add their beauty to the world. Surely Sun can do this, for he houses many musicians and a flaming choir whose brilliance sheds light upon the earth. Choose the best among both and return to Earth with them.

"When you reach the shore of the ocean," Tezcatlipoca concluded, "you will find my three servants, Water Monster, Water Woman, and Cane and Conch. Command them to unite their bodies and create a bridge on which you can travel up to Sun."

Quetzalcoatl agreed. As he traveled across the face of Earth, he heard what Tezcatlipoca had described, either sad silence or harsh, <u>raucous</u> chatter. When he reached the seashore he found Tezcatlipoca's three servants, who created the bridge for him. Even with the bridge, it took all of his mighty breath to bring him to the house of Sun.

Sun's musicians strode about the halls in colors appropriate to the music they played. Those who played cradle songs and melodies for children wore gleaming white. Those who played songs accompanying the epics of love or war wore brilliant red. Those who wandered with their music as minstrels among the clouds wore bright blue, and those who sat in the golden rays of Sun playing their flutes wore radiant yellow. Quetzalcoatl could not find a musician dressed in a dark, sad color, for there were no sad songs.

As soon as the Father of All Life saw Quetzalcoatl, he exclaimed, "Musicians! I see Wind, that <u>turbulent</u> pest who annoys Earth, approaching our peaceful kingdom. Be silent! I want to hear no singing! I want to hear no playing of instruments! Whoever makes a sound when Wind speaks will have to return

GUIDED READING

What is Wind to do when he finds the house of Sun, Father of All Life?

GUIDED READING

What does Quetzalcoatl hear as he travels across the face of Earth?

---

3. **tumult.** Agitation

words for everyday use

tem • pes • tu • ous (tem pes′ chə wəs) *adj.*, stormy. *The <u>tempestuous</u> sea threatened to swallow the little boat.*

dis • po • si • tion (dis pə zi′ shən) *n.*, customary mood and attitude toward life. *Charlie is always smiling; he has a very happy <u>disposition</u>.*

rau • cous (rô′ kəs) *adj.*, loud and disorderly. *I couldn't find my friends in the <u>raucous</u> lunchroom.*

tur • bu • lent (tər′ byə lənt) *adj.*, causing unrest or disturbance. *The <u>turbulent</u> atmosphere knocked the small plane around.*

to Earth with him, and you will find no music there."

Wind climbed the stairways to the halls of Sun. As soon as he saw the musicians, he raised his deep voice and shouted, "Musicians! Singers! Come with me!"

Not one musician or singer replied to his call.

Wind shouted again, more harshly, "Come, musicians! Come, singers! The Supreme Lord of the Universe summons you to join him!"

Again, not one musician or singer replied to his call. They remained in frozen silence in obedience to the wishes of flaming Sun, like a colorful array of dancers suspended in the midst of their dance.

Then Tezcatlipoca, God of the Heavens, expressed his rage. From the four corners of the sky, flocks of black storm clouds rumbled <u>ominously</u> toward the house of Sun, <u>lashed</u> forward by the whip of their lord's lightning bolts. Mighty roars of thunder poured from the great god's throat, engulfing the house of Sun in <u>torrential</u> sound.

> **GUIDED READING**
>
> What causes Tezcatlipoca to express his rage?

The storm clouds swallowed Sun, Father of All Life, who drowned like a flaming beast. Shivering with terror, the musicians and singers flew into the lap of Wind, who lifted them gently—so as not to crush their music—and happily carried them down to Earth, who was waiting far below.

> **GUIDED READING**
>
> Why do the musicians and singers finally decide to go with Wind?

Meanwhile, Earth scanned the heavens with her dark eyes, watching for the first appearance of Wind. Her face shone with a special radiance and she smiled with delight upon seeing that Quetzalcoatl's quest had been successful. All life welcomed the wanderers. Trees lifted their leafy branches, birds fluttered their wings, people and animals raised their voices, and flowers and fruits lifted their faces in greeting.

Sun's musicians and singers landed happily upon Earth and wandered off in small groups. One could not travel to the most distant corners of the world without meeting singers and musicians all along the way. Even Wind was now happy. No longer did he sadly sigh, moan, and groan as he had in former days. He now sang along with the rest of all life, refreshing the trees of the forest, the meadows, and the ocean waters with his gentle breezes.

> **GUIDED READING**
>
> How does Wind change when the musicians and singers wander off to the most distant corners of the world?

So it came to pass that Tezcatlipoca and Quetzalcoatl helped one another to create music upon Earth. Music accompanied the awakening dawn. It inspired the dreaming man. It comforted the waiting mother. One could hear it in the wings of the bird overhead and in the waters of the nearby brook. From that time forth, every living thing could create its own kind of music.

---

words for everyday use

om • i • nous (ä′ mə nəs) *adj.,* threatening. *The <u>ominous</u> clouds signaled an end to our softball game.* **ominously,** *adv.*

lash (lash′) *v.,* move violently or suddenly. *The flames <u>lashed</u> out at the firefighters.*

tor • ren • tial (tó ren[t]′ shəl) *adj.,* violently rushing. *The <u>torrential</u> rains filled the streets with water.*

If there was no music in the world and you had the power to create it, how would you do it?

About *the* AUTHOR

Donna Rosenberg has taught mythology at all levels from kindergarten to adult. She became interested in mythology by looking at the stars. As she was teaching a youth group about the constellations, she began to research myths about the constellations, starting with the story of Orion, the Hunter. She began reading myths aloud to her students, and then went on to create her own retellings, always trying to preserve the spirit of the original myth. That desire has led to the writing of many books and anthologies on mythology. *World Mythology: An Anthology of the Great Myths and Epics* is her most recent anthology. In it, she says, " 'The Creation of Music' reveals the importance of music in the Aztec/Toltec culture. The language is unusually beautiful because the source of the myth is a poem." The anthology is used in high schools, colleges, and universities all over the world.

Bill Holm

WHALE
breathing

Bartlett Cove, Alaska

A fifty foot trombone blows

under the sea a mile away.

I saw the black horn dive

into its own music,

the spout of its sounding

shooting up after.

That noise left its own

visible ghost. The one

who made it dines

on shrimp so small

a helping would fit

on my fingernail.

Playing a grand piano now,

I wonder what I skim from the sea

delicate enough to let air

between the strings rise

into the room, let music be

visible as whale breathing. ■

Whale Watch, 1993. Arlinka Blair. Private Collection.

ABOUT THE RELATED READING

Bill Holm was born north of Minneota, Minnesota, in 1943. "Whale Breathing: Bartlett Cove, Alaska" is from his book of poetry entitled *The Dead Get by with Everything* (1991). He has also written *Boxelder Bug Variations: A Meditation on an Idea in Language and Music, The Music of Failure*—later reprinted as *Prairie Days*—and *Coming Home Crazy: An Alphabet of China Essays.* He taught school for over twenty years and was a Fulbright professor of American literature in Iceland. Holm is an accomplished musician as well as a writer and poet, and themes of music are often found in his writings.

Investigate, Inquire, and Imagine

Recall: GATHERING FACTS → **Interpret:** FINDING MEANING

1a. After observing that music is missing on Earth, what reason does Tezcatlipoca give for his heart being heavy with sadness?

1b. What is the meaning of this reason?

2a. What color do the musicians who play songs for the epics of love or war wear?

2b. Why might this color have been chosen?

3a. Ever since the time when Tezcatlipoca and Quetzalcóatl create music on Earth, what can every living thing do?

3b. What is meant by this?

Analyze: TAKING THINGS APART → **Synthesize:** BRINGING THINGS TOGETHER

4a. Identify what is heard on Earth before and after music is created.

4b. Predict sounds that will, in the end, be heard. What musical sounds can we hear from the earth if we listen closely?

Evaluate: MAKING JUDGMENTS → **Extend:** CONNECTING IDEAS

5a. In your opinion, how believable would this myth—about the creation of music—have been to the Aztec people of the 1400s and 1500s? How believable would it be to the people in industrial countries of the world today? Explain both of your answers.

5b. The poem "Whale Breathing: Bartlett Cove, Alaska" also describes music coming into being. In what way is the description in the poem similar to that in the Aztec myth?

Understanding *Literature*

MYTH. A **myth** is a story that explains the beginnings of things in the natural world. These natural objects or events are explained as the result of the action of some supernatural force or being. In "The Creation of Music," which action of a supernatural being seemed the most dramatic to you?

SETTING. The **setting** of a literary work is the time and place in which it happens. Writers create settings in many different ways. In drama, the setting is usually made plain by the stage set and the costumes. In fiction, setting is most often revealed by means of descriptions of landscape, scenery, buildings, furniture, clothing, the weather, and the season. It can also be revealed by how characters talk and behave. How is the setting on the sun created? How is the setting of the universe created?

Writer's Journal

1. Write a **fortune cookie insert** for Quetzalcóatl that predicts where Tezcatlipoca will send him.

2. Imagine you are person living on earth who lived at a time when music was created. For readers of history, write a **descriptive paragraph** about how the coming of music changed you.

3. Write a new **myth** for children everywhere about how the sun was created.

Skill Builders

Language, Grammar, and Style

FIGURE OF SPEECH. A **figure of speech** is a statement that has more than a straight-forward, literal meaning. Hyperbole, metaphor, personification, and simile are all figures of speech. A *hyperbole* is an exaggeration made for effect. A *metaphor* is a figure of speech in which one thing is spoken or written about as if it were another. This figure of speech invites the reader to make a comparison between the two things. *Personification* is a figure of speech in which something not human is described as if it were human. A *simile* is a comparison using the word *like* or *as*. See examples below:

EXAMPLES

Hyperbole: The mile-high ice cream cones slowly melted.
Metaphor: The bulldozer in the group of men finally lowered his voice.
Personification: As we approached, the river murmured a greeting.
Simile: The diamond glittered like a star.

Underline and label the figures of speech in the following phrases and sentences from "The Creation of Music":

1. The storm clouds swallowed Sun, Father of All Life, who drowned like a flaming beast.
2. Yet, in spite of such beauty, Earth is sick with sadness!
3. "You must travel high above to the roof of the universe."
4. They remained in frozen silence in obedience to the wishes of flaming Sun, like a colorful array of dancers suspended in the midst of their dance.
5. . . . flocks of black storm clouds rumbled ominously toward the house of Sun . . .
6. Even Wind was now happy.
7. He [Wind] now sang along with the rest of all life . . .
8. Mighty roars of thunder poured from the great god's throat, engulfing the house of Sun in torrential sound.
9. . . . the musicians and singers flew into the lap of Wind . . .
10. Wind shouted again, more harshly, "Come, musicians! Come, singers!"

Speaking and Listening & Collaborative Learning

LISTENING TO THE WORLD AROUND

You. With a partner, take a walk around your school and listen for as many sounds as possible. Be sure to listen in a great variety of places, such as classrooms, the media center, labs, hallways, gymnasium, practice rooms, locker rooms, the school office, and the school grounds and parking lot. Keep a running list describing the different sounds you hear. Then make a chart categorizing each sound under the following headings: Very Pleasant to Hear, Pleasant to Hear, Neutral to Hear, Unpleasant to Hear, and Very Unpleasant to Hear. When the chart is complete, take turns with your partner in reading the description of each sound. Use a voice with tone, volume, and rhythm that matches the kind of sound being read. Listen carefully to each other's words and voice. When listening to your partner's voice, if you can think of another way the voice could imitate the sound, give a signal and say the same thing in the new way.

Applied English & Study and Research

SUMMARY REPORT. Imagine that you work as an archeologist for the National Museum of Mexico. For thirty years, your work has concentrated on uncovering the remains of the Aztec people at the height of their civilization. You have been asked by the museum to prepare a summary report that includes a listing of the types of findings (for example: bones, tools) that have been excavated so far and the conclusions that have been made from those items. Research to learn about as many types of such findings and conclusions as possible. Use resources from your school's media center as well as the Internet. Then, write your report for the museum.

Very Pleasant to Hear	Pleasant to Hear	Neutral to Hear	Unpleasant to Hear	Very Unpleasant to Hear

Reader's *Journal*

Can you imagine a world where no one got old and everyone stayed young forever?

Reader's TOOLBOX

LYRICS. Lyrics are the words of a song. Many similarities exist between song lyrics and poetry. In fact, poetry can be defined as language used in special ways so that its sound reflects its meaning more powerfully than in ordinary speech and writing. *Lyric poetry* is verse that tells the emotions of a speaker, much like song lyrics do. How do the lyrics of "Forever Young" compare to a poem?

METAPHOR. A **metaphor** is a figure of speech in which one thing is spoken or written about as if it were another. This figure of speech invites the reader to make a comparison between the two things. As you read the selection find two examples of metaphor the speaker uses.

Prereading

"Forever Young" by Bob Dylan

Reader's Resource

- **MUSIC CONNECTION.** Bob Dylan is one of the most influential figures in the history of popular music. He is the writer of scores of classic songs and is generally regarded as the artist who brought a poetic quality to rock lyrics. Dylan has released over 45 albums since his 1962 debut and remains as vital an artist today as he was in his '60s heyday. Bands from the Beatles to Pearl Jam have cited Bob Dylan as a vital influence on their artistic development. His songs have been covered by some of the most important figures in music, including Peter, Paul, and Mary; The Byrds; The Rolling Stones; Eric Clapton; Joan Baez; and Bob Marley. In 1988, Dylan was inducted into the Rock and Roll Hall of Fame. In 1998, he was named one of the most influential artists of the 20th century by *Time* magazine. He has won a number of awards throughout his career, including a 1991 Grammy Lifetime Achievement Award.

- "Forever Young" is a song from Bob Dylan's 1974 album, *Planet Waves*. It is a simple folk song, representative of Dylan's early career, when he captivated New York audiences with his acoustic guitar in the coffeehouses of Greenwich Village.

Graphic *Organizer*

What ideas does Bob Dylan associate with being "forever young"?

busy hands — Forever Young — swift feet

Forever Young

Bob Dylan

GUIDED READING

How does the author wish you to interact with others?

May God bless and keep you always,
May your wishes all come true,
May you always do for others
And let others do for you.
May you build a ladder to the stars
And climb on every rung,
May you stay forever young,
Forever young, forever young,
May you stay forever young.

GUIDED READING

What does the author say about truth?

May you grow up to be righteous,
May you grow up to be true,
May you always know the truth
And see the lights surrounding you.
May you always be courageous,
Stand upright and be strong,
May you stay forever young,
Forever young, forever young,
May you stay forever young.

GUIDED READING

What does the author say about your hands and your feet?

May your hands always be busy,
May your feet always be swift,
May you have a strong foundation
When the winds of changes shift.
May your heart always be joyful,
May your song always be sung,
May you stay forever young,
Forever young, forever young,
May you stay forever young.

Do you wish you could stay forever young? Why, or why not?

About *the*
A U T H O R

Bob Dylan was born Robert Zimmerman in Minnesota in 1941. As a teen he performed the then new sound of rock 'n' roll with his friends. While a student at the University of Minnesota, he discovered folk music and began performing solo in coffeehouses, accompanying himself on acoustic guitar and harmonica. At 20, he moved to New York and quickly became the top artist in the folk music boom of the 1960s. His early songs, like "Blowin' in the Wind," spoke of contemporary issues of the Civil Rights movement and the Vietnam War. By 1964, his songs became introspective and surrealistic, including stream-of-consciousness lyrics influenced by French Symbolist poetry and the Beat Poets. Shortly after, he made a dramatic shift back to rock 'n' roll with his hit song "Like a Rolling Stone" and ever since he has performed both electric and acoustic music. Dylan became the first popular musician whose lyrics were discussed as poetry, and he is often cited as an influence by songwriters of many styles. A very private and enigmatic person, he has always stood outside trends in the music industry. His most acclaimed albums are *The Freewheelin' Bob Dylan* (1963), *Highway 61 Revisited* (1965), *Blood on the Tracks* (1975), and *Time Out of Mind* (1997). Besides his song lyrics, his only published writing is *Tarantula* (1965), an absurdist novel in prose and poetry.

ABOUT THE RELATED READING ➤
This related reading is from Fran Lantz's book, *Rock, Rap, and Rad: How to Be a Rock or Rap Star.*

Developing Your Chops

Fran Lantz

"Initially there's a feeling of potential, of power, when you strap on an electric guitar. And then you learn that what it's really about is controlling that power."

—U2's The Edge in *Rolling Stone*

At last you've got it in your hands. Your very own instrument. If you're like most beginners, you love just looking at it and touching it. Guitarist Michael Petracca remembers his first Gibson Les Paul electric guitar. "I was crazy about it," he says. "I used to take it out of the case and just look at it. I think I polished it about five times a day."

But you can't sit around swooning and sighing over your new instrument forever. Sooner or later, you're going to want to learn how to play it. But how?

Show Me How You Do That

Many young players get their first lesson from a friend or relative. Karl Warmé is a twenty-five-year-old drummer, guitarist, and keyboard player. During high school and college in Toronto, Canada, he played in both cover bands and originals-only groups. "I had a friend of mine teach me three chords," he remembers, "and from there I just filled in the blanks."

Beth Allen, from the punk band PMS, learned bass the same way. "A friend showed me a couple of things on bass. And there was a local cover band, and whenever they played a Ramones' song they'd let me come up and play. It was really easy—just three chords."

Other people learn by listening to records and the radio. In *Fleetwood: My Life and Adventures with Fleetwood Mac,* Mick Fleetwood says, "By the time I was thirteen . . . I was beginning to be obsessed by drums. Dad bought me my first set of drums that year. I taught myself to play by playing along with the radio."

Guitar hero Jeff Beck was the same way. "I was heavily influenced by James Burton with Ricky Nelson," he says in *The Guitar Greats*. "I used to put the needle back again and again, slow it down a few times, and hear it backwards and forwards and every way, just to learn all the different ways it could be done, which is really a good way of learning."

Kim Thayil, guitarist for Soundgarden, started at age eight by picking out the theme song to the Beatles' cartoon on television. "I never took a lesson—just the radio, jamming, serendipity," he told *Guitar Player*.

Kim Thayil

Learning to play by listening and repeating what you've heard is called "playing by ear." If you've got a good ear—or, wonder of wonders, perfect pitch (the ability to identify individual notes simply by hearing them)—consider yourself lucky. You probably won't need a lot of training to learn your instrument. You'll just pick it up by listening, observing, and practicing.

Most people, however, are only so-so at playing by ear. And some are practically tone-deaf. If you haven't got a great ear, you would do well to take a few lessons.

Finding Your Personal Pop Professor

Joe Broccoli has been playing the guitar professionally for over twenty-five years. He's performed in Top 40 bands and country bands in Rhode Island, Hawaii, California, and Texas. But his talent isn't all natural. He took lessons from age ten until he was sixteen.

Drummer Peter Markiewicz took lessons at school. Later, he studied with some real pros—Dave Garibaldi from the premier west coast funk band, Tower of Power, and L.A. studio drummer Ralph Humphrey.

Bill Payne, renowned sessions player and keyboardist with Little Feat, took piano lessons for thirteen years. Rocker Willie Nile studied classical piano as a child. And Will Calhoun, the drummer with Living Colour, studied percussion at Boston's Berklee School of Music.

Even some seasoned veterans feel the need for more lessons. After five albums and years of touring, New York rocker Marshall Crenshaw decided he needed to learn a few new tricks on the guitar. It paid off, too. "There's a song on my new album called 'Fantastic Planet of Love,' " he told *Musician*, "and it contains every chord I learned in guitar lessons."

For the beginning musician, the challenge is finding a teacher who knows his stuff and can really inspire you. Unfortunately, it doesn't always work out that way. "I think what happens a lot of times is you get these stuffy old teachers that just live in the neighborhood—like somebody's grandmother," Peter Markiewicz suggests, "and you need more out of it."

Or sometimes the teacher doesn't teach the kind of music you want to learn. "I was dying to take piano lessons," Karl Warmé remembers, "and when I finally got them I hated them. It wasn't what I imagined it was going to be—I guess because I wasn't playing Elvis Presley songs."

Try to keep your expectations realistic. Some young musicians think they're going to learn to play like Eddie Van Halen or Neil Peart in three lessons. Face it—your first few weeks of lessons will consist mainly of learning how to play individual notes and chords. Then you can graduate to simple two- or three-chord songs. The key is balance—look for a teacher who spends part of each lesson teaching you theory and part of it helping you learn how to play your favorite tunes.

To find your pop professor, ask around. Maybe one of your friends can lead you to a good teacher. Check out your local music stores; most of them offer lessons. Music teachers also advertise in the newspapers or post their names on bulletin boards in music shops. Some list their names in the Yellow Pages.

Before you sign up with a teacher, talk to him or her. Find out what style of music he teaches, what sort of lesson books he uses, what kind of music he plays at home. Tell him what style of music you want to learn to play. If you love heavy metal and your prospective teacher plays in a bluegrass band on the weekends, odds are you weren't cut out for each other.

When you finally do sign up for lessons, don't judge your teacher on the basis of one meeting. Give yourself at least three weeks to decide whether you like him or not. During the trial period, listen carefully to everything he says and practice hard. If after three weeks you decide you aren't hitting it off, quit and find a new teacher.

"Lessons really make you very self-disciplined," says guitarist Joe Broccoli. "They also give you a broader concept of what music is . . . what makes a jazz riff different from a blues riff or a rock riff."

Of course, not everyone has the time or money to take lessons. As a teenager growing up in Miami, Florida, singer Gloria Estefan was too busy caring for her ailing father to study music. So she found a way to take guitar lessons for free—she taught herself by reading songbooks she took out of the library.

Name That Note

If you take lessons, your teacher will probably want you to learn some music theory. Many musicians think reading music is an essential part of playing an instrument, especially if you hope to make music your career. "If you really want to get serious and be a studio musician, you can't do anything unless you can read music," Joe Broccoli insists. "If you have an hour to learn a track exactly the way it's written, the producer is not going to stand there while you try to figure out what the note is."

Other people disagree. "You don't need to know how to read music to play rock 'n' roll," Michael Petracca argues. "I used to give guitar lessons and I had students who were so bound by the formal rules of music they had learned that they couldn't relax and improvise."

Admittedly, many world-famous rock musicians can't read a note of music. But some wish they could. Paul Barrère, hotshot studio guitarist and a member of the influential band Little Feat, says that if he could live his career over again, "I would have learned how to read music. If you really have a working knowledge of music it opens up the doors to being a lot more creative."

Rapper Q-Tip of A Tribe Called Quest is another example. He knows how to play electric bass by ear, but that isn't enough for him. "Ya know what I really wanna do?" he told *Rap Express*. "I wanna go back to school and study music theory, and then I wanna learn how to play a *real* bass. . . ."

Woodshedding

Whether you learn the subtleties of music theory or just play by ear, the secret of success is practice, practice, practice. And don't think the rock 'n' roll greats didn't have to practice hard to learn their instruments. "I literally shut myself away for three or four years and learnt properly," Pete Townsend says in *The Guitar Greats.*

Jimi Hendrix's father, Al, says of his son, "He used to practice a lot. I'd come home from work and he'd be there *plunk, plunk, plunk.* . . . I used to hear it constantly."

Rappers need to practice, too. "I have a hard time memorizing raps," says Peno. "I say it over and over and keep the tune in my head that I have in mind for the rap. That helps me memorize it."

When you start out, you'll probably try to copy your idols. "Solos which affected me could send a shiver up my spine," says Jimmy Page in *The Guitar Greats*, "and I'd spend hours and in some cases days trying to get them off." One of his favorites was the solo on the Elvis Presley record, "Baby, Let's Play House."

But don't waste your time trying to emulate a player who is light years beyond you. You'll only become frustrated. Drummer Peter Markiewicz remembers being in sixth grade and listening to Buddy Rich. "The guy was so fast . . . to me it was more intimidating than inspiring."

Joe Broccoli kept his goals within reach. He listened to Gene Cornish, the guitar player with the sixties band The Young Rascals. "They were the easiest band to copy. You could sit there and listen to the band a couple of times and know exactly what the chord changes were."

And remember, no matter how famous you get, you still have to keep practicing. "I like to leave no longer than a week between playings," Grateful Dead guitarist Jerry Garcia told *Musician*. "Otherwise, my technique starts to slide to the point where it takes me three weeks to get it back up."

Kenny Jones has played drums with The Who and The Rolling Stones. But when he practices, he goes back to basics. "Whenever I'm just playing on my own, I generally play jazz . . . it's the only form of drumming where you get to use all your paradiddles and bits and bobs."

In short, if you want to make it in music, you have to pay your dues. It's like the joke where the young musician is walking down the street in New York and he stops an old guy to ask for directions. "How do you get to Carnegie Hall?" the young kid asks.

The old man just smiles. "Practice, my boy, practice."

Investigate, *Inquire,* and imagine

Recall: GATHERING FACTS

1a. What does the author wish the listener to do with a ladder?

2a. In verse 2, what does the author hope you see surrounding you?

3a. What does the author wish for you "when the winds of changes shift"?

Interpret: FINDING MEANING

1b. What do you think the author means by "climb on every rung"? What is the significance of this?

2b. What is this a metaphor for? How will this help you stay forever young?

3b. What do you think the author means by this? Why is it important to have a strong foundation during big changes?

Analyze: TAKING THINGS APART

4a. Compare the qualities of a young person to those of an older person. What are the differences in attitude, outlook, experience, mood, words, and actions between older and younger people?

Synthesize: BRINGING THINGS TOGETHER

4b. What qualities from a young person do you think an older person would want to keep? Why? What qualities from an older person do you think a young person might want? Why?

Evaluate: MAKING JUDGMENTS

5a. How does verse 2 begin and end with two opposite wishes? Does the author mean this literally or metaphorically?

Extend: CONNECTING IDEAS

5b. What do you think the author means when he wishes the listener to grow up to be righteous and true and at the same time to stay forever young? How is this possible?

Understanding *Literature*

LYRICS. Lyrics are the words of a song. Many similarities exist between song lyrics and poetry. In fact, poetry can be defined as language used in special ways so that its sound reflects its meaning more powerfully than in ordinary speech and writing. And *lyric poetry* is verse that tells the emotions of a speaker, much like song lyrics do. Describe the emotions and thoughts that may have driven Bob Dylan to write these lyrics. How do lyrics work with music to create meaning?

Writer's Journal

1. Write a **paragraph** describing your favorite instrument for your class. A guitar? a drum? a violin?

2. Dedicate "Forever Young" to someone special. Write a brief **dedication** explaining why this person is special to you and why you'd like him or her to listen to this song.

3. Take five of the qualities of youth you listed in question 4a, and create a **metaphor** for each.

Skill Builders

Speaking and Listening

INTERVIEWING. Do this activity with a partner. Pretend that one of you is a famous musician—Bob Dylan, or someone else that you like—and the other is a reporter for *Rolling Stone* or another music magazine. Prepare five questions for your famous musician to answer. As the musician, stay in character and be creative with your responses. You may want to tape record your interview and share it with the class.

Study and Research & Collaborative Learning

RESEARCHING PEOPLE. With a partner research a musician of your choosing. Find information on how he or she became interested in music and how he or she learned to play an instrument. How many albums has he or she produced? Which is your favorite, and why? Deliver your report to the class.

Media Literacy

RADIO PROGRAMMING. Imagine that you are a disc jockey on a local radio station. Design a radio program featuring some of your favorite musicians. Create a song list of all the songs you'll play, as well as a dialogue of what you'll say in between songs. Will you have a clip from an interview with one of the musicians? You could offer free tickets to a concert for the first caller who can answer one of your trivia questions.

Reader's *Journal*

Think of a person you haven't seen in awhile. What messages would you want to convey to that person if you could?

Reader's TOOLBOX

FOLK SONG. A **folk song** is a traditional or composed song typically made up of stanzas, a refrain, and a simple melody. Folk songs are expressions of commonly shared ideas or feelings and may be narrative or lyric in style. Traditional folk songs, such as "Scarborough Fair," are anonymous songs that have been passed down orally. "Scarborough Fair," in fact, probably came from an even earlier ballad, "The Elfin King," which was spoken or written in Middle English, and has many different variations. Why would people pass this song down through the generations?

BALLAD. A **ballad** is a simple poem that tells a story. Most ballads have four-line stanzas that have the rhyme scheme *abcb* (the second and fourth lines rhyme but the first and third do not). Sometimes the last line of a stanza is repeated. In music, a ballad is considered a song that tells a story, or a story told in song. In what ways does "Scarborough Fair" fit the definition of a ballad?

Prereading

"Scarborough Fair"

Reader's Resource

- Scarborough is a town in east-central England. Founded before the year 1000 by Viking raiders, the town developed mainly as a fishing center. As the town grew and became a major port, trade fairs became an important part of Scarborough life. From the 1200s to the 1700s, the Scarborough Fair was a six-week trading festival that attracted merchants and others from all over Europe. The fair ran from Assumption Day, the 15th of August, to Michaelmas Day, the 29th of September.

- Parsley, sage, rosemary, and thyme are some of the most commonly used herbs in cooking and in herbal remedies. Parsley is a biennial plant, meaning it grows for two years, blooming the second year. It has curly leaves and a distinctive flavor and scent that make it popular in cooking. In the Middle Ages, it was used as a remedy for stomach ailments. Sage is a large, woody plant with greyish-green leaves. It is often used in stuffings and was used in early Europe for many purposes. Rosemary is a hardy evergreen shrub. Its fresh leaves are used in a variety of dishes. Its oil has long been used in medicines. Thyme is a perennial plant that comes up every year. It has aromatic leaves and small purple flowers. Thyme has long been a popular cooking herb.

Graphic *Organizer*

For each stanza of "Scarborough Fair," make a sketch of the part of the story the stanza narrates.

Scarborough *Fair*

Where are you going? To Scarborough Fair?
    Parsley, sage, rosemary and thyme,
Remember me to a bonny lass there,
    For once she was a true love of mine.

Tell her to make me a cambric shirt,[1]
    Parsley, sage, rosemary and thyme,
Without any needle or thread work'd in it,
    And she shall be a true love of mine.

Tell her to wash it in yonder well,
    Parsley, sage, rosemary and thyme,
Where water ne'er sprung nor a drop of rain fell,
    And she shall be a true love of mine.

Tell her to plough me an acre of land,
    Parsley, sage, rosemary and thyme,
Between the sea and the salt sea strand,
    And she shall be a true love of mine.

Tell her to plough it with one ram's horn,
    Parsley, sage, rosemary and thyme,
And sow it all over with one peppercorn,
    And she shall be a true love of mine.

Tell her to reap it with a sickle[2] of leather,
    Parsley, sage, rosemary and thyme,
And tie it all up with a tom-tit's[3] feather,
    And she shall be a true love of mine.

Tell her to gather it all in a sack,
    Parsley, sage, rosemary and thyme,
And carry it home on a butterfly's back,
    And she shall be a true love of mine. ∎

GUIDED READING
How does the speaker want his shirt made?

GUIDED READING
Where should the acre of land be?

GUIDED READING
How should the harvest be carried home?

---

1. **cambric.** Fine thin white linen fabric
2. **sickle.** Cutting tool with a long, curved blade used in agriculture
3. **tom-tit's.** Small, active bird's

Why does the speaker demand so much of the one he loves?

INSIGHTS

Parsley, Sage, Rosemary and Thyme

"Scarborough Fair" is an English folk ballad that has been sung for hundreds of years. It has often been recorded by folk artists, especially in the 1960s and 1970s. Martin Carthy, Kim Robertson, the Gilmour Brothers, and Cathy Barton and Dave Para have recorded it. Among the most well-known folk artists to perform the ballad are Paul Simon and Art Garfunkel. "Scarborough Fair" is a song on Simon and Garfunkel's album _Parsley, Sage, Rosemary and Thyme,_ recorded in 1966.

About the ballad Simon said, "That's a gorgeous song. I learned it from Martin Carthy. 'Scarborough Fair' is like three hundred years old. Martin Carthy had a beautiful arrangement of it, and my arrangement was like my memory of his arrangement." The ballad is one of Garfunkel's favorite songs. "Scarborough is the most natural, effortless song we ever recorded. Really, it's as if it happened through us. We just got out of the way while the music god recorded that song."

Simon and Garfunkel began playing together as Tom and Jerry in the 1950s, after they met at Forest Hills High School in New York. Their career as the duo Simon and Garfunkel spanned much of the 1960s, during which they recorded a number of folk albums. Besides "Scarborough Fair," some of the pair's most famous songs include "Bridge over Troubled Water," "The Sounds of Silence," "I Am a Rock," and "Homeward Bound." Simon and Garfunkel were known for their beautifully harmonized voices and unique musical style. Today Paul Simon and Art Garfunkel both are following successful solo careers.

Paul Simon and Art Garfunkel

Investigate, *Inquire,* and **Imagine**

Recall: GATHERING FACTS

1a. Who is the speaker referring to in this ballad? Where is she to be found?

2a. How is the person supposed to plough the field? What is she supposed to sow, or plant?

3a. What tool should be used to reap the harvest? How is the harvested crop to be bundled?

→ **Interpret:** FINDING MEANING

1b. Who might the speaker be addressing?

2b. How easy or difficult is this task?

3b. Do you think the speaker truly means this? Explain.

Analyze: TAKING THINGS APART

4a. On a scale of one to ten, rate each task mentioned by the speaker, with one being a simple task and ten being impossible.

→ **Synthesize:** BRINGING THINGS TOGETHER

4b. Why does the speaker relate these tasks that he wants someone to fulfill? What does the speaker really want? What would make the person he is referring to "a true love of mine"?

Evaluate: MAKING JUDGMENTS

5a. Why do you think this ballad lasted for centuries? What do you think people like about it?

→ **Extend:** CONNECTING IDEAS

5b. Why do you think modern folk singers, like Simon and Garfunkel, decide to record old folk ballads like "Scarborough Fair"?

Understanding *Literature*

FOLK SONG. A **folk song** is a traditional or composed song typically made up of stanzas, a refrain, and a simple melody. A form of folk literature, folk songs are expressions of commonly shared ideas or feelings and may be narrative or lyric in style. Traditional folk songs, such as "Scarborough Fair," are anonymous songs that have been passed down orally. What does this folk song indicate to you about traditional English culture?

BALLAD. A **ballad** is a simple poem that tells a story. Most ballads have four-line stanzas that have the rhyme scheme *abcb* (meaning the second and fourth lines rhyme but the first and third do not). Sometimes the last line of a stanza is repeated. What repetition do you see in "Scarborough Fair"? How does that repetition affect the song? What rhyme patterns do you find in this song?

Writer's Journal

1. Write an additional **stanza** for "Scarborough Fair."

2. Imagine you are a trader at Scarborough Fair and write an **inventory** of the wares you are bringing to sell there.

3. Develop a short **short story** about the speaker and the bonny lass in "Scarborough Fair."

Skill Builders

Language, Grammar, and Style

TYPES OF SENTENCES. There are four main types of sentences: declarative, interrogative, imperative, and exclamatory.

A **declarative** sentence gives information.

> **EXAMPLE**   The herbs grew on the window sill.

An **interrogative** sentence asks a question and ends with a question mark.

> **EXAMPLE**   Did you pick some basil for the spaghetti sauce?

An **imperative** sentence gives orders or makes a request. It can end with a period or exclamation mark.

> **EXAMPLE**   Please weed the garden this weekend.

An **exclamatory** sentence expresses strong feelings and ends with an exclamation mark.

> **EXAMPLE**   I want to go to the fair now!

Identify each of the following sentences as declarative, interrogative, imperative, or exclamatory. Then modify each sentence to change its function. For example, you could turn an exclamatory sentence into an interrogative sentence, or a declarative sentence into an imperative sentence. See the Language Arts Survey 3.15, "Functions of Sentences," for more information.

> **EXAMPLE**   Did you pick some basil for the spaghetti sauce? (interrogative)
> *Pick some basil for the spaghetti sauce, please.* (imperative)

1. I plan to go to the Renaissance Fair next week.
2. Get that goat out of my garden!
3. Did you bring the fish from the market?
4. My stomach hurts!
5. Are you going to work in the field now?
6. My mother is sewing me a new shirt.
7. Will you please wash a load of clothes?
8. Don't forget the fabric softener.
9. What are your favorite herbs?
10. Sophie is a bonny lass.

Study and Research & Media Literacy

RESEARCHING WORLD FOLK MUSIC.
Using the Internet, look for information about the traditional folk music of at least three cultures. Compare and contrast the types of songs, the instruments commonly used in playing the music, and the ways in which the music has been brought into the 21st century. Write a summary of what you find for each of the three cultures you choose, and write a short comparison-contrast essay. Include in your summaries an evaluation of your search. How difficult was it to find information? How helpful were the sources you did find?

You may want to begin at the World Folk Music Association homepage at http://wfma.net/.

Collaborative Learning

LEARNING MORE ABOUT HERBS.
Form a small group and visit your local library. Find a book about the uses of herbs, such as rosemary, sage, parsley, and thyme. What foods are they commonly used in? If possible, find fresh or dried versions of herbs. What do they smell like? taste like? Choose a herb or herbs that you might want to use. Then find a recipe featuring the herb(s). Use your school's kitchen to prepare the recipe. How do herbs enhance the flavor of the food?

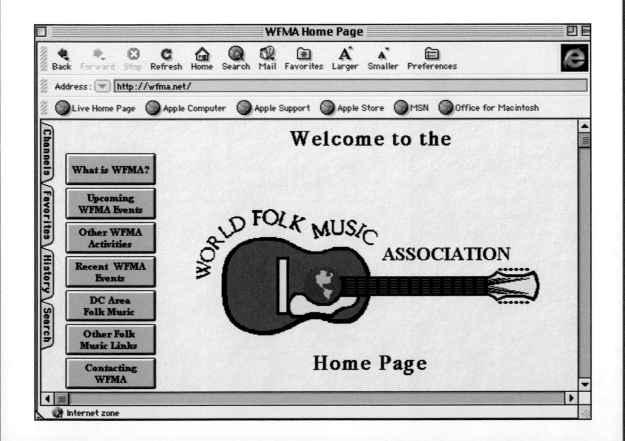

Reader's *Journal*

Describe one thing you already know about poetry and one thing you'd like to learn about it.

Reader's ~ Resource

- **CULTURAL CONNECTION.** Drums are musical instruments found in practically every culture. They are known to have existed since at least 6000 BC. Drums commonly have a strong ceremonial, sacred, or symbolic importance. A drum consists of one or two stretched membranes that are held taut across a frame and are sounded by striking the instrument with the hands or with sticks. The conga are single-headed drums of Afro-Cuban origin.

- **MUSIC CONNECTION.** In much of ballroom dance music the most basic rhythmic unit is the beat or pulse, which is a recurring time pattern that resembles the ticking of a clock. Individual beats are organized by larger recurring units called measures, which stress the first in a series of two or more beats: for example, ONE two, ONE two, or ONE two three, ONE two three. A "time signature" is a sign used in music to indicate the pattern in each measure.

Prereading

"NOTHING BUT DRUMS" by Oscar Hijuelos
and
"THREE/QUARTERS TIME" by Nikki Giovanni

Reader's T O O L B O X

REPETITION. Repetition is the use of a sound, word, or group of words more than once. As you read "Nothing but Drums" and "Three/Quarters Time," look for use of repetition.

RHYTHM. Rhythm is the pattern of beats in a line of poetry or prose. Stress, or accent, is the amount of emphasis given to a syllable. The pattern of stresses determines the poem's rhythm. Some syllables are described as being strongly or weakly stressed, and accented or unaccented. The strongly stressed syllables are marked with slash marks (/) placed directly above those syllables. After you've read "Three/Quarters Time" a few times, carefully identify and mark each of its stressed syllables. Try clapping out its rhythm, clapping louder on the stressed syllables. To help the hyphenated words in the poem sound as a unit, you'll need to clap them slightly faster while slowing down or prolonging the words between them. As you clap the rhythm of this poem a few more times, listen for a point where the rhythm changes, dividing the poem into sections. To show the rhythm visually in "Three/Quarters Time," make a graphic organizer like the one below.

Graphic *Organizer*

You may want to use color to highlight stressed syllables in the poem.

Dance with me	Dance with me	We are the song	We are the music	
Waltz me				

And now nothing but drums,
a <u>battery</u> of drums, the conga drums[1] jamming out,[2]
in a *descarga,*[3]
and the drummers lifting their heads and
shaking under some kind of <u>spell</u>.
There's rain drums, like pitter-patter pitter-patter
but a hundred times faster, and then
slamming-the-door-drums
and dropping-the-bucket-drums, kicking-the-car-fender
drums. Then circus drums,
then coconuts-falling-out-of-the-trees-and
thumping-against-the-ground-drums, then lion-skin
    drums,
then the-whacking-of-a-hand-against-a-wall drums
the beating-of-a-pillow drums, heavy-stones-against-a-
    wall drums,
then the-mountain-rumble drums, then the-little-birds-
    learning
to-fly drums and the big-birds-alighting-on-a-rooftop
and fanning-their-immense-wings drums, then a-boat
down-the-river-with
its-oars-dropping-heavily
into-the-water
drums.

NOTHING BUT DRUMS

Oscar Hijuelos

> **GUIDED READING**
> What kind of musical instruments are mentioned in this poem?

> **GUIDED READING**
> What are the drummers doing? What types of drums are mentioned?

---

1. **conga drums.** Tall barrel-shaped or tapering drums of Afro-Cuban origin that are played with the hands
2. **jamming out.** Holding an unrehearsed, spur-of-the-moment performance
3. ***descarga.*** (Spanish) Explosion or setting off, as with fireworks

words for everyday use

bat • ter • y (ba′ tə rē) *n.,* array; impressive or imposing group. *A <u>battery</u> of model airplanes decorates the walls of my brother's bedroom.*

spell (spel′) *n.* strong, compelling influence or attraction. *A mysterious <u>spell</u> seemed to cause Margo to sleepwalk into the backyard.*

The Dance, 1988. Paula Rego. Tate Gallery, London.

THREE /QUARTERS (TIME

Nikki Giovanni

Dance with me . . . dance with me . . . we are the song . . . we
are the music . . .
Dance with me . . .

Waltz[1] me . . . twirl me . . . do-si-do[2] please . . . peppermint
twist[3] me . . . philly
Squeeze[4]

Cha cha cha[5] . . . tango[6] . . . two step[7] too . . .
Cakewalk[8] . . . charleston[9] . . . bougaloo[10]

Dance with me . . . dance with me . . . all night long . . .
We are the music . . . we are the song . . .   ■

GUIDED READING

What main thing does the speaker request that some-one do?

GUIDED READING

For what length of time does the speaker suggest?

---

1. **Waltz.** Ballroom dance in 3/4 time with strong accent on the first beat and a basic pattern of step step-close
2. **do-si-do.** Dancing a figure in which two dancers pass each other right shoulder to right shoulder and circle each other back to back
3. **peppermint twist.** Song title from the 1960s based on a wildly popular dance called the Twist
4. **philly / Squeeze.** Dance related to a dance of the 1960s called the Philly Dog
5. **cha-cha.** Fast rhythmic ballroom dance of Latin-American origin with a basic pattern of three steps and a shuffle
6. **tango.** Ballroom dance of Latin-American origin in 2/4 time with a basic pattern of step-step step-step-close
7. **two step.** Ballroom dance in 2/4 or 4/4 time having a basic pattern of step-close-step
8. **Cakewalk.** Stage dance developed from walking steps and figures typically involving a high prance with backward tilt
9. **charleston.** Lively ballroom dance in which the knees are twisted in and out and the heels are swung sharply outward on each step
10. **bougaloo.** Hip-shaking dance with a slight bend at the waist and lots of shoulder action

Respond *to the* SELECTION

Write about a time in your life when you remember either drums being played or dancing with a partner.

About *the* AUTHORS

Oscar Hijuelos, of Cuban heritage, was born in New York City in 1951. He graduated from City College, and his first novel, *Our House in the Last World*, was published in 1985. Winner of the Pulitzer Prize for his best-selling *The Mambo Kings Play Songs of Love*, Hijuelos is one of the most beloved and celebrated writers in America. His honors include the 1985 Rome Fellowship in Literature of the American Academy and Institute of Arts and Letters, a Guggenheim Fellowship, and fellowships from the Ingram Merrill Foundation, the National Endowment for the Arts, and the New York State Foundation of the Arts. Hijuelos lives in New York.

Nikki Giovanni, born in 1943 in Knoxville, Tennessee, has written almost 50 books for young people and adults. The focus of Giovanni's work has changed frequently, reflecting her view that life itself is fluid and that change is necessary for growth. Two of her books published in 1968 capture the militant attitude of the Civil Rights movement during that time. Much of her later work focused on family and personal relationships. Giovanni's most recent works have stressed a global outlook. Her books and poems for children include the popular title *Ego-Tripping and Other Poems for Young People*.

 art smart

The Dance, 1988. Paula Rego. Tate Gallery, London.

Paula Rego (b.1935) was born in Portugal and now lives in England. She creates hypnotic scenes that imply psychological undercurrents. The narrative of the scene is left to the viewer's imagination. What do you think is happening?

Investigate, Inquire, and Imagine

Recall: Gathering Facts

1a. In "Nothing but Drums," what does the poet say the conga drums are doing?

2a. What are the drummers doing?

3a. How does the poet describe the "battery of drums"?

4a. What does the speaker in "Three/Quarters Time" say he or she and another person are?

5a. What is the title of Giovanni's poem?

→ Interpret: Finding Meaning

1b. Why might the poet be saying this?

2b. What might be meant by this?

3b. How does the unique name given to each drum serve another purpose?

4b. What might the poet mean by this?

5b. How does this title relate to the meaning of the poem?

Analyze: Taking Things Apart

6a. Identify Hijuelos's actual and suggested descriptions of drums. Identify Giovanni's actual and suggested descriptions of dance.

→ Synthesize: Bringing Things Together

6b. Based on your analysis above, integrate what Hijuelos and Giovanni are saying in these two poems.

Evaluate: Making Judgments

7a. Which of the two poems do you prefer or relate to more? Explain your answer.

→ Extend: Connecting Ideas

7b. Think about the impact of combining drums and dance. What different results can you imagine? How might the combination be a positive one? How might it be negative?

Understanding *Literature*

Repetition. **Repetition** is the use of a sound, word, or group of words more than once. For what purpose is repetition being used in each poem?

Rhythm. **Rhythm** is the pattern of beats in a line of poetry or prose. Stress, or accent, is the amount of emphasis given to a syllable. The pattern of stresses determines the poem's rhythm. Some syllables are described as being strongly or weakly stressed, and accented or unaccented. The strongly stressed syllables are marked with slash marks (/) placed directly above those syllables. Mark the stressed syllables in the poem "Three/Quarters Time." Clap out the rhythm of the poem several times, listening carefully each time. How does the poem's rhythm reinforce its meaning?

Writer's Journal

1. Write an **advertisement** for the public that promotes the jam session in "Nothing but Drums."

2. Write a **poetry review** that describes any strengths and any weaknesses in "Three-Quarters Time."

3. Imagine you are one of the drummers in an extremely long jam session. Write a **journal entry** for yourself about how you feel physically and emotionally.

Skill Builders

Speaking and Listening & Collaborative Learning

CHORAL READING. The sound of a poem contains part of its meaning. Form groups of five to eight members so that there is an even number of groups and then pair up. One group in each pair will work with "Nothing but Drums," and the other with "Three/Quarters Time." Each group should consider the ways individual members have marked the stresses in the poem they are analyzing. Discuss these and come to agreement on the version to use as a group. After everyone has a copy of that version, practice reading it aloud as a group. Once you are fairly comfortable with the group reading, discuss how to make the group voice more expressive. This might include variations in volume, pitch, rhythm, and tone. Practice and then exchange choral readings with the other group. Each group should listen closely as the other group is reading. After each reading, discuss how the group voice brought out the sound and meaning of the poem. If time allows, exchange poems and repeat.

Study and Research

STUDYING POEMS. In "Nothing but Drums," Hijuelos creates complex adjectives with strings of carefully chosen hyphenated words. In "Three/Quarters Time," Giovanni uses words in an unfamiliar way with "Waltz me" and "peppermint twist me." If done skillfully, using language in unexpected ways can be an excellent way to engage the reader. This technique can be found in many modern poems. Using resources from the school's library or media center, research contemporary poetry to gather a variety of examples that reflect the unexpected use of words. Look for coined words and phrases; departures from conventional spelling, punctuation, or capitalization; and other inventions or variations that may catch your eye. You can quickly check the work of many poets by searching in collections or anthologies of poetry. In preparing a report of your findings, present your examples by photocopying or typing them. For each example, write your interpretation of its purpose. Next, add two examples of your own creation. Conclude by giving your opinion about which example is the least and most effective and why.

Reader's *Journal*

Describe how you've explained to someone a new sound that had no name and that didn't sound like anything else.

Reader's *Resource*

- **HISTORY CONNECTION.** Jazz is a music form first developed by African Americans in New Orleans around 1900. The Jazz Age refers to the increased popularity of jazz in the 1920s. Jazz is generally considered a major contribution of the United States to the world of music.

- **MUSIC CONNECTION.** Jazz is characterized by free improvisation (music made up on-the-spot rather than by following written or memorized music), virtuoso (highly skilled) solo performances, syncopated rhythm (accents in unexpected places), and a variety of original vocal and instrumental styles of varying complexity: bebop, big band, cool, Dixieland, fusion, hot, modern, New Orleans, progressive, ragtime, and swing.

Prereading

FROM TO BE OR NOT TO BOP

by Dizzy Gillespie with Al Fraser

Reader's TOOLBOX

ONOMATOPOEIA. Onomatopoeia is the use of words or phrases like *meow* or *beep* that sound like what they name. As you read this selection and the Related Reading, look for examples of onomatopoeia.

MEMOIR. A **memoir** is a nonfiction narration that tells a story. Memoirs focus on a person's experiences and reactions to historical events. Memoirs can be autobiographical (about one's own life) or biographical (about someone else's life). They differ from strict autobiography or biography by stressing experiences and events rather than an individual's life. Dizzy Gillespie's memoir is autobiographical, but it includes many long quotations from other people. The quotations are *anecdotes,* which are short narratives of interesting or amusing incidents. Why do you think he included these quotations in his memoir?

Graphic *Organizer*

In what ways do people in this selection describe bebop?

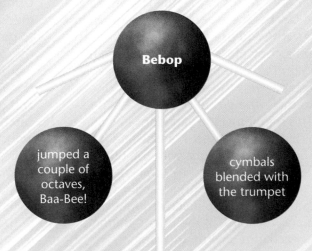

Bebop

jumped a couple of octaves, Baa-Bee!

cymbals blended with the trumpet

from
TO BE OR NOT TO BOP
Dizzy Gillespie

KENNY CLARKE[1] (percussion):
"I used to follow Diz around to all the jam sessions and hear him blow against other trumpet players. He was young and he was blowing. Everybody was asking me, "What is Diz playing?" I was just telling them to "Listen . . ." We were with Teddy Hill's[2] band together, Ella Fitzgerald,[3] Claude Hopkins,[4] so we've *been* <u>barnstorming</u>, early, you know.

"I noticed something unique about Dizzy's playing, that's why I was hanging out with him. His approach to modern <u>harmonies</u>, but rhythms, mostly. He could take care of all that harmony, but his rhythms interested me real <u>profoundly</u>, and I just had to find out about that gift he had hidden in him, the gift of rhythm. It wasn't only his trumpet playing, he was doing

GUIDED READING
What gift does Clarke say Dizzy had in him?

---

1. **Kenny Clarke.** American jazz percussion musician, especially drums and cymbals
2. **Teddy Hill.** American jazz bandleader and trombonist
3. **Ella Fitzgerald.** Acclaimed American jazz singer of the 1930s and 1940s
4. **Claude Hopkins.** American bandleader and pianist

words for everyday use

barn • storm (bärn' storm) *v.*, travel and stage performances. *The theater company spent March <u>barnstorming</u> Ohio.*

har • mo • ny (här' mə nē) *n.*, combination of musical notes and chords. *My sister and I can sing in perfect <u>harmony</u>.*

pro • found (prə faund') *adj.*, with depth and understanding. *Dogs have a <u>profound</u> sense of smell and a great instinct to track scents.* **profoundly,** *adv.*

a lotta other things that some people didn't see, but I saw the rhythmic aspect of it. The way he played and the way he would hum time and things like that. I knew it was avant-garde, ahead of time, so I just fell in line with what was going on.

"It was the idea of the cymbals, which blended with the trumpet. It was a certain way to play the cymbals, that Dizzy liked very well, and I just happened to be playing like that at the time. The cymbals and the trumpet have something in common, they're both brass. It's a perfect blend, and when the cymbals are played according to what the soloist is playing, something that corresponds, it's really beautiful. That's where the whole thing happens, right there.

> **GUIDED READING**
>
> What do the cymbals and the trumpet have in common?

LIONEL HAMPTON[5] (vibraharp, bandleader):

"I went down to the Apollo Theater,[6] somebody was singing, and Dizzy was playing some background behind him. That's where I first heard him. I was sitting behind the stage, man, and heard this guy playing all this trumpet, you understand. I said, 'I wanna hear him at this recording session.' I had a contract at this time, and these were all-star guys.

"He came out with a new style, came out with a bebop style. He came out with a different style than we'd ever heard before. A lot of people don't know that was the creation of bebop, the beginning of bebop. After that, he left Cab[7] and started hanging around Minton's, and him and Charlie Parker[8] got to playing, and then they got into it more, you understand. But the first time I noticed, the distinct style, something new coming in outta trumpet was that time in the recording session with 'Hot Mallets.'[9] You'll see it's a different style of playing. You know he left that Roy Eldridge[10] style and left the Louis style,[11] left all those guys' styles. It was a complete new style in trumpet playing.

> **GUIDED READING**
>
> What does Lionel Hampton notice in the recording session with "Hot Mallets"?

"It was new, and it was fresh, and here's a guy who was creating a crazy sump'n entirely new, but it was so inventive. The harmonies, the <u>chord</u> structure, and the skill with which it was being played. He had a part where he jumped a couple of <u>octaves</u>, 'Baa-Bee!' Like that. And it was really outstanding playing.

"It just amazed me, and I knew that Dizzy was gonna keep right in the style. This was the style he <u>cultivated</u>, and I was glad to see it. I like <u>execution</u>, and here's a guy playing fast as a cat playing a saxophone. On a trumpet. I mean, a fast saxophone player. Here's a guy (on trumpet) playing faster than the fastest saxophone player. Of course that first day I heard him, when he played on 'Hot Mallets,' he amazed

> **GUIDED READING**
>
> In what way does Hampton compare Dizzy's trumpet playing with a saxophone player's?

---

5. **Lionel Hampton.** American jazz bandleader and vibraharp musician

6. **Apollo Theater.** Famous theater in New York

7. **Cab.** Cab Calloway, American bandleader during the big band era of jazz

8. **Charlie Parker.** Outstanding and influential American jazz musician of the 1940s, often called greatest alto saxophonist and jazz improviser

9. **Hot Mallets.** Jam sessions held by Hampton in New York, to which he invited the biggest names in jazz

10. **Roy Eldridge.** American jazz trumpeter

11. **Louis style.** Jazz music played in the manner pioneered by Louis Armstrong, celebrated jazz trumpeter

---

words for everyday use

chord (kord′) n., three or more musical tones sounded simultaneously. *Summer strummed a few <u>chords</u> on her guitar.*

oc • tave (äk′ təv) n., musical interval spanning eight notes. *Joel's fingers could span an entire <u>octave</u> on the piano.*

cul • ti • vate (kəl′ ti vāt) v., foster or encourage the growth of. *We <u>cultivated</u> a five-acre garden last year.*

ex • e • cu • tion (ek sə kyü′ shən) n., performance. *Pete showed perfect <u>execution</u> on the race course.*

me, because that's about as fast as I've heard a trumpet played. I had never heard a trumpet played that fast before.

"The first time I heard bebop played on a trumpet—I mean that style later called bebop—was when Dizzy played 'Hot Mallets' with me."

BUDD JOHNSON:

"Now the way that word bebop came about to my way of thinking is when Dizzy would be trying to explain something or show you how to play it, he would hum it to you. And he would say, 'No, no, it goes like this—ump-de-be-de-bop-be-bop-be-doo-dop-de-de-bop.' So they would come up to Dizzy and say, 'Hey, play some more of that bebop music,' because he would be scatting[12] like that. See, and they just picked up that word and they'd say, 'Play some more of that bebop music.' This was the description, you know, this was the way—the only way they could identify it and tell him what they wanted to hear him play. And of course Dizzy, being as intelligent as he is, he just kept it going. So this thing went on and made him a fortune. . . .

> **GUIDED READING**
>
> What word do the other musicians pick up from Dizzy's scatting?

"When you have a lot of knowledge of music, and understand the <u>theory</u> and the new harmonic devices and everything, it's not very difficult to come out with a sound. But with a style of music, it's very difficult, man, because it's hard to play something that somebody has never played before. But, I mean, see this is what Diz had on all of these musicians. And he could sit down and play the piano so well. Even today, Dizzy says, 'Dig this, this little thing I wrote.' And the beautiful simplicity to it and with the way he is going harmonically, you say, 'Oh, wow, man isn't that pretty!' It's something that you haven't heard before. And of course, now, with his wide, wide world of traveling and picking up different sounds from different countries and really understanding their music, he can <u>incorporate</u> that into what he already knows and always have something new to present. . . .

> **GUIDED READING**
>
> How does Dizzy's traveling affect his music?

"On 'Salt Peanuts'[13] he had that all set up. The drum part worked like part of a jigsaw puzzle 'Bop-be-da' the little figures. He had little parts in there that had to work together, and this was all going a mile a minute, man. He worked this all out in his head. And, [if], you can't do it? He'd say, 'This is the way it goes,' sit down and play it, just the way he'd sit down at the piano and play what he wanted. Incredible!" ∎

> **GUIDED READING**
>
> What does Dizzy have all set up for "Salt Peanuts"?

---

12. **scatting.** Vocally imitating the sound and style of a horn playing

13. **'Salt Peanuts.'** Title of a musical composition written by Dizzy Gillespie

---

words for everyday use

the • o • ry (thē′ ə rē) n., principles of a body of fact, a science, or an art. *Glenndell studied art <u>theory</u> in college.*

in • cor • por • ate (in kôr′ pə rāt) v., blend. *After mixing the flour and the baking powder, I <u>incorporated</u> the dry mixture with the eggs and sugar.*

Would you have enjoyed being a part of the jazz scene in the 1940s? Explain your answer.

About *the* AUTHOR

Dizzy Gillespie, born John Birks Gillespie in Cheraw, South Carolina, in 1917, became one of the most influential jazz musicians of the 1940s. After playing trumpet in the big bands of Cab Calloway and Earl "Fatha" Hines, he ushered in a radically new style of music called bebop that revolutionized the jazz world. Known for his extraordinary speed and range and daring sense of harmony, Gillespie performed internationally through the 1980s. He died in 1993.

art smart.

Empress of the Blues, 1974. Romare Bearden.

In his artwork, Romare Bearden (1914–1988) mixes watercolor, paint, and collage elements cut out of magazines. What about the look of Bearden's style evokes the feeling of Sandburg's poem?

ABOUT THE RELATED READING

Carl Sandburg was one of the most important poets of the 20th century. Many of his poems dealt with the lives and issues of everyday American people. "Jazz Fantasia" is from the collection of poetry *Smoke and Steel,* published in 1922.

Empress of the Blues, 1974. Romare Bearden. National Museum of American Art, Washington, DC.

© Romare Bearden Foundation/Licensed by VAGA, New York.

JAZZ FANTASIA

Carl Sandburg

Drum on your drums, batter on your banjoes,
sob on the long cool winding saxophones.
Go to it, O jazzmen.

Sling your knuckles on the bottoms of the happy
tin pans, let your trombones ooze, and go husha-hush with the slippery sand-paper.

Moan like an autumn wind high in the lonesome treetops,
moan soft like you wanted somebody terrible, cry like
racing car slipping away from a motorcycle cop,
bang-bang! you jazzmen, bang altogether drums, traps,
banjoes, horns, tin cans—make two people fight on the
top of a stairway and scratch each other's eyes in a
clinch tumbling down the stairs.

Can the rough stuff . . . now a Mississippi steamboat
pushes up the night river with a hoo-hoo-hoo-oo . . . and
the green lanterns calling to the high soft stars . . . a red
moon rides on the humps of the low river hills . . . go to it,
O jazzmen.

Investigate, Inquire, and Imagine

Recall: GATHERING FACTS

1a. Who says "That's where the whole thing happens"?

2a. What does Lionel Hampton say a lot of people didn't know?

3a. What does Dizzy, being as intelligent as he is, do when the other musicians said, "Play some more of that bebop music"?

→ **Interpret:** FINDING MEANING

1b. What does he mean by that?

2b. In what respect does Hampton think people didn't know this?

3b. Why would Dizzy do this?

Analyze: TAKING THINGS APART

4a. Identify the ways bebop is defined in these excerpts.

→ **Synthesize:** BRINGING THINGS TOGETHER

4b. Based on the definitions above and what else you know about bebop, create an accurate definition of bebop.

Evaluate: MAKING JUDGMENTS

5a. Evaluate how well the excerpts give you a sense of Dizzy Gillespie as a person and as a musician. Support your evaluation with examples from the text.

→ **Extend:** CONNECTING IDEAS

5b. What and how does Carl Sandburg communicate about jazz in his poem "Jazz Fantasia"?

Understanding Literature

ONOMATOPOEIA. Onomatopoeia is the use of words or phrases like *meow* or *beep* that sound like what they name. For you, how effective was the use of onomatopoeia in the excerpts from Dizzy Gillespie's memoir? Did its use increase your understanding of the meaning of the reading? If so, how? Answer the same questions for Sandburg's "Jazz Fantasia."

MEMOIR. A **memoir** is a nonfiction narration that tells a story. Memoirs focus on a person's experiences and reactions to historical events. Memoirs can be autobiographical (about one's own life) or biographical (about someone else's life). They differ from strict autobiography or biography by stressing experiences and events rather than an individual's life. What event or situation in history does Gillespie's memoir address? How does hearing about this from the points of view of Gillespie and his friends lend insight to this event or situation?

Writer's Journal

1. Write a **short note** to a friend to let him or her know about a jam session the next night.
2. Write an **onomatopoeia**—in words state how you would hum or scat the sound and rhythms of a car horn for someone.
3. For yourself, write a **paragraph** or a **poem** to describe the sound of a musical instrument.

Skill Builders

Speaking and Listening & Collaborative Learning

DISCUSSING MEMORIES. We all have personal memories of many kinds, and we often relive some or all of the emotions we felt when we recall them. Think of a memory you'd like to share and recall how you felt at the time. Form small groups and take turns recounting the memories. At some point in telling the memory, allow your voice to convey how you felt by adjusting its tone, volume, and pace. As each member of the group is telling his or her memory, listen closely and try to determine how the person felt about it. After each telling, group members will share with the speaker what feelings they heard being expressed. If desired, the speaker can respond.

Study and Research

RESEARCHING A PERSON. Select a jazz musician or singer about whom you'd like to know more. Using library resources and the Internet, search for information about his or her life and career. What happened during the person's childhood and school years? What led the person to a career as a jazz musician or singer? What were some of the person's hopes and dreams? What challenges did the person have to face? What can you learn about the talents of and achievements by the person? Pay careful attention to the approximate dates when events occurred and record them in your research notes. Organize the information you've gained from various sources in chronological order. Present your findings by writing a short biography of the person. Include a time line that presents events in the person's life on the bottom and significant events in the world and in jazz along the top.

Applied English

FUNDRAISING. Imagine you work as a fundraiser for a school of jazz in a large city. The school wants to expand its facilities by adding more practice rooms, doubling the materials on jazz in the school library, and buying three new tour buses. Write a letter requesting contributions from prospective donors. Begin your letter with a simple statement of its purpose. Provide a brief introduction of the school, its reputation for quality, and its value to the city. Include the names of a few graduates who have become well-known jazz musicians. Then present the school's current plans for expansion and the estimated cost. Close with a respectful request for monetary donations and offer donors a complimentary CD or cassette of a recent performance by the students.

for your READING LIST

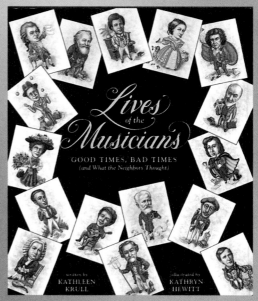

Lives of the Musicians: Good Times, Bad Times (and What the Neighbors Thought) by Kathleen Krull is a collection of anecdotes about nineteen famous men and women composers from various countries and historical periods. The profiles give brief descriptions of the composers' lives, as well as insights into the habits and hangouts, phobias and personalities of these often eccentric creative geniuses. You'll learn what they ate, what they wore, and what they were like as children. Throughout the book you will find obscure facts that are sure to catch your interest. For example, did you know that the two *Voyager* spacecraft, launched into the solar system in 1977, contain three musical compositions by Bach? Or that Sir William Gilbert (of Gilbert and Sullivan) wrote *The Gondoliers* based on his memories of being kidnapped and held for ransom in Italy when he was two years old? Or that George Gershwin banged the piano keys so hard during the first performance of his jazz orchestral work *Rhapsody in Blue* that his fingers bled on the keys? These stories will show you that the composers whom people today might call boring and "classic" shook up the times they lived in.

INTRODUCING A COMPOSER

After you have read *Lives of the Musicians*, select one of the composers to introduce to the rest of your class. You might wish to begin your presentation by playing a song written by the composer and see if the class can guess what the song is and who wrote it. You should summarize information from *Lives of the Musicians* for your presentation, but you might want to read some passages straight from the text. If possible, find photographs of the composer to show the class. After your presentation, ask the class if any of the information you provided surprised them, and why. You might lead a discussion about how this person influenced other musicians, or if his or her influence can be found in popular culture today in such venues as advertising, movies, or other music.

Other books you may want to read:
What I Had Was Singing: The Story of Marian Anderson by Jeri Ferris
A Century of Country: An Illustrated History of Country Music by Robert K. Oermann

Guided Writing

DESCRIBING YOUR FAVORITE MUSIC

Music is a part of life. Whether you are at home, school, the mall, or in the car, you experience music. It is difficult to think of an instance when music is not present. Sometimes you don't even notice it. At other times, you focus on it and shut out everything else. You probably have already developed likes and dislikes. Think about the music that you find enjoyable. What do you like about it? In this assignment, you are going to choose a favorite musical selection. Then you will listen and enjoy the music. While you're doing that, you'll think about that music and your enjoyment of it. Then you will put your ideas into words.

How you feel about music is a very personal thing. Therefore, your aim in this exercise will simply be to express your thoughts and feelings, not try to inform or persuade. In doing so, you will be using **expressive writing**. Expressive writing is primarily done for oneself, not necessarily for a reader. Before you begin, take a look at the Professional Model below.

Professional Model

from *To Be or Not to Bop* by Dizzie Gillespie with Al Fraser, pages 363–365

In the words of Kenny Clarke:

I noticed something unique about Dizzy's playing, that's why I was hanging out with him. His approach to modern harmonies, but rhythms, mostly. He could take care of all that harmony, but his rhythms interested me real profoundly . . .

It was the idea of the cymbals, which blended with the trumpet. It was a certain way to play the cymbals, that Dizzy liked very well, and I just happened to be playing like that at the time. The cymbals and the trumpet have something in common, they're both brass. It's a perfect blend, and when the cymbals are played according to what the soloist is playing, something that corresponds, it's really beautiful . . .

A **metaphor** is a figure of speech in which one thing is spoken or written about as if it were another. This figure of speech invites the reader to make a comparison between the two things. A **simile** also compares one thing to another, but while using the word *like* or *as*. *My skateboard is a rocket* is a metaphor, while *My skateboard is* _like_ *a rocket* is a simile.

"When I die, I leave you my music—It is music that followed rules that were not written, but I hope I have added something new to what was existing."

—Igor Stravinsky

Examining the Model

The model shows different ways the book's contributors, Kenny Clarke and Budd Johnson, respond to the music of Dizzy Gillespie. They describe both musical components and his emotional response. When the speaker says "the cymbal was keeping the rhythm, and my feet were playing something else," he uses *feet* as a metaphor for a musical instrument. One especially visual metaphor is Budd Johnson's reference to jazz people as being *cats*. The speakers have fun with sound words in this piece. *Bebop* is probably the most evident because it is the topic. The tune entitled "Buh De Daht" and the *boom* of the bass drum are also good examples of sound words.

Reference to *harmony* and *rhythms* illustrates the technical components the authors talk about. In addition, the authors use words and phrases to describe their emotional responses to the music. ". . . his rhythms interested me profoundly" and the "perfect blend" of cymbals and trumpet are two examples.

The cymbal was keeping the rhythm, and my feet were playing something else, but I knew where the rhythm was. But evidently—I don't know whether he was listening to the cymbal or listening for the bass drum, I think it was the latter—he was listening for the Boom-Boom-Boom—on the bass drum. . . .

The most important characteristic of this new style of playing was camaraderie, that was first because everybody, each musician, just loved the other one, just loved them so much they just exchanged ideas and would do everything together. That's one characteristic about it I like very much. Another word for that is unity. That's right, and I think that era of jazz had more enemies than any phase of jazz. Everybody knew it was good, but they couldn't figure out what it was. And when somebody doesn't understand a thing, he has a tendency to dislike . . .

In the words of Budd Johnson:

The thing that I wrote, Clyde Hart and me, was a tune called "Buh De Daht." Well, this was a beginning for this stuff being put down on paper because the cats used to just play it and teach each other . . .

Now the way that word bebop came about to my way of thinking is when Dizzy would be trying to explain something or show you how to play it, he would hum it to you. And he would say, "No, no, it goes like this—ump-de-be-de-bop-be-bop-be-doo-dop-de-de-bop." So they would come up to Dizzy and say, "Hey, play some more of that bebop music," because he would be scatting like that. See, and they just picked up that word and they'd say, "Play some more of that bebop music."

Prewriting

FINDING YOUR VOICE. This piece of writing is called expressive. That's the kind of writing you use when you're trying to figure out and to explain something for the first time. Your voice will be your natural, everyday, unpressured voice. It's the voice you use when you talk to someone you know very well. Which of the following examples uses that voice?

The dude was really shifty.

He was slipperier than a pan of eels.

One would be wise not to trust such an example of *Homo sapiens*.

IDENTIFYING YOUR AUDIENCE. First of all, write for yourself and to yourself. Later, you may decide to share with your peers in your class. You may also want to consider submitting your writing to your school newspaper. Sharing ideas with others who have similar musical tastes through web site access is another possibility. But start out with yourself as the audience.

WRITING WITH A PLAN. Your first task is to choose one of your favorite pieces of music, and then listen to it. As you listen, there are a number of things that you can focus upon.

Plan on listening to your music more than once. You may wish to focus on musical components in your first listening(s), and then with new 'ears', listen to the music again on an emotional level. Just notice what you enjoy and note it. Some people see colors in their minds when they listen to music. What do you see in your mind's eye? What type of emotions do you experience?

When it is time to start writing, remember that you will be incorporating similes, metaphors, and sound words into your final product. You may even need to make up a word or two to help you! Make it "soundsational!" Make it sing!

You may also find it interesting to find out what the artist was trying to express with writing the music.

After Lisa listened to her music the first time, she filled in the graphic organizer to help her keep track of her observations. She listened to the music again so she could notice even more.

Student Model—Graphic Organizer

Music I Listened To: "Sometimes"

I. Musical Components
Lyrics? Do you like their meaning?
What instruments/voices are being used? *Voices are used. I like Britney Spears's voice.*
Is the music upbeat or slow? *Both. In between, not really fast, but not slow either.*
Is the music loud or soft (invigorating or soothing?) *Pretty loud, but it's pretty soothing.*
What do you think of the melody (ies) or, main musical ideas? *I really like them, because they put out a good message not a gross one.*
What do you think of the supporting sounds (harmonies)? *The harmonies are great. You can really feel the music. It's not plain.*
Other
II. Mood and Emotion
What mood do you experience as you listen? *I listen to music when I'm in a bad mood (it puts me in a good mood).*
Can the music change your mood? *Yes*
Does the music remind you of a specific time or event? *Not really. I just like it.*
Do you think about the first time, or a special time when you heard this music? *It's not really special, but I heard it on the radio and instantly wanted to know who was singing.*
Does the music evoke any type of visual imagery? *No, it's just fun music.*
Other

Language, Grammar, and Style
Making Pronouns and Antecedents Agree

Pronouns must always agree with their antecedents in number and gender.

IDENTIFYING PRONOUN-ANTECEDENT AGREEMENT. The **antecedent** is the noun that the pronoun references. **Number** refers to singular and plural. If the antecedent is singular, the pronoun must also be singular; if the antecedent is plural, the pronoun must also be plural.

INCORRECT NUMBER
Has *everyone* found *their* music?

CORRECT NUMBER
Has *everyone* found *his* or *her* music?

INCORRECT NUMBER
One of the musicians lost *their* music.

CORRECT NUMBER
One of the musicians lost *his* music.

Gender is the form a pronoun takes to show whether it is masculine, feminine, or neither masculine nor feminine. The gender of the pronoun must match that of its antecedent.
- When the antecedent is masculine, the pronoun is masculine:
  The *boy* listened to *his* favorite music.

continued on page 374

- When the antecedent is feminine, the pronoun is feminine:

  Rhonda gave *her* recital today.

- When the antecedent is neutral, use the pronouns *it* or *its:*

  The music has shown its power.

- When the antecedent is a word that could stand for both men and women, the masculine pronoun or both the masculine and feminine pronoun can be used:

  Someone forgot *his* or *her* instrument.

FIXING PRONOUN-ANTECEDENT AGREEMENT PROBLEMS. Fixing pronoun antecedent problems in sentences requires that you find the antecedent first and then track down the pronoun referring to it. Then check if they agree in gender and number.

Consider the following sentences. Which pronouns are correct and which need changing?

Nobody expected to find his or her instrument in the storage room.

One of the musicians left their violin on the stage.

Everybody has their own taste in music.

Find the pronoun-antecedent problems in Lisa's first draft. How would you fix it?

Drafting

If your organizer is complete, you should be ready to sit down and write. Make sure that your first paragraph tells about the type of music you will be describing. If you know some background information, this would be a good place to include it.

Refer to your organizer for the body of your paper. Approach your interpretation from both an intellectual and emotional angle. Write down the musical components first. Try to describe what you hear. Then write about the second list, the mood and emotion part. Use metaphors, similes, and lots of sound words to help you with both parts. Try to capture your music and your enjoyment of it. If you aren't enjoying writing about your favorite music, you probably aren't doing it right. Try to open up and bring life into it. Feel that music again. Express it. Share it. Sing it.

Your conclusion, the last paragraph, should reflect your overall impressions of the music. It's like the last part of the piece that goes b-boom.

Student Model—Draft

Everyone has ~~their~~ favorite song. Mine *Title?* / ^"a" or "her"

is "Sometimes" by Britney Spears. This *Good—you identify the piece right away!*

song is considered "soft rock." Anyone

who wants to listen to electric guitars

playing crazy stuff and hear lyrics

~~they~~ can't understand can listen to ^she

regular rock and roll. Soft rock on the ^*sound of the drum*

other hand is understandable and ^

usually more se^ttle. This song, unlike *sp.* / ^*subtle*

some other soft rocks song I've heard,

has a positive influence. *What do you mean?*

Add some sound words! The lyrics of this song are clear

and understandable. As clear as a ——*frag*

bright sunny day. ^The meaning of the *"I don't want to be shy everytime I'm alone I wonder why"*

lyrics is like watching a good movie,

they pull you right in. ^The song is *Tell something about the lyrics … be specific … so I know what you mean.*
...*tinkly wood chimes*

between slow and fast. They are like *Who?*

watching someone jog past. You can

clearly hear the lyrics and understand them. The song is fairly loud, like a television on medium, but it's really soothing as a nice hot bath. I like the melody because it's like a pg movie, *[underlined twice]* none of that gross stuff. The harmonies ... singing bells *[note]* of this song are very clear and adds *[underlined]* a lot to the song. The harmony is like adding yeast to bread, without it the bread doesn't taste good (or rise). The same rules apply for music. *Good image here!*

Can you turn this into a metaphor?

When I'm in a bad mood I listen to music. The second the music starts it's like walking right away from what was bothering me. I just get in a good mood when I listen to music. The reason I started listening to this song I was listening to the radio and the song *A bit wordy here* started and automatically I liked the *You use some fresh similes. Good job.* song. It was like listening to your parents saying they're raising your allowance. I really like this song and I would definitely recommend Britney Spears to any kid who was looking for good CLEAN songs. *Is that the biggest reason you like it?*

I like the melody, beat and lyrics

Revising and Proofreading

Review your self- and peer evaluations. Revise your writing by incorporating any of the suggestions you received. Proofread for spelling errors. Check to make sure you are using pronouns and antecedents in agreement.

Using Pronoun-Antecedent Agreement. Read through your description searching for pronouns. Underline them. Now scan backward looking for the words to which they refer. Circle these words. Do the pronouns and antecedents agree in gender and number? Correct any problems so that your reader will be able to follow your description without being confused by disagreement between pronouns and antecedents.

Self- and Peer Evaluation
When your first draft is complete, answer the following questions about your writing.

- Where in the opening paragraph do I clearly identify the music I am writing about?
- Did I include details from my graphic organizer?
- Where have I included similes, metaphors, and sound words?
- Did I make my ideas clear by using good grammar and sentence structure?
- Where do I show my impressions of the music?
- Where, if anywhere, does my voice sound "off," that is, not like me?
- Where, if anywhere, have I made mistakes in pronoun-antecedent agreement?
- What words are especially lively? Are there dull words that could be replaced?

Lisa's draft with self- and peer editing marks is shown here for you.

Publishing and Presenting

You may be happy to simply save your writing in your writing folder. If you choose to, there are certainly other eager audiences for this piece. Think of all the others who enjoy music, many of them the same kind you have written about. Others may be led to appreciate your music because of what you have written. So consider having your writing published in the school newspaper or on the school web page.

Student Model—Revised

I Hear the Music

by Lisa Bourdon

The musical selection I chose is the song "Sometimes" by Britney Spears. This song is considered "soft rock." You can tell because regular rock and roll music often has electric guitars playing crazy stuff and lyrics you usually can't understand. Soft rock, on the other hand, is more understandable and subtle. The "boom - chick chick" of the drum set is gentler than heavy metal rock and roll. This song, unlike some other soft rock songs I've heard, has a positive effect on me.

The cymbals shimmer into the opening vocals. The lyrics of this song are clear and understandable. She sings, "I don't want to be so shy/Every time I'm alone I wonder why." I know people who must feel like that. One girl in my school talks so softly that you can hardly hear her. She must wonder why, too. The lyrics are like watching a good movie, they pull you right in. The tinkly wind chimes that I hear in the chorus add a breezy effect. This song is in between slow and fast. It jogs past me. The song is fairly loud, like a television on medium, but it's really as soothing as a nice hot bath. I like the melody because it's like a PG movie

- none of that gross stuff. I can hear the pinging bells gently playing the melody above Britney's voice. The harmonies of this song are very clear and add a lot to the song. The harmony is the yeast in the music; without it the music is flat.

When I'm in a bad mood I listen to music. The music is a wave that washes away what was bothering me. I just get in a good mood when I listen. I first heard this song on the radio, and automatically I liked it. It was like listening to your parents saying they're raising your allowance. I really like this song and I would definitely recommend Britney Spears to any kid who was looking for a good melody and beat wrapped around clear lyrics.

Reflecting
Have your listening to and writing about this music changed your appreciation of it? Why might that be? Do you have different "favorite" pieces of music—depending upon your mood? on what you are doing? on whether you are listening with someone or by yourself?

UNIT FIVE *review*

Review: Words for Everyday Use

Check your knowledge of the following vocabulary words. Choose ten words that you would like to add to your own daily language. For each word, write a short sentence that includes the word in context. To review a word, look back to the page number(s) indicated.

- barnstorm (363)
- battery (357)
- chord (364)
- cultivate (364)
- disposition (335)
- execution (364)
- harmony (363)

- incorporate (365)
- lash (336)
- octave (364)
- ominous (336)
- profound (363)
- raucous (335)
- reluctant (334)

- spell (357)
- tempestuous (335)
- theory (365)
- torrential (336)
- turbulent (335)

Review: Literary Tools

Define each of the following terms, giving concrete examples when possible. To review a term, refer to the page number(s) indicated.

- ballad (350)
- folk song (350)
- lyrics (342)
- memoir (362)

- metaphor (342)
- myth (333)
- onomatopoeia (362)
- repetition (356)

- rhythm (356)
- setting (333)

Reflecting *on your reading*

Theme

Music is organic, which means that it changes and grows and evolves naturally. Musicians are inspired by other musicians to create new sounds. That is how folk music influenced rock music, rap evolved from rock music, and bebop evolved from jazz. Music can also influence written words—poems, stories, and lyrics. What influence has music had on your life? What kinds of music do you prefer? Why?

Genre

Words have rhythm and beat, just like music. Poetry can have rhythm, which is often what makes it so stirring. Poetry is a combination of words and sounds—what the poem is saying and how it sounds when it says it. You can find poetry in music, in advertising, in simple phrases, in childhood games, and in many other places. Choose a song with lyrics that you really like. Find or write down the lyrics and try to identify as many elements of poetry as you can within the lyrics.

Media Literacy

With a partner, discuss how music is portrayed in the media. How, for example, is hip-hop portrayed differently from classical music? How do different types of media vary in the ways they portray music? How do certain publications or television shows or radio stations demonstrate a bias toward a certain type of music and against another? How much of an effect do media biases have on what kinds of music people listen to?

On Your Own

Find a piece of beautiful music, like classical or jazz. It should be music without lyrics, or words. As you listen to it, begin to write down words that the music inspires you to write. Let the music guide and influence your writing. Write about anything you want to. Don't try to edit the words, and don't be critical of what you are writing. For now, just listen and write. Afterwards, look at what you have written. How did the music effect what you wrote? You may find that you have written something different from anything you have written before. Now you can recopy it and make any changes or corrections, if needed. If you did this as a group, you can compare how each person interpreted the music. If you were on your own, you can share your writing with the rest of your class or your friends.

Rajah Gokul-Das Hunting, c.1810. Indian artist.

Fantastic Places

echoes

Now, little old ladies who sleep under trees in a dark wood are almost always fairies in disguise.

—*Jane Yolen*

I knew a ghost once who was afraid of the dark, so he always appeared at noon. He had a terrible time scaring anyone.

—*Patricia C. Wrede said by Morwen in* Calling on Dragons

We like to think we live in daylight, but half the world is always dark; and fantasy, like poetry, speaks the language of the night.

—*Ursula LeGuin*

Don't you know . . . that everybody's got a Fairyland of their own?

—*P. L. Travers, said by Mary Poppins in* Mary Poppins

The earth with its fearful covering of dark shadow swam out of view and they moved rapidly through the Milky Way. And there was the Thing again.

—*Madeleine L'Engle,* A Wrinkle in Time

The great instrument of moral good is the imagination.

—*Percy Bysshe Shelley*

She heard the sound of the music again, lovely and elusive, and she saw Will and Bran step together on to the bright road of light and move away, over the river, through the air, into the haze and towards the Lost Land.

—*Susan Cooper,* Silver on the Tree

Some dragons would just go stomping along, eyes glowing, smoke twirling from their nostrils, never giving a thought to being secret, to keeping out of sight.

—*Sarah Sargent,* Weird Henry Berg

The Chosen were the caretakers of the Ellcrys, the strange and wondrous tree that stood at the center of the Gardens—the tree, as the legends told, that served as protector against a primordial evil that had very nearly destroyed the Elves centuries ago . . .

—*Terry Brooks,* The Elfstones of Shannara

Prereading

from The Hobbit

by J. R. R. Tolkien

Reader's T O O L B O X

NARRATOR. A **narrator** is a person or character who tells a story. A narrator is usually used to draw the reader into the story. As you read this selection, determine if the narrator is a person outside of the story or a character from the story.

CHARACTER. A **character** is a person or animal who takes part in the action of a literary work. The *main character* is called the protagonist. A character who struggles against the main character is called an *antagonist*. Characters can also be classified as *major characters* or *minor characters*. Two major characters in *The Hobbit* are Bilbo Baggins and a creature named Gollum. Make a chart by "mapping" out the details of each character to help you distinguish between them. Start by drawing a large circle in the middle with the character's name. Surround the circle with details about that character. Finally, connect each detail by drawing a line to the name.

Graphic Organizer

Bilbo Baggins

Reader's Journal

If you could do magic, what one magical skill would you choose to have? Why?

Reader's Resource

- In this story, a hobbit becomes lost in a tunnel within a mountain. In order for him to find his way back out of the tunnel, he must win at a game of riddles against Gollum.

- **HISTORY CONNECTION.** In the past, riddles were often seen as important and serious. In ancient Greece, priests and priestesses called oracles spoke in puzzling riddles. The messages were so confusing that other holy people had to explain what each one meant. People thought that the gods were speaking through the oracles in these strange words. In Greek mythology, there was a creature called a Sphinx. This creature had a woman's head, a lion's body, a snake's tail, and a bird's wings. It terrorized the city of Thebes by posing a riddle to everyone who passed by and killing those who could not answer it. Here is the riddle: what has one voice and becomes four-footed, two-footed, and three-footed? A man named Oedipus finally answered the riddle. The answer is this: a person, because a person crawls on all fours as a baby, walks on two feet when grown, and uses two feet and a cane when old. When the Sphinx heard Oedipus, it became enraged that someone knew the answer, and it threw itself off a high rock to its death.

The Mountain-path, 1937. J. R. R. Tolkien. Private Collection.

from The Hobbit

J. R. R. Tolkien

The main character in the selection that you are about to read is named Bilbo Baggins. Bilbo is an imaginary creature called a hobbit. Early in his novel The Hobbit, *J. R. R. Tolkien describes hobbits in the following way:*

I suppose hobbits need some description nowadays, since they have become rare and shy of the Big People, as they call us. They are (or were) a little people, about half our height, and smaller than the bearded Dwarves. Hobbits have no beards. There is little or no magic about them, except the ordinary everyday sort which helps them to disappear quietly and quickly when large stupid folk like you and me come <u>blundering</u> along, making a noise like elephants which they can hear a mile off. They are inclined to be fat in the stomach; they dress in bright colors (chiefly green and yellow); wear no shoes, because their feet grow natural leathery soles and thick warm brown hair like the stuff on their heads (which is curly); have long clever brown fingers, good-natured faces, and laugh deep fruity laughs (especially after dinner, which they have twice a day when they can get it). Now you know enough to go on with.

> **GUIDED READING**
> What sort of magic do hobbits have?

When Bilbo opened his eyes, he wondered if he had; for it was just as dark as with them shut. No one was anywhere near him. Just imagine his fright! He could hear nothing, see nothing, and he could feel nothing except the stone of the floor.

Very slowly he got up and groped about on all fours, till he touched the wall of the tunnel; but neither up nor down it could he find anything: nothing at all, no sign of goblins, no sign of dwarves. His head was swimming, and he was far from certain even of the direction they had been going in when he had his fall. He guessed as well as he could, and crawled along for a good way, till suddenly his hand met what felt like a tiny ring of cold metal lying on the floor of the tunnel. It was a turning point in his career, but he did not know it. He put the ring in his pocket almost without thinking; certainly it did not seem of any particular use at the moment. He did not go much further, but sat down on the cold floor and gave himself up to complete miserableness, for a long while. He thought of himself frying bacon and eggs in his own kitchen at home—for he could feel inside that it was high time for some meal or other; but that only made him miserabler.

> **GUIDED READING**
> Why might finding this object be "a turning point" in Bilbo's career?

He could not think what to do; nor could he think what had happened; or why he had been left behind; or why, if he had been left behind, the goblins had not caught him; or even why his head was so sore. The truth was

he had been lying quiet, out of sight and out of mind, in a very dark corner for a long while.

"Go back?" he thought. "No good at all! Go sideways? Impossible! Go forward? Only thing to do! On we go!" So up he got, and trotted along with his little sword held in front of him and one hand feeling the wall, and his heart all of a patter and a pitter.

Now certainly Bilbo was in what is called a tight place. But you must remember it was not quite so tight for him as it would have been for me or for you. Hobbits are not quite like ordinary people; and after all if their holes are nice cheery places and properly aired, quite different from the tunnels of the goblins, still they are more used to tunneling than we are, and they do not easily lose their sense of direction underground—not when their heads have recovered from being bumped. Also they can move very quietly, and hide easily, and recover wonderfully from falls and bruises, and they have a <u>fund</u> of wisdom and wise sayings that men have mostly never heard or have forgotten long ago.

GUIDED READING

In what ways are hobbits different from humans?

I should not have liked to have been in Mr. Baggins' place, all the same. The tunnel seemed to have no end. All he knew was that it was still going down pretty steadily and keeping in the same direction in spite of a twist and a turn or two. There were passages leading off to the side every now and then, as he knew by the glimmer of his sword, or could feel with his hand on the wall. Of these he took no notice, except to hurry past for

fear of goblins or half-imagined dark things coming out of them. On and on he went, and down and down; and still he heard no sound of anything except the occasional whirr of a bat by his ears, which startled him at first, till it became too frequent to bother about. I do not know how long he kept on like this, hating to go on, not daring to stop, on, on, until he was tireder than tired. It seemed like all the way to tomorrow and over it to the days beyond.

Suddenly without any warning he trotted splash into water! Ugh! it was icy cold. That pulled him up sharp and short. He did not know whether it was just a pool in the path, or the edge of an underground stream that crossed the passage, or the brink of a deep dark <u>subterranean</u> lake. The sword was hardly shining at all. He stopped, and he could hear, when he listened hard, drops drip-drip-dripping from an unseen roof into the water below; but there seemed no other sort of sound.

"So it is a pool or a lake, and not an underground river," he thought. Still he did not dare to wade out into the darkness. He could not swim; and he thought, too, of nasty slimy things, with big bulging blind eyes, wriggling in the water. There are strange things living in the pools and lakes in the hearts of mountains: fish whose fathers swam in, goodness only knows how many years ago, and never swam out again, while their eyes grew bigger and bigger and bigger from trying to see in the blackness; also there are other things more slimy than fish. Even in the tunnels and caves the goblins have made for themselves there are other

GUIDED READING

What sorts of creatures live in the hearts of mountains?

---

words for everyday use

fund (fund′) *n.,* supply, wealth. *Because my mother's birthday present was more expensive than I had expected, I had to take some money from the <u>fund</u> I have been saving for a new bicycle.*

sub·ter·ra·ne·an (sub tə rā′ nē ən) *adj.,* underground. *The mole lives a primarily <u>subterranean</u> life, while its close cousin, the field mouse, often spends time above ground.*

things living unbeknown to them that have sneaked in from outside to lie up in the dark. Some of these caves, too, go back in their beginnings to ages before the goblins, who only widened them and joined them up with passages, and the original owners are still there in odd corners, slinking and nosing about.

Deep down here by the dark water lived old Gollum, a small slimy creature. I don't know where he came from, nor who or what he was. He was Gollum—as dark as darkness, except for two big round pale eyes in his thin face. He had a little boat, and he rowed about quite quietly on the lake; for lake it was, wide and deep and deadly cold. He paddled it with large feet dangling over the side, but never a ripple did he make. Not he. He was looking out of his pale lamplike eyes for blind fish, which he grabbed with his long fingers as quick as thinking. He liked meat too. Goblin he thought good, when he could get it; but he took care they never found him out. He just throttled them from behind, if they ever came down alone anywhere near the edge of the water, while he was prowling about. They very seldom did, for they had a feeling that something unpleasant was lurking down there, down at the very roots of the mountain. They had come on the lake, when they were tunneling down long ago, and they found they could go no further; so there their road ended in that direction, and there was no reason to go that way—unless the Great Goblin sent them. Sometimes he took a fancy for fish from the lake, and sometimes neither goblin nor fish came back.

Actually Gollum lived on a slimy island of rock in the middle of the lake. He was watching Bilbo now from the distance with his pale eyes like telescopes. Bilbo could not see him, but he was wondering a lot about Bilbo, for he could see that he was no goblin at all.

Gollum got into his boat and shot off from the island, while Bilbo was sitting on the brink altogether <u>flummoxed</u> and at the end of his way and his wits. Suddenly up came Gollum and whispered and hissed:

"Bless us and splash us, my preciousssss! I guess it's a choice feast; at least a tasty <u>morsel</u> it'd make us, gollum!" And when he said gollum he made a horrible swallowing noise in his throat. That is how he got his name, though he always called himself 'my precious.'

GUIDED READING

What is strange about Gollum's manner of speech?

The hobbit jumped nearly out of his skin when the hiss came in his ears, and he suddenly saw the pale eyes sticking out at him.

"Who are you?" he said, thrusting his dagger in front of him.

"What iss he, my preciouss?" whispered Gollum (who always spoke to himself through never having anyone else to speak to). This is what he had come to find out, for he was not really very hungry at the moment, only curious; otherwise he would have grabbed first and whispered afterwards.

GUIDED READING

Why does Gollum talk to himself?

"I am Mr. Bilbo Baggins. I have lost the dwarves and I have lost the wizard, and I don't know where I am; and I don't want to know, if only I can get away."

"What's he got in his handses?" said Gollum, looking at the sword, which he did not quite like.

"A sword, a blade which came out of Gondolin!"

"Sssss" said Gollum, and became quite polite. "Praps[1] ye sits here and chats with it a bitsy, my preciousss. It like riddles, praps it does, does it?" He was anxious to appear friendly, at any rate for the moment, and until he found out more about the sword and the hobbit, whether he was quite alone really, whether he was good to eat, and whether Gollum was really hungry. Riddles were all he could think of. Asking them, and sometimes guessing them, had been the only game he had ever played with other funny creatures sitting in their holes in the long, long ago, before he lost all his friends and was driven away, alone, and crept down, down, into the dark under the mountains.

"Very well," said Bilbo, who was anxious to agree, until he found out more about the creature, whether he was quite alone, whether he was fierce or hungry, and whether he was a friend of the goblins.

> **GUIDED READING**
> What does Bilbo want to know about Gollum?

"You ask first," he said, because he had not had time to think of a riddle.

So Gollum hissed:

What has roots as nobody sees,
Is taller than trees,
*   Up, up it goes,*
*   And yet never grows?*

"Easy!" said Bilbo. "Mountain, I suppose."

"Does it guess easy? It must have a competition with us, my preciouss! If precious asks, and it doesn't answer, we eats it, my preciousss. If it asks us, and we doesn't answer, then we does what it wants, eh? We shows it the way out, yes!"

> **GUIDED READING**
> What are the rules of the game that Bilbo and Gollum play?

"All right!" said Bilbo, not daring to disagree, and nearly bursting his brain to think of riddles that could save him from being eaten.

Thirty white horses on a red hill,
*   First they champ,*
*   Then they stamp,*
Then they stand still.

That was all he could think of to ask—the idea of eating was rather on his mind. It was rather an old one, too, and Gollum knew the answer as well as you do.

"Chestnuts,[2] chestnuts," he hissed. "Teeth! teeth! my preciousss; but we has only six!" Then he asked his second:

Voiceless it cries,
Wingless flutters,
Toothless bites,
Mouthless mutters.

"Half a moment!" cried Bilbo, who was still thinking uncomfortably about eating. Fortunately he had once heard something rather like this before, and getting his wits back he thought of the answer. "Wind, wind of course," he said, and he was so pleased that he made up one on the spot. "This'll puzzle the nastly little underground creature," he thought:

An eye in a blue face
Saw an eye in a green face.
"That eye is like to this eye"
Said the first eye,
"But in low place,
Not in high place."

"Ss, ss, ss," said Gollum. He had been underground a long long time, and was forgetting this sort of thing. But just as Bilbo was beginning to hope that the wretch would not be able to answer, Gollum brought up memories of ages and ages and ages before,

---

1. **Praps.** Short form of "perhaps"
2. **Chestnuts.** Old, frequently repeated riddles or puzzles

when he lived with his grandmother in a hole in a bank by a river, "Sss, sss, my preciouss," he said. "Sun on the daisies it means, it does."

But these ordinary aboveground everyday sort of riddles were tiring for him. Also they reminded him of days when he had been less lonely and sneaky and nasty, and that put him out of temper. What is more they made him hungry; so this time he tried something a bit more difficult and more unpleasant:

> *It cannot be seen, cannot be felt,*
> *Cannot be heard, cannot be smelt.*
> *It lies behind stars and under hills,*
> *And empty holes it fills.*
> *It comes first and follows after,*
> *Ends life, kills laughter.*

Unfortunately for Gollum Bilbo had heard that sort of thing before; and the answer was all round him any way. "Dark!" he said without even scratching his head or putting on his thinking cap.

> *A box without hinges, key, or lid,*
> *Yet golden treasure inside is hid.*

He asked to gain time, until he could think of a really hard one. This he thought a dreadfully easy chestnut, though he had not asked it in the usual words. But it proved a nasty poser for Gollum. He hissed to himself, and still he did not answer; he whispered and spluttered.

After some while Bilbo became impatient. "Well, what is it?" he said. "The answer's not a kettle boiling over, as you seem to think from the noise you are making."

GUIDED READING
What effect do the riddles have on Gollum?

"Give us a chance; let it give us a chance, my preciouss—ss—ss."

"Well," said Bilbo, after giving him a long chance, "what about your guess?"

But suddenly Gollum remembered thieving from nests long ago, and sitting under the river bank teaching his grandmother, teaching his grandmother to suck—"Eggses!" he hissed. "Eggses it is!" Then he asked:

> *Alive without breath,*
> *As cold as death;*
> *Never thirsty, ever drinking,*
> *All in mail never clinking.*

He also in his turn thought this was a dreadfully easy one, because he was always thinking of the answer. But he could not remember anything better at the moment, he was so flustered by the egg-question. All the same it was a poser for poor Bilbo, who never had anything to do with the water if he could help it. I imagine you know the answer, of course, or can guess it as easy as winking, since you are sitting comfortably at home and have not the danger of being eaten to disturb your thinking. Bilbo sat and cleared his throat once or twice, but no answer came.

GUIDED READING
Why does Bilbo have difficulty answering this riddle? Why is it so simple for Gollum?

After a while Gollum began to hiss with pleasure to himself: "Is it nice, my preciouss? Is it juicy? Is it scrumptiously crunchable?" He began to peer at Bilbo out of the darkness.

"Half a moment," said the hobbit shivering. "I gave you a good long chance just now."

"It must make <u>haste</u>, haste!" said Gollum, beginning to climb out of his boat on to the shore to get at Bilbo. But when he put his

words for everyday use

haste (hāst') *n.,* act of hurrying; quickness of motion. *The hiker descended the hazardous mountain in* <u>haste</u> *because the sun was already setting and she did not want to spend the night on the dangerous slopes.*

long webby foot in the water, a fish jumped out in a fright and fell on Bilbo's toes.

"Ugh!" he said, "it is cold and clammy!"—and so he guessed. "Fish! Fish!" he cried. "It is fish!"

Gollum was dreadfully disappointed; but Bilbo asked another riddle as quick as ever he could, so that Gollum had to get back into his boat and think.

No-legs lay on one-leg, two-legs sat near on three-legs, four-legs got some.

It was not really the right time for this riddle, but Bilbo was in a hurry. Gollum might have had some trouble guessing it, if he had asked it at another time. As it was, talking of fish, "no-legs" was not so very difficult, and after that the rest was easy. "Fish on a little table, man at table sitting on a stool, the cat has the bones" that of course is the answer, and Gollum soon gave it. Then he thought the time had come to ask something hard and horrible. This is what he said:

This thing all things <u>devours</u>:
Birds, beasts, trees, flowers;
Gnaws iron, bites steel;
Grinds hard stones to meal;
Slays king, ruins town,
And beats high mountain down.

Poor Bilbo sat in the dark thinking of all the horrible names of all the giants and ogres he had ever heard told of in tales, but not one of them had done all these things. He had a feeling that the answer was quite different and that he ought to know it, but he could not think of it. He began to get frightened, and that is bad for thinking. Gollum began to get out of his boat. He flapped into the water and paddled to the bank; Bilbo could see his eyes coming towards him. His tongue seemed to stick in his mouth; he wanted to shout out: "Give me more time! Give me time!" But all that came out with a sudden squeal was:

"Time! Time!"

Bilbo was saved by pure luck. For that of course was the answer.

Gollum was disappointed once more; and now he was getting angry, and also tired of the game. It had made him very hungry indeed. This time he did not go back to the boat. He sat down in the dark by Bilbo. That made the hobbit most dreadfully uncomfortable and scattered his wits.

"It's got to ask uss a quesstion, my preciouss, yes, yess, yesss. Jusst one more quesstion to guess, yes, yess," said Gollum.

But Bilbo simply could not think of any question with that nasty wet cold thing sitting next to him, and pawing and poking him. He scratched himself, he pinched himself; still he could not think of anything.

"Ask us! ask us!" said Gollum.

Bilbo pinched himself and slapped himself; he gripped on his little sword; he even felt in his pocket with his other hand. There he found the ring he had picked up in the passage and forgotten about.

"What have I got in my pocket?" he said aloud. He was talking to himself, but Gollum thought it was a riddle, and he was frightfully upset.

> **GUIDED READING**
>
> What is Bilbo's last riddle?

"Not fair! not fair!" he hissed. "It isn't fair, my precious, is it, to ask us what it's got in its nassty little pocketses?"

---

 words for everyday use

de • vour (dē vowr') *v.,* swallow or engulf hungrily. *The hungry lion <u>devours</u> its food.*

Bilbo seeing what had happened and having nothing better to ask stuck to his question, "What have I got in my pocket?" he said louder.

"S-s-s-s-s," hissed Gollum. "It must give us three guesseses, my preciouss, three guesseses."

"Very well! Guess away!" said Bilbo.

"Handses!" said Gollum.

"Wrong," said Bilbo, who had luckily just taken his hand out again. "Guess again!"

"S-s-s-s-s," said Gollum more upset than ever. He thought of all the things he kept in his own pockets: fishbones, goblins' teeth, wet shells, a bit of bat-wing, a sharp stone to sharpen his fangs on, and other nasty things. He tried to think what other people kept in their pockets.

"Knife!" he said at last.

"Wrong!" said Bilbo, who had lost his some time ago. "Last guess!"

Now Gollum was in a much worse state than when Bilbo had asked him the egg-question. He hissed and spluttered and rocked himself backwards and forwards, and slapped his feet on the floor, and wriggled and squirmed; but still he did not dare to waste his last guess.

"Come on!" said Bilbo. "I am waiting!" He tried to sound bold and cheerful, but he did not feel at all sure how the game was going to end, whether Gollum guessed right or not.

"Time's up!" he said.

"String, or nothing!" shrieked Gollum, which was not quite fair—working in two guesses at once.

"Both wrong," cried Bilbo very much relieved; and he jumped at once to his feet, put his back to the nearest wall, and held out his little sword. He knew, of course, that the riddle-game was sacred and of immense <u>antiquity</u>, and even wicked creatures were afraid to cheat when they played at it. But he felt he could not trust this slimy thing to keep any promise at a pinch. Any excuse would do for him to slide out of it. And after all that last question had not been a genuine riddle according to the ancient laws.

GUIDED READING

Does Bilbo trust Gollum to keep his promise? Would Gollum be justified in not keeping his promise? Why, or why not?

But at any rate Gollum did not at once attack him. He could see the sword in Bilbo's hand. He sat still, shivering and whispering. At last Bilbo could wait no longer.

"Well?" he said. "What about your promise? I want to go. You must show me the way."

"Did we say so, precious? Show the nasty little Baggins the way out, yes, yes. But what has it got in its pocketses, eh? Not string, precious, but not nothing. Oh no! gollum!"

"Never you mind," said Bilbo. "A promise is a promise."

"Cross it is, impatient, precious," hissed Gollum. "But it must wait, yes it must. We can't go up the tunnels so hasty. We must go and get some things first, yes, things to help us."

"Well, hurry up!" said Bilbo, relieved to think of Gollum going away. He thought he was just making an excuse and did not mean to come back. What was Gollum talking about? What useful thing could he keep out on the dark lake? But he was wrong. Gollum did mean to come back. He was angry now and hungry. And he was a miserable wicked creature, and already he had a plan.

Not far away was his island, of which Bilbo knew nothing, and there in his hiding-place

---

words for everyday use

an • tiq • ui • ty (an tik′ wə tē) *n.*, quality of being ancient or old; great age. *The <u>antiquity</u> of the pottery shard was confirmed by the anthropologist who said it was probably created in the first century* BC.

he kept a few wretched <u>oddments</u>, and one very beautiful thing, very beautiful, very wonderful. He had a ring, a golden ring, a precious ring.

GUIDED READING

What is Gollum going to fetch from his island?

"My birthday-present!" he whispered to himself, as he had often done in the endless dark days. "That's what we wants now, yes; we wants it!"

He wanted it because it was a ring of power, and if you slipped that ring on

GUIDED READING

What power does the ring have?

your finger, you were invisible; only in the full sunlight could you be seen, and then only by your shadow, and that would be shaky and faint.

"My birthday-present! It came to me on my birthday, my precious." So he had always said to himself. But who knows how Gollum came by that present, ages ago in the old days when such rings were still at large in the world? Perhaps even the Master who ruled them could not have said. Gollum used to wear it at first, till it tired him; and then he kept it in a pouch next his skin, till it <u>galled</u> him; and now usually he hid it in a hole in the rock on his island, and was always going back to look at it. And still sometimes he put it on, when he could not bear to be parted from it any longer, or when he was very, very, hungry, and tired of fish. Then he would creep along dark passages looking for stray goblins. He might even <u>venture</u> into places where the torches were lit and made his eyes blink and smart; for he would be safe. Oh yes, quite safe. No one would see him, no one would notice him, till he had his fingers on their throat. Only a few hours ago he had worn it, and caught a small goblin-imp. How it squeaked! He still had a bone or two left to gnaw, but he wanted something softer.

"Quite safe, yes," he whispered to himself. "It won't see us, will it, my precious? No. It won't see us, and its nassty little sword will be useless, yes quite."

That is what was in his wicked little mind, as he slipped suddenly from Bilbo's side, and flapped back to his boat, and went off into the dark. Bilbo thought he had heard the last of him. Still he waited a while; for he had no idea how to find his way out alone.

Suddenly he heard a screech. It sent a shiver down his back. Gollum was cursing and wailing away in the gloom, not very far off by the sound of it. He was on his island, scrabbling here and there, searching and seeking in vain.

"Where is it? Where iss it?" Bilbo heard him crying. "Losst it is, my precious, lost, lost! Curse us and crush us, my precious is lost!"

"What's the matter?" Bilbo called. "What have you lost?"

"It mustn't ask us," shrieked Gollum. "Not its business, no, gollum! It's losst, gollum, gollum, gollum."

"Well, so am I," cried Bilbo, "and I want to get unlost. And I won the game, and you promised. So come along! Come and let me out, and then go on with your looking!" Utterly miserable as Gollum sounded, Bilbo could not find much pity in his heart, and he had a feeling that anything Gollum wanted so much could hardly be something good. "Come along!" he shouted.

"No, not yet, precious!" Gollum answered. "We must search for it, it's lost, gollum."

"But you never guessed my last question, and you promised," said Bilbo.

"Never guessed!" said Gollum. Then suddenly out of the gloom came a sharp hiss.

words for everyday use

odd • ments (äd′ mənts) *n.*, various miscellaneous objects. *The* <u>oddments</u> *on Gabriel's window included a hawk's feather, a medieval coin, and a ticket stub from a Celtics game.*

gall (gôl′) *v.*, irritate, annoy. *It* <u>galled</u> *Gerald to think that after he had studied so hard the test had been cancelled.*

ven • ture (ven′ chər) *v.*, undertake the risk of going. *Rita curled up on the couch because she did not want to* <u>venture</u> *out into the snowstorm.*

"What has it got in its pocketses? Tell us that. It must tell first."

As far as Bilbo knew, there was no particular reason why he should not tell. Gollum's mind had jumped to a guess quicker than his; naturally, for Gollum had brooded for ages on this one thing, and he was always afraid of its being stolen. But Bilbo was annoyed at the delay. After all, he had won the game, pretty fairly, at a horrible risk. "Answers were to be guessed not given," he said.

> **GUIDED READING**
> What guess do you think Gollum has made?

"But it wasn't a fair question," said Gollum. "Not a riddle, precious, no."

"Oh well, if it's a matter of ordinary questions," Bilbo replied, "then I asked one first. What have you lost? Tell me that!"

"What has it got in its pocketses?" The sound came hissing louder and sharper, and as he looked towards it, to his alarm Bilbo now saw two small points of light peering at him. As suspicion grew in Gollum's mind, the light of his eyes burned with a pale flame.

"What have you lost?" Bilbo persisted.

But now the light in Gollum's eyes had become a green fire, and it was coming swiftly nearer. Gollum was in his boat again, paddling wildly back to the dark shore; and such a rage of loss and suspicion was in his heart that no sword had any more terror for him.

Bilbo could not guess what had maddened the wretched creature, but he saw that all was up, and that Gollum meant to murder him at any rate. Just in time he turned and ran blindly back up the dark passage down which he had come, keeping close to the wall and feeling it with his left hand.

"What has it got in its pocketses?" he heard the hiss loud behind him, and the splash as Gollum leapt from his boat. "What have I, I wonder?" he said to himself, as he panted and stumbled along. He put his left hand in his pocket. The ring felt very cold as it quietly slipped on to his groping forefinger.

The hiss was close behind him. He turned now and saw Gollum's eyes like small green lamps coming up the slope. Terrified he tried to run faster, but suddenly he struck his toes on a snag in the floor, and fell flat with his little sword under him.

In a moment Gollum was on him. But before Bilbo could do anything, recover his breath, pick himself up, or wave his sword, Gollum passed by, taking no notice of him, cursing and whispering as he ran.

> **GUIDED READING**
> Why does Gollum pass Bilbo?

What could it mean? Gollum could see in the dark. Bilbo could see the light of his eyes palely shining even from behind. Painfully he got up, and <u>sheathed</u> his sword, which was now glowing faintly again, then very cautiously he followed. There seemed nothing else to do. It was no good crawling back down to Gollum's water. Perhaps if he followed him, Gollum might lead him to some way of escape without meaning to.

---

words for everyday use **sheathe** (shēth') v., enclose or protect with a cover or case. *Because the kitchen knife was sharp, Julio <u>sheathed</u> it in a protective layer of plastic before packing it for the trip to his new apartment.*

"Curse it! curse it! curse it!" hissed Gollum. "Curse the Baggins! It's gone! What has it got in its pocketses? Oh we guess, we guess, my precious. He's found it, yes he must have. My birthday-present."

Bilbo pricked up his ears. He was at last beginning to guess himself. He hurried a little, getting as close as he dared behind Gollum, who was still going quickly, not looking back, but turning his head from side to side, as Bilbo could see from the faint glimmer on the walls.

"My birthday-present! Curse it! How did we lose it, my precious? Yes, that's it. When we came this way last, when we twisted that nassty young squeaker. That's it. Curse it! It slipped from us, after all these ages and ages! It's gone, gollum."

Suddenly Gollum sat down and began to weep, a whistling and gurgling sound horrible to listen to. Bilbo halted and flattened himself against the tunnel-wall. After a while Gollum stopped weeping and began to talk. He seemed to be having an argument with himself.

"It's no good going back there to search, no. We doesn't remember all the places we've visited. And it's no use. The Baggins has got it in its pocketses; the nassty noser has found it, we says.

"We guesses, precious only guesses. We can't know till we find the nassty creature and squeezes it. But it doesn't know what the present can do, does it? It'll just keep it in its pocketses. It doesn't know, and it can't go far. It's lost itself, the nassty nosey thing. It doesn't know the way out. It said so.

"It said so, yes; but it's tricksy. It doesn't say what it means. It won't say what it's got in its pocketses. It knows. It knows a way in, it must know a way out, yes. It's off to the back-door. To the back-door, that's it.

"The goblinses will catch it then. It can't get out that way, precious.

"Ssss, sss, gollum! Goblinses! Yes, but if it's got the present, our precious present, then goblinses will get it, gollum! They'll find it, they'll find out what it does. We shan't ever be safe again, never, gollum! One of the goblinses will put it on, and then no one will see him. He'll be there but not seen. Not even our clever eyeses will notice him; and he'll come creepsy and tricksy and catch us, gollum, gollum!

"Then let's stop talking, precious, and make haste. If the Baggins has gone that way, we must go quick and see. Go! Not far now. Make haste!"

With a spring Gollum got up and started shambling off at a great pace. Bilbo hurried after him, still cautiously, though his chief fear now was of tripping on another snag and falling with a noise. His head was in a whirl of hope and wonder. It seemed that the ring he had was a magic ring: it made you invisible! He had heard of such things, of course, in old old tales; but it was hard to believe that he really had found one, by accident. Still there it was: Gollum with his bright eyes had passed him by, only a yard to one side.

On they went, Gollum flip-flapping ahead, hissing and cursing; Bilbo behind going as softly as a hobbit can. Soon they came to places where, as Bilbo had noticed on the way down, side-passages opened, this way and that. Gollum began at once to count them.

> **GUIDED READING**
>
> How does Bilbo feel when he realizes that he has found a magic ring?

---

words for everyday use

sham • ble (sham' bəl) v., walk in a clumsy manner. *At the rest stop, Hank shambled out of the car to stretch his legs.*

"One left, yes. One right, yes. Two right, yes, yes. Two left, yes, yes." And so on and on.

As the count grew he slowed down, and he began to get shaky and weepy; for he was leaving the water further and further behind, and he was getting afraid. Goblins might be about, and he had lost his ring. At last he stopped by a low opening, on their left as they went up.

"Seven right, yes. Six left, yes!" he whispered. "This is it. This is the way to the back-door, yes. Here's the passage!"

He peered in, and shrank back. "But we durstn't go in, precious, no we durstn't. Goblinses down there. Lots of goblinses. We smells them. Ssss!

"What shall we do? Curse them and crush them! We must wait here, precious, wait a bit and see."

So they came to a dead stop. Gollum had brought Bilbo to the way out after all, but Bilbo could not get in! There was Gollum sitting humped up right in the opening, and his eyes gleamed cold in his head, as he swayed it from side to side between his knees.

Bilbo crept away from the wall more quietly than a mouse; but Gollum stiffened at once, and sniffed, and his eyes went green. He hissed softly but <u>menacingly</u>. He could not see the hobbit, but now he was on the alert, and he had other senses that the darkness had sharpened: hearing and smell. He

> **GUIDED READING**
>
> How does Gollum know Bilbo is near if Gollum can't see Bilbo?

seemed to be crouched right down with his flat hands splayed on the floor, and his head thrust out, nose almost to the stone. Though he was only a black shadow in the gleam of his own eyes, Bilbo could see or feel that he

was tense as a bowstring, gathered for a spring.

Bilbo almost stopped breathing, and went stiff himself. He was desperate. He must get away, out of this horrible darkness, while he had any strength left. He must fight. He must stab the foul thing, put its eyes out, kill it. It meant to kill him. No, not a fair fight. He was invisible now. Gollum had no sword. Gollum had not actually threatened to kill him, or tried to yet. And he was miserable, alone, lost. A sudden understanding, a pity mixed with horror, welled up in Bilbo's heart: a glimpse of endless unmarked days without light or hope of betterment, hard stone, cold fish, sneaking and whispering. All these thoughts passed in a flash of a second. He trembled. And then quite suddenly in another flash, as if lifted by a new strength and resolve, he leaped.

> **GUIDED READING**
>
> What emotion makes Bilbo change his mind about killing Gollum?

No great leap for a man, but a leap in the dark. Straight over Gollum's head he jumped, seven feet forward and three in the air indeed, had he known it, he only just missed cracking his skull on the low arch of the passage.

Gollum threw himself backwards, and grabbed as the hobbit flew over him, but too late: his hands snapped on thin air, and Bilbo, falling fair on his sturdy feet, sped off down the new tunnel. He did not turn to see what Gollum was doing. There was a hissing and cursing almost at his heels at first, then it stopped. All at once there came a bloodcurdling shriek, filled with hatred and despair. Gollum was defeated. He dared go no further. He had lost: lost his prey, and lost, too, the only thing he had ever cared for, his precious. The cry brought Bilbo's heart to his

words for everyday use

men • ac • ing (men' əs iŋ) *adj.*, threatening. *The <u>menacing</u> monster stepped forward and growled.* **menacingly,** *adv.*

mouth, but still he held on. Now faint as an echo, but menacing, the voice came behind:

"Thief, thief, thief! Baggins! We hates it, we hates it, we hates it for ever!"

GUIDED READING

Do you think Gollum's shriek frightens Bilbo or makes him feel pity for Gollum? Explain.

Then there was a silence. But that too seemed menacing to Bilbo. "If goblins are so near that he smelt them," he thought, "then they'll have heard his shrieking and cursing. Careful now, or this way will lead you to worse things."

GUIDED READING

What now threatens Bilbo?

The passage was low and roughly made. It was not too difficult for the hobbit, except when, in spite of all care, he stubbed his poor toes again, several times, on nasty jagged stones in the floor. "A bit low for goblins, at least for the big ones," thought Bilbo, not knowing that even the big ones, the orcs of the mountains, go along at a great speed stooping low with their hands almost on the ground.

Soon the passage that had been sloping down began to go up again, and after a while it climbed steeply. That slowed Bilbo down. But at last the slope stopped, the passage turned a corner, and dipped down again, and there, at the bottom of a short incline, he saw, filtering round another corner—a glimpse of light. Not red light, as of fire or lantern, but a pale out-of-doors sort of light. Then Bilbo began to run.

Scuttling as fast as his legs would carry him he turned the last corner and came suddenly right into an open space, where the light, after all that time in the dark, seemed dazzlingly bright. Really it was only a leak of sunshine in through a doorway, where a great door, a stone door, was left standing open.

Bilbo blinked, and then suddenly he saw the goblins: goblins in full armor with drawn swords sitting just inside the door, and watching it with wide eyes, and watching the passage that led to it. They were aroused, alert, ready for anything.

They saw him sooner than he saw them. Yes, they saw him. Whether it was an accident, or a last trick of the ring before it took a new master, it was not on his finger. With yells of delight the goblins rushed upon him.

A pang of fear and loss, like an echo of Gollum's misery, smote Bilbo, and forgetting even to draw his sword he struck his hands into his pockets. And there was the ring still, in his left pocket, and it slipped on his finger. The goblins stopped short. They could not see a sign of him. He had vanished. They yelled twice as loud as before, but not so delightedly.

"Where is it?" they cried.

"Go back up the passage!" some shouted.

"This way!" some yelled. "That way!" others yelled.

"Look out for the door," bellowed the captain.

Whistles blew, armor clashed, swords rattled, goblins cursed and swore and ran hither and thither, falling over one another and getting very angry. There was a terrible outcry, to-do, and disturbance.

Bilbo was dreadfully frightened, but he had the sense to understand what had happened and to sneak behind a big barrel which held drink for the goblin-guards, and so get out of the way and avoid being bumped into, trampled to death, or caught by feel.

GUIDED READING

How does Bilbo avoid being caught by the goblins?

"I must get to the door, I must get to the door!" he kept on saying to himself, but it was a long time before he ventured to try. Then it was like a horrible game of blindman's-buff. The place was full of goblins running about, and the poor little hobbit dodged this way and that, was knocked over by a goblin who could not make out what he had bumped into, scrambled away on all fours, slipped

between the legs of the captain just in time, got up, and ran for the door.

It was still ajar, but a goblin had pushed it nearly to. Bilbo struggled but he could not move it. He tried to squeeze through the crack. He squeezed and squeezed, and he stuck! It was awful. His buttons had got wedged on the edge of the door and the door-post. He could see outside into the open air: there were a few steps running down into a narrow valley between tall mountains; the sun came out from behind a cloud and shone bright on the outside of the door—but he could not get through.

Suddenly one of the goblins inside shouted: "There is a shadow by the door. Something is outside!"

> **GUIDED READING**
> What gives away Bilbo's presence to the goblins?

Bilbo's heart jumped into his mouth. He gave a terrific squirm. Buttons burst off in all directions. He was through, with a torn coat and waistcoat, leaping down the steps like a goat, while bewildered goblins were still picking up his nice brass buttons on the doorstep.

Of course they soon came down after him, hooting and hallooing,[3] and hunting among the trees. But they don't like the sun: it makes their legs wobble and their heads giddy. They could not find Bilbo with the ring on, slipping in and out of the shadow of the trees, running quick and quiet, and keeping out of the sun; so soon they went back grumbling and cursing to guard the door. Bilbo had escaped. ■

> **GUIDED READING**
> Why did the goblins quit their hunt for Bilbo?

---

3. **hallooing.** Shouting or calling out

Respond *to the* SELECTION

If you were Bilbo, would you have killed Gollum when you had the chance, or would you have tried to escape without killing him? Why?

About *the* AUTHOR

John Ronald Reuel (J. R. R.) Tolkien (1892–1973) was an English author, born in Bloemfontein, South Africa. He taught for 35 years at Oxford University in England. As a teacher and scholar, Tolkien's field was the languages and literature of the Middle Ages. Tolkien borrowed heavily from folk tales and legends from the Middle Ages to write his famous fantasy stories. Those stories are full of elves, fairies, dragons, and goblins like Gollum. Tolkien wrote a series of books about hobbits, imaginary creatures who live in a place called Middle-earth. If you enjoyed this selection from *The Hobbit,* the first in the series, you might want to read the rest of the book and try Tolkien's three other novels about Middle-earth, *The Lord of the Rings, The Two Towers,* and *The Return of the King.*

Investigate, Inquire, and Imagine

Recall: GATHERING FACTS

1a. What does Bilbo find on the ground as he crawls along through the tunnel?

2a. What kind of game did Bilbo and Gollum play? What will happen if Bilbo can't answer Gollum's riddle? What will happen if Gollum can't answer Bilbo's riddle?

3a. How does Bilbo escape from Gollum?

→ **Interpret:** FINDING MEANING

1b. What did the narator mean by saying that "finding it was a turning point in his career"?

2b. Why do think Bilbo and Gollum agree to play?

3b. Why does Bilbo decide to jump over Gollum and run away instead of killing him with his sword?

Analyze: TAKING THINGS APART

4a. How would you describe Bilbo's character? List his qualities.

→ **Synthesize:** BRINGING THINGS TOGETHER

4b. Based on your description of Bilbo's character, predict what he would do or how he would react if Gollum won the riddle game.

Evaluate: MAKING JUDGMENTS

5a. Pretend you are a judge. How would you rule Bilbo's last riddle? Do you think it was a fair question? Why, or why not?

→ **Extend:** CONNECTING IDEAS

5b. In what ways would the story be different if Gollum kept his word and simply showed Bilbo out of the tunnel? Do you think their relationship would be different compared to the way it ended in the story? Why, or why not?

Understanding *Literature*

NARRATOR. A **narrator** is a person or character who tells a story. A narrator is usually used to draw the reader into the story. Does the narrator of *The Hobbit* seem to take part in the action of the story, or is he or she an outside witness?

CHARACTER. A **character** is a person or animal who takes part in the action of a literary work. The main character is called the *protagonist.* A character who struggles against the main character is called an *antagonist.* Characters can also be classified as *major characters* or *minor characters.* The two major characters in this selection are Bilbo Baggins and a creature named Gollum. Which is the protagonist? Which is the antagonist? How do you know?

Writer's Journal

1. Imagine you are Bilbo. Write a **postcard** to your family, describing the place in which you are lost. Include how you feel about being lost.

2. Imagine you are Gollum, who has lost all his friends. Write a **journal entry** about how you feel now that there is no one to talk to.

3. Pretend you are a goblin. As a goblin, you know your way around the tunnels. Go back to the text and write down **directions** for Bilbo to help him find his way out of the tunnel.

Skill Builders

Language, Grammar, and Style

USING COMMAS AND QUOTATIONS MARKS. The use of commas and quotation marks helps readers to understand what part is narration and what part is conversation/dialogue within a story. Rewrite the sentences below, placing commas and quotation marks in their proper places and capitalizing where necessary.

1. Bilbo said give me a moment to think about the answer.
2. I don't know the way home Bilbo cried miserably.
3. Curse it! Curse it! screamed Gollum. Curse Bilbo!
4. As he shook his head in shame, he said I lost the game.
5. I don't think so Bilbo replied.

Speaking and Listening

DEBATING. With a partner, debate the question, "Was Bilbo's last riddle fair?" Back up your position with references to the text. For more information, see the Language Arts Survey 4.21, "Participating in a Debate."

Study and Research

RESEARCHING CREATURES. The author of *The Hobbit*, J. R. R. Tolkien, borrowed heavily from mythology and folklore from the Middle Ages in creating his stories. These stories include elves, goblins, fairies, and dragons. Pick one of these creatures to research. Then write a short paper that describes your creature in detail. If you want to be creative, draw a picture of your creature.

Collaborative Learning

DEVELOPING A SETTING. The setting of a literary work is the time and place in which it happens. Writers create settings in many ways. In drama, a setting is usually revealed through stage directions, props, and costumes. Get into groups of three or four people. Pretend you are asked to write a scene for a horror film. The first step, however, is to establish setting. Write a setting that creates suspense.

Reader's Journal

Have you ever felt pressured by your friends to do something you didn't want to do? How did you respond to the pressure?

Reader's Resource

- **CULTURAL CONNECTION.** In Liverpool, England, there is an underground web of tunnels built by Joseph Williamson (1769–1840). For most of the 20th century, these tunnels were only rumors. Williamson was not known as an architect. He was actually a wealthy tobacco agent with a compassionate heart. After the Napoleonic Wars, England was in deep recession. Unwilling to see families starve, he hired unemployed men to build huge brick arches behind his house in return for an honest wage. Word got out that this man was giving men work at a good wage, so Williamson kept hiring more and more men. The result was the creation of an enormous underground tunnel system, or labyrinth. After over 150 years of exploration, scholars are still unable to map out the underground system, because it has not all been explored yet. The labyrinth has been found to be too complex and too vast to figure out. However, that has not stopped them from trying.

Prereading

"THE TUNNEL"
by Sarah Ellis

Reader's TOOLBOX

PLOT. A **plot** is a series of events related to a central conflict, or struggle. A plot usually involves the introduction of a conflict, its development, and its eventual resolution. The parts of a plot usually include the exposition (or introduction), the inciting incident, the climax, and the resolution—although some plots contain additional elements. The *exposition* sets the tone or mood, introduces the characters and the setting, and provides background information. The *inciting incident* introduces the central conflict. The *climax* is the high point of interest or suspense in the plot. The *resolution* is the point at which the central conflict is ended, or resolved. As you read "The Tunnel," try to identify these elements of the plot.

CONFLICT. Conflict is a struggle between people or things in a literary work. A plot is formed around conflict. The conflict can be internal or external. A plot usually involves the introduction of a conflict, its development, and eventual resolution. As you read "The Tunnel" see if you can discover where the plot moves from introduction into development, and then to resolution.

FLASHBACK. Flashback is a part of a story, poem, or play that presents events that happened at an earlier time. As you read the story, look for examples of flashback, and think about how they help develop the central conflict.

Graphic *Organizer*

Fill in each block with notes about the corresponding part of the plot.

Climax

Inciting Incident   Resolution

Exposition

THE TUNNEL

Sarah Ellis

When I was a kid and I imagined myself older and with a summer job, I thought about being outdoors. Tree planting, maybe. Camping out, getting away from the parents, coming home after two months with biceps[1] of iron and bags of money. I used to imagine myself rappelling[2] down some mountain with a geological[3] hammer tucked into my belt. At the very worst I saw myself sitting on one of those tall lifeguard chairs with zinc ointment on my lips.

GUIDED READING

What is the worst thing the speaker can imagine doing for a summer job, before he winds up babysitting?

I didn't know that by the time I was sixteen it would be the global economy and there would be no summer jobs, even though you did your life-skills analysis as recommended by the guidance counselor at school. Motivated! Energetic! Computer literate![4] Shows initiative! Workplace-appropriate hair! What I never imagined was that by the time I got to be sixteen the only job you could get would be baby-sitting.

I sometimes take care of my cousin Laurence. Laurence likes impersonating trucks and being held upside down. I am good at assisting during these activities. This evidently counts as work-related experience.

Girls are different.

Elizabeth, who calls herself Ib, is six and one-quarter years old. I go over to her place at 7:30 in the morning and I finish at one o'clock. Then her dad or her mom or her gran (who is not really her gran but the mother of her dad's ex-wife) takes over. Ib has a complicated family. She doesn't seem to mind.

GUIDED READING

How old is Elizabeth?

Ib has a yellow plastic suitcase. In the suitcase are Barbies. Ib would like to play with Barbies for five and one-half hours every day. In my baby-sitting course at the community center they taught us about first aid, diapering, nutritious snacks, and how to skip to my Lou. They did not teach Barbies.

GUIDED READING

What does Ib keep in her plastic suitcase?

"You be Wanda," says Ib, handing me a nude Barbie who looks as though she is having a bad hair life.

I'm quite prepared to be Wanda if that's what the job requires. But once I *am* Wanda I don't know what the heck to do.

Ib is busy dressing Francine, Laurice, Betty, and Talking Doll, who is not a Barbie at all, but a baby doll twice the size of the Barbies.

"What should I do?" I ask.

Ib gives me the Look, an unblinking stare that combines impatience, scorn, and pity.

"*Play*," she says.

When you have sixteen-year-old guy hands, there is no way to hold a nude Barbie without violating her personal space. But all her clothes seem to be made of extremely form-fitting stretchy neon stuff, and I can't get her rigid arms with their poky fingers into the sleeves.

Playing with Barbies makes all other activities look good. The study of French irregular verbs, for example, starts to seem attractive. The board game Candyland, a favorite of Cousin Laurence, and previously condemned by me as a sure method for turning the human brain to tofu,[5] starts to seem like a laff riot.

---

1. **biceps.** Large muscles at the front of the upper arm
2. **rappelling.** Moving down the face of a cliff while tied to ropes anchored at the cliff top
3. **geological.** Related to the study of the earth's crust, including rock types
4. **Computer literate.** Knowledgeable or capable with computers
5. **tofu.** Bland, cheeselike food made from soybeans

words for everyday use

in • i • tia • tive (i ni′ shə tiv) *n.*, action of taking the first step or move. *I took the initiative by asking the first question.*

im • per • son • ate (im pur′ sən āt) *v.*, represent; act like. *Chad impersonates Elvis at parties.*

scorn (skorn′) *n.*, extreme contempt or dislike for someone or something. *Todd does notice the scorns of people who dislike him.*

I look at my watch. It is 8:15. The morning stretches ahead of me. Six weeks stretch ahead of me. My life stretches ahead of me. My brain is edging dangerously close to the idea of <u>eternity</u>.

I hold Wanda by her hard, clawlike plastic hand and think of things that Laurence likes to do. We could notch the edge of yogurt lids to make deadly star-shaped weapons for a Ninja attack, but somehow I don't think that's going to cut it with Ib. She's probably not going to go for a burping contest, either.

A warm breeze blows in the window, a small wind that probably originated at sea and blew across the beach, across all those glistening, slowly browning bodies, before it ended up here, trapped in Barbie World. I'm <u>hallucinating</u> the smell of suntan oil. I need to get outside.

I do not suggest a walk. I know, from Laurence, that "walk" is a four-letter word to six-year-olds. Six-year-olds can run around for seventy-two hours straight, but half a block of walking and they suffer from life-threatening exhaustion. I therefore avoid the *W* word.

"Ib, would you like to go on an exploration mission?"

Ib thinks for a moment. "Yes."

We pack up the Barbies.

"It's quite a long way," I say. "We can't take the suitcase."

"I need to take Wanda."

We take Wanda.

We walk along the overgrown railway tracks out to the edge of town. Ib steps on every tie.[6] The sun is behind us and we stop

> **GUIDED READING**
> What does playing Barbies make the speaker think about?

> **GUIDED READING**
> What do they do by the tracks in the sun?

every so often to make our shadows into letters of the alphabet.

("And what sort of work experience can you bring to this job, young man?"

"Well, sir, I spent one summer playing with Barbie dolls and practicing making my body into a *K*."

"Excellent! We've got exciting openings in that area.")

We follow the tracks as the sun rises high in the sky. Ib walks along the rail holding my hand. My feet crunch on the sharp gravel and Ib sings something about ducks. I inhale the dusty smell of sun-baked weeds and I'm pulled back to the summer that we used to come out here, Jeff and Danielle and I. That was the summer that Jeff was a double agent planning to blow up the enemy supply train.

> **GUIDED READING**
> What does Ken smell that reminds him of his past trips to the tunnel?

The sharp sound of a pneumatic[7] drill rips through the air and Ib's hand tightens in mine.

"What's that?"

I remember. "It's just a woodpecker."

There was a woodpecker once back then, too.

Machine-gun attack!" yelled Jeff. And I forgot it was a game and threw myself down the bank into the bushes. Jeff laughed at me.

No little ducks came swimming back." Ib's high, thin voice is burrowing itself into my brain and there is a pulse

---

6. **tie.** Wooden strips between railroad tracks
7. **pneumatic.** Operating by compressed air

---

words for everyday use

e • ter • ni • ty (i tər′ nə tē) *n.*, long period of time that seems endless. *I had to wait what seemed like an <u>eternity</u> for my bus.*

hal • lu • ci • nate (hə lü′ sə nāt) *v.*, experience sights or sounds that are not actually present. *Sometimes patients who are heavily medicated will <u>hallucinate</u>.*

above my left eye. I begin to wish I had brought something to drink. Maybe it's time to go back.

GUIDED READING

What does Ken begin to wish he'd brought along?

And then we come to the stream. I hear it before I see it. And then I remember what happened there.

Ib jumps off the tracks and dances off toward the water.

I don't want to go there. "Not that way, Ib."

"Come *on*, Ken. I'm exploring. This is an exploration mission. You said."

I follow her. It's different. The trees—dusty, scruffy-looking cottonwoods—have grown up and the road appears too soon. But there it is. The stream takes a bend and disappears into a small culvert[8] under the road. Vines grow across the entrance to the drainage pipe. I push them aside and look in. A black hole with a perfect circle of light at the end.

It's so small. Had we really walked through it? Jeff and Danielle and finally me, terrified, shamed into it by a girl and a double dare.

I take a deep breath and I'm there again. That smell. Wet and green and dangerous. There I was, feet braced against the pipe, halfway through the tunnel, at the darkest part. I had kept my mind up, up out of the water where Jeff said that blackwater bloodsuckers lived. I kept my mind up until it went into the weight of the earth above me. Tons of dirt and cars and trucks and being buried alive.

Dirt pressing heavy against my chest, against my eyelids, against my legs which wouldn't move. And then, above the roaring in my ears, I heard a high snatch of song, two notes with no words. Calling. I pushed against the concrete and screamed without a sound.

And then Jeff yelled into the tunnel, "What's the matter, Kenny? Is it the bloodsuckers? Kenton,

Kenton, where are you? Ve vant to suck your blood." Jeff had a way of saying "Kenton" that made it sound like an even finkier name than it is. By this time I had peed my pants and I had to pretend to slip and fall into the water to cover up. The shock of the cold. The end of the tunnel. Jeff pushed me into the stream because I was wet anyway. Danielle stared at me and she knew.

GUIDED READING

What did Danielle do when she first saw Ken come out of the tunnel?

"Where does it go?" Ib pulls on my shirt. And I'm big again. Huge. Like Talking Doll.

"It goes under the road. I walked through it once."

"Did you go to that other place?"

"What other place?"

Ib gives me the Look. "Where those other girls play. I think this goes there."

Yeah, right. The Barbies visit the culvert.

Ib steps right into the tunnel. "Come on, Kenton."

I grab her. "Hey! Hold it. You can't go in there. You'll…you'll get your sandals wet. And I can't come. I don't fit."

GUIDED READING

What does Ken say will happen if Ib goes into the tunnel?

Ib sits down on the gravel and takes off her sandals. "I fit."

Blackwater bloodsuckers. But why would I want to scare her? And, hey, it's just a tunnel. So I happen to suffer from claustrophobia.[9] That's my problem.

"Okay, but look, I'll wait on this side until you're halfway through and then I'll cross over the road and meet you on the other side. Are you sure you're not scared?"

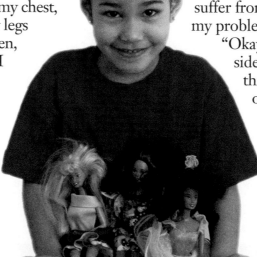

---

8. **culvert.** Pipelike drain that passes under a road, railroad track, or through an embankment

9. **claustrophobia.** Abnormal fear of being in an enclosed space

Ib steps into the pipe and stretches to become an X. "Look! Look how I fit!"

I watch the little X splash its way into the darkness. "Okay, Ib, see you on the other side. Last one there's a rotten egg." I let the curtain of vines fall across the opening.

I pick up the sandals and climb the hill. It's different, too. It used to be just feathery horsetail[10] and now skinny trees grow there.

I grab on to them to pull myself up. I cross the road, <u>hovering</u> on the center line as an RV rumbles by and then I slide down the other side, following a small avalanche of pebbles. I kneel on the top of the pipe and stick my head in, upside down.

"Hey, rotten egg, I beat you."

Small, echoing, dripping sounds are the only answer.

I peer into the darkness. She's teasing me. "Ib!"

Ib, Ib, Ib—the tunnel throws my voice back at me. A semitrailer roars by on the road. I jump down and stand at the pipe's entrance. My eyes adjust and I can see the dim green *O* at the other end. No outline of a little girl. A tight heaviness grips me around the chest.

"Ibbie. Answer me right now. I mean it." I drop the sandals.

She must have turned and hidden on the other side, just to fool me.

GUIDED READING

What feelings does Ken have when he can't find Ib?

I don't remember getting up the hill and across the road, except that the noise of a car horn rips across the top of my brain.

She isn't there. Empty tunnel.

"Elizabeth!"

She slipped. She knocked her head. Child drowns in four inches of bathwater.

GUIDED READING

Where does he think she is?

I have to go in. I try walking doubled over. But my feet just slip down the slimy curved concrete and I can only shuffle. I drop to my hands and knees.

Crawl, crawl, crawl, crawl.

GUIDED READING

What does Ken do after he discovers it's too slippery to walk in the tunnel?

The sound of splashing fills my head. Come back, Elizabeth.

Do not push out against the concrete. Just go forward, splash, splash.

Do not think up or down.

Something floats against my hand. I gasp and jerk upward, cracking my head. It's Wanda. I push her into my shirt. My knee bashes into a rock and there is some sobbing in the echoing tunnel. It is my own voice.

And then I grab the rough ends of the pipe and pull myself into the light and the bigness.

Ib is crouched at the edge of the stream pushing a floating leaf with a stick. A green light makes its way through the trees above.

She looks up at me and sees Wanda poking out of my shirt. "Oh, good, you found her. Bad Wanda, running away."

My relief explodes into anger.

GUIDED READING

When he emerges from the tunnel what does Ib see poking out of Ken's shirt?

"Ib, where were you?"

"Playing with the girls."

"No, quit pretending. I'm not playing. Where were you when I called you from the end of the tunnel? Were you hiding? Didn't you hear me call?"

"Sure I heard you, silly. That's how they knew my name. And I was going to come back but it was my turn. They never let me play before, but this time they knew my name and I got to go into the circle. They were dancing.

---

10. **horsetail.** Plants with hollow jointed stems and scalelike leaves

words for everyday use

hov • er (həs′ vər) *v.*, stay suspended in the air near one place. *The eagle was <u>hovering</u> over its victim.*

Like ballerinas. Except they had long hair. I get to have long hair when I'm in grade two."

My head is buzzing. I must have hit it harder than I realized. I hand Wanda to Ib and grab at some sense. "Why didn't you come when I called you?"

"They said I wasn't allowed to go, not while I was in the circle, and they were going to give me some cake. I saw it. It had sprinkles on it. And then you called me again but you said 'Elizabeth.' And then they made me go away."

Ib blows her leaf boat across the stream. And then she starts to sing.

"Idey, Idey, what's your name,
What's your name to get in the game."

That song, the two-note song. The sweet high voice calling to me in the tunnel. The sound just before Jeff yelled at me. The sound just before Jeff called me back by my real name.

The final puzzle piece of memory slides into place. They wanted me. They wanted Ib. I begin to shiver.

I find myself sitting on the gravel. The stream splashes its way over the lip of the pipe into the tunnel. I stare at Ib, who looks so small and so solid. My wet jeans with their slime-green knees begin to steam in the sun. A crow tells us a thing or two.

GUIDED READING

What does Ken feel after he feels relief that Ib is safe?

"Ken?"

'Yes?"

"I don't really like those girls."

"No, they don't sound that nice. Do you want to go home?"

"Okay."

I rinse off my hands and glance once more into the darkness.

"Put on your sandals, then."

Ib holds on to the back belt loops of my jeans and I pull her up the hill, into the sunshine. ∎

Respond *to the* SELECTION

What do you think happens in the tunnel?

About *the* AUTHOR

Sarah Ellis has been a librarian, a book reviewer, a columnist, a storyteller, a teacher of children's literature, and an award-winning children's author. Her novels take place mainly in Vancouver, British Columbia, where she has lived most of her life. Many of the events in her stories are taken from her past; the people and places that were a part of her childhood often appear. She grew up in a family where sharing stories and reading books were daily activities. Although she didn't think about becoming a writer, her love for reading led her to study librarianship. While in college, she became interested in children's literature. When she began her first novel, she never told anyone. Ellis has published six books and is known throughout Canada and the world as an accomplished author.

Rabbit Among the Fairies, 1880. John Anster Fitzgerald. Private Collection.

The Stolen Child

W. B. Yeats

Where dips the rocky highland
Of Sleuth Wood in the lake,
There lies a leafy island
Where flapping herons wake
5   The drowsy water-rats;
There we've hid our faery vats,
Full of berries
And of reddest stolen cherries.
Come away, O human child!
10 *To the waters and the wild*
With a faery, hand in hand,
For the world's more full of weeping than you
*   can understand.*

Where the wave of moonlight glosses
The dim grey sands with light,
15 Far off by furthest Rosses

We foot it all the night,
Weaving olden dances,
Mingling hands and mingling glances
Till the moon has taken flight;
20 To and fro we leap
And chase the frothy bubbles,
While the world is full of troubles
And is anxious in its sleep.
Come away, O human child!
25 *To the waters and the wild*
With a faery, hand in hand,
For the world's more full of weeping than you
     can understand.

Where the wandering water gushes
From the hills above Glen-Car,
30 In pools among the rushes
That scarce could bathe a star,
We seek for slumbering trout
And whispering in their ears
Give them unquiet dreams;
35 Leaning softly out
From ferns that drop their tears
Over the young streams.
Come away, O human child!
To the waters and the wild
40 *With a faery, hand in hand,*
For the world's more full of weeping than you
     can understand.

Away with us he's going,
The solemn-eyed:
He'll hear no more the lowing
45 Of the calves on the warm hillside
Or the kettle on the hob
Sing peace into his breast,
Or see the brown mice bob
Round and round the oatmeal-chest.
50 *For he comes, the human child,*
To the waters and the wild
With a faery, hand in hand,
From a world more full of weeping than he can
     understand. ■

Investigate, Inquire, and Imagine

Recall: GATHERING FACTS → **Interpret:** FINDING MEANING

1a. What is Ken's relationship with Elizabeth?

1b. What does Ken think about his responsibilities in this role?

2a. What does Ken remember as he and Elizabeth walk along the railroad tracks?

2b. What did Ken's relationship with Jeff and Danielle seem to be like?

3a. What does Elizabeth tell Ken about her experience in the tunnel?

3b. Why do Ken and Elizabeth agree that the girls are not nice?

Analyze: TAKING THINGS APART → **Synthesize:** BRINGING THINGS TOGETHER

4a. Compare Ken's experience with his friends at the tunnel with Ib's experience in the tunnel.

4b. Do you think Ib will remember this day at the tunnel differently than Ken remembered his previous experience there? Why, or why not?

Perspective: LOOKING AT OTHER VIEWS → **Empathy:** SEEING FROM INSIDE

5a. In what ways does Ken let his feelings and fears control his actions? Why did he allow Ib to go into the tunnel in the first place?

5b. Imagine yourself in Ken's position. Consider the fear he's overcoming while searching for Ib. Is his fear only in his mind? Would you have been fearful?

Understanding Literature

PLOT. A **plot** is a series of events related to a central conflict, or struggle. The parts of a plot include the *exposition* (or introduction), the *inciting incident*, the *climax*, and the *resolution*. What did you learn from the exposition of "The Tunnel"? What background information was not included in the exposition? What was the inciting incident of the story? What part of the story was the climax? How was the plot resolved?

CONFLICT. A **conflict** is a struggle between two people or things in a literary work. A conflict can be external or internal. An **external conflict** is a struggle between a character and some outside force such as another character, society, or nature. An **internal conflict** is a struggle that takes place inside the mind of a character. Consider the conflict or conflicts in "The Tunnel." What external conflicts take place? What inner struggles does Ken face?

FLASHBACK. A **flashback** is a part of a story that presents events that happened at an earlier time. Locate the flashbacks in "The Tunnel." How do they help form the plot?

Writer's Journal

1. Imagine you are Ken and are faced with the decision to accept or decline a dare. As Ken, write a **letter** to a good friend describing what happened, the decision you made, and why you made it.

2. Imagine that you are baby-sitting a six-year-old child who wants very badly to do something you feel is unsafe. Write a **paragraph** describing how you would tell her no, even if she insisted on having her way.

3. Imagine you are Ken and that you've just returned home from your experience with Ib at the tunnel. Write a **journal entry** describing your feelings about what happened there and what it meant to you.

Skill Builders

Speaking and Listening

ROLE-PLAY. Imagine you are Ken and you've gone back to school after the summer with a fresh perspective on friendship. Imagine that Jeff and Danielle join him at his lunch table and what their conversations with him might be like. How does Ken respond to them now? Is he distant or does he tell them a thing or two? Is he cordial? Role-play this gathering and prepare a script showing Ken in a new light.

Study and Research & Media Literacy

RESEARCHING. Go to the library and read up on claustrophobia and how it affects people's lives. Conduct a talk show interview with someone from the class portraying himself as Ken, and have him inform the audience on claustrophobia and panic and how people can overcome their fears.

Applied English

LOOKING AT JOBS. Research summer jobs in your community. Find out if there are outdoor jobs that include rock climbing or camping out somewhere. Prepare a summer newsletter for students seeking summer work outdoors.

Language, Grammar and Style

USING COMMAS. A comma separates words or groups of words within a sentence. Review the rules for using commas correctly in the Language Arts Survey 3.77, "Commas," and then rewrite the sentences below, placing commas in the correct places.

1. The baby-sitting course taught first aid diapering nutritious snacks and how to skip to my Lou.
2. The study of French irregular verbs for example could even seem attractive.
3. "It's quite a long way to the park" I told her.
4. She was busy dressing Francine Laurice Betty and Talking Doll.
5. With water dripping from my pants I climbed the hill.
6. Ken I want to go home now.
7. Where are you Ib?
8. No I don't want to play dolls.

Prereading

"Dragon, Dragon"

by John Gardner

Reader's T O O L B O X

FAIRY TALE. A **fairy tale** is a type of European folk tale containing supernatural events and imaginary creatures such as elves, giants, and fairies. For example, a supernatural event in *Cinderella* is the turning of the pumpkin into a stagecoach and an imaginary creature is the fairy godmother. As you read this selection, find one example of a supernatural event and one example of an imaginary creature.

CHARACTERIZATION. Characterization is the act of creating or describing a character. Writers use three major techniques to create a character: by showing what characters say, do, and think; by showing what other characters say about them; and by showing what physical features, dress, and personality the characters display. As you read this selection, find the characterization of the major characters. Use the graphic organizer below to help you organize your information. Write the name of the character. Then list details that describe the character by using the three techniques mentioned above.

Graphic
Organizer

Dragon: clever, mischievous, funny

Knights: cowardly, frightened

Wizard: forgetful

Reader's
Journal

If you were a king, what would you do if an evil dragon were violently destroying your kingdom?

Reader's
Resource

- What makes the fairy tale unique is its use of magic. Contrary to popular belief, however, the supernatural characters in fairy stories are not always fairy godmothers or winged spirits like Tinker Bell in *Peter Pan*. They may be magicians, ogres, dragons, brownies, elves, goblins, gnomes, or leprechauns. More often, fairy tales involve ordinary people who have experiences of a supernatural kind and are affected by charms, disguises, spells, or other fantastic occurrences. Although the stories were told centuries ago to entertain children, many were originally written for adults. In the 20th century psychologists sometimes use fairy tales to interpret and examine universal fears and desires. The enduring appeal and popularity of the tales, however, is a result of their continued ability to entertain.

- The author of "Dragon, Dragon" is popular for poking fun at old-fashioned fairy tales. For example, the hero in "Dragon, Dragon" is so weak and puny that he can't lift his sword and the wizard can't remember his magic.

Peaceful City, 1339. Ambrogio Lorenzetti. Palazzo Pubblico, Siena Italy.

Dragon, Dragon

John Gardner

There was once a king whose kingdom was <u>plagued</u> by a dragon. The king did not know which way to turn. The king's knights were all cowards who hid under their beds whenever the dragon came in sight, so they were of no use to the king at all. And the king's

GUIDED READING

Why are the king's knights of no use to the king at all?

wizard could not help either because, being old, he had forgotten his magic spells. Nor could the wizard look up the spells that had slipped his mind, for he had unfortunately misplaced his wizard's book many years before. The king was at his wit's end.

Every time there was a full moon the dragon came out of his lair and <u>ravaged</u> the

words for everyday use

plague (plāg') v., afflict with disease or disaster. *Locusts <u>plagued</u> our wheat last year.*

rav • age (rav' ij) v., wreak havoc on. *The bear <u>ravaged</u> our garbage bins every weekend.*

Judicial Proceeding, c.1400s. Portuguese artist. Arquivo Nacional da Torre do Tombo, Lisbon, Portugal.

countryside. He frightened maidens and stopped up chimneys and broke store windows and set people's clocks back and made dogs bark until no one could hear himself think.

He tipped over fences and robbed graves and put frogs in people's drinking water and tore the last chapters out of novels and changed house numbers around so that people crawled into bed with their neighbors' wives.

He stole spark plugs out of people's cars and put firecrackers in people's cigars and stole the clappers from all the church bells and sprung every bear trap for miles around so the bears could wander wherever they pleased.

And to top it all off, he changed around all the roads in the kingdom so that people could not get anywhere except by starting out in the wrong direction.

"'That,'" said the king in a fury, "'is enough!'" And he called a meeting of everyone in the kingdom.

Now it happened that there lived in the kingdom a wise old cobbler who had a wife and three sons. The cobbler and his family came to the king's meeting and stood way in back by the door, for the cobbler had a feeling that since he was nobody important there had probably been some mistake, and no doubt the king had intended the meeting for everyone in the kingdom except his family and him.

GUIDED READING

Why does the cobbler stand way in back by the door?

"Ladies and gentlemen," said the king when everyone was present, "I've put up with that dragon as long as I can. He has got to be stopped.'"

All the people whispered amongst themselves, and the king smiled, pleased with the impression he had made.

But the wise cobbler said gloomily, "'It's all very well to talk about it—but how are you going to do it?'"

And now all the people smiled and winked as if to say, "Well, King, he's got you there!"

The king frowned.

"It's not that His Majesty hasn't tried,'" the queen spoke up loyally.

"Yes,'" said the king, "I've told my knights again and again that they ought to slay that dragon. But I can't *force* them to go. I'm not a tyrant."

"Why doesn't the wizard say a magic spell?" asked the cobbler.

"'He's done the best he can," said the king.

The wizard blushed and everyone looked embarrassed. "I used to do all sorts of spells and chants when I was younger," the wizard explained. "But I've lost my spell book, and I begin to fear I'm losing my memory too. For instance, I've been trying for days

GUIDED READING

Why can't the wizard say a magic spell and get rid of the dragon?

to recall one spell I used to do. I forget, just now, what the deuce it was for. It went something like—

Bimble,
Wimble,
Cha, Cha
CHOOMPF!

Suddenly, to everyone's surprise, the queen turned into a rosebush.

"Oh dear," said the wizard.

"Now you've done it," groaned the king.

"Poor Mother," said the princess.

"I don't know what can have happened,'" the wizard said nervously, "but don't worry, I'll have her changed back in a jiffy." He shut his eyes and racked his brain for a spell that would change her back.

But the king said quickly, "You'd better leave well enough alone. If you change her into a rattlesnake we'll have to chop off her head."

Meanwhile the cobbler stood with his hands in his pockets, sighing at the waste of time. "About the dragon . . ." he began.

"Oh yes," said the king. "I'll tell you what I'll do. I'll give the princess' hand in marriage to anyone who can make the dragon stop."

"It's not enough," said the cobbler. "She's a nice enough girl, you understand. But how would an ordinary person support her? Also, what about those of us that are already married?"

"In that case," said the king, "I'll offer the princess' hand or half the kingdom or both—whichever is most convenient."

The cobbler scratched his chin and considered it.

"It's not enough," he

GUIDED READING

What does the king offer to do for anyone who can make the dragon stop?

said at last. "It's a good enough kingdom, you understand, but it's too much responsibility."

"Take it or leave it," the king said.

"I'll leave it," said the cobbler. And he shrugged and went home.

But the cobbler's eldest son thought the bargain was a good one, for the princess was very beautiful and he liked the idea of having half the kingdom to run as he pleased. So he said to the king, "I'll accept those terms, Your Majesty. By tomorrow morning the dragon will be slain."

"Bless you!" cried the king.

GUIDED READING

Who is the first one to accept the king's offer?

"Hooray, hooray, hooray!" cried all the people, throwing their hats in the air.

The cobbler's eldest son beamed with pride, and the second eldest looked at him enviously. The youngest son said timidly, "Excuse me, Your Majesty, but don't you think the queen looks a little unwell? If I were you I think I'd water her."

"'Good heavens," cried the king, glancing at the queen who had been changed into a rosebush, "I'm glad you mentioned it!"

Now the cobbler's eldest son was very clever and was known far and wide for how quickly he could multiply fractions in his head. He was perfectly sure he could slay the dragon by somehow or other playing a trick on him, and he didn't feel that he needed his wise old father's advice. But he thought it was only polite to ask, and so he went to his father, who was working as usual at his cobbler's bench, and said, "Well, Father, I'm off to slay the dragon. Have you any advice to give me?"

The cobbler thought a moment and replied, "When and if you come to the dragon's lair, recite the following poem.

Dragon, dragon, how do you do? I've come from the king to murder you.

GUIDED READING

What advice does the cobbler give to his eldest son?

Say it very loudly and firmly and the dragon will fall, God willing, at your feet."

"How curious!" said the eldest son. And he thought to himself, "The old man is not as wise as I thought. If I say something like that to the dragon, he will eat me up in an instant. The way to kill a dragon is to out-fox him." And keeping his opinion to himself, the eldest son set forth on his quest.

When he came at last to the dragon's lair, which was a cave, the eldest son slyly disguised himself as a peddler and knocked on the door and called out, "Hello there!"

"There's nobody home!" roared a voice.

The voice was as loud as an earthquake, and the eldest son's knees knocked together in terror.

"I don't come to trouble you," the eldest son said meekly. "I merely thought you might be interested in looking at some of our brushes. Or if you'd prefer," he added quickly, "I could leave our catalogue with you and I could drop by again, say, early next week."

"I don't want any brushes," the voice roared, "and I especially don't want any brushes next week."

"Oh," said the eldest son. By now his knees were knocking together so badly that he had to sit down.

Suddenly a great shadow fell over him, and the eldest son looked up. It was the dragon. The eldest son drew his sword, but the dragon <u>lunged</u> and swallowed him in a single gulp, sword and all, and the eldest son found himself in the dark of the dragon's belly. "What a fool I was not to listen to my wise old father!" thought the eldest son. And he began to weep bitterly.

"Well," sighed the king the next morning, "I see the dragon has not been slain yet."

"I'm just as glad, personally," said the princess, sprinkling the queen. "I would have had to marry that eldest son, and he had warts."

Now the cobbler's middle son decided it was his turn to try. The middle son was very strong and was known far and wide for being able to lift up the corner of a church. He felt perfectly sure he could slay the dragon by simply laying into him, but he thought it would be only polite to ask his father's advice. So he went to his father and said to him, "Well, Father, I'm off to slay the dragon. Have you any advice for me?"

lunge (lunj') *v.,* thrust or lean forward suddenly. *The baserunner <u>lunged</u> toward home plate.*

The cobbler told the middle son exactly what he'd told the eldest.

"When and if you come to the dragon's lair, recite the following poem.

Dragon, dragon, how do you do? I've come from the king to murder you.

Say it very loudly and firmly, and the dragon will fall, God willing, at your feet."

Saint George and the Dragon, c.1400s.
Spanish artist. Biblioteca Nacional, Madrid, Spain.

"What an odd thing to say," thought the middle son. "The old man is not as wise as I thought. You have to take these dragons by surprise." But he kept his opinion to himself and set forth.

When he came in sight of the dragon's lair, the middle son spurred his horse to a gallop and thundered into the entrance swinging his sword with all his might.

But the dragon had seen him while he was still a long way off, and being very clever, the dragon had crawled up on top of the door so that when the son came charging in he went under the dragon and on to the back of the cave and slammed into the wall. Then the dragon chuckled and got down off the door, taking his time, and strolled back to where the man and the horse lay unconscious from the terrific blow. Opening his mouth as if for a yawn, the dragon swallowed the middle son in a single gulp and put the horse in the freezer to eat another day.

"What a fool I was not to listen to my wise old father," thought the middle son when he came to in the dragon's belly. And he too began to weep bitterly.

That night there was a full moon, and the dragon ravaged the countryside so terribly that several families moved to another kingdom.

"Well," sighed the king in the morning, "still no luck in this dragon business, I see."

"I'm just as glad, myself," said the princess, moving her mother, pot and all, to the window where the sun could get at her. "The cobbler's middle son was a kind of humpback."

Now the cobbler's youngest son saw that his turn had come. He was very upset and nervous, and he wished he had never been born. He was not clever, like his eldest brother, and he was not strong, like his second eldest brother. He was a decent, honest boy who always minded his elders.

He borrowed a suit of armor from a friend of his who was a knight, and when the youngest son put the armor on it was so heavy he could hardly walk. From another knight he borrowed a sword, and that was so heavy that the only way the youngest son could get it to the dragon's lair was to drag it along behind his horse like a plow.

When everything was in readiness, the youngest son went for a last conversation with his father.

"Father, have you any advice to give me?" he asked.

GUIDED READING
What happens to the cobbler's eldest and middle sons when they go to visit the dragon?

The Lord and Lady in Their Castle, c.1400s. Portuguese artist. Arquivo Nacional da Torre do Tombo, Lisbon, Portugal.

"Only this," said the cobbler. "When and if you come to the dragon's lair, recite the following poem.

Dragon, dragon, how do you do? I've come from the king to murder you.

Say it very loudly and firmly, and the dragon will fall, God willing, at your feet."

"Are you certain?" asked the youngest son uneasily.

"As certain as one can ever be in these matters," said the wise old cobbler.

And so the youngest son set forth on his quest. He traveled over hill and dale and at last came to the dragon's cave.

The dragon, who had seen the cobbler's youngest son while he was still a long way off, was seated up above the door, inside the cave, waiting and smiling to himself. But minutes passed and no one came thundering in. The dragon frowned, puzzled, and was tempted to peek out. However, reflecting that patience seldom goes unrewarded, the dragon kept his head up out of sight and went on waiting. At last, when he could stand it no longer, the dragon <u>craned</u> his neck and looked. There at the entrance of the cave stood a trembling young man in a suit of armor twice his size, struggling with a sword so heavy he could lift only one end of it at a time. At sight of the dragon, the cobbler's youngest son began to

crane (krān') *v.*, stretch (the neck) toward an object of attention. *Sylvia* <u>*craned*</u> *her neck to see the horses in the parade.*

tremble so violently that his armor rattled like a house caving in. He heaved with all his might at the sword and got the handle up level with his chest, but even now the point was down in the dirt. As loudly and firmly as he could manage, the youngest son cried—

Dragon, dragon, how do you do?
I've come from the king to murder you!

"What?" cried the dragon, flabbergasted. "You? *You? Murder Me???*" All at once he began to laugh, pointing at the little cobbler's son. "*He he he ho ha!*" he roared, shaking all over, and tears filled his eyes. "*He he he ho ho ho ha ha!*" laughed the dragon. He was laughing so hard he had to hang onto his sides, and he fell off the door and landed on his back, still laughing, kicking his legs helplessly, rolling from side to side, laughing and laughing and laughing.

GUIDED READING
Which of the cobbler's three sons decides to follow his father's advice and recite the poem to the dragon?

The cobbler's son was annoyed. "I *do* come from the king to murder you," he said. "A person doesn't like to be laughed at for a thing like that."

GUIDED READING
What does the dragon do when the cobbler's youngest son recites the poem his father quotes to him?

"*He he he!*" wailed the dragon, almost sobbing, gasping for breath. "Of course not, poor dear boy! But really, *he he*, the *idea* of it, *ha ha ha!* And that simply *ridiculous poem!*" Tears streamed from the dragon's eyes and he lay on his back perfectly helpless with laughter.

"It's a good poem," said the cobbler's youngest son loyally. "My father made it up." And growing angrier he shouted, "I want you to stop that laughing, or I'll—I'll—" But the dragon could not stop for the life of him. And suddenly, in a terrific rage, the cobbler's son began flopping the sword end over end in the direction of the dragon. Sweat ran off the youngest son's forehead, but he labored on, blistering mad, and at last, with one supreme

heave, he had the sword standing on its handle a foot from the dragon's throat. Of its own weight the sword fell, slicing the dragon's head off.

"*He he ho huk,*" went the dragon—and then he lay dead.

The two older brothers crawled out and thanked their younger brother for saving their lives. "We have learned our lesson," they said.

Then the three brothers gathered all the treasures from the dragon's cave and tied them to the back end of the youngest brother's horse, and tied the dragon's head on behind the treasures, and started home. "I'm glad I listened to my father," the youngest son thought. "Now I'll be the richest man in the kingdom."

GUIDED READING
What do the three brothers do once the dragon has been killed?

There were hand-carved picture frames and silver spoons and boxes of jewels and chests of money and silver compasses and maps telling where there were more treasures buried when these ran out. There was also a curious old book with a picture of an owl on the cover, and inside, poems and odd sentences and recipes that seemed to make no sense.

When they reached the king's castle the people all leaped for joy to see that the dragon was dead, and the princess ran out and kissed the youngest brother on the forehead, for secretly she had hoped it would be him.

"Well," said the king, "which half of the kingdom do you want?"

"My wizard's book!" exclaimed the wizard. "He's found my wizard's book!" He opened the book and ran his finger along under the words and then said in a loud voice, "Glmuzk, shkzmlp, blam!"

Instantly the queen stood before them in her natural shape, except she was soaking wet from being sprinkled too often. She glared at the king.

"Oh dear," said the king, hurrying toward the door.

Respond _to the_ SELECTION

If you were one of the cobbler's sons, would you have followed your father's advice and recited the poem to the dragon?

About _the_ AUTHOR

John C. Gardner was a poet, novelist, dramatist, translator, and teacher who died in 1982. Gardner was raised just outside of Batavia, New York, attended school through eleventh grade in Alexander, New York, and graduated from Batavia High School in 1951. The author of many novels, he also wrote three influential works on the art of writing— _On Becoming a Novelist, The Art of Fiction,_ and _On Moral Fiction._ Many of his students, such as Raymond Carver and Charles Johnson, have had successful publishing careers. Additionally, Gardner translated texts from the Middle Ages, wrote fairy tales (such as "Dragon, Dragon") and plays (including _Days of Vengeance_ written for his mother, Priscilla), composed operas and librettos, and played the French horn.

Investigate, *Inquire,* and Imagine

Recall: Gathering Facts

1a. How does the cobbler himself respond when the king offers the princess's hand in marriage and half of the kingdom or both to the person who can stop the dragon?

2a. How does the dragon respond to the youngest son when he recites the poem his father told him?

Interpret: Finding Meaning

1b. Why do you think the cobbler responds this way while his sons decide to accept the offer? Why doesn't the cobbler follow his own advice and kill the dragon? What does this tell you about the cobbler?

2b. Do you think this is the response the cobbler had in mind when he advised his sons to recite the poem? Why, or why not?

Analyze: Taking Things Apart

3a. Compare and contrast the characters in this story to the same kinds of characters in traditional fairy tales. How are the knights in this tale different from the knights in traditional fairy tales? How is the wizard different? How would you describe the dragon?

Synthesize: Bringing Things Together

3b. Why do you think Gardner has decided to present his characters this way? What significance does this have to what ultimately happens at the end of the tale? Do you like this kind of twist on the traditional fairy tale?

Evaluate: Making Judgments

4a. Examine reasons why the cobbler's two eldest sons refuse to follow their father's advice. What kind of people do you think they are? How is the youngest son different from his two older brothers?

Extend: Connecting Ideas

4b. Why do you think the author chose to have the two oldest sons disobey their father? What kind of point is the author trying to make? What do you think the two eldest sons would say to their father when they return?

Understanding *Literature*

Fairy Tale. A **fairy tale** is a type of European folk tale containing supernatural events and imaginary creatures such as elves, giants, and fairies. Why do you think fairy tales are so popular?

Characterization. Characterization is the act of creating or describing a character. Writers use three major techniques to create a character: by showing what characters say, do, and think; by showing what other characters say about them; and by showing what physical features, dress, and personality the characters display. Describe the character of the dragon, the wizard, the king, and the cobbler's youngest son.

Writer's Journal

1. Imagine that you are one of the cobbler's sons. Write a short **paragraph** explaining why you think it is wise to follow or not to follow your father's advice.

2. Imagine that you are the king and you want to convince people to attempt to stop the dragon. Design a short **advertisement** offering the princess's hand in marriage or half the kingdom to the person who can stop the dragon first.

3. Write a short **dialogue** between the eldest and middle sons, discussing the dragon's reaction to their attempts to threaten him.

Skill Builders

Language, Grammar, Style

USING VIVID VERBS. "Dragon, Dragon" uses very vivid verbs to capture the attention of the reader and help him or her visualize what is happening in the story. For example, in the beginning of the story when the wizard accidentally turns the queen into a rose, he "shut his eyes and racked his brain for a spell that would change her back." The author uses the verb *racked* instead of *searched* because it is more vivid. Look through the story and find five other places where the author uses a vivid verb that helps the reader visualize the action. What alternatives can you think of for the following verbs?

1. The sun was so bright it <u>hurt</u> my eyes.
2. The snow <u>blew</u> through the air so fast that we couldn't see anything in front of us.
3. On our hiking trip, we watched a beautiful eagle <u>fly</u> across the blue sky above.
4. After playing soccer all day, we were so hungry we <u>ate</u> dinner in no time.

Speaking and Listening

INTERVIEWING. Imagine that you are a reporter and you've just heard that the cobbler's youngest son has slain the dragon, rescued his older brothers, and returned all the lost treasures to the kingdom. Get together with a partner and role-play an interview between the cobbler's youngest son and a reporter. If you are the reporter, make a list of important questions you'd like this new hero to answer for the people of the kingdom. If you are the son, imagine how you feel now that you are a hero and how this might affect the way you answer questions. Will you brag or be modest with your answers?

Applied English

MAKING AN ADVERTISEMENT. Imagine that you are the king in "Dragon, Dragon" and you've decided to fire all the knights who were cowards. Once the cowardly knights have been fired, you are faced with the challenge of hiring new ones. Create an advertisement requesting applications to these new positions for knights in the king's court. Make sure your advertisement is very clear about what skills and experiences you are looking for in a knight. How much are you willing to pay these new knights? How many hours will they be required to work? Discuss your design with other classmates.

Prereading

"The Rebellion of the Magical Rabbits"

by Ariel Dorfman

Reader's TOOLBOX

PARABLE. A parable is a story told to communicate a moral. Usually, the parable is a very simple story that attempts to teach the reader a larger and more complicated truth. "The Rebellion of the Magical Rabbits" at first seems to be simply about a magical land of rabbits, wolves, and monkeys. As you read the story, keep in mind that the plot represents the plight of the people of Chile under the dictatorship of Augusto Pinochet, and think about what the moral of the story might be.

CHARACTERIZATION. Characterization is the act of creating or describing a character. Writers use three major techniques to create a character: showing what characters say, do, and think; showing what other characters say about them; and showing what physical features, dress, and personality the characters display. As you read the story, pay attention to which of the three techniques the author uses for characterization.

Graphic Organizer

Using what you know about the definition of a parable, the life of Ariel Dorfman, and the characters in "The Rebellion of the Magical Rabbits," create a mind map of links and phrases. Start with the following and add to it.

wolves conquer land of the rabbits

they announce that rabbits don't exist

"The birds . . . insist that they have seen some . . ."

Reader's Journal

How would you respond to life in a country where expressing your true thoughts and beliefs might get you arrested?

Reader's Resource

- **HISTORY CONNECTION.** This story is set in the country of Chile, a long thin strip of land on the Pacific coast of South America. Chile was controlled for seventeen years (1973–1990) by the dictator Augusto Pinochet, who used violence and terror to influence the political beliefs and activities of the country's citizens. Pinochet was known for the frequent and unexpected arrest of any citizen who gave the slightest indication of having unfashionable political ideals. This technique, which Pinochet called "disappearance," was responsible for a mass terror that swept through the people of Chile. People were afraid to speak about anything that may have them arrested. Pinochet was proud of his efforts and declared his country to be "an island of tranquility" in a world of violence.

- The author of this story, Ariel Dorfman, was living in Chile in 1973 and working for President Allende when Augusto Pinochet and his army succeeded in overthrowing the government and taking control of the country. Dorfman was known as an author with political beliefs in opposition to Pinochet's and therefore he was in danger of being arrested. Dorfman was forced to live in exile, first in Argentina and then in the United States, where he lives today.

Howl, 1977. Luis Jimenez. National Museum of American Art, Washington, DC.

The Rebellion of the Magical Rabbits

Ariel Dorfman

When the wolves conquered the land of the rabbits, the first thing the leader of the pack did was to proclaim himself King. The second was to announce that the rabbits had ceased to exist. Now and forever it would be forbidden to even mention their name.

Just to be on the safe side, the new Wolf King went over every book in his realm with a big black pencil, crossing out words and tearing out pictures of cottontails until he was satisfied that not a trace of his enemies remained.

But an old gray fox who was his counselor brought bad news.

"The birds, Your Wolfiness, <u>insist</u> that they have seen some . . . some of those creatures. From on high."

"So how come I don't see anything from way up here, on my throne?" asked the Wolf.

"In times like these," answered the fox, "people have got to see to believe."

"Seeing is believing? Bring me that monkey who takes photos, the one who lives nearby. I'll teach those birds a lesson."

The monkey was old and weak.

GUIDED READING

Why does the wolf ask to see the monkey who takes photos?

"What can the Wolf of all Wolves want with me?" he asked, looking at his wife and daughter.

The little girl had an answer. "He must want you to take a picture of the rabbits, Dad."

"Quiet, quiet," said her mother. "Rabbits don't exist."

words for everyday use

in • sist (in sist´) v., persist or demand. *The doctor <u>insists</u> that I eat an apple a day.*

But the little monkey knew that rabbits did exist. It was true that, since the howling wolves had invaded the country, the rabbits no longer came to visit her as they had before. But in her dreams she continued hearing the green rain of their voices singing nearby, reflecting in her head as if she were a pond under the moonlight, and when she awoke there was always a small gift beside her bed. Walls and closed doors were like water for the rabbits.

"That's why I sleep well," said the little girl. "That's why that General Wolf must need the photo. To keep nightmares away. You'll bring me a picture of them someday, won't you, Dad?"

The monkey felt fear crawl up and down his fur. "Send this little girl to her room," he told his wife, "until she understands that there are certain things we just don't talk about."

The King of the Wolves was not in the best of moods when the monkey came in. "You're late. And I'm in a hurry. I need photographs of each important act in my life. And all my acts, let me tell you, are supremely important. . . . Can you guess what we're going to do with those pictures? You can't? We're going to put one on every street, inside every bush, in every home. I'll be there, watching each citizen with my very own eyes. You'd better pity those who don't have the latest events of my life hung up on their walls. And you know who is going to distribute each picture? You don't know?"

> **I need photographs of each important act in my life.**

GUIDED READING

Why does the King of Wolves want to photograph each important act in his life?

The monkey was trembling so hard that no words came out.

"The birds, ugly monkey. Now they'll bite their own beaks before they twitter around with any nonsense about rabbits. And we'll tie an endless cord to their legs, so they can't escape. Understand?"

The monkey understood so well that his trembling paw immediately clicked the shutter of the camera, taking the first picture.

"Go," roared the Wolf, "and develop it. I want it on every wall in the kingdom."

But when the photographer returned some minutes later, he did not dare to enter the throne room, and asked one of the soldiers to call the counselor. Without a word, the monkey passed him the picture he had just taken.

The fox blinked once, and then blinked again. In a corner of the photo, far from the muscular, ferocious figure of the King—who had both arms up in the air as if he had just won a boxing championship—appeared what was without any doubt the beginning of an ear, the ear of someone who had insolently come to spy on the whole ceremony.

GUIDED READING

What do the monkey and the fox discover in the first picture?

"You blind monkey!" fumed the fox. "How come you didn't notice that this . . . this thing was there? Can't you focus that camera of yours?"

"If it could get into the picture," the monkey answered, "it was because you and your guards let it get close."

"It won't happen again," the counselor promised. "Rub out that . . . ear before His Wolfishness finds out."

From his bag, the monkey took out a special liquid that he used to erase any detail that might bother a client. The intruding ear began to disappear as if it had never existed.

The King of the Wolves was pleased with the portrait and ordered it sent all over the realm. Two hours later he personally went on an inspection tour to make sure that not a window was without a picture of his large, gleaming, dangerous grin. "Not bad," he said, "but this photo is already getting old. People should see my latest deeds. Take another. Quick. Show me scaring these pigeons—right away. And bring it to me immediately. You took too long last time."

But the monkey wasn't able to comply this time either. Once again he had the counselor called secretly.

"Again?" asked the fox. "It happened again?"

Except that now it was worse than an indiscreet ear. A whole corner of the new picture was filled with the unmistakable face of . . . yes, there was no denying it, of a rabbit winking an eye in open <u>defiance</u> of the nearby guards.

GUIDED READING

What do the monkey and fox discover in the second picture of the wolf?

"We've got to tighten security," muttered the fox. "Meanwhile, erase that invader."

"Wonderful," shouted the King Wolf when finally he was given the picture. "Look at the frightened faces of the pigeons trying to escape. I want a million copies. I want them on milk cartons and on the coupons inside cereals. . . . Onward. Onward. Let's go and smash up a dam. Come on, monkey. Fame awaits us both."

The beavers had been working summer and winter for three years on a beautiful dam that would allow them to irrigate a distant valley.

The Wolf of Wolves climbed a tree. "I want you to shoot the precise moment when my feet crash into the middle of the dam, monkey. If you miss the shot, next time I'll fall on top of you and then I'll have to get myself another photographer. Are you ready?"

Not only was the monkey ready, so was the counselor. The fox was breathing down the old monkey's back, peering over his shoulder, watching, listening. Nothing could escape those vigilant, darting eyes. Not a fuzzy ear would dare to make its appearance.

So neither the monkey nor the fox could believe it when, a bit later, they saw at the bottom of the picture a rabbit <u>lolling</u> on his side as if he were relaxing at a picnic. Next to him, another rabbit had raised her paw and was boldly thumbing her nose.

"This is an epidemic," said the fox. "And let me tell you, our lives are in danger."

"Let's start erasing," the monkey said wearily.

"You erase. I'll get a squadron of buzzards and hawks. They see all animals, even the quick and the small."

His Wolfhood the King yelped with pleasure when he saw the picture. It portrayed him at the exact moment he was breaking the backbone of the beavers' dam. In the distance, families of beavers could be seen fleeing. There was not a single shadow of a rabbit.

"Send it out! A strong country is an educated country, a country that always is tuned in to the latest news. What are we going to do now for some fun?"

"We could rest," the monkey suggested, his paws peeling from the harsh erasing fluid.

The Wolf looked at him as if he were a stone.

---

words for everyday use

de • fi • ance (di fī′ əns) n., act of resistance or challenge. *Tommy screamed in <u>defiance</u> when his mom said, "Be quiet."*

loll (läl′) v., be in a relaxed posture; hang or droop. *The boys were <u>lolling</u> against the wall, waiting for the bus to come.*

"And who asked you for an opinion? I'm in charge here. That's why I was born with these teeth, and you'd better pray you never have to feel them crunching your bones. Onward. We are the future, the morrow, the dawn! We'll go on until there's no more light."

But in each new photo, the rabbits became more plentiful, <u>audacious</u>, and <u>saucy</u>. His Wolfinity the King destroyed sugar mills, shook squirrels out of their trees and hid their nuts, stripped ducks of their feathers, drove sheep off cliffs, drilled holes in the road so that horses would break their legs, unveiled new cages and old dungeons . . . and the more his frightening yellow eyes flickered, the more innumerable were the rabbits of every color that frolicked in the margins of the photographs. Even the clouds seemed full of fur and whiskers and cottontails.

"Hey, birdie," jeered the Supreme Wolf, grabbing a swallow about to fly off with a bag overflowing with pictures, "what tune are you singing now, featherhead? Who's that in the center of the picture, huh? Who's the King?"

The bird held his beak tight, so that not even a peep could come out.

"Lights, camera, action, monkey!" the Monarch demanded. "Call this: WOLF KING RECEIVES <u>HOMAGE</u> FROM A MESSENGER."

The monkey obeyed, but could hardly hide his despair. Though nobody ever saw the rebels when the photos were taken, they were always there when it was time to show them, nibbling lettuce at the very feet of the biggest and baddest of wolves.

"Exterminate them," hissed the fox, who had ordered a stronger, more acid liquid. "Don't leave even a twitch of a nose."

But the pictures were beginning to look defective. There were blank spaces everywhere. The monkey knew that the only solution was to convince His Wolfiness to sit up high on an elevated throne. Since rabbits live underground, they wouldn't be able to wiggle their way into the frame of the photograph.

GUIDED READING

What does the monkey convince the wolf to do in an effort to keep rabbits out of the pictures?

The King, fortunately, was delighted with the idea. "I'll look more impressive up here. And I can keep an eye on those birds. What a surprise for my subjects when they find my new picture at breakfast, right? So get here early, monkey, do you hear?"

When the exhausted monkey dragged himself home, his fingers hurting from the terrible liquid, the latest photograph of the King had just been plastered on the front door of his house. Just at that moment, a soldier was leaving.

"No cause for alarm, Mr. Monkey," the soldier laughed. "Just a routine inspection to see if anybody is sabotaging His Wolfhood's pictures."

GUIDED READING

Why is there a soldier visiting the house when the monkey returns home?

The monkey rushed inside. "Our daughter? Is she all right? Did she say anything?"

"I'm fine, Dad," the little girl said. "Those wolves are gone, aren't they? And you brought me that special photo—you know, the one I asked you for?"

The monkey felt as if from all four walls, from all four pictures on the four walls, the eight eyes of the Biggest of Wolves were watching each word he might say.

"Let your father rest," said her mother. "The only pictures he's taken are the ones we've put up in the house, like good citizens."

---

words for everyday use

au • da • cious (ô dā′ shəs) *adj.*, state of being adventurous or bold. *Exploring space is an <u>audacious</u> act.*

saucy (sô′ sē) *adj.*, impudent; bold; forward. *The lawyer gave a <u>saucy</u> look at the judge.*

hom • age (ä′ mij) *n.*, expression of respect or high regard. *Lisa paid <u>homage</u> to her tennis coach when she won the tournament.*

But the next morning, the monkey was awakened by his child's kiss. She put her lips near his ears and whispered something so softly that only he could hear it: "Thank you. It's the best present you could ever give me. You're a magical dad."

"Thanks? Thanks for what?"

She motioned almost imperceptibly toward the wall from which the photo of the Wolf King ruled. Her father opened his eyes wide. In one of the corners of that picture, like the sun rising over the mountains, he could just glimpse, in the act of making their gradual but glorious appearance, a pair of, yes, of course, a pair of soft, pink, pointed ears.

The monkey jumped out of bed. The liquid he had applied did not work permanently. The rabbits had needed the whole night to sneak back into the pictures, but somehow they had managed it.

"I think they knew I was scared," the little girl murmured, "and came to see me while I slept."

Her father dressed in less time than it takes a chill to run up a spine and scurried to the palace without stopping for breakfast. Was this happening only at their house or could the same invasion have taken place everywhere in the kingdom? If so, how could the rabbits be removed from so many portraits?

His Wolfiness was still in bed, but the counselor was already pacing about, biting the tip of his tail. "It's a plague," he said, "but, fortunately, it is already under control. The

GUIDED READING

What does the monkey's daughter whisper the next morning into her father's ear?

GUIDED READING

What does the monkey discover has happened overnight to the pictures?

offending pictures have been burned. As for you . . ."

"I swear that I—"

"Not a word from you," interrupted the fox. "It's lucky those creatures don't exist. Imagine the damage they'd cause if they really existed. But enough talk. What we need now is a new photo to replace the ones that are contaminated."

They rushed to the new throne, which was now set up on top of four colossal wooden legs, out of reach of the spreading virus of the mischievous ears.

"I want two shots," His Wolfhood demanded, "one of me <u>ascending</u> my throne and another of me sitting on it, enjoying the fresh air. And send them abroad too, so those silly foreign papers will stop attacking me."

This time, when the photos were developed, there was no trouble. Not so much as a carrot of a sign of a rabbit.

"Didn't I tell you? Didn't I tell you they don't exist?" The counselor was jubilant. "It was just a matter of your focusing the camera properly."

For the next few days, there were no more unpleasant surprises. The Wolf of Wolves felt happy, high above the heads of the multitude. He let his lieutenants run things while he posed for pictures giving commands, delivering speeches, signing laws. He examined the shots carefully, however. "Congratulations,"

---

words for everyday use

as • cend (ə send′) v., rise upward to a higher level or position. *The prince will <u>ascend</u> to the throne after the king dies.*

he said. "You're being more careful, monkey. It seems you're learning your trade just by being near me. I don't see any more of those whitish spots that spoiled my first pictures."

But one morning, the monkey was again awakened by his daughter's voice. "They're back, Dad," she whispered in his ears. "Those pictures you took sure are magical."

In one set of photos, at the foot of the towering throne, a small army of rabbits was biting, chewing, and splintering the wooden legs. Their teeth worked patiently, and they stopped their work only now and again to wave to the spectators.

Those pictures you took sure are magical.

The counselor was waiting. The monkey could see his fur ruffling and swelling like a swarm of bees.

"How many this time?" the monkey asked.

"The photos are being taken care of," the fox said grimly. "But the birds have got wind of what happened, and now they're telling everyone that those . . . those awful animals exist. And His Wolfinity is beginning to suspect something. 'Why are those birds so happy, so shrill?' he asks. I told him they're just a bunch of featherbrains, full of hot air."

GUIDED READING

What happens to the two photos of the wolf ascending to and sitting on his throne?

GUIDED READING

What do the birds do when they find out about the rabbits in the photos?

"What did he answer?" asked the monkey.

The King had announced that balloons are full of hot air too and that they could be popped. If those birds didn't keep quiet, he would make them disappear.

But the counselor had another idea: The Wolf of All Wolves should tie a recording of one of his latest speeches around the necks of the birds. They would have to carry not only the photos, but also the King's words, all over his kingdom. Nobody would be able to hear any of their songs.

"Hearing is believing," trumpeted His Wolfiness. "We'll give them a taste of some hymns, some military marches, some lessons in history, economics, and ethics."

GUIDED READING

What does the Wolf do to the birds in order to stop them from telling people that the rabbits exist?

The old monkey's life became unbearable. Not even the recorded howls of the King and his chorus of warlike beasts could stop the timid appearance, in the next photo, of an inquisitive nose, a pair of furry ears, some white whiskers, and something hungry gnawing away at the legs of the throne.

The fox replaced the chief officer of the royal guard with a boa constrictor straight from the jungle of a neighboring country. He put small, hundred-eyed spiders in strategic places throughout the Wolfdom. One day he ordered half the population to shave off their shiny fur so that no spy could hide in it. To punish the cows, accused of uttering subversive moos, he commanded that their milk be soured. And finally, he raised the volume of the King's broadcasts. But in spite of these efforts, there began to be heard a persistent, rowdy, merry sound, the clicking of thousands of tiny teeth, the burbling of an underground stream.

The monkey felt dizzy.

The rhythm was maddening. During the night, the legs of the throne, spindlier by the minute, were reinforced grudgingly by

woodpeckers who would have much preferred to take the throne apart. The monkey had to rely on every photographic trick of the trade, now erasing, now trimming with scissors, disguising ears so they looked like shadows and shadows so they looked like wallpaper. He even began using old portraits of the King, trying to make them seem like recent ones.

Until one night, when it was very late, the old monkey was awakened by an angry hand that shook him from his slumber. It was the counselor, flanked by a fierce escort of soldiers. The Lord Wolf had sent for him.

The whole house was up by now. The little girl watched her father begin dressing.

"Say hello to His Foxcellency," said the monkey.

"Dad," she said, and it was astonishing that she did not speak in a low, fearful voice anymore, as if the armed guards were not even there, "today you've got to bring me that picture I asked for."

"A picture?" The counselor showed interest. "A picture of what, of whom?"

The child continued to ignore him. "Today you'll bring me a photo of the rabbits, right, Dad? For my wall?"

GUIDED READING

What does the Counselor Fox overhear the monkey's daughter asking the monkey for?

The mother monkey touched the girl's head as if she had fever. "Hasn't your father told you that rabbits don't exist? Haven't we shut you up in your room for telling lies?"

"They exist," the girl announced. "Everybody knows they exist."

GUIDED READING

What does the monkey's daughter announce about the rabbits?

"Just as I suspected," said the counselor. "Let's go."

The Wolfiest of Wolves was waiting for them atop his throne. Around each leg, hundreds of guards and snakes kept watch.

"Monkey, you are a traitor," thundered the King. "Your photos are being used by people who say that strange and malicious creatures—who are nonexistent as everyone knows—are conspiring this very night to overthrow my rule. They say my throne trembles and my dynasty will topple. Is there any evidence that my throne trembles? Does anybody dare say so?" And he yowled like a hundred jet fighters in the air. "We'll start by making a recording of that sound. And you, you monkey, you're going to help me stamp out these rumors. Touching is believing. You are going to make me a wide-angle, three-dimensional picture that will cover all walls. In color. Because I am going to crown myself Emperor of the Wolves, the Supreme Wolferor. And if a single wretched rabbit shows its snout, I will make you eat the photos, one by one, a million of them, and then I'll eat you and not only you, but your wife and your daughter, and all the monkeys in this country. Now. Take that picture."

The monkey stuck his quaking head under the black cloth behind his camera and focused on the throne. He let out a little moan. Up till then, the rabbits had appeared only later, when the picture was developed. But here they were now, directly in front of his lens, ungovernable and carefree, gnawing away, biting not only the wood of the throne, but also the swords of the astonished guards and the very rattles of the rattlesnakes.

"What's the matter?" bellowed the future Wolferor, who was not looking downward so his profile would be perfect for posterity.

The monkey moved the camera nearer the throne, hoping the rabbit army would not come out in the picture. The rabbits moved faster than he did. They were clambering up the legs, one on top of the other as if they were monkeys or birds. The soldiers tried to frighten them away in silence, unwilling to attract the attention of the King, but the invaders were too agile. The Wolves kept bumping into one another and hitting each other over the head. The monkey realized that a contingent of birds had arrived from above, winging freely through the air, without a cord tied to them or a recording.

"Hurry up!" ordered the Wolf of all Wolves.

The monkey closed his eyes very tightly. It was better not to witness what was going to happen. At the very moment he clicked the shutter, he heard a deafening noise. He knew what he was going to see when he opened his eyes, but still could not believe it: Like an old elm tree rotten to the core, the throne had come crashing to the ground along with the King of Wolves, guards, snakes, counselor, and all. The monkey blinked. There at the foot of his tripod lay the Biggest, Baddest, the Most Boastful Wolf in the Universe. His ribs were broken, his black fur was torn by the fall, his yellow eyes were reddened, and he was wailing in pain.

GUIDED READING
What does the wolf accuse the monkey of being, and what does he make the monkey do?

GUIDED READING
What does the monkey see through the lens of the camera when he attempts to take a three-dimensional photo?

GUIDED READING
What happens to the throne when the monkey clicks the shutter of the camera?

"Monkey," squeaked the would-be Wolferor of the World, "this picture . . .you have my permission not to publish it."

At that moment, all the lights in the palace went out. The monkey was <u>paralyzed</u>. He did not know where to go. Then, as if someone in the darkness were suddenly shining a light on a pathway, he knew what he must do. He grabbed his camera and his bag, and clutching them to his chest like a treasure, he fled.

His daughter was waiting for him at the door of the house.

"Wait," he said to her. "Wait. I've brought you something." And without another word, he raced into his darkroom to develop the last picture as quickly as possible.

When he came out a few minutes later, his daughter and wife were standing on chairs, taking down the pictures of the Wolf King.

"Here," the old monkey said to his daughter, blinking in the bright light. "Here, this is the picture you've been asking for all this time. I've finally brought you your present."

"Thanks, Dad," the little girl said. "But I don't need it anymore."

She pointed around the room and toward the street and across the fields where the sun was beginning to rise.

The world was full of rabbits. ∎

GUIDED READING

Why does the monkey's daughter no longer need the picture she has been asking for?

Respond *to the* SELECTION

If you were the monkey, how would you handle the discovery that rabbits were appearing in the photographs? Would you erase them? Would you show them to the wolf? Why?

About *the* AUTHOR

Ariel Dorfman is currently the Walter Hines Page Research Professor of Literature in Latin America Studies for Duke University. He has taught at the Universidad de Chile, the Sorbonne, and the University of Amsterdam. He is the winner of numerous awards for his writings, especially his plays. One of his most famous plays, *Death and the Maiden*, was made into a film by the renowned director Roman Polanski. His most recent book is *The Nanny and the Iceberg*, which was published in 1999.

words for everyday use

par • a • lyze (pār′ ə līz) *v.*, stun; make speechless. *Ben was <u>paralyzed</u> when he heard that he won the poetry contest.*

Investigate, *Inquire,* and Imagine

Recall: GATHERING FACTS

1a. How does the King Wolf make the citizens of the country deny the existence of rabbits?

2a. What do the monkey and his wife do when their daughter insists that the King Wolf must want pictures of the rabbits to keep nightmares away?

3a. What is the King Wolf doing each time he has a photograph taken?

→ **Interpret:** FINDING MEANING

1b. Why do you think the King Wolf wants the citizens not to talk about or acknowledge the existence of rabbits? How successful do you think this technique is?

2b. Why do you think the little monkey continues to speak about the rabbits even when her parents tell her to be quiet? Who else in the story does the daughter remind you of?

3b. Why does the King Wolf want pictures of himself throughout the streets and homes of his country? How is he trying to make the citizens of the country feel?

Analyze: TAKING THINGS APART

4a. Examine the character of the King Wolf by his words and actions. How do his actions help you understand the kind of person that he is? How does he feel about the citizens of his country?

→ **Synthesize:** BRINGING THINGS TOGETHER

4b. How do the King Wolf's words and actions reflect his own perception of himself? How does this contribute to his eventual downfall at the end of the story?

Perspective: LOOKING AT OTHER VIEWS → **Empathy:** SEEING FROM INSIDE

5a. Why do you think the rabbits go as far as they do to rebel against the King Wolf? Why don't they just remain in the ground, out of view, and pretend they do not exist as the King Wolf would like them to do?

5b. Imagine yourself as one of the rabbits in the story. How would you respond to the King Wolf's actions against you and the other rabbits? Would you understand why the other animals living around you are afraid to acknowledge your existence?

Understanding *Literature*

PARABLE. A **parable** is a story told to communicate a moral. Usually, the parable is a very simple story that attempts to teach the reader a larger and more complicated truth. What is the moral in this story?

CHARACTERIZATION. Characterization is the act of creating or describing a character. Writers use three major techniques to create a character: showing what characters say, do, and think, showing what other characters say about them; and showing what physical features, dress, and personality the characters display. Which techniques does the author use most in "The Rebellion of the Magical Rabbits"? Which technique reveals the most about the king? the monkey? the fox?

Writer's Journal

1. Write **captions** for the monkey's photographs described in the story.
2. Imagine that you are the King Wolf. Write a brief **speech** to the citizens, explaining what you intend to do as their new leader.
3. Write a brief **radio news report**, informing the rabbit citizens of the invasion of the wolves.

Skill Builders

Language, Grammar, and Style

COMBINING SENTENCES. One way of linking words and phrases in a sentence is to use a transition of cause and effect such as *because*. For example, *I stayed home from school today because I have the flu*. In a sentence expressing cause and effect, the word *because* can be placed in one of two places. See the Language Arts Survey 3.23, "Working with Inverted Sentences," and 3.34, "Combining and Expanding Sentences."

EXAMPLE *I moved to Seattle because I got a job there. Because I got a job there, I moved to Seattle.*

Link the following pairs of sentences together using the word *because*.
1. In this story, "The Rebellion of the Magical Rabbits," the wolf attempts to erase all rabbits from the land. He thinks that rabbits are his enemy.
2. Ariel Dorfman decided to write his story as a parable. He wanted his story to have a moral.
3. Ariel Dorfman was forced to leave Chile and live in exile. Augusto Pinochet wanted him arrested for writing about his ideas and beliefs.
4. The wolf puts pictures of himself in the homes of all the citizens. He wants them to feel like he is watching them at all times.
5. The rabbits rebel against the wolf's attempt to erase them. They want to express their existence and live freely.

Speaking and Listening

SPEECH. Imagine that you are one of the rabbits in the story and you are speaking to a group of other rabbits about how you are being forced to live under the dictatorship of the King Wolf. Write and perform a short speech designed to inspire your fellow rabbits and call them to action. What persuasive words and phrases will you use to make the other rabbits want to band together and overthrow the throne of the mighty Wolf? Deliver your speech to the class.

Critical Thinking

THINKING ABOUT THE AUTHOR'S IDEAS. Consider the following excerpt from Ariel Dorfman's essay "Memory and Truth."

Memory is a constant obsession for me. I deal often with people who are fighting against those who would obliterate others, who would forget them, ignore them, neglect them, erase them from the earth. Somehow the voices come out. I am not their voice: I make a space for those voices, a bridge.

How does the above statement help explain Dorfman's desire to write the story "The Rebellion of the Magical Rabbits"? How is Dorfman like one of the rabbits in the story?

Collaborative Learning & Vocabulary

USING VOCABULARY IN A STORY. In small groups, write a collaborative story using the following words from "The Rebellion of the Magical Rabbits." If you wish, develop a parable together, deciding on a moral you wish to communicate.

- proclaim
- cease
- forbid
- insist
- defiance
- loll
- audacious
- saucy
- jeer
- homage
- ascend
- imperceptible
- contaminate
- conspire
- agile

for your READING LIST

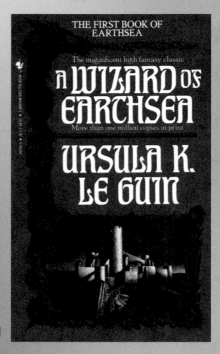

In the cold dawn when Ogion woke, Ged was gone. Only he had left in wizardly fashion a message of silver-scrawled runes on the hearthstone, that faded even as Ogion read them: "Master, I go hunting."

The boy Ged, or Sparrowhawk, as he is more commonly known, has the makings of a great sorcerer. The main character in Ursula K. LeGuin's **A Wizard of Earthsea** (the first of her novels in The Earthsea Cycle), learns a painful lesson about the perils of ignorantly reaching beyond one's powers. Ged studies hard at the school for wizards on Roke Island and makes progress unexpected even of one of his natural talents. Feeling overconfident and wanting to prove himself to an older student, Ged attempts a spell for raising the dead that even Master Sorcerers would not have dared to touch. The spell goes horribly wrong, and Ged almost gets killed in the process. With the help of his true friend, Estarriol, and his first Master, Ogion, Ged will attempt to send the dark presence back from where it came.

HOSTING A BOOK CLUB

Review the Language Arts Survey 1.8, "Guidelines for Discussing Literature in a Book Club." Gather with members of your book club after everyone has finished reading the book. As you discuss the book, make sure everyone has a chance to share his or her thoughts and opinions about it. You may want to use these questions to spark your discussion.

- Who is Ged? How would you describe his character?
- Who has the most influence on Ged?
- Which part of the book has the most suspense? How would you describe the climax?
- What were the most compelling parts of the plot? What, if anything, was too long or boring?
- What do you think the other books in the collection are about? Are you interested in reading them? Why, or why not?

Other books you may want to read:
The Tombs of Atuan, The Farthest Shore, Tehanu—the other books in The Earthsea Cycle by Ursula K. LeGuin
The Hobbit by J. R. R. Tolkien
The Chronicles of Narnia series by C. S. Lewis

Guided Writing

> "When the characters start talking to each other or to me, I know it's time to begin the first draft."
>
> —Monica Hughes

DEVELOPING A CHARACTER

It seems there is no limit to the kinds of creatures that have appeared on this spinning earth. Under ancient seas, all manner of critters scuttled and swam. For untold years, these animals of every size, color, and description reproduced, filling the seas and devouring one another. Only more recently did life follow on land. There, life in every imaginable form materialized—new forms with wonderful abilities to see and hear, to communicate, to flee or fight, to eat and reproduce—and populated the earth.

Yet, when people appeared on the earth, they were not content to merely create stories about all the mysterious and wonderful creatures that occupied the flowing waters, the ice and snow, the land and trees, and the swirling skies around them. While these real world creatures found their way into tales, they were often accompanied by totally imaginary creatures born entirely within the imagination of the storyteller. From fire-breathing dragons in fairy tales to the one-eyed Cyclops in myths, there is no end to the kinds of fantasy characters that may occupy stories, and more recently, comic books, toy shelves, and computer games.

Just as other storytellers have done throughout time, you too can create a fantasy character who lives in a world of your making. For this assignment, you will develop your own character and then write a character sketch.

Professional Model

from *The Hobbit* by J. R. R. Tolkien on page 387

Deep down here by the dark water lived old Gollum, a small slimy creature. I don't know where he came from, nor who or what he was. He was Gollum—as dark as darkness, except for two big round pale eyes in his thin face. He had a little boat, and he rowed about quite quietly on the lake; for lake it was, wide and deep and deadly cold. He paddled it with large feet dangling over the side, but never a ripple did he make. Not he. He was looking out of his pale lamplike eyes for blind fish, which he grabbed with his long fingers as quick as thinking. He liked meat too. Goblin he thought good, when he could get it; but he took care they never found him out. . . .

Examining the Model

In this excerpt from *The Hobbit*, Tolkien introduces the character Gollum. Within this short description, the reader learns many things about Gollum—what he looks like, where he lives, how he acts, what he says, and how he reacts to Bilbo. Notice that Tolkien does not just tell this information about Gollum. Instead, he weaves it into the situation when Gollum first saw Bilbo. Which words and phrases work best to create a picture of Gollum in your mind? What do the actions and speech that Tolkien includes tell us about this character?

Actually Gollum lived on a slimy island of rock in the middle of the lake. He was watching Bilbo now from the distance with his pale eyes like telescopes. Bilbo could not see him, but he was wondering a lot about Bilbo, for he could see that he was no goblin at all.

Gollum got into his boat and shot off from the island, while Bilbo was sitting on the brink altogether flummoxed and at the end of his way and his wits. Suddenly up came Gollum and whispered and hissed:

"Bless us and splash us, my preciousssss! I guess it's a choice feast; at least a tasty morsel it'd make us, gollum!" And when he said gollum he made a horrible swallowing noise in his throat. That is how he got his name, though he always called himself 'my precious.'

Prewriting

FINDING YOUR VOICE. No matter how imaginative a fantasy becomes, a good writer can keep the story believable by using a convincing voice. As you develop your sketch, think about the words that you will use to describe your character. Using specific and definite words will help to create a real picture. Even made-up words can sound believable if they are used to name or describe things that are made to seem real. Read the following sentences. Why does a "Scandalon" seem real? What words help the reader to create a picture of this character?

> A single Scandalon is nothing but long green limbs that grow in all directions along the ground. It looks like the spokes coming out from the hub of a bicycle wheel.

The attitude you have toward your writing can also make your fantasy character convincing. If you express yourself as if you are convinced that your character is real, your reader will be convinced too. Read the following sentence. How does the writer's attitude about viewing the Scandalon help to convince the reader that it is real?

> When Dusty looked with a magnifying glass, the mystery of the Scandalon came into focus.

WRITING WITH A PLAN. A character sketch is a short piece of writing. The sketch needs to be long enough to give a complete description of your character—who or what it is, what it looks like, how it acts and treats others, and what it says. However, your sketch does not tell a complete story. Instead it gives just a look into your character and its world.

To develop your sketch, you will first need to decide on a character. Since your character is to be an imaginary creature, you have many choices. Brainstorm a list of at least twenty possibilities for your character. Discuss your list with a few classmates, considering the possibilities for each character. Then

IDENTIFYING YOUR AUDIENCE. You and your classmates have seen and read about many imaginary characters in movies, books, toys, and video games. What makes these characters seem real to you? Ask your classmates what makes the characters seem real to them. Now, imagine yourself reading your character sketch to your classmates. What will you need to say in order for your classmates to believe your fantasy character? Be sure to include in your sketch the types of details and information your classmates will be expecting.

Steps for developing a character:

- describe what the character looks like
- describe the character's setting
- tell what the character does
- tell what the character says
- show how the character reacts to others
- describe a situation that the character is in

Language, Grammar, and Style
Clear and Unclear Sentences

Sometimes writers think that adding more words to a sentence will make the meaning clearer. But often, adding more words makes the sentence more difficult to understand. Well-written sentences are clear and to the point. They use simple and specific words. Sentences with too many unnecessary, complicated, and general words are wordy sentences.

IDENTIFYING WORDY SENTENCES.
Read the following two sentences. Which sentence is wordy because it contains unnecessary words?

> I really do appreciate very much that you were thoughtful enough to go out of your way to sending me the best wishes greeting card for my recent success in making the gymnastics team.

> Thank you for the card with best wishes for being on the gymnastics team.

FIXING WORDY SENTENCES.
Look at the following sentences from Jon's first draft. On your own paper, rewrite each sentence, getting rid of unnecessary words that complicate the sentence.

> The first Scandalons that ever, ever came to the earth were dropped

continued on page 441

select one. Before you write your character sketch, you can use several steps for developing—or getting to know—the character you have selected.

To begin, list words that describe what your character looks like. Does your character have a face, arms, or legs? What type of body does it have? Does it stand, sit, or lie on the ground? What color is it? Is it hairy? Does it have skin? Use your list of descriptions to write at least three sentences that describe what your character looks like.

Second, describe where the character lives. Just as your own room and the way it looks say something about you, telling about where your character lives says something about who or what it is. Make a list of details. Is it on the ground, above the ground, or below the ground? Is it big or small, open or closed-up, light or dark, warm or cold? What possessions are in it? Use your list to either draw a picture of where the character lives or write at least two sentences that describe it.

The third way to describe a character is to tell what the character does. Consider what you do during the day. You get up, eat breakfast, go to school, interact with other students and teachers, play sports, do chores, and many other things. What does your character's day look like? Does it sleep, eat, interact with other living things, hunt, roam, hide, or explore? List at least ten things that your character does. Next to each activity on the list, write a few words that explain how or why your character does this.

How does your character talk? What does it say? Dialogue is the fourth way that you can describe your character. Suppose your character meets you, an enemy, a friend, or a stranger as it is leaving the place where it lives. What does your character say? How does your character say it? What language, tone of voice, or emotions does the character use? Pick several words from the following list. Then write a short dialogue between the two characters using the words from the list to help describe how your character speaks.

declared	suggested	argued	questioned
bragged	asked	ordered	sighed
smiled	blurted	mumbled	warned
snapped	advised	glared	reminded
retorted	gulped		

A fifth way to develop a character is to show how your character reacts to another character. This may include dialogue, but it also the physical actions that your character takes. How does it stand or move? Is it aggressive or shy, demanding or submissive, courageous or cowardly? Suppose a stranger barges into the place where your character lives. Write at least three sentences that show how your character reacts. Try to include details about facial expressions, movement, posture, and your character's thoughts and feelings.

By now, you should have a good understanding of your character. You are ready to write your character sketch—a complete description of your character at a moment in time in its world. Your character sketch will combine all the steps you have practiced to describe your character. Remember that a character sketch is not a complete story; you are only describing one situation that shows your character in action.

Jon used the following graphic organizer to organize the information he wanted to include in his character sketch.

Student Model—Graphic Organizer

Character: Scandalon
The situation: meets a human

<u>What the Scandalon looks like</u>
long green limbs like bicycle wheel spokes
tiny, sparkly bumps on the limbs
rows of lights that change colors

<u>Where the Scandalon lives</u>
seeds were on the tail of a passing comet
on the ground, in the dirt with other weeds

<u>What the Scandalon does</u>
grows on the earth
waits, watches, and listens
decides to tell humans about it

<u>What the Scandalon says; how it says it</u>
strange voice
short and choppy sentences
Hello human. You are the contact. Listen carefully.

<u>How the Scandalon reacts</u>
afraid, wants to hide
curious
thinks about what might happen

Copy the graphic organizer onto your own paper and complete the information for your character and situation.

Drafting

Use your graphic organizer and the descriptions you wrote while developing your character as you begin your rough draft. Place your character in the situation and begin describing what your character looks like, how it acts, what it says, and how it reacts to others. Use ideas about where your character lives to help develop the setting for your situation. Do not focus on grammar or spelling at this time. You can go back later and check for errors. Your first draft should focus on creating a picture of your character.

accidentally by chance off the tail of a passing comet going by the earth.

The lights were changing colors back and forth from one color to another and forming designs.

Review Jon's draft. Find at least two more wordy sentences and correct them.

USING CLEAR AND DIRECT SENTENCES. Review your character sketch. Which sentences, if any, use unnecessary, overly complicated, or general words? Rewrite these sentences so that the meaning is clear and direct.

• • • • • • • • •

Reflecting

Each day you interact with many different types of people. If you have pets or live on a farm, you may interact with different animals as well. What makes these people or animals memorable to you? What causes you to like or dislike them? Is it the way they look or dress? Is it the things they say or do? Is it how they react or interact with you? The qualities and traits that make humans and animals memorable are the same qualities and traits that make characters memorable. Spend some time reflecting on the things that make people and animals memorable to you. You can use these ideas to develop your character.

Self- and Peer Evaluation

After you finish your first draft, complete a self-evaluation of your writing. If time allows, you may want to get one or two peer evaluations. See the Language Arts Survey 2.37–2.40 for more details about self-evaluation and peer evaluation.

As you evaluate your character sketch or that of a classmate, answer the following questions:

- What does the character look like? Which descriptions give the clearest picture? Which descriptions could be improved to create a better picture?
- How do the character's actions show what the character is like? Which actions best show what the character is like? Which actions, if any, don't seem to fit the character?
- What does the character's speech tell about the character? How do the words and the way the character speaks them help to develop a picture of the character?
- Which descriptions of the setting reveal information about the character? How could the setting be developed to tell more about the character?
- How do the character's reactions help to describe the character? What reactions could be developed more fully?

continued on page 443

Student Model—Draft

The first Scandalons that ever, ever came to the earth were dropped accidentally by chance off the tail of a passing comet going by the earth. The Scandalons weren't alive on the comet's tail. Only the seeds were on the comet. The seeds were asleep. But inside the seeds was the memory of another world. One day they would wake up and grow on the earth. *[wordy sentence]*

A Scandalon has limbs that grow in all directions every which way along the ground. It looks like the spokes of a bicycle wheel. A full sized Scandalon is the size of a large bicycle wheel. When Dusty passed by the Scandalon, he thought the creature was just a weed. But the Scandalon was there waiting, watching, and listening.

For some reason ~~that he couldn't explain to himself or any one else~~, Dusty stopped and bent over to look at the Scandalon. Dusty saw the bumps all along the Scandalon's limbs. When Dusty looked with a magnifying glass, the mystery of the Scandalon came into focus. What had looked like a plant now looked like rows and rows of Christmas tree lights. The lights were changing colors back and forth, from one color to another and forming designs. *[what did they look like?]* *[wordy sentence]*

The Scandalon saw Dusty looking at it, and it grew afraid. The Scandalon wanted to curl its limbs close around itself, but it didn't want Dusty to see it move. So it waited and waited to see what Dusty would do to it. Then the Scandalon became curious. It studied Dusty's face. Maybe this was its time to finally tell humans about the Scandalons. The Scandalon decided to speak. The voice that came out sounded how? (strange. The Scandalon said, "Hello human. I want to tell you about the Scandalons."

When the Scandalon saw Dusty's reaction, it grew afraid again. But when Dusty didn't hurt it, the Scandalon said, "The Scandalons came to earth millions of years ago. We have watched and waited for the right time to make contact. This is the time. You are the contact. Listen carefully."

- How convincing is the character description? What words make the character seem real? What attitude toward the character does the writing have?
- Which sentences, if any, are wordy? Which words could be deleted to make the sentences easier to read?

Revising and Proofreading

Read your character sketch out loud, picturing the description of your character in your mind. Then review your self-evaluation and peer evaluation comments. Which comments focus on problems you recognize as you read your character sketch? Which comments help you identify other areas that could be improved? How will you improve these areas? Revise your writing based on your answers to these questions. Then proofread your draft for errors in spelling, grammar, punctuation, capitalization, and other details. See the Language Arts Survey 2.45 for a proofreading checklist.

Student Model—Revised

The first Scandalons were dropped accidentally off the tail of a passing comet. The Scandalons weren't alive on the comet's tail. Only the star shaped seeds were on the comet. The seeds were asleep. But inside the seeds was the memory of another world. One day they would wake up and grow on the earth. A Scandalon has only long green limbs that grow in all directions along the

Write or print a final copy of your character sketch. You might want to draw a picture of your character and include it with your final copy. Share your character sketch with your classmates by taking turns reading them out loud. As you read your sketch, watch your classmates' reactions. Does the character in your sketch seem believable to them?

ground. It looks like the spokes of a bicycle wheel. A full sized Scandalon is the size of a large bicycle wheel. When Dusty passed by the Scandalon, he thought the creature was just a weed lying in the dirt with the other weeds and ants. But the Scandalon was there waiting, watching, and listening.

For some reason, Dusty stopped and bent over to look at the Scandalon. Dusty saw the tiny, sparkly bumps all along the Scandalon's long green limbs. When Dusty looked with a magnifying glass, the mystery of the Scandalon came into focus. What had looked like a plant now looked like rows of Christmas tree lights. The lights were changing colors and forming designs.

The Scandalon saw Dusty looking at it, and it grew afraid. The Scandalon wanted to curl its long green limbs close around itself, but it didn't want Dusty to see it move. So it waited. Then the Scandalon became curious. It studied Dusty's face. Maybe this was its time to finally tell humans about the Scandalons. The Scandalon decided to speak. The voice that came out sounded strange. It was high pitched and mechanical. The Scandalon blurted out, "Hello human. I want to tell you about the Scandalons."

When the Scandalon saw Dusty's reaction, it grew afraid again. But when Dusty didn't hurt it, the Scandalon gulped a breath and continued. "The Scandalons came to earth millions of years ago. We have watched and waited for the right time to make contact. This is the time. You are the contact. Listen carefully."

UNIT SIX *review*

Review: Words for Everyday Use

Check your knowledge of the following vocabulary words. Choose ten words that you would like to add to your own daily language. For each word, write a short sentence that includes the word in context. To review a word, look back to the page number indicated.

- antiquity (391)
- ascend (429)
- audacious (428)
- blunder (385)
- crane (418)
- defiance (427)
- devour (390)
- eternity (403)
- flummox (387)
- fund (386)
- gall (392)

- hallucinate (403)
- haste (389)
- homage (428)
- hover (405)
- impersonate (402)
- initiative (402)
- insist (425)
- loll (427)
- lunge (416)
- menacing (395)
- morsel (387)

- oddments (392)
- paralyze (433)
- plague (413)
- ravage (413)
- saucy (428)
- scorn (402)
- shamble (394)
- sheathe (393)
- subterranean (386)
- venture (392)

Review: Literary Tools

Define each of the following terms, giving concrete examples when possible. To review a term, refer to the page number(s) indicated.

- character (383)
- characterization (411, 423)

- conflict (400)
- fairy tale (411)
- flashback (400)

- narrator (383)
- parable (423)
- plot (400)

Reflecting on your *reading*

Theme & Genre

In each selection of this unit, something magical happens. These selections are part of a type of literature called fantasy. Fantasy is imaginative fiction often set in other worlds or other times and often including magical characters, such as fairies, elves, goblins, dwarves, and magic animals. There are strange tunnels; characters become invisible; and things happen that may seem unreal in the world as we know it. What types of things in fantasy generally *do* remain "normal"? What magical elements do these fantasy stories have in common?

Critical Thinking

In each selection in this unit, the main character is afraid of something. Compare the characters to one another. You can imagine that their fear is like a tunnel. When they are in the middle is when they are most afraid, and they are relieved to be out of it at the end. Why do they experience this fear, and how do they resolve it in the end?

Character	Tunnel of Fear	Resolution
Bilbo Baggins		
Ken		
The Monkey		

Group Project

As a group, create a magic world or village. Brainstorm to come up with a group "vision" of the place, including all the elements of setting. Make a poster of your magical world or village using paint, collage, markers, or any other medium. What does your fantasy setting look like? Who lives in it? What are their homes like? What are the public buildings like? What about it is magical?

On Your Own

Review the definition of a parable in the Handbook of Literary Terms, and then write a short parable of your own. It could be a parable of a situation you are familiar with—for example, fear of the first day of school, or of getting in trouble—or something you have read about, like homelessness or an endangered species.

Media Literacy

Look for elements of fantasy in different types of media, including magazines, films, television shows, radio programs, art, computer-generated art on the Internet, books, and comic books. Look for elements of fantasy that cross borders, appearing in different types of media. Can you find similar characters? settings? plots? themes? What common images can you find? Write a summary of your findings, including specific examples. You may wish to attach photocopies of stories, articles, book covers, and pictures. If time permits, give a presentation of your findings to your classmates.

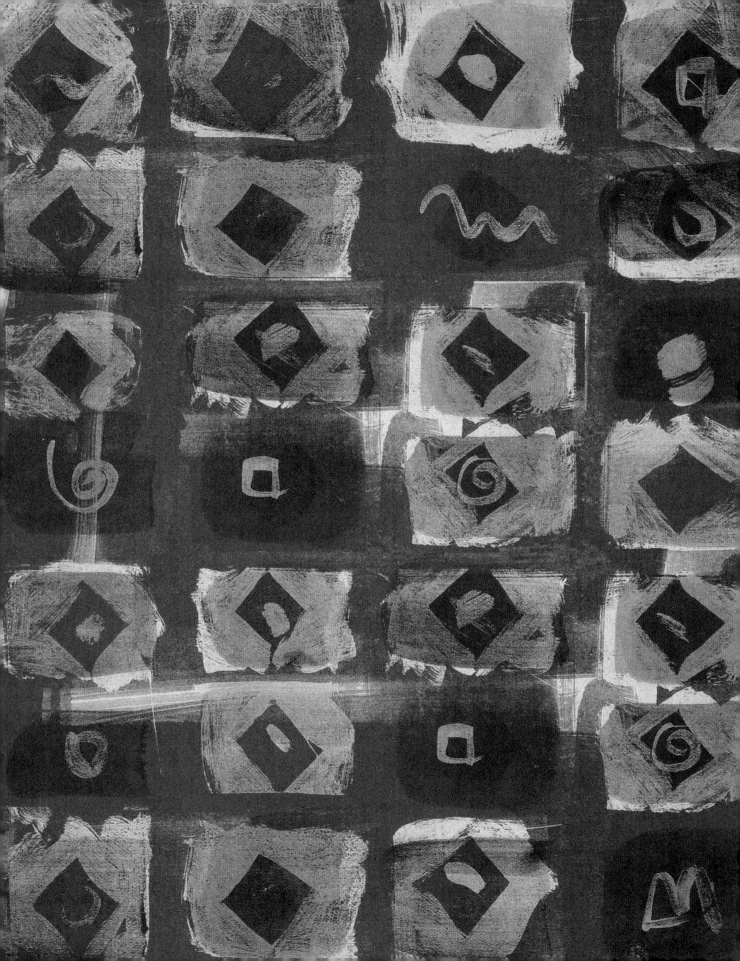

Genres in Literature
PART TWO

Bayeux Tapestry, c.1070. English artist. Bayeux, France.

PASS IT ON

The Oral Tradition

ELEMENTS of THE ORAL TRADITION

Long before people invented writing, they were telling stories, reciting poetry, and singing songs about their beliefs, dreams, and experiences. Many stories were passed down by word of mouth from one generation to the next. The passing of stories, poems, and songs by word of mouth became an important element in forming a group's culture. Together, these works made up what is known as a culture's oral tradition. Eventually many of these stories, poems, and songs were written down and have become an important part of literature. Some of the common forms of traditional oral literature are defined below.

Folk tales are stories passed by word of mouth from generation to generation. Although the term *folk tale* is often used to describe any type of story in the oral tradition, it also refers specifically to stories that could have taken place anywhere and at any time and that are considered anonymous (created by an unknown person). "Hansel and Gretel" and "Little Red Riding Hood" are two well-known folk tales. **Fairy tales** are folk tales that contain supernatural beings, such as fairies, dragons, ogres, and animals with human qualities. Well-known fairy tale characters include Cinderella, Puss in Boots, and Snow White. **Tall tales** are colorful stories that depict the exaggerated wild adventures of North-American folk heroes. Many of these heroes and stories revolve around the American frontier and the Wild West. Some tall tales offer explanations for how certain mountains, lakes, and other geographical features came to exist. Common characters in tall tales include Paul Bunyan, Calamity Jane, Pecos Bill, Davy Crockett, Annie Oakley, and Johnny Appleseed.

Folk songs typically have structured stanzas, a refrain, and a relatively simple melody. They often express a group's shared ideas or feelings. "Yankee Doodle" is an example of a folk song. Narrative folk songs often tell of adventure, war, or everyday life. **Ballads** are short narrative folk songs that are often sung while dancing. They often contain repeated words, lines, or phrases.

Parables are short stories that illustrate a moral or a spiritual truth. Many parables are found in religious writings such as the Christian Bible, the Hebrew Torah, and the Islamic Koran.

Fables are like parables in that they contain a moral. They are also like fairy tales because they have characters that are animals or inanimate objects that speak and act like humans. "The Tortoise and the Hare" is a fable.

Legends are stories that have been passed down through time. These stories are popularly thought of as historical but without evidence to verify that the events occurred. Stories about King Arthur and about Robin Hood are legends.

Myths are traditional stories that explain objects or events in the natural world. These explanations revolve around the actions of supernatural forces, such as gods. Every early culture around the world produced its own myths. This unit contains a variety of myths from around the world. Learning about these myths can help you better understand the cultures from which they stem. Myths also provide a way to compare and contrast the beliefs and attitudes of different traditional cultures. Characters, events, and ideas from myths often appear in contemporary literature. Words derived from mythological characters and places also appear in modern English. Becoming familiar with myths from around the world will help you identify these references in other works and in everyday life.

Prereading
"The Creation"
by Joseph Bruchac

Reader's Resource

- Many early cultures developed myths to explain the beginnings or creation of the earth. These creation myths often formed a basis for the religious beliefs of a culture group. Many American Indian creation myths focus on the roles of nature and of animals in forming the world as Native Americans knew it.

- **HISTORY CONNECTION.** In the early 1600s, five Native American groups joined together and became known as the Iroquois. The group, or federation, was called the Five Nations. They were the Mohawk, Oneida, Onondaga, Cayuga, and Seneca, all of the region that is now upper New York State. In 1722 the Tuscarora joined the group, which became the Six Nations. Each of the Six Nations sent representatives to a main council, which acted as the government of the federation. The organization of the Iroquois may have served as a model for the writers of the U.S. Constitution. Women played an important role in tribal politics. They nominated members of the tribal council and could also remove them from the council. During the French and Indian Wars (1754–1763) and the American Revolution (1775–1783), the Iroquois fought mainly on the side of the British. Many of their settlements were destroyed, and many Iroquois moved west or north into Canada. The headquarters of the Iroquois federation are at Onondaga Reservation near Syracuse, New York.

Reader's Journal

How do you believe the earth began?

Reader's TOOLBOX

MYTH. A **myth** is a story that explains objects or events in the natural world. What specific aspects of nature does this myth explain?

POINT OF VIEW. Point of view is the vantage point from which a story is told. If a story is told from the *first-person point of view*, the narrator uses the pronouns *I* and *we* and is a part of or a witness to the action. When a story is told from the *third-person point of view*, the narrator is outside the action; uses words such as *he, she, it,* and *they*; and avoids the use of *I* and *we*. Is this story told from the first-person point of view or from the third-person point of view? How do you know?

THE CREATION

Joseph Bruchac

Before this world came to be,
there lived in the Sky-World
an ancient chief.
In the center of his land
grew a beautiful tree
which had four white roots
stretching to each
of the four directions:
North, South, East and West.
From that beautiful tree,
all good things grew.

GUIDED READING

Who existed before the world came to be?

art smart.

Sky Woman, 1936. Ernest Smith. Rochester Museum and Science Center, Rochester, NY.

A member of the Seneca tribe, Ernest Smith (1907–1975) illustrated a creation story that has been retold for thousands of years. In this first scene of the long and complex story, Sky Woman falls toward the waters where the world will be created on the back of a turtle. What type of oral literature do you think Smith is illustrating?

Then it came to be
that the beautiful tree
was uprooted and
through
the hole it made in the
Sky-World
fell the youthful wife
of the ancient chief,
a handful of seeds,
which she grabbed from the tree
as she fell, <u>clutched</u> in her hand.
Far below there were only water
and water creatures
who looked up as they swam.
"Someone comes," said the duck.
"We must make room for her."

The great turtle swam up
from his place in the depths.

"There is room on my back,"
the great turtle said.

"But there must be earth
where she can stand," said the duck

GUIDED READING

How did the young woman fall from the Sky-World?

words for everyday use

clutch (kluch') v., grasp or hold tightly; snatch. *The eagle <u>clutched</u> the rattlesnake in its talons and rose soundlessly toward its nest.*

and so he dove beneath the waters,
but he could not reach the bottom.

"I shall bring up earth,"
the loon then said and he dove too,
but could not reach the bottom.

"I shall try," said the beaver
and he too dove but
could not reach the bottom.

Finally the muskrat tried.
He dove as deeply as he could, swimming
until his lungs almost burst.
With one paw he touched the bottom,
and came up with a tiny speck of earth
clutched in his paw.

"Place the earth on my back,"
the great turtle said,
and as they spread
the tiny speck of earth it grew
larger and larger and larger
until it became the whole world.
Then two swans flew up
and between their wings
they caught the woman
who fell from the sky.
They brought her gently
down to the earth
where she dropped her handful
of seeds from the Sky-World.

Then it was that the first plants grew
and life on this new earth began. ■

GUIDED READING

What does the young woman drop?

Respond *to the* SELECTION

What do you think could happen after life on earth begins? What developments could have taken place next?

About *the* AUTHOR

Joseph Bruchac (b.1942) often draws on his Native American (Abenaki) heritage in his writing and storytelling. He has written several books of folk tales, including *Thirteen Moons on Turtle's Back.* His original stories and poems have appeared in more than 400 periodicals and anthologies. He has won several prizes, including one for a storytelling tape of traditional Abenaki tales and another for his work in promoting children's literature. Besides being a poet and writer, Bruchac is editor and publisher of a literary magazine. He lives in Greenfield Center, New York.

Investigate, Inquire, and Imagine

Recall: GATHERING FACTS

1a. When does this story take place? Where does the action begin?

2a. How does the wife of the ancient chief happen to fall from the Sky-World?

3a. What danger or problem does the falling woman face? Who worries about her and decides to help?

4a. How does the earth form? How do the first plants come to be?

→ **Interpret:** FINDING MEANING

1b. How is the Sky-World like our world? Consider who and what live there.

2b. Why might this event be disastrous to the wife of the ancient chief? to the Sky-World?

3b. Why might these beings be concerned? What does their concern say about them?

4b. What is significant about how these things happen?

Analyze: TAKING THINGS APART

5a. What characters in this myth go out of their way to help another?

→ **Synthesize:** BRINGING THINGS TOGETHER

5b. What does this myth say about the relationship between humans and animals? Explain your answer.

Evaluate: MAKING JUDGMENTS

6a. How realistic is this view of the connection between animals and people?

→ **Extend:** CONNECTING IDEAS

6b. How do you view the relationship between humans and animals?

Understanding *Literature*

MYTH. A **myth** is a story that explains objects or events in the natural world. How did the creators of this myth incorporate what they did know about the world into an explanation of the world's beginnings?

POINT OF VIEW. Point of view is the vantage point from which a story is told. If a story is told from the *first-person point of view*, the narrator uses the pronouns *I* and *we* and is a part of or a witness to the action. When a story is told from the *third-person point of view*, the narrator is outside the action; uses words such as *he, she, it,* and *they*; and avoids the use of *I* and *we.* If this story had been told from the first-person point of view, how would it differ? Which characters in the story might have been able to tell it from the first-person point of view?

Writer's Journal

1. Write the text for a **bumper sticker** that promotes the protection and preservation of the environment. Use a catchy phrase to catch people's attention.

2. Think of an aspect of nature you could explain—such as why it rains, why no two snowflakes are alike, why the sun goes down at night, or why caterpillars turn into butterflies—and write a short **myth** to explain it.

3. Create **names** for all the characters in this myth.

Skill Builders

Applied English

CREATING A POSTER. Earth Day is an annual holiday that is celebrated on April 20. On this day, people celebrate the earth and learn about ways to help preserve and protect the environment. Imagine that you work in the environmental science department of a college or university. Create a poster encouraging students to attend an Earth Day celebration on campus. Be sure to include on the poster the date, time, and location. You may also want to include a phone number for people to call for more information or to volunteer to help.

Language, Grammar, and Style

PRONOUNS AND ANTECEDENTS. When you use pronouns in your writing, be sure that they agree with their antecedents in number and gender. Review these rules in the Language Arts Survey 3.42, "Getting Pronouns and Antecedents to Agree." Then for each sentence below, choose the pronoun in parentheses that agrees with its antecedents in number and gender.

1. Emily often wondered where the clouds went when (he, she) went to bed.
2. Once Victor and Sue stayed up to look at the stars from (his or her, their) kitchen window.
3. Many women share (her, their) tips on how to succeed in the business world.
4. Every environmentalist has a deep respect for the earth and dedicates (his or her, their) work to preserve it.
5. Every time the tide comes in, the people on the beach move (his or her, their) belongings farther from the water.
6. How many people are curious about (his or her, their) environment?
7. I enjoyed listening to the speaker because (she, they) was interesting.
8. Kevin claims to have spoken to a seal who asked (him, them) if he was a friend or foe.
9. The seal waved (his or her, its) flipper and said, "Welcome to the Land of Oceana!"
10. Jorge has always been quite trustworthy, but I'm not sure if we should believe (him, her) this time.

Prereading

"The Twelve Labors of Hercules"
by Walker Brents

Reader's Resource

- **HISTORY CONNECTION.** Greek culture began to develop thousands of years ago. For centuries, people thought that the story of the Trojan War (1250 BC) was simply a myth, but in the 1800s, the ruins of Troy were discovered. The oral tradition thrived, led by Homer, who is credited for two great epic poems, the *Iliad* and the *Odyssey*, which told of the tale of the return of the hero Odysseus from the Trojan War to his home in Ithaca. During the 400s BC, the Greeks made major contributions in art, philosophy, theater, and literature.

- Hercules was known as the son of Zeus, the leader of the Olympian gods, the god of the sky, and the god of thunder. His mother was Alcmena, a mortal human. Hera, wife of Zeus and queen of the gods, was jealous of Alcmena. Ares, the god of war, and Hebe, the goddess of youth, sprang from the union of Hera and Zeus. Hera alone gave birth to Hephaistos, the god of fire. Apollo, the god of poetry and music, was the son of Zeus and Leto. Athena, another daughter of Zeus, was the goddess of wisdom, justice, and peace.

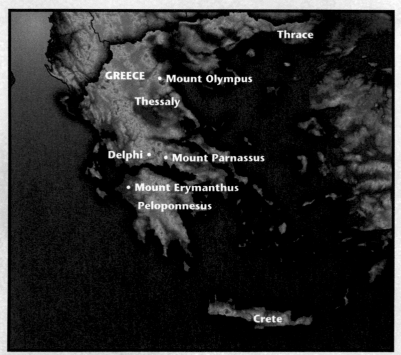

The Olympian gods lived on Mount Olympus in Thessaly. Crete, the island of King Minos, is the largest of the Greek islands.

Reader's Journal

If you had to choose between being very strong and very intelligent, which would you choose? Why?

Reader's TOOLBOX

MYTH. A **myth** is a story that explains objects or events in the natural world. These objects or events are explained as being caused by some supernatural force or being, often a god. Greek mythology portrayed gods as figures who participated in daily life alongside people. Look for examples in this story of how the actions of gods affected the workings of the world.

CHRONOLOGICAL ORDER. Events arranged in order of the time when they happened are said to be in **chronological order**. This method of organization is used in most literary works, whether they are fiction or nonfiction. Why do you think this selection is told in chronological order?

The Twelve Labors of

Walker Brents

HERCULES

The goddess Hera hated Hercules from the moment of his birth. In his infancy she sent two

giant serpents to kill him as he slept, but Hercules strangled them instead. His parents rushed

into the room to find the baby shaking the dead bodies of the snakes as if they were rattles.

This was an early indication of his great strength, but this strength was not always used well.

Once Hera sent madness and insanity into the consciousness of Hercules. His thoughts became scrambled. Under the delusion[1] that he was at war, he mistook his nephews and nieces for enemies, and killed them. When the madness passed and he saw what he had done he was overwhelmed with grief and guilt. Terrible <u>remorse</u> drove him to the oracle[2] of the god Apollo at Delphi, and he asked the priestesses there what he could do to <u>expiate</u> his terrible deed. They told him, "Go to King Eurystheus, and undertake the labors he will put upon you."

GUIDED READING

How does Hera try to kill baby Hercules?

GUIDED READING

What drives Hercules to the oracle of Apollo?

Hercules went to Tiryns, the land ruled by King Eurystheus. He stood before the throne. Eurystheus said to him, "Go to Nemea, where a fierce lion terrorizes the people. No weapon can pierce through its terrible skin. Kill this lion, remove its skin, carry it here and show it to me." Eurystheus was shrewd, calculating, cunning, and cowardly. Each task he was to set before Hercules was designed to be impossible, but the determination of Hercules was to overcome the impossible. He followed the lion's tracks to a deep dark cave hidden in a hillside. He saw the bones strewn at the cave's entrance, and entered in. In such a darkness he could not see his hand before his face, the <u>dank</u> air was filled with the smell of blood. The lion had just killed, and had carried its prey to this place which was its very den. Hercules leapt upon the lion and wrestled with it. His tremendous club and sharp knife were of no use, for the lion's hide

GUIDED READING

How does King Eurystheus design the tasks for Hercules?

was too thick. Hercules grasped the lion's neck with his hands, and held it against the cave wall until the lion's thrashings ceased, and it was dead. Then he dragged the lion into the light of day, skinning it with one of its own claws. He draped the skin over his shoulders, its head over his head like a helmet, and hurried back to the palace of King Eurystheus, who saw him approach from a distance and was so frightened at the sight that he hid in a giant olive jar. He sent his servants to Hercules to tell him of the next task. "Go to the swamp of Lerna and defeat the hydra,[3] who lives at the <u>confluence</u> of the three springs."

Hercules and one of his surviving nephews, Iolaus, found the monster in the depths of the swamp, at the confluence of three springs. Hercules shot his arrows as the monster so as to anger it enough to attack, and come close enough for him to fight it with his oaken club. The monster had nine heads, and came toward them screaming with rage, belching great gouts[4] of poison bloody mud. Hercules began to knock off the creature's heads, but saw that three heads grew back from where one was knocked off! Iolaus lit the branch of a tree with fire, and held this torch against the neck-stubs where Hercules knocked the heads off. The burnt blood prevented the heads from growing back. With this the tide of the battle turned. The creature was weakening. Finally, Hercules tore off the central head, the primary one. He carried it away and buried it in the ground with a great rock over it, so that it could not rejoin the

---

1. **delusion.** Persistent false psychotic belief
2. **oracle.** Shrine where a god shares knowledge
3. **hydra.** Serpent monster with regrowable heads
4. **gouts.** Masses of fluid

words for everyday use

re • morse (ri mors') *n.,* gnawing distress over guilt. *Marta felt growing <u>remorse</u> over having lied to her mother.*

ex • pi • ate (ek' spē āt) *v.,* make amends for. *Gina hoped the peace offering would <u>expiate</u> her wrongdoings.*

dank (daŋk') *adj.,* unpleasantly moist. *The <u>dank</u>, dark basement smelled like mildew.*

con • flu • ence (kän' flü əns) *n.,* a coming together or gathering. *The meeting resulted in a confluence of ideas about how the organization's research should continue.*

body and come alive again. Then Hercules dipped his arrow points in the poison blood of the hydra, which lay in pools all around, so as to make them deadly.

GUIDED READING

How does Hercules make poisonous arrows?

Other labors followed, and they took Hercules far and wide. In the forest of Ceryneia he chased a deer with golden antlers for an entire year, caught it and carried it alive to King Eurystheus, then returned to Ceryneia and let the deer go. Earlier, he had gone to the land of King Augeias, who kept a stable filled with thousands upon thousands of cattle, which had never been cleaned. Eurystheus, gleefully imagining Hercules carrying baskets and baskets of dung, had ordered him to clean those stables. But Hercules <u>diverted</u> the course of two rivers and sent them through the stables so that they were entirely cleaned in one day.

GUIDED READING

How does Hercules clean the stables?

On Mount Erymanthus there lived a great boar. Searching amid the lower slopes of this mountain Hercules met an old friend of his, Pholos the centaur,[5] who lived in a village of centaurs. Hercules shared a meal with his friend, but accidentally spilled a drop or two of wine upon the ground. The smell of the wine drove the centaurs insane, and they attacked Hercules, who responded with a volley of arrows tipped with the hydra's poison blood. Many were killed. Pholos was burying their bodies when an arrow came loose from one of them, fell down and pierced the flesh near his hoof. The poison entered his veins and killed him. By this time, Hercules was on the upper part of the mountain hunting for the boar but when he heard of his friend's death he returned to the centaur village and in great sadness helped with the funeral. But he had made enemies with some of the centaurs, and one of them, Nessus, swore revenge. Hercules returned to the hunt for the boar and chased it into deep snowdrifts, where he caught it. After that he went to the land of Thrace and fought against Diomedes, killing him and his man-eating horses.

GUIDED READING

What kills Pholos?

Another labor brought Hercules to the marshes of Stymphalus. Somewhere in these vast marshes there lived grotesque vicious birds that shot their feathers like arrows into people. Then they tore the people into pieces and carried their chunks of flesh away into the marshes where they devoured them. No one could get to the place from which they came. Hercules came very close to their <u>lair</u>, but not close enough. The <u>foliage</u> was so thick not even he could hack through it with his sword, so that his forward motion was stopped, and he sat upon the ground in despair. Here an ally came to him, the goddess Athena. She helped him. She caused a set of brazen cymbals to appear upon the ground next to his feet, and spoke these words into his consciousness: "Strike the cymbals together. The sound of their brassy clashing will startle the birds from their branches and nests. They will fly into the air and become targets for your arrows." Hercules followed her instructions. As fast as the birds flew up his arrows pierced them. Most were killed

GUIDED READING

How does Athena help Hercules?

---

5. **centaur.** Creature that is half man and half horse

words for everyday use

di • vert (dī vərt′) v., turn from one course to another. *Father <u>diverted</u> the conversation from football to homework.*

lair (lār′) n., resting place. *The boy accidentally wandered up to the bear's <u>lair</u>.*

fo • li • age (fō′ lē ij) n., leaves, flowers, and branches. *Mrs. Simms trimmed the <u>foliage</u> in her yard with a hedge clipper.*

and those who lived flew away and never returned.

He came to Themiscyra, where the river Thermodon flowed into the sea, in a place of many cliffs and rocky hiding places. This was the land of the Amazons, woman-warriors, whose queen, Hippolyte, had a sword-belt made of bronze and <u>iridescent</u> glass, given to her by the god of war, Ares. Hercules was to take this belt from them. Expecting a battle, he was surprised when Hippolyte gave it to him freely, but outside their meeting place, the goddess Hera filled the minds of the Amazons with rumors of war, so that as Hercules left he was suddenly attacked by battalions of Amazons. Once more his poison arrows did their deadly work, and, with the belt, he made his escape.

GUIDED READING

With what does Hera fill the minds of the Amazons?

In Crete he carried away the bull Poseidon gave to King Minos. On the island of Erytheia, he killed Geyron, a giant man-monster with one head and three bodies, and his two-headed dog, Orthrus. He took the herd of cattle they guarded—cattle whose hides were red as the rays of the setting sun. Helios the sun-god caused a floating golden cup to appear in the sea, and Hercules drove the bull of Crete and the red cattle onto this cup and floated back to Tiryns.

"Your next to last task requires that you find the garden beyond the world. There, in the Garden of the Hesperides, grow the golden apples upon the branches of a tree guarded by the serpent that never sleeps. Bring back those apples." Hercules had no sooner heard these orders than he was off. At the world's edge he met Atlas, the giant who holds up the sky. "The three sisters who live there are my own daughters. Let me bring back the apples. I am the only one they will let have them. But you must hold up the sky while I am gone." So Atlas said as he waited for Hercules to climb atop the high mountain preparatory to taking upon himself the burden of the sky. Once the load was transferred, Hercules stood with the sky upon his back, watching Atlas stride away, already waist-deep in the ocean that encircles the world. Some few moments, hours, days, or months later Atlas returned, holding a branch with three golden apples. "Let me take the apples back to Eurystheus. You go on holding up the sky, for I am tired of it." Atlas was getting ready to go when Hercules said, "Friend, let me do just one thing before you're off. That lion's skin lying there—I carry it with me wherever I go. It would make a good pad to cushion my shoulders against this mighty burden. Kindly take up the sky again for a moment as I gather it up. Then you can return the load to me." Atlas agreed to do so, but once the sky was returned to his keeping Hercules took the branch and walked away, ignoring Atlas' angry cries for him to return.

GUIDED READING

Who does Hercules meet at the edge of the world? What does this person say?

GUIDED READING

How does Hercules trick Atlas?

The final labor required Hercules to go down to the world of the dead and bring back Cerberus, the fierce three-headed dog. The gods Hermes and Athena met him at the river between the two worlds and helped him. He carried Cerberus back to Tiryns and showed it to King Eurystheus. The three heads barked at him and bared their teeth, and Eurystheus died of fright.

words for everyday use   **ir • i • des • cent** (ir ə des' ənt) *adj.*, showing a play of colors that produces rainbow effects. *The <u>iridescent</u> bubbles floated upward.*

Hercules had many other adventures besides these twelve labors. He did many terrible things and many wonderful things. His earthly father was Amphitryon, but his father in the skies was Zeus. As time went on, the events in his life brought that to clear realization. Hercules was returning from the land of Calydonia with his bride Deianeira when they were faced with a rain-swollen raging river. Hercules was unconcerned about his own ability to swim across this river, but how Deianeira would cross was another matter. Just then the centaur Nessus approached them. He spoke to them very courteously: "Ah Hercules, I congratulate your marriage. Do you remember me? I am Nessus. I was there in the village at Mount Erymanthos that awful day. It is a wonder your deadly arrows did not kill me, though I was wounded. I apologize on behalf of all us centaurs, for our <u>deranged</u> behavior then. Please allow me to carry Deianeira across this river. I am a most excellent swimmer." Hercules <u>assented</u> to this, and as Nessus clattered down into the water, with Deianeira on his back, he threw his bow and arrows across the water, and vaulted in. Reaching the other side he was startled by cries. He turned and saw Nessus farther down the riverbank crossing onto land, attempting to carry Deianeira away. "Nessus," he uttered as he placed an arrow against the bowstring and drew it back, "haven't you felt enough of the hydra's poison?" With that he let the arrow fly. It pierced Nessus' back as he fled and the point <u>protruded</u> through his chest. Coughing up blood he tumbled to the ground as Deianeira, an experienced rider, rolled free. He

> **GUIDED READING**
>
> Who greets Hercules and Deianeira?

staggered up again but lost his footing and fell down the riverbank into the shallow waters, gasping and choking. With his dying words he requested that Deianeira take a few drops of his blood spilled onto the sand and save it. "Let my death keep your love strong. Take this blood and rub it into anything your husband wears. My blood is charmed. It will renew his love whenever and wherever he puts such clothes on as have been touched with this blood." He died just before Hercules arrived upon the scene. Deianeira told him nothing about what had been said. Little did either one know of the actual reasons behind Nessus' bequest.[6]

> **GUIDED READING**
>
> What does Nessus say to Deianeira as he is dying?

Years later, Hercules went to a distant land and conquered it. He sent a message back home after the final battle was won. "Send me my best robe to wear for the sacrifices I will make to the gods, in gratitude for our victory here." Among the captives that had earlier arrived was a woman, Iole, whose love, once long before, Hercules had tried to win. When Deianeira saw her she was reminded of that time, and began to worry. She resolved to put the blood-charm of Nessus into the robe she would send him. She gave it to the messenger, who carried it to Hercules, waiting upon a high mountain to begin the ceremony.

> **GUIDED READING**
>
> What does Deianeira decide to do with the robe?

It was just a few moments after Hercules had donned[7] the robe and begun the sacrifice that the true nature of the charm revealed itself. A terrible burning began to spread through his limbs all the way into his heart.

---

6. **bequest.** Item given by will to another
7. **donned.** Put on

---

words for everyday use

de • range (di rānj′) v., disturb. *The speaker tried to <u>derange</u> the audience with taunts and threats.* **deranged,** adj.

as • sent (ə sent′) v., agree. *My mother <u>assented</u> to the increase of my allowance.*

pro • trude (prō trüd′) v., stick out. *Cyrano's nose <u>protruded</u> at least six inches from the rest of his face.*

The hydra's blood had returned to the one who had sent it out on so many arrows before. He clutched at the robe to pull it off, but it stuck fast in some places and in others great chunks of skin clung to it as it was torn free, revealing his bones. He screamed in rage and pain, stumbling through the forest, farther up the mountain. At the summit, a <u>semblance</u> of calm came to him, and he began to build his own funeral pyre.[8] When it was finished he commanded someone among those around him to set it alight. No one would. Hercules offered a shepherd's son passing by, Philoctetes, his bow and arrows if he would ignite the pyre. Philoctetes agreed to, and

Hercules climbed to its very top, placed upon it the skin of the Nemean Lion as a blanket, and the oaken club as a pillow, and laid himself down there in a state of <u>serene composure</u>. The torch was lit and handed to Philoctetes, who put it to the bier,[9] which was soon engulfed. As the flames did their work, the earthly form of Hercules disintegrated, but his godly form became more clear. The skies opened up and a chariot came down and took him away. In the heavens, Hera reconciled herself to him, and he took his place amid the company of the gods.

> **GUIDED READING**
>
> What does Philoctetes agree to do?

---

8. **pyre.** Place for burial fire
9. **bier.** Coffin stand

Respond *to the* SELECTION

What do you think about Nessus and his revenge on Hercules? Did Hercules deserve this? Why, or why not?

About *the* AUTHOR

Walker Brents (b.1959) is a poet and storyteller who has loved folklore and myths since he discovered at the age of five the myths of Hercules and the Greek gods. After majoring in English and philosophy at Drury College in Springfield, Missouri, Brents worked with the Jesuit Volunteer Corps in the early 1980s. It was while working at a refugee center in southern California that he was able to listen to the many stories of Vietnamese, Romanian, Laotian, and Cambodian refugees. Brents now tells Hindu and Japanese myths and folktales at the Asian Art Museum in San Francisco and teaches at Berkwood Hedge School in Berkeley. He has published poetry in a number of literary magazines, including the *Berkeley Review of Books, Moksha Journal,* and *Galley Sail Review.*

words for everyday use

sem • blance (sem' bləns) *n.*, appearance, likeness. *Amid the hubbub, the school production showed a <u>semblance</u> of control and calm.*

se • rene (sə rēn') *adj.*, calm. *I looked out at the calm beauty of the <u>serene</u> lake.*

com • po • sure (kəm pō' zhər) *n.*, self-controlled mind or appearance. *Horace maintained his <u>composure</u> throughout the stressful day.*

GETTING INTO STORYTELLING

On the Telling of Myths, Legends, and Stories

Walker Brents

I tell stories at Berkwood Hedge School in Berkeley, California, and at the Asian Art Museum in San Francisco. In the past, I have told stories in many various schools and at the Children's Folk Theater. I have also performed at parties, at fundraisers, in cafes, and in healthcare facilities. I have been telling stories this way since 1985.

Recollecting how I became a storyteller, in memory I see myself at twenty or twenty-one, standing in the public library in Springfield, Missouri, a small city on the edge of the Ozark Plateau, surrounded by vertical stacks of books, towering over me in all direction. In my hands was a copy of Jeremiah Curtin's *Myths and Folklore of Ireland,* a book published in the early 1900s, or maybe it was Joseph Jacob's *Celtic Folk Tales*, from the end of the 1800s. Standing there—it was springtime, the clover was blooming yellow flowers, and I could hear the warm winds blow across the windows and see the shadows of tree leaves move across the spines of the books—I suddenly imagined myself carrying these tales in my mind to a place where I would speak them aloud.

When I was fourteen, filled with thoughts of Huck Finn's adventures, I stood beside the Missouri River, the black earth beneath my feet, the sunlight on my hands, and the wind blowing from across the river. I knew this beauty in sight and thought and feeling, and my sense of appreciation for what was around me was deepened by what was within me: thoughts of the story, its atmosphere, and the words it contained. I knew then that if my speech could be so living as all this, I would be happy.

Sometimes, though, I was less than happy. When I was very young, four or five, I was frightened of the backyard garden of my grandparents' house, of what was back there, and of what came out of hiding when the evening shadows fell. By day it was wild and mysterious, with the tall oak trees and their leaves so nobly shaped and the rough hungry thistles as tall as me, with all their clawed leaves and bristly stems. I knew this place in my childhood imagination as a place of cowboys, spacemen, ancient warriors, and gods. But at night, in the sinister dark, there were scarier monsters, and how would I see them before they saw me?

At various times in childhood, my brother and I held enchanted conversations, peopling our bedroom dark with fantastical and whimsical figures, such as The Rhino, a rhinoceros with an "R" on its sweatshirt; Rumbles, faceless gorillas who lived in the windows; Trido Men with their animals, Lightning Tridoes, who lived in the bedsheets; each a unique creature, fanciful and familiar both.

As I grew older, the winds of summer blew hotter, and those of winter blew colder. The ice in the silvery branches of February was as overwhelmingly beautiful as the April, May, and June wildflowers. It became more and more urgent that I understand myself. I guess that's when literature became to me as a lantern, to light my way. Doors opened into adventures, filled with possibilities of hopes fulfilled and disappointments faced. The days and nights of the world, its lights and darknesses—how could such truths be expressed in words and gestures? Myths, legends, and tales form a room in the imagination, wherein we ponder the way things are and how they seem to be. In language, each one puts their thoughts together differently; it is simple at times and laborious at others. There is a time in the learning of a story when its qualities take on their own life.

The process of learning tales and myths, and understanding in a personal way their ideas, lessons, symbols, and designs, is a vast journey. Any kind of speech only approaches its edges. Saint Patrick exclaimed, "An intricate business is story-telling!" By that he means that the more you look, the more you will see. It may take time and what you set out to learn may be changed in the learning. What comes to someone else from a story may be different than what you have cherished or received.

If you are interested in storytelling, study and tell mysterious stories. See what thoughts and moods your imagination leads you to, and consider how they relate to what you see, hear, read, or feel. Each time you tell a story, you'll receive something new from it; sometimes a wordless hint, sometimes a great phrase or profound insight, sometimes a joke, sometimes all these things. Navigate your way through legends and myths with a sense of the doors that each one opens for you. In the world of legend and mythology, you can reanimate events and scenes of the past with your own thoughts and imaginations. You have felt the rays of the same sun and moon as the ancient creators. The characters in the myths share problems, hopes, and dreams with people in your own world.

Your imagination will help you understand yourself. Imaginative conceptions are windows through which the heart looks and sees. Myth, legend, and story are houses of such windows. When children say to me, after I have related a fantastical sequence of events, "That's not true!" I reply, "The outside may or may not be true, but the inside is mysteriously true." Mystery and beauty are the very fabric of the universe, and we make them come alive through oral literature.

Investigate, *Inquire,* and Imagine

Recall: GATHERING FACTS

1a. Why does Hercules go to Tiryns to see King Eurystheus?

2a. What does Hercules do with his arrows after killing the hydra?

3a. What does Nessus swear on Mount Erymanthus?

4a. Whom does Hercules meet at the edge of the world? What does that person do for him?

5a. What happens when Hercules and Deianeira are at the river?

Interpret: FINDING MEANING

1b. Why does King Eurystheus give orders that are difficult to carry out?

2b. How does this act eventually harm Hercules himself?

3b. How does he fulfill this vow?

4b. How does Hercules trick this person?

5b. Why does Nessus offer his assistance?

Analyze: TAKING THINGS APART

6a. List the twelve labors of Hercules. Then order them according to what you think is the most to least difficult.

Synthesize: BRINGING THINGS TOGETHER

6b. How do you think Hercules feels after accomplishing the twelve labors? Why do you think Hercules chooses to live such an adventuresome and dangerous life? How do his actions in life work against him at the end of the story?

Evaluate: MAKING JUDGMENTS

7a. Who do you think is responsible for Hercules' death—Nessus, Deianeira, Hercules, Hera, or Eurystheus? Or is his death a result of a combination of people's actions? Explain your answer.

Extend: CONNECTING IDEAS

7b. Describe in your own words what kind of mythological figure Hercules is. How would such a person fare in today's world?

Understanding *Literature*

MYTH. A **myth** is a story that explains objects or events in the natural world. These objects or events are explained as being caused by some supernatural force or being, often a god. Greek mythology creates a world in which the gods are as active and important in day-to-day experiences in the world as people are. Why do you think the Greeks created such a sophisticated web of mythology to explain events in the natural world and in their own history?

CHRONOLOGICAL ORDER. Events arranged in order of the time when they happened are said to be in **chronological order**. This method of organization is used in most stories, whether they are fiction or nonfiction. Is the chronological order of the twelve labors of any real importance? Which events in the story must be presented in chronological order so that the story makes sense?

Writer's Journal

1. Imagine you are a director of a play about Hercules. Write a **character description** of Hercules for the costume designer, the makeup artist, and the actor playing the part.

2. If the story of Hercules' twelve labors were set in the modern era rather than in ancient Greece, what tasks might the hero be given? Write a **list of twelve labors** for a modern-day Hercules.

3. Write a **speech** that Hercules might have given before dying.

Skill Builders

Vocabulary

ANTONYMS. An antonym is a word of opposite meaning. Match each of the words on the left with the word that most closely resembles its antonym on the right. If you wish, you may use a dictionary or thesaurus.

assent	arid
cunning	daft
dank	dissent
divert	dull
iridescent	focus
protrude	giddy
serene	sink

Study and Research

INVESTIGATING GREEK GODS. With the help of a librarian, find resources that you can use to study the gods in Greek mythology. Choose a particular god or goddess to focus on. Find descriptions of the god's actions, physical appearance, and relationships to other gods. Look for pictures of the god. What stories did he or she play a part in? With what historic events was he or she involved? Prepare a report for your class, including pictures, descriptions, and stories.

Reader's Journal

Describe a time in your life when magic could have saved you from a big disappointment, from embarrassment, from fear, or from suffering.

Reader's Resource

- "The Singing, Springing Lark" is a folktale that includes enchanted characters, supernatural events, and magic spells.

- **CULTURAL CONNECTION.** Jacob and Wilhelm Grimm, known as the Brothers Grimm, were the first collectors of folklore to recognize that folk tales can be a source for the scientific study of the culture that produced them.

- The Grimm brothers noted great similarity in themes and characters among German and other European folktales. Later folklorists discovered resemblances between European folktales and those of other continents.

Prereading

"The Singing, Springing Lark"

by Jacob and Wilhelm Grimm, translated by Jack David Zipes

Reader's TOOLBOX

PERSONIFICATION. Personification is a figure of speech in which something not human is described as if it were human. "The Singing, Springing Lark" contains many uses of personification. As you read, look for the uses of personification.

FOLK TALE AND FAIRY TALE. A **folk tale** is a story passed by word of mouth from generation to generation. A **fairy tale** is a type of European folk tale containing supernatural events and often imaginary creatures such as elves, giants, fairies, dragons, and animals with human qualities. Fairy tales often are set in medieval times (also called the Middle Ages, from about 500 to 1350).

Graphic Organizer

Keep track of the magical elements of this fairy tale, using clusters like these.

lion

can talk

really a prince

Mary Hall in the Character of Una, 1771. Benjamin West.
Wadsworth Atheneum, Hartford, Connecticut.

The Singing, Springing Lark

Jacob and Wilhelm Grimm

Once upon a time there was a man who was about to go on a long journey, and right before his departure he asked his three daughters what he should bring back to them. The oldest wanted pearls, the second, diamonds, but the third said, "Dear Father, I'd like to have a singing, springing lark."

"All right," said the father. "If I can get one, you shall have it."

So he kissed all three daughters good-bye and went on his way. When the time came for his return journey, he had purchased pearls and diamonds for the two oldest, but even though he had looked all over, he had not been able to find the singing, springing lark for his youngest daughter. He was particularly sorry about that because she was his favorite. In the meantime, his way took him through a forest, in the middle of which he discovered a magnificent castle. Near the castle was a tree, and way on top of this tree he saw a lark singing and springing about.

GUIDED READING

Where does the father find a lark?

"Well, you've come just at the right time," he said, quite pleased, and he ordered his servant to climb the tree and catch the little bird. But when the servant went over to the tree, a lion jumped out from under it, shook himself, and roared so ferociously that the leaves on the trees trembled.

"If anyone tries to steal my singing, springing lark," he cried, "I'll eat him up."

"I didn't know that the bird belonged to you," said the man. "I'll make up for my trespassing and give you a great deal of gold if only you'll spare my life."

"Nothing can save you," said the lion, "unless you promise to give me the first thing you meet when you get home. If you agree, then I'll not only grant you your life, but I'll also give you the bird for your daughter."

At first the man refused and said, "That could be my youngest daughter. She loves me most of all and always runs to meet me when I return home."

But the servant was very scared of the lion and said, "It doesn't always have to be your daughter. Maybe it'll be a cat or dog."

GUIDED READING

What does the servant say to persuade the man?

The man let himself be persuaded and took the singing, springing lark. Then he promised the lion he would give him the first thing that met him when he got home.

Upon reaching his house, he walked inside, and the first thing that met him was none other than his youngest and dearest daughter: she came running up to him, threw her arms around him, and kissed him. When she saw that he had brought her a singing, springing lark, she was overcome with joy. But her father could not rejoice and began to cry.

GUIDED READING

Who or what first meets the father when he arrives home?

"My dearest child," he said. "I've had to pay a high price for that bird. In exchange I was <u>compelled</u> to promise you to a wild lion, and when he gets you, he'll tear you to pieces and eat you up." Then he went on to tell her exactly how everything had happened and begged her not to go

words for everyday use

com • pel (kəm pel´) v., cause to do something by overwhelming pressure. *The wonderful weather <u>compelled</u> me to go the beach instead of to the library.*

there, no matter what the consequences might be. Yet she <u>consoled</u> him and said, "Dearest Father, if you've made a promise you must keep it. I'll go there, and once I've made the lion nice and tame, I'll be back here safe and sound."

The next morning she had her father show her the way. Then she took leave of him and walked calmly into the forest. Now, it turned out that the lion was actually an enchanted[1] prince. During the day he and his men were lions, and during the night they assumed their human form.

GUIDED READING

Who actually was the lion?

When she arrived there, she was welcomed in a friendly way, and they conducted her to the castle. When night came, the lion became a handsome man, and the wedding was celebrated in <u>splendor</u>. They lived happily together by remaining awake at night and asleep during the day. One day he came to her and said, "Tomorrow there will be a celebration at your father's house since your oldest sister is to be married. If you wish to attend, my lions will escort you there."

She replied that, yes, she would very much like to see her father again, and she went there accompanied by the lions. There was great rejoicing when she arrived, for they all had believed that she had been torn to pieces by the lions and had long been dead. But she told them what a handsome husband she had and how well off she was. She stayed with them just as long as the wedding celebration lasted. Then she went back to the forest.

When the second daughter was about to be married, she was again invited to the wedding, but this time she said to the lion, "I don't want to go without you."

However, the lion said it would be too dangerous for him because he would be changed into a dove and have to fly about with the doves for seven years, if the ray of a burning candle were to fall upon him.

GUIDED READING

What will change the lion into a dove?

"Please, come with me," she said. "I'll be sure to take good care of you and protect you from the light."

So they went off together and took their small child with them. Once there she had a hall built for him, so strong and thick that not a single ray of light could <u>penetrate</u> it. That was the place where he was to sit when the wedding candles were lit. However, its door was made out of green wood, and it split and developed a crack that nobody saw. The wedding was celebrated in splendor, but when the wedding <u>procession</u> with all the candles and torches came back from church and passed by the hall, a ray about the width of a hair fell upon the prince, and he was instantly transformed. When his wife entered the hall to look for him, she could find only a white dove sitting there, and he said to her, "For seven years I shall have to fly about the world, but for every seven steps you take I shall leave a drop of red blood and a little white feather to show you the way. And, if you follow the traces, you'll be able to set me free."

Then the dove flew out the door, and she followed him. At every seventh step she took, a drop of blood and a little white feather would fall and show her the way. Thus she went farther and farther into the wide world and never looked about or stopped until the

---

1. **enchanted.** Influenced by charms or incantations

words for everyday use

con • sole (kən sōl´) v., comfort. *Father <u>consoled</u> Sonia after she fell off her bike.*
splen • dor (splen´ dər) n., magnificence, pomp. *The shining castle stood in <u>splendor</u> the day of the great ceremony.*
pen • e • trate (pen´ ə trāt) v., pass through. *The sword easily <u>penetrated</u> the dragon's scaly tail.*
pro • ces • sion (prə sesh´ ən) n., group of individuals moving along in a ceremonial way. *The funeral <u>procession</u> followed the police motorcycle onto the highway.*

seven years were almost up. She was looking forward to that and thought they would soon be free. But, they were still quite far from their goal.

Once, as she was moving along, she failed to find any more feathers or drops of blood, and when she raised her head, the dove had also vanished. *I won't be able to get help from a mortal,*[2] she thought, and she climbed up to the sun and said to her, "You shine into every nook and cranny. Is there any chance that you've seen a white dove flying around?"

"No," said the sun, "I haven't, but I'll give you a little casket. Just open it when your need is greatest."

GUIDED READING

What does the sun give to the youngest daughter?

She thanked the sun and continued on her way until the moon came out to shine in the evening. "You shine the whole night through and in all the fields and meadows. Is there any chance that you've seen a white dove flying around?"

"No," said the moon, "I haven't, but I'll give you an egg. Just crack it open when your need is greatest."

GUIDED READING

What does the moon give to the young woman?

She thanked the moon and went farther until the Night Wind shifted and started to blow at her. "You blow over every tree and shake every leaf. Is there any chance that you've seen a white dove flying around?"

"No," said the Night Wind, "I haven't, but I'll ask the three other winds. Perhaps they've seen one."

The East Wind and the West Wind came and reported they had not seen a thing, but the South Wind said, "I've seen the white dove. It's flown to the Red Sea[3] and has become a lion again, for the seven years are over. The lion's now in the midst of a fight with a dragon that's really an enchanted princess."

Then the Night Wind said to her, "Here's what I would advise you to do: Go to the Red Sea, where you'll find some tall reeds[4] growing along the shore. Then count them until you come to the eleventh one, which you're to cut off and use to strike the dragon. That done, the lion will be able to conquer the dragon, and both will regain their human form. After that, look around, and you'll see the griffin[5] sitting by the Red Sea. Get on his back with your beloved, and the griffin will carry you home across the sea. Now, here's a nut for you. When you cross over the middle of the sea, let it drop. A nut tree will instantly sprout up

GUIDED READING

What does the Night Wind give to the young lady?

out of the water, and the griffin will be able to rest on it. If he can't rest there, he won't be strong enough to carry you both across the sea. So if you forget to drop the nut into the sea, he'll let you fall into the water."

She went there and found everything as the Night Wind had said. She counted the reeds by the sea, cut off the eleventh, and struck the dragon with it. Whereupon[6] the lion conquered the dragon, and both immediately regained their human form. But when the princess, who had previously been a dragon, was set free from the magic spell, she picked the prince up in her arms, got on the griffin, and carried him off with her. So the poor maiden, who had journeyed so far, stood alone and <u>forsaken</u> again, and sat down to cry.

---

2. **mortal.** Human being
3. **Red Sea.** Sea between Saudi Arabia and northeastern Africa
4. **reeds.** Tall, slender grasses growing in wet places
5. **griffin.** Mythical animal typically having the head, forepart, and wings of an eagle and the body, hind legs, and tail of a lion.
6. **Whereupon.** Closely following in sequence

words for everyday use

for • sake (fôr sāk´) *v.*, abandon. *I will <u>forsake</u> all my wealth for a chance to marry the maiden.* **forsaken,** *adj.*

Eventually, she took heart and said, "I'll keep going as far as the wind blows and so long as the cock crows until I find him." And off she went and wandered a long, long, way until she came to the castle where the two were living together. Then she heard that their wedding celebration was soon to take place. "God will still come to my aid," she remarked as she opened the little casket that the sun had given her. There she found a dress as radiant as the sun itself. She took it out, put it on, and went up to the castle. Everyone at the court and the bride herself could not believe their eyes. The bride liked the dress so much she thought it would be nice to have for her wedding and asked if she could buy it.

GUIDED READING
What does the dragon become?

GUIDED READING
What does the little casket contain?

"Not for money or property," she answered, "but for flesh and blood."

The bride asked her what she meant by that, and she responded, "Let me sleep one night in the bridegroom's room."

The bride did not want to let her, but she also wanted the dress very much. Finally, she agreed, but the bridegroom's servant was obliged to give him a sleeping potion. That night when the prince was asleep, she was led into his room, sat down on his bed, and said, "I've followed you for seven years. I went to the sun, the moon, and the four winds to find out where you were. I helped you conquer the dragon. Are you going to forget me forever?"

But the prince slept so soundly that it merely seemed to him as if the wind were whispering in the firs. When morning came, she was led out again and had to give up her golden dress.

Since her ploy had not been of much use, she was quite sad and went out to a meadow, where she sat down and wept. But as she was sitting there, she remembered the egg that the moon had given her. She cracked it open, and a hen with twelve chicks came out, all in gold. The peeping chicks scampered about and then crawled under the mother hen's wings. There was not a lovelier sight to see in the world. Shortly after that she stood up and drove them ahead of her over the meadow until they came within sight of the bride, who saw them from her window. She liked the little chicks so much that she came right down and asked if she could buy them.

GUIDED READING
What comes out of the egg?

"Not with money or possessions, but for flesh and blood. Let me sleep another night in the bridegroom's room."

The bride agreed and wanted to trick her as she had done the night before. But when the prince went to bed, he asked his servant what had caused all the murmuring and rustling during the night, and the servant told him everything: that he had been compelled to give him a sleeping potion because a poor girl had secretly slept in his room, and that he was supposed to give him another one that night.

GUIDED READING
What does the servant tell the prince?

"Dump the drink by the side of my bed," said the prince.

At night the maiden was led in again, and when she began to talk about her sad plight, he immediately recognized his dear wife by her voice, jumped up, and exclaimed, "Now I'm really free from the spell! It was all like a dream. The strange princess had cast a spell over me and made me forget you, but God has delivered me from the spell just in time."

That night they left the castle in secret, for they were afraid of the princess's father, who was a sorcerer.[7] They got on the griffin, who carried them over the Red Sea, and when they were in the middle, she let the nut

GUIDED READING

What happens when the nut is dropped in the middle of the Red Sea?

drop. Immediately a big nut tree sprouted, and the griffin was able to rest there. Then he carried them home, where they found their child, who had grown tall and handsome. From then on they lived happily until their death. ∎

---

7. **sorcerer.** Wizard; a person who uses power from evil spirits

Respond *to the* SELECTION

As a modern-day young person reading an old fairy tale, what do you find most interesting about this fairy tale?

About *the* AUTHORS

Jacob Ludwig Karl Grimm (1785–1863) and **Wilhelm Karl Grimm** (1786–1859) were born at Hanau, in Hesse-Cassel, Germany. They grew up in a family with four other children and were educated at the University of Marburg. At first studying law, they became fascinated by the medieval history and language of Germany and gradually turned their focus to in-depth research and study of the German language, its history, and its structure. During this time they uncovered stories that country people knew by heart, and they began collecting these old German folk tales from many sources. They first published their collection in two volumes, entitled *Household Tales* (1812–1815). In the early 1830s, each brother became a professor of old German literature, and they were considered gifted teachers. The brothers also steadily published an astonishing number of scholarly works. Jacob wrote on topics including German mythology and the history of the German language. His most highly acclaimed scientific work was a German grammar. Wilhelm's published works focused on medieval German literature and folklore. In 1854 they published the first volume (through the letter *F*) of the monumental standard German dictionary (other scholars completed the work in the 1900s). Then, in 1857, they published an expanded version of their collection, *Grimm's Fairy Tales*. Wilhelm died two years later, and Jacob, six years later.

Investigate, *Inquire,* and Imagine

Recall: GATHERING FACTS

1a. What does the father promise the lion he will do?

2a. What does the youngest daughter think that causes her to climb up to the sun for help?

3a. What kind of spell did the strange princess cast over the prince?

→ Interpret: FINDING MEANING

1b. What causes him to promise this?

2b. Why might she think this?

3b. How could the wife's voice break the spell?

Analyze: TAKING THINGS APART

4a. From the youngest daughter's point of view, tally the approximate number of times supernatural events and magic move the folk tale in a positive direction. Do the same for the number of times they move it in a negative direction. Which is greater?

→ Synthesize: BRINGING THINGS TOGETHER

4b. Think about the early German people who created this story and began telling it orally to others. Why would they include supernatural events and magic in the story? From where would they have gotten their ideas? What do you think was their purpose in creating such a tale?

Evaluate: MAKING JUDGMENTS

5a. Evaluate the use of the supernatural in this tale. Is it believable? Is it supposed to be believable? How does it add to the mood of the story?

→ Extend: CONNECTING IDEAS

5b. Think about the obstacles that couples face in real life. How do people overcome these obstacles?

Understanding *Literature*

PERSONIFICATION. Personification is a figure of speech in which something not human is described as if it were human. How might personification in folk tales—such as the talking sun—be viewed and understood by early listeners of the story?

FOLK TALE AND FAIRY TALE. A **folk tale** is a story passed by word of mouth from generation to generation. A **fairy tale** is a type of European folk tale containing supernatural events and often imaginary creatures such as elves, giants, fairies, and animals with human qualities. Fairy tales often use medieval settings. What well-known fairy tales can you think of that include magical creatures and supernatural events or situations?

Writer's Journal

1. Imagine you are the singing, springing lark, and write the words to a **song** you've been singing to the lion under the tree you are in.

2. Imagine you are a cook in this tale. Write a **recipe**, to be given to the bridegroom's servant, for your best sleeping potion. Be sure to include the name of the potion, the amount of each ingredient, and instructions on how to combine them.

3. Imagine you are a mortal in this tale and you happen to see the lion and dragon regain their human form and fly off on the griffin. In a **letter** to the king, write about what you saw, felt, and did.

Skill Builders

Study and Research & Collaborative Learning

STUDYING TRADITIONAL TALES. Fairy tales (and some folk tales) from different countries and cultures are often similar to one another. To find evidence that supports that statement, form small groups to research and compare fairy tales. First, using resources from the media center, a public library, or the Internet, collect fairy tales or folk tales from around the world. You may want to pick a subject on which to focus your search, such as dragons, giants, princes and princesses, or magic objects. Each group member should select a tale to read carefully. Then research to find additional information about the people in the time and place where the tale was developed. Investigate the geography of the region and the traditional beliefs and values of the people. Take notes on any information that might connect with your tale. In another class period, rejoin your group and take turns reading the tales and presenting the information in your notes. Discuss the similarities and differences of the tales.

Applied English

SCRIPT WRITING. Imagine you work as a script writer for a movie studio that is making a movie out of "The Singing, Springing Lark." Your job is to add a twist to the ending of the story line, structuring it so that you can still use the last sentence—"From then on they lived happily until their death." So far you have the wife forgetting to drop the nut in the middle of the Red Sea and the griffin having no place to rest, running out of strength, and dropping the wife and the prince in the sea about three-quarters of the way across it. Continue your rewrite using three supernatural events or magic spells.

Prereading

"The Magic Mortar"

by Yoshiko Uchida

Reader's Resource

- **CULTURAL CONNECTION.** Shinto, the ancient native religion of Japan, originally centered around the worship of *kami*, gods that were believed to reside in trees, mountains, waterfalls, and other natural objects. Shrines were constructed in peaceful, natural spots as places for people to worship the *kami* and give them offerings of food. A Shinto shrine appears in the story you are about to read. Although Shinto traditions are very different from those in the past, many shrines can be found throughout Japan.

- The Japanese New Year, or *O shogatsu*, is a very important holiday. People celebrate *O shogatsu* on the same day as our New Year's Day—January 1. On New Year's Eve, Japanese people typically visit a local shrine to make an offering of coins. On New Year's Day, they gather with their families for a special meal, which often includes fish, and *mochi*, or rice cakes. Some people dress in traditional *kimono*, or silk robes, on New Year's Day. The story you are about to read takes place on the New Year.

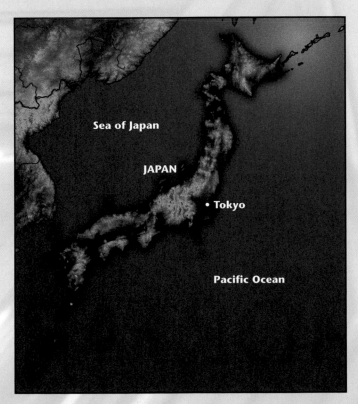

Sea of Japan

JAPAN

• Tokyo

Pacific Ocean

Reader's Journal

Write about a time when you were jealous of something a friend or sibling had.

Reader's TOOLBOX

MORAL. A **moral** is a practical or moral lesson, usually relating to the principles of right and wrong, found in a story or other work of literature. As you read, determine what lessons, or morals, appear in this selection.

POINT OF VIEW. Point of view is the vantage point from which a story is told. If a story is told from the first-person point of view, the narrator uses the pronouns *I* and *we* and is a part of or witness to the action. If a story is told from the third-person point of view, the narrator is outside the action and uses words such as *he, she, it,* and *they*. From what point of view is "The Magic Mortar" told?

Yoshiko Uchida

The Magic MORTAR

Suwa Lake, c.1800. Katsushika Hokusai.
Private Collection.

L ong, long ago, in a small village <u>nestled</u> beside the sea of Japan, there lived two brothers. The older brother was very wealthy and owned many things, but the younger brother was poor and had nothing.

One day, toward the end of December, when the people of the land were preparing to welcome the New Year, the younger brother went to his brother's home to borrow some rice.

"We have no rice for New Year's breakfast," he said. "Will you lend me just a little? I shall return it as soon as I can."

But the older brother was greedy, and he did not want to lend even a small amount of rice. "I haven't any to spare," he said, and he turned his brother away.

GUIDED READING

What worries the younger brother as he returns home from visiting his brother?

The young brother was sad and disappointed. He walked slowly down the narrow dirt road that led back to his house. What would be say to his wife, coming home empty-handed? What would they eat on New Year's Day? He looked out at the cold blue sea, beating against the shore. He looked up at the murky skies full of the promise of snow, but he found no comfort anywhere. Scuffling along silently, he felt the wind sweep down from the mountains beyond, and thought of his empty charcoal bucket. It would be cold without coals in his hibachi.[1]

As he walked along, he saw an old man with a long white beard working in the fields beside the road. He leaned against his hoe and called out, "Say there, young man! Why are you walking with your head down, looking so sad?"

---

1. **hibachi.** Brazier, or small charcoal stove, used for heat and cooking

words for everyday use

nest • le (nes′ əl) *v.,* settle snugly. *The deer* <u>nestle</u> *among the brush, out of sight from the path.* **nestled,** *adj.*

"You would be sad too," the young man answered. "I am cold and hungry and my own brother will not even lend me rice for the New Year. The world is a sad and selfish place!"

"Come, now," the old man answered. "All the world is not so bad."

Then he handed the young man a small cake. "Here," he said. "Take this wheat cake and go to the shrine[2] in the woods beyond. Behind the shrine you will see a big hole, and nearby will be many dwarfs. They will ask you for your wheat cake, but don't give it to them on any account, unless they agree to give you their stone mortar[3] in exchange."

> **GUIDED READING**
> What instructions does the farmer give the young man?

The young man thanked the farmer, and carrying the wheat cake carefully, he set off for the shrine in the woods. Just as the old man had said, behind the shrine was a big hole, and nearby were many dwarfs climbing in and out, tumbling and stumbling over each other. They were trying to lift a big log into their hole, and shouted and pushed as they got in each other's way. The young man bent down and picked up the log.

"Here, let me help you," he said, and lifting the log with one hand, he pushed it into the hole for them.

All at once, he heard a cry like the whine of a tiny mosquito. "Help! Murderer!" He looked down in alarm, and saw a tiny dwarf caught under his wooden clogs. He quickly picked him up, and as he did so, the tiny dwarf saw the wheat cake.

"What delicious thing is this?" he asked, sniffing hungrily. "It smells like all the good things I've ever eaten all rolled into one!"

"Why, this is just a wheat cake given to me by an old farmer," answered the young man.

"Please," begged the tiny dwarf. "Let me have that wheat cake. It will make a lovely dinner."

But the young man remembered what the farmer had said. "No, no," he said, shaking his head. "I can never let you have this wheat cake. It is very precious to me." Soon, the other dwarfs clustered around. "Give us your wheat cake," they begged. But still the young man shook his head.

Then the dwarfs brought out big bags of gold. "Here," they said. "We will give you all this gold if you will just let us have that wheat cake."

But again, the young man shook his head. "No, no," he said, "I'll not trade this wheat cake for all the gold in the world."

"Not for all the gold in the world? Why, this must be a very special and most wonderful wheat cake," the dwarfs said. "What do you want for it, if you will not take gold?"

> **GUIDED READING**
> What do the dwarfs believe about the wheat cake?

"Well, let me see," the young man said, looking around. Then, he saw the stone mortar the old man had told him about. "I will give you my wheat cake if you will give me that stone mortar," he said.

The dwarfs put their heads together and talked noisily. At last, they agreed. "All right," they said. "Although it is a very special mortar, we will let you have it in exchange for your wheat cake."

Then the tiny dwarf spoke up. "This is a magic mortar, you know. It will give you anything you ask for if you turn it to the right. Then, when you've had enough, turn it to the left and it will stop."

> **GUIDED READING**
> What instructions does the tiny dwarf give the young man?

The young man thanked the dwarfs for the mortar and gave them his wheat cake. Before he could even turn around, they had gathered about the cake and were making a great

---

2. **shrine.** Place where one prays to a saint or god
3. **mortar.** Sturdy bowl in which food or other material is pounded or ground up with a club-shaped tool called a pestle

<u>commotion</u> that sounded like a thousand mosquitoes buzzing in the air. The young man slipped away quietly and set off for home. This time, he walked with his head up, whistling a gay tune. He looked up at the tall cedar trees that reached out to the sun, and his own glad heart soared into the sky with them.

When he got home, his wife was waiting anxiously for him in the cold house. "What were you doing for so long?" she asked. "I have been waiting and waiting for you to bring home the rice!"

"But I have brought home something even better than a bag of rice," the young man said, and he told his wife about the old man with the white beard, and about the mortar the dwarfs had given him.

"Hurry then," the wife said. "Let's see if the mortar really works."

So they spread a clean mat on the tatami[4] and placed the mortar in the center.

"Now," the young man said. "What would you like first?"

The wife thought for only a moment. "Oh, I would like some rice," she said, "so I can make rice cakes for New Year's Day."

The young man slowly turned the mortar to the right. "Mortar, mortar, make some rice!" he called out, and slowly, slowly, the mortar began to fill with clean white rice. It was soon so full, it overflowed, and rice spilled out everywhere. The young man let the mortar make enough rice to last the whole new year, and then, turning it to the left, he told it to stop.

Next, he decided he would like some wine.

"Mortar, mortar, make some wine!" he

commanded, and as he turned it, the mortar filled with clear white wine.

One after the other, he produced all kinds of wonderful things from the mortar, until he had enough to have a great feast on New Year's Day.

"What an amazing thing the dwarfs gave me," the young man thought happily. And the next morning, he decided to ask for a bigger house, for he now had so many wonderful things his little house could not hold them all.

"Mortar, mortar, please give us a bigger house," he said.

Suddenly, there was a blinding flash. The young man and his wife blinked their eyes, and when they opened them again, they found themselves sitting inside a beautiful, big mansion. Outside, there was a lovely garden with a wooden bridge that curved over a glistening pond. There was even a stable with many fine horses that stood swishing their tails, waiting for someone to ride on them. The young man and his wife looked wonderingly at their new home, and decided they would invite all their friends to visit this beautiful estate.

"Make rice! Make wine! Make fish and chicken and lotus root!"[5] they said to the mortar, and then they invited their friends and neighbors to a big celebration. Everyone came dressed in their best kimonos,[6] and looked with curious eyes at the house and all the good things to eat.

GUIDED READING

What does the mortar do for the young man and his wife?

---

4. **tatami.** Mat woven from rushes, laid on the floor in traditional Japanese homes

5. **lotus root.** Root of a species of water lily, which is good to eat

6. **kimonos.** Japanese robes, the traditional clothing of Japan. Today they are most often made of silk and worn only on special occasions.

words for everyday use

com • mo • tion (kə mō′ shən) *n.*, disturbance, noisy confusion. *There was much <u>commotion</u> in the classroom when the students learned that school was canceled for the rest of the day.*

"How strange it is," they said to one another. "How can it be, when only yesterday they didn't even have rice for the New Year?" But even as they wondered, they were glad for the young brother, for he had always been a good and kind man.

GUIDED READING

What do the young man's friends think about his new wealth?

Because he was also forgiving and generous, he had even invited his older brother who had been so unkind to him the day before.

The older brother came and looked about in amazement. "This is very strange indeed," he said to himself, and over and over he asked the younger brother how he had suddenly become so wealthy.

"Tell me how it happened," he asked.

But the younger brother merely smiled and said, "I was very lucky, that's all."

When the guests were about to leave, the young brother thought he would like to give each of them some sweet cakes to take home. He opened the cupboard, took out the magic mortar and told it to make some cakes. Just as he was doing this, the older brother passed by and saw what he was doing.

"So!" he said to himself. "That is how my poor brother suddenly got so much money and food!" And he went off into the garden to think of a way in which he could get his brother's mortar.

When all the guests had gone, the older brother asked if he might spend the night there. "The night is cold, and I do not like to walk home in the darkness. Let me stay with you tonight," he asked.

And so the younger brother spread an extra quilt on the floor, and the older brother lay down, pretending to go to sleep. He waited until the others were sound asleep, and then he tiptoed to the cupboard, stole the magic mortar, and slipped out into the dark night. He ran with the mortar under his arm until he came to the edge of the sea. There he found a little boat on the beach.

"Just what I need to help me get away," he said, and he jumped into the boat. Then he decided he would row out to one of the little islands in the sea. There he would use the mortar and become the wealthiest man of the land.

GUIDED READING

What does the older brother plan to do with the mortar?

"Ah, I shall live a good life," he thought happily.

But as he rowed on, his arms began to ache and grow weary. He decided to stop and have something to eat, but all he could find in the bundle he brought along were a few unsalted rice cakes. He looked about, wishing he had brought along some salt, when suddenly he remembered the stone mortar he had stolen.

"Now is the time to test it," he thought, and turning it to the right, as he had seen his brother do, he said, "Mortar, mortar, make some salt!"

Slowly, the mortar began to fill with salt, and soon it overflowed into the boat.

"That's enough! Stop!" cried the older brother, but he didn't know how to make the mortar stop. Soon, the whole boat was filled with salt, and as it grew heavier it sank deeper and deeper into the water.

GUIDED READING

What doesn't the older brother know about the mortar?

"Help! The boat will sink!" the older brother shouted, but there was no one out in the middle of the sea to hear him. The waves lapped higher and higher and soon swallowed the little boat, taking the mortar and the brother down to the very bottom of the sea.

On top of the water, only a mass of white bubbles gleamed in the moonlight, but down at the bottom of the sea, the mortar continued to make salt. Because no one ever went down to turn it to the left and tell it to stop, salt still flows from the mortar. And that is why, they say, the sea is salty even today.

GUIDED READING

What effect does the mortar finally have?

Do you think the older brother deserves what happens to him at the end of the story? Explain.

About *the* AUTHOR

Yoshiko Uchida (1921–1992) grew up in Berkeley, California, as a *Nisei*, or second-generation Japanese American. She often wrote about the experience of Asian Americans, sometimes exposing the prejudice Americans have showed Asians. Prejudice and misunderstanding between cultures bothered Uchida. She wrote, "With so much in all of us that is alike, it is a pity people the world over have continued to find so much in each other that is different and strange."

Uchida became interested in retelling folk tales because she believed that "the universal qualities of the folk tale can bring the children of the world closer together," and that "a further sharing of common ideas and hopes will eventually bring them closer together as adults." She published several collections of Japanese folk tales. This story is from a collection entitled *The Magic Listening Cap.*

Investigate, Inquire, and Imagine

Recall: GATHERING FACTS

1a. What does the young man ask of his older brother? How does his brother respond?

2a. What unusual encounter does the younger brother have on his way home? What does he bring home to his wife, and what is special about this object? What do they do the next day?

3a. What plans does the older brother make when he discovers his brother's secret? Do his plans succeed or fail? Explain. What natural phenomenon does this myth explain?

→ **Interpret:** FINDING MEANING

1b. What does the older brother's response reveal about his character?

2b. Why were the dwarfs willing to trade their prize possession? How does the possession change the lives of the young brother and his wife?

3b. Why does the older brother's plan have the results it has?

Analyze: TAKING THINGS APART

4a. Compare the way the younger brother treats his older brother on New Year's Day with the way his older brother treated him the day before. What do their different actions reveal about the two brothers? How does the older brother's response to his brother's new situation differ from the response of the young man's friends?

→ **Synthesize:** BRINGING THINGS TOGETHER

4b. What qualities do you think the creator of this tale valued? What qualities did he or she dislike?

Evaluate: MAKING JUDGMENTS

5a. Do you think the punishment of the older brother fits the crime in this instance? Why, or why not? If you could rewrite this folk tale, how would you have the older brother punished?

→ **Extend:** CONNECTING IDEAS

5b. How might this story be different if the older brother had acted differently at the beginning? at the end? Explain. For example, how do you think the story would have continued if the older brother had asked to borrow the mortar?

Understanding *Literature*

MORAL. A **moral** is a practical or moral lesson, usually relating to the principles of right and wrong, found in a story or other work of literature. What lessons or morals do you think this story teaches? Why are these lessons important? What do these morals reveal about Japanese culture and Japanese values?

POINT OF VIEW. Point of view is the vantage point from which a story is told. How would this story be different if it were told from a different point of view?

Writer's Journal

1. Write a brief **character sketch** of each brother, imagining you need to provide this sketch to a company planning an animated movie about "The Magic Mortar."

2. Imagine you are the director of a play adapted from "The Magic Mortar." Write **stage directions** that describe the setting of this story.

3. In the selection you have just read, instructions play an important role. Imagine that you are the old farmer in the story and are going to give the younger brother written instructions for how to get the magic mortar from the dwarfs. Write **step-by-step instructions** for him.

Skill Builders

Study and Research

EXAMINING THE OCEANS. "The Magic Mortar" gives an explanation for why the sea is salty. What explanation do you think modern scientists would give? Use the Internet or library to find out. Why are oceans and seas salty? What percentage of salt is in most bodies of salt water? Name five examples of aquatic life that can only live in salt water. As an alternative, you may be interested in researching the Dead Sea, which is located between Israel and Jordan in the Middle East. If you were to swim there, you could not sink because the water is so thick with salt. What makes the Dead Sea so salty? Why is it called "Dead"?

Language, Grammar, and Style

COMMON SPELLING ERRORS. Some words have irregular plural forms. For example, in the selection you just read, the word *dwarf* was written in the plural form *dwarfs*. However, the plural can also be spelled *dwarves*. Other words that have this irregular plural are *knife* and *life*. *Knife* and *life* must be written *knives* and *lives* in their plural form. Read the Language Arts Survey 3.91 and 3.92, "Using Spelling Rules." Then find the misspelled words in the following sentences. Spell them correctly on your own paper.

1. The younger brother is hopeing that his usualy selfish brother will lend him some rice.
2. The older brother has many richs, but he is the greedyest man in Japan.
3. As the younger brother gos home he looks up at the skys and starts cryeing.
4. His luck changs when he finds some dwarfs stumbleing around and is able to decieve them and get the magic mortar.
5. The old farmer tells him how to succede in takeing the mortar.
6. The young man and his wife recieve many valueable gifts from the mortar.
7. They need a biger house and invite all their friendes for a big feast.
8. The older brother spys on the younger brother.
9. He is a theif and procedes to steal the mortar.
10. However, the older brother eventualy meets his fatful end, dieing at the bottom of the sea.

Reader's *Journal*

Describe a time in your life when you experienced or witnessed something unfair. How did you feel? What did you do?

Reader's *Resource*

• "The Cow of No Color" is a type of folk story called a **justice tale**, in which the villain is taught a lesson. In justice tales, the reader is asked to think about what is truly fair in a given situation.

• **HISTORY CONNECTION.** Africa has a rich and varied oral literature, which has grown since the beginnings of African societies and continues to flourish today. Many African folktales draw on the value systems of African cultures—a strong work ethic, the powers of beauty, perseverance, peace, harmony, and humor. Storytelling in Africa was a way not only of entertaining but also of passing on history, values, and family traditions.

Prereading

"THE COW OF NO COLOR"
by Nina Jaffe and Steve Zeitlin

Reader's T O O L B O X

AIM. A writer's (or speaker's) **aim** is his or her purpose, or goal. People may write or speak with the following aims:

• to inform (expository/informative writing);
• to tell a story, either true or invented, about an event or sequence of events (narrative writing);
• to reflect (personal/expressive writing);
• to share a perspective by using an artistic medium—such as fiction or poetry—to entertain, enrich, or enlighten (imaginative writing);
• to persuade readers or listeners to respond in some way, such as to agree with a position, change a view on an issue, reach an agreement, or perform an action (persuasive/argumentative writing).

As you read "The Cow of No Color," look for evidence that helps you determine the aim or aims of the tale.

SUSPENSE. Suspense is a feeling of anxiousness or curiosity. Writers create suspense by raising questions in the reader's mind and by using details that create strong emotions. As you read "The Cow of No Color," notice how suspense is created. When do you feel anxious or curious? What questions are raised in your mind? What details create strong emotions?

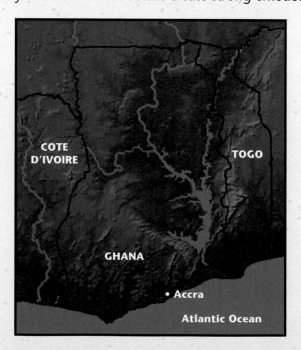

Untitled, 1992. Cyprien Tokoudagba. Private Collection.

THE COW OF NO COLOR

Nina Jaffe and Steve Zeitlin

Once among the Ewe people[1] of Ghana[2] there lived a wise woman named Nunyala. For miles around, people would come to her asking for advice, and she always found a way to help them. Her fame spread till it reached the ears of the chief, who became very jealous. He called her to the palace, and when she appeared, he said to her, through his spokesman:

GUIDED READING

How does the chief feel when he hears about the wise woman Nunyala?

"I hear you are Nunyala, the wise woman."

"That may be, and that may not be," she replied. "It is what some people say."

"If you are so wise," said the chief, "surely I can ask you to do one simple thing for me."

"If it is simple or not," she replied, "I will do my best."

"All you have to do to prove how wise you are," the chief said to her, "is to bring me a cow."

Nunyala thought to herself: "A cow. That is not difficult. My village is full of cows."

And she was just about to leave when the chief added, "Now listen well. Yes, I wish you to bring me a cow. But this cow cannot be black, and it cannot be white. It cannot be brown, or yellow, or spotted, or striped. In fact, this cow cannot be of any color at all!

---

1. **Ewe people.** People of southeastern Ghana who make up 13 percent of its total population
2. **Ghana.** West African country (formerly known as Gold Coast) with its southern border along the Gulf of Guinea

Bring me a cow of no color in three days' time—or you will be executed[3] without delay!"

Nunyala returned to her village and sat in her hut. She thought to herself: Should I be executed because some people say I am wise as the chief? Should I lose my own life for his jealousy? Is this a wise leader's approach to justice? She had to answer the chief's impossible request, but how?

Nunyala sat and thought for three days and three nights, and at the end of that time, she sent a child from her village to the chief with a message. The chief sat on his stool,[4] waiting to hear

what the child had to say. These were his words: "O Chief, Nunyala, the wise woman of our village, has sent me to repeat these words to you. This is her message. She has said, 'I have your cow of no color. It is in my house. You can come and take it.

" 'But don't come in the morning. Don't come in the evening. Don't come at dawn. Don't come at twilight. Don't come at midnight. Don't come any time. You can have your cow of no color—at no time at all!' "

The boy turned and left the palace, while the chief sat speechless on his stool, to <u>ponder</u> the words of Nunyala, wise woman of the Ewe. ■

---

3. **executed.** Put to death
4. **stool.** Seat used in southern Ghana as a symbol of a chief's authority and power

Respond *to the* SELECTION

How would you have responded to the chief? Would you have tried to meet his challenge?

About *the* AUTHORS

Nina Jaffe teaches at the Bank Street College of Education. She has authored many books for young readers, including *A Voice for the People: The Life and Work of Harold Courlander* and *Patakin: World Tales of Drums and Drummers.* Folklorist **Steve Zeitlin** is director of City Lore, which documents and presents the living cultural heritage of New York City. In addition to co-authoring *The Cow of No Color: Riddle Stories and Justice Tales from Around the World,* from which this selection comes, Jaffe and Zeitlan collaborated on the highly acclaimed *While Standing on One Foot,* which won the Anne Izard Storyteller's Choice Award and Belgium's prestigious Prix Versele.

words for everyday use

pon • der (pän' dər) *v.,* think about quietly and deeply. *I <u>pondered</u> all weekend whether to join the chess club or the soccer team.*

Investigate, Inquire, and Imagine

Recall: GATHERING FACTS

1a. When Nunyala appears before the chief, by what means does he speak to her?

2a. What is the chief's full description of the cow Nunyala is to bring?

3a. How does Nunyala deliver her response to the chief?

→ **Interpret:** FINDING MEANING

1b. Why might the chief have done this?

2b. Why might the chief have made such a request?

3b. Why might she have done this?

Analyze: TAKING THINGS APART

4a. Identify places in the story where Nunyala shows her wisdom.

→ **Synthesize:** BRINGING THINGS TOGETHER

4b. What approach to justice do you think a wise leader would take?

Evaluate: MAKING JUDGMENTS

5a. Evaluate how effectively this story communicates ideas about fairness and justice. In your opinion, what about the story makes it effective or not effective?

→ **Extend:** CONNECTING IDEAS

5b. What ideas about fairness and justice did you learn from this story? Describe how you could apply these ideas when you face unfair situations in the future.

Understanding Literature

AIM. A writer's **aim** is his or her purpose, or goal. People may write or speak with the following aims:

- to inform (expository/informative writing);
- to tell a story, either true or invented, about an event or sequence of events (narrative writing);
- to reflect (personal/expressive writing);
- to share a perspective by using an artistic medium—such as fiction or poetry—to entertain, enrich, or enlighten (imaginative writing);
- to persuade readers or listeners to respond in some way, such as to agree with a position, change a view on an issue, reach an agreement, or perform an action (persuasive/argumentative writing).

What is the main aim of "The Cow of No Color"? What do you as a reader appreciate most about the story?

SUSPENSE. Suspense is a feeling of anxiousness or curiosity. Writers create suspense by raising questions in the reader's mind and by using details that create strong emotions. How did the suspense in this story add to or relate to its aim(s)? How might the suspense itself encourage creative thinking in a reader or listener?

Writer's Journal

1. Imagine you are one of the people in Nunyala's village. Write a **thank-you note** to her for some wise advice she gave you.
2. Imagine you are Nunyala and write a **paragraph** about your beliefs about justice.
3. Write the **description** of a particularly involved or difficult task that you have accomplished.

Skill Builders

Media Literacy & Study and Research

ANALYZING MEDIA. Working in small groups, research various types of media, looking for messages about justice or fairness. Explore books, magazines, newspapers, TV shows, movies, speeches, songs, bumper stickers, slogans, and cartoons. Pool your findings and classify them by filling in a chart like the one below.

Type of Media	Its Message about Justice/Fairness	The Aim or Purpose and Type of Writing

When the chart is complete, think about what conclusions you can draw from the data. From the examples collected, do any of the media stand out as being more effective or more able in handling issues of fairness and justice? How are the messages from the media the same as or different from the themes and ideas in "The Cow of No Color"?

Speaking and Listening & Collaborative Learning

PUTTING ON A PLAY. Enact "The Cow of No Color" by forming groups of five, with each member taking on the role of one of the five characters: narrator, Nunyala, chief, chief's spokesman, and message boy. As a group, read through the story and identify what each character will say and do. Practice your parts individually and then practice together, acting out the story as a group. Remember to stay in character, letting variations in your voice and body language communicate as well as the words you say. When ready, team up with another group of five. One group will present their enactment while the other group listens, then the groups will switch places. When listening, imagine you are a young child hearing the story for the first time. Pay attention to each actor's part and listen closely for details that help bring out the meaning of the story. After both enactments are complete, take turns discussing how it felt to be a part of the drama and how it felt to listen to the drama. When did you feel the effect and meaning of the story more—when acting or when listening?

Prereading

"Don't Step on a Crack"

by Lila Perl

Reader's Resource

- Superstitions have long been part of the oral tradition. People have historically gone to great lengths to do things that would ensure good luck or to avoid things that could bring bad luck. Many superstitions have been passed along through so many generations that their origins are long forgotten. A number of superstitions that are still passed on today date from the Middle Ages (about 500 to 1350).

- Omens are signs of things to come. In a superstition, a particular action may be an omen. For example, finding a four-leaf clover is a good omen—it supposedly means favorable luck in the future. Hearing an owl hoot when you are sick supposedly is a bad omen, signaling that the listener will die. Many omens appear to people in their dreams.

Graphic Organizer

Keep track of the superstitions mentioned in this selection and the historical explanations behind them.

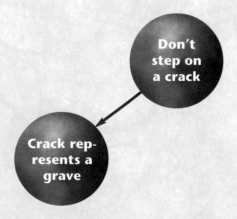

Don't step on a crack

Crack represents a grave

Reader's Journal

What signs mean good luck to you? Which mean bad luck?

Reader's TOOLBOX

ORAL TRADITION. An **oral tradition** is works, ideas, or customs of a culture, passed by word of mouth from generation to generation. Works found in the oral traditions of peoples around the world include *folk tales, fables, fairy tales, tall tales, nursery rhymes, proverbs, legends, myths, parables, riddles, charms, spells,* and *ballads.* What other material could be considered oral tradition?

Don't Step on a Crack

Lila Perl

Step on a crack, break your mother's back. Step in a hole, break your mother's sugar bowl.

Have you ever walked along the sidewalk being very careful not to step on the cracks in the paving? Perhaps the old rhyme above came to mind. Experts who study folklore and folk sayings think that the "crack" represents an opening in the earth that leads to a grave. The "hole" is the grave itself.

Nobody really knows why stepping on a crack should bring bad luck to one's mother rather than some other person. Even worse, the broken back is often interpreted to mean death. And the broken sugar bowl is definitely a bad omen.

From quite early times, it was the custom of some peoples to bury their dead with articles of crockery. But first they would "kill" the "spirit" that lived in the bowl or plate. They did so either by driving an opening through its center or smashing the entire piece to bits. This ancient practice may well be the reason for the connection between a "hole," or grave, and a broken sugar bowl.

> **GUIDED READING**
> What burial custom was common in early times?

Most of us, of course, don't believe in the superstitious rhyme about avoiding cracks and holes. If it were true, we would all become motherless orphans at a very tender age. Similarly, we say that if we step on an ant, it will rain (possibly as a punishment for having killed an innocent creature). But if every ant or beetle crushed underfoot caused even a drizzle, the Earth would have been flooded eons ago.

> **GUIDED READING**
> What superstition involves ants?

One of the real hazards of trying to avoid cracks, holes, and crawling insects when we venture forth is that we may stumble.

Stumbling or tripping is supposed to be a dangerous sign. Stumbling as we leave the house is said to be caused by evil spirits who live on our doorstep. Some people think it is a warning not to go any further. We can try, though, to change our luck by doing and saying the following:

I turn myself three times about,
And thus I put bad luck to rout.

That *should* take care of the demons lurking in our doorways. But not always. One reason given for the old custom of the groom carrying his bride across the threshold of their new home is to keep her from tripping. Such an accident would invite bad luck at the very start of their life together. No one, though, ever seems to have given a thought as to what might happen if the heavily burdened groom were to trip!

> **GUIDED READING**
> What is one reason for the custom of grooms carrying brides over the threshold?

Sometimes another reason is offered for the bride's being carried over the threshold. It goes way back to the days of "bride capture," when a wife-to-be was stolen from an enemy and carried into the cave or hut of her captor. She was his property from then on.

When it comes to stumbling, theater people are probably the most superstitious of all. Some actors believe that to trip as one walks onto the stage is lucky because it gets the evil happening out of the way. Others say it is a bad sign that will be followed by the actor's missing a cue or forgetting a line.

But stage people never disagree about the danger of wishing one another "good luck" just before they face an audience. They feel these words are a sure invitation for mischievous forces to do their worst. So instead, they say just the opposite: "Break a leg." In the German theater, especially at the opera, performers go a step further. As they are about to set foot on the stage, they tell one another, *"Hals und Beinbruch,"* or 'Break your neck *and* legs!"

GUIDED READING
What do stage people say instead of "good luck"?

In recent times there has been a new theory about stumbling. Human-behavior specialists say it is caused by something in ourselves that does not *want* to go forward. So, if you stumble out of the house some morning on your way to school or work, don't blame the wicked sprites on your doorstep. Your mind may be simply telling your body that it wishes it would go back to bed.

Once you *are* out and about, you may encounter even more hazards—for instance, a tall ladder leaning against the side of a building. Few of us will boldly walk under a ladder, for we've always heard that this is bad luck. But why? There is, naturally, the danger that a can of paint, a heavy tool, or some other object may fall on our heads. But there's a less obvious reason for this superstition.

GUIDED READING
What practical reasons exist for not walking under a ladder?

In and of themselves, ladders are considered lucky symbols. The ancient Egyptians often placed small ladders in the tombs of their loved ones to help the souls of the dead "climb" heavenward in the afterlife. But a leaning ladder, or even an open stepladder, that forms a triangle with the ground is another matter. The three sides are said to represent the basic family unit, the very means by which life goes on. In the Christian faith, Joseph, Mary, and Jesus are called the "holy family." The much older religion of ancient Egypt had several holy families composed of father, mother, and child. Probably the best known was that of the god Osiris, the goddess Isis, and their son Horus.

GUIDED READING
What do the three lines created by an open ladder and the ground represent?

So, walking under a ladder is said to bring bad luck because passing through the triangle violates the unity of the family. However, if you should unthinkingly find yourself under a ladder, you can still try to save yourself by crossing your fingers or by spitting three times between the rungs. On the other hand, if you decide to go *around* the ladder, be careful when walking out into the traffic. You don't want to invite some other calamity!

On a really "unlucky" day, you might not only stumble over your doorstep and walk under a ladder, but a black cat might also cross your path.

Cats were not always thought to be unlucky. The ancient Egyptians worshiped the cat and even had a goddess named Bast who was the patroness of cats. It's quite easy to understand the Egyptian fondness for cats. They were not only house pets, they also hunted and killed the rats and mice that would otherwise have overrun the storehouses in which the Egyptians kept their grain. Cats were often honored in ancient Egypt by being mummified after they died. Thus their bodies were preserved just like those of Egypt's kings and other important people.

GUIDED READING
How did ancient Egyptians feel about cats?

Step on a crack, break your mother's back.

In parts of Europe, however, by the time of the Middle Ages, people began to believe that witches could change themselves into cats. So the black cat became a spooky symbol of Halloween. And all black cats came to be feared as witches in disguise!

There are many myths about cats that have probably led to our thinking of them as supernatural creatures. It isn't true, though, that cats can see in complete darkness or that they have nine lives. They do, however, have good coordination and a flexible spine, so they are less likely to hurt themselves in falls and other accidents.

There doesn't seem to be much we can do to counteract the bad omen of seeing a black cat. But it may be a comfort to know that in England black cats are considered lucky, and *white* cats are feared. Some people think this is because of the mummified cats that British archeologists found in ancient Egyptian tombs and brought back to England. All of the "lucky" Egyptian cats were black, as a result of the drying-out process used to make mummies. This left the British with only white cats to worry about!

GUIDED READING

How are cat superstitions different in England than in other areas?

Certain objects that we are likely to handle almost every day, both inside and outside our houses, are also said to have the power to bring us bad luck. Who hasn't heard that breaking a mirror can lead to seven years of misfortune?

Although breakable glass mirrors probably weren't widely known until around the 1300s, people have long feared having their image

GUIDED READING

When did mirrors become widely known?

shattered. The very first "mirrors" were quiet pools of water. People looked into them, saw their reflection, and believed they were seeing their soul, or life force. If an enemy came by and threw a stone in the pool, the reflection broke up. This meant an evil fate was in store. If the soul was taken away completely, the person would die.

With the increased use of glass mirrors, many new superstitions came along. Some people believed that all mirrors had to be covered in a house where a death had taken place. Otherwise, the soul of the dead person might be caught in the mirror and would not find its way to heaven. A different reason for covering the mirrors was to prevent the mourners from seeing their haggard and tear-stained faces. If they did, they might be tempted to stop weeping for their dead before the mourning period was up.

Some say that a baby should never be held up to a mirror during the first year of its life. Infancy is a time of great danger and the child's soul might be captured by the angel of death or by an evil spirit. The worst fear of all among superstitious people is that they will look into a mirror and not see any reflection at all. This is a sure sign that death is very near.

GUIDED READING

What danger is associated with infants and mirrors?

What about the "seven years of bad luck" said to follow the breaking of a mirror? This superstition probably has something to do with the so-called magical properties of the number seven. One long-held belief is that the cells of the body renew themselves completely every seven years. So, at the end of that period, we are not the same person we were at the beginning. Therefore, we cannot

Step in a hole, break your mother's sugar bowl.

be affected any longer by the "curse" of the broken mirror.

Unfortunately, there is no truth to the seven-year theory about our body cells. There may be another explanation, though, for the penalty we are said to pay for breaking a mirror. When glass mirrors first appeared they were so costly that it might well have taken seven years to save enough money to replace a broken one!

Respond *to the* SELECTION

Have you ever done something because it could bring you good luck? Have you ever avoided doing something that could bring bad luck?

About *the* AUTHOR

Lila Perl was born in Brooklyn, New York. She read a lot, but it never occurred to her that she would eventually become a writer. She began to write for young people when her own kids were in the fourth or fifth grades. She has written both fiction and nonfiction. Her early books included those in the Fat Glenda series, *Pieface and Daphne; Don't Ask Miranda,* and many others. Her nonfiction titles include *Slumps, Grunts, and Snickerdoodles: What Colonial America Ate and Why; Mummies, Tombs, and Treasure: Secrets of Ancient Egypt;* and *Don't Sing Before Breakfast, Don't Sleep in the Moonlight: Everyday Superstitions and How They Began,* the book from which this selection was taken. Her most recent publication is *Four Perfect Pebbles: A Holocaust Story,* which she co-authored with Marion Blumenthal Lazan.

Investigate, *Inquire,* and Imagine

Recall: GATHERING FACTS

1a. What superstition is associated with stepping on a crack? stepping in a hole? What do experts think these superstitions stem from?

2a. What superstition is common among theater people? What is the reasoning behind the phrase they say to one another?

3a. According to the superstition, why is it unlucky to walk under a ladder?

4a. What were the first "mirrors"?

→ **Interpret:** FINDING MEANING

1b. Why might people have passed on this superstition?

2b. Why would they choose this particular phrase?

3b. What kind of bad luck might this bring? Why can you supposedly save yourself by crossing your fingers or spitting three times?

4b. What reasons could exist for people long having feared having their image shattered?

Analyze: TAKING THINGS APART

5a. How many of the superstitions mentioned deal with bad luck? How many deal with good luck?

→ **Synthesize:** BRINGING THINGS TOGETHER

5b. Why do you think people pass along superstitions or act in certain ways because of superstitions?

Evaluate: MAKING JUDGMENTS

6a. Are there good reasons to believe in superstitions? Why, or why not?

→ **Extend:** CONNECTING IDEAS

6b. Have you ever acted a certain way to avoid bad luck or to bring on good luck? Explain your answer.

Understanding *Literature*

ORAL TRADITION. An **oral tradition** is works, ideas, or customs of a culture, passed by word of mouth from generation to generation. Works found in the oral traditions of peoples around the world include folk tales, fables, fairy tales, tall tales, nursery rhymes, proverbs, legends, myths, parables, riddles, charms, spells, and ballads. Why do you think people pass down superstitions? In what ways do superstitions—as well as other forms of the oral tradition—continue to be part of our culture today?

Writer's Journal

1. Write down a **superstition** that you know about. Then write your reaction to it.

2. Write a **list of questions** you would like to find answers to regarding early cultures that created superstitions.

3. An epitaph is the writing on a grave marker or another brief statement honoring the dead. Write an **epitaph** for a mummified Egyptian cat, dug up by British archeologists and about to be reburied.

Skill Builders

Collaborative Learning & Speaking and Listening

CREATING AND ACTING OUT A PLAY.

In small groups, choose one of the superstitions from the selection to use as a starting point. Together, brainstorm and come up with a basic plot about a person who has an interesting experience with the superstition. After you have created the basic plot, write the story in drama form, using stage directions and dialogue. As you write, add in details about the character(s), scenery, and action. After you finish writing your play, decide who will act in the play, who will design the scenery and costumes, and who will be in charge of props, lighting, and sound. When everything is assembled, practice your play until you feel confident performing it in front of an audience. Then, hold a performance for the rest of your class.

Applied English

CREATING A CHILDREN'S COMIC BOOK. Make sketches showing some of the superstitions explained in this selection. If you wish, research the subject to come up with additional ideas. After you have compiled a good group of sketches, refine your ideas into finished drawings. Carefully write captions for the drawings. Photocopy your pages and compile in sets. Bind the sets of pages into books with a stapler, or sew or glue them together. Distribute your comic books to children's libraries in your area.

for your READING LIST

The Cow of No Color: Riddle Stories and Justice Tales from Around the World by Nina Jaffe and Steve Zeitlin is a multicultural collection of folk tales that ask the basic question: What is fair? The book tackles such issues as poetic justice, deciding guilt or innocence, balancing justice and mercy, and settling disputes. You will read a story from Ireland about a young man who teaches his father that what goes around comes around. In a story from Laos you will read about a young woman who understands that justice must include mercy. You will also read a tale about two college students who think they can outwit their professor. As each story draws to its conclusion, you are asked to figure out how justice will be served. As you read tales from ancient to modern times, you must closely examine justice from many different angles and use your wits to outsmart evil sultans, corrupt government officials, and clever thieves.

Nina Jaffe & Steve Zeitlin
THE COW OF NO COLOR

Riddle Stories and Justice Tales from Around the World

Pictures by Whitney Sherman

PERFORMING JUSTICE PLAYS

Form small groups with other students and select one of the stories to read and then act out for the rest of the class. One member of your group should act as the narrator, while the others should choose a character from the story to play. You may choose to have the narrator read the story while the actors perform a pantomime or you may wish to rewrite the story to perform as a play. Whatever method you choose, the narrator should stop the performance once the problem is presented and ask the class to come up with solutions themselves. After this discussion, conclude your performance with the solution from the original tale. After your performance, you may wish to discuss whether everyone in the class agrees that justice was truly served.

Other books you may want to read:
Parzival: The Quest of the Grail Knight by Katherine Paterson
Gray Heroes: Elder Tales from Around the World by Jane Yolen
Fearless Girls, Wise Women, and Beloved Sisters: Heroines in Folktales from Around the World by Kathleen Ragan and Jane Yolen

Guided Writing

> "Words are things;
> and a small drop of ink,
>
> Falling like dew upon a
> thought, produces
>
> That which makes
> thousands, perhaps
> millions, think."
>
> —Lord Byron

CREATING A FABLE

Did you ever have an adult say to you, "Don't cry wolf"? If you were young, you might have wondered what that meant. But as you grew older, you probably heard the story behind the saying, and its meaning became clear. The wolf warning comes from a fable, a short story about a boy who gets bored while tending sheep and decides to play a trick on the village.

He cries out, "Wolf, wolf," and the people from the village run to protect the sheep. They search the hills and find no wolf. The boy thinks this is fun, so a few days later, he cries "wolf" again. And the villagers run up again to the flock of sheep, looking for the wolf.

The people tire of the boy's game and grumble about him. Meanwhile a real wolf comes to kill and eat the sheep and the boy, in a panic, runs down the hill to the village for help. But no one will listen by now—no one believes him—and the sheep are lost. The story has a moral or a lesson at the end: No one believes a liar, even when he tells the truth.

Fables are an ancient form intended to teach a lesson. Famous fables include those of Æsop and La Fontaine. These stories are still popular today and hold a special power to show us human nature and to guide us with humor and wisdom.

Your assignment in this lesson is to write an original fable.

Professional Model

"The Fox and the Goat" from Æsop's Fables

A Fox one day fell into a deep well and could find no means of escape. A Goat, overcome with thirst, came to the same well, and seeing the Fox, inquired if the water was good. Concealing his sad plight under a merry guise, the Fox indulged in a lavish praise of the water, saying it was excellent beyond measure, and encouraging him to descend. The Goat, mindful only of his thirst, thoughtlessly jumped down, but just as he drank, the Fox informed him of the difficulty they were both in and suggested a scheme for their common escape. "If," said he, "you will place your forefeet upon the wall and bend your head, I will run up your back and escape, and will help you out afterwards." The Goat readily assented and the Fox leaped upon his back.

Examining the Model

Just as Æsop's wolf tale did, this fable has a moral or lesson to teach. Some fables teach us right from wrong, while others show us a fact of life. Some fables have multiple meanings. The moral of this story is "look before you leap." How else could you state the moral or morals this fable suggests?

Fables frequently use animal characters that represent different kinds of people. You learn about these characters, not by their actions, but by what they say through dialogue. What do you learn about the fox and the goat through what they say? How would you describe the animal characters in this story? What kind of people do they represent?

Steadying himself with the Goat's horns, he safely reached the mouth of the well and made off as fast as he could. When the Goat upbraided him for breaking his promise, he turned around and cried out, "You foolish old fellow! If you had as many brains in your head as you have hairs in your beard, you would never have gone down before you had inspected the way up, nor have exposed yourself to dangers from which you had no means of escape."

Look before you leap.

Prewriting

FINDING YOUR VOICE. Voice is the way a writer uses language to reflect his or her attitude toward the topic, form, and audience. Since fables are intended to teach and entertain, you might want to adopt a "narrator's" voice with a touch of humor.

IDENTIFYING YOUR AUDIENCE. Fables come from an old oral tradition when people sat together and told stories. Because they are short and easy to follow, fables still make excellent pieces to tell aloud. You could read your fable to your class or share it with a class of younger students. If you write for a group of younger children, keep in mind what topics and language they would enjoy and understand.

WRITING WITH A PLAN. For some writers, it helps to know the moral of the tale before they start to write their fable. Others find it easier to play with character types first.

Either way, consider the qualities of a fable as you begin your prewriting.
Fables often have:
- several stereotyped, animal characters
- natural interference like a storm, hot sun, or rain

Fables always have:
- more dialogue than action
- a moral or lesson, sometimes called an aphorism

Marvin filled out the graphic organizer below to get ideas for his story. He originally thought he wanted to write about cheating, but changed his mind as he wrote. Copy the graphic organizer shown on the next page onto your own paper and list ideas for a story.

Language, Grammar, and Style
Using Quotation Marks Correctly

When you use a person's exact words in your writing, you are using a direct quotation. The same is true for the words of a character in a fictional story. Enclose the words of a direct quotation in **quotation marks**.

IDENTIFYING QUOTATION MARKS. Look at the example below from the student model. What are the words that the character said?

EXAMPLE
The crow shrugged her feathers and said, "Why do you ask me? You're the cat."

Direct quotations always begin with a capital letter. When you break up a sentence in the direct quotation with he said or she said, capitalize the beginning of the speaker's sentence, but not the second half.

EXAMPLE
"No," the cat said, "you might fly away."

Separate a direct quotation from the rest of the sentence with a comma, question mark,

continued on page 504

"Plot grows out of character."
—Anne Lamott

or exclamation point. Do not use a period to separate the quotation from the rest of the sentence.

Incorrect

"There are some things I can't see on the ground." the crow said.

"Well, what do you want." the cat asked

Correct

"There are some things I can't see on the ground," the crow said.

"Well, what do you want?" the cat asked.

All punctuation marks that belong to the direct quotation should be placed inside the quotation mark. That means if the quotation starts out the sentence, the comma goes inside the last quotation mark. If the direct quotation ends the sentence, the period goes inside the last quotation mark.

If the direct quotation is broken in two parts, put the comma after the first part of the direct quotation inside the quotation marks. Put another comma after the word *said* and the period just before the last quotation mark.

EXAMPLE

Comma before the quotation mark:

"There are some things I can't see on the ground," the crow said.

Period before the quotation mark:

The crow shrugged her

continued on page 505

Student Model—Graphic Organizer

HUMAN TRAITS
What human behaviors do you admire or dislike? List at least ten.

Admire:	Dislike:
loyalty; honesty — people who don't play games; being friendly; getting along with everyone	cheating; lying; stealing; bullying or being mean; being greedy; being a hog; loudmouths; saying you'll do something and then not following through; stingy people

ANIMAL CHARACTERS/HUMAN TRAITS
Name some animals that could represent these or other human characteristics.

fox — smart, mean	cat — cruel, sneaky
raccoon — thief	crow — smart, loudmouth
dog — trusting, loyal	fish — minds his own business

DIALOGUE
Now imagine what these characters might say to each other if they met one day. Pick two characters and jot ideas for their dialogue.
cat — asks a crow to help him find dinner
crow — says no way
cat — says he'll do something for the crow
crow — says to help him find dinner
cat — says no way
they argue for a long time and the cat doesn't get his dinner

NATURAL INTERFERENCE
What small, natural interference could happen: a wind, an impassable river, a farmer going to market?
a wind could come along and blow the cat and crow away or night could fall and they are still arguing
What lessons might this story teach the reader? Write at least three possible morals.
It doesn't pay to be unfriendly.
If you are stubborn, you lose more than you win.
If you won't share what you know, you won't get nothing back.

Drafting

Using your characters from your graphic organizer, or two new ones you have since developed, begin a rough draft of your fable. Don't be surprised if your ideas for your story change as you write the dialogue. This is natural when you are drafting. Because fables are short, you can easily write yours over several times until you are satisfied.

Once your dialogue is complete, try this prewriting exercise again: write three possible morals for your story. Look them over and cross out any sayings you have heard before. Spend some time playing with words, trying to find a short and memorable statement to finish your piece.

Student Model—Draft

A ^wily cat came down the road looking for something to eat. When he came upon a[use dialogue?] ^n old crow in a tree, he asked where he might find some mice to feast on. The crow shrugged her feathers and said "why do you ask me? You're the cat."

"Because you fly. You see everything," the cat said.

The crow stretched her wings. "That's true. I do see most everything. But why would I tell you[add question mark]

"Well what do you want?" [who said this?]

"You tell me where I can find fresh baked bread to steal" the crow said [lower case] "And I'll tell you about the fattest mice you ever saw."

The cat licked his lips. "It's a deal. I know where a baker cools his bread on a windowsill. You tell me about the mice first."

The crow laughed "Ha! and have you run off before telling me? No, you go first."

feathers and said, "Why do you ask me? You're the cat."

Comma after *said,* and period before the last quotation mark:
"No," the cat said, "you might fly away."

FIXING ERRORS IN DIRECT QUOTATIONS. Look at these sentences from the rough draft of Marvin's paper. Find the errors in punctuation and capitalization. Copy the sentences onto your own paper and fix the errors. Briefly explain the changes you made.

The crow flapped her wings and said "I don't know".

I do see things. But why would I tell you? Give me a reason. said the crow.

"There are some things." the crow said that I can see.

USING DIRECT QUOTATIONS. Go through your paper to see that you have punctuated your dialogue correctly. Poorly punctuated dialogue is almost impossible to understand, and you will be glad you made corrections when it comes time to read your piece aloud.

In addition to punctuation, paragraphing makes the dialogue clear. Help yourself and your reader to know when each character is speaking by making a new paragraph every time the speaker changes.

> So the two argued. Soon it was dark. "Now neither of us shall eat dinner," said the crow. And flew off to roost hungry for the night.

can you add details?

Self- and Peer Evaluation

Once you have a rough draft, complete a self-evaluation of your writing. Try to get several peer evaluations as well.

As you evaluate your fable or that of a classmate, answer the following questions:

- What human traits do each of the characters in the fable represent?
- Which parts of the dialogue show the reader the character's traits? Is there any dialogue that does not fit the character? What changes would make the character more consistent?
- Is there a natural interference in this story? How does it add to or take away from the story?
- What is the moral of the story? Is it a catchy well-written phrase or has the writer used a cliché? What other ways of stating the moral can you think of?
- Has the dialogue been punctuated correctly? Are there quotation marks around direct quotations? Do the direct quotations begin with capital letters? What about commas? Are they placed before the quotation mark? Which sentences need editing?
- Is there a new paragraph every time the speaker changes?

Revising and Proofreading

Based on responses to your self- and peer evaluations, decide where you want to make changes in your story. Check to see if the parts of your fable all fit together. Look at the dialogue again. Do you need to add or get rid of dialogue that doesn't match the moral you are striving for?

Write your moral statement many different ways until you discover a short, snappy way to say it.

In Marvin's first draft, he wrote a moral that contained a grammatical error and sounded awkward. He wrote and rewrote his moral, reading it aloud, until he came up with a clear statement.

First draft of moral: If you won't share what you know, you won't get nothing back.

Final draft of moral: Without trust you learn nothing.

Read Marvin's rough draft and note other changes Marvin made.

Student Model—Revised

by Marvin Johnson

A wily cat crept down the road looking for something to eat. When he came upon a crow in an old tree, he asked, "Tell me, Crow, where is a fat family of mice that I might feast on?"

The crow shrugged her feathers and said, "Why do you ask me? You're the cat."

"Because you fly. You see everything," the cat said.

The crow stretched her wings. "That's true. I do see most everything. But why would I tell you? Give me a reason to help."

"Well, what do you want?" the cat asked.

"You tell me where I can find fresh-baked bread to steal," the crow said, "and I'll tell you about the fattest mice you ever saw."

The cat licked his lips and quivered. "It's a deal. I know where a baker cools his bread on a windowsill. You tell me about the mice first."

The crow laughed. "Ha! And have you run off before telling me? No, you go first."

"No," the cat said, "you might fly away. You go first."

And so the two stood arguing while the day grew old and the moon rose in the sky. The mice crawled off to their nests. The baker pulled the bread off the sill and put it away. It wasn't until dark that the cat and crow realized their loss.

"Now neither of us shall eat dinner," said the cat in disgust. And off flew the crow to roost, hungry for the night.

Moral: Without trust, you learn nothing.

Publishing and Presenting

Write or print a final copy of your story. Consider reading these to your class and/or classes of younger students. You may want to illustrate your fable and bind the final copy and drawings in a book to share with other students.

Reflecting

What are some lessons that you learned as a child from fables? What lessons did your classmates try to teach? Are the fables written long ago still true for us now? Do you think the fables you and your classmates wrote will be true for people 100 years from now? Why, or why not? What is the value of knowing the lessons taught in morals?

UNIT SEVEN *review*

Review: Words for Everyday Use

Check your knowledge of the following vocabulary words. Choose ten words that you would like to add to your own daily language. For each word, write a short sentence that includes the word in context. To review a word, look back to the page number(s) indicated.

- assent (464)
- clutch (455)
- commotion (483)
- compel (472)
- composure (465)
- console (473)
- dank (461)
- derange (464)
- divert (462)

- expiate (461)
- forsake (474)
- foliage (462)
- iridescent (463)
- lair (462)
- nestle (481)
- oblige (475)
- penetrate (473)
- plight (475)

- ploy (475)
- ponder (490)
- procession (473)
- protrude (464)
- remorse (461)
- semblance (465)
- serene (465)
- splendor (473)

Review: Literary Tools

Define each of the following terms, giving concrete examples when possible. To review a term, refer to the page number(s) indicated.

- aim (488)
- chronological order (459)
- fairy tale (470)
- folk tale (470)

- moral (479)
- myth (453, 459)
- oral tradition (493)

- personification (470)
- point of view (453, 479)
- suspense (488)

Reflecting *on your reading*

Theme

Since ancient times people have tried to explain the natural phenomena of the earth and cosmos. The need to know is strong in people. Some things, however, could not and still cannot be explained. So people made up stories about origins and nature. Stories explain, for example, how the earth began, how the sky is held up, and why the ocean is salty.

Genre

Fairy tales, folk tales, and myths are some of the ways that people tell stories to explain nature, or to teach moral lessons. These stories often include an element of magic, the supernatural, or of superstition. What makes them "folk" tales are the people who began telling them, who were often simple, country people, or "folk."

Critical Thinking

In many of the selections, the main character is given detailed and often complicated and difficult instructions he or she has to carry out in order to achieve something. Look back at the selections and recall what the characters had to do in order to succeed. Using the graphic organizer below as a sample, do this for the following characters: Hercules, the youngest daughter of "The Singing, Springing Lark," and the younger brother of "The Magic Mortar." What qualities do the main characters have that allow them to succeed?

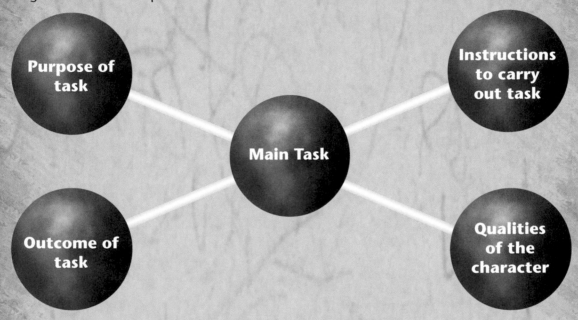

Group Project

In a small group, discuss the importance of fairy tales. Recall the fairy tales you listened to when you were a small child. Share these fairy tales with each other. Which ones did you like the best? Why did you like them? Which ones frightened you? Why? Were there any that you did not like? What did you enjoy about fairy tales when you were small? Do you think listening to fairy tales is valuable for children? Why? Listen carefully and respectfully to each other as you carry on your group discussion.

On Your Own

Think of an aspect of nature, and write a myth or fairy tale to explain it. For example, how does the moon wax and wane each month? Why does the sun rise and set? Why are there seasons? Why do lakes freeze in the winter? Your myth or fairy tale can be situated in a magic setting, such as an enchanted castle, or high in the clouds above the earth. The characters can be princes and princesses, dwarves or gnomes, or mythological gods.

Montparnasse Station, 1914. Giorgio de Chirico. Museum of Modern Art, New York.

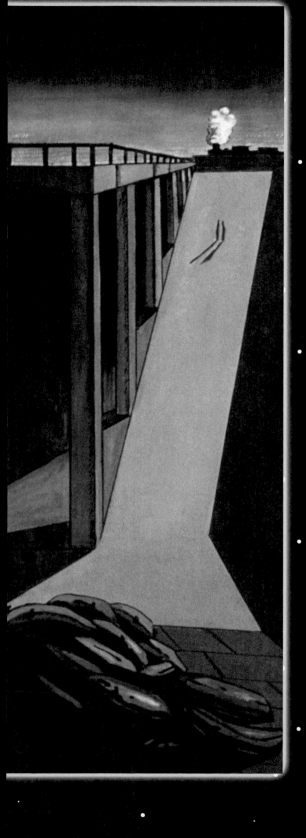

Stories to TELL

FICTION

ELEMENTS of FICTION

FICTION. Fiction is prose created from the imagination. Prose is writing that uses straightforward language and that differs from poetry in that it doesn't have a rhythmic pattern. Fiction is usually narrative. Narrative writing is that which tells a story. Works of fiction usually contain the elements of character, plot, setting, and theme.

CHARACTER. A **character** is a person (or sometimes an animal) who takes part in the action of a literary work. A *protagonist* is the main character in a story. An *antagonist* is a character who struggles against the main character. A *major character* is one who plays an important role in a literary work. A *minor character* is one who plays a lesser role. A *one-dimensional character*, or flat character, reveals only one quality or character trait. A *three-dimensional character* seems to have all the complexities of an actual human being.

Characters come alive in fiction through **characterization**. Characterization is the act of creating a character. A writer creates characters in three ways—1) by showing what characters say, do, and think; 2) by showing what other characters say about them and 3) by showing what physical features, dress, and personality the characters display.

PLOT. The **plot** of a work of fiction is the series of events or situations related to a *central conflict*, or struggle. The conflict can be internal or external. An *internal conflict* takes place within a character. An *external conflict* is a struggle between a character and an outside force, such as another character, society, or nature.

A plot usually contains the introduction of a conflict, its development, and its eventual resolution. A story may begin with *exposition*—the introduction of the setting and characters. The *inciting incident* is the event that introduces the central conflict. The highest point of suspense in the story is the *climax*. The *crisis*, or turning point, is the point in the story where something happens to decide the future course of events. The *resolution* is the point at which the central conflict ends. The *dénouement* is any final material that finishes the story. Plots are often illustrated using a pyramid.

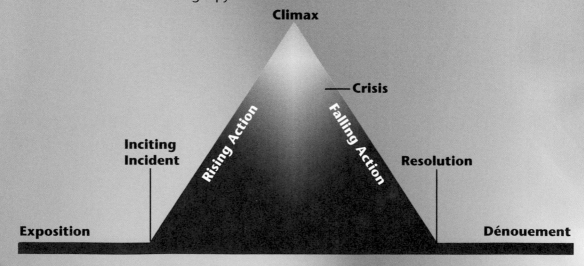

SETTING. The **setting** of a work of fiction (or any other literary work) is the time and place in which it happens. In fiction, the setting is often revealed through the description of the landscape, buildings, rooms, scenery, weather, and season. Setting reveals important information about the time period, geographical location, cultural environment, and physical conditions in which the characters live. These distinctions affect how the reader interprets a character's views and actions. For example, a scene with teenagers dancing in public would seem surprising in 17th-century New England but not in 20th-century Chicago.

THEME. A **theme** of a work of fiction is a central idea. Theme is different from subject. A subject of a work is its topic, such as "horses," "friendship," or "tornadoes." A theme is a broad statement about a topic, such as "animals can be our most loyal companions," "friends are worth more than money," or "tornadoes might destroy buildings but not communities." Many stories share the same subject but have different themes because they make unique statements about that subject.

In identifying a story's theme, keep the following things in mind. A story may have more than one theme. Two readers of the same story may state its theme or themes in different ways, and both may be correct. Describing theme can be a useful means of clarifying your thinking about the story.

OTHER ELEMENTS. Other elements that influence and shape a work of fiction include mood and point of view. *Mood*, or atmosphere, is the emotion created in the reader by a piece of writing. A writer creates a mood by using *concrete details*—words describing how something looks, sounds, smells, tastes, or feels. *Point of view* is the vantage point from which a story is told.

TYPES OF FICTION. Short stories, novels, and novellas are all types of fiction. A **short story** is a brief work of fiction that contains a definite beginning, middle, and end. Although it contains all the main elements of fiction—character, setting, plot, and theme—it may not fully develop each element. Many short stories use characterization to develop the plot and create a theme. A **novel** is a long work of fiction that usually has more complex elements than a short story. Its longer format allows the elements of fiction to be more fully developed. A **novella** is a work of fiction that is longer than a typical short story but shorter than a typical novel. The main elements of fiction are usually more fully developed than in a short story yet not as developed as in a full-length novel.

Some people view fiction in terms of subject matter and define short stories and novels as works of historical fiction, science fiction, westerns, romances, or any of a number of additional categories.

Reader's *Journal*

Imagine that you are describing the sun to someone who has never seen or felt it before. In what way would you describe the sun? To what could you compare it?

Reader's TOOLBOX

PLOT. A **plot** is a series of events related to a central conflict, or struggle. A plot includes the introduction of a conflict, its development, and its resolution. In a short story, the events in the plot usually lead from one to the next. Review the parts of a plot on page 512. Try to identify the climax as you read "All Summer in a Day."

SCIENCE FICTION. Science fiction is imaginative literature based on scientific principles, discoveries, or laws. Science fiction writers often suspend or alter elements of reality to teach the reader something about our planet or ourselves. As you read, compare Bradbury's picture of Venus with what scientists actually know about that planet (as shown in Reader's Resource).

Prereading

"All Summer in a Day"

by Ray Bradbury

Reader's Resource

- **SCIENCE CONNECTION.** Venus is the second planet from the Sun and the second brightest object in our nighttime sky. (The moon is the brightest.) Often called Earth's sister planet, Venus is similar to Earth in size and mass. Venus is covered by a nine-mile-thick layer of clouds, is much too hot for water to form, and has an atmosphere made up mostly of carbon dioxide. Life as we know it cannot exist under such conditions. Venus's heavy clouds trap great amounts of solar heat as the result of what is known as "the greenhouse effect." In fact, Venus is so hot that its rocks glow red with heat.

- **BIOLOGY CONNECTION.** You may have heard about the "wintertime blues" or noticed that some people seem happier and more energetic in spring, summer, and early fall than they do in winter. All people react to seasonal changes to some degree. For some people, however, winter and its decreased sunlight can cause serious emotional problems. People affected by Seasonal Affective Disorder, or SAD, feel very depressed and tired in winter. They often retreat from family and friends and have trouble concentrating. Doctors have found that controlled exposure to bright light can make people with SAD happier and more productive.

Graphic Organizer

SIMILES AND METAPHORS. A **simile** is a comparison using *like* or *as*. A **metaphor** is a figure of speech in which one thing is spoken or written about as if it were another. Look for similes and metaphors as you read "All Summer in a Day."

Simile or Metaphor?	Example	What does it mean?
M	storms so heavy they were tidal waves	the storms were exceptionally heavy

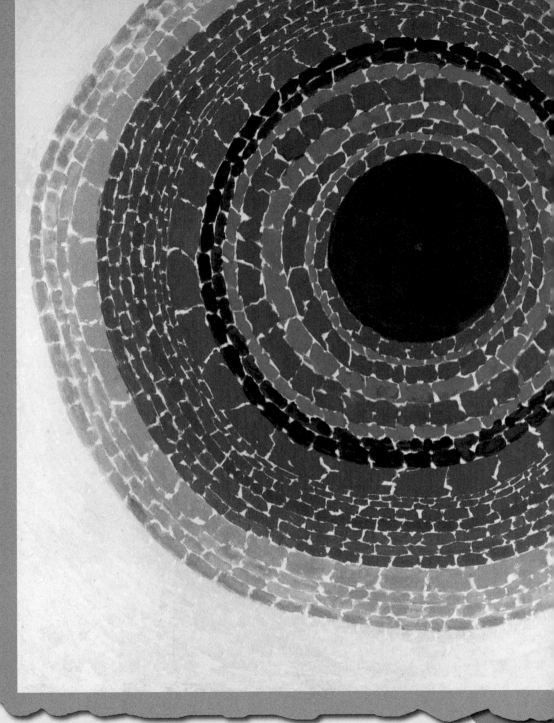

The Eclipse, 1970. Alma Thomas. National Museum of American Art, Washington, DC.

All SUMMER in a Day

Ray Bradbury

"Ready?"

"Ready."

"Now?"

"Soon."

"Do the scientists really know? Will it happen today, will it?"

"Look, look; see for yourself!"

The children pressed to each other like so many roses, so many weeds, intermixed, peering out for a look at the hidden sun.

GUIDED READING

What is the weather like? How long has the weather been this way?

It rained.

It had been raining for seven years; thousands upon thousands of days compounded and filled from one end to the other with rain, with the drum and gush of water, with the sweet crystal fall of showers and the <u>concussion</u> of storms so heavy they were tidal waves come over the islands. A thousand forests had been crushed under the rain and grown up a thousand times to be crushed again. And this was the way life was

GUIDED READING

Where does this story take place?

forever on the planet Venus, and this was the schoolroom of the children of the rocket men and women who had come to a raining world to set up civilization and live out their lives.

"It's stopping, it's stopping!"

"Yes, yes!"

Margot stood apart from them, from these children who could never remember a time when there wasn't rain and rain and rain. They were all nine years old, and if there had been a day, seven years ago, when the sun came out for an hour and showed its face to the stunned world, they could not recall. Sometimes, at night, she heard them stir, in remembrance, and she knew they were dreaming and remembering gold or a yellow crayon or a coin large enough to buy the world with. She knew that they thought they remembered a warmness, like a blushing in the face, in the body, in the arms and legs and trembling hands. But then they always awoke to the tatting drum, the endless shaking down of clear bead necklaces upon the roof, the walk, the gardens, the forest, and their dreams were gone.

All day yesterday they had read in class about the sun. About how like a lemon it was, and how hot. And they had written small stories or essays or poems about it:

I think the sun is a flower
That blooms for just one hour.

That was Margot's poem, read in a quiet voice in the still classroom while the rain was falling outside.

"Aw, you didn't write that!" protested one of the boys.

"I did," said Margot. "I *did*."

"William!" said the teacher.

I think the
sun is a flower
That blooms for
just one hour.

---

words for everyday use

con • cus • sion (kən kush' ən) *n.,* strong shaking; collision. *John's head hit the cement with such force that he suffered a* <u>concussion</u>.

But that was yesterday. Now, the rain was <u>slackening</u>, and the children were crushed to the great thick windows.

"Where's teacher?"

"She'll be back."

"She'd better hurry; we'll miss it!"

They turned on themselves, like a feverish wheel, all tumbling spokes.

Margot stood alone. She was a very frail girl who looked as if she had been lost in the rain for years and the rain had washed out the blue from her eyes and the red from her mouth and the yellow from her hair. She was an old photograph

GUIDED READING
What does Margot look like?

dusted from an album, whitened away, and if she spoke at all, her voice would be a ghost. Now she stood, separate, staring at the rain and the loud, wet world beyond the huge glass.

"What're *you* looking at?" said William.

Margot said nothing.

"Speak when you're spoken to." He gave her a shove. But she did not move; rather, she let herself be moved only by him and nothing else.

They edged away from her; they would not look at her. She felt them go away. And this was because she would play no games with them in the echoing tunnels of the underground city. If they tagged her and ran, she stood blinking after them and did not follow. When the class sang songs about happiness and life and games, her lips barely moved. Only when they sang about the sun and the summer did her lips move, as she watched the drenched windows.

And then, of course, the biggest crime of all was that she had come here only five years ago from Earth, and she remembered the sun and the way the sun was and the sky was when she was four, in Ohio. And they, they had been on Venus all their lives, and they had been

GUIDED READING
Why do the other children dislike Margot?

only two years old when last the sun came out and had long since forgotten the color and heat of it and the way that it really was. But Margot remembered.

"It's like a penny," she said, once, eyes closed.

"No, it's not!" the children cried.

"It's like a fire," she said, "in the stove."

"You're lying; you don't remember!" cried the children.

But she remembered and stood quietly apart from all of them and watched the patterning windows. And once, a month ago, she had refused to shower in the school shower rooms, had clutched her hands to her ears and over her head, screaming that the water mustn't touch her head. So after that, dimly, dimly, she sensed it; she was different, and they knew her difference and kept away.

There was talk that her father and mother were taking her back to Earth next year; it seemed vital to her that they do so, though it would mean the loss of thousands of dollars to her family. And so the children hated her for all these reasons, of big and little consequence. They

GUIDED READING
What are Margot's parents planning to do for her?

hated her pale, snow face, her waiting silence, her thinness, and her possible future.

"Get away!" The boy gave her another push. "What're you waiting for?"

Then, for the first time, she turned and looked at him. And what she was waiting for was in her eyes.

"Well, don't wait around here!" cried the boy, savagely. "You won't see nothing!"

Her lips moved.

words for everyday use
slack • en (slak′ ən) v., lessen; let up. "*Slacken* that rope before it snaps!" cried Petunia.

"Nothing!" he cried. "It was all a joke, wasn't it?" He turned to the other children. "Nothing's happening today. *Is* it?"

They all blinked at him and then, understanding, laughed and shook their heads. "Nothing, nothing!"

"Oh, but," Margot whispered, her eyes helpless. "But, this is the day, the scientists predict, they say, they *know*, the sun . . ."

"All a joke!" said the boy, and seized her roughly. "Hey, everyone, let's put her in a closet before teacher comes!"

"No," said Margot, falling back.

They <u>surged</u> about her, caught her up and <u>bore</u> her, protesting and then pleading and then crying, back into a tunnel, a room, a closet, where they slammed and locked the door. They stood looking at the door and saw it tremble from her beating and throwing herself against it. They heard her muffled cries. Then, smiling, they turned and went out and back down the tunnel, just as the teacher arrived.

"Ready, children?" She glanced at her watch.

"Yes!" said everyone.

"Are we all here?"

"Yes!"

The rain slackened still more.

They crowded to the huge door.

The rain stopped.

It was as if, in the midst of a film concerning an avalanche, a tornado, a hurricane, a volcanic eruption, something had, first, gone wrong with the sound <u>apparatus</u>, thus muffling and finally cutting off all noise, all of the blasts and repercussions and thunders, and then, secondly, ripped the film from the projector and inserted in its place a peaceful tropical slide which did not move or tremor. The world ground to a standstill. The silence was so <u>immense</u> and unbelievable that you felt that your ears had been stuffed or you had lost your hearing altogether. The children put their hands to their ears. They stood apart. The door slid back, and the smell of the silent, waiting world came in to them.

The sun came out.

It was the color of flaming bronze, and it was very large. And the sky around it was a blazing blue tile color. And the jungle burned with sunlight as the children, released from their spell, rushed out, yelling, into the summertime.

"Now, don't go too far," called the teacher after them. "You've got only one hour, you know. You wouldn't want to get caught out!"

But they were running and turning their faces up to the sky and feeling the sun on their cheeks like a warm iron; they were taking off their jackets and letting the sun burn their arms.

It was the color of flaming bronze, and it was very large.

> **GUIDED READING**
> What do the children tell their teacher?

> **GUIDED READING**
> How long will the sunlight last?

> **GUIDED READING**
> How do the children react to the sun?

words for everyday use

surge (sərj´) *v.,* suddenly push forward in a violent way. *The waves <u>surged</u> forward into the weakened dock.*

bear (bār´) *v.,* carry; transport. *The crew will <u>bear</u> the cargo to the warehouse.* **bore,** past tense

ap • pa • ra • tus (ap ə rat´ əs) *n.,* machine; instrument. *Gina knows how to fix the ship's <u>apparatus</u>.*

im • mense (im mens´) *adj.,* very large; enormous. *The <u>immense</u> tower loomed over the island.*

"Oh, it's better than the sunlamps, isn't it?"

"Much, much better!"

They stopped running and stood in the great jungle that covered Venus, that grew and never stopped growing <u>tumultuously</u>, even as you watched it. It was a nest of octopuses, clustering up great arms of flesh-like weed, wavering, flowering in this brief spring. It was the color of rubber and ash, this jungle, from the many years without sun. It was the color of stones and white cheeses and ink.

The children lay out, laughing, on the jungle mattress and heard it sigh and squeak under them, <u>resilient</u> and alive. They ran among the trees, they slipped and fell, they pushed each other, they played hide-and-seek and tag; but most of all they squinted at the sun until tears ran down their faces, they put their hands up at that yellowness and that amazing blueness, and they breathed of the fresh air and listened and listened to the silence which suspended them in a blessed sea of no sound and no motion. They looked at everything and <u>savored</u> everything. Then, wildly, like animals escaped from their caves, they ran and ran in shouting circles. They ran for an hour and did not stop running.

And then—

In the midst of their running, one of the girls wailed.

Everyone stopped.

The girl, standing in the open, held out her hand.

> **GUIDED READING**
> Why does the girl wail?

"Oh, look, look," she said, trembling.

They came slowly to look at her opened palm.

In the center of it, cupped and huge, was a single raindrop.

She began to cry, looking at it.

They glanced quickly at the sky.

"Oh. Oh."

A few cold drops fell on their noses and their cheeks and their mouths. The sun faded behind a stir of mist. A wind blew cool around them. They turned and started to walk back toward the underground house, their hands at their sides, their smiles vanishing away.

A boom of thunder startled them, and like leaves before a new hurricane, they tumbled upon each other and ran. Lightning struck ten miles away, five miles away, a mile, a half mile. The sky darkened into midnight in a flash.

They stood in the doorway of the underground for a moment until it was raining hard. Then they closed the door and heard the gigantic sound of the rain falling in tons and avalanches everywhere and forever.

"Will it be seven more years?"

"Yes. Seven."

Then one of them gave a little cry.

"Margot!"

"What?"

"She's still in the closet where we locked her."

"Margot."

They stood as if someone had driven them, like so many stakes, into the floor.

> **GUIDED READING**
> What do the children realize?

They looked at each other and then looked away. They glanced out at the world that was raining now and raining and raining steadily. They could not meet each other's glances. Their faces were solemn and pale.

They looked at their hands and feet, their faces down.

"Margot."

words for everyday use

tu • mul • tu • ous (tōō mul' chōō əs) *adj.*, wild and disorderly. *The <u>tumultuous</u> crowd stormed the exits of the hall.* **tumultuously**, *adv.*

re • si • lient (ri zil' yənt) *adj.*, flexible and springy. *The <u>resilient</u> mesh showed no sign of damage from the goat's rampage.*

sa • vor (sā' vər) *v.*, take great pleasure in. *I <u>savored</u> every bite of the delicious meal.*

One of the girls said, "Well . . . ?"

No one moved.

"Go on," whispered the girl.

They walked slowly down the hall in the sound of cold rain. They turned through the doorway to the room, in the sound of the storm and thunder, lightning on their faces, blue and terrible. They walked over to the closet door slowly and stood by it.

Behind the closet door was only silence.

They unlocked the door, even more slowly, and let Margot out. ■

Respond *to the* SELECTION

About *the* AUTHOR

Ray Bradbury (b.1920) was born in Illinois. He is best known for his science fiction and fantasy stories. He has published more than 20 books, including novels, children's books, and collections of short stories, poetry, and plays. Bradbury's science fiction stories offer social criticism and warnings against the dangers of uncontrolled technological development. For science fiction and fantasy writing, he has won the World Fantasy Award for lifetime achievement and the Grand Master Award from the Science Fiction Writers of America.

Investigate, *Inquire,* and Imagine

Recall: GATHERING FACTS → **Interpret:** FINDING MEANING

1a. What is the weather like on Venus? What is supposed to happen on this particular day?

1b. Why are the other children unable to remember the sun? How does Margot feel about the weather on Venus?

2a. What makes Margot different from the other children?

2b. Why does this difference cause the other children to dislike Margot?

3a. What do the children remember when it starts to rain again?

3b. How do the children feel when it starts to rain again? How do they feel about what they have done to Margot?

Analyze: TAKING THINGS APART → **Synthesize:** BRINGING THINGS TOGETHER

4a. Find examples that reveal how the other children feel about Margot.

4b. Before the children see the sun, they hate Margot "for . . . reasons, of big and little consequence." After the children see the sun, they feel terrible about what they have done to Margot. How has seeing the sun changed the children?

Evaluate: MAKING JUDGMENTS → **Extend:** CONNECTING IDEAS

5a. What do you think the sun is a metaphor for in this story?

5b. If Bradbury's central theme involves the children's intolerance of someone they perceive as "different," why does he use a science fiction setting to make this point?

Understanding *Literature*

PLOT. A **plot** is a series of events related to a central conflict, or struggle. What is the central conflict in "All Summer in a Day"? How is it introduced? Give one example of how the plot is developed toward the climax. What is the climax? How is the conflict resolved?

SCIENCE FICTION. Science fiction is imaginative literature based on scientific principles, discoveries, or laws. Science fiction writers often suspend or alter elements of reality to teach the reader something about our planet or ourselves. Review the Reader's Resource information at the beginning of the selection about the planet Venus. How does Bradbury's picture of Venus differ from what scientists actually know about the planet? What elements of this story are not strictly realistic? What elements of this story are realistic? What do you think Bradbury is trying to teach us about ourselves? Explain.

SIMILES AND METAPHORS. A **simile** is a comparison using *like* or *as*. A **metaphor** is a figure of speech in which one thing is spoken or written about as if it were another. Margot uses a metaphor in her poem when she writes about the Sun as if it were a flower. Identify two similes and a metaphor from "All Summer in a Day."

Writer's Journal

1. Write one sentence describing the weather using a **simile** and another sentence describing it using a **metaphor**.
2. Write a **short poem** in which you express your feelings about a rainbow, a sunset, an eclipse, or other natural event.
3. Write a **science fiction scene** about a Martian in a zoo, life on a space station, or using flying automobiles.

Skill Builders

Collaborative Learning

CLASS DISCUSSION. Think about how the children treat Margot because she is new and because she is different. How does it feel or how do you think it might feel to be new in a school? Discuss the way you have treated new students to your school or have been treated as a new student. In small groups, develop a plan for welcoming new students to your school. If there are students new to your school, try implementing your plan.

Study and Research

PLANET REPORT. In recent years scientists have discovered information about the various planets such as their topography and atmospheric conditions. Select one of the planets to research. How far away is this planet from Earth? from the sun? Is it hot or cold on this planet? What have scientists discovered about its atmosphere and surface? How did scientists find out this information? Early scientists predicted that Venus was covered with swampy plant life—are there any myths associated with the planet you are researching? Compile your information into a written report.

Prereading

"The Woman and the Wolf"

by Farley Mowat

Reader's TOOLBOX

SETTING. The **setting** of a literary work is the time and place in which it happens. Writers create settings in many different ways. In drama, the setting is usually made plain by the stage set and the costumes. In fiction, setting is most often revealed by means of descriptions of landscape, scenery, buildings, furniture, clothing, the weather, and the season. It can also be revealed by how characters talk and behave. As you read "The Woman and the Wolf," make note of the setting. How does the author create a setting the reader can visualize? How many different adjectives and phrases does the author use to create a picture in the reader's mind of where this story takes place? Use the Graphic Organizer below to help you organize your findings about setting.

CONFLICT. A **conflict** is a struggle between two people or things in a literary work. A plot involves the introduction, development, and resolution of a conflict. A conflict can be internal or external. A struggle that takes place between a character and some outside force such as another character, society, or nature is called an *external conflict*. A struggle that takes place within a character is called an *internal conflict*. As you read "The Woman and the Wolf," think about what conflict or conflicts are taking place. Do you encounter internal or external conflict(s)?

Graphic *Organizer*

Keep track of words the author uses to describe the setting.

The Woman and the Wolf

wastelands

stark plains country of the Barren Lands

Reader's Journal

Describe a special bond you've seen between an animal and a person—maybe it was yourself, a friend, someone you read about in a book, or someone in a movie. What made this relationship special?

Reader's Resource

- This short story features a husky dog. Huskies are working dogs. With their heavy coats, they easily endure the harsh climate of the Arctic north. Huskies are also intelligent and friendly.

- **CULTURAL CONNECTION.** The Inuit are a group of indigenous people that live in the Arctic regions of Greenland, Canada, Alaska, and a small part of Siberia. In the winter, they traditionally traveled through the cold hunting for food.

The Woman and the Wolf

Farley Mowat

The people built the little snowhouse and departed into the western lands. They went from the place singing laments for the dying, and they left nothing behind them except the old man. They took Arnuk, the dog, that being the old man's wish, for Arnuk was the last gift an old man could make to his son and to his grandson and to his people.

It had been a hard time—those long, hungry months before the spring—and in the camp there had been the cries of children who were too young to know that starvation must be faced in silence. There had been death in the camp, not of men but of those who were of the utmost importance to the continuance of human life. The dogs had died, one by one, and as each was stilled so men's hopes for the future shrank.

GUIDED READING

Who or what was dying at the camp?

Though it had been a harsh time, no word had been spoken against the folly of feeding one old and useless human body. Maktuk, the son, had shared his own meager rations equally between his aged father and his hungry child who also bore the name that linked the three together. But one dark April day the old man raised himself slowly from the sleeping ledge and gazed for a little while at his grandchild. Then out of the depths of a great love, and a greater courage, old Maktuk spoke:

"I have it in my heart," he said, "that the deer await you at the Western Lakes, but I stay here. You shall take Arnuk with you so that in the years ahead you will remember me."

GUIDED READING

Why does the old man tell his son to leave and take Arnuk with him? What does the old man plan to do?

The old man had his rights, and this was his final one. In the morning the people were gone, and behind young Maktuk's sled the dog Arnuk tugged <u>convulsively</u> at her tether and turned her head backward to stare at a small white mound rising against the snow ridges.

Arnuk had been born two winters earlier, but she was the ninth pup of the litter and so there was little food for her. If the old man had not taken it upon himself to feed and care for her, she would have died before her life truly began. With his help she saw warm days come and tasted the pleasures of long days romping with other young dogs by the side of the great river where the summer camp was pitched. When she grew tired she would come to the skin tent and push against the old man's knees until he opened his eyes and smiled at her.

So she grew through the good times of youth and the people in the camp looked at her with admiration for she became beautiful and of a size and strength surpassing that of any other dog in the camp. Maktuk, the elder, gave her the name she bore, Arnuk—The Woman—for she was wife and daughter to him in the autumn of his years.

> **GUIDED READING**
>
> What does Arnuk's name mean? Why is it significant?

Because there can be no death while there is birth, old Maktuk decided in mid-winter that his dog should be mated, although famine had already struck the camp. It was arranged, and so Arnuk bore within her the promise of a strength which would be the people's strength in years to come. When Maktuk, the elder, felt the throb of new life in the womb[1] of The Woman, he was content.

Hunger grew with the passing days. The older dogs died first, then even Arnuk's litter mates lay silent in the snows. But Arnuk's strength was great; and when there was some scrap of bone or skin the people could spare, she received it—for in her womb lay the hopes of years to come.

This was the way things stood when the people turned from the little snowhouse and set their faces to the west, dragging the sleds with their own failing muscles.

The ties that bind man and his dog can be of many strengths, but the ties that bound Arnuk to old Maktuk were beyond human power to <u>sunder</u>. Arnuk went with the people, but resisting stubbornly. On the third night of the journey she gnawed through the rawhide[2] tether and vanished into the swirling ground drift. In the morning Maktuk, the son, held the frayed tether in his hand and his face was shadowed by <u>foreboding</u>. Yet when he spoke to his family it was with these words:

> **GUIDED READING**
>
> Where did Arnuk go after breaking free from Maktuk?

"The Woman has gone to my father and she will be with him when the Snow Walker comes. But my father's spirit will know of our need, and perhaps the day will dawn when he will return The Woman to us."

Arnuk reached the little igloo before daybreak and when the old man opened his eyes to see if it was the Snow Walker, he saw the dog instead. He smiled and laid his bony hand upon her head, and once more he slept.

The Snow Walker was late in coming, but on the third day he came unseen; and when he passed from the place, the bond between man and dog was broken. Yet Arnuk lingered beside her dead for another day, and then it was

> **GUIDED READING**
>
> Who is the Snow Walker?

---

1. **womb.** Uterus. The dog is pregnant.
2. **rawhide.** Leather

con • vul • sive (kən vul′ səv) *adj.*, producing an uncontrolled fit. *The frightened chickens sounded a <u>convulsive</u> uproar when the fox appeared.* **convulsively,** *adv.*

sun • der (sun′ dər) *v.*, break apart or sever. *Mr. Harris <u>sundered</u> his ties to the company when he sold company secrets to a competitor and got caught.*

fore • bod • ing (fôr bod′ iŋ) *n.*, omen or prediction of coming evil. *A sense of <u>foreboding</u> overtook Pompeii before the volcano erupted.*

perhaps the wind that whispered the unspoken order: "Go to the people. Go!"

When she emerged from the snowhouse she found the plains newly scoured by a blizzard. For awhile she stood in the pale winter sun, her <u>lambent</u> coat gleaming against the blue shadows, then she turned her face with its broad ruff[3] and wide-spaced amber eyes toward the west. That way lay her path, and within her the voices of the unborn generations echoed the voice of the wind but with greater urgency. "Go to the places of men," they told her. "Go!"

Head down and great plume held low, she moved westward into the pathless spaces and only once did she pause to turn and stare at her back trail, waiting for some final sign. There was no sign, and at length she turned away.

This was the beginning of her journey. Death had released her from the ties that held her to one man, but she was still bound fast to Man. Through untold generations stretching back through the long dim sweep of time before the Eskimos drifted east across the island chain from Asia, the fate of her kind had been one with that of Man. Arnuk was one with the people and her need of them was as great as their need of her.

She did not halt when darkness swept the bleak plains into <u>obscurity</u>. At midnight she came to the place where she had chewed her way free of young Maktuk's sled. She knew it was the place only by an inner sense, for the snow had levelled all signs and drifted in all trails. Uncertainty began to feed upon her as she circled among the hard drifts, whining miserably. She climbed a rock ridge to test the night air for some sign

that men were near. A scent came to her—the odor of an arctic hare that had fled at her approach. But there was no scent of man.

Her whines rose to a <u>crescendo</u>, pleading in the darkness, but there was no answer except the rising mutter of the wind. Unable to endure the weight of her hunger and loneliness, she curled up in the shelter of a drift and lost herself in dreams.

So the dog slept in the heart of the great plains. But even as she dozed restlessly, a profound change was taking place in the secret places of her body. She lay with her nose outstretched on her

GUIDED READING

What did Arnuk find when she returned to the spot where she left Maktuk?

---

3. **ruff.** Long, thick fur on the neck

words for everyday use

lam • bent (lam′ bənt) *adj.,* softly bright or radiant. *The restaurant's <u>lambent</u> lighting created a romantic atmosphere.*

ob • scu • ri • ty (əb skür′ i tē) *n.,* state of being shrouded or hidden in darkness. *My neighbor followed the backyard path into the <u>obscurity</u> of the woods.*

cre • scen • do (krə shen′ dō) *n.,* gradual increase in volume. *The baby's cries rose to a <u>crescendo</u> when it had to wait for me.*

broad forepaws and her muscles twitched with <u>erratic</u> impulses. Saliva flowed in her mouth and had the taste of blood. In her mind's eye she laid her stride to that of the swift deer, and her teeth met in the living flesh and she knew the ecstasy of the hunter.

From out of time the ageless instincts which lie in all living cells were being revitalized so that the dog, and the new life within her, would not perish. When Arnuk raised her head to the dawn light, the thing was done, the change complete.

The dawn was clear, and Arnuk, her perceptions newly honed, tested the wind. When she found the warm aroma of living flesh she went to seek it out.

A Snowy Owl, dead white and shadowless in the pre-dawn, had swept across the plains with great eyes staring. The owl had seen and fallen on a hare so swiftly that the beast had known nothing until the inch-long talons[4] took life from him. For a little time the great bird chose to savor its hunger; and while it sat <u>complacently</u> crouched above the hare, it did not see the flow of motion behind a nearby drift.

Arnuk was a weasel easing up on a lemming, a fox drifting toward a ptarmigan. Skills she had never fully known had come alive within her. She inched forward soundlessly over the hard snows. When she was still a few yards from the owl, it raised its head and the yellow eyes stared with expressionless intensity full into Arnuk's face. Arnuk was the stillness of death, yet every muscle vibrated. When the owl turned back to its prey, Arnuk leapt. The owl saw the beginning of the leap and threw itself

GUIDED READING

What did Arnuk seek when she woke the next morning?

backward into its own element with a smooth thrust of mighty wings. Those wings were a fraction slow and the hurtling form of the dog, leaping six feet into the air, struck flesh beneath the feathers.

Arnuk slept afterwards while white feathers blew into the distance and tufts of white fur moved like <u>furtive</u> living things in the grip of the wind. When she woke again the age-old voices within her had quieted. Once more she was man's beast, and so she set out again into the west, unconscious yet directly driven.

The people whom she sought were wanderers on the face of a plain so vast that it seemed limitless. The dog could not <u>envisage</u> the odds against her finding them, but in her memory was the image of the summer camp by the wide river where she had spent her youth. She set her mind upon that distant place.

GUIDED READING

What far-distant place did Arnuk hope to find?

The days passed and the sun stood a little higher in the sky after each one faded. Time passed under the dog's feet until the explosion of spring overwhelmed the tundra. The snows melted and the rivers awoke and thundered seaward. Flights of ravens hung like eddies[5] of burned leaves in a white and glaring sky, and on the thawing ponds the first ducks mingled with raucous flocks of gulls.

Life quickened in the deep moss where the lemmings tunnelled and on the stony ridges where cock ptarmigan[6] postured before their mates. It was in all living things and in all places, and it was within the womb of the

---

4. **talons.** Claws
5. **eddies.** Whirlpools
6. **cock ptarmigan.** Male ptarmigan, grouselike birds of northern regions, distinguished by feathered feet

words for everyday use

er • ra • tic (ir a′ tik) adj., with lack of consistency or regularity. *Martha's <u>erratic</u> behavior included wild mood swings.*

com • pla • cent (kəm plā′ sənt) adj., self-satisfied; unconcerned. *Greg seemed <u>complacent</u> in math after getting an A on the test.* **complacently,** adv.

fur • tive (fər′ tiv) adj., secret; stolen. *The <u>furtive</u> cat hid daily in the rafters.*

en • vis • age (en vis′ əj) v., have a mental picture of. *I could not <u>envisage</u> a mall where the park is now.*

dog. Her journey had been long and her broad paws were crusted with the dried blood of many stone cuts. Her coat was matted and lustreless[7] under the spring suns. Still she drew upon her indomitable will and went forward into the western plains.

GUIDED READING

How did Arnuk look at this point in her journey?

Gaunt and hot eyed she brought her quest to an end on a day in June. Breasting a long ridge she saw before her the glittering light of sun on roaring water and she recognized the river.

Whining with excitement she ran clumsily down the slope, for her body had grown awkward in these last days. Soon she was among the rings of weathered boulders where, in other summers, men's tents had stood.

No tents stood there now. There were no living men to welcome the return of the lost one. Only the motionless piles of rocks on nearby ridges, that are called *Inukok*, Men of Stone, were there to welcome Arnuk. She understood that the place was abandoned yet for a time she refused to believe it. She ran from old tent ring to old meat cache,[8] sniffing each with a despairing hope, and finding nothing to give her heart. It was dusk before she curled herself in a hollow beside the place where Maktuk, the elder, had once held her at his knees, and gave herself up to her great weariness.

Yet the place was not as deserted as it looked. While Arnuk was making her fruitless search she was too preoccupied to realize that she was being watched. If she had glanced along the river bank she might have seen a lithe shape that followed her every move with eyes that held in them a hunger not born of the belly. She would have seen and recognized a wolf, and her hackles would have risen and her teeth been bared. For the dogs of men and the dogs of the wilderness walk apart, theirs being the hostility of brothers who deny their common blood.

GUIDED READING

Who was watching Arnuk search the empty camp?

The wolf was young. Born the preceding season, he had stayed with his family until, in the early spring of this year, the urge to wander had come over him and he had forsaken his clan's territory. Many adventures had befallen him and he had learned, at the cost of torn flanks and bleeding shoulders, that each wolf family guards its own land and there is no welcome for a stranger. His tentative approaches had been met with bared teeth in the lands of three wolf clans before he came to the river and found a place where no wolves were.

It was a good place. Not far from the empty Inuit camp the river flared over a shallow stretch of jagged boulders to lose itself in the beginning of an immense lake, and here for centuries the caribou had forded the shallows during their migrations. Two or three times a year they crossed the river in untold thousands, and not all escaped the river's surge. Drowned bodies of dead deer lay among the rocks at the river mouth, giving food to many foxes, ravens, and white gulls. The wolves of the country did not visit the place because it belonged to man, and that which man

GUIDED READING

Why didn't other wolves live at the campsite?

---

7. **lustreless (lusterless).** Dull
8. **cache.** Hiding place, especially for food

---

words for everyday use

in • dom • i • ta • ble (in dô′ mə tə bəl) *adj.*, unconquerable. *The army was unable to subdue the indomitable protesters.*

lithe (līth′) *adj.*, characterized by flexibility and grace. *The lithe gymnast showed great skill on the uneven bars.*

for • sake (fər sāk′) *v.*, give up or abandon. *I would forsake everything for a chance to follow my dreams.*

claims to himself is <u>abhorrent</u> to the great wild dogs.

Knowing nothing of this tabu, the young male wolf, the wanderer, had taken up his home by the river; and here he nursed his loneliness, for even more than dogs, wolves are social beings.

When the young wolf saw and smelled Arnuk, he was filled with conflicting emotions. He had seen no dog before but he sensed that the golden-coated beast below him was somehow of his blood. The smell was strange, and yet it was familiar. The shape and color were strange, and yet they roused in him a warmth of memory and desire. But he had been <u>rebuffed</u> so many times that he was cautious now.

When Arnuk woke she did not at first see the stranger, but her nostrils told her of the nearness of deer meat. Her hunger was overpowering. She leapt to her feet and flung herself upon a ragged haunch[9] of caribou that had been dragged to within a few yards of her sleeping place. Only when she had satisfied her first hunger did she glance up . . . to meet the still gaze of the young wolf.

He sat motionless a hundred feet from her and did not even twitch an ear as Arnuk's hackles[10] lifted and the threat took form deep in her throat. He remained sitting quietly but tense to spring away, and after a long minute Arnuk again dropped her head to the meat.

This was the way of their first meeting, and this is what came of it.

Arnuk could no longer resist the insistent demands of her heavy body. Once again the hidden force within her took command. Ignoring the young wolf, who still cautiously kept his distance, Arnuk made a tour of the familiar ground beside the river. She carefully examined the carcasses of five drowned deer and chased away the screaming gulls and guttural[11] ravens, for this meat was hers now by right of greater strength. Then, satisfied with the abundant food supply, she left the river and trotted inland to where a rock outcrop had opened its flanks to form a shallow cave. Here, as a pup, Arnuk had played with the other dogs of the camp. Now she examined the cave with more serious intent. The place was dry and protected from the winds. There was only one thing wrong, and that was the smell.

GUIDED READING

What did Arnuk find waiting for her when she woke? Who left it for her?

---

9. **haunch.** Hip or hindquarter
10. **hackles.** Stiff hairs along the neck and back, especially of a dog
11. **guttural.** Articulated in the throat

---

words for everyday use

ab • hor • rent (ǝb hōr' ǝnt) *adj.*, repulsive. *Jessica finds <u>abhorrent</u> the smell of chopped liver.*

re • buff (ri buf') *v.*, reject or criticize sharply. *Dad <u>rebuffed</u> my pleas with a firm "No."*

The rock cleft was <u>pervaded</u> with a potent and unpleasant stench that caused Arnuk to draw back her lips in anger and distaste—a wolverine[12] had bedded in the cave during the winter months.

GUIDED READING

What was the problem with the cave that Arnuk found? What caused the problem?

Arnuk's nose told her that the wolverine had been gone for several weeks, and there seemed little likelihood that he would return until the winter gales again forced him to seek shelter. She scratched earth and sand over the unclean floor, then set about dragging moss into the deepest recess. Here she hid herself and made surrender to her hour.

Arnuk's pups were born on a morning when the cries of the white geese were loud in the spring air. It was the time of birth, and the seven squirming things that lay warm against the dog's fur were not alone in their first day of life. On the sand ridges beyond the river, female ground squirrels suckled naked motes of flesh;[13] and in a den by a ridge a mile distant, an arctic fox thrust his alert face above the ground while the feeble whimpers of the pups his mate was nursing warned him of the tasks ahead. All living things in the land by the river moved to the rhythm of the demands of life newborn or soon to be born. All things moved to this rhythm except the outcast wolf.

During the time Arnuk remained hidden, the young wolf underwent a torment that gave him no peace. Restless and yearning for things he had never known, he haunted the vicinity of the cave. He

GUIDED READING

How did the wolf feel during Arnuk's three days of hiding?

did not dare go too close, but each day he carried a piece of deer meat to within a few yards of the cave mouth and then drew back to wait hopefully for his gift to be accepted.

On the third day, as he lay near the cave snapping at the flies which hung in a cloud about his head, his keen ears felt the faintest tremors of a new sound. He was on his feet instantly, head thrust out and body tense with attention. It came again, so faint it was felt rather than heard—a tiny whimper that called to him across the ages and across all barriers. He shook himself abruptly and with one quick, <u>proprietary</u> glance at the cave mouth, he trotted out across the plain — no longer a solitary outcast but a male beginning the evening hunt that would feed his mate and pups. So, simply and out of his deep need, the young wolf filled the <u>void</u> that had surrounded him through the torturing weeks of spring.

Arnuk did not so easily accept the wolf in his newly assumed role. For several days she kept him at a distance with bared teeth, although she ate the food he left at the cave mouth. But before a week was out she had come to expect the fresh meat—the tender ground squirrels, arctic hares, and plump ptarmigan. From this acceptance it was not a very long step to complete acceptance of the wolf himself.

Arnuk sealed the compact with him during the second week after the pups were born, when, coming to the den mouth one morning, she found part of a freshly killed caribou fawn lying ready for her, and the sleeping form of the young wolf only a few feet away.

---

12. **wolverine.** Carnivorous member of the weasel family, known for strength
13. **suckled . . . flesh.** Nursed their young

---

words for everyday use

per • vade (pər vād′) v., spread through every part of. *A feeling of excitement <u>pervaded</u> the holiday party.*

pro • pri • e • tar • y (prə prī′ ə ter ē) *adj.*, relating to or characteristic of an owner. *Richie had <u>proprietary</u> feelings about the treehouse he always played in.*

void (voyd′) *n.*, emptiness. *After their children had moved away, the Johnsons felt a <u>void</u> in their home.*

The wolf had made a long, hard hunt that night, covering most of the hundred square miles of territory he had staked out for his adopted family. Exhausted by his efforts, he had not bothered to retire the usual discreet distance from the den.

For a long minute Arnuk stared at the sleeping wolf and then she began to stalk him. There was no menace in her attitude and when she reached the wolf's side her great plumed tail went up into its husky curl and her lips lifted as if in laughter.

GUIDED READING

How did the wolf know that Arnuk accepted him?

The wolf woke, raised his head, saw her standing over him and knew that here at last was the end to loneliness. The morning light blazed over the den ridge as the two stood shoulder to shoulder looking out over the awakening plains.

Life was good by the banks of the river during the days that followed. There was no emptiness now in Arnuk's heart. And for the wolf there was the swelling pride with which he lay in the sun outside the den while the pups tussled with his fur and chewed at his feet.

Time passed until the pups were in their seventh week. Midsummer had come to the barrens and the herds of deer were drifting southward again. The crossing place was once more <u>thronged</u> and calves grunted beside their ragged mothers while old bucks, their velvet-covered antlers reaching to the skies, moved <u>aloofly</u> in the van.[14]

One evening a hunger for the chase came over Arnuk, and in the secret ways men know nothing of, she made her desire known to the wolf. When the late summer dusk fell, Arnuk went out alone into the darkening plains, secure in the knowledge that the wolf would steadfastly guard the pups until she returned.

She did not intend a long absence, but several miles from the river she came on a band of young buck deer. They were fine beasts, and fat, which at this time of the year was unusual. Arnuk was tired of lean meat and she circled the resting herd, filled with an <u>ardent</u> appetite.

A change of the uncertain breeze betrayed her and the startled deer

GUIDED READING

What kept Arnuk away for so long?

sprang to their feet and fled. Arnuk was hungry and the night was a hunter's night. She took up the long chase.

The hours drove the brief darkness from the land and when the early winds of dawn rose in the north the young wolf roused himself from his vigil at the cave mouth. An ill-defined uneasiness made him turn to the den and thrust his head and shoulders into the entrance. All was well, and the pups were rolled together in a compact ball, jerking their sturdy legs in sleep. Yet the prickle of anxiety persisted in the wolf's mind and he turned toward the river where the gray light picked out the long rolls of distant ridges.

Perhaps he was worried by Arnuk's long absence; or perhaps he had been disturbed by senses unknown to man. He trotted away from the den sniffing at the cold trail of the dog, hoping to see her approaching across the lightening plains.

He had gone no more than a quarter of a mile when the vague sense of something amiss took concrete form. A <u>vagrant</u> eddy brought the north breeze to his nostrils and instantly he knew what had disturbed him when he woke. He sprinted back toward the cave with startling speed.

---

14. **van.** Caravan, moving group of animals

 words for everyday use

throng (thrän′) v., crowd or pack. *The meeting participants <u>thronged</u> the hall, waiting to enter the auditorium.* **thronged,** *adj.*

a • loof (ə lüf′) *adj.,* indifferent. *Sandra looked <u>aloof</u> whenever the rest of us discussed our problems.* **aloofly,** *adv.*

ar • dent (är′ dənt) *adj.,* very eager. *Ian has an <u>ardent</u> desire to go to the amusement park.*

va • grant (vā′ grənt) *adj.,* wandering about; random. *A <u>vagrant</u> skunk wandered up to our camper.*

As he breasted the slope beside the den the stink of wolverine filled his nostrils and he was transformed by an elemental fury. He came down the slope in half a dozen gigantic leaps, ears flat to his skull and his throat rumbling with incoherent rage.

> **GUIDED READING**
>
> What made the wolf return to the cave?

The wolverine which had wintered in the cave where Arnuk's pups now whimpered in their sleep was a sixty-pound male, a little past his prime, and more than a little short of temper. That spring he had methodically searched for a mate across hundreds of miles of the surrounding country and had found none. During the night of Arnuk's hunt he had returned to the ford by the river where he expected to find a good store of drowned deer. Instead he had found nothing but clean bones and the evidence that a wolf and a dog had preempted what he considered to be his private larder. His mood grew worse, and when his wrinkling nostrils caught the faintest trace of pup smell from the direction of the old winter lair, he did not hesitate. His belly rumbling with hunger he turned from the river in the grey dawn light and circled upwind until he found a rock outcrop that gave him cover and from which he could observe the den. Here he waited until he saw the young wolf trot away from the den mouth toward the inland plains.

Cautiously the wolverine moved in upon the den, pausing to reassure himself that the pups were undefended. His massive body hugged the rough ground as he drew closer and now, certain of success, he could foretaste the pleasure of the killing and the salt warmth of blood.

There was blood enough for him to taste that dawn.

The young wolf's furious rush was so swift that the wolverine had only time to slew[15] about and take the weight of the attack upon his side. It was enough to save him for the moment. Although the wolf's teeth sank into the tough skin, they missed their intended hold upon the throat, meeting instead in the muscles of the wolverine's shoulder. On any lesser beast it would have been a good hold, but on this beast it was not good

> **GUIDED READING**
>
> What part of the wolverine's body did the wolf sink its teeth into? On what part of the wolverine's body would a bite have been fatal?

enough. Aflame with an incandescent[16] anger, he swung the wolf clean off its feet as he whirled in a savage counter-thrust.

Had the wolf been older and more experienced he might have released his grip and sidestepped that lunge, but he was young and blinded by the allegiance he had so freely given to the pups he had not sired.[17] He held his grip and did not slacken it even when the wolverine's teeth and claws raked deep into his flank.

They fought in silence. On the eastern rim of the horizon the red sun seemed <u>pallid</u> beside the glare of blood upon the rocks. Drawn to the cave mouth by the first <u>onslaught</u>, the pups watched for an instant and then, terrified by the fury of the struggle, retreated to crouch trembling in the dark earth. Only the gulls witnessed the duel's end.

The gulls warned Arnuk. As she trotted wearily homeward in the warmth of the morning, she saw them circling and heard their <u>strident</u> screams.

> **GUIDED READING**
>
> How did Arnuk know to come home?

---

15. **slew.** Turn or pivot
16. **incandescent.** White or glowing with heat; demonstrating great zeal
17. **sired.** Fathered

words for everyday use

pal • lid (pa′ lǝd) *adj.,* dull, lacking color. *Marion's <u>pallid</u> face showed that she wasn't feeling well.*

on • slaught (än′ slät) *n.,* especially fierce attack. *The king's army led the <u>onslaught</u> against the enemy.*

stri • dent (strī′ dǝnt) *adj.,* loud, harsh, and insistent. *Rover's <u>strident</u> barking alerted me to the burglar.*

They eddied ominously above the rocks where the den lay and, weary as she was, anxiety gave her new strength and she came on at a gallop. And so she found them. The wolverine had dragged himself toward the river before he bled to death. But the wolf, his belly ripped raggedly so that his entrails sprawled around him, lay stiffening beside the entrance to the cave.

The bodies still lay where they had died when, a few days later, the voices of men echoed once more along the shores of the river, and young Maktuk bent down to the dark opening and gently thrust his hand under the timid pups while Arnuk, half wild with old emotions, stood trembling by his side. Maktuk was a man who could read much that is never written and he understood all there was to know of what had taken place beneath those shattered rocks.

On an evening in late summer he took his son to the bank of the river and placed the boy's hand on the head of the saffron-coated dog.

"Maktuk, my son, in a little time you also shall be a man and a hunter, and the wide plains will know your name. In those days to come you will have certain friends to help you in the hunt, and of these the foremost you shall always call *Arnuk*; and then my father will know that we received his gift and he will be at ease. And in those times to come, all beasts shall fall to your spear and bow, save one alone. Never shall your hand be raised against the white one—against *Amow*, the wolf—and so shall our people pay their debt to him." ■

GUIDED READING

What gift has Maktuk's father left him and his family?

Respond *to the* SELECTION

How would you feel at the end of the story if you were Maktuk's son?

About *the* AUTHOR

Farley Mowat has written more than 30 books; more than 14 million copies of them have been sold worldwide. Mowat was born in Belleville, Ontario, Canada, in 1921. During his childhood, he lived in many places throughout Canada. Mowat served in the Canadian army during World War II (1939–1945), rising from private to captain. After the war, Mowat moved around frequently and visited nearly every corner of Canada and many places outside that country. His fascination in northern Arctic lands led him to write about them. Mowat's books include *The People of the Deer, My Discovery of America, Farfarers: Before the Norse,* and *The Snow Walker,* from which this short story was taken.

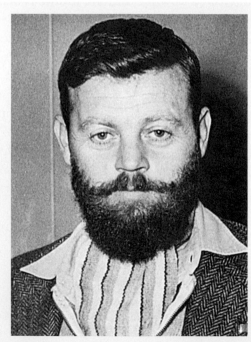

Investigate, Inquire, and Imagine

Recall: GATHERING FACTS → **Interpret:** FINDING MEANING

1a. What profound change took place in Arnuk while she slept at the place where she had chewed her way free of Maktuk's sled?

1b. Why was this change important? What may have happened to Arnuk if the change had not taken place?

2a. What did the wolf hear on the third day of lying near the cave that put his unease to an end?

2b. Why did this sound create such a change in the wolf?

3a. When did the husky finally accept the wolf?

3b. Why did she do this?

4a. Maktuk tells his son never to hurt what animal?

4b. Why did Maktuk tell his son this?

Analyze: TAKING THINGS APART → **Synthesize:** BRINGING THINGS TOGETHER

5a. Identify places in the story where we learn what is important to Arnuk. Think about her feelings towards the old man; the conflicts she faces to keep her pups (both before and after their birth) alive; and her acceptance of the wolf. What words would you use to describe Arnuk?

5b. Why is Arnuk the most precious gift the old man could leave his son and his people?

Evaluate: MAKING JUDGMENTS → **Extend:** CONNECTING IDEAS

6a. How effective is the author's use of setting in the story?

6b. Find an example of another story—either in a book or in a movie—in which the setting plays an important role. Compare its effectiveness to "The Woman and the Wolf."

Understanding *Literature*

SETTING. The **setting** of a literary work is the time and place in which it happens. Writers create settings in many different ways. In drama, the setting is usually made plain by the stage set and the costumes. In fiction, setting is most often revealed by means of descriptions of landscape, scenery, buildings, furniture, clothing, the weather, and the season. It can also be revealed by how characters talk and behave. Look back at your Graphic Organizer. How does Farley Mowat create a setting? How is the setting important to understanding the old man's gift to his son and his people?

CONFLICT. A **conflict** is a struggle between two people or things in a literary work. A *plot* involves the introduction, development, and resolution of a conflict. A conflict can be internal or external. A struggle that takes place between a character and some outside force such as another character, society, or nature is called an *external conflict.* A struggle that takes place within a character is called an *internal conflict.* What kind of conflict did you encounter in "The Woman and the Wolf"? How was the conflict resolved?

Writer's Journal

1. Write a **paragraph** describing the setting of your classroom.

2. Pretend you are away from home and you just witnessed a woman get mugged. Before the mugger could get very far with the woman's purse, a dog chased the mugger, retrieved the purse, and brought it back to the woman. Write an **e-mail message** to a friend describing this event and its effect on you.

3. A paraphrase is a rewriting of a passage in different words. **Paraphrase** the last paragraph of "The Woman and the Wolf" in which Maktuk speaks to his son.

Skill Builders

Critical Thinking

DESCRIBING SETTING. Think about your own neighborhood or city. Imagine that you have to write a story about a person who lives in the same place you do. How would you describe the setting? The words you choose make up the setting of your story. Use a graphic organizer like the one on page 523. In the inner circle, write *My Neighborhood/City.* Fill in the spaces between the "spokes" with words you would use to describe the setting where you live. Think of as many ways as possible to describe your neighborhood or city. Exchange your graphic organizer with a partner in your class and discuss the similarities and differences between your work and your partner's.

Study and Research

RESEARCHING NATIVE AMERICANS. Using library resources and the Internet, research the similarities

and differences between two North American Indian groups. For example, look at the Inuit and the Navajo. Where does each group live? What language does each group speak? Do they share the same hunting techniques? the same spiritual beliefs? the same ceremonies? Share your findings with the class.

Collaborative Learning

RECREATING A SETTING. Get together in groups of three. Each person in your group should take charge of one setting: the place where Arnuk left Maktuk, the deserted summer camp, and the cave where the pups were born. Decide how you want to represent your setting. You could make a collage, paint the scene, or collect photocopies of photographs that depict your setting. Once you've each recreated your setting, paste each of your creations onto one piece of poster board, or other big piece of paper. Talk about the similarities of the settings and what makes each setting different.

Prereading

"I, Hungry Hannah Cassandra Glen . . ."

by Norma Fox Mazer

Reader's T O O L B O X

POINT OF VIEW. Point of view is the vantage point from which a story is told. If a story is told from the **first-person point of view**, the narrator uses words such as *I* and *we* and is a part of or a witness to the action. When a story is told from the **third-person point of view**, the narrator is outside the action, uses words such as *he, she, it,* and *they*; and avoids the use of *I* and *we*. As you read this story, find evidence that shows it is told from the first-person point of view. How does using this point of view affect the story?

CHARACTERIZATION. Characterization is the act of creating or describing a character. Writers use three main techniques to create a character:

- showing what characters say, do, and think;
- showing what other characters say about them;
- showing what physical features, dress, and personality the characters display.

As you read, use a chart like the one shown below and write down specific examples of techniques the author uses to create the characters of Hannah and Crow.

Graphic Organizer

THREE WAYS AUTHORS CREATE CHARACTERS

Techniques Used:	Hannah	Crow
Words, actions, and thoughts		
Other characters' words	• "wake up, Hannah dreamer"	
Physical features, dress, and personality		• high cheekbones • dark, shining eyes

Reader's Journal

How do you feel and what do you do when you are extremely hungry?

Reader's Resource

- Funerals have long been part of the grieving ritual for human beings. The ceremonies and gathering associated with honoring the dead have religious, social, and psychological meaning. Four major symbols are associated with funerals around the world. First, the color black is widely associated with funerals in many cultures. Secondly, social get-togethers are often held as part of the funeral service or after the funeral service. Techniques to preserve the body of the dead are also widespread. Lastly, in many cultures, mourners shave their heads or leave their hair disheveled.

- A birthmark is an unusual mark or blemish on the skin at birth. Of the nearly four million children born in the U.S. each year, 10 percent— or 400,000—will be born with an abnormal birthmark. Ninety percent of these birthmarks will disappear by age one, but others need to be treated by a doctor.

I, HUNGRY
Hannah Cassandra Glen...

Norma Fox Mazer

When Mr. Augustus Francher's heart burst, I told Crow we were going to the service at Bascind's Funeral Home because, afterward, at Mrs. Francher's house, there would be food.

"How are we supposed to get in? Nobody asked us," he said.

"They will. First we go to the service—to show respect, you know. Mrs. Francher sees us there and she says, 'You two fine young people must come over to my house after the funeral and have some delicious food.' "

"Safety Pin Francher says that? Wake up, Hannah dreamer."

"Maybe she won't say it exactly that way," I admitted.

"Maybe she won't." Crow mocked. "Forget it. I don't want to go." He scraped his Adidas on the curb.

"You never want to go anywhere." Just because of his face. He had to go to school, he couldn't get out of that, but he didn't like to go anyplace else where there were a lot of people.

"You go," he said.

"Not without you." We went everywhere together. We had been friends since we were four years old. "Just think of all that food," I urged Crow. I bet there'll be those little tiny fancy hot dogs with toothpicks stuck in them. You know how

good they smell? And a baked ham stuck all over with cloves and slices of pineapple on top. There's got to be a cake—maybe a three-layer chocolate cake with chocolate icing—and ice cream and tons of cookies. She's got the whole store to choose from."

I talked about food until Crow couldn't stand it. "I'll go, I'll go, since you want to do it so much."

"Just for me. Big-hearted you."

Crow was always hungry. His elbows stuck out like sticks. His stepfather, Willie, was on half time at the Buffalo Chemical Works, but even when he was on full time and they had more money, Crow was hungry.

Willie said workingmen had to get fed first. (That was Willie.) Then, said Willie, came the littlest kids, Jay, Mike, Chris, and Kelly. After that came the women—Crow's mother and Willie's two daughters, Lisa and Janet. After that, said Willie, came older boys. That was Crow. His mom always saved him something, but he never got enough to eat.

In the funeral parlor, we signed our names in the guest book. David James Alpern.

GUIDED READING

What reason does the narrator give for going to the service at Bascind's Funeral Home?

GUIDED READING

What types of places does Crow want to avoid?

Hannah C. Glen. We followed two men into the chapel and Crow sat down in the last row. If there'd been a darkest corner, he would have chosen that. I sat down next to him.

In the front row, Mrs. Francher sniffled loudly. She was tall and shaped like a summer squash, skinny on top and swelling out on the bottom. In the store she always wore a dark green smock held together with safety pins. Today she had on a black dress and black hat, no safety pins anywhere in sight.

Crow's stomach rumbled and then mine did, like a two-piece band. "What'd you have for breakfast?" I whispered. He shrugged. I had had two grape jelly sandwiches and a glass of instant milk. After she got laid off at the paper-bag factory, my mother began buying powdered milk instead of whole milk. She said it was cheaper and just as good for us. Every day she went out looking for work. As soon as she found a job, we'd have real milk again and plenty of eggs. At night, instead of macaroni and cheese,

we'd have hamburgers that sizzled delicious-smelling fat all over the stove and vegetables cooked with hunks of margarine. And for dessert we'd have cookies and freestone[1] peaches in thick syrup.

A man wearing a peppermint-striped tie passed us and then came back. I thought he was going to say something about Crow. Once, on a bus, a man said in a loud voice to the woman with him that Crow's parents should do something about his face. Mostly, people just stared.

"You, young lady," Peppermint Tie said, "shouldn't be chewing gum in here."

I spit the gum out into my hand. As soon as Peppermint Tie went by I put it up under my upper lip to save for later. Crow said it made him hungrier to chew gum. It was just the opposite for me.

Sometimes I thought that if Crow didn't have that stuff on his face he would be prettier than a girl. He had high cheekbones and his eyes were dark and shining, but it was hard to notice because his face looked as if it had been splashed with gobs of rusty paint. A splash like a map of Tennessee covered half his forehead, wandered down over his left eye, and dribbled out onto his cheek. Another splash around his mouth and chin looked like a mushy baked apple, and a splash on his neck looked like a four-legged spider.

A minister came into the chapel from a side door and stood near the open coffin. He cleared his throat. "Good afternoon, friends." He began talking about Mr. Francher. "Augustus Francher has left us. He was a fine, upstanding man."

No, I thought, that's wrong. He was a fine man, but he didn't stand up any more than he had to. Mr. Francher was fat, his face was round and yellow as a lemon pie, and he wheezed when he talked. If he and Mrs. Francher were both in the store, she waited on the customers and Mr. Francher sat on a high stool in front of the cash register. He always wore big soft shoes, a white shirt with a little bow tie, and baggy black pants.

---

1. **freestone.** Fruit having a pit that doesn't cling to it

---

"He lived a good life," the minister said. "He had <u>charity</u> in his heart and we are saddened that he has been struck down in his prime." Mrs. Francher sniffled loudly and called out, "Oh, Augustus, Augustus."

Mr. and Mrs. Francher's grocery store was in the front of their house. Dried salamis hung in the window over dusty stacks of Campbell's baked beans and Diet Pepsi. Lots of mornings when Crow and I walked past on the way to school, Mr. Francher's round yellow face would be in the window, between the salamis, and he would wink at me.

At the end of the month when my mom was short of money, she'd send me to Francher's Groceteria for half a pound of bologna and a can of spaghetti for supper. "Tell Francher to put it on the bill, Hanny," she'd say.

And I'd go off, hoping and hoping that it would be Mr. Francher in the store. If it was Mrs. Francher, she'd finger a safety pin on her smock, click her tongue, and look up

© Wayne Thiebaud/Licensed by VAGA, New York.

Salads, Sandwiches, and Desserts, 1962. Wayne Thiebaud.
Sheldon Memorial Art Gallery, Lincoln, Nebraska.

what we owed in her account book. "Twenty-five dollars and seventy-six cents. You'd better pay something on that." And she'd hold out her hand as if I had money in my pocket. I would try not to look at the tub of creamy-

> **GUIDED READING**
>
> What does Hannah's mother do at the end of the month when she is short of money?

art s m a r t.

Salads, Sandwiches, and Desserts, 1962. Wayne Thiebaud.

Wayne Thiebaud (b.1920) is a realist painter whose favorite subject is cafeteria food. He uses the thick oil paint to imitate the actual surface of the object. How do you think he achieves the three-dimensional quality of his paintings?

words for everyday use   **char • i • ty** (chãr' ə tē) *n.,* generosity; good will toward humankind. *Grandma's <u>charity</u> is evident through her volunteer work.*

looking potato salad in the case or the round of cheese on the counter with the sharp cheese knife lying next to it. "Go home and see what your mother wants to pay on account," she'd order.

But if it was Mr. Francher, he'd put his hand on my shoulder, look right at me with his brown eyes that were bright as a chipmunk's, and say, "Now, daughter, just tell your mother not to forget she should pay up soon." And he'd pull the can of spaghetti down from the shelf. Once he'd told me that long ago he'd had a little sister who died, and her name, too, was Hannah. "A nice old-fashioned name," he said. He was shorter than his wife and, sitting on his stool, he would munch on cream-filled doughnuts, then wash them down with long sips from a bottle of soda. My mother said he was his own best customer.

> **GUIDED READING**
>
> What does Mr. Francher say about Hannah's name?

The minister was through talking about Mr. Francher and everybody stood up to walk around the coffin where he lay, wearing a dark suit and tie, his hands folded together over his big round stomach. I stopped in surprise. He looked like a baby in a crib, a huge baby who would, at any moment, open his eyes and chuckle. His cheeks were puffed out and shining.

Mrs. Francher stood off to one side with another woman, also in black. They were holding hands. I walked slowly past the coffin, looking back at Mr. Francher over my shoulder. Was he really gone?

Was it true that when I went to Francher's the next time, there would be no Mr. Francher to say, "Now, daughter…"? No Mr. Francher anymore to wink at me through the salamis? My eyes filled. Just then I understood that he was dead and what it meant.

Behind me, Crow jabbed his finger into my back, reminding me why we were there. "Mrs. Francher," I said. Her eyes were dark and puffy. She looked at me, through me. I didn't think she recognized me.

It was the other woman who answered. "Yes?" She was not as tall as Mrs. Francher, but she was shaped the same: summer squash. "What is it, dear?" she said. "What do you want?"

I—can we—I'm sorry about Mr. Francher," I said. "I wish—I'm sorry."

Mrs. Francher's eyes focused. "You're the Glen girl." She reached up to the neck of her dress and a glimmer of surprise (that there was no safety pin there?) seemed to cross her face. I thought she was going to ask when my mother would pay up.

And fast, not so brave now that I was face-to-face with her, I said, "Can we, can Crow and—can David and I come after the funeral to your house?"

She grabbed my arm and bent close to me. "You came to the service. I didn't know you loved him so much."

I nodded dumbly. She smelled of chocolate mints and mothballs.

"And him?" Flapping her hand in Crow's direction, she looked away from him, but the other woman stared.

> **GUIDED READING**
>
> What does Mrs. Francher do and say when Hannah asks if she and Crow can come to her house after the funeral?

A man reached past me and pressed Mrs. Francher's shoulder. "My sympathies, Berenice."

"Thank you, Jack. Do you know my sister? This is my sister, Celia. Come to the house," she said. "You're coming to the house after, aren't you?"

"We'll be there," he said. "Jane made a meat pie."

"Move on, dear, move on," Mrs. Francher's sister said. She was all in black, too. "People are waiting. Move, children."

My mouth watered. A meat pie! "Thank you, we'll come to your house," I said, sort of low and fast, as we walked by Mrs. Francher and her sister.

Outside, cars with headlights on were lined up for the drive to the cemetery. Mrs. Francher and her sister got into Bascind's long black limousine. A chauffeur with a black peaked cap drove.

"I'm not going to die the way old Francher did," Crow said as we walked down the street. "I'm not going to wait around for it to come get me. When I'm ready, I'm going to do it myself."

"You mean kill yourself?"

He nodded. "I've thought about it a lot. I might do it soon."

"Soon? Now that is truly dumb. I never heard anything so magnifico dumb."

"Give me one good reason."

"I'll give you ten good reasons. You're too young. You don't know what you're saying. You get these ideas in your head and you think they mean something. Sometimes you make me so mad!"

GUIDED READING

What reasons does Hannah give to Crow for not killing himself soon?

"Now there's a good reason."

"Besides," I said coldly, "it's against the law."

"Oh, dear, dear, dear. I forgot that. After I stick my head in the oven some night, they're going to arrest my corpse and send it to jail for life."

"Would you please knock it off! I don't want you dead. So just forget it."

"Even if I leave you my track shoes?" He held up a foot temptingly.

"Oh, your brothers would get them."

"I'll make a will," he said. "I'll leave them to you in my will."

We sat on the stoop in front of my house where we could watch down the block to see when Mrs. Francher arrived back from the cemetery.

"Go get us some paper and pencils," Crow said.

"You want to play tic-tac-toe? Again?" It was his favorite game and no wonder, he always won.

"I'm going to write my will. You can do yours, too. Everybody should have a will."

"Not kids."

"Who says? Putting my track shoes in my will makes it official. You get them, nobody else."

GUIDED READING

Why does Crow want Hannah to get them some paper and pencils?

"I don't want your track shoes, and I don't want to make a will. I'm not going to die."

"Well, not right away," he agreed. "But you never know. I bet Mr. Francher didn't think he was going to drop dead. Give me your key, I'll go in and get the stuff if you're too lazy."

"You are one magnifico pest." I went into the apartment, tore paper out of my notebook, and grabbed two pencil stubs from the coffee tin in the kitchen. I didn't want to use up my ball-point pen.

"Make sure you leave me something good," Crow said when I sat down next to him again. He smoothed out his piece of paper on his knee.

"This is dumb," I said. Crow was already scribbling away. "I don't even know how to start."

"Don't be difficult, Hanny." He held up his paper and read out, " 'I, David James Alpern, being of exceptionally sound mind and not so good body, do <u>hereby</u> make my last will and testament.' That's the way you begin. That's all there is to it. Then 'I leave to etcetera, etcetera.' "

After a while, I wrote. "I, the hungry Hannah Cassandra Glen, being of possibly

words for everyday use   **here • by** (hēr bī') *adv.,* by this means. *After completing the ceremony, the minister said, "I <u>hereby</u> pronounce you husband and wife."*

sound mind and <u>passably</u> sound body, do hereby make my last will. I leave—"

But I couldn't think of anything I had that anyone would want. No, that was a lie. I didn't want to give my things away. I fingered the string of blue coral[2] around my neck and thought of the green and white afghan[3] on my bed, which my grandmother had made years before for my mother. It always somehow made me think of a spring day. I had never told anyone that, not even Crow. Then there were the six little glass chicks that my father had sent me when I was five, the last thing he ever sent me. The chicks sometimes marched across the top of my <u>bureau</u>, bumping into the jam jar in which I kept barrettes, shoelaces, and rubber bands, and sometimes made a magic circle on the floor at the side of my bed where I could see them as soon as I woke.

I peered over Crow's shoulder. He had just left an extra toilet plunger to his stepfather. I thought about putting down that I left a terrifico job making magnifico money (maybe as a private secretary to a very important person) to my mother. "Aren't you done yet?" I asked.

"In a minute." He kept writing and crossing out and writing.

My stomach rumbled. What if Mrs. Francher and her sister wouldn't let us in? No way, you kids, all you want is food, you don't care about poor Mr. Francher being dead.

I cleaned my fingernails and cuffed up the bottom of my Levis. They were my best pair. My mother

> **GUIDED READING**
> Why does Hannah have a hard time thinking of what to put in her will?

> **GUIDED READING**
> How does Hannah describe her jeans?

had found them in a church rummage sale. "Not even worn at the knees, Hanny!"

Crow turned over his paper to write on the other side. "Anyone would think you're serious about this," I said.

"I am." He covered his paper with his arm. "No peeking. I'll read it to you when I'm done."

I wrote down that I left Crow my afghan, but I crossed it out. How could I give that up? I was ashamed of my greediness and willed him my glass chicks. He probably wouldn't even like them.

Finally he stopped writing. "Okay. *Fini*."[4]

"What now?" I said. "You get out there in traffic and let a car run over you so I can get your track shoes?"

"I wouldn't do it that way. It's not sure enough. Let me tell you, when I do it, I'm not <u>botching</u> it up."

"Read me your will or shut up."

"I, David James Alpern (aka[5] Crow)," he read, "being of exceptionally sound mind and not so good body, leave to my best friend, Hannah Glen, my mighty brain, including all the words she doesn't know—"

"Thanks a lot."

"—a lifetime supply of Tootie Frooty gum—"

"Gimme a break!"

He stopped reading. "Are you going to listen?"

"I'll listen, I'll listen."

"—a lifetime supply of Tootie Frooty gum and my track shoes. To my mother, M*A*S*H[6] reruns forever and a quiet day. An

---

2. **coral.** Skeleton of the coral, a sea-dwelling polyp colony
3. **afghan.** Knitted blanket of colored wool
4. *Fini.* (Latin) Finished
5. **aka.** Also known as
6. **M*A*S*H.** Television series from the 1970s

---

words for everyday use

pass • a • ble (pa′ sə bəl) *adj.*, just good enough. *Although Henry's knees were dirty, his appearance was <u>passable</u>.* **passably,** *adv.*

bu • reau (byur′ ō) *n.*, low chest of drawers for use in a bedroom. *My bedroom has a bed, a desk, and a <u>bureau</u>.*

botch (bäch) *v.*, foul up hopelessly. *I tried to make Sammy a birthday cake, but I forgot the baking soda and <u>botched</u> the whole thing up.*

extra toilet plunger to my stepfather, Willie. To my brothers, Jay and Mike, snot-free noses—shut up please so people can sleep! birthdays at Burger King, and a snow shovel so you can make some money in the winter. To my sisters, Kelly and Chris, all the tangerines y'all want, a box full of chocolate chip cookies that never goes empty, and Wonder Woman tee shirts, red for Kelly, green for Chris. To Lisa and Janet, getting out of the house safe, thanks for the sandwich under the door, and winning all their volleyball games. And finally to all those others, teachers, acquaintances, enemies, and strangers, good good goodby, y'all, I'm not sorry to leave."

He glanced at me, the way he does, quick and sideways, so you don't get a good look at his face. "Like it? Think it was funny?"

I had to admit leaving a toilet plunger to his stepfather was fairly hilarious. "That's humor."

"Also there was some serious stuff in there," he said. "Like thanking Lisa and Janet. I thought that was important because when I die they might not know that I really like them. Read me yours."

GUIDED READING

How does Crow describe what he put in his will about Lisa and Janet?

"Nothing to read." I was hungry and that always made me feel mean.

"Didn't you leave me anything?"

"No." I tore up the paper and stuffed the scraps in my pocket. "Why aren't they back yet?" I said and I had a terrible thought. What if Mrs. Francher and her sister were going to have the food part of the funeral someplace else, not in their apartment behind the store? I thought about eating bread and jelly again for lunch and crackers and <u>pasty</u> milk for supper.

Just then the long black funeral car passed us. It stopped in front of Francher's Groceteria and Mrs. Francher and her sister got out. Other cars pulled up, one after the other. People spilled out, a whole crowd, all of them going into Mrs. Francher's house.

I spit on my fingers and scrubbed at my cheeks. "Do I look okay? Is my face clean? You better pull up your pants so you don't step on them."

"Maybe we shouldn't go, Hanny," Crow said all of a sudden.

GUIDED READING

When the funeral procession arrives at the house, what does Hannah do and say about her and Crow's appearance?

"What? Now you say it? After all this? I know you, you're getting cold feet just because there's going to be a bunch of people there. Who cares, Crow? There's going to be *food*. Don't be gutless."

"If you're so brave, go yourself."

"I will," I shouted, "but you can just forget about eating any of that food, because I'm not bringing any back for you, Mr. Crow David Gutless."

"Shut up, Hanny, you have a big fat mouth!"

We went down the street, not speaking. The cars were gone. The store was locked and dark. In the window a sign said CLOSED ON ACCOUNT OF A DEATH IN THE FAMILY. Were they eating up all the food, the meat pies and the baked ham and the cookies and cakes? I led the way around the side and knocked on the door.

Nobody came. I knocked again. There was a white lace curtain on the window of the door. "You and your ideas. They're not going to let us in," Crow said, and the door swung open.

words for everyday use

pas • ty (pās' tē) *adj.*, resembling paste; unhealthy in appearance. *The old woman's pasty complexion was lined with wrinkles.*

"We're here," I said to Mrs. Francher. She was in her stocking feet. She looked at me, then at Crow, as if she expected people, all right, but not us two. "We came to—" I almost said *eat*. I put my hand over my mouth and said, "We came to pay our respects."

"What?"

"Pay our respects." Behind me I sensed Crow moving away, disappearing down the path.

Mrs. Francher's sister appeared and they stood in the doorway, side by side. They seemed to me like two swollen black balloons. From the room behind them, wonderful smells of meat and cooked fruit drifted toward me. I wanted to cry. "We're here," I said again.

Mrs. Francher looked at her sister. "Oh . . . You take care of it, Celia." She walked away, a funny duck-footed walk in her stocking feet.

"Well . . . well . . ." Mrs. Francher's sister said. "Just you?"

"No, me and my friend. Cr—David," I yelled to him. My mouth was full of saliva and I smiled hard and said, "We were both friends of Mr. Francher's. We were always friends."

A long table, loaded with food, took up almost the whole dining room.

GUIDED READING

What does Hannah sense is happening as she tells Mrs. Francher she and Crow have come to pay their respects?

Mrs. Francher's sister sighed and looked over her shoulder and finally said, "I suppose you can come in, then."

The living room was warm and crowded. People stood around in little clumps with glasses in their hands, talking. The curtains were drawn and there were pictures and little statues everywhere, on tables, on top of the TV, and on little hanging shelves above the couch.

A long table, loaded with food, took up almost the whole dining room. I squeezed Crow's hand. Our quarrel was forgotten. In the center of the table were two crystal bowls, one filled with apples, pears, grapes, and bananas, the other brimming with a fizzing red punch. There were platters of roast beef, ham, turkey, and salami, little <u>fluted</u> cups filled with butter, a wooden board with a

words for everyday use

flut • ed (flü′ təd) *adj.*, having grooves. *It is hard to wash all the grooves in this <u>fluted</u> casserole.*

cutting knife, and different kinds of cheeses. There was applesauce and fruit salad, baked potatoes wrapped in silver paper, tomatoes and cucumbers, bread and rolls and cakes and all kinds of hot casseroles.

GUIDED READING

What kinds of food are on the table in the dining room?

"What should we do?" Crow whispered.

"Eat," I said, but first I slipped an apple and a pear and slices of ham and roast beef into my pockets. How surprised my mother would be tonight when she came home and found the refrigerator full. "Oh, Hanny," she'd say, "you shouldn't have done that, that's not nice." But she'd eat a slice of roast beef (her favorite) and then polish an apple on her shirt and cut it in half to share with me.

GUIDED READING

What does Hannah do just before she starts eating?

Crow and I filled plates with food. We found a place near a window away from people and began eating as fast as possible. We ate everything on our plates and went back to the table for more. People talked and laughed and no one bothered with us.

GUIDED READING

How long do Hannah and Crow eat?

Crow's cheeks and lips were shiny with grease. We ate without stopping until neither of us could eat any more.

When we left, I was wonderfully full. Crow rubbed his bulging stomach and whispered, "Well, guess I'll go on living a little longer." And hearing that, I thought without shame how glad I was that Mr. Francher had died and left us this feast. I imagined him looking like a great baby in his coffin, winking at me and saying in his wheezy voice, which had always sounded to me like dark rough honey, "Now, daughter, now, daughter . . ."

GUIDED READING

What does Hannah think when Crow says he's going to go on living a little longer?

Respond *to the* SELECTION

Would you have made the same choices that Hannah did in this story? Why, or why not?

About *the* AUTHOR

Norma Fox Mazer is an award-winning author of books for young people. Her books—including *When She Was Good, A Figure of Speech, Saturday, the Twelfth of October,* and *Taking Terri Mueller*—are enormously popular because the stories are realistic, showing how people interact, deal with problems, and come to terms with change. Although she knew since the age of 13 that she wanted to be a writer, she wasn't very good at writing as a student. Mazer began writing seriously at the age of 28. She and her husband, Harry Mazer—who is also a writer—live in Jamesville, New York.

"Ideas come in every possible way you could imagine. I've had ideas come to me from dreams, from memories, conversations, news articles, letters, and certainly from plain old garden variety daydreams or fantasies," Mazer says. "Sometimes an idea hits me between the eyes—it's just there waiting for me, and believe me I take it and run." She has always worked hard at writing. "Really," she emphasizes, "I had to do what everyone has to do to master anything in this world—which is work, to keep at it, not give up, believe in myself, and believe that what I wanted so much—to be a real writer—was possible."

Investigate, Inquire, and Imagine

Recall: GATHERING FACTS

1a. Why is Crow always hungry?

2a. How does Hannah come to realize that Mr. Francher is dead and what it means?

3a. Why can't Hannah think of anything to put in her will?

→ **Interpret:** FINDING MEANING

1b. How does Hannah feel about Crow? Describe some things she says and does that support your answer.

2b. In what ways had Mr. Francher been important to Hannah?

3b. Why doesn't Hannah want to use up things, like her ballpoint pen, or give her things away?

Analyze: TAKING THINGS APART

4a. Compare and contrast how Mr. and Mrs. Francher each react when Hannah asks to put some bologna and a can of spaghetti on the Glen's bill at the end of the month.

→ **Synthesize:** BRINGING THINGS TOGETHER

4b. Why you think they react as they do?

Evaluate: MAKING JUDGMENTS

5a. In your opinion, are Hannah and Crow justified in saying they are paying respects to Mr. Francher in order to eat a lot at the gathering after the funeral?

→ **Extend:** CONNECTING IDEAS

5b. Think of a time when someone who was kind to you moved away or died. How did you feel? Did you think about it much? Did you talk to anybody about it? How had that person helped you?

Understanding Literature

POINT OF VIEW. Point of view is the vantage point from which a story is told. If a story is told from the **first-person point of view**, the narrator uses words such as *I* and *we* and is a part of or a witness to the action. When a story is told from the **third-person point of view**, the narrator stands outside the action; uses words such as *he, she, it,* and *they;* and avoids the use of *I* and *we.* How would some of the scenes in this story have been different if it had been told from the vantage point of a third person?

CHARACTERIZATION. Characterization is the act of creating or describing a character. Writers use three main techniques to create character:
• showing what characters say, do, and think;

- showing what other characters say about them;
- showing what physical features, dress, and personality the characters display.

Look at your chart, on which you recorded specific examples of techniques the author used to create Hannah's and Crow's characters. What kind of a person is Hannah? Which details tell you the most about her? What do you know about Crow? Which character is developed more fully? What else, in your opinion, would be interesting or helpful to know about either of these characters?

Writer's Journal

1. Imagine you are Mrs. Francher. Make a **list** of the Groceteria's ten best-selling foods that need to be reordered from the supplier to restock the shelves.

2. Write a section of your own **will,** modeled after those in the story. Give at least six of your possessions away to others.

3. Imagine you are Hannah. Write an **essay** about the green and white afghan, including why it makes you think of a spring day and why you don't want to part with it by giving it away in your will.

Skill Builders

Language, Grammar, and Style

WORKING WITH NEGATIVES. Review the Language Arts Survey 3.25, "Working with Negatives." The easiest mistake when using negatives—words like *not, nobody, none, hardly, barely, can't, don't, won't,* and *isn't*—is to use more than one in a sentence. Read the following sentences. Fix those that contain more than one negative with editing marks, as shown in the examples.

EXAMPLES You never want to go ~~no~~*any*where.
  My mother ~~didn't buy~~ no fresh fruit.
      bought

1. Crow hardly never got enough to eat.
2. I don't care about nothing Mrs. Francher says.
3. Tell your mother not to forget the money.
4. I didn't have no idea about your problem.
5. I would try not to look at no potato salad or cheese.
6. Hannah's not going to wait around for nobody.
7. He probably wouldn't like the glass chicks.
8. These jeans don't even have no holes.
9. The shop owners aren't letting in no one.
10. I'm not bringing back no food for you!

Prereading

"RAYMOND'S RUN"

by Toni Cade Bambara

Reader's T O O L B O X

POINT OF VIEW. Point of view is the vantage point from which a story is told. Stories are often written from a **first-person point of view**, in which the narrator uses words such as *I* and *we*. They can also be told from a **third-person point of view**, in which the narrator uses words such as *he, she,* and *they*, and avoids the use of *I* and *me*. As you read, identify the point of view from which this story is told.

CHARACTER. A **character** is a person or animal who takes part in the action of a literary work. The main character is called the *protagonist*. In this story, Squeaky is the protagonist. A character who struggles against the main character is called an *antagonist*. Characters can also be classified as major characters or minor characters. *Major characters* are ones who play important roles in a work. *Minor characters* are ones who play less important roles. As you read "Raymond's Run," try to determine who is the antagonist. Then, think about which characters are major characters and which are minor characters.

HYPERBOLE. A **hyperbole** is an exaggeration made for effect. An example of hyperbole is the statement "I'm hungry enough to eat a horse." Look for examples of hyperbole as you read through this story and think about the effect the writer was trying to achieve with these examples. Use the graphic organizer to record your thoughts.

Graphic Organizer

Hyperboles
"And tomorrow I'm subject to run the quarter-meter relay all by myself and come in first, second, and third."

Reader's Journal

Which of your skills make you proudest and most confident?

Reader's Resource

- **SCIENCE CONNECTION.** People in most countries in the world measure distances using the metric system. The metric system is used in the United States in science and in track and field sports. The basic unit in the metric system is the meter, which is about three and a half feet. A thousand meters is a kilometer, which is equal to about two-thirds of a mile.

- Squeaky, the main character in "Raymond's Run," is an extremely fast runner. Some runners compete in short races called sprints. A sprinter must reach his or her highest speed very quickly but does not need to keep that speed for long. Other races can be as long as 10,000 meters. Runners plan such long races carefully. They usually want to save some energy for a fast finish.

Raymond's RUN

Toni Cade Bambara

I don't have much work to do around the house like some girls. My mother does that. And I don't have to earn my pocket money by hustling; George runs errands for the big boys and sells Christmas cards. And anything else that's got to get done, my father does. All I have to do in life is mind my brother Raymond, which is enough.

Sometimes I slip and say my little brother Raymond. But as any fool can see he's much

GUIDED READING

What one task does the narrator have to do?

bigger and he's older too. But a lot of people call him my little brother cause he needs looking after cause he's not quite right. And a lot of smart mouths got lots to say about that too, especially when George was minding him. But now, if anybody has anything to say to Raymond, anything to say about his big head, they have to come by me. And I don't play the dozens[1] or

GUIDED READING

How do you think the narrator feels about her brother Raymond?

---

1. **the dozens.** Game in which players insult one another

believe in standing around with somebody in my face doing a lot of talking. I much rather just knock you down and take my chances even if I am a little girl with skinny arms and a squeaky voice, which is how I got the name Squeaky. And if things get too rough, I run. And as anybody can tell you, I'm the fastest thing on two feet.

There is no track meet that I don't win the first place medal. I used to win the twenty-yard dash when I was a little kid in kindergarten. Nowadays it's the fifty-yard dash. And tomorrow I'm subject to run the quarter-meter relay all by myself and come in first, second, and third. The big kids call me Mercury[2] cause I'm the swiftest thing in the neighborhood. Everybody knows that—except two people who know better, my father and me.

He can beat me to Amsterdam Avenue with me having a two fire-hydrant headstart and him running with his hands in his pockets and whistling. But that's private information. Cause can you imagine some thirty-five-year-old man stuffing himself into PAL[3] shorts to race little kids? So as far as everyone's concerned, I'm the fastest and that goes for Gretchen, too, who has put out the tale that she is going to win the first place medal this year. Ridiculous. In the second place, she's got short legs. In the third place, she's got freckles. In the first place, no one can beat me and that's all there is to it.

> **GUIDED READING**
> Are Squeaky's reasons that Gretchen won't beat her sensible? Why, or why not?

I'm standing on the corner admiring the weather and about to take a stroll down Broadway so I can practice my breathing exercises, and I've got Raymond walking on the inside close to the buildings cause he's subject to fits of <u>fantasy</u> and starts thinking he's a circus performer and that the curb is a tight-rope strung high in the air. And sometimes after a rain, he likes to step down off his tightrope right into the gutter and slosh around getting his shoes and cuffs wet. Or sometimes if you don't watch him, he'll dash across traffic to the island in the middle of Broadway and give the pigeons a fit. Then I have to go behind him apologizing to all the old people sitting around trying to get some sun and getting all upset with the pigeons fluttering around them, scattering their newspapers and upsetting the waxpaper lunches in their laps. So I keep Raymond on the inside of me, and he plays like he's driving a stagecoach, which is O.K. by me so long as he doesn't run me over or interrupt my breathing exercises, which I have to do on account of I'm serious about my running and don't care who knows it.

Now some people like to act like things come easy to them, won't let on that they practice. Not me. I'll high prance down 34th Street like a rodeo pony to keep my knees strong even if it does get my mother uptight so that she walks ahead like she's

> **GUIDED READING**
> How does Squeaky feel about practicing?

not with me, don't know me, is all by herself on a shopping trip, and I am somebody else's crazy child.

Now you take Cynthia Procter for instance. She's just the opposite. If there's a test tomorrow, she'll say something like, "Oh, I guess I'll play handball this afternoon and watch television tonight," just to let you

---

2. **Mercury.** Messenger of the gods in Roman mythology, known for his speed
3. **PAL.** Police Athletic League

words for everyday use

fan • ta • sy (fant' ə sē) *n.*, daydream; imagined image. *Doug had <u>fantasies</u> of becoming a professional basketball player.*

know she ain't thinking about the test. Or like last week when she won the spelling bee for the millionth time, "A good thing you got 'receive,' Squeaky, cause I would have got it wrong. I completely forgot about the spelling bee." And she'll clutch the lace on her blouse like it was a narrow escape. Oh, brother.

But of course when I pass her house on my early morning trots around the block, she is practicing the scales on the piano over and over and over and over. Then in music class, she always lets herself get bumped around so she falls accidently on purpose onto the piano stool and is so surprised to find herself sitting there, and so decides just for fun to try out the ole[4] keys and what do you know— Chopin's[5] waltzes just spring out of her fingertips and she's the most surprised thing in the world. A regular <u>prodigy</u>. I could kill people like that.

GUIDED READING

In what way is Cynthia Procter dishonest?

I stay up all night studying the words for the spelling bee. And you can see me anytime of day practicing running. I never walk if I can trot and shame on Raymond if he can't keep up. But of course he does, cause if he hangs back someone's <u>liable</u> to walk up to him and get smart, or take his allowance from him, or ask him where he got that great big pumpkin head. People are so stupid sometimes.

So I'm strolling down Broadway breathing out and breathing in on counts of seven, which is my lucky number, and here comes Gretchen and her sidekicks—Mary Louise who used to be a friend of mine when she first moved to Harlem from Baltimore and got beat up by everybody till I took up for her on account of her mother and my mother used to sing in the same choir when they were young girls, but people ain't grateful, so now she hangs out with the new girl Gretchen and talks about me like a dog; and Rosie who is as fat as I am skinny and has a big mouth where Raymond is concerned and is too stupid to know that there is not a big deal of difference between herself and Raymond and that she can't afford to throw stones. So they are steady coming up Broadway and I see right away that it's going to be one of those Dodge City scenes cause the street ain't that big and they're close to the buildings just as we are. First I think I'll step into the candy store and look over the new comics and let them pass. But that's chicken and I've got a reputation to consider. So then I think I'll just walk straight on through them or over them if necessary. But as they get to me, they slow down. I'm ready to fight, cause like I said I don't feature a whole lot of chit-chat, I much prefer to just knock you down right from the jump and save everybody a lotta precious time.

"You signing up for the May Day races?" smiles Mary Louise, only it's not a smile at all.

A dumb question like that doesn't deserve an answer. Besides, there's just me and Gretchen standing there really, so no use wasting my breath talking to shadows.

GUIDED READING

Why doesn't Mary Louise's question deserve an answer?

"I don't think you're going to win this time," says Rosie, trying to signify[6] with her hands on her hips all salty, completely

---

4. **ole.** Slang for old
5. **Chopin.** Frédéric François Chopin (1810–1849), Polish pianist and composer
6. **signify.** Urban slang for insult or taunt

---

prod • i • gy (präd' ə jē) *n.*, person of highly unusual talent. *Beethoven's father wanted him to be a child <u>prodigy</u> like Mozart, but Beethoven was a late bloomer.*

li • a • ble (lī' ə bəl) *adj.*, likely. *If Waylon doesn't hurry, he is <u>liable</u> to miss his brother Skip who is leaving on a flight for Copenhagen in fifteen minutes.*

forgetting that I have whupped her many times for less salt than that.

"I always win cause I'm the best," I say straight at Gretchen who is, as far as I'm concerned, the only one talking in this ventriloquist[7]-dummy routine.

Gretchen smiles but it's not a smile and I'm thinking that girls never really smile at each other because they don't know how and don't want to know how and there's probably no one to teach us how cause grown-up girls don't know either. Then they all look at Raymond who has just brought his mule team to a standstill. And they're about to see what trouble they can get into through him.

GUIDED READING

In what way might Gretchen's smile be "not a smile"?

"What grade you in now, Raymond?"

"You got anything to say to my brother, you say it to me, Mary Louise Williams of Raggedy Town, Baltimore."

GUIDED READING

In what way does Squeaky protect her brother?

"What are you, his mother?" sasses Rosie.

"That's right, Fatso. And the next word out of anybody and I'll be their mother too." So they just stand there and Gretchen shifts from one leg to the other and so do they. Then Gretchen puts her hands on her hips and is about to say something with her freckle-face self but doesn't. Then she walks around me looking me up and down but keeps walking up Broadway, and her sidekicks follow her. So me and Raymond smile at each other and he says, "Gidyap" to his team and I continue with my breathing exercises, strolling down Broadway toward the ice man on 145th with not a care in the world cause I am Miss Quicksilver herself.

I take my time getting to the park on May Day because the track meet is the last thing on the program. The biggest thing on the program is the May Pole dancing, which I can do without, thank you, even if my mother thinks it's a shame I don't take part and act like a girl for a change. You'd think my mother'd be grateful not to have to make me a white <u>organdy</u> dress with a big satin sash and buy me new white baby-doll shoes that can't be taken out of the box till the big day. You'd think she'd be glad her daughter ain't out there prancing around a May Pole getting the new clothes all dirty and sweaty and trying to act like a fairy or a flower or whatever you're supposed to be when you should be trying to be yourself, whatever that is, which is, as far as I am concerned, a poor black girl who really can't afford to buy shoes and a new dress you only wear once a lifetime cause it won't fit next year.

GUIDED READING

Why does Squeaky not hurry to the park?

I was once a strawberry in a Hansel and Gretel pageant when I was in nursery school and didn't have no better sense than to dance on tiptoe with my arms in a circle over my head doing umbrella steps and being a perfect fool just so my mother and father could come dressed up and clap. You'd think they'd know better than to encourage that kind of nonsense. I am not a strawberry. I do not dance on my toes. I run. That is what I am all about. So I always come

GUIDED READING

Why does Squeaky believe her parents should "know better than to encourage that kind of nonsense"?

---

7. **ventriloquist.** Person who speaks so that the voice seems to come from some source other than the speaker

words for everyday use   **or • gan • dy** (ôr' gən dē) *n.*, sheer, crisp cotton fabric used for dresses. *Rita decided to make a party dress out of pale pink organdy.*

late to the May Day program, just in time to get my number pinned on and lay in the grass till they announce the fifty-yard dash.

I put Raymond in the little swings, which is a tight squeeze this year and will be impossible next year. Then I look around for Mr. Pearson, who pins the numbers on. I'm really looking for Gretchen if you want to know the truth, but she's not around. The park is jam-packed. Parents in hats and <u>corsages</u> and breast-pocket handkerchiefs peeking up. Kids in white dresses and light blue suits. The parkees unfolding chairs and chasing the rowdy kids from Lenox as if they had no right to be there. The big guys with their caps on backwards, leaning against the fence swirling the basketballs on the tips of their fingers, waiting for all these crazy people to clear out the park so they can play. Most of the kids in my class are carrying bass drums and glockenspiels[8] and flutes. You'd think they'd put in a few bongos or something for real like that.

Then here comes Mr. Pearson with his clipboard and his cards and pencils and whistles and safety pins and fifty million other things he's always dropping all over the place with his clumsy self. He sticks out in a crowd cause he's on stilts. We used to call him Jack and the Beanstalk to get him mad. But I'm the only one that can outrun him and get away, and I'm too grown for that silliness now.

"Well, Squeaky," he says checking my name off the list and handing me number seven and two pins. And I'm thinking he's got no right to call me Squeaky, if I can't call him Beanstalk.

GUIDED READING

Why doesn't the narrator want Mr. Pearson to call her "Squeaky"?

"Hazel Elizabeth Deborah Parker," I correct him and tell him to write it down on his board.

"Well, Hazel Elizabeth Deborah Parker, going to give someone else a break this year?" I squint at him real hard to see if he is seriously thinking I should lose the race on purpose just to give someone else a break.

"Only six girls running this time," he continues, shaking his head sadly like it's my fault all of New York didn't turn out in sneakers. "That new girl should give you a run for your money." He looks around the park for Gretchen like a periscope[9] in a submarine movie. "Wouldn't it be a nice gesture if you were . . . to ahhh . . ."

I give him such a look he couldn't finish putting that idea into words. Grownups got a lot of nerve sometimes. I pin number seven to myself and stomp away—I'm so burnt. And I go straight for the track and stretch out on the grass while the band winds up with "Oh the Monkey Wrapped His Tail Around the Flag Pole," which my teacher calls by some other name. The man on the loudspeaker is calling everyone over to the track and I'm on my back looking at the sky trying to pretend I'm in the country, but I can't, because even grass in the city feels hard as sidewalk and there's just no pretending you are anywhere but in a "concrete jungle" as my grandfather says.

GUIDED READING

What does Mr. Pearson seem to be suggesting Squeaky do? How does Squeaky feel about this suggestion?

---

8. **glockenspiels.** Percussion instruments with flat metal bars that produce bell sounds when struck with a hammer

9. **periscope.** Optical instrument with a system of lenses and mirrors that a person can look through on one end and see objects reflected on the other end; allows a person to see objects above the level of normal sight

words for everyday use

cor • sage (kôr säzh´) *n.,* small bouquet of flowers worn pinned to the shoulder of a garment. *Remembering that Rita's dress would be pink, her brother bought her a <u>corsage</u> of white roses.*

The twenty-yard dash takes all of the two minutes cause most of the little kids don't know no better than to run off the track or run the wrong way or run smack into the fence and fall down and cry. One little kid, though, has got the good sense to run straight for the white ribbon up ahead, so he wins. Then the second-graders line up for the thirty-yard dash and I don't even bother to turn my head to watch cause Raphael Perez always wins. He wins before he even begins by <u>psyching</u> the runners, telling them they're going to trip on their shoelaces and fall on their faces or lose their shorts or something, which he doesn't really have to do since he is very fast, almost as fast as I am. After that is the forty-yard dash, which I use to run when I was in first grade. Raymond is hollering from the swings cause he knows I'm about to do my thing cause the man on the loudspeaker has just announced the fifty-yard dash, although he might just as well be giving a recipe for angel food cake cause you can hardly make out what he's saying for the static. I get up and slip off my sweat pants and then I see Gretchen standing at the starting line kicking her legs out like a pro. Then as I get into place I see that ole Raymond is in line on the other side of the fence, bending down with his fingers on the ground just

GUIDED READING

What is Raymond doing as the race begins?

like he knew what he was doing. I was going to yell at him but then I didn't. It burns up your energy to holler.

Every time, just before I take off in a race, I always feel like I'm in a dream, the kind of dream you have when you're sick with fever and feel all hot and weightless. I dream I'm flying over a sandy beach in the early morning sun, kissing the leaves of the trees as I fly by. And there's always the smell of apples, just like in the country when I was little and use to think I was a choo-choo train, running through the fields of corn and chugging up the hill to the orchard. And all the time I'm dreaming this, I get lighter and lighter until I'm flying over the beach again, getting blown through the sky like a feather that weighs nothing at all. But once I spread my fingers in the dirt and crouch over for the Get on Your Mark, the dream goes and I am solid again and am telling myself, Squeaky you must win, you must win, you are the fastest thing in the world, you can even beat your father up Amsterdam if you really try. And then I feel my weight coming back just behind my knees then down to my feet then into the earth and the pistol shot explodes in my blood and I am off and weightless again, flying past the other runners, my arms pumping up and down and the whole world is quiet except for the crunch as I zoom over the

GUIDED READING

What does the narrator feel at the beginning of a race?

words for everyday use

psych (sīk′) v., cause to feel nervous or less self-confident. *Our soccer team's confident attitude <u>psyched</u> the other team, making them uncertain of victory.*

gravel in the track. I glance to my left and there is no one. To the right a blurred Gretchen, who's got her chin jutting out as if it would win the race all by itself. And on the other side of the fence is Raymond with his arms down to his side and the palms tucked up behind him, running in his very own style and the first time I ever saw that and I almost stop to watch my brother Raymond on his first run. But the white ribbon is bouncing toward me and I tear past it racing into the distance till my feet with a mind of their own start digging up footfuls of dirt and brake me short. Then all the kids standing on the side pile on me, banging me on the back and slapping my head with their May Day programs, for I have won again and everybody on 151st Street can walk tall for another year.

GUIDED READING

What is Raymond doing as the narrator races?

"In first place . . ." the man on the loudspeaker is clear as a bell now. But then he pauses and the loudspeaker starts to whine. Then static. And I lean down to catch my breath and here comes Gretchen walking back for she's overshot the finish line too, huffing and puffing with her hands on her hips taking it slow, breathing in steady time like a real pro and I sort of like her a little for the first time. "In first place . . . " and then three or four voices get all mixed up on the loudspeaker and I dig my sneaker into the grass and stare at Gretchen who's staring back, we both wondering just who did win. I can hear old Beanstalk arguing with the man on the loudspeaker and then a few others running their mouths about what the stop watches say.

GUIDED READING

Why can't the girls tell who won the race?

Then I hear Raymond yanking at the fence to call me and I wave to shush him, but he keeps rattling the fence like a gorilla in a cage like in them gorilla movies, but then like a dancer or something he starts climbing up

nice and easy but very fast. And it occurs to me, watching how smoothly he climbs hand over hand and remembering how he looked running with his arms down to his side and with the wind pulling his mouth back and his teeth showing and all, it occurred to me that Raymond would make a very fine runner. Doesn't he always keep up with me on my trots? And he surely knows how to breathe in counts of seven cause he's always doing it at the dinner table, which drives my brother George up the wall. And I'm smiling to beat the band cause if I've lost this race, or if me and Gretchen tied, or even if I've won, I can always retire as a runner and begin a whole new career as a coach with Raymond as my champion. After all, with a little more study I can beat Cynthia and her phony self at the spelling bee. And if I bugged my mother, I could get piano lessons and become a star. And I have a big rep as the baddest thing around. And I've got a roomful of ribbons and medals and awards. But what has Raymond got to call his own?

GUIDED READING

Why does the thought of coaching Raymond make Squeaky smile?

So I stand there with my new plan, laughing out loud by this time as Raymond jumps down from the fence and runs over with his teeth showing and his arms down to the side, which no one before him has quite mastered as a running style. And by the time he comes over I'm jumping up and down so glad to see him—my brother Raymond, a great runner in the family tradition. But of course everyone thinks I'm jumping up and down because the men on the loudspeaker have finally gotten themselves together and compared notes and are announcing "In first place—Miss Hazel Elizabeth Deborah Parker." (Dig that.) "In second place—Miss Gretchen P. Lewis." And I look over at Gretchen wondering what the P stands for. And I smile. Cause she's good, no doubt about it. Maybe she'd like to help me coach

Raymond; she obviously is serious about running, as any fool can see. And she nods to congratulate me and then she smiles. And I smile. We stand there with this big smile of respect between us. It's about as real a smile as girls can do for each other, considering we don't practice real smiling every day you know, cause maybe we too busy being flowers or fairies or strawberries instead of something honest and worthy of respect . . . you know . . . like being people. ■

Respond *to the* SELECTION

Based on what you've learned about Squeaky's personality in this story, do you think you would like to have her as a friend? Why, or why not?

About *the* AUTHOR

Toni Cade Bambara (1939–1995) was born in New York City. She received her bachelor's degree from Queens College and her master's degree from City College of the City University of New York. In addition, she studied drama and mime in Europe as well as dance in the United States. She is best known for her short stories, articles, essays, and screenplays that focus on African-American people and issues. She held a variety of positions including welfare investigator, director of community programs, college teacher, lecturer, and editor. Bambara, who was active in civil rights efforts for many years, presented in her writing a realistic, courageous, and sensitive picture of contemporary African-American life.

Investigate, *Inquire,* and Imagine

Recall: GATHERING FACTS

1a. Of what ability is Squeaky most proud? How does she include her brother Raymond in her training? What is different about Raymond?

2a. Why does Squeaky get to the park late on May Day? Under what name does she register for the race? Is she confident or nervous about winning?

3a. Who catches Squeaky's attention as they wait to find out who won the race? What does Squeaky realize then? What does Squeaky decide to do next, no matter who has won the race?

Interpret: FINDING MEANING

1b. How does Squeaky feel about her job of taking care of Raymond? How does she deal with people who make fun of Raymond?

2b. Why doesn't Squeaky like dressing up in costumes or fancy dresses?

3b. Why does she think that Raymond can be a fine runner some day? Why does Squeaky laugh out loud and jump up and down?

Analyze: TAKING THINGS APART

4a. What event provides suspense near the end of the story? Why do you think the writer added the suspense?

Synthesize: BRINGING THINGS TOGETHER

4b. At the end of the story, Squeaky and Gretchen smile at each other honestly. Why do they begin to respect and like each other? Do you agree with Squeaky that girls aren't really used to smiling honestly? Do you think that girls' relationships with other girls are less straightforward than boys' relationships with one another? Explain.

Evaluate: MAKING JUDGMENTS

5a. What makes Cynthia Procter's approach to her talent different from Squeaky's? Is Squeaky interested in doing well in anything besides running? Explain.

Extend: CONNECTING IDEAS

5b. In the story, Squeaky reveals several strategies she practices to help fulfill her dream of winning running races. She will "high prance…like a rodeo pony" to strengthen her knees, she runs every chance she gets, she practices breathing exercises, and she practices positive thinking, telling herself that she can win the race. Have you ever used any of these strategies to pursue a special interest? If so, which ones, and why? What other strategies have you used?

Understanding *Literature*

POINT OF VIEW. Point of view is the vantage point from which a story is told. As you read in the Reader's Toolbox at the beginning of the selection, stories may be written from a *first-person point of view* or a *third-person point of view*. From which point of view is this story written? How does this point of view help you to understand the main character?

HYPERBOLE. A **hyperbole** is an exaggeration made for effect. An example of hyperbole is the statement, "The water in the hot tub was boiling." Obviously the water wasn't really boiling (212 degrees Fahrenheit) or you would be instantly and severely burned. But with this use of hyperbole, the writer relays his or her message that the water was *really* hot. Find two examples of hyperbole in "Raymond's Run," and explain what effect the writer was trying to achieve.

CHARACTER. A **character** is a person or animal who takes part in the action of a literary work. The main character is called the *protagonist*. In this story, Squeaky is the protagonist. A character who struggles against the main character is called an *antagonist*. A *one-dimensional character*, or *flat character*, is one who exhibits a single quality, or character trait. A *three-dimensional character*, or *rounded character*, is one who seems to have all the complexities of an actual human being. Indicate which of the following characters are major characters and which are minor characters. Then indicate which are one dimensional and which are three dimensional.

	Major Character	Minor Character	One Dimensional	Three Dimensional
Squeaky				
Raymond				
Cynthia Procter				
Gretchen				
Mary Louise				
Rosie				
Mr. Pearson				

Writer's Journal

1. A hyperbole is an exaggeration made for effect. Write a short **description** of a competitive event you have seen and include a **hyperbole** to describe one of the participants, a team, the setting, the weather, or something else.

2. Imagine that after the race Squeaky is asked to give a very brief **speech** at an awards banquet. Write this speech for Squeaky.

3. A personal memoir is a self-reflective, autobiographical essay, written about some occasion in a person's life. Write a **personal memoir** about a time when you learned a lesson about winning or losing.

Skill Builders

Language, Grammar, and Style

VERBS. A **verb** expresses action or a state of being. There are three different types of verbs: **action verbs, linking verbs**, and **helping verbs**. Review the Language Arts Survey 3.8, 3.10, and 3.56 on verbs. Then identify the verbs in the following sentences and indicate whether they are action verbs, linking verbs, or helping verbs. If a verb is a helping verb, identify both the main verb and the helping verb.

1. My mother cooked that.
2. He can beat me to Amsterdam Avenue.
3. I am the fastest.
4. Gretchen is competing in the races.
5. What grade are you in now, Raymond?
6. I will win this year.
7. She sounded confident and secure.
8. My brother is a real champ.
9. Mary Louise has moved here from Raggedy Town, Baltimore.
10. I squint at him real hard.
11. The twenty-yard dash takes all of two minutes.
12. Just before the race, I always feel as if I'm in a dream.

Speaking and Listening & Collaborative Learning

ROLE-PLAY. Imagine what would happen if the track coach told Squeaky that she could not compete in the race this year because it is only open to new runners. Get together with a partner to role-play this scene. Take turns playing each part and critique each other's performances. In what way did your individual interpretations of the characters differ? Remember to think about the dialogue, tone of voice, gestures, and facial expression that each character would use. Review the Language Arts Survey 4.7, "Communicating with Another Person," for help.

Applied English

THANK-YOU NOTE. Imagine that you have just interviewed with the track coach at the local high school for the part-time position of track team assistant. Review the Language Arts Survey 6.5, "Writing a Personal Letter." Then write a thank-you note to the track coach, thanking him or her for taking the time to meet with you. (Use your imagination to make up a name for the track coach.) Keep in mind that any correspondence with a potential employer should have a formal tone. Address the person who interviewed you as Mr., Mrs., or Ms., and sign the note using a formal closing such as "Sincerely" or "Yours truly."

Study and Research

FAMOUS RUNNER BIOGRAPHY. Choose a famous track star from history. Research biographical information about this individual. What races did he/she typically run? Did he/she break any records? Was this runner in the Olympics? Did he/she win any medals? At what point in his/her life did this runner decide to focus on running? What were some of this runner's keys to a training regimen and competition? Write a report based on the information you find.

Prereading

"The Boy Who Talked with Animals"

by Roald Dahl

Reader's T O O L B O X

THEME. A **theme** is a central idea in a literary work. Theme is different from subject or topic. The themes of a literary work are the statements the work makes about life, society, human behavior, or the world. Sometimes the theme of a work is directly stated, but most often the reader must explore the elements of the literary work—characters, setting, and plot—to discover the theme or themes. Literary works commonly address universal topics that people around the world share—things like friendship, compassion, honesty, family, and determination. Think about the story of the three little pigs. The two pigs who build unstable houses because they don't want to do the work it takes to build a strong house end up losing their homes to the big bad wolf. The theme of that story could be stated as, "It pays off in the end to work hard and do the job right." As you read "The Boy Who Talked with Animals," consider the topics of the story and the possible themes that relate to those topics.

CONFLICT. A **conflict** is a struggle between two people or things in a literary work. A struggle that takes place between a character and some outside force is called an *external conflict*. An *internal conflict* takes place within a character. As you read, think about what conflicts take place in this story. Who do they involve?

Reader's Journal

In what ways do some people show respect for nature and animals, and in what ways do some people show disrespect for nature and animals?

Reader's Resource

- **GEOGRAPHY CONNECTION.** Jamaica is an island nation of the West Indies. Located south of Cuba in the middle of the Caribbean Sea, Jamaica is the third largest island in the Caribbean. Kingston, the capital, is a major seaport. Jamaica's developing economy is largely based on mineral exports and tourism.

- **BIOLOGY CONNECTION.** The turtle is a toothless, slow-moving reptile that has a shell to protect itself. Many turtles have sturdy, short feet. Marine turtles, however, like the one in this story, have paddle-like flippers. These flippers suit them to life in the ocean. There are 200 to 250 species of turtles, most of which live in or near the tropics. Today, many of the world's turtle species are threatened with extinction. The causes of turtle extinction are many but include loss of habitat, disturbance of nesting sites such as beaches, ocean pollution, and hunting of turtles for their meat, eggs, and shells.

The BOY
Who Talked with Animals
Roald Dahl

Not so long ago, I decided to spend a few days in the West Indies. I was to go there for a short holiday. Friends had told me it was marvelous. I would laze around all day long, they said, sunning myself on the silver beaches and swimming in the warm green sea.

I chose Jamaica, and flew direct from London to Kingston. The drive from Kingston airport to my hotel on the north shore took two hours. My room in the hotel had a little balcony, and from there I could step straight down onto the beach. There were tall coconut palms growing all around, and every so often an enormous green nut the size of a football would fall out of the sky and drop with a thud on the sand. It was considered foolish to linger underneath a coconut palm because if one of those things landed on your head, it would smash your skull.

The Jamaican girl who came in to tidy my room told me that a wealthy American called Mr. Wasserman had met his end in precisely that manner only two months before.

"You're joking," I said to her.

"Not joking!" she cried. "No, *suh!* I sees it happening with my very own eyes!"

"But wasn't there a terrific fuss about it?" I asked.

"They hush it up," she answered darkly. "The hotel folks hush it up and so do the newspaper folks because things like that are very bad for the tourist business."

Tropical Flora Along a Path in Jamaica. Franklin McMahon. Private Collection.

"And you say you actually saw it happen?"

"I actually saw it happen," she said. "Mr. Wasserman, he's standing right under that very tree over there on the beach. He's got his camera out and he's pointing it at the sunset. It's a red sunset that evening, and very pretty. Then all at once, down comes a big green nut right smack onto the top of his bald head, *wham!* And that," she added with a touch of relish, "is the very last sunset Mr. Wasserman ever did see."

"You mean it killed him instantly?"

"I don't know about *instantly,*" she said. "I remember the next thing that happens the camera falls out of his hands onto the sand. Then his arms drop down to his sides and hang there. Then he starts swaying. He sways backward and forward several times ever so gentle, and I'm standing there watching him, and I says to myself the poor man's gone all dizzy and maybe he's going to faint any moment. Then very very slowly, he keels right over and down he goes."

"Was he dead?"

"Dead as a doornail," she said.

"Good heavens."

"That's right," she said. "It never pays to be standing under a coconut palm when there's a breeze blowing."

"Thank you," I said. "I'll remember that."

On the evening of my second day, I was sitting on my little balcony with a book on my lap and a tall glass of punch in my hand. I wasn't reading the book. I was watching a small green lizard stalking another small green lizard on the balcony floor about six feet away. The stalking lizard was coming up on the other one from behind, moving forward very slowly and very cautiously, and when he came within reach, he flicked out a long tongue and touched the other one's tail. The other one jumped round, and the two of them faced each other, motionless, glued to the floor, crouching, staring, and very tense. Then suddenly, they started doing a funny little hopping dance together. They hopped up in the air. They hopped backward. They hopped forward. They hopped sideways. They circled one another like two boxers, hopping and prancing and dancing all the time. It was a queer thing to watch, and I guessed it was some sort of a courtship ritual they were going through. I kept very still, waiting to see what was going to happen next.

But I never saw what happened next because at that moment I became aware of a great <u>commotion</u> on the beach below. I glanced over and saw a crowd of people clustering around something at the water's edge. There was a narrow canoe-type fisherman's boat pulled up on the sand nearby, and all I could think of was that the fisherman had come in with a lot of fish and that the crowd was looking at it.

A haul of fish is something that has always fascinated me. I put my book aside and stood up. More people were trooping down from the hotel <u>veranda</u> and hurrying over the beach to join the crowd on the edge of the water. The men were wearing those frightful Bermuda shorts that come down to the knees, and their shirts were <u>bilious</u> with pinks and oranges and every other clashing color you could

GUIDED READING

How did Mr. Wasserman meet his untimely fate? What did the hotel people do about it?

GUIDED READING

Of what does the maid warn the narrator?

GUIDED READING

What does the narrator think of the way in which the men are dressed? the women?

words for everyday use

com • mo • tion (kə mō′ shən) *n.*, noisy rushing about. *I could not concentrate on my test because of the <u>commotion</u> in the hallway.*

ve • ran • da (və ran′ də) *n.*, open porch, usually roofed, along the outside of a building. *During the storm Mr. Smithers sat outside his cottage on the <u>veranda</u> where he could feel the misty breeze without getting wet.*

bil • ious (bil′ yəs) *adj.*, sick in appearance. *The park ranger will care for the <u>bilious</u> raccoon who is huddled in the bushes.*

think of. The women had better taste, and were dressed for the most part in pretty cotton dresses. Nearly everyone carried a drink in one hand.

I picked up my own drink and stepped down from the balcony onto the beach. I made a little detour around the coconut palm under which Mr. Wasserman had supposedly met his end and strode across the beautiful silvery sand to join the crowd. But it wasn't a haul of fish they were staring at. It was a turtle, an upside-down turtle lying on its back in the sand. But what a turtle it was! It was a giant, a mammoth. I had not thought it possible for a turtle to be as enormous as this. How can I describe its size? Had it been the right way up, I think a tall man could have sat on its back without his feet touching the ground. It was perhaps five feet long and four feet across, with a high domed shell of great beauty.

The fisherman who had caught it had tipped it onto its back to stop it from getting away. There was also a thick rope tied around the middle of its shell, and one proud fisherman, slim and black and naked except for a small loincloth, stood a short way off holding the end of the rope with both hands.

GUIDED READING

How does the narrator feel about the turtle? What is special about this creature?

Upside down it lay, this magnificent creature, with its four thick flippers waving frantically in the air, and its long wrinkled neck stretching far out of its shell. The flippers had large sharp claws on them.

"Stand back, ladies and gentlemen, please!" cried the fisherman. "Stand well back! Them claws is *dangerous*, man! They'll rip your arm clear away from your body!"

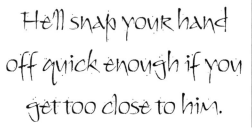

He'll snap your hand off quick enough if you get too close to him.

The crowd of hotel guests was thrilled and delighted by this spectacle. A dozen cameras were out and clicking away. Many of the women were squealing with pleasure and clutching onto the arms of their men, and the men were demonstrating their lack of fear and their masculinity by making foolish remarks in loud voices.

GUIDED READING

What does the narrator think of the way in which the men are talking?

"Make yourself a nice pair of horn-rimmed spectacles out of that shell, hey Al?"

"Darn thing must weigh over a ton!"

"You mean to say it can actually float?"

"Sure it floats. Powerful swimmer, too. Pull a boat easy."

"He's a snapper, is he?"

"That's no snapper. Snapper turtles don't grow as big as that. But I'll tell you what. He'll snap your hand off quick enough if you get too close to him."

"Is that true?" one of the women asked the fisherman. "Would he snap off a person's hand?"

"He would right now," the fisherman said, smiling with brilliant white teeth. "He won't ever hurt you when he's in the ocean, but you catch him and pull him ashore and tip him up like this, then man alive, you'd better watch out! He'll snap at anything that comes in reach!"

"I guess I'd get a bit snappish myself," the woman said, "if I was in his situation."

One idiotic man had found a plank of driftwood on the sand, and he was carrying it toward the turtle. It was a fairsized plank, about five feet long and maybe an

GUIDED READING

Why does the narrator call this man "idiotic"?

inch thick. He started poking one end of it at the turtle's head.

"I wouldn't do that," the fisherman said. "You'll only make him madder than ever."

When the end of the plank touched the turtle's neck, the great beast whipped around and the mouth opened wide and *snap*, it took the plank in its mouth and bit through it as if it were made of cheese.

"Wow!" they shouted. "Did you see that! I'm glad it wasn't my arm!"

"Leave him alone," the fisherman said. "It don't help to get him all stirred up."

A <u>paunchy</u> man with wide hips and very short hairy legs came up to the fisherman and said, "Listen, feller. I want that shell. I'll buy it from you." And to his plump wife, he said, "You know what I'm going to do, Mildred? I'm going to take that shell home and have it polished up by an expert. Then I'm going to place it smack in the center of our living room! Won't that be something?"

GUIDED READING

What does the paunchy man want to do with the turtle?

"Fantastic," the plump wife said. "Go ahead and buy it, baby."

"Don't worry," he said. "It's mine already." And to the fisherman, he said, "How much for the shell?"

"I already sold him," the fisherman said. "I sold him shell and all."

"Not so fast, feller," the paunchy man said. "I'll bid you higher. Come on. What'd he offer you?"

"No can do," the fisherman said. "I already sold him."

"Who to?" the paunchy man said.

"To the manager."

"What manager?"

"The manager of the hotel."

"Did you hear that?" shouted another man. "He's sold it to the manager of our hotel!

GUIDED READING

What might happen to the turtle?

And you know what that means? It means turtle soup, that's what it means!"

"Right you are! And turtle steak! You ever have turtle steak, Bill?"

"I never have, Jack. But I can't wait."

"A turtle steak's better than a beefsteak if you cook it right. It's more tender and it's got one heck of a flavor."

"Listen," the paunchy man said to the fisherman. "I'm not trying to buy the meat. The manager can have the meat. He can have everything that's inside including the teeth and toenails. All I want is the shell."

"And if I know you, baby," his wife said, beaming at him, "you're going to get the shell."

I stood there listening to the conversation of these human beings. They were discussing the destruction, the <u>consumption</u> and the flavor of a creature who seemed, even when upside down, to be <u>extraordinarily</u> dignified. One thing was certain. He was senior to any of them in age. For probably one hundred and fifty years he had been cruising in the green waters of the West Indies. He was there when George Washington was President of the United States and Napoleon was being clobbered at Waterloo.[1] He would have been a small turtle then, but he was most certainly there.

GUIDED READING

What alarms the narrator? What does he understand that the other people present do not understand?

---

1. **Napoleon . . . Waterloo.** Napoleon Bonaparte (1769–1821) was a French general and emperor who was defeated at the Battle of Waterloo in 1815.

---

words for everyday use

paunch • y (pônch′ ē) *adj.*, having a potbelly. *Tyler felt a bit <u>paunchy</u>, so he decided to do some situps.*

con • sump • tion (kən sump′ shən) *n.*, eating up, devouring. *Have you been lowering your <u>consumption</u> of sweets and fatty foods?*

ex • tra • or • di • nary (ik stror′ dən er ē) *adj.*, very unusual, remarkable. *Mia's talent at the trumpet is <u>extraordinary</u>.* **extraordinarily**, *adv.*

Marina at Captiva Island. Franklin McMahon. Private Collection.

And now he was here, upside down on the beach, waiting to be translated into soup and steak. He was clearly alarmed by all the noise and the shouting around him. His old wrinkled neck was straining out of its shell, and the great head was twisting this way and that as though searching for someone who would explain the reason for all this ill treatment.

"How are you going to get him up to the hotel?" the paunchy man asked.

"Drag him up the beach with the rope," the fisherman answered. "The staff'll be coming along soon to take him. It's going to need ten men, all pulling at once."

"Hey, listen!" cried a muscular young man. "Why don't we drag him up?" The muscular young man was wearing magenta and pea-green Bermuda shorts and no shirt. He had an exceptionally hairy chest, and the absence of a shirt was obviously a calculated touch. "What say we do a little work for our supper?" he cried, rippling his muscles. "Come on, fellers! Who's for some exercise?"

"Great idea!" they shouted. "Splendid scheme!"

The men handed their drinks to the women and rushed to catch hold of the rope. They ranged themselves along it as though for a tug-of-war, and the hairy-chested man appointed himself anchorman[2] and captain of the team.

GUIDED READING

Why is the muscular young man not wearing a shirt?

---

2. **anchorman.** Person who stands at the end

"Come on, now, fellers!" he shouted. "When I say *heave*, then all heave at once, you understand?"

The fisherman didn't like this much. "It's better you leave this job for the hotel," he said.

"Nonsense!" shouted hairy-chest. "*Heave*, boys, *heave!*"

They all heaved. The giant turtle wobbled on its back and nearly toppled over.

"Don't tip him!" yelled the fisherman. "You're going to tip him over if you do that! And if he gets back onto his legs again, he'll escape for sure!"

"Cool it, laddie," said hairy-chest in a <u>patronizing</u> voice. "How can he escape? We've got a rope round him, haven't we?"

"That old turtle will drag the whole lot of you away with him if you give him a chance!" cried the fisherman. "He'll drag you into the ocean, every one of you!"

"Heave!" shouted hairy-chest, ignoring the fisherman. "Heave, boys, heave!"

And now the gigantic turtle began very slowly to slide up the beach toward the hotel, toward the kitchens, toward the place where the big knives were kept. The womenfolk and the older, fatter, less athletic men followed alongside, shouting encouragement.

"Heave!" shouted the hairy-chested anchorman. "Put your back into it, fellers! You can pull harder than that!"

Suddenly I heard screams. Everyone heard them. They were screams so high-pitched, so shrill and so urgent they cut right through everything. "No-o-o-o-o!" screamed the scream. "No! No! No! No! No!"

The crowd froze. The tug-of-war men stopped tugging and the onlookers stopped shouting and every single person present turned toward the place where the screams were coming from.

Half walking, half running down the beach from the hotel were three people, a man, a woman and a small boy. They were half running because the boy was pulling the man along. The man had the boy by the wrist, trying to slow him down, but the boy kept pulling. At the same time, he was jumping and twisting and wriggling and trying to free himself from the father's grip. It was the boy who was screaming.

"Don't!" he screamed. "Don't do it! Let him go! Please let him go!"

GUIDED READING

Who is screaming and why?

The woman, his mother, was trying to catch hold of the boy's other arm to help <u>restrain</u> him, but the boy was jumping about so much, she didn't succeed.

"Let him go!" screamed the boy. "It's horrible what you're doing! Please let him go!"

GUIDED READING

What does the boy try to get the people to do?

"Stop that, David!" the mother said, still trying to catch his other arm. "Don't be so childish! You're making a perfect fool of yourself."

"Daddy!" the boy screamed. "Daddy! Tell them to let him go!"

"I can't do that, David," the father said. "It isn't any of our business."

The tug-of-war pullers remained motionless, still holding the rope with the gigantic turtle on the end of it. Everyone stood silent and surprised, staring at the boy. They were all a bit off balance now. They had the slightly hangdog[3] air of people who have

---

3. **hangdog.** Ashamed, guilty

been caught doing something that was not entirely honorable.

GUIDED READING
Why do the people have a "hangdog air"?

"Come on now, David," the father said, pulling against the boy. "Let's go back to the hotel and leave these people alone."

"I'm not going back!" the boy shouted. "I don't want to go back! I want them to let it go!"

"Now, David," the mother said.

"Beat it, kid," the hairy-chested man told the boy.

"You're horrible and cruel!" the boy shouted. "All of you are horrible and cruel!" He threw the words high and shrill at the forty or fifty adults standing there on the beach, and nobody, not even the hairy-chested man, answered him this time. "Why don't you put him back in the sea?" the boy shouted. "He hasn't done anything to you! Let him go!"

"Why don't you put him back in the sea?"

The father was embarrassed by his son, but he was not ashamed of him. "He's crazy about animals," he said, addressing the crowd. "Back home he's got every kind of animal under the sun. He talks with them."

"He loves them," the mother said.

Several people began shuffling their feet around in the sand. Here and there in the crowd it was possible to sense a slight change of mood, a feeling of uneasiness, a touch even of shame. The boy, who could have been no more than eight or nine years old, had stopped struggling with his father now. The father still held him by the wrist, but he was no longer restraining him.

"Go on!" the boy called out. "Let him go! Undo the rope and let him go!" He stood very small and erect, facing the crowd, his eyes shining like two stars and the wind blowing in his hair. He was magnificent.

GUIDED READING
What does the narrator think of the boy and why?

"There's nothing we can do, David," the father said gently. "Let's go on back."

"No!" the boy cried out, and at that moment he suddenly gave a twist and wrenched his wrist free from the father's grip. He was away like a streak, running across the sand toward the giant upturned turtle.

"David!" the father yelled, starting after him. "Stop! Come back!"

The boy dodged and swerved through the crowd like a player running with the ball, and the only person who sprang forward to <u>intercept</u> him was the fisherman. "Don't you go near that turtle, boy!" he shouted as he made a lunge for the swiftly running figure. But the boy dodged round him and kept going. "He'll bite you to pieces!" yelled the fisherman. "Stop, boy! Stop!"

GUIDED READING
Of what does the fisherman warn the boy?

But it was too late to stop him now, and as he came running straight at the turtle's head, the turtle saw him, and the huge upside-down head turned quickly to face him.

words for everyday use **in • ter • cept** (in tər sept′) *v.*, seize or stop on the way. *My dog Barney will <u>intercept</u> the tennis ball if you throw it across the yard.*

The voice of the boy's mother, the <u>stricken</u>, agonized wail of the mother's voice rose up into the evening sky. "*David!*" it cried. "*Oh, David!*" And a moment later, the boy was throwing himself onto his knees in the sand and flinging his arms around the wrinkled old neck and hugging the creature to his chest. The boy's cheek was pressing against the turtle's head, and his lips were moving, whispering soft words that nobody else could hear. The turtle became absolutely still. Even his giant flippers stopped waving in the air.

A great sigh, a long soft sigh of relief went up from the crowd. Many people took a pace or two backward, as though trying perhaps to get a little farther away from something that was beyond their understanding. But the father and mother came forward together and stood about ten feet away from their son.

GUIDED READING
Why do the people back away? What don't they understand?

"Daddy!" the boy cried out, still caressing the old brown head. "Please do something, Daddy! Please make them let him go!"

"Can I be of any help here?" said a man in a white suit who had just come down from the hotel. This, as everyone knew, was Mr. Edwards, the manager. He was a tall, beaknosed Englishman with a long, pink face. "What an extraordinary thing!" he said, looking at the boy and the turtle. "He's lucky he hasn't had his head bitten off." And to the boy, he said, "You'd better come away from there now, sonny. That thing's dangerous."

"I want them to let him go!" cried the boy, still cradling the head in his arms. "Tell them to let him go!"

"You realize he could be killed any moment," the manager said to the boy's father.

"Leave him alone," the father said.

"Rubbish," the manager said. "Go in and grab him. But be quick. And be careful."

"No," the father said.

"What do you mean, no?" said the manager. "These things are <u>lethal</u>! Don't you understand that?"

"Yes," the father said.

"Then for heaven's sake, man, get him away!" cried the manager. "There's going to be a very nasty accident if you don't."

"Who owns it?" the father said. "Who owns the turtle?"

"We do," the manager said. "The hotel has bought it."

"Then do me a favor," the father said. "Let me buy it from you."

The manager looked at the father but said nothing.

GUIDED READING
What offer does the boy's father make and why?

"You don't know my son," the father said, speaking quietly. "He'll go crazy if it's taken up to the hotel and slaughtered. He'll become hysterical."

"Just pull him away," the manager said. "And be quick about it."

"He loves animals," the father said. "He really loves them. He communicates with them."

The crowd was silent, trying to hear what was being said. Nobody moved away. They stood as though hypnotized.

"If we let it go," the manager said, "they'll only catch it again."

"Perhaps they will," the father said. "But those things can swim."

GUIDED READING
What prediction does the hotel manager make?

"I know they can swim," the manager said. "They'll catch him all the same. This is a

---

words for everyday use

strick • en (strick' ən) *adj.*, wounded; distressed. *The <u>stricken</u> marathon runner massaged her severe leg cramp before she finished the race.*

lethal (lē' thəl) *adj.*, fatal or deadly. *Luckily, vaccines and medicines have been invented to cure many formerly <u>lethal</u> illnesses.*

Rum Cay, c.1898. Winslow Homer. Worcester Art Museum and School, Massachusetts.

valuable item, you must realize that. The shell alone is worth a lot of money."

"I don't care about the cost," the father said. "Don't worry about that. I want to buy it."

The boy was still kneeling in the sand beside the turtle, caressing its head.

The manager took a handkerchief from his breast pocket and started wiping his fingers. He was not keen to let the turtle go. He probably had the dinner menu already planned. On the other hand, he didn't want another gruesome accident on his private beach this season. Mr. Wasserman and the coconut, he told himself, had been quite enough for one year, thank you very much.

The father said, "I would <u>deem</u> it a great personal favor, Mr. Edwards, if you would let me buy it. And I promise you won't regret it. I'll make quite sure of that."

The manager's eyebrows went up just a fraction of an inch. He had got the point. He was being offered a bribe. That was a different matter. For a few seconds he went on wiping his hands with the handkerchief. Then he shrugged his shoulders and said, "Well, I suppose if it will make your boy feel any better . . ."

"Thank you," the father said.

> **GUIDED READING**
> What changes the manager's mind? What sort of person is the manager?

words for everyday use

deem (dēm′) v., think, believe, judge. *Most people <u>deem</u> Mr. Ortiz one of the best teachers in our school.*

"Oh, thank you!" the mother cried. "Thank you so very much!"

"Willy," the manager said, beckoning to the fisherman.

The fisherman came forward. He looked thoroughly confused. "I never seen anything like this before in my whole life," he said. "This old turtle was the fiercest I ever caught! He fought like a devil when we brought him in! It took all six of us to land him! That boy's crazy!"

GUIDED READING

What reason does the fisherman give for not letting the turtle go?

"Yes, I know," the manager said. "But now I want you to let him go."

"Let him go!" the fisherman cried, aghast. "You mustn't ever let this one go, Mr. Edwards! He's broke the record! He's the biggest turtle ever been caught on this island! Easy the biggest! And what about our money?"

"You'll get your money."

"I got the other five to pay off as well," the fisherman said, pointing down the beach.

About a hundred yards down, on the water's edge, five black-skinned almost naked men were standing beside a second boat. "All six of us are in on this, equal shares," the fisherman went on. "I can't let him go till we got the money."

"I guarantee you'll get it," the manager said. "Isn't that good enough for you?"

"I'll underwrite[4] that guarantee," the father of the boy said, stepping forward. "And there'll be an extra bonus for all six of the fishermen just as long as you let him go at once. I mean immediately, this instant."

The fisherman looked at the father. Then he looked at the manager. "Okay," he said. "If that's the way you want it."

"There's one condition," the father said. "Before you get your money, you must promise you won't go straight out and try to catch him again. Not this evening, anyway. Is that understood?"

"Sure," the fisherman said. "That's a deal." He turned and ran down the beach, calling to the other five fishermen. He shouted something to them that we couldn't hear, and in a minute or two, all six of them came back together. Five of them were carrying long thick wooden poles.

The boy was still kneeling beside the turtle's head. "David," the father said to him gently. "It's all right now, David. They're going to let him go."

The boy looked round, but he didn't take his arms from the turtle's neck, and he didn't get up. "When?" he asked.

"Now," the father said. "Right now. So you'd better come away."

"You promise?" the boy said.

"Yes, David, I promise."

The boy withdrew his arms. He got to his feet. He stepped back a few paces.

"Stand back, everyone!" shouted the fisherman called Willy. "Stand right back, everybody, please!"

The crowd moved a few yards up the beach. The tug of war men let go the rope and moved back with the others.

Willy got down on his hands and knees and crept very cautiously up to one side of the turtle. Then he began untying the knot in the rope. He kept well out of the range of the big flippers as he did this.

When the knot was untied, Willy crawled back. Then the five other fishermen stepped

"Go, turtle, go!" . . . "Go back to the sea!"

---

4. **underwrite.** Guarantee

forward with their poles. The poles were about seven feet long and immensely thick. They wedged them underneath the shell of the turtle and began to rock the great creature from side to side on its shell. The shell had a high dome and was well shaped for rocking.

"Up and down!" sang the fishermen as they rocked away. "Up and down! Up and down! Up and down!" The old turtle became thoroughly upset, and who could blame it? The big flippers lashed the air frantically, and the head kept shooting in and out of the shell.

"Roll him over!" sang the fishermen. "Up and over! Roll him over! One more time and over he goes!"

The turtle tilted high up onto its side and crashed down in the sand the right way up.

But it didn't walk away at once. The huge brown head came out and peered cautiously around.

"Go, turtle, go!" the small boy called out. "Go back to the sea!"

The two hooded black eyes of the turtle peered up at the boy. The eyes were bright and lively, full of the wisdom of great age. The boy looked back at the turtle, and this time when the boy spoke, his voice was soft and intimate. "Goodbye, old man," he said. "Go far away this time." The black eyes remained resting on the boy for a few seconds more. Nobody moved. Then, with great dignity, the massive beast turned away and began waddling toward the edge of the ocean. He didn't hurry. He moved sedately over the sandy beach, the big shell rocking gently from side to side as he went.

The crowd watched in silence.

> **GUIDED READING**
>
> What does the boy call the turtle? Why?

He entered the water.

He kept going.

Soon he was swimming. He was in his element now. He swam gracefully and very fast, with the head held high. The sea was calm, and he made little waves that fanned out behind him on both sides, like the waves of a boat.

It was several minutes before we lost sight of him, and by then he was halfway to the horizon.

The guests began wandering back toward the hotel. They were curiously subdued. There was no joking or bantering now, no laughing. Something had happened. Something strange had come fluttering across the beach.

I walked back to my small balcony and sat down. . . . I had an uneasy feeling that this was not the end of the affair.

> **GUIDED READING**
>
> Why are the guests subdued? What strange thing had "come fluttering across the beach"?

The next morning at eight o'clock, the Jamaican girl, the one who had told me about Mr. Wasserman and the coconut, brought a glass of orange juice to my room.

"Big big fuss in the hotel this morning," she said as she placed the glass on the table and drew back the curtains. "Everyone flying about all over the place like they was crazy."

"Why? What's happened?"

"That little boy in number twelve, he's vanished. He disappeared in the night."

"You mean the turtle boy?"

"That's him," she said. "His parents is raising the roof and the manager's going mad."

> **GUIDED READING**
>
> What do you think might have happened to the boy?

 words for everyday use

in • ti • mate (in' tə mət) *adj.*, personal, private. *The film star was angry when the tabloid newspaper shared intimate details about her life.*

se • date (si dāt') *adj.*, quiet, calm. *Martin yawned and strolled across the sedate beach.* **sedately,** *adv.*

sub • dued (sub dood') *adj.*, controlled or repressed emotionally. *Celia was surprised that her parents' reaction to her bad news was so calm and subdued.*

"How long's he been missing?"

"About two hours ago his father found his bed empty. But he could've gone any time in the night I reckon."

"Yes," I said. "He could."

"Everybody in the hotel searching high and low," she said. "And a police car just arrived."

"Maybe he just got up early and went for a climb on the rocks," I said.

Her large, dark, haunted-looking eyes rested a moment on my face, then traveled away. "I do not think so," she said, and out she went.

I slipped on some clothes and hurried down to the beach. On the beach itself, two native policemen in khaki uniforms were standing with Mr. Edwards, the manager. Mr. Edwards was doing the talking. The policemen were listening patiently. In the distance, at both ends of the beach, I could see small groups of people, hotel servants as well as hotel guests, spreading out and heading for the rocks. The morning was beautiful. The sky was smoke blue, faintly glazed with yellow. The sun was up and making diamonds all over the smooth sea. And Mr. Edwards was talking loudly to the two native policemen, and waving his arms.

I wanted to help. What should I do? Which way should I go? It would be pointless simply to follow the others. So I just kept walking toward Mr. Edwards.

About then, I saw the fishing boat. The long wooden canoe with a single mast and a flapping brown sail was still some way out to sea, but it was heading for the beach. The two natives aboard, one at either end, were paddling hard. They were paddling very hard. The paddles rose and fell at such a terrific speed they might have been in a race. I

stopped and watched them. Why the great rush to reach the shore? Quite obviously they had something to tell. I kept my eyes on the boat. Over to my left, I could hear Mr. Edwards saying to the two policemen, "It is perfectly ridiculous. I can't have people disappearing just like that from the hotel. You'd better find him fast, you understand me? He's either wandered off somewhere and got lost or he's been kidnapped. Either way, it's the responsibility of the police. . . ."

GUIDED READING

Is Mr. Edwards really worried about the boy's safety? How do you know?

The fishing boat skimmed over the sea and came gliding up onto the sand at the water's edge. Both men dropped their paddles and jumped out. They started running up the beach. I recognized the one in front as Willy. When he caught sight of the manager and the two policemen, he made straight for them.

"Hey, Mr. Edwards!" Willy called out. "We just seen a crazy thing!"

The manager stiffened and jerked back his neck. The two policemen remained <u>impassive</u>. They were used to excitable people. They met them every day.

GUIDED READING

What do you think the fisherman have seen?

Willy stopped in front of the group, his chest heaving in and out with heavy breathing. The other fisherman was close behind him. Their black skins were shining with sweat.

"We been paddling full speed for a long way," Willy said, excusing his out-of-breathness. "We thought we ought to come back and tell it as quick as we can."

"Tell what?" the manager said. "What did you see?"

"It was crazy man! Absolutely crazy!"

---

words for everyday use

im • pas • sive (im pas′ iv) *adj.*, not feeling or showing emotion. *The jurors' faces were <u>impassive</u>, so it was impossible to tell how they felt about the newly introduced evidence.*

"Get on with it, Willy, for heaven's sake."

"You won't believe it," Willy said. "There ain't nobody going to believe it. Isn't that right, Tom?"

"That's right," the other fisherman said, nodding vigorously. "If Willy here hadn't been with me to prove it, I wouldn't have believed it myself!"

"Believed what?" Mr. Edwards said. "Just tell us what you saw."

"We'd gone off early," Willy said, "about four o'clock this morning, and we must've been a couple of miles out before it got light enough to see anything properly. Suddenly, as the sun comes up, we see right ahead of us, not more'n fifty yards away, we see something we couldn't believe not even with our own eyes. . . ."

"What?" snapped Mr. Edwards. "For heaven's sake, get on!"

"We sees that old monster turtle swimming away out there, the one on the beach yesterday, and we sees the boy sitting high up on the turtle's back and riding him over the sea like a horse!"

GUIDED READING

What did the fisher-man see?

"You gotta believe it!" the other fisherman cried. "I sees it too, so you gotta believe it!"

Mr. Edwards looked at the two policemen. The two policemen looked at the fishermen. "You wouldn't be having us on, would you?" one of the policemen said.

"I swear it!" cried Willy. "It's the gospel truth![5] There's this tiny little boy riding high up on the old turtle's back and his feet isn't even touching the water! He's dry as a bone and sitting there comfy and easy as could be! So we go after them. Of course we go after them. At first we try creeping up on them very quietly, like we always do when we're catching a turtle, but the boy sees us. We aren't very far away at this time, you understand. No more than from here to the edge of the water. And when the boy sees us,

he sort of leans forward as if he's saying something to that old turtle, and the turtle's head comes up and he starts swimming like the clappers of hell! Man, could that turtle go! Tom and me can paddle pretty quick when we want to, but we've no chance against that monster! No chance at all! He's going at least twice as fast as we are! Easy twice as fast, what you say, Tom?"

"I'd say he's going three times as fast," Tom said. "And I'll tell you why. In about ten or fifteen minutes, they're a mile ahead of us."

"Why on earth didn't you call out to the boy?" the manager asked. "Why didn't you speak to him earlier on, when you were closer?"

"We never stop calling out, man!" Willy cried. "As soon as the boy sees us and we're not trying to creep up on them any longer, then we start yelling. We yell everything under the sun at that boy to try and get him aboard. 'Hey boy!' I yell at him. 'You come on back with us! We'll give you a lift home! That ain't no good what you're doing there, boy! Jump off and swim while you got the chance and we'll pick you up! Go on, boy, jump! Your mammy must be waiting for you at home, boy, so why don't you come on in with us?' And once I shouted at him, 'Listen, boy! We're gonna make you a promise! We promise not to catch that old turtle if you come with us!'"

"Did he answer you at all?" the manager asked.

"He never even looks round!" Willy said. "He sits high up on that shell and he's sort of rocking backward and forward with his body just like he's urging the old turtle to go faster and faster! You're gonna lose that little boy, Mr. Edwards, unless someone

GUIDED READING

Why do you think the boy never even looked around? Why doesn't he want to return?

5. **gospel truth.** Something, such as an idea, accepted without question

gets out there real quick and grabs him away!"

The manager's normally pink face had turned white as paper. "Which way were they heading?" he asked sharply.

"North," Willy answered. "Almost due north."

"Right!" the manager said. "We'll take the speedboat! I want you with us, Willy. And you, Tom."

The manager, the two policemen and the two fishermen ran down to where the boat that was used for water skiing lay beached on the sand. They pushed the boat out, and even the manager lent a hand, wading up to his knees in his well pressed white trousers. Then they all climbed in.

I watched them go zooming off.

Two hours later, I watched them coming back. They had seen nothing.

All through that day, speedboats and yachts from other hotels along the coast searched the ocean. In the afternoon, the boy's father hired a helicopter. He rode in it himself, and they were up there three hours. They found no trace of the turtle or the boy.

For a week, the search went on, but with no result.

And now, nearly a year has gone by since it happened. In that time, there has been only one significant bit of news. A party of Americans, out from Nassau in the Bahamas, were deep-sea fishing off a large island called Eleuthera. There are literally thousands of coral reefs and small uninhabited islands in this area, and upon one of these tiny islands, the captain of the yacht saw through his binoculars the figure of a small person. There was a sandy beach on the island, and the small person was walking on the beach. The binoculars were passed around, and everyone who looked through them agreed that it was a child of some sort. There was, of course, a lot of excitement on board, and the fishing lines were quickly reeled in. The captain steered the yacht straight for the island. When they were half a mile off, they were able, through the binoculars, to see clearly that the figure on the beach was a boy, and although sunburned, he was almost certainly white-skinned, not a native. At that point, the watchers on the yacht also spotted what looked like a giant turtle on the sand near the boy. What happened next, happened very quickly. The boy, who had probably caught sight of the approaching yacht, jumped onto the turtle's back, and the huge creature entered the water and swam at great speed around the island and out of sight. The yacht searched for two hours, but nothing more was seen either of the boy or the turtle.

GUIDED READING

What is the result of the search for the boy?

GUIDED READING

What do the boy and the turtle do when they are spotted?

There is no reason to disbelieve this report. There were five people on the yacht. Four of them were Americans and the captain was a Bahamian from Nassau. All of them in turn saw the boy and the turtle through the binoculars.

To reach Eleuthera Island from Jamaica by sea, one must first travel northeast for two hundred and fifty miles and pass through the Windward Passage between Cuba and Haiti. Then one must go north-northwest for a further three hundred miles at least. This is a total distance of five hundred and fifty miles, which is a very long journey for a small boy to make on the shell of a giant turtle.

Who knows what to think of all this?

One day, perhaps, he will come back, though I personally doubt it. I have a feeling he's quite happy where he is. ■

GUIDED READING

Why might the narrator doubt that the boy will come back?

About *the*
AUTHOR

Roald Dahl (1916–1990) lived a life of adventure before becoming a writer. Born in Llandaff, South Wales, he was educated in English schools, where he did poorly. His first job involved travel across Tanganyika (now Tanzania) in Africa. During World War II, he was a fighter pilot with the Royal Air Force until injuries forced him to take a desk job in Washington, DC. There he began writing stories for American magazines. He wrote one book for children during the war but did not concentrate on writing for young readers until he began writing for his own children. Dahl was married twice and had five children. His books include *James and the Giant Peach* and *Charlie and the Chocolate Factory.*

Turtles taken off the menu in Brazil

Protection lets tourism thrive
Knight Ridder

Praia do Forte, Brazil
Sea turtles used to mean no more to Ulisses Santana, a skinny fisherman in this small coastal village, than an occasional hot meal and a bit of shark bait.

Today he reveres them. Two large concrete turtles mark the path to the small house he built selling papier-mache turtles to US and European tourists who flock here by the thousands. On most afternoons, you can find the former predator slopping strips of newspaper over a turtle-shaped mold.

"Turtles have become a big part of my life," Santana, 47, said solemnly. "Today, if I or any other fisherman sees a turtle sick on the shore, we stop and try to help it."

Santana's ecological conscience is the result of the dogged efforts of a pioneering project called Tamar—short for "tartaruga marinha," Portuguese for sea turtle. Dedicated to saving the five endangered species of sea turtles that nest on Brazil's Atlantic Coast, it has won international raves for its achievements.

In the past 18 years, Tamar employees have helped release 2.8 million turtle hatchlings to the sea. They have reeducated hunters who once raided nests, supervised a growing tourist industry, drawn key government and business support, and made the huge, clumsy sea turtle a lovable and even trendy figure in Brazil.

Last year, Tamar shared the J. Paul Getty Wildlife Conservation Award with two Asian groups. Brazilian Environment Minister Gustavo Krause has praised it as "a landmark in the history of Brazilian marine conservation."

Sea turtles have been on Earth for about 150 million years, having proved hardier than dinosaurs. But specialists said the population has been reduced by half since the 1970s, mostly due to unrestricted poaching. Today, seven of the world's eight known species of sea turtles are considered endangered.

Female turtles are easy prey when they leave the sea by night to nest. Every three years or so, they return faithfully to the same stretch of coastline, even if it means traveling thousands of miles. The lumbering creatures, which can weigh 1,000 pounds or more, fall into a kind of trance, ignoring the danger from hunters eager to devour their meat and eggs and sell their shells for jewelry.

To help protect the vulnerable giants, Tamar oversees 620 miles of coastline north and south of Praia do Forte, with 400 residents on the payroll as part-time beach monitors. Throughout the nesting season, each monitor takes charge of about 2 miles of beach, watching over eggs where they are laid or, if the nests are vulnerable to animals or birds, taking them to hatcheries.

Praia do Forte, 750 miles northeast of Rio de Janeiro, hosts Tamar's headquarters and the largest of its 21 stations along the coast. A visitors' center, equipped with a museum and several turtles in tanks, receives 300,000 guests each year, many of whom buy turtle paraphernalia, including T-shirts, hats, shorts, key chains and stuffed animals made by residents.

Tamar's founders, a married couple of oceanographers named Neca and Guy Guagni dei Marcovaldi, are considering expanding tourism. Environmentalists are watching to see if they can create a $5 million sea-turtle theme park in this fishing village of 2,000 people without sacrificing their ecological values.

Ecotourism can be a tricky business, though.

In recent years, tour operators have stuck the label on everything from simple nature walks to huge resorts to ecologically incorrect rides on dolphin-chasing speedboats.

Yet here in Praia do Forte, blessed with beautiful beaches, coral reefs and natural pools, ecotourism seems a natural, and profitable, choice. Although the streets remain unpaved, 15 hotels and several restaurants have sprouted up to serve travelers attracted by the turtles.

The revenue already has won over former predators such as Santana, the papier-mache craftsman, and Antonio Vasconcellos, 62, a fisherman whose eyes still gleam at the memory of turtle stew.

"It was truly delicious, but this is better," Vasconcellos said. "Today I never have trouble selling my fish." Moreover, he said, all 12 of his children are working at tourism-related jobs.

Investigate, *Inquire,* and Imagine

Recall: GATHERING FACTS

1a. What is the crowd staring at on the beach? What remarks do the people on the beach make?

2a. What does David want the crowd to do?

3a. Why does the hotel manager agree to sell the turtle to David's father?

→ Interpret: FINDING MEANING

1b. What do these people's remarks reveal about them?

2b. Why doesn't the turtle bite David?

3b. Why do you think David calls the turtle "old man"?

Analyze: TAKING THINGS APART

4a. Compare and contrast David and his family to the other people in the story. How are the tourists different from David and his family? How are the native Jamaicans different from David and his family?

→ Synthesize: BRINGING THINGS TOGETHER

4b. Why do you think David decides to go with the turtle?

Evaluate: MAKING JUDGMENTS

5a. When David confronts the crowd and insists that the turtle be freed, the writer indicates that "it was possible to sense a slight change of mood, a feeling of uneasiness, a touch even of shame" among the crowd. What do you think this change says about the people involved?

→ Extend: CONNECTING IDEAS

5b. Throughout history, individuals and groups of people have effected change by standing up for issues they believe in. What cause might you be willing to take a stand on?

Understanding *Literature*

THEME. A **theme** is a central idea in a literary work. Theme is different from subject or topic. The themes of a literary work are the statements the work makes about life, society, human behavior, or the world. Sometimes the theme of a work is directly stated, but most often the reader must explore the elements of the literary work—characters, setting, and plot—to discover the theme or themes. Literary works commonly address universal topics that people around the world share—things like friendship, compassion, honesty, family, and determination. What topics does "The Boy Who Talked with Animals" explore? One possible topic is the relationship between humans and wild animals. Work through the graphic organizer on the next page to develop ideas about themes associated with that topic. After you have finished, you may want to try it again using a different topic you find in the story.

Graphic Organizer

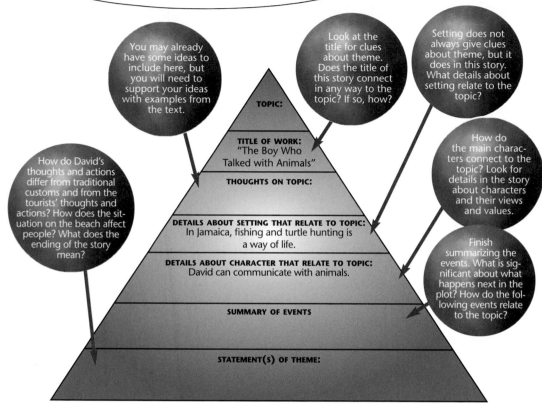

You may already have some ideas to include here, but you will need to support your ideas with examples from the text.

Look at the title for clues about theme. Does the title of this story connect in any way to the topic? If so, how?

Setting does not always give clues about theme, but it does in this story. What details about setting relate to the topic?

How do David's thoughts and actions differ from traditional customs and from the tourists' thoughts and actions? How does the situation on the beach affect people? What does the ending of the story mean?

How do the main characters connect to the topic? Look for details in the story about characters and their views and values.

Finish summarizing the events. What is significant about what happens next in the plot? How do the following events relate to the topic?

TOPIC:

TITLE OF WORK: "The Boy Who Talked with Animals"

THOUGHTS ON TOPIC:

DETAILS ABOUT SETTING THAT RELATE TO TOPIC: In Jamaica, fishing and turtle hunting is a way of life.

DETAILS ABOUT CHARACTER THAT RELATE TO TOPIC: David can communicate with animals.

SUMMARY OF EVENTS

STATEMENT(S) OF THEME:

CONFLICT. A **conflict** is a struggle between two people or things in a literary work. A struggle that takes place between a character and some outside force is called an **external conflict**. In this selection, the external conflict is David's struggle against the other characters—the crowd on the beach—to have the turtle released. David undergoes another type of conflict, too. This type of struggle is called an **internal conflict**, which takes place within a character. Given the ending of the story, what do you think was David's internal conflict?

Writer's Journal

1. Many environmental organizations exist today for the purpose of preserving birds and animals and their natural habitats. Write your own **bumper sticker** regarding the freedom and well-being of animals or a specific animal in danger of extinction.

2. Write an **itinerary** for what you think would be the ideal vacation. Include for each day the activities you would plan and the time of day each activity would occur.

3. A sequel is a continuation of a literary work or film. Write a **sequel** to the story "The Boy Who Talked with Animals."

Skill Builders

Language, Grammar, and Style

SIMPLE AND COMPOUND SENTENCES. A simple sentence consists of one main clause. A compound sentence consists of two or more main clauses connected by a semicolon or a comma and a coordinating conjunction. Then identify each of the following sentences as either simple or compound.

1. I decided to spend a few days in the West Indies.
2. I chose Jamaica, and my friend and I flew direct from London to Kingston.
3. On the evening of my second day, I sat on my little balcony.
4. The women had better taste and were dressed for the most part in pretty cotton dresses.
5. David's father wanted to set the turtle free, so he offered to buy it.
6. David begged and begged the fishermen to let the turtle go, but they refused.
7. His old wrinkled neck was straining out of its shell.
8. The crowd froze.
9. The boy dodged and swerved through the crowd like a player running with the ball, and the only person to intercept him was the fisherman.
10. The tug-of-war pullers remained motionless.

Applied English

MEMORANDUM. A memorandum, or memo, is a means of communication often used in businesses, schools, and other organizations. Imagine that you are one of the police officers in the story "The Boy Who Talked with Animals." Write a memo that you would send to other districts to let them know about the boy's disappearance. Remember to include any clues or leads that you have which might be helpful in the search. Also include a description of the boy. Refer to the Language Arts Survey 6.7, "Writing a Memo," for a sample memo format.

Study and Research & Speaking and Listening

ENDANGERED ANIMALS CLASS PROJECT. Many animals, like the sea turtle, are in danger of becoming extinct due to extensive hunting or fishing of their species or due to a loss of habitat. Using information on the Internet and from books or periodicals at the library, find a list of endangered animals and choose one you wish to study. Try to answer the following questions. What is this animal's habitat? Why is it endangered? What steps are being taken to prevent its extinction? Prepare an oral report and present your findings to the class. Then, as a class, you could select one animal that you all wish to support. Perhaps you could hold a bake sale or other fundraising activity to raise money to send to an environmental group working to save this animal. You could write letters to government representatives or letters to the editor of your local newspaper to discourage activities that cause habitat destruction. Or you could make posters to hang in your community making others aware of the animal's plight.

Reader's Journal

Describe a piece of artwork—such as an illustration in a book, a painting in a museum, or a sculpture in a park—and comment on the thoughts and feelings you have when viewing it.

Reader's Resource

- The Louvre Museum is a famous fine arts museum in Paris, France. Before it was a museum, the Louvre was a fortress and then it became the home to the kings of France. It was built in 1200.

- Paulus Potter was a Dutch painter and etcher who lived from 1625 to 1654. His father, like himself, was an artist. Paulus Potter is most famous for his paintings of animals. He was one of the first artists to paint them as prominent subjects of his compositions. Paulus died from tuberculosis at the age of 28.

Prereading

"Potter's Gray" by Joan Aiken

Reader's TOOLBOX

THEME. A **theme** is a central, or main, idea in a literary work. A theme is a statement about a topic in the literary work. For example, if a topic within a story is honesty, "honesty strengthens friendships" could be a possible theme in that story. Use the Graphic Organizer below to help you organize your findings about theme in "Potter's Gray."

FORESHADOWING. Foreshadowing is the act of hinting at events that will happen later in a poem, story, or play. As you read "Potter's Gray," look for passages that may hint at something to come.

Graphic

Divide the story into roughly six parts. Determine the main topic of each section and write it down in a slice of the pie chart. When you are finished, reread your six topics. Think about the topics and how they relate to one another. What statements can you make about these topics?

Grig and Anna go to the Louvre

POTTER'S Gray

Joan Aiken

They were hurrying through the cold, windy streets of Paris to the Louvre Museum—young

Grig Rainborrow, and the au pair[1] girl, Anna. They visited the Louvre two or three times every

week. Grig would far rather have gone to one of the parks, or walked along by the river, but Anna

had an arrangement to meet her boyfriend, Eugène, in the Louvre; so that was where they went.

---

1. **au pair.** Foreign girl who works for a family in exchange for room and board and the opportunity to learn the family's language

Alongside one of the big main galleries, where hung huge pictures of battles and shipwrecks and coronations,[2] there ran a linked series of much smaller rooms containing smaller pictures. Here visitors seldom troubled to go; often the little, rather dark rooms would be empty and quiet for a half hour at a time. Anna and Eugène liked to sit side by side, holding hands, on a couple of stiff upright metal chairs, while Grig had leave to roam at will through the nest of little rooms; though Anna tended to get fidgety if he wandered too far away, and would call him back in a cross voice, "Grig! Grig, where are you? Where have you got to? Come back here now!" She worried about kidnappers, because of the importance of Grig's father, Sir Mark. Grig would then trail back reluctantly, and Eugène would grin at him, a wide, unkind grin, and say, "*Venez vite, petit mouton!*"[3] Grig did not like being called a sheep, and he detested Eugène, who had large untrustworthy mocking black eyes, like olives; they were set so far apart in his face that they seemed able to see around the back of his head. He had a wide, oddly shaped mouth; his curling lips were thick and strongly curved like the crusts of farmhouse bread, and his mouth was always twisting about; it never kept still. Grig had once made some drawings of Eugène's mouth, but they looked so nasty that he tore them up before Anna could see them; he thought they might make her angry.

"Hurry up!" said Anna, jerking at Grig's hand. "We're going to be late. Eugène will be waiting; he'll be annoyed." Grig did not see why it would hurt Eugène to wait a few minutes, he never seemed to have anything to

GUIDED READING

Why do Anna and Grig go the Louvre two or three times each week?

GUIDED READING

How does Grig feel about Eugène?

do but meet Anna in the Louvre museum. That was where they had met in the first place.

Standing waiting to cross the Rue de Rivoli at a traffic light, Grig was sorry that he lacked the courage to say, "Why do we have to meet hateful Eugène almost every day?"

But he knew that his courage was not up to that. Anna could be quite fierce. She had intense blue eyes the color of marbles, but they weren't very good for observing. Grig noticed a million more things than Anna did, he was always saying, "Look, Anna—" And she would say, "Oh, never mind that! Come along!" But the stare of her eyes was so piercing when she lost her temper, they were like two gimlets[4] boring right through him, and she had such a way of hissing, "You *stupid* child!" making him feel pulpy,[5] breathless, and flattened, that he did not say what he felt about Eugène. He kept quiet and waited for the lights to change, while French traffic poured furiously past in a torrent of steel, rubber, and glass.

"Come on! There's a gap—we can go," said Anna, and jerked at Grig's hand again.

They hurled themselves out, in company with a French girl who had a small child in a stroller and, bounding on the end of his lead, a large Alsatian dog that the girl could only just control. As they crossed, the stroller veered one way, the dog tugged the other—it seemed amazing that the trio had survived among the traffic up to this day. A tall thin white-haired man in pink-tinted glasses

GUIDED READING

Why does Grig keep quiet about his feelings for Eugène?

---

2. **coronations.** Crowning ceremonies
3. **"Venez vite, petit mouton!"** (French) Hurry up, little sheep!
4. **gimlets.** Small tools for boring holes
5. **pulpy.** Soft and shapeless

observed their <u>plight</u>, and turned to give the girl a helping hand with her <u>wayward</u> stroller; a sharp gust of wind blew just at that moment, the dog tugged, the stroller swerved crazily, and the pink-tinted glasses were jerked off the man's face to spin away into the middle of the road, just as a new wave of traffic surged forward.

With a cry of <u>anguish</u>, the white-haired man tilted the stroller over the curb, hurriedly passing its handle into the mother's grasp, and then turned back to retrieve his glasses. Too late—and a terrible mistake: a motorcyclist, twisting aside to avoid him, collided with a taxi, and a Citroën[6] following too close behind the cycle struck the elderly man on the shoulder and flung him onto the sidewalk, where he lay on his face without moving.

GUIDED READING

How does the old man get hit by a car?

If he had been wearing his glasses at that moment, they would have been smashed, Grig thought.

The mother with the stroller let out a horrified wail, "*Oh, oh, c'est le vieux Professeur Bercy!*"[7] and she ran to kneel by him, while, out in the road, all was confusion, with brakes squawking and horns braying, and a general tangle and snarl of traffic coming too suddenly to a stop.

Police, blowing their whistles, were on the spot in no time—there are always plenty of police near the Louvre.

"Come along, Grig!" snapped Anna. "We don't want to get mixed up in all this, your father wouldn't be a bit pleased—" for Sir Mark, Grig's father, was the British Ambassador[8] in Paris. But it wasn't easy to get away; already the police were swarming around, asking everybody there if they had seen the accident.

"Oh, I do *hope* the poor man is not badly hurt!" cried the distraught young mother. "It is Professor Bercy, the physicist—I have often seen his face in the papers and on TV—It was so kind of him to take my baby carriage—oh, it will be terrible if he is badly injured, and all because he stopped to help me—"

GUIDED READING

Who is the old man who was hit by a car?

A gendarme[9] was talking to Anna, and, while she snappishly but accurately gave an account of what had happened, Grig slipped out into the street and picked up the professor's glasses, which he had noticed lying—astonishingly, quite unharmed—about six feet out from the edge of the road, among a glittering sprinkle of somebody's smashed windshield.

"*Grig! Will* you come out of there!" yelled Anna, turning from the cop to see where he had got to, and she yanked his arm and hustled him away in the direction of the Louvre entrance, across the big quadrangle,[10] before he could do anything about giving the pink-tinted glasses to one of the policemen.

"But I've got these—"

"Oh, who cares? The man's probably dead, he won't want them again. If he hears that you got mixed up in a street accident your father will be hopping mad. And Eugène will be upset — he'll be wondering where we've got to."

---

6. **Citroën.** French-made car
7. **"*c'est le vieux Professeur Bercy!*"** (French) It is old Professor Bercy!
8. **Ambassador.** Government representative in another country
9. **gendarme.** French police officer
10. **quadrangle.** Four-sided enclosure surrounded by buildings

---

plight (plīt′) *n.*, bad condition or state. *Henry was in a lot of trouble, but no one knew of his <u>plight</u>.*

way • ward (wā′ wərd) *adj.*, following one's own foolish inclinations. *The <u>wayward</u> boy never listened to anyone's advice.*

an • guish (aŋ′ gwish) *n.*, extreme distress or pain. *Mr. Glim told of the <u>anguish</u> he felt after his wife died.*

It seemed to Grig that the last of these three statements was the real reason why Anna didn't want to hang around at the scene of the accident. He pulled back from her grasp and twisted his head round to see if an ambulance had arrived yet;

GUIDED READING

Why does Grig think Anna doesn't want to hang around at the scene of the accident?

yes, there it went, shooting across the end of the square with flashing lights. So at least the poor man would soon be in the hospital.

Well, it was true that if he was unconscious—and he had looked dreadfully limp—he wouldn't be needing his glasses right away.

Maybe he only wore them outdoors.

I'll ask mother to see that he gets them, Grig decided. She'll be able to find out which hospital he has gone to, and make sure that the glasses are taken to him. Mother was fine at things like that; she always knew what must be done, and who was the best person to do it. She understood what was important. And—Grig thought—the glasses must be *very* important to Professor Bercy, or he would hardly have risked his life in the traffic to try to recover them. Could they be his only pair? Surely not. If he was such an important scientist, you'd think he'd have dozens of pairs!

The glasses were now in Grig's jacket pocket, safely cradled in his left hand; the right hand was still in the iron grip of Anna, who was hauling him along as if the Deluge had begun and they were the last two passengers for the Ark.[11]

GUIDED READING

What does Grig do with the glasses?

Eugène was there before them, waiting in the usual room; but, surprisingly, he didn't seem annoyed at their lateness, just listened to Anna's breathless explanation with his wide frog-smile, said it was quite a little excitement they'd had, and did the man bleed a lot? Then, even more surprisingly, he produced a small patissier's[12] cardboard carton, tied with shiny string, and said to Grig,

"Here, *mon mouton,* this is for you. For your *petit manger.* A cake."

Grig generally brought an apple to the Louvre. Indeed, he had one today, in his right-hand pocket. Eugène called the apple Grig's *petit manger*—his little snack. While Anna and Eugène sat and talked, Grig was in the habit of eating his apple slowly and <u>inconspicuously</u>, as he walked around looking at the pictures.

"Go on," repeated Eugène. "The cake's for you."

Grig did not want to appear rude or doubtful or suspicious at this unexpected gift; but just the same he *was* suspicious. Eugène had never before showed any friendly feelings; the things he said to Grig were generally sharp or spiteful or teasing; why, today,

GUIDED READING

Why is Grig suspicious of Eugène's gift?

should he have brought this piece of patisserie—rather expensive it looked, too, done up so carefully with a gold name on the side of the box. Eugène was always shabby, in worn jeans and a rubbed black-leather jacket, and his sneakers looked as if they let in water. Why should he suddenly bring out such an offering?

"Say thank you!" snapped Anna. "It's very kind of Eugène to have brought you a cake!"

---

11. **Deluge...Ark.** Biblical reference to the story of Noah and the Ark
12. **patissier's.** Pastry shop's

---

words for everyday use

in • con • spic • u • ous (in kən spi′ kyə wəs) *adj.,* unnoticeable. *Tip picked an <u>inconspicuous</u> spot in which to hide his treasure.*

"Thank you," said Grig. He added doubtfully, "But I don't think people are allowed to eat in here."

"Oh, don't be silly. Who's going to see? Anyway, you always eat your apple—here, I'll undo the string."

It was tied in a hopelessly tight, hard knot—Anna nibbled through it with her strong white teeth, and Eugène made some low-voiced remark, in French too quick for Grig to catch, which made her flush and laugh, though she looked rather cross. Once the string was undone, the little waxed box opened out like a lily to <u>disclose</u> a gooey glistening brown cake in a fluted paper cup.

"Aren't you lucky; it's a rum baba,"[13] said Anna.

As it happened, a rum baba was Grig's least favorite kind of cake: too syrupy, too squashy, too scented. He wasn't greatly surprised, or disappointed; he would have expected Eugène to have a nasty taste in cakes, or anything else. He thanked Eugène again, with great politeness, then strolled away from the pair at a slow, casual pace, looking at the pictures on the walls as he went.

GUIDED READING

Why isn't Grig surprised that Eugène's gift is a rum baba?

"Eat that up fast, now, or it'll drip syrup all over everywhere," Anna called after him sharply, and then she began talking to Eugène, telling him some long story, <u>gabbling</u> it out, while he listened without seeming to take in much of what she said, his eyes <u>roving</u> after Grig, who wandered gently into the next room, and then into the one after that, wondering, as he went, if it would be

GUIDED READING

What is Eugène doing while Anna talks to him?

possible to slip the pastry into a litter bin without being noticed.

"Don't go too far now—" he could hear Anna's voice, fainter in the distance behind him.

As usual, there weren't any other people in the suite of small dark rooms. Grig supposed that the pictures here were not thought to be very important, though some of them were his particular favorites.

There was one of an astronomer with a globe; Grig always liked to look at that; and another of a woman making lace on a pillow; she wore a yellow dress, and had a contented, absorbed expression that reminded Grig of his mother while she was working on her embroidery. There was a picture that he liked of a bowl and a silver mug, with some apples; and

GUIDED READING

What is Grig reminded of while looking at the woman making lace on a pillow?

another of a china jug with bunches of grapes and a cut-up pomegranate[14] that he deeply admired. Grig intended to be a painter himself by and by; he always stood before this picture for a long, long time, wondering how many years it took to learn to paint like that—so that you could actually see the bloom on the grapes and the shine on the pearl handle of the knife, and the glisten on the red seeds of the pomegranate. Then there was a picture of a boy about Grig's age, sitting at a desk, playing with a spinning top. The boy was really a bit old to be playing with a childish toy such as a top; you could see that he had just come across it, maybe among some forgotten things at the back of his desk,

---

13. **rum baba.** Rich cake soaked in rum and sugar syrup
14. **pomegranate.** Thick-skinned reddish fruit full of seeds. People eat the red juicy flesh around the seeds.

---

words for everyday use

dis • close (dis klōz′) v., reveal. *Ms. Hartmon was unable to disclose that private information.*

gab • ble (ga′ bəl) v., talk fast or foolishly. *Ned gabbled constantly about that silly cartoon.*

rove (rōv′) v., roam. *I roved through town, looking for something to do.*

The Boy with a Spinning Top, 1741. Jean-Baptiste Chardin. Louvre, Paris, France.

She paused beside Grig and glanced out through the window into the big central courtyard. What she saw there seemed to surprise her very much and arouse her disapproval too. She let out several exclamations—*"Oh, la la! Tiens! Quel horreur!"*[15]— put on a pair of long-distance glasses to take a better look at what was going on outside, stared frowningly for a moment or two more, then muttered some grumbling comment to herself, in which Grig caught several references to Napoleon III;[16] then, shaking her head in a <u>condemning</u> manner, she went stomping on her way.

and had taken it out to give it a spin because he was bored and had nothing better to do just then; he was watching it thoughtfully, consideringly, in fact he had the same intent expression as that on the face of the woman working at the lace on her pillow. Perhaps, thought Grig, that boy grew up to be some kind of scientist or mathematician (he must have lived long ago, for he wore an old-fashioned satin jacket) and at the sight of the spinning top, some interesting idea about speed or circles or patterns or time had come into his head. The boy with the top was one of Grig's favorite pictures, and he always stood in front of it for quite a while.

Then he was about to move on to his very favorite of all, when his attention was caught by an old lady, who had been walking through the rooms in the <u>contrary</u> direction.

After waiting until she was out of sight, Grig put a knee on the leather window seat and hoisted himself up to look out, in order to see what was happening outside that aroused such feelings of outrage in the old girl.

What he saw in the quadrangle made him surprised that he had not noticed it as they made their way in; but he remembered that then he had been looking back for the ambulance, and worrying about Professor Bercy's glasses; that must have been why he did not take in the oddness of the scene.

GUIDED READING

Why hadn't Grig noticed what was happening in the quadrangle on his way into the museum?

---

15. *"Oh, la la! Tiens! Quel horreur!"* (French) Oh! Look at that! What a shame!
16. **Napoleon III.** French emperor 1852–1871

---

words for everyday use

con • trary (kän′ trer ē) *adj.,* opposite. *Whenever Jill spoke, her sister cut in saying something <u>contrary</u>.*

con • demn (kən dem′) *v.,* pronounce guilty; doom. *Horace was <u>condemned</u> by the principal and suspended for shooting spitballs.* **condemning,** *adj.*

A wooden barricade had been built around the central part of the quadrangle, and it seemed that digging was going on inside this fence, a big excavator with its grabbing jaw could be seen swinging its head back and forth, dumping soil and rubble in a truck that stood by the paling.[17]

Then, outside the barrier—and this was probably what had shocked the old lady—three fullsize chestnut trees lay, crated up, on huge towing trucks, the sort that usually carry heavy machinery, or sardinelike batches of new cars. The trees all had their leaves on, and their roots too; the roots had been carefully bundled up in great cylindrical containers made from wooden slats—like flower tubs, only a million times bigger, Grig thought. It appeared that the trees had been dug up from the central area and were being taken away, perhaps to be replanted somewhere else, just like geraniums or begonias in the public gardens. What on earth could Napoleon III have to do with it? Grig wondered, thinking of the old lady. Had he planted the trees, perhaps? They looked as if they could easily be over a hundred years old. Napoleon III had done a lot to beautify Paris, Grig knew. Perhaps among the roots of the trees, now <u>parceled</u> up like bean sprouts, there might be coins, francs and centimes[18] from 1850, or medals or jewels, or all kinds of other relics. I'd love to have a closer look at them, thought Grig, and his left hand happened to touch Professor Bercy's sunglasses in his jacket pocket at the moment this thought came to him; he absentmindedly pulled out the glasses and perched them on his nose.

> **GUIDED READING**
>
> What does Grig see that he figures is what shocked the old lady?

They fitted him quite well. He could feel that the earpieces were made out of some light, strong, springy material that clung, of its own accord, not uncomfortably, to the sides of his head. The lenses, squarish in shape, were very large; in fact they almost entirely covered his face, so that he could see nothing except through their slightly pinkish screen. For a moment they misted over, after he had put them on; then they began to clear, and he looked through them, out of the window and into the courtyard.

For years and years and years afterward, Grig went over and over that scene in his memory, trying to recall every last detail of it. When he had grown up, and become a painter, he painted it many times—the whole scene, or bits of it, small fragments, different figures from it—over and over and over again. "Ah, that's a Rainborrow," people would say, walking into a gallery, from thirty, forty feet away, "You can always tell a Rainborrow."

> **GUIDED READING**
>
> What would Grig do in the future?

What did he see? He would have found it almost impossible to give a description in words. "*Layers*," he thought. "It's like seeing all the layers together. Different levels. People now—and people *then*. People when? People right on back to the beginning. How many thousands of years people must have been doing things on this bit of ground! And, there they all are!"

As well as the people *then*, he could see the people *now*; several students, a boy riding a bicycle, a policeman, and the three great chestnut trees, tied on their trucks like

---

17. **paling.** Picket fence
18. **francs and centimes.** French coins

par • cel (pär′ səl) *v.*, wrap. *I will <u>parcel</u> my belongings and leave the hotel.* **parceled,** *adj.*

invalids on stretchers. And, sure enough, in among the roots of the trees, Grig could catch a glimpse of all kinds of objects, knobby and dusty, solid and sparkling; perhaps that was what Professor Bercy had been coming to look at? The glasses must have had a fairly strong magnifying power, as well as this other mysterious ability they had, to show the layers of time lying one behind another.

What else could they show?

The Piebald Horse, 1653. Paulus Potter. Louvre, Paris, France.

GUIDED READING

What do the glasses allow Grig to see?

Grig turned, carefully, for he felt a little dizzy, to look inward at the room behind him. The first thing that caught his gaze, as he turned, was Eugène's gift, the rum baba, which he still clutched awkwardly in his right hand. Through Professor Bercy's pink-tinted glasses the cake looked even nastier than it had when seen by the naked eye. It was darker in color—the dark blood-brown, oozy and horrible; embedded in the middle of it he now saw two pills, one pink, one yellow. The pills hadn't been visible before, but through the pink lenses Grig could see them quite distinctly; sunk in the wet mass of dough they were becoming a bit mushy at the edges, beginning to wilt into the surrounding cake.

GUIDED READING

What does Grig see in his cake from Eugène?

Why should Eugène want to give him cake with pills in it? What in the world was he up to? With a jerk of disgust, Grig dropped the little patisserie box on the floor. Nobody else was in the room. With his heel, he slid box and cake out of view under the window seat, then wiped his fingers—the syrup had already started to ooze through the carton—wiped his fingers vigorously, again and again, on a tissue. He glanced behind him to make sure that his action had not been seen by Anna or Eugène—but no, thank goodness, they were still safely out of sight, several rooms away.

GUIDED READING

What does Grig do with the cake?

Turning in the opposite direction, Grig walked quickly into the next room, where his favorite picture of all hung.

This was a painting of a horse, by an artist called Potter. Grig always thought of it as Potter's Gray. The picture was not at all large: perhaps one foot by eighteen inches, if as much; and the horse was not particularly handsome, rather the contrary. It was a gray, with some blobby dark dappled spots. Grig could hardly have said why he liked it so much. He was sure that the painter must have

GUIDED READING

Who is Potter?

been very fond of the horse. Perhaps it belonged to him. Perhaps he called it Gray, and always gave it an apple or a carrot before sitting down with his easel and his tubes or pots of paint. The picture was over three hundred years old; a label said that Potter had been a Dutchman who lived from 1625 to 1654. He was only twenty-nine when he died, not old. Mother, who knew all sorts of things, once told Grig that Potter died of tuberculosis,[19] which could have been cured these days. Grig thought that very sad. If Potter had lived now, he could have painted many more pictures of horses, instead of having his life cut off in the middle.

Anyway, this Gray was as good a horse as you could wish to meet, and, on each visit to the Louvre, Grig always walked to where his portrait hung, on the left of the doorway, between door and window, and—after first checking to make certain no one else was in the room—stood staring until his whole mind was filled with pleasure, with the whole <u>essence</u> of the horse; then he would pull the apple out of his pocket, take a bite of it himself, hold the rest up on the palm of his hand as you should when feeding a horse, and say, "Have a bite, Gray."

He did so now. But this time, something happened that had never happened before.

Gray put a gentle, silvery muzzle with soft nostrils sprouting white hairs out of the picture *and took the apple from Grig's hand.*

Then he withdrew his head into the frame and ate the apple with evident satisfaction.

Grig gasped. He couldn't help it—he was so pleased that he felt warm tears spring into his

> **GUIDED READING**
> What happens when Grig, wearing the glasses, offers the apple to the horse?

eyes. Blinking them away, he looked rapidly around the small gallery—and saw, without any particular surprise, that every picture was alive, living its life in its own way as it must have done when the artist painted it: a fly was buzzing over the grapes that lay beside the china jug, some men were hauling down the sail of a ship, the woman, winding the bobbins of her lace pillow, carefully finished off one and began another. Then she looked up and gave Grig an absent-minded smile.

There were other people in the room too, outside the pictures, walking about—people in all kinds of different clothes. Grig wished, from the bottom of his heart, that he could hear what they were saying, wished he could speak to them and ask questions—but Professor Bercy's glasses were only for seeing, they couldn't help him to hear. You'd want headphones too, Grig thought, straining his ears nonetheless to try and catch the swish of a dress, the crunch of Gray finishing the apple—but all he heard was the angry note of Anna's voice, "*Grig!* Where in the *world* have you *got* to?" and the clack of her wooden-soled shoes on the polished gallery floor as she came hurrying in search of him. Grig couldn't resist glancing back at Potter's horse—but the apple was all finished, not a sign of it remained—then he felt Anna's fingers close on his wrist like pincers, and she was hurrying him toward the exit, angrily gabbling into his ear. "What in heaven's name have you been *doing* with yourself all this

> **GUIDED READING**
> What does Grig hear when he's trying to hear the sounds he can see while wearing the glasses?

---

19. **tuberculosis.** Contagious disease that affects the lungs

es • sence (es′ səns) *n.*, permanent, ultimate nature of a thing, as opposed to its immediate existence. *The <u>essence</u> of the environment is more than trees, grass, water, and animals.*

time? Can't you see it's started to rain and we'll be late, we'll have to take a taxi—"

All this time she was hurrying Grig through one gallery after another, and Eugène was walking beside them, looking a little amused, and calmly indifferent to Anna's scolding of her charge.

Grig himself was still dizzy, shaken, confused, and distracted. Firstly, he would have liked to stop and stare with <u>minute</u> attention at each of the huge canvases they were now passing in the main galleries. Because—just *look* at what was happening in that coronation scene with Emperor Napoleon putting the crown on his queen's head, and the Pope behind him—and those people struggling to keep on the raft which was heaving about among huge waves—but some of them were dead, you could see—and the lady lying twiddling her fingers on a sofa—and the man on a horse— they were all alive, it was like looking through a series of windows at what was going on beyond the glass.

But also, Grig was absolutely horrified at what he saw when he looked across Anna at Eugène; the sight of Eugène's face was so extremely frightening that Grig's eyes instantly flicked away from it each time; but then he felt compelled to look back in order to convince himself of what he had seen.

All the *workings* were visible: inside the skull the brain—inside the brain, memory, feelings, hopes and plans. The memories were all dreadful ones, the hopes and plans were all wicked. It was like, from the height of a satellite, watching a great storm rage

> **GUIDED READING**
> What would Grig rather be doing than hurrying out of the Louvre?

> **GUIDED READING**
> What does Grig see when he looks at Eugène?

across a whole continent; you could see the whirl of cloud, the flash of lightning; you could guess at uprooted trees, flooded rivers, and smashed buildings. You could see that Eugène planned to do an enormous amount of damage; and it was plain that, here and now, he hated Grig and had a plan about him; what kind of a plan Grig didn't exactly know, but little details of it that came to him in flashes made him shudder.

"Come on, hurry up," said Anna, buttoning her raincoat, when they reached the entrance lobby. "Button your jacket, put your scarf around. Eugène's getting a taxi, and he'll drop us at the embassy and go on—"

"*No!*" said Grig. He didn't intend going with Eugène in any taxi. And he knew well that Eugène had no plans at all to drop them at the embassy.

> **GUIDED READING**
> Why won't Grig go anywhere with Eugène?

"What do you mean, *no?*" said Anna furiously. "What in the world are you *talking* about? Don't act like a baby. You'll do as I say, or else—"

"*No,*" repeated Grig <u>doggedly</u>, and yanked at the wrist which she still grasped in an unshakable grip. He looked at Anna and saw that she was not wicked like Eugène, but stupid all through, solid like a block of marble or plaster. It would be useless to argue with her and say,

> **GUIDED READING**
> What does Grig see when he looks at Anna?

"Eugène is bad. He has some awful plan. Why did he put pills in that cake?"

Grig was still terribly confused and distracted by the complicated sights, the layers and layers of different happenings that were taking place all around him. But at last he realized what he must do. With his free

---

words for everyday use

mi • nute (mī nüt') *adj.*, marked by close attention to details. *Celia's showed <u>minute</u> care in her peer evaluation of my essay.*

dog • ged (däg' əd) *adj.*, marked by stubborn determination. *Marsha persistently followed a grueling, <u>dogged</u> exercise routine.* **doggedly,** *adv.*

hand he pulled the pink-tinted glasses off his face, and said, "Please, Anna. Put these on for a moment."

"Oh, don't be so *silly!* Why in the world should I? Where ever did you *get* those glasses?" She had forgotten all about the accident, and Professor Bercy. "What is this, anyway, some kind of silly joke?"

"Please put them on, Anna. If you don't—" What could he do, what could he possibly do? Then, with a gulp of relief, he remembered some practical advice that his mother had once given him. "It sounds babyish," she had said, "but if ever you are in a tight corner, *yell*. It attracts attention; people will come running, and that will give you time to think, so never mind that you may feel a fool, just do it, just yell."

> **GUIDED READING**
>
> What advice had Grig's mother given him?

"If you don't put them on," said Grig, "I shall scream so loud that people will think I've gone mad. I mean it, Anna."

"I think you already *have* gone mad," she said, but she looked at him, saw that he did mean it, and put on the glasses. At that moment Eugène came back through the glass entrance door, his black leather jacket shiny with rain, and on his face a big false smile. Without the glasses, Grig could no longer see the evil workings of Eugène's brain—which was in every way a relief—but just the same, he knew exactly how false that smile was.

"Okay," said Eugène, "*venez vite, tous les deux*—"[20] and then Anna, looking at him, started to scream. Her scream was far, far louder than any yell that Grig could have raised, he had no need even

> **GUIDED READING**
>
> What does Anna do when she sees Eugène while wearing the glasses?

to open his mouth. The smile dropped from Eugène's face like paper off a wet window, he stared at Anna first with shock, then with rage. "*Come* on, girl, what *is* this?" he said, trying to grab her hand, but she twisted away from him, still shrieking like a machine that has blown off its safety valve. "No—no—no—get away—get away—you're *horrible*—"

By this time, as Mother had <u>prophesied</u>, people were running toward them; people were staring and exclaiming and pushing close, trying to discover what was the matter with Anna. Now Eugène's nerve suddenly broke. He let out a couple of wicked, hissing swearwords, turned on his heel, went out the glass doors, and vanished from view. At the same moment Anna, furiously dragging the tinted glasses from her face, flung them on the stone floor as if they were poisoned, trampled them into fragments, and burst into hysterical sobs.

> **GUIDED READING**
>
> What does Anna do with the glasses?

"Would you please telephone my father?" Grig said to a uniformed woman who seemed like someone in a position of authority. "I think my *gouvernante*[21] has been taken ill. My father is the British Ambassador," and he gave her the embassy number.

So they went home in a taxi after all.

"Please, can you take me to see Professor Bercy in the hospital?" Grig asked his mother, the next day, when Anna was under sedatives and the care of a doctor, and a new au pair girl was being advertised for, and in the meantime Lady Julia Rainborrow was leaving

> **GUIDED READING**
>
> What happens to Anna?

---

20. *venez vite, tous les deux.* (French) Hurry up, both of you
21. *gouvernante.* (French) governess: woman or girl who supervises children

---

words for everyday use

prophesy (prä′ fə sī) *v.*, predict. *Grant <u>prophesied</u> that math would be easy this year, and he was right.*

her ambassadorial duties to take her son for an airing.

But she said, "Darling, no; I'm afraid I can't. It was on the news this morning. He died last night in the hospital; he never recovered consciousness."

"Oh," said Grig. "Oh."

He had dreaded having to tell Professor Bercy that his glasses had been smashed; but this was far worse.

I wonder if they *were* his only pair? Grig thought, plodding along the street beside Lady Julia. Or if other people—the other scientists who worked with him—knew about them too?

"Where would you like to go?" Grig's mother asked him. "It's not a very nice day— I'm afraid it looks like rain again."

"Can we go to the Louvre?"

"Are you sure you want to go there?" she said doubtfully.

GUIDED READING

Where does Grig want to go with his mother?

"Yes, I would like to," said Grig, and so they walked in the direction of the Louvre, finding it hard to talk to each other, Grig very unhappy about Professor Bercy, dead before he had finished his life's work—and what work!—while Lady Julia worried about Grig. But what can you do? You can't look after somebody twenty-four hours a day. Ambassadors' sons have to take their chances, like everybody else.

Going quickly through the suite of dark little galleries, Grig came to the picture of Potter's Gray. He stood and stared at the dappled horse, very lovingly, very intently, and thought: Yesterday I gave you an apple, and you put out your head and took it from my hand, and I stroked your nose. I shall come back tomorrow, and next week, and the week after, and that will never, never happen again. But it *did* happen, and I remember it.

Do you remember it, Gray?

He thought that the gray horse looked at him very kindly.

Respond *to the* SELECTION

What would you have liked to look at if you had the glasses that Grig had a chance to wear?

About *the* AUTHOR

Born in 1924 in Sussex, England, **Joan Aiken** grew up telling stories. She and her brother exchanged stories about made-up fantasy lands as they walked in the countryside near the family's home. Aiken was fascinated with mysterious places and happenings and loved to read stories by Charles Dickens, an author whose style rubbed off on her, as well as books by Rudyard Kipling, Edgar Allan Poe, and Jane Austen.

When Aiken died in 2004, she had written a total of 92 books, 65 of them for young people. She strove to write material that made young people think, that treated them respectfully, and that included the problems and dilemmas they faced in real life. Her two children were her favorite reviewers and critics.

Investigate, Inquire, and Imagine

Recall: GATHERING FACTS → **Interpret:** FINDING MEANING

1a. What does Grig notice about Eugène's eyes?

1b. How is this important later in the story?

2a. Because Professor Bercy risks his life to try to recover them, Grig realizes what about the glasses?

2b. How does this turn out to be true?

3a. What happens to Professor Bercy?

3b. What does this mean to Grig? Why is it far worse than having to tell Professor Bercy that his glasses had been smashed?

4a. Where does Grig want to go with his mother?

4b. Why would she be surprised by this?

Analyze: TAKING THINGS APART → **Synthesize:** BRINGING THINGS TOGETHER

5a. In what ways have the glasses helped Grig to see life differently?

5b. Do you predict Grig will continue to see life differently without the glasses? Why, or why not?

Perspective: LOOKING AT OTHER VIEWS → **Empathy:** SEEING FROM INSIDE

6a. What do you think Eugène had been planning to do with Grig? Why is he interested in Anna?

6b. What would you have done about Eugène if you were Anna or Grig?

Understanding Literature

THEME. A **theme** is a central, or main, idea in a literary work. A theme is a statement about a topic in the literary work. With a partner, brainstorm and list some possible themes, based on the topics in your graphic organizer. Choose the one you think is the best to share with the class. As a class, discuss the theme ideas suggested and come up with a final theme that everyone can agree with.

FORESHADOWING. Foreshadowing is the act of hinting at events that will happen later in a poem, story, or play. Skimming, reread the story to locate examples of foreshadowing. You may find foreshadowing where you didn't notice it the first time you read the story. What effect does the use of foreshadowing have on the story?

Writer's Journal

1. List three alternative **titles** for "Potter's Gray."

2. Imagine you are a pastry baker moving to Paris. You do not care for traditional pastries such as rum baba and want to introduce different treats in your new pastry shop. Write a **menu** of items you will sell there.

3. Pretend you are Anna, recovering in the hospital after seeing Eugène's mind at work. Write a short **diary entry** explaining what you saw and how it made you feel.

Skill Builders

Collaborative Learning

FINDING SOLUTIONS. You have just learned that your city or town is planning to clear away trees that are more than 100 years old in order to add more parking. In groups of four or five, list three or four concrete ideas you could carry out to try to stop the plans. For example, you could hold a protest, or you could write a letter to the city council, explaining your concerns. Discuss the pros and cons of each idea, using a chart like the one below your plan. Choose one of your ideas and make a detailed plan of how you would carry it out.

Study and Research

STUDYING ART. Use library resources or take a visit to a museum to study a piece of art. Jot down your interpretations of the piece and note how it makes you feel and the mood it sets. Then find out as much as you can about the piece. When was it created? Who is the artist? What else has the artist done? What impact has the piece had on the public? Write up a short report on your findings. Remember to include your own opinions as well as the factual information you find.

PROS AND CONS		
Ideas to stop tree destruction		
	Pros	**Cons**
1		
2		
3		
4		

for your READING LIST

The View from Saturday by E. L. Konigsburg tells the story of four students who surprise the entire state of New York by becoming the first sixth-grade team ever to win the Academic Bowl. Through separate narrations, Noah, Nadia, Ethan, and Julian tell how they came to be part of this champion team. The stories may seem unrelated, but you will see how they, and the characters, fit together like the pieces of a jigsaw puzzle. Drawn together by common threads—and a little bit of magic, the four students, who call themselves "The Souls," decide to take on the project of helping their teacher, Mrs. Olinski, to "stand on her own two feet" after a car accident leaves her confined to a wheelchair. Mrs. Olinski thinks that she has chosen "The Souls" to be her Academic Bowl team, but the truth is actually a lot more complicated than that.

BOOK CLUB

After everyone in the group has finished reading *The View from Saturday*, decide on a time to meet for discussion. Before you meet, you might want to distribute a list of discussion prompts, such as the ones given here, so the members of your group have a chance to think about the questions and make note of passages in the book that might be helpful in answering the questions.

- Did the story seem believable to you? Why, or why not? You might want to focus on the plot, the characters, and the setting.
- Discuss the ways that Noah, Ethan, Nadia, Julian, and their families are interconnected. List as many connections as you can.
- What problems do each of "The Souls" face throughout the book? How do they solve these problems?
- How does Mrs. Olinski feel about returning to teaching? What challenges does she face?
- What do you think motivates Hamilton Knapp to behave the way he does?
- Why is it so important to "The Souls" to win the state Academic Bowl championship?
- How did Mr. Singh know that Mrs. Olinski almost selected Hamilton Knapp to be a member of the team, even though she never told anyone about this?
- Discuss the conversation between Mr. Singh and Mrs. Olinski on the way home from the championship round. According to Mr. Singh, what journey did each member of "The Souls" make? Do you agree with Mr. Singh?
- Did Mrs. Olinski choose the team, or did they choose her? Explain.
- What does the title "The View from Saturday" mean?

Other books you may want to read:
A Jar of Dreams by Yoshiko Uchida
Tangerine by Edward Bloor

> "Stuff your eyes with wonder. Live as if you'd drop dead in ten seconds. See the world. It's more fantastic than any dream made up or paid for in factories."
>
> —Ray Bradbury

Examining the Model

In the opening of this essay the writer introduces his two favorite authors and then identifies two websites for his authors on the Internet. The main idea for his paper is stated in the last sentence of the opening: "Both of these sites have background information on the authors and their books, links to other sites, and extra information that a person wanting to know more about an author would want to read."

Now the reader knows what the paper will be about. What do you expect the writer to tell you in the body of the paper?

In the body of the piece, the writer compares and contrasts the two sites using the categories listed in his main idea: background information

continued on page 599

Guided Writing

COMPARING AND CONTRASTING AUTHOR WEBSITES

Did you ever wonder about the person who wrote your favorite book? Chances are good that your author — or a fan of your author — has created a website. And chances are also good that your author's website contains information you've never heard before.

In this paper, you compare and contrast two websites related to an author of your choosing. By observing ways that sites are alike and different, you can learn more about your topic and, at the same time, begin to think about which sites are useful and which are not.

Student Model

from "Live Ideas" by Darnell Graham

My two favorite authors this year are Ray Bradbury and Roald Dahl. When I looked them up on the Internet, I found that lots of other people like them too. There are many websites for each author, but I chose two sites that have more information than the others I saw: The Ray Bradbury Page at www.brookingsbook.com/bradbury/index.htm and The Roald Dahl Home Page at www.roalddahl.org/index2.htm. Both of these sites have background information on the authors and their books, links to other sites, and extra information that a person wanting to know more about an author would want to read.

For starters, both websites give information about the authors' lives. The Bradbury site has a category for biography that you can click on. The biography is written like a story. I learned from the biography that an Apollo astronaut named the Dandelion Crater on the moon after Bradbury's book *Dandelion Wine*. In the biography are photographs of Bradbury that match the story. Also, you can click on the names of his books in the biography and find out more about them. Like the Bradbury Page, The Roald Dahl Home Page gives information about the author. On the first page, next to a picture of Dahl, is a short summary of his life and books. There is also a biography category to click on, but it is less complete than the Bradbury one. The biography is only two pages long, but I did learn some interesting facts about Dahl. He once faked appendicitis so that he could go home from boarding school. And when he was at another school, he got to test chocolates for a local chocolate factory. That's what gave him the idea for *Charlie and the Chocolate Factory*.

Example of point-by-point organization:

> The Bradbury website has twenty-eight links.

> The Dahl site has twenty-seven links.

Look at this statement about the Bradbury site. Read over the essay and find a parallel statement from the Dahl site.

Bradbury Site

> The Bradbury site has a lot of publishing information about each book.

Dahl Site

>

Prewriting

FINDING YOUR VOICE. Use your natural voice, one that shows that you are interested in your topic. Since you want your opinion to be heard, your voice should be reasonable and appropriate to your audience.

For example, using slang to describe websites neither convinces your reader nor instills confidence in your analytical abilities.

This does not mean you should use an overly formal voice. Do include original and fresh descriptions, humor, or other language that shows honesty and conviction. Compare the two sentences below to see which has a more appropriate voice.

I never knew you could find so much information about an author on the Internet.

I found out some way cool info. on these guys.

IDENTIFYING YOUR AUDIENCE. Your class could create a collection of website critiques to post in the classroom or school library as a research resource. In these cases, the audience would be other students and perhaps teachers. Or you might want to offer your essay to an Internet website where your audience would be readers and fans of all ages.

on the authors and their books, links, and extra information.

Read through the essay and find the statement that talks about the background information on Bradbury. Now find the statement that talks about the background information on Dahl. This is called point-by-point organization.

With point-by-point organization, you jump back and forth from one item to the other. First you might make a point about the biography in website #1 and then compare or contrast it to the biography in website #2. Next, you might make a point about the kind of links in website #1 and then discuss the links in website #2. Think of point-by-point organization as small boxes.

Language, Grammar, and Style
Modifiers

Using modifiers correctly in your writing will make your meaning clearer. What are modifiers? Modifiers are words used to describe other words.

EXAMPLES

small book — The word *small* describes or modifies the word *book*.

ran quickly — The word *quickly* describes or modifies the word *ran*.

continued on page 600

IDENTIFYING COMPARATIVE AND SUPERLATIVE MODIFIERS.

When you are making comparisons, modifiers show the amount or degree of comparison. Each modifier has a positive, comparative, and superlative form of comparisons. Note how the form of the modifiers changes.

Positive:
small, smooth, fast

Comparative:
smaller, smoother, faster

Superlative:
smallest, smoothest, fastest

Most one-syllable modifiers and some two-syllable modifiers form comparative and superlative degrees by adding *–er* and *–est*.

Positive:
sweet, tall, happy

Comparative:
sweeter, taller, happier

Superlative:
sweetest, tallest, happiest

Other two-syllable modifiers and all modifiers of more than two syllables use *more* and *most* to form the comparative and superlative degrees.

Positive:
active, complicated, quickly

Comparative:
more active, more complicated, more quickly

Superlative:
most active, most complicated, most quickly

continued on page 601

Student Model—Graphic Organizer

Darnell used this graphic organizer to compare and contrast his two author sites. Create a chart on your paper like the one below. Choose three categories from the list at left to help you compare and contrast your websites. Fill in each square with information about the websites.

Darnell used "biographical information," "links," and two categories he found in his sites that were not listed above. You will want to choose categories that fit your sites.

Website #1 (give web name and address) Ray Bradbury Home Page www.brookingsbook.com/bradbury/ index.htm	**Website #2** (give web name and address) The Roald Dahl Home Page www.roalddahl.org/index2.htm
Biographical Information 2 pages well written story with photographs	**Biographical Information** less than one page unfinished, but interesting no photographs on the page
Links 28 links to other sites about the book & discussion groups	**Links** 27 links to other sites
Student Information e-mail address for questions	**Student Information** several pages of student help paper topics, sources, readers for your paper
Author quotes lots of quotes	**Author quotes** lots of quotes

With your chart filled in, you are ready to write a statement that describes what you have found in your websites. This statement or main idea may change as you write your paper, so consider it a beginning.

Writing with a Plan. Choose an author you enjoy reading who is respected and well known. This could be one of the authors studied in class or some other author of literary significance.

One way to find websites about your author is simply to enter the author's name into a search engine and scan the list that results. You may also want to try combinations of words such as "arts and literature" or "author biographies." Consider using several search engines—Lycos, AltaVista, Yahoo—because each one offers a slightly different result.

Darnell easily found his author websites by using the Netscape Directory. He clicked on "Literature," then "Authors," and finally the letter *B* for Bradbury and the letter *D* for Dahl. It was that simple.

Look over the websites that refer to your authors and pick one for each. Note the Internet address at the top of each page and the title of the site.

Take notes on what you find in the website and how the website looks. Most author websites contain topics you can click on for more information. What kind of information is included in the website and how is it presented? Are there graphics and pictures?

Once you have carefully observed your two author websites, you are ready to begin sorting your information.

Most author sites include one or more of these:
- biographical information
- upcoming appearances by the author
- articles about the author or book reviews
- interviews
- short examples (excerpts) from an author's poems, articles, or fiction
- a list of works by the author and where you can purchase them
- information about the person or persons who posted the site—individuals and organizations have many reasons for publishing information on the Internet. Is someone trying to sell books? There is nothing wrong with this. But it helps you understand the site better when you understand who posted it.
- graphics, photographs
- links to other sites
- other (category not listed here)

Drafting

With your main idea as a starting point, write a draft that compares and contrasts two websites. Your completed chart from the graphic organizer provides facts, evidence, and reasons for your opinion. Put these in the body of your piece. Use point-by-point organization for your paper.

Don't worry about making a perfect draft at this point. Just try to get your most important points in writing.

To show a decrease in the quality of a modifier, form the comparative and superlative degrees by using *less* and *least*.

Positive:
sweet, complicated

Comparative:
less sweet, less complicated

Superlative:
least sweet, least complicated

Use comparative degree when you are comparing two things.

EXAMPLE Jack was the taller of the two brothers.

Use superlative degree when comparing more than two things.

EXAMPLE Jack was the tallest boy on the team.

Note: Some modifiers—like *bad, worse,* and *worst*—don't follow these rules exactly. They are irregular comparisons. If you are unsure about the comparison of a modifier, check the dictionary.

Look through Darnell's final draft and find examples of comparative and superlative modifiers. Did Darnell use the correct form for the modifier? Why, or why not?

Fixing Incorrect Modifiers. In Darnell's rough draft, he found these sentences with modifiers used incorrectly. Identify and correct the errors in the following passages:

continued on page 602

The Dahl website has the most information for students compared to the Bradbury site.

The Bradbury site has big photographs you can see quicklier than the Dahl site.

The Dahl site has the most variety of photographs compared to Bradbury's.

USING MODIFIERS. Search through your own essay looking for modifiers used in comparison. Check to see if the modifiers are one or two syllables. Have you used the right form? Since you are comparing two websites, many of your modifiers will be in the comparative, rather than superlative, degree. Read your sentences aloud to see that your modifiers have the correct endings. Make the necessary changes to improve the readability of your paper.

Student Model—Draft

abrupt start

Now my two favorite authors are Ray Bradbury and Roald Dahl. They seem to be two of the popularist authors on the Internet too. There are many websites. *fix modifier*

I chose two that had (most) information, *modifier ok?*
include site names
www.brokingsbook.com/bradbury/index and www.roalddahl.org/index2.htm. Both have

more specific
background information, links to other sites, and extra information as well, like information about the authors' lives.——— *use for next par.*

Student Model—Revised

Live Ideas by Darnell Graham

My two favorite authors this year are Ray Bradbury and Roald Dahl. When I looked them up on the Internet, I found that lots of other people like them too. There are many websites for each author, but I chose two sites that have more information than the others I saw: The Ray Bradbury Page at www.brookingsbook.com/bradbury/index.htm and The Roald Dahl Home Page at www.roalddahl.org/index2.htm. Both of these sites have background information on the authors and their books, links to other sites, and extra information that a person wanting to know more about an author would want to read.

For starters, both websites give information about the authors' lives. The Bradbury site has a category for biography that you can click on. The biography is written like a story. I learned from the biography that an Apollo astronaut named the Dandelion Crater on the moon after Bradbury's book *Dandelion Wine*. In the biography are photographs of Bradbury that match the story. Also, you can click on the names of his books in the biography and find out more about them.

Like the Bradbury site, The Roald Dahl Home Page gives information about the author. On the first page, next to a picture of Dahl, is a short summary of his life and books. There is also a biography category to click on, but it is less complete than the Bradbury one. The biography is only two pages long, but I did learn some interesting facts about Dahl. He once faked appendicitis so that he could go home from boarding school. And when he was at another school, he got to test chocolates for a local chocolate factory. That's what gave him the idea for *Charlie and the Chocolate Factory*.

The two websites also have lists of books written by the authors. The Bradbury site has a lot of publishing information about each book and short plot summaries. The Dahl site has less publishing information, but longer plot summaries.

Both sites have excellent links to other sites. The Bradbury website has twenty-eight links. The Dahl site has twenty-seven links. You can click on addresses for fan clubs and other interesting sites.

The Bradbury and Dahl sites have basically the same kinds of information. But the two sites do have some differences. The Bradbury site has nothing special for students. The Dahl site has pages of materials for students of all ages. This site gives you a category called Homework Frequently Asked Questions. In this category you can find ideas for writing about Roald Dahl, where and how to find the information you need, and who you can discuss your paper with. The person who wrote this site seems to really want to help students. Maybe she was once just a student herself.

Even though the Bradbury site has no

Self- and Peer Evaluation
Use the questions below to guide you in making revisions on your first draft. If time allows, have another student evaluate your paper.

- Does the paper have a statement in the opening that clearly states a main idea? What is the statement?
- What reasons, facts, or evidence does the paper use to support the statement?
- Which examples are the strongest and why?
- Which examples are least effective and why?
- Identify any places where the organization could be clearer.
- Look for transitions between points. Are there places where the paper could use a transition to guide the reader from one idea to the next?
- What about voice? Are there parts of the paper where the language does not sound convincing or real?

materials for students, it does have something the Dahl site doesn't: quotations from the author. My favorite is a quote from Ray Bradbury about writing: "My stories run up and bite me in the leg—I respond by writing down everything that goes on during the bite. When I finish, the idea lets go and runs off."

I never knew you could find so much information about an author on the Internet. And not all sites have the same information. So if you want to know every thing about an author, you should look at many sites.

Reflecting

Think about when you already use the thinking skill of comparing and contrasting in your daily life. How does the skill help you? How might you benefit from this skill in the future? Your ability to evaluate websites by comparing and contrasting can serve you well. What did you learn about yourself as a writer as you prepared this lesson? How might comparison and contrast help you use and judge the masses of information you see every day?

Revising and Proofreading

Based on the responses to your self- and peer evaluations, make changes in your essay that will help your reader better understand your point of view. Don't hesitate to play with your main idea until it reflects exactly what you want to say. A clear main idea is the glue that holds your paper together and the body of your essay will fall into place once you have it.

Think about adding more evidence to weak points and getting rid of repetitious ones. Insert transitions where necessary.

When you are finished revising, proofread your paper for errors in capitalization, spelling, punctuation, and grammar usage such as modifiers that show comparative and superlative degrees of comparison.

Publishing and Presenting

Print a final copy of your essay and combine it with your classmates' essays into a website resource book. Your class could add graphics and a table of contents to create an attractive and readable handbook. Consider placing this resource in the school library for other students to use.

Another option for publishing is to post your essay on the Internet. Some websites and online magazines are looking for manuscripts about the Internet and may welcome your essay. You might even find that the websites you analyzed are eager to read your assessment of their site.

UNIT EIGHT *review*

Review: Words for Everyday Use

Check your knowledge of the following vocabulary words. Choose ten words that you would like to include in your own daily language. For each word, write a short sentence that includes the word in context. To review a word, look back to the page number(s) indicated.

- abhorrent (530)
- aloof (532)
- anguish (585)
- apparatus (518)
- ardent (532)
- bear (518)
- bilious (564)
- botch (543)
- bureau (543)
- charity (540)
- commotion (564)
- complacent (528)
- concussion (516)
- condemn (588)
- consumption (566)
- contrary (588)
- convulsive (526)
- corsage (554)
- crescendo (527)
- deem (571)
- disclose (587)
- dogged (592)
- envisage (528)
- erratic (528)
- essence (591)
- extraordinary (566)

- fantasy (551)
- fluted (545)
- foreboding (526)
- forsake (529)
- furtive (528)
- gabble (587)
- hereby (542)
- immense (518)
- impassive (574)
- inconspicuous (586)
- indomitable (529)
- intercept (569)
- intimate (573)
- lethal (570)
- liable (552)
- lithe (529)
- minute (592)
- obscurity (527)
- onslaught (533)
- organdy (553)
- pallid (533)
- parcel (589)
- passable (543)
- pasty (544)
- patronizing (568)
- paunchy (566)

- pervade (531)
- plight (585)
- prodigy (552)
- prophesy (593)
- proprietary (531)
- psych (555)
- rebuff (530)
- resilient (519)
- restrain (568)
- rove (587)
- savor (519)
- sedate (573)
- slacken (517)
- stricken (570)
- strident (533)
- subdued (573)
- surge (518)
- throng (532)
- tumultuous (519)
- upstanding (539)
- vagrant (532)
- veranda (564)
- void (531)
- wayward (585)

Review: Literary Tools

Define each of the following terms, giving concrete examples when possible. To review a term, refer to the page number(s) indicated.

- character (549)
- characterization (537)
- conflict (523, 561)
- foreshadowing (582)

- hyperbole (549)
- metaphor (514)
- plot (514)
- point of view (537, 549)

- science fiction (514)
- setting (523)
- simile (514)
- theme (561, 582)

Reflecting on your reading

Theme

In each story of this unit, the main characters had to summon up deep inner strength in order to preserve something vital to their existence and even to their survival. They all showed gumption, courage, and grit.

Genre

Short stories often have complex plots that show the characters in a conflict. The conflict usually reaches a peak, and then the characters move toward some kind of resolution of that conflict. The conflict is what makes short stories exciting to read. It is what makes us read faster, and turn the pages quickly. The resolution, or outcome, of the conflict is sometimes happy, sometimes not.

On Your Own

Think of things that you can't live without. Make two lists:
1) things that are vital to your survival on earth, such as water, food, or the sun.
2) things that are crucial for your self-image, your beliefs, your conscience, or your well-being, such as love, a peaceful environment, or, like Squeaky and her running, to be able to express your best skill. Choose one element from either list and write a short essay describing why it is essential in your life.

Critical Thinking

In the chart below fill in the element that is, indeed, vital to the main character's existence. Then think about what the conflict was in the story, and how it was resolved.

Character	Vital Element	Conflict	Resolution
Margot	The Sun	She was locked in a closet while the sun was out	She was only let out after the sun went away
Arnuk the Wolf			
Hungry Hannah			
Squeaky (Hazel)			
David, who spoke to animals			
Grig Rainborrow			

Group Project

The short stories in this unit could have complex interpretations. When you have completed the chart above choose, as a group, one story that you would like to discuss in more depth. Discuss the following questions:

1. What circumstances did the main character face that allowed him or her to get into the conflict?
2. What qualities did the main character have that helped him or her find a solution, or not, to the conflict?
3. What obstacles did the character have to face?
4. Were the obstacles greater than the main character could cope with?
5. What outside assistance came to the aid of the main character?

Report the ideas your group came up with to the rest of the class.

Suzy's Sun (for Judy Tyler), 1957. Joseph Cornell. North Carolina Museum of Art, Raleigh.

Words in Motion

POETRY

ELEMENTS *of* POETRY

The main elements of poetry are imagery, shape, sound, and meaning.

IMAGES AND IMAGERY. An **image** is language that creates a concrete representation of an object or an experience. An image is also the vivid mental picture created in the reader's mind by that language. The images in a literary work are referred to, when considered together, as the work's **imagery**. Poets use colorful, vivid language and figures of speech to create imagery. **Colorful language** is precise and lively words and phrases that help to create clear pictures in the reader's mind. A **figure of speech** is language meant to be understood imaginatively instead of literally. Metaphor, simile, and personification are figures of speech. A **metaphor** is a figure of speech in which one thing is spoken or written about as if it were another. A **simile** is a comparison using *like* or *as*. **Personification** is describing something not human as if it were human.

SHAPE. The shape of a poem is how it looks on the page. A **concrete poem,** or shape poem, is one with a shape that suggests its subject.

SOUND. The sound of a poem is created through the use of rhyme, rhythm, alliteration, assonance, onomatopoeia, and repetition. **Rhyme** is the repetition of sounds at the ends of words, like _locks_, _box_, and _socks_. **Rhythm** is the pattern of beats in a line of poetry or prose. **Alliteration** is the repetition of consonant sounds at the beginnings of syllables, as in _Peter Piper picked a peck of pickled peppers_. **Assonance** is the repetition of vowel sounds in stressed syllables that end in different consonant sounds, as in _lime light._ **Onomatopoeia** is the use of words or phrases like *meow* or *beep* that sound like what they name. **Repetition** is more than one use of a sound, word, or phrase.

MEANING. Meaning in poetry is created in many ways. The use of symbols, appeals to emotion, and techniques such as *dialogue* and *flashback* can add meaning to a poem. A **symbol** is a thing that stands for or represents both itself and something else.

FORMS OF POETRY. Poetry comes in two main forms: narrative and lyric. A **narrative poem** is a verse that tells a story. A **lyric poem** is highly musical verse that expresses the emotions of a speaker and does not tell a story. Lyric poems focus on ideas. **Haiku** is a highly specialized form of lyric poetry—a traditional Japanese three-line poem. It has five syllables in the first line, seven in the second, and five in the third. Haiku and other poems written in languages besides English must be translated so that people can read them in English.

Getting into Poetry

Donnie Belcher is a 15-year-old student in the tenth grade at North High School in Minneapolis, Minnesota. She has been writing poetry since she was in the sixth grade. Her

poem "America" was published in the poetry anthology *Peaceful Reveries*. Here, she answers some questions about herself, poetry, and her work.

What do you like most about poetry?
Poetry allows me to be free. It allows me to express myself in ways that would otherwise be impossible. In the beginning, there was the word and there always will be the word. Poetry gives me a unique and distinct voice. It allows me to be me with no restrictions and no limitations. Poetry makes me feel a lot of things. The most relevant is power. Nothing compares to the feeling I have after having completed a poem. It makes me feel very good. Sort of like opening gifts at Christmas time or winning a contest.

What process do you use in writing your poems?
There really is no process. It usually starts with something I see, hear, or feel. Then the idea just lingers around in my head until it is written down. I've been writing for so long that the words just flow out onto the page. So I guess you can say living is my process.

What motivates you to write poetry? How did you get started?
My motivation for writing is the truth. With my poetry, I try to educate, entertain, and enlighten—not only myself, but those who come into contact with my words. I started my poetry writing with a poem titled, "Respect." It took two months to write and it started with an attitude. I was being disrespected everyday and the poem sort of "told" how I felt. I was going through all these changes, my body was transforming, and everything seemed so complicated inside of me. Writing allowed me to deal with all my issues. Poetry got me through some difficult years.

Who or what has influenced you the most in your writing of poems? Who is your favorite poet?
My influence has come from many writers who have come before me including: Alice Walker, Zora Neale Hurston, Terry McMillan, Gwendolyn Brooks, Ann Petry, Toni Morrison, Sonya Sanchez, and the greatest influence— Maya Angelou. As you notice, these are all phenomenal African-American women writers. They are my influence because they've been where I'm at and they're at where I'm trying to go. They have all elevated something I am doing. My favorite poet is Maya Angelou. She is so well respected and so wise. I can relate to her words the most. My initial impulse came from hearing her poem, "Phenomenal Woman."

What subject matter do you like to write about?
I would have to say history and love. Love is something so simple, yet complicated. If you don't know your past, you can't determine your future, so I love writing about African-American history and culture.

What are your career goals?
My career goals are to go to college and major in English or creative writing. And one day, I would like to own a big writing and publishing business that does everything from production to performing.

Power of the Pen
Donnie Belcher

NEVER
Underestimate
The power
Of the pen.
Profoundly liberating,
What's within.
Invoking feelings,
And emotions.
Wider than seas,
Deeper than oceans.
They haunt you until released,
Like holding in a laugh,
Or a sneeze.
Can be delayed,
But will manifest!
Like a secret
That lingers
In your head until . . .
Confessed.
NEVER
Underestimate
The power
Of the pen.
Profoundly liberating,
What's
Within!

Prereading

"in Just-" and "Spring is like a perhaps hand"

by E. E. Cummings

Reader's Resource

- **SCIENCE CONNECTION.** Spring begins around March 20 and ends around June 21. In the Northern Hemisphere, daytime temperatures are generally warm during spring, hot during summer, cooler during autumn, and cold during winter. When it is winter in the Northern Hemisphere, it is summer in the Southern Hemisphere. Near the equator, temperatures remain warm year-round, although there might be a rainy season and a dry season. In polar regions, temperatures remain cold for most of the year.

- **SOCIAL STUDIES CONNECTION.** In many cultures, spring traditionally has been celebrated with festivals. The Aztecs of Central America centered their most important ceremonies on the planting and harvesting seasons. They worshiped several hundred deities, one of whom was Xipe Totec, god of springtime, planting, and growth. The ancient Greeks observed two major spring festivals: the Eleusinia, held in honor of Demeter, the goddess of grain, and the Great Dionysia, held in honor of Dionysus, the god of the vine. May Day celebrations have been held throughout European history. Often these celebrations involved dancing around a May pole and crowning a May queen.

Graphic Organizer

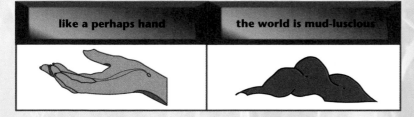

| like a perhaps hand | the world is mud-lusclous |

Reader's Journal

Which season is your favorite? What do you like best about that season?

Reader's TOOLBOX

IMAGE AND IMAGERY. An **image** is language that creates a concrete representation of an object or an experience. An image is also the vivid mental picture created in the reader's mind by that language. The images in a literary work are referred to, when considered all together, as the work's **imagery.** As you read these poems, think about the pictures in your head created by the words you read. You may want to draw the images you see as shown in the graphic organizer below. Use the specific words you envision as captions for your pictures.

DESCRIPTION. Description is a type of writing that portrays a character, object, or scene. Descriptions make use of *sensory details*—words and phrases that describe how things look, sound, smell, taste, or feel. Effective descriptions contain precise—or concrete—nouns, verbs, adverbs, and adjectives. Descriptions often use imagery and figurative language. Figurative language includes figures of speech, such as similes, and other ways of inventing creative words and phrases. A *simile* is a comparison using *like* or *as*. How do the descriptions of spring in these two poems work to create a certain mood?

613

First Days of Spring in the Country, 1912. Pierre Bonnard. Pushkin Museum, Moscow.

in Just-
E. E. Cummings

in Just-
spring   when the world is mudluscious the little
lame balloonman

5   whistles   far
    and wee

and eddieandbill come
running from marbles and
piracies and it's
spring

10   when the world is puddle-wonderful

the queer
old balloonman whistles
far   and   wee
and bettyandisbel come dancing

15   from hop-scotch and jump-rope and

it's
spring
and
    the

20   goat-footed

balloonMan   whistles
far
and
wee ■

GUIDED READING
How does the speaker describe "Just-spring"?

GUIDED READING
What does the balloonMan do?

Spring
E. E. Cummings
is like a perhaps hand

Spring is like a perhaps
    hand
(which comes carefully
out of Nowhere)arranging
a window,into which people look(while

5   people stare
arranging and changing placing
carefully there a strange
thing and a known thing here)and

changing everything carefully

10   spring is like a perhaps
Hand in a window
(carefully to
and fro moving New
    and
Old things,while

15   people stare carefully
moving a perhaps
fraction of flower here placing
an inch of air there)and

without breaking anything. ■

GUIDED READING
How does the spring come?

GUIDED READING
What does spring move to and fro?

How do you view spring? Which poem more closely describes spring as you see it?

About *the* AUTHOR

Edward Estlin (E. E.) Cummings was born in Cambridge, Massachusetts, in 1894. He studied literature and languages at Harvard University and volunteered as an ambulance driver during World War I (1914–1918). During the war he was jailed in France for writing letters that criticized the war. He later became a writer and artist. Cummings developed a unique style and broke many traditional rules in his poetry. He made up words and used unconventional spelling, punctuation, grammar, and capitalization, even spelling his own name all in lowercase letters—e. e. cummings. Before his death in 1962, Cummings wrote a number of books, including *The Enormous Room*, a novel he wrote about his experiences while wrongly jailed in France, *i: SIX NON LECTURES*, a book of essays, and *No Thanks*, a book of poetry. Many of his poems have been published in anthologies, such as *100 Selected Poems*, which was published in 1999.

Investigate, Inquire, and Imagine

Recall: GATHERING FACTS	→	**Interpret:** FINDING MEANING

1a. In "in Just-," what do "eddieandbill" do? What do "bettyandisbel" do?

1b. How do their activities help show that it is "Just-/spring"?

2a. What does the balloonman do?

2b. Why do you think he does this?

3a. In "Spring is like a perhaps hand," where does spring come from?

3b. What does this mean?

4a. What is spring compared to? How do people react to seeing this thing?

4b. What does this comparison mean?

Analyze: TAKING THINGS APART	→	**Synthesize:** BRINGING THINGS TOGETHER

5a. In what different ways do people in these two poems react to the arrival of spring? Compare and contrast the people's attitudes toward spring.

5b. In what ways does spring act like hand arranging a shop window? In what ways does it cause people to act differently than they do in winter?

Evaluate: MAKING JUDGMENTS	→	**Extend:** CONNECTING IDEAS

6a. How well does "in Just-" describe how it feels when spring comes? How well does "Spring is like a perhaps hand" portray spring's arrival?

6b. Which of the two poems better matches your feelings about spring?

Understanding *Literature*

IMAGE AND IMAGERY. An **image** is language that creates a concrete representation of an object or experience. An image is also the vivid mental picture created in the reader's mind by that language. The images in a literary work are referred to, when considered altogether, as the work's **imagery**. In your own words, describe the imagery in "in Just-" and in "Spring is like a perhaps hand."

DESCRIPTION. Description is a type of writing that portrays a character, object, or scene. Descriptions make use of *sensory details*—words and phrases that describe how things look, sound, smell, taste, or feel. Effective descriptions contain precise—or concrete—nouns, verbs, adverbs, and adjectives. Descriptions often use imagery and figurative language. Figurative language includes figures of speech, such as similes, and other ways of inventing creative words and phrases. A *simile* is a comparison using *like* or *as.* Think about the descriptions of spring offered in "in Just-" and "Spring is like a perhaps hand." How do they make use of sensory details? How do they use concrete language? What similes or other creative invented words or phrases can you find in the poems?

Reader's *Journal*

How do you part with a friend or family member? What do you usually say?

Reader's *Resource*

- **LANGUAGE CONNECTION.** The term *goodbye* came about in the late 1500s. It is an alteration of the phrase "God be with you." Many languages have terms that mean the same as goodbye. For example, in Spanish, goodbye is *adios*. The Japanese word *sayonara* also means goodbye. Some languages do not have a term equal to goodbye. In French, the closest term, *au revoir*, means "until we see each other again." In German, *auf Wiedersehen* means "until I see you again."

Prereading

"There Is No Word for Goodbye" by Mary TallMountain and *"If You Should Go"* by Countee Cullen

Reader's T O O L B O X

IMAGERY. Taken together, the images in a poem or passage are called its **imagery**. An *image* is the language that creates a concrete representation of an object or an experience. An image is also the vivid mental picture created in the reader's mind by that language. Imagery can create mental pictures not only of things that can be seen, such as springtime or children playing, but also of ideas. How do these poems create imagery from the idea of saying goodbye to someone you care about?

SPEAKER. The **speaker** is the voice that speaks, or narrates, a poem. The speaker and the writer of a poem are not necessarily the same person. Think about the speaker of each of these two poems. Who does the speaker address in "There Is No Word for Goodbye"? Whom does the speaker address in "If You Should Go"?

Graphic *Organizer*

Use a graphic organizer like this one to keep track of the main ideas in each poem.

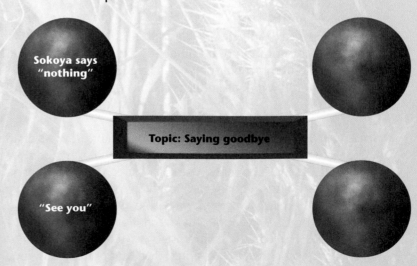

Sokoya says "nothing"

Topic: Saying goodbye

"See you"

There Is No Word for *Goodbye*

Mary TallMountain

Sokoya,[1] I said, looking through
    the net of wrinkles into
    wise black pools
    of her eyes.

5   What do you say in Athabaskan[2]
    when you leave each other?
    What is the word
    for goodbye?

    A shade of feeling rippled
10   the wind-tanned skin.
    Ah, nothing, she said,
    watching the river flash.

    She looked at me close.
    We just say, Tłaa. That means,
15   See you.
    We never leave each other.
    When does your mouth
    say goodbye to your heart?

    She touched me light
20   as a bluebell.
    You forget when you leave us,
    You're so small then.
    We don't use that word.

    We always think you're coming back,
25   but if you don't,
    we'll see you some place else.
    You understand.
    There is no word for goodbye. ■

GUIDED READING

What question does the speaker ask?

GUIDED READING

Why do speakers of Athabaskan not have a word for goodbye?

---

1. **Sokoya.** (Athabaskan) Aunt or mother's sister
2. **Athabaskan.** Family of native North American languages, including Chipewyan, Hupa, and Navajo

If You Should Go

Countee Cullen

Love, leave me like the light,
    The gently passing day;
We would not know, but for the night,
    When it has slipped away.

Go quietly; a dream,
    When done, should leave no trace
That it has lived, except a gleam
    Across the dreamer's face.

GUIDED READING

What should a dream do? In what ways is love like a dream?

Respond *to the* SELECTION

When you leave someone, how is that person still with you?

About *the* AUTHORS

Mary TallMountain (1918–1994), whose mother was stricken with tuberculosis, was adopted when she was three years old. A member of the Koykon-Athabaskan people, she was taken away from the village where she had been born to another place in Alaska. She moved to San Francisco in 1945 to run her own business. She later changed jobs many times before finding her calling in writing.

Countee Cullen (1903–1946) was born in New York City and given the name Countee Leroy Porter. He was adopted by the Reverend Frederick Cullen in 1918. He studied at New York University and at Harvard University. Cullen served as editor of the magazine *Opportunity: Journal of Negro Life*, taught French in a high school, and wrote and published children's books. He also wrote novels and many poems. His works include *Color, Copper Sun, The Ballad of the Brown Girl, One Way to Heaven,* and *On These I Stand.*

Investigate, Inquire, and Imagine

Recall: GATHERING FACTS

1a. In "There Is No Word for Goodbye," what does the speaker compare Sokoya's eyes to?

2a. What does "Tłaa" mean?

3a. In "If You Should Go," how does the speaker want "Love" to leave?

4a. What should a dream leave behind?

→ **Interpret:** FINDING MEANING

1b. What does this description suggest about the speaker's relationship to Sokoya?

2b. Why do you think Sokoya's people "never leave each other"? Why don't they say goodbye?

3b. Why might a person feel that way about a loved one leaving?

4b. What does this mean? How is a dream like a loved one?

Analyze: TAKING THINGS APART

5a. What specific views does Sokoya have about people leaving one another? What specific thoughts about this does the speaker have in "If You Should Go"?

→ **Synthesize:** BRINGING THINGS TOGETHER

5b. Does Sokoya see departures as permanent? sad? hopeful? How does the speaker in "If You Should Go" view a loved one's departure? How does he or she hope the loved one goes? Why might he feel this way?

Perspective: LOOKING AT OTHER VIEWS →

6a. What does Sokoya's answer to the question "What is the word for goodbye?" say about her worldviews? How does she probably view relationships between and among people? What do the speaker's words in "If You Should Go" indicate about his or her views about relationships? What does he or she hope to avoid if the relationship with his or her loved one should end?

Empathy: SEEING FROM INSIDE

6b. How might Sokoya respond to the speaker in "If You Should Go"? How might that speaker respond to Sokoya's words in "There Is No Word for Goodbye"?

Understanding *Literature*

IMAGERY. Taken together, the images in a poem or passage are called its **imagery**. An *image* is the language that creates a concrete representation of an object or an experience. An image is also the vivid mental picture created in the reader's mind by that language. Write down specific images you find in each of the two poems. How do the words create pictures in your mind? What imagery is created in the poem "There Is No Word for Goodbye"? What imagery is created in "If You Should Go"?

SPEAKER. The **speaker** is the voice that speaks, or narrates, a poem. The speaker and the writer of a poem are not necessarily the same person. Think about the speaker of each of these two poems. How would you describe the speakers in these two poems? Do you think the speaker of "There Is No Word for Goodbye" is the author? Why, or why not? Do you think the speaker of "If You Should Go" is the author? Why, or why not?

Critical Thinking

- What does "There Is No Word for Goodbye" reveal about Sokoya's philosophy of life? her culture?
- How do you say *goodbye?* Why do you use the word or phrase you use? What does it say about your philosophy of life?
- Think about other people in your life. Do they say *goodbye* or do they use a different word or phrase? Why do you think they use these words or phrases?

Reader's Resource

"The Sidewalk Racer, or On the Skateboard"

by Lillian Morrison

- **HISTORY CONNECTION.** Skateboards have gone through many changes in the past century. In the early 1900s, a typical skateboard was made of roller skate wheels, a two-by-four wood plank, and a milk crate with handles—resembling a scooter. In 1963, Larry Stevenson's company, Makaha, designed the first professional skateboards, and a team was formed to promote the design. Now there are skateboarding parks all over the United States. The popularity of skateboarding has had its peaks and valleys. Safety concerns have highly contributed to the valleys. However, the sport remains much safer than football, rollerblading, or hockey, when looking at the percentage of participants injured.

- The most basic move in skateboarding is called the Ollie. If you can't do the Ollie, you can forget about competitive skateboarding. The Ollie is done while skating along on a flat surface at a moderate speed. You hit the tail, or end of the board, on the ground with your feet. At this time, your body and board are lifted in the air for a brief moment. As you come down, bend your knees and skate on.

Reader's TOOLBOX

CONCRETE POEM. A **concrete poem**, or shape poem, is one with a shape that suggests its subject. Poets develop concrete poems as visual images of the words they contain. Concrete poems can convey powerful images using few words. What image does the shape of "The Sidewalk Racer or On the Skateboard" suggest?

IMAGERY. Taken together, the images in the poem make up the poem's **imagery**. What imagery is created in "The Sidewalk Racer, or On the Skateboard"?

The following is an example of a simple concrete poem. Using a simple word or passage, create a concrete poem of your own.

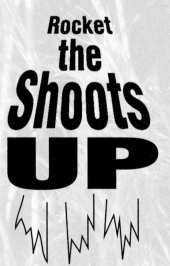

Reader's Journal

How does it feel to be moving really fast with the wind on your face, as when on a bicycle, skis, or a roller coaster?

The Sidewalk Racer, or On the Skateboard

Lillian Morrison

Skimming
an asphalt sea
I swerve, I curve, I
sway; I speed to whirring
sound an inch above the
ground; I'm the sailor
and the sail, I'm the
driver and the wheel
I'm the one and only
single engine
human auto
mobile. ■

GUIDED READING

In what way is the speaker the driver and the wheel?

words for everyday use

skim (skim') *v.*, glide over lightly. *Her waterskis skimmed the surface of the lake.*

as • phalt (as' fôlt') *n.*, dark rocky mixture used for paving. *My dad poured new asphalt on our driveway.*

whir • ring (hwur' iŋ) *adj.*, whizzing or buzzing. *The whirring sound of a helicopter caught my attention.*

What activities in your life bring you the most joy and excitement?

About *the* AUTHOR

Lillian Morrison (b.1917) writes poems filled with rhythm and active movement. Born in Jersey City, New Jersey, Morrison spent nearly forty years of her life working in the New York Public Library. She has written several books of poetry, including *The Breakdance Kids* and *The Sidewalk Race and Other Poems of Sports and Motion*. As these titles suggest, Morrison is drawn especially to the body movements and rhythms shown by athletes and dancers.

Investigate, Inquire, and Imagine

Recall: GATHERING FACTS

1a. What is the speaker skimming?

2a. What does the speaker say in lines 7 and 8?

3a. What kind of "auto mobile" does the speaker claim to be?

→ **Interpret:** FINDING MEANING

1b. In what way does this surface suggest both skateboarding and a water sport?

2b. What does the speaker mean by this?

3b. How would you describe that "vehicle"? Check the dictionary for the meanings of *auto* and *mobile*.

Analyze: TAKING THINGS APART

4a. What motion words does the speaker use? What do these words have in common? What sort of motion do they describe?

→ **Synthesize:** BRINGING THINGS TOGETHER

4b. What do these words and phrases suggest about the speaker's feelings while skateboarding?

Evaluate: MAKING JUDGMENTS

5a. How does the shape of this poem contribute to its meaning?

→ **Extend:** CONNECTING IDEAS

5b. What activity causes you to imagine you could just as easily be doing something bigger, stronger, faster, or more intense? What shape would you outline to represent this activity and your feelings about it?

Understanding *Literature*

CONCRETE POEM. A **concrete poem**, or shape poem, is one with a shape that suggests its subject. Poets develop concrete poems as visual images of the words they contain. Concrete poems can convey powerful images using few words. How does the shape of this poem affect the way you read it?

IMAGERY. Taken together, the images in the poem make up the poem's **imagery**. Describe the images you visualize as you read this poem. How does the poem's shape influence this imagery?

Writer's Journal

1. Imagine it is spring and write a **shopping list** of all the things you might need for spring cleaning, planting, and other activities.

2. Imagine that a close friend is moving to another town. Write a **personal letter** to the friend, sharing your thoughts on how the two of you can remain friends despite the distance between you.

3. With a partner, write an **advice column** question regarding a relationship and the response to that question.

Skill Builders

Study and Research

RESEARCHING GREETINGS. Using library resources, research greetings in different languages. You may decide to focus on one greeting—such as *hello* or *goodbye*—or you may want to look at many types of greetings. Find words or phrases in other languages that correspond with the greeting or greetings you are researching. Share your findings with your class.

Media Literacy

REPRESENTATIONAL MEDIA. Think about the four seasons and what images they bring about to you. For example, maybe summer conjures up images of a lazy river in the sun or of a high-energy soccer game. Jot down a couple of ideas for each of the four seasons. Then choose types of media in which to search for those images. You may want to look for magazine pictures; Internet pages; songs; paintings, advertisements, television shows, films, maps, or other media. Use your imagination, and find images that correspond with your ideas about each season.

Vocabulary

THESAURUS. One way to build your vocabulary is to learn a new word with a meaning similar to a word you already know. Use a thesaurus to find other words with meanings similar to *love*. For each word that you find, write a sentence that uses the word. There may be subtle differences in the meanings of the words that correspond to *love*. You may want to consult a dictionary to determine how each word should be used. Follow this same procedure for the following terms:

- perhaps
- arrange
- strange
- light
- close
- forget
- pass
- go

Prereading

"The Eagle: A Fragment" and "Break, Break, Break"
by Alfred, Lord Tennyson

Reader's T O O L B O X

RHYTHM. Rhythm is the pattern of beats, or stressed syllables, in a line of poetry or prose. *Stress,* or accent, is the amount of emphasis given to a syllable. The pattern of stresses in a poem determines its rhythm. A strongly stressed syllable receives a strong emphasis and a weakly stressed syllable receives a weak one. As you read the following poems, note which syllables are strongly stressed. You may want to use a graphic organizer like the one below to determine the rhythm of each line of the poems.

RHYME. Rhyme is the repetition of sounds at the ends of words. As you read these poems, look for rhyming words at the ends of lines.

Graphic

Make a grid like this one and write the lines of the poems, with each syllable in its own box. Place stress marks over the strongly stressed syllables.

He	clasps	the	crag	with	crook	–ed	hands
Close	to	the	sun	in	lone	–ly	lands
Ringed	with	the	a	–zure	world	he	stands

Keep track of rhyming words at the ends of the lines by writing the last words of each line in a column.

1st line	break
2nd line	sea
3rd line	utter
4th line	me

Reader's Journal

What elements in nature do you find most interesting or awe-inspiring? Why?

Reader's Resource

- *Eagle* is a common name for a number of different birds of prey. The golden eagle can be found in many areas in the Northern Hemisphere. It is known for its large size, amazing flying skills, and preference for nesting in high-up places. Sea eagles live in coastal regions and near lakes and streams in North America. The bald eagle—darkly colored with a white head—is a member of this group. Tropical eagles, such as the harpy eagle, Philippine eagle, and serpent eagle, live near the equator.

- Tennyson composed the poem "Break, Break, Break" after his good friend died. He wrote about the sea, which he could have seen as a symbol of the endless circle of life and death. The sea could also symbolize the indifference of the world to one small death—the sea continues to "break, break, break," as always, even though Tennyson's friend had died. In the first stanza, the poet seems troubled by his inability to put his feelings and thoughts into words. In the second and third stanzas, he sees life going on around him, even after such a tragedy occurred. The indifferent children and the ship do as they have always done, not paying attention to the tragedy. In the fourth stanza, he realizes that he will never again see his friend.

629

The Eagle: A Fragment

Alfred, Lord Tennyson

He clasps the crag[1] with crooked hands;

Close to the sun in lonely lands,

Ringed with the azure world, he stands.

The wrinkled sea beneath him crawls:

He watches from his mountain walls,

And like a thunderbolt he falls. ∎

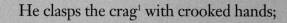

> **GUIDED READING**
>
> Where does the eagle watch from? How does he fall?

---

1. **crag.** Steep, tall rugged rock

Jabberwocky

Lewis Carroll

'Twas brillig, and the slithy toves
    Did gyre and gimble in the wabe;
All mimsy were the borogoves,
    And the mome raths outgrabe.

5   "Beware the Jabberwock, my son!
    The jaws that bite, the claws that catch!
Beware the Jubjub bird, and <u>shun</u>
    The frumious Bandersnatch!"

He took his vorpal sword in hand;
10   Long time the manxome foe he <u>sought</u>—
So rested he by the Tumtum tree,
    And stood awhile in thought.

And, as in uffish thought he stood,
    The Jabberwock, with eyes of flame,
15   Came whiffling through the tulgey wood,
    And burbled as it came!

One, two! One, two! And through and through
    The vorpal blade went snicker-snack!
He left it dead, and with its head
20   He went galumphing[1] back.

"And hast thou slain the Jabberwock?
    Come to my arms, my beamish boy!
O frabjous day! Callooh! Callay!"
    He chortled[2] in his joy.

25   'Twas brillig, and the slithy toves
    Did gyre and gimble in the wabe;
All mimsy were the borogoves,
    And the mome raths outgrabe. ■

Wood engraving from ***Through the Looking Glass***, 1865. Sir John Tenniel.

> **GUIDED READING**
>
> What does the son do to the Jabberwock?

---

1. **galumphing.** Moving with a clumsy, heavy tread
2. **chortled.** Laughed with satisfaction

words for everyday use

shun (shən') *v.*, avoid deliberately and habitually. *Choua <u>shuns</u> the library, preferring to study outdoors.*

seek (sēk') *v.*, search for. *Dan went from store to store <u>seeking</u> the perfect gift for Milla.* **sought,** *past tense*

You are old, Father William

Lewis Carroll

"You are old, Father William," the young man said,
    "And your hair has become very white;
And yet you <u>incessantly</u> stand on your head—
    Do you think, at your age, it is right?"

5   "In my youth," Father William replied to his son,
    "I feared it might injure the brain;
But now that I'm perfectly sure I have none,
    Why, I do it again and again."

"You are old," said the youth, "as I mentioned before,
10   And have grown most uncommonly fat;
Yet you turned a back-somersault in at the door—
    Pray, what is the reason of that?"

"In my youth," said the sage,[1] as he shook his grey locks,
    "I kept all my limbs very <u>supple</u>
15   By the use of this ointment—one shilling the box—
    Allow me to sell you a couple."

"You are old," said the youth, "and your jaws are too weak
    For anything tougher than suet;[2]
Yet you finished the goose, with the bones and the beak—
20   Pray, how did you manage to do it?"

---

1. **sage.** Person distinguished for wisdom
2. **suet.** Hard fat in beef and mutton

words for everyday use

incessant (in se' sənt) *adj.*, continuing without interruption, unceasing. *The <u>incessant</u> dripping of the faucet kept me awake.* **incessantly,** *adv.*

supple (sə' pəl) *adj.*, limber, without stiffness. *She kneaded the dough until it was <u>supple</u> enough to be formed into rolls.*

Wood engraving from *Alice's Adventures in Wonderland,* 1865. Sir John Tenniel.

"In my youth," said his father, "I took to the law,
    And argued each case with my wife;
And the muscular strength which it gave to my jaw
    has lasted the rest of my life."

25   "You are old," said the youth; "one would hardly suppose
        That your eye was as steady as ever;
Yet you balanced an eel on the end of your nose—
        What made you so awfully clever?"

    "I have answered three questions, and that is enough,"
30   Said his father; "don't give yourself <u>airs</u>!
Do you think I can listen all day to such stuff?
        Be off, or I'll kick you down stairs!" ■

GUIDED READING

What does Father William tell his son?

words for everyday use

airs (ārz′) *n.,* artificial or affected manners. *Milo sometimes puts on <u>airs</u> to hide his lack of confidence.*

When is it appropriate to question authority?

About the
AUTHOR

Lewis Carroll was born Charles Lutwidge Dodgson, the oldest of his ten siblings, in 1832 in Daresbury, England. As a young man, he had a sharp and questioning mind and was fascinated by the mechanics of things. Some of his typical childhood projects included building his own miniature train complete with railway stations, performing magic tricks, and writing plays performed by marionettes that he made and manipulated. In 1850, Carroll entered Oxford College, where he studied mathematics and became a teacher. He also became a clergyman. Carroll is perhaps best known for writing *Alice in Wonderland*, which began as a story told one day to three young girls during a boat ride on the Thames River on July 3, 1862. Carroll went on to publish many books, but that wasn't the only writing he did. From the time he was 28, Carroll kept a record of all the letters he wrote. When he died at the age of 66, the record listed 98,721 letters!

The MINDWORKS of Lewis Carroll

Charles Lutwidge Dodgson, who used the famous pen name Lewis Carroll, had a stutter and deafness in one ear that made him shy and awkward around adults. However, when he was around children, he felt comfortable and relaxed. He always seemed happiest when spending time with his nieces and nephews or his friends' children, telling them stories and teaching them games. It was during a session of storytelling that the idea for *Alice in Wonderland* was born. Dodgson decided to take Alice Liddell and her two sisters for a leisurely boat ride on the Thames River. To pass the time, he told the youngsters about a girl named Alice who fell down a rabbit hole. At the end of the trip, Alice Liddell asked Dodgson to write out the story he told for her. Three and a half years later, *Alice's Adventures in Wonderland* was published.

Alice's Adventures in Wonderland and *Through the Looking-Glass*—the sequel to *Alice*—are Carroll's most well-known books and are full of puzzles, games, and nonsense language. Ever since he was a young boy, Carroll had been fascinated with language and writing. He began to write letters at the age of twelve while he was at Richmond School, a school nine miles from his home. Even at this age, his writing was imaginative and nonsensical. For example, a letter he wrote to his sister Elizabeth said, "I am glad to hear of the six rabbits. For the new name, after some consideration, I recommend Parellelopipedon. It is a nice and easy one to remember, and the rabbit will soon learn it."

As an adult, Carroll continued to follow his out-of-the-ordinary imagination. For example, he only wrote with purple colored ink. And when he would write at his writing desk, he preferred to stand, rather than sit. He invented a system of mnemonics (technique of improving memory) for remembering names and dates, and a system for writing in the dark. Carroll had another passion: mathematics. He constantly invented "tricks" for computing arithmetic. For example, he invented a trick for division and for finding the day of the week for any given date. He also loved to dabble in cryptology—the study of code-making and code-breaking.

All these interests eventually found their way into Carroll's stories. A perfect example is the poem "Jabberwocky" from *Through the Looking-Glass*. To begin with, the first stanza of the poem is written backward, in what Carroll calls "looking-glass letters" because one had to use a mirror to read it:

Jabberwocky
'Twas brillig, and the slithy toves
Did gyre and gimble in the wabe:
All mimsy were the borogoves,
And the mome raths outgrabe.

"Jabberwocky" also contains words that seem to have no meaning. However, Carroll created these words with both logic and imagination. Listed on the following page are some words from the poem as Humpty Dumpty interprets them in chapter six of *Through the Looking-Glass*. Many of these words are derived from Old English words.

brillig (derived from the verb *bryl* or *broil*). Four o-clock in the afternoon—the time of broiling dinner

slithy (compounded of *slimy* and *lithe*). Smooth and active

toves. Animals like badgers, lizards, and corkscrews that make nests under sundials and eat cheese

gyre. Go round and round like a gyroscope

gimble (taken from *gimlet*). Screw out holes in something

wabe. Grass plot around the sundial

mimsy (derived from *flimsy* and *miserable*). Unhappy

borogoves. Thin shabby-looking birds with feathers sticking out all around; like live mops

outgrabe. Past tense of *outgribe*, meaning to make a noise like something between bellowing and whistling, with a kind of sneeze in the middle

Carroll was infamous for using word games and puzzles in his letters and in his stories. You can log onto Doublets at Thinks.com at http://thinks.com/puzzles/doublets.htm to learn how to play word games such as doublets. To learn more about Carroll, visit the Lewis Carroll Home Page at http://www.lewiscarroll.org/carroll.html.

The impact of Lewis Carroll and his stories on our society has been and continues to be phenomenal. The Alice stories (*Alice's Adventures in Wonderland* and *Through the Looking-Glass*) have been adapted to many different art forms—plays, ballets, symphonies, sculptures, animation, and movies.

The language of *Jabberwocky* has found its way to television scripts, where lines spoken by characters from *The Muppet Show, Doctor Who,* and *Star Trek* use words and phrases from the poem. There is even a frisbee sport called "Jabberwock Ultimate" and a video game called "Secret of Mana" with the main enemy named Jabberwock. Although Carroll's stories are more than a century old, his works continue to give joy and pleasure to children and adults all around the world.

Investigate, *Inquire,* and Imagine

Recall: GATHERING FACTS

1a. What is Father William sure he doesn't have?

2a. What does Father William say about answering three questions?

3a. What does the son in "Jabberwocky" do despite his father's warning? What happens when the young man finds the Jabberwock?

4a. How does the father react when the son returns home?

→ Interpret: FINDING MEANING

1b. Why would Father William say this to his son?

2b. What does Father William think about his son's line of questioning?

3b. Does the son seem frightened? Why does he stop along the way? How does he feel on his way home?

4b. Why does he react this way?

Analyze: TAKING THINGS APART

5a. Identify examples in each poem of how the father communicates with his son. Then find specific examples showing how the son acts and how he communicates with his father.

→ Synthesize: BRINGING THINGS TOGETHER

5b. Develop a character description for the father and the son in "You Are Old, Father William." Do the same for the father and the son in "Jabberwocky."

Evaluate: MAKING JUDGMENTS

6a. Summarize and cite the positive elements of the father-son relationships in both poems.

→ Extend: CONNECTING IDEAS

6b. Which poem more fully describes the father-son relationship? Which father-son relationship is more believable? Which relationship is more intimate? Explain your answers.

Understanding *Literature*

MOOD. Mood, or atmosphere, is the emotion a writer creates in a literary work. A writer creates a mood by using concrete details. Describe the mood of "You Are Old, Father William." Describe the mood of "Jabberwocky." How does the mood shift or change in that poem?

BLEND. A blend is a new word created by joining together two old ones, as in *smog*, from the words *smoke* and *fog*; or *brunch*, from the words *breakfast* and *lunch*. Write the words from "Jabberwocky" you think are blends. Then look up those words in the dictionary to see if the entry indicates that the word is a blend of two other words. Keep in mind that many of Carroll's made-up words do not appear in the dictionary.

RHYME. Rhyme is the repetition of sounds at the ends of words. Rhyme can enhance the musical quality of a poem. Many poems reveal a pattern of rhyming words that appear at the ends of lines. These are called *end rhymes. Internal rhymes* are rhymes within the line. The regular pattern of rhymes in a poem is its *rhyme scheme.* To identify a poem's rhyme scheme, assign letters of the alphabet to the end of each line. The first line would have an *a*, as would any lines that rhyme with the first line. When you find a new rhyme, assign it the letter *b*. Any line that rhymes with line b should be assigned the same letter. Continue using letters of the alphabet to identify patterns of rhyme until you get to the end of the poem. See the graphic organizer for an example. Copy down two other stanzas from "You Are Old, Father William" and mark their rhyme schemes. Do they match the first stanza? Does the entire poem use the same rhyme scheme? Copy several stanzas from "Jabberwocky" and identify its rhyme scheme.

Graphic *Organizer*

"You are old, Father William," the young man said,	a
"And your hair has become very white;	b
And yet you incessantly stand on your head—	a
Do you think, at your age, it is right?"	b

Prereading

"Stopping by Woods on a Snowy Evening"
by Robert Frost

Reader's T O O L B O X

RHYME. Rhyme is the repetition of sounds at the ends of words. The rhymes in this poem are end rhymes—they occur at the ends of lines. Notice how the lines are grouped into stanzas. There are four stanzas in the poem. Within each stanza, which words rhyme? You may want to use a graphic organizer like the one below to help keep track of your answers.

REPETITION. Repetition is more than one use of a sound, word, or phrase. What words are repeated in this poem? What line is repeated?

Graphic Organizer

Write the last word of each line in the graphic organizer. Then mark a star next to the words that rhyme.

Stanza 1	know
	_____
	_____
	_____

Reader's Journal

What do you think is the most fascinating scene in the natural world—mountains, storms, waterfalls, prairies, ice floes, or something else? Write about the scene that most fascinates you.

Reader's Resource

- More than 95 percent of the native forests in the United States have been logged. In the lower 48 states (all but Alaska and Hawaii), more than 99 percent of the forests have been logged. Very few woodlands exist in large enough blocks to sustain wildlife. Clearcutting—a common method of harvesting trees—involves mowing down all the trees at once on a tract of land. Clearcutting destroys wildlife habitats and causes flooding, as the land can no longer absorb water very well. Spotted owls, bald eagles, black bears, and many other species are dwindling as their habitats disappear.

- A **symbol** is a thing that stands for or represents both itself and something else. Poetry commonly contains symbols. A rose, for example, might represent beauty, love, or romance. A dove might stand for peace. Poets often use the cycle of the seasons as a source of symbols. Springtime, when plants begin growing, is often used as a symbol of youth. Autumn, when leaves turn brown and fall, is frequently used as a symbol of advancing age. Winter, the end of the year, with its ice and snow and cold, can symbolize death, the end of life. Another traditional symbol of death is sleep.

Winter, 1890. Ivan Shishkin. State Russian Museum, St. Petersburg, Russia.

Stopping by Woods on a
Snowy Evening

Robert Frost

Whose woods these are I think I know.
His house is in the village though;
He will not see me stopping here
To watch his woods fill up with snow.

5   My little horse must think it queer
To stop without a farmhouse near
Between the woods and frozen lake
The darkest evening of the year.

GUIDED READING

Where does the speaker stop and why?

GUIDED READING

At what time of year is the poem set?

He gives his harness bells a shake
10 To ask if there is some mistake.
The only other sound's the sweep
Of easy wind and <u>downy</u> flake.

The woods are lovely, dark and deep,
But I have promises to keep,
15 And miles to go before I sleep,
And miles to go before I sleep. ∎

GUIDED READING

What does the speaker feel about the woods? Why can't he stay there?

Respond *to the* SELECTION

Would you stop to watch such a scene despite the cold, the lateness of the day, and the long journey ahead? Why, or why not?

About *the* AUTHOR

Robert Frost (1874–1963) was born in San Francisco. Frost's father died when the boy was eleven. He and his mother then moved to New England, where Frost lived for most of the rest of his life. He attended high school in Lawrence, Massachusetts, and graduated at the top of his class, sharing the position of valedictorian with Elinor White, whom he later married. After attending Dartmouth and Harvard and working as a teacher and farmer in New Hampshire, Frost moved with his family to England where, in 1913, he published his first book of poetry, *A Boy's Will.* In this book and in later volumes such as *North of Boston, Mountain Interval, New Hampshire, West-Running Brook,* and *A Further Range,* Frost wrote about the people and landscape of New England in verse that made him the most popular poet of this century. In later years, Frost taught at various universities and gave many public readings of his works. He received honorary doctorates from Cambridge and Oxford and was invited to read a poem at the inauguration of President John F. Kennedy.

words for everyday use

down • y (down' ē) *adj.,* like down, the soft, fine inner feathers of an adult bird or outer feathers of a young bird. *The baby's stuffed animal is soft and <u>downy</u>.*

Investigate, Inquire, and Imagine

Recall: GATHERING FACTS

1a. What does the speaker say about the owner of the woods?

2a. What does the horse think is queer and perhaps a mistake?

3a. What sounds are described in this poem?

→ **Interpret:** FINDING MEANING

1b. Why might he be concerned about where the owner is?

2b. Is there good reason for the horse to be restless and anxious? Why, or why not? Compare his attitude to that of the speaker.

3b. What do these sounds suggest about the atmosphere in this place?

Analyze: TAKING THINGS APART

4a. What two contradicting thoughts does the speaker voice in the last stanza?

→ **Synthesize:** BRINGING THINGS TOGETHER

4b. Why might the speaker want to stay? Why must the speaker move on?

Evaluate: MAKING JUDGMENTS

5a. How well does the author create a specific mood in this poem? How would you describe the mood?

→ **Extend:** CONNECTING IDEAS

5b. If you were writing about winter, what mood would you try to create? How would you do it?

Understanding *Literature*

RHYME. Review your graphic organizer. Look for rhyme patterns in each stanza. Do all the stanzas have the same pattern? Is there any connection between the third line of a stanza and the first, second, and fourth lines of the following stanza?

REPETITION. Repetition is more than one use of a sound, word, or group of words. What line is repeated in this poem? Why do you think Frost wanted to repeat that line?

"Life Doesn't Frighten Me"

by Maya Angelou

Reader's TOOLBOX

REPETITION. Repetition is more than one use of a sound, word, or group of words. Repetition is used in poetry to create rhythmic effects. It also is used to emphasize ideas. What examples of repetition are found in "Life Doesn't Frighten Me"?

RHYME AND SLANT RHYME. Rhyme is the repetition of sounds at the ends of words. A **slant rhyme** is a rhyme in which the sounds are almost but not exactly alike, like in *green sleeve*. What rhymes can you find in this poem? What slant rhymes can you find?

Graphic Organizer

Write inside circles each pair of words that creates a rhyme or slant rhyme. Connect the pair with a solid line if it creates a rhyme. Connect the pair with a dotted line if it creates a slant rhyme.

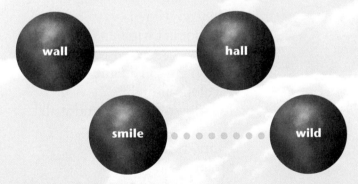

Reader's Journal

What situations frighten you? What do you do to overcome your fear?

Reader's Resource

- Stress resulting from threatening or unfamiliar situations can have a major effect on mental health. Milder stress-related symptoms might include a headache, a cough, or a rash, while more severe stress-related symptoms might include stomach ulcers and high blood pressure. Learning how to relax as well as taking the time to exercise and rest sufficiently have been identified as important techniques for handling stress and helping to maintain mental and emotional health.

- Anxiety is a feeling of dread or worry that can be related to stress or difficult situations. Anxiety differs from fear in that it is not closely associated with any one thing. Fear of the dark is a common fear in young children that usually disappears with time. Responding to dangerous or frightening situations requires courage or fearlessness. Being able to face one's fears is the first step in overcoming them. People have many different ways of overcoming or dealing with their fears.

Life Doesn't Frighten Me

Maya Angelou

Little Sweet, 1944. William H. Johnson.
National Museum of American Art.

Little Sweet, 1944. William H. Johnson.

William H. Johnson (1901–1970) painted in a style
that he identified as "primitive" although he had a
great deal of training as an artist. He was inspired by
his childhood in rural South Carolina and by African-
American folk painting. Do you think the attitude of
the girl in the painting is like that of the speaker in
the poem? Why, or why not?

Shadows on the wall
Noises down the hall
Life doesn't frighten me at all
Bad dogs barking loud
Big ghosts in a cloud
Life doesn't frighten me at all.

Mean old Mother Goose
Lions on the loose
They don't frighten me at all
Dragons breathing flame
On my counterpane
That doesn't frighten me at all.

I go boo
Make them shoo
I make fun
Way they run
I won't cry
So they fly
I just smile
They go wild
Life doesn't frighten me at all.

GUIDED READING

What does the
speaker do to con-
front scary things?

Tough guys in a fight
All alone at night
Life doesn't frighten me at all.

Panthers in the park
Strangers in the dark
No, they don't frighten me at all.

That new classroom where
Boys all pull my hair
(Kissy little girls
With their hair in curls)
They don't frighten me at all.

Don't show me frogs and snakes
And listen for my scream.

If I'm afraid at all
It's only in my dreams.

I've got a magic charm
That I keep up my sleeve,
I can walk the ocean floor
And never have to breathe.

Life doesn't frighten me at all
Not at all
Not at all.
Life doesn't frighten me at all ■

GUIDED READING

If the speaker is ever afraid, when is it?

GUIDED READING

What does the speaker keep up her sleeve?

Respond *to the* SELECTION

What thoughts about life do you have?

About *the* AUTHOR

Born Marguerite Johnson in St. Louis in 1928, **Maya Angelou** was raised by her grand-mother in segregated Arkansas from the ages of three to seven. Angelou was influenced at an early age by the work of writers like Shakespeare and Paul Laurence Dunbar. In the 1960s she was sought out by Dr. Martin Luther King, Jr. to be the northern coordinator for the Southern Christian Leadership Conference, an organization dedicated to using nonviolent protest to end racism and achieve civil rights for African Americans. In 1993, at the request of President Clinton, she wrote and read a poem for his inauguration. Angelou says the basic message in that poem is fundamental to all her work: "What I try to say is that as human beings we are more alike than we are unalike."

Investigate, Inquire, and Imagine

Recall: GATHERING FACTS

1a. How does the speaker confront scary things?

2a. What in the new classroom does the speaker mention?

3a. What does the speaker keep up her sleeve?

Interpret: FINDING MEANING

1b. How do these tactics help the speaker?

2b. How might these things be scary?

3b. How could that object help her?

Analyze: TAKING THINGS APART

4a. Identify all the things in the poem that the speaker is not frightened of.

Synthesize: BRINGING THINGS TOGETHER

4b. How does the speaker avoid being frightened of these things? What quality or characteristic does the speaker have that allows her to feel unafraid?

Evaluate: MAKING JUDGMENTS

5a. In making the point that life doesn't frighten her at all, she mentions certain things that could possibly be scary. What do you think about the items she mentions? Do you think this is a good representation of scary things in life? Why, or why not?

Extend: CONNECTING IDEAS

5b. If you were to write a poem similar to this one, what items would you use to make the point that life doesn't frighten you at all?

Understanding *Literature*

REPETITION. Repetition is more than one use of a sound, word, or group of words. Repetition is used in poetry to create rhythmic effects. It also is used to emphasize ideas. How does repetition affect the rhythm of this poem? What ideas are repeated? How does repeating these ideas create a particular mood?

RHYME AND SLANT RHYME. Rhyme is the repetition of sounds at the ends of words. A **slant rhyme** is a near rhyme in which the sounds are almost but not exactly alike, like in *green sleeve*. How does rhyme work with repetition in this poem?

Prereading

"Cynthia in the Snow" by Gwendolyn Brooks

Reader's T O O L B O X

ONOMATOPOEIA. Onomatopoeia is the use of words or phrases like *meow* or *beep* that sound like what they name. In poetry, words are chosen to create a combination of sounds. With onomatopoeia, the sounds themselves create meaning. As you read "Cynthia in the Snow," look for examples of onomatopoeia.

ALLITERATION. Alliteration is the repetition of consonant sounds at the beginnings of syllables, as in *bats in the belfry* or *dead as a doornail.* Alliteration is based on sound rather than spelling. For example, *ginger jelly* and *keen car* show alliteration, but *ginger* and *gumdrop* do not. Look for examples of alliteration in this poem.

Graphic *Organizer*

Arrange your findings of alliteration visually.

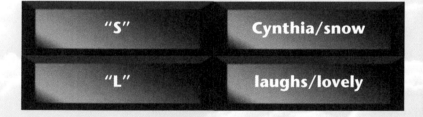

| "S" | Cynthia/snow |
| "L" | laughs/lovely |

Reader's *Journal*

What do you like about snow? What don't you like about it?

Reader's *Resource*

- **SCIENCE CONNECTION.** Snowflakes are made up of tiny transparent ice crystals. These crystals cling together as they thaw in the atmosphere, forming large puffs of snow as they fall. Snow crystals develop in hexagonal forms. Most of them fall under one of four types—needle, columnar, platelike, or star-shaped. Every snow crystal is unique, however, because each crystal forms under different precise weather conditions.

The Snow in Louveciennes, c.1874. Alfred Sisley. Musée d'Orsay, Paris.

Cynthia
in the Snow
Gwendolyn Brooks

It SHUSHES.
It hushes
The loudness in the road.
It flitter-twitters,
And laughs away from me.
It laughs a lovely whiteness,
And whitely whirs away,
To be
Some otherwhere,
Still white as milk or shirts.
So beautiful it hurts. ∎

art smart.

The Snow in Louvenciennes, 1874. Alfred Sisley.

The Impressionists were interested in reproducing the light and color of nature. They were especially fond of the effects of different weather. Alfred Sisley (1839–1899) made several paintings of this scene in winter, under different conditions. How are the intentions of the painter similar to those of poet Gwendolyn Brooks in "Cynthia in the Snow"?

Respond *to the* SELECTION

What have you ever seen that you could describe as "so beautiful it hurts"?

About *the* AUTHOR

Gwendolyn Brooks (1917–2000) was born in Topeka, Kansas, but lived most of her life in Chicago. She began rhyming at a young age and published her first poem, called "Eventide," when she was thirteen. Much of Brooks's writing draws from her experiences growing up in the inner city neighborhood of Bronzeville. Her collection of poems *Annie Allen,* about a black girl growing up in Chicago, won the Pulitzer Prize for poetry in 1949, making her the first African American to receive that famous award.

In 1968, she was named the official poet, or Poet Laureate, of Illinois. From 1985–1986, she was the first African-American woman to become the Poetry Consultant to the Library of Congress, the national library of the United States. Brooks went to teach as professor of English at Chicago State University in 1990. In her honor, the university formed and built the Gwendolyn Brooks Center. The center's mission is to promote literature and creative writing, and to encourage people to learn about African-American writers.

Investigate, Inquire, and Imagine

Recall: GATHERING FACTS

1a. How does the snow laugh?

2a. Where does the snow "whir away" to?

Interpret: FINDING MEANING

1b. How can snow seem to do this?

2b. What causes the snow to "whir"?

Analyze: TAKING THINGS APART

3a. In this poem, the snow is mainly described by its actions. List the verbs used to describe the snow's actions.

Synthesize: BRINGING THINGS TOGETHER

3b. How does this description show characteristics about the snow? Does it make the snow seem powerful, full of life, meek, angry, or playful? Explain your answer.

Perspective: LOOKING AT OTHER VIEWS

4a. How does the speaker (probably Cynthia) feel about snow? Does she like it? How do you know?

Empathy: SEEING FROM INSIDE

4b. If you, like Cynthia, were out in the snow, what would you do?

Understanding Literature

ONOMATOPOEIA. Onomatopoeia is the use of words or phrases like *meow* or *beep* that sound like what they name. Some onomatopoeias are established words in the English language. Others can be made-up words and phrases. Which onomatopoeias in this poem are words you could find in a dictionary? Which are more unconventional?

ALLITERATION. Alliteration is the repetition of consonant sounds at the beginnings of syllables, as in <u>b</u>ats in the <u>b</u>elfry or <u>d</u>ead as a <u>d</u>oornail. Alliteration is based on sound rather than spelling. For example, <u>g</u>inger <u>j</u>elly and <u>k</u>een <u>c</u>ar show alliteration, but *ginger* and *gumdrop* do not. What examples of alliteration did you find in "Cynthia in the Snow"? What effect do they have on the poem?

Writer's Journal

1. The line "And like a thunderbolt he falls" is a simile. A simile is a comparison using *like* or *as*. Write a **simile** about the sea.

2. Create **onomatopoeias** for the following sounds: an airplane flying overhead, a whale's call, a pencil writing, and paper tearing.

3. Write a short **nonsense verse** in which the words that end each line rhyme.

Skill Builders

Study and Research

RESEARCHING THE POET. At your library, find information about Alfred, Lord Tennyson. Try to locate a biography or use the Internet to search for information about the poet's life. Look for answers to some of these questions, or make up a list of questions you would like to answer. Present your findings in class along with a list of the resources you used.

- Where was Tennyson born? What was his life like as a boy? When did he begin writing?
- Who was Henry Hallam? Why was he an important figure in Tennyson's life?
- Who was Emily Sellwood? How did Tennyson meet her?
- What besides poetry did Tennyson write?
- How did Tennyson get the title "lord"? What did that title mean?

Speaking and Listening & Collaborative Learning

RECITING POETRY. Choose one of the poems in this first section of the unit to practice reciting aloud to a partner. Take turns with your partner, practicing reading the poem you have chosen until you can recite it without tripping over any of the words. Then, practice reading the poem with some emotion and drama. Think about your pace, volume, expressions, gestures, and tone of voice. After your partner's turn reciting, share constructive criticism with him or her. Let your partner know what he or she did very well, what he or she could improve on, and what ideas you may have that could improve their oral reading. For more information, review the Language Arts Survey 4.19, "Oral Interpretation of Poetry."

Media Literacy

EVALUATING AN INTERNET SITE. Use a computer with an Internet connection and go to the site Voices from the Gaps at http://voices.cla.umn.edu/. Browsing by name, look at several author entries, including those of Maya Angelou and Gwendolyn Brooks. What kinds of information can you find about the authors featured at this site? Who put the site together? Why? How is this site unique? What value does the site have?

Reader's Resource

- **HISTORY CONNECTION.**
Automats became popular in the 1930s and 1940s. Automat machines were comparable to modern-day vending machines, with one exception: the food in automats was prepared daily. A typical automat customer would walk up to a wall of glass windows. He or she would put his or her coins in a slot and get freshly prepared food—anything from a roll with butter to an entree such as lasagna to a slice of pie. Horn & Hardarts was the first automat restaurant chain. Automats diminished in popularity in the 1950s as fast food restaurants began to appear. Horn & Hardarts still continues to restore old automat machines, especially for those people who like to collect antiques.

- Japan has more than five million vending machines (one for every 24 people). You can buy dry rice, pantyhose, comic books, and even insects. Kabutomushi, or horned beetles, are the featured items in some vending machines. Customers place $3.40 into a slot and open a small door to acquire a pair of three-inch beetles in a box. These insects are kept as pets and are extremely popular among Japanese children.

Prereading

"TWO GIRLS . . ."
by Charles Reznikoff

Reader's TOOLBOX

AIM. A writer's **aim** is his or her purpose, or goal. People may write for one or more of the following purposes: to inform (informative writing); to tell a story (narrative writing); to reflect (personal writing); to share a perspective, entertain, enrich, or enlighten (imaginative writing); or to persuade readers to respond in some way (persuasive writing). What do you think the author's main aim is in this poem?

FREE VERSE. Free verse is poetry that does not use regular rhyme, rhythm, or division into stanzas. In this type of verse, which is very common in modern poetry, sound patterns are created through selective pauses or through the normal rhythms of language. Although "Two Girls…" is an example of free verse, a couple of lines do contain rhymes. Try to identify them as you read.

METAPHOR. A **metaphor** is a figure of speech in which one thing is spoken or written about as if it were another. This figure of speech invites the reader to make a comparison between the two things. What metaphor can you find in this poem?

Reader's Journal

Do you buy things from vending machines? Why, or why not?

art smart

Horn & Hardart Automat, 1967. Richard Estes.

Richard Estes (b.1936) paints in a style identified as "photorealism" or "superrealism." He is particularly interested in the complex pattern of reflections on glass. Why do you think he would choose to paint the scene rather than take a photograph of it?

© Richard Estes/Licensed by VAGA, New York.

Horn & Hardart Automat, 1967. Richard Estes. Private Collection.

TWO GIRLS...

Charles Reznikoff

Two girls of twelve or so at a table
in the Automat, smiling at each other
and the world; eating sedately.
And a tramp, wearing two or three tattered coats,
dark with dirt, mumbling, sat down beside them—
Miss Muffit's spider.
But, unlike her, they were not frightened away,
and did not shudder as they might if older and look <u>askance</u>.
They did steal a glance
at their dark companion and were slightly amused:
in their shining innocence seeing
in him only another human being. ■

words for everyday use

askance (ə skans´) *adv.,* with disapproval or distrust. *The doctor looked <u>askance</u> when I said that I had taken all the medication.*

How do you react when you see someone very different from yourself?

About *the* AUTHOR

Charles Reznikoff was born on August 31, 1894, in Brooklyn, New York. His parents were Russian Jews who emigrated to the United States around the time of his birth. His family was forced to move throughout the city due to the anti-Semitism with which they were faced. Reznikoff later wrote about the times he would rush home from high school in order to avoid taunts from other kids. But despite his insecurities, Reznikoff was an excellent student. He finished grammar school three years ahead of his class and graduated from high school at the age of fifteen. By age sixteen, Reznikoff knew he wanted to be a writer. However, he went on to law school and practiced for a brief period before becoming a full-fledged writer. During the 1920s, his poetry began to be published commercially. His reputation grew—resulting in becoming one of the major influences to form the Objectivist group of poets. He died from a heart attack on January 22, 1976.

Investigate, Inquire, and Imagine

Recall: GATHERING FACTS

1a. Where are the two girls? What are they doing?

2a. Who enters this place? What does he do?

3a. What don't the girls do when they see the newcomer?

→ **Interpret:** FINDING MEANING

1b. Why do you think they are there? Why are they smiling?

2b. Why might he have entered this place?

3b. Why do you think they don't?

Analyze: TAKING THINGS APART

4a. In what ways does the speaker say the girls might have reacted but didn't?

→ **Synthesize:** BRINGING THINGS TOGETHER

4b. What do the girls do in reaction to the newcomer? How does the speaker explain their reaction? What is the speaker's main idea in this poem?

Understanding Literature

AIM. A writer's **aim** is his or her purpose, or goal. People may write for one or more of the following purposes: to inform (informative writing); to tell a story (narrative writing); to reflect (personal writing); to share a perspective, entertain, enrich, or enlighten (imaginative writing); or to persuade readers to respond in some way (persuasive writing). What is the author's main purpose, or goal, in writing this poem? What does he want the reader to think about?

FREE VERSE. Free verse is poetry that does not use regular rhyme, rhythm, or division into stanzas. In this type of verse, which is very common in modern poetry, sound patterns are created through selective pauses or through the normal rhythms of language. Where in this free verse poem is there a hint of traditional rhyming? What effect does this have on the poem?

METAPHOR. A metaphor is a figure of speech in which one thing is spoken or written about as if it were another. This figure of speech invites the reader to make a comparison between the two things. What does the metaphor in this poem compare? Is this metaphor effective? Why, or why not?

Writer's Journal

1. Imagine you are Charles Reznikoff, and turn the poem "Two Girls . . ." into a **short story**.

2. Write a possible **dialogue** that could have taken place between the two girls.

3. Create a new **title** for the poem you just read. Explain why you chose the title.

Skill Builders

Speaking and Listening

FIND A PARTNER. Select one person to be the interviewer and the other to be Charles Reznikoff. In this project, the interviewer will be asking Charles Reznikoff about his life, his work, and what inspired him to write the poem "Two Girls . . . ." The other person will respond. To find the information you need to form appropriate questions and answers, you will need to do some research on Charles Reznikoff. Then write a list of questions that link with the information you have gathered. You may need to make up some of the answers, but try to be as factual as possible. After practicing, videotape or audiotape your interview and share it with the rest of the class. For more help on conducting an interview, refer to the Language Arts Survey 4.14 "Conducting an Interview."

Study and Research

REVISITING NURSERY RHYMES. In "Two Girls . . . ," Charles Reznikoff creates a metaphor using a character from the Mother Goose rhyme (Miss Muffit's spider) to describe the stranger who sits near the two girls. Find a Mother Goose character. The library or the Internet should have plenty of information on characters in the Mother Goose tales. Then go somewhere where you can "people watch." Write a poem about the people you see, comparing each of them to characters from the Mother Goose tales. Refer back to other poems you have read in the unit for ideas on rhyme and meter. After you have finished your poem, take turns reading the poems out loud with other members of your class. Make sure you use appropriate expression in your voice as you read.

Prereading

"Ox Cart Man" by Donald Hall

Reader's TOOLBOX

NARRATIVE POEM. A **narrative poem** is a verse that tells a story. Like a work of fiction, a narrative poem has a character or characters, a setting, a plot, and a theme. This narrative poem describes a yearly cycle in the life of one person. The poem tells the reader about the ox cart man's life from October to November, but in doing so, reveals how the man works through the rest of the year. As you read, look for information about what the ox cart man does in the winter, spring, and summer.

CONCRETE LANGUAGE. A **concrete word**, like *cloud* or *airplane*, names something that can be directly seen, tasted, touched, heard, or smelled. **Concrete language** is particularly effective when it is as specific and detailed as possible. For example, the phrase *Charlie collapsed on the wobbly stool* is more precise than *the boy sat down on the chair*. By carefully choosing specific words to describe objects and actions, a writer can portray a much more vivid picture of what is happening in a poem or story. Look at the first two lines of "Ox Cart Man." What specific information does the poet offer?

Graphic Organizer

Use a graphic organizer like this to keep track of what the ox cart man does during each season of the year.

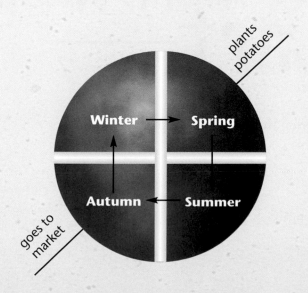

plants potatoes

Winter → Spring

Autumn ← Summer

goes to market

Reader's Journal

What routines do you follow?

Reader's Resource

- Donald Hall wrote this poem after hearing the story about the ox cart man from a cousin in their hometown of Wilmot, New Hampshire. According to Hall, this is how it happened: "Paul was a great storyteller. His face would crinkle a little bit and the corners of his mouth would turn up. You'd know he was thinking of a story. So Paul said, 'Did you ever hear the story about the fella used to live around here? Every autumn he loaded up his cart,' and then told me pretty much that story. My spine shivered. I don't know if I knew at that moment that I was going to write about it, but I began the next morning and I took about a year making that little poem."

- Donald Hall admires the cyclical life of the ox cart man. He says, "A life of productive work that sustains itself by expending itself is also the life of a perennial plant that dies down in the fall and comes up again in the spring."

A Rocky Landscape with an Ox Cart, c.1600s. Jan Both. National Gallery, London.

Ox Cart MAN

Donald Hall

In October of the year, he counts potatoes dug from the brown field,
counting the seed, counting
the cellar's portion out,
and bags the rest on the cart's floor.

He packs wool sheared in April, honey in combs, linen, leather
tanned from deerhide,

GUIDED READING

When was the wool sheared?

and vinegar in a barrel
hooped[1] by hand at the forge's fire.

He walks by his ox's head, ten days
to Portsmouth Market, and sells potatoes,
and the bag that carried potatoes,
flaxseed, birch brooms, maple sugar, goose
feathers, yarn.

GUIDED READING

Where does the
man go? What
does he do there?

When the cart is empty he sells the cart.
When the cart is sold he sells the ox,
harness[2] and yoke,[3] and walks
home, his pockets heavy
with the year's coin for salt and taxes,

GUIDED READING

What does the
man have as he
walks home?

and at home by fire's light in November cold
stitches new harness for next year's ox in the barn,
and carves the yoke, and saws planks
building the cart again. ∎

---

1. **hooped.** Bound and fastened with a hoop
2. **harness.** Leather gear that fastens to a draft animal for pulling a cart
3. **yoke.** Wooden bar that rests on a draft animal's shoulders

Respond *to the* SELECTION

What do you think about the ox cart man's life?

About *the* AUTHOR

Donald Hall was born in 1928 in Hamden, Connecticut. He has written more than ten books of poetry. In 1975 Hall and his wife Jane Kenyon moved back to Hall's childhood home on Eagle Pond Farm in Wilmot, New Hampshire. As a child, Hall had written his first poetry on the farm. From 1984 to 1989, Hall was the Poet Laureate of New Hampshire. He has also written plays, essays, short stories, and children's books. About writing, Hall advises, "Don't ever hold anything back. Put everything out that can possibly belong in that poem or story. Don't save anything for the next one." He says, "That's the only way to work. It's the only way to live, really."

Investigate, Inquire, and Imagine

Recall: GATHERING FACTS

1a. What does the ox cart man do in October?

2a. Where does the man walk to? How far is it?

3a. What does the man do in November?

→ **Interpret:** FINDING MEANING

1b. Why is this work done in October?

2b. How do you think he acquired everything he sold? Why do you think he sells the cart, ox, harness, and yoke?

3b. What is he preparing for?

Analyze: TAKING THINGS APART

4a. In "Ox Cart Man," some of the man's actions are described directly. Others are only implied. For example, if the man is counting potatoes, the reader can probably assume that the man planted the potatoes and then harvested them. List the actions that are directly described and then list those that are implied.

→ **Synthesize:** BRINGING THINGS TOGETHER

4b. Describe in your own words the ox cart man's lifestyle.

Perspective: LOOKING AT OTHER VIEWS →

5a. Do you think the ox cart man is happy with his life? Why, or why not?

Empathy: SEEING FROM INSIDE

5b. Would you be satisfied with a life like that of the ox cart man? Why, or why not?

Understanding Literature

NARRATIVE POEM. A **narrative poem** is a verse that tells a story. Like a work of fiction, a narrative poem has a character or characters, a setting, a plot, and a theme. This narrative poem describes a yearly cycle in the life of one person. What does the poem imply about the previous year in the man's life? about the following year?

CONCRETE LANGUAGE. A **concrete word**, like *cloud* or *airplane*, names something that can be directly seen, tasted, touched, heard, or smelled. **Concrete language** is particularly effective when it is specific and detailed. What specific, concrete language do you find in "Ox Cart Man"? How does this language create meaning in the poem? Would the poem be as interesting if the poet used more general language? Why, or why not?

Prereading

"One Time" by William Stafford

Reader's TOOLBOX

NARRATIVE POEM. A **narrative poem** is a verse that tells a story. The story a narrative poem tells can be long or short. Some longer narrative poems fill entire books and are broken down into sections or chapters. Others, like this one, are quite short. What is the story this poem tells? Who are the characters? What is the setting?

SENSORY DETAILS. Sensory details are words and phrases that describe how things look, sound, smell, taste, or feel. What sensory details can you find in "One Time"? Use the graphic organizer below to keep track of the sensory details you find.

Graphic *Organizer*

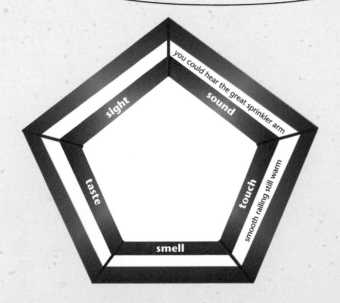

sight

sound — you could hear the great sprinkler arm

touch — smooth railing still warm

taste

smell

Reader's *Journal*

If you lost one of your senses, how might you differently use those you still had?

Reader's Resource

- The National Federation of the Blind, founded in 1940, is the nation's largest organization of blind persons. The federation's purpose is to help blind persons achieve self-confidence and self-respect and to serve as a tool for blind people to use to express their thoughts, concerns, and ideas. The federation provides public information about blindness, scholarships, aids and appliances, services, job opportunities, and protection of civil rights. The American Federation for the Blind is a leading national resource for people who are blind or visually impaired. Founded in 1921, the organization strives to enable people who are blind or visually impaired to achieve equality of access and opportunity. It collects and makes available information, promotes governmental and educational policies that aid people with blindness or visual impairment, and produces and distributes talking books and other audio materials.

- Braille is a series of raised dots that can be read with the fingers by people who are blind or visually impaired. Teachers, parents, and others who are not visually impaired ordinarily read braille with their eyes.

One time

William Stafford

When evening had flowed between houses
and paused on the schoolground, I met
Hilary's blind little sister following
the gray smooth railing still warm from the sun
with her hand; and she stood by the edge
holding her face upward waiting
while the last light found her cheek
and her hair, and then on over the trees.

You could hear the great sprinkler arm
of water find and then leave the pavement,
and pigeons telling each other their dreams
or the dreams they would have. We were
deep in the well of shadow by then, and I
held out my hand, saying, "Tina, it's me—
Hilary says I should tell you it's dark,
and, oh, Tina, it is. Together now—"

And I reached, our hands touched,
and we found our way home.

GUIDED READING

Who does the speaker meet?

GUIDED READING

What is happening to the daylight?

What mood does this poem create? Draw a picture of Tina, showing how she feels.

About *the* AUTHOR

William Stafford (1914–1993) was a poet and a writer with an extraordinary ability to absorb and reflect on the world around him and on human nature. His ability to listen—to the sounds of the natural world, to spoken words, and to the interplay of silence and noise—was surpassed only by his ability to communicate his thoughts. Stafford said that he greeted his ideas with the words, "Come in, come in!" He seemed to feel the same way about his readers. His poems and stories are ones with which many people feel they can really connect. His books, including *Down in My Heart, Even in Quiet Places,* and *Learning to Live in the World: Earth Poems,* have received many awards, including the National Book Award and the Award in Literature of the American Academy and Institute of Arts and Letters.

Investigate, *Inquire,* and Imagine

Recall: GATHERING FACTS

1a. What is Hilary's sister doing when the speaker finds her?

2a. What does the speaker say you could hear the pigeons doing?

3a. What does the speaker tell Tina?

4a. What do the speaker and Tina do after they grasped one another's hand?

→ **Interpret:** FINDING MEANING

1b. Why do you think she is doing this?

2b. How could the speaker have heard this?

3b. How does she respond?

4b. How would it have been a challenge to do this?

Analyze: TAKING THINGS APART

5a. Note the words and passages in this poem that reveal the passing of time.

→ **Synthesize:** BRINGING THINGS TOGETHER

5b. By the last lines of the poem, how is the speaker equally as challenged as Tina?

Evaluate: MAKING JUDGMENTS

6a. How does Stafford create a unique image of a sunset in this poem?

→ **Extend:** CONNECTING IDEAS

6b. How would you try to create a unique image of a sunset in a poem? What sensory details might you focus on?

Understanding *Literature*

NARRATIVE POEM. A **narrative poem** is a verse that tells a story. What story does this poem tell? How much time elapses in the poem? How much does the reader learn about the characters and setting?

SENSORY DETAILS. Sensory details are words and phrases that describe how things look, sound, smell, taste, or feel. How are sensory details especially important in this poem?

Writer's Journal

1. Write a short **narrative poem** about an experience you have had helping someone.

2. Write a **routine** for the responsibilities you have around the house, such as caring for siblings or pets, cleaning, or lawn care.

3. Imagine you are looking for someone and finally find the person. Write a half page of **dialogue** between you and the person you find.

Skill Builders

Speaking and Listening

TELLING A STORY. "One Time" is a narrative poem—a poem that tells a story. Write a story for the poem. You may need to add more detail to the poem to turn it into a story. For example, your story may offer detailed information on who the speaker is, why he or she is meeting Tina, where the speaker is coming from to meet Tina, and the speaker's friendship with Tina and Hilary. In other words, your story should expand the poem by filling in details that are missing from the poem. After you have written your story, tell it to the class. For more help on telling a story, refer to the Language Arts Survey 4.20, "Telling a Story."

Language, Grammar, and Style

ADJECTIVES. Adjectives modify nouns by telling specific details about them. Make a list of adjectives from "One Time" and "Ox Cart Man." Write the noun being modified along with the adjective or adjectives that modify it. Look at each example. How specific are the words? How would the poem be different if the adjectives were less specific? Create a piece of writing that narrates a story, using as many specific adjectives as possible. Omit any adjectives that are too general to reveal information to the reader. For more information, see the Language Arts Survey 3.63, "Adjectives."

Reader's Journal

Do you consider yourself more of a city person or more of a country person? What do you prefer about urban or rural settings?

Reader's Resource

• Edna St. Vincent Millay often wrote poetry based on her own life. "English Sparrows (Washington Square)" was written about a scene in Greenwich Village, a neighborhood in New York City where Millay lived in the early 1900s. Washington Square is at the heart of Greenwich Village. The "arch" mentioned in the poem is the Washington Memorial Arch, which overlooks Washington Square. This arch is one of the features that make Greenwich Village distinctive. The neighborhood is also known for its narrow, winding streets and old buildings, as well as SoHo, its famous shopping district. "City Trees" also probably is set in Greenwich Village.

Prereading

"English Sparrows (Washington Square)" and "City Trees"
by Edna St. Vincent Millay

Reader's TOOLBOX

LYRIC POEM. A lyric poem is a highly musical verse that expresses the emotions of a speaker and does not tell a story. Lyric poems got their name from a musical instrument known as the lyre. Lyres are stringed instruments that are similar to harps. In ancient Greece, short poems that revealed intense thoughts or feelings were either spoken or sung to the music of the lyre. Today, lyric poems may not be sung or chanted to music, but they do focus on thoughts and emotions, just as they did in ancient Greece. We also get our term for the words sung to music, or *lyrics*, from the lyre. As your read, think about the emotions each lyric poem reveals. You should also jot down on a separate sheet of paper words or phrases that seem musical to you.

MOOD. Mood, or atmosphere, is the emotion created by the writer in a literary work. A writer creates a mood by using sensory details. Create a chart like the one below on your own paper. As you read both poems by Edna St. Vincent Millay, note groups of words that create a definite mood in the left-hand column and identify the mood the words create in the right-hand column.

Graphic Organizer

"English Sparrows (Washington Square)"	
Group of Words	**Mood**
"sweet the sound in the city an hour before sunrise"	Peaceful, tranquil

"City Trees"	
Group of Words	**Mood**

English Sparrows

(Washington Square)
Edna St. Vincent Millay

Washington Square, 1900. Paul Cornoyer. Museum of the City of New York.

How sweet the sound in the city an hour before sunrise,
When the park is empty and gray and the light clear and so lovely
I must sit on the floor before my open window for an hour with my arms on
    the sill
And my cheek on my arm, watching the spring sky's
Soft <u>suffusion</u> from the roofed horizon upward with palest rose,
<u>Doting</u> on the charming sight with eyes
Open, eyes closed;
Breathing with quiet pleasure the cool air cleansed by the night, lacking all will
To let such happiness go, nor thinking the least thing ill
In me for such <u>indulgence</u>, pleased with the day and with myself. How sweet
The noisy chirping of the urchin sparrows from crevice and shelf
Under my window, and from down there in the street,
Announcing the advance of the roaring competitive day with city bird-song.

A bumbling bus
Goes under the arch. A man bareheaded and alone
Walks to a bench and sits down.
He breathes the morning with me; his thoughts are his own.
Together we watch the first <u>magnanimous</u>
Rays of the sun on the tops of greening trees and on houses of red brick and of stone. ∎

words for everyday use

suf • fuse (sə fyüz′) *v.,* spread over or through. *Light <u>suffused</u> the thin curtain.* **suffusion,** *n.*

dote (dōt′) *v.,* be lavish or excessive in one's attention or affection. *My brother <u>doted</u> on his pet cat, carrying it wherever he went.*

in • dul • gence (in dəl′ jəns) *n.,* unrestrained pleasure in something. *My favorite <u>indulgence</u> is ice cream.*

mag • nan • i • mous (mag na′ nə məs) *adj.,* showing lofty or courageous spirit. *Forest's <u>magnanimous</u> spirit helped him regain his health.*

City TREES

Edna St. Vincent Millay

The Sweeper, c.1902. Alfred Stieglitz. Private Collection.

The trees along this city street,

    Save for[1] the traffic and the trains,

Would make a sound as thin and sweet

    As trees in

    country lanes.

> **GUIDED READING**
> What would the city trees be able to do? What stops them from doing this?

And people standing in their shade

    Out of a shower, undoubtedly

Would hear such music as is made

    Upon a country tree.

Oh, little leaves that are so dumb[2]

    Against the shrieking city air,

I watch you when the wind has come,

    I know what

    sound is there. ■

> **GUIDED READING**
> What does the city air do?

---

1. **save for.** Except for
2. **dumb.** Lacking the power of speech

The Sweeper, c.1902. Alfred Stieglitz.

Alfred Stieglitz (1864–1946) was an important figure in the early development of photography. He and his associates argued for photography to be accepted as art. They often manipulated their photographs to imitate painting or charcoal drawing, as with this scene. Do you think photographs should be considered art?

Respond *to the* SELECTION

What are your own feelings about viewing sunrises or trees blowing in the wind? What emotions do such scenes create in you?

About *the* AUTHOR

Edna St. Vincent Millay (1892–1950) was a poet and playwright best known for her lyrical poetry. Millay, who was called Vincent by her close friends, grew up fatherless after the age of seven. Her mother believed that women should strive to be independent. She passed this philosophy on to Millay by encouraging her to be self-sufficient and ambitious. Millay's upbringing led her to attend college at Vassar, where she became serious about poetry and theater. In 1922, her play *The Harp Weaver* received the Pulitzer Prize. She continued to write plays and lyrical poems until her death in 1950.

Investigate, Inquire, and Imagine

Recall: GATHERING FACTS

1a. What time of day is described in the first stanza of "English Sparrows (Washington Square)"? What does the speaker do, see, and hear at this time of day?

2a. In the second stanza of "English Sparrows (Washington Square)," what does the speaker see a man do? What do both the speaker and the man watch?

3a. In "City Trees," what sound does the speaker say the trees would have made in country lanes? What would people standing beneath them in a rainstorm hear? What sounds are heard in the city instead of these sounds?

→ **Interpret:** FINDING MEANING

1b. How does the speaker seem to feel about this time of day and what she does, sees, and hears?

2b. In what way do the speaker and the man seem to be alike?

3b. Explain whether the speaker is satisfied just knowing the sound that the trees would make in a country setting or whether she wishes she were in the country.

Analyze: TAKING THINGS APART

4a. In stanza 1, how does the speaker of "English Sparrows (Washington Square)" seem to feel about her time alone? In stanza 2, what does she share with the man on the bench? In what ways are they together, and in what ways are they apart? In "City Trees" what would people hear when it showers? What does the speaker watch? What does the speaker know?

→ **Synthesize:** BRINGING THINGS TOGETHER

4b. Based on what you have read about the speaker of these two poems, explain what the speaker's attitude might be toward being alone.

Perspective: LOOKING AT OTHER VIEWS → **Empathy:** SEEING FROM INSIDE

5a. Based on the two poems you have read, explain how you think the speaker feels about the city in which she lives.

5b. Explain whether you would enjoy the sights, sounds, and smells of the city the speaker describes.

Understanding Literature

LYRIC POEM. A **lyric poem** is a verse that tells the emotions of a speaker and does not tell a story. In a sentence or two, sum up the emotions revealed in each poem.

MOOD. Mood, or atmosphere, is the emotion created in the reader by a piece of writing. Explain what mood is created in each poem. How are the moods similar? How are they different?

Writer's Journal

1. Write a **descriptive paragraph** about a time of day that you enjoy. What are the sights, sounds, smells, tastes, or feelings you associate with this time of day?
2. Imagine that you are an advice columnist. You receive a letter from a person who lives in the city and is homesick for the country. Write an **advice column** in which the person explains his or her problem and you give some helpful advice.
3. Write four or five lines of your own **lyric poem** about how you feel in a certain setting.

Skill Builders

Language, Grammar, and Style

CAPITALIZATION OF PLACE NAMES. The names of specific places are capitalized, while names of general places are not. For example, Washington Square is capitalized because it is the name of a specific square, but if you are writing about town squares in general, *squares* should be lowercase. For more information on proper capitalization of place names, see the Language Arts Survey 3.84, "Editing for Capitalization Errors." Read the sentences below, and choose the correct word from the pair in parentheses.

1. Edna St. Vincent Millay lived in (Greenwich Village, greenwich village).
2. She explored her thoughts about living in a (City, city).
3. Did you know the capital of (new york, New York) is (albany, Albany), not (New York City, new york city)?
4. Millay lived in a (Neighborhood, neighborhood) filled with narrow, winding (Streets, streets).
5. Head (west, West) to the (brooklyn bridge, Brooklyn Bridge).

Speaking and Listening

EXPERIMENTING WITH ALLITERATION. In the poems you have read, Millay uses a stylistic technique known as alliteration. **Alliteration** is the repetition of consonant sounds at the beginnings of syllables, as in "How sweet the sound in the city an hour before sunrise." Read aloud "English Sparrows (Washington Square)" and "City Trees" with a partner. Together, list at least five examples of alliteration from these poems. Then, write five phrases or sentences of your own that make use of alliteration. Try out the phrases or sentences by reading them aloud to one another.

Reader's *Journal*

What is your favorite food? What do you like about it?

Reader's TOOLBOX

IMAGE, SENSORY DETAILS, AND IMAGERY. An **image** is language that creates a concrete representation of an object or experience. An image is also the vivid mental picture created in the reader's mind by that language. The words and phrases that describe how things look, sound, smell, taste, or feel are known as **sensory details**. The images in a literary work are referred to, when considered altogether, as the work's **imagery**. As you read "Good Hot Dogs," identify images, or words and phrases that contain sensory details. Some images may appeal to more than one sense. For example, the word *lemon* may appeal to sight, touch, smell, and taste. On your own paper, make symbols to represent each of the five senses. Then, rewrite each sensory detail next to each of the symbols that apply.

Prereading

"Good Hot Dogs" and "Buenos Hot Dogs"

by Sandra Cisneros

Reader's Resource

- Translation is the art of rewording speech or writing into a different language. A translator cannot just sit down with a Spanish-English dictionary, look up the meaning of each Spanish word, and write down its meaning in English. Nor could a person do this to translate from English to Spanish. A literal translation out of a dictionary would create a lot of gibberish. Words and phrases in one language may be meaningless or have a completely altered meaning when translated literally. For example, if you were to say, "That new kid is cool," and someone translated that sentence literally into another language, without thinking about slang and shades of meaning, those hearing the translation might believe that you are talking about a chilly newborn goat.

- Translating poetry is even more difficult than translating prose or speech because the translator has to worry about preserving in his or her translation the poetic techniques the author used. It can be very difficult to keep a poem's rhyme and rhythm when translating it, and sometimes translators have to sacrifice the use of these techniques in their translations. Translators also have their own ideas about what is important to preserve in a literary work. Two different translators could create two very different translations of the same poem.

- The poem "Good Hot Dogs" was first written by Sandra Cisneros in English. Cisneros translated the poem herself into the Spanish "Buenos Hot Dogs." Many of her works in English include Spanish terms that lend a cultural flavor and an authentic feeling to the stories and poems.

Graphic *Organizer*

the store/ that smelled like steam

Good Hot Dogs

Sandra Cisneros

for Kiki

Fifty cents apiece
To eat our lunch
We'd run
Straight from school
Instead of home
Two blocks
Then the store
That smelled like steam
You ordered
Because you had the money
Two hot dogs and two pops[1] for here
Everything on the hot dogs
Except pickle lily
<u>Dash</u> those hot dogs
Into buns and splash on
All that good stuff
Yellow mustard and onions

And french fries piled on top all
Rolled up in a piece of wax
Paper for us to hold hot
In our hands
Quarters on the counter
Sit down
Good hot dogs
We'd eat
Fast till there was nothing left
But salt and poppy seeds even
The little burnt tips
Of french fries
We'd eat
You humming
And me swinging my legs

---

1. **pops.** Soda pops, soft drinks

words for everyday use

dash (dash′) *vt.*, throw. *In frustration with her team's losing streak, Georgina <u>dashed</u> her baseball mitt to the ground.*

Buenos Hot Dogs

Sandra Cisneros

para Kiki

Cincuenta centavos cada uno
Para comer nuestro lonche
Corríamos
Derecho desde la escuela
En vez de a casa
Dos cuadras
Después la tienda
Que olía a vapor
Tú pedías
Porque tenías el dinero
Dos hot dogs y dos refrescos para comer aquí
Los hot dogs con todo
Menos pepinos
Hecha esos hot dogs
En sus panes y salpícalos
Con todas esas cosas buenas

Mostaza amarilla y cebollas
Y papas fritas amontonadas encima
Envueltos en papel de cera
Para llevarlos calientitos
En las manos
Monedas encima del mostrador
Sientate
Buenos hot dogs
Comíamos
Rápido hasta que no quedaba nada
Menos sal y semillas de amapola hasta
Las puntitas quemadas
De las papas fritas
Comíamos
Tú canturreando
Y yo columpiando mis piernas ■

What types of meals do you like to share with your friends?

About *the*
AUTHOR

Sandra Cisneros had a hard childhood. Her parents were from Mexico, and they would move between Mexico City and Chicago frequently, never settling in one place for very long. This and the fact that she had six brothers and no sisters made for a lonely childhood. Loneliness and poverty drove her to reading books. She saw stories as a way of escape from reality. Cisneros began to write poetry in high school, but it wasn't until her first creative writing class in college that she started to take writing seriously. Because of her background, her writing is different from that of other American writers. She believes that she has something to say that most American writers don't know about, especially on subjects of feminism, love, oppression, and religion.

Investigate, *Inquire,* and Imagine

Recall: GATHERING FACTS

1a. What do the speaker and his or her companion do right after school? Where do the two go? What do they get?

2a. In what way is the lunch served?

3a. At what speed do the two eat? What is left? What do they do as they eat?

→ **Interpret:** FINDING MEANING

1b. How can you tell that the speaker and his or her companion are eager to go to this place and make their order?

2b. How do the speaker and his or her companion feel about the way the food is served?

3b. Explain whether the speaker and his or her companion enjoy the meal? How can you tell?

Analyze: TAKING THINGS APART

4a. What signs are there about the ages of the speaker and his or her companion in the poem? How old do you think the speaker and his or her companion are?

→ **Synthesize:** BRINGING THINGS TOGETHER

4b. How do you think the speaker might feel as an adult looking back on this memory?

Evaluate: MAKING JUDGMENTS

5a. Who do you think the speaker's companion is in relation to the speaker? How does the speaker seem to feel about this person? Who do you think the person named Kiki mentioned in the dedication might be?

→ **Extend:** CONNECTING IDEAS

5b. Twenty years from now, to whom do you think you might like to dedicate a poem? What memory might you share in this poem?

Understanding *Literature*

IMAGE, SENSORY DETAILS, AND IMAGERY. An **image** is language that describes something that can be seen, heard, touched, tasted, or smelled. The words and phrases that describe how things look, sound, smell, taste, or feel are known as **sensory details**. The images in a literary work are referred to, when considered altogether, as the work's **imagery**. Review your graphic organizer. To what senses does the imagery in the poem most appeal? Explain whether this makes sense, given the poem's title.

Writer's Journal

1. Pretend you are a hot dog stand owner. Write a **list** of "fixings" that people can choose to put on their hot dogs.

2. Recall a time you ate something you really like. Describe that experience in a **letter** to a friend, using three examples of sensory detail.

3. Imagine you are opening your own restaurant. Make a **menu** of the items you would serve there. Include prices and descriptions.

Skill Builders

Language, Grammar, and Style

SENTENCE FRAGMENTS. The poem you just read has many fragments—phrases that do not express complete thoughts. In other words, a fragment is an incomplete sentence. For example, the phrase "Everything on the hot dogs" is a fragment because it doesn't have a subject or verb. To complete this fragment, you need to add a subject and a verb: "Sandra and Miguel put everything on the hot dogs." Review the Language Arts Survey 3.31, "Correcting Sentence Fragments." For the sentences below, fix the fragments by adding a subject, predicate, and/or a verb.

1. Straight home from school
2. Smelled like fried chicken
3. Quarters on the counter
4. Good hot dogs
5. The little girls
6. In our hands
7. Looking for the lost dog
8. Helping me put away the dishes
9. The fierce wind
10. Six classes a day

Media Literacy & Collaborative Learning

MAKING A TELEVISION COMMERCIAL. Imagine you work in the marketing department for a fast food restaurant. In groups of four, create a commercial that appeals to as many of the five senses as possible. The shorter the commercial, the better. In your description, use vivid and succinct words to describe food items. You may want to include music in your commercial to catch consumers' attention. As you prepare to videotape your commercial, make sure the person who is describing the item uses expression in his or her voice since he or she will not be seen. Include a picture big enough to show the minute details of a food item to the television viewer.

for your READING LIST

Joyful Noise by Paul Fleischman is a collection of 14 poems that celebrate insects. That alone is unusual, but what makes this book truly unique is that the author wrote the poems to be read aloud by two readers at once, sometimes alternating, sometimes simultaneous, but always in the style of the insect described. From the dizzying dance of the whirligig beetles to the brief life of the mayfly, the poems capture the essence of these intriguing members of the insect world. You will read about the love life of book lice and the unfair working conditions of honeybees. Some of the poems are sad, some are funny, some are loud, and some are quiet, but all will captivate you with their "joyful noise."

TROPHY NEWBERY

Winner of the 1989 Newbery Medal

JOYFUL NOISE

Poems for Two Voices

PAUL FLEISCHMAN

illustrated by Eric Beddows

PERFORMING POETRY READINGS

After you have read *Joyful Noise*, select one of the poems to perform for your class. If several people want to perform poems, you may wish to divide the class into groups such as the following, based on each person's individual interest: Readers, Illustrators, Costume Designers, and Special-effects Technicians. Remember that you will need two readers for each poem. Students who enjoy drawing can create illustrations of the insects to display as you perform your poem. Other students might prefer to make soundtracks for the readings, selecting music to accompany the performance or recreating the sounds made by the insects in your poem. If you wish, students can create costumes for the performers in each poem, or find props to use during the readings. Since each reader has to concentrate not only on what he or she is reading but also on what his or her partner is reading, as well as keeping the timing and rhythm consistent, each group will need plenty of time to rehearse.

Other books you may want to read:
A Visit to William Blake's Inn: Poems for Innocent and Experienced Travelers by Nancy Willard
The Dream Keeper and Other Poems by Langston Hughes
The Other Side: Shorter Pieces by Angela Johnson
Cool Salsa: Bilingual Poems on Growing Up Latino in the United States, ed. Lori Carlson

Guided Writing

> "Poetry might be defined as a kind of language that says more and says it more intensely than does ordinary language."
>
> —Laurence Perrine

COMPOSING A POEM

Have you ever had moments in your life when words just didn't seem able to describe what you saw or felt? These are the moments made for poetry. A poem can tell a story or capture a moment in time in a way no other form of writing can.

Poetry is about looking with your whole body—paying attention to an object, an event, a feeling. Poetry lets you play with language, with the rich sounds and meanings of words, and in the process express the inexpressible.

Professional Model

"Cynthia in the Snow"

It SHUSHES.
It hushes
The loudness in the road.
It flitter-twitters,
And laughs away from me.
It laughs a lovely whiteness,
And whitely whirls away,
To be
Some otherwhere,
Still white as milk or shirts.
So beautiful it hurts.

— Gwendolyn Brooks

Prewriting

FINDING YOUR VOICE. In this writing assignment, you will want to be playful and free to express new ideas that come to you. This is the attitude inside you that enjoys living. Let that come out in your voice in this poem.

IDENTIFYING YOUR AUDIENCE. You will be writing for yourself and other classmates who would enjoy your subject. You may want to publish your poem in a class anthology or in the school newspaper or literary supplement.

WRITING WITH A PLAN. The power of poetry is in its concentrated language. That means ideas and descriptions are condensed into a few words or phrases. For example, in her

Examining the Model

This poem by Gwendolyn Brooks describes a moment in the snow. Look for the ideas and feelings behind the imagery. How does the speaker feel about this moment in the snow? What words tell you this is not a sad or uncomfortable moment? Brooks uses images like "hushes the loudness in the road" and figures of speech like "white as milk" to show you her meaning. Look at this line where the snow is personified: "It laughs a lovely whiteness." By describing the snow as though it were human, the poet helps the reader understand her experience.

Brooks plays with several techniques of sound in her poem, and the musical language adds to the meaning as well. Read this line aloud and listen for **alliteration**, or repetition of initial consonant sounds: "And whitely whirls away." What other examples of alliteration can you find in the

continued on page 684

poem? What does alliteration add to this piece?

Another technique that Brooks uses is **onomatopoeia**—the use of words like *bang* or *beep* that sound like what they mean. Can you find an example of onomatopoeia in the poem?

What about **rhyme?** Which lines rhyme and what does rhyme do for this poem?

If overused, alliteration, onomatopoeia, and rhyme can take away from the meaning in your poem. But if you use them to emphasize important ideas, they can add a strong, musical element to your writing.

Some of the most visual language in this poem are verbs such as *flitter-twitters*. Read the line that holds this verb. Why do you think the poet chose *flitter-twitters* over words like *falls* or *is coming down?*

poem, "Cynthia in the Snow," Gwendolyn Brooks could have explained snow this way:

Snow is a really happy and gorgeous thing with all the little white stuff coming down and whirling all around you.

But this explanation doesn't have nearly as much power as the concentrated language that Brooks *did* use:

It laughs a lovely whiteness,
And whitely whirls away

How do we condense language? You do it every day when you make comparisons between one thing and another. Comparisons are a quick way to communicate a lot of information.

When you say "Hank is as shy as a hedgehog," you are transferring one quality of a hedgehog—shyness—to Hank. We call this a simile. **Similes** are comparisons that use *like* or *as* in their construction. When you leave out the part about being shy and say "Hank is a hedgehog," you create a metaphor. **Metaphors** make comparisons without telling you what qualities the items share.

You make up metaphors all the time and probably don't even realize it. In poetry, metaphors are an essential ingredient, a way to communicate unusual connections between ideas in just a few words.

For your poem, you will create images, similes, and metaphors around a color.

BRAINSTORMING: THE FIVE SENSES, PLUS ONE. Choose a color. Consider the following categories. Spend three minutes on each of the categories, quickly writing the first ideas that come to mind.

SEE: Write a list of everything you have ever seen that is your color. After three minutes, move on to the next sense.

HEAR: Imagine your color as a sound. What sound would it be? For example, what does pink sound like—a cat purring, a new rain? What does orange sound like—a dog yapping, a car door slamming? What does brown sound like? A cello or a saxophone?

SMELL: What does your color smell like? Kerosene? Apples?

TASTE: What does your color taste like? Don't worry about whether a food is the same color. You might think an orange tastes purple.

TOUCH: What does your color feel like? Slimy, cold, or like the bristles on a broom?

FEELINGS: This last sense uses your heart. Think back on three times when you felt a strong emotion. Maybe you were happy or mad or amused. For these memories, write complete sentences that contain your color:

When I won the first prize for archery at camp and everybody clapped, that felt green to me.

When my grandmother died and my mom had to tell me in the car home from school, that felt orange to me.

Whenever my brother cheats at cards, that feels red to me.

Student Model—Graphic Organizer

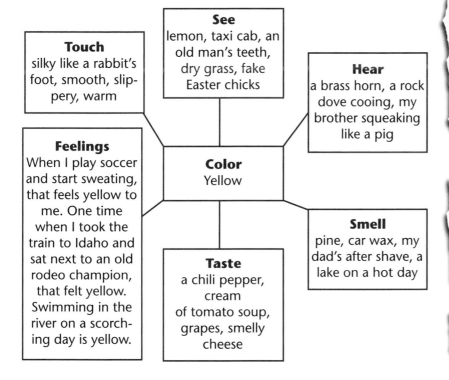

See
lemon, taxi cab, an old man's teeth, dry grass, fake Easter chicks

Touch
silky like a rabbit's foot, smooth, slippery, warm

Hear
a brass horn, a rock dove cooing, my brother squeaking like a pig

Color
Yellow

Feelings
When I play soccer and start sweating, that feels yellow to me. One time when I took the train to Idaho and sat next to an old rodeo champion, that felt yellow. Swimming in the river on a scorching day is yellow.

Taste
a chili pepper, cream of tomato soup, grapes, smelly cheese

Smell
pine, car wax, my dad's after shave, a lake on a hot day

Drafting

Try to tell about experiences from your life by comparing them to your color. You will find many descriptive words and comparisons from your prewriting that you can use in your poem. You will also think of others as you write the first draft.

In every line, put strong images that appeal to the sense of sight, smell, taste, touch, hearing, or feelings. Use at least one image from each sense in the poem. Expand on some of your metaphors. Instead of saying "Scarlet is a cold drink," you could say "Scarlet is cold berry juice after running hard up a hill."

Don't focus yet on line breaks or techniques of sound like alliteration and rhyme. And don't worry about whether or not your poem makes sense. The surprising and delightful language of poetry often comes from letting your inner ear play with words.

Here's a little exercise to help you find fresh and unusual verbs. Imagine that the color you choose is an animal. Write the animal's name at the top of your paper and then quickly write 15 verbs that describe actions your animal does. For example, for a bear, you might list the verb *scratch*.

Now look through your poem for state of being verbs like *is* or general verbs like *go* or *went*. Is there a place where you can put in one of the animal verbs instead? Can you replace *goes* with the more visual verb *ambles*?

"Poets are in love with language. They weigh and treasure the sound and meaning of words; they relish the use of language by other writers and have a compulsion, a necessity, for working with words."

—Ruth Whitman

Language, Grammar, and Style
Verb Functions

Verbs are essential to sentences. They tell whether the action is finished, or continuing, or will happen and all kinds of conditions for the action. Verbs can be one to four words long.

EXAMPLES

I <u>run</u>.

I <u>have run</u>.

I <u>could have run</u>.

I <u>should have been running</u>.

The added words change the meaning or condition of the action.

IDENTIFYING VERBS.
Action Verbs

Action verbs are the words that describe things you can do.

EXAMPLES

eat, laugh, jump, sew, have

Transitive verbs are one kind of action verb. Transitive verbs have completers. That is, the action is directed toward a person or thing in the sentence. If a verb has a direct object, it is a transitive verb.

EXAMPLE

Sara ate the Dutch pancake.

The subject is *Sara* and the verb is *ate*. To find out if this is a transitive verb, ask *Sara ate what?* The answer is *pancake*, so *pancake* is the direct object. Because the verb has a direct object it is transitive.

continued on page 687

Student Model—Draft

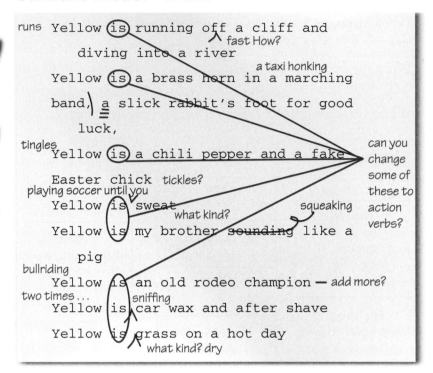

Self- and Peer Evaluation

Once you have a rough draft of your poem, read it aloud several times. This helps you hear the music of the lines. If you can, get someone else to read it aloud as well. After you and your peer editor discuss the following questions, you should have a good idea about how to revise your piece.

- What feelings or thoughts are expressed in the poem and what words communicate this feeling?
- Images refer to things we can see, hear, smell, touch and taste. Which images in the poem are specific and strong? Which are general and weak?
- Which similes and metaphors make unusual and fresh comparisons? Which ones could be more interesting?
- Which lines or phrases sound musical? Where could the writer use techniques of sound to emphasize meaning?
- Do any lines sound awkward? Are there places where the writer has used obvious rhymes or too much alliteration? How could those lines be improved?
- Are there any places where breaking the line would help the rhythm or meaning?
- Which verbs are active and strong? Which verbs could be changed from state of being to action verbs?

Revising and Proofreading

Based on your self- and peer edit, make changes to your draft. Add action verbs, delete extra words, and play with the sound of your poem. Trust your ear to tell you when you need a shorter word or a longer line.

Some forms of poetry require certain rhyme patterns or a specific number of syllables in a line. But since you are writing a free verse form, you get to decide whether to use rhyme at all and how long or short your lines will be.

How do poets decide where to break their lines? Most let their ears and eyes tell them. When you want to slow down parts of your poem, use long lines. When you want to speed up parts, use short lines.

In Mack's first draft he wrote this long line that wrapped around to the next line:

Yellow is a brass horn in a marching band, a slick rabbit's foot for good luck, and a taxi honking

When he revised his poem, he broke the line apart. Now the lines have a faster beat and move more smoothly.

Yellow is a brass horn in a marching band
A slick rabbit's foot for good luck
A taxi honking

After you have made changes to your poem, read over your draft for errors in spelling and punctuation. In poetry, you are often dealing with lines instead of sentences, so capitalization and punctuation become a matter of choice. However you decide to capitalize or punctuate, stick to a pattern from start to finish so that your format is clear to the reader.

Student Model—Revised

Mack played with the language and created many versions of the poem. He worked until he was satisfied that the words, images, and sounds that he wrote down were just what he wanted.

```
Yellow runs fast off a cliff

And into a blue river on a hot day

Yellow is a brass horn in a marching
    band

A slick rabbit's foot for good luck

A taxi honking

Yellow tingles like chili pepper and

Tickles like a fake Easter chick

Yellow is playing soccer until you
```

Intransitive verbs are another kind of action verb. These are verbs that do not have completers.

EXAMPLE
Sara laughed all night.

The subject is *Sara* and the verb is *laughed*. When we ask the direct object question *Sara laughed what?*, there is no answer. *Laughed* is an intransitive verb.

State of Being Verbs

State of being verbs indicate that something exists. These are all the forms of *to be*, such as *is, am, are, was, were, been, have been, should have been*.

Read through the poem "Cynthia in the Snow" and find all the verbs. What kinds of verbs has Gwendolyn Brooks chosen to use in her piece?

FIXING VERBS. Because verbs are the words that complete your statements, you want to make them strong and clear. One way to do this is to use action verbs—either transitive or intransitive—in your writing.

In a color poem, there is a temptation to use state of being verbs like *is* and *was* for every statement. While there is nothing wrong with a few state of being verbs here and there, it's action verbs that will give your poetry images the reader can see, hear, smell, taste, and feel.

Gwendolyn Brooks could have said "Snow is great,"

continued on page 688

but that statement doesn't get at how a beautiful snowfall moves and delights. So she used verbs like *hushes*, *laughs*, and *whirls* instead.

In the rough draft of Mack's poem, he began every line with *Yellow is*. Help him to improve his poem by changing *is* to action verbs in one of the lines. Look what happens to the meaning and music of the line when you do this.

Yellow is a chili pepper and a fake Easter chick

USING VERBS. Too many state of being verbs can weaken your writing. So can vague or general verbs like *went* or *go* or *do*. Find the verbs in your poem and change state of being verbs and general verbs into strong, specific action verbs.

```
    sweat

Sniffing aftershave or car wax

It's an old man on a train

Who won the bullriding championship

Twice

Yellow sounds like my brother laughing

In dry grass
```

Publishing and Presenting

Poetry is best when shared either out loud or as a printed piece of art. To share your poetry out loud, consider reading to a small group of students. To publish your poem as a work of art, create a small poster by printing the poem in a way that suggests the color and content of the poem. Add art and designs that also draw out the ideas in the poem. You may want to publish your poem in the school newspaper or literary supplement. A beautiful rainbow of poetry from your whole class could be created by putting all the poems together in one book.

Reflecting

"The magic of literary art, especially poetry," says writer Martin Angoff, "consists in suggesting with words what words cannot possibly say."

Do you see how poetry suggests new meanings and ways of understanding? What happened when you started comparing your sense observations to color? Which sense surprised you or gave you the most unusual images and comparisons?

Consider how the language of poetry offers a way to express ourselves, play with words, and entertain and enlighten others. Which of these would you say your poem strives for? In addition to color, what other topics might you explore in poetry?

UNIT NINE *review*

Review: Words for Everyday Use

Check your knowledge of the following vocabulary words. Choose ten words that you would like to add to your own daily vocabulary. For each word, write a short sentence that includes the word in context. To review a word, look back to the page number indicated.

- airs (637)
- askance (657)
- asphalt (625)
- dash (677)
- dote (671)

- downy (645)
- incessant (636)
- indulgence (671)
- magnanimous (671)
- seek (635)

- shun (635)
- skim (625)
- suffuse (671)
- supple (636)
- whirring (625)

Review: Literary Tools

Define each of the following terms, giving concrete examples when possible.
To review a term, refer to the page number(s) indicated.

- aim (656)
- alliteration (651)
- blend (634)
- concrete language (661)
- concrete poem (624)
- description (613)
- free verse (656)

- image (613, 676)
- imagery (613, 618, 624, 676)
- lyric poem (670)
- metaphor (656)
- mood (634, 670)
- narrative poem (661, 665)

- onomatopoeia (651)
- repetition (643, 647)
- rhyme (629, 634, 643, 647)
- rhythm (629)
- sensory details (665, 676)
- slant rhyme (647)
- speaker (618)

Reflecting *on your* *reading*

Theme

Poetry can be written on any topic whatsoever, or even on no topic at all. Poetry can simply be words that try to capture a certain feeling or create an image. Some poets write to try to convey an experience they have had that they want the reader to experience as well.

Genre

There is no one kind of poetry. Poems can be written in so many different ways, long or short, detailed or brief. Narrative poems tell a story; lyric poems create images. There are poems with complex patterns and forms, poems that rhyme, and "free verse" poems that don't.

Critical Thinking

Review the poems in this unit and notice what a wide range of topics they have. In your notebook, using the graphic organizers below as samples, record the images or themes that stand out the most for you. Once you have organized the images, think about what they might mean to you. How can you interpret, or understand, the poems based on these images?

perhaps hand

mudluscious

window arrange-ment

Spring

puddle-wonderful

hopscotch and jumprope

single engine human auto mobile
skim swerve curve sway
speed
falls like a thunderbolt
we'd run/we'd eat fast

Group Project

Find poems with images and themes you really like. (Go to the library and do some reading, or get some poetry anthologies to flip through.) You can even use the poems in this unit. Read the poems out loud to each other. Copy and decorate them to make artistic posters. Now, hang or place your posters in appropriate places. For example, you might put a poster with Sandra Cisneros's poem about hot dogs in the school cafeteria (with your principal's permission, of course). You might put "in Just—" by E. E. Cummings on the window or on a balloon.

On Your Own

1. Make a drawing based on one of the poems in this unit. Draw what it is that the poem makes you see.
2. Write a poem. You can model it after a poem from this unit, if you would like. You can make your poem rhyme, like Alfred, Lord Tennyson's poem. You can write about someone you know. You can describe an experience you have had, like eating a hot dog, or a feeling, like courage. You can write a concrete poem. The possibilities are endless.
3. What topics do you like to read about in poetry? Maybe you like sports poems or poems about nature, music, family, friends, cars, animals, or the seasons. Choose a topic and find at least five poems that address your topic. Think of an object that represents your topic, such as a soccer ball, family photo, or piece of birchbark. Write or reproduce your selected poems on the object.

Crispin and Scapin, c.1864. Honoré Daumier. Musée d'Orsay, Paris.

Turning Words into Action: DRAMA

ELEMENTS *of* DRAMA

DRAMA. A **drama,** or **play,** is a story told through characters played by actors. Early groups of people around the world enacted ritual scenes related to hunting, warfare, or religion. From these drama arose. Western drama as we know it first began in ancient Greece.

THE PLAYWRIGHT AND THE SCRIPT. The author of a play is the **playwright.** A playwright has limited control in deciding how his or her work is presented. Producers, directors, set designers, and actors all interpret a playwright's work and present their interpretations to the audience.

A **script** is the written text from which a drama is produced. Scripts are made up of stage directions and dialogue. Scripts may be divided into long parts called *acts* and short parts called *scenes*.

STAGE DIRECTIONS. **Stage directions** are notes included in a play to describe how something should look, sound, or be performed. Stage directions can describe lighting, costumes, music, sound effects, or other elements of a play. They can also describe entrances and exits, gestures, tone of voice, or other elements related to the acting of a play. Stage directions sometimes provide historical or background information. In stage directions, the parts of the stage are described from the actors' point of view, as shown on the diagram below. As you read the plays in this unit, pay attention to the suggestions the playwright has given for the set, the lighting, and props. Also notice the important role that stage directions have throughout this play.

Up Right	Up Center	Up Left
Right Center	Center	Left Center
Down Right	Down Center	Down Left

The parts of the stage are often referred to in abbreviated form, such as UR for Up Right and C for Center.

The speech of the actors in a play is called **dialogue.** A speech given by one character is called a **monologue.** In a play, dialogue appears after the names of characters.

An **act** is a major part of a play. One-act, three-act, and five-act plays are all common. A **scene** is a short section of a literary work, one that happens in a single place and time. There may be any number of scenes in each act, and the number of scenes may vary from act to act.

THE SPECTACLE. The **spectacle** includes all the elements of the drama that are presented to the audience's senses. The set, props, special effects, lighting, and costumes are part of the spectacle.

All the World's a Stage

from *As You Like It*

by William Shakespeare

Jaques.   All the world's a stage,
And all the men and women merely players;
They have their exits and their entrances,
And one man in his time plays many parts,
His acts being seven ages. At first, the infant,
Mewling and puking in the nurse's arms.
Then the whining schoolboy, with his satchel
And shining morning face, creeping like snail
Unwillingly to school. And then the lover,
Sighing like furnace, with a woeful ballad
Made to his mistress' eyebrow. Then a soldier,
Full of strange oaths and bearded like the pard,
Jealous in honor, sudden and quick in quarrel,
Seeking the bubble reputation
Even in the cannon's mouth. And then the justice,
In fair round belly with good capon lined,
With eyes severe and beard of formal cut,
Full of wise saws and modern instances;
And so he plays his part. The sixth age shifts
Into the lean and slippered pantaloon,
With spectacles on nose and pouch on side;
His youthful hose, well saved, a world too wide
For his shrunk shank, and his big manly voice,
Turning again toward childish treble, pipes
And whistles in his sound. Last scene of all,
That ends this strange eventful history,
Is second childishness and mere oblivion,
Sans teeth, sans eyes, sans taste, sans everything.

Reader's Journal

What is more important to you—outer or inner beauty? Provide some reasons for your answer.

Reader's Resource

- This play is based on a fairy tale, a type of story that was originally passed down through the oral tradition. Fairy tales often take place in medieval settings and feature magical transformations and events. A Danish writer named Hans Christian Andersen wrote the fairy tale called "The Ugly Duckling" on which this play is based, as well as a number of others you may know, such as "The Little Mermaid," "The Snow Queen," and "Thumbelina." The ugly duckling has an extremely hard time until he finally sees three beautiful white swans swimming and flies over to them, assuming that the birds will kill him because of his ugliness. When the duckling bends his head down to the water, awaiting the swans to put an end to his misery, he sees his reflection in the water and realizes that he too is a swan and has grown to be beautiful and graceful. As you read, think about why A. A. Milne chose the same title for his play as Hans Christian Andersen did for his fairy tale. In what ways are the Princess Camilla and the ugly duckling alike?

Prereading

THE UGLY DUCKLING

by A. A. Milne

Reader's TOOLBOX

CHARACTERIZATION. Characterization is the act of creating or describing a character. Writers create characters in three major ways: by showing what characters say, do and think; by showing what other characters say about them; and by showing what physical features, dress, and personality the characters display. As you read *The Ugly Duckling*, jot down on a separate piece of paper words and groups of words you think help to create the characters.

PLOT. A **plot** is a series of events related to a central conflict, or struggle. A plot usually involves the introduction of a conflict, its development, and its eventual resolution. The following terms are used to describe the parts of a plot:

- The *exposition*, or introduction, sets the tone or mood, introduces the characters and the setting, and provides necessary background information.
- The *inciting incident* is the event that introduces the conflict.
- The *climax* is the high point of interest or suspense in the plot.
- The *resolution* is the point at which the central conflict is ended, or resolved.
- The *dénouement* is any material that follows the resolution and that ties up loose ends.

The parts of a plot are often shown on a pyramid like the one below. Draw a copy of this pyramid on your own paper. As you read, write down at the appropriate points on the pyramid what you think the exposition, inciting incident, climax, resolution, and dénouement are.

Graphic Organizer

The king and queen have had a hard time finding a husband for their daughter, Princess Camilla, because she is plain. The king and queen believe that Great-Aunt Malkin caused Camilla to be plain.

Climax

Crisis

Rising Action

Falling Action

Inciting Incident

Resolution

Exposition

Dénouement

THE UGLY DUCKLING

A. A. Milne

CHARACTERS

THE KING   DULCIBELLA

THE QUEEN   PRINCE SIMON

THE PRINCESS CAMILLA   CARLO

THE CHANCELLOR[1]

(*The* SCENE *is the Throne Room of the Palace; a room of many doors, or, if preferred, curtain-openings: simply furnished with three thrones for Their Majesties*[2] *and Her Royal Highness*[3] *the* PRINCESS CAMILLA—*in other words, with three handsome chairs. At each side is a long seat: reserved, as it might be, for His Majesty's Council (if any), but useful, as today, for other purposes. The* KING *is asleep on his throne with a handkerchief over his face. He is a king of any country from any storybook, in whatever costume you please. But he should be wearing his crown.*)

A VOICE. (*Announcing*) His Excellency[4] the Chancellor! (*The* CHANCELLOR, *an elderly man in hornrimmed spectacles, enters, bowing. The* KING *wakes up with a start and removes the handkerchief from his face.*)

KING. (*With simple dignity*) I was thinking.

CHANCELLOR. (*Bowing*) Never, Your Majesty, was greater need for thought than now.

KING. That's what I was thinking. (*He struggles into a more _dignified_ position.*) Well, what is it? More trouble?

GUIDED READING

What is the king doing just before the chancellor enters?

---

1. **Chancellor.** Official secretary or nobleman of the king
2. *Their Majesties.* Titles used when speaking of kings and queens
3. *Her Royal Highness.* Term used when referring to a ruler, especially royalty
4. **His Excellency.** Title of honor given to a man in an important position

---

words for everyday use

dig • ni • fied (dig' nə fīd) *adj.,* showing nobility. *Jackson had a _dignified_ look as he sat in his tuxedo.*

CHANCELLOR. What we might call the old trouble, Your Majesty.

KING. It's what I was saying last night to the Queen. "Uneasy lies the head that wears a crown,"[5] was how I put it.

CHANCELLOR. A profound and original thought, which may well go down to <u>posterity</u>.

KING. You mean it may go down well with posterity. I hope so. Remind me to tell you some time of another little thing I said to Her Majesty: something about a fierce light beating on a throne.[6] Posterity would like that, too. Well, what is it?

CHANCELLOR. It is in the matter of Her Royal Highness's wedding.

KING. Oh . . . yes.

CHANCELLOR. As Your Majesty is aware, the young Prince Simon arrives today to seek Her Royal Highness's hand in marriage. He has been traveling in distant lands and, as I understand, has not—er—has not—

GUIDED READING

Who is arriving in the kingdom that day? What is the purpose of the visit?

KING. You mean he hasn't heard anything.

CHANCELLOR. It is a little difficult to put this <u>tactfully</u>, Your Majesty.

KING. Do your best, and I will tell you afterwards how you got on.

CHANCELLOR. Let me put it this way. The Prince Simon will naturally assume that Her Royal Highness has the customary—so customary as to be, in my own poor opinion, slightly monotonous—has what one might

GUIDED READING

Why is the chancellor worried?

call the <u>inevitable</u>—so inevitable as to be, in my opinion again, almost mechanical—will assume, that she has the, as *I* think of it, faultily faultless, icily regular, splendidly—

KING. What you are trying to say in the fewest words possible is that my daughter is not beautiful.

CHANCELLOR. Her beauty is certainly <u>elusive</u>, Your Majesty.

KING. It is. It has eluded you, it has eluded me, it has eluded everybody who has seen her. It even eluded the Court Painter. His last words were, "Well, I did my best." His successor is now painting the view across the water-meadows from the West Turret. He says that his doctor has advised him to keep to landscape.

CHANCELLOR. It is unfortunate, Your Majesty, but there it is. One just cannot understand how it can have occurred.

KING. You don't think she takes after *me*, at all? You don't detect a likeness?

CHANCELLOR. Most certainly not, Your Majesty.

KING. Good. . . . Your predecessor did.

CHANCELLOR. I have often wondered what happened to my predecessor.

KING. Well, now you know. (*There is a short silence.*)

CHANCELLOR. Looking at the bright side, although Her Royal Highness is not, strictly speaking, beautiful—

---

5. **"Uneasy lies the head . . . crown."** From William Shakespeare's play *King Henry IV*

6. **something about a fierce light beating on a throne.** From a quotation by the poet Alfred, Lord Tennyson

---

words for everyday use

pos • ter • i • ty (päs ter´ə tē) *n.*, future generations. *We will save pictures and mementos for <u>posterity</u>.*

tact • ful (takt´ fəl) *adj.*, having or showing good sense of what to say and do. *Gina answered the question with a <u>tactful</u> response.* **tactfully,** *adv.*

in • ev • i • ta • ble (in ev´i tə bəl) *adj.*, unavoidable. *Getting wet is <u>inevitable</u> when wind blows the rain.*

e • lu • sive (ē lo͞o´siv) *adj.*, not easily seen or understood. *The <u>elusive</u> wolf has only been spotted twice.*

KING. Not, truthfully speaking, beautiful—

CHANCELLOR. Yet she has great beauty of character.

KING. My dear Chancellor, we are not considering Her Royal Highness's character, but her chances of getting married. You observe that there is a distinction.

CHANCELLOR. Yes, Your Majesty.

KING. Look at it from the <u>suitor's</u> point of view. If a girl is beautiful, it is easy to assume that she has, tucked away inside her, an equally beautiful character. But it is impossible to assume that an unattractive girl, however elevated in character, has, tucked away inside her, an equally beautiful face. That is, so to speak, not where you want it—tucked away.

CHANCELLOR. Quite so, Your Majesty.

KING. This doesn't, of course, <u>alter</u> the fact that the Princess Camilla is quite the nicest person in the Kingdom.

CHANCELLOR. (*Enthusiastically*) She is indeed, Your Majesty. (*Hurriedly*) With the exception, I need hardly say, of Your Majesty—and Her Majesty.

KING. Your exceptions are tolerated for their loyalty and <u>condemned</u> for their extreme fatuity.[7]

CHANCELLOR. Thank you, Your Majesty.

KING. As an adjective for your King, the word "nice" is ill-chosen. As an adjective for Her Majesty, it is—ill-chosen. (*At which moment* HER MAJESTY *comes in. The* KING *rises. The* CHANCELLOR *puts himself at right angles.*)

QUEEN. (*Briskly*) Ah. Talking about Camilla? (*She sits down.*)

KING. (*Returning to his throne*) As always, my dear, you are right.

QUEEN. (*To* CHANCELLOR) This fellow, Simon—What's he like?

CHANCELLOR. Nobody has seen him, Your Majesty.

QUEEN. How old is he?

CHANCELLOR. Five-and-twenty, I understand.

QUEEN. In twenty-five years he must have been seen by somebody.

KING. (*To the* CHANCELLOR) Just a fleeting glimpse.

CHANCELLOR. I meant, Your Majesty, that no detailed report of him has reached this country, save that he has the usual personal advantages and qualities expected of a Prince, and has been traveling in distant and dangerous lands.

> **GUIDED READING**
> What do people know about the prince?

QUEEN. Ah! Nothing gone wrong with his eyes? Sunstroke or anything?

CHANCELLOR. Not that I am aware of, Your Majesty. At the same time, as I was venturing to say to His Majesty, Her Royal Highness's character and disposition are so outstandingly—

QUEEN. Stuff and nonsense. You remember what happened when we had the Tournament of Love last year.

CHANCELLOR. I was not myself present, Your Majesty. I had not then the honor of— I was abroad, and never heard the full story.

---

7. **fatuity.** Stupidity

suit • or (süt´ər) *n.*, man who is seeking a romantic relationship with a woman. *In that old movie, the <u>suitor</u> brought the young woman a bouquet of daisies.*

al • ter (ôl´tər) *v.*, change. *The waves will <u>alter</u> the shape of the sand castle.*

con • demn (kən dem´) *v.*, disapprove of. *My club chooses to <u>condemn</u> all acts of vandalism in the neighborhood.*

QUEEN. No; it was the other fool. They all rode up to Camilla to pay their homage—it was the first time they had seen her. The heralds blew their trumpets, and announced that she would marry whichever Prince was left master of the field when all but one had been unhorsed.[8] The trumpets were blown again, they charged enthusiastically into the fight, and—(*The* KING *looks nonchalantly at the ceiling and whistles a few bars.*)—don't do that.

GUIDED READING

What was the purpose of the Tournament of Love? What happened at the Tournament of Love?

KING. I'm sorry, my dear.

QUEEN. (*To* CHANCELLOR) And what happened? They all simultaneously fell off their horses and assumed a posture of defeat.

KING. One of them was not quite so quick as the others. I was very quick. I proclaimed him the victor.

QUEEN. At the Feast of Betrothal[9] held that night—

KING. We were all very quick.

QUEEN. The Chancellor announced that by the laws of the country the successful suitor had to pass a further test. He had to give the correct answer to a riddle.

CHANCELLOR. Such undoubtedly is the fact, Your Majesty.

KING. There are times for announcing facts, and times for looking at things in a broad-minded way. Please remember that, Chancellor.

CHANCELLOR. Yes, Your Majesty.

QUEEN. I invented the riddle myself. Quite an easy one. What is it which has four legs and barks like a dog? The answer is, "A dog."

KING. (*To* CHANCELLOR) You see that?

CHANCELLOR. Yes, Your Majesty.

KING. It isn't difficult.

QUEEN. He, however, seemed to find it so. He said an eagle. Then he said a serpent; a very high mountain with slippery sides; two peacocks; a moonlight night; the day after tomorrow—

KING. Nobody could accuse him of not trying.

QUEEN. *I* did.

KING. I *should* have said that nobody could fail to recognize in his attitude an appearance of doggedness.

QUEEN. Finally he said "Death." I nudged the King—

KING. Accepting the word "nudge" for the moment, I rubbed my ankle with one hand, clapped him on the shoulder with the other, and congratulated him on the correct answer. He disappeared under the table, and, personally, I never saw him again.

QUEEN. His body was found in the moat[10] next morning.

CHANCELLOR. But what was he doing in the moat, Your Majesty?

KING. Bobbing about. Try not to ask needless questions.

CHANCELLOR. It all seems so strange.

QUEEN. What does?

---

8. **unhorsed.** Thrown from a horse
9. **Betrothal.** Engagement or promise to marry
10. **moat.** Ditch dug around a castle and filled with water, used to protect against invaders

words for everyday use

hom • age (häm´ij) *n.,* something done to show honor or respect. *We would like to pay* homage *to volunteers in the community.*

non • cha • lant (nän´shə länt) *adj.,* unconcerned or uninterested. *Because Fatima was an enthusiastic football fan, she could not understand why her brother was* nonchalant *about the outcome of the game.* **nonchalantly,** *adv.*

as • sume (ə soom´) *v.,* take on. *I would like the children to* assume *more household responsibilities.*

dog • ged • ness (dôg´id nes) *n.,* stubbornness. *It is difficult to argue with my sister because of her* doggedness.

CHANCELLOR. That Her Royal Highness, alone of all the Princesses one has ever heard of, should lack that <u>invariable attribute</u> of Royalty, supreme beauty.

QUEEN. (*To the* KING) That was your Great-Aunt Malkin. She came to the christening. You know what she said.

KING. It was <u>cryptic</u>. Great-Aunt Malkin's besetting weakness. She came to *my* christening—she was one hundred and one then, and that was fifty-one years ago. (*To* CHANCELLOR) How old would that make her?

CHANCELLOR. One hundred and fifty-two, Your Majesty.

KING. (*After thought*) About that, yes. She promised me that when I grew up I should have all the happiness which my wife deserved. It struck me at the time—well, when I say "at the time," I was only a week old—but it did strike me as soon as anything could strike me—I mean of that nature—well, work it out for yourself, Chancellor. It opens up a most interesting field of speculation. Though naturally I have not liked to go into it at all deeply with Her Majesty.

QUEEN. I never heard anything less cryptic. She was wishing you extreme happiness.

KING. I don't think she was *wishing* me anything. However.

CHANCELLOR. (*To the* QUEEN) But what, Your Majesty, did she wish Her Royal Highness?

QUEEN. Her other godmother—on my side—had promised her the dazzling beauty for which all the women in my family are famous—(*She pauses, and the* KING *snaps his fingers* <u>surreptitiously</u> *in the direction of the* CHANCELLOR.)

CHANCELLOR. (*Hurriedly*) Indeed, yes, Your Majesty. (*The* KING *relaxes.*)

QUEEN. And Great-Aunt Malkin said—(*To the* KING)—what were the words?

KING. I give you with this kiss
A wedding-day surprise.
Where ignorance is bliss
'Tis folly to be wise.

I thought the last two lines rather neat. But what it *meant*—

QUEEN. We can all see what it meant. She was given beauty—and where is it? Great-Aunt Malkin took it away from her.

> **GUIDED READING**
>
> What does the queen believe is Camilla's "wedding-day surprise"?

words for everyday use

in • var • i • a • ble (in ver´ē ə bəl) *adj.*, constant. *Extremely hot temperatures are <u>invariable</u> in most countries near the equator.*
at • tri • bute (a´ trib yüt) *n.*, quality or characteristic. *Herman's sense of honesty was his finest <u>attribute</u>.*
cryp • tic (krip´tik) *adj.*, having hidden or mysterious meaning. *Frank was bothered by the <u>cryptic</u> message left on his answering machine.*
sur • rep • ti • tious (sər´əp tish´əs) *adj.*, secret, sneaky. *Marvin had a <u>surreptitious</u> way of learning people's secrets.*
surreptitiously, *adv.*

The wedding-day surprise is that there will never be a wedding day.

KING. Young men being what they are, my dear, it would be much more surprising if there *were* a wedding day. So how— (*The* PRINCESS *comes in. She is young, happy, healthy, but not beautiful. Or let us say that by some trick of make-up or arrangement of hair she seems plain to us: unlike the* PRINCESS *of the storybooks.*)

PRINCESS. (*To the* KING) Hallo, darling! (*Seeing the others*) Oh, I say! Affairs of state? Sorry.

KING. (*Holding out his hand*) Don't go, Camilla. (*She takes his hand.*)

CHANCELLOR. Shall I withdraw, Your Majesty?

QUEEN. You are aware, Camilla, that Prince Simon arrives today?

PRINCESS. He has arrived. They're just letting down the draw-bridge.

KING. (*Jumping up*) Arrived! I must—

GUIDED READING

Who has arrived? How does the king react to this news?

PRINCESS. Darling, you know what the drawbridge is like. It takes at *least* half an hour to let it down.

KING. (*Sitting down*) It wants oil. (*To the* CHANCELLOR) Have *you* been <u>grudging</u> it oil?

PRINCESS. It wants a new drawbridge, darling.

CHANCELLOR. Have I Your Majesty's permission—

KING. Yes, yes. (*The* CHANCELLOR *bows and goes out.*)

QUEEN. You've told him, of course? It's the only chance.

KING. Er—no. I was just going to, when—

QUEEN. Then I'd better. (*She goes to the door.*) You can explain to the girl; I'll have her sent to you. You've told Camilla?

KING. Er—no. I was just going to, when—

QUEEN. Then you'd better tell her now.

KING. My dear, are you sure—

QUEEN. It's the only chance left. (*Dramatically to heaven*) My daughter! (*She goes out. There is a little silence when she is gone.*)

KING. Camilla, I want to talk seriously to you about marriage.

GUIDED READING

About what does the king want to have a serious talk?

PRINCESS. Yes, father.

KING. It is time that you learnt some of the facts of life.

PRINCESS. Yes, father.

KING. Now the great fact about marriage is that once you're married you live happy ever after. All our history books <u>affirm</u> this.

PRINCESS. And your own experience too, darling.

KING. (*With dignity*) Let us confine ourselves to history for the moment.

PRINCESS. Yes, father.

KING. Of course, there *may* be an exception here and there, which, as it were, proves the rule; just as—oh, well, never mind.

PRINCESS. (*Smiling*) Go on, darling. You were going to say that an exception here and

---

words for everyday use

grudge (gruj´) *v.*, not give willingly. *The company owner <u>grudged</u> bonuses and raises to even hard-working employees.*

af • firm (ə furm´) *v.*, prove. *The way the defendant averted his eyes served only to <u>affirm</u> his guilt from the prosecutor's point of view.*

there proves the rule that all princesses are beautiful.

KING. Well—leave that for the moment. The point is that it doesn't matter *how* you marry, or *who* you marry, as long as you *get* married. Because you'll be happy ever after in any case. Do you follow me so far?

PRINCESS. Yes, father.

KING. Well, your mother and I have a little plan—

PRINCESS. Was that it, going out of the door just now?

KING. Er—yes. It concerns your waiting-maid.[11]

PRINCESS. Darling, I have several.

KING. Only one that leaps to the eye, so to speak. The one with the—well, with everything.

PRINCESS. Dulcibella?

> **GUIDED READING**
>
> Who is Dulcibella?

KING. That's the one. It is our little plan that at the first meeting she should pass herself off as the Princess—a harmless <u>ruse</u>, of which you will find frequent record in the history books—and allure Prince Simon to his—that is to say, bring him up to the—in other words, the wedding will take place immediately afterwards, and as quietly as possible—well, naturally in view of the fact that your Aunt Malkin is one hundred and fifty-two; and since you will be wearing the family bridal veil—which is no doubt how the custom arose—the surprise after the ceremony will be his. Are you following me at all? Your attention seems to be wandering.

> **GUIDED READING**
>
> What is the plan of the king and queen?

PRINCESS. I was wondering why you needed to tell me.

KING. Just a <u>precautionary</u> measure, in case you happened to meet the Prince or his attendant before the ceremony; in which case, of course, you would pass yourself off as the maid—

PRINCESS. A harmless ruse, of which, also, you will find frequent record in the history books.

KING. Exactly. But the occasion need not arise.

A VOICE. (*Announcing*) The woman Dulcibella!

KING. Ah! (*To the* PRINCESS) Now, Camilla, if you will just <u>retire</u> to your own apartments, I will come to you there when we are ready for the actual ceremony. (*He leads her out as he is talking; and as he returns calls out.*) Come in, my dear! (DULCIBELLA *comes in. She is beautiful, but dumb.*) Now don't be frightened, there is nothing to be frightened about. Has Her Majesty told you what you have to do?

DULCIBELLA. Y-yes, Your Majesty.

KING. Well now, let's see how well you can do it. You are sitting here, we will say. (*He leads her to a seat.*) Now imagine that I am Prince Simon. (*He curls his moustache and puts his stomach in. She giggles.*) You are the beautiful Princess Camilla whom he has never seen. (*She giggles again.*) This is a serious moment in your life, and you will find that a giggle will not be helpful. (*He goes*

> **GUIDED READING**
>
> What does the king ask Dulcibella to pretend?

11. **waitingmaid.** Person whose job is to assist a queen or princess

---

words for everyday use

ruse (rōōz′) v., trick. *Queen Fatima knew that the enemy's apparent surrender was merely a <u>ruse</u> to draw her own troops out into the open.*

pre • cau • tion • ar • y (prē kô′shən ar ē) adj., safety. *Many car companies are installing air bags in their vehicles as <u>precautionary</u> devices.*

re • tire (ri tīr′) v., go away. *The servant said that since he was no longer needed, he would like to <u>retire</u> for the evening.*

to the door.) I am announced: "His Royal Highness Prince Simon!" That's me being announced. Remember what I said about giggling. You should have a far-away look upon the face. (*She does her best.*) Farther away than that. (*She tries again.*) No, that's too far. You are sitting there, thinking beautiful thoughts—in maiden <u>meditation</u>, fancy-free, as I remember saying to Her Majesty once . . . speaking of somebody else . . . fancy-free, but with the mouth definitely shut—that's better. I advance and fall upon one knee. (*He does so.*) You extend your hand graciously—*graciously;* you're not trying to push him in the face—that's better, and I raise it to my lips—so—and I kiss it—(*He kisses it warmly.*)—no, perhaps not so <u>ardently</u> as that, more like this (*He kisses it again.*), and

I say, "Your Royal Highness, this is the most—er—Your Royal Highness, I shall ever be—no—Your Royal Highness, it is the proudest—" Well, the point is that he will say it, and it will be something complimentary, and then he will take your hand in both of his, and press it to his heart. (*He does so.*) And then—what do you say?

DULCIBELLA. Coo!

KING. No, *not* Coo.

DULCIBELLA. Never had anyone do *that* to me before.

KING. That also strikes the wrong note. What you want to say is, "Oh, Prince Simon!" . . . Say it.

DULCIBELLA. (*Loudly*) Oh, Prince Simon!

words for everyday use

med • i • ta • tion (med ə tā′ shən) *n.,* deep and continued thought. *Pamela spent hours in <u>meditation</u> before deciding whether to have an operation or not.*

ar • dent (är′dent) *adj.,* passionate. *Senator Johnson made an <u>ardent</u> plea to his colleagues about the need to increase the education budget.* **ardently,** *adv.*

KING. No, no. You don't need to shout until he has said "What?" two or three times. Always consider the possibility that he *isn't* deaf. Softly, and giving the words a dying fall, letting them play around his head like a flight of doves.

DULCIBELLA. (*Still a little overloud*) O-o-o-o-h, Prinsimon!

KING. Keep the idea in your mind of a flight of *doves* rather than a flight of panic-stricken elephants, and you will be all right. Now I'm going to get up and you must, as it were, <u>waft</u> me into a seat by your side. (*She starts wafting.*) *Not* rescuing a drowning man, that's another idea altogether, useful at times, but at the moment <u>inappropriate</u>. Wafting. Prince Simon will put the necessary muscles into play—all you require to do is to indicate by a gracious movement of the hand the seat you require him to take. Now! (*He gets up, a little stiffly, and sits next to her.*) That was better. Well, here we are. Now, I think you give me a look: something, let us say, half-way between a worshipful attitude and wild <u>abandonment</u>, with an undertone of regal dignity, touched, as it were, with good comradeship. Now try that. (*She gives him a vacant look of bewilderment.*) Frankly, that didn't quite get it. There was just a little something missing. An absence, as it were, of all the qualities I asked for, and in their place an odd resemblance to an unsatisfied fish. Let us try to get at it another way. Dulcibella, have you a young man of your own?

DULCIBELLA. (*Eagerly, seizing his hand*) Oo, yes, he's ever so smart, he's an archer, well not as you might say a real archer, he works in the armory, but old Bottlenose, *you* know who I mean, the Captain of the

Guard, says the very next man they ever has to shoot, my Eg shall take his place, knowing Father and how it is with Eg and me, and me being maid to Her Royal Highness and can't marry me till he's a real soldier, but ever so loving, and funny like, the things he says, I said to him once, "Eg," I said—

GUIDED READING

Who is Eg?

KING. (*Getting up*) I rather fancy, Dulcibella, that if you think of Eg all the time, *say* as little as possible, and, when thinking of Eg, see that the mouth is not more than partially open, you will do very well. I will show you where you are to sit and wait for His Royal Highness. (*He leads her out. On the way he is saying*) Now remember—*waft*—*waft*—not *hoick*.[12] (PRINCE SIMON *wanders in from the back unannounced. He is a very ordinary-looking young man in rather dusty clothes. He gives a deep sigh of relief as he sinks into the* KING's *throne. . . .* CAMILLA, *a new and strangely beautiful* CAMILLA, *comes in.*)

GUIDED READING

What does Prince Simon look like?

PRINCESS. (*Surprised*) Well!

PRINCE. Oh, hallo!

PRINCESS. Ought you?

PRINCE. (*Getting up*) Do sit down, won't you?

PRINCESS. Who are you, and how did you get here?

PRINCE. Well, that's rather a long story. Couldn't we sit down? You could sit here if you liked, but it isn't very comfortable.

PRINCESS. That is the King's Throne.

---

12. *hoick.* Hunter's call

words for everyday use

waft (wäft') *v.,* cause to move as if by the action of waves. *Sylvia dropped a feather from the bridge, leaving it <u>waft</u> down to the surface of the river.*

in • ap • pro • pri • ate (in ə prō′ prē it) *adj.,* not proper. *Many people feel it is <u>inappropriate</u> for companies to use animals for the testing of their products.*

a • ban • don • ment (ə ban′ dən mənt) *n.,* impulsiveness and freedom of action. *Samantha was delighted that the band played her favorite songs with <u>abandonment</u>.*

PRINCE. Oh, is that what it is?

PRINCESS. Thrones are not meant to be comfortable.

PRINCE. Well, I don't know if they're meant to be, but they certainly aren't.

PRINCESS. Why were you sitting on the King's Throne, and who are you?

PRINCE. My name is Carlo.

PRINCESS. Mine is Dulcibella.

GUIDED READING

How do the prince and the princess introduce themselves to each other?

PRINCE. Good. And now couldn't we sit down?

PRINCESS. (*Sitting down on the long seat to the left of the throne, and, as it were, wafting him to a place next to her*) You may sit here, if you like. Why are you so tired? (*He sits down.*)

PRINCE. I've been taking very <u>strenuous</u> exercise.

PRINCESS. Is that part of the long story?

PRINCE. It is.

PRINCESS. (*Settling herself*) I love stories.

PRINCE. This isn't a story really. You see, I'm attendant on Prince Simon who is visiting here.

GUIDED READING

What has the prince heard about the princess?

PRINCESS. Oh? I'm attendant on Her Royal Highness.

PRINCE. Then you know what he's here for.

PRINCESS. Yes.

PRINCE. She's very beautiful, I hear.

PRINCESS. Did you hear that? Where have you been lately?

PRINCE. Traveling in distant lands—with Prince Simon.

PRINCESS. Ah! All the same, I don't understand. Is Prince Simon in the Palace now? The drawbridge *can't* be down yet!

PRINCE. I don't suppose it is. *And* what a noise it makes coming down!

PRINCESS. Isn't it terrible?

PRINCE. I couldn't stand it any more. I just had to get away. That's why I'm here.

PRINCESS. But how?

PRINCE. Well, there's only one way, isn't there? That beech tree, and then a swing and a grab for the battlements, and don't ask me to remember it all—(*He shudders.*)

GUIDED READING

How was the prince able to get to the palace even though the drawbridge was not yet down?

PRINCESS. You mean you came across the moat by that beech tree?

PRINCE. Yes. I got so tired of hanging about.

PRINCESS. But it's terribly dangerous!

PRINCE. That's why I'm so exhausted. Nervous shock. (*He lies back and breathes loudly.*)

PRINCESS. Of course, it's different for *me*.

PRINCE. (*Sitting up*) Say that again. I must have got it wrong.

PRINCESS. It's different for me, because I'm used to it. Besides, I'm so much lighter.

PRINCE. You don't mean that *you*—

PRINCESS. Oh yes, often.

PRINCE. And I thought I was a brave man! At least, I didn't until five minutes ago, and now I don't again.

---

words for everyday use

stren • u • ous (stren′ yü əs) *adj.*, requiring hard work and energy. *Rocco was out of shape, and swimming just a few laps had become <u>strenuous</u> for him.*

PRINCESS. Oh, but you are! And I think it's wonderful to do it straight off the first time.

PRINCE. Well, *you* did.

PRINCESS. Oh no, not the first time. When I was a child.

PRINCE. You mean that you crashed?

PRINCESS. Well, you only fall into the moat.

PRINCE. Only! Can you *swim*?

PRINCESS. Of course.

PRINCE. So you swam to the castle walls, and yelled for help, and they fished you out and walloped you. And next day you tried again. Well, if *that* isn't <u>pluck</u>—

PRINCESS. Of course I didn't. I swam back, and did it at once; I mean I tried again at once. It wasn't until the third time that I actually did it. You see, I was afraid I might lose my nerve.

PRINCE. Afraid she might lose her nerve!

PRINCESS. There's a way of getting over from this side, too; a tree grows out from the wall and you jump into another tree—I don't think it's quite so easy.

PRINCE. Not quite so easy. Good. You must show me.

PRINCESS. Oh, I will.

PRINCE. Perhaps it might be as well if you taught me how to swim first. I've often heard about swimming but never—

PRINCESS. You can't swim?

GUIDED READING

Why did the princess fall into the moat once? How did she get out? How does the prince react to this story?

PRINCE. No. Don't look so surprised. There are a lot of other things which I can't do. I'll tell you about them as soon as you have a couple of years to spare.

PRINCESS. You can't swim and yet you crossed by the beech tree! And you're *ever* so much heavier than I am! Now who's brave?

PRINCE. (*Getting up*) You keep talking about how light you are. I must see if there's anything to it. Stand up! (*She stands obediently and he picks her up.*) You're right, Dulcibella. I could hold you here forever. (*Looking at her*) You're very lovely. Do you know how lovely you are?

GUIDED READING

What compliment does the prince pay the princess?

PRINCESS. Yes. (*She laughs suddenly and happily.*)

PRINCE. Why do you laugh?

PRINCESS. Aren't you tired of holding me?

PRINCE. Frankly, yes. I <u>exaggerated</u> when I said I could hold you forever. When you've been hanging by the arms for ten minutes over a very deep moat, wondering if it's too late to learn how to swim—(*He puts her down.*)—what I meant was that I should *like* to hold you forever. Why did you laugh?

PRINCESS. Oh, well, it was a little private joke of mine.

PRINCE. If it comes to that, I've got a private joke too. Let's exchange them.

PRINCESS. Mine's very private. One other woman in the whole world knows, and that's all.

---

words for everyday use

pluck (pluk´) *n.*, courage and strength. *The boxer showed a lot of <u>pluck</u> by continuing to fight even after his opponent had knocked him down.*

ex • ag • ger • ate (eg zaj´ər āt) *v.*, make something seem greater than it really is. *No one believed Luther when he said he owned 20 rare pets because they knew he loved to <u>exaggerate</u>.*

PRINCE. Mine's just as private. One other man knows, and that's all.

PRINCESS. What fun. I love secrets. . . . Well, here's mine. When I was born, one of my godmothers promised that I should be very beautiful.

PRINCE. How right she was.

PRINCESS. But the other one said this:

> I give you with this kiss
> A wedding-day surprise.
> Where ignorance is bliss
> 'Tis folly to be wise.

And nobody knew what it meant. And I grew up very plain. And then, when I was about ten, I met my godmother in the forest one day. It was my tenth birthday. Nobody knows this—except you.

PRINCE. Except us.

PRINCESS. Except us. And she told me what her gift meant. It meant that I *was* beautiful—but everybody else was to go on being ignorant, and thinking me plain, until my wedding day. Because, she said, she didn't want me to grow up spoiled and willful and <u>vain</u>, as I should have done if everybody had always been saying how beautiful I was; and the best thing in the world, she said, was to be quite sure of yourself, but not to expect admiration from other people. So ever since then my mirror has told me I'm beautiful, and everybody else thinks me ugly, and I get a lot of fun out of it.

> **GUIDED READING**
>
> What does the godmother's gift mean? When did the princess find out what it meant?

PRINCE. Well, seeing that Dulcibella is the result, I can only say that your godmother was very, very wise.

PRINCESS. And now tell me *your* secret.

PRINCE. It isn't such a pretty one. You see, Prince Simon was going to woo Princess Camilla, and he'd heard that she was beautiful and haughty and <u>imperious</u>—all *you* would have been if your godmother hadn't been so wise. And being a very ordinary-looking fellow himself, he was afraid she wouldn't think much of him, so he suggested to one of his attendants, a man called Carlo, of extremely attractive appearance, that *he* should pretend to be the Prince, and win the Princess's hand; and then at the last moment they would change places—

> **GUIDED READING**
>
> What secret does the prince first share with the princess?

PRINCESS. How would they do that?

PRINCE. The Prince was going to have been married in full armor—with his visor[13] down.

PRINCESS. (*Laughing happily*) Oh, what fun!

PRINCE. Neat, isn't it?

PRINCESS. (*Laughing*) Oh, very . . . very . . . very.

PRINCE. Neat, but not so terribly *funny.* Why do you keep laughing?

PRINCESS. Well, that's another secret.

PRINCE. If it comes to that, *I've* got another one up my sleeve. Shall we exchange again?

PRINCESS. All right. You go first this time.

PRINCE. Very well. . . . I am not Carlo. (*Standing up and speaking dramatically*) I am

---

13. **visor.** In a suit of armor, a movable part of the helmet that can be lowered to cover the face

---

words for everyday use

vain (vān´) *adj.,* being too concerned with one's own looks or possessions. *We did not compliment Reggie on his new wardrobe because he was too <u>vain</u> already.*

im • per • i • ous (im pēr´ē yus) *adj.,* commanding; marked by arrogant assurance. *Sheila's <u>imperious</u> behavior caused others to shy away from her.*

Simon!—ow! (*He sits down and rubs his leg violently.*)

PRINCESS. (*Alarmed*) What is it?

PRINCE. Cramp. (*In a mild voice, still rubbing*) I was saying that I was Prince Simon.

PRINCESS. Shall I rub it for you? (*She rubs.*)

PRINCE. (*Still hopefully*) I am Simon.

PRINCESS. Is that better?

PRINCE. (*Despairingly*) I am Simon.

PRINCESS. I know.

PRINCE. How did you know?

PRINCESS. Well, you told me.

PRINCE. But oughtn't you to <u>swoon</u> or something?

PRINCESS. Why? History records many similar ruses.

PRINCE. (*Amazed*) Is that so? I've never read history. I thought I was being profoundly original.

PRINCESS. Oh, no! Now I'll tell you *my* secret. For reasons very much like your own, the Princess Camilla, who is held to be extremely plain, feared to meet Prince Simon. Is the drawbridge down yet?

PRINCE. Do your people give a faint, surprised cheer every time it gets down?

PRINCESS. Naturally.

PRINCE. Then it came down about three minutes ago.

PRINCESS. Ah! Then at this very moment your man Carlo is declaring his passionate love for my maid, Dulcibella. That, I think,

GUIDED READING

What is the second secret the prince shares?

is funny. (*So does the* PRINCE. *He laughs heartily.*) Dulcibella, by the way, is in love with a man she calls Eg, so I hope Carlo isn't getting carried away.

PRINCE. Carlo is married to a girl he calls "the little woman," so Eg has nothing to fear.

PRINCESS. By the way, I don't know if you heard, but I said, or as good as said, that I am the Princess Camilla.

PRINCE. I wasn't surprised. History, of which I read a great deal, records many similar ruses.

PRINCESS. (*Laughing*) Simon!

PRINCE. (*Laughing*) Camilla! (*He stands up.*) May I try holding you again? (*She nods. He takes her in his arms and kisses her.*) Sweetheart!

PRINCESS. You see, when you lifted me up before, you said, "You're very lovely," and my godmother said that the first person to whom I would seem lovely was the man I should marry; so I knew then that you were Simon and I should marry you.

GUIDED READING

When did the princess realize on her own that Carlo was Simon? Why did she realize this?

PRINCE. I knew directly I saw you that I should marry you, even if you were Dulcibella. By the way, which of you *am* I marrying?

PRINCESS. When she lifts her veil, it will be Camilla. (*Voices are heard outside.*) Until then it will be Dulcibella.

PRINCE. (*In a whisper*) Then good-bye, Camilla, until you lift your veil.

---

words for everyday use

swoon (swo͞on') *v.*, faint; feel powerful emotion. *Frank will <u>swoon</u> when he gets a visit from his hero.*

PRINCESS. Good-bye, Simon, until you raise your visor. (*The* KING *and* QUEEN *come in arm-in-arm, followed by* CARLO *and* DULCIBELLA *also arm-in-arm. The* CHANCELLOR *precedes them, walking backwards, at a loyal angle.*)

PRINCE. (*Supporting the* CHANCELLOR *as an accident seems inevitable*) Careful! (*The* CHANCELLOR *turns indignantly round.*)

KING. Who and what is this? More accurately who and what are all these?

CARLO. My attendant, Carlo, Your Majesty. He will, with Your Majesty's permission, prepare me for the ceremony. (*The* PRINCE *bows.*)

KING. Of course, of course!

QUEEN. (*To* DULCIBELLA) Your maid, Dulcibella, is it not, my love? (DULCIBELLA *nods violently.*) I thought so. (*To* CARLO) She will prepare Her Royal Highness. (*The* PRINCESS *curtsies.*)

KING. Ah, yes. Yes. *Most* important.

PRINCESS. (*Curtsying*) I beg pardon, Your Majesty, if I've done wrong, but I found the gentleman wandering—

KING. (*Crossing to her*) Quite right, my dear, quite right. (*He pinches her cheek, and takes advantage of this kingly gesture to say in a loud whisper*) We've pulled it off! (*They sit down; the* KING *and* QUEEN *on their thrones,* DULCIBELLA *on the* PRINCESS'S *throne.* CARLO *stands behind* DULCIBELLA, *the* CHANCELLOR *on the right of the* QUEEN, *and the* PRINCE *and* PRINCESS *behind the long seat on the left.*)

CHANCELLOR. (*Consulting documents*) H'r'm! Have I Your Majesty's authority to put the final test to His Royal Highness?

QUEEN. (*Whispering to* KING) Is this safe?

KING. (*Whispering*) Perfectly, my dear. I told him the answer a minute ago. (*Over his shoulder to* CARLO) Don't forget, *Dog.* (*Aloud*) Proceed, Your Excellency. It is my desire that the affairs of my country should ever be conducted in a strictly constitutional manner.

CHANCELLOR. (*Oratorically*) By the constitution of the country, a suitor to Her Royal Highness's hand cannot be deemed successful until he has given the correct answer to a riddle. (*Conversationally*) The last suitor answered incorrectly, and thus failed to win his bride.

KING. By a coincidence he fell into the moat.

CHANCELLOR. (*To* CARLO) I have now to ask Your Royal Highness if you are prepared for the <u>ordeal</u>?

CARLO. (*Cheerfully*) Absolutely.

CHANCELLOR. I may mention, as a matter, possibly, of some slight historical interest to our visitor, that by the constitution of the country the same riddle is not allowed to be asked on two successive occasions.

KING. (*Startled*) What's that?

CHANCELLOR. This one, it is interesting to recall, was <u>propounded</u> exactly a century ago, and we must take it as a fortunate <u>omen</u> that it was well and truly solved.

KING. (*To* QUEEN) I may want my sword directly.

GUIDED READING

What is the prince's final test? Why is the king not worried about the prince passing the test?

---

words for everyday use

or • deal (ôr dēl´) *n.*, difficult experience. *Benedict considered sitting quietly for twenty minutes to be the most difficult* <u>ordeal</u> *imaginable.*

pro • pound (prə pound´) *v.*, propose. *The city council chose the occasion of the big parade to* <u>propound</u> *its new zoning policies.*

o • men (ō´mən) *n.*, sign of a future event. *The black clouds that Gertrude saw before she left for school seemed to her a bad* <u>omen</u> *for a test day.*

CHANCELLOR. The riddle is this. What is it which has four legs and mews like a cat?

CARLO. (*Promptly*) A dog.

KING. (*Still more promptly*) Bravo, bravo! (*He claps loudly and nudges the* QUEEN, *who claps too.*)

CHANCELLOR. (*Peering at his documents*) According to the records of the occasion to which I referred, the correct answer would seem to be—

PRINCESS. (*To* PRINCE) Say something, quick!

CHANCELLOR. —not dog, but—

PRINCE. Your Majesty, have I permission to speak? Naturally His Royal Highness could not think of justifying himself on such an occasion, but I think that with Your Majesty's gracious permission, I could—

KING. Certainly, certainly.

PRINCE. In our country, we have an animal to which we have given the name "dog," or, in the local dialect of the more mountainous districts, "doggie." It sits by the fireside and purrs.

CARLO. That's right. It purrs like anything.

PRINCE. When it needs milk, which is its <u>staple</u> food, it mews.

CARLO. (*Enthusiastically*) Mews like nobody's business.

PRINCE. It also has four legs.

CARLO. One at each corner.

PRINCE. In some countries, I understand, this animal is called a "cat." In one distant country to which His Royal Highness and I

GUIDED READING

What was the correct answer to the question? How does the prince try to correct the situation?

penetrated, it was called by the very curious name of "hippopotamus."

CARLO. That's right. (*To the* PRINCE) Do you remember that ginger-colored hippopotamus which used to climb on to my shoulder and lick my ear?

PRINCE. I shall never forget it, sir. (*To the* KING) So you see, Your Majesty—

KING. Thank you. I think that makes it perfectly clear. (*Firmly to the* CHANCELLOR) You are about to agree?

CHANCELLOR. Undoubtedly, Your Majesty. May I be the first to congratulate His Royal Highness on solving the riddle so accurately?

sta • ple (stā′pəl) *adj.,* most important. *In many countries, rice is the <u>staple</u> crop.*

KING. You may be the first to see that all is in order for an immediate wedding.

CHANCELLOR. Thank you, Your Majesty. (*He bows and withdraws. The* KING *rises, as do the* QUEEN *and* DULCIBELLA.)

KING. (*To* CARLO) Doubtless, Prince Simon, you will wish to retire and prepare yourself for the ceremony.

CARLO. Thank you, sir.

PRINCE. Have I Your Majesty's permission to attend His Royal Highness? It is the custom of his country for Princes of the royal blood to be married in full armor, a matter which requires a certain adjustment—

KING. Of course, of course. (CARLO *bows to the* KING *and* QUEEN *and goes out. As the* PRINCE *is about to follow,* the KING *stops him.*) Young man, you have a quality of quickness which I admire. It is my pleasure to reward it in any way which commends itself to you.

GUIDED READING What does the king admire about the prince?

PRINCE. Your Majesty is ever gracious. May I ask for my reward *after* the ceremony? (*He catches the eye of the* PRINCESS, *and they give each other a secret smile.*)

KING. Certainly. (*The* PRINCE *bows and goes out. To* DULCIBELLA) Now, young woman, make yourself scarce. You've done your work excellently, and we will see that you and your—what was his name?

DULCIBELLA. Eg, Your Majesty.

KING. —that you and your Eg are not forgotten.

DULCIBELLA. Coo! (*She curtsies and goes out.*)

PRINCESS. (*Calling*) Wait for me, Dulcibella!

KING. (*To* QUEEN) Well, my dear, we may congratulate ourselves. As I remember saying to somebody once, "You have not lost a daughter, you have gained a son." How does he strike you?

GUIDED READING What does the queen think about Carlo, who she believes will be marrying her daughter?

QUEEN. Stupid.

KING. They made a very handsome pair, I thought, he and Dulcibella.

QUEEN. Both stupid.

KING. I said nothing about stupidity. What I *said* was that they were both extremely handsome. That is the important thing. (*Struck by a sudden idea*) Or isn't it?

QUEEN. What do *you* think of Prince Simon, Camilla?

PRINCESS. I adore him. We shall be so happy together.

KING. Well, of course you will. I told you so. Happy ever after.

QUEEN. Run along now and get ready.

PRINCESS. Yes, mother. (*She throws a kiss to them and goes out.*)

KING. (*Anxiously*) My dear, have we been wrong about Camilla all this time? It seemed to me that she wasn't looking *quite* so plain as usual just now. Did *you* notice anything?

GUIDED READING What does the king notice about his daughter on her wedding day? What does the queen say is the reason for the change in Camilla?

QUEEN. (*Carelessly*) Just the excitement of the marriage.

KING. (*Relieved*) Ah, yes, that would account for it. ■

Do you think Great-Aunt Malkin's gift to Camilla was a good idea? Why, or why not? How might Camilla's life have been different if her beauty had not been hidden?

About *the*
AUTHOR

Alan Alexander (A. A.) Milne
(1882–1956) was born in London, England. Milne began his writing career working for newspapers and magazines. From 1906 to 1914, he worked as an assistant editor and writer for a British humor magazine called *Punch*. Milne is best known for the children's verses and stories he wrote after the birth of his son, Christopher Robin. Milne's storybooks *Winnie-the-Pooh* (1926) and *The House at Pooh Corner* (1928) are about the adventures of his son and his son's favorite stuffed animals. His books of poetry for children are *When We Were Very Young* (1924) and *Now We Are Six* (1927). For adults, Milne wrote novels, several popular comedy plays, and an autobiography called *It's Too Late Now* (1939).

Investigate, *Inquire,* and Imagine

Recall: GATHERING FACTS

1a. What problem does the chancellor want to discuss with the king at the beginning of the play? What does the king say about his daughter's looks and personality?

2a. What did Great-Aunt Malkin say at Camilla's christening? What does Camilla learn from Great-Aunt Malkin on her tenth birthday?

3a. What does the king decide to do to make sure his daughter marries Prince Simon? What does Prince Simon decide to do to make sure he marries Princess Camilla? What do Camilla and Simon discuss when they accidentally meet?

→ Interpret: FINDING MEANING

1b. Why is the chancellor uncomfortable discussing this subject with the king? Why does the king believe it is more important for a princess to be beautiful than have a wonderful personality?

2b. Explain what the king and queen think Great-Aunt Malkin's words mean? What do they really mean?

3b. Explain whether Prince Simon and Princess Camilla are a good match. In what ways are they similar? What do they admire about each other?

Analyze: TAKING THINGS APART

4a. What attitudes are presented in this play about outer beauty? about inner beauty? Focus your response on the attitudes of the chancellor, the king and queen, Great-Aunt Malkin, the princess herself, and Prince Simon.

→ Synthesize: BRINGING THINGS TOGETHER

4b. What do you think is this play's theme about beauty and judging others using one standard, or idea, of beauty?

Evaluate: MAKING JUDGMENTS

5a. The king says that the great fact about marriage is "that once you're married you live happy ever after." Explain whether the king bases this statement on his own experience. How happy do the king and queen seem together? How can you tell?

→ Extend: CONNECTING IDEAS

5b. Based on what you have learned about Princess Camilla, Prince Simon, and how the two of them get along, explain how you think their marriage will compare with that of Camilla's parents.

Understanding *Literature*

CHARACTERIZATION. Characterization is the act of creating or describing a character. Writers create characters in three major ways: by showing what characters say, do, and think; by showing what other characters say about them; and by showing what physical features, dress, and personality the characters display. Explain the way each of the following characters has been characterized: the king, the queen, Dulcibella, Princess Camilla, Carlos, and Prince Simon. Try to sum up each of their characters in a brief description.

PLOT AND CONFLICT. A **plot** is a series of events related to a central conflict, or struggle. A plot usually involves the introduction of a conflict, its development, and its eventual resolution. A **conflict** is a struggle between two people or things in a literary work. Conflicts may be internal or external. What are some of the conflicts that take place in this play? Which ones are internal and which ones are external? Which conflict would you say is the central one? How is it resolved?

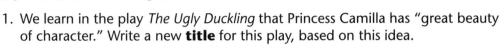

Writer's Journal

1. We learn in the play *The Ugly Duckling* that Princess Camilla has "great beauty of character." Write a new **title** for this play, based on this idea.
2. Write a **list** of the ways the world would be changed if everyone looked exactly the same.
3. Write a brief **personal essay** about the way you think your society's standards of beauty have affected you and your classmates.

Skill Builders

Applied English
WRITING A PRESS RELEASE.
Companies try to promote a favorable image to the public to help support their business. Imagine that you have just opened a new store, restaurant, beauty salon, or sporting goods store. Write a press release announcing the opening of your business. You should try to create a positive image of your business to make it a success. For more information on writing a press release, see the Language Arts Survey, 6.9, "Delivering a Press Release."

Language, Grammar, and Style

CAPITALIZATION OF TITLES OF
PERSONS. Titles like *king, queen,* and *princess,* as well as professional titles like *doctor, vice-president,* or *governor* are either capitalized or lowercased depending on their use. If the title is being used generally, such as "Richard III was a terrible king," the title is lowercased. When the title is used as part of a specific person's name, it is capitalized: "Some people say King Richard III was terrible." Remember that it doesn't matter how close to a person's name in a sentence the title

appears. Unless the title is a part of the person's name, it should be lowercased. "We gave our insurance card to Doctor Jane Doe," *but* "Jane Doe, a doctor, took our insurance card." Words that indicate family relations, such as *Grandpa* or *Mom,* follow the same rule. They are only capitalized when they are used as the name or part of the name of a particular person. For more information on capitalization and titles of persons, refer to the Language Arts Survey 3.87, "Family Relationships and Titles of Persons." Then read the sentences below, and choose the correct word from the pair of words in parentheses.

1. While nobody could see her outer beauty, (princess, Princess) Camilla was confident of her own inner beauty.
2. Princess Camilla told her (Dad, dad) that she was happy to marry Simon.
3. Nobody could see Camilla's outer beauty because of a spell cast by (Great-Aunt, great-aunt) Malkin.
4. Because of (prince, Prince) Simon's trick, Camilla's parents think that Carlos is the (prince, Prince).
5. Unlike the (Queen, queen) in the play, (Queen, queen) Elizabeth I was a real ruler who held the throne without a king at her side.

Reader's *Journal*

Write about a time when you were frightened by something you heard or saw at night.

Reader's TOOLBOX

DIALOGUE. Dialogue is conversation involving two or more people or characters. Plays are made up of dialogue and stage directions. In a play, dialogue appears after the names of characters. As you begin to read, pay attention to what parts of the play are actual speech between characters.

STAGE DIRECTIONS. Stage directions are notes included in a play or script to describe how something should look, sound, or be performed. Often stage directions appear in parentheses and italic type to set them apart from dialogue. While dialogue is made up of the words delivered aloud on stage, stage directions are not read or delivered aloud and are intended as notes for the director and actors. As you read the beginning of the play, keep track in a chart like the one at right of what is dialogue and what are stage directions. Focus on that part of the play from the doctor's first words to the bottom of the page.

Prereading

IN THE FOG   by Milton Geiger

Reader's Resource

- **APPLIED ENGLISH CONNECTION.** Screenwriters put to paper the words that form the basis of movies and television shows. First, a screenwriter creates an outline describing the plot of the film or show in one or two pages. Then a screenwriter writes what is called a treatment, or a more full detailed description of the film or television show containing dialogue. Finally, the screenwriter writes the actual screenplay. Screenplays consist of dialogue, or the words actors speak, as well as stage directions describing actions, settings, or the way something is performed. Unlike traditional dramas or plays, screenplays may also include instructions about how the camera should move or how the film should be edited. *In the Fog* is a screenplay. As you read, you will discover instructions about how the camera should move and what it should film.

- **AMERICAN HISTORY CONNECTION.** The screenplay you are about to read is set at Gettysburg, Pennsylvania. This place was the site of one of the most bloody American Civil War battles. The Civil War was fought between the northern states, known as the Union, and the southern states, known as the Confederacy. The Civil War took place between 1861 and 1865, and the Battle of Gettysyburg took place from July 1 to July 3, 1863. Although the battle was an important victory for the Union, many soldiers of both sides died during the three days of fighting. President Lincoln dedicated a soldiers' cemetery at Gettysburg and gave his famous Gettysburg Address there.

Graphic Organizer

Character	Stage Directions	Dialogue

IN THE FOG

Milton Geiger

CHARACTERS

THE DOCTOR

ZEKE

EBEN

FILLING STATION ATTENDANT

(SETS: *A signpost on Pennsylvania Route 30. A rock or stump in the fog. A gas station pump.*)

(FADE IN: *Exterior. Night. At first we can only see fog drifting across a dark scene devoid of detail. Then, to weird minor music, the camera dollies[1] in slowly so that out of the fog there emerges toward us a white roadside signpost with a number of white painted signboards pointing to right and to left. The camera continues to dolly in until it has in closeup the state route marker fastened below the signs on the post. The marker is a Pennsylvania State Route—marked characteristically "PENNA-30." Now, a light as from a far headlight sweeps the signs.*)

(SOUND: *Automobile approaching on road. The car pulls up close. We hear the car door open and slam and a man's footsteps approaching on the concrete. Now the signs are lit up again by a more localized, smaller source of light. The light grows stronger as the man, off-stage, approaches. The* DOCTOR *enters the shot, holding a flashlight before him. He* <u>scrutinizes</u> *the road marker. He flashes his light up at the arrows, the camera moving up with the light. We see the legends on the markers. Pointing off right there are markers that read: York, Columbia, Lancaster; pointing left the signs read: Fayetteville, McConnellsburg, Pennsylvania Turnpike.*)

(CUT TO: *Another angle. We shoot into the* DOCTOR's *perplexed and annoyed face as he turns his flashlight on a folded road map. He is a bit lost in the fog. Then his flashlight fails him. It goes out!*)

> **GUIDED READING**
>
> What happened to the doctor?

DOCTOR. Darn! (*He fumbles with the flashlight in the gloom. Then a voice is raised to him from off-scene.*)

EBEN. (*Off-scene, strangely*) Turn around, mister . . . (*The* DOCTOR *turns sharply to stare off-scene. His face is lit by a bobbing light from off-scene.*)

ZEKE. (*Off-scene*) You don't have to be afraid, mister . . .

(CUT TO: *What* DOCTOR *sees. Two men are slowly approaching out of the fog,* <u>grotesque</u> *in the distorting gloom. One carries a lantern below his knees. The other holds a heavy rifle of dim manufacture. Their features are utterly indistinct as they approach and the rifleman holds up his gun with quiet threat.*)

> **GUIDED READING**
>
> What is threatening about the two men?

(CUT TO: *Group shot, angling past* DOCTOR's *shoulder, at their faces.*)

EBEN. You don't have to be afraid.

DOCTOR. (*More* <u>indignant</u> *than afraid*) So you say! Who are you, man?

EBEN. We don't aim to hurt you none.

DOCTOR. That's reassuring. I'd like to know just what you mean by this? This gun business! Who *are* you?

ZEKE. (*Mildly*) What's your trade, mister?

DOCTOR. I . . . I'm a doctor. Why?

ZEKE. (*to* EBEN) Doctor.

EBEN. (*Nods; then to* DOCTOR) Yer the man we want.

ZEKE. Ye'll do proper, we're thinkin.'

EBEN. So ye'd better come along, mister.

---

1. **dollies.** Moves on a low, wheeled platform

words for everyday use
scru • ti • nize (scrōot' ən īz) *v.*, look at very carefully. *Before Malachai signed the contract he* <u>scrutinized</u> *the fine print.*

gro • tesque (grō tesk´) *adj.*, fantastic; bizarre; strange. *The flickering light of the campfire cast* <u>grotesque</u> *shadows.*

in • dig • nant (in dig´nənt) *adj.*, feeling or expressing anger in reaction to an injustice, ingratitude, or meanness. *Mona was* <u>indignant</u> *when someone made fun of her painting.*

ZEKE. Aye.

DOCTOR. Why? Has—anyone been hurt?

EBEN. It's for you to say if he's been hurt nigh[2] to the finish.

GUIDED READING
What do the two men want from the doctor?

ZEKE. So we're askin' ye to come along, doctor.

(CUT TO: *Another angle, favoring* DOCTOR. *He looks from one to another in indecision and puzzlement.*)

EBEN. In the name o' mercy.

ZEKE. Aye.

DOCTOR. I want you to understand—I'm not afraid of your gun! I'll go to your man all right. Naturally, I'm a doctor. But I demand to know who you are.

ZEKE. (*Patiently*) Why not? Raise yer lantern, Eben. . . .

EBEN. (*Tiredly*) Aye.

(EBEN *lifts his lantern. Its light falls on their faces now and we see that they are terrifying. Matted beards, clotted with blood; crude head bandages, crusty with dirt and dry blood. Their hair, stringy and disheveled. Their faces are lean and hollow-cheeked; their eyes sunken and tragic. The* DOCTOR *is shocked for a moment—then bursts out—*)

DOCTOR. Good Lord!—

ZEKE. (*Impassively*) That's Eben, I'm Zeke.

DOCTOR. What's happened? Has there been an accident or . . . what?

ZEKE. Mischief's happened, stranger.

EBEN. Mischief enough.

DOCTOR. (*Looks at the rifle at his chest*) There's been gunplay—hasn't there?

ZEKE. (*Mildly ironic*) Yer tellin' us there's been gunplay!

DOCTOR. And I'm telling you that I'm not at all frightened! It's my duty to report this and report it I will!

GUIDED READING
What is Zeke's reaction to the doctor's threat of notifying the authorities?

ZEKE. Aye, mister. You *do* that.

DOCTOR. You're arrogant about it now! You don't think you'll be caught and dealt with. But people are losing patience with you men. . . .

(CUT TO: *Close two-shot.* ZEKE *and* EBEN.)

DOCTOR'S VOICE. (*off-scene*) . . . You . . . you moonshiners![3] Running wild . . . a law unto yourselves . . . shooting up the countryside!

GUIDED READING
What does the doctor think of Zeke and Eben?

ZEKE. Hear that, Eben? Moonshiners.

EBEN. Mischief's happened, mister, we'll warrant that . . .

DOCTOR. And I don't like it!

ZEKE. Can't say we like it better'n you do, mister . . .

EBEN. (*Strangely sad and remote*) What must be, must.

ZEKE. There's not changin' or goin' back and all 'at's left is the wishin' things were different.

EBEN. Aye.

DOCTOR. And while we talk your wounded man lies bleeding I suppose—worthless though he may be. Well? I'll have

---

2. **nigh.** Nearly; almost
3. **moonshiners.** People who make and sell whiskey illegally

i · ron · ic (ī rän´ ik) *adj.*, meaning the opposite of what is expressed. *"Nice weather we're having," said Mona in an ironic tone of voice as the blizzard raged outside the house.*

ar · ro · gant (ar´ə gənt) *adj.*, full of unwarranted pride and self-importance. *The arrogant man thought that he was always right.*

to get my instrument bag, you know. *(Nods off-scene)* It's in the car.

(EBEN and ZEKE part to let DOCTOR pass between them. DOCTOR leaves shot grimly as they watch him, off-scene.)

(SOUND: Car door opens off-scene. Pause. Slams.)

(The DOCTOR re-enters the shot, carrying his medical bag.)

DOCTOR.   I'm ready. Lead the way.

(EBEN lifts his lantern a bit and goes first. ZEKE prods the DOCTOR ever so gently and apologetically but firmly with the rifle muzzle. The DOCTOR leaves the shot next. ZEKE strides off slowly after them.)

(DISSOLVE TO: Exterior, night. Medium shot of a wounded man lying against a section of stone fence or a boulder or a tree trunk. He, too, is bearded though very young and wears some sort of unidentifiable tunic like the other men. His shirt is dark with blood. He breathes stertorously[4] but never stirs otherwise. The light of EBEN's bull's-eye[5] falls on him, bobbingly. EBEN enters the shot followed by the DOCTOR and ZEKE.)

(SOUND: Owl, far off, from time to time.)

ZEKE.   Ain't stirred a mite since we left 'im.

DOCTOR.   Let's have that lantern here! *(The DOCTOR tears the man's shirt for better access to the wound.)*

(CLOSE UP: DOCTOR's face. Appalled.)

DOCTOR.   *(Softly)* Dreadful! Dreadful! . . .

ZEKE'S VOICE.   *(Off-scene)* Reckon it's bad in the chest like that, hey?

DOCTOR.   *(Taking pulse)* His pulse is positively racing! . . .

(Tight group shot.)

DOCTOR.   How long has he been this way?

ZEKE.   A long time, mister. A *long* time. . . .

DOCTOR.   *(To EBEN)* You! Hand me my bag.

(EBEN puts down lantern and hands bag to DOCTOR. The DOCTOR opens bag and takes out a couple of retractors.[6] ZEKE holds lantern close now.)

DOCTOR.   Lend me a hand with these retractors. *(He works on man, hiding wound from camera with his body.)* All right . . . when I tell you to draw back on the retractors—draw back.

EBEN.   Aye.

ZEKE.   How is 'e, mister?

DOCTOR.   *(Preoccupied)* More retraction. Pull them a bit more. Hold it. . . .

EBEN.   Bad, ain't he?

DOCTOR.   Bad enough. The bullet didn't touch any lung tissue far as I can see right now. There's some pneumothorax[7] though. All I can do now is plug the wound. There's some cotton and gauze wadding in my bag. Find it. . . .

(ZEKE probes about silently in the bag and comes up with a small dark box of gauze.)

DOCTOR.   That's it. *(Works a moment in silence.)* I've never seen anything quite like it.

EBEN.   Yer young, doctor. Lots o' things you've never seen.

DOCTOR.   Adhesive tape!

(ZEKE finds a roll of three-inch tape and hands it to the DOCTOR who tears off strips and, unseen to camera, slaps them on the dressing[8]

GUIDED READING

How long has the wounded man been this way?

4. *stertorously.* With loud, raspy, obstructed breathing
5. *bull's-eye.* Type of lantern
6. *retractors.* Surgical instruments for drawing back part of an organ, such as the skin at the edge of an incision
7. **pneumothorax.** Presence of air in the chest cavity as a result of a puncture in the lungs
8. *dressing.* Bandages applied to wounds

and pats and smooths them to the man's chest. EBEN *replaces equipment in* DOCTOR'*s bag and closes it with a hint of the finality to come. A preview of* <u>dismissal</u> *so to speak.*)

DOCTOR. *(At length)* There. So much for that. Now then—*(Takes man's shoulders)* Give me a hand here.

ZEKE. *(Quiet suspicion)* What fer?

DOCTOR. We've got to move this man.

ZEKE. What fer?

DOCTOR. *(Stands; indignantly)* We've got to get him to a hospital for treatment; a thorough cleansing of the wound; irrigation.[9] I've done all I can for him here.

ZEKE. I reckon he'll be all right, 'thout no hospital.

DOCTOR. Do you realize how badly this man's hurt!

GUIDED READING

What does the doctor say they must do? What do the two men say?

EBEN. He won't bleed to death, will he?

DOCTOR. I don't think so—not with that plug and the pressure dressing. But bleeding isn't the only danger we've got to—

ZEKE. *(Interrupts)* All right, then. Much obliged to you.

DOCTOR. This man's *dangerously* hurt!

---

9. **irrigation.** Washing out a wound

words for everyday use **dis • miss • al** (dis mis´ əl) *n.,* act of causing someone to go. *The yearbook staff was given an early* <u>dismissal</u> *from class on picture day.*

ZEKE. Reckon he'll pull through now, thanks to you.

DOCTOR. I'm glad you feel that way about it! But I'm going to report this to the Pennsylvania State Police at the first telephone I reach!

ZEKE. We ain't stoppin' ye, mister.

EBEN. Fog is liftin', Zeke. Better be done with this, I say.

ZEKE. *(Nods, sadly)* Aye. Ye can go now, mister . . . and thanks.

(Group shot. Another angle, favoring ZEKE, *then* EBEN.*)*

ZEKE. *(Continues)* We never meant a mite o' harm, I can tell ye. If we killed, it was no wish of ours.

> **GUIDED READING**
>
> What do Zeke and Eben say about the "gunplay" that injured their companion?

EBEN. What's done is done. Aye.

EBEN. Ye can go now, stranger. . . .

*(*EBEN *hands* ZEKE *the* DOCTOR's *bag.* ZEKE *hands it gently to the* DOCTOR.*)*

DOCTOR. Very well. You haven't heard the last of this, though!

ZEKE. That's the truth, mister. We've killed, aye; and we've been hurt for it. . . .

EBEN. Hurt bad.

(Group shot. Another angle, favoring DOCTOR *in close shot. His face puckered with doubt and strange apprehension.)*

ZEKE. We're not alone, mister. We ain't the only ones. *(Sighs)* Ye can go now, doctor . . . and our thanks to ye. . . .

(The camera moves with the DOCTOR *as he leaves the other two, still gazing at them in strange* enchantment *and wonder and a touch of* indignation. *Camera takes his body from waist up as he walks against neutral, featureless background wreathed with some tendrils of fog.)*

EBEN'S VOICE. *(Off-scene)* Thanks, mister. . . .

ZEKE'S VOICE. In the name o' mercy . . . We thank you. . . .

(Cut to: Close up: ZEKE *and* EBEN, *their faces* grizzled *like the faces of monuments in the park in winter; their eyes unhappy and suffering. The fog drifting across them.)*

EBEN. In the name o' mercy.

ZEKE. Thanks, mister. . . .

EBEN. In the name o' kindness. . . .

(The camera pulls back for a group shot of the two men standing; their wounded comrade at their feet—like a group statue in the park . . . grizzled and time-worn. The fog thickens across the scene.)

> **GUIDED READING**
>
> What do the three men look like?

(MUSIC: *Eerie, sad.*)

(SOUND: *Far off the long, sad wail of a locomotive whimpers in the dark. Then fades.*)

(FADE OUT.)

(FADE IN: *The illuminated translucent glass globe atop a gasoline pump. The camera pulls back to show the young* ATTENDANT *standing in front of the pump taking a reading and recording it in a book as he prepares to close up. Lights sweep him. He turns as he hears the car approach on the gravel drive.)*

(SOUND: *Car approaching. Crunches on gravel and stops. Door opens and slams shut.* DOCTOR's *feet crunch on gravel, approaching swiftly.*)

(DOCTOR *enters shot.*)

---

words for everyday use

en • chant • ment (en chant´ mənt) *n.*, magical spell or charm. *The book told the tale of a forest full of magic and* enchantment.

griz • zled (griz´əld) *adj.*, partly gray. *Grampa's* grizzled *beard was covered in frost when he came in from the cold.*

ATTENDANT. (*Pleasantly*) Good evening, sir. (*Nods off at off-scene car*) Care to pull 'er up to this pump, sir? Closing up.

DOCTOR. (*Impatiently*) No. Where's your telephone, please? I've just been held up!

ATTENDANT. Pay-station inside, sir. . . .

DOCTOR. Thank you! (*The* DOCTOR *starts to go past the* ATTENDANT.)

ATTENDANT. Excuse me, sir. . . .

DOCTOR. (*Stops*) Eh, what is it, what is it?

ATTENDANT. Uh . . . what sort of looking fellows were they?

DOCTOR. Oh . . . two big fellows with a rifle; faces and heads bandaged and smeared with dirt and blood. Friend of theirs with a gaping hole in his chest. I'm a doctor so they forced me to attend to him. Why?

ATTENDANT. *Those* fellers, huh?

DOCTOR. Then you know about them!

ATTENDANT. I guess so.

DOCTOR. They're armed and they're desperate!

ATTENDANT. That was about two or three miles back, would you say?

DOCTOR. (*Fumbling in pocket*) Just about—I don't seem to have the change. I wonder if you'd spare me change for a quarter? . . .

ATTENDANT. (*Makes change from metal coin canister at his belt*) Certainly, sir. . . .

DOCTOR. What town was that back there, now?

ATTENDANT. (*Dumps coins in other's hand*) There you are, sir.

DOCTOR. (*Impatient*) Yes, thank you. I say—what town was that back there, so I can tell the police?

(*Two shot. A new angle favoring* ATTENDANT. *His eyes are serious and candid; matter-of-fact and very steady.*)

ATTENDANT. That was . . . Gettysburg, mister. . . .

(MUSIC: *Softly, eerily poignant. "Dixie" and "Battle Hymn of the Republic" in minor counterpoint.*)

GUIDED READING
Where did the doctor see the armed men?

(*Camera slowly trucks around for two-shot that slowly favors* DOCTOR.)

DOCTOR. Gettysburg? . . .

ATTENDANT. Gettysburg and Gettysburg battlefield . . . (*Looks off.*) When it's light and the fog's gone, you can see the gravestones. Meade's men . . . Pickett's men, Robert E. Lee's. . . .

(*The* DOCTOR *is looking off with the* ATTENDANT; *now he turns his head slowly to stare at the other man.*)

ATTENDANT. (*continues*) On nights like this— well—you're not the first those men've stopped...or the last. (*Nods off*) Fill 'er up, mister?

GUIDED READING
What are the men the doctor has seen?

(*Camera dollies in slowly on the rapt face of the* DOCTOR.)

DOCTOR. Yes, fill 'er up. . . .

(FADE OUT.)

(MUSIC FINISHES.)

■

If you were the doctor, what would you do after talking to the gas station attendant?

About *the* AUTHOR

Milton Geiger of Northridge, California, was a radio script writer and a screenwriter. Some of his plays for radio theater include *Twilight Show* and *In the Fog*. He began his career in radio before moving to television, where he regularly wrote scripts for *Climax, You Are There, Eternal Light,* and *Stoney Burke*. He wrote the play *Edwin Booth*, which opened in New York in 1958, featuring actor Jose Ferrer. Geiger also wrote poetry. "I Will Not Go Back" is one of his most well-known poems.

Investigate, Inquire, and Imagine

Recall: Gathering Facts → Interpret: Finding Meaning

1a. What makes the doctor stop and get out of his car? Who approaches him when he stops? What do these people want the doctor to do?

1b. Why might the setting make the doctor nervous? Why do the two men make the doctor nervous?

2a. Where do the two men lead the doctor? What does the doctor do when he gets there?

2b. Explain how the doctor and the two men differ in opinion toward what should be done to the two men's friend.

3a. What does the doctor say to the gas station attendant about what has happened? Where does the gas station attendant say the doctor has been? What does he say about the two men?

3b. How do you think the doctor feels about what the gas station attendant says to him?

Analyze: Taking Things Apart → Synthesize: Bringing Things Together

4a. What does the doctor think at first of the two men who stop him? What explanation does he provide for what he sees? Based on what the gas station attendant says, what is the story of the two men? What clues in the story help support the gas station attendant's words?

4b. Explain whose explanation you think is right—the doctor's or the gas station attendant's? Do you think the gas station attendant changed the doctor's mind? Why, or why not? If you were a police chief in the town, how would you explain the events that happened to the doctor?

Perspective: Looking at Other Views → Empathy: Seeing from Inside

5a. Explain whether you can understand the doctor's assumptions and attitudes toward Zeke and Eben at the beginning of the screenplay.

5b. Explain what Zeke and Eben try to tell the doctor about the killing they have done. Why might they have had to act as they did in their situation? How do they seem to feel about their behavior?

Understanding Literature

DIALOGUE. Dialogue is conversation involving two or more people or characters. Plays are made up of dialogue and stage directions. In a play, dialogue appears after the names of characters. Through which character's dialogue do you learn the most about the two men the doctor meets? Explain.

STAGE DIRECTIONS. Stage directions are notes included in a play or script to describe how something should look, sound, or be performed. Explain how the stage directions help create the scary, mysterious mood or feeling of this screenplay.

Writer's Journal

1. Write a brief and spooky **description** of a scene at night or in the fog.
2. Imagine that you are a reporter writing about the strange experience that the doctor and others like him have experienced at Gettysburg. Write a **news article** about Zeke and Eben and the people who have encountered them.
3. Imagine you encounter a ghost from a historical time period. Write a **dialogue** between you and the ghost, in which you try to learn about that time period.

Skill Builders

Language, Grammar, and Style

DIALECT. A **dialect** is a version of a language spoken by people of a particular place, time, or group. Geiger uses dialect in *In the Fog* to emphasize that Zeke and Eben are from another time. Rewrite the examples of dialect below from "In the Fog" into the dialect of your own place, time, and group.

1. We don't aim to hurt you none.
2. Ye'll do proper, we're thinkin'.
3. It's for you to say if he's been hurt nigh to the finish.
4. Reckon it's bad in the chest like that, hey?
5. We never meant a mite o' harm, I can tell ye.

Collaborative Learning & Speaking and Listening

PRODUCING A SCREENPLAY. *In the Fog* is a screenplay, which is meant to be enacted. Work in groups of six to create a production of *In the Fog.* One student should be the director, and the others should take the parts of the doctor, Zeke, Eben, the wounded soldier, and the attendant. You can also work in larger groups and have other students take charge of providing and designing costumes, props (items that can be carried on and off stage by actors), and special effects.

Collaborative Learning

READING WITH A BOOK CLUB. Join together with a group of four to five other students to form a book club. Together your book club should choose another eerie play or screenplay to read. For example, you might try to find another eerie story from shows that were popular toward the mid-20th century, such as *The Twilight Zone, Alfred Hitchcock Presents,* or *The Outer Limits.* Each group member should then read the play or screenplay independently. The group should then meet to discuss what they thought of the play or screenplay. Group members should take notes on ideas discussed.

Reflecting
on your *reading*

Theme

The element of surprise is often used in drama (plays, film, television) because all the information is conveyed through dialogue, setting, and character, so the viewer slowly begins to make connections. One play in this unit is very funny, because not all of the characters know what is going on. One scene is profoundly sad and dramatic, because it is slowly revealed to represent a tragic episode in our history. What themes can you find in these two dramas?

Genre

Drama is different from a short story in that all information about plot and character are conveyed through dialogue, setting, and action. In what other ways is drama different from fiction?

Group Project

How much information can be conveyed about characters through dialogue alone? As a group, write a short play or scene. Define your characters and write dialogue that will convey information about the characters and their situation. Let the dialogue reveal their situation and who they are. Reveal, for example, age, feelings, profession, and personality. Which character is cruel? lonely? secretly in love? brave? honest? dishonest? How are they related to each other? Which character is a school dropout or an A student? Which one is a professional business person? Which is a truck driver? How do you know? Let your audience get to know these characters through dialogue, dress, and stage setting. Perform your scene in front of the class and ask classmates to describe the characters you have created.

On Your Own

Be the author of your own one-act play. Create a setting and characters. Write the stage directions and dialogue. From curtain up, to curtain down, write a short, complete play.

Conference at Night, 1949. Edward Hopper.

Telling It as it Is

Nonfiction

ELEMENTS *of* NONFICTION

NONFICTION. Nonfiction is writing about real people, places, things, and events. Essays, autobiographies, biographies, new stories, speeches, and documentary writing are all types of nonfiction writing.

AIM. Aim is a writer's reason for writing. A writer may write to inform readers or report to them about something that has taken place. This **mode** or type of writing is called **informative writing.** News articles, reports, scientific essays, and speeches are frequently forms of informative writing. A writer may write to entertain, amuse, or enlighten readers. This type of writing is called **imaginative writing**. Poems, short stories, novels, and plays are often examples of imaginative writing. A writer may write to share a story. This type of writing is called **narrative writing.** Biographies and autobiographies are examples of narrative writing. A writer may write to reflect on his or thoughts and emotions about something that is personal to him or her. This type of writing is known as **personal** or **expressive writing.** Diary entries and personal letters are examples of this type of writing. Finally, a writer may want to persuade readers to share his or her view on a particular subject. This type of writing is called **persuasive or argumentative writing,** as the writer's goal is to persuade the reader. Newspaper editorials and petitions are examples of this kind of writing. A writer can have more than one aim in creating a work. A biographical essay, for example, can be both narrative and informative. An essay that offers an opinion about a vacation site may be both expressive, revealing the author's personal reactions to the place, and persuasive, offering arguments for or against visiting the place.

AUTOBIOGRAPHY. An **autobiography** is the story of a person's life told by that person. Autobiographical works are told from the first-person point of view. Personal letters, personal essays, journal entries, and memoirs are all examples of autobiography, along with book-length works of autobiography that tell a complete life story.

BIOGRAPHY. A **biography** is the story of a person's life told by another person. Biographies are told from a third-person point of view, although writers of biography may also include autobiographical excerpts so that the reader may gain some firsthand knowledge about the person whose life story is being told.

ESSAY. An **essay** is a short nonfiction work that expresses a writer's thoughts about a single subject. A well-written essay clearly presents information organized into an introduction, body, and conclusion. There are many types of essays. A *personal or expressive essay,* for example, is a short nonfiction work on a single topic related to the life of the writer. The author of a personal essay may tell a story or an anecdote or reflect on and share thoughts and feelings about something in his or her life. In a *scientific essay,* the writer's main goal is to inform the reader and to communicate specific scientific information.

SPEECH. A **speech** is a public address. Although speeches are delivered orally, most speeches are written first—and many famous historical speeches are passed on through writing. Speeches may be delivered to a wide and varied audience or to a small audience of people with similar interests and experiences. Most speeches address a specific issue or event, although some may encompass several topics. A speech can inform an audience, tell a story, persuade an audience, or reflect on an idea.

DOCUMENTARY WRITING. Documentary writing is writing that records an event in accurate detail. News articles and research reports are both examples of documentary writing.

Prereading

"MADAM C. J. WALKER"

by Jim Haskins

Reader's TOOLBOX

BIOGRAPHY. A **biography** is the story of a person's life, told by another person. As you read, you will learn about the life of Madam C. J. Walker. Think about why the writer wanted to tell the story of her life.

INTRODUCTION AND CONCLUSION. An **introduction** should capture the reader's attention and present the subject of the work. A **conclusion** should sum up the ideas presented in the piece and give the reader a sense of resolution. Pay special attention to the introduction and conclusion of this selection.

Graphic  Organizer

Make a time line like the one below to keep track of important dates and events in Walker's life.

1867   1927

December 23,
Sarah Breedlove
(Madam Walker) born
in Delta, Louisiana

Reader's Journal

Write about a goal that you have and how you will face the obstacles to reaching your goal.

Reader's Resource

- **HISTORY CONNECTION.** *Reconstruction* refers to the rebuilding period that followed the American Civil War. Although slavery had ended, many African Americans were forced into sharecropping because they did not have land or jobs. A sharecropper provided farm labor in return for a share in the profits from the crop produced. The landowner provided the land, equipment, animals, and seed, as well as living accommodations for the sharecroppers and their families. The landowner deducted the costs of these things from the sharecroppers' share of the profits. Often sharecroppers were left with no money or even went into debt.

- An entrepreneur is a person who starts and manages a business. The entrepreneur takes financial risk in hopes of making a profit. Madam C. J. Walker was a successful entrepreneur who became a millionaire from her hair-care products.

Madam C. J. WALKER

Jim Haskins

Madam C. J. Walker was the first American woman to earn a million dollars. There were American women millionaires before her time, but they had inherited their wealth, either from their husbands or from their families. Madam Walker was the first woman to earn her fortune by setting up her own business and proving that women could be financially independent of men. The company she started in the early years of this century is still in operation today.

Madam C. J. Walker was born Sarah Breedlove on December 23, 1867. She grew up in the South under very racist conditions. Her parents, Owen and Minerva Breedlove, had been slaves until President Abraham Lincoln's Emancipation Proclamation and the Union victory in the Civil War had freed the slaves.

After the war, few <u>provisions</u> were made to help former slaves become independent. They did not receive money to help them get started in their new lives. They were uneducated, they had few skills except the ability to grow crops, and many were unaware of what freedom meant. Like the majority of former slaves, the Breedloves remained on the

GUIDED READING

What obstacles did many former slaves face?

THE MADAM C.J. WALKER'S
TRADE MARK REGISTERED
VEGETABLE SHAMPOO
A SPLENDID
FOOD FOR DANDRUFF AND
SORE SPOTS FOR SCALP
AND SKIN
PRICE 50 CENTS

Directions

words for everyday use

pro·vi·sion (prō vizh' ən) *n.,* arrangement made for the future. *Thelma made <u>provisions</u> for the children's well-being during her upcoming vacation.*

Burney family plantation in Delta, Louisiana. They had little choice but to stay on the same land where they had been slaves, only now they were sharecroppers.

Sharecroppers farm land for a landowner. In return, they receive a place to live and part of the crop. But since they must buy what they cannot grow from the landowner, when they harvest the crop they find themselves owing whatever is their share to the landowner anyway.

The Breedloves sharecropped cotton. Like her brothers and sisters, Sarah was working in the cotton fields by the time she was six. By the time she was seven, both her parents were dead, and she moved in with her older sister, Louvenia. A few years later, they moved across the river to Vicksburg, Mississippi.

Sarah had little schooling. Like other sharecroppers' children, she had a chance to go to school only when there were no crops to be planted or harvested, which totaled about four months out of the year. She also had little happiness in her childhood. Not only was she an orphan, but she also suffered at the hands of her sister's cruel husband. Sarah was just fourteen when she married a man named McWilliams to get away from her sister's household.

By the time Sarah got married, conditions in the South for blacks were actually worse than they had been during slavery. This was the time when Jim Crow laws were passed, segregating southern blacks from whites in nearly every area of life. It was the time when white supremacy groups like the Ku Klux Klan achieved their greatest power, and lynchings[1] of blacks were common.

GUIDED READING

Why were things worse when Sarah was married than during slavery?

Sarah and her husband lived with the terror of being black as best they could. In 1885 their daughter, Lelia, was born, and her parents dreamed of making a better life for their little girl. Then, when Lelia was two, McWilliams was killed by a lynch mob.[2]

Sarah was a widow at the age of twenty, and the sole support of a two-year-old daughter. She took in laundry to earn a living and was determined to leave the South. With Lelia, she made her way up the Mississippi River and settled in St. Louis, where she worked fourteen hours a day doing other people's laundry. She enrolled Lelia in the St. Louis public schools and was pleased that her daughter would get the education that had been denied to her. But she wanted more for her daughter and for herself.

Not long after they moved to St. Louis, Sarah McWilliams realized that her hair was falling out. She did not know why, but it is likely that the practice of braiding her hair too tightly was part of the cause. At the time, few hair-care products were available for black women. The ideal was straight, "white," hair, and to achieve this effect black women divided their hair into sections, wrapped string tightly around each section, and then twisted them. When the hair was later combed out, it was straighter. But this procedure pulled on the scalp and caused the hair to fall out.

Sarah was not the only black woman to suffer from hair loss. But she was one who refused to accept the idea that there was nothing she could do about it. For years she

---

1. **lynchings.** Acts of hanging someone by a mob, without a proper trial or other due process of law
2. **McWilliams . . . mob.** No documentation actually proves that he died this way.

words for everyday use

seg • re • gate (seg' rə gāt') v., separate; set apart. We segregated the grapes into groups based on freshness.

tried every hair-care product available. But nothing worked.

Then one night she had a dream. As she told the story many years later, in her dream "a black man appeared to me and told me what to mix up for my hair. Some of the remedy was grown in Africa, but I sent for it, mixed it, put it on my scalp, and in a few weeks my hair was coming in faster than it had ever fallen out." Sarah never publicly <u>revealed</u> the formula of her mixture.

Sarah's friends remarked on what a full and healthy head of hair she had, and she gave some of her mixture to them. It worked on them, too, so she decided to sell it. She later said that she started her "Hair Grower" business with an investment of $1.50.

She had not been in business long when she received word that a brother who lived in Denver, Colorado, had died, leaving a wife and daughters. Her own daughter, Lelia, was attending Knoxville College, a private black college in Tennessee, and did not need her around all the time. Sarah decided to go to Denver to live with her sister-in-law and nieces.

In Denver, Sarah began to sell her special haircare product and did well. But she realized she needed to advertise to get more customers. Six months after arriving in Denver, she married C. J. Walker, a newspaperman who knew a lot about selling by mail order. With his help, she began to advertise her product, first in black newspapers across the state and later in black newspapers nationwide, and to make more money.

But soon her marriage was in trouble. As Sarah Walker later said of her husband, "I had business disagreements with him,

GUIDED READING

About what did Sarah Walker disagree with her second husband?

for when we began to make ten dollars a day, he thought that amount was enough and that I should be satisfied. But I was convinced that my hair preparations would fill a longfelt want, and when we found it impossible to agree, due to his narrowness of vision, I embarked in business for myself."

In addition to helping her learn about advertising, her marriage gave Sarah Breedlove McWilliams Walker the name she would use for the rest of her life—Madam C. J. Walker. The "Madam" part was an <u>affectation</u>, but Sarah liked the way it sounded. She thought it would be good for her business. By 1906 her business was so well that she was able to stop doing laundry for a living and devote all her time to her hair-care company. Her products by this time included "Wonderful Hair Grower," "Glossine" hair oil, "Temple Grower," and "Tetter Salve" for the scalp.

Madam Walker was very proud of being a woman, and she was convinced that she could make it in the business world without the help of men. Almost from the start she determined that her business would be run by women. In 1906 she put her twenty-one-year-old daughter, Lelia, in charge of her growing mail-order business. She herself

GUIDED READING

How was Madam Walker determined to run her business?

started traveling throughout the South and East selling her preparations and teaching her methods of hair care. She was so successful that two years later she and Lelia moved to Pittsburgh, Pennsylvania, and started Lelia College, which taught the Walker System of hair care.

Once again, Lelia ran the business while her mother traveled thousands of miles to

---

words for everyday use

re • veal (ri vēl') v., show; make known. *The millionaire <u>revealed</u> all the secrets of her success.*

af • fec • ta • tion (af' ek tā' shən) n., artificial behavior meant to impress others. *Everyone knew that Robert's British accent was simply an <u>affectation</u>.*

spread the word. Madam Walker realized that the normal outlets for her products—white department stores and pharmacies—were not open to her. These stores would not stock black products because they did not want black customers. In addition to advertising, mostly in black newspapers, Madam Walker had to depend on the institutions in the black communities, the black churches, and the black women's clubs.

Madam Walker's lectures on hair culture were widely attended. She was an excellent speaker and a commanding woman, nearly six feet tall, who was always beautifully dressed and coiffed.[3] She made a lasting impression wherever she went.

Her travels, and her personality, brought her into contact with many important black people. She joined the National Association of Colored Women and through that organization met the educator Mary McLeod Bethune. She also met Ida B. Wells-Barnett, who worked for the right of women to vote, and against lynching in the South. She formed friendships with these women, who helped her spread the word about her business.

Although she lacked the formal education that most of these women had, Madam Walker never felt ashamed of her shortcomings in that area. She taught herself as much as she could and was not afraid to ask someone to define a word she did not know or explain something she did not understand.

GUIDED READING

How did Madam Walker deal with her lack of formal education? What does this behavior say about her?

There were other black hair-care companies in business at this time. A couple of companies were owned by whites. But they stressed hair straightening. Madam Walker emphasized hair care. Most of the products she developed were aimed at producing healthy hair, not straight hair. She did design a steel comb with teeth spaced far enough apart to go through thick hair, but its main purpose was not hair straightening.

Madam Walker also wanted black women to go into business. Why should they toil over hot laundry tubs and clean white people's houses when they could be in business for themselves? Helping other black women also helped the Walker Company, and with this goal in mind Madam Walker recruited and trained scores of women to use and sell Walker products. Many of them set up salons in their own homes. Others traveled door-to-door selling Walker products and demonstrating the Walker System. Madam Walker insisted that her agents sign contracts promising to abide by her strict standards of personal hygiene—long before various states passed similar laws for workers in the cosmetics field. By 1910 the Walker Company had trained around 5,000 black female agents, not just in the United States but in England, France, Italy, and the West Indies. The company itself was taking in $1,000 a day, seven days a week.

GUIDED READING

Why did Madam Walker help other black women?

That same year, Madam Walker's travels took her to Indianapolis, Indiana, a city that impressed her so much that she decided to move her headquarters there. She put a man in charge of her operations, which was a departure from her usual philosophy, but

---

3. **coiffed.** Styled; specifically hair

---

words for everyday use

short • com • ing (shôrt′ kum′ iŋ) *n.,* less than what is expected or required. *Gerta realized that her greatest shortcoming was not getting her work done on time.*

re • cruit (ri′ krōōt′) *v.,* hire or engage the services of. *Peter wants to recruit Naomi for the talent show.*

hy • giene (hī′ jēn) *n.,* cleanliness and sanitary practices. *Vanessa's personal hygiene was so important to her that she constantly washed her hands.*

Freeman B. Ransom was, in her opinion, an unusual man.

She had met him in her travels when he was working as a train porter summers and during school vacations, while working his way through Columbia University Law School. He impressed her with his <u>ambition</u> and with his vision of progress for blacks. When he finished school, she put him in charge of her Indianapolis headquarters.

In 1913 Lelia moved from Pittsburgh to New York to expand the Walker Company's East Coast operations. Madam Walker built a <u>lavish</u> town house in Harlem at 108–110 West 136th Street and installed a completely equipped beauty parlor.

Lelia had become an <u>astute</u> businesswoman herself, although she did not have the drive of her mother. Lelia, who changed her name to A'Lelia, liked to enjoy the fruits of their success. The Walker town house soon became the "in" place for parties in Harlem, attended by wealthy and artistic people, black and white.

Madam Walker also enjoyed spending the money she made. In 1917 she built a $250,000 mansion on the Hudson River in upstate New York. She hired the black architect Vertner Tandy to design it and named it Villa Lewaro. She drove around in an electric car, dressed in the finest clothing, and was said to have spent $7,000 on jewelry in a single afternoon.

Madam Walker also gave generously to charity. She had a strong interest in education and took time out of her busy schedule to be tutored by Booker T. Washington, founder of Tuskegee Institute in Alabama. She became an avid reader of literature and American history. She encouraged her friend Mary McLeod Bethune and later gave money to Mrs. Bethune to establish her Daytona Normal and Industrial Institute for Negro Girls in Daytona, Florida. When the National Association of Colored Women decided to pay off the mortgage on the home of the late black abolitionist Frederick Douglass, Madam Walker made the largest single contribution.

GUIDED READING

How did Madam Walker demonstrate her interest in education?

Madam Walker did not have much of a private life. She spent her time thinking of new ways to increase her business. The friends she had were people who could help her.

By 1917 the years of traveling and overwork began to take their toll on her. She developed high blood pressure, and in 1918 her doctors warned her that she had to slow down. She turned over her responsibilities in the business to her daughter, to Freeman B. Ransom, and to other trusted associates, and retired to her mansion, Villa Lewaro. There, she tried to relax, but her mind was always on her business. She died quietly of kidney failure resulting from hypertension in May 1919.

In her will, Madam Walker left the bulk of her estate and the business to her daughter, A'Lelia. But she also provided generously for a variety of educational institutions run by black women, including $5,000 to Dr. Bethune's school. She established a trust fund for an industrial and mission school in West Africa and provided <u>bequests</u> to Negro orphanages, old people's homes, and Negro YWCA branches. In addition, she made bequests to many friends and employees.

---

words for everyday use

am • bi • tion (am bish' ən) *n.*, drive to succeed. *Lucy was known for her driving <u>ambition</u> to succeed.*

la • vish (lav' ish) *adj.*, abundant, rich. *The ancient Romans were known for their <u>lavish</u> feasts.*

as • tute (ə stoot') *adj.*, having or showing a clever mind; crafty. *Clara has an <u>astute</u> mind and she always says clever things.*

be • quest (bē kwest') *n.*, anything handed down or passed on. *The piano was a <u>bequest</u> from my grandmother.*

Also in her will, Madam Walker insisted that the Madam C. J. Walker Company always be headed by a woman, and her wishes were carried out. Her daughter, A'Lelia, became president of the company after her death and presided at the dedication of the new company headquarters in Indianapolis in 1927, fulfilling a long-held dream of her mother's.

Times have changed greatly since Madam C. J. Walker made her millions. Drugstores and department stores owned by both whites and blacks now stock hair- and skin-care products for black women. Many more companies, white and black, manufacture such products. In the midst of all that competition, the Walker Company is not as active as it once was, although it still sells some of the products Madam developed. The Walker Building is being renovated as part of the rejuvenation of downtown Indianapolis. Now called the Madam Walker Urban Life Center, it houses professional offices and a cultural center.

> **GUIDED READING**
>
> In what way is the current use of the Walker Company headquarters appropriate to Madam Walker's life and goals?

Madam C. J. Walker, the daughter of former slaves, with little education, overcame the barriers of being black and a woman and succeeded beyond everyone's expectations but her own. ∎

Respond *to the* SELECTION

What kind of legacy has Madam Walker left? What kind of legacy would you like to leave?

About *the* AUTHOR

Jim Haskins (b.1941) graduated from New York University in 1968. He has worked as a stock market trader in New York City and as a teacher. He has written many books for adults and children. His children's books include *Black Dance in America: A History Through Its People, Black Music in America, Get on Board: The Story of the Underground Railroad,* and *Outward Dreams: Black Inventors and Their Inventions.* "Madam C. J. Walker" was taken from *One More River to Cross: The Stories of Twelve Black Americans.*

words for everyday use

ren • o • vate (ren′ ə vāt′) v., clean up; replace worn and broken parts. *Last summer, we renovated our old bathroom.*

Investigate, Inquire, and Imagine

Recall: GATHERING FACTS

1a. What was Sarah Breedlove doing by the age of six?

2a. What inspired Sarah to create her first hair-care product? What did she gain from her second husband?

3a. In what area was Madam Walker lacking?

→ **Interpret:** FINDING MEANING

1b. What effect did sharecropping have on her life?

2b. Why did Madam Walker continue to build her business?

3b. How did she minimize the effect of this shortcoming?

Analyze: TAKING THINGS APART

4a. Identify difficulties Madam Walker faced as an African American woman living in the 19th century.

→ **Synthesize:** BRINGING THINGS TOGETHER

4b. How did Walker help others who faced similar difficulties? In what ways did she make a difference so that others might not face such a struggle?

Evaluate: MAKING JUDGMENTS

5a. "Madam C. J. Walker . . . succeeded beyond everyone's expectations but her own." Explain why you think Walker was successful.

→ **Extend:** CONNECTING IDEAS

5b. What advice do you think Madam Walker would give to a young person struggling to achieve a goal today?

Understanding Literature

BIOGRAPHY. A **biography** is the story of a person's life, told by another person. Why do you think the author chose to write a biography of Madam C. J. Walker? What ideas does he convey about her?

INTRODUCTION AND CONCLUSION. An **introduction** should capture the reader's attention and present the subject of the work. A **conclusion** should sum up the ideas presented in the piece and give the reader a sense of resolution. How does the author capture the reader's attention in the introduction? What main idea is presented? How are the ideas in the conclusion related to the ideas in the introduction?

Writer's Journal

1. Make a **list** of personal goals. Choose one goal, cite possible barriers to reaching that goal, and indicate ways you might get around those barriers.
2. Write a **jingle** for one of Madam C. J. Walker's hair-care products. Use concise but catchy language.
3. Write a brief **biography** of a person you admire. It can be a famous figure or somebody you know personally. Research your subject and identify the main idea you want to convey about this person.

Skill Builders

Media Literacy
ANALYZING ADVERTISEMENTS.
Review advertisements for several beauty products. What do you learn about each product from the advertisement? What—if any—important information is missing? What methods does the advertisement use to sell the product?

Study and Research & Speaking and Listening
RESEARCHING AN INVENTOR.
Research the life and works of another inventor. Look for biographical information and for information on what the person invented. Search for pictures of those inventions. Then give a short presentation to your class. Use graphs, posters, or other visual media to show the inventions the person created, where he or she lived, and what he or she looked like.

Collaborative Learning
PLANNING A BUSINESS. If you were going to start a business, what would you want to do? Working with a small group, create a plan for a business. Determine the purpose of your business and decide on a name. Brainstorm what you would need to start the business, how you would advertise, and what challenges you might face. Write a proposal that outlines your plan.

Reader's Journal

Write about a person whose skills you admire.

Reader's Resource

- **HISTORY CONNECTION.** With one exception—"Fleet" Walker in 1884—African-American baseball players were banned from competing in the major leagues until 1947. Black players formed teams made up of entirely African-American players. These teams made up the Negro National League and the Negro American League. The Negro Leagues held an annual World Series until 1950.

- Jackie Robinson became the first African-American player in the major leagues, when he joined the Brooklyn Dodgers in 1947. His success opened the door for others. In 1948, at over 40 years of age, Satchel Paige finally got to play in the major leagues.

Prereading

"Satchel Paige" by Bill Littlefield

Reader's TOOLBOX

BACKGROUND INFORMATION. Background information is information provided in a literary work, often at the beginning, to explain the situation to the reader. A writer may include background information to explain the central conflict, the relationships between the characters, the setting, or any other part of the work. Bill Littlefield, the author of "Satchel Paige," provides background information to help the reader understand why Satchel Paige did not get a chance at major league baseball until he was past his prime. What else does the background information tell the reader about Paige?

CHRONOLOGICAL ORDER. Events arranged in order of the time when they happened are said to be in **chronological order**. This method of organization is often used in biographical pieces like "Satchel Paige." In this biography, the background information is provided as an introduction before the chronological organization begins. As you read, make a time line of events in the life of Satchel Paige. Even if you do not know the specific date for something, put the major events down in chronological order.

Graphic Organizer

1906	194?		1982
Paige is born	Paige gets the name "Satchel" carrying bags at the train station		

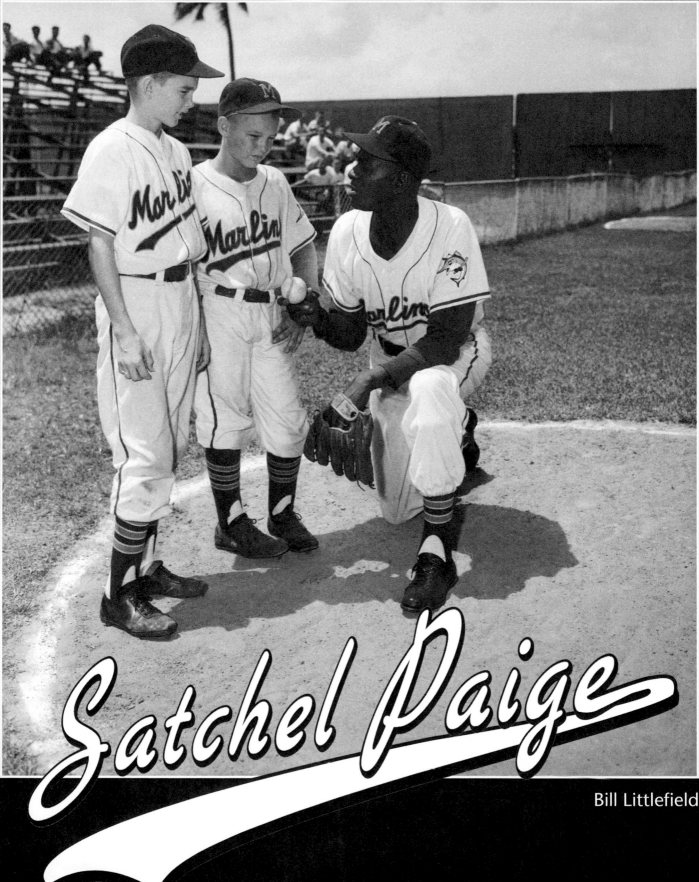

Satchel Paige

Bill Littlefield

Leroy "Satchel" Paige, perhaps the greatest pitcher ever, came out of the Negro leagues, where there'd been a Babe Ruth named Josh Gibson and a Rickey Henderson[1] named James "Cool Papa" Bell. By the time the major leagues finally allowed him to play, in 1948, Paige should have been too old, too slow, and too beat up to get anybody out. But for a few remarkable and <u>flamboyant</u> seasons with Cleveland and St. Louis, he showed folks what they'd been missing during all those years of segregated baseball. Maybe Satchel was lucky to finally have his chance, but the fans who saw him take advantage of it were luckier, and none of them ever forgot it.

Late in the afternoon of July 9, 1948, Leroy "Satchel" Paige began the long walk from the bullpen to the mound at Cleveland's Municipal Stadium. He didn't hurry. He *never* hurried. As he said himself, he "kept the juices flowing by jangling gently" as he moved. The crowd roared its appreciation. This was the fellow they'd come to see.

When Satchel finally reached the mound, Cleveland manager Lou Boudreau took the ball from starting pitcher Bob Lemon, who would eventually be voted into the Hall of Fame but had tired that day, and gave it to Paige. Probably he said something like, "Shut 'em down, Satchel." Whatever he said, Paige had no doubt heard the words a thousand times. Though he was a rookie with the Indians that year, no pitcher in the history of baseball had ever been more thoroughly prepared for a job. He kicked at the rubber, looked in for the sign, and got set to throw. In

GUIDED READING

Who was luckier than Paige? Why?

a moment, twenty-odd years later than it should have happened, Satchel Paige would deliver his first pitch in the big leagues.

GUIDED READING

When did Paige deliver his first pitch in the "big leagues"?

The tall, skinny kid named Leroy Paige became Satchel Paige one day at the railroad station in Mobile, Alabama. He was carrying bags for the folks getting on and off the trains, earning all the nickels and dimes he could to help feed his ten brothers and sisters. Eventually it occurred to him that if he slung a pole across his narrow shoulders and hung the bags, or satchels, on the ends of the pole, he could carry for more people at once and collect more nickels and dimes. It worked, but it looked a little funny. "You look like some kind of ol' satchel tree," one of his friends told him, and the nickname stuck.

Even in those days, before he was a teenager, Satchel Paige could throw hard and accurately. Years later, Paige swore that when his mother would send him out into the yard to get a chicken for dinner, he would brain the bird with a rock. "I used to kill *flying* birds with rocks, too," he said. "Most people need shotguns to do what I did with rocks."

It was not a talent that would go unnoticed for long. He was pitching for the semipro Mobile Tigers before he was eighteen . . . or maybe before he was sixteen, or before he was twelve. There is some confusion about exactly when Satchel Paige was born, and Satchel never did much to clarify the matter. But there never has been any confusion about whether he could pitch. His first steady job in

---

1. **Babe Ruth . . . Rickey Henderson.** The author is comparing Negro League players to famous major league players to show the skill of the lesser-known Negro League players.

flam • boy • ant (flam boi′ ənt) *adj.,* showy, extravagant. *People stared at Nia's <u>flamboyant</u> outfit.*

baseball was with the Chattanooga Black Lookouts. He was paid fifty dollars a month. In the seasons that followed he would also pitch for the Birmingham Black Barons, the Nashville Elite Giants, the Baltimore Black Sox, the Pittsburgh Crawfords, and the Kansas City Monarchs, among other teams.

GUIDED READING

About what was there some confusion? About what was there no confusion?

If those names are not as familiar sounding as those of the New York Yankees, the Los Angeles Dodgers, or the Boston Red Sox, it's because they were all clubs in the Negro leagues, not the major leagues. Today the presence of black baseball players in the big leagues is taken for granted. Hank Aaron is the greatest of the home run hitters, and Rickey Henderson has stolen more bases than any other big leaguer. But before 1947, neither of them would have had the opportunity to do what they have done. Until Brooklyn Dodger general manager Branch Rickey signed Jackie Robinson, black players had no choice but to play for one of the all-black teams, and making that choice, they faced hardships no major-leaguer today could imagine.

Players in the Negro leagues crowded into broken-down cars and bumped over <u>rutted</u> roads to makeshift ball fields with lights so bad that every pitch was a potential weapon. Then they drove all night for an afternoon game three hundred miles away. On good days they played before big, appreciative crowds in parks they'd rented from the major league teams in Chicago, New York, or Pittsburgh. On bad days they learned that the team they were playing for was too broke to finish the season, and they would have to look

Satchel Paige with the Kansas City Monarchs, 1942.

for a healthier team that could use them, or else find a factory job.

It took talent, hard work, and a sense of humor to survive in the Negro leagues, and Satchel Paige had a lot of all three. But he didn't just survive. He <u>prospered</u>. Everybody knows about the fastball, the curve, and the slider. But Satchel threw a "bee" ball, which, he said, "would always *be* where I wanted it to *be*." He featured a trouble ball, which, of course, gave the hitters a lot of trouble. Even the few who could see it couldn't hit it. Sometimes he'd come at them with his hesitation pitch, a delivery so mysterious that the man at the plate would sometimes swing before the ball left Satchel's hand.

words for everyday use

rut • ted (rut′ əd) *adj.*, bumpy and marked by tracks made by wheels. *The car jolted over the <u>rutted</u> dirt road.*

pros • per (präs′ pər) *v.*, succeed, thrive. *The plant <u>prospered</u> in the sunny spot.*

Nor was pitching his sole triumph. Early in his career Satchel Paige began building a reputation as a storyteller, a spinner of tall tales as well as shutouts. He particularly liked to recall an occasion upon which he was asked to come on in relief of a pitcher who'd left men on first and third with nobody out. "It was a tight situation," Satchel would say.

GUIDED READING

In addition to pitching, what skill was Paige known for?

We only had a one-run lead, and that was looking mighty slim. But I had an idea. When I left the bench, I stuck a baseball in my pocket, so when the manager gave me the game ball on the mound, I had two. I went into my stretch just like usual. Then I threw one ball to first and the other to third. It was a good pickoff move, you see, and it fooled the batter, too. He swung, even though there was no ball to swing at. Those boys at first and third were both out, of course, and the umpire called strike three on the batter, so that was it for the inning. It's always good to save your strength when you can.

Major-leaguers today make enough money so that they don't have to work over the winter, but it hasn't always been so. Big-leaguers and Negro-leaguers alike used to make extra money after their regular seasons ended by putting together makeshift teams and playing each other wherever they could draw a paying crowd. This practice was called barnstorming, and Satchel Paige was the world champion at it. For thirty years, from 1929 to 1958, he played baseball summer and winter. When it was too cold to

GUIDED READING

What was barn-storming?

play in the Negro league cities, he played in Cuba, Mexico, and the Dominican Republic. In Venezuela he battled a boa constrictor in the outfield, or so he said, and in Ciudad Trujillo he dodged the machine-gun fire of fans who'd bet on the losing team.

Throughout the early years of these adventures, the years of Satchel's prime, he often barnstormed against the best white ballplayers of his day. St. Louis Cardinal great Dizzy Dean once told him, "You're a better pitcher than I ever hope to be." Paige beat Bob Feller and struck out Babe Ruth. And when Joe DiMaggio, considered by some the most multitalented ballplayer ever, beat out an infield hit against Paige in 1936, DiMaggio turned to his teammates and said, "Now I know I can make it with the Yankees. I finally got a hit off of ol' Satch."

Everywhere these <u>confrontations</u> took place, Satchel Paige would hear the same thing: "If only you were white, you'd be a star in the big leagues." The fault, of course, was not with Satchel. The fault and the shame were with major league baseball, which stubbornly, stupidly clung to the same prejudice that characterized many institutions in the United States besides baseball. Prejudice has not yet disappeared from the game. Black players are far less likely than their white counterparts to be hired as managers or general managers. But today's black players can thank Robinson, Paige, and a handful of other pioneers for the opportunities they enjoy.

GUIDED READING

What prejudice do black players still face?

Though the color line prevented Satchel Paige from pitching in the company his talent and hard work should have earned for him, he was not bitter or defeated. Ignorant white

words for everyday use

con • fron • ta • tion (kän frun tā' shən) *n.,* heated opposition. *The <u>confrontation</u> might have led to a fight if Ms. Marquez hadn't stepped in.*

fans would sometimes <u>taunt</u> him, but he kept their insults in perspective. "Some of them would call you [names]," he said of his early years on the road, "but most of them would cheer you." Years later he worked to shrug off the pain caused by the restaurants that would not serve him, the hotels that would not rent him a room, the fans who would roar for his bee ball but would not acknowledge him on the street the next day. "Fans all holler the same at a ball game," he would say, as if the racists and the racist system had never touched him at all.

GUIDED READING

What did Paige shrug off?

When he finally got the chance to become the first black pitcher in the American League at age forty-two (or forty-six, or forty-eight), he made the most of it. On that first day in Cleveland, Satchel Paige did the job he'd never doubted he could do. First he smiled for all the photographers. Then he told the butterflies in his stomach to leave off their flapping around. Then he shut down the St. Louis Browns for two innings before being lifted for a pinch hitter.

And still there were doubters. "Sure," they said to each other the next day when they read the sports section. "The old man could work two innings against the Browns. Who couldn't?"

But Satchel Paige fooled 'em, as he'd been fooling hitters for twenty-five years and more. He won a game in relief six days later, his first major league win. Then on August 3 he started a game against the Washington Senators before 72,000 people. Paige went seven innings and won. In his next two starts he threw shutouts against the Chicago White

Satchel Paige pitching for the Kansas City Athletics, 1965.

Sox, and through the <u>waning</u> months of that summer, his only complaint was that he was "a little tired from underwork." The routine on the major league level must have been pretty leisurely for a fellow who'd previously pitched four or five times a week.

Satchel Paige finished the 1948 season with six wins and only one loss. He'd allowed the opposing teams an average of just over two runs a game. Paige was named Rookie of the Year, an honor he might well have achieved twenty years earlier if he'd had the chance. The sportswriters of the day agreed that without Satchel's contribution, the

GUIDED READING

What honor did Paige win twenty years after he might have?

words for everyday use

taunt (tônt) v., jeer, mock. *Jose ignored the <u>taunts</u> and the names Irwin called him.*

wan • ing (wān' iŋ) adj., approaching the end. *During the <u>waning</u> hours of the day, the setting sun turns the sky a rosy color.*

Indians, who won the pennant, would have finished second at best. Many of the writers were <u>dismayed</u> when Satchel appeared for only two-thirds of an inning in the World Series that fall. Paige, too, was disappointed that the manager hadn't chosen to use him more, but he was calm in the face of what others might have considered an insult. The writers told him, "You sure take things good." Satchel smiled and said, "Ain't no other way to take them."

Satchel Paige outlasted the rule that said he couldn't play in the big leagues because he was black. Then he made fools of the people who said he couldn't get major league hitters out because he was too old. But his big league numbers over several years—twenty-eight wins and thirty-two saves—don't begin to tell the story of Paige's unparalleled career. Playing for teams that no longer exist in leagues that came and went with the seasons, Satchel Paige pitched in some 2,500 baseball games. Nobody has ever pitched in more. And he had such fun at it. Sometimes he'd accept offers to pitch in two cities on the same day. He'd strike out the side for three innings in one game, then fold his long legs into his car and race down the road toward the next ballpark. If the police could catch him, they would stop him for speeding. But when they recognized him, as often as not they'd escort him to the second game with sirens howling, well aware that there might be a riot in the park if Satchel Paige didn't show up as advertised. Once he'd arrived, he'd instruct his infielders and outfielders to sit down for an inning, then he'd strike out the side again.

GUIDED READING
What would Paige tell the infielders and outfielders?

For his talent, his energy, and his showmanship, Satchel Paige was the most famous of the Negro league players, but when he got some measure of recognition in the majors, he urged the writers to remember that there had been lots of other great ballplayers in those Negro league games. He named them, and he told their stories. He made their <u>exploits</u> alive and real for generations of fans who'd never have known.

GUIDED READING
What did Paige urge people to remember?

In 1971, the Baseball Hall of Fame in Cooperstown, New York, inducted Satchel Paige. The action was part of the Hall's attempt to remedy baseball's shame, the color line. The idea was to honor Paige and some of the other great Negro league players like Josh Gibson and Cool Papa Bell, however late that honor might come. Satchel Paige could have rejected that gesture. He could have told the baseball establishment that what it was doing was too little, too late. But when the time came for Satchel Paige to speak to the crowd gathered in front of the Hall of Fame to celebrate his triumphs, he told the people, "I am the proudest man on the face of the earth today."

GUIDED READING
What could Paige have done upon being inducted into the Hall of Fame? What did he do instead?

Satchel Paige, whose autobiography was entitled *Maybe I'll Pitch Forever*, died in Kansas City in 1982. He left behind a legend as large as that of anyone who ever played the game, as well as a long list of achievements celebrated in story and song—and in at least one fine poem, by Samuel Allen:

words for everyday use

dis • may (dis mā') v., afraid because of a fear of danger or trouble. *We were <u>dismayed</u> to see the team performing poorly at practice before the big game.*

ex • ploit (eks' ploit) n., bold deed. *The crook's <u>exploits</u> made the front page of the newspaper.*

To Satch   Samuel Allen

Sometimes I feel like I will *never* stop
Just go on forever
'Till one fine mornin'
I'm gonna reach up and grab me a handfulla stars
Swing out my long lean leg
And whip three hot strikes burnin' down the heavens
And look over at God and say
How about that!

Respond *to the* SELECTION

What do you think of Satchel Paige as a player? as a person?

About *the* AUTHORS

Bill Littlefield has written numerous articles, reviews, and essays for a publications such as the *Boston Globe* and *Los Angeles Times*. He was the guest editor for the 1998 edition of Houghton Mifflin's *Best American Sports Writing.* His books include *Baseball Days, Prospect,* and *Champions: The Stories of Ten Remarkable Athletes.* He is currently a professor in the at Curry College in Milton, Massachusetts, where he has taught writing and literature courses since 1976. He is also the host of "Only a Game," a radio show aired on WBUR and National Public Radio in Boston.

Samuel Allen is a poet known for merging African and African-American culture in his poetry. He attributes the heritage of black people, African-American oral tradition, and the Southern black church as the major influences in his poetry. Allen is also a prominent figure both in Africa and in the United States as a reviewer, translator, editor, and lecturer of African and African-American literature. He has taught literature and writing at Tuskegee Institute in Alabama, Wesleyan University, Boston College, and Rutgers University. He also lectures about black affairs at national and international conferences.

Investigate, Inquire, and Imagine

Recall: GATHERING FACTS

1a. When did Satchel Paige throw his first pitch in the big leagues? In what league had he played before?

2a. What "idea" does Paige describe in his story about a tight situation?

3a. What do the numbers tell you about Paige? What don't they tell you?

→ **Interpret:** FINDING MEANING

1b. Why didn't Satchel Paige get the recognition he deserved as a young ball player?

2b. What do you learn about Paige from this story?

3b. What do Paige's antics suggest about his character?

Analyze: TAKING THINGS APART

4a. What difficulties did African-American players face during the years of segregation?

→ **Synthesize:** BRINGING THINGS TOGETHER

4b. How did Paige react in the face of these difficulties?

Evaluate: MAKING JUDGMENTS

5a. What do you think are the main characteristics of Paige's personality?

→ **Extend:** CONNECTING IDEAS

5b. Explain what qualities of Paige's personality are reflected in the poem "To Satch."

Understanding *Literature*

BACKGROUND INFORMATION. Background information is information provided in a literary work, often at the beginning, to explain the situation to the reader. Reread the background information at the beginning of this selection. What is the main point of this information? How does the author reinforce this point throughout the selection?

CHRONOLOGICAL ORDER. Events arranged in order of the time when they happened are said to be in **chronological order**. Look at the time line your created of the events in Satchel Paige's life. In a separate color, mark where Satchel Paige should have started his major league career and when he could have won Rookie of the Year.

Writer's Journal

1. Write a **headline** about one of Paige's exploits. It might be about a game he won, how he got his team out of a tricky situation, how he pitched two games at the same time, or some other story.
2. The stories Paige told often contained elements that seemed overstated or larger than life. This is often true of tall tales. Write a **tall tale** about an exploit of your own.
3. Write a **poem** about a person who has influenced you in some way.

Skill Builders

Language, Grammar, and Style

AVOIDING DOUBLE NEGATIVES. A negative is a "no" word. The use of two negatives in a sentence is called a double negative. Check your writing to be sure that you have not used two negative words such as *no, not, nobody, none, nothing, hardly, barely, can't, doesn't, won't, isn't,* or *aren't* together. Change double negatives by deleting one negative or by replacing it with a positive word. Rewrite the following sentences, correcting any errors in the use of negatives.

1. No African-American players weren't allowed to play in the major leagues until the mid-1940s.
2. Before Jackie Robinson, there weren't no African-American players in the major leagues.
3. Satchel Paige did not play for no major league team until he was over 40.
4. People thought that he was too old, but nobody couldn't say he wasn't a great player.
5. Paige didn't let nobody talk him out of playing.

Speaking and Listening

STORYTELLING. Satchel Paige was known as an excellent storyteller. Storytelling involves having an interesting tale to tell and sharing in a way that engages the audience. Choose a brief story. Practice telling the story. Think about using gestures and facial expressions, raising and lowering your voice, and speeding up and slowing down your speech to help convey the story. Then, tell the story to your class.

Study and Research

USING ALMANACS AND YEARBOOKS. Use an almanac or yearbook to answer the following questions:

1. Who won the 1989 World Series?
2. What team has won more World Series than any other?
3. What teams played in the 1991 World Series?
4. What Negro League pitcher entered the hall of fame in 1999?
5. Who won the Cy Young Awards in 1999? What was each pitcher's ERA?

Reader's *Journal*

If you were writing the story of your life, what would you want people to understand about you?

Reader's *Resource*

- Geronimo was an Apache. The name *Apache* comes from a Zuni word meaning "enemy." The Apaches call themselves N'de or Dineh, which means "the people." Originally, the Dineh were part of a larger group of native people called the Athapascans.

- The Dineh were nomadic, meaning they traveled from place to place as they hunted. Dineh men were great warriors and hunters. Dineh women were skilled artisans who wove beautiful, complex baskets.

- The Dineh shared their land peacefully with white settlers at first. As the U.S. and Mexican armies took more and more of their land, the Dineh began raiding settlers. In the 1870s, the United States government moved Dineh tribes from their homelands to reservations. Geronimo led a group who escaped the reservation many times. Geronimo and his followers surrendered to U.S. General Nelson Miles on September 4, 1886.

Prereading

FROM GERONIMO'S STORY OF HIS LIFE
by Geronimo

Reader's TOOLBOX

AUTOBIOGRAPHY. An **autobiography** is the story of a person's life, written by that person. As you read, pay attention to the details Geronimo tells you about his life. Think about why he may have written his autobiography.

POINT OF VIEW. Point of view is the vantage point from which a story is told. In a story told from the *first-person point of view*, the narrator takes part in the action and refers to himself or herself using words such as *I* and *we*. Autobiographies are usually told from the first-person point of view, since the narrator is writing about himself or herself. Would this selection have the same effect if it were written by somebody else?

Graphic *Organizer*

In this selection, Geronimo tells us about himself, but also about the Apache way of life. Using a cluster chart like this one, keep track of the information you learn about Apache customs.

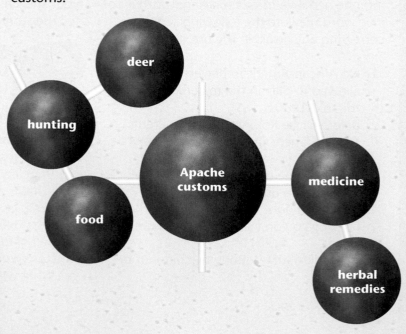

FROM
GERONIMO'S
STORY OF HIS LIFE

Geronimo

Council between Geronimo and General Crook, 1886.

"I WAS BORN IN NO-DOYOHN CAÑON, ARIZONA, JUNE, 1829."

I was born in No-doyohn Cañon, Arizona, June, 1829.

In that country which lies around the headwaters of the Gila River I was reared. This range was our fatherland. Among these mountains our wigwams[1] were hidden. The scattered valleys contained our fields. The boundless prairies, stretching away on every side, were our pastures. The rocky caverns were our burying places.

GUIDED READING

Why was the country around the Gila River important to Geronimo?

I was fourth in a family of eight children—four boys and four girls. Of that family, only myself; my brother, Porico (White Horse); and my sister, Nah-da-ste, are yet alive. We are held as prisoners of war in this Military Reservation (Fort Sill).

As a babe, I rolled on the dirt floor of my father's tepee, hung in my *tsoch* (Apache name for *cradle)* at my mother's back, or suspended from the bough of a tree. I was warmed by the sun, rocked by the winds, and sheltered by the trees as other Indian babes.

When I was a child, my mother taught me the legends of our people; taught me of the sun and sky, the moon and stars, the clouds and storms. She also taught me to kneel and pray to Usen the spirit father, for strength, health, wisdom, and protection. We never prayed against any person; but if we had aught[2] against any individual, we ourselves took vengeance. We were taught that Usen does not care for the petty quarrels of men.

GUIDED READING

What did Geronimo's mother teach him about Usen?

My father had often told me of the brave deeds of our warriors, of the pleasures of the chase, and the glories of the warpath.

With my brothers and sisters, I played about my father's home. Sometimes we played hide-and-seek among the rocks and pines; sometimes we loitered in the shade of the cottonwood trees or sought the *shudock* (a kind of wild cherry) while our parents worked in the field. Sometimes we played that we were warriors. We would practice stealing upon some object that represented an enemy, and in our childish imitation often performed the feats of war. Sometimes we would hide away from our mother to see if she could find us, and often when thus concealed go to sleep and perhaps remain hidden for many hours.

GUIDED READING

What games did the Apache children play?

When we were old enough to be of real service, we went to the field with our parents, not to play, but to toil. When the crops were to be planted, we broke the ground with wooden hoes. We planted the corn in straight rows, the beans among the corn, and the melons and pumpkins in irregular order over the field. We cultivated these crops as there was need.

GUIDED READING

What did the children in Geronimo's family do when they were older?

Our field usually contained about two acres of ground. The fields were never fenced. It was common for many families to cultivate land in the same valley and share the burden of protecting the growing crops from destruction by the ponies of the tribe, or by deer and other wild animals.

GUIDED READING

What did the Apache families share with one another?

---

1. **wigwams.** Traditional dwellings of Native American people of North America, consisting of a dome-shaped framework of poles covered with mats or sheets of bark
2. **aught.** Anything whatsoever

---

words for everyday use

sus • pend (sə spend′) v., hang by or support from above. *The acrobat was suspended by the trapeze far above the heads of her audience.*

loi • ter (loit′ ər) v., spend time idly. *The convenience store put up a sign that warned people not to loiter in front of the store.*

toil (toil′) v., work hard. *The farmer toiled in his fields.*

Melons were gathered as they were <u>consumed</u>. In the autumn, pumpkins and beans were gathered and placed in bags or baskets; ears of corn were tied together by the husks, and then the harvest was carried on the backs of ponies up to our homes. Here the corn was shelled, and all the harvest stored away in caves or other <u>secluded</u> places to be used in winter.

We never fed corn to our ponies; but if we kept them up in the winter time, we gave them fodder[3] to eat. We had no cattle or other domestic animals except our dogs and ponies. . . .

Besides grinding the corn (by hand with stone mortars and pestles) for bread, we sometimes crushed it and soaked it; and . . . made from this juice a *tiswin*, which . . . was very highly prized by the Indians. This work was done by the squaws and children. When berries or nuts were to be gathered, the small children and the squaws would go in parties to hunt them, and sometimes stay all day. When they went any great distance from camp, they took ponies to carry the baskets.

I frequently went with these parties, and upon one of these excursions a woman named Cho-ko-le got lost from the party and was riding her pony through a thicket in search of her friends. Her little dog was following as she slowly made her way through the thick underbrush and pine trees. All at once a grizzly bear rose in her path and attacked the pony. She jumped off and her pony escaped, but the bear attacked her; so she fought him the best she could with her knife. Her little dog, by snapping at the bear's heels and distracting his attention from the woman, enabled her for some time to keep pretty well out of his reach. Finally the grizzly struck her over the head, tearing off almost her whole scalp. She fell, but did not lose consciousness, and while <u>prostrate</u> struck him four good licks with her knife; and he retreated. After he had gone, she replaced her torn scalp and bound it up as best she could. Then she turned deathly sick and had to lie down. That night her pony came into camp with his load of nuts and berries, but no rider. The Indians hunted for her, but did not find her until the second day. They carried her home, and under the treatment of their medicine man all her wounds were healed.

GUIDED READING

How did Cho-ko-le demonstrate bravery?

The Indians knew what herbs to use for medicine, how to prepare them, and how to give the medicine. This they had been taught by Usen in the beginning, and each succeeding generation had people who were skilled in the art of healing.

In gathering the herbs, in preparing them, and in <u>administering</u> the medicine, as much faith was held in prayer as in the actual effect of the medicine. Usually about eight persons worked together in making medicine, and there were forms of prayer and incantations[4] to attend each stage of the process. Four attended to the incantations, and four to the preparation of the herbs.

GUIDED READING

How did the people work together to make the medicine?

Some of the Indians were skilled in cutting out bullets, arrowheads, and other missiles with which warriors were wounded. I myself have done much of this, using a common dirk or butcher knife.

---

3. **fodder.** Coarse food for cattle, horses, and sheep, such as hay, straw, and cornstalks
4. **incantations.** Verbal charms

words for everyday use

con • sume (kən soom′) v., eat or drink up. *The class <u>consumed</u> all of the party food.*

se • cluded (si klood′ ed) adj., shut off or kept away from others. *Their cottage was in a <u>secluded</u> area of the woods, far away from any neighbors.*

pro • strate (prä′ strāt) adj., lying face down. *After missing the hurdle, I landed <u>prostrate</u> on the track.*

ad • min • is • ter (əd mi′ nə stər) v., dispense or give. *The nurse can <u>administer</u> aspirin to students.*

Small children wore very little clothing in winter and none in summer. Women usually wore a primitive skirt, which consisted of a piece of cotton cloth fastened about the waist, and extending to the knees. Men wore breech cloths and moccasins. In winter they had shirts and leggings in addition.

Frequently when the tribe was in camp, a number of boys and girls, by agreement, would steal away and meet at a place several miles distant, where they could play all day free from tasks. They were never punished for these frolics; but if their hiding places were discovered, they were ridiculed. To celebrate each noted event, a feast and dance would be given. Perhaps only our own people, perhaps neighboring tribes, would be invited. These festivities usually lasted for about four days. By day we feasted; by night, under the direction of some chief, we danced. The music for our dance was singing led by the warriors, and accompanied by beating the *esadadedne* (buck-skin-on-a-hoop). No words were sung—only the tones. When the feasting and dancing were over, we would have horse races, foot races, wrestling, jumping, and all sorts of games.

GUIDED READING

What games were played as part of Apache festivities?

Among these games, the most noted was the tribal game of *Kah* (foot). It is played as follows: Four moccasins are placed about four feet apart in holes in the ground dug in a row on one side of the camp, and on the opposite side a similar parallel row. At night a camp fire is started between these two rows of moccasins; and the players are arranged on sides, one or any number on each side. The score is kept by a bundle of sticks, from which each side takes a stick for every point won.

First one side takes the bone, puts up blankets between the four moccasins and the fire so that the opposing team cannot observe their movements, and then begins to sing the legends of creation. The side having the bone represents the feathered tribe; the opposite side represents the beasts. The players representing the birds do all the singing, and while singing, hide the bone in one of the moccasins. Then the blankets are thrown down. They continue to sing; but as soon as the blankets are thrown down, the chosen player from the opposing team, armed with a war club, comes to their side of the camp fire and with his club strikes the moccasin in which he thinks the bone is hidden. If he strikes the right moccasin, his side gets the bone, and in turn represents the birds, while the opposing team must keep quiet and guess in turn. There are only four plays: three that lose and one that wins. When all the sticks are gone from the bundle, the side having the largest number of sticks is counted winner.

This game is seldom played except as a gambling game, but for that purpose it is the most popular game known to the tribe. Usually the game lasts four or five hours. It is never played in daytime.

After the games are all finished, the visitors say, "We are satisfied," and the camp is broken up. I was always glad when the dances and feasts were announced. So were all the other young people.

Our life also had a religious side. We had no churches, no religious organizations, no Sabbath day, no holidays, and yet we worshiped. Sometimes the whole tribe would <u>assemble</u> to sing and

GUIDED READING

What does Geronimo say about the religious side of his life? Were services always the same?

words for everyday use

as • sem • ble (ə sem′ bəl) v., gather in a group. *The students <u>assembled</u> in the gymnasium for a pep rally.*

pray; sometimes a smaller number, perhaps only two or three. The songs had a few words, but were not formal. The singer would occasionally put in such words as he wished instead of the usual tone sound. Sometimes we prayed in silence; sometimes each one prayed aloud; sometimes an aged person prayed for all of us. At other times, one would rise and speak to us of our duties to each other and to Usen. Our services were short.

When disease or pestilence <u>abounded</u>, we were assembled and questioned by our leaders to <u>ascertain</u> what evil we had done, and how Usen could be satisfied. Sometimes sacrifice was deemed necessary. Sometimes the offending one was punished.

If an Apache had allowed his aging parents to suffer for food or shelter, if he had neglected or abused the sick, if he had <u>profaned</u> our religion, or had been unfaithful, he might be <u>banished</u> from the tribe.

> **GUIDED READING**
> What crimes were considered punishable?

The Apaches had no prisons as white men have. Instead of sending the criminals into prison, they sent them out of their tribe. These faithless, cruel, lazy, or cowardly members of the tribe were excluded in such a manner that they could not join any other tribe. Neither could they have any protection from our unwritten tribal laws. Frequently these outlaw Indians banded together and committed depredations[5] which were charged against the regular tribe. However, the life of an outlaw Indian was a hard lot, and their bands never became very large. Besides, these bands frequently provoked the

> **GUIDED READING**
> How did the Apache punish criminals?

wrath of the tribe and secured their own destruction.

When I was about eight or ten years old, I began to follow the chase; and to me this was never work.

Out on the prairies, which ran up to our mountain homes, wandered herds of deer, antelope, elk, and buffalo, to be slaughtered when we needed them.

Usually we hunted buffalo on horseback, killing them with arrows and spears. Their skins were used to make tepees and bedding; their flesh, to eat.

It required more skill to hunt the deer than any other animal. We never tried to approach a deer except against the wind. Frequently we would spend hours in stealing upon grazing deer. If they were in the open, we would crawl long distances on the ground, keeping a weed or brush before us, so that our approach would not be noticed. Often we could kill several out of one herd before the others would run away. Their flesh was dried and packed in vessels, and would keep in this condition for many months. The hide of the deer was soaked in water and ashes and the hair removed, and then the process of tanning continued until the buckskin was soft and pliable. Perhaps no other animal was more valuable to us than the deer.

In the forests and along the streams were many wild turkeys. These we would drive to the plains, then slowly ride up toward them until they were almost tired out. When they began to drop and hide, we would ride in upon them and by swinging from the sides of our horses, catch them. If one started to fly, we would ride swiftly under him and kill him

---

5. **depredations.** Acts of robbing or plundering

words for everyday use

a • bound (ə bound′) v., be plentiful. *The lake once <u>abounded</u> with fish, but now they are scarce.*
as • cer • tain (as′ ər tān′) v., find out with certainty. *Hank was unable to <u>ascertain</u> whether or not the famous basketball star had really been spotted in a local restaurant.*
pro • fane (prō fān′) v., show disrespect for sacred things. *One of the most terrible crimes to the Dineh was to <u>profane</u> their religion.*
ban • ish (ba′ nish) v., drive out or remove from a place. *We were <u>banished</u> from the kitchen while our parents wrapped Christmas gifts.*

with a short stick, or hunting club. In this way we could usually get as many wild turkeys as we could carry home on a horse.

There were many rabbits in our range, and we also hunted them on horseback. Our horses were trained to follow the rabbit at full speed, and as they approached them, we would swing from one side of the horse and strike the rabbit with our hunting club. If he was too far away, we would throw the stick and kill him. This was great sport when we were boys, but as warriors we seldom hunted small game.

There were many fish in the streams, but as we did not eat them, we did not try to catch or kill them. Small boys sometimes threw stones at them or shot at them for practice with their bows and arrows. Usen did not intend snakes, frogs, or fishes to be eaten. I have never eaten of them.

There are many eagles in the mountains. These we hunted for their feathers. It

> **GUIDED READING**
>
> Why did the Apache not fish?

required great skill to steal upon an eagle; for beside having sharp eyes, he is wise and never stops at any place where he does not have a good view of the surrounding country.

I have killed many bears with a spear, but was never injured in a fight with one. I have killed several mountain lions with arrows, and one with a spear. Both bears and mountain lions are good for food and valuable for their skin. When we killed them, we carried them home on our horses. We often made quivers for our arrows from the skin of the mountain lion. These were very pretty and very durable.

During my minority,[6] we had never seen a missionary or a priest. We had never seen a white man. Thus quietly lived the Be-don-ko-he Apaches. ∎

> **GUIDED READING**
>
> What had Geronimo never seen during his youth?

---

6. **minority.** Childhood years

Respond *to the* SELECTION

How would you feel about living with Geronimo's people?

About *the* AUTHOR

Geronimo (1829–1909), whose Dineh name was Goyathlay, or "one who yawns," became one of the greatest Native American leaders. He led a group of over 400 Chiricahua soldiers in a revolt against the U.S. Army that lasted ten years. Geronimo and his men surrendered in 1886. Geronimo was told he would be allowed to return to his native lands after a brief term of imprisonment in Florida and Alabama. This promise, however, turned out to be one of the many false promises the United States government made to native peoples. Geronimo never regained the freedom he so highly prized. In 1894, he was sent to Fort Sill, Oklahoma, to live out the rest of his life as a captive. It was at Fort Sill, in 1906, that Geronimo dictated his autobiography to Stephen M. Barrett.

Investigate, *Inquire,* and Imagine

Recall: GATHERING FACTS

1a. Where did Geronimo grow up? What games did he play with his brothers and sisters?

2a. What happened to Cho-ko-le? According to Geronimo, who taught the people the ways to use herbs and make medicine?

3a. What word does Geronimo use to describe the life of the Be-don-ko-he Apaches during his childhood? What does he say his people had not seen at that time?

→ **Interpret:** FINDING MEANING

1b. Why were the games Geronimo played important?

2b. Why was "as much faith . . . held in prayer as in the actual effect of the medicine"?

3b. What does Geronimo imply, or hint, about the coming of the white people and the missionaries?

Analyze: TAKING THINGS APART

4a. List some things that might cause somebody to be banished from the tribe.

→ **Synthesize:** BRINGING THINGS TOGETHER

4b. Why was banishment an effective form of punishment? What effect did it have on the tribe?

Evaluate: MAKING JUDGMENTS

5a. Judge the form of punishment used by Geronimo's people. Do you think it is fair to punish people this way?

→ **Extend:** CONNECTING IDEAS

5b. What do you think of forms of punishment used in our society? Explain whether you think fines, prison, or the death penalty are good ways to punish people for crimes. You may wish to think about the effectiveness and the morality of these means.

Understanding *Literature*

AUTOBIOGRAPHY AND POINT OF VIEW. Geronimo uses the first-person point of view to tell his story. How would your thoughts about and reaction to the story change if it were written from the point of view of another person—a missionary, for example? How do you think the story might differ?

Writer's Journal

1. Write a **descriptive paragraph** about an activity that you enjoyed when you were younger. Write about how you played, who you played with, and why you enjoyed this activity.

2. Imagine Geronimo were still alive. How do you think he would react to life today? Write a **journal entry** that Geronimo might write in the year 2005.

3. Geronimo gives detailed descriptions of the lands on which his people live. Write a **descriptive paragraph** about the place where you live.

Skill Builders

Critical Thinking

TECHNICAL WRITING. Geronimo describes different procedures that he and his people follow to perform certain tasks or to play games. Write a set of **rules** or **instructions** for a game that you enjoy. Begin by identifying any items you need to play the game. Then explain the purpose of the game, and present the rules in a logical order.

Collaborative Learning

WORKING AS A RESEARCH TEAM. Working in a small group, research an aspect of Native American culture and society. You might focus on art, economics, history, the calendar, language, literature, clothing, medicine, religion, social issues, or warfare. Learn about this aspect as it applies to the Apache, or Dineh, and to two other groups. Compare and contrast the groups' beliefs about the subject you chose.

Language, Grammar, and Style

PREPOSITIONS, CONJUNCTIONS, AND INTERJECTIONS. Identify the underlined word in each sentence as a preposition, conjunction, or interjection.

1. <u>Among</u> these mountains our wigwams were hidden.
2. His only living family members are his brother Porico and his sister Nah-da-ste, <u>yet</u> he still thinks about his family often.
3. "<u>Well</u>," exclaimed White Horse, "I did not expect you to arrive back here so soon."
4. *Kah* is a game we played when we were <u>among</u> friends.
5. <u>After</u> the games are finished, the camp is broken up.

Prereading

from *Gorillas in the Mist*

by Dian Fossey

Reader's Resource

- Documentary writing is writing based on field notes. *Field notes* are a person's observations, reactions to, and analysis of the subject matter they are studying. *Fieldwork* is work done in the native environment of the subject—for example, studying rain forest insects in the Amazon, studying ice in Antarctica, or studying ancient Asian herbal remedies in Cambodia. *Ethology*, the study of animal behavior, is the scientific work that Fossey undertook. Ethology combines work in laboratories and in the field.

- The Virunga Mountains (also known as the Mufumbiro Mountains) rise in east-central Africa, extending across the borders of Uganda, Congo, and Rwanda. In Uganda, several national park reserves protect the mountain wildlife. Two of these, Mgahinga National Park and Bwindi National Park are home to mountain gorillas. Mountain gorillas also live in Virunga National Park in Zaire and in Volcanoes National Park in Rwanda. These parks are home to nearly all the surviving mountain gorillas in the world. The Karisoke Research Centre, near Volcanoes National Park, is where Dian Fossey studied gorillas. Research groups still work there. The parks have long attracted people from around the world who come to see these gorillas, but in recent years, acts of violence have curbed tourism.

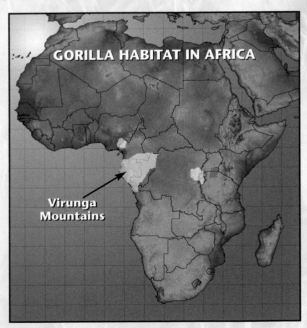

GORILLA HABITAT IN AFRICA

Virunga Mountains

Reader's Journal

What animal would you like to study, and why?

Reader's TOOLBOX

ANECDOTE. An **anecdote** is a usually short narrative of an interesting, amusing, or biographical incident. An anecdote is commonly told to make a point or to emphasize a specific event. What is the aim, or purpose, of this anecdote from *Gorillas in the Mist*?

CONCRETE DETAILS. Concrete details are specific words that name objects or actions or provide descriptions of those objects or actions. These specific details help to provide the reader with clear, concise, and in-depth information. Using concrete details in place of more general words helps the reader really understand the situation or event being discussed. As you read, look for concrete details that make the situation seem more real or personal. What words does Fossey use to provide specific (rather than general) information?

from Gorillas in the Mist

Dian Fossey

Often I am asked about the most rewarding experience I have ever had with gorillas. The question is extremely difficult to answer because each hour with the gorillas provides its own return and satisfaction. The first occasion when I felt I might have crossed an <u>intangible</u> barrier between human and ape occurred about ten months after beginning the research at Karisoke. Peanuts, Group 8's youngest male, was feeding about fifteen feet away when he suddenly stopped and turned to stare directly at me. The expression in his eyes was <u>unfathomable</u>. Spellbound, I returned his gaze—a gaze that seemed to combine elements of inquiry and of acceptance. Peanuts ended this unforgettable moment by sighing deeply, and slowly resumed feeding. Jubilant, I returned to camp and cabled Dr. Leakey[1] I'VE FINALLY BEEN ACCEPTED BY A GORILLA.*

GUIDED READING

What does the cable to Dr. Leakey say?

Two years after our exchange of glances, Peanuts became the first gorilla ever to touch me. The day had started out as an ordinary one, if any day working from Karisoke might be considered ordinary. I felt unusually compelled to make this particular day outstanding because the following morning I had to leave for England for a seven-month period to work on my doctorate. Bob Campbell and I had gone out to contact Group 8 on the western-facing Visoke slopes. We found them feeding in the middle of a shallow ravine of densely growing herbaceous vegetation. Along the ridge leading into the ravine grew large *Hagenia* trees that had always served as good lookout spots for scanning the surrounding terrain. Bob and I had just settled down on a comfortable moss-cushioned *Hagenia* tree trunk when Peanuts, wearing his "I want to be entertained" expression, left his feeding group

GUIDED READING

Why does Fossey feel compelled to make the day outstanding?

to <u>meander</u> toward us. Slowly I left the tree and pretended to munch on vegetation to reassure Peanuts that I meant him no harm.

Peanuts' bright eyes peered at me through a latticework of vegetation as he began his strutting, swaggering approach. Suddenly he was at my side and sat down to watch my "feeding" techniques as if it were my turn to entertain him. When Peanuts seemed bored with the "feeding" routine, I scratched my head, and almost immediately, he began scratching his own. Since he appeared totally relaxed, I lay back in the <u>foliage</u>, slowly extended my hand, palm upward, then rested it on the leaves. After looking intently at my hand, Peanuts stood up and extended his hand to touch his fingers against my own for a brief instant. Thrilled at his own daring, he gave vent to his excitement by a quick chestbeat before going off to rejoin his group. Since that day, the spot has been called *Fasi Ya Mkoni*, "the Place of the Hands." The contact was among the most memorable of my life among the gorillas.

GUIDED READING

What does Peanuts sit down to watch Fossey do?

GUIDED READING

What does Peanuts touch?

*Nine years after Dr. Leakey's death in 1972 I learned that he had carried the cable in his pocket for months, even taking it on a lecture tour to America. I was told that he read it proudly, much as he once spoke to me of Jane Goodall's outstanding success with chimpanzees. ∎

---

1. **Dr. Leakey.** Scientist and colleague of Fossey's who encouraged her to study gorillas

---

words for everyday use

un • fath • om • a • ble (un faʼ thə mə bəl) *adj.*, impossible to comprehend. *The number of stars in the sky is <u>unfathomable</u>.*

me • an • der (mē anʼ dər) *v.*, follow a winding course or wander. *The bubbly stream <u>meanders</u> through the hillside.*

fo • li • age (fōʼ lē əj) *n.*, cluster of leaves, flowers, and branches. *Derek stared in awe at the dazzling emerald <u>foliage</u> in the park.*

Describe an interaction with an animal that you would find memorable.

About *the* AUTHOR

Dr. Dian Fossey was born in Fairfax, California, in 1932. Her strong interest in animals led her to enter college as a pre-veterinary student. Soon, however, she switched to occupational therapy and obtained her degree from San Jose State College. Through friends, Fossey became interested in Africa and made a six-week trip there in 1963. She became determined to work with gorillas and gained support to start a research program in Rwanda, where she established Karisoke Research Centre in 1967. Intense observation over thousands of hours enabled Fossey to earn the trust of the wild gorilla groups she studied. She contributed volumes of new knowledge about gorillas and their behavior. When poachers attacked and killed a young male named Digit, to whom she had grown especially attached, she began a public campaign against gorilla poaching. Contributions from around the world allowed Fossey to establish the Digit Fund (renamed the Dian Fossey Gorilla Fund in 1992) and to dedicate the rest of her life to the protection of the gorillas.

Dr. Fossey obtained her Ph.D. at Cambridge University and in 1980 accepted a position at Cornell University that enabled her to begin writing *Gorillas in the Mist.* The book brought even more attention to the plight of mountain gorillas, whose numbers had dwindled to 250. She returned to Karisoke to continue her work to ensure the survival of the mountain gorilla and to stop the practice of poaching. Dr. Fossey was murdered in her cabin at Karisoke on December 26, 1985. Her death is a mystery yet unsolved. The last entry in her diary reads: "When you realize the value of all life, you dwell less on what is past and concentrate on the preservation of the future." Dian Fossey's dream still lives on in the work of the Dian Fossey Gorilla Fund and of the dedicated researchers and Rwandan staff at Karisoke. Today, the mountain gorilla population is making steady gains in the Virunga Volcano area.

ABOUT THE RELATED READING ➤
Chris Nelson is a student at St. Olaf College in Northfield, Minnesota.

Gorillas

Chris Nelson

Dian Fossey was 31 years old, living in California, and working at a hospital as a children's therapist, but she wanted to do other things with her life. She longed to go to Africa to study the mountain gorillas she had read so much about. With money borrowed from the bank and friends she set out on a six-week safari. Her travels would eventually take her to a far-off mountain range, the last home of the mysterious gorillas that would become her obsession and her work for nearly 13 years. (Mowat 6)

Fossey fell in love with the gentle giant apes on that first visit and returned a few years later to become the first person to do a long-term study of their behavior. During her time spent closely observing the gorillas, she learned many important things about them. The information she gathered may help the gorillas survive despite being hunted almost to extinction and losing their homeland to farmers. Gorillas are the largest of the primates, a group that includes monkeys, chimpanzees, orangutans, and even humans. In fact, gorillas are more like humans than any other animal.

In the mid-1800s, Thomas Savage, a missionary in Africa, became the first westerner to document gorillas. The ones he saw were Western lowland gorillas. People at first portrayed gorillas as savage and cruel. Stories were told of gorillas hoisting men up into trees and strangling them. Of course, gorillas usually don't climb trees and are rarely aggressive, but no one had really studied the gorillas

in depth. (Schaller 9) In 1902 Oscar von Beringe discovered the mountain gorilla in the Virunga Mountains, the thickly forested volcanic region where Fossey would later set up her scientific study. The scientific name for these gorillas, *Gorilla gorilla beringei,* comes from von Beringe's name. (Schaller 10)

Carl Akeley was the first person to truly study gorillas. He hunted them on an expedition in 1921 and went back to observe them five years later. His study caught the interest of many scientists, and led them to learn more about these great apes. The information they discovered showed people for the first time what gorillas are really like. (Schaller 11)

Adult mountain gorillas are huge. Females can reach 200 pounds. Males weigh up to 400 pounds, twice as much as the females. When they are first born, gorilla babies are tiny, weighing only four pounds, but they grow twice as fast as human babies. The newborn gorillas have pinkish-gray skin and patches of brown or black hair on their bodies. As they get older, they develop a thick coat of black hair.

A baby's limbs are very weak and thin at first, so its mother carries it under her chest. There, the baby can cling to its mother for safety and drink her milk when it gets hungry. Within a few months, a gorilla baby is strong enough to hitch a ride on its mother's back.

Other immature gorillas—especially females—often try to play with young babies. This teaches the baby how to interact and how to behave around other gorillas. It also teaches younger female gorillas how to take care of children. Some mothers, however, are possessive of their babies and won't let young females near, especially if the younger female is not related to the mother.

As gorillas grow, differences between males and females start to appear. Although both males and females like to roughhouse, females begin to spend more time trying to take care of the older females' babies, while males begin to learn how to protect and lead a gorilla family.

The leader of a gorilla family is always a silverback. A silverback is a male gorilla, usually at least twelve years old, that has a saddle-shaped patch of silver hair on his back. This patch gets bigger as the gorilla gets older. (Gorillafund par. 4) Some ancient silverbacks have been seen with silver hair spreading all the way from their cheeks to their lower hind legs. Younger males, called blackbacks, are between eight and twelve years old and lack the silver patch on their backs. (Gorillafund par 8)

If the oldest silverback in a group dies, then the next oldest silverback— usually the son of the old leader— takes over leadership of the group. If the old leader's sons are too young or too weak, the other silverbacks in a family group will fight to see who is the strongest, and the winner will become the new leader. If a family group is especially large, with many females for the silverbacks to share, one or two other silverbacks may stay to help the leader take care of the family. Usually, however, the younger silverbacks will leave to try and start a new family somewhere else. These lone silverbacks may band together temporarily with other lone silverbacks, but their goal is to find females from other gorilla families that will join them and become their mates.

Lone silverbacks often cause problems for other gorilla groups. When a silverback and an established family group meet, the resulting contest of strength between the lone male and the silverback leader of the family can quickly grow into a fight. First they will face each other from a distance and give a *hootseries*. "The hootseries, a vocalization given by silverbacks during interactions, may carry for nearly a mile throughout the forest." (Fossey 66) Then the two gorillas will beat their chests with their fists, making a loud *pok pok pok* sound. This is the typical image of gorillas found in old stories and movies, but gorillas will only chestbeat when they are angry or frightened. Next, the gorillas may race from side to side, grunting, breaking small trees and ripping leaves. All of these actions are intended to scare the other silverback and impress his females. If the lone silverback gives a good display of his strength, some of the young females from the family may join him and become his family.

This type of challenge between silverbacks can sometimes turn into a fight, especially if one is young and doesn't know how to bluff (pretend to be big and powerful without actually fighting), but this is uncommon. Silverback fights can be extremely violent. The strong apes will try to wrestle and bite each other until one of them gives up. Sometimes one of the silverbacks will take so many injuries that he dies, but this does not happen very often. Most of the time, one will quickly give up the fight and run away.

When a silverback wins a fight and manages to gain new females from another family group, he moves them to his home range, an area of 10 to 15 square miles that he lives in and travels around during the year. The gorillas will then have babies, which ensure the future of the family and provide a sense of closeness for the new father and mother.

In a typical day, gorillas awake late, sometimes hours after sunrise. Their first instinct is to eat. Gorillas are mainly herbivores, or plant-eaters, but they have been known to eat insects, slugs, snails, and grubs as well. They eat massive quantities of food each day to support their giant bodies. Gorillas eat fruit when they can get it, and a certain kind of bracket fungus is also a favorite snack, but mainly they eat leaves, flowers, vines, and ripe young bamboo. (Fossey 49)

After a few hours of foraging and eating, the gorillas settle down for noon playtime and naps. Younger gorillas stage rowdy tumble sessions, playfully wrestling with each other and climbing all over the sleeping bodies of the older gorillas. Sometimes they find large round fruits and play a catching game or kick the fruit like a soccer ball. They swing on vines and trees until they are too big. Anything can become a toy to a young gorilla.

Besides sleeping, older gorillas take this time to develop stronger family bonds. Playing, grooming, and other group activities help strengthen these bonds. A group whose members have strong connections is more likely to survive, since it means they will help each other with raising young and defending the family and not fight amongst themselves.

After resting, gorillas feed once more late in the day and then begin to prepare for the night. Gorillas sleep in nests on the ground or, for the younger, lighter gorillas, in low hanging branches. Often they will sleep inside huge hollow trees, where they are protected from rain and cold. To make a nest, a gorilla will find an area with many low-lying plants, grab the plants, and bend their stems under him or herself. It will then rotate around, bending down plants until it has a firm cushion underneath and a supporting ring surrounding them to keep the nest together. Smaller gorillas will share a nest with their mothers until they learn how to make their own. Naturalist George Schaller, watching a group of gorillas preparing to settle down for the night, observed, "Within minutes, at half-past five, all movement had ceased, and the dark forms of the gorillas fused with the night." (Schaller 18)

Gorillas are in danger of disappearing permanently. Poacher hunting practices, the loss of living space, and diseases brought in by human tourists have put their existence in jeopardy. In 1999 scientists figured there were about 650 mountain gorillas left in the wild, with none living in zoos or private collections. This makes them extremely endangered, although their population has been growing.

Many Africans do not know of laws protecting gorillas. Others hunt the gorillas and sell their parts for money to survive. Tourists from around the world buy gorilla heads and hands as souvenirs, even though they know the gorilla was illegally killed. In addition, much of the mountain rainforest where the gorillas live has been given to farmers to cut down and plow for farming, and this makes it hard for the gorillas to find food or to have enough forest to roam in. Finally, although tourists bring in a lot of money to help save gorillas, they also bring in diseases—like measles, influenza, or even colds, which can kill a gorilla.

People in the countries where the gorillas live are learning more about these majestic animals. Scientists like Dian Fossey hope that education will keep gorillas around for future generations to admire, but it will be a long time before the gorillas can live in peace and safety.

Bibliography

Fossey, Dian. *Gorillas in the Mist.* Boston: Houghton Mifflin Co., 1983

Norton, Boyd. *The Mountain Gorilla.* Stillwater, MN: Voyageur Press, Inc., 1990

Mountain Gorilla Fact File. 11 paragraphs. 6/29/1999. http://www.awf.org/wildlives/149

Schaller, George B. Introductory Essay. *Gorilla: Struggle for Survival in the Virungas.* By Michael Nichols. Ed. Nan Richardson. New York: Aperture Foundation, Inc., 1989. 9–26

Investigate, Inquire, and Imagine

Recall: GATHERING FACTS

1a. What question do people frequently ask Fossey? Why is it difficult to answer?

2a. What look is Peanuts "wearing" as he approaches Fossey and Bob Campbell?

3a. What does Fossey do to reassure Peanuts?

4a. What does Peanuts do that is so extraordinary?

Interpret: FINDING MEANING

1b. Why do you think she follows this with the anecdotes about Peanuts?

2b. How might this expression actually have looked? How would Peanuts demonstrate this desire?

3b. Why would this action reassure a gorilla?

4b. Why is this action so extraordinary?

Analyze: TAKING THINGS APART

5a. Make a list of all the ways that Fossey and Peanuts demonstrate interest in one another.

Synthesize: BRINGING THINGS TOGETHER

5b. How does this anecdote describe a landmark event in Fossey's study of gorillas? Why is Fossey's developing interaction with Peanuts important?

Evaluate: MAKING JUDGMENTS

6a. Consider Fossey's techniques for fostering trust and friendship in Peanuts. How well do they work? What other techniques do you think she might have used?

Extend: CONNECTING IDEAS

6b. Using what you have learned about gorillas from the related reading, "Gorillas," explain some of the behaviors that Peanuts demonstrates in the selection from *Gorillas in the Mist*.

Understanding Literature

ANECDOTE. An **anecdote** is a usually short narrative of an interesting, amusing, or biographical incident. An anecdote is commonly told to make a point or to emphasize a specific event. Why do you think Fossey includes this anecdote in her book?

CONCRETE DETAILS. **Concrete details** are specific words that name objects or actions or provide descriptions of those objects or actions. These specific details help the piece of writing to provide clear, concise, and in-depth information to the reader. Using specific details in place of more general words helps the reader really understand the situation or event being discussed. Find examples of concrete details that provide specific information about what happens between Peanuts and Fossey.

Writer's Journal

1. Write a **poem** about one of Fossey's encounters with Peanuts.
2. Write a **title** for the short selection from *Gorillas in the Mist.*
3. Imagine you are a researcher at Karisoke. Write a day's worth of **field notes** about your experiences with gorillas.

Skill Builders

Applied English

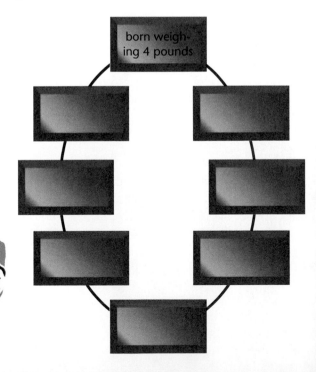

PLANNING A TRIP. The Virunga Mountains are a prime location for what is known as ecotourism, a type of travel that takes people to environmentally sensitive locations to witness the beauty and splendor of the wildlife and fauna. Research the area's parks and reserves and the activities offered in them. Locate travel guides or use the Internet to find information. Plan a trip to the area, mapping out where you would go, what you would do, how you would get there, and where you would sleep.

Study and Research

EXTENDING YOUR LEARNING. Using the Internet, find out more about gorilla research. Start at the Dian Fossey Gorilla Fund site at http://www.gorillafund.org/. Then use the site's links to find additional information. Prepare a report about your findings, and inform the rest of your class on what you learned about gorilla research today.

Collaborative Learning

CREATE A POSTER. Reread the research report, "Gorillas," on page 771. In small groups, fill out a graphic organizer like the one to the right. Each square should represent one stage in the life cycle of a gorilla. Sketch a picture, diagram, or symbol in each square until you have completed the circle. Then, create a poster using the ideas you created here. Draw the squares on poster board and fine-tune your visuals within the squares. Create a title for the poster and add any other text you wish to include. Ask your teacher if you can display your poster in your classroom or in another location in your school.

born weighing 4 pounds

Reader's *Journal*

What would you like to know about the universe?

Reader's *Resource*

- People have always wondered at the worlds that surrounded the Earth. They especially have marveled at the night sky when many celestial bodies, such as stars, the moon, and some planets, were visible. Over the years, people have come up with many explanations about the universe and the bodies within it. This selection focuses on some early ideas.

- **SCIENCE CONNECTION.** We now know that there are nine planets in our solar system: Mercury, Venus, Earth, Mars, Jupiter, Saturn, Uranus, Neptune, and Pluto. For many years, people believed that the planets revolved around the Earth. Nicholas Copernicus (1473–1543), a Polish astronomer, proved that the planets, including Earth, revolve around the sun. Within our solar system there are also many moons, asteroids, comets, and other matter. Scientists have also discovered other solar systems.

Prereading

"THE FIVE 'WANDERERS' OF THE ANCIENT SKIES"
by Dennis Brindell Fradin

Reader's T O O L B O X

COHERENCE AND TRANSITIONS. Coherence is the logical arrangement and progression of ideas in speech or writing. **Transitions** help create coherence. They are words, phrases, or sentences that connect ideas in writing and help the reader move from one thought to the next.

IMAGE AND IMAGERY. An **image** is language that describes something that can be seen, heard, touched, tasted, or smelled. The images in a literary work are referred to as **imagery.** Imagery is widely associated with poetry and fiction, but nonfiction writers use imagery, too. Images make writing more vivid and create a response in the reader. Keep track of images you notice as you read.

Graphic

List the images you find in the left column and the senses those images appeal to in the right column.

Image	Sense It Appeals To
huge yellow orb	sight

Man Looking into Outer Space, c.1500s. French artist.

THE
FIVE 'WANDERERS'
OF THE ANCIENT SKIES

Dennis Brindell Fradin

Aristarchus was accused of evil teachings. He refused to acknowledge that the Earth is at the center of the Universe. Instead, he claimed that it moves in an orbit [around the Sun] and at the same time spins on its axis.

Ancient description of the Greek astronomer Aristarchus, who lived about 2,300 years ago

GUIDED READING

What belief caused Aristarchus to be accused of evil teachings?

On a clear night, in a place far from city lights, a person with good vision can see about 3,000 stars in the sky. A few stars are so bright that they dazzle the eye, but many others are barely visible. There are white stars and blue stars, orange stars and red stars, yellow stars and stars that seem to change color as they twinkle. Many people who view the starfilled sky for the first time are almost hypnotized by its splendor. Whether children or adults, they are likely to wonder: How many stars are there and how far away are they? Do stars extend forever in space or is there a place where they end? Are we alone in the Universe, or do beings on other worlds look up at their night sky with the same sense of awe that we feel?

People have undoubtedly asked these questions for most of our two million years on Earth. Some of the oldest known <u>relics</u> created by human beings have astronomical significance. Ten thousand-year-old bones on which people recorded the cycles of the Moon have been found in Africa and Europe. Cliff drawings and stone monuments found in many places also prove that people have been <u>intrigued</u> by the objects in the heavens since prehistoric times.

GUIDED READING

What are some of the signs that people have studied the skies for thousands of years?

Our ancient ancestors observed that seven <u>celestial</u> objects behave differently than the stars in the night sky. One of them, the huge yellow orb we call the Sun, appears only by day and seems to take the light away when it sets each evening. The second unusual object was the large body we call the Moon, which seems to change shape during a cycle lasting about thirty days.

The other five unusual objects resemble bright stars, yet differ from them in two important ways. First, a star twinkles "like a diamond in the sky," as the nursery rhyme says, while the five special objects shine with a steady light. Also, the relative positions of the stars change so slowly over long periods of time that the ancients made up imaginary star pictures called constellations that look nearly the same today as they did thousands of years ago. On the other hand, the five unusual objects do not remain in fixed positions, but move through the constellations from month to month and year to year.

Ancient people generally worshiped the seven unusual heavenly bodies as gods and goddesses. The Greeks believed that the Sun was the god Helios and the Moon his sister Selene. They referred to the five bright objects that moved among the constellations as *planetae*, meaning "wanderers." Although the Greeks did not understand the nature of the "wanderers," their word *planetae* lives on in our modern name for the objects: *planets*.

GUIDED READING

What does the word from which we get the word *planet* mean?

The Romans coined the names still applied to the five known planets of ancient times. The fast-moving orange planet that always remained near the Sun they named *Mercury*, for their fleet-footed messenger of the gods who wore magic sandals. The brilliant white planet that outshone every heavenly body except the Sun and the Moon they called *Venus*, for their goddess of love. The red planet reminded the Romans of blood, so they named it *Mars*, for their god of war. The yellow planet that wandered slowly through the constellations the Romans named *Jupiter*,

words for everyday use

rel • ic (rel' ik) n., object that has survived from the past. *I was amazed by the <u>relics</u> from the ancient Egyptians I saw at the museum.*

in • trigue (in trēg') v., excite the interest or curiosity of. *Many people are <u>intrigued</u> by comets and falling stars.*

ce • les • tial (sə les' chel) adj., of the sky or universe. *The moon and sun are two visible <u>celestial</u> bodies.*

with a man's body and a bird's head. The Babylonians, who lived in what is now Iraq, worshiped Jupiter as Marduk, their king of the gods who killed a dragon and created the sky and the oceans out of its body. Mexico's Maya and Aztec Indians referred to Venus as Quetzalcoatl, a god who also took the form of a feathered serpent. The Masai people of Africa claimed that the Sun and the Moon were a husband and wife who had a fight. The Sun god was so ashamed of his bruises that he made himself bright to keep people from looking at him, but when we gaze upon the Moon goddess's face, we can see her injuries.

GUIDED READING

According to the Masai story, why is the sun bright? What features of the moon does the story explain?

Ancient Jewish people did not <u>associate</u> the heavenly bodies with gods and goddesses, for their religion, Judaism, taught that there is only one God. Yet they believed that each planet influenced a part of the human body and a day of the week. For example, Mars was associated with the right ear and the day we call Tuesday, and Mercury's influence extended to the left nostril and Friday. The Chinese identified each planet with an important substance. They called Mercury *Shui Xing*, the Water Star, and Venus *Jin Xing*, the Gold Star. The red planet, Mars, was *Huo Xing*, the Fire Star, while Jupiter was *Mu Xing*, the Wood Star, and Saturn was *Tu Xing*, the Earth Star.

The Moon, Sun, and five planets known to the ancients influenced our language, calendar, and other aspects of our daily life. Seven is considered a lucky number to this day because of the seven unusual heavenly

for their king of the gods who was also known as Jove. The golden planet that moved even more slowly than Jupiter they named *Saturn*, for Jupiter's father. The Romans worshiped the Moon as Luna, a goddess who drove across the night sky in her chariot,[1] and identified the Sun with Apollo, the god of musicians and poets.

GUIDED READING

With whom did the Romans identify the moon and the sun?

Other people had their own beliefs about the seven special heavenly bodies. To the people of ancient India the Sun was Surya, a god who was driven across the sky by a seven-headed horse. The ancient Egyptians believed that the planets Mars, Jupiter, and Saturn were various forms of Horus, a god

---

1. **chariot.** Wheeled vehicle, drawn by horses

---

words for everyday use

as • so • ci • ate (ə sō′ shē āt) *v.,* connect. *Do you* <u>associate</u> *the beginning of baseball season with the beginning of spring?*

Personification of the days of the week.

bodies, and the week has seven days for the same reason. Each of our days is named for one of the objects. *Sunday* and *Monday* are old words meaning "the Sun's Day" and "the Moon's Day." *Tuesday, Wednesday,* and *Thursday* come from old words meaning "the Day of Mars," "the Day of Mercury," and "the Day of Jupiter." *Friday* is "the Day of Venus," and *Saturday* is "Saturn's Day."

Helium, an element used to fill balloons, was named for the Sun god, Helios. Because the god and planet Mercury moved so quickly, the element used in thermometers was named mercury, and individuals whose moods quickly change are called "mercurial." People who are gloomy or slow to act are sometimes described as "saturnine" for the slow-moving planet, while good-natured individuals are called "jovial" in honor of Saturn's son, King Jupiter or Jove. Long ago, nations took time out from wars during the winter, because the cold weather could claim more lives than the battles. They resumed fighting when the weather turned warmer, which was why the first month of spring was named *March* for Mars, the god of war.

> **GUIDED READING**
>
> How did the month March get its name?

The Moon inspired the custom of dividing the year into twelve segments. Each of these periods roughly corresponds to the Moon's thirty-day cycle and is called a *month*, a word related to *Mene*, meaning "Moon" in Greek. The Moon also figures in many old superstitions, including the belief that it could transform people into werewolves or wolf-men. To this day, mentally ill people are sometimes called *lunatics*, as a result of the ancient belief that the Moon and its goddess, Luna, could do strange things to the human mind.

> **GUIDED READING**
>
> What superstitions revolve around the moon?

Except for a handful of individuals considered in their own time to be lunatics, ancient people shared a completely false view of the Universe. They thought that all of the heavenly bodies circled the Earth, which stood motionless at the center of everything. There seemed to be a simple "proof" of this. At night the Moon, stars, and planets traveled across the sky in an arc from east to west, and each day the Sun did the same. All a person had to do was watch a planet rise over a treetop in the east or a star set behind a mountain in the west to see "evidence" that the heavenly bodies circled the Earth from east to west.

The Greek astronomer Aristarchus was one of the very few ancient scientists who differed with this theory. About 2,300 years ago, Aristarchus claimed that the heavenly bodies only *appear* to circle overhead because our Earth spins like a top. He also suggested that the Earth orbits the Sun— not the other way around. Aristarchus was accurate on both counts, but for many centuries his ideas were <u>ridiculed</u>.

GUIDED READING

What idea was ridiculed?

Ptolemy, a Greek astronomer who was born about 100 AD, led the attack on Aristarchus's theories. "If the Earth actually rotated to the east," reasoned Ptolemy, "wouldn't winds always blow westward and clouds always move westward?" Ptolemy became the most famous spokesman for the false idea that the Earth stands still and is the center of the Universe, a theory that became known as the "Ptolemaic System." Its followers, called "Ptolemaists," developed numerous arguments to explain why the Earth couldn't possibly spin. One was that a spinning Earth would make us feel constantly dizzy. They also argued that if the Earth really rotated, a rock or ball hurled into the sky would be left far behind rather than coming down near where it was thrown.

One thing disturbed the Ptolemaists, however. Certain movements of the planets could best be explained if in fact they orbited the Sun rather than the Earth. At times some planets make backward loops in the sky. This *retrograde[2] motion* is due to the Earth overtaking the other "wanderers" as the

GUIDED READING

What disturbed the Ptolemaists?

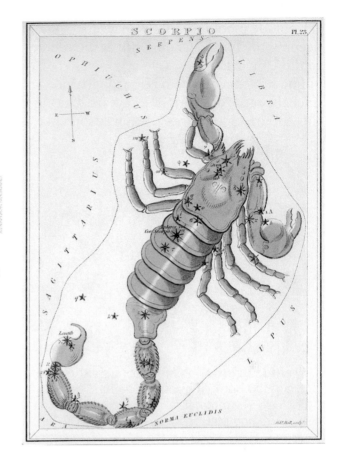

planets all orbit the Sun, much as a car traveling 50 miles per hour on a highway can appear to be moving backward if you are whizzing past it at 60 miles per hour. Ptolemy <u>concocted</u> another explanation for the planets' backward loops. He claimed that the planets travel in large circles around the Earth, but that they sometimes also move in extra small circles called *epicycles*. Although completely wrong, this explanation won acceptance because it accounted for the

GUIDED READING

What explanation did Ptolemy concoct?

---

2. **retrograde.** Having a direction contrary to the general motion of similar bodies in space

---

words for everyday use

rid • i • cule (rid′ i kyool) *v.*, make the object of laughter, make fun of. *Shelby <u>ridiculed</u> Stasia's idea, but stopped laughing when he saw the invention work.*

con • coct (kən käkt′) *v.*, invent or put together a plan. *Coach <u>concocted</u> a new strategy for the big game.*

retrograde motion of the "wanderers" while keeping the Earth standing still at the center of the Universe.

The Ptolemaic System <u>reigned</u> virtually unchallenged for nearly 1,400 years. During those fourteen centuries the Earth spun like a top (as Aristarchus claimed) half a million times, Mercury orbited the Sun five thousand times, and Saturn made fifty trips around the Sun—yet all the while humanity continued to believe that we stood motionless at the center of creation.

Respond *to the* SELECTION

Do you think we are alone in the universe? Explain your response.

About *the* AUTHOR

Dennis Brindell Fradin has published more than 300 books for young people. The titles include *The Internet for Kids, Astronomy, Comets and Meteor Showers, Is There Life on Mars?, Samuel Adams, the Father of American Independence,* and a number of books about the fifty states. Many of these books can be found in your school library.

Investigate, *Inquire,* and Imagine

Recall: GATHERING FACTS

1a. What were the seven celestial objects that ancient people noticed behaved differently than the stars?

2a. What superstitions are related to the moon?

3a. What is the Ptolemaic System? What problem disturbed the Ptolemaists?

→ **Interpret:** FINDING MEANING

1b. Why do you think people worshiped these seven objects?

2b. Why might the moon, and not other celestial bodies, be associated with superstitions?

3b. On what was Ptolemy's belief based?

Analyze: TAKING THINGS APART

4a. Analyze the different stories about the sun and the moon. What characteristics are attributed to each body?

→ **Synthesize:** BRINGING THINGS TOGETHER

4b. What are the differences between these stories? What are the similarities?

Evaluate: MAKING JUDGMENTS

5a. Evaluate the arguments made by the Ptolemaists in defense of their system.

→ **Extend:** CONNECTING IDEAS

5b. Evaluate a current theory about the universe, our solar system, or another planet.

Understanding *Literature*

COHERENCE AND TRANSITIONS. Coherence is the logical arrangement and progression of ideas in writing or speech. **Transitions** help create coherence. They are words, phrases, or sentences that connect ideas in writing and help the reader move from one thought to the next. Identify three transitions and the ideas they connect. What element from the introduction and the conclusion helps create coherence?

IMAGE AND IMAGERY. An **image** is language that describes something that can be seen, heard, touched, tasted, or smelled. The images in a literary work are referred to as **imagery**. What effect do the images you noticed have on you? Why might imagery be important even in nonfiction?

Writer's Journal

1. Stars are often associated with wishes. Write a **wish** that you might make on a star.

2. A hypothesis is an educated guess about the cause of something. Aristarchus and Ptolemy both developed hypotheses about the movements of the earth and sun. Write a **hypothesis** stating a belief you have about the universe, the sun, or the earth.

3. Write a **children's story** about the solar system. You may write a myth-like story or you may write a story that includes scientific details about the solar system.

Skill Builders

Collaborative Learning

MAKING A MOBILE. Find a diagram or picture of the solar system. You might want to try The Nine Planets: A Multimedia Tour of the Solar System by Bill Arnett, an Internet site at http://seds.lpl.arizona.edu/nineplanets/nineplanets/overview.html. After you have a good idea of what the planets look like and how they are positioned around the sun, gather materials for the mobile. For the planets, you may want to cut out cardboard circles or find round styrofoam balls in different sizes. You will also need markers or paint, fishing line or thread, and sturdy wire. Make the planets, then arrange them around the sun. Attach a piece of thread or fishing line to each planet with a staple, a pin, or a tack. Attach the other end of the thread to a piece of wire. Arrange the wires so that the planets surround the sun.

Vocabulary

TEST-TAKING SKILLS. In many standardized tests, students are asked to choose a word or phrase closest to the meaning of the word in the question. Practice your test-taking skills by answering the following questions. For each question, choose the answer that best matches the meaning of the underlined word.

1. My love is <u>fickle</u> like the moon.
   a. unchanging b. crescent-shaped
   c. not constant

2. Stella was overwhelmed by the <u>multitude</u> of stars in the sky.
   a. color b. large number c. brightness

3. Earth is considered a <u>terrestrial</u> planet, but Jupiter, a largely gaseous planet, is not.
   a. consisting of solid land b. alien
   c. made of gas

4. Grandpa's old farmhouse is full of interesting <u>relics</u>.
   a. toys b. vehicles c. antiques

5. Stories about aliens and UFOs really <u>intrigue</u> Morris.
   a. bore b. interest c. anger

Prereading

"*Night*"

by Jerry Spinelli

Reader's TOOLBOX

AIM. A writer's **aim** is his or her purpose, or goal. People may write to inform (informative/expository writing); to tell a story, either true or invented (narrative writing); to reflect (personal/expressive writing); to share a perspective (imaginative writing); or to persuade readers to respond in some way (persuasive/argumentative writing). Writing may have more than one aim. As you read, try to determine Spinelli's aim or aims.

ALLITERATION. Alliteration is the repetition of consonant sounds at the beginnings of syllables. The following sentence is an example because the *y* sound is repeated: "Yes, I know how to yo-yo," yawned Yolanda, "and I yearn to be as good as you." Alliteration is often used in poetry, but here Spinelli uses it in nonfiction. Look for examples as you read.

REPETITION. Repetition is more than one use of a sound, word, or group of words. A writer may use repetition for many reasons, such as to stress an idea, to achieve coherence, or to create rhythm.

Graphic *Organizer*

As you read, think about how the author associates different things with nighttime. Write words and phrases identifying these things in a graphic organizer like the one below. Then, write how the author reacts to each of those things.

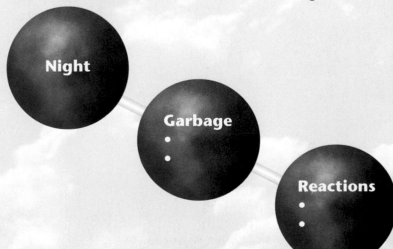

Reader's *Journal*

Write about a time that you were afraid of the dark.

Reader's *Resource*

- Being afraid of the dark is a common kind of fear, especially among young people. Darkness makes things seem bigger and louder than they normally are. Shadows distort the shape and appearance of people and objects, and it is difficult to see what is there in the darkness. In this selection, Spinelli explains why he was sometimes afraid of the darkness.

- Trains once played a key role in transporting people and cargo all over the country. However, with the growth of travel by car, bus, and plane, fewer people travel by train than in the past. Items that used to be transported by trains are now often shipped by truck or plane instead. But trains still do transport people and goods all over the country. In the past, trains had steam engines that were powered by coal or wood. Now most trains use diesel engines.

Dead End, 1942. Lyonel Feininger. Worcester Art Museum, Massachusetts.

Night

Jerry Spinelli

chh

It always began as a solitary chuffing, a sudden explosive snort as if a night beast rising in the distance, down in Conshohocken[1] maybe, had cleared its snout. So faint and faraway was it, so alien, that I usually <u>persuaded</u> myself that it wasn't there. But sooner or later, again, it was.

chh

It seemed to enter my night room from below, catching on the antenna of my bedsprings, running up the coils, whispering through the mattress, the sheet, making an ear of my entire body.

chh

Then the furious flurry.

chhchhchhchhchhchh

My eyes were wide, <u>groping</u> for light, but I could not even see the pillow. I wished I had the nerve to run for the light switch. I wished my room was not at the back of the house, nearest the tracks.

The sound was still far off, along the Schuylkill (SKOO-kul) River,[2] somewhere in the East End, but it had movement now, direction. It was coming. The breath of the night beast beat faster and louder. It was passing the DeKalb Street station now, turning from the river, behind the empty dark Garrick Theater, under the erector set[3] Airy Street bridge, Marshall Street now, between the black and white striped crossing gate, bell tinkling, red light blinking—louder and louder—past the sand place, where I went with my father to bring home a wagonful; past the shoebox-shaped Orange Car store, where my mother could buy a bagful

GUIDED READING

What does the train pass after passing the crossing gate?

of Florida in February; crossing Elm, bending with the creek—louder, louder, *chhchh chhchhchhchhchh*—behind the ice plant now, Astor Street, the stone piles, the dump—louder still—the iron beast pouring sooty blackness into all the world, creating night—how loud can something be?—coming around the curve at the dead end of Chain CHHCHHCHHCHHCHHCHHCHHC HHCHHCHHCHHCHHCHHCHH HCHHCHHCHH—into my room, the bedsprings under me singing like the fiddle strings of Hell . . .

Did it really happen? In morning's comforting sunshine I could never be sure—

---

1. **Conshohocken.** City in Pennsylvania, near Philadelphia
2. **Schuylkill River.** River in Pennsylvania
3. **erector set.** Toy for building

---

words for everyday use

per • suade (pər swād′) v., convince. *Lia <u>persuaded</u> Mr. Morgan to give her a discount on the book because the cover was torn.*

grope (grōp′) v., feel for blindly. *Ramon stumbled in the dark as he <u>groped</u> for the light switch.*

Nighttime lent a horror not only to trains but also to garbage.

until I ran my finger along the clothesline or over the yellow face of a pansy in the backyard, and the tiny black particles of grit confirmed: yes, a train—a coal-fired, smoke-belching locomotive—had passed the night before.

GUIDED READING

What is the proof that a train passed the night before?

Nighttime lent a horror not only to trains but also to garbage. Garbage had status in those days. Garbage was garbage, and trash was everything else. Garbage had a can of its own, basically an oversize metal pail with a lid. The garbage pail could be found in the back of the backyard. To lift the lid off the garbage can was to confront all the horrors of the creepiest movie: dead, rotting matter; <u>teeming</u> colonies of pale, slimy creeping things; and a stench that could be survived only in the smallest whiffs.

GUIDED READING

What did it mean to take the lid off the garbage can?

<u>Ironically</u>, the garbage can was never more disgusting than the day *after* garbage collection—for the collection was never quite complete. The garbage man would snatch the can from our curbside and overturn it into the garbage truck's unspeakable <u>trough</u>. He would bang it once, maybe twice, against the trough wall. This would dislodge most of the garbage, including a rain of maggots, but not the worst of it, not the very bottom of it, the most persistent, the oldest, the rottenest, the <u>vilest</u>. I held my breath while putting the lid back on. Sometimes I pushed the can all the way to the backyard with my foot.

When garbage met darkness, the potential for horror doubled.

Emptying the garbage after dinner was a frequent chore of mine, but only one particular instance do I remember. My mother had dumped the leftovers into a cake batter bowl and sent me off. The season was winter; it was already dark outside. The light from the back door petered out halfway down the yard, leaving me to moonlight. At the garbage can I went through my usual ritual: I curled my fingers around the metal handle of the lid, took a deep breath, held it, and with an almost audible winching of willpower, yanked the lid off. Careful not to look directly into the can, I overturned the

GUIDED READING

What is the narrator's usual garbage ritual?

batter bowl. I tapped it against the can to loosen any stragglers—and discovered I had a problem.

Whatever we had had for dinner that night must have been sticky, because half of it was still clinging to the bowl. I tapped harder.

words for everyday use

teem • ing (tēm′ iŋ) *adj.,* swarming. *The fallen popsicle was* <u>teeming</u> *with ants.*

i • ron • ic (ī rän′ ik) *adj.,* directly opposite of what one might expect. *It was* <u>ironic</u> *that the bus came just after Hermoine walked off, tired of waiting.* **ironically,** *adv.*

trough (trôf) *n.,* long, narrow, open container. *Yuri filled the* <u>trough</u> *with collected scraps of food for his pig.*

vile (vīl) *adj.,* loathsome, disgusting. *The cousins competed to make the* <u>vilest</u> *mixture.*

Still the stuff stuck. Risking breakage, I banged the bowl against the can. Nothing came loose. My chest was getting tight, my lungs demanded breath. In the moonlight I caught a glimpse of white worms. I panicked. I dropped the bowl into the garbage can, slammed down the lid, and raced for the house. I waited until I was inside to gasp for air, as I was sure that the garbage can, open so uncommonly long, must have fouled all outdoors. When my mother asked about the missing bowl several days later, I said I knew nothing about it.

Though night at various times <u>conspired</u> with a locomotive or a garbage can or a pup tent to frighten me, at other times night did not scare me at all.

GUIDED READING

Was the narrator always afraid of the dark?

We used to play a game called outs. It was the major leagues of hide-and-seek games. The kid who was It covered his eyes and counted to a hundred while everyone else ran and hid. If the It kid found you, he yelled "You're out!" and then the two of you were It and went seeking the others, and so on, until all were It but one—the winner.

There were no boundaries. You could hide anywhere. Popular hiding places included the stone piles, Red Hill, alleys, assorted backyards. As if the hiding needed to be made any easier, we always played outs after dark.

My favorite hiding place was behind a stone pile near the creek. I would crouch silently for an hour or more in utter darkness. The dark did not scare me when playing outs. What scared me was being found.

GUIDED READING

When wasn't the narrator afraid of the dark? What scared him instead?

One night I heard the Its coming close to my hiding place. I slipped away down the path to the park and trotted up past the state hospital. I didn't stop until I was more than a mile west of town, in Jeffersonville. By the time I got back home my parents were calling my name down the dark alleys and streets. All the other players were home in bed.

Night was at its best once a week: outdoor movies in the park. After dinnertime and baseball games and Popsicles for dessert, kids from all over town headed for the band shell. Little kids sat in the cement-anchored benches that still form the stage's permanent seats. On the hill behind, older kids pulled up wooden benches or just sat on the grass. One night I must have been thinking I was older than I was. As I made myself at home on a wooden bench on the hill, several teenagers decided that was where they wanted to sit. They lifted the bench at one end, and off I slid to the grass.

GUIDED READING

When was night the best?

The movies were usually in black and white. Occasionally we got through the show without the projector breaking down or the film snapping. More often than not the movie was about Francis the talking mule.

Afterward everyone scattered, across the fields to the East End, North End, West End. We George Streeters walked through the American Legion field and over the granite bridge spanning Stony Creek and turned left. Sometimes we took the dirt path, sometimes the tracks.

On moonlit nights the tracks looked like silver ribbons. Behind me, ahead of me, I could hear the voices of other kids. I could see their dark shadows. Atop the ten-foot clay

---

words for everyday use

con • spire (kən spīr´) v., plan and act together. *Norbert and Ismene <u>conspired</u> to play a trick on Lester.*

bluff to the right was the spear field, then the dump, then Red Hill. A bald, packed dome of eraser-colored clay, Red Hill was said to be the home of the Devil, the clay's color coming from the infernal fires burning below. I always looked to see if it was true that at night you could see the hill glowing. Once, I thought, it was.

Always glowing, however, was the dead end, the faint "Welcome home" from the last streetlight. From the path, from the tracks we funneled onto George, the after-dark, midsummer band shell park movie kids. You could always bet that someone would face the row house windows and do his best imitation of a talking mule.

And somewhere beyond the East End a locomotive was moving through the night . . .

chh

GUIDED READING

What would you most likely hear after the movie?

Respond *to the* SELECTION

Do you like nighttime? Why, or why not?

About *the* AUTHOR

Jerry Spinelli was born in Norristown, Pennsylvania. You can read all about his childhood in this town in his autobiography *Knots in My Yo-yo String,* from which "Night" is taken. He has written 23 books, including *Maniac Magee,* which won the Newbery Medal in 1991, and *Wringer,* which was named a Newbery Honor book in 1998. If he could recommend only one of his books, he would recommend *Maniac Magee* "for its message, story, and the language." He says that ideas for his books come easy for him, but *good* ideas are hard. When students ask where he gets his ideas for his books, Spinelli replies, "From you. You're the funny ones."

Investigate, Inquire, and Imagine

Recall: Gathering Facts → **Interpret:** Finding Meaning

1a. What sound did the narrator hear at night? What made this sound?

1b. How did this sound make the narrator feel? Why did he have such a reaction?

2a. When was the garbage can most disgusting? What did the narrator do when he had to take out the garbage?

2b. Why did the narrator have such a strong reaction on the night he had a problem with the garbage?

3a. What game did the narrator play in the evenings?

3b. How did the narrator feel when he was out after dark to play this game?

Analyze: Taking Things Apart → **Synthesize:** Bringing Things Together

4a. Analyze the different ways night and darkness are portrayed in this selection.

4b. Overall, how does the narrator feel about night and darkness?

Evaluate: Making Judgments → **Extend:** Connecting Ideas

5a. Evaluate the speaker's attitude about his childhood.

5b. Compare and contrast the attitude the narrator has toward his childhood with the attitude Geronimo reveals about his in the selection from *Geronimo's Story of His Life* (on page 759).

Understanding *Literature*

Aim. A writer's **aim** is his or her purpose, or goal. What is Spinelli's aim in this selection? How do you know?

Alliteration. Alliteration is the repetition of consonant sounds at the beginnings of syllables. Find three examples of alliteration. Why does Spinelli use this technique—usually reserved for poetry—in this selection?

Repetition. Repetition is more than one use of a sound, word, or group of words. What elements are repeated in the first segment of this selection? How are these elements connected to the rest of the selection? What purpose does this repetition serve?

Writer's Journal

1. Write a **letter** to a friend reminding him or her of a game you played when you were younger or sharing some other memory you have in common.

2. Write a **description** of your room, your home, or your street at night. How does it differ from daytime? How do you feel about this place at night?

3. Write a **horror story** about either the train or the garbage can that Spinelli describes.

Skill Builders

Collaborative Learning

ORAL INTERPRETATION. Work in groups of four to prepare an oral interpretation of this selection. Divide the selection into four sections: the train, the garbage, playing "outs," and movie night. Each person should be responsible for a section. Practice reading your section aloud, varying your tone, pitch, pace, and volume to convey the mood of the piece. Offer one another constructive criticism and try to present the best possible reading you can give.

Critical Thinking

GIVING DIRECTIONS. Spinelli talks about "outs," a game he used to play in his neighborhood. Think about a game you like to play. It may be a very simple game like "outs." Write a set of directions for this game. Arrange the rules and directions in a logical order and use clear, simple language. Compile the directions with others from your class to create a book of games.

Language, Grammar, and Style

GETTING SUBJECTS AND VERBS TO AGREE. Review the Language Arts Survey 3.38, "Getting Subject and Verb to Agree." Rewrite each sentence correcting errors in subject-verb agreement.

1. Trains and garbage scares Spinelli at night.
2. When he plays outs with his friends, he are not afraid.
3. One night he goes so far to hide, his parents is looking for him when he gets back.
4. Two nighttime activities he enjoys is playing outs and watching movies.
5. In the end, the train come back to haunt him.

Speaking and Listening

CONDUCTING AN INTERVIEW. Interview a parent or other older person about what it was like growing up when he or she was a child. Prepare a list of questions before the interview. Here are some ideas to get you started: What was school like? What kinds of games did you play? What was your favorite activity? Add some questions of your own. As the person you are interviewing answers the questions, you may come up with some additional follow-up questions. For example, if the person you are interviewing says she liked to play marbles, you might ask: How do you play?, or, Were you good at that game? Remember that listening is an important part of interviewing. When you have completed the interview, write a brief biographical sketch about your subject.

Prereading

"A Breath of Fresh Air?"
by Alexandra Hanson-Harding

Reader's T O O L B O X

ARTICLE. An **article** is a brief nonfiction work on a specific topic. Encyclopedia entries, newspaper reports, and nonfiction magazine pieces are examples of articles. This article was published on the Junior Scholastic Online Internet site on April 11, 1997. What is the topic of the article? What is the main idea?

CONCLUSION. The **conclusion** of an article or essay should sum up the ideas presented in the body and give the reader a sense of resolution.

Graphic *Organizer*

Keep a chart to show the main ideas in this article.

Thesis:	
Supporting Points:	
Conclusion:	

Reader's *Journal*

How do you feel when you see signs of air pollution?

Reader's *Resource*

- The U.S. Environmental Protection Agency (EPA) was set up to protect not only the environment but also human life. People rely on air, water, and the land to live, so when these resources are threatened, human life is endangered. The EPA enforces federal laws designed to protect these natural resources.

- Air pollution is a major problem in the United States and in many other areas of the world. Air pollution can lead to respiratory or breathing problems for many people. It can also cause problems for animals and plants. Pollution from the air can also get into water supplies and cause additional problems.

A Breath of Fresh Air?

Alexandra Hanson-Harding

It started with a dark, soupy haze that hung in the sky during the week of October 25, 1948. When it left, 5,900 people were seriously ill. Twenty more were dead.

It was not a horror movie. It really happened in Donora, Pennsylvania. Back then, many people in the U.S. were struck down by polluted air. In New York City, smog caused 700 more deaths than normal in 1953, 1963, and 1966 combined. Throughout the 1950s, schools and businesses in Los Angeles were closed on a regular basis because of Stage 3 "smog alerts." The air was so dirty, said Edward Camerena, a Los Angeles chemist, "You'd blow your nose and it would be black."

> **GUIDED READING**
> What happened on a regular basis in the 1950s?

Cleaning Up Our Act

The U.S. has come a long way since then. In 1970, Congress passed the Clean Air Act. This law required private businesses and state and local governments to make changes to decrease air pollution. Carmakers had to build cars that leaked fewer harmful gases. Power plants were required to put special "scrubbers" in their smokestacks. These changes—and those required by later laws—have made the air we breathe much cleaner.

> **GUIDED READING**
> What did the Clean Air Act of 1970 require?

Not Clean Enough

Is the air today clean enough to protect people's health? The Environmental Protection Agency (EPA), the government agency that regulates air pollution, says no. Last November, Carol Browner, head of the EPA, announced that the EPA plans to set even tougher standards. After examining hundreds of studies, the EPA found that U.S. standards for two major pollutants were not tough enough. It also says that these two pollutants are costing the U.S. billions of dollars in hospital visits and days lost from work and school. Even worse, the EPA estimates that more than 40,000 people a year die prematurely (earlier than normal) because of dirty air.

The Culprits

What are the two pollutants? The first is ground-level ozone; the second, something called fine particulates.

Ground-level ozone is an odorless, colorless gas that is formed when sulfates react with sunlight. (Sulfates are chemicals released when coal is burned.) Ozone that occurs naturally in the upper atmosphere helps to protect Earth, but ground-level ozone, which is worse on hot days, makes it harder for people to breathe. If people inhale too much of it over time, it can damage their lungs. Children are more likely to be harmed by ozone than adults, because their lungs are

GUIDED READING

What two pollutants are the focus of EPA action?

growing at a faster rate. People with lung problems also are at high risk.

GUIDED READING

What problems does ground-level ozone cause? Who is especially at risk?

The second pollutant, fine particulates, are tiny particles that hang in the air. Some larger particulates are solid pieces of dust or soot. But the EPA is more concerned about the tiniest particulates, which can be inhaled more deeply into the lungs, damaging them. These particulates also contribute to haziness in the air. At some national parks, haze has decreased visibility by more than 77 percent on some days.

Together, ozone and fine particulates cause more than 1.5 million incidents of major breathing and lung problems a year, says the EPA. Such problems include the loss of lung capacity and the <u>aggravation</u> of asthma in both adults and children.

Adam Buchoff, 10, knows the problem first hand. He has asthma, and has to use inhalers (devices used to convey medicine to the lungs). "Sometimes it feels like a gorilla is on your chest," he told *JS*. "It can be tough."

Are Changes Needed?
The EPA has called for tougher standards for both pollutants. Ozone comes mostly from car exhausts and smokestack <u>emissions</u> on hot, sunny days. Particulate matter is caused mostly by power plants and large incinerators.

GUIDED READING

What are the major causes of each of these types of pollution?

The EPA says that the proposed new standards would reduce serious breathing problems in children by 250,000 cases per year. "The EPA proposal would give new protection to nearly 133 million Americans, including 40 million children," says Carol Browner. "We will use the very best science to do what is necessary to protect public health in commonsense, cost-effective ways."

Too Strict?
However, more than 500 organizations are fighting the new regulations, including many carmakers, oil companies, and power-plant owners. More than a hundred members of Congress are siding with them.

GUIDED READING

Who is fighting the EPA's measures?

Why? Some opponents say that the new regulations will be expensive, and that companies will pass the costs on to consumers. The Automobile Manufacturers Group, for instance, estimates that the price of putting additional air-pollution controls on cars will be $2,000 per car. Low-pollutant gasoline could cost an extra five to ten cents a gallon, according to Al Mannato of the American Petroleum Institute (API).

Mannato says that we need to give the latest Clean Air Act, passed in 1990, time to work. Some <u>provisions</u> of the law have not yet taken effect, such as new standards on diesel vehicles and reformulated gas. "Pollution will go down in the future because of regulations that are already in place," he told *JS*.

GUIDED READING

What does Al Mannato say we have to do?

Most of all, he says that scientists do not agree on the effects of these pollutants. Also, says Mannato, there have not been enough studies of fine particulates to make a fair conclusion.

"The science isn't there, and air pollution will continue to go down in the future," Mannato says. "Therefore, the cost associated with these proposals is unjustified."

---

words for everyday use

ag • gra • va • tion (ag rə vā′ shən) *n.,* worsening. *The <u>aggravation</u> of Lindsay's allergies occurs in the summer when pollen counts are high.*

e • mis • sion (ē mish′ ən) *n.,* gas or other substance that is let out. *Cars have to be tested to make sure their <u>emissions</u> are at acceptable levels.*

pro • vi • sion (prō vizh′ ən) *n.,* condition. *The <u>provisions</u> of the law require businesses to make changes.*

Setting Tough Standards

Dave Ryan of the EPA disagrees. He says that the vast majority of studies agree with the EPA's conclusions. "The weight of scientific evidence is with us," he says. "Science is always evolving. The EPA has a mandate [requirement] from Congress to make a decision every five years based on the best science available. That's what we've done."

GUIDED READING
What is the EPA's mandate?

Ryan says that the benefits of the new standards will drastically outweigh the costs. "In the year 2007," says Ryan, "the cost of implementing this for each American will be in a range from $26 to $34 per person. The total price tag will be between $6.5 and $8.8 billion a year. But the benefits per year will range from $70 to $120 billion. Obviously, that's an incredible payback."

A Fierce Battle Ahead

What will happen next? The EPA will complete its regulations in June. Then, Congress will review the new rules. If Congress decides that the plan is too expensive, it can reject it. The battle between opponents and supporters of the new standards is expected to be fierce.

But it is not just up to Congress, says Ryan. Individuals also can make a difference. Turning down the thermostat in cold weather, using cars less often, and recycling are just three ways people can use less energy and send fewer pollutants into the air. That will help kids like Adam Buchoff to breathe more easily. ■

GUIDED READING
What things can individuals do to make a difference?

Respond *to the* SELECTION

Do feel like you can make a difference in cutting pollution?

About *the* AUTHOR

Alexandra Hanson-Harding is a writer for Scholastic Here, she talks a bit about her background and answers a couple of questions.

I grew up in Wilbraham, Massachusetts, and like many kids, I did want to grow up to be a writer. I kept journals since I was 14, and I still do. I have 105 volumes of journals now. After I graduated from college, I moved to New York City to work in publishing. I have been working at Scholastic for 11 years now. I am a Senior Editor for Junior Scholastic, and my main job there is writing stories for 6th to 8th grade kids. It is a very interesting job and I feel quite lucky to have it. I think those are very important years in kids' lives and I feel very honored to create things for them. I am also married to an English teacher, Brian, and I have two sons, Moses, 10, and Jacob, 7, and I live in New Jersey. I have written 8 books for kids and teachers.

As a writer for Scholastic, do you get to write about the things that most interest you? How do you select topics?
I work with my editor and other staff members to develop story ideas. I do get to write about subjects I'm interested in, like history and politics. Lately I've become more interested in the economy and have been able to write some stories about that as well.

When writing an article like "A Breath of Fresh Air?," how do you research your topic?
For "A Breath of Fresh Air?" I did research by reading newspapers, magazines, and material on the Internet. Then I wrote down questions and did interviews with experts and with people who suffered the effects of air pollution. I try to make sure I get different perspectives when I do an article, especially one about a controversial subject. Sometimes the people I enjoy talking to most are the ones who have opinions that are the most different than my own personal opinions.

Investigate, Inquire, and Imagine

Recall: GATHERING FACTS

1a. What kinds of events were common before the Clean Air Act of 1970?

2a. What does the Clean Air Act require of businesses? What would new EPA proposals require?

3a. What can individuals do to help keep the air clean?

Interpret: FINDING MEANING

1b. Why do you think it took so long to do something about such events?

2b. Why do many businesses oppose the EPA proposal?

3b. Are the efforts of individuals as effective as the changes made by businesses? Explain your response.

Analyze: TAKING THINGS APART

4a. Writers use many techniques to engage an audience. Some of these techniques include presenting statistics, using anecdotes or stories, and including quotations or dialogue. Identify three methods the author uses to get the reader to accept her point of view and give an example for each.

Synthesize: BRINGING THINGS TOGETHER

4b. How does each example contribute to the author's main point? What is the author's main point?

Evaluate: MAKING JUDGMENTS

5a. Evaluate whether either industry or individuals are likely to make changes that will help reduce air pollution.

Extend: CONNECTING IDEAS

5b. What arguments do you think are most likely to prompt a change in industry? in individuals?

Understanding Literature

ARTICLE. An **article** is a brief nonfiction work on a specific topic. Encyclopedia entries, newspaper reports, and nonfiction magazine pieces are examples of articles. What is this article trying to persuade readers to believe or do? Is it successful? Why, or why not?

CONCLUSION. The **conclusion** of an article or essay should sum up the ideas presented and give the reader a sense of resolution. Identify the conclusion of this article. How does the author sum up the ideas of the article?

Writer's Journal

1. Write a **slogan** that reflects the main idea of this article.
2. Write a **description** of a place that is polluted. Use vivid details to show how pollution has affected the place.
3. Choose an issue that you care deeply about. Write a **persuasive article** that presents your point of view about this issue.

Skill Builders

Speaking and Listening & Collaborative Learning

STAGING A MOCK RADIO TALK SHOW. Hold a radio talk show about pollution. One or two students should act as the host(s) and moderate the discussion. These students should prepare an introduction to the topic and then open up the phones to questions from listeners. Other students can "call in" to express their opinions on the topic. Some students might also serve as experts in a particular field related to the subject.

Applied English

BUSINESS LETTER. Review the Language Arts Survey 6.6, "Writing a Business Letter." Then, write a letter to the Environmental Protection Agency (EPA) expressing your concern or opinion on air pollution or on another environmental issue.

Study and Research

USING REFERENCE MATERIALS. At your school or local library, look for information about pollution, using the following reference materials: encyclopedias, almanacs, yearbooks, and atlases. What specific information about pollution can you find in each of these sources? Make a bibliography of the reference books you use, and summarize your findings from each one.

for your READING LIST

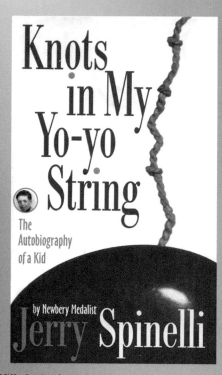

Newbery Medal-winning author Jerry Spinelli was speaking to a group of students in Fargo, North Dakota, when a young boy asked, "Do you think being a kid helped you to become a writer?" In his autobiography, ***Knots in My Yo-yo String,*** Spinelli explores the answer to that question by recalling memories from the first sixteen years of his life as a boy growing up in a tight-knit neighborhood in Norristown, Pennsylvania. Although the sports-crazy Spinelli never thought about becoming a writer, from an early age his love of words and his ability to observe the world around him laid the foundation for his future career. As he remembers the people and places that helped shaped his character, Spinelli touches on themes that are familiar to everyone: love, fear, dreams, and disappointment. From laugh-out-loud humor describing his antics as a "cowboy" to a somber discussion about prejudice, Spinelli's honest examination of his own life encourages others to realize that they too can fulfill their dreams.

BOOK CLUB

After everyone in your literature circle has finished reading *Knots in My Yo-yo String*, set a time and place for discussion. You may wish to review the Language Arts Survey 1.8, "Guidelines for Discussing Literature in a Book Club," for more assistance. The following questions may help you get started:

- What did Jerry dream of becoming when he grew up? Do you think he regrets not fulfilling these early dreams? Why, or why not?
- Would you want to be friends with Jerry? Why, or why not?
- In what ways is Jerry like you? In what ways is he unlike you?
- What chapter did you like best in the book? Which did you like least? Why?
- Which incidents or people do you think had the strongest influence on Jerry?
- What does Jerry mean when he says that he was "king"? How was he dethroned?
- What do you think made Jerry want to become a writer?
- If you were going to write about your life, what experiences would you include?

Other books you may want to read:
Little by Little by Jean Little
Woman of Hope: African Americans Who Made a Difference by Joyce Hansen
Spy by Richard Platt

Guided Writing

To paraphrase means to express someone else's ideas in your own words.

WRITING AN INFORMATIVE RESEARCH PAPER

LOOKING AT THE INFORMATIVE MODE. Just as you depend on others for information, others will, at times, depend on you for accurate information. Teachers, and even future employers, may also require you to present researched information. One way you can present clear information to others is by writing an informative research paper. Before you write the paper, you must first research information from a variety of reliable sources. Then you present the information in a clear and logical way for your readers.

Professional Model

from "Gorillas" by Chris Nelson, pages 771–773

During her time spent closely observing the gorillas, she [Fossey] learned many important things about [the gorillas]. The information she gathered may help the gorillas survive despite being hunted almost to extinction and losing their homeland to farmers....

In a typical day, gorillas awake late, sometimes hours after sunrise. Their first instinct is to eat. Gorillas are mainly herbivores, or plant-eaters, but they have been known to eat insects, slugs, snails, and grubs as well. They eat massive quantities of food each day to support their giant bodies. Gorillas eat fruit when they can get it, and a certain kind of bracket fungus is also a favorite snack, but mainly they eat leaves, flowers, vines, and ripe young bamboo. (Fossey 49)

After a few hours of foraging and eating, the gorillas settle down for noon playtime and naps. Younger gorillas stage rowdy tumble sessions, playfully wrestling with each other and climbing all over the sleeping bodies of the older gorillas. Sometimes they find large round fruits and play a catching game or kick the fruit like a soccer ball. . . .

After resting, gorillas feed once more late in the day and then begin to prepare for the night. Gorillas sleep in nests on the ground or, for the younger, lighter gorillas, in low hanging branches. Often they will sleep inside huge hollow trees, where they are protected from rain and cold. To make a nest, a gorilla will find an area with many low-lying plants, grab the plants,

Examining the Model

In the Professional Model, the writer describes a typical day for mountain gorillas. The writer uses specific examples to help readers understand how the gorillas eat, play, and sleep. The author also uses active verbs to bring the gorillas daily activities to life. Find at least one specific example and the active verb that is used in the example.

The first paragraph of the excerpt provides an introduction to the research paper. It starts with a **thesis statement**, the main idea of the entire paper. The thesis statement gives readers an overview of what the paper will be about. In the excerpt, the thesis statement lets readers know that what Dian Fossey learned about the gorillas may help them survive. The rest of the sentences in the excerpt tell readers some of the things she learned. Find the thesis statement in the introductory paragraph.

Did you notice in the fourth paragraph how the writer includes direct words from

continued on page 802

George Schaller's essay? The writer puts the words in quotation marks and includes Schaller's name and the page number where the words are found in parentheses. The writer also paraphrases some of Dian Fossey's ideas in the second paragraph. Paraphrasing is a form of borrowing, so the writer credits Fossey for this information by putting her name and the page number where the information is found in parentheses. The bibliography following the excerpt shows the complete reference for George Schaller's essay and Dian Fossey's book along with several Internet sites that were used for research.

The last paragraph provides a conclusion to the paper. The writer restates the thesis statement in different words and gives the reader something to think about—when the gorillas will be able to live in peace and safety.

and bend their stems under him or herself. It will then rotate around, bending down plants until it has a firm cushion underneath and a supporting ring surrounding them to keep the nest together. Smaller gorillas will share a nest with their mothers until they learn how to make their own. Naturalist George Schaller, watching a group of gorillas preparing to settle down for the night, observed, "Within minutes, at half past five, all movement had ceased, and the dark forms of the gorillas fused with the night." (Schaller 18) . . .

People in the countries where the gorillas live are learning more about these majestic animals. Scientists like Dian Fossey hope that education will keep gorillas around for future generations to admire, but it will be a long time before the gorillas can live in peace and safety.

Bibliography

Mountain Gorilla Fact File. 29 June 1999.
   <http://www.awf.org/wildlives/149

Schaller, George B. Introductory Essay. *Gorilla: Struggle for Survival in the Virungas.* By Michael Nichols. Ed. Nan Richardson. New York. Aperture Foundation, Inc., 1989, 9–26.

Prewriting

IDENTIFYING YOUR AUDIENCE. The audience for your research paper will partly depend on your topic. Jacob could write about the local steelhead fishing for other members of the fishing club or he could write for a panel of language arts and science teachers. If he decides to write for members of the club, he could use words and concepts that they already understand. If he chooses to write for his teachers, he might need to define specific fishing terms and explain basic fishing concepts.

WRITING WITH A PLAN. Leah didn't have a topic to write about at first. Then she remembered her experience using chopsticks at her friend Shannon's house. It was difficult for Leah to use the chopsticks at first, but Shannon showed her how to hold them and how to place them on the chopstick rest. At the time, Leah wondered about where chopsticks had come from and why they were used. So, she decided to research and write a paper about chopsticks.

What topics come to mind from the personal experiences you have had? What topics are you learning about in science, art, social studies, language arts, music, and math? On another piece of paper, brainstorm a list of topics that you could research. Select the topic that is the most interesting to you.

After you have selected your topic, check to see if you have several resources available at the library. You can also check the Internet for reliable web sites which often provide primary and secondary sources of information.

A primary source is a firsthand account. Leah, for example, found a book called *Cooking the Korean Way* in the library. It is written by Okwha Chyung who was born in South Korea. In the book, the author describes how to use and hold chopsticks. Her account is a primary source since she has used chopsticks for many years. Leah also used a book that simply explained the history of chopsticks. That book is a secondary source.

You should try to use at least one primary source. If you do not have three of four good sources of information including at least one primary source, you may need to think of a different topic.

Leah knew that she had to focus her research paper, so she filled in the graphic organizer below with four questions she wanted to research about chopsticks.

Student Model—Graphic Organizer

Topic: Chopsticks
4 Important Questions to Research
Question 1: How do you use chopsticks?
Question 2: What is the history of chopsticks?
Question 3: What are chopsticks made of?
Question 4: What rules are there for using chopsticks?

Copy the graphic organizer onto your own paper. Fill in your topic. Then write four questions that are important to answer in your informative research paper.

LEARNING TO PARAPHRASE. To paraphrase means to use your own words. When you paraphrase what an author has written, you put it in your own words. Read the paragraph below copied directly from the Cuisenet web site at: http://www.cuisinet.com/digest/region/china/chopsticks.shtml.

Unlike Chinese chopsticks, which are squared-off and blunt at the end, the Japanese utensils are rounded and tapered to a point. It has been suggested that this is in order to facilitate the removal of bones from fish, which makes up a great part of the Japanese diet.

"To treat your facts with imagination is one thing; to imagine your facts is another."

—John Burroughs
in The Heart of Burroughs' Journal

FINDING YOUR VOICE. Your readers expect to learn accurate and interesting information as they read your research paper, so you will want to use a voice that reflects an informed attitude toward your subject. Although you need to write facts and not opinions in your informative research paper, you can still use a voice that shows your enthusiasm for your topic. The voice you use needs to show your readers that the topic is important to you and to them.

Look at the two sentences below. Which one has an informed and enthusiastic voice?

There are some well-known local fish.

Local steelhead are famous for their size and taste as well as their fight when they are hooked.

KEEPING TRACK OF YOUR SOURCES. Take your graphic organizer to the library and collect your reference materials. On a separate piece of paper, write down the title, author, publishing company, place and date of publication, location and call number for each book. Write down the addresses of any reliable Internet web sites you plan to use. Record the names of articles in magazines, along with the magazine titles and dates. You will need your list of sources when you write your bibliography.

See the Language Arts Survey 5.42, "Paraphrasing, Summarizing, and Quoting," for more information.

Language, Grammar, and Style
Documentation

When you use source materials, you need to give credit to the authors for the information you use in your research. For example, if you quote directly from Jenny Ridgwell's book *A Taste of Japan,* published by Thomson Learning in New York, you would need to enclose her exact words in quotation marks. Then you would put her last name and the page number where you found those words in parentheses.

(Ridgwell 25)

You would also need to include this source in your bibliography at the end of your

Which of the following examples would be a good paraphrase of the paragraph above?

Japanese chopsticks are good for eating fish.

Chinese chopsticks are squared-off and blunt at the end. Japanese chopsticks are rounded and tapered at the end. This shape helps the Japanese to remove bones from their fish.

When you paraphrase an author's words in your research paper, you will need to give credit to the author in your paper for those ideas.

TAKING NOTES. Read the questions on your graphic organizer again. Look through each of your sources for the answers to your questions. When you find an answer, you can paraphrase, summarize, or quote the information on a piece of paper or on a note card. Do not copy the author's exact words unless you are quoting the author. To copy another person's words without crediting that person as your source is unethical. You want your research paper to reflect your clear and natural voice. Your notes should be specific, accurate, and brief. You will use your notes later to help you write your draft.

Use a separate card or piece of paper for each note your write. Include the question you are answering, the name of the source you are using, and the page number where you found the information.

USING QUOTATIONS. Try to include two or three important quotations from authors. Use just a few quotations so that the ones you use will be effective. Write the authors exact words on a note card and put quotation marks around them. Reference the quotation in your paper with the author's last name and the page number in parentheses.

ARRANGING THE INDEX CARDS. After you have answered your questions, you need to decide on the best order for presenting the information in your paper. To help decide the order, ask yourself what is the most important or logical thing for my audience to learn first, second, third, and fourth. Put a number 1 next to the question on your graphic organizer that you will write about first in your research paper. Put a number 2 on the question you plan to write about next. Put a number 3 on the third question and a number 4 on the last question.

Now gather all your notes cards together that go with question number 1. Arrange these cards in the order that you plan to use them. Number them as 1-1, 1-2, 1-3, etc.

Then do the same process for the note cards that go with question number 2. Arrange those cards in the order that you plan to use them and number them as 2-1, 2-2, 2-3, etc.

Continue to do the same process for the note cards that go with question number 3 and 4.

You can write your rough draft from your ordered note cards, or your teacher may want you to use your cards to write an outline. See the Language Arts Survey 2.28 for more information about outlines.

Drafting

WRITING THE THESIS STATEMENT AND THE INTRODUCTION. Leah was now ready to write a thesis statement, or main idea, for her informative research paper. To develop ideas for her thesis statement, Leah reviewed her cards. She wanted the thesis statement to give her readers an overview of what they would be learning about in the rest of the paper. She wrote this thesis sentence:

> Eating with chopsticks is not hard once you learn some basic techniques.

Next, Leah added several sentences to her introduction to clearly identify her topic.

> People in several countries have long used wooden chopsticks to eat their food. Eating with chopsticks is not hard once you learn some basic techniques. There are also some very definite manners you need to follow.

Begin your draft with the introductory paragraph, which includes your thesis statement.

WRITING THE BODY. Leah next used her ordered note cards to write the body of her research paper. She wrote at least one paragraph for each of her four questions. As she wrote each sentence, she tried to make sure it supported her thesis statement. She also made sure that each paragraph had a topic sentence.

Use your ordered note cards or your outline to write the body of the paper. Use active verbs, precise language, and smooth transitions between your ideas. Give specific examples that will make your research paper interesting to your readers.

WRITING THE CONCLUSION. Your paper will need to have a conclusion. Use the conclusion to summarize the main points in your paper. Include in your conclusion a summary statement about your thesis and the results of your research. You can restate your thesis statement using different words. Your conclusion could encourage your readers to discover more about your topic or other related topics.

paper. Your bibliography entry should read like this:

> Ridgwell, Jenny. *A Taste of Japan.* New York: Thomson Learning, 1993.

IDENTIFYING THE NEED FOR DOCUMENTATION. Read the following exact words from page 29 of Roz Denny's book *A Taste of China*, published by Thomson Learning in New York in 1994.

> It is considered polite to hold a small bowl of rice up to your mouth and scoop the rice in using chopsticks.

Explain how you would reference this quotation in your paper. Then explain how you would reference this source in your bibliography.

You will also need to reference an author's idea in your paper when you paraphrase it. Read the exact words from page 40 of Lesley Downer's book, *Japanese Food and Drink* published by The BookWright Company in New York in 1988. Then explain how you would paraphrase these words.

> Soup comes in a beautiful lacquered wooden bowl shaped like a large cup. Vegetables or fish are taken out with chopsticks and eaten, then the soup is drunk without using a spoon. It is good manners to slurp.

How would you reference this information in your paper? How would you reference this source in your bibliography?

continued on page 806

FIXING DOCUMENTATION. You need to document sources correctly. To reference a book in your paper, put the author's last name first and the page number where you found the information.

(Visser 179)

Explain how you would fix the documentation in each example below.

(Ridgwell, page 25)

(p. 183, Visser)

(Downer 19)

Look at the reference in Leah's partially revised draft and explain whether it is documented correctly.

USING DOCUMENTATION CORRECTLY. Read your informative research paper again. Are there any places where you paraphrased an author's ideas that you need to reference? Are there any exact quotations that you need to reference? Fix any documentation in the body of your paper. Then look at your bibliography. Be sure each source is documented correctly. For more information, see the Language Arts Survey 5.35, "Documenting Sources."

Student Model—Draft

Leah's draft is shown below. After you read her draft, revise your own draft.

Chopsticks

People in several countries have long used wooden chopsticks to eat their food. Eating with chopsticks is not hard once you learn some basic techniques. There are also some rules you need to follow. *add topic sentence* Chopsticks have been used in Japan since the fifth century. The Japanese call chopsticks *hashi* [italics], That means bridge [incomplete sentence] because chopsticks are like a bridge between the bowl and your mouth. The Chinese have used chopsticks for thousands of years. They call them [italics] K'uai-tzu which means "something fast." Traders called them chopsticks when they [When?] translated the Chinese into pidgin English. Because the word "chop" can mean "fast." [incomplete sentence] [use author's name or site name] (<http:www.cuisinet.com/digest/region/china/chopsticks/shtml>) They are not used to chop food. People in Korea and Vietnam use chopsticks, too. [run-on sentence] Chopsticks are most often made of wood or bamboo some are plastic or ivory. They come in different lengths and colors. Some are beautifully decorated. [lowercase] People in Japan eat a lot of [Because] fish, their chopsticks are rounded and tapered to a point so that they can

806 UNIT ELEVEN

remove the bones in their fish. Chinese chopsticks are squared off and blunt at the end. *use author or name of site* (<http:www.cuisinet.com/glossary/chopsticks.html>) Chinese food is prepared so that it may be easily handled with chopsticks. Chinese rice is sweet, *run-on* sticky, and slightly moist, they work really well for that. (Visser p. 179)

To hold chopsticks, place the thicker end of the first chopstick in the crook of your thumb. Rest the lower part of the chopstick against the inside of your ring finger. You do not move this chopstick when you eat. Put the second chopstick between *good directions!* the tips of your index finger and your middle finger. Hold it with your thumb. Now just move the outer chopstick by bending your index and middle fingers toward the inside chopstick. The tips of your sticks should come together it's sort of like pincers. If you practice, you can do it real well. (Chung 14)

There are definite rules for using chopsticks. Each person has a rice bowl and a pair of chopsticks. The rice is the main part of the meal. People are allowed to hold their rice bowls close to their mouths and to scoop the rice in. (Denny 29) You are supposed to eat every grain of rice. Rice represents all food, so it shouldn't be wasted.

Self- and Peer Evaluation
After finishing your rough draft, you can do a self-evaluation of your work. If time allows, you may also want to do peer evaluations. See the Language Arts Survey 2.37 for more details about self- and peer evaluation.

As you evaluate your research paper draft or that of a classmate, ask the following questions:

- Does the research paper inform the reader about an interesting topic?
- Does the introduction develop interest in the topic?
- Does the introduction include a thesis statement that identifies the research paper's main idea?
- Does the body of the research paper contain a separate paragraph for each idea?
- Does each paragraph have a topic sentence?
- Are specific examples included in each paragraph?
- Are there strong transitions between the ideas in the paragraphs?
- Are active verbs used? Which words could be improved?
- Does each sentence in the body of the paper support the thesis statement? Which ones need improvement?
- Is there a conclusion to the paper that restates the thesis statement?
- Is there adequate and accurate documentation in the paper? Does it contain a separate bibliography?

Revising and Proofreading

Review your self- and peer evaluations. Revise your writing after considering these comments. Check that each paragraph has a topic sentence that is related to your thesis statement. Also check that the details in each paragraph support the topic sentence.

Proofread your revised draft for errors in spelling and grammar. Be sure each source in your paper and in your bibliography is referenced correctly. See the Language Arts Survey 5.35, "Documenting Sources," for more information about documenting sources.

Leah kept her introduction the same, but she revised her next paragraph to include a topic sentence at the beginning of the paragraph. She combined a short sentence with a longer sentence. She took out the sentence about Korea and Vietnam since most of the paragraph was about Japan and China. She added transitional words to the seventh sentence. She also added two sentences to the end of the paragraph explaining where and why chopsticks are used.

(Downer 40). Serving bowls with meat *[incomplete sentence]* and vegetables in the center of the table. When you take something from the serving bowl, you should put it in your own rice bowl, not directly in your mouth. You must take exactly what you touch. There may also be pairs of chopsticks on the serving platters that can be used to bring the food to your bowl.

[topic sentence?] It's rude to point your chopsticks at someone while you're eating. No one should lick their chopsticks or spear food with the points. In Japan, people don't stick their chopsticks straight up in a rice bowl. That's a sign of mourning for the dead (Ridgwell ~~page~~ 22). There are many other rules and a Chinese proverb even says, "If you rattle your chopsticks against the bowl, you and your descendents will always be poor" (Visser 182).

Chopsticks have a long and interesting history. If you practice, you, too, can learn to use chopsticks correctly and to have good manners.

Bibliography

Chung, Okwha and Judy Monroe. *Cooking the Korean Way.* Minneapolis: Lerner
    Publications Company, 1988.

Denny, Roz. *A Taste of China.* New York: Thomson Learning, 1994.

Downer, Lesley. *Japanese Food and Drink*. New York: The Bookwright Press, 1988.

Ridgwell, Jenny. *A Taste of Japan*. New York: Thomson Learning, 1993.

Visser, *The Rituals of Dinner: The Origins, Evolution, Eccentricities, and Meaning of*
        Table Manners. New York: Grove Weidenfeld, 1991.

do these go together?

Diners Digest. ©Cyber Palate LLC. 1996

<http:www.cuisinet.com/digest/region/china/chopsticks.shtml>.

Publishing and Presenting
Write your final copy in ink or print it. Put the bibliography on a separate sheet of paper and attach it to the back of your paper. Add a title page to the front of the paper that includes the title, your name, and date. Include at least one illustration or chart in your research paper. Leah planned to include a four-part illustration showing someone holding chopsticks. Put your research paper in a folder and display it in the classroom for other students to read. Plan to read several of your classmates' papers.

Student Model—Revised

People in several countries have long used wooden chopsticks to eat their food. It's not hard to eat with chopsticks once you learn some basic techniques. There are also some very definite rules you need to follow.

Chopsticks have an interesting history. They have been used in Japan since the fifth century. The Japanese call chopsticks *hashi* which means *bridge*. The chopsticks are like a bridge between the bowl and your mouth. The Chinese have used chopsticks for thousands of years. They call them *k'uai-tzu* which means "something fast." Then in the 19th century, traders called them chopsticks when they translated the Chinese words into pidgin English. They called them chopsticks because the word "chop" can mean fast. (Diners Digest). Today, chopsticks are used not only by people in China and Japan, but in other countries as well. Chopsticks provide a fast and efficient way to eat.

Chopsticks are most often made of wood or bamboo. Some are plastic or ivory. They come in different lengths and colors. Some are beautifully decorated. Because people in Japan eat a lot of fish, their chopsticks are rounded and tapered to a point, so that they can remove the bones in their fish. Chinese chopsticks are squared off and blunt at the end. (Diner's Digest n. pag) Chinese food is prepared so that it may be easily handled with chopsticks. Chinese rice is sweet, sticky, and slightly moist, and the blunt chopsticks work really well for that. (Visser 179)

To hold chopsticks, place the thicker end of the first chopstick in the crook of your thumb. Rest the lower part of the chopstick against eat. Put the second chopstick between the tips of your index finger and your middle finger. Hold it with your thumb. Now just move the outer chopstick by bending your index and middle fingers toward the inside chopstick. The tips of your sticks should come together, sort of like pincers (Chung 14). If you practice, you can do it real well.

There are definite rules for using chopsticks. Each person has a rice bowl and a pair of chopsticks. The rice is the main part of the meal. People are allowed to hold their rice bowls close to their mouths and to scoop the rice in (Denny 29). You are supposed to eat every grain of rice. Rice represents all food, so it shouldn't be wasted (Downer 40). There are also serving bowls with meat and vegetables in the center of the table. When you take something from the serving bowl, you should put it in your own rice bowl, not directly in your mouth. You must take exactly what you touch. There may also be pairs of chopsticks on the serving platters that can be used to bring the food to your bowl.

Rules also dictate what not to do. It's rude to point your chopsticks at someone while you're eating. No one should lick their chopsticks or spear food with the points. In Japan, people don't stick their chopsticks straight up in a rice bowl. That's a sign of mourning for the dead (Ridgwell 22). A Chinese proverb even says, "If you rattle your chopsticks against the bowl, you and your descendents will always be poor." (Visser 182).

Chopsticks have a long and interesting history. If you practice, you, too, can learn to use chopsticks correctly and to have good manners.

Bibliography

Chung, Okwha and Judy Monroe. *Cooking the Korean Way*. Minneapolis: Lerner Publications Company, 1988.

Denny, Roz. *A Taste of China*. New York: Thomson Learning, 1994.

Downer, Lesley. *Japanese Food and Drink*. New York: The Bookwright Press, 1988.

Ridgwell, Jenny. *A Taste of Japan*. New York: Thomson Learning, 1993.

Visser, Margaret. *The Rituals of Dinner: The Origins, Evolution, Eccentricities, and Meaning of Table Manners*. New York: Grove Weidenfeld, 1991.

Diner's Digest. ©Cyber Palate LLC. 1996
    <http:www.cuisinet.com/digest/region/china/chopsticks.shtml>.

UNIT ELEVEN *review*

Review: Words for Everyday Use

Check your knowledge of the following vocabulary words. Choose ten words that you would like to incorporate into your own daily language. For each word, write a short sentence that includes the word in context. To review a word, look back to the page number(s) indicated.

- administer (761)
- abound (763)
- affectation (742)
- aggravation (796)
- ambition (744)
- ascertain (763)
- assemble (762)
- associate (779)
- astute (744)
- banish (763)
- bequest (744)
- celestial (778)
- concoct (781)
- confrontation (752)
- conspire (789)
- consume (761)
- dismay (754)
- emission (796)

- exploit (754)
- flamboyant (750)
- foliage (769)
- grope (787)
- hygiene (743)
- intangible (768)
- intrigue (778)
- ironic (788)
- lavish (744)
- loiter (760)
- meander (769)
- persuade (787)
- profane (763)
- prosper (751)
- prostrate (761)
- provision (740, 796)
- recruit (743)
- reign (782)

- relic (778)
- renovate (745)
- retrograde (781)
- reveal (742)
- ridicule (781)
- rutted (751)
- secluded (761)
- segregate (741)
- shortcoming (743)
- suspend (760)
- taunt (753)
- teeming (788)
- toil (760)
- trough (788)
- unfathomable (769)
- vile (788)
- waning (753)

Review: Literary Tools

Define each of the following terms, giving concrete examples when possible. To review a term, refer to the page number(s) indicated.

- aim (785)
- alliteration (785)
- anecdote (767)
- article (793)
- autobiography (758)
- background information (748)

- biography (739)
- chronological order (748)
- coherence (776)
- conclusion (739, 793)
- concrete details (767)
- image (776)
- imagery (776)

- introduction (739)
- point of view (758)
- repetition (785)
- transition (776)

Reflecting *on your* reading

Theme

Every person and every thing in the universe has a life story. Every animal, plant, and person has evolved, changed, and grown during his, her, or its life span in the universe. This unit offers a wide range of life stories: a wealthy woman, a black athlete, an Apache Indian, an animal, the planets, a young child. Each selection tells a unique story, from a unique point of view.

Genre

Autobiography is the story of a person's life, written by that person. When an author tells the story of their own life, it is written in the first person. The author remembers what happened to them and writes it down. Biography is the story of someone's life written by someone else. Often the author does quite a lot of research to get accurate facts and background on the person they are writing about.

Critical Thinking

What can we know from autobiography that we will never know from biography? Often an autobiography includes things a biographer might not have known. Using the graphic organizer below, interpret the quotes from the firsthand accounts in this unit. Why was it important for the author to write it? What do they want us to know? What does it say about the author?

Quote	Interpretation
Geronimo wrote "Usen [the spirit father] did not intend snakes, frogs, or fishes to be eaten. I have never eaten of them." (764)	
Dian Fossey said, "Often I am asked about the most rewarding experience I have ever had with gorillas. The question is extremely difficult to answer because each hour with the gorillas provides its own return and satisfaction." (768)	
Jerry Spinelli writes, "My eyes were wide, groping for light, but I could not even see the pillow. I wished I had the nerve to run for the light switch." (787)	

Group Project

As a group, choose an aspect of the earth, or of nature, or of the cosmos, and study its life history. You may choose to study the evolution of a mountain range or a river. You could study an animal species, perhaps an endangered species. You could tell the brief life story of a hurricane. You could study the moon or a well-known comet. Ask yourselves questions that will help you do research. What is its name? Was it discovered by someone? How did it change? When was it "born"? How old is it? What else do you want to know about your topic? Once your group has gathered information, create visual aids—photos, drawings, charts—that you can use to illustrate your presentation, and present your study to the rest of the class.

On Your Own

Interview an older member of your family, such as an aunt or uncle or a grandparent, or a close friend of your family. First, make a list of questions to ask this person, so that you will be prepared for the interview. Ask questions about his or her past, background, and family history. Ask the person to tell you stories about his or her life, accomplishments, and significant events. You may want to record the interview in order to capture it. After you think about the information, you may have more questions for the person you interviewed. You may want to conduct a follow-up interview. Once you feel happy with the information you have collected, write a biographical essay on the person's life.

Las Lavanderas, c.1990s. Angel Botello. Private Collection.

Reading between the Lines

INFORMATIONAL AND VISUAL MEDIA

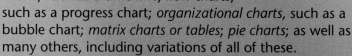

CHART. A **chart** is a visual representation of data that is intended to clarify, highlight, or put a certain perspective on the information presented. There are many types of charts, each with a different purpose or style. Types include *line charts*, such as a time line; *flow charts*, such as a progress chart; *organizational charts*, such as a bubble chart; *matrix charts or tables*; *pie charts*; as well as many others, including variations of all of these.

TABLE. A **table** is a type of chart, also called a *matrix chart*, in which data is placed by matching it with vertical and horizontal categories. Before calculators were invented, many people used multiplication tables instead of calculators to multiply numbers. If you were going to multiply 6 and 9, you would look up the horizontal row for 6 and the vertical column for 9. The number at the intersection of the two categories would be the answer for that multiplication.

GRAPH. A **graph** is a rectangular grid—with horizontal and vertical scales of numbers—that demonstrates change in a set of numbers. The horizontal and vertical scales have *axes* (plural of *axis*) that mark the zero value for that scale and thus cross at the point (0,0), called the *origin*. The horizontal axis is usually called the *x-axis*, and the vertical, the *y-axis*. Graphs have a *coordinate system* using numbers to indicate a point on the two axes. For example, a point with x-axis value 7 and y-axis value 3 would be located at the coordinates (7,3). The most common graph has a value scale (such as height) on the y-axis and time on the x-axis. This sort of graph can, for example, show how much a child grows in a year. The vertical column is marked with height in inches or centimeters, and the horizontal row is marked with the time in months. To figure out the height at a certain month, you simply go to that month on the x-axis and follow the column up until you get to the line of the graph. The value there will be the height of the child at that time.

MAP. A **map** is a representation, usually on a surface such as paper or a sheet of plastic, of a certain geographic area, showing various significant features of that area, depending on the purpose of the map. There are many different kinds of maps, including world, country, state, local, marine (of a body of water), topographical (of elevation), road, trail, and underwater. Maps can also be made of things other than the land, such as star maps, maps of the body, maps of the brain and other organs, or maps of the inner workings of machinery. Maps often have a key or legend to assist in their interpretation.

LEGEND. Similar to a key, a **legend** assists the reader in interpreting a map, graph, chart, diagram, or table by giving the title and subject of the graphic and explaining its significant symbols.

KEY. A **key** is a guide that aids in interpreting and identifying significant marks, especially on a map. Map keys are most often found in boxes in the corners or by the edges of maps. They contain explanations of map symbols and marks, such as boundary lines, roads, types of terrain such as deserts and forests, and other places of significance depending on the map's intended function. Keys can also be included on graphs, charts, diagrams, and tables, serving a similar function as those on maps.

ILLUSTRATION. An **illustration** is a photograph, drawing, or diagram that serves to make a concept clearer by providing a visual example. For example, an encyclopedia entry for the wooly mammoth would have a drawn illustration of what scientists think the mammoth looked like, and perhaps a photo illustration of a real fossilized mammoth skeleton.

DIAGRAM. A **diagram** is an illustration that serves to explain a concept or process, including the arrangement and relations of the various parts of the concept, object, or process.

PERSPECTIVE. **Perspective** is the technique of representing, in an image on a flat surface, the size and distance of objects as they might appear to the eye. This technique is achieved by making the lines of the image converge on one or two points to give the effect of depth—the "3-D" effect. Alternately, *perspective* can mean the point of view from which something is seen or understood.

DISTORTION. **Distortion** is the quality or state of having been twisted out of normal, natural, or original shape, or out of true meaning or proportion. For example, photographs can be distorted to emphasize or shrink elements or to make the image fuzzy or broken, among other effects. Computers are sometimes used to distort pictures for dramatic or humorous effect. *Distortion* can also be an altering of the truth of a piece of information, such as exaggerating a fact or a number.

INTERNET. The **Internet** is a vast system of interconnected computer networks. Network administrators cooperate and use certain *protocols*—or codes for working together—in order to allow information to pass among various otherwise incompatible systems. One of those protocols is HyperText Transfer Protocol (http), which begins the most common site addresses on the Internet.

- *Search Engines* are the tools of choice for navigating the massive, ever-growing Internet. A search engine is a listing of sites, registered in the browser's directory by each site's owner, which can be searched by entering keywords, or topics, pertaining to a subject. Engines can contain tens of millions of sites and are updated constantly.

- *Surfing* is a slang term that simply means browsing through Internet sites. It probably comes from the term *channel surfing*, which originated with the popularity of cable television. Cable gave people so many viewing choices that they would skip from channel to channel, "surfing" the stations for something interesting to watch. The Internet gives an enormous selection of topics and websites, and thus people end up "channel surfing" the Internet, much as they do with cable.

WEB PAGES. Web pages are the basic unit of the World Wide Web, an organizational structure that includes a large part of what is offered on the Internet. World Wide Web page addresses start with http://www.sitename. Their main purpose is to provide information, entertainment, or advertising. These electronic "pages" contain text, pictures, and sometimes animations related to a particular topic. A *web site* is a collection of pages grouped together to organize the information offered by the person, company, or group that owns it.

- The suffix of a web page indicates what type of person or group owns the page. The suffixes ".com" or ".net" are most often commercial organizations, though they can be private individuals as well. The suffix ".org" is used for not-for-profit organizations; ".gov" indicates a government site, ".edu" designates an educational site, and ".co.uk" uses the code for another country, in this case the United Kingdom.

- Web pages can contain "links," or connections to other pages within the site or completely different sites altogether. These connections are mostly in the form of "hotlinks" or "hyperlinks," which are addresses signaled by underlined blue text.

- Web sites, and their pages, are all collected under a domain, the name of the parent site that they belong to. For instance, rapper/actor Will Smith has his own official web site with its own domain, www.willsmith.net.

COMPUTER SOFTWARE. Computer software consists of programs and data that allow a computer to perform various functions. The actual physical components of the computer, such as the monitor and computer chips, are called *hardware*, in which "hard" implies that these are physical things that can be touched. Because programs and data are series of electrical impulses with no real physical substance, they are called "soft"ware.

NEWS ARTICLES. News articles are informational pieces of writing about a particular topic, issue, event, or series of events. News articles can be found in newspapers, magazines, journals, and Internet sites. Broadcast reporters on the radio and on television verbally present forms of news articles.

ADVERTISING. Advertising is the use of media—television, radio, Internet pages, newspapers, magazines, and other publishing formats—to promote a product or service. The intent of advertising is, in most cases, to get a product name out and into the minds of consumers so that they buy the product.

VISUAL ARTS. The **visual arts** include objects that may be two dimensional or three dimensional, stationary or moving. Forms of art include painting, sculpture, drawing, printmaking, collage, photography, video, computer-assisted art, and other forms. Art is a two-part process consisting of the creation by the artist and the interpretation by the viewer. It conveys meaning in ways that draw differing interpretations from different viewers. Concepts and uses of art differ greatly throughout the world and throughout history, but every culture has created objects that have no practical function other than to be visually pleasing and to convey ideas or meaning to viewers.

GETTING INTO MEDIA

Contests! *David LaRochelle*

David LaRochelle is an author and illustrator who has a wide variety of hobbies. Over the years, LaRochelle has entered thousands of contests and has won a few. Here, he answers some questions about contests.

When did you become interested in entering contests?
The first contest I remember entering was a coloring contest in first grade. I won a transistor radio. I've been hooked on contests ever since.

What other types of contests have you entered—and what have been the results?
I've entered a wide variety of contests: building sandcastles, carving watermelons, taking photographs, inventing ice cream flavors, designing new shapes for pasta, identifying songs on the radio, and writing jingles, poetry, and essays.

The prizes I've won have been as varied as the contests. They range from T-shirts, CDs, and a Big Mac belt buckle to furniture, televisions, exercise equipment, and trips. My largest prize to date is $10,000 and a home entertainment center, which I won for creating a video praising the merits of a laxative!

Which contests have been your favorites?
I entered an essay competition in which the object was to nominate a worthy person who brings relief to others. My nominee was the founder of an organization that sends upbeat mail to children with life-threatening diseases.

When my essay was selected as the grand prize winner, I received $10,000, and the woman I nominated received $25,000. It was a great feeling knowing that someone else also benefited from my good fortune.

Another favorite contest was one I entered when I was in seventh grade. Shasta soda pop sponsored a contest, asking entrants to describe in 30 words or less why their 14 flavors of pop were more fun than one. My entry was chosen as one of the first place winners and my prize was a seven-minute shopping spree at a grocery store. I was able to keep all the food that I could get back to the checkout counter within the time limit. The fact that this was my first national win and the unusual nature of the prize made it one of my most memorable contests.

What was your entry for the Shasta contest, and why do you think it won?
I wrote: Shasta's fabulous fourteen flavors are far more fantastic than one flat, foul, fickle, flop of a flavor. They're freezy, frosty, fizzy, and far-out. Finally, they're fun. I'm your fan forever.

The originality and humor of the alliteration probably made my entry stand out from the 75,000 other submissions. I used strong, descriptive language. Also, and very importantly, I followed the rules. I stayed within the 30-word limit and I answered the question of why I thought their fourteen flavors were more fun than one.

It sounds like you have been very successful with entering contests. Do you always win?
Heavens, no! Friends sometimes tell me, "David, you are so lucky! I never win anything." Well, I am lucky, but part of the reason for my luck is that I enter many, many contests. Most of them I don't win, but friends only hear about my successes, not all the times that I lose.

Why do contests appeal to you?
Contests are a great place to take creative risks. I can experiment with something unusual and bizarre, and if it doesn't win, so what? I enjoy the challenge of trying to come up with a unique idea that no one else will submit. And of course, it's always nice to receive an unexpected letter informing me that I've won a prize.

What opportunities have contests given you?
The producer of a locally created gardening show heard about my successes in a pumpkin-carving contest. He asked me to carve a few pumpkins for his television program, which in turn, were seen by the producers of *Good Morning America.* Those producers flew me out to New York City to carve pumpkins live on their show. In preparation, I was up all night carving examples. I'm sure it was the first time anyone used the luxury hotel suite where I was staying as a place to carve pumpkins! At 5 o'clock the next morning I was escorted across the street to the studio. During the show, I was interviewed while carving an intricate jack-o'-lantern. It was very exciting to appear on national television. Later in the day, when I was walking down Broadway in Times Square, several New Yorkers stopped me and

said, "I saw you on TV this morning—great pumpkins!" I felt like a celebrity, at least for the afternoon!

I also credit contests with the publication of my first book, *A Christmas Guest.* I originally wrote the story for a contest sponsored by a local writers' group. When the contest ended, a friend convinced me to send my manuscript to a publisher, where it was accepted as a children's story. That was the beginning of my career as a professional writer.

Is entering contests primarily something you do on your own, or does it involve teamwork?
Most of the contests I enter are solo affairs, but there have been some significant exceptions. For the sandcastle and video contests, I teamed up with a friend to create the winning entries.

Another favorite contest that required a great deal of teamwork was the National Scavenger Hunt sponsored by *GAMES* magazine. The object was to find as many of the thirty unusual objects as possible before the contest's deadline. My close friend Gary Nygaard and I worked together for several months trying to locate these items. I would have never been able to win on my own. Not only are two heads better than one when it comes to generating ideas, but when I was discouraged and ready to give up on ever finding a particular item, Gary's enthusiasm always got me interested again.

What sorts of things did you have to find for this contest?
A Boy Scout merit badge in atomic energy, a high school report card show-

ing both an A and an F grade, a coupon that expired on February 29, a folding paper fan with a picture of a giraffe, the manual from a Betamax VCR, an American Express card that expired in the 1980s.

One of the most challenging things we had to locate was a St. Patrick's Day card printed in German. We tried Irish pubs, greeting card companies, ethnic restaurants, as well as writing letters to our friends all across the country. Eventually we contacted a foreign language camp where somebody there had a relative in Germany who found a card and mailed it to us just days before the deadline.

We ended up winning first place. Our prizes were deluxe editions of Monopoly, Scrabble, and Chinese checkers which we sold for enough money for a trip to Paris.

How have contests sharpened your writing skills? Have they sharpened other skills as well?
Entering jingle and essay contests has taught me the importance of using strong, powerful language. When you are limited to 25 or 50 words, there is no room for any weak or unclear word choices. My editing skills have also improved. I often rewrite my entries many times before I am able to say what I want while staying within the word limit. These skills are particularly helpful in writing picture books, where the text is often sparse yet still needs to capture the reader's interest.

Contests have taught me other important skills too. Without a doubt the more contests I've entered, the more creative I've become. The scavenger hunt taught me valuable research skills, as well as the importance of teamwork and persistence. I've also learned that it never hurts to try. More than once I've been disappointed with an entry and thought, "Why did I even bother entering? I'll never win." Months later I may be surprised to discover that this entry won an honorable mention, or even first prize.

As you conduct writers' workshops for young authors, you encourage kids to enter contests. What advice do you give them?
These are my four tips for winning contests:

1. Enter. You'll never win unless you try.
2. Follow the rules. This includes paying attention to the deadline, word limit (if any), and judging criteria. It also means making sure your entry fits the contest's theme. If a contest asks you to tell how healthful a product is, for example, make sure that's the focus of your entry.
3. Be creative. Judges are often faced with thousands of entries. Unless your entry is somehow unique, it will be lost in the crowd. Creating an original contest entry usually requires time. The first idea that pops into your head will probably pop into the heads of thousands of other people as well. Take the time to brainstorm other possibilities, and also take the time to create the best entry you can.
4. Don't get hung up on one contest. When you are finished with your entry, move on to the next contest. This also means not being discouraged if you don't win. I've lost hundreds of contests, but the reason I've been successful is that I've continued to enter.

Explain your "55 words or less" contest that you conducted at a recent young authors conference for middle school students. Where did you get the idea? How many kids entered and what were the results?

This contest was inspired by Steve Moss's "Fifty-Five Fiction" writing contest. I had just finished reading his book *The World's Shortest Stories*, which contains many of the winning entries from this contest.

I decided to have students try their hands at writing a complete story in 55 words or less. Although they had very little time to work—not much longer than ten minutes—they came up with some impressive stories. About 40 students turned in finished entries, and these were the top three winners:

Writer's Block Battle • By Billy French • Wayzata Central Middle School

Lifting up my trusty pencil, I blocked my opponent's blow. A smirk of satisfaction crossed his face. Writer's Block was a deadly adversary, and was sure of uncreative victory. But as our swords clashed, words flew to the blank page. Before I knew it, I had a story! Author: 1, Writer's Block: 0.

Swimsuit • By Nellene Benhardus • St. Anthony Middle School

Brushing back my golden hair, I approach the beach. I notice eyes staring as I stride across the sand. Laying my towel out, I sit, absorbing the sun.

"Alli?"

"Yeah?"

"Finished yet?"

I step out of the dressing room and show Mom the suit I've selected.

She sighs. "Man, you're slow!"

[no title] • By Michelle Reinke • Wayzata Central Middle School

"I'll be right back."

The thought of fresh, chocolaty cookies filled my mind.

Racing over across the kitchen, I grabbed a chair, dragging it along the floor. Clambering up, my arms reached for the lid. I could smell it. I peered inside.

Empty?!?

My mom came back and I spied the crumbs on her face.

These students were winners because they demonstrated the traits of a successful contestant: they entered, followed the rules, and had original, creative ideas. Not only are they successful contestants, they are successful authors as well.

Prereading

Earth from Space

Reader's Resource

- **SCIENCE CONNECTION.** One of the important areas of study in America's space program is Earth. The National Aeronautics and Space Administration (NASA) uses space travel opportunities and technology to focus on the earth, its climate patterns, and shifts in its surface. Photographs taken from space allow scientists to examine the atmosphere, the water cycle, land-use trends, the ozone, storms such as hurricanes, and other natural disasters like earthquakes and tidal waves.

- NASA began its research in space in 1958. Since that time, great strides have been made in science, technology, and knowledge about space and about Earth. In the first ten years, NASA scientists made advances with rockets and satellites and saw Earth from space for the very first time. This global view allowed researchers to study earth sciences as a whole, collecting data about many aspects of the world from many different sites on the globe. A major highlight occurred in 1969, when astronauts walked on the moon for the first time. In the 1970s, Apollo missions, the Lunar Rover, and the Skylab made the headlines. In the 1980s, satellites put in space allowed technological advances in earth studies. Radar imaging and remote sensing became important in these studies. In the 1990s, further technological advances in earth studies added to longer missions in the solar system and in-depth studies of Mars and other planets.

- Many photos of Earth are taken from numerous space transportation system (STS) missions. These spacecraft are commonly known as space shuttles.

Reader's Journal

How would it feel to be out in space looking back on the earth?

Reader's TOOLBOX

PERSPECTIVE. Perspective is the technique of representing, in an image on a flat surface, the size and distance of objects as they might appear to the eye. This technique is achieved by making the lines of the image converge on one or two points to give the effect of depth—the 3-D effect. How do these photographs assist the viewer in understanding the perspective from which they are taken?

CONCRETE AND ABSTRACT IMAGES. Just as there are concrete words (red table, cold icicle) and abstract words (tired happiness, hopeful future), there are **concrete images** and **abstract images** in photographs like those on the following page. You can look at a picture of the sky, for example, and see white and gray clouds. Or you might see in the shapes of the clouds a picture of a car or a giraffe. As you view these photographs of Earth, look for continents, bodies of water, and clouds. What else do you see?

Earth
from Space

Mount Everest and the Himalayas, Tibet, and Nepal, taken from *Space Transportation System 66,* November 1994. ▼

▲ Earth partly covered in clouds, taken from *Apollo 16,* April, 1972.

▲ Earth over the lunar north pole, taken from *Clementine,* March 1994.

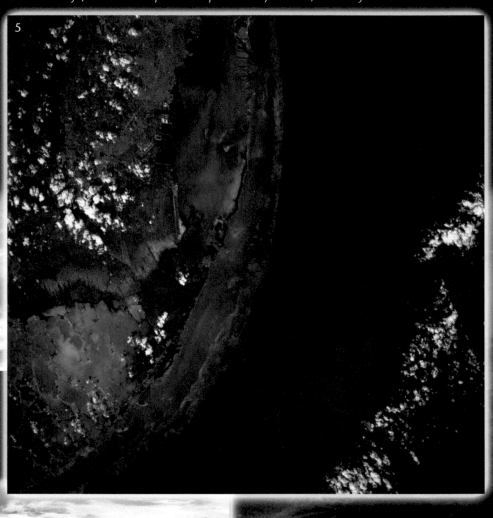

▼ Florida Keys, taken from *Space Transportation System 75,* February 1996.

5

◄ Colorado, Nevada, Utah, and Wyoming, taken from *Space Transportation System 62,* March 1994.

Critical Thinking
- From what perspective are the pictures taken?
- How are picture #2 and picture #3 different?
- What concrete images do you see in picture #4?
- What abstract images can you picture in your mind from picture #5?

What abstract figures or "pictures" do you see in these photos of the earth?

RELATED READING   May Swenson

ORBITER 5 SHOWS
HOW EARTH LOOKS FROM THE MOON

There's a woman in the earth, sitting on
her heels. You see her from the back, in three-
quarter profile. She has a flowing pigtail. She's
holding something
in her right hand—some holy jug. Her left arm is thinner,
in a gesture like a dancer. She's the Indian Ocean. Asia is
light swirling up out of her vessel. Her pigtail points to Europe
and her dancer's arm is the Suez Canal. She is a woman
in a square kimono,
bare feet tucked beneath the tip of Africa. Her tail of long hair is
the Arabian Peninsula.   A woman in the earth.

A man in the moon.

Investigate, *Inquire,* and Imagine

Recall: GATHERING FACTS

1a. From what perspective is picture #1 taken? What evidence can you see that the picture is of the earth?

2a. What geographical forms do you see in picture #2? in picture #3? How do the images differ?

3a. How do pictures #4 and #5 differ?

Interpret: FINDING MEANING

1b. How is this perspective different than the perspective in which you see the earth?

2b. Why do you think NASA scientists and other people who study the earth need both kinds of pictures?

3b. How would you know about these differences without the captions?

Analyze: TAKING THINGS APART

4a. Compare and contrast the five pictures of the earth shown on pages 824–825. In what major ways do they differ from one another? What do they have in common?

Synthesize: BRINGING THINGS TOGETHER

4b. Besides concrete representations of the earth, what other images are suggested in these pictures? How do these pictures help society? How do you think these pictures have influenced the American public?

Evaluate: MAKING JUDGMENTS

5a. How much or how little information do you think people can gather from photographing the earth from space? What non-scientific value do these pictures have?

Extend: CONNECTING IDEAS

5b. In "Orbiter 5 Shows How Earth Looks from the Moon," how does May Swenson describe the picture of Earth she had seen? How can abstract images in photographs lend themselves to the creation of poetry? Think of another type of photograph about which a poem could be written.

Understanding *Media*

PERSPECTIVE. Perspective is the technique of representing, in an image on a flat surface, the size and distance of objects as they might appear to the eye. This technique is achieved by making the line of the image converge on one or two points to give the effect of depth—the 3-D effect. After analyzing and observing these photos, from what perspective are the photos taken? How do the photographers use size and distance to convey their perspective?

CONCRETE AND ABSTRACT IMAGES. Just as there are concrete words (red table, cold icicle) and abstract words (tired happiness, hopeful future), there are **concrete images** and **abstract images** in photographs like those on pages 824–825. What concrete images did you see in the photos? What abstract images did you see? What images are created in your mind as you read the poem, "Orbiter 5 Shows How Earth Looks from the Moon"?

Writer's Journal

1. Write a **short story** using one of the photos on pages 824–825 as the setting for your story.

2. Imagine that an astronaut is coming to visit your school. Write five **interview questions** to ask him or her that would help you gain insight on both the Earth and the moon from the astronaut's experience.

3. Create a **title** or **heading** for two of the photos that reflect the images portrayed in the photos.

Skill Builders

Applied English

PHOTOGRAPHY. Editors and publishers who make books, magazines, and journals often have to come up with ways to illustrate literary works. Find or compile a short collection of poems that you would like to illustrate. Brainstorm a list of images that you think would best illustrate each poem. Then, with a camera, set out to capture those images on film. Will you want to use black-and-white or color film? Will you shoot outdoors or indoors, where you will need a flash? Will you photograph people, objects, or scenes? After taking your pictures and developing your film, choose one photograph to accompany each poem. Then, compile the poems and photos into a book.

Study and Research & Collaborative Learning

PLANET RESEARCH. Gather into groups of four or five people. Choose a planet that your group would like to learn more about. Use the Internet and library materials to help you find information on your planet. Include information about geography, climate, size, the position from the sun, and other information that makes the planet unique from all the other planets. Then present your information to the rest of the class in an oral presentation. You may want to use visual aids to make your presentation more interesting and more engaging for your audience. Refer to Language Arts Survey 6.11, "Displaying Effective Visual Information."

Prereading

from *Dear Ms. Demeanor*
by Mary Mitchell

Reader's Resource

- **MEDIA LITERACY CONNECTION.** The first recognizable columnist in America was Benjamin Franklin (1706–1790). The year was 1722, the place, Boston, Massachusetts. Franklin was 16 years old when he slipped articles under the printing house door of his brother's newspaper company. Franklin disguised himself under the pen name Silence Dogood, who he described as a young widow. He did this because he felt that his brother, James, wouldn't publish anything with the name "Benjamin Franklin" on it. The trick succeeded, resulting in 14 Dogood letters published in the *New England Courant* from April to October 1722. James eventually found out the true authorship of the articles, so he fired Benjamin, who was working as an apprentice at the time. Benjamin left Boston and ended up in Philadelphia, where he became a success writing numerous columns.

- Advice columnists Abigail Van Buren and Ann Landers are household names. In 1918 Abigail Van Buren was born Pauline Esther Friedman and Ann Landers, Esther Pauline Friedman. As twin sisters, they not only resemble each other in looks, but they also resemble each other in their careers and in their commitments to humanity. They both began to write advice columns around the same time in the mid-1950s.

- The word *demeanor* means "way of behaving toward others" or "manners." The word *etiquette* means "social code of correct behavior" or "good manners." Mary Mitchell, using the name Ms. Demeanor, writes a popular newspaper advice column for kids. Her down-to-earth explanations of basic polite behavior answer young people's real concerns about social situations in their daily lives.

Reader's Journal

Do you like to read advice columns in the newspaper or magazines? Why, or why not?

Reader's TOOLBOX

ACTIVE VERBS. Active verbs express meaning more emphatically and vigorously than passive verbs such as the verb form of *be* (*be, am, is, are, was, were, been*). As you read, look for examples of active verbs in Ms. Demeanor's responses.

TONE AND REGISTER. Tone is a writer's or speaker's attitude toward the subject and audience. **Register** is a subset of language usage specific to a particular relationship between people. An author chooses a specific register, such as formal, informal, polite, firm, or humorous. Tone is reflected in the author's word choices and in more subtle ways to create a piece that is friendly, enthusiastic, helpful, remorseful, or that reveals another tone. In deciding on a level of formality, a writer considers both the subject and the audience. For most professional writing, such as a school paper or a letter of application for a job, some degree of formality is appropriate. It would be a mistake to sound too casual and relaxed. But for private letters, articles in popular magazines, or advice columns, casual and informal language can be more appropriate. Slang is informal vocabulary that expresses the solidarity of a group. As you read, point out three examples of slang words or phrases used in Ms. Demeanor's column. Also point out three examples of formal word choices.

Dear Ms. Demeanor

Mary Mitchell

Apologies

Q. I hit a baseball through my neighbor's window. He was really upset and angry. He's really old, too, and when I tried to apologize, he just grumbled. What should I do?

A. Oops. Poor guy can hardly be blamed for being upset, can he? Sometimes older folks find communicating with young people frustrating because their hearing isn't sharp or the person they're trying to communicate with doesn't speak clearly. Since the personal approach wasn't successful, try writing.

You must apologize and make amends. Send a letter and apologize again for the trouble you caused. It might read something like this:

Dear Mr. Smith:
   Please accept my apology for breaking your window the other day. It was careless of me, and I feel bad about it. I know all the trouble it has caused you. If you would like, I will repair the window myself. If you have made other arrangements, please send me the bill so that I can pay for the damage.
                                    Sincerely,
                                    Bobby Jones

Remember that there is more to a letter than just words. Be sure that you use clean stationery. Write in ink, not pencil. Make a

GUIDED READING

What does Ms. Demeanor suggest to the letter writer?

scratch copy first if you feel clumsy about writing.

The date should be at the top, on the right side of the paper. Start the "Dear Mr. Smith" below the date and at the left, a little in from the edge of the paper. Indent the first word of each paragraph about one inch. The all-purpose closing for just about any kind letter is, *Sincerely*. It is especially appropriate for a letter of apology to someone older than you, or in a formal letter such as a business letter.

GUIDED READING

What is the all-purpose closing for any letter?

You'll probably want to deliver your letter by hand, since he is a neighbor. Even so, write your name, street address, and city and state with zip code at the top left corner on the front of the envelope. Your neighbor's full name, such as Mr. John Smith, goes in the center of the front of the envelope with your city and state underneath. Don't abbreviate the state name.

Properly addressing anything you send is a way to show respect for the person who will receive it. Never omit honorifics—*Mr.*, *Mrs.*, *Ms.*, or *Miss*—from an envelope. The only other word which can be abbreviated on an address is *Dr.* for *Doctor*. Write everything else out in full.

Condolences

Q. My friend's father died. I went to the funeral, but now I want to send her a letter, too. How should I do it and what should I say?

A. Regardless of whatever else you have done—attended the funeral, sent flowers, paid a visit to your friend's home, telephoned—the condolence letter is a must. You should be congratulated for

thinking of it. Such letters are comforting and diverting for those who have suffered a loss. Some even become part of a family history to be passed down to future generations. Forget about buying sympathy cards or condolence cards. They are impersonal and the easy way out.

GUIDED READING

What does Ms. Demeanor say about buying cards? What is her reason?

Write your letter in ink. Use a fountain pen if you have one. A ballpoint will do if you don't, but it isn't very refined. Try to use black ink. If you own personal note paper, use it. If not, ask your parents for some good stationery. If your handwriting is hard to read, go ahead and type the letter or have someone type it for you. Sign it in ink.

What you write depends on how you feel. Write from the heart. Don't try to be formal; it comes out wooden and impersonal. At the very least, acknowledge your friend's loss. Say how sad you are about it. If you and your friend's father shared time together, mention that and any special memories of it. Say how much he will be missed. Offer your friend your help. The condolence letter is the place to recall in more detail the special characteristics of the deceased, visits to your home, lessons learned from that person, good times shared, etc. Such reminiscences celebrate the life of the deceased rather than being morbid and depressing about the loss. The shared memories of that life and times become treasured by the family of the person who has died.

GUIDED READING

What does Ms. Demeanor say about being formal?

Pen Pals

Q. I have a pen pal in Australia who lives on a vineyard. He writes the greatest letters. They are so good, I read them to my parents and friends. But I live in Raleigh, North Carolina, and I think my letters are boring. How can I make my letters more interesting?

A. First of all, Raleigh probably sounds pretty interesting to your pen pal because it is so far away. Don't give yourself a bad rap that you don't deserve. America is probably as interesting to him as Australia is to you. Also, the very fact that you have a pen pal indicates you probably are an interesting and curious individual. You probably communicate that about yourself without being aware of it. The funny thing about letter writing is that we all love to receive them, but we all think they're a chore to write. The easiest way to get started is to write the way you talk. Think of a letter as a one-sided conversation. Write the things you would say or ask your pen pal if you were together in person.

I think the surest way to make a reader yawn from the start is to write "How are you? I am fine." There are many interesting ways to start a letter. You might want to begin with something like "Last night I saw a television program about vineyards, and you came to mind. Your letters make me feel like I have real inside information." The goal of letter writing is to draw the reader into your written conversation as quickly as you can. You can tell your friend something you did that was exciting, fun, or wonderful; for example, "Today I went to Sea World and petted a dolphin for the first time. It would have been great if you could have been there, too. Do they have a Sea World where you live?"

It is much more interesting to write specific questions. They make the reader feel part of your conversation. Think about how you would feel if someone wrote to you and asked, "Have you recovered from the flu yet? What did you do when you had to stay in? Did you see anything special on TV? Read anything great?"

By comparison, think about how you would respond to "How are you? I'm fine." Both are basically the same questions. The difference is in how you ask.

Go ahead and use exclamation points to underline sentences or phrases if you want. In a personal letter these devices convey your enthusiasm. Steer clear of apologies for not writing sooner. They only make your letter sound like you're writing to fulfill an obligation rather than writing for the fun of it. Make your letter enthusiastic and full of your own personality. That will make your pen pal feel your letter was worth waiting for.

RSVP

Q. I got an invitation to a party. At the bottom of the invitation it said, "regrets only." What does that mean, and what should I do about it?

A. *Regrets only* written at the bottom of an invitation means (strictly speaking) that if you cannot attend, you are expected to tell the host in advance. If you plan to attend, you don't have to call to accept the invitation.

However, if you were a host planning a party, wouldn't you want your guests to let you know one way or the other? Wouldn't you like to know that they were pleased to be invited and looking forward to coming? I know I would, so go ahead and do it.

> **GUIDED READING**
> What is the surest way to make a reader yawn?

> **GUIDED READING**
> What does *regrets only* mean?

Call the host and tell him or her that you received the invitation, how excited you are about the party, and that you plan to attend. If you cannot attend, do the same thing. Explain that you won't be there. Respond immediately to any invitation and be sure to stick to your commitment. Nothing is worse than holding out until the last possible moment in case you receive a "better offer."

RSVP is used most often on invitations. It is a request for a reply. It means "Respond if you

please" in French (not, "Roast skunk very possible," as in the comic strip "L'il Abner"). If the RSVP is followed by a telephone number, just call the host. Sometimes the letters are followed by the host's address. In that case, send the host a short note right away. Indicate whether you'll be able to attend.

These guidelines will serve you well for most informal invitations sent today, the kind with casual wording on colorful, printed, fill-in-the-blank cards. Formal invitations are a different story. They require a bit more homework. ∎

Respond *to the* SELECTION

With which advice do you agree? With which don't you agree? Why? Do you think Ms. Demeanor gives good advice? Why, or why not?

About *the* AUTHOR

Mary Mitchell is the syndicated etiquette columnist otherwise know as Ms. Demeanor. Mitchell's advice column on manners for children and teens evolved from a class she taught in an urban school. She is also the owner of a corporate training firm in Philadelphia called Uncommon Courtesies. Her company gives advice on business manners in and out of the boardroom and practical etiquette advice for the use of e-mail, faxes, pages, cell phones, and handshakes.

Her book, *The Complete Idiot's Guide to Business Etiquette,* reflects these ideas. In her role as Ms. Demeanor, Mitchell has corresponded with children from all over the country and has answered questions about what to do in all kinds of social situations. She compiled her correspondences into a book called *Dear Ms. Demeanor: The Young Person's Etiquette Guide to Handling Any Social Situation with Confidence and Grace,* from which this selection is taken.

Investigate, _Inquire,_ and Imagine

Recall: GATHERING FACTS

1a. When the boy tried to apologize, how did the old man respond?

2a. What are some things you can do for a friend who has experienced the death of a loved one?

3a. Name three ways to make a letter interesting.

4a. According to Ms. Demeanor, how should a person respond to an invitation?

→ **Interpret:** FINDING MEANING

1b. What are some of the advantages of writing an apology instead of verbalizing an apology?

2b. Why does Ms. Demeanor say that a "condolence letter is a must"?

3b. How do these things liven up a letter?

4b. Why is it important to respond this way?

Analyze: TAKING THINGS APART

5a. List the different suggestions and tips Ms. Demeanor offers to letter writers. Which seem most important?

→ **Synthesize:** BRINGING THINGS TOGETHER

5b. Altogether, what do these tips and suggestions mean? How might you summarize Ms. Demeanor's ideas about letter writing?

Evaluate: MAKING JUDGMENTS

6a. How is the language used by Ms. Demeanor different from that of most adults? Why do you think she writes this way?

→ **Extend:** CONNECTING IDEAS

6b. Compare Ms. Demeanor's advice with advice you have gotten from a parent or another adult. How is it similar? How is it different?

Understanding _Media_

ACTIVE VERBS. Newspaper columnists continually try to stimulate the reader's eye with catchy language. **Active verbs** express meaning more emphatically and vigorously than passive, or inactive, verbs such as the verb form of _be_ (_be, am, is, are, was, were, being, been_). Identify five places in which Ms. Demeanor uses active verbs instead of inactive verbs.

TONE AND REGISTER. Tone is a writer's or speaker's attitude toward the subject and toward the reader. **Register** is a subset of language usage specific to a particular relationship between people. An author chooses a specific register, such as formal, informal, polite, firm, or humorous. Tone is reflected in the author's word choices and in more subtle ways to create a piece that is friendly, enthusiastic, helpful, remorseful, or that reveals another tone. In deciding on a level of formality, a writer considers both the subject and the audience. For the following forms of writing, write an *F* if it requires the use of formal language, or an *I* if informal language is acceptable.

Graphic

Personal narrative	I
Book review for the *New York Times*	
Thank-you note to a neighbor	
Letter of condolence to a friend	
Paper on nuclear war	
Step-by-step procedures to a chemistry experiment	
Résumé	
Obituary for the newspaper	
Journal entry in a diary	
Testament in a will	

Writer's Journal

1. Imagine you damaged a neighbor's property and want to apologize. Write a **letter of apology** indicating how you plan to make amends.

2. Write a **letter to the editor** about one of the advice columnists in your local newspaper. Do you agree or disagree with the advice he or she gave concerning a specific question? Should he or she continue to give advice? Why, or why not?

3. Write a semiformal **invitation** to a party. Include the purpose, date, and time.

Skill Builders

Media Literacy

ANALYZING ADVICE COLUMNS. Many advice columns deal with issues related to growing up, family, relationships, etiquette, and social problems. Not only does the advice offered reflect the values of the person giving the advice, but it also reflects the cultural values of a society. At your local library or on the Internet, find advice columns published in countries other than the United States. Foreign newspapers, magazines, and Internet sites publish advice columns similar to the popular ones in the United States. Ask Zesi (Kenya), Agony Aunt (Britain), and Hassling Heather (Australia) are some popular advice columnists.

Read some of the questions you find in foreign publications, and respond from your point of view, keeping in mind your own cultural values. Then read the answers given by the foreign advice columnists. How do your responses differ from theirs? How do the differences in responses reflect the differences in culture? What do the similarities in the responses suggest about each culture?

Language, Grammar, and Style

ACTIVE AND PASSIVE VOICE. Active verbs express meaning more emphatically and vigorously than passive verbs, such as forms of the verb *be (be, am, is, are, was, were, being, been)*. Active verbs make the point more forcefully and clearly. Review the Language Arts Survey 3.35, "Making Passive Sentences Active." The following sentences are all written in the passive voice. Rewrite each sentence so that it is in the active voice by replacing inactive verbs with active verbs. You may also need to rearrange the words in the sentence. Write the new sentence on a separate sheet of paper. The first one is done for you.

EXAMPLE   We were headed toward the field.
             We jogged toward the field.

1. The fly ball was caught by Hernando.
2. The campfire was put out by the ranger.
3. The operation is managed by Dr. Ahmed.
4. Players were booed by fans on both sides of the rink.
5. Julia was failed by her driving instructor.
6. Fireworks were exploded by pranksters.
7. The tree was struck by lightning.
8. I am greeted by my dog.
9. I was being attacked by the stray cat.

Prereading

BEADS & BANGLES

Reader's Resource

- **CULTURAL CONNECTION.** In Africa, more than in any other part of the world, beads have played an integral role in the daily life of Africans. Even today, beads are worn for protection, for tribal identification, and to indicate status, wealth, power, and age. Before the arrival of traders in the late 1400s, ornaments were crafted from many materials: berries, animal teeth, stones, shell, and bone. After trade began, multicolored glass beads from Bohemia and Venice were traded in Africa for gold, spices, ivory, and slaves.

- **CULTURAL CONNECTION.** Everyone has seen Native American beadwork in earrings, necklaces, watchbands, belts, purses, and other items. Because of its popularity, however, American Indian beadwork is often imitated by factories and sold inexpensively. Nevertheless, traditional beading is still done by Native American artisans. For example, they still make beads from bone, sea shells, stone, turquoise, and other semi-precious stones, and the process has not been affected by modern technology. Artisans create most of the finest beadwork only for relatives and as gift giveaways, because of the enormous amount of work that goes into it. For example, to fully bead the upper sleeves of a buckskin dance dress, it takes 20 pounds of tiny seed beads and about a year of work. Women wear these dresses for dancing in a powwow—a highly religious and traditional ceremony in some Native American tribes.

Graphic Organizer

Pick out three different kinds of beads from the catalog and fill in the information in the chart below.

Name/Description of Item	Style #	Color	Quantity	Price
1.				
2.				
3.				

Reader's Journal

If you could make beaded jewelry, which would you choose to make? Why?

Reader's TOOLBOX

ILLUSTRATION. An **illustration** is a photograph, drawing, or diagram that serves to make a concept clearer by providing a visual example. For example, if you look up the word *kite* in a dictionary, there may be a picture of a kite to illustrate how it looks. In this selection, how does the illustration of the beads help you in deciding which beads you would choose to order?

ORDER FORM. An **order form** is a printed or typed document with blank spaces for insertion of required or requested information. People fill out order forms for many things. For example, when people want to buy music or clothes from a catalog, they must fill out an order form. In this selection, what kind of information is asked of the customer in the order form?

BEADS and CORDING

Red Horn Bead

#25-171   Irregular 4mm Red Horn Bead
2.50/strand   20.00/10 strand

NEW! Bone Bead Sample Assortment

#45-390   1 pair of *each* of the new Carved Bone
Tubes, Donuts, Horns, and *Claws.*
30 beads total. These bone beads are all hand carved,
so will vary slightly in size and pattern. Assortments
are made with colors currently in stock. Some pairs
may be antiqued, others will be natural bone color.

$16.00/per assortment pack
(Average cost per bead: 53¢)

1mm Lace Adjuster

#25-001   Porcelain 1mm Double Lace Adjustor
Designed to make adjustable or double strand
necklaces or bracelets, using 1mm cord.

White or Brown   3.00/doz   15.00/100

Turquoise Nuggets
with Extra Large Hole

At the time we sent this to the printer,
we didn't have these in yet, so we couldn't
price them . . . By the time you see this,
however, they will be in stock and priced.
If interested, please call for prices.

#20-486   9-15mm Blue (with Matrix) Turquoise Nuggets
1/8" Hole; easily fits 2mm cord.

Imitation Sinew

- New stock numbers
- New quantity and price
- Flat 1/8" (2.5mm) sturdy light brown cord
- Great for heavy ceramic beads, trade beads, and "mountain man" designs
- When twisted, will fit beads with 1mm hole

NYMO BEAD CORD
size "B" (medium weight)

#61-129   Size "B" Nymo Bead Cord
A bit thicker than "A" and "O" listed in our
Spring catalog.
See Brass Wire Needle or Big Eye Needle,
page 15, Spring catalog, or use
"Sharps," found in most craft or fabric stores.

.60/each   6.00/doz   24.50box (80 bobbins)

#61-600	60 foot bobbin	1.25
#61-604	4 oz (150 yard spool)	4.50
#61-608	8 oz (300 yard spool)	7.00

BASIC GLASS BEADS and NEW COLORS

AB and Iris Round Glass Beads

#23-244   4mm Round Glass Beads, Fancy Colors
1.75/100   15.00/Mass

Colors Available

Ruby AB   Emerald AB   Crystal AB
Sapphire AB   Amethyst AB
Blue Iris   Purple Iris

#23-246   6mm Round Glass Beads, Fancy Colors
2.75/100   25.00/Mass

Colors Available

Emerald AB   Sapphire AB
Crystal AB   Amethyst AB

Cobalt Blue and Ruby Islamic Beads

#22-860   Islamic Glass Beads
with embossed Gold Moon and Stars.
The new ruby and dark cobalt
are beautiful in sunlight!

Cobalt or Ruby   9.00/50   16.00/100

We're still out of the original black (which was on
page 76 in the Spring catalog), but we'll keep you
updated on in-stock colors.

BEADS & BANGLES

200 N. Front - Suite 6
P.O. Box 410
Spokane, WA 99210-00450

FAX 509 555 2602
✆ Phone (509) 555-8565

Toll Free Order Line
1 (800) 555-2156

LEAVE THIS BLANK	T	P	Rcvd
			Pmt

Name of Business _The Bead Corner_
Name of Individual _Frances Graceful Bear_
Street _3100 Euclid Avenue_
City _Cleveland_
Phone Number (_800_) _555-3460_ State _OH_ Zip _44115_
Date _10/19/xx_

❑ Is this your first order?
❑ Is this a change of address?

❑ COD ☒ Open Acct. ❑ Prepaid ❑ VISA ❑ MasterCard ❑ Other

Bankcard # _____

Signature _____ Exp. Date _____

SHIP VIA
☒ UPS
❑ UPS 2nd Day Air
❑ Other
❑ Parcel Post
❑ 1st Class Mail

Quantity	Unit	Style Number	Color	Description of Item	Unit Price	Total
2	doz	61-129		Nymo bead cord	6.00	
1	50	22-860	Ruby	Islamic glass beads	9.00	
3	mass	23-246	Crystal	6mm round glass beads	25.00	
4	strand	25-171		Red horn bead	2.50	

Critical Thinking

- What would you do if you wanted to buy turquoise nuggets? Why?
- In which colors are the Islamic glass beads available?
- How many ounces of sinew are in a 150-yard spool?
- How could you order from Beads & Bangles if you did not have an open account? What are the other payment options?
- How many bobbins of Nymo bead cord is Frances Graceful Bear ordering for The Bead Corner?

Respond to the SELECTION

If you were going to order from this catalog, which beads would you choose? What type of cording would you select? Why?

Investigate, *Inquire,* and **Imagine**

Recall: GATHERING FACTS

1a. What are the different quantities of Nymo Bead Cord you can order?

2a. Describe the Cobalt Blue and Ruby Islamic Beads based on the textual description.

3a. List the different ways in which your order can be shipped.

→ **Interpret:** FINDING MEANING

1b. Why do you think that three different quantities are listed?

2b. How does the illustration of the beads give more or different information than the textual description?

3b. Why do you think there are so many different ways to ship your order?

Analyze: TAKING THINGS APART

4a. List the information you would need in order to fill out the order form.

→ **Synthesize:** BRINGING THINGS TOGETHER

4b. Summarize in paragraph form the things listed from question 4a.

Evaluate: MAKING JUDGMENTS

5a. As a customer, is the catalog appealing to you? Does it make you want to buy the company's products? Why, or why not?

→ **Extend:** CONNECTING IDEAS

5b. Pretend you are employed in the marketing department for Beads and Bangles. What changes in the layout of the catalog would you make? Would you change the illustrations? the headings? How could you make the brochure more customer friendly?

Understanding *Media*

ILLUSTRATION. An **illustration** is a photograph, drawing, or diagram that serves to make a concept clearer by providing a visual example. For example, if you look up the word *kite* in a dictionary, there may be a picture to illustrate what a kite looks like. What kinds of detail can an illustration offer that a worded description leaves out? What kinds of detail can a worded description offer that an illustration leaves out?

ORDER FORM. An **order form** is a printed or typed document with blank spaces for required or requested information, used by consumers to buy merchandise or services. Order forms are generally included in catalogs. How would you order merchandise without an order form? How would you organize the request shown in the order form on page 839 on a blank piece of paper?

Writer's Journal

1. Pretend you make your own beaded jewelry. Write an **advertisement** to sell the beaded jewelry you made.

2. Create a **billboard** for Beads and Bangles. Be creative in your illustrations and headings.

3. Pretend your family pet is lost. Write up a "Lost Dog" or "Lost Cat" **notice,** describing what your dog or cat looks like. You will not be able to include a photograph, so be as detailed as possible.

Skill Builders

Applied English

LEARNING ABOUT ADVERTISING. Find out more information about a company in which you are interested. Interview a marketing representative for that company, asking him or her what kind of process the company uses in advertising their products or services. How do they decide what pictures to use? Who creates the illustrations? What forms of advertisement do they use? Why? Present your findings to the class in an oral speech. Provide examples of advertisements the company uses in marketing their products.

Collaborative Learning

PLACING AN ORDER. Pretend you are budgeting for your company. You need to order stock for next year, but you must be within the budget. Your company needs twice as many beads as string/cording. And your bill must be within the range of $150–$200. In your group of four or five people, fill out the order form meeting these stipulations. For this project, pretend that there is no extra fee for shipping.

Reader's *Journal*

How important is your hearing? your sight? your other senses?

Reader's TOOLBOX

CAUSE AND EFFECT. Cause is defined as a condition or an action that brings about a particular result. **Effect** is a result of a particular action, or cause. In a cause and effect essay or article, the writer presents one or more causes followed by one or more effects. In some cases, the effects are presented before the causes are revealed. In this selection, the article discusses hearing loss and the events that lead up to it. As you read, find one cause and effect relationship in the article.

STATISTICS. Statistics are numerical facts or data. You most commonly see statistics in sporting events. Batting averages, free throw percentages, and win-loss ratios are all examples of statistics that athletes and spectators use to keep track of how well the athletes are performing. Your grade point average (GPA) is also a statistic. In this magazine article, find two instances where the journalist uses statistics to emphasize the point he wants to make.

Prereading

"HEARING UNDER SIEGE"

by Bob Ludlow

Reader's Resource

- **SCIENCE CONNECTION.** Sound is produced when air is disturbed by a vibrating object. For example, in a bass speaker, the air immediately in the front of the speaker is compressed, causing a slight increase in air pressure. It then moves back past its resting position and causes a reduction in air pressure. This process continues so that a wave of alternating high and low pressure is radiated away from the speaker, resulting in the production of sound. Sound is measured by decibels.

- **BIOLOGY CONNECTION.** The ear is made up of three parts: the outer ear, middle ear, and inner ear. The outer ear is comprised of the auricle, or pinna (cartilage part of the ear), the ear canal, and the outer layer of the eardrum. Sound enters the ear canal. At the eardrum, sound energy (change in air pressure) is transformed into eardrum movement. The middle ear serves as a transformer, concentrating the sound energy of the air in the ear canal. In this process, the hammer, which is attached to the eardrum, receives vibrations from the eardrum, passes them to the anvil, which then moves the stirrup. The inner ear is where the last energy transformation occurs. A ribbon-like structure, the basilar membrane, holds the spiral-shaped organ of Corti. Thousands of hairlike projections on the organ of Corti receive the sound vibrations from the middle ear and send them to the brain, where they are recognized and interpreted as specific sounds.

Graphic *Organizer*

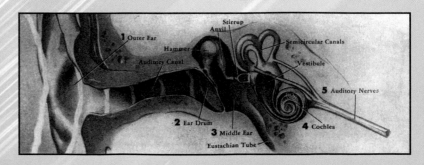

Hearing
UNDER SIEGE

Bob Ludlow

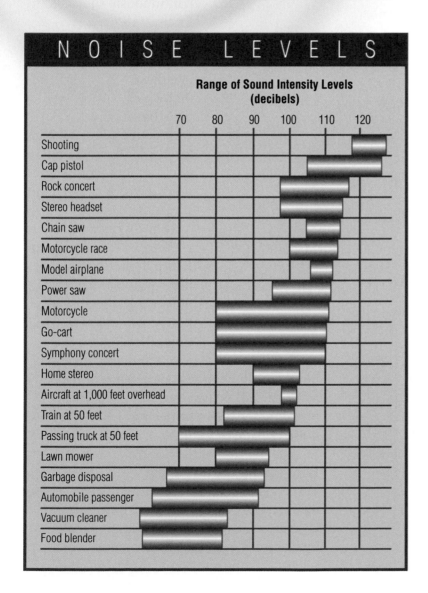

NOISE LEVELS

Range of Sound Intensity Levels (decibels)

	70	80	90	100	110	120
Shooting						▬
Cap pistol					▬	
Rock concert				▬		
Stereo headset				▬		
Chain saw				▬		
Motorcycle race				▬		
Model airplane				▬		
Power saw				▬		
Motorcycle		▬				
Go-cart		▬				
Symphony concert		▬				
Home stereo			▬			
Aircraft at 1,000 feet overhead			▬			
Train at 50 feet		▬				
Passing truck at 50 feet	▬					
Lawn mower		▬				
Garbage disposal	▬					
Automobile passenger	▬					
Vacuum cleaner	▬					
Food blender	▬					

Whether it's rock or Bach, music that's played too loud can put more than a temporary damper on your hearing. At most rock concerts and many night clubs, the sound intensity is high enough to cause irreversible damage to the delicate sensor cells lining the inner ear. Car and home stereo equipment and headphones can also harm your hearing when the volume is cranked up too high.

GUIDED READING

In what situations could sound intensity damage hearing?

Noted noise-pollution expert William Clark, Ph.D., a researcher at the Central Institute for the Deaf, in St. Louis, is especially troubled by reports of teenagers' music listening habits. He cites recent studies of personal stereo use that indicate 5% to 10% of these young people are risking significant hearing loss. In his testimony before Congress, Clark called for mandatory warning labels to be placed on stereo equipment as well as red warnings on volume controls.

But loud music is only one of the threats to good hearing that abound in everyday life. Workplace noise has long been recognized as a major cause of permanent hearing loss. And outside of work, many kinds of home and recreational equipment have the potential to damage your hearing. Power saws, leaf blowers, model airplanes, all-terrain vehicles, and firearms—especially firearms—are cause for concern. So are the high noise levels at automobile races, motorcycle races, and other crowded sporting events.

Know the Signs

Hearing experts recommend a simple "talk test" as a practical means of safeguarding your hearing. They say that the noise level is too high if it's hard to carry on a conversation with someone who is three feet away from you.

Experts also tell people to beware of temporary changes in hearing, such as ringing or a "stuffy" feeling in the ears. These symptoms are not just harmless annoyances but signs that the wispy nerve endings called "hair cells" have been traumatized.

GUIDED READING

How do you know if the noise level in a given situation is too high?

How Loud and How Long

The intensity, or loudness, of sound is measured in units called decibels. A whisper,

Most hearing loss in noisy industrial societies is gradual and becomes noticeable only as people age. That is why it is widely believed that aging is the major cause of hearing loss. However, studies have found excellent hearing in older people who live in quiet, tribal societies.

which is at the lower end of the scale, registers about 20 decibels, while normal speech comes in at a comfortable 60. Sound begins to get "uncomfortable" at about 70 decibels, and it becomes potentially harmful when it reaches 85 or 90 decibels. A typical rock concert assaults your ears with 100 to 120 decibels.

GUIDED READING

At what point are sound levels potentially harmful?

The damage done by noise depends not only on how loud it is but also on the length of time you're exposed to it. Many workers are continuously subjected to levels above 85 decibels on a daily basis. The

GUIDED READING

What besides loudness determines whether noise can be harmful?

cumulative effects of high levels of industrial and environmental noise add up to some very alarming statistics.

By age 65, for instance, 20% to 30% of the people in the United States will have difficulty hearing normal conversational levels. To reduce the risks to workers, federal agencies as well as private industry have set limits on allowing noise exposure in the workplace. But there are no regulations providing effective protection from everyday noise outside of work.

Bang, Bang, You're Deaf

When noise levels are extremely high, severe damage can occur from just a single, brief exposure. Clark puts such risks in perspective by firing off a round of high-powered scientific "ammunition." "A shot from a 357

Rooftops (No.1, This is Harlem), 1943. Jacob Lawrence. Hirshhorn Museum and Sculpture Garden, Washington, DC.

Magnum (165 decibels) is the acoustic equivalent of working in a noisy factory for a week," he explains. "Firing a box of shells is like working in that same factory for a year. Much of the hearing loss that's been blamed on the workplace actually comes from hunting and target shooting. Our research showed that people who worked in a noisy plant but didn't shoot had better hearing than a similar group who worked in a quiet office and did shoot."

And guns don't have to be real to cause real harm. Children's cap pistols (105 to 125 decibels), when fired close to the ear, are not safe toys.

Sensible Precautions

Experts in hearing conservation offer several common sense guidelines that can help you preserve good hearing throughout your lifetime.

- Always wear protective devices, such as earplugs or specially designed earmuffs, when working in noisy settings or with loud equipment.
- Never use firearms without effective hearing protection.
- Spend less time in noisy environments, and give your ears frequent breaks from periods of continuous noise exposure. Consider carrying and using earplugs the way you use sunglasses.

GUIDED READING

When should people use devices to protect their hearing?

The chart on page 843 lists decibel levels for some common activities and equipment. Clark and other experts aren't saying you have to avoid all noisy activities—just be aware of noise levels and take sensible precautions.

Critical Thinking

- Which has the potential to be louder, a model airplane or a chain saw?
- Could a home stereo ever be louder than a go-cart? Explain your answer.
- If sound can be harmful at 85 to 90 decibels, how many items in this chart have the potential to harm your hearing?

Respond *to the* SELECTION

After reading this article, will you be more cautious about the type of environment in which you will work or "hang out"? Why, or why not?

About *the* AUTHOR

Bob Ludlow was born on May 26, 1939, in Chicago. He grew up in Orlando, Florida, which is his current residence. He wrote this article while working as a fitness editor for *Cooking Light* magazine. He currently is employed in the Brevard County Public Schools as a behavior therapist. Here, he answers some questions about his life and his work.

As a young person, did you like to read and write? If so, what did you like to read and write? How did you develop your skills?
I began reading good literature on my own while I was in high school. Reading became almost an obsession during the two years I spent in the Navy after high school. Beginning with the works of Mark Twain, I read hundreds of novels by American and English authors. I also read some poetry and philosophy.

I began writing some poetry and essays in high school to express my thoughts about the meaning of life. I admired good writing and wanted to see what I could do.

Following my military service, I began taking courses at a junior college in Orlando. At first I tended to miss assignments and turn work in late. Of course my grades suffered accordingly. One incident I do remember was staying up all night to complete a short story for an English class. Later the teacher told me

he thought it was good enough to submit to the *Atlantic Monthly!* Wow, did hearing that mean a lot to me! It probably was the first time I really believed I could be a good writer.

How did you become involved in magazine writing?
My first published writing was an outgrowth of my passion for chess. I was appointed editor of the *Florida Chess News*, a quarterly newsletter published by the Florida Chess Association. I must say I got carried away and took that little publication to new heights, transforming it into an attractive and literate magazine! This was my first experience with deadlines, editing others' works, and preparing copy for press.

A later opportunity came in the form of a regional running magazine published in Orlando. I was an avid distance runner, and I wrote a piece for the magazine about my Boston Marathon experience in 1982. Based on that, the publisher asked me to become editor of the magazine, which was a shoe-string operation. In my spare time, I plunged into that task with a passion, until my wife and I moved away from Orlando. I still believe the pieces I wrote for the running magazine are my best work, probably because of my intense interest in health, fitness, and running and the creative freedom I enjoyed. I later became fitness editor for *Cooking Light* magazine, my first real job in publishing, which I held for almost three years.

Investigate, *Inquire,* and Imagine

Recall: GATHERING FACTS

1a. What does William Clark want placed on all stereo equipment?

2a. What are some temporary changes in hearing?

3a. What are the two factors in hearing damage?

→ **Interpret:** FINDING MEANING

1b. Why do you think he wants this done?

2b. What do these changes signify? What alarm could they send to the person affected by the changes?

3b. Which of the two factors is more damaging? Why?

Analyze: TAKING THINGS APART

4a. List possible precautions you can take to preserve good hearing.

→ **Synthesize:** BRINGING THINGS TOGETHER

4b. If society became as concerned about hearing loss as it is about other issues—such as smoking, drinking, exercise, and diet—how do you think our world might change? What precautions would go into effect?

Evaluate: MAKING JUDGMENTS

5a. The warnings in this article are based on facts. Knowing this, why do you think people ignore warnings like these? What does this say about human nature?

→ **Extend:** CONNECTING IDEAS

5b. If you were writing this article, what additional information would you include? what facts? what precautions? What, if anything, would you omit?

Understanding *Media*

STATISTICS. Statistics are numerical facts or data. How does the use of statistics make the article stronger? How does it make the journalist's argument more valid?

CAUSE AND EFFECT. Cause is defined as a condition or an action that brings about a particular result. **Effect** is a result of a particular action, or cause. In a cause and effect essay or article, the writer presents one or more causes followed by one or more effects. What causes are mentioned in this article? what effects?

Writer's Journal

1. A Surgeon General's Warning is placed on cigarettes because they cause lung cancer. Write a similar type of **warning** for a rock concert, informing attendees that going to the rock concert could damage their hearing.

2. Write five **sentences** that include basic statistics about hearing issues.

3. Imagine you manage a large industrial factory, where noise levels are frequently at or near 100 decibels. Create a **poster** reminding employees to wear their ear plugs.

Skill Builders

Language, Grammar, and Style

USING CAUSE AND EFFECT LANGUAGE. In the selection you read, the article discussed hearing loss and the events that led up to it—creating a cause and effect relationship. When writing cause and effect paragraphs, you may find it useful to use certain linkers, or transitional words and phrases, for the reader to clarify cause and effect relationships. These words and phrases include *after this, as a result, because, consequently, if/then, in order that, since, so, then, therefore, thus, while.* They can help signal a cause and effect relationship for the reader. For each of the following sentences, underline the cause and circle the effect.

1. My grandpa died of lung cancer because he smoked cigarettes since he was 20 years old.
2. The wind was so cold that I had to wear earmuffs.
3. Because of a broken toe, I had to sit out the rest of the football season.
4. I ended up losing my voice because I screamed so loud at the horse races.
5. The much needed rain helped produce a healthy crop of corn.
6. I was tired all day because I was up all night studying.
7. The dog got into the garbage and made our house stink.
8. The sad movie made my mom cry.
9. Dad's brand new white shirt turned pink because I accidentally washed it with my red dress.
10. As a result of being late for practice, I had to run ten laps around the track.

Using these linkers, write a paragraph illustrating a cause and effect relationship. You may want to write about the results of a natural disaster, the effects of people's attitudes on others, weather's effects on plants, how diet affects health, or any other such topic.

Prereading

from The Adventures of Tintin: The Black Island
by Hergé

Reader's Resource

- **ARTS CONNECTION.** Comic strips are a sequence of drawings that tell a story. They typically have dialogue printed in balloons and are arranged in horizontal strips. The first comic strip introduced to the United States was the German comic strip, "Max and Moritz," by Wilhelm Busch in 1865. Almost 30 years later in 1894, the first color newspaper page was published in the *New York Recorder*. Three years later, *Yellow Kid* by Richard Felton Outcault began publication as part of the Sunday comic supplement in *Journal American*. By the early 1930s, *Little Orphan Annie, Dick Tracy, Popeye, Little Nemo, Buster Brown*, and *Krazy Kat were* all in publication. Action comics were introduced in the late 1930s. The most popular action comic was *Superman*. In 1939 *Batman* came on the scene. Throughout the century, comic strips expanded to explore science fiction, crime, and horror.

- The materials used in drawing comics are very different from the materials used in everyday drawing. They require paper and pencils like other types of drawings. However, the paper and pencils are designed specifically for cartoon drawing. For example, comics are drawn on two-ply bristol, which is thick, durable paper available only in art supply stores. Another type of paper comic artists use is called Vellum paper. Vellum paper is like tracing paper. It is used for artists who redraw a lot since erasing over and over can wear down paper. Cartoonists also use special art pencils when they draw. They range from 6H to 6B. *H* pencils have hard leads. They require less sharpening and produce a faint but sharp line. *B* pencils have soft leads. They wear down more quickly and produce a darker but fuzzier line than *H* pencils. However, *B* pencils are easier to erase than *H* pencils. Another type of pencil that most cartoonists cannot live without is called the non-photo blue pencil. These pencils contain a particular shade of light blue that is not picked up by cameras used in most black-and-white printing processes or by copy machines. Therefore, cartoonists don't have to erase every time they print or make copies.

- The two police officers who appear in the section of *The Adventures of Tintin: The Black Island* shown here are Thompson and Thomson. The only way you can distinguish one from another is by their mustaches. Thompson has a pointy mustache, and Thomson has a more rounded mustache. Their relationship with Tintin is curious in that they never hesitate to arrest him, yet they call him "old boy" and are quick to be his friend.

Reader's Journal

Think back to a time when you were accused of something you did not do. How did you react?

Reader's TOOLBOX

END PUNCTUATION. The period, the question mark, and the exclamation point are all examples of **end punctuation**. End marks tell the reader where a sentence ends. They also show the purpose of the sentence. A period ends all sentences except for direct questions or genuine exclamations. As you read through this selection, pick out three sentences—one that uses a period, one that uses a question mark, and one that uses an exclamation mark.

CHRONOLOGICAL ORDER. Chronological order puts events in the order in which they happen. In writing, transition words such as *first, second, next, then,* and *finally* are used to connect a series of events. In this selection, however, chronological order is represented by the order of pictures, not by the use of transition words. As you read the comic strip, notice the order in which the pictures are placed. How do you know which picture frame is next? How is this similar to reading?

© Hergé/Moulinsart 2000

© Hergé/Moulinsart 2000

If you were Hergé, what would you draw in the next picture frame? Why?

About *the*
AUTHOR

Hergé is the pen name for Georges Remi. He was born in the Etterbeek district of Brussels, Belgium on May 22, 1907. As a child, Remi was rambunctious and loud. His parents found two ways to keep him quiet: spankings and allowing him to draw. The latter proved to assure many hours of peace and quiet, because Remi loved to draw. By the age of seven, he was already drawing picture stories at the bottom of his exercise books in school. When he was 21 years old, his parents enrolled him in art school. It took only one day for him to despise art school. His artistic training has been entirely self-taught. Year after year, Hergé would buy books to improve himself on different techniques of drawing. Today, the Tintin series has been translated into more than 30 languages and is sold all over the world. The series follows the adventures of Tintin and his dog, Snowy, from Europe to faraway places like South America and China. *The Black Island* takes place in Scotland.

Investigate, Inquire, and Imagine

Recall: GATHERING FACTS

1a. What does Tintin see in the corridor?

2a. What does Snowy, the dog, do to help Tintin?

3a. What two things does the man find in Tintin's pockets?

→ **Interpret:** FINDING MEANING

1b. Why do you think Tintin runs after the person?

2b. What does this say about Snowy?

3b. Why are the items suspicious?

Analyze: TAKING THINGS APART

4a. Outline the main action of the story in short phrases. Complete sentences are unnecessary.

→ **Synthesize:** BRINGING THINGS TOGETHER

4b. Summarize in paragraph form the main events in the comic strip.

Evaluate: MAKING JUDGMENTS

5a. Refer to question 4b. How does the paragraph version of the story differ from the comic strip version of the story? Which do you think is better?

→ **Extend:** CONNECTING IDEAS

5b. Pretend you are an author. Would you rather be an author of novels or of comic books? Why? What does this say about your interests? Your abilities?

Understanding Media

CHRONOLOGICAL ORDER. Chronological order puts events in the order in which they happen or should be done. In writing, transition words such as *first, second, next, then,* and *finally* are used to connect a series of events. In this selection, however, chronological order is represented by the order of pictures, not by the use of transition words. Now that you have read the comic strip, consider how the story would be different if the pictures were not in chronological order. What does this convey about the importance of chronological order when telling a story through pictures?

END PUNCTUATION. The period, the question mark, and the exclamation point are all examples of end punctuation. These end marks tell the reader where a sentence ends. They also show the purpose of the sentence. A *period* is used to declare or state something. It ends all sentences except for direct questions or genuine exclamations. A *question mark* is used in direct questions. An *exclamation point* is used to express exceptional feeling or to put special emphasis on something. In what type of writing do you find the most variety in end punctuation—narration, description, dialogue, informative, or persuasive writing? Why do you think that is?

Writer's Journal

1. Pretend you are a cartoonist for your town newspaper. Create a **comic strip** that consists of five frames.
2. Your friend needs **directions** to your house. As you write, use transition words such as *first, second, next, then, finally* in your directions.
3. Imagine you are one of the Thompson and Thomson team. Write a **police report** about what took place on the train in Scotland.

Skill Builders

Language, Grammar, and Style

END PUNCTUATION. The period, the question mark, and the exclamation point are all examples of end punctuation. These end marks tell the reader where a sentence ends. Read the following sentences, and complete them by filling in the appropriate end marks. For more information on end marks, refer to the Language Arts Survey 3.75, "Editing for Punctuation Errors."

1. I am so full
2. Will you please pass the salt
3. Why are you late
4. I passed my math test
5. Stop it Stop doing that
6. Wow The movie was really funny
7. Can you help me with my homework
8. Emily Dickinson was a poet
9. When did you say your appointment was
10. That was the best party ever

Collaborative Learning & Media Literacy

CREATING A COMIC STRIP. Gather into groups of three or four students. Brainstorm ideas for the characters, setting, and plot for a comic strip. The comic strip should have at least 20 picture frames.

Begin by sketching out your ideas in storyboard fashion. Jot down ideas for dialogue next to each square. Then assemble a more polished version of your comic strip, and fine tune it until everyone is satisfied. After you have finished, display your comic strip in class for others to see. For help in creating your own comic strip, search the Internet for sites that give step-by-step instruction on how to write and draw comic strips.
The How-To Guide to Comics at http://www.teleport.com/~ennead/ampersand/how_to.html
The Cartoonist's Fountain of Knowledge at http://www.spirit.com.au/~pat/fountain.html
Art Tips by Gerry Alanguilan at http://www.laguna.net/~timawa/tips.htm

Study and Research

RESEARCHING HERGÉ AND TINTIN. Locate books in your library or use the Internet to find more information about Hergé and the Tintin comics. Try to find out how popular the comics are around the world and why they are so popular. What criticisms have the comics received, and why? How, over time, did Hergé modify his comics? Why did he do so?

for your READING LIST

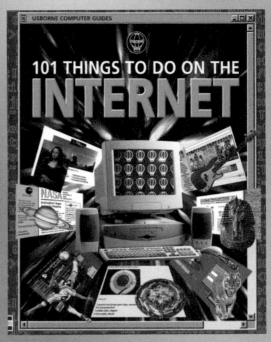

101 Things to Do on the Internet is part of the Computer Guide Series created by Mark Wallace. This kid-friendly volume describes a series of Internet projects, most of which involve visiting a web site. The book gives clear instructions on using the Internet—from the most simple tasks, such as getting online, to more difficult tasks, such as designing your own web page. This book also provides helpful step-by-step instructions that guide readers to browse web pages about sports, music, dinosaurs, moviemaking, travel, and more. The book even helps you find web pages that can help you with your homework! Most of the illustrations in this book are taken from the Internet.

TRYING IT OUT

Find a partner. Read the Table of Contents of the book. Then scan through the book, looking at the various Internet activities the book has to offer. As you will see, there is a wealth of information on the web. Choose five activities to try from the book. For example, you may choose to:

- Find biographical information on your favorite sports star or movie star,
- Check out the weather of the country or state your friends or relatives live,
- Find a recipe for your favorite entrée or dessert,
- Send an e-mail postcard or greeting card to a friend overseas or to a friend right in your own town,
- Go on an interactive art exhibit through an online museum.

Before you begin with these activities, you may want to read through the Language Arts Survey 5.25, "Using the Internet," 5.26, "Browsing versus Searching on the Internet," and 5.34, "How to Understand Internet Sites." After you and your partner have completed the five activities you chose, discuss the following questions with your partner:

1. What new information did you acquire as you worked on this project?
2. What did you learn about the process of Internet search and use?
3. What are the advantages and disadvantages of using the Internet?
4. What Internet site did you find most interesting?

> "Your best perceptions and thoughts are always going to be tied up in whatever is really occupying you, and that is also where your energy is."
>
> —Peter Elbow

Examining the Model

In "Hearing Under Siege," Bob Ludlow explains a simple cause and effect relationship—too much noise can cause hearing loss. To help the reader understand, he elaborates on the causes and the effect. He identifies two causes for this type of hearing loss—sounds above a certain decibel level and sounds that last over long periods of time. The hearing loss is the result of damage to the sensory cells that line the ear.

continued on page 857

Guided Writing

WRITING A CAUSE AND EFFECT ESSAY

Reese loved the science experiment that he and Emily planned to present to the class. He had used the same experiment before, but that wouldn't stop him from enjoying the "oohs" and "ahs" that his classmates would exclaim as they watched the experiment unfold.

First, Reese and Emily constructed a model of a volcano. They hid a small cup filled with baking soda inside the top of the volcano. Then they prepared the information for the class to explain what causes a volcano to erupt and what might be expected from a volcanic eruption. Right before presenting their experiment to the class, Emily set a small cup of vinegar behind their volcano. Then, as Reese described how lava often comes out of the top and flows down the sides of the volcano, Emily poured the vinegar into the hidden baking soda. Within seconds, lava was bubbling up and flowing down the sides. Another volcanic success!

Reese and Emily knew that they could rely on their experiment because pouring vinegar into baking soda always causes the same effect—a bubbling solution.

The result of pouring vinegar into baking soda is one example of a cause and effect relationship. For this assignment, you will write an essay that explains a different cause and effect. You may use a diagram or picture to make it easier for another person to understand the cause and effect relationship.

Professional Model

from "Hearing Under Siege" by Bob Ludlow, page 843

Whether it's rock or Bach, music that's played too loud can put more than a temporary damper on your hearing. At most rock concerts and many night clubs, the sound intensity is high enough to cause irreversible damage to the delicate sensory cells lining the inner ear. Car and home stereo equipment and headphones can also harm your hearing when the volume is cranked up too high. . . .

But loud music is only one of the threats to good hearing that abound in everyday life. Workplace noise has long been recognized as a major cause of permanent hearing loss. And outside of work, many kinds of home and recreational equipment have the potential to damage your hearing. Power saws, leaf blowers, model airplanes, all-terrain vehicles, and firearms—especially firearms—are cause for concern. . . .

The damage done by noise depends not only on how loud it is but also on the length of time you're exposed to it. Many workers are continuously subjected to levels above 85 decibels on a daily basis. The cumulative effects of high levels of industrial and environmental noise add up to some very alarming statistics.

Reflecting

Some difficulties that people experience are the result of cause and effect relationships. For example, not getting enough sleep (cause) might make it difficult for a student to pay attention in class (effect). Or, not eating breakfast (cause) might lead to running out of energy before lunchtime (effect). Consider some of the cause and effect relationships that happen in peoples' lives. How might changing the cause affect what happens?

Prewriting

FINDING YOUR VOICE. As you read Ludlow's article, it becomes evident that he is serious about hearing loss and that he wants the reader to take hearing loss seriously, too. He develops this voice through his word choice, sentence structure, tone, and style.

You also want your readers to appreciate the importance of the cause and effect relationship you have chosen to write about. You can do this by allowing your unique personality to shine through, choosing your words carefully, arranging your sentences logically, and using a style that matches the message you are sending.

IDENTIFYING YOUR AUDIENCE. Your audience for this assignment will depend on your topic. As you select your topic, decide which audience will benefit from learning about the cause and effect relationship that you are explaining. After you decide on an audience, consider your audience's needs. For example, if you were going to explain to young children how striking a piano key causes a musical note to play, you might use easy words, short sentences, and a simple diagram. If you were explaining the same process to your peers, you could use more precise words, longer sentences, and a more detailed diagram.

WRITING WITH A PLAN. Each day, you see and experience many cause and effect relationships. Which one might make a good topic for your essay? On your own paper, make a list of cause and effect relationships. You might consider events that happen in everyday living, weather, sports, geology, animal life, plant life, machinery, and inventions for ideas.

Consider what you already know about these topics and what you'd be interested in finding out. Put a star next to the two topics that seem the most interesting to you. Freewrite about

Ludlow gives specific examples of the causes—music, workplace noise, guns, and all-terrain vehicles—and uses a chart to show the decibel levels of many other noises. He also gives specific examples of the effects—10 percent of young people with hearing loss and 30 percent of people experiencing difficulty hearing a normal conversation.

Besides giving specific examples, Ludlow chooses words—irreversible damage, delicate sensory cells, and alarming statistics—that show the seriousness of this cause and effect relationship. Even the title, "Hearing Under Siege" reinforces this idea. Ludlow also uses words that show cause and effect, words such as *major cause, is only one, depends, cumulative effect,* and *add up to.*

Finally, Ludlow presents his ideas in a logical order. First, he gives general information about hearing loss and identifies the cause and the effect relationship. Next, he develops the information with examples and other factual information. Last, since the effect is harmful, he tells how to avoid this cause and effect relationship.

"Freewriting teaches you to write without thinking about writing."

—Peter Elbow

Words that show cause and effect relationships:

after this
as a result
because
consequently
if
in order that
since
so
then
therefore
thus
while

How can you tell a cause from an effect?

A cause makes something happen. The effect is what happens.

Putting the cookie dough in the hot oven bakes the cookies.

Putting the cookie dough in the hot oven is the cause. The *baked cookies* is the effect.

Sometimes an effect becomes a cause. For example, the *freshly baked cookies* might cause someone to finish dinner in order to have a cookie.

"Ultimately, if the process is good, the end will be good. You will get good writing."
—Natalie Goldberg

each of these topics. For one topic, use the sentence starter, *Sometimes people wonder why.* . . . For the other topic, use the sentence starter, *Whenever this happens.* . . . Which freewriting presents the most intriguing and challenging information? Choose this as your topic.

After you've selected your topic, generate a list of all the causes for this topic and all of the effects. You may need to do some research to understand the causes, effects, and the interaction between them to write about your topic. Also, list specific examples and other factual information that can be used to elaborate on your topic. You will use these lists as you organize how you will present the cause and effect relationship.

Andy was fascinated by hailstorms. He used the sentence starter *Sometimes people wonder why . . .* to freewrite about hailstorms. Through his freewriting, he realized that people wonder why hail forms, why it falls to the ground, and why some hailstones get so big. Andy also realized that while he knew the effect—hailstones—he didn't understand the causes. So, he researched hailstorms, listing the causes and effects. He also discovered and listed some interesting facts and examples to use, including the size of the biggest hailstone ever recorded.

Next, Andy used a graphic organizer to list and show the relationship between the causes and effects for hail.

Student Model—Graphic Organizer

How Hailstorms Happen

Causes
• *strong air currents inside thunderclouds*
• *cold temperatures inside the cloud*
• *water droplets in the cloud*

Interaction
• *air currents force water droplets up*
• *cold air freezes them*
• *air currents force water droplets down*
• *frozen droplets collect moisture, making a larger droplet*
• *air currents force droplets with more moisture up*
• *cold air freezes them*
• *air currents force water droplets down*
• *larger droplets collect more moisture and make a larger droplet*
• *the ice drops get so heavy that the air currents can't hold them up*

Effect
• *hail drops to the ground*

Copy the graphic organizer onto your own paper. Think about the causes, the interactions, and the effects that you are going to explain. Then fill in the cause and effect relationships on the graphic organizer.

Drafting

Start by identifying the causes. Continue by explaining each of the interactions between the causes and effects.

Present the cause and effect statements in a brief, but logical way. Try to use specific words to clarify your explanation. For example, words like *as, when, before, after, if, then, first, second, finally, because, since, so,* and *therefore* can help your readers understand a cause and effect relationship.

Using specific names for parts and identifying them as *the first, second, left, right, top, bottom, upper,* or *lower parts* also helps to form a clear explanation. Other descriptive words—*short, long, rough, smooth, fat, small,* and *tall*—help to provide precise information.

Weave the specific examples and other factual information that you listed earlier into your draft. These details make your writing more interesting and help the reader get a better understanding of your topic.

After you are satisfied with your draft, create a visual—perhaps a diagram or a chart—to show the cause and effect relationship.

Student Model—Draft

We all remember last year's storm . . .
ice on the ground in the summer!   *Can you give it a title?*

Have you ever wondered how hail stones

are formed? Or how they get so big? *Start off with the*

Do you think hailstorms are   *reason you chose this topic.*

dangerous to you? Are hailstorms

dangerous at all?

Combine first two sentences

Hail is a form of precipitation. Rain

Hail, like rain and snow, is a form of precipitation.

and snow are forms of precipitation too.

Although they are all forms of

precipitation they are formed very

differently. Rain and snow are formed

when clouds are ~~to~~ saturated. Then the
      too

water in them is forced out of the

clouds in the form of rain or snow.

Whether that water is rain or snow *Combine these to have less choppiness*

depends on the temperature.

Hail on the other hand is formed

when clouds become saturated. The water

Language, Grammar, and Style
Sentence Types

To keep your writing lively, try using different lengths and structures for the sentences you write.

A **simple sentence** has a subject and a predicate (verb phrase). Look at the example below.

> The thundercloud is moving quickly.

You can combine two or more simple sentences to make a **compound sentence.** The simple sentences are usually combined with a **coordinating conjunction.** A coordinating conjunction is a connecting word such as *and, but, for, nor, or,* or *yet.* A comma is usually placed before the connecting word in a compound sentence. Read the example below,

> The thundercloud is moving quickly, but the storm hasn't arrived yet.

The two simple sentences are joined together with the coordinating conjunction *but.*

IDENTIFYING DIFFERENT TYPES OF SENTENCES. Look at the two simple sentences in the example below. Combine them into a compound sentence using one of the following conjunctions: *and, but, for, nor, or,* or *yet.*

> I wanted to play outside. I waited for the storm.

continued on page 860

Next, identify a compound sentence in the student model that uses a coordinating conjunction.

Another way to create sentence variety is to combine a simple sentence with a dependent clause. This forms a **complex sentence**. Look at the example below.

> When the thunderclouds roll in, I want to run outside to watch.

The dependent clause is *When the thunderclouds roll in.* The simple sentence is *I want to run outside to watch.*

Words that are used to begin dependent clauses are called **subordinating conjunctions:** *after, although, as, as if, because, before, even if, even though, if, if only, rather than, since, that, though, unless, until, when, where, where as, wherever, whether, which, while.*

Combine each simple sentence with the dependent clause in the examples below.

> When hail pours down. I run for cover.

> Hail can damage cars and crops. Because the hailstones are so large.

Next, identify a complex sentence from the student model that uses a subordinating conjunction.

The dependent clause may either begin or end a complex sentence, but when it begins the sentence, a comma must follow it.

---

falls. But first it's tossed <u>back and</u>
Do you mean "up and down?"
<u>forth</u> from air currents to freezing

altitudes. As the water is sent <u>back</u>

More <u>and forth</u> it freezes. Then it gathers
detail *Mention updrafts and downdrafts*
needed more and more water that freezes also.
here When the stone gets too heavy to get

tossed <u>back and forth</u> any longer it

falls to the ground.
Can you define?
Hail can only form in <u>cumulonimbus</u>
they are the large, puffy clouds that become dark gray with water.
clouds with a lot of water in them.

Hail is often times mixed up with *Maybe sleet*
is off the
sleet. But sleet is smaller and *topic.*

doesn't get tossed back and forth like

hail does. Hail can be about the size

of a baseball at times. But sleet is
Conclusion? Answer your question from the 1st ¶! Are hailstones dangerous?
much smaller. *Yes - to livestock and cars and people*

Self- and Peer Evaluation

After you finish your rough draft, you can do a self-evaluation of your work. If time allows, ask a member of your intended audience to do a review of your work as well. See the Language Arts Survey 2.37 for more details about self-evaluation and peer evaluation. As you evaluate your draft, ask yourself these questions:

- How well does the essay explain the cause and effect relationship? Which parts are explained best? Which parts need a clearer or easier explanation?
- Which cause and effect words illustrate the relationships? What additional cause and effect words are needed to show the relationships?
- How clearly does the essay present the order of the steps in the process? How clear is the cause and effect sequence?
- Which specific names for parts are needed to clarify the explanation?
- What specific examples and facts elaborate on the information? What specific examples and facts are still needed to further elaborate on the information?
- How appealing is the information and the layout design? What changes might make it more interesting and enjoyable?
- Check the writing for sentence variety. What additional sentence styles would improve the rhythm and fluency in the writing?

Student Model—Revised

Take Cover!

By Andy Lipski

We all remember that hailstorm last year. Though it was the middle of summer, the ground was covered in ice! Have you ever wondered how those hailstones were formed? Or how they got so big? Have you ever considered whether hailstorms can be dangerous?

Hail, like rain and snow, is a form of precipitation. Although they are all forms of precipitation they are formed very differently. Rain and snow are formed when clouds are too saturated and the water in them is forced out of them. Whether that water is rain or snow depends on the temperature.

Hail, on the other hand, is formed when summer clouds become saturated and the water falls. But now, instead of falling to the ground as rain, something different happens. Strong winds, called updrafts, force the water drops up into the top of the cloud. The air is colder at the top of the cloud. It's freezing, in fact. The water drop therefore becomes covered in ice.

Other strong winds, called downdrafts, cause the water, now an ice drop to fall. Another updraft will take it to the top again. As a result, it becomes bigger and bigger with another ice coating. The water drop, now an ice ball, is tossed up and down from air current to air current. As the water is sent up and down, it freezes and gathers more and more water that also freezes. Eventually, the stone gets too heavy to get tossed up and down any longer. It then falls to the ground as hail.

FIXING SENTENCE VARIETY. Read the sentences below. Rewrite the sentences using compound and complex sentence structures to create sentence variety.

Thunderclouds move quickly. Thunderclouds change their shapes. Strong air currents move thunderclouds. The tops of thunderclouds are freezing cold. Water droplets inside thunderclouds freeze. Air pushes them up. Air forces them down. Water droplets grow. Water droplets get heavier. They fall to the ground.

Select one paragraph in the student essay. What various sentence structures are used? How could you change sentences in this paragraph to make it more interesting?

USING A VARIETY OF SENTENCES. Look at your essay and examine the kinds of sentences that you have used. If you have several short, choppy sentences, try combining them into compound sentences or complex sentences.

Check to see if the rhythm or pattern of your sentences lacks variety. You can check the rhythm and flow of your writing by reading your essay out loud. One way to increase sentence variety is to move part of a sentence to a different location. For example, you can put dependent clauses at the beginning of some sentences and at the end of other sentences. Finally, alternate short and long sentences to vary the rhythm.

Revising and Proofreading

As you consider your self-evaluation and the evaluations from members of your intended audience, think about what will make your essay more effective. Be sure your text clearly explains the cause and effect relationships. Check to see if your text and your visual component work well together. Make all your revisions. Then proofread your writing for errors in spelling, grammar, usage, punctuation, and capitalization. See the Language Arts Survey 2.45, "A Proofreading Checklist," and 6.11, "Displaying Effective Visual Information," for help.

After reviewing his essay and considering all of the evaluation notes, Andy revised his essay.

Publishing and Presenting

Write or print the final draft for your essay. You might arrange the text of your essay around your visual. Include a title, labels, numbers, arrows, and a key as needed.

Display your finished essay and visual in your classroom. Take turns presenting your essay and visual to your classmates. If you have written your essay for a younger audience, tell your peers how that decision influenced your text and your choice of a visual component.

Hail can only form in cumulonimbus clouds. Those clouds are the huge, puffy ones that have gotten dark gray and are full of water. Hailstones form only in summer when warm air provides the strong updrafts and downdrafts that push the raindrops into and out of the freezing temperatures. Hail can be about the size of a baseball, or even bigger.

So, yes, hail can be dangerous. Larger hailstones can dent cars, hurt livestock in pastures, and hurt you if you are unlucky enough to get caught in a this kind of summer storm.

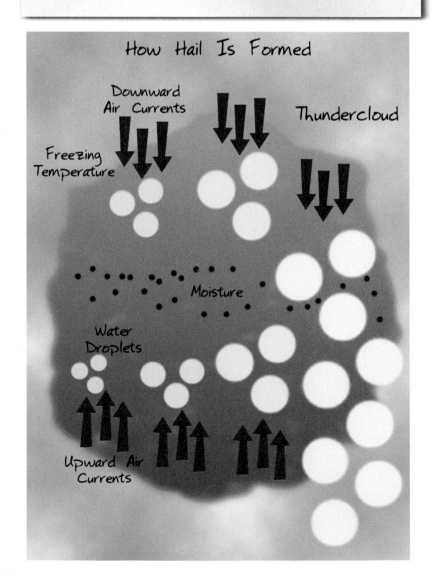

How Hail Is Formed

UNIT TWELVE *review*

Review: Literary Tools

Define each of the following terms, giving concrete examples when possible. To review a term, refer to the page number indicated.

- abstract images (823)
- active verbs (829)
- cause and effect (842)
- chronological order (849)

- concrete images (823)
- end punctuation (849)
- illustration (837)
- order form (837)

- perspective (823)
- register (829)
- statistics (842)
- tone (829)

Reflecting *on your reading*

Theme

"A picture is worth a thousand words." Often a graphic representation of a topic is more effective than trying to write about it. Each selection in this unit has provided a unique visual way to convey information to the reader, or viewer, whether it is through photography, charts and graphs, poetry, or an interview or advice column which is easily recognized by its format. What types of visuals help you to grasp concepts?

Genre

Informational and Visual Media is everywhere these days. You find advertisements on buses, on billboards, and posted on walls and kiosks. Information is on all product packaging. Messages are written on bumper stickers, t-shirts, shop windows, and even on airplane banners. You listen to the radio, watch television, log onto the Internet, read newspapers and magazines, and write e-mail. What do you think the future holds for informational media?

Group Project

As a group, find a selection of visual materials. Look in a number of different sources: newspapers, magazines, the Internet. Be creative. Look at cereal boxes, shampoo bottles, concert tickets, CD covers. These visual materials are trying to give information, and often trying to get you to do something, like buy the product. As a group, choose images that work, that you all agree are great. Also choose some that are not so great, that don't really work. Compare them. Try to find out, in your group, what makes these visual materials effective or not. Present your ideas, as well as the visual materials, to the class.

Language Arts Survey:
A Handbook of Essential Skills
PART THREE

READING
Resource

INTRODUCTION TO READING

1.1 Purposes of Reading

You as a reader read for different purposes. You might **read for experience**—for insights into ideas, other people, and the world around you. You can also **read to learn**. This is the kind of reading done most often in school. Third, you can **read for information** using reference materials, tables, databases, and diagrams.

1.2 Reading Independently

Learning to know and value your own response to what you read is one of the rewards of becoming an independent reader.

SCANNING. When you **scan**, you look through written material quickly to locate particular information. To scan, simply run your eye down the page, looking for a key word. When you find the key word, slow down and read carefully.

SKIMMING. When you **skim**, you glance through material quickly to get a general idea of what it is about. Skimming is useful for previewing a chapter in a textbook, for surveying material to see if it contains information that will be useful to you, and for reviewing material for a test or essay. When skimming, look at titles, headings, and words in boldface or colored type. Read topic sentences of paragraphs, first and last paragraphs of sections, and any summaries or conclusions.

SLOW AND CAREFUL READING. When you **read slowly and carefully**, you look at each sentence, taking the time to absorb its meaning before going on. Slow and careful reading is appropriate when reading for pleasure or when studying a textbook chapter for the first time. If you encounter unfamiliar words, try to figure them out from context or look them up in a dictionary. When reading for school, take notes using a rough outline form. Writing the material will help you to remember it. For more information, see the Language Arts Survey 5.16, "Taking Notes, Outlining, and Summarizing Information."

READING FOR EXPERIENCE

1.3 Reading Literature: Educating Your Imagination

The most important reason to read literature is to educate your imagination. Reading literature will train you to think and feel in new ways.

1.4 Educating Your Imagination as an Active Reader

Reading literature actively means thinking about what you are reading as you are reading it. Here are some important strategies for reading actively:

ASK QUESTIONS AS YOU READ
- How does what I am reading make me feel?
- What is the setting of this work? How do things look, sound, taste, feel, or smell?
- Do I identify with any of the characters? What would I do if I were in their place?
- Does what I am reading involve a conflict? If so, what is it? How might it be resolved?
- What main images, ideas, symbols, or themes appear in the work?
- What can I learn from the experiences of these characters?

MAKE PREDICTIONS AS YOU READ. Think about what will come next, how situations might turn out, and what characters might do.

SUMMARIZE PARTS AS YOU READ. Especially when reading longer works, stop, perhaps at the end of each chapter or section, to summarize on paper what you have read so far.

1.5 Keeping a Reader's Journal

Keeping a reader's journal will help you get the most out of your experience with literature. A reader's journal can act as a log in which you record the title and author of the selection, along with a brief summary. You can write a journal response to questions such as those in the Reader's Journal and Respond to the Selection features in this textbook.

1.6 Reading Silently versus Reading Out Loud

When reading independently, you will make the most progress by reading silently. However, you may find it helpful to read difficult passages out loud, even if softly. Hearing the words spoken can help make sense of complex passages. By reading poetry aloud, you will hear the rhythm and rhyme. Plays are intended to be performed. Reading them out loud can be particularly helpful when different people take on the roles of different characters.

1.7 Reading with a Book Club or Literature Circle

The experience that you have when reading a particular story, poem, or play will always be different from the experiences of each of your classmates. That's what makes discussing literature with others so interesting.

In a classroom literature circle or book club, a small group of students meets to exchange insights, interpretations, and questions about literature they have read independently. They may discuss a selection and work together to understand it. The following section gives some guidelines to help your book club get started.

1.8 Guidelines for Discussing Literature in a Book Club

BEFORE THE SESSION
- Finish reading the assignment on time.
- Write down ideas in your reader's journal to help yourself get ready for the discussion.
- Mark places in the reading that you don't understand or want to discuss with your group. Also mark passages that you like, disagree with, or find especially worth remembering.
- Bring the literature to school on discussion day.

DURING THE SESSION
- Share your ideas and offer suggestions.
- Speak clearly, loudly, and slowly.
- Make eye contact with others.

- Answer questions other people ask.
- Ask questions to help other members clarify or expand on their points.
- Help keep the group on track and focused.
- Encourage others to talk.
- Disagree respectfully when you find it necessary.
- Give reasons for your opinions.

AFTER THE SESSION
- Evaluate your contribution to the group.
- Evaluate the overall success of your group.
- List ways to improve the next time.

READING TO LEARN

When you are reading to learn, you have two main goals: to expand your knowledge about a topic and to remember the information. When you read to learn, you will often work with textbooks, nonfiction library books, newspapers, and newsmagazines.

1.9 Reading Textbooks and Nonfiction

Textbooks provide a broad overview of a course of study. Textbooks should provide as much material as possible in an objective, factual way.

THE PARTS OF A BOOK. When previewing a book, first glance at all of its parts. Every book will have some or all of the following parts:

THE PARTS OF A BOOK

Title page: Gives the title, author, and publisher

Copyright page: Gives information regarding the publication of the book and the copyrights protecting it from being copied or sold illegally

Table of contents: Lists the units, chapters, and/or subjects of the book and the page numbers where they are found

Preface, introduction, or foreword: Introduces the book

Text: Contains main part of the book

Afterword or epilogue: Gives conclusion or tells what happened later

Appendix: Gives additional information about subjects covered in the book, often in chart or table form

Glossary: Lists key words used in the book and their definitions

Bibliography: Lists sources used in writing the book or sources for further study

Index: Lists in alphabetical order the subjects mentioned in the book and pages where these subjects are treated

1.10 Reading Newspapers, Journals, and Newsmagazines

Newspapers, journals, and newsmagazines contain an enormous amount of information. Few people have time to read everything that appears in a newspaper each day. Nonetheless, staying aware of the news is important.

To get an overview of a newspaper, journal, or newsmagazine, skim the headlines and leads (the first sentence in a news story that explains the who, what, where, when, why, and how of the story). Read any news summaries. Then read in depth any stories that seem particularly important or interesting.

When reading news stories and editorials, make sure to distinguish between facts and opinions. **Facts** are statements that can be proved by observation or by consulting a reliable and objective source. **Opinions** are predictions or statements of value or belief. Sound opinions are supported by facts. For more information, see the Language Arts Survey 5.2, "Distinguishing Fact from Opinion."

1.11 "Reading" Art and Photographs

In today's visually stimulating world, books and news media rely on art, photographs, and other visuals as well as the printed word to convey ideas. Being able to understand and interpret graphic images is important. Visual arts offer insights into our world in a different way than print does.

Carefully examining a painting can lead you to discover meaning in it and to compare and contrast the painting's meaning with that of a written work. The same thing happens with photographs. Learning to interpret other graphics or images—drawings, diagrams, charts, and maps—will help

you to understand how things work, what things mean, and how things compare.

1.12 Seeking Knowledge as an Active Reader

Reading actively means thinking about what you are reading as you read it. Slow and careful reading—and sometimes rereading—is necessary to understand new and complex material. There are five key skills required for active reading.

ASK QUESTIONS. Questioning allows you to realize what you understand about what you are reading. Before you read, think about your prior knowledge about the subject. After reading, think about what you have learned and identify the questions you still have.

BEFORE READING
- What is this going to be about?
- What do I already know about the topic?
- What's my purpose for reading this?

DURING READING
- What does the author want me to know?
- What is the significance of what I am reading?
- What do I need to remember from this material?

AFTER READING
- What have I learned?
- What else do I want to know about this topic?

USE YOUR PRIOR KNOWLEDGE TO MAKE INFERENCES AND PREDICTIONS. While you are reading, use what you already know about the topic to make inferences about what the author is saying. As you read, try to make predictions about the next section.

KNOW WHAT YOU DO NOT KNOW. Recognizing when you do not understand something is as important as knowing that you do understand it. Form questions about the material you do not understand. Reread the text. Explain the topic to another student. Teaching someone else makes you understand the material in deeper ways.

SUMMARIZE OR SYNTHESIZE TEXT. Summarizing what you read helps you understand the main and supporting points in the text and helps you retrieve the information from long-term memory.

ADAPT YOUR READING APPROACH. If you realize that you are not comprehending the material, try another approach. Experiment with different tactics: speed up, slow down, reread, stand up and read, read the same material from another book, read with a dictionary in your lap, or generalize or visualize what you are reading.

1.13 Strategies for Reading to Learn: SQ3R

A five-step reading strategy called SQ3R can help you reduce your study time and increase your ability to understand essential information. The main steps of SQ3R are SURVEY, QUESTION, READ, RECALL, and REVIEW.

SURVEY
- Preview the organization of material.
- Glance at visuals and assess how they contribute to the meaning of the text.
- Skim headings and introductory paragraphs.
- Notice words in italics, boldface, and other terms that stand out.
- Ask yourself: What is the scope of the reading task? What should I learn from this material?

QUESTION
- Turn chapter titles and headings into questions.
- Ask yourself what the text is offering and what the author is saying.
- Ask yourself what you should know about the material and what you already know about it.
- Question graphics and visual materials. Translate the information they offer into your own words.
- Use words like *who, what, when, where, why,* and *how.*

READ
- Read and interact with the text.
- Underline or copy in your journal the main points.
- Make note of unusual or interesting ideas.
- Jot down words you need to define.
- Write your reactions to what you read.

RECALL
- Condense the major points of the text by writing recall cues.
- Summarize the material you have read. Reread any sections you don't clearly remember.

- Use graphic organizers to visualize or map out the material.
- Reread the text aloud if you need help recalling.

REVIEW
- After you have finished your reading, reread main headings and compare them to your notes.
- Review your notes, summaries, and definitions. Answer any questions you wrote.
- Ask yourself: What do I now understand? What is still confusing?

READING FOR INFORMATION

1.14 Reading Internet Materials, Reference Works, Graphic Aids, and Other Visuals

When you read for information, you are looking for information that answers a specific, immediate question; that teaches you to do something; or that will help you make a decision or draw a conclusion. You must learn to access, process, and think about the vast amount of information available on the Internet and in print reference works, graphic aids, and other visuals.

DETERMINE YOUR SPECIFIC PURPOSE FOR READING. State your purpose for reading as clearly as you can. Are you searching the Internet for a review of the movie you're unsure whether to see? Are you learning to operate a computer program? Are you researching data to determine the cost of a pet?

DETERMINE THE AUTHOR'S PURPOSE. Ask yourself what the writer wants the reader to think, believe, or do. Ask yourself if the author has bias on the topic that is affecting his or her views. If you are on the Internet, ask the following: Who is sponsoring the site? What hyperlinks are embedded in the site? Can you contact the site's author? When was the content written?

USE THE SEARCH APPROACH. Although your reading strategies should vary and relate directly to your purpose for reading, you may find the SEARCH method helpful when you are reading for information. SEARCH stands for SCAN, EXAMINE,

ACT, REVIEW, CONNECT, and HUNT.

SCAN
- Look over the text and determine how the material is structured.
- Look for a table of contents, a glossary, an index, and other helpful sections.
- On an Internet site, look for a site map.

EXAMINE
- Are there step-by-step directions on diagrams? Do directions reveal exactly what to do or do you need to experiment a little?
- Is there a pattern in headings or icons?
- Are there any references to other sources of information?

ACT
- Explore the procedures you are reading and learn by doing.
- If you are seeking data, take notes about the information. Is it exactly what you were looking for, or do you need to keep looking?

REVIEW
- Revisit the steps of a procedure to make sure you have them clear in your head.
- Compare similar resources and read any additional references or links provided.

CONNECT
- Connect the information to what you previously knew about the topic. How did you build on what you knew?
- Connect text with visual aids. How do the visual aids add to the text?

HUNT
- Look up the meanings of any new words.
- Use the help feature on a computer program to find answers to your questions.
- Make a diagram of a procedure to will help you remember it.

1.15 Using Graphic Aids

Graphic aids are maps, illustrations, charts, graphs, diagrams, spreadsheets, and other visual materials that present information. Information presented in tables, charts, and graphs can help you find information, see trends, discover facts, and uncover patterns. For a complete description of graphic aids, see "Elements of Informational and Visual Media" on pages 816–818.

Here are guidelines for working with graphics:

BEFORE READING
- Determine the subject of the graphic by reading the title, headings, and other clues.
- Determine how the data is organized, classified, or divided by reading the labels along rows or columns.
- Ask yourself: Why am I reading this document? What do I need to find? Where in this graphic is that information located?

DURING READING
- Survey the data and look for trends.
- Compare columns and rows, noting changes among information fields, look for patterns, or navigate map sections using keys and legends.
- Use legends, keys, and other helpful sections.
- Ask yourself: How does the data I need compare to other data on the graphic?

AFTER READING
- Check footnotes or references for additional information about the data and its sources.
- Ask yourself: Did this graphic answer my questions? If so, what are the answers? If not, where do I go to find the answers?

DEVELOPING YOUR VOCABULARY

1.16 Using Context Clues to Estimate Word Meaning

If you come across an unfamiliar word, you can often figure out its meaning by using context clues.

One type of context clue is **restatement**. The author may tell you the meaning of the word by using different words to express the same idea in another sentence.

EXAMPLE

The dog snarled at Donald malevolently. It looked mean and spiteful.

The restatement provides a context clue that *malevolently* means "maliciously, with intent to do harm."

Another type of context clue is **apposition**. An apposition renames something in different words.

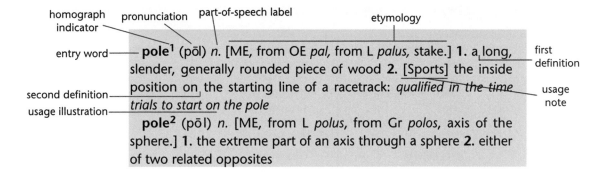

homograph indicator pronunciation part-of-speech label etymology

entry word

first definition

second definition

usage note

usage illustration

pole[1] (pōl) *n.* [ME, from OE *pal,* from L *palus,* stake.] **1.** a long, slender, generally rounded piece of wood **2.** [Sports] the inside position on the starting line of a racetrack: *qualified in the time trials to start on the pole*

pole[2] (pōl) *n.* [ME, from L *polus,* from Gr *polos,* axis of the sphere.] **1.** the extreme part of an axis through a sphere **2.** either of two related opposites

Look for a word or phrase in the sentence that clarifies the word you do not know.

EXAMPLE

Evan's conclusion was based on a fallacy, a false idea about how Maggie felt toward him.

Examples given in a sentence can also be used as context clues.

EXAMPLE

The words *dad, radar, noon,* and *tenet* are all palindromes.

1.17 Using a Dictionary

Dictionary entries provide much more information about words than just their spelling and definitions.

The **pronunciation** is given immediately after the entry word. You can find a complete key to pronunciation symbols in the dictionary's table of contents. In some dictionaries, a simplified key is provided at the bottom of each page.

An abbreviation of the **part of speech** usually follows the pronunciation. This label tells the ways in which a word can be used (see the Language Arts Survey 3.46–3.78, "Parts of Speech Summary").

An **etymology** is the history of a word. In the first entry, the word *pole* can be traced back through Middle English (ME) and Old English (OE) to the Latin (L) word *palus,* which means "stake."

Each **definition** in the entry gives a different meaning of the word. When a word has more than one meaning, the different definitions are numbered. The first definition in an entry is the most common meaning of the word. Sometimes the entry will include a list of **synonyms**.

1.18 Using Glossaries and Footnotes

A **glossary** is an alphabetized list of defined words at the end of an article, chapter, or book.

Footnotes appear at the foot, or bottom, of a page. Sometimes they cite a source of information. Other times they define annotated words in order of appearance.

1.19 Learning Base Words, Prefixes, and Suffixes

Many words are formed by adding prefixes or suffixes to base words. (See the Language Arts Survey 3.95, "Using Spelling Rules I.") If you are unfamiliar with a word that is formed with a prefix or a suffix, see if you recognize the meaning of the base word and the meaning of its prefix or suffix. See the Prefixes and Suffixes table on the following page.

1.20 Learning Synonyms, Antonyms, and Homonyms

A **synonym** is a word that has the same or nearly the same meaning as another word.

EXAMPLES   discover, find, locate, pinpoint

An **antonym** is a word that means the opposite of another word.

EXAMPLES   discover, conceal
give, take
success, defeat

A **homonym** is a word that has the same pronunciation as another word but a different meaning, origin, and usually, spelling.

EXAMPLES   bight, bite, byte

1.21 Exploring Word Origins and Word Families

The English language gains new words from many different sources. One source is the names of people and places. For example, the hamburger takes its name from the city of Hamburg, Germany.

prefix	meaning	example	meaning
anti–	"against"	antibacterial	against bacteria
dis–	"not, opposite"	disagreeable	not agreeable
hyper–	"over, excessively"	hyperactive	excessively active
im–, un–	"not"	unusual	not usual
post–	"after"	postseason	after the season
re–	"again"	reprint	print again

suffix	meaning	example	meaning
–er, –or	"one who"	narrator	one who narrates
–ful	"full of"	graceful	full of grace
–ish	"like"	childish	like a child
–ity, –ty	"state of, quality"	captivity	state of being captive
–less	"without"	fearless	without fear
–ment	"act of, state of"	achievement	act of achieving

Acronyms are words formed from the first letter or letters of the major parts of terms.

EXAMPLES sonar, from sound navigation ranging; NATO, from North Atlantic Treaty Organization; NASA, from National Aeronautic and Space Administration

Some words in the English language are **borrowed** from other languages.

EXAMPLES deluxe (French), Gesundheit (German), kayak (Eskimo)

Many words are formed by **shortening** longer words.

EXAMPLES ad, from advertisement; auto, from automobile; lab, from laboratory

Brand names are often taken into the English language. People begin to use these words as common nouns, even though most of them are still brand names.

EXAMPLES Scotch tape, Rollerblade, Walkman

1.22 Jargon and Gobbledygook

Jargon is the specialized vocabulary members of a profession use. It tends to be difficult for people outside the profession to understand. A plumber may speak of a "hubless fitting" or a "street elbow" (kinds of pipe). A computer programmer may talk of "ram cache" (part of computer memory). Jargon is useful to writers who want to authentically describe certain situations. For example, a novel about fighter pilots might feature aviation jargon.

Gobbledygook is unclear, wordy jargon used by bureaucrats, government officials, and others. A bureaucrat might say, "We are engaged in conducting a study with a view to ascertaining which employees might be assigned to the mobility pool and how we might create revenue enhancement" when he means, "We plan to cut jobs and increase taxes."

1.23 Clichés and Euphemisms

A **cliché** is an expression that has been used so often it has become a cliché. Clichés instantly make writing dull.

EXAMPLES quick as a wink, pretty as a picture

A **euphemism** is an inoffensive term that substitutes for one considered harsh or offensive.

EXAMPLES aerial mishap (for "plane crash") building engineer (for "janitor")

1.24 Connotation and Denotation

A **denotation** of a word is its dictionary definition. A **connotation** of a word is all the associations it has in addition to its literal meaning. For example, the words *cheap* and *economical* both denote "inexpensive," but *cheap* connotes shoddy and inferior while *economical* connotes a good value for the money. Writers and speakers should be aware of the connotations as well as the denotations of the words they use.

INTRODUCTION TO WRITING

2.1 The Writing Process

The most important action that you can take to shape a successful future for yourself is to learn how to write clearly and effectively. Almost anyone can learn to write well by learning the writing process. The writing process is simply the steps that a person takes to put together a piece of writing.

SEVEN STAGES IN THE PROCESS OF WRITING	
STAGE	**TASKS**
1. Prewriting	Plan your writing; choose a topic, audience, purpose, and form; gather ideas; and arrange them logically.
2. Drafting	Get your ideas down on paper.
3. Self- and Peer Evaluation	Evaluate, or judge, the writing piece and suggest ways to improve it. Judging your own writing is called **self-evaluation**. Judging a classmate's writing is called **peer evaluation**.
4. Revising	Work to improve the content, organization, and expression of your ideas.
5. Proofreading	Check your writing for errors in spelling, grammar, capitalization, and punctuation. Correct these errors, make a final copy of your paper, and proofread it again.
6. Publishing and Presenting	Share your work with an audience.
7. Reflecting	Think through the writing process to determine what you learned as a writer, what you accomplished, and what you would like to strengthen the next time you write.

While writing moves through these seven stages, it is also is a continuing cycle. You might need to go back to a previous stage before going on to the next step. Returning to a previous stage will strengthen your final work. Note also that the Reflecting stage can be done between any of the other steps. The more you reflect on your writing, the better your writing will become.

UNDERSTANDING THE WRITING PROCESS

2.2 Prewriting

In the **prewriting** stage of the writing process, you make a writing plan. You decide on a purpose, audience, form, and topic. You also begin to discover your voice and gather and organize ideas.

THE PARTS OF A WRITING PLAN

Purpose	A **purpose**, or **aim**, is the goal that you want your writing to accomplish.
Audience	An **audience** is the person or group of people intended to read what you write.
Form	A **form** is a kind of writing. For example, you might write a paragraph, an essay, a short story, a poem, or a news article.
Topic	A **topic** is simply something to write about. For example, you might write about a sports hero or about a cultural event in your community.

2.3 IDENTIFYING YOUR PURPOSE. A **purpose**, or **aim**, is the goal that you want your writing to accomplish. For example, you might write to inform, to entertain, to tell a story, to reflect, or to persuade. Your writing might have more than one purpose. For example, a piece of writing might inform about an important event while persuading the audience to respond in a specific way.

MODES AND PURPOSES OF WRITING

MODE	PURPOSE	EXAMPLE
expository/informative writing	to inform	news article, research report
imaginative writing	to entertain, enrich, and enlighten by using a form such as fiction or poetry to share a perspective	poem, short story
narrative writing	to make a point by sharing a story about an event	biography, family history
personal/expressive writing	to reflect	diary entry, personal letter
persuasive/argumentative writing	to persuade readers or listeners to respond in some way, such as to agree with a position, change a view on an issue, reach an agreement, or perform an action	editorial, petition

2.4 IDENTIFYING YOUR AUDIENCE. An **audience** is the person or group of people intended to read what you write. For example, you might write for yourself, for a friend, for a relative, or for your classmates. The best writing usually is intended for a specific audience. Choosing a specific audience beforehand will help you make important decisions about your work. For example, for an audience of young children, you would use simple words and ideas. For an audience of fellow members of a technology club, you would use jargon and other specialized words that the members already know. For more information, see the the Language Arts Survey 3.3, "Register, Tone, and Voice."

THINKING ABOUT YOUR AUDIENCE

- What people would be most interested in my topic?
- How much does the audience that I am considering already know about the topic?
- How much background information do I need to provide?
- What words, phrases, or concepts in my writing will my audience not understand? For which ones will I have to provide clear explanations?
- What can I do at the beginning of my writing to capture my audience's interest?

2.5 FINDING YOUR VOICE. Voice is the quality of a work that tells you that one person in particular wrote it. Voice makes a person's writing unique. Beginning with the prewriting stage and continuing through the rest of the writing process, a writer discovers his or her own unique voice. For more information, see the section about voice in the Language Arts Survey 3.3, "Register, Tone, and Voice."

2.6 CHOOSING A FORM. Another important decision that a writer needs to make is what form his or her writing will take. A **form** is a kind of writing. For example, you might write a paragraph, an essay, a short story, a poem, or a newspaper article. The following chart lists some forms of writing that you might want to consider.

FORMS OF WRITING

Adventure	Dialogue	Journal entry	Rap
Advertisement	Directions	Letter	Recipe
Advice column	Dream report	Magazine article	Recommendation
Agenda	Editorial	Memorandum	Research report
Apology	Epitaph	Menu	Résumé
Appeal	Essay	Minutes	Schedule
Autobiography	Eulogy	Movie review	Science fiction
Biography	Experiment	Mystery	Short story
Book review	Fable	Myth	Slide show
Brochure	Family history	Narrative	Slogan
Calendar	Fantasy	Newspaper article	Song lyric
Caption	Greeting card	Obituary	Speech
Cartoon	Headline	Parable	Sports story
Character sketch	History	Paraphrase	Statement of belief
Cheer	Human interest story	Petition	Summary
Children's story	Instructions	Play	Tall tale
Comedy	Interview questions	Police/Accident report	Thank-you note
Consumer report	Invitation	Poster	Tour guide
Debate	Itinerary	Proposal	Want ad
Detective story	Joke	Radio or TV spot	Wish list

2.7 CHOOSING A TOPIC. A **topic** is simply something to write about. For example, you might write about a sports hero or about a cultural event in your community. Here are some ideas that may help you to find interesting writing topics:

WAYS TO FIND A WRITING TOPIC

Check your journal	Search through your journal for ideas that you jotted down in the past. Many professional writers get their ideas from their journals.
Think about your experiences	Think about people, places, or events that affected you strongly. Recall experiences that taught you important lessons or that you felt strongly about.
Look at reference works	Reference works include printed or computerized dictionaries, atlases, almanacs, and encyclopedias.
Browse in a library	Libraries are treasure houses of information and ideas. Simply looking around in the stacks of a library can suggest good writing ideas.

CONTINUED

WAYS TO FIND A WRITING TOPIC

Use the mass media	Newspapers, magazines, radio, television, and films can suggest good writing topics. For example, a glance at listings for public television programs might suggest topics related to the arts, to history, or to nature.
Talk to people	Friends, relatives, teachers, and other people you know make great sources for writing topics.
Do some freewriting	Simply put your pen or pencil down on a piece of paper and write about whatever pops into your mind. Write for two to five minutes without pausing to worry about whether your writing is perfect. Then look back over what you have written to see if you can find any good topics there.
Ask "What if" questions	Ask questions beginning with "What if" to come up with topics for creative writing. For example, you might ask, "What if a kid with a ham radio set received a message from space? Would people believe her?"
Make a cluster chart	Write some general subject such as music or sports in the middle of a piece of paper. Circle this subject. Then, around it, write other ideas that come into your mind as you think about the subject. Circle these and draw lines to connect the outer circles to the inner one.

2.8 FOCUSING A TOPIC. Sometimes a topic is too broad to be treated in a short piece of writing. When you have a topic that is too broad, you must **focus**, or limit, the topic. Try to break the topic into parts. Try asking questions about the topic, making a cluster chart, or freewriting.

GATHERING IDEAS

Once you have made your writing plan by identifying your purpose, form, audience, and topic, the next step in the prewriting stage is to **gather ideas**. There are many ways to gather ideas for writing. This section will introduce you to some of the most useful ones.

2.9 BRAINSTORMING. When you **brainstorm,** you think of as many ideas as you can, as quickly as you can, without stopping to evaluate or criticize the ideas. In brainstorming, anything goes. Sometimes even silly-sounding ideas can lead to productive ones. When you brainstorm in a group, often one person's idea will help another person to build on that concept. It is a good way to come up with creative, new ideas and innovative solutions to problems. Welcome all ideas with an encouraging response. Be sure to get contributions from everyone in your group and to record all ideas so they can be considered and judged later.

2.10 LEARNING FROM PROFESSIONAL MODELS. Professional models are works by published authors. They can be an excellent way to gather your own ideas. For more information, see the way professional models are used in the Guided Writing lessons at the end of each unit in this textbook.

2.11 KEEPING A JOURNAL. A **journal** is a record of your ideas, dreams, wishes, and experiences. Composition books, spiral notebooks, looseleaf binders, and bound books with blank pages all make excellent journal books. Some people even keep electronic journals on computers. You may want to use a journal to write thoughts, collect ideas for writing, organize tasks, or keep a learning log.

2.12 FREEWRITING. Freewriting is simply taking a pencil and paper and writing whatever comes into your mind. Try to write for several minutes without stopping and without worrying about spelling, grammar, usage, or mechanics. If you get stuck, just repeat the last few words until something new pops into your mind. To gather ideas about a specific topic, you might want to try **focused freewriting**. In a focused freewrite, you still write nonstop for a few minutes, but you stick with one topic and write whatever comes to mind as you think about that topic.

2.13 CLUSTERING. Another good way to tap what you already know is to make a **cluster chart**. To make a cluster chart, draw a circle in the center of your paper. In it write a topic you want to explore. Draw more circles branching out from your center circle, and fill them with subtopics related to your main topic.

SAMPLE CLUSTER CHART

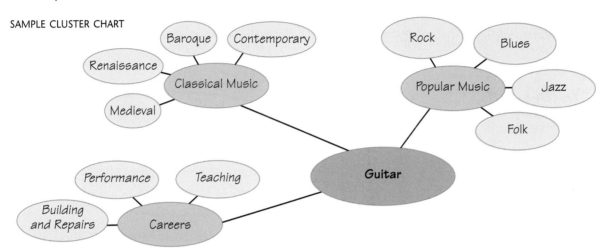

2.14 QUESTIONING: USING THE 5 Ws AND AN H. Using the 5 Ws and an H means asking the **reporting questions** who, what, where, when, why, and how about your topic. This questioning strategy is especially useful for gathering information about an event or for planning a story.

USING QUESTIONING (TOPIC: COWBOY POETRY)	
Who	Cowboy poets from the United States and other parts of the world
What	The Cowboy Poetry Festival, where cowboy poets gather
Where	Elko, Nevada
When	Held annually the last week in January
Why	So cowboys who love performing their songs, poetry, and stories can share them with others
How	This happens because of the huge interest in cowboy poetry and because of the major help from volunteers; the Western Folklife Center in Elko is a major organizer.

2.15 IMAGINING: ASKING "WHAT IF" QUESTIONS. If you are doing imaginative or creative writing, ask questions that begin with the words *what if*. "What if" questions can spark your imagination and lead you down unexpected and interesting paths. It can also help you see another side of things and strengthen your own when writing a persuasive piece.

What if I could run school for a week? What changes would I make?

What if I could go back in time to speak with a historical figure?

What if the greenhouse effect melted the polar icecaps and raised the levels of the oceans around the world? How would people respond?

2.16 COMPLETING VENN DIAGRAMS. If you are writing a comparison and contrast essay, one of the best ways to gather ideas is by completing a Venn diagram. A **Venn diagram** shows two slightly overlapping circles. The outer part of each circle shows what aspects of two things are different from each other. The inner, or shared, part of each circle shows what aspects the two things share.

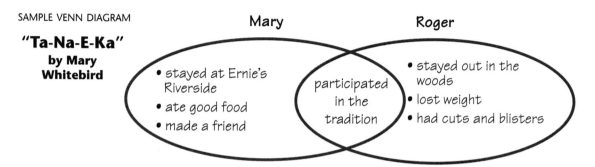

SAMPLE VENN DIAGRAM

"Ta-Na-E-Ka" by Mary Whitebird

Mary
- stayed at Ernie's Riverside
- ate good food
- made a friend

participated in the tradition

Roger
- stayed out in the woods
- lost weight
- had cuts and blisters

2.17 ANALYZING. To **analyze** is to break something down into its parts and then think about how the parts are related. Analyzing is a way to sort out information about a topic.

2.18 SENSORY DETAIL CHARTS. Most people have the use of five major senses: sight, sound, touch, taste, and smell. The larger the number of these senses you use to observe something, the more you will notice about it. A **sensory detail chart** can help you to collect information about something so that you can describe it thoroughly.

SENSORY DETAILS OF A MARATHON				
SIGHT	**SOUND**	**TOUCH**	**TASTE**	**SMELL**
hundreds of runners of all ages	starting gun	hot, sore feet from standing so long	hot dogs and lemonade from vendor carts	hot asphalt
news reporters and onlookers	crowds clapping			perspiration
running clothes	running shoes slapping on asphalt	stinging face from sun and wind		

2.19 TIME LINES. A **time line** can be useful when you are planning to write a story or a historical account. It gives you an overview of the sequence of events during a particular time period. To make a time line, draw a line on a piece of paper and divide it into equal parts. Label each part with a date or a time. Then add key events at the right places along the time line.

Confucius lived — 500 BC

Building of the Great Wall began — 200 BC

Huns invaded China — AD 250

Marked developments in literature and the arts — AD 1000

2.20 STORY MAPS. A **story map** is a chart that shows the various parts of a fable, myth, tall tale, legend, short story, or other fictional work. Most story maps include the following elements:

ELEMENTS OF A STORY MAP	
ELEMENT	**DESCRIPTION**
Setting	The time and place in which the story occurs
Mood	The emotion created in the reader by the story
Conflict	A struggle between two forces in the story
Plot	The series of events taking place in the story
Characters	The people (or sometimes animals) who play roles in the story
Theme	The main idea of the story

2.21 PRO AND CON CHARTS. A **pro and con chart** shows arguments for and against taking a particular position on some issue. To create a pro and con chart, begin by writing a statement, called a **proposition**, at the top of a piece of paper. Under the proposition, make two columns, one labeled *Pro* and the other, *Con*. In the pro column, list arguments in favor of the proposition. In the con column, list arguments against the proposition.

PRO AND CON CHART	
Proposition: All students should take an hour of physical education each day.	
Pro	**Con**
—would keep students in good physical condition —improved health would also improve students' ability to think clearly and work hard	—would take time away from academic studies —the same ends might be achieved in less time per day

2.22 INTERVIEWING. In an **interview**, you meet with someone and ask him or her questions. Interviewing experts is an excellent way to gain information about a particular topic. When planning an interview, list the questions you would like to ask, including some about the person's background as well as about your topic. Other questions might occur to you as the interview proceeds. See the Language Arts Survey 4.14, "Conducting an Interview."

2.23 RESEARCHING FOR IDEAS. No matter what your subject, you can probably find information about it by doing research in reference works. **Reference works** include encyclopedias, dictionaries, almanacs, atlases, indexes, Internet sites, and more. For additional information about reference materials and how to find them, see the Language Arts Survey 5.19, "Using Reference Works," and 5.36, "Keeping a Research Journal."

ORGANIZING IDEAS

2.24 WRITING PARAGRAPHS. After you have gathered ideas for a piece of writing, the next step is to organize these ideas in a useful way. The most basic organization of ideas occurs in paragraphs. A good paragraph is a carefully organized unit of writing. It develops a sequence in narrative writing or develops a particular topic in informational or persuasive writing.

PARAGRAPHS WITH TOPIC SENTENCES. Many paragraphs include a topic sentence that presents a main idea. The topic sentence can be placed at the beginning, middle or end of the paragraph. Topic sentences usually appear early on in the paragraph and are commonly followed by one or more supporting sentences. Often these supporting sentences begin with transitions that relate them to the other sentences or to the topic sentence. This type of paragraph may end with a clincher sentence, which sums up what has been said in the paragraph.

PARAGRAPHS WITHOUT TOPIC SENTENCES. Most paragraphs do not have topic sentences. In a narrative piece of writing, many paragraphs state a series of events, and no sentence in the paragraph sums up the events. In good narrative writing, the sequence of events appears in chronological order. Descriptive writing may contain paragraphs organized spatially—in the order in which the speaker or narrator sees, hears, feels, smells, and tastes things in a given situation.

PARAGRAPH UNITY. The ideas in a paragraph should be tightly linked, or "together." They should be ordered and linked in a logical and easily understandable way. You can organize a paragraph in the order of time (chronologically), in the order of importance, or in order to achieve a specific purpose, such as describing or comparing and contrasting. To link the ideas in a paragraph, use connective words and phrases. In informational or persuasive paragraphs, *for example, as a result, finally, therefore,* and *in fact* are common connectives. In narrative and descriptive paragraphs, words like *first, then, suddenly, above, beyond, in the distance,* and *there* are common connectives. In comparison-contrast paragraphs, common phrases include *similarly, on the other hand,* and *in contrast.* In cause-and-effect paragraphs, linkers include *one cause, another effect, as a result, consequently, finally,* and *therefore.*

2.25 WRITING A THESIS STATEMENT. One way to start organizing your writing, especially if you are writing an informative essay, is to identify the main idea of what you want to say. Present this idea in the form of a sentence or two called a thesis statement. A **thesis statement** is simply a sentence that presents the main idea or the position you will take in your essay.

EXAMPLE   The ecosystem at Lost Dutchman State Park is mainly made up of plants and animals that thrive in a hot, dry climate.

2.26 WRITING MAIN IDEAS AND SUPPORTING DETAILS. Once you have a thesis statement, the next step is to select several main ideas to support your thesis statement. Begin by writing your thesis at the top of a piece of paper. Then list the main points that you will use to support your thesis. For each main idea, list several supporting details—statements, facts, examples, quotes, and illustrations that explain or demonstrate your idea.

THESIS: The ecosystem at Lost Dutchman State Park is mainly made up of plants and animals that thrive in a hot, dry climate.

- Desert plants
  —cacti, succulents, low-moisture shrubs, and some trees
  —provide nutrients for desert animals

—can hold in moisture to use in times of drought
—bloom when enough rain occurs

- Desert animals
—coyotes, rabbits, chipmunks, wolves, hedgehogs, prairie dogs, foxes, bats, javelinas
—lizards, geckoes, snakes, salamanders, tarantulas, millipedes
—roadrunners, sparrows, hummingbirds, cactus wrens

- Interaction among animals and plants
—Ocotillo shrub and hummingbirds
—teddy bear cactus and cactus wrens
—prickly pear cactus and javelina

2.27 CHOOSING A METHOD OF ORGANIZATION. Writing can be organized in different ways.

METHOD	DESCRIPTION
Chronological Order	Give events in the order in which they happen or should be done; connect events by using transition words such as *first, second, next, then,* and *finally.* Chronological organization would be a good method for giving a recipe, writing a how-to article on building a bird-feeder, or to describe a process, such as what happens when a volcano erupts.
Spatial Order	Describe parts in order of their location in space, for example, from back to front, left to right, or top to bottom; connect your descriptions with transition words or phrases such as *next to, beside, above, below, beyond,* and *around.* Spatial order would be a useful form for an article describing a kitchen renovation, or a descriptive passage in a science fiction story set in a space station.
Order of Importance	List details from least important to most important or from most important to least important; connect your details with transition phrases such as *more important, less important, most important,* and *least important.* A speech telling voters why they should elect you class president could be organized from the least important reason and build to the most important reason.
Comparison and Contrast Order	Details of two subjects are presented in one of two ways. In the first method, the characteristics of one subject are presented, followed by the characteristics of the second subject. This method would be useful to organize an essay that compares and contrasts two fast-food chains. You could use this method to say why one is superior to another. "BurgerWorld has the most restaurants. They broil their hamburgers, and offer a line of low-fat meals. Ma's Burgers has far fewer restaurants, fries their hamburgers, and offers no low-fat choices." In the second method, both subjects are compared and contrasted with regard to one quality, then with regard to a second quality, and so on. An essay organized according to this method could compare the platforms of two political parties, issue by issue: the environment, the economy, and so on.

Cause and Effect Order	Ideas are connected by transitional words and phrases that indicate similarities or differences, such as *likewise, similarly, in contrast,* and *another difference.* One or more causes are presented followed by one or more effects, or one or more effects are presented followed by one or more causes. A public health announcement warning about the dangers of playing with fire would be usefully organized by cause and effect. An essay discussing the outbreak of World War I and the events that led up to it could be organized by effect and causes. Transitional words and phrases that indicate cause and effect include *one cause, another effect, as a result, consequently,* and *therefore.*
Part-by-Part Order	Ideas are presented according to no *overall* organizational pattern. However, each idea is connected logically to the one that precedes it and/or to the one that follows it. A letter to a friend might be organized part by part. One paragraph might discuss a party the writer just attended and the next could focus on the writer's feelings about a person he or she met there. After chronological order, this is the most common method for organizing ideas in writing.

2.28 OUTLINING. An **outline** is an excellent framework for highlighting main ideas and supporting details. Rough and formal outlines are the two main types of outlines writers commonly use.

2.29 ROUGH OUTLINES. To create a **rough outline**, simply list your main ideas in some logical order. Under each main idea, list the supporting details set off by dashes.

2.30 FORMAL OUTLINES. A **formal outline** has headings and subheadings identified by numbers and letters. One type of formal outline is the **topic outline**. Such an outline has entries that are words or phrases rather than complete sentences.

What Is a Myth?

I. Definition of myth
    A. Ancient story involving gods
        1. Multiple gods in mythology
        2. Gods given human characteristics
    B. Often about origins
        1. Reflect prescientific worldview
        2. Gods and humans actively participate
    C. Often about heroes
II. Origin myths
    A. Arachne and the origins of spiders
    B. Phaëthon and the origins of deserts
III. Hero myths
    A. Theseus and the Minotaur
    B. Herakles and the twelve labors

2.31 Drafting

After you have gathered your information and organized it, the next step in writing is to produce a draft. A **draft** is simply an early attempt at writing a paper. When working on a draft, keep in mind that you do not have to get everything just right the first time through. You can rework it many times until you are happy with the final product.

Different writers approach drafting in different ways. Some prefer to work slowly and carefully, perfecting each part as they go. Producing such a **careful draft** can be rewarding because you get to see a finished, polished piece emerging part by part. However, many writers find that perfecting each part as they come to it bogs down the process. These writers prefer to write a discovery draft, getting all their ideas down on paper in rough form and then going back over the paper to work it into shape. When writing a **discovery draft**, you do not focus on spelling, grammar, usage, and mechanics. You can take care of those matters during revision.

2.32 DRAFTING AN INTRODUCTION. The purpose of an introduction is to capture your reader's attention and establish what you want to say. An effective introduction can start with a quotation, a question, an anecdote, an intriguing fact, or a description that hooks the reader to keep reading. An effective introduction can open with a quote, a question, an anecdote, a fact, or a description.

2.33 DRAFTING BODY PARAGRAPHS. When writing the body of an essay, refer to your outline. Each heading in your outline will become the main idea of one of your paragraphs. To move smoothly from one idea to another, use transitional words or phrases. As you draft, you may want to include evidence from documented sources to support the ideas that you present. For more information, see 2.24, "Writing Paragraphs."

2.34 DRAFTING A CONCLUSION. In the conclusion, bring together the main ideas you included in the body of your essay and create a sense of closure to the issue you raised in your thesis. There is no single right way to conclude a piece of writing. Possibilities include:

- making a generalization
- restating the thesis and major supporting ideas in different words
- summarizing the points made in the rest of the essay
- drawing a lesson or moral
- calling on the reader to adopt a view or take an action
- expanding on your thesis or main idea by connecting it to the reader's own interests
- linking your thesis to a larger issue or concern.

2.35 USING TRANSITIONS EFFECTIVELY. Transitions are words and phrases that help you move smoothly from one idea to the next in your writing. The transition words themselves depend on the method of organization you are using in your paper. For lists of these words and when to use them, see the Language Arts Survey 2.27, "Choosing a Method of Organization."

2.36 WRITING NARRATIVE, DIALOGUE, DESCRIPTION, AND EXPOSITION. Some writing purposes do not require a thesis or a formal outline. They rely on other types of writing to present their ideas effectively. These types include description, dialogue, narration, and exposition. **Narration** tells a story or describes events using time, or *chronological order*, as a way of organization. **Dialogue** presents words as they were actually spoken by people. Quotation marks are usually used to set off direct speech. **Description** portrays a character, an object, or a scene. Descriptions make use of sensory details—words and phrases that describe how things look, sound, smell, taste, or feel. Descriptive writing frequently uses *spatial order* as a way of organization. **Exposition** presents facts or opinions in an organized manner. There are many ways to organize exposition. Among the most common are the following:

- **Analysis** breaks something into its parts and shows how the parts are related.
- **Cause and Effect** identifies and analyzes the causes and effects of something.
- **Classification** involves placing subjects into categories, or classes, according to their properties or characteristics. These groups are then presented, one-by-one, in some reasonable order.
- **Comparison and Contrast Order** is a method of organization in which details about the similarities and differences between two subjects are presented.
- **Definition** explains a concept or idea and examines its qualities.
- **Problem/Solution** writing analyzes a problem and proposes possible solutions. It can be objective or persuasive.
- **Process/How-to** writing presents the steps in a process or gives the reader directions on how to do something.

2.37 Self- and Peer Evaluation

When you evaluate something, you examine it carefully to find its strengths and weaknesses. Evaluating your own writing is called **self-evaluation**. A **peer evaluation** is an evaluation of a piece of writing done by a classmate, or peer.

2.38 How to Evaluate a Piece of Writing. A good evaluation practice is to read through the piece of writing three times:

- First, check for content. If you are evaluating your own writing, make sure that you have said all that you want to say, that you have not left out important details, and that you have not included unimportant or unrelated details. If you are evaluating a peer's writing, make sure the content is clear, that nothing is missing to prevent the work from carrying the reader forward, and that the writer has not included any unrelated details.
- Second, check for organization. Present your ideas in the writing in a reasonable order.
- Third, check the style and language of the piece. Make sure that the language is appropriately formal or informal, that the tone is appropriate, and that the writer has defined any key or unfamiliar terms.

As you check the writing piece, make notes about what the writer needs to revise, or change. See the Language Arts Survey 2.42, "A Revision Checklist," for further information on what to look for as you evaluate your or a peer's writing.

2.39 How to Deliver Helpful Criticism

- Be focused. Concentrate on content, organization, and style. Do not concentrate at this point on proofreading matters such as spelling and punctuation; they can be fixed later.
- Be positive. Let the writer know what he or she has done right. Show how the paper could be improved by making the changes that you are suggesting.
- Be specific. Give the writer concrete ideas for improving his or her work. For example, if you think that two ideas seem unconnected, suggest a way in which they might be connected clearly.
- Be tactful. Consider the other person's feelings, and use a pleasant tone of voice. Do not criticize the writer. Instead, focus on the writing.

2.40 How to Benefit from Helpful Criticism

- Tell your evaluator specific concerns. For example, if you are wondering whether something you have written is clear, ask the evaluator if he or she understands that part of what you have written.

- Ask questions to clarify comments that your evaluator makes.
- Accept your evaluator's comments graciously. Remember that criticisms can be helpful. If you think that a given suggestion will not truly improve your writing, you do not have to follow it.

2.41 Revising

After identifying weaknesses in a draft through self-evaluation and peer evaluation, the next step is to **revise** the draft. Here are four basic ways to improve meaning and content.

ADDING OR EXPANDING. Sometimes writing can be improved by adding details, examples, or transitions to connect ideas. Often a single added adjective, for example, can make a piece of writing clearer or more vivid.

UNREVISED

Wind whistled through the park.

REVISED

A **bone-chilling** wind whistled through the park.

At other times, you will find you will need to add details to back up your main idea.

UNREVISED

Everyone uses the park so its destruction would be a major loss to the community.

REVISED

Of the 653 people who responded to the survey, 85 percent said they would consider the destruction of the park a major loss to the community.

CUTTING OR CONDENSING. Often writing can be improved by cutting unnecessary or unrelated material.

UNREVISED

Watson was firmly determined to find the structure of the DNA molecule.

REVISED

Watson was determined to find the structure of the DNA molecule.

REPLACING. Sometimes weak writing can be replaced with stronger writing that is more concrete, more vivid, or more precise.

UNREVISED

Chandra lived in a house down the street.

REVISED

Chandra lived in a Garrison colonial down Mulberry Street.

MOVING. Often you can improve the organization of your writing by moving part of it so that related ideas appear near one another.

UNREVISED

Mince the garlic in very fine pieces. Then cook in olive oil in a small skillet. Stir it with a wooden spoon and saute just until it starts to brown. Then remove it. Oh—before you put it in the skillet, heat some oil. Use about a tablespoon. Olive oil is best. Use medium-low heat.

Mince the garlic in very fine pieces. Heat a tablespoon of olive oil in a small skillet at a medium-low temperature. When the oil is hot, add the garlic. Stir it with a wooden spoon and saute it just until it starts to brown. Then remove the garlic.

When you mark a piece of writing for revision, use the standard proofreading symbols. The symbols for adding, cutting, replacing, and moving are the first four symbols in the Language Arts Survey 2.44, "Using Proofreader's Marks."

2.42 A REVISION CHECKLIST. The following chart lists some questions to ask yourself whenever you are revising your writing.

REVISION CHECKLIST	
Content	• Does the writing achieve its purpose?
	• Are the main ideas clearly stated and supported by details?
Organization	• Are the ideas arranged in a sensible order?
	• Are the ideas connected to one another within paragraphs and between paragraphs?
Style	• Is the language appropriate to the audience and purpose?
	• Is the mood appropriate to the purpose of the writing?

2.43 Proofreading

When you **proofread** your writing, you read it through to look for errors and mark corrections. When you mark corrections to your writing, use the standard proofreading symbols.

2.44 USING PROOFREADER'S MARKS. Consult the chart below for standard proofreading marks.

PROOFREADER'S SYMBOLS	
Symbol and Example	**Meaning of Symbol**
The very first time	Delete (cut) this material.
cat cradle	Insert (add) something that is missing.
George	Replace this letter or word.
All the horses king's	Move this word to where the arrow points.
french toast	Capitalize this letter.
the vice-President	Lowercase this letter.
housse	Take out this letter and close up space.
book keeper	Close up space.
gebril	Change the order of these letters.
end. "Watch out," she yelled.	Begin a new paragraph.
Love conquers all	Put a period here.
Welcome friends.	Put a comma here.

Symbol and Example	Meaning of Symbol
Get the stopwatch	Put a space here.
Dear Madam◇	Put a colon here.
She walked‸he rode.	Put a semicolon here.
name═brand products	Put a hyphen here.
cats meow	Put an apostrophe here.
cat's cradle (stet)	Let it stand. (Leave as it is.)

2.45 A PROOFREADING CHECKLIST. After you have revised your draft, make a clean copy of it and proofread it for errors in spelling, grammar, and punctuation. Use the following proofreading checklist.

PROOFREADING CHECKLIST

Spelling	• Are all words, including names, spelled correctly?
Grammar	• Does each verb agree with its subject?
	• Are verb tenses consistent and correct?
	• Are irregular verbs formed correctly?
	• Are there any sentence fragments or run-ons?
	• Have double negatives been avoided?
	• Have frequently confused words, such as *affect* and *effect*, been used correctly?
Punctuation	• Does every sentence end with an end mark?
	• Are commas used correctly?
	• Do all proper nouns and proper adjectives begin with capital letters?

2.46 PROPER MANUSCRIPT FORM. After proofreading your draft, you will want to prepare your final manuscript. Follow the guidelines given by your teacher or the guidelines given here. After preparing a final manuscript according to these guidelines, proofread it one last time for errors.

- Keyboard your manuscript using a typewriter or word processor, or write it out neatly using blue or black ink.
- Double-space your paper. Leave one blank line between every line of text.
- Use one side of the paper.
- Leave one-inch margins on all sides of the text.
- Indent the first line of each paragraph.
- Make a cover sheet listing the title of the work, your name, the date, and the class.
- In the upper right corner of the first page, put your name, class, and date. On every page after the first, include the page number in the heading.

2.47 Publishing and Presenting Your Work

In the **publishing and presenting stage**, you share your work with an audience.

2.48 MAINTAINING A WRITING PORTFOLIO. A **writing portfolio** is a collection of your writing. Usually, a portfolio is a file folder with your name on it and your writing in it. Your teacher may ask you to keep a complete portfolio, that includes all the pieces that you write, or a selected portfolio that contains only your very best pieces of writing. From time to time, you and your teacher will evaluate, or examine, your portfolio. You will meet in a student-teacher conference and talk about your pieces of writing. Your teacher will help you to find strengths and weaknesses in your writing. He or she also will help you to make plans for improving your writing in the future.

2.49 SHARING YOUR WORK WITH OTHERS. Some writing is done just for one's self. Journal writing usually falls into that category. Most writing, however, is meant to be shared with others. There are many ways in which to share your work. Here are several ways in which you can publish your writing or present it to others:

- Find a local publication that will accept your work. (A school literary magazine, a school newspaper, or a community newspaper are possibilities.)
- Submit the work to a regional or national publication.
- Enter the work in a contest. Your teacher may be able to tell you about writing contests for students.
- Read your work aloud to classmates, friends, or family members.
- Work with other students to prepare a publication—a brochure, online literary magazine, anthology, or newspaper.
- Prepare a poster or bulletin board, perhaps in collaboration with other students, to display your writing.
- Make your own book by typing or word processing the pages and binding them together. Or copy your work into a blank book.
- Hold a reading of student writing as a class or schoolwide project.
- Share your writing with other students in a small writers' group.

2.50 Reflecting on Your Writing

In the **reflecting** stage, you think through the writing process to determine what you learned as a writer, what you accomplished, and what skills you would like to strengthen the next time you write. Reflection can be done in a journal, on a self-evaluation form for writing, in small group discussion, or simply in your own thoughts. Here are some questions to ask as you reflect on the writing process and yourself as a writer.

- What have I learned in writing about this topic?
- What have I learned in writing for this purpose?
- What have I learned by using this form?
- How do I perceive my audience? What would I like my audience to gain from my writing?
- What kind of voice does my writing have?
- How have I developed as a writer while writing this piece?
- What strengths have I discovered in my work?
- What aspects of my writing do I want to strengthen? What can I do to strengthen them?

LANGUAGE, GRAMMAR, AND STYLE Resource

LANGUAGE HANDBOOK

3.1 Appropriate Uses of English

Language is a powerful and complex tool for conveying meaning. To communicate clearly, you must make choices—whether to use formal or informal English; what tone to use; the effects of irony, sarcasm, and rudeness; and how dialect affects the message.

3.2 Formal and Informal English

Depending on the situation, you might use either formal English or informal English when you speak or write. Formal English is used for school essays, newspaper and magazine articles, some literary works, oral or written reports, and test answers. Informal English is used when speaking with a friend or writing personal letters or notes; it can also be used in some literary works.

Informal English allows grammatical constructions that would not be acceptable in formal English. Many of these constructions will be described in the Grammar Handbook (where they are labeled "nonstandard"). Informal English also uses colloquialisms and slang.

A **colloquialism** is a word or phrase used in everyday conversation.

EXAMPLES

You guys must be sick of doing the same thing day after day.

He was **totally turned off** by the movie.

Slang is a form of speech made up of invented words or old words that are given a new meaning.

EXAMPLES

You'd better **chill out** for a while—you're too angry to talk to him now.

She has a real **hang-up** about mushrooms on her pizza.

3.3 Register, Tone, and Voice

To understand the concept of register, imagine that all the different kinds of usage in a language—both formal and informal—form one large set. A **register** is the set of language used in communicating with a particular person or group. In talking to a friend, you speak in a register that is casual, warm, and open. In speaking to a young child, you speak in a register that is simple to understand. In speaking to an official such as a police officer or a government clerk, you speak in a register that is polite—the same register that person should use with you. The language you use will change depending on the register you are using.

Tone is a writer's or speaker's attitude toward a subject. The tone of a message should reflect the speaker's attitude toward the subject and his or her audience. The speaker shapes the tone of a message by carefully choosing words and phrases. **Diction**, or choice of words, can affect your tone. You could say, "Your new product is so disgusting that I'll never buy anything you make ever again" or "I am concerned with the danger your new product poses to young children." The tone you convey will depend greatly upon word choice.

Voice makes a spoken or written work unique. The voice of a work may have to do with a writer's or speaker's attitude toward people, events, objects, or ideas. If this voice is consistent, the writer has established a sense of individuality in the work. In your own speaking and writing, aim to develop your own unique voice.

3.4 Irony, Sarcasm, and Rudeness

The standard definition of *rude* means bad-mannered, impolite, or inconsiderate. Interrupting someone else's conversation, cursing, or forgetting to say "please," "thank you," or "excuse me" is being rude. It is easy to confuse sarcasm or irony with rudeness. **Verbal irony** is present when someone says or writes the opposite of what he or she means, either to be funny or to make a point. It can be funny or serious. For example, if someone pushes to the front of a line, and someone else says, "What polite behavior," the speaker is using verbal irony. **Sarcasm** is similar to verbal irony; the difference is the speaker's intentions. Sarcastic people say the opposite of what they mean in order to criticize, hurt, or humiliate someone. Sarcasm differs from other forms of irony because it is always unkind.

3.5 Dialects of English

A **dialect** is a version of a language spoken by people of a particular place, time, or group. Dialects have differences in pronunciation, word choice, grammar, and accent. They are usually based on regional differences or on social differences. In the United States, the major regional dialects are northern, southern, midland, and western. Everyone speaks with some type of dialect.

A **standard** dialect exists in the United States. It uses traditional words, phrases, and pronunciations. News media, school resources, and government documents usually use this standard form of language.

Differences in dialect show up especially in the terms people use to refer to things. For example, the generic term for a carbonated beverage is "soda" in Florida and Washington, DC, "pop" in Ohio and Minnesota, "coke" in Georgia and Tennessee, and "tonic" in Boston.

GRAMMAR HANDBOOK

In English, the basic unit of meaning is the sentence. In this section, you will examine sentences to determine what they mean. This should help you to be a better reader and more skillful writer. The approach explained in this section may be new to you, so here are a series of charts and references to help you as you begin. Do not memorize these charts. The more you use them, the less you will need them. With time, you will develop a feeling for the way language works so you will not need them at all.

3.6 Identifying the Parts of Speech

Each word in a sentence has one of four basic functions: it **names**, **modifies**, **expresses action or state of being**, or **links**. A fifth function is to **interrupt** for effect. English also has words that can work as more than one part of speech. These are called **hybrids**. Following is an overview of the parts of speech. For a more detailed description of what each part of speech does, see the Parts of Speech Summary on page 902.

3.7 Grammar Reference Chart—Parts of Speech Overview

PARTS OF SPEECH	EXAMPLE(S)
NAMERS (nouns and pronouns) are subjects and objects.	
NOUN. A **noun** names a person, place, thing, idea	Adam, journalist, mountain, India, rose, motorcycle, honesty, feeling
PRONOUN. A **pronoun** is used in place of a noun to name a person, place, thing, or idea.	I bought the bricks and used **them** to build a wall. Take Kareem to the ice cream shop and buy **him** (used in place of Kareem) a cone.
EXPRESSERS (verbs) name an action or state of being plus the conditions around it.	
VERB. A **verb** expresses action or state of being.	bake, glance, give, build, compose, think, look, feel, am
MODIFIERS (adjectives and adverbs) make other parts of speech more specific.	
ADJECTIVE. An **adjective** modifies, or changes the meaning of, a noun or pronoun.	**gray** skies, **deep** water, **eerie** laughter
ADVERB. An **adverb** modifies a verb, an adjective, or another adverb.	Leanne gripped the wheel **nervously.** Ray peered over the cliff **very cautiously.**
LINKERS (prepositions and conjunctions) join all the constructions of the English language.	
PREPOSITION. A **preposition** is used to show how a noun or a pronoun is related to other words in the sentence. Common prepositions are *in, after, among, at, behind, beside, off, through, until, upon,* and *with.*	Pablo enjoyed the concert **at** the Wang Center. Theresa squeezed **through** the opening of the cave and crawled **into** the narrow passage.
CONJUNCTION. A **conjunction** joins words or groups of words. Common conjunctions are *and, but, for, nor, or, so,* and *yet.*	Wilhelm plays the guitar, **but** Leonard plays drums. Wilhelm **and** Leonard play loudly.
INTERRUPTERS (interjections and other constructions) interrupt a sentence for emphasis.	
INTERJECTION. An **interjection** is a word used to express emotion. Common interjections are *oh, ah, well, say,* and *wow.*	**Hey!** What are you doing in there? **Oh well**, I didn't expect to win the election anyway.
APPOSITIVE. An **appositive** is an interrupter that renames a noun.	My friend **Yang Yardley** did a beautiful project on birds. Mrs. Cokely, **my favorite teacher**, will retire.
NOUN OF DIRECT ADDRESS. A noun of direct address says the name of the person or group spoken to and is never the subject of the sentence.	Wait until dark, **Audrey.**
HYBRIDS (possessive nouns, pronouns, and verbals) can function as more than one part of speech.	
POSSESSIVE NOUNS AND PRONOUNS. Possessive nouns and **pronouns** are nouns and	Angela read **Scott's** essay. (*Scott's* is a possessive noun modifying *essay*.)

CONTINUED

| pronouns that function as adjectives. | Angela read **his** essay. (*His* is a possessive pronoun modifying *essay*.) |
| **VERBALS. Verbals** are verb forms such as participles, gerunds, and infinitives that can function as adjectives, nouns, and adverbs. | I love the **swimming** pool. (*Swimming* is a verbal called a participle, and acts as an adjective.)
 Swimming is my favorite sport. (*Swimming* is a verbal called a gerund, and acts as a noun.)
 I like **to swim**. (*To swim* is a verbal called an infinitive.) |

To understand how a sentence works, here are other groups of words that you should know about.

3.8 Helping Verbs

A **helping verb** helps a main verb to express action or a state of being. Common helping verbs are *can, could, may, might, must, shall, should, will, would,* and forms of the verb *to be (am, are, is, was being, been),* to have *(has, have, had)* and *to do (do, does, did).*

3.9 The Verb *To Be*

Most languages use the verb *to be* more than any other verb, because its forms have so many uses. *To be* can be the main verb of a sentence, used to express existence. It can also be a helping verb, one that helps a main verb. Here are some forms of *to be.*

PRESENT
  am, is are

PAST
  was, were, has been, had been

FUTURE
  will be; shall be; will have been; shall have been

OTHER EXPRESSIONS AND FORMS THAT USE *BE*
  being; can be; could be; could have been; would be; would have been; might be; might have been; must be; must have been

3.10 Linking Verbs

A **linking verb** connects a noun with another noun, a pronoun, or adjective that describes it or identifies it. The most common linking verb is *to be (am, are, is, was,* and *been).* Other words that can be used as linking verbs include *seem, look, sound, smell, taste, feel, stay, remain, become,* and *grow.*

3.11 Grammar Reference Chart— Prepositions

These are the most commonly used prepositions. Remember, though, that any word on this list may not always be used as a preposition. If it is a preposition, it will always have an object.

PREPOSITIONS

aboard	at	concerning	off	until
about	before	down	on	up
above	behind	during	over	upon
across	below	except	past	with
after	beside	for	since	within
against	besides	from	through	without
along	between	in	throughout	
amid	beyond	into	to	
among	but	like	under	
around	by	of	underneath	

3.12 What Is Grammar?

The word *grammar* has two meanings. First, **grammar** is the rules and standards that careful speakers use to write and speak. Second, a **grammar** is the description of a language. Learning about grammar will show you how the rules of the English language are applied.

English is a **syntactic language**. This means that **syntax**, or word order, is the most important factor to understand an English sentence.

3.13 The Importance of Syntax

Gina walks to work today.

Notice how the words are arranged: the sentence tells who (Gina) and then what that person did (walked to work). But look what happens when the word order is changed:

> To walks Gina today work.
> To work Gina today walks.
> Gina to today work walks.
> Today Gina walks to work.

None of the sentences has the same meaning, or makes much meaning at all, except the last one. But even this isn't the same as "Gina walks to work today," because in English, the most important idea comes first.

3.14 The Sentence: The Basic Building Block of the English Language

From the time you entered school, you have been writing and speaking in sentences, because they are the basic units of meaning. A sentence is a group of words that express a complete thought. A sentence is organized to tell 1) *who* or *what* a speaker is talking about, and 2) information about that *who* or *what*.

3.15 Functions of Sentences

Four different kinds of sentences express four different kinds of complete thoughts:

- A **declarative sentence** gives facts. It ends with a period.

- An **interrogative sentence** asks a question. It ends with a question mark.

- An **imperative sentence** gives orders or makes a request. It ends with a period or exclamation mark.

- An **exclamatory sentence** expresses strong feeling. It ends with an exclamation mark.

DECLARATIVE	Tom got a new bicycle.
INTERROGATIVE	Did Tom get a new bicycle?
IMPERATIVE	Get a new bicycle.
EXCLAMATORY	I really want a new bicycle!

3.16 Subjects and Verbs: The Basic Building Blocks in a Sentence

A basic language tool is knowing how to identify the parts of a sentence. The parts of a sentence are the building blocks of meaning.

3.17 Finding the Complete Subject and Complete Predicate in a Sentence

Simple sentences can be divided into two parts: the **subject** and the **predicate**. In the most common English sentences, the first part of the sentence tells us what or who the sentence is about. This is the **complete subject**. Then it gives us information about the subject; this second part of the sentence is called the **complete predicate**. In the following examples, the complete subject is underlined once. The complete predicate is underlined twice.

EXAMPLES

One of my brothers fixed his own car.
Sharyl and Ken will be presenting Friday's history lesson.
Lala might have been given a wrong classroom number.

NOTE: Every word in every sentence is a part of the complete subject or the complete predicate.

3.18 Finding the Simple Subject and Simple Predicate in a Sentence

Most people find the complete subject and complete predicate too general. To find basic meaning, you need to get down to the most basic sentence units—the **simple subject** and the **simple predicate** (more often called the **verb**).

To find the simple subject and verb of a sentence, first find the complete subject and predicate and then remove the extra words until you are left with only the simple subject and verb. What remains is absolutely necessary for basic meaning. The simple subject is the complete subject without any extra words.

EXAMPLES

A little fuzzy gray **kitten** walked across our back yard.
I worked for hours on my homework.
Jed's **grandfather** lived by the lake.

The **verb** is the predicate without any complements, linkers, or modifiers. Verbs may have more than one word and as many as four. Each of the following is one verb:

EXAMPLES

walked (one word)
is walking (two words)
has been walking (three words)
may have been walking (four words)

3.19 Finding the Simple Subject and Verb

The following **four-step method** will help you to find the simple subject and the verb in a sentence.

SAMPLE SENTENCE
My little sister might not attend school for the rest of the week.

1) Ask, "What is the action of this sentence?" The action is *attend*.

2) Go to the list of helping verbs in 3.9. Check some of the words around the action word. In this sentence, check *might* and *not*. When you look up these words, *might* is on the list; *not* isn't. Only *might* is a helping verb. The word *not* only describes the action. Therefore, the verb of the sentence is *might attend*.

3) You've found the verb. To find the subject, ask, "Who (or what) did this action?" Ask yourself, "Who might attend?" The answer is *my little sister*.

4) Finally, what words aren't necessary for the simplest meaning? Read the sentence. You can leave out *my*, because *little sister* makes sense. So does just *sister*. You can leave out

little. *Sister* is the simple subject of the sentence because *my* and *little* are not necessary for basic meaning.

3.20 Completers for Action Verbs: Direct and Indirect Objects

A sentence must have a subject and verb, but sometimes a sentence has other parts that complete the meaning. The completers for action verbs are **direct objects** and **indirect objects**.

3.21 DIRECT OBJECTS. Not all sentences have objects. Here are some examples of sentences without objects. There are no receivers of the action.

EXAMPLES

Birds fly south.
Work fast.
I have been walking.

Notice that the following sentences do have receivers of the action. These receivers are called **direct objects**. A **direct object** receives the action in the sentence. In each case, once the verb is found, the direct object answers the question *what*? about the verb.

EXAMPLES

Birds ate grain. (Birds ate what? *grain*)
Work the problems fast. (Work what? *problems*)
I walked the dog. (Walked what? *dog*)

The last step was to get rid of any modifiers. That tells you what the direct object itself is. Also note that the direct object is *never* in a prepositional phrase.

3.22 INDIRECT OBJECTS. Sometimes the direct object is received by someone or something. This receiver is called the **indirect object**. A sentence without a direct object cannot have an indirect object.

EXAMPLE   Mike gave me a red pencil.

What is the *action* (the verb)? *gave*
Who gave? (the subject) *Mike*
What did he give? (the direct object) *pencil*

To find the indirect object, check to see if the direct object had a receiver. Who got the direct object? In this sentence we ask, "Who got the pencil?" The answer is *me*.

Who received the pencil? (the indirect object) *me*

SUBJECTS AND VERBS: PROBLEM CONSTRUCTIONS

Because we like variety, we English speakers often rearrange our sentences or use different kinds of sentences. Some of these constructions can be very tricky!

3.23 Working with Inverted Sentences

A sentence is **inverted** when all or part of the complete predicate comes before the verb.

> **EXAMPLES**
>
> Will you walk my dog? (The sentence is inverted because the helping verb *will*, which is part of the verb *will walk*, is in front of the subject *you*.)
>
> After the dance was the party. (The sentence is inverted because *after the dance was*, the complete predicate, is in front of the subject *party*.)
>
> Here are the books. (The sentence is inverted because *Here are*, the complete predicate, is in front of the subject *books*.)

Notice in the following examples how the complete subject and complete predicate can be pared down to the simple subject and verb.

> **EXAMPLES**
>
> You will walk my dog.
> You will walk
>
> We went to the party after the dance.
> We went
>
> All of the students will be needing their books.
> All will be needing

3.24 Working with Compound Subjects, Verbs, and Sentences

One way to achieve sentence variety is through compounds—**compound subjects**, **compound verbs**, and **compound sentences**.

Subjects are compound if a sentence has more than one subject.

> **EXAMPLE**
>
> Mike and Harry washed the dishes.

Verbs are compound if a sentence has more than one verb.

> **EXAMPLE**
>
> Harry washed, dried, and put away the dishes.

A sentence can have both a compound subject and a compound verb.

> **EXAMPLE**
>
> Mikka and Juan made and ate their own dinner.

Sentences are compound when two sentences are connected by a semicolon or a by a coordinating conjunction and a comma. Each part of the compound has its own subject and verb.

> **EXAMPLES**
>
> The intermediate swim class practiced front dives; the advanced class practiced back somersaults.
>
> The intermediate swim class practiced front dives, and the advanced class practiced back somersaults.

3.25 Working with Negatives

Negatives such as *not* and *never* frequently affect verbs. They are adverbs, because they add to the meaning of the verb. The verb tells what an action is, and the negative says that the writer or speaker means the opposite of that.

> **EXAMPLES**
>
> I play basketball.
> Negative: I do not play basketball.

Make sure to use only one negative in each sentence. Check your writing to be sure that you have not used a negative word such *as not, nobody, none, nothing, hardly, barely, can't, doesn't, won't, isn't,* or *aren't* with another negative word.

> **DOUBLE NEGATIVE (NONSTANDARD)**
>
> I hardly never eat my lunch at school.
>
> Didn't Joyce never go to Chicago?
>
> It doesn't make no difference!
>
> Why wasn't Jerry hurt no worse when the car was destroyed?
>
> **CORRECTED SENTENCES (STANDARD)**
>
> I hardly ever eat my lunch at school.
>
> Didn't Joyce ever go to Chicago?
>
> It doesn't make any difference!

Why wasn't Jerry hurt any worse when the car was destroyed?

3.26 Using Contractions

Contractions combine two words by shortening and joining them with an apostrophe.

EXAMPLES

isn't, aren't, don't, can't

When you are trying to determine subjects and verbs in a sentence, contractions need to be written out into the two words that they represent. After the contraction is written out, each word should be considered separately. Each of the contractions above contains a negative. Remember that a negative is an adverb, not part of the verb.

CONTRACTION	WORDS CONTRACTED	PARTS OF SPEECH
isn't	is not	is (verb or helping verb), not (negative; adverb)
aren't	are not	are (verb), not (negative; adverb)
don't	do not	do (verb), not (negative; adverb)
can't	can not	can (helping verb), not (negative; adverb)

3.27 Identifying Prepositional Phrases

No basic part of the sentence is ever in a prepositional phrase, so before determining the subject and verb of a sentence, cross out the prepositional phrases. See 3.11, "Prepositions," for a list of common prepositions. If the word is on the list, find its object. If it has an object, it is a prepositional phrase.

EXAMPLE

She fell off her roller skates.

Is *off her roller skates* a prepositional phrase? Look up *off* on the list in section 3.11. *Off* is on the list. Now ask yourself, "Off what?" The answer is

off her roller skates. The word *off* has an object—*roller skates*. Therefore, *off her roller skates* is a prepositional phrase.

3.28 Understood Subjects

Sentences that make requests or give commands frequently have an understood subject. The subject is *you*, but it is not written or spoken.

EXAMPLE

Open your books.

What is meant is *You* open your books. The verb is *open*; the simple subject is *you*.

3.29 *There* Sentences

Frequently *there* is used to begin or serve as one of the first few words in a sentence. It is a modifier, so it will be not part of the simple subject or verb in the sentence. Cross out *there* before determining parts of the sentence. Note: Treat sentences that start with the word *here* in a similar way.

EXAMPLE

There are six classes scheduled every day. *Classes* (simple subject) are *scheduled* (verb)

Have there been any lost coats returned? *Coats* (simple subject) *have been returned* (verb)

3.30 Nouns of Direct Address

When you speak to someone, sometimes you say that person's name. This is called a **noun of direct address**. It is not the subject of the sentence; instead, it is an interjection.

EXAMPLES

Kent, take your paper from the pile. (The subject is *you*, not *Kent*.)

Tita, has Sam returned his paper yet? (The subject is *Sam*, not *Tita*.)

WRITER'S WORKSHOP: BUILDING EFFECTIVE SENTENCES

3.31 Correcting Sentence Fragments

A sentence contains a subject and a verb and should express a complete thought. A **sentence fragment** is a phrase or clause that does not express a complete thought but has been punctuated as though it did.

SENTENCE FRAGMENT

Looking for the lost little girl.

COMPLETE SENTENCE

The searchers combed the woods looking for the lost little girl.

3.32 Correcting Sentence Run-ons

A **sentence run-on** is made up of two or more sentences that have been run together as if they were one complete thought. You can fix a run-on by dividing it into two separate sentences. Mark the end of each idea with a period, question mark, or exclamation point. Capitalize the first word of each new sentence.

RUN-ON

Jason tried to jump across the swollen stream he slipped in the mud on the other side.

TWO SENTENCES

Jason tried to jump across the swollen stream. He slipped in the mud on the other side.

3.33 Correcting Wordy Sentences

As you write, use only words necessary to make your meaning clear to a reader. Edit your sentences so that they are not wordy and complicated. Replace complicated or general words with simple and specific words.

WORDY

I certainly am appreciative of your thoughtful gesture of bringing chicken soup for me to eat when I was sick and didn't feel like getting out of bed.

CLEAR AND DIRECT

Thank you for bringing chicken soup when I was sick.

3.34 Combining and Expanding Sentences

If you use several short sentences in a paragraph, your writing might sound choppy, and your reader might have trouble understanding how ideas are connected. **Combining** and **expanding sentences** can bring two sentences

together that deal with the same main idea. If you are able to combine short sentences, your writing will sound smooth and clear. The reader will see how ideas are connected to one another.

A good way to combine sentences is to take a word or phrase from one sentence and insert it into another sentence. You might need to change the form of the word.

BORING, SHORT SENTENCES

The thief ducked into the alley. The alley was dark.

COMBINED SENTENCE

The thief ducked into the dark alley.

An effective way to expand sentences is to merge two related sentences into one sentence that states both ideas. Your two sentences can be combined with a comma and a conjunction.

GIVEN SENTENCES

Alex jacked up the car. Margie changed the tire.

COMBINED SENTENCE

After Alex jacked up the car, Margie changed the tire.

3.35 Making Passive Sentences Active

A verb is **active** when the subject of the verb performs the action. It is **passive** when the subject of the verb receives the action.

ACTIVE

Caroline delivered a powerful speech.

PASSIVE

A powerful speech was delivered by Caroline.

Poor writing uses too many passive verbs. Use active verbs unless you have a good reason for using the passive voice. In the examples that follow, note how the active verbs make the writing more natural and interesting.

WITH PASSIVE VERBS

The school was flooded with requests from students for a longer vacation. It was not decided by the school board until later to give them a hearing. The meeting was begun by the student council. The vote was unanimous to extend spring break an extra week. It was considered an unprecedented move favoring all students suffering spring fever.

WITH ACTIVE VERBS

Students flooded the school with requests for a longer vacation. The school board did not decide until later to give them a hearing. The student council began the meeting. Everyone voted to extend spring break an extra week. The unprecedented move favored all students suffering spring fever.

Note that the writer could still combine and expand these sentences to give them more variety. Making sentences active instead of passive, however, is a good start toward livelier writing.

3.36 Achieving Parallelism

A sentence has **parallelism** when it uses the same grammatical forms to express ideas of equal, or parallel, importance. When you edit your sentences during revision, check to be sure that your parallelism is not faulty.

FAULTY

I really like to play chess, walking my dog, and vacations in Florida.

PARALLEL

I really like *playing* chess, *walking* my dog, and *taking* vacations in Florida.

3.37 Adding Colorful Language to Sentences

When you write, use words that tell your reader exactly what you mean. Precise and lively nouns, verbs, and modifiers make your writing more interesting to your reader.

EXAMPLES

The *people* made *noise*.
The *mob* made an *uproar*.

He *took* the pitcher and *drank* the cool water.
He *grabbed* the pitcher and *gulped* the cool water.

The *cold* wind blew *hard*.
The *frigid* wind blew *furiously*.

EDITING FOR GRAMMAR AND USAGE ERRORS

3.38 Getting Subject and Verb to Agree

A word that describes or stands for *one* person, place, thing, or idea is **singular**. A word that describes or stands for *more than one* person, place, thing, or idea is **plural**.

SINGULAR NOUNS	prize, child, instrument
PLURAL NOUNS	prizes, children, instruments

In a sentence, a verb must be singular if its subject is singular and plural if its subject is plural. A verb must agree in number with its subject.

SINGULAR AGREEMENT

Charles needs forty dollars more.

PLURAL AGREEMENT

They need forty dollars more.

Some verbs have special forms. The verb forms *is* and *was* are singular. The forms *are* and *were* are plural. The verb form *has* is singular. The verb form *have* is plural.

SINGULAR	Vivian is at the mall.
PLURAL	Vivian and Debbie are at the mall.
SINGULAR	This car has dual airbags.
PLURAL	These cars have dual airbags.

3.39 Using Irregular Verbs

To write about something that happened in the past, use past-tense verbs (*tense* means "time" in grammar). For regular verbs, add –*ed* or –*d* to the present form of the verb. For more information, see the Language Arts Survey 3.60, "Verb Tenses."

EXAMPLES

The bandit *guarded* the hideout.
guard (base form) + *ed*

Carmen *gazed* at the distant mountains.
gaze (base form) + *d*

Irregular verbs often have different past-tense forms and are formed using a different spelling. The following chart lists some of the most common irregular verbs.

IRREGULAR VERBS

begin/began	grow/grew
bring/brought	have/had
burst/burst	hurt/hurt
choose/chose	know/knew
come/came	lay/laid
cut/cut	make/made
do/did	ride/rode
draw/drew	run /ran
drink/drank	see/saw
eat/ate	sing/sang
fall/fell	take/took
feel/felt	teach/taught
fly/flew	wear/wore
give/gave	write/wrote
go/went	

When using irregular verbs in the perfect tense (with *has* or *have*), make sure you do not use the past form instead of the past participle.

NONSTANDARD

I *have knew* him since I was in middle school.

STANDARD

I *have known* him since I was in middle school.

Another error to avoid is using the past-participle form without a helping verb, or mistaking the past participle for the past.

NONSTANDARD	I *flown* this plane dozens of times.
STANDARD	I *have flown* this plane dozens of times.
NONSTANDARD	I *done* all I could do to convince him.
STANDARD	I *did* all I could do to convince him.

Finally, do not add *–d* or *–ed* to the past form of an irregular verb.

| NONSTANDARD | I *ated* an apple. |
| STANDARD | I *ate* an apple. |

3.40 Avoiding Split Infinitives

In the English language, the infinitive is often in the form of two words, *to* and the base word.

EXAMPLES   to catch, to succeed, to entertain

Under traditional rules of grammar, the infinitive should not be "split." In other words, adverbs or other sentence components should not come between *to* and the base word.

NONSTANDARD

Irving begged me to immediately show him the photos.

STANDARD

Irving begged me to show him the photos immediately.

3.41 Using *I* and *Me*

Before you use the words *I* and *me* in a sentence, remember that *I* is always the subject of a verb and *me* is always the object of a verb or of a preposition. *I* is the subject in both of these sentences:

I went sailing in Florida. Amber and *I* went sailing in Florida.

In both of these sentences, *me* is the object of the verb *helped*.

Lester helped *me* set up for the party.
Lester helped Brianna and *me* set up for the party.

If you are not sure which pronoun to use, try each part of your sentence separately.

EXAMPLE

Sam and (I, me) went sledding at the golf course.

After dropping out *Sam:*
I went sledding at the golf course. OR *Me* went sledding at the golf course.

Correct: Sam and *I* went sledding at the golf course.

EXAMPLE

Please apologize for Carol and (I, me).

After dropping out *Carol:*
Please apologize for *me*. OR Please apologize for *I*.

Correct: Please apologize for Carol and *me*.

3.42 Getting Pronouns and Antecedents to Agree

Make sure pronouns in your writing agree with their antecedents in number and gender. The

antecedent is the noun that the pronoun references.

Number refers to singular and plural. If the antecedent is singular, the pronoun must also be singular; if the antecedent is plural, the pronoun must also be plural.

INCORRECT NUMBER

If a customer needs help, direct *them* to the service counter.

CORRECT NUMBER

If a customer needs help, direct *him or her* to the service counter.

Gender is the form a pronoun takes to show whether it is masculine, feminine, or neither masculine nor feminine. The pronoun must match its antecedent in terms of gender.

INCORRECT GENDER

Bessie the cow rubbed *her* head and swished *its* tail.

CORRECT GENDER

Bessie the cow rubbed *her* head and swished *her* tail.

3.43 Recognizing Other Problems with Modifiers

Them is a personal pronoun. *Those* is a demonstrative pronoun, which means it points out a particular person, place, or thing.

NONSTANDARD   Them cars have four-wheel drive.
STANDARD   Those cars have four-wheel drive.

The words *bad* and *badly* often confuse writers. Use *bad* as an adjective, and *badly* as an adverb. The adjective *bad* should follow a linking verb such as *feel, see, smell, sound,* or *taste.*

NONSTANDARD

Reports of the forest fire sounded badly.

STANDARD

Reports of the forest fire sounded bad.

NONSTANDARD

Ricky behaved bad for the babysitter.

STANDARD

Ricky behaved badly for the babysitter.

The words *good* and *well* also tend to confuse writers. *Good* is an adjective used to modify a person, place, thing, or idea, not an action verb. *Well* is an adverb meaning "successfully" or "skillfully" and an adjective meaning "healthy" or "of a satisfactory condition."

NONSTANDARD

Allen swims good.

STANDARD

Allen swims well.

Allen is a good swimmer.

Each modifier has a **positive, comparative,** and **superlative** form of comparison. Most one-syllable modifiers and some two-syllable modifiers form comparative and superlative degrees by adding *–er* and *–est.* Other two-syllable modifiers, and all modifiers of more than two syllables, use *more* and *most* to form these degrees.

	POSITIVE	COMPARATIVE	SUPERLATIVE
ADJECTIVES	hungry	hungrier	hungriest
	daring	more daring	most daring
ADVERBS	late	later	latest
	fully	more fully	most fully

To show a decrease in the quality of any modifier, form the comparative and superlative degrees by using *less* and *least.*

EXAMPLES

dense, less dense, least dense
skeptically, less skeptically, least skeptically

Some modifiers form comparative and superlative degrees irregularly. Check the dictionary if you are unsure about the comparison of a modifier.

EXAMPLES

good, better, best
well, better, best
bad, worse, worst

Use the comparative degree when comparing two things. Use the superlative degree when comparing more than two things.

COMPARATIVE

Santha was the **more easily** intimidated of the two sisters.

SUPERLATIVE

The skin is the **largest** organ of the human body.

3.44 Correcting Common Usage Problems

Watch for these words and learn their correct usage as you edit your own writing.

accept, except. To *accept* is to "welcome something" or to "receive something willingly." To *except* is to "exclude or leave something out." *Except* is also used as a preposition meaning "but."

The Tigers *accept* our challenge to a rematch.

I will eat any vegetable *except* collard greens.

advice, advise. *Advice* is a noun meaning "guidance or recommendation regarding a decision." To *advise* is to "recommend or inform."

I took your *advice* about the movie.

I would *advise* you to avoid the sequel.

affect, effect. *Affect* is a verb meaning "have an effect on." Effect is a noun meaning "the result of an action."

The short story *affected* me strangely.

The short story had a strange *effect* on me.

altogether, all together. *Altogether* is an adverb meaning "thoroughly." Something done *all together* is done as a group or mass.

She was *altogether* frustrated waiting all day.

We were *all together* awaiting news of the surgery.

among, between. Use the word *between* when you are talking about two people or things at a time. Use the word *among* when you are talking about a group of three or more.

Oscar and Lucas had five dollars *between* them.

There was disagreement *among* the team members.

can, may. The word *can* means "able to do something." The word *may* is used to ask or give permission.

Can you swim across Gull Pond?

You *may* go swimming when you finish mowing the lawn.

fewer, less. *Fewer* refers to the number of units of something. *Less* refers to bulk quantity.

I have *fewer* than eight items.

I have *less* energy when it is very humid.

in, into. The preposition *in* indicates location. The preposition *into* indicates direction from the outside to the inside.

The meeting is being held *in* the gym.
The students are going *into* the gym now.

its, it's. The word *its* is a possessive pronoun. The word *it's* is a contraction of *it is*.

The turtle dug *its* nest.
The sun will be up by the time *it's* over.

lay, lie. *Lay* means to "put" or to "place." It always takes a direct object. *Lie* means to "rest" or to "be in a lying position." *Lie* never takes a direct object. (Note that the past tense of *lie* is *lay*.)

Lay the map on the table.
Gretchen *laid* the map on the table.
Lie down and keep quiet.
Oliver *lay* down and kept quiet.

like, as. *Like* is a preposition meaning "similar to." *Like* usually introduces a phrase. *As* should be used as a conjunction. *As* usually introduces a clause that has a subject and a verb.

NONSTANDARD
The sun came out earlier, just *like* I had hoped.

STANDARD
The sun came out earlier, just *as* I had hoped.

NONSTANDARD
Rodney has been acting *as* a spoiled brat.

STANDARD
Rodney has been acting *like* a spoiled brat.

their, they're, there. These three homonyms (words that sound alike but that have different spellings and meanings) can be very confusing. The word *their* is a possessive pronoun. The word *they're* is the contracted form of *they are.* The word *there* refers to a place.

Marsupials carry *their* young in a pouch.
They're complaining about the noise.
The lamp should go over *there*.

to, too, two. *To* is a preposition that can mean "in the direction of." *Too* is an adverb that means both "extremely, overly" and "also." *Two* is the spelling for the number 2.

> Take the basket *to* Granny's house.
> Ivan has *too* many fish in his tank.
> Sharon is invited, *too*.
> I have *two* wishes left.

your, you're. *Your* is a possessive pronoun. *You're* is the contracted form of *you are*.

> *Your* mittens are in the dryer.
> *You're* the winner!

PARTS OF SPEECH SUMMARY

As you have seen, the meanings of words often depend upon their positions in a sentence. As their positions change, both meaning and function change. By looking at the relationship of one word to the rest of the words in a sentence, you can determine what the word does.

3.45 Namers—Nouns and Pronouns

Namers are nouns and pronouns. They name or refer to people, places, ideas, and things. You can tell what they are by what they do. Nouns and pronouns are subjects and objects—direct objects, indirect objects, or objects of prepositions.

3.46 Types of Nouns

A **noun** is a word that names a person, place, thing, or idea.

NOUNS
Cornelius (person), New Orleans (place), wagon (thing), optimism (idea)

3.47 COMMON NOUNS. A common noun names any person, place, thing, or idea.

COMMON NOUNS
plumber, city, bottle, satisfaction

3.48 PROPER NOUNS. A proper noun names a specific person, place, or thing and begins with a capital letter.

PROPER NOUNS
Luke Baldwin, Alaska, Thanksgiving

3.49 COMPOUND NOUNS. A compound noun is a noun made up of two or more words. Some compound nouns are written as one word, some as two words, and some as hyphenated words.

COMPOUND NOUNS
porthole, pancake, fire escape, Groundhog Day, mother-in-law

3.50 CONCRETE NOUNS. A concrete noun names a thing that can be touched, seen, heard, smelled, or tasted.

CONCRETE NOUNS
telephone, carpet, peanut butter

3.51 ABSTRACT NOUNS. An abstract noun names something that cannot be seen, heard, touched, smelled, or tasted.

ABSTRACT NOUNS
excellence, mathematics, despair

3.52 Types of Pronouns

A **pronoun** is used in place of a noun. Sometimes a pronoun refers to a specific person or thing. The most commonly used pronouns are personal pronouns, interrogative pronouns, indefinite pronouns, and relative pronouns. Speakers also use possessive pronouns, but they are hybrids. They have pronoun forms but act as modifiers. Hybrids are discussed in their own section.

3.53 PERSONAL PRONOUNS. A personal pronoun is used in place of the name of a person or thing. The personal pronouns are *I, me, we, us, he, she, it, him, her, you, they,* and *them*. Personal pronouns refer to three groups of speakers: first, second, and third person.

FIRST PERSON	the speaker or speakers talk about themselves: *I, me, we, us*
SECOND PERSON	the speaker talks about the person talked to: *you*
THIRD PERSON	the speaker talks about someone or something else: *he, she, it, they*

All personal pronouns require clear **antecedents**, or nouns that come before the pronoun. That means that the person or thing that the pronoun refers to must be obvious.

EXAMPLE

Have you seen *Mary?* Yes, I saw <u>her</u> yesterday. (*Mary* is the antecedent of *her*.)

3.54 INTERROGATIVE PRONOUNS. An **interrogative pronoun** asks a question. *Who, whose, what, whom,* and *which* are the interrogative pronouns.

EXAMPLES

Which movie would you like to see?
Whose sweater is on the chair?
To *whom* am I speaking?

3.55 Expressers—Verbs

Verbs are the **expressers** of the English language. They tell of an action and tell whether the action is finished, continuing, or will happen. English verbs can be from one to four words long.

EXAMPLES

I *study* English.
I *have studied* English.
I *could have studied* English.
I *should have been studying* English.

Each of the additional words changes the meaning or condition of the action. The same verb may fit into several classes, depending on its use in different sentences.

3.56 ACTION VERBS. Action verbs are the words that refer to actions and to things you can do.

EXAMPLES   have, get, drive, run, get, sleep

3.57 STATE OF BEING VERBS. State of being verbs indicate that something exists. These are all the forms of the verb *to be* that are listed in 3.9, "The Verb *To Be*."

3.58 TRANSITIVE VERBS. Transitive verbs are action verbs that have completers. If a verb has a direct object, it is a transitive verb.

EXAMPLE

The teacher shows movies twice this week.

In this sentence the simple subject is *teacher;* the verb is *has shown*. If you ask the question, *The teacher has shown what?*, the answer is *movies*, so *movies* is a direct object. Because the verb has an object, it is **transitive**.

3.59 INTRANSITIVE VERBS. Intransitive verbs are action verbs that do not have completers.

EXAMPLE   The wind blows all day long.

In this sentence the subject is *wind*, and the verb is *blows*. When we ask the direct object question, *Wind blows what?*, there is no answer. *Blows* is an **intransitive verb**.

3.60 Verb Tenses

Verbs carry a concept of time, called **tense**. The simple tenses express simple past, present, and future. The perfect tenses give information about actions that take place over time. The progressive form uses *be* with the present participle.

3.61 SIMPLE TENSES. Present tense shows that something is happening now. **Past tense** verbs talk about something that happened before now, and **future tense** verbs talk about something that will happen in the future.

PRESENT TENSE

Today I *eat* chocolate ice cream.
Today I *do eat* chocolate ice cream.
Today I *am eating* chocolate ice cream.

Notice that the past tense in English also uses the same three forms as present tense.

PAST TENSE

Yesterday I *ate* strawberry ice cream.
Yesterday I *did eat* strawberry ice cream.
Yesterday I *was eating* strawberry ice cream.

There are only two future tense forms.

FUTURE TENSE

Tomorrow I *will eat* vanilla ice cream.
Tomorrow I *will be eating* vanilla ice cream.

3.62 Modifiers

Adjectives and adverbs—two kinds of **modifiers**—describe or add meaning to nouns, adjectives, verbs, and adverbs. To determine whether the work is an adjective or adverb, follow the following procedure:

1. Look at the word that is modified.

2. Ask yourself, "Is this modified word a noun or pronoun?"

If the answer is yes, the modifier is an adjective. Adjectives modify only nouns and pronouns.

If the answer is no, the modifier is an adverb. **Adverbs** modify verbs, adjectives, and other adverbs.

3.63 ADJECTIVES. **Adjectives** modify nouns by telling specific details about them.

NOUN	woman
A LITTLE MORE SPECIFIC	*young* woman
MORE SPECIFIC YET	*red-haired young* woman
EVEN MORE SPECIFIC	*smiling, red-headed young* woman

3.64 ADVERBS. **Adverbs** modify anything that isn't a *namer* (noun or pronoun.) Adverbs can modify verbs, adjectives, and other adverbs. Many times they will tell us where or when; nouns and pronouns tell us who or what.

ADVERBS MODIFY VERBS

Scotty ran home *quickly*.

Quickly tells how Scotty ran.

ADVERBS MODIFY ADJECTIVES

She wore really new shoes.

New modifies *shoes; really* modifies the modifier, *new*. Since *new* is an adjective, not a noun or pronoun, and *really* modifies *new, really* has to be an adverb.

ADVERBS MODIFY OTHER ADVERBS

Scotty ran home *really fast*.

Fast modifies the verb *ran; really* modifies *fast*. Here one adverb modifies another.

3.65 Linkers

Conjunctions and prepositions are the linkers of the English language. These words join words and phrases to create compound sentences. Because many kinds of links need to be made, there are many kinds of linkers.

3.66 PREPOSITIONS. **Prepositions** always have objects. Look at the Grammar Reference Chart 3.11, "Prepositions." If you find one of these words in a sentence, find its object. If it has an object, then the preposition and its object(s) form a prepositional phrase.

EXAMPLE

I went *to* the store *for* a loaf *of* sandwich bread.

In this sentence, three words are on the preposition list: *to, for,* and *of*. Does *to* have an object? Ask, "*to* what?" The answer is *the store. To* has an object, so it is a preposition. *To the store* is a prepositional phrase. After we apply the same test to *for* and *of*, we find that they are both prepositions and that the sample sentence has three prepositional phrases. These are *to the store, for a loaf,* and *of sandwich bread*.

3.67 COORDINATING CONJUNCTIONS. **Coordinating conjunctions** join words and groups of words. The most common coordinating conjunctions are *and, or, nor, for, but,* and *so*. Coordinating conjunctions link words or word groups to make them equally important in the sentence.

EXAMPLE

Her morning schedule included math *and* history *and* music *and* home room.

Joining a series of words using coordinating conjunctions between them is perfectly acceptable grammar. Most writers, however, use commas and save multiple conjunctions for sentences with special emphasis. Note that all but the last could be replaced by commas:

EXAMPLE

Her morning schedule included math, history, music, and home room.

When coordinating conjunctions plus commas join two or more complete thoughts that could be separate sentences, the resulting structure is called a **compound sentence**.

EXAMPLE

I wanted to go to a movie, but nothing sounded very good.

Here a comma plus *but* joins two short, complete, independent thoughts. Each of the two parts could be a sentence of its own:

EXAMPLE

I wanted to go to a movie. Nothing sounded very good.

3.68 CORRELATIVE CONJUNCTIONS. **Correlative conjunctions** travel in pairs that belong together. Some of these pairs are *both/and, either/or, neither/nor,* and *not only/but also*.

Both her sisters *and* her brothers had talent.

Neither her mother *nor* her father had played sports in school.

She *either* takes drafting *or* art this semester.

He *not only* passed French *but also* aced math.

3.69 Interrupters

Sometimes you will want to interrupt the flow of a sentence and thought by adding an **interrupter**, a word or phrase for emphasis. Most interrupters are set off from the rest of the sentences by commas because they are not basic building blocks of meaning. Interrupters include *interjections, parenthetical expressions, nouns of direct address,* and *appositives.* Another interrupter, *intensifying pronouns,* is discussed in 3.72, "Hybrids."

Interrupters are always set off from other parts of the sentence by commas or, in some cases, dashes or exclamation marks. Interrupters are not basic building blocks of meaning.

3.70 INTERJECTIONS. Interjections are parts of speech that express strong feeling.

EXAMPLES

Yes, I finally finished my homework.
Good grief, you did what again?
Wow! Sam got a new car for his birthday.
Huh! I don't understand.

Yes, good grief, wow, and *huh* are all interjections. Notice that leaving them out does not affect the meaning of the sentence. Each interjection is set off from the rest of the sentence either by a comma or an exclamation point.

3.71 Nouns of Direct Address

Nouns of direct address say the name of the person or group spoken to. A noun of direct address is *never* the subject of the sentence. This becomes especially tricky when the subject is understood (not stated), as in commands.

EXAMPLES

The grass needs to be cut, *Jenna*, and you must start cutting it now.

Class, listen to the instructions.

3.72 Hybrids

Hybrids are words usually thought of as one part of speech that occasionally function as another. Because word forms are labeled according to what they do, each should be labeled according to what it does in the sentence. Common hybrids include *possessive nouns, possessive pronouns, intensifying pronouns,* and a group of verb forms called *verbals.*

3.73 Possessive Nouns and Pronouns

Possessive nouns are noun forms that modify other words. To form a possessive noun, an apostrophe plus an *–s* is added to a singular noun, and an apostrophe is added to a plural noun. Notice how the possessive noun uses a noun form, but with the suffix, it becomes a modifier.

EXAMPLE

Drew dropped *Mary's* book.

Mary's modifies *book.* This construction is a hybrid; it looks like a noun, but it functions as an adjective.

Possessive pronouns act much the same way. Many possessive forms look like other pronouns, while a few pronoun forms are uniquely possessive. Forms that are always possessive include *my, mine, your, yours, hers, his, its, our, ours, their,* and *theirs.*

EXAMPLES

The book is *yours.*
This is *your* book.
The book is *hers.*
Don't lay the book on *its* side.

One other possessive form, *her*, is not always possessive. It can also serve as a noun, direct object, and indirect object.

EXAMPLES

Give the book to *her*. (In this sentence, *her* serves as a noun and indirect object.)

This is her *book.* (In this sentence, *her* serves as a possessive pronoun and adjective.)

3.74 Verbals

Verbals are verb forms that act as namers or modifiers. There are three different forms of verbals.

These include **participles** (*–ing* or *–ed* verb forms that act as modifiers), **gerunds** (*–ing* verb forms that act like nouns), and **infinitives** (*to* verb forms that can act like nouns, adjectives, and adverbs).

Participles are action adjectives.

Jana jumped off the *diving* board.
A *watched* pot never boils.

Gerunds are action nouns.

Swimming is good exercise.
Mary has improved her *reading*.

Infinitives are formed by adding the word to to a verb.

I want *to go* home.
Have you ever been given a test *to take*?

STYLE HANDBOOK

3.75 Editing for Punctuation Errors

Several punctuation errors to avoid are the misuse of end marks, commas, and semicolons.

3.76 END MARKS. End marks tell the reader where a sentence ends. They also show the purpose of the sentence. The three end marks are the period, question mark, and exclamation point.

A **declarative sentence** ends with a period.

DECLARATIVE

Friedrich's cousins live in Switzerland.

An **interrogative sentence** ends with a question mark.

INTERROGATIVE

When did World War I begin?

An **exclamatory sentence** ends with an exclamation point.

EXCLAMATORY

The view from the top is breathtaking!

3.77 COMMAS. A comma separates words or groups of words within a sentence. Commas tell the reader to pause at certain spots in the sentence. These pauses help keep the reader from running certain words and phrases together when they should be kept apart. You should always use commas to separate items in a series. Three or more words make a series.

Choices include *carrots, green beans, corn*, and *asparagus*.

Use commas when you combine sentences using *and, but, or, nor, yet, so,* or *for*. Place the comma before these words.

Joanna will sing in the talent show, *and* Margaret will accompany her.

Use a comma to set off words or phrases that interrupt sentences. Use two commas if the word or phrase falls in the middle of the sentence. Use one comma if the word or phrase comes at the beginning or at the end of a sentence.

Hercules, *a hero of classical mythology*, was said to be the strongest man on earth.

After the first quarter, the Knicks dominated the game.

Use commas to separate the parts of a date. Do not use a comma between the month and the year.

The Germans surrendered on *May 8, 1945*.

My appointment is on *Wednesday, January 7*.

Use commas to separate items in addresses. (Do not put a comma between the state and the ZIP code.)

Francisco was born in *Caracas, Venezuela*.
They live at 210 *Newfield Road, DeWitt, New York* 13214.

3.78 SEMICOLONS. You have seen how two related sentences can be combined into one using a conjunction such as *and, but, so,* and *or*. Another way to join two related sentences into one is to use a **semicolon**. The semicolon can be used in place of the comma and the conjunction.

A fin was spotted moving through the water, so the bathers scrambled onto the beach.

A fin was spotted moving through the water; the bathers scrambled onto the beach.

3.79 COLONS. Use a **colon** to introduce a list of items.

Don't forget the following items for the hike: water bottle, food, first-aid kit, extra sweater, and rain gear.

You should also use a colon between numbers that tell hours and minutes.

1:07 P.M.   6:00 A.M.   9:54 P.M.

A colon is often used after the greeting in a business letter.

Dear Sirs: Dear Ms. Flanagan:

3.80 APOSTROPHES. An **apostrophe** is used to form the possessive of nouns. To form the possessive of a singular noun, you should add an apostrophe and an *s* to the end of the word.

The sun's diameter is about 864,000 miles.

Isaac's room is plastered with posters of the Pacers.

The women's volleyball team is undefeated.

If the plural noun ends with an *–s*, you only need to add an apostrophe.

The Vikings' star quarterback is on the injured list. (Vikings + ' = Vikings')

3.81 UNDERLINING AND ITALICS. Italics are a type of slanted printing used to make a word or phrase stand out. In handwritten documents, underlining is used. You should underline or italicize the titles of books, magazines, works of art, movies, and plays.

BOOKS
The Cay, Old Yeller; <u>The Cay</u>, <u>Old Yeller</u>

MAGAZINES
Reader's Digest, Sports Illustrated, <u>Reader's Digest</u>, <u>Sports Illustrated</u>

WORKS OF ART
The Thinker, The Starry Night, <u>The Thinker</u>, <u>The Starry Night</u>

MOVIES
The Lion King, Dances with Wolves, <u>The Lion King</u>, <u>Dances with Wolves</u>

PLAYS
The Mousetrap, Hamlet, <u>The Mousetrap</u>, <u>Hamlet</u>

3.82 QUOTATION MARKS. When you use a person's exact words in your writing, you are using a **direct quotation**. Enclose the words of a direct quotation in **quotation marks**.

"It looks as if the rain is coming," Sylvia remarked.

Pietro said, "It's good to be back home."

A direct quotation should always begin with a capital letter. Separate a direct quotation from the rest of the sentence with a comma, question mark, or exclamation point. Do not separate the direct quotation from the rest of the sentence with a period. All punctuation marks that belong to the direct quotation itself should be placed inside the quotation marks.

"Your golf game has really improved," Avram remarked.

Victor lamented, "I wish Uncle Don were here."

Joy asked, "Have you seen my red blouse?"

"Hey," Allison called, "Wait for me!"

Use quotation marks to enclose the titles of short works such as short stories, poems, songs, articles, and parts of books.

SHORT STORIES
"Joyriding," "Eleven"

POEMS
"Ox Cart Man," "Two Girls . . ."

SONGS
"Forever Young," "Silent Night"

ARTICLES, ESSAYS
"Night," "Hearing Under Seige"

3.83 HYPHENS AND DASHES. A **hyphen** is used to make a compound word.

four-year-old boy, great-grandmother, run-of-the-mill, seventh-grade student, three-time winner

A **dash** is used to show a sudden break or change in thought.

Juan surprised his teacher—and himself—by getting an *A* on the science test.

3.84 Editing for Capitalization Errors

To avoid capitalization errors, you should know how to capitalize proper nounds and adjectives; geographical names, directions and historical names; and titles of artworks and history books.

3.85 PROPER NOUNS AND ADJECTIVES. Using capital letters is called **capitalization**. Always capitalize proper nouns and adjectives. A proper noun names a specific person, place, or thing. A **proper adjective** is an adjective formed from a proper noun. Make sure to capitalize the many kinds of proper nouns and proper adjectives.

PROPER NOUNS
Lebanon, Queen Elizabeth, Democrat

PROPER ADJECTIVES
Lebanese, Elizabethan, Democratic

There are many different kinds of proper nouns. The chart below should help you to recognize some of them.

TITLES USED WITH NAMES
Dr. Stetson, Ms. Dixon, Mr. Meletiadis

MONTHS, DAYS, HOLIDAYS
January, Wednesday, Labor Day

RELIGIONS
Hinduism, Catholicism, Buddhism

SACRED WRITINGS
the Bible, the Great Spirit, the Koran, the Vedas

CITIES, STATES, COUNTRIES
Seattle, Louisiana, Peru

NATIONALITIES
Danish, Brazilian, Greek

STREETS, BRIDGES
Highland Street, Tappan Zee Bridge

BUILDINGS, MONUMENTS
World Trade Center, USS *Arizona* Memorial

CLUBS, ORGANIZATIONS, BUSINESSES
Kiwanis Club, National Audubon Society, Sears Roebuck

3.86 *I* AND FIRST WORDS. Capitalize the first word of every sentence.

EXAMPLES   Did you see that meteor?
             The river rose over its banks.

Capitalize the word *I* whenever it appears.

EXAMPLES   Janice and *I* will buy the present.
             Whenever *I* see horses, *I* think of
             Uncle Sherman.

3.87 FAMILY RELATIONSHIPS AND TITLES OF PERSONS. A word for a family relation such as *Mom, Dad*, or *Grandpa* should be capitalized if it is used as the name or part of the name of a particular person. Do not capitalize a word for a family relation if a modifier such as *the, a, my*, or *your* comes before it.

CAPITALIZED
When they were children, Dad, Aunt Polly, and Uncle Richard went to the Grand Canyon.

NOT CAPITALIZED
My grandma has a cousin who lives in Germany.

Capitalize the official title of a person when it is followed by the person's name or when it is used instead of a name in direct address.

President James Polk, Queen Mary, Sir Winston Churchill, Pope Paul
"I am honored to meet you, Ambassador."

Do not capitalize references to occupations.

the electrician, the doctor, the sergeant, the judge, the chef, the editor

3.88 GEOGRAPHICAL NAMES, DIRECTIONS, AND HISTORICAL NAMES. Capitalize the names of specific places, including terms such as *lake, mountain, river*, or *valley* if they are used as part of a name.

BODIES OF WATER
Colorado River, Black Sea

CITIES AND TOWNS
Kansas City, Fayetteville

COUNTIES
Cayuga County, Kosciusko County

COUNTRIES
Switzerland, Indonesia

ISLANDS
Ellis Island, Isle of Wight

MOUNTAINS
Pike's Peak, Mount Rainier

STATES
Montana, South Carolina

STREETS AND HIGHWAYS
Erie Boulevard, Route 71

Capitalize historical events, special events, and recognized periods of time.

HISTORICAL EVENTS
Continental Congress, Boxer Rebellion

HISTORICAL PERIODS
Paleozoic Era, Industrial Age

SPECIAL EVENTS
Empire State Games, Rose Bowl

Capitalize geographical directions if they are part of a specific name or a commonly recognized region. Do not capitalize words such as *east(ern)*, *west(ern)*, *north(ern)*, and *south(ern)* if they are used only to indicate direction.

CAPITALIZED
Western Samoa, *East* Africa, *South* Bend, *Northern* Ireland

NOT CAPITALIZED
west of Denver, *eastern* face of the mountain, *south* side of the city, *northern* regions

3.89 TITLES OF ARTWORKS AND LITERARY WORKS.
Apply title capitalization to titles of artworks and literary works. In title capitalization, capitalize the first word, the last word, and all other words except articles *(a, an,* and *the)* and prepositions.

EXAMPLES
Raphael's *The School of Athens*, Matisse's *Joy of Life*, Jackson Pollock's *Autumn Rhythm*, Shakespeare's *The Taming of the Shrew*, Faulkner's *The Sound and the Fury*, Ray Bradbury's "All Summer in a Day"

3.90 Editing for Spelling Errors

3.91 USING SPELLING RULES I. Always check your writing for spelling errors, and try to recognize the words that give you more trouble than others. Adding prefixes and suffixes often causes spelling errors. A **prefix** is a letter or a group of letters added to the beginning of a word to change its meaning. When adding a prefix, do not change the spelling of the word itself.

EXAMPLES
dis + similar = dissimilar
un + necessary = unnecessary

A **suffix** is a letter or group of letters added to the end of a word to change its meaning. The spelling of most words is not changed when the suffix *–ness* or *–ly* is added.

EXAMPLES
even + ness = evenness
usual + ly = usually

If you are adding a suffix to a word that ends with *y*, and that *y* follows a vowel, you should usually leave the *y* in place. (*Vowels* are the letters *a, e, i, o,* and *u.*)

EXAMPLES
employ + ment = employment
stay + ing = staying
destroy + ed = destroyed

If you are adding a suffix to a word that ends with *y*, and that *y* follows a consonant, you should usually change the *y* to *i*. (*Consonants* are all letters that are not vowels.)

EXAMPLES
silly + est = silliest
sticky + ness = stickiness
cry + ed = cried
cheery + ly = cheerily

If you are adding a suffix that begins with a vowel to a word that ends with a silent *e*, you should usually drop the *e*.

EXAMPLES
shave + ing = shaving
value + able = valuable
rose + y = rosy
take + ing = taking

If you are adding a suffix that begins with a consonant to a word that ends with a silent *e*, you should usually leave the *e* in place.

EXAMPLES
tire + less = tireless
sincere + ly = sincerely
fate + ful = fateful
place + ment = placement

3.92 USING SPELLING RULES II. When a word is spelled with the letters *i* and *e* and has the long / ē / sound, it is spelled *ie* except after the letter *c*.

EXAMPLES
thief, relieve, yield, pierce
ceiling, conceive, receipt, deceive

The only word in the English language that ends in *–sede* is *supersede*. Only the following three words end in *–ceed: exceed, proceed*, and *succeed*. Every other word that ends with the / sēd / sound is spelled *cede*.

EXAMPLES
precede, recede, concede, accede

Most noun plurals are formed by simply adding *–s* to the end of the word.

EXAMPLES
stairs, ducklings, kites, rockets

The plurals of nouns that end in *o, s, x, z, ch*, or *sh* should be formed by adding *–es*.

EXAMPLES
tomatoes, classes, taxes, topazes

An exception to the rule above is that musical terms (and certain other words that end in *o*) are usually pluralized by adding *–s*.

EXAMPLES
pianos, solos, concertos, sopranos

Form the plurals of nouns that end in *y* following a vowel by adding *–s*.

EXAMPLES
toys, donkeys, Thursdays, rays

Form the plurals of nouns that end in *y* following a consonant by changing the *y* to an *i* and adding *–es*.

EXAMPLES
ponies, spies, countries, stories

3.93 COMMON SPELLING ERRORS. Some English words are often misspelled. Here is a list of 75 commonly misspelled words. If you master this list, you will avoid many errors in your spelling.

COMMONLY MISSPELLED ENGLISH WORDS

absence	behavior	fulfill	nickel	rhythm
accidentally	breathe	guidance	niece	schedule
accommodate	business	independent	noticeable	separate
across	committee	irresistible	nutritious	succeed
adequately	conscious	judgment	obedience	surprise
advisable	descend	league	occasion	temperature
all right	desperate	license	occurrence	tomorrow
a lot	eighth	lightning	parallel	transparent
ancient	embarrass	liquefy	permanent	twelfth
anonymous	environment	manageable	pleasant	vacuum
apparent	excellent	miniature	privilege	vehicle
attendance	exhaust	misspell	prove	villain
beautiful	existence	mysterious	receive	weird
beggar	fascinate	necessary	responsibility	whistle
beginning	forfeit	neighbor	restaurant	yield

SPEAKING AND LISTENING Resource

THE POWER OF COMMUNICATION

Communication is a form of behavior that fulfills the basic human need to connect and interact with other individuals in society. Because democratic government requires the free exchange of ideas, communication is also fundamental to the political way of life in the United States.

4.1 Verbal and Nonverbal Communication

Human beings use both verbal and nonverbal communication to convey meaning and exchange ideas. When a person expresses meaning through words, he or she is using **verbal communication**. When a person expresses meaning without using words, for example by standing up straight or shaking his or her head, he or she is using **nonverbal communication**. When you speak to another person, you may think that the meaning of what you say comes chiefly from the words you use. However, as much as 60 percent of the meaning of a message may be communicated nonverbally.

ELEMENTS OF VERBAL COMMUNICATION

ELEMENT	DESCRIPTION	GUIDELINES FOR SPEAKERS
Volume	loudness or softness	Vary your volume, but make sure that you can be heard.
Melody, Pitch	highness or lowness	Vary your pitch. Avoid speaking in a monotone (at a single pitch).
Pace	speed	Vary the speed of your delivery to suit what you are saying. Excitement, for example, can be communicated by a fast pace, and seriousness can be communicated by slowing down and saying something forcefully.
Tone	emotional quality	Suit your tone to your message, and vary it appropriately as you speak. For example, you might use a light tone for a happy message and a heavier one for a sad message.
Enunciation	clearness with which words are spoken	When speaking before a group, pronounce your words more precisely than you would in ordinary conversation.

CONTINUED

ELEMENTS OF NONVERBAL COMMUNICATION

ELEMENT	DESCRIPTION	GUIDELINES FOR SPEAKERS
Eye contact	Looking audience members in the eye	Make eye contact regularly with people in your audience. Include all audience members.
Facial expression	Using your face to show your emotions	Use expressions to emphasize your message—raised eyebrows for a question, pursed lips for concentration, eyebrows lowered for anger, and so on.
Gesture	Meaningful motions of the arms and hands	Use gestures to emphasize points. Be careful, however, not to overuse gestures. Too many can be distracting.
Posture	Position of the body	Keep your spine straight and head high, but avoid appearing stiff. Stand with your arms and legs slightly open, except when adopting other postures to express particular emotions.
Proximity	Distance from audience	Keep the right amount of distance between yourself and the audience. You should be a comfortable distance away, but close enough for the audience to hear you.

LISTENING SKILLS

Learning to listen well is essential for success in personal life, in school, and, later, on the job.

4.2 Active versus Passive Listening

Effective—or active—listening requires skill and concentration. Active listeners focus on what a speaker is trying to communicate. Ineffective listeners view listening as a passive activity, something that simply "happens" without any effort on their part.

4.3 Listening to a Lecture or Demonstration

- Think of creative reasons to listen. Think of reasons why the information is important by asking yourself: How can I use this information?

- As you listen, show the speaker that you are involved. Maintain an attentive posture by sitting up straight, making eye contact, and nodding when you understand.

- Listen for major ideas. Identify the speaker's main points and the facts offered to support them.

You may want to briefly note on paper the major ideas and related details.

- When you do not understand something that the speaker is saying, make a note. Save questions and comments for when the speaker invites questions. Then raise your hand before asking your question or making your comment.

- Do not let yourself become distracted. Avoid daydreaming, focusing on the speaker's delivery, or listening to background noise.

4.4 Listening in Conversations

- Do not monopolize the conversation. Give the other person plenty of opportunities to speak.

- When the other person is speaking, pay attention to what he or she is saying. Show through eye contact, body language, and facial expressions that you are attentive.

- Avoid mentally debating the other person while he or she is speaking. This may distract you from truly hearing what the person has to say. Withhold judgment until the other person has finished.

- Ask the other person questions. Respond to what the other person has been saying.

4.5 Listening to the Media

- Television, movies, and radio programs can contain subtle messages. As you watch or listen, think critically and evaluate what you see or hear.

- When watching or listening, distinguish facts from opinions. Facts are statements that can be proved by checking a reference work or by making observations. Opinions express beliefs. An opinion may express positive or negative attitudes toward a person, object, or idea.

- When watching or listening to an entertainment program, evaluate its quality. Consider the quality of the acting, directing, and writing. Also consider the production qualities—the lighting, sound effects, staging, camera work, costumes, props, and music.

- Set standards about what you will watch or listen to. Turn off a program if it does not meet your standards.

4.6 Adapting Listening Skills to Specific Tasks

Just as different situations require different types of listening, different tasks or goals may also require different listening strategies and skills.

Listening for comprehension means listening for information or ideas other people communicate. For example, you listen for comprehension when you try to understand directions to a friend's house or your teacher's explanation of how to read a poem. Focus on getting the main points of a message.

Listening critically means listening to a message to comprehend and evaluate it. When listening critically, you will judge the arguments in a message to decide whether to accept or reject them. Critical listening is most useful when you encounter a persuasive message such as a sales pitch, advertisement, campaign speech, or news editorial. When evaluating a persuasive message, consider the following: Is the speaker trustworthy and qualified to speak about this subject? Does the speaker present logical arguments supported by solid facts? Does the speaker use unproven assumptions to make a case? Does the speaker use

questionable motivational appeals, such as appeals to fear or to prejudice? These questions can help you decide whether or not to be convinced by a persuasive message.

Listening to learn vocabulary involves a very different kind of listening because the focus is on learning new words and how to use them. For instance, if you were to hear a presentation on hip-hop music, the speaker might introduce some of the many terms used in this musical style and explain what they mean. Sometimes it is possible to figure out what an unfamiliar word means simply by how the word is used in a sentence. Once you learn a new word, try to use it several times so you become comfortable using it.

Listening for appreciation means listening purely for enjoyment or entertainment. You might listen appreciatively to a singer, a comedian, a storyteller, or a humorous speaker.

COMMUNICATING WITH OTHERS

4.7 Communicating with Another Person

Daily human interactions involve a great deal of **interpersonal communication**, or communication between two individuals. These guidelines will help you to communicate more effectively in such interactions.

- Make eye contact and maintain a relaxed posture.

- Provide feedback as you listen. Smile or nod to show understanding or agreement. Ask questions or make comments. Try not to interrupt or to finish the speaker's sentences for him or her.

- Rephrase what the speaker has said to make sure that you understand him or her. For example, suppose that the speaker says, "Crazy Horse never allowed anyone to take his photograph." You could reflect back, "So, nobody ever photographed Crazy Horse? That's interesting."

- Control your emotions. If you become angry while listening to the speaker, take a deep breath and count to ten. Make sure you haven't misunderstood by rephrasing the statement that angered you. If you can contain your anger, express your objections calmly. If you cannot contain your anger, end your conversation and say that you would like to continue it at another time.

- Distinguish between facts and opinions. Facts are statements that can be proven true, whereas opinions are expressions of personal belief that may or may not be true. Ask if you are unsure whether another person is stating a fact or opinion.

4.8 Communicating in a Small Group

Much human activity takes place in small groups. Here are additional guidelines to consider when more than two people are involved.

- Understand group roles. Individual members are likely to fulfill particular roles in a group based on what they do best. Successful group members attempt to fulfill positive and constructive roles within the group and encourage others to do so.

- Take turns participating. Good group members contribute to the discussion but also allow others to participate. If a person dominates the discussion, help others join in. You might say, "I've been interested in what you have to say. What do other people think about this issue?"

- Help to foster a positive group climate. **Group climate** refers to the degree of warmth or coldness that group members feel toward each other. Positive or warm group climates are characterized by trust, cooperation, and concern for others. Negative or cold group climates are characterized by suspicion, competition, and selfishness. You can help to create a positive and warm climate by supporting others' ideas, treating others as equals, and remaining flexible and open to new ideas and information.

- Establish group goals. Some groups have difficulty accomplishing anything because they lack clear-cut goals. Help your group establish clear goals at the beginning.

4.9 Communicating in a Large Group

Generally, the larger the size of the group, the less opportunity there is for each individual to participate. However, there are still principles that can help you communicate in large groups.

- Share group roles. In large groups, many members may have the skills needed for any one role.

Sharing roles can allow everyone to contribute.

- Focus on key relationships. It may not be possible to get to know everyone well in a large group. Identify key people in the group with whom you will need to carry out your assignments, and focus on getting to know them well.

- Emphasize group identity, norms, and goals. As groups become larger in size, they are likely to become less cohesive. **Cohesiveness** refers to the level of commitment and connection members feel to each other and the group.

- Stand up when speaking. Make sure that everyone in the room can see and hear you. If there is a microphone available, use it. Speak in a normal tone 4 to 6 inches from the microphone.

- Avoid the pressure to conform. In large groups, individuals are less comfortable speaking out if they disagree with an idea or decision. If you disagree with an expressed idea or decision, speak out and share your reservations.

- Foster responsibility. In large groups, it is relatively easy for individual members to avoid responsibility. Take responsibility yourself, and encourage others in the group to carry out their assigned duties.

4.10 Asking and Answering Questions

In many situations you will find it useful to ask questions of a speaker, or you will be asked questions. Often a formal speech or presentation will be followed by a question-and-answer period.

ASKING QUESTIONS
- Wait to be recognized. In most cases, it is appropriate to raise your hand if you have a question.

- Make questions clear and direct. The longer your question, the less chance a speaker will understand it.

- Do not debate or argue. If you disagree with a speaker, the question-and-answer period is not the time to hash out an argument. Ask to speak with the speaker privately after the presentation is over, or agree on a later time and place to meet.

- Do not give a speech. Sometimes audience members are more interested in expressing their own opinion than in asking the speaker a question.

- Come prepared for a question-and-answer period. Although you can never predict the exact questions that people will ask you, you can anticipate many questions that are likely to be asked. Rehearse aloud your answers to the most difficult questions.

- Be patient. Give the audience time to ask questions about your speech. Don't run back to your seat the minute your speech is over.

- Be direct and succinct. Be sure to answer the question directly and to provide a short but clear answer.

- Rephrase difficult questions. If you are not sure what an audience member's question is, repeat the question back to them to clarify. You may also want to repeat the question if not everyone in the audience could hear it.

- Be courteous. Sometimes audience members will ask a question you have already answered in your speech. Be tactful in such situations. Briefly repeat the information from your speech in case the audience member did not hear or understand you the first time.

- Handle difficult audience members gracefully. Some audience members may hog the stage or try to pick a verbal fight with a speaker. In such situations, keep your cool and gently suggest that the audience member talk to you privately after the presentation.

COMMUNICATION STYLES AND CULTURAL BARRIERS

4.11 Being Considerate of Other Cultures and Communication Styles

Communication styles and behaviors vary greatly among people of different cultures—even those who live in the same country. There are many possible sources of miscommunication between cultural groups. In some cultures, for example, two people in conversation may stand very close together. In other cultures, standing close is considered an intrusion on personal space. When interacting with a person from another culture, respect the other individual's cultural practices and behaviors.

4.12 Overcoming Barriers to Effective Multicultural Communication

The following guidelines and suggestions will help you to overcome some common barriers and stumbling blocks to communicating with people of different cultural backgrounds.

- Treat people as individuals. Do not assume that everyone is "the same" as you are, or even that people with similar cultural backgrounds are the same.

- Seek common ground. People from different cultures may have difficulty communicating if they focus on differences rather than similarities.

- Accept others as they are. Avoid evaluating or judging the behavior, beliefs, feelings, or experiences of others. Instead, learn to accept differences as valid, even if you personally disagree with what someone else thinks or feels.

- Avoid provoking language. Racial, ethnic, or gender slurs or swearing is unacceptable. You-statements ("You are not listening to me," "You should not do that," "You don't know what you're talking about") can feel like an attack, even when they are well intentioned. People often react to you-statements by becoming defensive or hostile. Try to use I-statements instead ("I feel like you aren't listening to me," "I don't think you should do that," "I'm not sure I agree with you").

4.13 Collaborative Learning and Communication

Collaboration is the act of working with one or more other people to achieve a goal. Many common learning situations—such as small group work, tutoring, book clubs, or peer evaluations—involve collaboration. In collaborative learning situations, remember to listen attentively, be polite, participate, and help keep discussion focused.

4.14 Conducting an Interview

In an interview, you meet with someone and ask him or her questions. Interviewing experts is an excellent way to gain information about a particular topic. When planning an interview, do some background research on your subject. Write out a list of questions. Other questions might occur to you during the interview.

Set up a time for the interview. Be sure the person you are interviewing knows what you want to find out and why you need to know it. This will help him or her to answer your questions in a useful way. Ask open-ended questions. Open-ended questions cannot be answered with a simple "yes" or "no" nor a brief statement of fact. One of the most valuable questions to ask at the end of the interview is, "What would you like to add that I haven't asked about?"

If possible, tape-record the interview. Be sure to ask the person you are interviewing permission to tape-record the session. Take notes during the interview, whether or not you are also tape-recording it. Write down the main points and key words to help you remember details. Record the person's most important statements word for word. Clarify spelling and get permission for quotes. End the interview on time. Thank the person for his or her help. Write up the results of the interview as soon as possible. Over time, what seemed like a very clear note may become unclear.

PUBLIC SPEAKING

4.15 Giving a Speech

The fear of speaking in public can be overcome by preparing a speech thoroughly and by practicing positive thinking and relaxation.

4.16 Types of Speeches

Here are the three main types of speeches:

- **Impromptu speech**. This is a speech given without any advance preparation. If you were surprised by a gift or an award, you might be asked to give a brief, unrehearsed speech.

- **Memorized speech**. This is a speech that has been written out and memorized word for word.

- **Extemporaneous speech**. This is a speech in which the speaker refers to notes occasionally. Most professional speakers prefer to deliver extemporaneous speeches because they combine the liveliness of an impromptu speech with the careful preparation of a memorized speech. The speaker creates an overall plan for the speech, records important points on cards, and rehearses until comfortable.

4.17 Steps in Preparing an Extemporaneous Speech

1. Choose a topic for your speech. Consider the audience, occasion, and your own strengths and weaknesses when choosing a topic.

2. Do prewriting to identify what you know or think about the topic. As you write, think about different ways to approach the topic.

3. Research the topic. Use a variety of source materials, including newspapers, magazines, books, interviews, Internet sources, and personal experience.

4. Determine your specific purpose. What are you trying to accomplish in speaking to your audience? Are you trying to demonstrate something to them? compare and contrast two things or ideas? strengthen their commitment to something? spur them to take action?

5. Organize your material. Use a clear, logical, and interesting organizational strategy that suits your specific purpose, audience, and occasion. You may want to stick to three or four main points.

6. Create visual aids. Some material is best presented visually. Visual aids should be neat, attractive, visible from a distance, and relevant to your speech. For more information, see the Language Arts Survey 6.11, "Displaying Effective Visual Information."

7. Prepare note cards. Note cards should be no larger than 4" x 6" inches and should contain as much information as you need to present your speech, but not so much that you are tempted to read word for word. Write clearly and legibly so you can easily read your notes.

8. Rehearse with your note cards. Practice what you will say in front of a live audience or by using a mirror or recording device. Rehearse with visual aids if you are using them.

4.18 Guidelines for Giving a Speech

A speech should always include an introduction, body, and conclusion. The introduction of your speech should spark the audience's interest, present your central idea, and briefly preview your main points. The body of your speech should expand upon each of your main points in order to support the central idea. The conclusion of your speech should be memorable and give your audience a sense of completion.

4.19 Oral Interpretation of Poetry

Oral interpretation is the art of presenting a literary work aloud to an audience. In the past, people often entertained one another by reading poems aloud. After analyzing what the poem is about, make a copy of the poem and mark it to show:

- the emotions that you will express
- places where you will increase or decrease your pace
- places where you will raise or lower your volume
- the gestures and facial expressions that you will use to communicate emotions
- any different voices that you will use when reading (if dramatizing different characters)

When a poem contains more than one voice, such as the voices of a narrator and characters, make each voice sound different from the others. Excellent ways to differentiate voices when reading include changing your tone (the emotion expressed) and pitch (the highness or lowness of your voice) and looking in a different direction each time you change voices.

To memorize a poem, work line by line. Look at one line. Look away and repeat it. Then check to see that you got it right. Once you get that line right, add a second line. Look away and repeat both lines. Then check them. Continue in this manner until the entire poem is memorized. Have a partner look at a copy of the poem while you recite it out loud. This person can prompt you when you forget a line. Memorize the poem thoroughly before you begin working on the qualities of your reading.

Rehearse your interpretation using a tape recorder or a video recorder. You might also want to rehearse in front of a mirror so that you can view your facial expressions and gestures.

4.20 Telling a Story

When telling a story, consider these elements:

- Decide on your purpose. Every story has a purpose. Sometimes the purpose is simply to entertain or to share a personal experience, but often there is a moral or lesson that the storyteller hopes listeners will learn from.
- Select a focus. The focus for your story will depend largely on your purpose in telling it. For example, if you were telling the story of Abraham Lincoln's life, and your purpose was to show how someone could rise from humble roots to a position of greatness, you would probably choose a broad focus for the story. You might begin with Lincoln's birth in a Kentucky log cabin and end with his eventual rise to the position of president of the United States and his many accomplishments in office. If your purpose was to show that perseverance is an important virtue, you might choose a narrower focus. Your story could ignore Lincoln's early life and instead focus on his long political career and his many defeats on the way to the presidency.
- Choose your point of view. You can speak in the first person, either as a direct participant in the events or as an observer (real or imagined) who witnessed the event. You can use the third person voice to achieve greater objectivity.
- Determine sequence of events. The **sequence of events** refers to the order in which they are presented. Although it might seem obvious that stories should "begin at the beginning," this is not always the best approach. Some narratives begin with the turning point of the story to create a sense of drama. Others begin at the end of the story and present the events leading up to the point. Wherever you begin your story, you should present events in a logical way and establish a clear sense of direction for your listeners.
- Select details. Carefully chosen details should keep the story focused. A well-constructed story should flow smoothly and not get bogged down by unnecessary details.
- Choose characters. All stories need to include real, believable characters. Provide your listeners with vivid, concrete descriptions of the important characters in the story.

- Create dialogue. Although it is possible to tell a story in which the characters do not speak directly, conversation and dialogue add life to a story. Dialogue should sound authentic, relate to the main action of the story, and advance the plot. When telling a story, you might choose to enact the characters by creating an individual voice for each one.

4.21 Participating in a Debate

A **debate** is a contest in which two people or groups of people defend opposite sides of an issue in an attempt to convince a judge or audience to agree with their views.

EXAMPLES

Whether or not to have year-round schools

Whether imagination is more important than knowledge

Whether or not to prohibit pets from using public parks

The two sides in a debate take opposite stances on the issue. Sometimes you may find that you are defending a side of an issue that you do not personally agree with. For example, you may be asked to support year-round schools, even if you believe the idea is a poor one. Defending a position you do not believe in will allow you to better understand the position of those who disagree with you. Although you may not change your stance, you may come to appreciate why others see the issue differently.

Typically, both sides in a debate are allowed an equal amount of time to state their cases.

Once the debate is finished, the audience or judge considers the arguments of both sides and votes for which side made the more persuasive case.

4.22 Preparing a Multimedia Presentation

Multimedia technology can add an important visual element to a presentation. Consider the following guidelines when creating a multimedia presentation:

- Ensure that audio-visual elements enhance understanding. The multimedia elements of your presentation should add to the verbal elements, not replace them. Be sure the content of the presentation is easy to understand and that the amount of information will not overwhelm audience members.

- Make sure the presentation is clearly audible and visible. Video clips or graphics may appear blurry on a projection screen, or may not be visible to audience members in the back or at the sides of the room. Audio clips may sound muffled or may echo in a large room. Be sure the presentation can be easily seen and heard from all parts of the room.

- Become familiar with the equipment. Well before the presentation, know how to operate the equipment you will need. Have a backup plan in case the equipment malfunctions. Make sure that you can operate the equipment while speaking at the same time. If you will need to turn off the room lights, make sure you can operate the equipment in the dark and can still see your note cards.

- Be sure the room can accommodate your needs. Once you know where you will make your presentation, be sure the necessary electrical outlets and extension cords are available, that lights can be dimmed or turned off as needed, and that the room can accommodate the equipment you will use.

STUDY AND RESEARCH Resource

THINKING SKILLS

This section gives you some tips that can greatly improve your ability to make decisions, to solve problems, and to learn and think critically.

5.1 Making Decisions and Solving Problems

MAKING DECISIONS. When making a decision, you often must weigh several factors. You can compare your options by making a **pros and cons** chart on paper. First make a list of all your options. For each option list the reasons for choosing it (the pros) and the reasons for not choosing it (the cons). Then compare the lists.

PROS AND CONS		
Painting Yearbook Illustration or Drawing It in Pencil		
	Painting	**Drawing in Pencil**
Pros	colorful	easier less expensive
Cons	more expensive more difficult	not colorful

SOLVING PROBLEMS. There are many ways to solve problems. To solve a complex problem, you will probably need to use more than one strategy. Here are two approaches you can try:

Trial and error. Sometimes when you have to solve a problem, you just make a guess and see if it works. In a **trial-and-error approach**, you try one possible solution and if it doesn't work you try

another. If you don't know how to solve a particular math problem, you could guess the answer, plug it back into the problem, and then revise your answer as necessary.

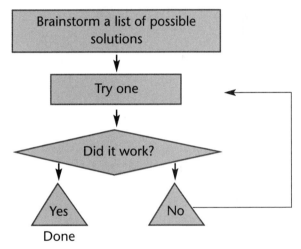

Divide and conquer. Another strategy for problem solving is to divide the problem into parts and then solve each part one at a time in a logical sequence. Here is an example:

PROBLEM

A friend is coming to stay at your house for a few days and you need to prepare a room for him.

SOLUTION

Break down the job into small, manageable goals:

STRATEGY

(1) Move desk and computer from spare room.
(2) Remove storage boxes from closet and put in basement.
(3) Clean the room.
(4) Put cot in room and make bed.

5.2 Distinguishing Fact from Opinion

What is the difference between the following statements?

> The language with the greatest number of speakers, over nine hundred million, is Mandarin Chinese.

> Mandarin Chinese is the greatest language in the world.

The first statement expresses a fact. You can prove this fact by looking in a reference book. The second statement expresses an opinion. This statement can be supported but not proved.

A **fact** is a statement that, at least in principle, could be proved by direct observation. Every statement of fact is either true or false. An opinion is a statement that expresses not a fact about the world but rather an attitude or desire.

An **opinion** can express an attitude toward something. Such statements often include judgment words such as *good, worthless, valuable, ugly, wonderful, nice,* or *excellent.*

An opinion can also tell not what is but what someone believes should be. Such statements usually include words such as *should, should not, ought to, ought not to, must,* or *must not.*

Some opinions make statements about the future. Because the future is unpredictable, most predictions can be considered opinions.

EXAMPLES

> People will live longer in the future.
> Tomorrow will be partly cloudy.

EVALUATING FACTS AND OPINIONS. When evaluating a statement, ask yourself whether it can be proved through direct observation or by checking a reliable source such as a reference work or an unbiased expert. An opinion is as good as the facts that support it. The opinion that Mandarin Chinese is the greatest language in the world is supported by such facts as the number of speakers that it has. However, others might argue that English is the greater language because it is spoken more widely around the globe. But no facts would prove or disprove these opinions.

Usually, you can make a stronger case by using facts in place of opinions. For example, instead of saying, "This was a wonderful day," you could say something like, "Today the sun was shining, it was 74 degrees outside, and I got an *A* on my math test. That's what made it a great day." When you express an opinion, especially in writing, include facts to back up or support that opinion.

When reading or listening, be critical about the statements that you encounter. Ask yourself, "Is this a fact or an opinion?" If it is a statement of fact, consider whether it can be proved or seems likely. If it is an opinion, consider whether it is supported by facts.

5.3 Avoiding False Arguments and Propaganda

Another very important thinking skill is learning to use good logic. Not only do you need good facts, but you also need to know how to put those facts together to come up with the right conclusions. Learning how to think clearly will enable you to avoid errors in logic and to arrive at true conclusions. It will also help you to recognize the faulty thinking of others (especially advertisers) who might be trying to persuade you. The intentional use of false arguments to persuade others is called **propaganda**. Here are some of the faulty arguments of which you should be aware:

GLITTERING GENERALITIES AND "SPIN." Glittering generalities are statements given to make something sound more appealing. Such statements can be hard to prove, as they appeal to the emotions.

EXAMPLE

> These trading cards are the best ever in this limited-time collection!

ANALYSIS

> Nothing in this statement tells the listener why the trading cards are the best ever. Adding "limited-time collection" to the statement vaguely implies that the trading cards will be available for only a short while, and that the listener should buy them quickly before they are unavailable.

Spin is a technique used to slant public perception of the news. Public relations firms and advertisers use this technique to create a favorable perception of a product or organization. Spin can be hard to recognize.

The accident was a minor incident because only 25 people were injured.

ANALYSIS

The fact is that 25 people were injured. This does not make it a minor incident; someone is merely interpreting the accident as minor.

STEREOTYPES. An overgeneralization about a group of people is known as a **stereotype**. Stereotypes are one of the most dangerous of all overgeneralizations. Stereotyping is based on lack of knowledge or experience.

UNSOUND OPINIONS. A sound opinion is one that can be supported by facts. An **unsound opinion** is one that cannot be supported by facts. Be sure that you can back up your opinions with facts.

FACT

Miss Rivers won this year's award for excellence in teaching.

OPINION

Miss Rivers is the best teacher at Adams Middle School.

ANALYSIS

The statement that "Miss Rivers is the best teacher at Adams Middle School" is someone's personal feeling about her. However, it is probably a sound opinion because it is backed up by the fact that she received the award for excellence in teaching.

CIRCULAR REASONING. **Circular reasoning** is the error of trying to support an opinion by restating it in different words. You can avoid circular reasoning by always backing up your opinions with facts.

EXAMPLE

That adventure book was exciting because it was full of action.

ANALYSIS

The "reason" the speaker gives for saying that the book was exciting is really just another way of saying it was exciting. He or she should mention some specific examples to show what makes the story exciting.

LOADED WORDS. In trying to argue for or against something, people will often use **loaded words**, or words that stir up strong feelings, whether positive or negative. Be careful not to let your feelings interfere with your understanding of the facts.

EXAMPLE

Representative Philbert is a lazy, good-for-nothing imbecile.

ANALYSIS

This statement, an emotional attack on the representative, uses loaded words that will stir up feelings against him. It is not a reasonable evaluation of his policies or actions in office.

BANDWAGON APPEAL. **Bandwagon appeal** plays to your desire to be part of the crowd—to be like everyone else and to do what everyone else is doing. Beware of advertisements or arguments that try to get you to think or act like everyone else. Just because "everybody" believes or does something does not make it good or right for you.

EXAMPLE

Those who want to be cool wear Star jeans.

ANALYSIS

This statement suggests that you aren't really part of the "in" crowd unless you wear this brand of jeans. It does not prove, or even say, anything about the quality of the clothing.

5.4 Classifying

One of the many higher-level thinking skills you can develop is the ability to classify. To **classify** is to put into categories. Items in the same category should share one or more characteristics. For example, whales are classified by their method of eating as either baleen or toothed whales. The key step in classifying is choosing categories that fit your purpose.

5.5 Generalizing

To **generalize** is to make a broad statement based on one or more observations. For example, suppose that you observe that several cats like to stare through windows. You might generalize, based on this discovery, that "cats like to stare through windows." Such generalizations are also called **inferences**. People have learned most of what they know about the world by making generalizations based on their experiences.

Generalizing is an extremely important thinking tool but it is not a perfect one. Generalizations can be proved false by only one exception. Avoid making generalizations based on too little evidence. Keep an open mind and be willing to revise your ideas based on new experiences.

5.6 Making Inferences, Predictions, and Hypotheses

From careful observation, it is possible to make generalizations, or **inferences**, about the world around us. From there it is possible to **predict** what will happen and to form hypotheses. A **hypothesis** is an educated guess about a cause or an effect. A prediction based on a theory is a hypothesis. A possible explanation for an observed event is also a hypothesis. A hypothesis always needs to be tested against experience. Theories and hypotheses can change if a discovery shows that something is otherwise.

5.7 Estimating and Quantifying

To support an argument, you need to provide facts, and often facts are strengthened by numbers or quantities. If you claim, for instance, that too many people are without health insurance, you should **quantify** your claim by stating how many. The numbers you need may be available in reference works. If not, you might be able to **estimate**, or find the approximate quantity. Sometimes you will have only enough knowledge to estimate a range within which the actual number actually falls. If you need to estimate, always make clear that you are doing so.

QUANTIFYING

The science fair had 314 registered participants.

ESTIMATING

The science fair was attended by about 300 students and their parents.

5.8 Analyzing and Synthesizing

When you **analyze** something, you break it down into parts and then think about how the parts are related to each other and to the whole. You might analyze a short story by describing its conflict, plot, characters, setting, and theme. You might analyze a movie by describing its acting, directing, writing, settings, and costumes.

When you **synthesize** something, you bring everything that you were considering together into a whole.

5.9 Comparing and Contrasting

Comparing and contrasting are closely related processes. When you **compare** one thing to another, you describe similarities between the two things. When you **contrast** two things, you describe their differences. To compare and contrast, begin by listing the features of each subject. Then go down both lists and check whether each feature is shared or not. You can also show similarities and differences in a Venn diagram. For more information, see the Language Arts Survey 2.16, "Completing Venn Diagrams."

5.10 Evaluating

When you evaluate, you make a judgment about something. You may be asked to compare two things to determine which is more valuable or effective. Evaluate questions use such words as *evaluate, judge, justify, critique, determine whether, decide the effectiveness of,* and *appraise.*

5.11 Extending

When you extend your knowledge, you connect one experience to another. In the study of literature, you extend your knowledge by making connections between two pieces of literature, between the literary work and your own experience, or between a literary work and a cultural or current event. Extend questions use such words as *extend your knowledge, connect, relate,* and *apply.*

5.12 Perspective, Empathy, and Self-Understanding

When you are asked to use perspective, empathy, and self-understanding to answer a question, you are exercising an important ability to connect the experience of one person or group to your own. Such thinking allows you to see multiple perspectives, generate alternative viewpoints, and understand another person's ideas.

STUDY SKILLS

5.13 Developing Good Study Habits

Success in a future career depends largely on success in school. You can improve your performance enormously by developing good study habits.

Homework is best done in a special study area. Choose a quiet location, away from distractions such as conversation, television, or loud music. Choose a place that is well lit and comfortable. Adequate lighting will help you to avoid eyestrain and headaches. Choose a study area that is available at regular times. Set aside a specific time each day for study. Have all the tools that you will need, such as paper, pencils, textbooks, handouts, and reference works, ready and at hand.

Many of your assignments will be due on the following day. Others will be long-term projects. At the end of each school day, make a habit of looking over your assignments. Decide what tasks you need to complete for the following day. Break longer assignments down into specific steps that need to be completed by specific times.

5.14 Keeping an Assignment Notebook

Keeping track of assignments in your head can be dangerous because of the possibility of forgetting important details. Instead, write down all your assignments in an assignment notebook. For each assignment, record:

- the name of the subject
- details of the assignment, including what, precisely, you need to do

- the date of the assignment
- the date when the assignment is due

5.15 Understanding the Assignment

Understanding an assignment depends on your ability to follow directions.

FOLLOWING SPOKEN DIRECTIONS. Often teachers give assignments orally. When listening to spoken directions, make sure you do the following:

- Listen carefully. Write down the directions as you hear them.
- Notice what steps are involved in the assignment. Also notice the order of these steps.
- Listen for the key word in each step. A key word is one that tells you what to do. Examples are *read*, *write*, *organize*, and *memorize*.
- If you do not understand the directions, ask your teacher to explain them.

FOLLOWING WRITTEN DIRECTIONS. Directions for tests usually are written down. Assignment directions also sometimes appear in written form on the board, on overhead transparencies, or on handouts. Make sure to:

- Read all the directions completely before you begin the assignment.
- Ask questions to clarify any points not covered in the directions.
- Divide the assignment into steps. Put these steps in a logical order.
- Decide what materials you will need, and assemble them before you begin.
- Reread each step before you actually do it.

5.16 Taking Notes, Outlining, and Summarizing Information

When **taking notes** in class or while conducting research, you may find it helpful to use a **rough outline**. Write the main ideas, and beneath the main ideas, write related ideas, set off by dashes.

Major Cultures in N. Amer., 1492

  —Eastern woodland (incl. Iroquois & Algonquians)
  —Southeastern (incl. Cherokee & Chicasaw)
  —Plains (incl. Dakota, Pawnee, & Kiowa)
  —Southwestern (incl. Navajo, Hopi, & Apache)
  —Great Basin (incl. Ute & Paiute)
  —Plateau (incl. Nez Perce & Yakima)
  —Northwestern (incl. Chinook & Yurok)
  —California (incl. Shasta, Pomo, & Chumash)

Origins

  —Came to Amer. by land bridge across Bering Strait
  — ~ 35,000 bc
  —May have followed herds, mammoths, musk oxen, etc.

To review the material, you might find it helpful to read over your notes and outline and then **summarize** what you have learned. Writing reinforces your memory of what you have learned.

RESEARCH SKILLS

Mastering research skills will help you both in school and in real-life situations outside school. Research is the process of gathering ideas and information. One of the best resources for research is the library.

5.17 How Library Materials Are Organized

Each book in a library is assigned a unique number, called a **call number.** The call number is printed on the **spine** (edge) of each book. The numbers serve to classify books as well as to help the library keep track of them.

Libraries commonly use one of two systems for classifying books. Most school and public libraries use the **Dewey Decimal System.** Most college libraries use the **Library of Congress Classification System** (known as the LC system).

5.18 How to Locate Library Materials

If you know the call number of a book, you can usually go to the bookshelves to obtain the book. Use the signs at the ends of the rows to locate the section you need. Then find the particular shelf that contains call numbers close to yours.

Library collections include many other types of publications besides books, including magazines, newspapers, audio and video recordings, and government documents. Ask a librarian to tell you where to find the materials you need.

To find the call numbers of books that will help you with your research, use the library's catalog. The catalog lists all the books in the library (or group of libraries in a larger system).

COMPUTERIZED CATALOGS. Many libraries today use computerized catalogs. Systems differ from library to library, but most have computer terminals you may use to search through the library's collection. You can usually search by author, title, subject, or key word. To search by author, type the last name first. Type as much of the name as you know.

EXAMPLE

taylor, mildred d

To search by title, omit articles such as *a, an,* or *the* at the beginning of titles.

EXAMPLE

red badge of courage

To search by subject, use the subjects provided by the library. To search by key words, use related topics or specific words or names.

EXAMPLE

civil war; racism; great depression; union

A librarian can help you to master the system. On the next page is a sample book entry screen from a computerized catalog.

CARD CATALOGS. Like a computerized catalog, a card catalog contains basic information about each book in the library. In a card catalog the information is typed on paper cards, and the cards are arranged alphabetically in drawers. For each book there is a title card, one author card for each author, and at least one subject card. All of these cards show the book's title, author, and call number, so you can search for a book by title, author, or subject. The following illustration shows a typical title card.

A TITLE CARD

333.78   The Quetzal and the Macaw : the story of
Costa Rica's national parks.
Wallace, David Rains, 1945–
The Quetzal and the Macaw : the story of
Costa Rica's national parks.—San
Francisco: Sierra Club Books, 1992
xvi, 222 p. : maps : 24 cm.
1. National parks and reserves—Costa Rica—
History. 2. Costa Rica. Servicio de
Parques nacionales—History. 3. Nature
conservation—Costa Rica—History. I. Title.
ISBN 0-394-57456-7

INTERLIBRARY LOANS. Many libraries are part of larger library networks. In these libraries, the computerized catalog covers the collections of several libraries. If you want a book from a different library, you will need to request the book at the library's request desk or by using its computer.

5.19 Using Reference Works

Most libraries have an assortment of reference works in which information is organized so that you can find it easily. Usually, reference works cannot be checked out of the library.

5.20 TYPES OF DICTIONARIES. You will find many types of dictionaries in the library reference section. The most common is a dictionary of the English language. Examples include *Merriam Webster's Collegiate Dictionary*, *Merriam Webster's New World Dictionary*, and the multivolume *Oxford English Dictionary*. Other dictionaries focus on slang, abbreviations and acronyms, English/foreign language translation, and spelling. For more information on using a dictionary to look up specific words in English, see the Language Arts Survey 1.17, "Using a Dictionary."

5.21 USING A THESAURUS. A thesaurus is a reference book that groups synonyms, or words with similar meanings. Suppose that you are writing an essay and have a word that means

almost but not quite what you want, or perhaps you find yourself using the same word over and over. A thesaurus can give you fresh and precise words to use. For example, if you look up the word *sing* in a thesaurus, you might find the following synonyms listed:

> sing (v.) carol, chant, croon, hum,
> vocalize, warble, yodel

5.22 USING ALMANACS, YEARBOOKS, AND ATLASES. Almanacs and **yearbooks** are published each year. An almanac provides statistics and lists, often related to recent events. In an almanac you can find facts about current events, countries of the world, famous people, sports, entertainment, and many other subjects. An overview of the events of the year can be found in a yearbook.

Some of the more widely used almanacs and yearbooks are *The Guinness Book of World Records*, *World Almanac and Book of Facts,* and *World Book Yearbook of Events*.

An **atlas** is a collection of maps and other geographic information. Some atlases show natural features such as mountains and rivers; others show political features such as countries and cities. If you need to locate a particular feature on a map in an atlas, refer to the gazetteer—an index that lists every item shown on the map.

5.23 USING BIOGRAPHICAL REFERENCES, ENCYCLOPEDIAS, AND PERIODICALS. A **biographical reference** contains information on the lives of famous people. Examples include *Who's Who*, *Dictionary of American Biography*, and *Contemporary Authors*. Biographical reference books are usually organized in alphabetical order.

Encyclopedias provide a survey of knowledge. General encyclopedias, such as *World Book*, contain information on many different subjects. Specialized encyclopedias, such as the *LaRousse Encyclopedia of Mythology*, contain information on one particular area of knowledge.

The topics in an encyclopedia are treated in articles, which are usually arranged in alphabetical order. If you look up a topic and do not find it, check the index (usually in the last volume). The index will tell you where in the encyclopedia your topic is covered.

A **periodical** is a publication that comes out regularly, usually once a week, once a month, or four times a year. Magazines and newspapers are periodicals. Because they are published frequently, periodicals are an excellent source of up-to-date news and information, but they may not be as accurate as some other sources.

5.24 Using Tables of Contents, Indexes, Appendices, and Glossaries

Most books contain a table of contents and an index. These two tools can be used to find information that you may be seeking. You will probably want to examine the **table of contents** to scan the entire content of a book, to find a section or chapter of the book, or to find out if a particular topic is covered in depth in the book. The **index** is useful in finding a specific reference to a topic, in locating a chart or table, or in determining whether a certain name appears anywhere in the book. If you don't find what you are looking for in one of these areas, try the other. Look in the table of contents to answer questions like these:

- Does this book have a glossary?
- Does this computer book have a section on the Internet?
- Do I recognize many of the poems in this poetry anthology?

Look in the index to answer questions like these:

- Are there any poems by Robert Frost in this poetry anthology?
- Does this woodworking book have any information about sanding?
- Where is that chart showing the nutritional values of foods?

An **appendix** contains supplemental material at the end of the book. An appendix can include charts, graphs, tables, or other graphic information; lists of addresses, Internet sites, or telephone numbers; book lists for additional reading; or other items. A **glossary** is a list of vocabulary words used in the book and their definitions.

5.25 Using the Internet

The **Internet** is a vast collection of computer networks that can provide you with a great wealth of information from libraries, government agencies, high schools and universities, nonprofit and educational organizations, museums, user groups, and individuals around the world. The Internet provides a valuable way to do research—if you know how to use it. Here are some guidelines.

5.26 BROWSING VERSUS SEARCHING ON THE INTERNET. Browsing means sifting through Internet sites through an Internet browser. **Searching** means conducting focused research by using an Internet search engine. By both browsing and searching, you can gain access to the information you want. Browsing allows you to navigate through different sites, either before or after you have conducted a search. Searching allows you to narrow and expand your research in a focused way to find the particular information you need.

5.27 CONDUCTING AN INTERNET SEARCH. Some of the most popular search engines are:

Fast Search: All the Web, All the Time at
http://www.alltheweb.com

Altavista at
http://www.altavista.digital.com

Infoseek at
http://www.infoseek.com

and Yahoo at
http://yahoo.com.

When searching, use keywords to narrow or broaden your topic. Browse your results, their links, and links suggested by the search engine. Use different search engines for different results.

To keep track of your Internet research, see the Language Arts Survey 5.40, "Documenting and Mapping Internet Research."

5.28 USING BOOLEAN SEARCH STRATEGIES. Boolean logic refers to the logical relationship among search terms. It is named for the mathematician George Boole. Boolean operators such as AND, OR, and NOT, allow you to limit or expand the scope of your topic. Some search engines use other terms or symbols to modify search topics. Refer to each search engine's help feature to learn about these.

5.29 Evaluating Information and Media Sources

To conduct your research efficiently, you need to evaluate your sources and set priorities among them. Ideal sources are unbiased, authoratative, timely, and written at the right level for you to understand and learn from. Ask these questions when evaluating a source:

- Does the author present the material evenly, acknowledging differing points of view and revealing all sides of an issue? Does he or she have a personal stake in what people think about the subject?

- What is the author's background? What makes him or her an expert on the subject? What kind of reputation does he or she have?

- When was the material published? Is it out of date?

- Is the reading level too high or too low to be helpful to you? Does the source cover the material in too much depth or too superficially?

5.30 How to Read a Newspaper or Newsmagazine. Newspapers and newsmagazines contain enormous amounts of information. Few people have the time to read all or most of what appears in a newspaper each day. Nonetheless, reading the news is important.

To get the most out of a newspaper, skim the headlines and leads for world, national, state, and local news stories. Read any news summaries included in your paper. Then read in depth any articles, editorials, or features that seem particularly important or interesting.

When reading news stories and editorials, make sure to distinguish between facts and opinions. When you encounter opinions in a newspaper, try to determine whether these opinions are sound. Sound opinions are ones supported by facts. For more information on distinguishing between facts and opinions, see the Language Arts Survey 5.2, "Distinguishing Fact from Opinion."

5.31 How to Evaluate a Film. A great film gives us insight into the lives of others and so expands our understanding and our sympathies. Some films, however, are created solely for the purpose of making money through exploitation of sensational elements or gimmicks. Decide in advance which films you would like to see. Don't settle for just any movie that happens to be playing at your local theater or on television. Listen, watch, and read what the critics have to say. Take their views into consideration to help you decide which movies to see. Once you have

seen the movie, decide for yourself whether you agree or disagree with a particular critic.

Be aware of previews. These are designed by the production company's marketing department to motivate you to see their film. Previews can make a film seem more humorous, exciting, and powerful than it really is by showing only the best dialogue and action. Never see a film adaptation of a literary work as a substitute for reading the work itself.

5.32 How to Evaluate Radio and Television. Plan your television and radio time. Rather than accepting whatever program happens to be on, look at broadcast listings and choose programs that are of interest to you. Question what you see and hear. What criticisms do you have about a program's quality, message, originality, depth, and reliability? Remember that advertisers pay for most broadcast programs. They also control the content of the programs they sponsor and pay for your attention because they want to sell you something. Listen to and watch advertisements and programs critically. Read the Language Arts Survey 5.2, "Distinguishing Fact from Opinion," for tips on evaluating information critically.

5.33 How to Evaluate Advertisements. Advertising messages in the media are everywhere. To sharpen your skills in evaluating them, see the Language Arts Survey 5.2, "Distinguishing Fact from Opinion," and 5.3, "Avoiding False Arguments and Propaganda."

5.34 How to Evaluate Internet Sites. Most published print materials have been checked carefully before publication. But anyone can publish something on the Internet—without having to verify facts or guarantee quality. When you use the Internet for research, be careful to evaluate your sources. Consider the resource's domain name. Documents that end with ".edu" and ".gov" are generally reliable, since they come from educational and governmental organizations. Commercial sites end in ".com." They can be reliable, too, but watch for biases that favor the company's product. Sites ending in ".org" or ".net" can be trusted if they are from a reliable organization, but watch for special interest group sites that slant or "spin" information to their advantage. Evaluate the content. Examine the content for accuracy. Look for links, source information, and date of publication. Consider the author's reliability and look for a way to contact him or her. Ask yourself whether the information is biased or unbiased.

5.35 Documenting Sources

As you use your research in your writing, you must document your sources of information. Remember to:

- Credit the sources of all ideas and facts that you use.
- Credit original ideas or facts that are expressed in text, tables, charts, and other graphic information.
- Credit all artistic property, including works of literature, song lyrics, and ideas.

5.36 KEEPING A RESEARCH JOURNAL. A research journal can help you track your research. A research journal is a notebook, electronic file, or other means to track the information you find as you conduct research.

5.37 USING YOUR RESEARCH JOURNAL FOR DOCUMENTATION. As you conduct your research, use your research journal to take notes on the sources you find and your evaluation of them.

5.38 INFORMAL AND FORMAL NOTE-TAKING. Informal Note-Taking. Take informal notes when you want information for your own use only and when you will not need to quote or document your sources. You would take informal notes when preparing materials to use in studying, for instance. Informal note-taking is much like outlining (see 2.29, "Outlining: Rough Outlines"). Use important ideas as headings, and write relevant details below.

Formal Note-Taking. Take formal notes when you may need to quote or document your sources. When you are keeping formal notes for a project—for example, for a debate or a research paper—you should use 4" x 6" index cards.

Preparing Note Cards
- Identify the source at the top right corner of the card. (Use the source numbers from your bibliography cards.)
- Identify the subject or topic of the note on the top line of the card.
- Use a separate card for each fact or quotation.
- Write the pertinent source page number or numbers after the note.

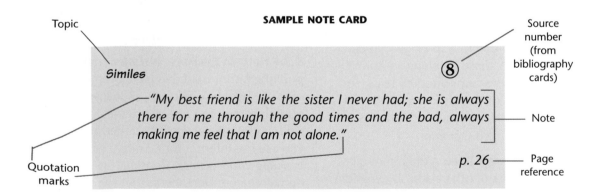

SAMPLE NOTE CARD

Topic

Similes ⑧ Source number (from bibliography cards)

"My best friend is like the sister I never had; she is always there for me through the good times and the bad, always making me feel that I am not alone." — Note

Quotation marks

p. 26 — Page reference

5.39 MAKING BIBLIOGRAPHIES AND BIBLIOGRAPHY CARDS. If you are writing a research paper, your teacher will ask you to include a bibliography to tell where you got your information. A **bibliography** is a list of sources that you used for your writing. A **source** is a book, a magazine, a film, or any other written or audio-visual material that you use to get information. As you work on your paper, you should be writing down on note cards the information for each source that you use. For each source that you use, you should prepare an index card with complete bibliographic information. Include all of the information shown on the sample bibiography card.

Forms for Bibliography Entries

- **A book**
  Douglass, Frederick. *Escape from Slavery: The Boyhood of Frederick Douglass in His Own Words*. New York: Alfred A. Knopf, 1994.

- **A magazine article**
  Reston, James, Jr. "Orion: Where Stars Are Born." *National Geographic*. December 1995: 90–101.

- **An encyclopedia entry**
  "Lewis and Clark Expedition." *Encyclopedia Americana*. Jackson, Donald. 1995 ed.

- **An interview**
  Campbell, Silas. Personal interview. 6 February 1997.

- **An Internet page**
  Heasley, Michael. Producer. "At the Tomb of Tutankhamen." 1998. <http://www.nationalgeographic.com/egypt>.

SAMPLE BIBLIOGRAPHY CARD

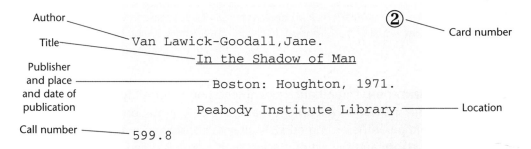

5.40 Documenting and Mapping Internet Research. Your research journal is an excellent tool for tracking how you find information, especially for documenting and mapping Internet research. As you browse and search on the Internet, it can be easy to jump from one site to the next and to lose track of how you got from place to place. Here is one way to map your path.

- Write a brief statement of the topic of your research.
- Write key words or phrases that will help you search for this information.
- Note the search engines that you will use.
- As you conduct a search, note how many "hits" or Internet sites the search engine has accessed. Determine whether you need to narrow or expand your search. Write down new key words accordingly, and the results of each new search.
- When you find promising sites, write them down.
- Access each promising site. Evaluate its information using the guidelines in 5.34, "How to Understand Internet Sites."
- Once you find information to include in your work, document it carefully. For more information on how to document Internet sites, see the Language Arts Survey 5.39, "Making Bibliographies and Bibliography Cards."

5.41 Avoiding Plagiarism. Plagiarism is taking someone else's words or thoughts and pretending that they are your own. Plagiarism is a very serious problem and has been the downfall of many students and even famous people. Whenever you

use someone else's writing to help you with a paper or a speech, you must be careful either to put the ideas in your own words or to use quotation marks. In either case, you must give credit to the person whose ideas you are using.

Giving such credit to others is called documenting your sources.

5.42 PARAPHRASING, SUMMARIZING, AND QUOTING. As you do research, you notes will include paraphrases, and summaries, and quotations.

TYPE OF NOTE	WHEN TO USE	WHAT TO WATCH FOR
Quotation	When the exact wording of a primary source is important to your topic When you are providing a definition	Copy spelling, capitalization, punctuation, and numbers exactly as in the source. Place quotation marks around all direct quotations.
Paraphrase	When the wording of a secondary source is particularly memorable or insightful Most of the time	Record, when appropriate, explanatory background information about the speaker or the context of a quotation. Focus on your main purpose, and note only points related to your topic. Place quotation marks around any quoted words or phrases.
Summary	When the point you are making does not require the detail of a paraphrase	Reread the source after writing your summary to be sure that you have not altered the meaning.

5.43 PARENTHETICAL DOCUMENTATION. Parenthetical documentation is currently the most widely used form of documentation. To use this method to document the source of a quotation or an idea, place a brief note identifying the source in parentheses immediately after the borrowed material. This type of note is called a **parenthetical citation**, and the act of placing such a note is called **citing a source**.

The first part of a parenthetical citation refers the reader to a source in your bibliography. The second part of the citation refers the reader to a specific page or place within the source. If the source is clearly identified in the text, omit it from the citation and give only the page number.

SAMPLE PARENTHETICAL CITATIONS

- **For works listed by author or editor, use the author's or editor's last name.**

  Sample bibliographic entry

  Galt, Margot Fortunato. *Up to the Plate: The All-American Girls Professional Baseball League*. Minneapolis: Lerner, 1995.

  Sample citation

  "Still very much a pitcher's league in 1945, the All American Girls pushed back the base paths from 60 to 68 feet and the mound-to-home plate distance from 40 to 42 feet" (Galt 37).

- **For works listed by title, use the title (abbreviate if necessary).**

  Sample bibliographic entry

  ```
  "Baseball." Encyclopedia Britannica. 2000 ed.
  ```

  Sample citation

  ```
  "The AAGBL was an American sports organization that, between 1943 and
  its dissolution in 1954, grew from a stopgap wartime entertainment to a
  professional showcase for women baseball players" ("Baseball" 854).
  ```

- **When the author's name is used in the text, cite only the page number.**

  ```
  Galt says that the teams were organized so that no one team had more
  talent than any other (15).
  ```

5.44 FOOTNOTES AND ENDNOTES. The method of documentation described in Section 5.43 is the most common of many accepted systems. Footnoting and endnoting are two other methods.

Instead of putting citations in parentheses within the text, you can place them at the bottom or foot of the page. These are **footnotes**. In this system, a number or symbol is placed in the text where the parenthetical citation would otherwise be, and a matching number or symbol at the bottom of the page identifies the citation. *Literature and the Language Arts* uses numbered footnotes in the literature selections to define obscure words and to provide background information.

Many books use endnotes instead of footnotes. **Endnotes** are like footnotes in that a number or symbol is placed within the text, but the matching citations are compiled at the end of the book, chapter, or article rather than at the foot of the page.

Footnote and endnote entries begin with the author's (or editor's) name in its usual order (first, then last) and include publication information and a page reference.

SAMPLE FOOTNOTE OR ENDNOTE CITATIONS

A BOOK WITH ONE AUTHOR	[1]Wilson Rawls, *Where the Red Fern Grows* (New York: Delacorte Press, 1996) 105–106.
A BOOK WITH AN EDITOR AND NO SINGLE AUTHOR	[2]Liz Rosenberg, ed., *The Invisible Ladder: An Anthology of Contemporary American Poems for Young Readers* (New York: Henry Holt and Co., 1996) 85–87.
A MAGAZINE ARTICLE	[3]Marissa Nuñez, "Climbing the Golden Arches," *Cicada,* February 1999: 124.

5.45 Preparing for Tests

Tests are a common part of school life. These guidelines will help you to prepare for and take a test.

PREPARING FOR A TEST

- Know exactly what you will be tested on. If you have questions, ask your teacher.
- Make a study plan to allow yourself time to go over the material. Avoid last-minute cramming.
- Review the subject matter. Use your notes, your SQ3R strategy, and any study questions given by your teacher.
- Make lists of important names, dates, definitions, or events. Ask a friend or family member to quiz you on them.
- Try to predict questions that may be on the test. Make sure you can answer them.
- Get plenty of sleep the night before the test and eat a nutritious breakfast on the morning of the test.

TAKING A TEST

- Survey the test to see how long it is and what types of questions are included.
- Read all directions and questions carefully. Make sure that you know exactly what to do.
- Plan your time. Answer easy questions first. Allow extra time for complicated questions. If a question seems too difficult, skip it and go back to it later. Work quickly, but do not rush.
- Save time for review. Once you have finished, look back over the test. Double-check your answers, but do not change answers too often. Your first ideas are often the correct ones.

5.46 Taking Objective Tests

Objective tests require simple right-or-wrong answers. This chart describes the kinds of questions you may see on objective tests.

QUESTIONS FOUND ON OBJECTIVE TESTS	
Description	**Guidelines**
True/False. You are given a statement and asked to tell whether the statement is true or false.	• If any part of a statement is false, then the statement is false. • Words like *all, always, never,* and *everyone* often appear in false statements. • Words like *some, usually, often,* and *most* often appear in true statements.
Matching. You are asked to match items in one column with items in another column.	• Check the directions. See if each item is used only once. Also check to see if some are not used at all. • Read all items before starting. • Match those you know first. • Cross out items as you match them.
Multiple Choice. You are asked to choose the best answer from a group of answers given.	• Read *all* choices first. • Rule out incorrect answers. • Choose the answer that is most complete or accurate. • Pay particular attention to choices such as *none of the above* or *all of the above.*
Short Answer. You are asked to answer the question with a word, a phrase, or a sentence.	• Read the directions to find out if you are required to answer in complete sentences. • Use correct spelling, grammar, punctuation, and capitalization. • If you cannot think of the answer, move on. Something in another question might remind you of the answer.

5.47 Strategies for Taking Standardized Tests

Standardized tests are given to many students. You may already have taken a standardized test, such as the Iowa Test of Basic Skills, and you will take more during your school career. Learning how to take standardized tests well can help you to achieve your academic and career goals. When selecting an answer on a standardized test, remember these points.

- If you do not know the answer, try to rule out some choices and then guess from those remaining.
- If a question seems too difficult, skip it and go back to it later. Be aware, however, that most tests allow you to go back to questions only within a section.
- Always follow the instructions of the test monitor.

5.48 ANALOGY QUESTIONS. Analogy questions ask you to find the relationship between a pair of words and then to recognize a similar relationship between another pair of words. In an analogy question, the symbols : and :: mean "is to" and "as," respectively. The example below would be "Mare is to horse as . . ." when read aloud. To answer an analogy question, think of a sentence that relates the two words. For example, you might say "A *mare* is a female *horse*." Then look for another pair of words that would make sense in that sentence: "A *doe* is a female *deer*."

EXAMPLE ANALOGY QUESTIONS
MARE : HORSE ::
(A) lamb : sheep
(B) man : woman
(C) boy : girl
(D) bee : wasp
(E) doe : deer

The answer is E.

5.49 SYNONYM AND ANTONYM QUESTIONS. A synonym or antonym question gives you a word and asks you to select the word that has the same meaning (synonym) or the opposite meaning (antonym). You must select the best answer, even if none is exactly correct. Try all the choices to see which one works best. Always know whether you are looking for a synonym or an antonym, because you will usually find both among the answers.

5.50 SENTENCE COMPLETION QUESTIONS. Sentence-completion questions present you with a sentence that has two words missing. You must select the pair of words that best completes the sentence.

5.51 READING COMPREHENSION QUESTIONS. Reading comprehension questions give you a short piece of writing and then ask you several questions about it. The questions may ask you to figure out something based on information in the passage.

STEPS IN ANSWERING READING COMPREHENSION QUESTIONS

- Read all the questions quickly.
- Read the passage with the questions in mind.
- Reread the first question carefully.
- Scan the passage, looking for key words related to the question. When you find a key word, slow down and read carefully.
- Answer the first question.
- Repeat this process to answer the rest of the questions.

5.52 Taking Essay Tests

An **essay** is a short piece of writing that expresses the writer's thoughts about a particular subject. To answer an essay question, follow these guidelines.

- Analyze each question. First, read the *entire* question carefully. Look for key words in the question that tell you what is expected. Underline these words or write them on your own note paper. Then make sure to answer *all* parts of the question.

- Organize your answer. Allow time for planning, writing, and reviewing. Before you begin writing, create a rough outline of the main points you will make. Include main points and key details. Later, if you find yourself running out of time, try at least to state your remaining main points and to add a conclusion.

- Write a clear introduction. This will help to keep you on track as you write each paragraph. Your introduction should state the thesis, or main idea, of your essay and should briefly answer the question. In the rest of the essay, you can provide evidence to support your answer.

- Reviewing your answer. Before you turn in your completed essay, take time to proofread.

APPLIED ENGLISH Resource

THE IMPORTANCE OF APPLIED ENGLISH

Applied English is English in the world of work. When you apply English skills to real-world situations, you are using your reading, writing, speaking, and listening abilities for practical reasons.

6.1 Filling Out Forms

Entering a new school, going to a new doctor, registering computer software, applying for a job—these are but a few of the thousands of activities that involve filling out forms. The following guidelines will help you to complete a form in a way that will make a good impression.

GUIDELINES FOR COMPLETING FORMS

- Get an extra copy or make a photocopy of the form so that you can complete a practice form.

- Read through the directions and the form itself before completing it.

- Gather the information you will need to complete the form. This information may include former addresses, dates of events, or a social security number.

- Complete the form neatly. Avoid smudges or cross-outs.

- Do not leave any lines blank. Use N.A. for "not applicable" if a request for information does not apply to you. For example, if you have always lived at the same address, you would write N.A. in the blank following "Previous Addresses."

- Proofread your information for errors in punctuation, spelling, or grammar. Make sure all information is correct.

- Submit the form to the appropriate person or address. Use an envelope or folder to keep the form neat and clean.

- Keep a copy of the form for your own records.

6.2 Following Directions

Every day people face the challenge of doing something they have never done before. Despite their inexperience, people succeed because they can follow directions. At the same time, someone must be able to give them clear, precise directions. Consider these guidelines before following or giving directions.

GUIDELINES FOR FOLLOWING DIRECTIONS

- If the directions are being given in written form, read them carefully before beginning the procedure. If they are being given in spoken form, take notes as you listen. Ask for clarification if something is confusing.

- Take your time and make sure you have performed each step carefully and accurately before proceeding to the next step.

- If you get stuck following directions, either retrace your steps or reread the step you are on.

6.3 Giving Directions

GUIDELINES FOR GIVING DIRECTIONS

- Think through the directions completely, from start to finish, before you begin.

- Give each step in the correct order and include all necessary steps. Do not assume that your reader or listener already knows any part of the directions unless you are absolutely sure that this is the case.

- Do not include any unnecessary steps. Use simple, clear language.

- Use transition words such as *first, second, third, next, then,* and *finally* to connect your ideas. When possible, use a similar sentence structure for each part of the directions.

- When giving directions orally, ask the listener to repeat the directions to you when you have finished. This way you can check to make sure that your directions have been understood.

- If the directions that you are giving are complicated, put them into writing. Number each direction to help you and your reader to keep the steps separate and clear. You may also wish to include a map, diagram, or other illustration. For more information, see the Language Arts Survey 6.11, "Displaying Effective Visual Information."

6.4 Writing a Step-by-Step Procedure

A **step-by-step procedure** is a how-to or process piece that uses directions to teach someone something new. Written procedures include textual information and sometimes graphics. Spoken procedures can include textual and graphic information and other props. Examples of step-by-step procedures include an oral demonstration of how to saddle a horse, instructions on how to treat a sprained ankle, or a video showing how to do the perfect lay-up in basketball.

To write a step-by-step procedure, review the Language Arts Survey 6.3, "Giving Directions," and 6.11, "Displaying Effective Visual Information." Use these tips to give a demonstration.

GUIDELINES FOR A DEMONSTRATION

- If you are showing how to make something, create several different samples to show each step of the procedure. You might also want to have a sample showing a variation.

- Be prepared. The best way to prevent problems is to anticipate and plan for them. Rehearse an oral demonstration several times. If you are preparing the procedure in written form, go through your directions as if you knew nothing about the process. See if you can follow your own directions. Or have a friend work through the procedure and offer suggestions for improvement.

- Acknowledge mistakes. If you are showing a procedure "live" as an oral demonstration, tell your audience what has gone wrong, and why. Handle the situation in a calm, direct way.

- Know your topic well. The better you know it, the better you will be able to teach others.

6.5 Writing a Personal Letter

One of the easiest and most efficient ways of communicating and practicing your writing skills is to compose personal letters. You may want to write to a friend about your experiences on a vacation, to a relative about a school play or big sports event, or to a pen pal about simple everyday things. Letter writing allows for a lot of creativity. When you write a letter, keep in mind the following points.

GUIDELINES FOR A LETTER

- In addition to descriptions of your topic, include in your letter your reactions and emotions and beliefs about your topic.

- Use concrete, specific language to create the most meaningful and vivid descriptions.

- Consider the recipient of your letter. What background information does he or she need? What does he or she already know about your topic?

- Begin your letter with the date. Under the date, write a salutation, such as "Dear Grandma," or "Dear Julie:" and then follow with your letter. End the letter with your name.

6.6 Writing a Business Letter

A business letter is usually addressed to someone you do not know personally. Therefore, a formal tone is appropriate for such a letter.

Following appropriate form is especially important when writing business letters. If you follow the correct form and avoid errors, your letter will sound professional and make a good impression.

A business letter includes the same parts as a personal letter. In addition, an inside address appears above the salutation. The inside address includes the name and title of the person to whom you are writing and the name and address of that person's company or organization.

One common form for a business letter is the block form. In the block form, each part of the letter begins at the left margin. The parts are separated by linespaces.

Begin the salutation with the word *Dear*, followed by the courtesy or professional title used in the inside address, such as *Ms., Mr.,* or *Dr.,* and a colon. If you are not writing to a specific person, you may use a general salutation such as *Dear Sir or Madam.*

In the body of your letter, use a polite, formal tone and standard English. Make your points clearly, in as few words as possible.

End with a standard closing such as *Sincerely*, *Yours truly*, or *Respectfully yours*. Capitalize only the first word of the closing. Type your full name below the closing, leaving three or four blank lines for your signature. Sign your name below the closing in blue or black ink (never in red or green). Proofread your letter before you send it. Poor spelling, grammar, or punctuation can ruin an otherwise well written business letter.

498 Blue Key Rd.
Charleston, SC 89943

May 3, 2001

Mr. Davy Jones, Owner
Deep Sea Divers, Inc.
73 Ocean St.
Charleston, SC 89943

Dear Mr. Jones:

Please consider me for a position as a part-time clerk in your store for the coming summer. I understand that in the summer your business increases considerably and that you might have need for a conscientious, reliable, hard-working clerk. I can offer you considerable knowledge of snorkeling and diving equipment and experience working in a retail shop.

I will be available for work three days per week between June 1 and August 12. I am enclosing a resumé and references. Please contact me if you wish to set up an interview.

Sincerely,

Jorge Alvarez
Jorge Alvarez

6.7 Writing a Memo

In businesses, schools, and other organizations, employees, students, and others often communicate by means of memoranda, or memos. For example, the director of a school drama club might write a memo to the editor of the student newspaper announcing tryouts for a new play. A memo begins with a header. Often this header contains the word *memorandum* (the singular form of *memoranda*) and the following words and abbreviations: TO, FR (meaning from), DT (meaning date), RE (meaning regarding), and C (meaning copy).

MEMORANDUM

TO: Lisa Lowry
FR: Jack Hart   C: Ms. Wise
RE: Tryouts for the spring production of *Oklahoma!*
DT: February 12, 2001

Please include the following announcement in the upcoming issue of the *Wheaton Crier:* Tryouts for the Wheaton Drama Club's spring production of *Oklahoma!* will be held on Friday, February 26, at 6:00 P.M. in the Wheaton Middle School Auditorium. . . .

Thank you.

6.8 Writing a Proposal

A **proposal** outlines a project that a person wants to complete. You would write a proposal if you wanted funding for an art project that would benefit your community, if your friends wanted to help organize a summer program for teens your age, or if your student council wanted to hold a clothing drive for disaster relief. A good proposal presents a summary of an idea, the reasons why the idea is important, and an outline of how the project would be carried out. A proposal is both informative and persuasive.

GUIDELINES FOR A PROPOSAL

- Use standard, formal English. Keep the tone positive, courteous, and respectful. State your purpose and rationale briefly and clearly.

- Give your audience all necessary information. A proposal with specific details makes it clear what you want approved, and why your audience—often a committee or someone in authority—should approve it.

- Format your proposal with headings, lists, and schedules to make your proposed project easy to understand and approve.

6.9 Delivering a Press Release

A **press release** is an informative piece intended for publication in local news media. A press release is usually written to promote an upcoming event or to inform the community of a recent event.

GUIDELINES FOR A PRESS RELEASE

- Use the 5 *Ws* and an *H*—*who, what, where, why, when,* and *how*—questioning strategy to convey the important information at the beginning of the piece. (For help, see the Language Arts Survey 2.14.)

- Keep it brief. Local media are more likely to publish or broadcast your piece if it is short and to the point.

- Include contact information: your name, phone number, and times you can be reached, either for the media representative or, if applicable, for the reading public.

- Type your press release using conventional manuscript form. At the top of the press release, type the date.

- Check a previous newspaper for deadline information or call the newspaper office to make sure you get your material there on time. Address the press release to the editor.

6.10 Writing a Public Service Announcement

A **public service announcement**, or PSA, is a brief, informative article intended to be helpful to the community. PSAs are written by nonprofit organizations and concerned citizens for print in local newspapers, for broadcast by television and radio stations, and available on the Internet.

EXAMPLES

an article by the American Cancer Society outlining early warning signs of cancer

an announcement promoting Safety Week

an informative piece telling coastal residents what to do during a hurricane

To write a public service announcement, follow the same guidelines you would for a press release.

6.11 Displaying Effective Visual Information

People frequently learn things best and remember more when information is presented visually. Whenever possible, use charts, tables, pictures, slides, photographs, models, and art to express key points. Depending on their use, visuals can detract from a presentation or enhance it.

GUIDELINES FOR DISPLAYING VISUALS

- Keep visual information simple. Do not clutter your visual display with too many small images or too much textual or graphic information.

- Design your visual display in a way that the viewer's eye will naturally follow. Include a title or caption, labels for different parts, and simple, main points when needed.

- Make the visual visible. Type or graphics that are too small can make the best visual presentation useless. If the display is for a speech or exhibit, stand back and see if you can see it from the back of the room or wherever your audience members will be.

- Use bullets or numbering to organize your text.

- Use color carefully. Color can add visual interest, but it can also be distracting.

- Document all sources of graphic information. The ideas in visual information are someone's intellectual property, just like the ideas in text material. Make sure you give proper credit for all work not your own.

6.12 Working on a Team

Working on a team, or doing collaborative learning, is an essential Applied English skill that depends on a strong ability to communicate. Refer to the Speaking and Listening Resource for more information.

Handbook of Literary Terms

ABSTRACT. An **abstract** word, like *hope* or *pride*, names something that cannot be directly seen, touched, tasted, heard, or smelled. See *concrete*.

ACRONYM. An **acronym** is a word made from the first letters of a group of words. The word *laser* is an acronym. Many organizations, such as SADD, have names that are acronyms.

laser = **L**ight **A**mplication **S**timulated by **E**mission **R**adiation

SADD = **S**tudents **A**gainst **D**runk **D**riving

ACT. An **act** is a major part of a play. Long plays are often divided into several acts. Sometimes acts are divided into scenes. See *scene*.

ACTOR. An **actor** is someone who plays a character. Actors perform in theater, television, and films. They also do readings and story-telling. Today, the word *actor* is used to speak about both male and female performers.

AIM. A writer's **aim** is his or her purpose, or goal. People may write with the following aims:

- to *inform* (expository/informative writing);
- to *tell a story*, either true or invented, about an event or sequence of events (narrative writing);
- to *reflect* (personal/expressive writing);
- to *share a perspective* by using an artistic medium, such as fiction or poetry, to enter-tain, enrich, or enlighten (imaginative writing);
- to *persuade* readers or listeners to respond in some way, such as to agree with a position, change a view on an issue, reach an agree-ment, or perform an action (persuasive/argu-mentative writing).

Here are examples of writing that reflect these five aims:

expository/informative
    news article, research report
narrative
    biography, family history
personal/expressive
    diary entry, personal letter

imaginative
    poem, short story
persuasive/argumentative
    editorial, petition

ALLITERATION. **Alliteration** is the repetition of consonant sounds at the beginnings of syllables, as in <u>b</u>ats in the <u>b</u>elfry or <u>d</u>ead as a <u>d</u>oornail. "Cynthia in the Snow" by Gwendolyn Brooks (Unit 9) contains examples of alliteration.

ALLUSION. An **allusion** is a reference in literature to something famous. The thing referred to may be a person, an object, an event, a work of art, a liter-ary work, or anything else that is well known.

ANALOGY. An **analogy** is a comparison of things that are alike in some ways but different in others.

ANALYSIS. **Analysis** is the act of dividing a subject into parts and then thinking about how the parts are related. For example, an analysis of a short story might consider these parts: the plot, the setting, the characters, and the theme, or main idea.

ANECDOTE. An **anecdote** is a usually short narra-tive of an interesting, amusing, or biographical incident. Although anecdotes are often the basis for short stories, an anecdote differs from a short story in that it lacks a complicated plot and relates a single episode. The selection from *To Be or Not to Bop* by Dizzy Gillespie (Unit 5) contains various anecdotes about Gillespie.

ANTAGONIST. In a story, a character who struggles with the main character is called an **antagonist**. In "Priscilla and the Wimps" by Richard Peck (Unit 2), Mighty Monk is the antagonist.

APPOSITION. An **apposition** is a renaming of something in different words. The following sentence includes an apposition:

Cleveland Amory, the author of *Ranch of Dreams*, was an animal lover.

ARTICLE. An **article** is a brief nonfiction work on a specific topic. Encyclopedia entries, newspaper reports, and nonfiction magazine pieces are examples of articles.

ASSONANCE. **Assonance** is the repetition of vowel sounds in stressed syllables that end in different consonant sounds.

ATMOSPHERE. See *mood*.

AUTOBIOGRAPHY. An **autobiography** is the story of a person's life, written by that person.

BACKGROUND INFORMATION. **Background information** is information provided in a literary work, often at the beginning, to explain the situation to the reader. A writer may include background information to explain the central conflict, the relationships between the characters, the setting, or any other part of his or her work.

BALLAD. A **ballad** is a simple poem that tells a story. Most ballads have four-line stanzas that have the rhyme scheme *abcb*. Sometimes the last line of a stanza is repeated. "Scarborough Fair" in Unit 5 is an English folk ballad.

BIBLIOGRAPHY. A **bibliography** is a list of books, magazines, or other sources of information. A writer may include a bibliography at the end of his or her work to show where he or she got the information that appears in the work. A complete bibliography entry for a book gives its author, its title, its place of publication, its publisher, and its date of publication.

BIOGRAPHY. A **biography** is the story of a person's life, told by another person. "Satchel Paige" by Bill Littlefield (Unit 11) is a biography.

BLEND. A **blend** is a new word created by joining together two old ones, as in *smog*, from the words *smoke* and *fog;* or *pixel*, which is a dot on a computer screen, from the words *picture* and *element*.

CAPTIONS. **Captions** explain in writing a visual item such as a photo or drawing.

CENTRAL CONFLICT. A **central conflict** is the main problem or struggle in the plot of a poem, story, or play. In "Ta-Na-E-Ka" by Mary Whitebird (Unit 1), the central conflict revolves around the traditional rite of passage of the Kaw Indians. See *conflict* and *plot*.

CHARACTER. A **character** is a person or animal who takes part in the action of a literary work. The main character is called the *protagonist*. A character who struggles against the main character is called an *antagonist*. Characters can also be classified as *major characters* or *minor charac-* *ters*. Major characters are ones who play important roles in a work. Minor characters are ones who play less important roles. A *one-dimensional character, flat character,* or *caricature* is one who exhibits a single quality, or character trait. A *three-dimensional, full,* or *rounded character* is one who seems to have all the complexities of an actual human being.

CHARACTERIZATION. **Characterization** is the act of creating or describing a character. Writers create characters using three major techniques: by showing what characters say, do, or think; by showing what other characters say or think about them; and by describing what physical features, dress, and personality the characters display. See *character*.

CHRONOLOGICAL ORDER. Events arranged in order of the time when they happened are said to be in **chronological order**. This method of organization is used in most stories, whether they are fiction or nonfiction. Chronological order is also used in informative nonfiction writing that describes processes and cause-and-effect relationships.

CLICHÉ. (klē shā') A **cliché** is an overused expression such as *happy as a lark* or *time is money*. Most clichés begin as vivid, colorful expressions but become uninteresting because of overuse.

CLIMAX. The **climax** is the point of highest interest and suspense in a literary work. The climax sometimes signals the turning point of the action in a story or play. See *plot*.

COHERENCE. **Coherence** is the logical arrangement of ideas in speech or writing. Writers achieve coherence by presenting their ideas in a logical order and by using transitions to show how their ideas are connected to one another. See *transition*.

COINED WORDS. **Coined words** are ones that are intentionally created, often from already existing words or word parts. Examples of recently coined words include *modem* (from modulator + demodulator), *sitcom* (situation + comedy), and *videophone*.

CONCRETE. A **concrete** word, like *cloud* or *airplane*, names something that can be directly seen, tasted, touched, heard, or smelled. Concrete language is particularly effective when it is as specific and detailed as possible. See *abstract*.

CONCRETE POEM. A **concrete poem**, or **shape poem**, is one with a shape that suggests its subject.

CONFLICT. A **conflict** is a struggle between two people or things in a literary work. A *plot* is formed around conflict. A conflict can be internal or external. A struggle that takes place between a character and some outside force such as another character, society, or nature is called an *external conflict*. A struggle that takes place within a character is called an *internal conflict*. See *central conflict* and *plot*.

CONNOTATION. A **connotation** is an emotional association attached to a word or statement. For example, the word *unique* has positive emotional associations, while the word *strange* has negative ones, even though the two words denote, or refer to, something highly unusual. See *denotation*.

CRISIS. The **crisis**, or **turning point**, is the point in a plot when something happens to determine the future course of events and the eventual fate of the main character. See *plot*.

CRITICISM. **Criticism** is the act of explaining or judging a literary work.

DENOTATION. A **denotation** is the basic meaning, or dictionary definition, of a word. See *connotation*.

DESCRIPTION. **Description** is a type of writing that portrays a character, object, or scene. Descriptions make use of *sensory details*—words and phrases that describe how things look, sound, smell, taste, or feel. Effective descriptions contain precise—or concrete—nouns, verbs, adverbs, and adjectives. Descriptions often use imagery and figurative language. In "The Woman and the Wolf" by Farley Mowat (Unit 8), the author uses vivid descriptions to portray the arctic setting of the story.

DIALECT. A **dialect** is a version of a language spoken by people of a particular place, time, or group. Writers often use dialect to give their works a realistic flavor. Dialect is shown in *In the Fog* by Milton Geiger (Unit 10).

DIALOGUE. **Dialogue** is conversation involving two or more people or characters. Plays are made up of dialogue and stage directions. Fictional works are made up of dialogue, narration, and description. In a play, dialogue appears after the names of characters. In fiction, dialogue is enclosed in quotation marks (" ") and is often accompanied by tag lines, words and phrases such as *he said* or *she replied* that tell who is speaking.

DIARY. A **diary** is a day-to-day record of a person's life, thoughts, or feelings.

DRAMA. A **drama**, or **play**, is a story told through characters played by actors. The script of a drama typically consists of characters' names, dialogue spoken by the characters, and stage directions. Drama is meant to be read or performed before an audience. When a person reads a drama, he or she should imagine what it would be like to see and hear the action. The spectacle of a drama includes everything that the audience sees and hears, such as lighting, costumes, makeup, props, set pieces, music, sound effects, and the movements and expressions of actors. Drama also differs from other types of literature in being a collaborative effort involving the author as well as a director, actors, and others involved in the production. *A Woman Called Truth* by Sandy Asher (Unit 2) and *The Ugly Duckling* (Unit 10) are plays. *In the Fog* by Milton Geiger (Unit 10) is a screenplay—a drama written for television.

EDITORIAL. An **editorial** is a short piece of persuasive writing that appears in a newspaper, magazine, or similar work.

ESSAY. An **essay** is a short nonfiction work that expresses a writer's thoughts about a single subject. A good essay develops a single idea, or *thesis*, and is organized into an introduction, a body, and a conclusion. A *personal essay* is a short nonfiction work on a single topic related to the life of the writer. A personal essay is written from the author's point of view using the pronouns *I* and *me*. A *narrative essay* tells a true story to make some point. An *informative* essay is written to communicate facts. A *persuasive essay* is written to advance an opinion. "Pompeii" by Robert Silverberg (Unit 3) is an informative essay.

EXPOSITION. The **exposition** is the part of a plot that introduces the setting and the major characters.

EXPRESSIVE WRITING. See *aim*.

EXTERNAL CONFLICT. An **external conflict** is a struggle that takes place between a character and something outside that character. In "Rikki-tikki-tavi" by Rudyard Kipling (Unit 4), the external conflict pits Rikki-tikki-tavi against a pair of snakes. See *conflict* and *internal conflict*.

FABLE. A **fable** is a brief story that frequently includes animal characters and a moral.

FAIRY TALE. A **fairy tale** is a type of European folk tale containing supernatural events and often imaginary creatures such as elves, giants, and fairies. "Cinderella" and "The Little Mermaid" are famous examples.

FANTASY. A **fantasy** is a very unrealistic or imaginative story. Fantasy is often contrasted with *science fiction*, in which the unreal elements are given a scientific or pseudoscientific basis. See *science fiction*.

FICTION. **Fiction** is prose writing about imagined events or characters. The primary forms of fiction are the short story, the novella, and the novel.

FIGURE OF SPEECH. A **figure of speech** is writing or speech meant to be understood imaginatively instead of literally. Many writers, especially poets, use figures of speech to help readers to see things in new ways. Figures of speech, also called figurative language, includes such literary techniques as *apostrophe*, *hyperbole*, *irony*, *metaphor*, *oxymoron*, *paradox*, *personification*, and *simile*.

FIRST-PERSON POINT OF VIEW. In a story told from the **first-person point of view**, the narrator takes a part in the action and refers to himself or herself using words such as *I* and *we*. See *point of view*. "The Goodness of Matt Kaizer" by Avi (Unit 1) is written in the first-person point of view.

FLASHBACK. A **flashback** is a part of a story, poem, or play that presents events that happened at an earlier time. Writers use flashbacks for many purposes. One common technique is to begin a work with a final event and then to tell the rest of the story as a flashback that explains how that event came about. Another common technique is to begin a story in the middle of the action and then to use a flashback to fill in the events that occurred before the opening of the story. "The Tunnel" by Sara Ellis (Unit 6) contains flashbacks.

FOLK SONG. A **folk song** is a traditional or composed song typically made up of *stanzas*, a refrain, and a simple melody. A form of folk lit-erature, folk songs are expressions of commonly shared ideas or feelings and may be narrative or lyric in style. Traditional folk songs are anonymous songs that have been passed down orally. Examples include the ballad "Bonny Barbara Allan," the children's song "Row, Row, Row Your Boat," the railroad song "Casey Jones," and the cowboy song "The Streets of Laredo." Contemporary composers of songs in the folk tradition include Bob Dylan, Joan Baez, Pete Seeger, and Joni Mitchell. See *ballad*.

FOLK TALE. A **folk tale** is a story passed by word of mouth from generation to generation. Famous collections of folk tales include the fairy tales collected by the Brothers Grimm and Zora Neale Hurston's collection of African-American folk tales in *Mules and Men*. "The Magic Mortar" by Yoshiko Uchida (Unit 7) is a folk tale. See *oral tradition*.

FORESHADOWING. **Foreshadowing** is the act of hinting at events that will happen later in a poem, story, or play.

FREE VERSE. **Free verse** is poetry that does not use regular rhyme, rhythm, or division into stanzas. "One Time" by William Stafford (Unit 9) is an example of free verse.

GENRE. A **genre** is a type of literary work. The main types are *drama*, *fiction*, *poetry*, and *nonfiction*. Some terms used to name literary genres in more specific ways include *autobiography*, *biography*, *drama*, *essay*, *novel*, *poetry*, *short story*, and *tragedy*. Literary works are sometimes classified into genres based on subject matter. Such a classification might describe *fantasy*, *mystery*, *adventure*, *romance*, *western*, and *science fiction* as different genres of fiction.

HAIKU. (hī' kü') A **haiku** is a traditional Japanese three-line poem. It has five syllables in the first line, seven in the second, and five in the third. A traditional haiku presents an *image* in order to arouse in the reader a specific emotional state.

HISTORICAL FICTION. **Historical fiction** tells a story that is partly based on actual historical events and is partially made up. Writers of historical fiction use specific details to make the past come alive in the reader's imagination.

HYPERBOLE. (hī pər' bə lē) A **hyperbole** is an exaggeration made for effect. "The Twelve Labors of Hercules" by Walker Brents (Unit 7) contains examples of hyperbole.

IMAGE. An **image** is language that creates a concrete representation of an object or an experience. An image is also the vivid mental picture created in the reader's mind by that language. The images in a literary work are referred to, when considered altogether, as the work's *imagery*. "Spring is like a perhaps hand" and "in Just-" by E. E. Cummings (Unit 9) contain vivid images.

IMAGERY. Taken together, the images in a poem or passage are called its **imagery**. See *image*.

IMAGINATIVE WRITING. See *aim*.

INCITING INCIDENT. The **inciting incident** is the event that introduces the central conflict, or struggle, in a poem, story, or play. The inciting incident in "The Rebellion of the Magical Rabbits" by Ariel Dorfman (Unit 6) is the wolf's demand that the monkey to take pictures. See *plot*.

INFORMATIONAL WRITING. See *aim*.

INTERNAL CONFLICT. An **internal conflict** is a struggle that takes place inside the mind of a character. See *conflict*.

IRONY. **Irony** is a difference between appearance and reality. In "All Summer in a Day" by Ray Bradbury (Unit 8), it is ironic that Margot, the only student who remembered the sun, did not get to see it.

IRONY OF SITUATION. See *irony*.

JOURNAL. A **journal**, like a *diary*, is a day-to-day record of a person's life, thoughts, or feelings.

LEGEND. A **legend** is a story coming down from the past, often based on important real events or characters.

LIGHT VERSE. **Light verse** is poetry meant to be humorous.

LIMERICK. A **limerick** is a five-line light verse. The first, second, and fifth lines end with one rhyme. The third and fourth lines end with another. The rhyme scheme is *aabba*.

> There was an old man who supposed
> That the street door was partially closed;
> But some very large rats
> Ate his coats and his hats,
> While that futile old gentleman dozed.
>
> —Edward Lear

LIMITED POINT OF VIEW. A literary work is written from a **limited point of view** if everything is seen through the eyes of a single character. The short story "Eleven" by Sandra Cisneros (Unit 1) is written from a limited point of view.

LYRIC POEM. A **lyric poem** is highly musical verse that expresses the emotions of a speaker and does not tell a story. Lyric poems are often contrasted with *narrative poems*, which have telling a story as their main purpose. The poems by Edna St. Vincent Millay (Unit 9) are examples of lyric poems.

MAIN CHARACTER. A **main character** is the most important figure in a literary work. See *character*.

MAJOR CHARACTER. A **major character** is one who plays an important role in a literary work. See *character*.

MEMOIR. A **memoir** is a nonfiction narration that tells a story. A memoir can be *autobiographical* (about one's own life) or *biographical* (about someone else's life). Memoirs are based on a person's experiences and reactions to historical events.

METAPHOR. A **metaphor** is a figure of speech in which one thing is spoken or written about as if it were another. This figure of speech invites the reader to make a comparison between the two things. A metaphor works because the things to be compared have one or more qualities in common. A simile also compares one thing to another, but while using the word *like* or *as*. *My skateboard is a rocket* is a metaphor, while *My skateboard is _like_ a rocket* is a simile.

METER. The **meter** of a poem is its overall rhythm, or pattern of beats. To chart, or scan, the meter of a poem, mark each stressed syllable with a (/) and each unstressed one with a (‿). See *stress*.

MOOD. **Mood,** or **atmosphere**, is the feeling or emotion the writer creates in a literary work. By working carefully with descriptive language, the writer can evoke in the reader an emotional response such as fear, discomfort, longing, or anticipation.

MORAL. A **moral** is a practical or moral lesson, usually relating to the principles of right and wrong, to be drawn from a story or other work of literature.

MOTIVATION. A **motivation** is a force that moves a character to think, feel, or behave in a certain way.

MOTIVE. A **motive** is a reason for acting in a certain way.

MYTH. A **myth** is a story that explains objects or events in the natural world. These objects or events are explained as being caused by some supernatural force or being, often a god.

NARRATIVE POEM. A **narrative poem** is a verse that tells a story. See *ballad*.

NARRATIVE WRITING. See *aim*.

NARRATOR. A **narrator** is a person or character who tells a story. Works of fiction almost always have a narrator. The narrator in a work of fiction may be a major or minor character or simply someone who witnessed or heard about the events being related. In "The Tunnel" by Sara Ellis (Unit 6), the narrator is the main character. See *point of view*.

NONFICTION. **Nonfiction** is writing about real people, places, things, and events. Essays, autobiographies, biographies, and news stories are all types of nonfiction. See *prose*.

NOVEL. A **novel** is a long work of prose fiction. Often novels have involved plots; many characters, both major and minor; and numerous settings.

NOVELLA. A **novella** is a work of fiction shorter than a novel but longer than a short story.

OMNISCIENT POINT OF VIEW. A story is written from an **omniscient point of view** if the narrator, or storyteller, knows everything and can see into the minds of all the characters. In "The Woman and the Wolf" by Farley Mowat (Unit 8), the narrator stands outside the action and is omniscient, or all-knowing. See *point of view* and *narrator*.

ONOMATOPOEIA. **Onomatopoeia** is the use of words or phrases like *meow* or *beep* that sound like what they name. Gwendolyn Brooks uses onomatopoeia in "Cynthia in the Snow" (Unit 9).

ORAL TRADITION. An **oral tradition** is works, ideas, or customs of a culture, passed by word of mouth from generation to generation. Works found in the oral traditions of peoples around the world include *folk tales, fables, fairy tales, tall tales, nursery rhymes, proverbs, legends, myths, parables, riddles, charms, spells,* and *ballads.* The selections in Unit 7 are from the oral tradition.

OXYMORON. An **oxymoron** is a word or a phrase that contradicts itself, such as *bittersweet, pretty ugly,* or *act natural.*

PARABLE. A **parable** is a story told to communicate a moral.

PARALLELISM. **Parallelism** is the expression of similar ideas in a similar way.

PARAPHRASE. A **paraphrase** is a rewriting of a passage in different words. See *summary*.

PERIODICAL. A **periodical** is a newspaper, magazine, or newsletter that is published regularly (once a month, for example).

PERSONAL ESSAY. A **personal essay** is a short non-fiction work on a single topic related to the life of the writer. A personal essay is written from the author's point of view, using the pronouns *I* and *me*. See *essay*.

PERSONAL WRITING. See *aim*.

PERSONIFICATION. **Personification** is a figure of speech in which something not human is described as if it were human. Jacob and Wilhelm Grimm use personification in "The Singing, Springing Lark" (Unit 7).

PERSUASIVE WRITING. See *aim*.

PLAGIARISM. **Plagiarism** is the act of presenting someone else's work as if it were your own. To avoid plagiarism, always give credit to a source from which you have taken information. In addition, use quotation marks around material picked up word for word from a source.

PLOT. A **plot** is a series of events related to a central conflict, or struggle. A plot usually involves the introduction of a conflict, its development, and its eventual resolution. The following terms are used to describe the parts of a plot:

- The **exposition**, or **introduction**, sets the tone or mood, introduces the characters and the setting, and provides necessary background information.
- The **inciting incident** is the event that introduces the central conflict.
- The **climax** is the high point of interest or suspense in the story.
- The **crisis**, or **turning point**, often the same event as the climax, is the point in the plot where something happens to decide the future course of events and the eventual working out of the conflict.
- The **resolution** is the point at which the central conflict is ended, or resolved.

- The **dénouement** is any material that follows the resolution and that ties up loose ends.

Note that some plots do not contain all of these parts. See *conflict.*

POETRY. Poetry is language used in special ways so that its sound reflects its meaning more powerfully than in ordinary speech and writing.

POINT OF VIEW. Point of view is the vantage point from which a story is told. If a story is told from the *first-person point of view*, the narrator uses the pronouns *I* and *we* and is a part of or a witness to the action. "Raymond's Run" by Toni Cade Bambara (Unit 8) is written from the first-person point of view. When a story is told from a *third-person point of view*, the narrator is outside the action; uses words such as *he, she, it,* and *they*; and avoids the use of *I* and *we.* "The Boy Who Talked with Animals" by Roald Dahl (Unit 8) is written from the third-person point of view.

PREFACE. A preface is a statement made at the beginning of a literary work that serves as an introduction.

PROSE. Prose is the word used to describe all writing that is not drama or poetry. Prose includes fiction and nonfiction. Novels, short stories, essays, news stories, biographies, autobiographies, and letters are written in prose.

PROTAGONIST. A protagonist is the main character in a story. The protagonist faces a struggle or *conflict.* The protagonist in "Potter's Gray" by Joan Aiken (Unit 8) is Grig.

PSEUDONYM. (sü′ də nim) A **pseudonym** is a name used by a writer instead of his or her real name.

REPETITION. Repetition is more than one use of a sound, word, or group of words.

RESOLUTION. The resolution is the point in a poem, story, or play in which the *central conflict*, or struggle, ends. The resolution of "Dragon, Dragon" by John Gardner (Unit 6) occurs when the youngest brother slays the dragon.

REVIEW. A review is a piece of writing that describes and judges a work of art, a performance, or a literary work.

RHYME. Rhyme is the repetition of sounds at the ends of words. Maya Angelou makes use of rhyme in "Life Doesn't Frighten Me Now" (Unit 9).

RHYME SCHEME. A rhyme scheme is the pattern of rhyming lines used in a poem. The rhyme scheme is usually represented with letters. For example, if every other line rhymes, the rhyme scheme is *abab.*

RHYTHM. Rhythm is the pattern of beats in a line of poetry or prose. See *meter* and *stress.*

SCENE. A scene is a short section of a literary work, one that happens in a single place and time.

SCIENCE FICTION. Science fiction is imaginative literature based on scientific principles, discoveries, or laws. It is similar to fantasy in that it deals with imaginary worlds, but differs from fantasy in having a scientific basis.

SET. A set is the collection of objects on a stage that create a scene.

SETTING. The setting of a literary work is the time and place in which it happens. Writers create settings in many different ways. In drama, the setting is usually made plain by the stage set and the costumes. In fiction, setting is most often revealed by means of descriptions of landscape, scenery, buildings, furniture, clothing, the weather, and the season. It can also be revealed by how characters talk and behave.

SIMILE. A simile is a comparison using *like* or *as.*

SLANT RHYME. A slant rhyme, or **half rhyme**, is one that is almost but not completely exact, as in *step* and *stop* or *rot* and *rock.*

SPEAKER. The speaker is the voice that speaks, or narrates, a poem. The speaker and the writer of a poem are not necessarily the same person.

STAGE DIRECTIONS. Stage directions are notes included in a play to describe how something should look, sound, or be performed. Stage directions describe setting, lighting, music, sound effects, entrances and exits, properties, and the movements of characters. They are usually printed in italics and enclosed in brackets or parentheses.

STANZA. A stanza is a group of lines in a poem. Stanzas are usually separated by spaces from other groups of lines.

STEREOTYPE. A stereotype is an unexamined, false idea about a type of person or group of people.

STRESS. **Stress**, or **accent**, is the amount of emphasis given to a syllable. The pattern of stresses in a poem determines its rhythm. Some syllables are described as being strongly or weakly stressed, and accented or unaccented. When you read a line of poetry, a strongly stressed syllable receives a strong emphasis and a weakly stressed syllable receives a weak one.

SUMMARY. A **summary** is a rewriting of a passage in different and fewer words. See *paraphrase*.

SUSPENSE. **Suspense** is a feeling of anxiousness or curiosity. Writers create suspense by raising questions in the reader's mind and by using details that create strong emotions. Mary O'Hara builds suspense in "My Friend Flicka" (Unit 4) by allowing the reader to wonder what will happen to Flicka.

SYMBOL. A **symbol** is a thing that stands for or represents both itself and something else. Some traditional symbols include doves for peace; the color green for jealousy; the color purple for royalty; winter, evening, or night for old age; roses for beauty; roads or paths for the journey through life; and owls for wisdom.

TAG LINE. A **tag line** is a phrase like *she said* used in a story to tell who is speaking. See *dialogue*.

TALL TALE. A **tall tale** is a lighthearted or humorous story with many exaggerated elements. Many tall tales depict the adventures of American folk heroes of the frontier and the Wild West, and offer explanations as to how certain mountains, lakes, or other geographical features came to exist.

THEME. A **theme** is a central idea in a literary work. The theme of "The Boy Who Talked with Animals" by Roald Dahl could be that people should respect animals.

THESIS. A **thesis** is a main idea in a work of nonfiction such as an essay. The thesis of "A Breath of Fresh Air?" is that more action needs to be taken to ensure that the air we breathe is safe.

THIRD-PERSON POINT OF VIEW. In a story told from the **third-person point of view**, the narrator does not take part in the action and tells the story using words such as *he* and *she* and avoiding the use of *I* and *we*. See *point of view*.

TONE. **Tone** is a writer's or speaker's attitude toward the subject or the reader. For example, a writer might use a lighthearted tone when writing about something happy or funny, and a heavier one when writing about something sad. The tone of the selection from *How to Eat like a Child* by Delia Ephron (Unit 1) is light and humorous. The tone that Geronimo uses in *Geronimo's Story of His Life* (Unit 11) is more serious and reflective. See *voice*.

TRANSCRIPTION. **Transcription** is the act of writing down words originally on audiotape or in another format.

TRANSITION. A **transition** is a word, phrase, sentence, or paragraph used to connect ideas and to show relationships between them. Transitions to show chronological order include *at, finally, first, next*, and *then*. Transitions that show spatial order include *above, behind, next to, to the left*, and *on top of*. Transitions that show order of importance are *less important, more important*, and *most importantly*.

TRANSLATION. **Translation** is the act of changing speech or writing into another language. Many works are translated into different languages so that people around the world can read them. "Good Hot Dogs" was written by Sandra Cisneros in English. She then translated the poem into Spanish.

UNDERSTATEMENT. An **understatement** is a statement that treats something important as though it were not important. "When George returned home, he was mildly surprised to find his house had burned to the ground," is an understatement.

UNITY. **Unity** is the use in a piece of writing of details related to the main idea, or theme. An essay with unity, for example, is one in which all the parts help to support the thesis statement, or main idea. See *essay*.

VERBAL IRONY. A statement that says one thing but means the opposite is an example of **verbal irony**. For example, if someone pushes to the front of a line, and someone else says, "What polite behavior," that is an example of verbal irony. See *irony*.

VOICE. **Voice** is the way a writer uses language to reflect his or her unique personality and attitude toward topic, form, and audience. A writer expresses voice through tone, word choice, and sentence structure.

GLOSSARY
Of Words For Everyday Use

PRONUNCIATION KEY

VOWEL SOUNDS

a	hat	i	sit	o͞o	blue, stew	ə	extra
ā	play	ī	my	oi	boy		under
ä	star	ō	go	ou	wow		civil
e	then	ô	paw, born	u	up		honor
ē	me	o͝o	book, put	ü	blue, stew		bogus

CONSONANT SOUNDS

b	but	j	jump	p	pop	th	the
ch	watch	k	brick	r	rod	v	valley
d	do	l	lip	s	see	w	work
f	fudge	m	money	sh	she	y	yell
g	go	n	on	t	sit	z	pleasure
h	hot	ŋ	song, sink	th	with		

a • ban • don • ment (ə ban′dən mənt) n., impulsiveness and freedom of action.

a • bate (ə bāt′) v., decrease.

ab • hor • rent (əb hôr′ ənt) adj., repulsive.

a • bound (ə bound′) v., be plentiful.

ab • rupt (ə brəpt′) adj., without preparation or warning; unexpected. abruptly, adv.

ac • cus • tomed (ə kəs′ təmd) adj., customary, habitual, usual.

ad • a • mant (ad′ ə mənt) adj., unyielding, inflexible.

ad • journ (ə jərn′) v., postpone or defer to a future time.

ad • min • is • ter (əd mi′ nə stər) v., dispense or give.

af • fa • ble (a′ fə bəl) adj., gracious, friendly.

af • fec • ta • tion (af′ ek tā′ shən) n., artificial behavior meant to impress others.

af • firm (ə furm′) v., prove.

ag • gra • va • tion (ag rə vā′ shən) n., worsening.

airs (ārz′) n., artificial or affected manners.

al • be • it (ol bē′ ət) conj., even though.

al • le • giance (ə lē′ jəns) n., devotion or loyalty to a person or a cause.

a • loof (ə lüf′) adj., indifferent.

al • ter (ôl′tər) v., change.

am • bi • tion (am bish′ ən) n., drive to succeed.

an • guish (aŋ′gwish) n., extreme pain or distress.

an • tic • i • pate (an ti′ sə pāt) v., look forward to, expect.

an • tiq • ui • ty (an tik′ wə tē) n., quality of being ancient or old; great age.

an • xious (aŋk′ shəs) adj., worried or eager.

ap • pall (ə pál′) v., overcome with dismay. appalled, adj.

ap • pa • ra • tus (ap ə rat′ əs) n., machine; instrument.

ar • dent (är′ dənt) adj., very eager.

ar • ro • gance (ar′ ə gəns) n., feeling or impression of superiority.

ar • ro • gant (ar′ə gənt) adj., full of unwarranted pride and self-importance.

ar • tic • u • late (är tik′ yo͞o lāt) v., speak clearly.

as • cend (ə send′) v., rise upward to a higher level or position.

as • cer • tain (as′ ər tān′) v., find out with certainty.

askance (ə skans′) adv., with disapproval or distrust.

as • phalt (as′ fôlt′) n., dark rocky mixture used for paving.

as • sem • ble (ə sem′ bəl) v., gather in a group.

as • sent (ə sent′) v., agree.

as • so • ci • ate (ə sō′ shē āt) v., connect.

as • sume (ə so͞om′) v., take on.

as • tute (ə sto͞ot′) adj., having or showing a clever mind; crafty.

at • mo • spher • ic (at məs fir′ ik) adj., relating to or occurring in the atmosphere.

at • tri • bute (a′ trib yüt) n., quality or characteristic.

au • da • cious (ô dā′ shəs) adj., state of being adventurous or bold.

au • da • ci • ty (ô da′ sə tē) n., excessive boldness and pride.

au • di • ble (ä′ də bəl) adj., pertaining to the sense of hearing.

aus • pi • cious (äs pish′ əs) adj., favorable.

bad • ger (baj′ ər) v., bother.

ban • ish (ba′ nish) v., drive out or remove from a place.

bar (bär′) v., confine; keep out or exclude.

barn • storm (bärn′ storm) v., travel and stage performances.

bat • ter • y (ba′ tə rē) n., array; impressive or imposing group.

bear (bār′) v., carry; transport.

be • guile (bi gīl′) v., amuse or charm; delight. beguiling, adj.

be • half (bi haf′) n., interest or aid of someone.

belch (belch′) v., throw forth contents rapidly.

be • quest (bē kwest′) n., anything handed down or passed on.

be • reft (bi reft′) adj., deprived or lacking something needed; wanting.

be • tray (be trā′) v., lead astray, mislead. betrayal, n.

be • wil • der (bi wil′dər) v., confuse. bewildered, adj.

bick • er (bik′ ər) v., quarrel. bickering, n.

bil • ious (bil′ yəs) adj., sick in appearance.

blun • der (blun′ dər) v., act carelessly, foolishly.

bolt (bōlt′) v., move or break away suddenly or rapidly.

botch (bäch′) v., foul up hopelessly.

bu • reau (byur′ ō) n., low chest of drawers for use in a bedroom.

cache (kash′) n., hiding place for preserving necessities.

cal • cu • la • tion (kal kyo͞o lā′ shən) n., plan; estimate.

ca • tas • tro • phe (kə tas′trə fē) n., any great or sudden disaster or misfortune.

ca • vort (kə vort′) v., prance or engage in extravagant behavior.

ce • les • tial (sə les′ chel) adj., of the sky or universe.

cha • grined (shə grind′) adj., ashamed.

char • ac • ter (kar′ ək tər) n., person's behavior, thoughts, and personality.

char • i • ty (chār′ ə tē) n., generosity; good will toward humankind.

cher • ish (cher′ ish) v., hold dear, treasure.

chord (kord′) n., three or more musical tones sounded simultaneously.

cleft (kleft′) adj., split; divided.

clutch (kluch′) v., grasp or hold tightly; snatch.

coax (kōks′) v., try to persuade with a gentle manner.

com • mod • i • ty (kə mä′ də tē) n., something useful or valued.

com • mo • tion (kə mō′ shən) n., disturbance, noisy confusion.

com • pel (kəm pel′) v. cause to do something by overwhelming pressure.

com • pla • cent (kəm plā′ sənt) adj., self-satisfied; unconcerned.

com • po • sure (kəm pō′ zhər) n., self-controlled mind or appearance.

com • pres • sion (kəm pre′ shən) n., act of pressing together.

com • rade (käm′ rad) n., friend.

con • cil • i • a • to • ry (kən sil′ ye tōr ē) adj., friendly or agreeable.

con • coct (kən käkt′) v., invent or put together a plan.

con • cus • sion (kən kush′ ən) n., strong shaking; collision.

con • demn (kən dem′) v., pronounce guilty; doom.

con • fide (kən fīd′) v., have confidence or trust in something.

con • fron • ta • tion (kän frun tā′ shən) n., heated opposition.

con • geal (kən jēl′) v., turn fluid into a more solid state; solidify.

con • science (kän′ shəns) n., thoughts and feelings about right and wrong.

con • sole (kən sōl′) v. comfort.

con • sol • i • date (kən sä′ lə dāt) v., join together into one whole. **consolidated,** adj.

con • spir • a • to • ri • al (kən spir ə tōr′ ē əl) adj., plotting, conspiring, scheming. **conspiratorially,** adv.

con • spire (kən spīr′) v., plan and act together.

con • struct (kən′ strəkt) n., something constructed by the mind, concept.

con • sume (kən soom′) v., eat or drink up.

con • sump • tion (kən səm[p]′ shən) n., act of eating or drinking.

con • trary (kän′ trer ē) adj., opposite.

con • verse (kən vərs′) adj., reversed in order or action. **conversely,** adv.

con • vul • sive (kən vul′ səv) adj., producing an uncontrolled fit.

cor • don (kor′ dən) v., form a protective or restrictive barrier.

cor • sage (kôr säzh′) n., small bouquet of flowers worn pinned to the shoulder of a garment.

cow • er (kou′ ər) v., shrink and tremble as from someone's anger, threats, or blows.

crane (krān′) v., stretch (the neck) toward an object of attention.

cre • scen • do (krə shen′ dō) n., gradual increase in volume.

crit • i • cal (krit′ ĭ kəl) adj., of or forming a crisis or turning point.

cryp • tic (krip′tik) adj., having hidden or mysterious meaning.

cul • ti • vate (kəl′ ti vāt) v., foster or encourage the growth of.

cyn • i • cal (si′ ni kəl) adj., having an attitude of distrust or pessimism.

dank (daŋk′) adj., unpleasantly moist.

dash (dash′) v., throw.

de • ci • pher (dē sī′ fər) v., to make out the meaning.

deem (dēm′) v., think, believe, judge.

de • fault (də fäwlt′) v., fail to fulfill an agreement.

de • fi • ance (də fī′ əns) n., open disregard to authority.

de • ject • ed (di jek′ təd) adj., be cast down in spirits, depressed. **dejectedly,** adv.

de • lir • i • ous (di lir′ ē əs) adj., the state of being confused, having disordered speech and hallucinations.

dense (den[t]s′) adj., compact; crowding together of parts.

de • range (di rānj′) v., disturb.

de • spair (di spār′) n., lack of hope.

de • test (dē test′) v., hate.

dev • as • tate (de′ və stāt) v., overwhelm with grief; destroy violently.

de • vour (dē vowr′) v., swallow or engulf hungrily.

dig • ni • fied (dig′ nə fīd) adj., showing nobility.

di • lap • i • dat • ed (də la′ pə dāt əd) adj., decayed or deteriorated through neglect or misuse.

dire (dīr′) adj., terrifying, desperately urgent.

dis • close (dis klōz′) v., reveal.

dis • cre • tion (dis kre′ shən) n., individual choice or judgment.

dis • dain • ful (dis dān′ fəl) adj., to be full of scorn or contempt. **disdainfully,** adv.

dis • grace (dis grās′) v., humiliate oneself; be a source of shame by your actions.

dis • in • fect • ant (dis in fec′ tənt) n., substance that prevents infection.

dis • may (dis mā′) v., afraid because of a fear of danger or trouble.

dis • miss • al (dis mis′əl) n., act of causing someone to go.

dis • po • si • tion (dis pə zi′ shən) n., customary mood and attitude toward life.

dis • traught (di strôt′) adj., extremely troubled.

di • verse (dī vərs′) adj., differing from one another.

di • vert (dī vərt′) v., turn from one course to another.

do • cile (dä′ səl) adj., easily led or managed.

dog • ged (däg′ əd) adj., marked by stubborn determination.

dog • ged • ness (dôg′ id nes) n., stubbornness.

dote (dōt′) v., be lavish or excessive in one's attention or affection.

down • y (down′ ē) adj., like down, the soft, fine inner feathers of an adult bird or outer feathers of a young bird.

ear • nest (ər′ nest) adj., serious, not joking.

eddy (ed′ ē) n., whirlwind; whirlpool.

e • lec • tron • ics (i lek′ trä niks) n., electronic devices or equipment.

e • lu • sive (ē loo′siv) adj., not easily seen or understood.

e • ma • ci • at • ed (ē mā′ shē āt əd) adj., abnormally thin, as from disease or starvation.

em • i • grant (e′ mi grənt) n., someone who left their country to live elsewhere.

e • mis • sion (ē mish′ ən) n., gas or other substance that is let out.

em • pha • tic (im fa′ tik) adj., strongly expressive, using emphasis to make a point. **emphatically,** adv.

en • chant • ment (en chant′mənt) n., magical spell or charm.

en • close (en klōz′) v., contain; shut in.

en • gulf (in gulf′) v., swallow up; overwhelm.

en • tranced (en transt′) adj., absorbed; filled with wonder.

en • vis • age (en vis′ əj) v., have a mental picture of.

en • vi • sion (en vizh′ ən) v., imagine.

equate (ē kwāt′) v., make equal.

erode (i rōd′) v., wear away or cause deterioration.

er • ra • tic (ir a′ tik) adj., with lack of consistency or regularity.

es • sence (es′ səns) n., permanent, ultimate nature of a thing, as opposed to its immediate existence.

e • ter • ni • ty (i tər′ nə tē) n., long period of time that seems endless.

e • thi • cal (e′ thi kəl) adj., conforming to accepted practices of conduct.

et • i • quette (e′ ti kət) n., conduct prescribed by authority to be observed in social life.

eu • phe • mism (yü′ fə mi zəm) n., substitution of inoffensive expression for one that may be unpleasant.

ex • ag • ger • ate (eg zaj′ər āt) v., make something seem greater than it really is.

ex • ca • va • tion (eks kə vā′shən) n., something unearthed by digging.

ex • e • cu • tion (ek sə kyü′ shən) n., performance.

ex • pi • ate (ek′ spē āt) v., make amends for.

ex • ploit (eks′ ploit) n., bold deed.

ex • traor • di • nary (ik stror′ dən er ē) adj., very unusual, remarkable.

ex • u • ber • ant (ig zü′ bə rənt) adj., joyously unrestrained and enthusiastic.

fa • nat • i • cal (fə nat' ik əl) *adj.*, unreasonably enthusiastic or determined.

fan • ta • sy (fant' ə sē) *n.*, daydream; imagined image.

fate (fāt') *n.*, inevitable outcome or end; destiny.

fa • vor • it • ism (fā' vər ti zəm) *n.*, showing of special favor.

fend (fend') *v.*, provide for, support.

fi • er • y (fī' rē) *adj.*, easily provoked, full of emotion or spirit.

fi • nite (fī' nīt) *adj.*, having definite limits.

flail (flāl') *v.*, whip.

flam • boy • ant (flam boi' ənt) *adj.*, showy, extravagant.

flu • id (flü' əd) *adj.*, changing or shifting smoothly.

fluke (flük') *n.*, chance occurrence.

flum • mox (flum' əks) *v.*, confuse.

flush (fləsh') *v.*, blush; be lively. **flushed**, *adj.*

flut • ed (flü' təd) *adj.*, having grooves.

fo • li • age (fō' lē ij) *n.*, leaves, flowers, and branches.

fore • bod • ing (fôr bod' iŋ) *n.*, omen or prediction of coming evil.

for • sake (fôr sāk') *v.*, give up or abandon.

fraud (frod') *n.*, person who is not what he or she pretends to be.

fruit • less (frōōt'ləs) *adj.*, without results.

fund (fund') *n.*, supply, wealth.

fur • tive (fər' tiv) *adj.*, secret; stolen.

gab • ble (ga' bəl) *v.*, talk fast or foolishly.

gall (gôl') *v.*, irritate, annoy.

gal • va • nize (gal' və nīz) *v.*, stimulate or excite.

gau • dy (gäw' dē) *adj.*, tastelessly ornamented. **gaudily**, *adv.*

gaunt (gänt') *adj.*, excessively thin and angular.

ghast • ly (gast' lē) *adj.*, frightening, terrifying.

glib (glib') *adj.*, marked by ease and informality, nonchalant.

gre • gar • i • ous (gri gar' ē əs) *adj.*, sociable; seeks companionship.

grim (grim') *adj.*, somber, gloomy. **grimly**, *adv.*

griz • zled (griz´əld) *adj.*, partly gray.

groom (grōōm') *v.*, clean and comb.

grope (grōp') *v.*, feel for blindly.

gro • tesque (grō tesk') *adj.*, misshapen, distorted.

grudge (gruj´) *v.*, not give willingly.

guf • faw (gu fə') *v.*, laugh loudly and suddenly.

hal • lu • ci • nate (hə lü' sə nāt) *v.*, experience sights or sounds that are not actually present.

hap • haz • ard (hap'haz´ərd) *adj.*, not planned; casual.

har • bor (här' bər) *v.*, hold on to, especially in the mind.

har • mo • ny (här' mə nē) *n.*, combination of musical notes and chords.

haste (hāst') *n.*, act of hurrying; quickness of motion.

here • by (hēr bī') *adv.*, by this means.

her • i • tage (her' ə tij) *n.*, something that is passed onto an heir; tradition.

hin • drance (hin' drəns) *n.*, something that interferes.

hom • age (häm´ij) *n.*, something done to show honor or respect.

hos • pi • ta • li • ty (häs pə ta' lə tē) *n.*, generous and pleasant treatment or reception.

hos • ti • li • ty (hä sti' lə tē) *n.*, strong feeling of ill will towards something.

hov • er (hə' vər) *v.*, stay suspended in the air near one place.

hy • giene (hī' jēn) *n.*, cleanliness and sanitary practices.

im • mense (i mens') *adj.*, very large; enormous.

im • mune (i myūn') *adj.*, having a high degree to resistance to disease or illness.

im • pas • sive (im pas' iv) *adj.*, not feeling or showing emotion.

im • per • i • ous (im pēr'ē yus) *adj.*, commanding; marked by arrogant assurance.

im • per • son • ate (im pər' sən āt) *v.*, represent; act like.

im • plor • ing (im plô' riŋ) *adj.*, to cry or call out earnestly, to beg.

im • pos • ing (im pō'ziŋ) *adj.*, making a strong impression

because of great size or strength.

im • pro • vis • er (im' prə vīz ər) *n.*, one who makes or invents things offhand.

im • pulse (im' puls) *n.*, sudden wish or desire.

in • ap • pro • pri • ate (in ə prō´prē it) *adj.*, not proper.

in • ca • pac • i • tate (in kə pa' sə tāt) *v.*, become incapable or disabled.

incessant (in se' sənt) *adj.*, continuing without interruption, unceasing.

in • ci • den • tal • ly (in sə den' təl ē) *adv.*, by way of interjection, by the way.

in • con • spic • u • ous (in kən spi' kyə wəs) *adj.*, unnoticeable.

in • cor • por • ate (in kōr' pə rāt) *v.*, blend.

in • del • i • ble (in de' lə bəl) *adj.*, lasting; unerasable.

in • dig • nant (in dig´nənt) *adj.*, feeling or expressing anger in reaction to an injustice, ingratitude, or meannesss.

in • dom • i • ta • ble (in dô' mə tə bəl) *adj.*, unconquerable.

in • dul • gence (in dəl' jəns) *n.*, unrestrained pleasure in something.

in • ev • i • ta • ble (in ev´i tə bəl) *adj.*, unavoidable.

in • flec • tion (in flek' shən) *n.*, change of form words undergo to distinguish case, gender, number, tense, person, or mood.

in • fu • ri • ate (in fyur' ē āt) *v.*, make furious.

in • ge • nious (in jēn' yəs) *adj.*, clever.

in • im • i • ta • ble (in im' i tə bəl) *adj.*, unique.

in • i • tia • tive (i ni' shə tiv) *n.*, action of taking the first step or move.

in • or • di • nate (i nor' dən ət) *adj.*, exceeding reasonable limits.

in • sist (in sist') *v.*, persist or demand.

in • stinc • tive (in stiŋk' tiv) *adj.*, prompted by natural instinct or spontaneity. **instinctively**, *adv.*

in • tan • gi • ble (in tan' jə bəl) *adj.*, not able to be seen or touched.

in • tel • lect (in' təl ekt') *n.*, capacity for thinking and gaining knowledge.

in • ten • si • ty (in ten' sə tē) *n.*, great energy, a feeling of high degree.

in • ter • cept (in tər sept') *v.*, seize or stop on the way.

in • ti • mate (in' tə mət) *adj.*, personal, private.

in • trigue (in trēg') *v.*, excite interest or curiosity.

in • var • i • a • ble (in ver´ē ə bəl) *adj.*, constant.

ir • i • des • cent (ir ə des' ənt) *adj.*, showing a play of colors that produces rainbow effects.

i • ron • ic (ī rän´ ik) *adj.*, meaning the opposite of what is expressed.

iron • i • cal • ly (ī rä' nik lē) *adv.*, curiously or surpisingly.

lac • er • a • tion (la sə rā' shən) *n.*, deeply cut wound.

la • dle (lā' dəl) *v.*, take or dip using a ladle or oversized spoon.

lair (lār') *n.*, resting place.

lash (lash') *v.*, move violently or suddenly.

la • vish (lav' ish) *adj.*, abundant, rich.

leer (lēr') *n.*, knowing, wanton look.

lethal (lē' thəl) *adj.*, fatal or deadly.

li • a • ble (lī' ə bəl) *adj.*, likely.

lit • er • al • ly (li' tə rə lē) *adv.*, actually.

lithe (līth') *adj.*, characterized by flexibility and grace.

loi • ter (loit' ər) *v.*, spend time idly.

loll (läl') *v.*, be in a relaxed posture; hang or droop.

lu • gu • bri • ous (lə gōō' brē əs) *adj.*, very sad, especially in an exaggerated way.

lunge (lunj') *v.*, thrust or lean forward suddenly.

lurch (lərch') *v.*, roll or tip abruptly; stagger.

mag • nan • i • mous (mag na' nə məs) *adj.*, showing lofty or courageous spirit.

ma • nip • u • late (ma nip' yōō lāt) *v.*, handle or use.

me • an • der (mē an' dər) *v.*, follow a winding course or wander.

me • di • o • cre (mē dē ō' kər) *adj.*, of moderate or low quality, value, ability or performance.

med • i • ta • tion (med ə tā´shən) n., deep and continued thought.

men • ac • ing (men´ əs iŋ) adj., threatening.

mi • nute (mī nüt´) adj., marked by close attention to details.

mol • ten (mōl´tən) adj., melted or liquefied by heat.

mo • nop • o • ly (mə näp´ə lē) n., exclusive possession or control over something.

mo • not • o • nous (mə nät´ ən əs) adj., of a single unchanging tone.

mor • sel (mor´ səl) n., small bite or portion of food.

mor • ti • fied (mor´ tə fīd) v., feel severe embarrassment or shame.

mo • tive (mo´ təv) n., something that causes a person to act a certain way.

myth • i • cal (mith´ i kəl) adj., having qualities suitable to myth.

nar • ra • tive (nar´ ə tiv) n., story or account of events and experiences.

nest • le (nes´ əl) v., settle snugly.

nom • i • nal (nä´ mə nəl) adj., insignificant.

non • cha • lant (nän´shə länt) adj., unconcerned or uninterested.

oblige (ə blīj´) v., force or require.

o • blige (ə blīj´) v., compel or force.

ob • scu • ri • ty (əb skür´ i tē) n., state of being shrouded or hidden in darkness.

oc • tave (äk´ təv) n., musical interval spanning eight notes.

odd • ments (äd´ mənts) n., various miscellaneous objects.

o • men (ō´mən) n., sign of a future event.

om • i • nous (äm´ə nəs) adj., threatening.

on • slaught (än´ slät) n., especially fierce attack.

or • deal (ôr dēl´) n., difficult experience.

or • gan • dy (ôr´ gən dē) n., sheer, crisp cotton fabric used for dresses.

pal • lid (pa´ləd) adj., dull, lacking color.

par • a • lyze (pār´ ə līz) v., stun; make speechless.

par • cel (pär´ səl) v., wrap.

pass • a • ble (pa´ sə bəl) adj., just good enough. **passably,** adv.

pas • ty (pās´ tē) adj., resembling paste; unhealthy in appearance.

pa • tron • iz • ing (pā´ trən īz iŋ) adj., haughty or snobbish.

paunch • y (pônch´ ē) adj., having a potbelly.

pe • dan • tic (ped an´ tik) adj., paying to much attention to unimportant details.

pen • e • trate (pen´ ə trāt) v., pass through.

per • pet • u • al (pər pə´ chə wəl) adj., continuing forever.

per • son • age (pər´ sən ij) n., person of fame.

per • suade (pər swād´) v., convince.

per • vade (pər vād´) v., spread through every part of.

plague (plāg´) v., afflict with disease or disaster.

plight (plīt´) n., bad condition or state.

ploy (ploi´) n., scheme or trick.

pluck (pluk´) n., courage and strength.

po • di • um (pō´ dē əm) n., small platform for a speaker or conductor.

poised (poizd´) adj., dignified, self-confident.

pon • der (pän´ dər) v., think hard upon something.

pore (pôr´) v., study thoroughly.

pos • ter • i • ty (päs ter´ə tē) n., future generations.

pre • cau • tion • ar • y (prē kô´shən ar ē) adj., safety.

pres • sure (presh´ ər) n., force pressing down.

pres • tige (pres tēzh´) n., reputation, fame.

prev • a • lent (pre´ və lənt) adj., widespread; generally accepted or practiced.

prim (prim´) adj., stiffly formal and proper.

pro • ces • sion (prə sesh´ ən) n., group of individuals moving along in a ceremonial way.

prod • i • gy (präd´ ə jē) n., person of highly unusual talent.

pro • fane (prō fān´) v., show disrespect for sacred things.

pro • found (prə faünd´) adj., with depth and understanding.

pro • ject (prō jekt´) v., throw or hurl forward.

prom • i • nent (prä´ mə nənt) adj., standing out; conspicuous.

prophesy (prä´ fə sī) v., predicted.

prop • o • si • tion (prä pə zi´ shən) n., act of offering or suggesting something to be considered.

pro • pound (prə pound´) v., propose.

pro • pri • e • tar • y (prə prī´ ə ter ē) adj., relating to or characteristic of an owner.

pro • spec • tive (prə spek´ tiv) adj., expected; would be.

pros • per (präs´ pər) v., succeed, thrive.

pros • per • ous (präs´ per əs) adj., successful.

pros • trate (prä´ strāt´) adj., lying face down.

pro • trude (prō trüd´) v., stick out.

prov • i • dence (präv´ ə dəns) n., valuable gift, godsend.

pro • vi • sion (prə vi´ zhən) n., stock of supplies or arrangement made for the future.

psych (sīk´) v., cause to feel nervous or less self-confident.

pun (pən´) n., humorous use of a word as to suggest two or more meanings.

quiz • zi • cal (kwi´ zi kəl) adj., questioning or puzzled expression. **quizzically,** adv.

ram • i • fi • ca • tion (ra´ mə fə kā´ shən) n., consequence or outgrowth of something.

range (rānj´) n., land for grazing cattle, sheep, or horses.

rant (rant´) v., talk in a noisy, excited, wild manner.

rasp • ing (ras´ piŋ) adj., producing a harsh, irritating sound.

rau • cous (rô´ kəs) adj., loud and disorderly.

rav • age (rav´ ij) v., wreak havoc on.

rea • son • a • ble (rē´ zən ə bəl) adj., agreeable; logical. **reasonably,** adj.

re • bel • lious (ri bel´ yəs) adj., defiant.

re • buff (rī buf´) v., reject or criticize sharply.

re • cep • tion (rē sep´ shən) n., act of being received.

re • cruit (ri´ kroot´) v., hire or engage the services of.

reign (rān´) v., rule.

re • lent • less (ri lent´ ləs) adj., showing no sign of decrease in intensity, strength, or pace.

rel • ic (rel´ ik) n., object that has survived from the past.

re • lin • quish (ri lin´ kwish) v., give up possession or control; release.

re • luc • tant (ri lək´ tənt) adj., not in the mood, disinclined.

rem • nant (rem´ nənt) n., small surviving group; trace remaining.

re • morse (ri mors´) n., gnawing distress over guilt.

ren • o • vate (ren´ ə vāt´) v., clean up; replace worn and broken parts.

re • pu • ta • tion (re pyə tā´ shən) n., overall character as seen or judged by people.

res • i • dence (re´ zə dən[t]s) n., place where one lives or dwells.

re • si • lient (ri zil´ yənt) adj., flexible and springy.

re • strain (ri strān´) v., hold back from action.

re • tire (ri tīr´) v., go away.

re • treat (ri trēt´) v., draw or lead back, withdraw.

re • treat (ri trēt´) n., act or process of withdrawing.

re • veal (ri vēl´) v., show; make known.

re • vol • ting (ri vōl´ tiŋ) adj., extremely offensive.

rid • i • cule (rid´ i kyool) v., make the object of laughter, make fun of.

rove (rōv´) v., roam.

rue (rü´) v., repent over or regret bitterly.

ruse (rooz´) v., trick.

rut • ted (rut´ əd) adj., bumpy and marked by tracks made by wheels.

sa • cred (sā´ krəd) adj., highly valued, important.

sauc • y (sô´ sē) adj., impudent; bold; forward.

saun • ter (sôn´ tər) v., walk slowly or casually.

sa • vor (sā´ vər) v., take great pleasure in.

scorn (skorn´) n., extreme contempt or dislike for someone or something.

scru • ti • nize (scroot´ ən īz) v., look at very carefully.

se • cluded (si klood´ ed) adj., shut off or kept away from others.

se • date (si dāt´) adj., quiet, calm.

seek (sēk') v., search for.

seg • re • gate (seg' rə gāt') v., separate; set apart.

sem • blance (sem' bləns) n., appearance, likeness.

se • rene (sə rēn') adj., calm.

sham • ble (sham' bəl) v., walk in a clumsy manner.

sheathe (shēth') v., enclose or protect with a cover or case.

short • com • ing (shôrt' kum' iŋ) n., less than what is expected or required.

shrewd (shrūd') adj., clever, having a high degree of commom sense.

shrewd • ness (shrōōd´nəs) n., cleverness.

shroud (shroud') n., something that covers or protects.

shun (shən') v., avoid deliberately and habitually.

skep • ti • cal (skep' ti kəl) adj., being doubtful or uncertain.

skim (skim') v., glide over lightly.

skir • mish (skər' mish) n., minor fight in war.

slack • en (slak' ən) v., lessen; let up.

slith • er (sli' thər) v., slide like a snake.

sluice (slōōs') n., valve through which water is run.

smite (smīt') v., hit or strike hard.

smug (sməg') adj., overly confident. **smugly,** adv.

sol • emn (sä' ləm) adj., serious; somber.

spec • ta • cle (spek' ta kəl) n., eye-catching display of drama that is unusual or entertaining.

spell (spel') n. strong compelling influence or attraction.

spite (spīt') v., harm, annoy, or frustrate.

splen • dor (splen' dər) n., magnificence, pomp.

spon • ta • ne • i • ty (spän tə nā' ə tē) n., voluntary or undetermined action or movement.

sta • ple (stā´pəl) adj., most important.

sto • i • cal (sto' i kəl) adj., showing no feeling.

stren • u • ous (stren´yü əs) adj., requiring hard work and energy.

strick • en (strick' ən) adj., wounded; distressed.

stri • dent (strī' dənt) adj., loud, harsh, and insistent.

sub • dued (sub dood') adj., controlled or repressed emotionally.

sub • ter • ra • ne • an (sub tə rā' nē ən) adj., underground.

sub • tle (sə' təl) adj., delicate or refined.

suf • fuse (sə fyüz') v., spread over or through.

suit • or (süt´ər) n., man who is seeking a romantic relationship with a woman.

sulky (səl' kē) adj., indicating a moody silence.

sul • try (səl' trē) adj., expressing strong sexual desire or passion.

sup • ple (sə' pəl) adj., limber, without stiffness.

surge (sərj') v., suddenly push forward in a violent way.

sur • rep • ti • tious (sər´əp tish´əs) adj., secret, sneaky. **surreptitiously,** adv.

sus • pend (sə spend') v., hang by or support from above.

sus • tain (sə stān') v., bear or withstand.

swoon (swōōn') v., faint; feel powerful emotion.

sys • tem • a • tic (sis tə ma' tik) adj., methodical in procedure or plan.

tact • ful (takt' fəl) adj., having or showing good sense of what to say and do.

taunt (tônt') v., jeer, mock.

teem • ing (tēm' iŋ) adj., swarming.

tem • per • a • ment (tem' prə mənt) n., distinguishing mental or physical character or quality.

tem • pes • tu • ous (tem pes' chə wəs) adj., stormy.

te • nac • i • ty (tə na'sə tē) n., quality of being firm, tough.

the • o • ry (thē' ə rē) n., principles of a body of fact, a science, or an art.

throng (thräŋ') v., crowd or pack.

toil (toil') v., work hard.

tor • ren • tial (tó ren[t]' shəl) adj., violently rushing.

tran • quil • li • ty (traŋ kwil´ə tē) n., quality or state of being calm.

tran • si • ent (tran' sē ənt) adj., passing quickly into and out of existence.

trek (trek') v., go on a journey.

tress (tres') n., hair.

tri • um • phant (trī um' fənt) adj., overjoyed with success.

trough (trôf') n., long, narrow, open container.

tu • mul • tu • ous (tōō mul' chōō əs) adj., wild and disorderly.

tur • bu • lent (tər byə lənt) adj., causing unrest or disturbance.

un • fath • om • a • ble (un fa' thə mə bəl) adj., impossible to comprehend.

uni • son (yü' nə sən) n., at the same time, in perfect agreement.

un • mer • ci • ful (un mər' si fəl) adj., without mercy, without stopping.

un • re • len • ting (ən ri len' tiŋ) adj., not letting up or yielding in determination.

un • rul • y (un rōō´lē) adj., hard to control.

un • sight • ly (un sīt' lē) adj., not pleasing to see.

up • stand • ing (up stand' iŋ) adj., marked by integrity and good character.

va • grant (vā' grənt) adj., wandering about; random.

vain (vān') adj., being too concerned with one's own looks or possessions.

veer (vir') v., change direction.

ven • ture (ven[t]' shər) v., undertake and be exposed to risks and dangers.

ve • ran • da (və ran' də) n., open porch, usually roofed, along the outside of a building.

vile (vīl') adj., loathsome, disgusting.

vin • tage (vin' tij) adj., being old-fashioned, dating from the past.

vir • tue (vər' chü) n., quality; merit.

vis • cer • al (vi' sə rəl) adj., felt deeply in the heart, not intellect.

vi • tal • i • ty (vī tal´ə tē) n., energy; life.

viv • id (viv' id) adj., bright.

void (voyd') n., emptiness.

waft (wäft') v., cause to move as if by the action of waves.

wan • ing (wān' iŋ) adj., approaching the end.

war • rant (wär' ənt) v., give a guarantee or promise.

wary (wār' ē) adj., watchful, careful.

wa • ver (wā' vər) v., sway unsteadily.

way • ward (wā' wərd) adj., following one's own foolish inclinations.

whir • ring (hwur' iŋ) adj., whizzing or buzzing.

wince (wins') v., shrink back involuntarily from pain, flinch.

win • some (win' səm) adj., charming.

zingy (ziŋ' ē) adj., pleasantly stimulating.

INDEX
Of Titles and Authors

INDEX Of Skills

comparing and contrasting, 598–604, 881–882

conclusion, 322, 883

criticism, 884–885

description, 25, 59, 184, 492, 559, 726, 792, 799, 883

dialogue, 17, 140, 220, 262, 270, 422, 660, 669, 726

diary entry, 44, 596

documentary writing, 738

drafting, 64–65, 143–144, 218–219, 322–324, 374, 441, 505, 601, 685, 730, 805, 859, 873–884

expository writing, 874, 883–884

fable, 502–507

forms of writing, 875

freewriting, 876–877

imaginative writing, 874

informative writing, 874

interview, 879

journals, 200, 361, 399, 410, 766, 876

letter, 25, 31, 200, 410, 478, 628, 681, 792, 835, 935–936

lists, 102, 177, 248, 469, 500, 548, 681, 715, 747

main idea, 880–881

manuscript preparation, 887

metaphor, 216, 349, 522, 684

narrative writing, 218–223, 874, 883

onomatopoeia, 369, 655

organization, 881–882

outline, 44, 882

paragraph, 318, 340, 349, 369, 410, 422, 492, 536, 675, 766, 879–880

paraphrase, 802–803

peer evaluation, 66, 144–145, 220–221, 375, 442–443, 506, 603, 686, 733, 807, 860, 873, 884–885

personal essay, 715

personal writing, 874

persuasive essay, 142–146

persuasive writing, 738, 799, 874

poetry, 306, 369, 522, 660, 669, 675, 683–688, 757, 775

point-by-point organization, 599

presenting, 67, 146, 223, 326, 376, 444, 507, 688, 733, 862, 873, 888

prewriting, 62–63, 143, 218–219, 321, 372–373, 438–441, 503, 599, 683–685, 729, 802–803, 857, 873–882

process, 320–326

proofreading, 67, 145–146, 221, 324–326, 375, 443, 506, 686–687, 732, 808, 862, 873, 886–887

proposition, 879

publishing, 67, 146, 223, 326, 376, 444, 507, 688, 733, 862, 873, 888

purpose, 874

questioning strategy, 877–878

questions, 31, 209

reflecting, 146, 326, 377, 441, 507, 688, 733, 857, 873, 888

research paper, 801–810

review, 728–733

revising, 65–67, 145–146, 221, 324–326, 375, 443, 506, 686–687, 732, 808, 862, 873, 885–886

self-evaluation, 66, 144–145, 220–221, 375, 442–443, 506, 603, 686, 733, 807, 860, 873, 884–885

sensory detail chart, 878

short story, 354, 660, 828

simile, 25, 220, 655, 684

spatial order, 881, 883–884

speech, 162, 469, 559

story map, 879

tall tale, 757

technical writing, 766

thesis statement, 801–802, 880

topic, 875–876

topic sentence, 31, 880

transitions, 883

Venn diagram, 878

voice, 63, 143, 219, 321, 372, 439, 503, 599, 683, 729, 803, 857, 875

writing plan, 62–63, 143, 219–220, 322–323, 373, 438–441, 503–504, 601, 683–684, 729, 802–803, 857–858

writing portfolio, 888

LANGUAGE, GRAMMAR, AND STYLE

active voice, 897–898

adjectives, 44–45, 184, 669, 891, 904

adverbs, 44–45, 184, 891, 904

antecedents, 902–903

antonyms, 469, 871

apostrophe, 907

appositives, 891

base words, 871

brand names, 872

capitalization, 209, 675, 715, 908–909

cliches, 871

colloquialism, 889

colons, 907

colorful language, 898

commas, 324–326, 399, 410, 906

complete predicate, 893

complete subject, 893

conjunctions, 44–45, 216, 766, 859–860, 891, 904–905

connotation, 872

context clues, 870

dash, 907–908

denotation, 872

dialect, 726

dictionary, 870–871

direct objects, 894

documentation in research papers, 804–806

end marks, 853–854, 906

etymology, 871

euphemisms, 871

family relationships, 908

figure of speech, 340, 941

future tense, 144–146

geographical names, 908–909

gerunds, 906

historical names, 908–909

homonyms, 871

hybrids, 891–892, 905

hyphen, 907–908

I and me, 899

indirect objects, 894

infinitives, 906

interjections, 44–45, 216, 766, 891, 905

interrupters, 905

italics, 907

linking verbs, 892

modifiers, 599–602, 900, 903–904

negatives, 548, 757, 894

noun of direct address, 891, 896, 905

nouns, 44–45, 221–223, 289–290, 891, 902, 905

onomatopoeia, 59

parallelism, 898

parts of speech, 44–45, 871, 890–892, 902–906

passive voice, 897–898

predicate, 64–65, 893

prefixes, 871, 909

prepositions, 44–45, 216, 766, 891, 892, 896, 904

Fine Art

Internet Sites

ACKNOWLEDGMENTS

ART ACKNOWLEDGMENTS
Cover *Rooftops (No. 1, This is Harlem)* [Detail], 1943. Jacob Lawrence. Hirshhorn Museum and Sculpture Garden, Smithsonian Institution, Gift of Joseph H. Hirshhorn, 1966. Photo by Ricardo Blanc. © Gwendolyn Knight Lawrence, courtesy of the Jacob and Gwendolyn Lawrence Foundation **Cover** *Saint George and the Dragon* [Detail], c.1400s. Spanish artist. © Archivo Iconografico, S.A./CORBIS **Cover** *The Fate of Animals* [Detail], 1913. Franz Marc. Offentliche Kunstsammlung, Basle, Switzerland/ Bridgeman Art Library, London/New York **Cover** *Tornado Over Kansas* [Detail], 1929. John Stuart Curry. Hackley Picture Fund, Muskegon Museum of Art, Muskegon, Michigan; **2** Planet Art; **7** PhotoDisc; **15** AP/Wide World Photos; **20** Planet Art; **27** Anne Frank Fonds, Basel/Archive Photos; **34** © Archivo Iconografico, S.A./CORBIS; **47** © Tom Wesselman/Licensed by VAGA, New York. © Burstein Collection/CORBIS; **49** PhotoDisc; **51** PhotoDisc; **53** PhotoDisc; **55** Photograph by Don Perkins; **56-57** All: PhotoDisc; **70** National Museum of American Art, Washington, D.C./Art Resource; **84** AP/Wide World Photos; **85** AP/Wide World Photos; **92** © Kevin Fleming/CORBIS; **105** Library of Congress; **105** PhotoDisc; **128** © 1991 Faith Ringgold; **130** © Kevin Fleming/CORBIS; **135** © Ed Eckstein/CORBIS; **150** Hackley Picture Fund, Muskegon Museum of Art, Muskegon, Michigan; **154** Scott Polar Research Institute; **157** Scott Polar Research Institute; **159** Scott Polar Research Institute; **160** First Light Studios; **165** Photo by Jennifer Wreisner; **167** Photo by Jennifer Wreisner; **171** Photo by Jennifer Wreisner; **175** Robert and Jane Meyerhoff Collection, Gift in Honor of the 50th Anniversary of the National Gallery of Art, © 2000 Board of Trustees, National Gallery of Art, Washington, D.C.; **179** © Estate of Ben Shahn/Licensed by VAGA, New York. © Philadelphia Museum of Art/CORBIS; **186** © James L. Amos/CORBIS; **188** © James L. Amos/CORBIS; **191** © James L. Amos/CORBIS; **195** © James L. Amos/CORBIS; **202** © National Gallery Collection; By kind permission of the Trustees of the National Gallery, London/CORBIS; **205** Library of Congress; **206** AP/World Wide Photos; **211** Sheldon Memorial Art Gallery, Nebraska Art Association Collection; **213** ©Jim Winkley Ecoscene/CORBIS; **214** AP/World Wide Photos; **226** Offentliche Kunstsammlung, Basle, Switzerland/Bridgeman Art Library, London/New York; **235** Museum and Sculpture Garden, Smithsonian Institution. Gift of Joseph H. Hirshhorn, 1966. Photo: Lee Stalsworth.; **239** PhotoDisc; **241** PhotoDisc; **242** PhotoDisc; **245** Estate of Mary O'Hara; **250** Melissa Poussard; **255** Melissa Poussard; **260** © Underwood & Underwood/CORBIS; **264** Illustrations by Maurice Sendak from *Zlateh the Goat and Other Stories* by Isaac Bashevis Singer © 1966. Reproduced by permission of HarperCollins Publishers.; **268** © Bettmann/CORBIS; **272** © Paul A. Souders/CORBIS; **286** © Roger Ressmeyer/CORBIS; **292** © Francis G. Mayer/CORBIS; **303** © Hulton-Deutsch Collection/CORBIS; **304** Whitney Museum of American Art, New York.; **308** PhotoDisc; **313** Jan Dean; **316** AP/World Wide Photo; **330** Planet Art; **334** © Danny Lehman/CORBIS; **338** © Jonathan Blair/CORBIS; **343** © Gianfranco Gorgoni/Contact Press Images/PictureQuest; **344** © Bettmann/CORBIS; **345** © Neal Preston/CORBIS; **352** © Hulton-Deutsch Collection/CORBIS;

357 National Museum of American Art, Washington, D.C./Art Resource; **358** Tate Gallery, London/Art Resource; **359** © Bettmann/CORBIS; **359** Archive Photos; **363** © Bettmann/CORBIS; **366** © Derick A. Thomas; Dat's Jazz/CORBIS; **367** © Romare Bearden Foundation/Licensed by VAGA, New York. National Museum of American Art, Washington, D.C./Art Resource, NY; **380** © Burstein Collection/CORBIS; **384** From *Pictures* by J.R.R. Tolkien. © 1992 by HarperCollins Publishers. All rights reserved.; **388** PhotoDisc; **393** PhotoDisc; **397** © Bettmann/CORBIS; **401** PhotoDisc; **404** © Laura Dwight/CORBIS; **406** Photo by Melanie Ray; **407** © John Anster Fitzgerald/Wood River Gallery/PictureQuest; **412** © Archivo Iconografico, S.A./CORBIS; **414** © Archivo Iconografico, S.A./CORBIS; **417** © Archivo Iconografico, S.A./CORBIS; **418** © Archivo Iconografico, S.A./CORBIS; **424** National Museum of American Art, Washington, D.C./Art Resource/© 2000 Luis Jimenez Artists Rights Society (ARS), New York.; **431** © Roger Tidman/CORBIS; **450** © Gianni Dagli Orti/CORBIS; **455** Rochester Museum and Science Center, Rochester, NY.; **456** Courtesy of Joseph Bruchac; **461** Bridgeman Art Library; **465** © Robert Fried / Robert Fried Photography; **466** © Robert Fried / Robert Fried Photography; **467** © Robert Fried / Robert Fried Photography; **471** © Francis G. Mayer/CORBIS; **480** © Asian Art & Archeology, Inc./CORBIS; **485** Bancroft Library, UC Berkeley, Berkley, CA.; **489** © Contemporary African Art Collection/CORBIS; **494** PhotoDisc; **498** Courtesy of Lila Perl; **510** © Burstein Collection/CORBIS; **515** National Museum of American Art, Washington, D.C.; **520** Library of Congress; **524** © Layne Kennedy/CORBIS; **527** © Kennan Ward/CORBIS; **530** © Museum of Flight/CORBIS; **534** Archive Photos; **540** © Wayne Thiebaud. Sheldon Memorial Art Gallery NAA-Thomas C. Woods Memorial; **550** © Robert Maass/CORBIS; **555** PhotoDisc; **563** © Franklin McMahon/CORBIS; **567** © Franklin McMahon/CORBIS; **571** © Burstein Collection/CORBIS; **577** Library of Congress; **578** © Buddy Mays/CORBIS; **583** © Adam Woolfitt/CORBIS; **588** Musee du Louvre, Paris/SuperStock; **590** Musee du Louvre, Paris/Lauros-Giraudon/SuperStock; **594** Photo by Rod Aiken; **608** © Joseph and Robert Cornell Memorial Foundation/Licensed by VAGA; © North Carolina Museum of Art/CORBIS; **614** © Alexander Burkatowski/CORBIS; **616** Library of Congress; **620** David David Gallery, Philadelphia/SuperStock; **624** Library of Congress; **625** © Karl Weatherly/CORBIS; **626** Photograph by Matilda Champagne.; **631** © Burstein Collection/CORBIS; **632** Library of Congress; **644** © The State Russian Museum/CORBIS; **645** Library of Congress; **648** National Museum of American Art. Washington, D.C./Art Resource; **649** © Bettmann/CORBIS; **652** Musee d'Orsay, Paris/SuperStock; **653** Library of Congress; **657** © Richard Estes/Licensed by VAGA, New York. © Burstein Collection/CORBIS; **658** Photo by Gerard Malanga. Courtesy of Black Sparrow Press.; **662** © National Gallery Collection; By kind permission of the Trustees of the National Gallery London/CORBIS; **663** Photo by Linden Frederick; **666** © Owen Franken/CORBIS; **667** Photo by Mike Markee. Estate of William Stafford.; **671** © Museum of the City of New York/CORBIS; **672** © CORBIS; **673** Library of Congress; **677** © Brent Bear/CORBIS; **678** © Brent Bear/CORBIS; **692** © Archivo Iconografico, S.A./CORBIS; **697** © Paul Almasy/CORBIS; **701** © Paul Almasy/CORBIS; **704** © Paul Almasy/CORBIS;

711 © Michael Busselle/CORBIS; 713 © E.O. Hoppé/CORBIS; 717 © Galen Rowell/CORBIS; 721 © Richard T. Nowitz/CORBIS; 724 Mrs. Milton Geiger; 734 © Francis G. Mayer/CORBIS; 738 A'Lelia Bundles / Walker Family Collection; 747 © Bettmann/CORBIS; 749 © Bettmann/CORBIS; 751 © Bettmann/CORBIS; 753 © L. Barry Hetherington; 755 © Bettmann/CORBIS; 757 © CORBIS; 762 Archive Photos; 766 © Karl Ammann/CORBIS; 768 © Yann Arthus-Bertrand/CORBIS; 769 © Kevin Schafer/CORBIS; 778 North Wind Picture Archive; 780 Photo by Judith Bloom Fradin; 784 © Burstein Collection/CORBIS/© 2000 Artists Rights Society (ARS), New York VG Bild-Kunst, Bonn; 792 © Philip James Corwin/CORBIS; 812 Christie's Images/SuperStock; 822-823 All: NASA; 830 SuperStock; 845 Hirshhorn Museum and Sculpture Garden, Smithsonian Institution, Gift of Joseph H. Hirshhorn, 1966. Photo by Ricardo Blanc. © Gwendolyn Knight Lawrence, courtesy of the Jacob and Gwendolyn Lawrence Foundation.

LITERARY ACKNOWLEDGMENTS

Samuel W. Allen. "To Satch" by Samuel W. Allen from *The Poetry of the Negro.* Langston Hughes and Arna Bontemps, p. 343. Doubleday. Compilation © 1993 by Lee Bennett Hopkins. Reprinted by permission of Samuel Allen, author. **The American Scholar.** "Big Wind" by Theodore Roethke, reprinted from *The American Scholar*, Volume 17, Number 1, Winter 1947–48. **Amistad Research Center.** "If You Should Go" by Countee Cullen. Copyrights held by the Amistad Research Center, Tulane University, New Orleans, Louisiana. Administered by Thompson and Thompson, New York City. Reprinted by permission. **Elizabeth Barnett.** "City Trees" by Edna St. Vincent Millay. From *Collected Poems*, HarperCollins. Copyright © 1921, 1948 by Edna St. Vincent Millay. All rights reserved. Reprinted by permission of Elizabeth Barnett, literary executor. "English Sparrows (Washington Square)" by Edna St. Vincent Millay. From *Collected Poems*, HarperCollins. Copyright © 1939, 1967 by Edna St. Vincent Millay and Norma Millay Ellis. All rights reserved. Reprinted by permission of Elizabeth Barnett, literary executor. **Susan Bergholz Literary Services.** "Eleven" from *Woman Hollering Creek* by Sandra Cisneros. Copyright © 1991 by Sandra Cisneros. Published by Vintage Books, a division of Random House, Inc., and originally in hardcover by Random House, Inc. Reprinted by permission of Susan Bergholz Literary Services, New York. All rights reserved. "Good Hot Dogs" from *My Wicked Wicked Ways.* Copyright © 1987 by Sandra Cisneros, published by Third Woman Press and in hardcover by Alfred A. Knopf. Reprinted by permission of Susan Bergholz Literary Services, New York. All rights reserved. **Black Sparrow Press.** "two girls of twelve or so at a table" by Charles Reznikoff. Copyright © 1977 by Marie Syrkin Reznikoff. Reprinted from *Poems 1918–1975: The Complete Poems of Charles Reznikoff* with the permission of Black Sparrow Press. **Georges Borchardt, Inc.** "Dragon, Dragon" by John Gardner. Copyright © 1975 by Boskydell Artists, Ltd. Reprinted by permission of Georges Borchardt, Inc., for the Estate of John Gardner. **Brandt & Brandt.** "Potter's Gray" from *Up the Chimney Down and Other Stories.* Copyright © 1984 by Joan Aiken Enterprises Ltd. Reprinted by permission of Brandt & Brandt Literary Agents, Inc. **Walker Brents.** "The Twelve Labors of Hercules", copyright 2000 by Walker Brents. **Gwendolyn Brooks.** "Cynthia in the Snow" by Gwendolyn Brooks. Reprinted by permission of the author. **Condé Nast Publications.** "Ox-Cart Man" from *Kicking the Leaves* by Donald Hall. Originally published in *The New Yorker.* Used by permission of Condé Nast Publications and the author. **Curtis Brown, London.** *The Ugly Ducking* by A. A. Milne. Reprinted by permission of Curtis Brown, London. Copyright © 1941 by A. A. Milne. **Candlewick Press.** "The Goodness of Matt Kaizer" from *What Do Fish Have to Do with Anything.* Text copyright 1997 Avi Wortis. Cover Illustration by Tracy Mitchell. Reproduced by permission of Candlewick Press, Inc. Cambridge, MA. **Ruth Cohen, Inc.** "The All-American Slurp", copyright © 1987 by Lensey Namioka, from *Visions,* ed. by Donald R. Gallo. All rights are reserved by the author. **Don Congdon Associates.** "All Summer in a Day" by Ray Bradbury. Copyright © 1954, renewed 1982 by Ray Bradbury. Reprinted by permission of Don Congdon Associates, Inc. **Cowboy Miner Productions.** "Gentle Hoss" from *Cowboy Poetry, Classic Rhymes* by Bruce Kiskaddon, compiled by Mason and Janice Coggin. Cowboy Miner Productions. Reprinted by permission. **Crossing Press.** " The Creation", retold by Joseph Bruchac from *Iroquois Stories: Heroes and Heroines, Monsters and Magic*, pp. 15–17. Copyright © 1985 by Joseph Bruchac. Reprinted by permission of Crossing Press. **David Black Literary Agency.** "Joyriding" by Jim Naughton from *Ultimate Sports*, edited by Donald R. Gallo. Used by permission of the author and the David Black Literary Agency. **Dramatic Publishing.** *A Woman Called Truth,* copyright MCMLXXXIX by Sandra Fenichel Asher. Printed in the United States of America. All rights reserved. *The play printed in this anthology is not to be used as an acting script. All inquiries regarding performance rights should be addressed to Dramatic Publishing, 311 Washington St., Woodstock, IL 60098. Phone: 815-338-7170. Fax: 815-338-8981.* **Farrar, Straus & Giroux, LLC.** "Nothing But Drums" *(excerpt re-titled by Oscar Hijuelos)* from *The Mambo Kings Play Songs of Love* by Oscar Hijuelos. Copyright © 1989 by Oscar Hijuelos. Reprinted by permission of Farrar, Straus & Giroux, LLC. **Dorothy R. Geiger.** *In the Fog* by Milton Geiger. Copyright © R423688 by Dorothy R. Geiger. Reprinted by permission. **Graywolf Press.** "One Time" copyright 1982, 1998 by the Estate of William Stafford. Reprinted from *The Way It Is: New & Selected Poems* with the permission of Graywolf Press, Saint Paul, Minnesota. **Groundwood Books/Douglas & McIntyre.** "The Tunnel" *from Back of Beyond: Tales of the Supernatural.* First published in Canada by Groundwood Books/Douglas & McIntyre. Reprinted by permission of the publisher. **Harcourt, Inc.** "Jazz Fantasia" from *Smoke and Steel* by Carl Sandburg, copyright 1920 by Harcourt, Inc. and renewed 1948 by Carl Sandburg, reprinted by permission of the publisher. "Shelter Shock" from *Lost and Found: Dogs, Cats, and Everyday Heroes at a Country Animal Shelter*, copyright © 1998 by Elizabeth Hess, reprinted by permission of Harcourt, Inc. **HarperCollins Publishers.** "Cynthia in the Snow", copyright © 1956 by Gwendolyn Brooks Blakely. Used by permission of HarperCollins Publishers. "Zlateh the Goat" from *Zlateh the Goat and Other Stories* by Isaac Bashevis Singer. Copyright © 1966 by Isaac Bashevis Singer. Used by permission of HarperCollins Publishers. **John Hawkins & Associates, Inc.** "My Friend Flicka" by Mary O'Hara. Copyright © 1941 by Mary O'Hara. Reprinted by permission of John Hawkins & Associates, Inc. **Diana Chang Herrmann.** "Saying Yes" by Diana Chang. Reprinted by permission of the author. **Bill Holm.** "Whale Breathing: Bartlett Cove, Alaska" by Bill Holm. Used by permission of the author. **Henry Holt and Company, LLC.** "The Cow of No Color" from *The Cow of No Color: Riddle Stories and Justice Tales* by Nina Jaffe and Steve Zeitland. © 1998 by Nina Jaffe and Steve

Zeitland. Reprinted by permission of Henry Holt and Company, LLC. "Buenos Hot Dogs" from *Cool Salsa*. Spanish language translation © 1994 by Lori M. Carlson, published by Henry Holt. Reprinted by permission of Henry Holt and Company. All rights reserved. "Fire and Ice" from *The Poetry of Robert Frost*, edited by Edward Connery Lathem. Copyright 1951 by Robert Frost. Copyright 1923, © 1969 by Henry Holt and Company, LLC. Reprinted by permission of Henry Holt and Company, LLC. "Stopping by Woods on a Snowy Evening" from *The Poetry of Robert Frost*, edited by Edward Connery Lathem. Copyright © 1951 by Robert Frost. Copyright 1923, © 1969 by Henry Holt and Company, LLC. Reprinted by permission of Henry Holt and Company, LLC. **Houghton Mifflin Company.** "Don't Step on a Crack" from *Don't Sing Before Breakfast, Don't Sleep in the Moonlight: Everyday Superstitions and How They Began* by Lila Perl. Text copyright © 1988 by Lila Perl. Reprinted by permission of Clarion Books/Houghton Mifflin Company. All rights reserved. From *Gorillas in the Mist* by Dian Fossey. Copyright © 1983 by Dian Fossey. Reprinted by permission of Houghton Mifflin Company. All rights reserved. From *The Hobbit* by J. R. R. Tolkien. Copyright © 1966 by J. R. R. Tolkien. Reprinted by permission of Houghton Mifflin Company. All rights reserved. **Sara Hyry.** "How Robin Hood Saved the Widow's Three Sons", copyright 2000 by Sara Hyry. **Alfred A. Knopf.** "The Boy Who Talked To Animals from *The Wonderful World of Henry Sugar and Six More* by Roald Dahl. Copyright © 1945, 1947, 1952, 1977 by Roald Dahl. Reprinted by permission of Alfred A. Knopf, a division of Random House, Inc. "Night" *from Knots in My Yo-Yo String* by Jerry Spinelli. Copyright © 1998 by Jerry Spinelli. Reprinted by permission of Alfred A. Knopf Children's Books, a division of Random House, Inc. **Francess Lantz/John Landsberg.** "Developing Your Chops" from *Rock, Rap and Rad* by Fran Lantz. Copyright © 1992 by Fran Lantz. Photographs by John Landsberg. Reprinted by permission of Francess Lantz and John Landsberg. **Little, Brown and Company.** "Satchel Paige" from *Champions: Stories of Ten Remarkable Athletes* by Bill Littlefield. Copyright © 1993 by Bill Littlefield. Reprinted by permission of Little, Brown and Company. "The Woman and the Wolf" from *The Snow Walker* by Farley Mowat. Copyright © 1975 by Farley Mowat Limited. Reprinted in the United States by permission of Little, Brown and Company (Inc.). **Liveright Publishing Corporation.** "in Just-" by E. E. Cummings. Copyright 1923, 1951, © 1991 by the Trustees for the E. E. Cummings Trust. Copyright © 1976 by George James Firmage, from *Complete Poems: 1904–1962* by E. E. Cummings, edited by George J. Firmage. Used by permission of Liveright Publishing Corporation. "Spring is like a perhaps hand" by E. E. Cummings. Copyright 1923, 1925, 1951, 1953, © 1991 by the Trustees for the E.E. Cummings Trust. Copyright © 1976 by George James Firmage. From *Complete Poems: 1904–1962* by E. E. Cummings, edited by George J. Firmage. Used by permission of Liveright Publishing Corporation. **McClelland and Stewart, Inc.** "The Woman and the Wolf" from *The Snow Walker* by Farley Mowat. Reprinted in Canada by permission of McClelland & Stewart, Inc. *The Canadian Publishers.* **Moose Music.** Lyrics to "The Wreck of the Edmund Fitzgerald" by Gordon Lightfoot. Copyright © 1976 by Moose Music. Reprinted by permission. **William Morrow & Company, Inc.** "Three/Quarters Time" from *Love Poems* by Nikki Giovanni. Text: Copyright © 1997 by Nikki Giovanni. By permission of William Morrow and Company, Inc. **Moulinsart SA.** From *The Adventures of Tintin: The Black Island* by Hergé. ©

Hergé/Moulinsart 2000. **NTC/Contemporary Publishing Group.** "The Creation of Music" from *World Mythology* by Donna Rosenberg. © 1999. Used with permission of NTC/Contemporary Publishing Group, Inc. From *Dear Ms. Demeanor* by Mary Mitchell. Copyright © 1995. Used with permission of NTC/Contemporary Publishing Group, Inc. **Penguin Putnam, Inc.** "How to Eat Like a Child", copyright © 1977, 1978 by Delia Ephron from *How to Eat Like a Child* by Delia Ephron. Used by permission of Viking Penguin, a division of Penguin Putnam, Inc. From *Ranch of Dreams* by Cleveland Amory, copyright © 1997 by Cleveland Amory. Used by permission of Viking Penguin a division of Penguin Putnam, Inc. **Ram's Horn Music.** "Forever Young" by Bob Dylan. Copyright © 1973, 1974 by Ram's Horn Music. All rights reserved. International copyright secured. Reprinted by permission. **Random House.** "Child on Top of a Greenhouse", copyright 1946 by Editorial Publications, Inc. from *The Collected Poems of Theodore Roethke* by Theodore Roethke. Used by permission of Doubleday, a division of Random House, Inc. "The Face of the Deep is Frozen" from *Shipwreck at the Bottom of the World* by Jennifer M. Armstrong. Copyright © 1998 by Jennifer M. Armstrong. Reprinted by permission of Crown Children's Books, a division of Random House, Inc. Map from *Shipwreck at the Bottom of the World* by Kayley LeFavier. Reprinted by permission of Crown Children's Books, a division of Random House, Inc. "I, Hungry Hannah Cassandra Glen…" by Norma Fox Mazer, copyright © 1984 by Norma Fox Mazer. From *Sixteen: Short Stories* by Donald R. Gallo, ed. Used by permission of Dell Publishing, a division of Random House, Inc. "Life Doesn't Frighten Me" from *And Still I Rise* by Maya Angelou. Copyright © 1978 by Maya Angelou. Reprinted by permission of Random House, Inc. "Priscilla and the Wimps" by Richard Peck, copyright © 1984 by Richard Peck. From *Sixteen: Short Stories by Outstanding Writers* by Donald R. Gallo, ed. Used by permission of Dell Publishing, a division of Random House, Inc. "Raymond's Run" from *Gorilla, My Love* by Toni Cade Bambara. Copyright © 1971 by Toni Cade Bambara. Reprinted by permission of Random House, Inc. "The Singing, Springing Lark" from *The Complete Fairy Tales of the Brothers Grimm* by Jack Zipes, Translator, Translation copyright © 1987 by Jack Zipes. Used by permission of Bantam Books, a division of Random House, Inc. From *Still Me* by Christopher Reeve. Copyright © 1998 by Cambria Productions. Reprinted by permission of Random House, Inc. From *To Be or Not to Bop: Memoirs—Dizzy Gillespie*. Copyright © 1979 by John Birks Gillespie and Wilmot Alfred Fraser. Used by permission of Doubleday, a division of Random House, Inc. "Why" from *Anne Frank's Tales From a Secret Annex* by Anne Frank. Copyright 1949, 1960 by Otto Frank. Copyright © 1982 by Anne Frank-Funds, Basel. English translation copyright © 1983 by Doubleday. Used by permission of Doubleday, a division of Random House, Inc. **Christopher Reeve.** Speech at the 1996 Democratic National Convention [transcript from CBS NEWS coverage of Democratic Nat'l Convention, Aug. 26, 1996]. Copyright © 1996 by Christopher Reeve. Reproduced by permission. **Marian Reiner.** "The Sidewalk Racer, or On the Sidewalk" from *The Sidewalk Racer and Other Poems of Sports and Motion* by Lillian Morrison. Copyright © 1965, 1967, 1968, 1977 by Lillian Morrison. Used by permission of Marian Reiner for the author. **Faith Ringgold.** "The Sunflower Quilting Bee at Arles" 1991 © Faith Ringgold. Reproduced by permission. **Sanga Music, Inc.** "The Springhill Disaster", words and music by Peggy Seeger. Copyright © 1960 (renewed) by Stormking Music, Inc.

Reprinted by permission. All rights reserved. **Scholastic, Inc.** "A Breath of Fresh Air" by Alexandra Hanson-Harding in *Junior Scholastic, 4/11/97.* Copyright © 1997 by Scholastic Inc. Reprinted by permission. "Madam C. J. Walker" from *One More River to Cross: The Story of Twelve Black Americans,* by Jim Haskins. Copyright © 1992 by James Haskins. Reprinted by permission of Scholastic, Inc. "Ta-Na-E-Ka," by Mary Whitebird. Published in *Scholastic Voice,* December 13, 1973. Copyright © 1973 by Scholastic, Inc. Reprinted by permission. **Simon & Schuster.** "Cat & the Weather", reprinted with the permission of Simon & Schuster Books for Young Readers, an imprint of Simon & Schuster Children's Publishing Division from *The Complete Poems to Solve* by May Swenson. Copyright © 1993 by the Literary Estate of May Swenson. "Orbiter 5 Shows How Earth Looks from the Moon" reprinted with the permission of Simon & Schuster Books for Young Readers, an imprint of Simon & Schuster Children's Publishing Division from *The Complete Poems to Solve* by May Swenson. Text copyright © 1993 The Literary Estate of May Swenson. "The Tunnel", reprinted in the United States with the permission of Margaret K. McElderry Books, an imprint of Simon & Schuster Children's Publishing Division, from *Back of Beyond: Tales of the Supernatural* by Sarah Ellis. Copyright © 1996 by Sarah Ellis. "'Wanderers' of the Ancient Skies" from *Planet Hunters* by Dennis Brindell Fradin. Reprinted with permission of Margaret K. McElderry Books, an imprint of Simon & Schuster Children's Publishing Division. Copyright © 1997 Dennis Brindell Fradin. **Southern Living.** "Hearing Under Siege", copyright © 1992 Cooking Light® Magazine. Reprinted by permission. **St. Martin's Press, LLC.** "Cat on the Go" from *All Things Wise and Wonderful* by James Herriot. Copyright © 1976, 1977 by James Herriot. Reprinted by permission of St. Martin's Press, LLC. **Tall Mountain Circle.** "There is No Word for Goodbye" by Mary Tallmountain. Copyright © by Mary Tallmountain. Previously published by American Indians Studies Center UCLA in *Light on the Tent Wall,* copyright © 1990. Reprinted by permission of Tallmountain Circle, Tenderloin Reflection & Education Center. **Thompson & Thompson.** "If You Should Go" by Countee Cullen. Published in: *On These I Stand* © 1947 Harper & Bros. NY. Renewed 1975 by Ida M. Cullen. Copyrights held by the Amistad Research Center, Tulane University, New Orleans, Louisiana. Administered by Thompson and Thompson, New York City. Reprinted by permission. **Tribune Media Services.** "Turtles Taken Off the Menu in Brazil. Reprinted with permission of Knight Ridder/Tribune Information Services. **University of California, Berkeley.** "The Magic Mortar" from *The Magic Listening Cap: More Folk Tales from Japan,* retold by Yoshiko Uchida. Copyright © 1955 by Yoshiko Uchida. Reprinted by permission of the Regents of the University of California, Berkeley. **Ralph M. Vicinanza, Ltd.** "Pompeii" from *Lost Cities and Vanished Civilizations,* by Robert Silverberg. Copyright © 1962 by Robert Silverberg. Published by permission of Robert Silverberg, c/o Ralph M. Vicinanza, Ltd. **Weekly Reader Corp.** "The Cutoff: The Story of the Donner Party" by Catherine Gourley, from *Read for Your Life: Tales of Survival.* Copyright © 1998. Reprinted by permission of Weekly Reader Corp. **The Wiley Agency, Inc.** "The Rebellion of the Magic Rabbits" by Ariel Dorfman. Copyright © 1990 by Ariel Dorfman, reprinted with the permission of The Wiley Agency, Inc.

We have made every effort to trace the ownership of all copyrighted material and to secure permission from copyright holders. In the event of any question arising as to the use of any material, we will be pleased to make the necessary corrections in future printings. Thanks are due to the aforementioned authors, publishers, and agents for permission to use the materials indicated.